D0200037

South Pacific

Geert Cole   Carolyn Hubbard
Leanne Logan   Korina Miller
Susannah Farfor   Mat Oakley
Michelle Bennett   Denis O'Byrne
Tione Chinula   Wendy Owen
Sally Dillon   Vincent Talbot
Tony Wheeler

LONELY PLANET PUBLICATIONS
Melbourne • Oakland • London • Paris

SOUTH PACIFIC

160°E · 170°E · 180° · 170°W

Wake Atoll (USA)

MARSHALL ISLANDS

Johnston Atoll (USA)

International Date Line

Pohnpei

Kosrae

Ratak Chain

Majuro Atoll

Palmyra Atoll (USA)

Tarawa Atoll

Howland Island (USA)
Baker Island (USA)

SAMOA
Kirikiti is a game very loosely based on cricket, but with a decidedly Pacific twist to the rules.

SOLOMON ISLANDS
This famous dive destination offers colourful coral reefs, exciting underwater topography and hundreds of sunken WWII wrecks. It's fantastic for snorkellers too.

TUVALU
The global warming frontline, if sea levels really do rise this could be the first country in the world to disappear.

Phoenix Islands

AMERICAN SAMOA
Ofu Beach is arguably the most beautiful beach in the world and offers the finest snorkelling in the territory.

Choiseul
Santa Isabel
New Georgia
Malaita
HONIARA

SOLOMON ISLANDS

TUVALU

FUNAFUTI ATOLL ✪

TOKELAU (New Zealand)

Northern Cook Islands

Guadalcanal
Makira
Rennell & Bellona
Santa Cruz Islands

M E L A N E S I A

WALLIS & FUTUNA (France)
MATA'UTU ✪
Futuna
Wallis Island

SAMOA
APIA ✪
Savai'i
'Upolu

AMERICAN SAMOA (USA)
PAGO PAGO ✪
Tutuila

VANUATU
On Pentecost Island, the *naghol* (land-diving) ceremony is carried out every year to ensure a good harvest and inspire the world's bungy jumpers.

Espiritu Santo
Malekula

VANUATU

Pentecost
Ambrym

FIJI

Vanua Levu

Lau Group

Niuas

P O L

Viti Levu
SUVA ✪

TONGA

Vava'u Group

ALOFI ✪

NEW CALEDONIA (France)

PORT VILA ✪ Efate
Erromango
Tanna

Kadavu Group

Ha'apai Group

NIUE

CORAL SEA

Loyalty Islands

NUKU'ALOFA ✪
Tongatapu

Grande Terre ✪
NOUMEA

NEW CALEDONIA
Canoe by moonlight down the tranquil Rivière Bleue through a spooky drowned forest to a shimmering lake.

FIJI
A haven for divers, nature lovers, adventurers and beach bums, this is one of the South Pacific's most popular destinations and home to a vibrant cultural mix.

TONGA
In the Ha'apai and Vava'u island groups you can snorkel with gentle humpback whales in waters where once they were hunted.

AUSTRALIA

Norfolk Island (Australia)

Lord Howe Island (Australia)

International Date Line

T A S M A N   S E A

Auckland ○

NEW ZEALAND

○ WELLINGTON

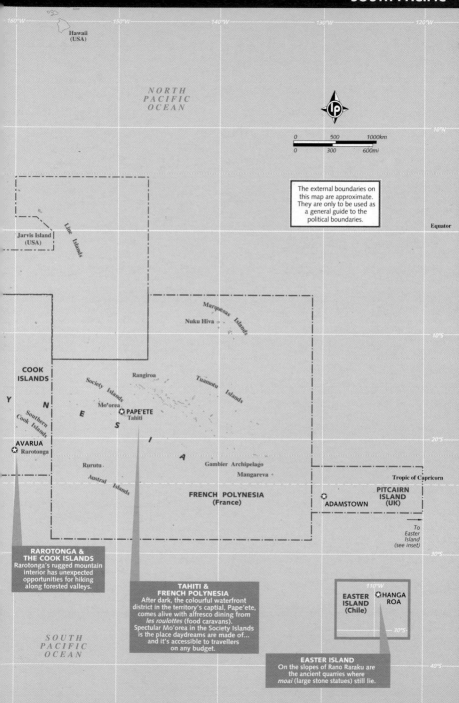

NORTH
PACIFIC
OCEAN

Hawaii
(USA)

160°W   150°W   140°W   130°W   120°W

10°N

0   500   1000km
0   300   600mi

The external boundaries on
this map are approximate.
They are only to be used as
a general guide to the
political boundaries.

Equator

Jarvis Island
(USA)

Line Islands

Marquesas Islands
Nuku Hiva

10°S

COOK
ISLANDS

Rangiroa

Society Islands

Tuamotu Islands

Mo'orea

PAPE'ETE
Tahiti

Southern
Cook Islands

AVARUA
Rarotonga

20°S

Rurutu

Gambier Archipelago
Mangareva

Austral Islands

Tropic of Capricorn

FRENCH POLYNESIA
(France)

ADAMSTOWN

PITCAIRN
ISLAND
(UK)

To
Easter
Island
(see inset)

**RAROTONGA &
THE COOK ISLANDS**
Rarotonga's rugged mountain
interior has unexpected
opportunities for hiking
along forested valleys.

30°S

**TAHITI &
FRENCH POLYNESIA**
After dark, the colourful waterfront
district in the territory's captial, Pape'ete,
comes alive with alfresco dining from
les roulottes (food caravans).
Spectular Mo'orea in the Society Islands
is the place daydreams are made of...
and it's accessible to travellers
on any budget.

110°W

EASTER
ISLAND
(Chile)

HANGA
ROA

30°S

SOUTH
PACIFIC
OCEAN

EASTER ISLAND
On the slopes of Rano Raraku are
the ancient quarries where
moai (large stone statues) still lie.

40°S

Contents – Text

4 Contents – Text

Contents – Maps

5

6 Contents – Maps

The Authors

Geert Cole
When Geert visited the South Pacific for the first time many moons ago, he could not have been further away from his homeland, Belgium. Frangipani, flashing smiles and timelessness – the beauty, culture and simplicity of everyday life in the Pacific entranced Geert as he sailed from New Zealand to Samoa. He shed his Western skin on the way and now, many years later, enjoys a similar relaxed lifestyle under subtropical Australian skies, with Leanne his partner and daughter Eleonor.

Leanne Logan
Leanne, a journalist from Australia, first tasted life in the South Pacific a decade ago when she updated Lonely Planet's *New Caledonia* guidebook. She's been back many times since, and on each visit falls in love, yet again, with Pacific hospitality, island time and green-coconut juice. When not travelling, Leanne can be found tending veggies, planting trees and watching wallabies with Geert, her partner, and daughter Eleonor, at their home in northern New South Wales, Australia.

Geert and Leanne were the book's coordinating authors.

Susannah Farfor
After growing up in Melbourne, Australia, Susannah set off to see if the world really was round. Five and a half years later, she finally ended up back where she started, surmising that the theory was sound. Susannah left glossy mags to work as an editor at Lonely Planet's Australia and US offices. She has been a contributing author on the *Australia*, *Queensland* and *Northern Territory* guidebooks.

Michelle Bennett
Raised on the edge of an open-cut mine in Driffield (Victoria, Australia), at 17 Michelle left the green pastures and headed for the big smoke of Melbourne to live it up (and study social geography). After graduating, she spent a couple of years in Asia and Europe before being lured back to Australia to work at a graphic design studio and, later, to run a jazz club. After gaining a Masters degree in tourism development, Michelle joined Lonely Planet, where she worked as an editor and writer, having authored on the *Vanuatu* and *Samoan Islands* guidebooks. The South Pacific is her latest obsession.

Tione Chinula
Tione grew up in Malawi before moving to New Zealand to study. After completing a French degree, she set off for France several years ago but only got as far as Tahiti. Seduced by the heady fragrance of *tiare* flowers, the translucent lagoon, breathtaking sunsets, and a Frenchman named Vincent, she fell in love with the Pacific. She swapped one idyllic lifestyle for another when she moved across the Pacific to New Caledonia in 1998. Tione now works as a journalist and spends most weekends tramping in New Caledonia's mountains, camping on its beaches, or out on its vast lagoon.

Sally Dillon

Sally fell in love with the islands of the South Pacific during five months of island hopping aboard the Tall Ship *Young Endeavour* on the final leg of its world voyage. Tahiti, the first landfall after almost a month at sea, retains a special place in her heart. She remembers fondly the sight of mountainous islands bursting out of azure waters, the smell of *tiare* garlands...plus the challenging hunt for a cheap beer, and that slide down a cliff while hiking around Tahiti Iti.

These days Sally does most of her travelling by bicycle, riding her mountain bike or penny farthing around the world with her husband Peter Hines. She turned this passion into a job, working as a cycling and walking guidebook editor for Lonely Planet for four years, when she also wrote *Cycling France*.

Carolyn Hubbard

A childhood in Australia, including a romp around the outback in a six-seater Cessna, schooling in Washington DC, followed by years in NYC and Barcelona, trips through Southeast Asia, North Africa and Mexico, and working as a senior editor at Lonely Planet in the USA and as an author on *Argentina* and *Chile* guidebooks: no amount of travels along these contours of the globe prepared Carolyn for the impact of rubbing a lone stone on a rugged beach – the navel of the world – on Rapa Nui.

Korina Miller

Korina spent the first 17 years of her life on Vancouver Island and has been on the move ever since. Her travels have taken her to many corners of the world, from Alaska to Sicily and Colombia to Scotland. She studied in Japan and Denmark; lived and worked with remote tribal peoples in India and southwestern China and ran a hotel in the mountains of Ecuador and arts organisations in Vancouver and London. En route, she picked up a degree in Communications, an MA in Migration Studies, and a Limey husband. Korina is co-author of LP's *Fiji*, *China*, *Southwest China* and author of *Beijing Condensed*.

Mat Oakley

After 18 years in Watford (which accounts for many personal problems) on the outer rim of London, Mat dumped an English degree in Leeds to travel the world – embarking on a rugged, dangerous journey that took him as far south as Watford, where he got stuck for another 18 months. Since finally leaving England's most ridiculed town, he has travelled through Africa and the Middle East, and lived and worked in Thailand, Laos and Australia. He currently lives in Fiji.

Denis O'Byrne

Born and raised in South Australia, Denis is now a resident of Darwin. After working in various mismatched jobs he realised that travel and writing about it were what he enjoyed doing most, so – taking a deep breath – he decided to become a full-time scribe. Since then Denis has worked on a number of Lonely Planet guidebooks including *South Pacific* 1 and two editions of *Vanuatu*. Darwin's tropical climate was good training for tripping around the Solomon Islands for this update.

Wendy Owen

Fascination with language drew Wendy to study English before joining Melbourne newspaper the *Age* as a journalist. This allowed her to get paid to participate in people's life stories, but courts and state party politics could not entirely satisfy her curiosity so she embarked on an odyssey of work and travel that lasted 17 years. After a glorious time as a freelance journalist, then several years as a stuff sub-editor for Reuters and for the *Independent* in London, she finally returned to home, where she joined Lonely Planet as an editor, then Publishing Manager of Upgrades. When she leapt back over the editorial fence she turned towards the Samoan Islands, which she'd got to know while editing *Samoa 3*.

Vincent Talbot

When he was 15, Vincent moved from France to Tahiti, where he discovered the wonderful world of surfing. He made local history as one of the first students at the French Pacific University in Pape'ete. Later he studied marine biology in South America and in the freezing waters of Antarctica. Armed with his PhD, he promptly headed back to the sunny tropics where he carried out research in the Tuamotu atolls of French Polynesia. He now lives in New Caledonia with his wife Tione and spends as much time as possible diving, surfing, boating, and exploring remote parts of New Caledonia.

Tony Wheeler

Tony Wheeler was born in England, but grew up in Pakistan, the Bahamas and the USA. In recent years he's travelled extensively in the Pacific, an activity which has led to two 'castaway' episodes, one on Nukufetau in the Tuvalu group and one on Futuna in Wallis & Futuna. Read all about it in *Lonely Planet Unpacked Again*.

FROM THE AUTHORS

From Geert & Leanne

Merci beaucoup to Pascal Nicomette, an invaluable and far-flung contact, for sharing her passion about Wallis & Futuna and its people.

On the home front, thanks to Eleonor for being happy with Sixy and Bluey as substitutes, and to Errol Hunt and our fellow *South Pacific* authors for being great to work with and not succumbing to 'island time'.

From Susannah

Utmost thanks to Ian for his unique brand of humour. A big 'thank you' to all the people along the way who gave their time and shared their knowledge, and to the other authors on this book for their assistance and information. Thanks also to all the readers who have written in with their invaluable comments, and to Errol Hunt for his Cook Islands tips.

From Michelle

Thanks especially to my darling Micky for being a terrific travel companion and support. Huge thanks also to dear Dad for accompanying me on yet another South Pacific adventure and for conversations I will always treasure.

Tank yu tumas to all the terrific people I met along the way who shared their perspective on Vanuatu and showed me a great time. Thanks in particular to Patrick Vurobaravu at the NTO for being incredibly helpful and patient, Timothy Takau for adopting me as his sister and making sure everything was always sorted and Dorah Wilson for being an ace friend. Thanks also to Roy Hills, Russell Nari, Michel Kalworai, Fred Tarisongtamate, Moana Matariki, Alix Crapper, Luwi, Dave Cross, Ralph Regenvanu, Eileen Boe, Jason Raubani, Mary Jane and Kim Dinh, Peter Whitelaw, Joy Wu, Tony Deamer, Glen Russell, Luke Tokar, Timmy Rovu, Anna Wells, the lovely crew of the *Soren Larsen* and the multitude of readers who wrote in with updates about Vanuatu.

On the home front, thanks a million to the LP delightfuls Jocelyn Harewood, Errol Hunt, Corie Waddell, Kath Dolan, Jon Murray, Leonie Mugavin, Lou McGregor, Jacqueline Nguyen and Cris Gibcus.

From Tione & Vincent
Merci beaucoup to all our friends in New Caledonia who helped with information, especially Luc Faucompré and Josette Neumayer. Special thanks to Sonia at the Noumea tourism office and Angel in Île des Pins. Thanks as well to Sylvie Cristofoli for the travel information.

From Sally
Thanks to Peter for cooking dinners, Errol Hunt at Lonely Planet for handling queries with his usual Kiwi good grace and humour, Hilary Rogers for the work she put into researching the *Tahiti* guidebook and Verly Atae from Tahiti Tourisme for patient responses to queries. Thanks also to Robert Thompson from Tahiti Tourisme, New Zealand.

From Carolyn
This update has been made possible by the dedicated work of Jeff Davis, the researcher for the Easter Island chapter in the *Chile* guidebook. Many thanks go to the people of Easter Island, who invited me in and shared the mystery of the island with me during my stay. *Un millòn de gracias a* Pablo Retamal, of CPT in Washington DC, for his assistance.

From Korina
Thank you to John and Marilyn in Levuka for the many tips and banana pancakes; to Andrea in Levuka for getting us on a boat to Leluvia; to Tom and his staff in Colo-i-Suva for the birthday cake; to Vasemaca in Suva for her help with statistics; to Bob and Lui on Vanua Levu for the their hospitality and the seaviews; to Jackie on the Tunuloa Peninsula for babysitting my book; to Bibi and his family on Taveuni for the herbal medicine from their garden; and to Morica, Tige, Chet and their crew for a very memorable tour. Many thanks to commissioning editor Errol for never being more than an email away, to Robyn and Leo, and to Corie for the mapping help. Thanks and love to Paul, my favourite travel crony. A special *vinaka* to the many beautiful Fijians we met on the road – your friendliness was the highlight of my trip.

From Mat
For Tonga, thanks to Steven Vete at the Forum for all the hints and pointers (and to 'Ulafala for the kava and trying to direct me into trouble);

Poluno, Tevita and Melenaite at the various TVBs for filling in the gaps, and Paul Johansson for countless tips (and stern food criticism!). In Vava'u, thanks to Benny, Mary, Mikio and Gunther for advice and in Tongatapu to Naoko for the priceless information, juicy gossip and shelter from the cyclone. And last, but most, to the peerless KT for all the help and more in Ha'apai and beyond.

For Niue, words cannot express my gratitude to the amazing Esther Pavihi, who managed to be in two places at once! Thanks also to Annie at Niue Dive for the lowdown.

And of course Hannah and Mae, for their patience.

From Denis
Many thanks to all those people who assisted me in one way or another during this update. I'd particularly like to thank Andrew Nihopara and Nelson Manepura of the Solomon Islands Visitors Bureau, as well as Benjamin Kaniotoku, Grant & Jill Kelly, Danny Kennedy, David Kera, Mary Poroaai, and Matias & Joyce Sake. Thanks also to Bob Johnson and Lee MacKinnon. I hope I've got the spelling right!

From Wendy
Much of the information in these chapters was provided by Michelle Bennett, whose initial research was so valuable. In Samoa, thanks to Mosie Su'a and his assistants at the Samoan Tourism Authority who were enormously helpful and good fun as well, and to Warren Jopling, for being so generous with his knowledge. The beautiful and talented Jackson Five – headed by Moelagi Jackson, were all magnificent and Uaea Laki Apelu demonstrated typical Samoan hospitality and trust by letting me use his computer 'after hours'. Steve, Ava, Sam and Pol made my work fun and their enthusiasm and willingness to share was much appreciated. In Pago Pago, thanks to John Wasco and the folk at the Tourism Office. Thanks also to Gordon MacLauchlan, who kept me amused (and sane) during write-up time.

From Tony
To James Conway on Funafuti, Peter Bennetts who dragged me around to almost every island in Tuvalu (and got marooned on Nukufetau with me for a week), Frank Mars and Emma Smallcombe (Dutch and English VSO volunteers on Vaitupu) and to the many other Tuvaluans and expats who were so helpful during my travels.

This Book

The first edition of *South Pacific* was coordinated by Errol Hunt. Contributing authors included Jean-Bernard Carillet (New Caledonia, French Polynesia), Robyn Jones and Leo Pinheiro (Fiji and Tuvalu), Nancy Keller (Cook Islands and Tonga), James Lyon (Easter Island), Rowan McKinnon (Solomon Islands), Denis O'Byrne (Vanuatu) and Tony Wheeler (French Polynesia, Niue, Pitcairn, Wallis & Futuna).

This second edition of *South Pacific* was coordinated by Geert Cole & Leanne Logan, who also updated the Regional Facts for the Visitor and Wallis & Futuna chapters. Susannah Farfor updated Facts about the South Pacific, Rarotonga & the Cook Islands, Pitcairn Island and the 'South Pacific Diving' special section. Tione Chinula & Vincent Talbot updated New Caledonia, Carolyn Hubbard updated Easter Island, Michelle Bennett updated Vanuatu, Sally Dillon updated Tahiti & French Polynesia, Korina Miller updated Fiji, Mat Oakley updated Tonga and Niue, Denis O'Byrne updated the Solomon Islands, Wendy Owen updated Samoa and American Samoa and Tony Wheeler updated Tuvalu. The 'South Pacific Arts' special section was updated by Errol Hunt, and Errol also updated Tokelau with help from Makalio Ioane. Leonie Mugavin worked wonders on the Getting There & Away and Getting Around chapters. Tony Horwitz updated the 'Captain James Cook' boxed text. And, last but not least, Quentin Frayne prepared the Language appendix.

FROM THE PUBLISHER

This second edition of *South Pacific* was commissioned in Lonely Planet's Melbourne office by Errol Hunt. Lou McGregor coordinated the editing and found the time to edit several chapters as well... Kim Hutchins, Simon Sellars, Suzannah Shwer, Julia Taylor, Daniel Caleo, Katrina Webb, Ilana Sharp and Carolyn Boicos all assisted with editing and proofreading. Nancy Ianni, Stephanie Pearson and Nick Stebbing assisted with indexing. Jacqueline Nguyen coordinated the cartography with assistance from Valentina Kremenchutskaya, Kusnandar, Helen Rowley and Anthony Phelan. This edition was project-managed by Charles Rawlings-Way and Eoin Dunlevy saw the book through the final days of production. Briefing was done with the help of Wayne Murphy and Corie Waddell (mapping). The cover was designed by Yukiyoshi Kamimura. Cris Gibcus laid the book out, designed the colour pages and expanded Lou's (rude) Dutch vocabulary. David Burnett and Mark Germanchis assisted with all the technical hitches along the way. Mark Robbins came to the rescue when Lou's computer blew up. Finally, thanks to the authors for hitting the ground at short notice, and to Robert Reid and Ryan Ver Berkmoes who allowed Errol to break all the rules to make sure this book actually happened (very Pacific Islands!).

THANKS
Many thanks to the travellers who used the last edition and wrote to us with helpful hints, advice and interesting anecdotes. Your names appear in the back of this book.

Foreword

ABOUT LONELY PLANET GUIDEBOOKS

The story begins with a classic travel adventure: Tony and Maureen Wheeler's 1972 journey across Europe and Asia to Australia. There was no useful information about the overland trail then, so Tony and Maureen published the first Lonely Planet guidebook to meet a growing need.

From a kitchen table, Lonely Planet has grown to become the largest independent travel publisher in the world, with offices in Melbourne (Australia), Oakland (USA), London (UK) and Paris (France).

Today Lonely Planet guidebooks cover the globe. There is an ever-growing list of books and information in a variety of media. Some things haven't changed. The main aim is still to make it possible for adventurous travellers to get out there – to explore and better understand the world.

At Lonely Planet we believe travellers can make a positive contribution to the countries they visit – if they respect their host communities and spend their money wisely. Since 1986 a percentage of the income from each book has been donated to aid projects and human rights campaigns, and, more recently, to wildlife conservation.

Although inclusion in a guidebook usually implies a recommendation we cannot list every good place. Exclusion does not necessarily imply criticism. In fact there are a number of reasons why we might exclude a place – sometimes it is simply inappropriate to encourage an influx of travellers.

UPDATES & READER FEEDBACK

Things change – prices go up, schedules change, good places go bad and bad places go bankrupt. Nothing stays the same. So, if you find things better or worse, recently opened or long-since closed, please tell us and help make the next edition even more accurate and useful.

Lonely Planet thoroughly updates each guidebook as often as possible – usually every two years, although for some destinations the gap can be longer. Between editions, up-to-date information is available in our free, monthly email bulletin *Comet* (W www.lonelyplanet.com/newsletters). You can also check out the *Thorn Tree* bulletin board and *Postcards* section of our website which carry unverified, but fascinating, reports from travellers.

Tell us about it! We genuinely value your feedback. A well-travelled team at Lonely Planet reads and acknowledges every email and letter we receive and ensures that every morsel of information finds its way to the relevant authors, editors and cartographers.

Everyone who writes to us will find their name listed in the next edition of the appropriate guidebook. The very best contributions will be rewarded with a free guidebook.

We may edit, reproduce and incorporate your comments in Lonely Planet products such as guidebooks, websites and digital products, so let us know if you don't want your comments reproduced or your name acknowledged.

How to contact Lonely Planet:
Online: e talk2us@lonelyplanet.com.au, W www.lonelyplanet.com
Australia: Locked Bag 1, Footscray, Victoria 3011
UK: 72-82 Rosebery Ave, London, EC1R 4RW
USA: 150 Linden St, Oakland, CA 94607

Introduction

The islands of the Pacific Ocean have enjoyed a reputation as an untouched paradise ever since 18th-century European explorers returned home with romantic tales about the South Sea islands and their people.

Modern visitors to the region are often surprised to discover bustling cosmopolitan cities and a plethora of tourist resorts. However, there are still places in the Pacific that conform to the tropical paradise myth: some seem entirely untouched by Western society and others unaffected by humans at all. From the mountain rainforests of the high islands to perfect beaches, underwater worlds and thriving coral reefs, the region's natural beauty is spectacular and accessible.

The Pacific Ocean is huge, as large as all the world's other oceans put together. Yet its landmasses are relatively small – tiny dots of land separated by enormous distances of open sea. It's hardly surprising then that the cultures of the South Pacific islands are so diverse, yet many similarities exist in their religion, languages and customs.

The history of oceanic voyaging that produced these similarities has amazed Westerners from the time of James Cook. Successive waves of settlement from as early as 1500 BC saw the Pacific Ocean criss-crossed by innumerable canoe journeys. Later, during the 18th and 19th centuries, these crossings were intersected by the paths of missionaries and curious or entrepreneurial Europeans.

The Pacific's history as a place of journeying is a tradition that has continued into our own age. Travel to the South Pacific these days is heavily focused on leisure, whether languidly soaking up paradise or taking advantage of the countless opportunities for yachting, kayaking, bushwalking, swimming, diving or snorkelling. There's no obligation to do any of these activities. The paralysis that afflicts Pacific travellers is legendary, and it doesn't take long to get used to lengthy spells reading a book or taking leisurely dips in the crystal-clear sea.

The South Pacific's natural beauty is unrivalled. Traditional cultures are strong and proudly displayed throughout the region; captivating dances, gastronomic feasts and time-honoured rites are performed, restating the vitality of these many cultures. Modern artists can be seen honouring their past, recreating and reinterpreting ancient themes in their artwork; these themes are also present in the ancient stone statues and monuments still standing in many places.

Whether you're setting out on an independent island-hopping odyssey or looking for that one special place in the sun, this book contains a wealth of information on the South Pacific's more popular islands, as well as its most remote. Convenient (and cost effective) package tours can be a great way to steady your South Pacific sea legs before adding extra time onto your holiday to travel independently in the region.

Wrap a fragrant flower behind your ear, don some floral clothing, sink your toes into soft sand, grab a mask and snorkel and plunge into everything the islands have to offer... or maybe just relax and do nothing for a while.

Facts about the South Pacific

HISTORY

It was about 50,000 years ago that people first reached the Pacific islands, arriving in New Guinea from Southeast Asia via Indonesia. These people, now known as Papuans, share ancestry with Australia's first Aboriginals. Moving slowly east, the Papuans were halted in the northern Solomon Islands about 25,000 years ago, due to the lack of technology and skills necessary to cross the increasingly wide stretches of open ocean. Subsequent people, collectively known as Austronesians, moved into the area from the west, mingling with the Papuans and eventually becoming the highly diverse group of people we conveniently group together as 'Melanesians'.

New Guinea and the Solomons were the only inhabited islands in the Pacific for many thousands of years.

The wider seas from the Solomons to Vanuatu were finally crossed in about 1500 BC. An Austronesian people now known as the Lapita (see the boxed text 'Lapita' in the South Pacific Arts special section) finally developed the technology and the skills to cross open seas and quickly expanded through New Caledonia, Fiji, Tonga and Samoa. The culture we now know as Polynesian was developed by the Lapita in Fiji, Tonga and Samoa.

The Melanesians of New Guinea and the Solomons mingled a little with the Lapita and

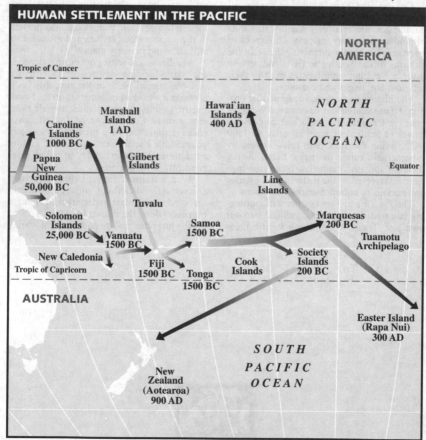

HUMAN SETTLEMENT IN THE PACIFIC

NORTH AMERICA

Tropic of Cancer

NORTH PACIFIC OCEAN

Hawai`ian Islands 400 AD

Marshall Islands 1 AD

Caroline Islands 1000 BC

Gilbert Islands

Papua New Guinea 50,000 BC

Equator

Line Islands

Tuvalu

Marquesas 200 BC

Solomon Islands 25,000 BC

Vanuatu 1500 BC

Samoa 1500 BC

Tuamotu Archipelago

New Caledonia

Tropic of Capricorn

Fiji 1500 BC

Tonga 1500 BC

Cook Islands

Society Islands 200 BC

AUSTRALIA

Easter Island (Rapa Nui) 300 AD

New Zealand (Aotearoa) 900 AD

SOUTH PACIFIC OCEAN

followed them east across the Pacific. Melanesians came to dominate New Guinea, the Solomons, Vanuatu, New Caledonia and Fiji.

The Lapitas' descendants, the Polynesians of Samoa and Tonga, 'paused' there for about a thousand years, until more advanced ocean vessels and skills were developed. They crossed the longer ocean stretches to the east to the Society and Marquesas island groups (in modern French Polynesia) some time around 200 BC. From there, voyaging canoes travelled southwest to Rarotonga and the southern Cook Islands, southeast to Rapa Nui (Easter Island; AD 300), north to Hawaii (AD 400) and southwest past Rarotonga to Aotearoa (New Zealand; AD 900).

Although the predominant direction of human movement was from west to east, population pressure and the occasional religious disagreement prompted constant movement of people across the oceans. There are Polynesians in Melanesia's eastern islands. Largely Melanesian, Fiji is also home to many Polynesians.

The settlement of the Pacific Ocean was the most remarkable feat of ocean sailing up to that time. All but the furthest-flung islands of the Pacific were colonised by 200 BC, 1200 years before the Vikings crossed the Atlantic.

Melanesians embarked on regular trade routes and some war missions, but Polynesians travelled the broader stretches of open ocean (see the boxed text 'Voyaging & Navigation' later). Almost no Pacific islands were cut off entirely from other cultures. The presence of the *kumara* (sweet potato) in the Pacific islands confirms that at least some journeys were made as far east as South America, probably from the Marquesas. Traditional stories also indicate exploratory journeys into Antarctic waters 'not seen by the sun'.

For further information about ancient Pacific cultures see Society and Religion later in this chapter.

European Explorers

Like Pacific islanders, European explorers came in search of resources (gold and spices initially), and were often driven by curiosity or national pride. However, Europeans were also inspired by one overpowering myth: the search for Terra Australis, the unknown Great Southern Continent.

Scientific philosophies since the time of Ptolemy predicted the presence of a huge landmass in the southern hemisphere to counter the Earth's northern continents. Otherwise, it was believed, the globe would be top heavy and fall over! Belief in this southern continent was unqualified; explorers were not asked to confirm its existence, but to chart its coasts and parlay with its people. In the absence of hard facts, Terra Australis was peopled with strange heathens and magical creatures, and rumoured to be rich in gold. The biblical tale of King Solomon required the presence of vast gold mines in some unknown location. What could be a better spot than Terra Australis?

Spanish In 1521 the Portuguese Ferdinand Magellan led a Spanish expedition that discovered, at the southern tip of the Americas, an entrance to the ocean he named 'Mar Pacifico', the Pacific Ocean, for the calmness of its seas. With extraordinary bad luck, and lacking the island-finding skills of Pacific islanders, Magellan saw only two small, uninhabited islands until he had sailed northwest across almost the entire ocean to Guam in Micronesia.

On Guam the first contact between Pacific islander and European followed a pattern that was to become all too familiar. The Micronesian (and Polynesian) attitude was that all property was shared. Guam's islanders helped themselves to one of the expedition's small boats and Magellan retaliated – seven islanders were killed. Magellan himself was killed two months later while in the Philippines, but not before he became the first person to circumnavigate the globe (having previously visited the Philippines from the other direction).

Spaniard Don Alvaro de Mendaña sailed west across the Pacific in search of Terra Australis in 1567. On the Solomon Islands, which he named for King Solomon's gold, conflict with the locals arose when islanders were unable to supply the resources Mendaña needed to reprovision.

It took Mendaña nearly 30 years to gain approval for his disastrous second voyage during 1595. An estimated 200 islanders were killed in the Marquesas when conflict broke out; there was even more conflict with locals when they reached the Solomons, and fighting also spread to the crew. Mendaña himself died of malaria, and the expedition returned to Peru under the command of the more humane Pedro Fernández de Quirós.

Voyaging & Navigation

Ancient Pacific islanders' voyages were motivated by war, trade, colonisation, the search for resources or sometimes merely by curiosity and pride. The Tongans, known as the 'Vikings of the Pacific', ruled Samoa, Niue and eastern Fiji with an iron fist, and raided from Tuvalu to the Solomon Islands, 2700km to the west!

At the time of European contact, prodigious feats of navigation and voyaging still occurred, although not on as grand a scale as previously. The navigator-priest Tupaia, who boarded Cook's *Endeavour* in Tahiti, could name around 100 islands between the Marquesas and Fiji, and he directed Cook's search for islands west of Tahiti. For the entire circuitous journey to Java in Indonesia, Tupaia could always point in the direction of his homeland.

Canoes
The term 'canoe' *(vaka* or *va'a)* is misleading. The same word describes small dugouts used for river navigation, giant war vessels accommodating hundreds of men and 25m-long ocean-voyaging craft. Ocean-voyaging craft, either double canoes or single canoes with outriggers, carried one (or more) masts and sails of woven pandanus. James Cook and contemporary observers estimated that Pacific canoes were capable of speeds greater than their own ships; probably 150km to 250km per day, so that trips of 5000km could be comfortably achieved with available provisions. See Books in the Regional Facts for the Visitor chapter for literature about Pacific canoes.

Navigation Techniques
Initial exploratory journeys would often follow the migratory flights of birds. Once a new land had been discovered, the method of rediscovery was remembered and communicated mostly by way of which stars to follow. Fine tuning of these directions was possible by observing the direction from which certain winds blew, the currents, wave fronts reflecting from islands and the flights of land birds.

European Theories
Many European explorers were unable to believe that a stone-age culture without a written language or use of the compass could have accomplished such amazing feats of navigation. Some assumed that an earlier, more advanced culture must have existed. They proposed that islanders were the barbaric survivors of this ancient empire, living on the mountain tops of the sunken continent of Mu.

Once the continent of Mu was discounted, a wide range of possible origins for Pacific islanders was considered, including India, Israel and the Americas. Others proposed that the islands had been settled quite accidentally, as fishermen were blown off course and lost at sea.

The majority of evidence, however, points towards mostly deliberate west to east migration. This conclusion rests on linguistic, genetic, anthropological and archaeological studies, vegetation patterns, computer modelling of wind and currents, and a study of oral traditions.

Quirós led another expedition to the Pacific in 1605, discovering the Tuamotu Islands and Vanuatu.

Dutch Le Maire and Schouten's 1616 expedition, again searching for Terra Australis, revealed to Europe the Tongan islands and Futuna. Jacob Roggeveen spotted Bora Bora in the Society Islands in 1722, and Tutuila and Upolu in Samoa. Abel Tasman, became the most famous Dutch explorer after charting Tasmania and the east coast of New Zealand in 1642, then sailing on to make contact with the islands of Tonga and Fiji.

English In 1767, Samuel Wallis – *still* searching for Terra Australis – landed on Tahiti and claimed it for England, but the greatest of the English explorers was James Cook (see the boxed text 'Captain James Cook').

Following the most famous of maritime mutinies, Fletcher Christian captained the *Bounty* to discover Rarotonga in the southern Cook Islands in 1789. See the boxed text 'Mutiny on the Bounty' in the Pitcairn Islands chapter.

French The most famous French explorer, Louis-Antoine de Bougainville, came upon

Voyaging & Navigation

Modern Voyaging

The voyaging skills of Pacific islanders may not match that of their ancestors, but the traditional knowledge of navigational methods is still being put to everyday use. Both small inter-island trips and long-distance voyages have been used to test many theories about ocean voyaging.

Probably the most famous such voyage, that of Thor Heyerdahl's *Kon Tiki* from South America to the Tuamotus in 1947, was made in an attempt to prove the now discredited theory that Polynesia was populated from South America.

Modern voyages along traditional routes have refined theories about canoe construction and navigational methods. Among such journeys, the 25m-long outrigger canoe *Tarratai* was sailed from Kiribati 2500km south to Fiji in 1976. That same year the voyage of the 20m *Hokule'a*, which used traditional navigation methods for the 4250km trip from Hawai'i to Tahiti, sparked a resurgence of interest in traditional navigation.

Other voyaging canoes include the 21m *Hawaiki Nui*, which sailed 4000km from Tahiti to Aotearoa in 1985. In 1995 *Te Au o Tonga*, captained by the former prime minister of the Cook Islands, Sir Thomas Davis (Papa Tom), sailed from Rarotonga to Tahiti, on to Hawai'i, and back to Rarotonga. Part of the cargo on the last leg was less than traditional: Papa Tom's new 1200cc Harley Davidson. The *Hokule'a* and *Te Au o Tonga*, among other great *vaka*, continue to make long voyages.

BY PERMISSION OF THE NATIONAL LIBRARY OF AUSTRALIA

'Pacific Ocean – a native canoe meeting strangers off the Murray Islands'. Painted by Edwin Augustus Porcher (watercolour, 1845). Driven by two sails and steered by paddle, this form of medium-sized canoe was used for inter-island travel.

Tahiti and claimed it for France in 1768. He went on to the Samoan islands, which he named the Navigator Islands for the skills of the canoeists sailing circles around his ship. He went on to Vanuatu and discovered Australia's Great Barrier Reef. Bougainville's impact was greater than dots on a map, however; his accounts of the South Pacific sparked massive interest in Europe and created the myth of a southern paradise.

In 1827 Dumont d'Urville sailed the Pacific searching for his lost countryman, the Comte de La Pérouse, who had sunk in the Solomon Islands in 1788. D'Urville's writings of this and another journey (ten years later) were to establish the concept of the three great subdivisions of the Pacific: Melanesia, Micronesia and Polynesia.

Missionaries

After a few largely unsuccessful Spanish Catholic forays into Micronesia during the 17th century, the first major attempt to bring Christianity to the Pacific was by English Protestants. Horrified – and inspired – by tales of cannibalism, human sacrifice, promiscuity and infanticide, the newly formed London Missionary Society (LMS) outfitted

Captain James Cook

If aliens ever visit earth, they may wonder what to make of the countless obelisks, faded plaques, and graffiti-covered statues of a stiff, wigged figure gazing out to sea from Alaska to Australia, from New Zealand to North Yorkshire, from Siberia to the South Pacific. James Cook (1728–79) explored more of the earth's surface than anyone in history, and it's impossible to travel the Pacific without encountering the captain's image and his controversial legacy in the lands he opened to the West.

For a man who travelled so widely, and rose to such fame, Cook came from an extremely pinched and provincial background. The son of a day labourer in rural Yorkshire, he was born in a mud cottage, had little schooling, and seemed destined for farm work – and for his family's grave plot in a village churchyard. Instead, Cook went to sea as a teenager, worked his way up from coal-ship servant to naval officer, and attracted notice for his exceptional charts of Canada. But Cook remained a little-known second lieutenant until, in 1768, the Royal Navy chose him to command a daring voyage to the South Seas.

In a converted coal ship called *Endeavour*, Cook sailed to Tahiti, then became the first European to land at New Zealand and the east coast of Australia. Though the ship almost sank after striking the Great Barrier Reef, and 40% of the crew died from disease and accidents, the *Endeavour* limped home in 1771 with eye-opening reports on curiosities including erotic Tahitian dances and, from Australia, a leaping, pouched quadruped so difficult for Europeans to classify that Cook's botanist called it an 'eighty-pound mouse'.

On a return voyage (1772–75), Cook became the first navigator to pierce the Antarctic Circle and circled the globe near its southernmost latitude, demolishing the ancient myth that a vast, populous, and fertile continent surrounded the South Pole. Cook also crisscrossed the Pacific from Easter Island to Melanesia, charting dozens of islands between. Though Maori killed and cooked ten sailors, the captain remained strikingly sympathetic to islanders. 'Notwithstanding they are cannibals,' he wrote, 'they are naturally of a good disposition'.

On Cook's final voyage (1776–79), in search of a Northwest Passage between the Atlantic and Pacific, he became the first European to visit Hawai'i, and coasted America from Oregon to Alaska. Forced back by Arctic pack ice, Cook returned to Hawai'i, where he was killed during a skirmish with islanders who had initially greeted him as Polynesian god. In a single decade of discovery, Cook had filled in the map of the Pacific and, as one French navigator put it, 'left his successors with little to do but admire his exploits'.

Cook's legacy extends far beyond his Pacific charts, some of them so accurate that they remained in use until the 1990s. His sails were the first true voyages of scientific discovery, aboard ships filled with trained observers: artists, astronomers, botanists – even poets. Their detailed observations helped lay the foundation for modern disciplines such as anthropology and museum science, and inspired Western writers and artists to romanticize the South Pacific as an innocent paradise. The plant and animal specimens Cook's men collected also revolutionized Western understanding of nature, seeding the notion of biodiversity and blazing a trail for Charles Darwin's voyage on the *Beagle*.

But Cook's travels also spurred colonisation of the Pacific, and within a few decades of his death, missionaries, whalers, traders and settlers began transforming – and often devastating-island cultures. As a result, many indigenous people now revile Cook as an imperialist villain who introduced disease, dispossession and other ills to the Pacific (hence the frequent vandalizing of Cook monuments). However, as islanders revive traditional crafts and practices, from tattooing to tapa, they have turned to the art and writing of Cook and his men as a resource for cultural renewal. For good and ill, a Yorkshire farm boy remains the single most significant figure in the shaping of the modern Pacific.

Tony Horwitz

Tony Horwitz is a Pulitzer-winning reporter and non-fiction author. In researching Blue Latitudes (or Into the Blue), Tony travelled the Pacific – 'boldly going where Captain Cook has gone before'.

missionary outposts on Tahiti and Tonga, and in the Marquesas in 1797. These first holy crusades were no roaring success – within two years the Tongan and Marquesan missions were abandoned. The Tahitian mission did survive but its success was limited. For a decade only a handful of islanders were tempted to join the new religion.

Other Protestant groups soon joined the battle. The new players were the Wesleyan Missionary Society (WMS), fresh from moderate victory in New Zealand, and the American Board of Commissioners for Foreign Missions (ABCFM), following great success in Christianising Hawaii. The WMS and ABCFM both failed miserably in the Marquesas, but fared marginally better in Tonga.

In the 1830s, French Catholic missions were established in the Marquesas and on Tahiti. Catholic missionaries were often as pleased to convert a Protestant as a heathen, and the fierce rivalry between the different denominations extended to their islander converts. Religious conflicts fitted easily into the already complex political melee of Pacific society, and local chiefs gleefully used the two Christian camps for their own purposes.

Despite the slow start, missionary success grew. By the 1820s missionary influence on Tahiti was enormous. The Bible was translated into Tahitian, a Protestant work ethic was being instilled, tattooing was discouraged, promiscuity was guarded against by nightly 'moral police' and the most 'heathen' practices such as human sacrifice were unknown. From Tahiti, Tonga and Hawaii, Christianity spread throughout the Pacific.

Missionaries' success was due to three major factors. Clever politics played a part, particularly the conversion of influential Tongan chief Taufa'ahau and the Tahitian Pomare family. Another factor was the perceived link between European wealth and Christianity: missionaries sought to 'civilise' as well as Christianise, and islanders desired European tools and skills. Finally, the message of salvation fell on especially attentive ears because of the massive depopulation occurring through the spread of disease.

Two rather remarkable missionaries had enormous influence on the Christianisation of the region: the 'plodding and laborious' John Thomas (WMS), who arrived in Tonga in 1826, and the extraordinary John Williams (LMS), who travelled between many islands from 1818 until his death in Vanuatu in 1839. Many Polynesian converts also took up missionary work themselves.

Missionaries changed the Pacific forever. While traditional culture was devastated and customs such as tattooing banned, human sacrifice and ritual warfare – ancient traditions about which it is harder to be nostalgic – were also curtailed. Missionaries shielded islanders from the excesses of some traders, and it was missionary pressure that finally put an end to the blackbirding trade (see later in this section). Putting Pacific languages into written form, initially in translations of the Bible, was another major contribution. While many missionaries deliberately destroyed 'heathen' Pacific artefacts and beliefs, others diligently recorded myths and oral traditions that would otherwise have been lost. A substantial portion of our knowledge of Pacific history and traditional culture comes from the work of missionary-historians.

Manoeuvrings by missionaries and islanders alike resulted in substantial political changes. Ruling dynasties in Tonga, Tahiti and Fiji all owed some of their success to missionary backing – just as missionary success owed a lot to those dynasties.

Trade

Whaling European whalers enthusiastically hunted in the Pacific from the late 18th century. The trade peaked in the mid-19th century, then declined rapidly as whale products were superseded by other materials. The effect on the Pacific's whale population was catastrophic, but the effect on Pacific islanders was complex. There were opportunities for trade as ships resupplied, and many Pacific islanders took the opportunity to travel on whaling ships. Some islanders, however, were forced to travel without consent, and conflict was common; whalers of the Pacific were not the most gentle of men.

Bêches-de-Mer Also known as trepang, sea cucumbers or sea slugs, the bêche-de-mer is a marine organism related to starfish and urchins. An Asian delicacy, Pacific bêches-de-mer were sought by early 19th century European traders to exchange for Chinese tea. Bêches-de-mer were relatively abundant, and important trading relations were forged with islanders. For the most part the trade was mutually beneficial, with islanders trading eagerly for metal, cloth, tobacco and muskets. The trade in bêches-de-mer was largely non-violent, in contrast with the sandalwood trade.

Sandalwood Nineteenth-century Europeans trading with China found another Pacific resource in fragrant sandalwood, used in China for ornamental carving and cabinet-making, as well as for burning as incense. By the 1820s traders had stripped the sandalwood forests of Hawaii, and forests on islands to the south were sought. Extensive sandalwood forests on Fiji, Vanuatu, the Solomons and New Caledonia became the focus for traders keen to satisfy the demands of the Chinese market.

On each new island, payment for sandalwood was initially low. A small piece of metal, a goat or a dog was sometimes sufficient to buy a boatload of the aromatic wood. But as the supply of slow-growing sandalwood dwindled, the price rose – islanders demanded guns, ammunition, tobacco or assistance in war as payment.

While the sandalwood trade in Fiji was fairly orderly under the supervision of local chiefs, spheres of chiefly influence in the Solomons, Vanuatu and New Caledonia were much smaller and traders had difficultly establishing lasting relationships with islanders. The sandalwood trade was the most violent of any trades in the Pacific, and the Melanesians' savage reputation in Europe was not improved. There were many attacks on ships' crews, sometimes motivated by a greed for plunder, but often these attacks were a response to previous white atrocities. Melanesians assumed that all Europeans belonged to the one kin-group, and thus were accountable for one-another's crimes.

The sandalwood trade was far from sustainable. Island after island was stripped of its forests, and the trade petered out in the 1860s with the removal of the last accessible stands.

Blackbirding

In the late 19th century, cheap labour was sought for various Pacific industries such as mines and plantations. Pacific islanders were also 'recruited' to labour in Australia, Fiji, New Caledonia, Samoa and Peru. Satisfying the demand for labour was a major commercial activity from the 1860s.

In some cases islanders were keen to sign up, seeking to share the benefits of European wealth. Often, though, islanders were tricked into boarding ships, either being deceived about the length of time for which they were contracted, or sometimes enticed aboard by sailors dressed as priests. In many cases no pretence was attempted: islanders were simply herded onto slaving ships at gunpoint.

The populations of many small, barely viable islands were devastated by blackbirders – Tokelau lost almost half its population to Peruvian slaving ships in 1863, while the Tongan island of 'Ata lost 40% of its population, and as a result is today uninhabited. People were also taken as slaves from Tuvalu, New Caledonia, Easter Island, Vanuatu and the Solomons.

Similar recruitment practices – trickery and deceit – were common when Indian labourers were transported to Fiji in the 1870s.

Blackbirding was finally halted at the end of the 19th century after persistent lobbying by missionaries. Their campaigns in the UK and Australia resulted in the banning of overseas-labour recruitment to Australia (in 1904), Samoa (in 1913) and Fiji (in 1916). Some islanders were restored to their homelands but many never returned. A sizeable Melanesian population remains in Australia's Queensland, and there is a huge Indian population in Fiji.

Epidemics & Depopulation

A population of a certain size is required for a contagious disease to establish itself. For the most part, Pacific islands lacked that population. The larger landmasses of Melanesia had (and still have) malaria, but the smaller islands of Polynesia knew only mild outbreaks of leprosy and filariasis (a form of elephantiasis).

The squalid cities of 17th-century Europe bred diseases (and resistant survivors) rather more effectively. The infection-ridden vessels of explorers, missionaries and traders brought diseases to which the peoples of the Pacific had little or no resistance: cholera, measles, smallpox, influenza, pneumonia, scarlet fever, chicken-pox, whooping cough, dysentery, venereal diseases and even the common cold all took a terrible toll on islanders.

Almost all Polynesian populations fell by at least half, while Melanesia's population suffered even more. Some of the islands of Vanuatu dropped to just 5% of their previous numbers.

Most recently, the post-WWI influenza epidemic of 1918 to 1919 devastated Tonga (killing 8% of the population), Fiji (5%) and Western Samoa, where 22% of the population died within a few months.

European Colonialism

Once European traders were established in the Pacific, many began agitating for their home countries to intervene and protect their interests. Some missionaries also lobbied for colonial takeover, hoping that European law would protect islanders from the lawless traders! Gradually, and sometimes reluctantly, European powers acted by declaring protectorates and then by annexing Pacific states.

Germany, one country which was *not* reluctant, annexed the northern Solomons and Western Samoa, along with parts of Micronesia, between 1878 and 1899. The treaty that gave Germany Western Samoa in 1899 ceded American Samoa to the US.

After annexing French Polynesia (1840s) and New Caledonia (1853), the French lost interest for a while before claiming Wallis & Futuna (1880s) and going into partnership with the UK in Vanuatu in 1906.

Contrary to popular opinion, Britain was a reluctant Pacific-empire builder. However, it ended up with the largest of all Pacific empires after being forced by various lobby groups to assume responsibilities for the Phoenix Islands in 1836, then Fiji, Tokelau, the Cooks, the Gilbert & Ellice Islands (modern Kiribati and Tuvalu), the southern Solomons and Niue between 1874 and 1900, and finally Vanuatu in 1906. Between 1900 and 1925, the UK happily offloaded the Cooks, Niue and Tokelau to eager New Zealand.

WWI & WWII

WWI had little effect in the Pacific, except to exchange German colonial rulers in Samoa for New Zealand rulers. Germany was more concerned with events in Europe and didn't resist this Pacific takeover.

In contrast, the Pacific was a major arena of conflict during WWII. The war with Japan was fought through the Micronesian territory Japan had won from Germany in WWI, in Papua New Guinea (PNG) and in the Solomon Islands.

Japan expanded south and southwest from its Micronesian territories almost unhindered until 1942, when it was turned back from PNG at the Battle of the Coral Sea and in the north Pacific at the Battle of Midway. From 1944 the US pushed the stubbornly defending Japanese back island by island – eventually right back to Japan. On 6 August 1945, the *Enola Gay* took off from Tinian in nearby Micronesia to drop an atomic bomb on Hiroshima. Days later another was dropped on Nagasaki, and the Pacific war was over.

Not surprisingly, the suffering of islanders during the Pacific war was immense. People were concentrated in areas without adequate food, thousands died from hunger and thousands more were executed by the Japanese as an Allied victory became apparent. It is difficult to establish the frequency of rape of islanders by both Japanese and Allied forces.

Many Pacific islanders participated in the war, fighting in the Pacific, Africa and Europe. Soldiers from Fiji, the Solomons, Western and American Samoa, Tonga, French Polynesia and New Caledonia served in the armed forces. Their valour cemented relations with white allies. Fijian Corporal Sefania Sukanaivalu was posthumously awarded the Victoria Cross in 1943.

WWII had a lasting effect on the region. There was a huge improvement in roads and other infrastructure on many islands. There was also an input of money, food and other supplies that contributed towards the development of so-called 'cargo cults' (see Religion later in this chapter).

WWII hastened the end of traditional colonialism in the Pacific, the relative equality between white and black US soldiers prompting islanders to question why they were still subservient to the British and the French. Many independence leaders were influenced by witnessing this more egalitarian group.

Postwar

From Western Samoa in 1962 through to Vanuatu in 1980, most of the Pacific island states gained independence (or partial independence) from their former colonial rulers. This was a relatively bloodless transition, with colonial masters as keen to ditch their expensive responsibilities as islanders were to gain independence. At the end of the 20th century only a handful of South Pacific territories were still in the hands of the US, France, Chile, and New Zealand. See Government & Politics later in this chapter.

GEOGRAPHY

The Pacific Ocean is huge – it covers 165,250,000 sq km (64,500,000 sq miles), which is a third of the world's surface, and is larger than all the Earth's land combined. The thousands of islands of the Pacific, however, have a total land area of less than 1,300,000 sq km – the bulk of which (1,100,000 sq km) is in the relatively massive islands of New Guinea, New Zealand and Hawaii.

The French explorer Dumont d'Urville conveniently divided the Pacific – largely along racial and cultural grounds – into three major subdivisions: Melanesia (Greek for the 'Black Islands'), composed of New Guinea, the Solomons, Vanuatu, New Caledonia and Fiji; Micronesia (Small Islands), the atolls and small islands north and northeast of New Guinea and the Solomons; and Polynesia (Many Islands), the huge triangle of islands bounded by Hawaii, Easter Island and New Zealand. Although the divisions are artificial, it is a useful and relevant partitioning of the Pacific. The characteristics of Polynesia and Melanesia are summarised in the introductions to the supra-chapters in this book.

Three main island types occur in the Pacific: continental, high and low. Large, continental islands exist only in Melanesia and New Zealand. And of the smaller islands, 'high' islands are usually the peaks of volcanoes, whether extinct or active, while 'low' islands are generally formed by coral growth on sinking submarine volcanoes (see the boxed text 'Coral Atolls' later in this chapter and 'How the Islands Formed' in the Tuvalu chapter).

GEOLOGY

The surface of the Earth is composed of seven large tectonic plates and several smaller ones, which float on the planet's molten mantle. The floor of the Pacific Ocean is largely composed of one enormous plate (called the Pacific plate). The much smaller Nazca plate is in the Pacific's southeastern corner.

The boundary between the two plates is an 8000km-long line of submarine volcanoes called a 'constructive fault', running roughly north–south at the longitude of Easter Island. From this fault, newly ejected material adds to the two plates. This pushes the Pacific plate northwest at about 17cm per year, and pushes the Nazca plate southeast.

Where the Pacific's oceanic plates meet neighbouring continental plates, the heavier oceanic plates are forced hundreds of kilometres down into the Earth's molten magma.

Coral Atolls

Submarine volcanoes are common on the ocean floor, and some of them grow above the sea's surface to become islands. Once an island exists, coral begins to grow around its coast. If subsequent plate movement causes the volcano to sink again, the coral continues to grow in order to stay close to the sea's surface (coral requires sunlight and cannot live in water deeper than 40m). As the central island sinks, a fringing lagoon forms between the island and the reef. A coral atoll is formed when the island finally sinks completely, leaving a ring of coral encircling an empty lagoon. The first person to recognise that atolls are made from coral growth built up around the edges of submerged volcanic mountain peaks was Charles Darwin. (See the boxed text 'How the Islands Formed' in the Tuvalu chapter.)

The long conversion of these coral islets to inhabitable islands begins when coral sitting above the sea's surface is broken up by waves, eventually forming a coarse, infertile soil. Seeds blown by the wind, carried by the sea or redistributed in bird droppings can then take root. Initially, only the most hardy of plants, such as coconut trees, can survive in this hostile, barren environment. Once the pioneering coconuts have established a foothold, rotting vegetative matter forms a more hospitable soil for other plants.

The people of the Pacific islands have learned how to eke out an existence from even the smallest of coral atolls. Vegetables brought from other islands, such as taro and *kumara*, supplement what grows naturally, and fish from the seas and the lagoon provide protein. However, atoll populations live a precarious existence. Resources are scarce and atolls are vulnerable to droughts, storms and tsunamis.

A coral atoll lifted entirely above the water's surface by geological activity is known as a *makatea*, after one such island in French Polynesia.

Deep trenches are formed along the seams. Molten, mineral-rich material from the diving plate rises to form volcanic archipelagos. The line where the Pacific plate meets the Indo-Australian plate can be followed north along the island chain of New Zealand to Tonga and Samoa, then northwest through Fiji and the other Melanesian islands.

A glance at a map of the Pacific reveals a number of parallel island chains. These are 'hot spot' volcano chains. Volcanoes form where hot spots exist in the Earth's mantle; then, as the ocean floor moves away to the northwest, these volcanoes become extinct, often sinking beneath the sea. In the Pacific's hot-spot island chains, the youngest, still-active volcanoes are in the southeast and older submarine volcanoes or coral atolls are in the northwest. The Australs in French Polynesia are classic examples of hot-spot island chains.

New volcanoes are constantly being formed – the most visible is Mt Yasur in Vanuatu.

The seismic activity of the area is also manifested in earthquakes and tsunamis, huge walls of water propelled by underwater earthquakes (often incorrectly called tidal waves). Tsunamis can do massive damage to low-lying islands and coastal towns.

CLIMATE

The tropical Pacific islands are humid and air temperatures here are high and generally uniform throughout the year (21°C to 28°C or 70°F to 83°F). The year is divided into a dry season and a wet season. South of the equator, the dry season is from May to October and the wet season (including the cyclone season in some regions) is from November to April. The level of rainfall in the region can vary between isolated showers and seasonal deluges – it's worth packing with rain in mind at any time of year. See Climate in the individual country chapters for specific details. Some Melanesian islands have cool highlands, while Easter Island and Pitcairn are temperate. See the appendix 'Climate Charts' at the back of this book.

Most Pacific islands are well-watered, but some drier regions can experience long droughts. Coral atolls, lacking rivers or streams and with little ground water, are particularly vulnerable to droughts.

In the tropics, air flowing towards the equator is deflected west by the Earth's rotation. Called the trade winds, these winds blow from the southeast in the southern hemisphere, and from the northeast in the northern hemisphere. The climate of islands facing these cool, rain-carrying trade winds changes from one side of the island to the other. Villages and towns on Pacific islands are more likely to be found on the sheltered leeward coast than the cloudier and wetter windward side.

The region where the trade winds meet at the equator gets little or no wind and is referred to as the doldrums. About Christmas time each year the prevailing easterlies of the trade winds weaken, then reverse for a time and blow from the west.

Tropical Cyclones

Called hurricanes in the Atlantic and typhoons in the western Pacific, tropical cyclones are large systems of winds rotating around a centre of low atmospheric pressure. Their winds, which can reach as high as 200km/h, torrential rains and high waves are a hazard to shipping and can cause extensive damage to crops and buildings.

Cyclones can occur at any time but are most common during the wet season, and only form in certain regions. Only Melanesia and western Polynesia are likely to experience cyclones. (However, patterns change with El Niño and La Niña events, and may be affected by global warming.)

It's worth checking for cyclones before you head off on a Pacific holiday, particularly if you're yachting. Try the websites of the **Joint Typhoon Warning Centre Hawai'i** (W *www.npmoc.navy.mil /jtwc.html*) or **Fiji Meteorological Service** (W *www.met.gov.fj*).

The worst year for cyclones in the region was 1996 to 1997, with a grand total of 38. Cyclone Zoe, which hit the Solomon Islands in 2003, was the most powerful cyclone ever recorded in the Pacific.

El Niño

In the tropical Pacific, the prevailing easterly trade winds, driven by the Earth's rotation, normally pile up the warmer surface water towards the western Pacific. The resulting warm water in the west causes more rain in that region, so that the western Pacific (Melanesia, Australia and New Zealand) experiences more rain than the east.

An El Niño (more correctly El Niño Southern Oscillation, or ENSO) event occurs when the annual Christmas-time reversal in wind direction combines with high air pressure in the western Pacific and low air pressure in the east. The self-perpetuating system that is created blows the warm surface water back towards the eastern Pacific.

As the warm water moves east, it carries rain with it. Western Pacific countries experience droughts while eastern islands suffer unusually heavy rains or cyclones. Although El Niño ('The Boy' or 'The Christ Child') develops in the Pacific, its effects are felt as far afield as Africa and India.

An El Niño usually lasts for about a year, and recurs irregularly about every four or five years. Although only recently understood, El Niño is no recent development. Evidence shows that El Niños have occurred for at least hundreds, and probably thousands, of years.

El Niño are often followed by a weaker related event called La Niña ('The Girl'), which reverses El Niño. La Niña brings storms to the western Pacific and droughts to the east.

ECOLOGY & ENVIRONMENT

The most severe ecological danger to the nations of the Pacific is attributed to the developed world (see the boxed text 'Global Warming' later in this chapter). Waste management of litter, from both the islands themselves and from rubbish drifting ashore, is another major concern.

Pacific Patrol Boats

It wasn't just altruism which pushed the big Asian fishing nations into paying tens of millions of dollars annually to some of the Pacific's smallest nations for fishing licences. At one time they simply didn't bother, knowing that these tiny countries didn't have a navy or coastal patrol capable of catching them. That all ended with a clever piece of Australian foreign aid. Between 1987 and 1997 Australia donated 22 patrol boats to 12 different Pacific nations. The islanders provide the crew and look after maintenance and operating costs and these miniature navies have proved highly effective. It only took a few high profile seizures of illegal fishing vessels to convince the fleet owners that paying for those fishing licences made a lot of sense.

Fishing

The Pacific Ocean's commercial fishing fleet catches about half of the world's annual 100 million tonnes of fish. While the ocean's vast size lulls many people into thinking of it as an infinite resource, others claim this catch is unsustainable. Critics point out that despite the ever increasing number of vessels in the world's fishing fleets, their annual catch is decreasing. A UN study, which found that most commercially exploited fisheries were being fished beyond their capacity to recover, said the industry is 'globally non-sustainable' and that 'major ecological and economic damage is already visible'.

If you want to avoid eating fish that are at risk, abstain from swordfish, marlin, southern bluefin tuna (albacore tuna is fine) and gemfish.

It is not only fish caught for consumption that are endangered; fishing fleets worldwide claim a 'bycatch' of almost 30 million tonnes per year. These are unwanted species, such as dolphins, sharks and turtles, that are pulled up along with the target species and then dumped. The infamous drift nets, which are legally limited to 2.5km in length but are often much longer, claim a huge bycatch.

Remnants of drift nets are often found wrapped around dead whales that wash ashore. Nets and lines that have broken loose continue to drift through the oceans, catching and killing as they go. Longlines drifting loose on the surface of the South Pacific have decimated albatross populations, bringing some species near to extinction. Closer to the coast, blast fishing and cyanide fishing – both illegal – kill everything nearby rather than just their target species.

To resource-poor Pacific islands, selling licences to fish their relatively large Exclusive Economic Zones (EEZ) is one of their few economic options. Governments' discussions in the Pacific Island Forum (PIF; see Government & Politics) raise concerns over the sustainability of the fisheries.

Mining

Melanesia's large continental islands are rich in minerals. New Caledonia and Fiji both have extensive mines providing an important income for those countries. (See Economy later in this chapter for further information.)

Global Warming

Since the Industrial Revolution in the 18th century, the concentration of greenhouse gases in the Earth's atmosphere has risen dramatically – particularly carbon dioxide from burning fossil fuels. These gases increase the Earth's natural greenhouse effect, reducing the loss of heat to space and raising the Earth's temperature. The predicted increase in average temperature may seem small – about 4°C in the next 100 years – but this rate of increase is vastly faster than any change in the last 10,000 years.

One of the most obvious effects of global warming will be a rise in sea level from thermal expansion of the oceans and the melting of polar icecaps – a 0.5m to 1m increase in the next 100 years is a conservative estimate. Other important effects are an increase in the severity of storms in some regions, an increase in the frequency of droughts in other areas, and coral bleaching (see Effects).

Although it is difficult to accurately calculate the causes and effects of global warming, there is no longer any doubt that it is occurring. It's accepted that global temperatures are increasing and polar ice breaking up, but claims of increasing storm severity and the exact cause of coral bleaching events are hotly debated. Some claim the Earth's warming is a natural event.

Some people express doubt about the whole issue of global warming and claim the risks are being exaggerated by extreme 'green' movements. However, these dire predictions are sourced from the United Nations Environment Programme, the Intergovernmental Panel on Climate Change, and the South Pacific Regional Environment Programme, and have been accepted by the international insurance community and even British Petroleum – hardly the lunatic left!

Effects

Rising sea levels will cause devastating sea flooding and coastal erosion in many Pacific countries, most disastrously on low-lying coral atolls. However, even on 'high' islands most agriculture, population centres and infrastructure tend to be in low-lying coastal areas. As well as the loss of land, higher seas will increase the effects of storms and cyclones, and the rising seawater table will poison crops and reduce the available fresh groundwater.

It has been found that even small increases in sea temperatures can kill off coral reefs (coral cannot survive in water warmer than 28°C). The first symptom of the process is known as **coral** bleaching, and involves the expulsion of the colourful symbiotic algae that lives within coral. Colourless, dead coral skeletons are left behind, causing the loss of precious fisheries. The absence of a coral reefs will decrease an islands' protection against storms already worsened by the rising sea level.

Freshwater contamination, land erosion, increased storms, lost fisheries and lost agricultural land will make some marginal, resource-poor atolls uninhabitable, forcing the relocation of large numbers of 'greenhouse refugees'.

'High' island countries, such as those in Melanesia, will be able to relocate people and infrastructure inland, although at enormous financial cost. Countries with both high and low islands, such as the Cook Islands, can relocate atoll dwellers to the higher islands. People in countries composed only of atolls and low-lying islands, such as Tuvalu, will have no choice but to emigrate entirely to other countries – risking the extinction of their unique cultures. These countries may not survive the next century.

Ironically, the developed Pacific rim countries that will probably bear the brunt of relocation (the US, Canada, Australia and New Zealand) are among the world's worst producers of greenhouse gasses per capita.

Deforestation

Rapa Nui (Easter Island) led the world in its efforts of deforestation a thousand years before Magellan sailed into the Pacific. The resources put into the famous statues of Easter Island turned the island into a desolate wasteland.

In modern times, many South Pacific countries are sacrificing long-term viability for short-term gains by intensive logging. Condoned by Pacific governments with few economic options, logging is often undertaken by offshore companies with few long-term interests in the island. Only the larger islands, such as the Solomons, Vanuatu, New Caledonia, Fiji and Samoa, have sufficient forestry reserves to hold the interest of such companies. However, even small-scale logging on the smaller islands can have a devastating effect.

As well as the loss of habitat for native birds and animals, the effects of deforestation include massive soil loss, particularly serious on small coral islands, such as Niue, which have never had good soil quality. Increased runoff from deforested land can lead to pollution of vital waterways and muddying of coastal waters can severely retard the growth of coral.

Nuclear Issues

The Pacific Ocean has seen more than its fair share of nuclear explosions. The world's only hostile use of nuclear weapons, on Hiroshima and Nagasaki in 1945, were launched from the Northern Marianas, in nearby Micronesia. Subsequently, US nuclear tests were conducted here.

The nuclear testing issue loomed large at the first meeting of the South Pacific Forum (SPF, now PIF) in 1971. The French certainly didn't reduce anti-nuclear sentiment in 1985, when they sank Greenpeace's *Rainbow Warrior* in Auckland's Waitemata Harbour, killing photographer Fernando Pereira. In 1986, the SPF's Treaty of Rarotonga established the South Pacific Nuclear-Free Zone, banning nuclear weapons and the dumping of nuclear waste. This was ratified ten years later by the nuclear powers France, the US and the UK.

France's Pacific nuclear testing programme commenced with atmospheric tests in 1966 at Mururoa and Fangataufa in French Polynesia. Their early atmospheric tests caused measurable increases in radiation in several Pacific countries – as far away as Fiji, 4500km to the west. Atmospheric testing was abandoned in 1974 under severe international pressure, but underground tests (totalling 127 on Mururoa and 10 on Fangataufa) continued until 1996, when France signed the comprehensive Test Ban Treaty.

The effects of atmospheric nuclear testing, which ceased in 1970, have rendered Rongelap and Bikini uninhabitable (although short-term visits are fine); their people live in unhappy exile on neighbouring islands. Fragile coral atolls were always a questionable place to detonate underground nuclear weapons, and the French have confirmed the appearance of cracks in the coral structure of

Mururoa and Fangataufa atolls, and leakage of plutonium at Mururoa. The effect of large amounts of radioactive material leaking into the Pacific Ocean would be catastrophic and far-reaching. Claims of high rates of birth defects and cancer on neighbouring islands are denied by the French, and are impossible to confirm because of the secrecy attached to government health records.

FLORA & FAUNA

Most species of vegetation and wildlife in the Pacific islands have historically moved across the ocean from west to east. This is confirmed by the reduction of numbers of species from the western to the eastern Pacific. In part the spread of flora was a natural process, with seeds and fruits borne across the sea by winds, in bird droppings and by ocean currents. But early Pacific settlers also deliberately carried with them many plants such as kava, coconut, breadfruit and taro.

Taro is the most important crop of many islands in the Pacific, and both its spinach-like leaves and the starchy corns are used as staple foods. The plantain also features in the diet of many Pacific islanders – the bananas are picked when green and cooked as a vegetable. Almost every part of the pandanus plant was used – providing food and medicine, and materials for housing, clothing, fishing and religious uses.

The higher islands (Samoa and Melanesia) have a greater diversity in flora and fauna. Smaller coral atolls and low islands, on the other hand, can be almost desolate.

Flora

Coconut If there is a symbol of the Pacific islands, it is the coconut tree. The coconut *(Cocos nucifera)* originated in Southeast Asia and its migration across the Pacific was probably a mixture of natural processes (coconut fruit floats freely) and deliberate introduction by ancient settlers.

Without the coconut tree many small Pacific atolls and islands would never have become inhabitable. Coconuts are tolerant of sandy soils and are the only large tree that will grow on a sandy atoll islet without human assistance. The plant broke the ground for later vegetation on many small coral atolls.

Coconuts historically provided drinking water for long ocean voyages, and the tree's wood was the main building material used for voyaging canoes. On land they were vital for

Facts about the South Pacific – Flora & Fauna 29

house and roofing materials, and the fibres were used for rope, weaving and fire-making. The coconut is still economically important to many Pacific countries, providing income from sales of crude oil, coconut cream and copra. A further use of the coconut in Polynesia can be seen whenever a group of boys or young men find themselves lacking a ball and wanting a quick game of rugby.

Kumara While most Pacific vegetables and trees originated in the west and migrated east, the *kumara (kumala* or *'umala)* or sweet potato originated in South America – it is known as *kumar* in Peru.

The east-to-west movement of the *kumara* was a foundation of the alternative theory that the Pacific was settled from the Americas. That theory quickly fell into disfavour as the bulk of other evidence mounted towards the west-to-east migration (see History earlier). It's now believed that the *kumara* was introduced to the Pacific by Polynesians, probably Marquesans, voyaging to South America. From the Marquesas it was carried westwards, reaching western Polynesia fairly quickly and Melanesia by the 16th century.

The *kumara* revolutionary effect on Pacific communities was enormous; it is easy to grow in tropical climates and to transport by canoe.

Fauna

Apart from possums in the Solomons, the flying fox, or fruit bat, is the only land mammal to make its own way to the Pacific islands. The domestic chicken, dog and pig were introduced on the canoes of settlers thousands of years ago. Since European contact, other introduced animals include cattle, horses, sheep, goats, dogs and cats.

Stowaways on voyaging canoes included the Polynesian rat and the geckos (small lizards) that are now ubiquitous in the region – that flicker of movement on the bedroom wall may not be a trick of the kava, it may be a lizard keeping the mosquito population under control. Apart from the geckos, land reptiles are confined to a few snakes and monitor lizards in western Melanesia. The Solomon Islands and Vanuatu have saltwater and freshwater crocodiles. Adult saltwater crocs can exceed 4m in length and have been known to supplement their fish diet with humans.

Birdlife is dominated by migratory seabirds. One of the more interesting bird types is the megapode; see the boxed text 'Megapodes' in the Solomon Islands chapter.

Domestic Animals As settlers moved into the Pacific, they were careful to bring domesticated dogs, chickens and pigs with them. As ready sources of protein, many of them probably did not survive the voyage, but enough arrived to spread the three species across the Pacific.

These animals were widespread by the time Europeans arrived, although on many islands one or more of the domestic trio was missing: only chickens made it to Easter Island and only dogs to New Zealand. Chickens, dogs and pigs were reserved for feasting in most societies.

Wild chickens still roam and forage throughout the Pacific islands and the pig now holds an important role in many Melanesian rituals. (See The Nimangki under Society in the Vanuatu chapter.) The Pacific dog, however, was wiped out by interbreeding and competition from European dog species.

The introduction of dogs and rats, as well as humans, had a major environmental impact on isolated islands. Birds that previously had no natural predators now contended with several. In many cases, extinction was the result. The later introduction of cats, very efficient killing machines, caused even more extinctions.

Marine Life Many thousands of species of fish live in the Pacific Ocean. It's impossible to describe here every species you might encounter; some guides to the marine life of the Pacific are listed under Books in the Regional Facts for the Visitor chapter. Also in that chapter, see the boxed text 'Venomous Marinelife' and Swimming under Dangers & Annoyances in the Regional Facts for the Visitor chapter for a few fish you might want to avoid.

Mammals Whales were plentiful in the Pacific until the arrival of whaling fleets in the 18th century. Their numbers are recovering, although this has been slowed by the continuing Japanese and Norwegian whaling industries. Attempts to establish a South Pacific whale sanctuary, in order to protect whales as they migrate through Pacific waters to mate and rear their young, continue despite strong opposition, and not only from the whaling nations. Pacific island countries such as the Solomon Islands are wary of a whale sanctuary, which would cut off whaling licences as a prospective source of income. In many Pacific countries, whale-watching tours are a win-win alternative (see the boxed text 'The Whale Debates' in the Tonga chapter).

Dolphins abound, and follow ships in the Pacific with the same enthusiasm they show elsewhere in the world. The source of the mermaid myth (those sea journeys must have been long indeed), the dugong, or sea cow, thrives in the western Pacific.

Reptiles Sea turtles (including hawksbills, green turtles and leatherbacks) are endangered species which inhabit Pacific waters. They've been an important native food for centuries, and both turtles and their eggs are still occasionally eaten, particularly on more remote islands.

Colourful sea snakes, highly venomous but non-aggressive, are common throughout the Pacific.

Coral Although coral looks and behaves like a plant, it's actually a tiny primitive carnivorous animal. Coral reefs are made up of millions of tiny rock-like limestone structures, which are coral skeletons. Coral draws calcium from the water, then excretes it to form a hardened shell to protect its soft body. As coral polyps reproduce and die, new polyps attach themselves in successive layers to the empty skeletons already in place. In this way, a coral reef grows by about 15cm per year. Only the outer layer of coral is alive; algae lives in a symbiotic relationship within the coral's tissue and gives it colour. So not only is it environmental vandalism to pluck vivid coral from the ocean, it's futile because it loses its colour when dead.

Coral is a fussy wee beast. It requires waters between 21°C and 28°C, and the algae needs abundant sunlight, so the water must be mud-free and relatively shallow (less than 40m). Coral reefs form in three ways: as a fringing reef close to the land, as a barrier reef separated from the land by a stretch of water, and as a coral atoll (see the boxed text 'Coral Atoll' earlier in this chapter). Coral reefs support throngs of fish and other marine life, and are one of the most biodiverse habitats found on earth. Thus, of course, they make excellent fishing grounds.

Corals catch their prey by means of stinging nematocysts (a specialised type of cell). Some corals can give humans a painful sting when touched. Despite the seemingly robust nature of many types, all corals are fragile and can be damaged by the gentlest touch. Take care to stay well back from coral

growths when diving or snorkelling on the reefs (see the boxed text 'Responsible Diving' in the South Pacific Diving special section), and avoid reef walking.

See the 'Global Warming' boxed text, earlier, for a discussion of coral bleaching.

National Parks

Parks and reserves are listed under individual country chapters. There are three Unesco-listed World Heritage Sites in the South Pacific: East Rennell Island (Solomons), Henderson Island (near Pitcairn) and the Parque Nacional Rapa Nui (Easter Island). With Rennell Island a stepping stone to the Lapita people's settlement of the Pacific, and Henderson and Easter among the last islands to be settled, these sites have important anthropological as well as ecological significance.

GOVERNMENT & POLITICS

After the rash of independence that broke out in the Pacific between 1962 and 1980 (see Postwar under History earlier in this chapter), Pacific island states largely adopted the British model of parliamentary government, incorporating varying degrees of traditional customs and hierarchies. Conflicts between traditional authorities (chiefs) and modern, elected officials are common.

One of the most traditional systems of government is that of Tonga. The Tongan royal family, descended from a chiefly line that is hundreds of years old, wields enormous power over that country's parliament. In Samoa, only *matai* (village elders) can be elected into parliament. In Fiji and Vanuatu, councils of chiefs have important roles in advising central government. In other countries, traditional chiefs wield their power at local government level. Even now, Pacific island politics are to a large degree dependent on kinship, family and *wantok* ties (see the boxed text 'The Wantok System' in the Solomon Islands chapter).

The representation of women in Pacific governments is minimal, except at a local government level. The situation is slightly better in Polynesia.

The only 'foreign' countries still administering or claiming South Pacific territories are Chile (Easter Island), France (French Polynesia, New Caledonia and Wallis & Futuna) and New Zealand (Tokelau). NZ also has some responsibilities for defence and foreign policy with Niue and the Cook Islands.

There is little agitation in Chile's Easter Island towards independence, while Tokelau is moving slowly but surely towards autonomy. In French Polynesia and New Caledonia, calls for more independence are finally being addressed by the French government. See History and Government & Politics in the New Caledonia chapter.

Secretariat of the Pacific Community (SPC)
The Secretariat of the Pacific Community, formerly the South Pacific Commission, was established in 1947 by the region's colonial powers to ensure the stability of the island nations and territories. Island governments became frustrated by colonial powers, particularly France's blocking of discussion of the nuclear testing issue, and formed the South Pacific Forum (SPF) in 1971. With the establishment of the SPF (now PIF, see following), the SPC was reduced to the role of an information agency, providing technical assistance, advice and training.

Pacific Island Forum (PIF)
Founded in 1971 (see the SPC entry), the PIF's 16 members are the heads of state of all the independent Pacific island countries, plus Australia and New Zealand. Unlike under the SPC, the UK, the US, France and France's Pacific colonies are not members, though New Caledonia has observer status because of its increasing autonomy.

Headquartered in Suva, the PIF meets annually to address issues of mutual interest, including environmental and social concerns, emergency relief and the status of Pacific territories remaining under colonial administration. Forum leaders signed the Treaty of Rarotonga in 1986, establishing the South Pacific Nuclear-Free Zone. Since the late 1980s the PIF has been lobbying the world's governments on the hazard posed to Pacific nations by global warming (see the 'Global Warming' boxed text earlier in this chapter). Unfortunately, Australia restrains these discussions just as France once blocked the SPC's efforts to discuss nuclear testing.

ECONOMY
The gross domestic product (GDP) per capita in Pacific countries varies widely, from as high as US$12,830 in New Caledonia and French Polynesia, to about US$1300 in Tuvalu and NZ$1000 (US$600) in Tokelau. In countries where foreign aid forms a

significant part of the economy, GDP is a poor indicator of the relative wealth of the people (eg, in Tokelau, where its NZ$4 million in annual aid is substantially greater than GDP).

Some of the larger Melanesian nations – Vanuatu, New Caledonia and Fiji – are in relatively strong economic positions. Rich in mineral resources, they have large areas available for agriculture and large Exclusive Economic Zones (EEZs) for fisheries. Their wide range of industries include forestry, agriculture, minerals, tourism and selling fishing rights.

At the other end of the scale, tiny Tuvalu has few resources and lacks the infrastructure to fully exploit their EEZs or tourism. Industry in such countries is largely subsistence agriculture and fishing.

The Solomon Islands is on the edge of bankruptcy and is being kept afloat by foreign aid. An armed coup in 2000 and subsequent ethnic tension caused many businesses to leave the country and few have returned. Inept and corrupt government is another major factor in the country's decline (for further information see the History section in the Solomon Islands' chapter).

Small Pacific island economies are particularly vulnerable to external influences, such as financial crises in other countries and particularly severe El Niño weather patterns. Individual islands can take years to recover from droughts, cyclones or tsunamis.

Agriculture
Although not as important as it has been historically, agriculture still forms a large part of all Pacific economies. This ranges from subsistence-level agriculture on the smaller islands to large scale growth of cocoa, vanilla, taro, kava and coconuts. The all-important coconut is vital to small (and some large) Pacific economies, forming a substantial proportion of export earnings from oil, cream and copra.

Fishing
In addition to feeding their own population, the relatively large EEZs of small Pacific nations provide an income from the licensing of international fishing fleets – about US$50 million per year. The importance of fisheries as a source of both food and income, makes it vital to ensure that they are managed in a sustainable manner; see Ecology & Environment earlier in this chapter.

Mining

The only long-term mining industries in the Pacific are in the larger Melanesian countries: New Caledonia (mostly nickel) and Fiji (gold), and there are some undeveloped mineral deposits in the Solomons.

On the Pacific sea bed, enormous deposits of minerals, including manganese, copper and nickel, have been discovered. However, the technology required to mine these deposits has not yet been developed.

Tourism

Tourism is a significant industry in many South Pacific countries. Tourism figures to the South Pacific islands topped 1.02 million in 1999. Significant tourist origins are the US, Australia, Korea, New Zealand and France. The most popular destinations are Fiji (410,000) and French Polynesia (218,800).

Tourism has many attractions for Pacific governments. Properly managed, it is sustainable, unlike logging or mining, and generates significant employment; over 20% of jobs in Fiji are generated by tourism. On the downside, interaction with affluent Western tourists introduces new social stresses, and tourism increases vulnerability to overseas economies. If not properly managed, tourism can also have severe environmental effects.

Aid & Remittances

In many South Pacific countries, trade imbalances are compensated for by foreign aid. It is difficult to put a figure on the amount paid: the definition of aid is nebulous, and the amount paid varies each year depending on needs in the Pacific and politics in the donor country. However, the South Pacific region receives the world's highest aid payments per capita – about US$200 per annum on average, and over US$1395 in some territories. The money is unevenly distributed; major donors are New Zealand (mostly to those Polynesian states with which it has historical links) and Australia (to PNG). The European Union, and organisations such as the UN and the PIF, provide development and emergency funds.

Many Pacific island emigrants living in the US, New Zealand and Australia, motivated by a strong family commitment, send a proportion of their earnings back home. Some Pacific countries depend heavily on these remittances.

Financial Miscellanea

Several Pacific islands have branched into 'financial services'. Vanuatu, the Cook Islands and Samoa offer tax havens for overseas businesses.

A handful of Pacific islands received something of a windfall with the popularity of the Internet. Countries that have profited from the sales of their top level domain (the last two letters in a URL or email address) include Niue (.nu), Tonga (.to) and Tuvalu (.tv). See the boxed text 'Dot tv' in the Tuvalu chapter.

In very small economies, such as those of Pitcairn or Tokelau, items such as handicrafts can form a significant proportion of the economy. Small, obscure countries have been able to profit from their own obscurity by the sales of postage stamps and coinage.

The public service is the major employer on many Pacific islands; such a large public service is often only made possible by foreign aid.

POPULATION & PEOPLE

The population of the South Pacific islands is around 1.9 million (1.4 million people in Melanesia and 500,000 Polynesia). Individual country populations range from Fiji at 856,000 to Pitcairn at 50.

Most populations are coastal – a trend that began in the 18th century when people migrated to coastal areas for easier access to trade with Europeans. Populations are also increasingly concentrated on one island or in one main town. Melanesian countries have the highest proportion of rural dwellers, eg, 80% in Vanuatu.

Pacific islanders have always been travellers, and a large number of them live abroad. About 15% of Pacific islanders live in other countries around the Pacific rim, in New Zealand (210,000), mainland US (154,000), and Australia (65,000). In many island nations, emigration relieves population pressure, but in some there is a net population loss; almost 90% of ethnic Niueans now live in New Zealand.

Islanders living abroad do their best to maintain both their community and language, and to maintain contact with family on their home island. The traffic between Pacific islands and developed nations, with islanders visiting overseas family as well as families getting an 'island fix', speeds the spread of Western influences through Pacific societies.

A group of *moai*, Ahu Akivi, Easter Island

Tahitian headdress

Rapa Nui man and child, Easter Island

The Mamanuca group, Fiji

Marovo Lagoon, Solomon Islands

Mt Yasur volcano, Tanna, Vanuatu

EDUCATION

Literacy rates in the South Pacific are high – above 90% in most countries, though hovering around 50% in countries such as the Solomon Islands, Vanuatu and Tuvalu.

University of the South Pacific (USP)

Established in 1968, the USP is jointly owned by 12 countries: the Cook Islands, Fiji, Kiribati, Marshall Islands, Nauru, Niue, Solomon Islands, Tokelau, Tonga, Tuvalu, Vanuatu and Samoa. The university is based in Suva, Fiji, with campuses in Vanuatu (law) and Samoa (agriculture); courses are taken either on campus or via satellite. Students also study humanities, science and economics. Learning in any particular discipline includes an emphasis on the Pacific region.

ARTS

The Pacific's premier cultural gathering is the Festival of Pacific Arts, where arts and crafts of all kinds, including dance, song, weaving and carving, are celebrated. Held every four years in a different country, the festival attracts large numbers of tourists from outside the region. See Special Events in the Regional Facts for the Visitor chapter.

Western artists influenced by the Pacific include Paul Gauguin, who lived in French Polynesia between 1890 and 1903. For information on the artist and his style, see the boxed text 'Paul Gauguin' in the Tahiti & French Polynesia chapter.

Object-based arts, such as sculpture, and information about common themes in Pacific arts are covered in the 'South Pacific Arts' special section.

Dance & Song

Traditional dance is still strong across the Pacific. The expectation of many tourists to see something like the Hawaiian hula has persuaded many islanders to adopt that familiar sway and wobble, but dancing for tourists also provides the young with a strong financial incentive to learn the ancient skill. Dances may be performed by groups or by individuals; group dancing is more common at large village ceremonies.

One of the most successful contemporary bands incorporating a Pacific feel into their songs recently has been the Tokelauan group Te Vaka, who are based in New Zealand but tour internationally (see W www .tevaka.com).

Literature

Pacific island authors are listed in the Institute of Pacific Studies' *South Pacific Literature – From Myth to Fabulation*. Contemporary Pacific island authors are listed under Books in the Facts for the Visitor sections of individual country chapters. Probably the most successful is the Samoan writer Albert Wendt.

Many 19th-century European authors were inspired to write about the Pacific islands. Among them James Michener and Jack London (see Books in the Regional Facts for the Visitor chapter). Other authors were moved enough to relocate to the islands themselves, either temporarily or permanently. Among them Robert Louis Stevenson, in Samoa. See that country's chapter for more information.

SOCIETY

Although the phrase *faka Pasifika* has been used to describe a Pacific culture, there are more differences between Pacific cultures than there are similarities. However, some common features resonate in both Melanesian and Polynesian cultures.

Traditional Culture

A huge diversity of cultures had evolved across the Pacific by the time of contact with Europeans. Not surprisingly, considering the poor resources of their island homes, Pacific islanders remained in a Stone-Age culture – it's difficult to run an iron foundry on a coral atoll. In the absence of metal tools, voyaging canoes, houses and artwork were fashioned largely with stone tools.

Only the design of ocean-going craft and navigation skills attained a high degree of scientific rigour (see the boxed text 'Voyaging & Navigation' earlier in this chapter). In the absence of modern technology, emphasis shifted to refining oral skills and cultural systems, creating rich mythologies and intricate cultural rules.

The status of women in traditional and modern Pacific societies seems to improve as you move east. In eastern Polynesia, chiefly titles are almost as likely to be held by women as by men, but there are very few female chiefs in the central Pacific, and almost none in Melanesia.

While European contact irreversibly changed the cultures of the Pacific, it did not lead to a complete loss of culture. Many traditional elements continue to be practised, or else they have been rejigged to accommodate the modern world of the Pacific.

Melanesia The remarkable cultural and linguistic diversity of Melanesia is partly a product of the region's many thousands of years of settlement. This has been attenuated by the rugged topographical nature of the islands: travel between villages even a short distance apart has always been made difficult by high mountain ranges and deep valleys.

Melanesian social groups were generally small – less than a few hundred people. Each group was (and still is) ruled by a man known as a 'bigman'. Hereditary factors were important in selecting a bigman, but the individual's ambition and skills in politics and war were equally important.

Men who displayed prowess in war or village affairs, or who showed a special affinity with the spirit world, could ascend the social hierarchy by stepping up through successive 'grades'. Feasting and displays of wealth were central to grade-taking ceremonies, which are still held today. See The Nimangki under Society in the Vanuatu chapter.

The concept of reciprocity is central to Melanesian culture. Assistance, whether in the form of food or labour, was given out of a sense of duty and was given with the expectation of the favour being returned in the future. Trade was a basis of the culture, and the relationships involved in exchange rituals between individuals and between clans were very complex. In a culture with many hundreds of languages spoken by small groups of people, allegiance to kin was paramount, and it was possible to include all speakers of one language in the wider group to which one owed allegiance. See the boxed text 'The Wantok System' in the Solomon Islands chapter for more details.

So-called 'ancestor worship' and sorcery pervaded every aspect of Melanesian life. Magical spells and rituals were necessary to guarantee success in war, fishing, agriculture and good health. Success in war was particularly important; the concept of reciprocity extended to an enthusiastic exacting of revenge for past wrongs. Headhunting was common and cannibalism (see the boxed text 'Dining on the Dead' in the Fiji chapter) was practised on a ritual basis as well as being a food source – in some areas as late as the 1950s.

More than other Pacific islanders, Melanesians have retained their culture in the face of Western influence. Around 86% of Solomon Islanders and Ni-Vanuatu still follow a subsistence-agriculture lifestyle. While Melanesians use modern technology for fishing, agriculture and other pursuits, this is still supplemented with sorcery and rituals. The concepts of *kastom* and reciprocity remain important in modern Melanesia, providing unique difficulties for Western businesses trying to operate there.

Kastom You will hear the word *kastom* (custom) used constantly in the Solomon Islands and Vanuatu when villagers refer to traditional beliefs and land ownership. If something is done in a certain way 'because of *kastom*', this means it has always been done this way, and people consider it right to continue doing it this way. Breaches of *kastom* are always deplored.

Maui's Fish

A common legend to many Pacific cultures features the demigod Maui – a trickster, fool, hero, Polynesian Prometheus and a damn fine fisherman.

In this traditional tale, Maui fishes one or more of the islands in the group up out of the ocean depths. Each island has its variations on the story: in Tokelau, Maui hauled up each of the three coral atolls in that group; while fishing up Rakahanga in the Cooks he is said to have baited his hook with coconuts and leaves; in Aotearoa (New Zealand) he used a fish-hook fashioned from the jawbone of his grandmother, and baited it with blood from his own nose; and on various islands of French Polynesia his bait was either his own ear or sacred crimson feathers. However the hook was baited, it was effective. The hook caught onto the largest fish ever seen.

Maui's struggles to haul this enormous catch to the surface were aided by various magical chants and spells – and his prize was a fish so large that it formed the island of Rakahanga or Tongatapu, or whichever island is appropriate to the teller of the tale.

Maui's other contributions to mankind include stealing fire from the gods, slowing the path of the sun and creating the first dog. One of his major appeals to Polynesian society seems to be the use of trickery to defeat force.

Polynesia Ancient Polynesian society was strongly hereditary, with seniority determined by descent through the male side of the family. The most senior male, the paramount chief or *ariki* (sometimes *ari'i* or *ali'i*), ruled over sub-chiefs and commoners. Chiefly families formed a class of their own, having minimal contact with lower classes. Proving chiefly genealogy was vital, and in the absence of a written language, oral histories evolved a high significance, with the ability to recite one's ancestry an important part of any political debate.

Along with the ruling chief, power was shared by a class of experts or priests known as *tohunga* (*tohu'a* or *kahuna*), who were the repository of knowledge and often the interpreter of the gods' wills for the village. Obviously, this was a position of some political power!

The degree to which Polynesian societies were stratified by hereditary class varied from island to island. In egalitarian Samoa, chiefs *(matai)* were selected on political nous and ability rather than on lines of descent. At the other end of the scale, social class in Hawaiian, Tongan and Tahitian societies was strictly hierarchical. Soon after European contact, all three of these latter cultures came to be ruled by single leaders.

Religious beliefs were remarkably consistent across ancient Polynesia. The worship of a pantheon of gods – ruled by Tangaroa (Tangaloa or Ta'aroa) – spread from the Society Islands throughout Polynesia. The gods shared responsibilities for the seas, the forests, war, cultivated crops and other departments.

The importance of warfare in Polynesian society was universal. The shortage of land was a contributing factor, and revenge was often demanded for long-remembered feuds. Cannibalism was common, and was the ultimate revenge against one's enemy.

Ancient hierarchies and the power of hereditary chiefs are diminished in modern Polynesia, although Tonga retains its powerful monarchy, and in Samoa (one of the most resilient Polynesian societies) only chiefs are eligible for election to parliament. The concepts of tapu and *mana* remain important.

Marae The word *marae* (or *malae*) varies in meaning in different Polynesian cultures. In western Polynesia, it refers to the grassy area at the centre of a village, the central point of village life. Towards the east, the same word is used for sacred sites and temples, such as

Marae Taputapuatea in French Polynesia. See also Production in the 'South Pacific Arts' special section.

Tapu

The concept of tapu (pronounced 'ta-bu' in many Pacific languages, and the source of the English word 'taboo') is common to all of Polynesia. There are many common themes, like the ability of women and cooked food to remove tapu, but there are also many variations. See the individual country chapters for local interpretations.

Mana

More important in Polynesia, the concept of *mana* (personal spiritual power) is common to many Pacific cultures. *Mana* is a quality possessed by all people (and things), and the degree of one's *mana* depends not only on hereditary factors but on one's achievements. A chief (or politician) without *mana* could not – and cannot – rule effectively.

RELIGION

Ancient Pacific religion is discussed in Traditional Society under Society earlier in this chapter. Ancestor worship and magic were prevalent in Melanesia, while a rich pantheon of gods ruled Polynesia. However, neither powerful ancestors nor Tangaroa were strong enough to resist the new religion that arrived in the early 19th century.

In many cases traditional religion has been incorporated into modern beliefs, but Christianity dominates religious life in the Pacific today. Only Fiji, with its large Hindu and Muslim Indo-Fijian population, has significant numbers of non-Christians.

Christianity

Following the efforts of missionaries in the Pacific in the last century, the islands of the South Pacific adopted Christianity with a passion, Polynesia especially. The area is famous now for the fervency of believers.

The Church of the Latter Day Saints (Mormon Church) arrived in the Pacific in 1888. They were at least partly inspired by the Book of Mormon's assertion that Pacific islanders are the children of the Israelite refugee Hagoth, who sailed into the Pacific from the American mainland in 53 BC. The Mormon Church has been fairly successful in the Pacific; it shares a family focus with islanders, allows believers to baptise heathen ancestors, and puts some effort and resources into schooling. Other Christian denominations include the Seventh Day Adventists, who arrived in Samoa in 1890.

Cargo Cults

During WWII, Pacific islanders were introduced to huge Western material wealth, but when US troops left the Pacific, most of this wealth disappeared with them (or was dumped into the sea in many cases). In Melanesia, cargo cults formed to encourage and prepare for the return of these riches, which were known as 'cargo'. One of the best known cargo cults is the Jon Frum movement in Vanuatu (see the boxed text 'The John Frum Movement' in that chapter).

LANGUAGE

The Austronesian family of languages is the most widely distributed in the world. It includes all Polynesian and Micronesian languages, many Melanesian and Southeast Asian languages as well as the Malagasy language from Madagascar, off the African coast. While the words for common concepts such as 'land', 'ancestors' or 'fish' are the same in many Pacific languages, there is also considerable diversity, particularly in ancient, culturally-diverse Melanesia, where over a thousand different languages exist.

In contrast, the last area to be settled, Polynesia, is the most linguistically homogenous. Here, inter-island voyaging ensured that the languages of Polynesia are almost dialects of one language. James Cook's Tahitian translator, Tupaia, had little trouble understanding Maori in the Cook Islands or New Zealand, and travellers to the Pacific may find that they have a head start in a new Polynesian language if they've already learned a few words in another.

Prior to the arrival of the missionaries, no written languages existed in the Pacific (with the possible exception of the *rongorongo* script of the Rapa Nui; see the boxed text 'Rongorongo' in the Easter Island chapter). Without a written language, oral traditions were very important in all Pacific cultures.

A common feature of Polynesian languages is the dropped consonant; an effect similar to that heard in the Cockney accent, where the letter 't' is not pronounced when it falls within a word. For example, 'butterfly' is pronounced 'bu-er-fly', and 'bottle' is pronounced 'bo-ul'. The space that's left in the word is called a glottal stop, and is written as an apostrophe. Thus in Tahiti, the place name Havaiki becomes Havai'i (ha-vai-ee) and *kumara* becomes *'umara*, when the 'k' sound is dropped. Cook Islanders drop 'h', so that Havaiki becomes 'Avaiki.

Another feature of Pacific languages that troubles English speakers is the soft 'ng' sound. This is pronounced as the 'ng' in the English word 'singer' – without pronouncing the hard 'g' as in 'finger'. For example the country name Tonga is pronounced 'tong-ah' not 'ton-gah'. To make it even more difficult, some Pacific languages spell this sound simply 'g' (the Samoan word *palagi* is pronounced 'pah-lang-i').

English is spoken widely across the Pacific, and will be understood in the main towns and cities of almost every country. Exceptions are the French territories (New Caledonia, Wallis & Futuna and French Polynesia, including Tahiti), where French is the first or second language.

The hundreds of languages of Melanesia have led to the development of 'business' or pidgin languages for communication across language barriers. Papua New Guinea, the Solomon Islands and Vanuatu all use pidgin languages that mix English, French and German with Melanesian words.

No Pacific languages use an 's' to denote plurals (as the English language does). Although this rule is happily broken almost everywhere – for example a Samoan hotel owner will offer to show you around their *fale* (huts), or a Vanuatuan trader will offer to sell you some *tamtams* (slit drums) – we have stuck to the rules in this book and relied on the context to make the meaning clear.

For useful phrases in Pacific languages, see the Language section in the individual country chapters. A little bit of French is very useful in the French territories; a basic French language guide is given in an appendix of this book.

For a more comprehensive overview of the languages of the region, get a copy of Lonely Planet's *South Pacific* and *Pidgin* phrasebooks.

South Pacific Arts

South Pacific art is very varied, and it can be incredibly beautiful and potent. Some objects of art from the South Pacific are highly sought after by collectors. However, this is not 'art' in the traditional Western sense of the word. Rather, in the Pacific islands, traditional art objects were (and often still are) practical items with a specific purpose, whether that be to invoke *mana* (spiritual power) in war, assist passage into the afterlife, forge relationships of exchange, bring juveniles into adulthood, or merely serve as a stool or a bowl.

The meanings that we look for in Pacific art are complicated, because it is necessary to look beyond the superficial appearance of the artwork and explore the social organisation and contexts in which the work was produced. Although artifice and decoration are traditional, art for its own sake is a new idea in most cultures of the Pacific islands.

PERCEPTIONS

Europe was abuzz when explorers returned with traditional artefacts and stories of South Sea islands in the late 18th century. The islands were described as places of loose morals and free love, as well as being earthly paradises uncorrupted by the modern world and its vices. These perceptions gave rise to the idea of the 'noble savage' who practised 'primitive art', and motivated many European artists and travellers to visit the Pacific or even settle there (including Paul Gauguin, W Somerset Maugham and Robert Louis Stevenson). Back in Europe, Picasso and Braque's cubism was greatly influenced by Pacific art pieces.

However, the patronising ideas of 'noble savage' and 'primitive art' do not provide us with any satisfying meanings of Pacific art. The term 'primitive art' is also a misnomer, because it refers to things that are not primarily art, but rather ceremonial objects, stories or motifs with real and immediate powers and vivid histories. In traditional Pacific societies all these objects of 'art' were interconnected, just as religion, culture, politics and tribal affairs were.

Traditionally, the manufacture of these art-objects was (and often still is) highly ceremonial and ritualised – in Melanesia, rigidly organised secret men's councils still build figures or masks to be presented in elaborate funerary rites or initiation ceremonies. Men and boys fell trees, prepare materials and build the artefacts under strict rules and according to their well-defined traditional roles. The production of art in these cultures is very unlike the way art is produced in the west.

CONTEXTS

In Melanesia, honouring ancestors was more important than honouring the gods, and the spirit world was ever present. 'Bigmen' (chiefs) provided feasts for the clan, and the display of wealth and the accumulation of ceremonial objects conferred much prestige upon the sponsor. Much Melanesian art was produced for these ceremonies (which were rites of passage for the living and the dead). Ancestors were powerful protectors and benefactors, whose presence was manifested in the process of producing art as well as in the artefact itself.

Title page: Mural fresco, Pouébo, Grande Terre, New Caledonia (Photograph by Jean-Bernard Carillet)

Lapita

The ancient race of people known as the Lapita are thought to be responsible for the wide distribution of Polynesian culture and Austronesian languages in the Pacific. Coming from the Bismark Archipelago in far-north Papua New Guinea (PNG) from around 1500 BC, they were the first to populate the islands from Vanuatu east to New Caledonia, Fiji, Samoa and Tonga. It was in Tonga and Samoa that the Lapita developed into the people we now call Polynesians.

The Lapita people had an enormous influence over a vast area of the Pacific from 1500 BC to 500 BC, where their influence can been traced through the reverberations of their unique pottery. Lapita pottery was tempered with sand and fired in open fires, and decorated with rows of curvilinear patterns stamped into the unfired clay. Polynesian tattooists took up these distinctive motifs, using chisels to scrape or puncture the skin, and tapa (bark-cloth) decoration across the Pacific also bears Lapita-like patterns. In some areas Lapita-style pottery is still produced.

The first Lapita ceramic fragments were discovered on Watom Island (PNG) by a missionary in 1909. The name Lapita comes from an archaeological dig at Lapita in New Caledonia in 1952. Shards of Lapita pottery have been found throughout Melanesia, in parts of Micronesia and in western Polynesia (Tonga, Samoa and Futuna). More recently, a distinctive Lapita style has been identified in certain adzes and other implements.

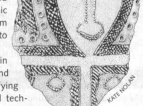

They were highly skilled sailors and navigators, able to cross hundreds of kilometres of open sea, and trade and settlement were important to their culture. They were also agriculturists and practised husbandry of dogs, pigs and fowls. Regarded as the first cultural complex in the Pacific, they were a highly organised people who traded obsidian (volcanic glass used in tool production) from New Britain (PNG) with people up to 2500km away in Tonga and Samoa.

Today Pacific art is dizzying in its variety of form, execution and purpose, but perhaps its most unifying thread is the patterns, motifs and techniques it inherits from these ancient people.

In most traditional cultures in the Polynesian region, the most noble of hereditary chiefs and *ariki* (aristocrats) were themselves semi-deities, and spiritual power and knowledge came to them through their splendid feather-worked regalia, fly-whisks and ornaments. In Polynesia, art was primarily produced for this elite group and objects of art were preserved and inherited by successive generations, bringing with them the *mana* (personal spiritual power) of their ancestors. These heirlooms had enormous prestige and power, and were preserved with much reverence.

PRODUCTION
War Objects

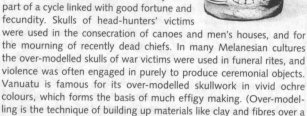

Warfare and killing were central to many Pacific cultures, and were often highly ritualised. In the Solomon Islands they were part of a cycle linked with good fortune and fecundity. Skulls of head-hunters' victims were used in the consecration of canoes and men's houses, and for the mourning of recently dead chiefs. In many Melanesian cultures the over-modelled skulls of war victims were used in funeral rites, and violence was often engaged in purely to produce ceremonial objects. Vanuatu is famous for its over-modelled skullwork in vivid ochre colours, which forms the basis of much effigy making. (Over-modelling is the technique of building up materials like clay and fibres over a skull. The surface is decorated with eyes, hair and teeth, and sometimes with ornaments like earrings and headbands.)

In Fiji and western Polynesia, warfare was associated with expansionism and rivalry. Marquesan war clubs, known as *u'u*, are highly prized among collectors and feature extraordinary fine-relief carving (often a double-sided human face, a Janus-figure form which proliferates through the Pacific). These weapons were carved from solid hardwoods and were very heavy, and very deadly. The massive Fijian *sali* (clubs) are recognisable by their 'lip' or barb, and a warrior wielding such an implement would have been very formidable indeed. Warriors from Kiribati wore full-body armour and helmets that were woven from vegetable fibres and human hair, and used swords of shark's teeth.

Weapons, shields and war canoes were decorated with motifs that imbued them with powers. Ancestors, spirits and legends assisted warriors in combat – coming alive in their tools.

BOTH ILLUSTRATIONS BY KATE NOLAN

Canoes

All Pacific cultures built and sailed canoes. It was (and in some places still is) the primary means of transport. Canoes traversed vast distances of open sea in the early migrations, plied trade routes and were used on fishing expeditions and for warfare. See the boxed text 'Voyaging & Navigation' in the Facts about the South Pacific chapter. Canoe prows were the subject of much creative energy, but many other parts of the canoe – paddles (both genuine and symbolic), sterns, bailers and splash boards – were decorated with symbolic motifs that conferred power and protection onto the craft and the voyage. The canoe is also an important element in mythology, and a recurring motif in Pacific art. The canoe shape – stylised, in profile and often bearing a mast – is represented in countless artworks.

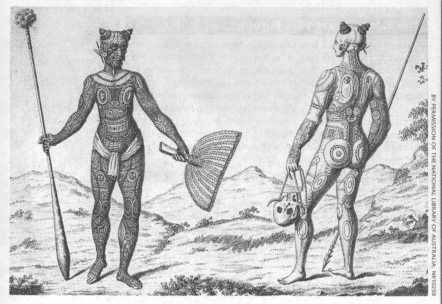

The Body

'Tattoo' is an Oceanic word, which comes from the Polynesian word *tatau*. Up until the 18th century, full-body tattoos were common through the Cook, Marquesas, Austral and Society Islands, mostly among high-ranked members of society (although some people of the highest rank were not tattooed at all). A person began acquiring tattoos in their childhood and initiation into adulthood was usually accompanied by special markings. Tattooing is a painful and arduous process, but this 'hardens' the body and the motifs have protective properties – warriors were often covered in motifs that inspired fear in their enemies and, like their weaponry, gave them the powers of their ancestors and spirits.

Polynesian tattooing reached its zenith in the war-torn Marquesas, where no part of a warrior's skin was left unembellished (even his eyelids and tongue were tattooed), giving him a second skin and a bewildering visual 'armour'. Marquesan warrior-tattoos featured an extraordinary density and number of designs. Marquesan noble people bore complex and elegant tattoos also, although theirs were not so all-covering. Tattooed skin was sometimes removed from a person after their death. In Tahiti, Samoa and Tonga tattoos were usually restricted to the buttocks and thighs. Here, dense areas of pigment were broken up with curvilinear designs and spots.

By the 20th century, missionary activity had virtually killed off Polynesian tattooing. The tradition remained strong in Samoa, however, and is now being revived in areas of French Polynesia and elsewhere. In Fiji, where tattooing had strong associations with sexuality, the repression by the Christian church means that a revival is unlikely.

Top: Inhabitants of Nuku Hiva (engraving by S Halle, 1810), shows Marquesan warriors' intricate 'clothing' of tattoos

The Tattoo Craze Hits Europe

Although tattooing had been practised in many cultures throughout the world, it only really took off in Europe after British officers and crewmen returned from Pacific voyages in the late 18th and early 19th centuries, and bared their flesh. Sir Joseph Banks had tattoos done in Tahiti, as did the *Bounty* mutineers. It became fashionable for seamen to have tattoos, and Europe's repressed underclasses took up the habit. Soon tattoos had become a furtive fashion among the European aristocracy – kings of England and Norway, Russian Tsars, Bourbons of France and many men and women of royal and social rank had themselves tattooed (some profusely).

Rather than tattooing, scarring of the body was more commonly practised in Melanesia where ochre pigments don't show so well against darker skin. Techniques varied somewhat but scarification (keloid decoration) served much the same role, in terms of bestowing symbols of rank and/or status, as tattooing did in lighter-skinned people.

Male Cults & Men's Houses in Melanesia

Throughout Melanesia secret councils of men convene to practise 'the arts'. The production of objects within these societies – for funerary rituals, initiations etc – is done in accordance with strict rules, and is itself highly ceremonial. Much Melanesian art was traditionally produced to allow rituals to be performed properly, and it was sometimes produced collectively or by a master and his apprentices.

Men's houses are widespread throughout Melanesia and, before the towering church edifices were built, were a village's dominant structure and often its most sacred place. In many places men still move through various grades or social ranks, and feasts, gifts, body adornment, sculpture, and song and dance remain components of these ceremonies. The best known grade-taking societies are on Ambrym, Malekula and Pentecost islands (all Vanuatu); see The Nimangki section under Society in the Vanuatu chapter. Males are allocated a place within the *nakamal* (men's club house) according to their rank, and they seriously transgress if they step into an area of a man of higher rank.

Nakamal contained the most sacred objects – often the revered over-modelled skulls of ancestors were kept here, although sometimes they were kept in other *tapu* (*tabu;* taboo) structures, such as the buildings in which canoes were housed. The structure of the men's houses universally symbolise woman and fecundity. They are often great artworks themselves with towering facades and detailed interiors, and are built using complex joinery without a nail or a screw. It's ironic, in a way, that all things exclusively male, magic and *tapu* to women happen inside a female form. The relationship between the exclusive men's council and the ever-present feminine symbol is very complicated, but connects with ideas of rebirth, grade-taking and initiation.

Marae in Polynesia

The principal social structure and meeting place in eastern Polynesia was the *marae* (or *malae*). It was very unlike a Melanesian men's club house (being gender neutral), but had a similar monumental status within the community. Villages might have several *marae*, each for a different function and devoted to different gods. Nobles and royal families would have their own *marae*.

In western Polynesia, on the other hand, *marae* were little more than village greens, sometimes merely a clearing marked off by walls. In the east they developed a religious significance and could be elaborate structures. The ancient *marae* in Easter Island, the Societies, Australs and Marquesas must have been extraordinary – they were massive open-air, paved temples with altars, carved-stone seating, platforms and walls. The scale of the remaining petroglyphs and carved-stone figures attest to some awesome temples.

In the Marquesas the *me'ae*, a structure of basalt blocks, was *tapu* to all but the most noble people and high priests. Here priests would engage in high religious acts involving sacrifice and cannibalism.

Women's Business – Tapa Cloth, Baskets & Mats

When the early European voyagers arrived in the Pacific, mulberry and breadfruit trees were plentiful and tapa anvils proliferated. Although tapa was ubiquitous, the early Europeans did not collect much. Women's art was largely undervalued and misunderstood. Weaving looms were not known outside of the Caroline Islands and the Santa Cruz Islands, although free-hand pandanus weaving was used to produce sleeping mats and sails for voyaging canoes.

Tapa was the only form of cloth and was used for garments as well as for mats. But its significance is wholly misunderstood if it's seen merely as a crude fibrous material – the importance of tapa cannot be overstated. In both Polynesia and Melanesia the exchange of tapa was (and often still is) crucial in forging relationships. By accepting gifts the receiver was indebted to the giver and was required, over time, to honour the debt. These relationships were bound not so much by the 'financial' transaction but by a moral contract that invoked spirits of ancestors or gods – the exchange of gifts was symbolic of a much more profound agreement. Certain kinds of tapa were valued in these exchanges above all other things.

Tapa, baskets and mats were

Bottom: An example of tapa design

PATRICK HORTON

often produced collectively; this was an important women's institution in much the same way (though not so grandiloquently) as men's councils were in producing their objects. Buka baskets, originally from Buka and Bougainville islands, PNG, are now emulated all over the Pacific and woven pandanus mats of various kinds are still commonly made.

Tapa was produced by great numbers of women in massive sheets for royal occasions and for the most sacred of ceremonies. Significantly, the most sacred Polynesian tapa cloths were fine, white and unadorned (similarly the most sacred demigod chiefs of Polynesia were usually not tattooed) – in some Pacific contexts, decoration is trivial. Meanings in Pacific art are not to be found in an object's motifs, but rather in the context in which the art is produced and the cultural structure in which it operates. When Tonga's Queen Salote said 'our history is written in our mats', she was referring to the role that tapa had always played in exchange and kinship relationships, rather than stories of Tonga's history being literally painted onto tapa.

In Tahiti, tapa was prepared in huge sheets – up to 3m wide and sometimes hundreds of metres long. These sheets were rolled up, stored and preserved in chiefs' houses. This way chiefs accumulated wealth, status and holy power – when they died, they and their mausoleums were wrapped in this sacred cloth for the duration of funerary rites.

The introduction of European calico quickly brought about the virtual abandonment of tapa making in much of Polynesia. However tapa is still produced in Melanesia, Tonga, Samoa (where it is called *siapo*), Wallis & Futuna and on 'Atiu (Cook Islands).

Money

Certain valuables act as currency in ceremonies (eg, bride price) or in trade. Currencies among interconnected Pacific peoples are complicated – a currency may be made by one group for use by another group, or it may only be valid tender in certain kinds of transactions. Money can enter a cyclical trade route between islands hundreds of kilometres apart, from which it never leaves.

The materials were usually hard to get, such as deep-water shells, obsidian and rare feathers, and were often worked on to produce the currency. Red-feather money, axe heads and shell money were traditional currencies in the Solomons, as were objects made from the teeth of dogs and dolphins. Rare shells (for example, deep-water oyster shells) would often be cut and ground into tiny discs and threaded along a string. Leaf money was widely used in Melanesia, and in New Caledonia a certain kind of women's skirt is still used as a traditional currency in particular transactions.

Ornament

In pre-European times Pacific chiefs and nobles wore splendid regalia that confirmed their status and imbued them with the powers of ancestors and spirits. Chiefs sat on artfully carved chiefly stools and ate from beautifully made vessels. The Polynesian nobles developed a penchant for delicate fly-whisks made from rare feathers, human hair and shells set on finely carved handles (it's commonly thought that the fly was introduced by Europeans). Nobles' staffs, feather capes and *lei* (*'ei*; necklaces) were not just stately symbols of prestige, but were vehicles through which the holy elite participated in the world of the gods – feathers were thought to be a particularly good conduit between the worlds. The feather capes and feather-god sculptures collected for European museums from the Marquesas and Hawaii are extraordinary – vividly coloured and made with the feathers of thousands of birds.

Shells were widely used in breastplates in Melanesia, and necklaces, armlets and ornaments associated with piercings in the earlobes and nose all displayed a person's status. The *kapkap*, an open-worked turtle shell over a white shell disc, is worn on the forehead or as a necklace, and is a classic form that appears in a vast area throughout the Solomons and New Ireland (PNG). The bones of animals, head-hunters' victims and ancestors had different spiritual properties, and were often carved into personal ornaments, or objects such as combs. The most splendid personal ornamentation was reserved for special ceremonies

Masks, Sculptures & Headdresses

The most abundant manifestation of aesthetic energy in the Pacific are masks and sculptures. Most 'masks' were never meant to be worn but were a form of iconographic sculpture representing a face. These objects were produced for a variety of reasons grounded in the local religion and mythology. Sometimes they were built to be destroyed in funeral pyres, and sometimes they were preserved for hundreds of years and used in on-going rituals. Sometimes masks were built to ward off malevolent spirits or to invoke benevolent ones. Some effigies and masks were built for long-dead ancestors to inhabit and watch over the clan – they were placed in special areas and had much tapu associated with them. Especially in Melanesia, the making of these kinds of artefacts was highly ritualised in secret men's councils.

Perhaps the world's most famous stone sculpture are the enormous *moai* of Easter Island (see that chapter). The *moai* show similarities to other eastern Polynesian statues, particularly the large stone *tiki* of the Marquesas and Tuamotu islands. The hands resting across the stomach is a common Polynesian design.

Right: A 19th-century wooden mask from Malekula in Vanuatu, designed to be worn by a dancer

Ceremonial activities were often accompanied by dancers in costumes and headdresses. Dancers were important to the rites performed at the ceremony, and were sometimes temporarily possessed by spirits. Such costumes are not likenesses of spirits, but, within the ceremony, they are the very embodiment of spirits in the real world.

COMMON THEMES

There are themes that echo through Pacific art, but they are more to do with the role of artefacts and their production than in any motifs and icons used. Objects were created for similar reasons (islanders were exposed to similar elements) and out of the same materials, but there is no identifiable style that represents Pacific art. Resonances of Lapita pottery decoration arguably exist in much Pacific art, particularly their curvilinear dot-rendered style and simple figurative renderings of humans.

Migrations, too, have made it complicated. People moved east first, but some Polynesians turned back west and northwest, and Micronesians came south to settle islands off northern PNG. With long sea journeys common, there was massive cross-pollination of stories, ideas, forms, motifs and meanings in Pacific art.

There are styles and forms attributable to islands and regions – Polynesian art is appreciably different to Melanesian art, and probably has a more unified 'look' to it (Polynesian settlement in the Pacific was relatively recent and contemporary Polynesian cultures are less diverse than those of Melanesia). Within many Polynesian cultures, the *tiki* figure is represented in various incarnations. It's much harder to find universal themes in Melanesian art. In terms of motifs, only the Janus figure (the double-headed human form) and the canoe shape (see the 'Canoes' boxed text earlier in this special section) are repeated right across the Pacific.

MODERN TRANSLATIONS

The influence and impact of European visitors on the production of art was remarked upon by Cook during his second and third voyages; tiki figures were much more widely available. Ever since, there's been a tourist trade of sorts and Europeans brought new metals, tools and materials that have long since been incorporated.

The influences on contemporary Pacific people are numerous, complicated and sometimes quite contradictory. Some purists might argue that Western society has 'contaminated' indigenous art, but that's a fairly patronising attitude, suggesting that Pacific islanders are unable to properly assess the value of their traditional forms, and meaningfully incorporate contemporary influences. As anywhere else on Earth, Pacific culture has not remained static, and few islanders are interested in being stone-age primitivists just to keep the purists happy.

Above: A Tahitian Janus figure – double-headed humans were a popular theme in Pacific sculpture, particulary in Tahiti

Missionaries killed off countless traditional art forms in their attempts to convert heathens, and reorganised people around different institutions. The production of some women's art – tapa, baskets, mats – is now often organised around Christian women's groups, and Christian motifs are incorporated in the design.

Oddly, modern textile designs have also taken on commercial images such as the Coca Cola and Pepsi emblems, and even the logos of banks and outboard motor manufacturers. Images of Western pop artists and film stars proliferate as T-shirt prints.

Tourist art (see the Buying Art section later) is produced in large volumes in places such as Fiji, New Caledonia and Tahiti, but elsewhere the tourist trade is too small to generate a proper industry. Many of the most attractive utilitarian objects – bowls, bags and mats – are made for other islanders and sold in the markets.

Although contemporary Pacific art still calls upon the histories and legends of islanders, its place in the culture has changed. The production of art is now often an individual activity instead of a collective one, and the notion of ownership of artworks has arisen. Some contemporary art is an adaptation of traditional forms, for example pottery and carving, but new media, materials and tools have been incorporated. Travelling exhibitions to Australia, Europe and the Americas have introduced a broad audience to Pacific art, and since the four-yearly Festival of Pacific Arts was inaugurated in 1972, the renaissance of Pacific art has become the source of great pride for islanders and the impetus for much regional tourism. National governments have been funding art schools, community groups and public works (mural art is popular in the Pacific).

Especially in Polynesia, where many traditional forms have been lost, the rebirth of creative energy has taken on new forms. Polynesian tapa is mostly a lost art, but these days *tivaevae* (or *tifaifai*) has supplanted tapa. These are appliqué works and the needlework technique was introduced by missionary wives from New England from the 1820s onwards. *Tivaevae* bear some designs and motifs that have been appropriated from traditional tapa cloth.

Tattooing has experienced a major rebirth in the Societies and Marquesas (French Polynesia) but the stories and meanings behind many of the traditional designs have been lost. This is true too in New Zealand where traditional Maori tattoos have become very popular, but in many cases their application has become more ad hoc and original meanings may be lost. Designs that were reserved for a chief or noble family may now exist in the public domain.

Nuclear testing in the Pacific is a strong theme in much modern art. In areas where independence and indigenous rights struggles are current (for example, in New Caledonia and French Polynesia) modern art is highly political.

Among the internationally recognised South Pacific artists are Eddie Daiding Bibimauri, from Malaita in the Solomons, a Honiara-based graphic artist and muralist; New Zealand-based John Pule, a Niuean artist who inventively reworks the traditional art of tapa; and painters Alio Pilioko and Nikolai Michoutouchkine from Vanuatu. Contemporary artists such as these rely on support from governments, cultural centres, art collectors and tourists.

BUYING ART

In the popular tourists destinations (Fiji, New Caledonia and Tahiti) artworks are abundant and specialist shops sell quasi-traditional arte-facts, T-shirts and various other souvenirs. In most other areas of the South Pacific there are not enough tourists to support this.

The biggest market for modern artists are the tourists that come and stay in the international hotels, and artists often sell works outside. Carvers and other traditional artists also sell pieces outside the hotels. Usually these are pieces produce d for sale to tourists, but that doesn't mean they're poorly made or trashy souvenirs – some of the objects are produced by masters using traditional forms or derivatives and honouring time-old traditions. Needless to say, there are plenty of poorly made trashy souvenirs too. Some local markets have artefacts for sale, and the bigger hotels often sell objects (at a substantial mark-up).

Out of the big cities and in the more remote places, artists and artefacts makers will often be hanging around the airport waiting for you to step off the plane, or they'll be waiting by the wharf. Some-times in these areas the vendor won't speak English well (if at all), but will have no trouble communicating the terms of the transaction.

You may prefer to buy one object that you really like, rather than countless small carvings and inferior pieces. This piece may be quite expensive, but it will be a much more potent and enduring reminder of your journey than a bunch of disposable souvenirs. Consider, too, how you will get it home in one piece – many carvings are heavy, unwieldy items that won't travel well. Or they might be incredibly delicate. Objects that are made from animal materials – skin, teeth, hair – will probably be subject to quarantine restrictions in your home country.

Look carefully at the details and the materials used. Inferior timbers are sometimes rubbed down with shoe polish or stain to pass them off as quality ebony (which is rare these days). Feel the weight in the timber and look carefully for the carver's deft touches in the details and the finish. Expect to pay for what you get – a good piece will be beautiful but it may be expensive.

Buying South Pacific Art

There are three important points about buying art in the South Pacific:
• If you buy from the maker rather than a shop owner, the maker collects the full-sale value. This is a good thing – in cash-poor communities your tourist dollars can make a real difference.
• Haggling about the price is considered extremely rude. Bargaining is not natural in the South Pacific (an exception is the Indian community in Fiji) and it's very rare for an artefact maker to over-inflate the price to give room for negotiation. While it is becoming increasingly common for artisans to offer a 'second price' in the bigger cities and around international hotels, protracted bargaining certainly won't meet with good-natured competitive banter, as in some countries in Asia. Here, it's downright rude, especially in Melanesia. If you can't afford it, buy something else.
• Don't buy objects that incorporate rare shells, corals or turtle shells.

JEAN-BERNARD CARILLET

LIZ THOMPSON

DENIS O'BYRNE

Top left: Traditional tattoo, French Polynesia

Top right: Tahitian man with traditional tattooing

Bottom: *Tamtam* (slit-drum) and *nakamal* (men's clubhouse), Ambrym, Vanuatu

LIZ THOMPSON

DEANNA SWANEY

JEAN-BERNARD CARILLET

JEAN-BERNARD CARILLET

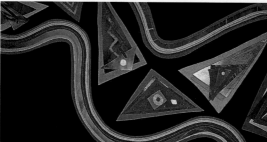

LEE FOSTER

Top left: *Siapo* (tapa) cloth designs, Samoa

Top right: Woven baskets, Tongatapu, Tonga

Middle left: Traditional wood carving, New Caledonia

Middle right: Traditional wood carving, Marquesas Islands, French Polynesia

Bottom: Appliqué design, 'Atiu, Cook Islands

Further Reading

There are many excellent books available on South Pacific art. Some that were published as early as the 1950s are out of print, but perhaps available from libraries.

The most comprehensive and beautifully presented pictorial book must be Anthony JP Meyer's hardback, two-volume *Oceanic Art* with explanatory text in English, French and German. Artefacts are singly photographed under studio lighting and there are various asides and archival photographs.

Anne D'Alleva's *Art of the Pacific* is also excellent. The fine colour pictures are secondary to the arguments developed in the text, which provide an excellent deconstruction of art in Pacific societies. This book provides some fascinating insights into the religious structures in which art was made.

From the World of Art series, *Oceanic Art*, by Nicholas Thomas, is splendid. Although it's an academic work, the book is very readable and the selection of pictures complements Thomas' compelling arguments.

Rowan McKinnon

Regional Facts for the Visitor

PLANNING
Despite appearances to the contrary, things can change quickly in the Pacific. A cyclone can knock out all accommodation (not to mention roads, electricity and telephones) and local disputes can close off an area.

The number one rule is to be flexible. The Pacific attitude to time is more relaxed than in many Western cultures, so you shouldn't set your heart on getting to destinations or getting things done in any great hurry. See the Time section later in this chapter.

When to Go
Most Pacific-islands tourists time their visit according to the weather. Specifically, they avoid the wet season. Being in the tropics, the temperature doesn't vary much – it's *always* hot – but during the wet season, heat, humidity and persistent rain can combine to make a holiday a bit uncomfortable. However, most of the rain falls at night, and the wet season is the time when other tourists will not accompany you in plague proportions.

South of the equator, the dry season runs from May to October and the wet season (including the cyclone season in some areas) is from November to April. In the individual country chapters, see Climate under Facts about the Country, and Planning or When to Go under Facts for the Visitor. Also use the appendix 'Climate Charts' to compare the weather in different destinations.

During peak tourist times, prices can be high, accommodation fully booked and the attractions packed. You'll find better deals and fewer crowds in the shoulder seasons (either side of the dry season) in October and May. Around Christmas many flights and boats are fully booked by islanders returning home to spend time with their families.

See Public Holidays & Special Events in this chapter and in the individual country chapters for information on holidays and festivities in your destination country.

Inter-Island Travel
Unlike in Europe or Africa, in the Pacific you usually can't just decide which country you'd like to visit next and arrange travel on the spot – unless, of course, you have your own yacht! If, like most Pacific tourists, you're travelling by aeroplane, the only reasonable way to get to more than one or

The Best & Worst

The Best
The Pacific is an enormous and diverse region and no list of highlights can hope to cover all of them. But it's fun to compile one anyway, so we asked our authors for their favourites. The results are as follows:

- Marvelling at nature's fireworks display on a night visit to Vanuatu's Mt Yasur, one of the world's most accessible volcanoes
- Staying with a Pacific family
- Hiking through Rarotonga's rugged mountain interior
- Participating in a game of *kirikiti* – a form of all-in cricket – in Samoa or Tokelau
- Attending a feast and cultural show and watching traditional dancing
- Diving in Rangiroa (French Polynesia), amongst soft corals (Fiji), the wreck of the SS *President Coolidge* (Vanuatu) – hell, diving anywhere in the Pacific!
- Soaking up the mystery of Easter Island's *moai* statues and birdman cult
- Watching the ancient *naghol* (land diving) ceremony on Pentecost Island in Vanuatu
- Getting a formal invite to a traditional kava-drinking ceremony

The Worst
It's not all kava & skittles. The authors were also asked to nominate the worst aspects of the South Pacific. Their list included:

- Mosquitoes!
- Piles of plastic trash, aluminium cans – and much much worse – littering beaches and lagoons
- Tinned meat and other highly processed foods and drinks
- Mosquitoes!
- Shonky sweatshops in American Samoa
- The relentless heat and humidity at certain times of the year
- Giant, brazen cockroaches
- Exorbitant prices in New Caledonia and French Polynesia

two countries is by buying an air pass (see Air in the Getting There & Away chapter). Otherwise, costs for inter-country flights will quickly break the bank.

Most air passes have to be bought well in advance, and many must be purchased before travel commences. So decide where you want to go before you do anything else.

Maps

No map covering a huge area like the South Pacific can provide enough detail of any one island to be really useful on the ground (or on the water). However, a map of the Pacific – there are several available – will put things into 'context' if that's important to you.

The maps in this book will help you get an idea of where you might want to go, and will be a useful first reference when you arrive in a country. However, if you're driving or cycling, proper road maps are essential. (See Planning under Facts for the Visitor in the individual country chapters for good local maps.) Tourist offices often provide free maps, while government lands departments put out better quality, more detailed maps.

France's **Institut Géographique National** *(IGN;* Ⓦ *www.ign.fr)* publishes an excellent range of maps for the French territories; and **Service Hydrographique et Océanographique de la Marine** *(SHOM;* Ⓦ *www.shom.fr)* has marine maps covering most of the South Pacific.

Maps on the Cook Islands and Tokelau (scale 1:25,000) can be downloaded from the **New Zealand government website** *(*Ⓦ *www.linz.govt.nz)*. **Hema Maps** *(*Ⓦ *www.hemamaps.com)* produces maps on Vanuatu, Samoa, Fiji and the Solomon Islands.

What to Bring

The Pacific is no shopping paradise. As the locals will tell you, it's difficult to find some items when you're not in the capital – and sometimes even when you are! The general rule of travelling, that it's better to start with too little rather than too much, doesn't apply quite so much in the Pacific. Clothes are easy to buy in large centres, but anything else you *need*, you should bring with you.

A backpack is still the most popular method of carrying gear, as it's convenient, especially for walking. However, a backpack doesn't offer much protection for your valuables, the straps can get caught on things and some airlines may refuse to accept responsibility if the pack is damaged or tampered with.

Travelpacks, a combination backpack/shoulder bag, are the best of both worlds. The backpack straps zip away inside the pack when they're not needed, and some packs have sophisticated shoulder-strap adjustments for increased comfort. Backpacks or travelpacks can be made slightly theft-proof with small padlocks.

As for clothing, the climate will dictate what you take. Remember that insulation works on the principle of trapped air, so several layers of thin clothing are warmer than a single thick one (and will be easier to dry). Be prepared for rain at any time of year.

A minimum packing list could include:

- underwear, socks and swimming gear
- a pair of long trousers and shorts or a skirt
- an ankle-length skirt for formal occasions
- a few T-shirts and shirts
- a warm pullover
- a pair of solid walking shoes
- sandals or thongs (flip flops) for showers and hot days
- a lightweight raincoat
- a medical kit and a sewing kit
- a padlock
- a Swiss Army-type knife
- soap and a light-weight towel
- toothpaste, toothbrush and other toiletries

A padlock is useful to lock your bag to a luggage rack in a bus; it may also be needed to secure your hostel locker. A Swiss Army-type knife comes in handy for all sorts of things but make sure it includes scissors, a bottle opener and strong corkscrew. Also, remember to pack it in your checked-in luggage prior to air travel to avoid the chance of it being confiscated. Soap, toothpaste and toilet paper are readily obtainable, but you'll need your own supply of paper in many public toilets and 'open air facilities' (behind a tree). Tampons are available at pharmacies and supermarkets in all but the most remote places. Condoms are similarly available (but if you prefer a favourite reliable brand, bring some from home).

A tent and sleeping bag are vital if you want to save money by camping, but see Accommodation later in this chapter for restrictions on camping in the Pacific. If you're not camping, don't bother bringing a sleeping bag.

Other optional items include a compass, a torch (flashlight), a pocket calculator for currency conversions, an alarm clock, an adapter plug for electrical appliances (such as a cup or immersion water heater to save on expensive tea and coffee), a universal bath/sink plug (a film canister sometimes works), portable short-wave radio, sunglasses and a few clothes pegs.

Also, consider using plastic carry bags or bin liners inside your backpack to keep things separate but also dry if the pack gets soaked.

RESPONSIBLE TOURISM
Being the perfectly responsible tourist sometimes feels like picking your way through a minefield. You may have to choose your battles and decide where you want to concentrate your efforts.

As background information for your crusade, you could read: Fishing, under Ecology & Environment in the Facts about the South Pacific chapter; Buying Art, in the 'South Pacific Arts' special section; and the boxed texts 'Responsible Bushwalking' (later in this chapter), 'Responsible Diving' in the 'South Pacific Diving' special section and finally 'Responsible Yachting' in the Getting Around the Region chapter. Phew!

TOURIST OFFICES
See the Facts for the Visitor sections of individual country chapters for local tourist offices.

The **South Pacific Tourism Organisation** *(SPTO; ☎ 330 4177, fax 330 1995;* Ⓦ *www.spto.org; 3rd floor, Dolphin Plaza, cnr Loftus St & Victoria Pde, Suva, Fiji)* is an intergovernmental organisation that fosters regional cooperation in the development and promotion of tourism in the Pacific. The SPTO serves as a tourist office for a few countries, however it doesn't offer a lot in the way of services to independent travellers.

VISAS & DOCUMENTS
For visa information, see Visas & Documents under Facts for the Visitor in the individual country chapters.

Travel Insurance
A travel insurance policy that covers theft, accidental loss and medical problems is vital. Some policies offer various medical-expense options; the higher ones are chiefly for countries, such as the US, that have extremely high medical costs. There is a wide variety of policies available, so make sure you check the small print.

Some policies exclude 'dangerous activities', which can include scuba diving,

motorcycling, even hiking. A locally acquired motorcycle licence is not valid under some policies.

You may prefer a policy that pays doctors or hospitals directly rather than you having to pay on the spot and claim later. If you have to claim expenses later, make sure you keep all documentation. Some policies ask you to call back (reverse charges) to a centre in your home country, where an immediate assessment of your problem is made.

Check that the policy covers ambulance transportation and/or an emergency flight home.

Driving Licence & Permits
Prior to travelling, check whether you need an International Driving Permit to drive in the countries you are visiting. Bring your scuba-certification card if you plan to do any scuba diving.

Copies
All important documents (passport data page and visa page, credit cards, travel insurance policy, air/bus/train tickets, driving licence etc) should be photocopied before you leave home. Leave one copy with someone at home and keep another with you, separate from the originals.

EMBASSIES & CONSULATES
See individual country chapters for the addresses of embassies and consulates.

Your Own Embassy
As a tourist, it's vitally important to realise what your own embassy – the embassy of the country of which you are a citizen – can and can't do.

Generally speaking, it won't be much help in emergencies if the trouble you're in is remotely your own fault. Remember that you are bound by the laws of the country you are in. Your embassy will not be sympathetic if you end up in jail after committing a crime locally, even if such actions are legal in your own country.

In genuine emergencies you might get some assistance, but only if other channels have been exhausted. For example, if you need to get home urgently, a free ticket home is exceedingly unlikely – the embassy would expect you to have insurance. If all your money and documents are stolen, it might assist with getting a new passport, but a loan for onward travel is out of the question.

CUSTOMS

If you are travelling with expensive camera- or computer-equipment, carry a receipt to avoid hassles when returning home. Bringing in vegetable matter, seeds, animals or dairy produce to isolated island nations can introduce diseases with the potential to lay waste to local agriculture. Importing such items without a licence is usually prohibited.

Naturally, taking firearms or drugs through customs is frowned upon everywhere. Many countries prohibit exporting coral, shells or artefacts. See the individual country chapters for any particular customs rules.

MONEY
Exchanging Money

The most easily exchanged currencies in the Pacific are the US, Australian and New Zealand dollars, and the Pacific franc (the Cour de Franc Pacifique; see the New Caledonia or Tahiti & French Polynesia chapters for exchange rates). Exactly which is best depends on the particular country (see Money in the individual country chapters).

You lose out through commissions and customer exchange rates every time you change money, so if you only visit American Samoa, for example, buy US dollars straight away if your bank at home can provide them. If banks charge a flat rate, you are better off changing larger amounts less frequently.

All Pacific currencies are fully convertible, but you may have trouble exchanging some of the lesser-known ones at small banks, while currencies of countries with high inflation face unfavourable exchange rates. Try not to have too many leftover notes of Pacific currencies at the end of your trip; no bank outside the Pacific will touch them.

Most airports and big hotels have banking facilities that are open outside normal office hours, sometimes on a 24-hour basis. Post offices often perform banking tasks and outnumber banks in remote places; they also tend to have extended hours of operation. Be aware, though, that while they always exchange cash, they might balk at handling travellers cheques.

The best exchange rates are offered at banks. *Bureaux de change* usually offer worse rates or charge a higher commission. Hotels are almost always the worst places to change money. American Express and Thomas Cook usually don't charge a commission for changing their own cheques, but may offer a less favourable rate than banks.

Getting money out from your home bank account via ATMs is probably the best way to access cash in many Pacific countries (see Plastic Cards & ATMs later in this chapter for details). To get money in an emergency see International Transfers.

Cash Nothing beats cash for convenience... or risk. If you lose it, it's gone forever and very few travel insurers will come to your rescue. Those that will, limit the amount to somewhere around US$300. A money belt under your clothes is not a bad precaution.

Travellers Cheques The main reason for carrying travellers cheques rather than cash is the protection they offer from theft, though they are losing their popularity as more travellers deposit their money in their bank at home and withdraw it as they go along through ATMs.

American Express and Thomas Cook travellers cheques are widely accepted and have efficient replacement policies. If you're going to remote places, stick to American Express, since small local banks may not accept other brands.

When you change cheques, don't look at just the exchange rate; ask about fees and commissions as well. There may be a service fee per cheque, a flat transaction fee or a percentage of the total amount irrespective of the number of cheques. Some banks charge fees (often exorbitant) to change cheques and not cash; others do the reverse.

Keep a record of cheque numbers; without them, replacement of lost cheques will be a slow and painful process. Many institutions charge a per-cheque fee, so most of your cheques should be in large denominations, say US$100. It's only at the end of your stay that you might want to change a US$10 or US$20 cheque just to get through the last day or two.

Plastic Cards & ATMs Ask your bank to explain the workings of credit, credit/debit, debit, charge and cash cards.

A major advantage of credit cards is that they allow you to pay for expensive items (eg, airline tickets) without your having to carry great wads of cash around. They also allow you to withdraw cash at selected banks or from the many ATMs that are linked up internationally. However, if an ATM in Fiji swallows a card that was issued in Germany, it can be a major headache.

Also, some credit cards aren't hooked up to ATM networks unless you specifically ask your bank to do this. ATMs are common in major Pacific centres, but unknown in the outer islands or rural areas.

Cash cards, which you use at home to withdraw money directly from your bank account or savings account, can be used at ATMs linked to international networks like Cirrus and Maestro.

Credit and credit/debit cards, such as Visa and MasterCard, are widely accepted. However, these cards often have a credit limit that is too low to cover major expenses like long-term car rental or airline tickets and can be difficult to replace if lost abroad. Also, a cash advance against your Visa or MasterCard credit card account incurs a transaction fee and/or finance charge. With some issuers, the fees can reach as high as US$10, *plus* interest per transaction, so it's best to check with your card issuer before leaving home and compare rates.

Charge cards like American Express (AmEx) have offices in many countries that will replace a lost card within 24 hours. However, AmEx offices in this part of the Pacific are limited to Australia, French Polynesia, New Caledonia and New Zealand. Charge cards are not widely accepted off the beaten track.

The best advice is not to put all your eggs in one basket. If you want to rely heavily on bits of plastic, go for two different cards – an AmEx along with a Visa or MasterCard. Better still is a combination of credit or cash card and travellers cheques so you have something to fall back on if an ATM swallows your card or the banks in the area are closed.

A word of warning: fraudulent shopkeepers have been known to quickly make several charge slip imprints with your credit card when you're not looking, and then simply copy your signature from the one that you authorise. Try not to let your card out of sight, and always check your statements upon your return.

International Transfers Telegraphic transfers are inexpensive but can be quite slow. Specify the name of the bank and the name and address of the branch where you'd like to pick it up.

In an emergency, it's much quicker and easier to have money wired via an American Express office (US$60 for US$1000). Western Union's Money Transfer system (available at post offices in some countries) and Thomas Cook's MoneyGram service are also popular. The money is available within minutes of being sent; you'll need identification when collecting it.

Costs
The Pacific is *not* a bargain paradise. Accommodation is relatively expensive; hostels may be fairly common in most regions but low-cost options such as camping are often not possible (see Accommodation later in this chapter). Much of the food is imported, and is therefore pricey. In remote areas transport costs force food prices up even further. The most expensive countries to visit are French Polynesia and New Caledonia, while the cheapest are Samoa and Fiji.

Costs vary enormously. About US$30 to US$40 per day will allow you to live like a monk (or a nun) in Tahiti (camping or staying in a guesthouse dormitory and eating bread and cheese), or have a pretty good time in Samoa (mid-range accommodation and some restauranting).

Because of the price of fuel, travel costs can be particularly high, whether by car, plane or speedboat. Some careful planning can reduce travel costs substantially. Hiring a bicycle or hitchhiking is worth considering.

One money-saving strategy is preparing your own meals; it's worth looking at accommodation with access to a kitchen. Avoid expensive tinned goods in favour of locally grown fruit and vegetables. Markets are usually the cheapest way to buy any kind of food. At the very least, avoid trendy tourist restaurants and look for the places catered by locals.

The more time you spend in any one place, the lower your daily expenses are likely to be as you get to know your way around. Travelling with someone else is another way to save money.

Activities such as scuba diving, organised tours and car hire will push costs up considerably.

A general warning about the prices we list in this book: they're likely to change, usually upward, but if the last holiday season was particularly slow, or the local economy crashes, they may remain the same or even come down a bit.

Tipping & Bargaining
Attitudes to tipping vary in the Pacific but in general, tipping is not expected and in some

cases it may cause offence. It's far better to keep your 'tip' to a smile of thanks. In Melanesian societies, a tip is a gift that creates an obligation that the receiver must reciprocate, and they can't do this if you're passing through. Tipping is becoming more common in cities like American Samoa's Pago Pago or French Polynesia's Pape'ete.

The Pacific is not Asia; bargaining is not the practice in any Pacific countries and may cause offence. Although bargaining is becoming more common in the tourist shops of major cities, village people will often take their produce back home from market rather than accept a lower price than what's asked. The exception to all this is Fiji where Indo-Fijians, as part of their culture, expect to bargain and will initiate it.

Occasionally, people in isolated areas will quote you grossly inflated prices for artefacts or accommodation, usually because they are not up to date with current prices. When this happens, explain that you can't afford that much and then tell them what it would cost in the city. If they don't accept it, you'll have to either pay the first price or try elsewhere.

POST & COMMUNICATIONS
Post
You can collect mail at poste restante counters at major post offices. Ask people writing to you to print your name and underline your surname. Then mark the envelope 'Poste Restante (General Delivery)' with the name of the city and country. When collecting mail, your passport may be required for identification and a fee may be charged. Check under your first name as well as your surname. Post offices usually hold letters for a month.

If you're arriving by yacht, letters should have the name of the vessel included somewhere in the address. Mail is normally filed under the name of the vessel rather than by surname.

Telephone
In some South Pacific countries, it's feasible to take a mobile phone on holiday; see Post & Communications under Facts for the Visitor in the individual country chapters. Public telephones can be a rarity, but it's usually not too hard to find a shop owner who will let you use their phone for a local call. Some top-end hotels charge pretty steeply for the privilege of using their phones.

International telephone codes are listed in an appendix of this book.

Email & Internet Access
The major international Internet service providers ISPs, such as **AOL** (W *www.aol.com*), **CompuServe** (W *www.compuserve.com*) and **IBM Net** (W *www.ibm.com*), have very few dial-in nodes in the South Pacific. This means it really isn't feasible to take a portable computer on holiday with you in order to stay in touch with life back home. You're better off relying on Internet cafés and other public access points – post offices, telecom offices, libraries, hostels, hotels or universities – to collect your mail. See Post & Communications under Facts for the Visitor in the individual country chapters for information about Internet access in that country.

If you use Internet cafés to access your home email account, you'll need three pieces of information: your incoming (POP or IMAP) mail server name, your account name and your password. Your ISP or network supervisor will provide these. With this information you should be able to access your account from any Internet-connected machine in the world, provided it runs some kind of email software (Netscape and Internet Explorer both have mail modules). Most ISPs also enable you to receive your emails through their website, which only requires you to remember your account name and password. It pays to become familiar with the process for doing this before you leave home. Another option for collecting mail through Internet cafés is to open a free web-based email account such as **HotMail** (W *www.hotmail.com*) or **Yahoo! Mail** (W *www.mail.yahoo.com*).

If you do decide to travel with a portable computer keep in mind that unless you know what you're doing it's fraught with potential problems. The power supply voltage in the countries you visit may vary from that at home – see Electricity later in this chapter. Also, your modem may not work once you leave your home country – you won't know for sure until you try. The best option is to buy a reputable 'global' modem before you leave home, or buy a local modem if you're spending an extended time in one country. Keep in mind that the telephone socket in each country you visit will probably be different from that at home, so take at least a US RJ-11 telephone adapter that works with your modem. (You can almost always find an adapter that will convert from RJ-11 to the local variety.) For more information on travelling with a portable computer, see W www.teleadapt.com or W www.igoproducts.com.

DIGITAL RESOURCES

The Internet is a rich resource for travellers. You can research your trip, hunt down bargain air fares, book hotels, check weather conditions or chat with locals and other travellers about the best places to visit (or avoid!).

Many airlines have their own websites; see Airlines in the Getting There & Away chapter. Tourist office websites are a good source for relevant links, see the individual country chapters. Some other useful and reliable websites are:

Australian National University (W www.sunsite .anu.edu.au/spin/wwwvl-pacific) Comprehensive collection of Pacific links

Greenpeace (W www.greenpeace.org) Details environmental issues including the greenhouse effect, nuclear testing and over-fishing

Lonely Planet (W www.lonelyplanet.com) There's no better place to start your explorations than the Lonely Planet website. Here you'll find succinct summaries on travelling to most places on earth, postcards from other travellers and the Thorn Tree bulletin board, where you can ask questions before you go or dispense advice when you get back. You can also find travel news and updates to many of our most popular guidebooks, and the subWWWay section links you to the most useful travel resources elsewhere on the Web.

Pacific Islands Development Programme (W www.pidp.eastwestcenter.org/pireport) Produces the daily Pacific Islands Report

Polynesian Voyaging Society (W www.leahi .kcc.hawaii.edu/org/pvs) The history of Polynesian voyaging and contemporary voyages

South Pacific Environment Programme (W www.sidsnet.org/pacific/sprep) Presents Pacific environmental issues

United Nations Environment Programme (W www.unep.ch/conventions) Looks at global warming, rising sea levels, coral reefs, biodiversity etc

University of the South Pacific (W www.usp bookcentre.com) Lists Pacific books and publications

World Climate (W www.worldclimate.com) Average climate data

BOOKS

Only the larger towns on main islands are likely to have much in the way of bookshops. It's also worth trying public and high school libraries. In the Pacific region you'll find large Pacific collections in libraries in Honolulu, Suva, Noumea and Auckland. Many South Pacific books can be ordered online through the **University of the South Pacific**

Book Centre (☎ 321 2500, fax 330 3265; W www.uspbookcentre.com; Suva). See the individual country chapters for more books.

Lonely Planet

A guidebook covering an area as vast as the South Pacific can only hope to scratch the surface. For more detailed information about your destination see Lonely Planet's comprehensive list of South Pacific titles. Single-country guidebooks of the region are *Rarotonga & the Cook Islands, Chile & Easter Island, Tahiti & French Polynesia, Samoan Islands, Tonga, Fiji, New Caledonia, Solomon Islands* and *Vanuatu*. In addition, we publish guides for the Pacific islands not included in this book: *Hawaii, Papua New Guinea, New Zealand* and the multicountry guide *Micronesia*.

Pacific travellers might also find Lonely Planet's phrasebook series useful: the *South Pacific* phrasebook includes Cook Islands Maori, Kanak, Niuean, Pitkern, Samoan, Tahitian and Tongan. The *Pidgin* phrasebook includes the languages of the Solomon Islands and Vanuatu.

Lonely Planet's Pisces series includes guides to *Great Reefs of the World, Sharks of Tropical & Temperate Seas, Venomous & Toxic Marine Life of the World* and *Watching Fishes*. Individual Pisces guides to diving and snorkelling in the Pacific islands are listed in the 'South Pacific Diving' special section.

Guidebooks

The natural history and environmental aspects of Pacific (and Caribbean) islands is given in Frederic Martini's *Exploring Tropical Isles and Seas*. Dick Watling's *Birds of Fiji, Tonga and Samoa* is excellent, and includes colour illustrations of all the region's endemic and migratory birds. A useful Melanesian bird guide is the *Field Guide to the Birds of the Solomons, Vanuatu and New Caledonia*, by Chris Doughty.

A guide to the marine life of the region is Ewald Lieske & Robert Myers' *Coral Reef Fishes*. Another good guide is *Sharks of Polynesia*, by RH Johnson. If you prefer killing fish to just looking at them, Peter Goadby's *Big Fish and Blue Water – Gamefishing in the Pacific* might be for you.

Travel

The first travelogue about the Pacific was Simon Winchester's *The Pacific* – an entertaining but rather hastily assembled account of his journalistic journeys around the region. Far superior is Julian Evans' *Transit of Venus – Travels in the Pacific* – a well written account of his shoestring journey by boat through the Pacific.

Slow Boats Home by Gavin Young is the sequel to his earlier book *Slow Boats to China*. These books recount the author's 1979 voyage around the world on a wide range of maritime transport. The second book includes the Pacific part of the journey.

The perpetually miserable Paul Theroux's *The Happy Isles of Oceania – Paddling the Pacific* is anything but 'happy'. Poor old Paul complained of a wretched time and eventually had to return to the US.

Fiction

After a flurry of novels about the Pacific islands at the start of the 20th century, other regions became more fashionable and it is now difficult to find a contemporary novel set in the region. Most famous among the oldies, *Tales of the South Pacific*, *Rascals in Paradise* and *Return to Paradise*, by James Michener, are collections of short stories and essays dealing with life in the South Pacific from WWII onward. The first title sparked a revival of Western interest in the Pacific, won a Pulitzer Prize, and was made into a Broadway show and a film; see the Films entry in this chapter.

Jack London (*South Sea Tales*; 1911), Somerset Maugham (*The Trembling of a Leaf*; 1921) and Robert Louis Stevenson (see Books in the Samoa chapter) were other European authors whose Pacific island short stories became famous.

Contemporary Pacific island novelists include Sir Thomas Davis (see First Settlers & Voyaging books), Albert Wendt (see Books in the Samoa chapter) and 'Epeli Hau'ofa (see the Tonga chapter).

The work of Pacific island authors is comprehensively described in the Institute of Pacific Studies' *South Pacific Literature – From Myth to Fabulation*.

General History

Ian Campbell's *A History of the Pacific Islands* is a good, short summary of the Pacific region from the time of the original inhabitants through to the 1980s. *Tides of History*, edited by KR Howe *et al*, is a superb collection of essays covering the same period, though from a variety of perspectives.

The Cambridge History of the Pacific Islands, edited by Donald Denoon *et al*, is an excellent recent study of the Pacific. Ferry Howe's popular *Where the Waves Fall* is a history of the islands from first settlement through to colonial rule.

First Settlers & Voyaging

The most comprehensive text on the Lapita precursors of Polynesians is Patrick Kirch's *The Lapita Peoples*. Peter Bellwood discusses the arrival and migration of the Polynesian islanders from Southeast Asia through the islands in his *Man's Conquest of the Pacific*.

A great compilation of Pacific mythology and legends is *Vikings of the Sunrise* by Te Rangi Hiroa (Sir Peter Buck).

One of the best books about ancient Pacific voyaging is *Polynesian Navigation*, edited by Jack Golson. Jeff Evans' *The Discovery of Aotearoa* describes the ancient journeys from the Society and Marquesas islands to New Zealand, and the modern journey of the *Hawaiki-Nui*, a traditional *vaka* (canoe), along the same route.

We, the Navigators and *The Voyaging Stars – Secrets of the Pacific Island Navigators*, both by meticulous researcher David Lewis, are excellent studies of traditional navigation methods, though difficult books to find. Lewis' more easily located *From Maui to Cook* is very readable. It includes European exploration in the Pacific and describes the modern journey of another traditional *vaka*, the *Hokule'a*.

Thor Heyerdahl's *Kon Tiki Expedition* is a rip-snorting adventure story of the author's 1947 journey from Peru to the Tuamotus in a balsa raft. While Heyerdahl's scientific methods may have been less than rigorous, he writes a good tale.

Vaka, by Sir Thomas Davis (Pa Tuterangi Ariki), is a fictional account of ancient Polynesian voyaging to the Cook Islands from Havaiki and Samoa. The author writes from personal experience: see the boxed text 'Voyaging & Navigation' in the Facts about the South Pacific chapter.

European Exploration & Contact

In *Blue Latitudes: Boldly Going Where Captain Cook has Gone Before* (2002; also sold as *Into the Blue:...*), Pulitzer-winning writer Tony Horwitz retraces the voyages of Captain Cook with a beer-swilling mate. It's a frustrating, funny and insightful read.

Glyndwr William's *The Great South Seas* is a fascinating and often amusing study of European explorers in the Pacific. Archibald Grenfell Price's *The Explorations of James Cook* is a worthy summary of Cook's journals. Miriam Estensen's *Discovery – The Quest for the Great South Land* is a good history of the search for *Terra Australis Incognita*.

An interesting work about 19th-century trade in the southwest Pacific is Dorothy Shinberg's *They Came for Sandalwood*. The blackbirding trade is described in *Slavers in Paradise* by HE Maude – an account of the tragic events surrounding the kidnapping of Pacific islanders by Peruvian slave traders in the early 1860s. The continuing effect of the blackbirding trade on Solomon Islander populations in Samoa is told in Malama Meleisea's short book *O Tama Uli – Melanesians in Western Samoa*.

One of the most influential books written on the impact of colonialism in the South Pacific, *The Fatal Impact – The Invasion of the South Pacific 1767–1840*, by Alan Moorehead, critically assesses the havoc wreaked on the Pacific by early European explorers and fortune-seekers. Much less pessimistic is Nicholas Thomas in *Colonialism's Culture* and *Entangled Objects*; he argues that despite the lasting impact of colonialism, Pacific cultures are resilient and that a complex system of cultural exchange took place (and continues to). Another book on this subject, Ron Crocombe's *The South Pacific – an Introduction*, discusses the potential of the Pacific nations as independent countries and the changes to their cultures and identities since white settlement.

For books about the mutiny on the *Bounty*, see the boxed text 'Mutiny on the Bounty' in the Pitcairn Island chapter.

Contemporary Issues

The definitive source for hard facts about Pacific countries is the comprehensive *Pacific Island Yearbook*, published by the University of the South Pacific (USP). However, despite the name, it is not an annual publication and such facts quickly become out of date.

A number of books have been written about the Pacific arena during WWII, including Eric Bergerud's *Touched With Fire – The Land War in the South Pacific*.

The USP's *Pacific Women – Roles and Status of Women in Pacific Societies* assesses the changing status of women in the Pacific.

Robert Stewart's *Pacific Profiles* is a fascinating compilation of very short stories by a hundred Pacific islanders. *Niu Waves* (2001), edited by Robert Nicole, is a contemporary collection of South Pacific short stories and poetry.

A modern and wide-ranging political guide is the USP's excellent *New Politics in the South Pacific*. Less up-to-date, David Robie's angry *Blood on Their Banner* describes nationalist struggles in New Caledonia, French Polynesia and Fiji.

Looking at France's role in the Pacific is *France's Overseas Frontier* by Robert Aldrich and John Connell. In the same genre is Stephen Henningham's *France & the South Pacific*, a very readable paperback dealing individually with each of the French territories, as well as with the issue of French nuclear testing. Henningham also wrote *The Pacific Island States*, which concentrates on conflict and security issues in the modern Pacific. *The French-Speaking Pacific* edited by Christian Jost looks at population, development and environmental issues associated with New Caledonia, French Polynesia, Wallis & Futuna and Vanuatu.

The nuclear testing programme in the Pacific is the topic of many books, including *Moruroa, Mon Amour* by Bengt Danielsson and Jane Dibblin's *Day of Two Suns*.

Global warming is discussed in John Houghton's *Global Warming – The Complete Briefing*, Ian Lowe's *Living in the Greenhouse*, Stewart Boyle and John Ardill's *The Greenhouse Effect* and many other books. If you have access to a good reference library, look for publications by the United Nations Environment Programme (UNEP) and the Intergovernmental Panel on Climate Change (IPCC). Some excellent websites giving up-to-date details about both nuclear testing and the greenhouse effect are listed earlier in this chapter under Digital Resources.

FILMS

The better-known Pacific films show little of Pacific culture and these days may be of more comedy value than social. Two of James Michener's novels were made into films: *Return to Paradise* (1953) and *South Pacific* (1958). The former was filmed in Samoa, where Return to Paradise Beach became a popular tourist destination. Fiji has also featured in several 'comedy-value' films: both the original 1948 *Blue Lagoon*, starring Jean Simmons, and the 1979 remake with Brooke Shields, were shot in the Yasawa islands; the 2001 blockbuster *Cast Away* with Tom Hanks, was filmed on Monuriki in the Mamanuca Group (Fiji).

See the boxed text 'Mutiny on the Bounty' in the Pitcairn Island chapter for movies about that famous mutiny.

The war film *The Thin Red Line* (1998) showcased the beautiful singing of the Solomon Islanders, and the stunning scenery of Guadalcanal. For a much less successful Hollywood production 'Rapa Nui', see the boxed text 'When Hollywood Came to Town' in the Easter Island chapter.

Recent short films by award-winning Sima Urale include *O Tamaiti* (The Children; 1996), and her innovative documentary *Velvet Dreams* – about kitschy velvet paintings of dusky Pacific maidens. *Tatau Samoa* by German director Glsa Schleelein retraces the life of Samoan tattoo master, Paulo Sulu'ape. Lonely Planet's *The Pacific Islands* video depicts Fiji, Vanuatu and the Solomon Islands. Other commercially available videos include *The Eastern Pacific*, in the OceanLife series; and *Wayfinders – A Pacific Odyssey*, a documentary about traditional voyaging and the *Hokule'a* canoe (see the film's website at W www.pbs.org/wayfinders).

NEWSPAPERS & MAGAZINES

If you want to keep up with issues in the Pacific, you could subscribe to the regionally published magazine, **Pacific Magazine** *(fax 808-537 6455; PO Box 913, Honolulu, Hawaii 96808)*. For further reading see Newspapers & Magazines in the individual country chapters.

RADIO & TV

In addition to the easy-listening music and Christian dogma of local stations, with a shortwave radio you can pick up several useful broadcasts across the Pacific. Some of the stations broadcasting international and Pacific news include:

BBC World Service (W www.bbc.co.uk/world service/freq)

Radio Australia (W www.abc.net.au/ra/hear)

Reseau France Outre-mer (W www.rfo.fr) French language

Radio New Zealand International (W www .rnzi.com) English and Pacific languages

Voice of America (W www.voa.gov)

Frequencies change depending on the time of day: higher frequencies (1MHz to 17MHz) are used during daylight hours, lower frequencies (6MHz to 7MHz) are used at night and intermediate frequencies (9MHz to 14MHz) are used during the early morning or evening (local time). Check broadcasters' websites, the magazine *Monitoring Times*, the annual *World Radio TV Handbook* or the *Passport to World Band Radio* for frequency schedules.

Television content is usually a combination of local programmes and foreign feeds. See Radio & TV in the individual country chapters for details.

PHOTOGRAPHY & VIDEO
Film & Equipment

The availability of film and photographic/video equipment varies from country to country. In most cases you will be able to buy film in the main town or city but not in more remote areas. Often though, even if film is available it is heinously expensive, so it's usually best to buy at least a few duty-free films, if not all your film, before you arrive.

Processing film is easy in the major cities of most countries although developing black-and-white print film and slide film may not be possible until you get home.

Useful equipment to bring includes a small flash, spare batteries, polarising filter, lens-cleaning kit and silica-gel packs to protect equipment from the high humidity. Film in the tropics needs to be protected from both heat and humidity. Sachets of silica crystals will protect your equipment from moisture, but it's more important to keep your camera and film in a cool place.

Technical Tips

Avoid taking pictures in the midday sun. The best times for photography are before 9.30am and after 4pm. Otherwise, you may have to underexpose your shots slightly to avoid glare.

Automatic cameras and light meters are often fooled by the Pacific's strong light. If your camera is automatic it may overcompensate, causing dark-skinned faces and rainforest views to come out shadowy. This can be a real problem if you're photographing subjects against a bright background, such as a white sand beach. In these situations, use manual settings. It's often best to deliberately overexpose by 1.5 stops (eg, use f11 instead of f16/22). It's a good idea to underexpose by the same amount if taking close-ups of dark-skinned faces and other dark subjects.

Slides have less latitude for using the wrong exposure. If you're taking slides, one option is to bracket exposures (take extra photos half a stop over and half a stop under the reading set by the camera's meter) as some guarantee of success.

Use a flash to take photos in house interiors, for close-ups in the jungle dimness and at evening dances (remember that kava makes the drinker's eyes sensitive to light, so go easy). A telephoto lens – 100mm is recommended – is invaluable when something interesting is going on but you'd prefer to remain unobtrusive. Use a polarising filter for dramatic effects and maximum colour saturation, particularly if shooting over the sea.

Underwater Photography

In recent years, underwater photography has become a much easier activity. There is a variety of reasonably priced and easy-to-use underwater cameras available. The cheapest and most convenient option is the disposable one-roll underwater camera. These cost around US$15 and will be available at only the biggest towns and cities in the region.

As with any basic camera, the best photos are likely to be straightforward snapshots. You are not going to get superb photographs of fish and marine life with a small, cheap camera; however, photos of your fellow snorkellers can be terrific.

More than with other types of photography, the results achieved underwater can improve dramatically if you spend more on equipment, particularly on artificial lighting. As you descend natural colours are quickly absorbed, starting at the red end of the spectrum. The deeper you go the more 'faded' and blue your photos will look. The brain fools us to some extent by automatically compensating for this colour change, but the camera doesn't lie. If you are at any depth, your photos will look cold and blue.

To put the colour back in, you need a flash, and to work effectively underwater it has to be a much more powerful and complicated flash than you'd use out of water. Thus newcomers to serious underwater-photography soon find that having bought a Nikonos camera, they have to lay out as much money again for flash equipment to go with it. With the right experience and equipment the results can be superb. Generally, the Nikonos cameras work best with 28mm or 35mm lenses;

longer lenses do not work so well underwater. Although objects appear closer underwater, with these short focal-lengths you have to get close to achieve good results. Underwater photography opens up a whole new field of interest to divers, and the results can be startling. Flash photography can reveal colours that simply aren't there for the naked eye.

TIME

Local time relative to Greenwich Mean Time (GMT; which is the same as UTC) is given in the boxed text 'At a Glance' at the start of individual country chapters. Since this is the tropics, there's no daylight saving (summer time) on most of the Pacific islands – the exceptions are Fiji, Cook Islands, Pitcairn Island and Easter Island.

Time zones in the Pacific are more complex by the International Date Line, which splits the region in half. Crossing from east to the west, you go forward one day. The Date Line runs along the 180-degree latitude, detouring 800km to the east around Fiji and Tonga.

Times that are valid at midday in Fiji:

country	time
American Samoa	1pm, previous day
Cook Islands	2pm, previous day
Easter Island	6pm, previous day
Gambier Archipelago	3pm, previous day
Hawaii	2pm, previous day
Marquesas Islands	2.30pm, previous day
New Caledonia	11am, same day
Niue	1pm, previous day
Pitcairn Island	3.30pm, previous day
Samoa	1pm, previous day
Society Islands including Tahiti	2pm, previous day
Solomon Islands	11am, same day
Tokelau	2pm, previous day
Tonga	1pm, same day
Tuvalu	midday, same day
Vanuatu	11am, same day
Wallis & Futuna	midday, same day

Some international hours at the same time:

country	time
Berlin	1am, same day
London	midnight, same day
Los Angeles	4pm, previous day
New Zealand	midday, same day
New York	7pm, previous day
Paris	1am, same day
Singapore	8am, same day
Sydney	10am, same day
Tokyo	9am, same day

It is worth checking your airline tickets and itinerary very carefully if a country on your route is either starting or finishing daylight saving.

Throughout the Pacific you'll hear such terms as 'Tongan time', 'Fijian time' or 'island time'. This could be translated to a wish for tourists to 'relax, it'll happen eventually'. The concept of time is a bit fluid in the tropics and you'll find it a lot less stressful to adopt the same relaxed approach rather than try to change the Pacific single-handedly. It's also worth building some flexibility into your plans; don't plan on split-second transfers from bus to ferry, and if you need government approval for anything, be prepared to wait for it.

ELECTRICITY

The electricity supply in each of the Pacific countries largely reflects its historical associations. The three plug shapes used in the Pacific are: Australasian (Australia and New Zealand), European (used everywhere in the west except in the UK and North America), and US-style. Many resorts have outlets for 240V or 110V shavers and hair dryers. The following gives a rundown on what's used where:

230/240V AC, 50Hz, Australasian-style plug (two or three flat blades) Cook Islands, Fiji, Niue, Pitcairn Island, Samoa, Solomon Islands, Tokelau, Tonga, Tuvalu, Vanuatu
220V AC, 60Hz, European-style plug (two round prongs) French Polynesia
220V AC, 50Hz, European-style plug (two round prongs) Easter Island, New Caledonia, Wallis & Futuna
110V/120V AC, 60Hz, US-style plug (two flat blades) American Samoa

A universal AC adapter will enable you to plug in anywhere without frying the innards of your equipment. You'll also need a plug adapter for each country you visit – they're often easier to buy before you leave home. While adapters can transform voltage or connect one type of plug with another type of socket, frequency (Hz) conversion is impractical, and a clock or computer designed for one frequency *will not operate* under another.

Power supply in some countries is extremely erratic – especially away from the main centres – and some form of surge protection is necessary to operate sensitive equipment. In some remote areas, generators and solar power are used; in other places people still live without any form of electricity.

WEIGHTS & MEASURES

The metric system (kilometres, kilograms and degrees Celsius) is used in all the South Pacific countries covered in this book with the exception of American Samoa which uses the American version of the imperial system (miles, pounds, degrees Fahrenheit). In some countries, old habits die hard so you may find elderly people still widely using imperial units – be aware of this when interpreting directions. For conversion information, see the table inside the back cover of this book.

TOILETS

Public toilets are rare or nonexistent in most Pacific towns and cities. In town you will be able to pop into hotels, restaurants and cafés if you ask permission; if you're travelling off the beaten track, you may on occasion have to nip behind a banyan tree (coconut trees can be hazardous due to falling coconuts, and filling out the travel insurance medical claim form would be embarrassing). Carry spare toilet paper with you, and bury your paper afterwards.

Although most of the toilets are of the Western sit-down variety, many villages still do not have flush toilets (the water is supplied in a separate container) or may just use the nearby bush or reef. Sustainable-development projects in several countries include the establishment of composting toilets.

HEALTH

How healthy you are while travelling depends on your own predeparture preparations, your daily health care and how you handle any medical problem that may develop. While the potential dangers can seem quite frightening, in reality few travellers experience anything more than an upset stomach.

Predeparture Planning
Immunisations Although there are no *required* vaccinations for travellers to any countries in the South Pacific, there are some that are recommended. Plan ahead for vaccinations: some require more than one injection, while some vaccinations should not

be given together. Note that some vaccinations should not be given during pregnancy or to people with allergies – discuss with your doctor.

Seek medical advice at least six weeks before travel. Be aware that there is often a greater risk of disease with children and during pregnancy. Carry proof of your vaccinations; this is sometimes needed to enter a country.

Discuss your requirements with your doctor, but vaccinations you should consider for this trip include the following: diphtheria & tetanus, polio, hepatitis A & B, typhoid, rabies, tuberculosis (TB) and malaria (for more details about the diseases themselves, see the individual disease entries later in this section).

Note that you would only need *all* of these vaccinations if you were going to every deep dark corner of the Pacific. For most travellers, tripping through healthy destinations such as Fiji, Rarotonga, Samoa, Tahiti and Tonga, you wouldn't need any vaccinations at all!

Travel Health Guides

If you're planning to be travelling in remote areas for a long period of time, you may like to consider taking a detailed health guide. Lonely Planet's *Healthy Travel – Australia, New Zealand & the Pacific* has everything you need to know about general travel health in the region.

There are also a number of excellent travel-health sites on the Internet. From Lonely Planet's home page, there are links at **w** www.lonelyplanet.com/subwwway/links to the World Health Organization (WHO) and the US Center for Disease Control & Prevention (CDC).

Other Preparations

Make sure you're healthy before you start travelling. If you are going on a long trip check that your dental health is OK. If you wear glasses take a spare pair and a copy of your prescription.

If you require a particular medication take an adequate supply; it may not be available locally. To make getting replacements easier, take part of the packaging showing the generic name rather than the brand. It's a good idea to have a legible prescription or letter from your doctor to show that you legally use the medication.

See Travel Insurance under Visas & Documents earlier in this chapter.

Medical Kit Check List

Following is a list of items you should consider including in your medical kit – consult your pharmacist for brands available in your country.

- ☐ **Aspirin or paracetamol (acetaminophen in the USA)** – for pain or fever
- ☐ **Antihistamine** – for allergies, eg, hay fever; to ease the itch from insect bites or stings; and to prevent motion sickness
- ☐ **Cold and flu tablets, throat lozenges and nasal decongestant**
- ☐ **Multivitamins** – consider for long trips, when dietary vitamin intake may be inadequate
- ☐ **Antibiotics** – consider including these if you're travelling well off the beaten track; see your doctor, as they must be prescribed, and carry the prescription with you
- ☐ **Loperamide or diphenoxylate** – 'blockers' for diarrhoea
- ☐ **Prochlorperazine or metaclopramide** – for nausea and vomiting
- ☐ **Rehydration mixture** – to prevent dehydration, which may occur, for example, during bouts of diarrhoea; particularly important when travelling with children
- ☐ **Insect repellent, sunscreen, lip balm and eye drops**
- ☐ **Calamine lotion, sting relief spray or aloe vera** – to ease irritation from sunburn and insect bites or stings
- ☐ **Antifungal cream or powder** – for fungal skin infections and thrush
- ☐ **Antiseptic (such as povidone-iodine)** – for cuts and grazes
- ☐ **Bandages, Band-Aids (plasters) and other wound dressings**
- ☐ **Water purification tablets or iodine**
- ☐ **Scissors, tweezers and a thermometer** – note that mercury thermometers are prohibited by airlines

Basic Rules

Food If you're worried about health, vegetables and fruit should be washed with purified water or peeled if possible. Beware of ice cream sold on the street or anywhere that it might have melted and been refrozen; if there's any doubt (eg, a recent power cut), steer well clear. Shellfish such as mussels, oysters and clams should be avoided as well as undercooked meat, particularly mince. Steaming does not make shellfish safe for eating.

If a place looks clean and well run and the vendor also looks clean and healthy, then the food is probably safe. In general, places that are packed with travellers or locals will be fine. The food in busy restaurants is cooked and eaten quite quickly, and is unlikely to have sat around or been reheated.

Water See Health in the individual country chapters for the local water-purity situation. If you're worried about the water, and don't know for certain that it's safe, assume it's not. Bottled water or soft drinks are almost always fine (bottles can be refilled with tap water but let's not get paranoid here!). Take care with fruit juice, particularly if water may have been added. Milk should be treated with suspicion as it is often unpasteurised, though boiled milk is fine. Tea or coffee should be OK, since the water will have been boiled.

Medical Problems & Treatment
Self-diagnosis and treatment can be risky, so you should always seek medical help. Ask an embassy, consulate or five-star hotel to recommend a local doctor or clinic.

Environmental Hazards
Heat Exhaustion & Heatstroke Dehydration and salt deficiency can cause heat exhaustion. Take time to acclimatise to high temperatures, drink sufficient liquids and do not do anything too physically demanding when you first get there. Salt deficiency is characterised by fatigue, lethargy, headaches, giddiness and muscle cramps; salt tablets may help, but adding extra salt to your food is better.

Heat exhaustion can also develop into heatstroke. This serious, and occasionally fatal, condition occurs when the body's heat-regulating mechanism breaks down and the body temperature rises to dangerous levels. The symptoms include feeling unwell, sweating very little (or not at all) and a high body temperature (39°C to 41°C, or 102°F to 106°F). When sweating ceases, the skin becomes flushed and red. Severe headaches and lack of coordination also occur, and the sufferer may be confused or aggressive. Eventually the victim can become delirious or convulse. Hospitalisation is essential, but in the interim get the victim out of the sun, remove his or her clothing, cover with a wet sheet or towel and fan continuously. Give fluids if the person is conscious.

Everyday Health
Normal body temperature is 37°C (98.6°F); more than 2°C (4°F) higher indicates a high fever. The normal adult pulse rate is 60 to 100 per minute (children 80 to 100, babies 100 to 140). As a general rule the pulse increases about 20 beats per minute for each 1°C (2°F) rise in fever.

Respiration (breathing) rate is also an indicator of illness. Count the number of breaths per minute: between 12 and 20 is normal for adults and older children (up to 30 for younger children, 40 for babies). People with a high fever or serious respiratory illness breathe more quickly than normal. More than 40 shallow breaths a minute may indicate pneumonia.

Prickly Heat This is an itchy rash caused by excessive perspiration trapped under the skin. It usually strikes people who have just arrived in a hot climate. Keeping cool, bathing often, drying the skin and using a mild talcum or prickly-heat powder may help as will resorting to air-conditioning.

Sunburn You can get sunburnt surprisingly quickly, even through cloud. Use sunscreen, a hat, and a barrier cream for your nose and lips. Snorkellers, distracted by the view below them, often get sunburnt. Calamine lotion or a commercial after-sun preparation are good for mild sunburn. Protect your eyes with good-quality sunglasses.

Diarrhoea Simple things like a change of water, food or climate can all cause a mild bout of diarrhoea, but a few rushed toilet trips with no other symptoms is not indicative of a major problem.

Dehydration is the main danger with any form of diarrhoea, particularly in children or the elderly as it can occur quite quickly. Under all circumstances *fluid replacement* is the priority. Weak black tea with a little sugar, soda water, or soft drinks allowed to go flat and diluted 50% with clean water are all good. With severe diarrhoea, a rehydrating solution is preferable to replace minerals and salts lost. Commercially available oral rehydration salts (ORS) are very useful; add them to boiled or bottled water. You need to drink at least the same volume of fluid that you are losing in bowel movements and vomiting. Urine is the best guide to the adequacy of replacement – if you have small amounts of concentrated urine, you need to drink more. Drink small amounts often, and stick to a bland diet as you recover.

Gut-paralysing drugs such as loperamide or diphenoxylate bring relief from the symptoms, but are not a cure for the problem. Only use these drugs if you do not have access to toilets, eg, if you *must* travel. These drugs are not recommended for children under 12.

In certain situations medical treatment may be required: diarrhoea with blood or mucus (dysentery), any diarrhoea with fever, profuse watery diarrhoea, persistent diarrhoea not improving after 48 hours and severe diarrhoea. These suggest a more serious cause and in these situations gut-paralysing drugs should be avoided.

Two other causes of persistent diarrhoea in travellers, particularly those travelling off the beaten track, are giardiasis and amoebic dysentery.

Giardiasis is caused by a common parasite, *Giardia lamblia*. Symptoms include stomach cramps, nausea, a bloated stomach, watery, foul-smelling diarrhoea and frequent gas. Giardiasis can appear several weeks after you have been exposed to the parasite. The symptoms may disappear for a few days and then return; this can go on for several weeks. Seek medical advice if you think you have giardiasis.

Amoebic dysentery is characterised by a gradual onset of low-grade diarrhoea, often with blood and mucus. Cramping abdominal pain and vomiting are less likely than in other types of diarrhoea, and fever may not be present. It will persist until treated and can recur and cause other health problems. As with giardiasis, seek medical advice if you suspect you have amoebic dysentery.

Infectious Diseases

Fungal Infections These occur more commonly in hot weather and are usually found on the scalp, between the toes (athlete's foot) or fingers, in the groin and on the body (ringworm). You get ringworm (which is a fungal infection, not a worm) from infected animals or other people. Moisture encourages these infections.

To prevent fungal infections wear loose, comfortable clothes, avoid artificial fibres, wash frequently and dry yourself carefully. If you do get an infection, wash the infected area

at least once daily with a disinfectant or medicated soap and water, and rinse and dry well. Apply an antifungal cream or powder such as tolnaftate. Try to expose the infected area to air and sunlight as much as possible and wash all towels and underwear in hot water, change them often and let them dry in the sun.

Hepatitis This is a general term for inflammation of the liver. There are several different viruses that cause hepatitis, and they differ in the way that they are transmitted. The symptoms are similar in all forms of the illness, and include fever, chills, headaches, fatigue, feelings of weakness and aches and pains, followed by loss of appetite, nausea, vomiting, abdominal pain, dark urine, light-coloured faeces, jaundiced (yellow) skin and yellowing of the whites of the eyes. People who have had hepatitis should avoid alcohol for some time after the illness, as the liver needs time to recover.

Hepatitis A is transmitted by contaminated food and drinking water. You should seek medical advice, but there is not much you can do apart from rest, drink lots of fluids, eat lightly and avoid fatty foods. Hepatitis E, transmitted in the same way as hepatitis A, can be particularly serious in pregnant women.

There are almost 300 million chronic carriers of hepatitis B. It is spread through contact with infected blood, blood products or body fluids, for example through sexual contact, unsterilised needles, blood transfusions or contact with blood via small breaks in the skin. Other risk situations include having a shave, tattoo or body piercing with contaminated equipment. The symptoms of hepatitis B may be more severe than type A, and the disease can lead to long-term problems such as chronic liver damage, liver cancer or a long-term carrier state. Hepatitis C and D are spread in the same way as hepatitis B and can also lead to long-term complications.

There are vaccines against hepatitis A and B, but there are currently no vaccines against the other types. Following the basic rules about food and water (hepatitis A and E) and avoiding risk situations (hepatitis B, C and D) are important preventative measures.

Intestinal Worms These parasites are most common in rural, tropical areas. The different worms have different ways of infecting people. Some may be ingested with food such as undercooked meat (eg, tapeworms) and some enter through your skin (eg, hookworms). Infestations may not show up for some time, and although they are generally not serious, if left untreated some can cause severe health problems later. Consider having a stool test when you return home to check for these and determine the appropriate treatment.

Tuberculosis TB is a bacterial infection usually transmitted from person to person by coughing but which may be transmitted through consumption of unpasteurised milk. Milk that has been boiled is safe to drink, and the souring of milk to make yoghurt or cheese also kills the bacilli. Travellers are usually not at great risk as close household contact with the infected person is usually required before the disease is passed on. You may need to have a TB test before you travel as this can help diagnose the disease later if you become ill.

Typhoid A dangerous gut infection, typhoid fever, is caused by contaminated water and food. Medical help must be sought.

In its early stages sufferers may feel they have a bad cold or flu on the way, as early symptoms are a headache, body aches and a fever that rises a little each day until it is around 40°C (104°F) or more. The victim's pulse is often slow relative to the degree of fever present – unlike a normal fever where the pulse increases. There may also be vomiting, abdominal pain, diarrhoea or constipation.

In the second week the high fever and slow pulse continue and a few pink spots may appear on the body; trembling, delirium, weakness, weight loss and dehydration may occur. Complications such as perforated bowel, pneumonia or meningitis may also occur.

Insect-Borne Diseases

Malaria This serious and potentially fatal disease is spread by mosquitoes. In the Pacific, malaria is only a problem for travellers in the Solomon Islands and Vanuatu (and Papua New Guinea). In these islands, it's extremely important to avoid mosquito bites (see the boxed text) and to take tablets to prevent this disease. Malaria's symptoms range from fever, chills and sweating, headache, diarrhoea and abdominal pains to a vague feeling of ill-health. Seek medical help immediately if malaria is suspected.

Avoiding Mosquito Bites

Travellers are best advised to prevent mosquito bites at all times to avoid potentially serious diseases such as malaria and dengue fever, and for their own comfort. The best advice is:

- Wear light-coloured clothing
- Wear long trousers and long-sleeved shirts
- Use mosquito repellents containing the compound DEET on exposed areas (prolonged overuse of DEET may be harmful, especially to children, but its use is considered preferable to being bitten by disease-transmitting mosquitoes)
- Avoid perfumes or aftershave
- Use a mosquito net impregnated with mosquito repellent (permethrin) – it may be worth taking your own net
- Impregnate clothes with permethrin to effectively deter mosquitoes and other insects

---

Dengue Fever This viral disease is transmitted by mosquitoes and is one of the top public health problems in the tropical world. Unlike the malaria mosquito, the mosquito which transmits dengue fever is most active during the day, and is found mainly in urban areas, in and around human dwellings.

Symptoms of dengue fever include a sudden onset of high fever, headaches, joint and muscle pains (hence its old name, 'breakbone fever') and nausea and vomiting. A rash of small red spots sometimes appears three to four days after the onset of fever. In the early phase of illness, dengue fever may be mistaken for other infectious diseases, including malaria and influenza. Minor bleeding such as nose bleeds may occur in the course of the illness. Recovery even from simple dengue fever may be prolonged, with tiredness lasting several weeks.

Seek medical attention as soon as possible if you think you may be infected. Aspirin should be avoided, as it increases the risk of haemorrhaging. There is no vaccine against dengue fever. The best prevention is to avoid mosquito bites at all times.

Filariasis This is a mosquito-transmitted parasitic infection found in many parts of the Pacific. Travellers aren't at risk – infection requires repeated exposure to the parasite over many, many years – but if you're wondering why some Pacific islanders have swollen ankles and legs, it's probably filariasis.

Cuts, Bites & Stings

Cuts & Scratches Wash and treat any cut with an antiseptic (for example povidone-iodine). If possible avoid bandages and elastic plasters, which can keep wounds wet.

Coral cuts are slow to heal and if they are not adequately cleaned, small pieces of coral can become embedded in the wound. Severe pain, redness, fever or general feelings of ill-health suggest an infection and the need for immediate antibiotics as coral cuts may result in serious infections. Avoid coral cuts by not walking on reefs and try not to touch coral when swimming or snorkelling.

Bites & Stings Bee and wasp stings are usually painful rather than dangerous. However, in people who are allergic to them severe breathing difficulties may occur and require urgent medical care. Calamine lotion or a sting-relief spray will give relief and ice packs will reduce the pain and swelling.

Centipedes can give a painful, irritating bite that may cause swelling. Avoid walking outside barefoot and, if you're sleeping on a mattress on the floor, check underneath it before jumping into bed.

There are various fish and other sea creatures that sting or bite (see the boxed text 'Venomous Marine Life' later in this chapter), or which are dangerous to eat – see Ciguatera, following.

Ciguatera This is a form of food poisoning that comes from eating fish. Reefs that have been disturbed, for example by urban development, are particularly prone to the micro-organism which becomes present in reef fish, which are themselves consumed by larger fish such as rock cod, trevally and sea perch. There are no outward signs that a fish is infected.

Symptoms include vomiting, diarrhoea, nausea, dizziness, joint aches and pains, fever and chills and tingling around the mouth, hands and feet. Seek medical attention if you experience any of these symptoms after eating fish. It's always best to seek local advice before eating any reef fish as any ciguatera outbreak will be well known.

Tetanus This disease is caused by a germ which lives in soil and in the faeces of horses and other animals. It enters the body via breaks in the skin. The first symptom may be discomfort in swallowing, or stiffening of the jaw and neck; this is followed by painful convulsions of the jaw and whole body. The disease can be fatal. It can be prevented by vaccination.

SOCIAL GRACES

Certain rules of etiquette have their origins in ancient custom, while others are the direct result of Christianity. Special allowances are made for visitors, especially in major cities and touristy centres, where many of the locals ignore established traditions themselves. Those who learn and respect local traditions, however, will be more readily accepted, especially in rural areas.

Clothes & Conduct

Few Pacific places are uptight about clothing standards, but complying with regional customs will get a much better reception from locals. Dressing like a slob won't endear you to anyone – it's rarely appropriate for men to go bare-chested in town, and women's dress conventions are even stricter (see Women Travellers later in this chapter).

Public displays of affection between men and women, even two tourists, are often inappropriate. Flirting with the locals can also get you into a *lot* of trouble; there are some very serious expectations attached to what may appear to be casual affairs. Despite the writings of Western visitors from Bougainville to Margaret Mead, the Pacific is *not* a playground of free love.

Avoid becoming visibly frustrated when things don't go your way. Causing someone to lose face because they have failed you is an unforgivable sin.

Both tipping for service and bargaining for better prices can cause offence in Pacific countries. See also Tipping & Bargaining under Money earlier in this chapter.

Visiting Villages

Many tourists wish to see traditional villages, and visitors are usually welcomed with remarkable hospitality. Bear in mind, though, that such visits can be extremely disruptive in a traditional society. Guidelines are often quoted in tourist publications in the islands, and some are repeated here for the benefit of intending visitors.

- Shoes are usually removed when entering a home
- Sit cross-legged on the floor, rather than with your feet pointing out
- Avoid entering a house during prayers

- On Sunday, observe local protocol. For example, it's best not to arrive in a village on this day of worship
- Avoid walking between two people in conversation
- Try to remain on a lower level than a chief.
- Refrain from eating food while walking around a village

Photographing People

The perfect 'people shot' poses some specific challenges in the Pacific. While most islanders will enjoy being photographed, others will be put off and some people may be superstitious about your camera or suspicious of your motives.

Some kids will bug you so hard to take their photo that you'll eventually resort to pretending to click the shutter just to keep them happy. Others will refuse unless they get something in return. Usually you'll find it hard to get a 'natural' shot, and people will want to pose for you – even to the point of changing into their best clothes before you take their photo!

Always respect the wishes of the locals. Ask permission to photograph if a candid shot can't be made and don't insist or snap a picture anyway if permission is denied.

WOMEN TRAVELLERS

Many Pacific customs, particularly in Melanesia, may look to Westerners like Draconian male chauvinism. Some of them might look like this to the local women too: domestic violence is a huge problem in many Pacific countries. The Secretariat of the Pacific Community (see Government & Politics in the Facts about the South Pacific chapter) has initiated studies to determine how widespread this problem is.

Safety Precautions

Rape and sexual assault are rare but do occur in the Pacific, as elsewhere. In general women travellers should have nothing to fear, but it's wise to exercise caution, as always when you are out of your element.

It's not uncommon for lone women to experience some harassment. Men sometimes assume you're fair game if travelling alone. Finding a travelling companion, seeking the company of local women, or even just wearing a wedding ring may reduce unwanted attention.

In some countries it is against local customs for young women to be out at night by themselves. So think *very* carefully before accepting an invite to go drinking alone with local men. If you are alone at night, remain in busy areas and use a taxi for transport. In some places, the Cook Islands for example, accepting an offer to go to the beach with a man at night is seen as consenting to sex. Lone female tourists swimming or sunbathing at isolated beaches may also attract local Romeos. And we do not recommend that women hitchhike by themselves.

Women travelling in some parts of the Pacific may encounter a phenomenon known as 'creeping' or 'window peeking'. This unnerving practise involves a male standing outside your window hissing, whistling or knocking on the glass. Keep curtains drawn and don't invite them inside if you're not after company overnight.

For more information, Rough Guide's *Women Travel* has a good section on women travelling in the Pacific.

What to Wear

Pacific islanders can be a conservative bunch. They are also usually more tolerant of the peculiar ways of Western males than of females. However, attitudes to women's dress are changing in the Pacific. It's common to see women wearing jeans or even longish shorts in many main centres. However, in more rural areas and outer islands the dress code is more severe.

Women showing their thighs in public is *tapu* (forbidden) in most areas, so shorts should be knee-length. Sleeveless shirts and short skirts are similarly frowned upon. You should never swim or sunbathe topless or in the nude, and in some places you should even consider knee-length shorts for swimming.

If you're visiting a church, your clothing should be even more modest. In resorts catering to Westerners, rules are considerably less strict: Western standards, or lack thereof, apply. Local fashions inevitably change at differing paces, so ask around and take note of what others are wearing.

The most fashionable frock in many Pacific countries, the frumpy full-length 'Mother Hubbard' dress, won't win you many admirers on the streets of Paris or New York but it will make you lots of friends in Port Vila or Nukunonu.

GAY & LESBIAN TRAVELLERS

Pacific attitudes to homosexuality are complex. Pacific cultures are conservative, and some more enthusiastic religious leaders occasionally whip themselves into a frenzy about homosexuality. However, in Polynesia at least, there is an ancient tradition of male 'cross-dressing', which is usually, but not always, associated with homosexuality. See the boxed text 'Fakaleiti' in the Tonga chapter.

Apart from the most popular tourist centres, such as Fiji, there is little in the way of clubs or other facilities for gays and lesbians. Exceptions are those Polynesian cultures where the *fakaleiti* tradition remains strong, in Tonga, Samoa and Tahiti. See individual country chapters for more details.

There's little problem with open displays of male gay affection in most Polynesian countries, although lesbians are much less open in public. Excessive public displays of both heterosexual and homosexual affection are frowned upon in many Pacific societies.

Male homosexuality is technically illegal (although this is rarely enforced) in many Pacific countries, including the Cook Islands, Fiji, Niue, the Solomon Islands, Tokelau, Tonga and Tuvalu. Female homosexuality only gets an official mention in Samoa, where it is also illegal. In the more liberal French colonies of New Caledonia and French Polynesia, homosexuality is legal.

DISABLED TRAVELLERS

Most Pacific nations have very poor facilities for disabled travellers. Getting around can be a real problem for wheelchair users – small domestic aeroplanes have narrow doors and shipping services may not have ramp access. What's more, hotels and guesthouses are not used to receiving disabled guests, and nautical and open-air activities are geared for the 'able-bodied'.

On the other hand, disabled people are simply part of the community in the Pacific, looked after if necessary but expected to play a useful role. You won't have people pretending you don't exist; where a Sydney taxi cab might just accelerate away, a Samoan bus driver will call someone over to help him carry you aboard.

Western resorts and hotels are more likely to have some facilities. If you intend staying at a particular resort, check if it suits your needs. It may be best to book a ground-level room until you verify the ramp situation.

For pre-trip planning advice, consult the Internet (W www.lonelyplanet.com/subwwway /links) and contact disabled people's associations in your home country.

SENIOR TRAVELLERS

Pacific cultures value the family above almost anything else, and the elderly are universally respected for their wisdom. You may find a holiday in the Pacific a terrifically uplifting experience.

Check with any relevant organisations before you leave home for advice and for discounted travel packages. Some countries have special discounts for senior citizens; ask at tourist offices in that country. Be aware that the medical facilities on some outer islands may be poor or nonexistent.

TRAVEL WITH CHILDREN

The climate, natural setting, aquatic games and lack of poisonous creatures make the Pacific a paradise for children. However, apart from major destinations such as Fiji, which is well set up for children, few travellers take their kids anywhere in the Pacific. In fact, some resorts and hotels ban small children for all or part of the year, so check when booking. Ask about kids' discounts on everything from hotels to air fares.

Smaller towns and outer islands may have few resources for Westerners wanting to pamper their kids. You will usually be able to buy disposable nappies (diapers), infant formula, long-life milk etc in the main town, but don't leave the capital without buying everything you need or checking the local situation.

Supervise your children when swimming or playing on beaches, and make sure they understand not to touch coral. Bring plenty of sunscreen, light clothes and a hat for sun protection. Make sure vaccinations are up to date and that your health and travel insurance also covers your child. It's important to keep small children well hydrated in a hot climate. Gastrolite helps prevent dehydration and also masks unpleasant tastes in the water. If your child is sensitive to the local water, boil drinking water or buy bottled water.

Children are highly valued in Pacific cultures. Locals will often be keen to talk to your kids, play with them and invite them to join activities or visit homes. However, local kids are expected to behave, so try (ha!) to curb your child's crying and tantrums if visiting a village. Child care is a shared responsibility in the Pacific, and locals will sometimes correct your children for you if they misbehave!

See Health earlier in this chapter for more advice. Lonely Planet's *Travel with Children* has useful information for travel with children anywhere in the world.

DANGERS & ANNOYANCES

The Pacific islands are safer than many places in the world, but a certain amount of common sense is still called for. In general, you will find most Pacific islands to be just as idyllic as the tourist brochures lead you to expect and the people to be some of the friendliest you will ever meet. As anywhere, crime does exist, but with minimal caution you should have no problems. In some of the larger cities of the Pacific there have been an increase of assaults, so be aware when walking around at night, even as a couple. See Women Travellers earlier in this chapter for hassles that women may encounter.

In some areas at peak season, the sheer number of tourists can be a nuisance. But you can hardly complain about that when you're one of the tourists, can you?

Theft

Like the European explorers before you, you might run into some different attitudes to personal property while you're in the Pacific. You'll also sympathise with Cook's dilemma:

it can be difficult to stay Zen about another culture's attitude to property when someone has just run off with the ship's sextant!

Keep copies of important documents somewhere safe (see Visas & Documents earlier in this chapter) and use a money belt under your clothes to carry your passport and travellers cheques. Belongings are normally safe in hotel rooms but bear in mind that privacy is far from a sacred right in the Pacific.

And remember what happened to Captain Cook. Don't let your over-reaction to the threat of stealing spoil your holiday.

Swimming

The safest ocean swimming is within the protected waters of lagoons. However, swimmers should still be aware of tides and currents, and particularly of the swift movement of water out of a lagoon and through a pass into the open sea. Avoid swimming alone, seek local advice about the conditions and stay alert for venomous marine life. The safest, and most responsible, approach to any sea life is to look but don't touch.

Venomous Marine Life

Probably the most dangerous thing you'll have to worry about when snorkelling over a reef is sunburn. However, there are several venomous critters worth mentioning because there's always the chance that you'll meet one.

The well-camouflaged stonefish spends much of its time on the sea floor pretending to be a weed-covered rock. If you tread on a stonefish's sharp, extremely venomous dorsal spines, you'll find that the pain is immediate and incapacitating. Bathing the wound in hot water reduces the pain and the effects of the venom, but medical attention should be sought urgently.

The lionfish, a relative of the stonefish, is a strikingly banded, brown and white fish with large, graceful dorsal fins containing venomous spines. Lionfish are obvious when they're swimming around, but they can also hide under ledges.

Lionfish

Then there's the cone shell, several species of which have highly toxic venom. The bad ones have a venomous proboscis – a rapidly extendible, dart-like stinging device that can reach any part of the shell's outer surface. Cone shell venom can be fatal. Stings should be immobilised with a tight pressure bandage (not a tourniquet) and splint. Get medical attention immediately.

Cone shell

Avoid contact with jellyfish, which have stinging tentacles – seek local advice. Dousing in vinegar will deactivate any stingers that have not 'fired'. Calamine lotion, antihistamines and analgesics may reduce the reaction and relieve the pain. Other stinging sea creatures include flame or stinging coral and sea urchins.

Generally speaking, the best way to avoid contact with any of the above while you're in the water is to look but don't touch. Shoes with strong soles will provide protection from stonefish, but reef walking damages the reef, so you shouldn't be doing it anyway – you could view the stonefish as a very enthusiastic environmental protection officer.

Attacks by shark are rare but not unknown in Pacific countries. It's wise to seek the advice of local people before taking to the water. Swimming inside a reef offers some protection from sharks but if you are approached, stay calm (as calm as possible, anyway) and swim steadily away.

Mosquitoes
Even in places where mosquito-borne malaria is not a risk, the bites of mosquitoes can still cause considerable discomfort. They are less of a problem around the coast where sea breezes keep them away, but inland they can be a pest. See the boxed text 'Avoiding Mosquito Bites' earlier in this chapter.

Conflict
Appropriately enough, the Pacific is a fairly peaceful region. However, there are exceptions. The Solomon Islands erupted in ethnic violence in 1999 (see the boxed text 'Ethnic Tension' in that country's chapter) and, in early 2003, travel on Guadalcanal was not recommended outside Honiara.

For details on Fiji's not-so-distant political troubles, see that country's History section. Conflicts in past trouble spots in New Caledonia and French Polynesia have been largely resolved.

LEGAL MATTERS
The only drug you are likely to come across (apart from the eminently legal kava, betel nut, alcohol, coffee and tobacco) is marijuana. This is illegal in all Pacific countries, so extreme caution should be exercised if you are thinking about supplementing that natural Pacific high.

BUSINESS HOURS
Business hours vary throughout the islands, but 8am to 4.30pm Monday to Friday is fairly common. Banking hours also vary, though 10am to 3pm Monday to Thursday, and to 5pm on Friday are usual. See individual country chapters for any local variations.

The last weeks of the year are often difficult for doing business. Not only do Christmas and New Year holidays and parties interfere, but many government employees have leftover annual leave that must be taken by the end of the year and take a quick vacation. This goes for the day after a holiday as well: people have a habit of extending their holiday.

Every second Friday is payday on some islands, so that people leave work early (if they show up at all) to line up at the bank; it can be a major challenge to find government workers on payday.

In the devoutly Christian Pacific, many countries effectively close down on Sunday. On Sunday morning especially there are often no businesses open, and travellers who have not planned ahead can find themselves waiting a long time for breakfast. Rules are often relaxed at resorts, so spending the day at a resort is one way to escape the Sunday blues. Another option is to join in; attend an island church and listen to the beautiful singing.

PUBLIC HOLIDAYS & SPECIAL EVENTS
The standard Western holidays are observed in the Pacific islands. For extra national holidays, check individual country chapters.

Easter includes Good Friday, Holy Saturday, Easter Sunday and Easter Monday. Many Catholic countries observe the Ascension 40 days after Easter Sunday; Whit Sunday (Pentecost) is seven weeks after Easter. The Assumption is celebrated on 15 August.

The US-influenced nations may celebrate Martin Luther King Day, US Independence Day, Columbus Day, Veterans' Day as well as Thanksgiving. French territories celebrate Labour Day, Bastille Day, All Saints' Day and Armistice Day. It's amusing to listen to children on the other side of the world from France practising *La Marseillaise* for 14 July, with its stirringly-militaristic lines about fertilising our fields with impure blood! Countries associated with New Zealand/Australia often celebrate Anzac Day.

The following is a list of some standard Western public holidays:

New Year's Day 1 January
Martin Luther King Day 3rd Monday in January
Easter March/April
Anzac Day 25 April
Labor Day (French) 1 May
Whit Sunday & Monday May/June (Pentecost)
US Independence Day 4 July
Bastille Day 14 July
Assumption Day 15 August
Columbus Day 2nd Monday in October
All Saints' Day 1 November
Veterans' (Armistice) Day 11 November
Thanksgiving 4th Thursday in November
Christmas Day 25 December
Boxing Day 26 December

If a public holiday falls on a weekend, the holiday is often taken on the preceding Friday or following Monday.

Local festivals that involve a few different countries are listed here. See this section in the individual country chapters for country-specific events and holidays.

Festival of Pacific Arts – Held every four years in October in a different Pacific country. The ninth festival will be in Palau (Micronesia) in 2004.

Hawaiki Nui Va'a – Held each November in French Polynesia. Canoes from many Pacific countries are raced between the islands of Huahine, Ra'iatea, Tahaa and Bora Bora

Pacific island sevens tournaments – Held annually in the Cook Islands, Fiji and Samoa. They feature as much dance and celebration as they do rugby.

South Pacific Games – Held every four years at a different location around the Pacific. The 2003 games were held in Fiji; in 2007 it's Samoa's turn.

ACTIVITIES

In the very Christian Pacific islands, many activities will not be appropriate on the Sabbath (Sunday), unless you're at a resort that is accustomed to the heathen ways of tourists, or in main cities.

Sailing

See the Getting Around the Region chapter for information about taking your own yacht to the Pacific or getting a berth on someone else's. Yacht clubs are a good first port of call (ho ho) for information about renting a yacht. In the individual country chapters, yacht clubs are listed under Sea section in the Getting Around the Region chapter, and yacht rental information is given under Activities in Facts for the Visitor.

Hiking

Although a hike from one side of the island to the other may be a matter of minutes on small coral atolls, on the higher Pacific islands there are opportunities to walk through some magnificent rainforest. Many tracks cross land under customary ownership, so ask around before heading off. You may need to ask someone's permission and you may be required to pay a small fee.

Bushwalking in the heat has the potential to be a truly miserable experience. It's better to undertake long walks in the cooler parts of the year. Check Climate under Facts for the Visitor in the individual country chapters. Take plenty of water for more information.

Water Sports

What the Pacific islands lack in landmass, they make up for in water. Snorkelling is a great introduction to the underwater world and there's no shortage of places to try it out; see Activities in the individual country chapters for details.

For information about scuba diving, see the 'South Pacific Diving' special section.

The sport of board surfing was invented first by the sea-loving cultures of Polynesia. The first recorded observations of surfing on a board come from Hawaii and Tahiti in the 1770s. Some 200 years later the Pacific is still popular among surfers. Apart from the most famous beaches in Hawaii, surfers flock to French Polynesia, Tonga and Fiji. See Activities in the relevant country chapters. Surfing over coral reefs is obviously dangerous and should only be attempted at high tide. As always, local knowledge is the best guide regarding both safety and where the best waves are to be found.

Kayaking is popular, and kayaks can be rented on several islands. There are also opportunities to windsurf and jet ski. Several islands have set up beach huts as very cheap accommodation especially to cater for the surfing crowd.

Fishing

Anglers will find paradise in the South Pacific. Many countries offer excellent fishing opportunities with catches of tuna, wahoo,

---

Surfing

Modern surfers will identify with James Cook's observations of a Tahitian surfer in 1777:

I could not help concluding that this man felt the most supreme pleasure while he was driven on so fast and so smoothly by the sea.

Frustrated surfers may also be interested to learn an ancient Hawai'ian chant used to make the surf rise:

Kumai!
Kumai!
Ka nalu nui mai Kahiki mai
(Arise! Arise! You great surfs from Tahiti)

Responsible Bushwalking

Bushwalking places great pressure on the natural environment. When bushwalking consider:

Rubbish

Carry out all your rubbish. Make an effort to carry out rubbish left by others.

Minimise the waste you must carry out by taking minimal packaging. If you can't buy in bulk, unpack small-portion packages and combine their contents in one reusable container.

Never bury your rubbish: digging disturbs soil and ground-cover and encourages erosion. Buried rubbish will more than likely be dug up by animals, causing injury or poisoning. It may also take years to decompose.

Don't rely on bought water in plastic bottles. Disposal of these bottles is a major environmental problem. Use iodine drops or purification tablets instead.

Carry out sanitary napkins, tampons and condoms. They burn and decompose poorly.

Human Waste Disposal

Contamination of water sources by human faeces can lead to the transmission of hepatitis, typhoid and intestinal parasites such as Giardia and roundworms. It can cause severe health risks not only to members of your party, but also to local residents and wildlife.

Where there are no toilets, bury your waste. Dig a small hole 15cm (6 inches) deep and at least 50m (55 yards) from any watercourse. Consider carrying a lightweight trowel for this purpose. Cover the waste with soil and a rock. Bury toilet paper with the waste.

If the area is inhabited, ask locals if they have any concerns about your chosen toilet site.

Washing

Don't use detergents or toothpaste in or near watercourses, even if they are biodegradable.

Wash at least 50m (55 yards) from a watercourse. Disperse the waste-water widely to allow the soil to filter it fully before it makes it back to the watercourse. For personal washing, use biodegradable soap. For cooking utensils use a scourer or sand instead of detergent.

Erosion

Hillsides and mountain slopes are prone to erosion. It is important to stick to existing tracks and avoid short cuts. If you blaze a new trail straight down a slope, it may turn into a watercourse with the next heavy rainfall and eventually cause soil loss and deep scarring.

If a well used track passes through a mud patch, walk through the mud: walking around the edge will increase the size of the patch.

Avoid removing the plant life that keeps topsoil in place.

Fires & Low Impact Cooking

Don't depend on open fires for cooking. Cook on a light-weight kerosene, alcohol or Shellite (white gas) stove; avoid those powered by disposable butane-gas canisters.

If you do light a fire, ensure that you fully extinguish it after use. Spread the embers and douse them with water. A fire is only safe to leave when you can comfortably place your hand in it.

Wildlife Conservation

Discourage the presence of vermin by not leaving food scraps behind. Place gear out of reach and tie packs to rafters or trees.

Do not feed the wildlife, as this can lead to animals becoming dependent on hand-outs.

Hiking in Populated Areas

Follow the social and cultural considerations when interacting with the local community. See Social Graces earlier in this chapter.

barracuda, sailfish and marlin common. For more information see Activities in the Tonga, Samoa, Solomon Islands and Rarotonga & Cook Islands chapters.

SPECTATOR SPORTS

Among Pacific women, netball is the most popular game. Other sports pursued in the Pacific are soccer, boxing, athletics, basketball, volleyball, pétanque (in the French territories) and American football. Rugby union is popular throughout the Pacific, as well as the faster version rugby sevens, in which Fiji is up there amongst the world's best.

The English influence can also be seen in cricket's popularity, as well as the local variation known as *kirikiti* (see the boxed text 'The Civilising Influence of Cricket' in the Samoa chapter).

Sailing and paddling contests pay tribute to islanders' voyaging past; international contests include the annual Hawaiki Nui *va'a* (canoe) race in French Polynesia. The premier multi-sport event is the South Pacific Games, held every four years at a different location in the Pacific (the next is in Samoa in 2007).

In Pacific rim countries, some of the highest profile Pacific islanders are those playing sport, such as the rugby players of New Zealand and Australia or the American football players of the US.

WORK

Generally it's hard to get a work visa for Pacific countries. To find out the rules and regulations regarding work in a particular country, contact the relevant embassy, consulate or immigration office, or check their website.

Volunteer work is an excellent way to get to know a country but it's not an option for the casual tourist: volunteer programmes require a serious and long-term commitment. Most organisations require volunteers to have tertiary qualifications or work experience in their particular field, and to hold residency in the organisation's base country. Volunteer organisations active in the Pacific region include:

Australian Volunteers International (☎ 03-9279 1788, W www.ozvol.org.au) PO Box 350, Fitzroy Vic 3065, Australia
United Nations Volunteers (☎ 0228-815 2000, W www.unv.org) Postfach 260 111, D-53153, Bonn, Germany
US Peace Corps (☎ 1 800 424 8580, W www .peacecorps.gov) 1111, 20th St NW, Washington DC 20526, USA

Volunteer Service Abroad (VSA) (☎ 04-472 5759, W www.vsa.org.nz) PO Box 12-246, Wellington 1, New Zealand
Voluntary Service Overseas (VSO) (☎ 020-8780 7200, W www.vso.org.uk) 317 Putney Bridge Rd, London SW15 2PN, UK; offices in Canada and the Netherlands

ACCOMMODATION

Accommodation options vary widely in the Pacific. Some countries with thriving tourist industries, such as Fiji, have a range of choices from expensive resorts to backpacker hostels. Countries with a small tourist trade have accordingly fewer options; see Accommodation in the individual country chapters for more information.

Camping

If you have your own tent, camping can be a cheap alternative. For example, it's an excellent way to save precious francs in Tahiti or New Caledonia. However, some countries actively discourage camping; check Facts for the Visitor in the individual country chapters. Before setting up your tent, it's important to seek permission from any customary owners of the land. In many cultures, camping near a village can cast shame on the villagers for failing to invite the strangers into their homes. If you do camp out, try to leave no trace of your visit; carry out everything you carry in.

Staying in Villages

The Pacific islands are famous for their hospitality, and in many countries it is almost inevitable that you will be invited to stay in the home of a local family. Not only does this provide you with an insight into local culture and lifestyle, it confers a degree of honour on the host family.

Staying with a family shouldn't be viewed as a cheap form of accommodation. Even the most welcome guest will eventually strain a family's resources, and although they may never ask you to leave, after a few days it may be more considerate to move on. When you leave, it is important to express your gratitude. Gather the family, offer your thanks with a short speech, and present a gift. Don't call it 'payment' or it may be refused. It may well be refused anyway, but you should do your best to leave it behind. Cash will not always be accepted, but kava, alcohol or shop goods (such as canned meat) may be. Souvenir items from your own homeland will be most popular.

See Social Graces earlier for advice about how to behave in traditional homes and villages. Bear in mind that many Pacific cultures have a relaxed attitude to property. It's best not to leave expensive gear lying around in homes unless you share that relaxed attitude.

FOOD

The traditional diet of Pacific islanders depended heavily on vegetables; coconuts, taro, breadfruit, bananas, papayas, yams and *kumara* provided the bulk of meals. Protein was largely gained from seafood and birds, with dogs, pigs and fowl kept in reserve for feasting and ceremonial occasions.

Since contact with Europeans, the diet of Pacific islanders has taken a turn for the worse. Canned foods, particularly canned meat, are popular, as are heavily processed foods and drinks. Health problems related to this diet include obesity and diabetes. Popular fast-food outlets have added to the problem.

Kava

Kava (*ava, yaqona* or *sakau*) is drunk throughout almost all of Polynesia and much of Melanesia.

Drinking kava has always been a very formal process. It is still a strong social tradition at evening time in many Pacific cultures. As well as being used as a form of welcome, it's also used to seal alliances, to start chiefly conferences, and to commemorate births, deaths and marriages. If you're asked to drink some at a village, consider yourself honoured. To decline kava when it is offered is to decline friendship – so even though it may taste disgusting, you've got to gulp it down and appear impressed.

Kava is made from the roots of the *Piper methysticum* shrub, which was deliberately carried from island to island from Melanesia eastwards into Polynesia. There are many varieties of the plant growing in Melanesia: some 40 subspecies thrive in Vanuatu. Eastern Polynesia has only a few varieties.

Kava is an important cash and cultural crop in a number of Pacific Islands. It has properties that combat depression, reduce anxiety, and even lower blood pressure, which is why it spread like wildfire through health-obsessed Western countries in the 1990s. When trade peaked in 1998, Fiji and neighbouring Vanuatu were exporting US$25 million worth of the stuff each year.

But the good times didn't last. A Germany study done in 2001 indicated that kava potentially caused liver damage and by 2002, most of Europe as well as Canada and the US had either banned or put harsh warnings and restrictions on kava. Trade disappeared. Reviews later revealed that the vast majority of individuals examined in the German study were using other drugs that affect the liver, yet the bans remain.

Ceremony

Traditionally, there are strict rules for preparing and drinking kava.

Preparation procedures vary throughout the Pacific. In the more traditional areas, kava root is washed then prepared by chewing into a mush and spitting the hard bits onto leaves. The mush is then placed in a container, water is added and the ingredients are stirred with the hands. Then the mud-coloured liquid is filtered through coconut fibres. In other areas, the root may simply be pounded in a plastic bucket, or the drink may be prepared from a commercially packaged powder. As saliva releases the root's active ingredients, kava prepared by chewing is more potent than that from pounding.

Once the liquid mixture is ready for drinking, it's poured into a bowl made from an empty half-coconut shell, which serves as a cup. The order in which kava is drunk varies. Usually the chief drinks it first, followed by any honoured guests. Then the other men drink in order of precedence. Usually kava drinkers consume two to three half-coconut cupfuls in a session.

Some cultures expect drinkers to down the kava in a single gulp, any remaining liquid being poured on the ground. Sometimes, kava is drunk in silence, but some cultures prefer a great deal of slurping to show appreciation. Sometimes your companions will quietly clap as you drink. Generally, while kava is being drunk, except for the clapping stage, conversation and loud noises are kept to a minimum. Islanders feel it's best imbibed when there's an atmosphere of quietness.

Kava makes the eyes sensitive to glare, so any strong lights, especially flashbulbs, are very intrusive. If you really want to take a photograph, ask permission and limit yourself to one or two shots.

Restaurants

In most cases, Pacific islanders themselves do not have the ready cash to patronise restaurants, so they are built to serve the tourist population. As a result of this, they are concentrated in areas with a high tourist population.

The restaurants of the French territories and ex-French territories can be superb. In general, vegetarians and vegans are not well catered for.

Self-Catering

There will be some form of shopping outlet in all but the smallest of villages. Depending on the level of isolation, the choice may be limited and the goods may be expensive. Markets are the source of the freshest and cheapest foodstuffs.

Umu

The *umu* earth/stone oven (*ahima'a* in French Polynesia; *lovo* in Fiji) is used throughout the

Kava

Experiential Effects

Kava has a pungent, muddy taste. If the brew is a strong one, your lips will go numb and cold, like after a dental injection. Then your limbs will feel heavy and your speech will become quiet and slow.

You'll begin to be affected within 10 to 25 minutes. Even if it's only a mild brew, you'll probably want to do nothing more than lie down and think about life, feeling sedated and a general sense of wellbeing. You may also experience some minor perceptual changes, both in emotions and vision. If the brew is a strong one, you'll probably experience a mild form of double vision, and want to sleep for a few hours.

Some islanders claim to have repeated religious experiences after drinking kava. Many religious visions have occurred at such times!

Social Effects

In many countries, kava has helped to retain ancient customs longer. Its rituals reinforce the traditional authority of chiefs, even when villagers have moved to the towns. Many people attribute a low crime rate to the calming effects of kava. Unlike alcohol, which often produces aggressive and irresponsible behaviour, kava produces amiability, peacefulness and acceptance of life.

Medicinal Uses

Some Melanesian subspecies of kava are too strong to drink, and are used as bush medicines.

In scientific terms, kava is an amalgam of up to 14 analgesics and anaesthetics, and has natural pain and appetite-suppressant features. The root also has antibacterial, relaxant, diuretic and decongestant properties. It's been recommended for cancer and asthma patients, and also for people suffering from stomach upsets.

No studies have fully established the effects of a lifetime of kava drinking. Plenty of elderly Pacific islanders and long-term expats who have drunk copious quantities on a daily basis for years appear to be well and mentally alert. However, some evidence points to heavy drinkers developing a scaly skin, hepatitis, weight loss, lung disease and/or impotence.

Female Kava Drinkers

In some parts of the Pacific, drinking kava is an exclusively male activity – some say the original kava plant sprang from the loins of a woman, hence the tapu. However, women are free to drink it along with the men in some areas. In major tourist areas, where customary rules are usually relaxed, an increasing number of local, expat and tourist women enjoy a regular shell

Men drinking from a kava bowl

Pacific. Variations are many but the common theme is that food, wrapped in wet cloth or leaves, surrounded by rocks heated red-hot in a fire and cooked under a layer of earth. The food is steamed slowly and takes on some of the flavour of the earth. A traditional *umu* meal is not hard to arrange in most Pacific centres.

Coconuts

The coconut is a vital resource in the Pacific. Each of the nut's five growth stages provides a different form of food or drink. The first stage is ideal for drinking, because as yet there's no flesh inside. During the next stage, tasty jellied flesh appears inside. The best eating stage is the third, when the flesh inside is firm but thin and succulent. After this, the flesh becomes thick and hard – ideal for drying into copra. At its fifth stage, the nut begins to shoot while the milk inside

goes crispy, making what is known throughout the Pacific as 'coconut ice cream'.

See Flora & Fauna in the Facts about the South Pacific chapter for more information about the coconut tree.

DRINKS

Tap water is not always safe to drink; see Health earlier in this chapter and in individual country chapters. Fresh coconut juice is a refreshing drink on a hot day. Any small town in the Pacific will have young drinking coconuts for sale somewhere, or you can prevail upon most small boys to climb up a tree for the right price (anything from a smile to a few coins). Make sure you get permission from the owner of the land, and you'll need a large knife to hack away the green husk – or a pocket knife and a lot of patience.

Alcoholic Drinks

Attitudes to alcohol vary. Some communities, seeing the detrimental effects of alcohol, such as domestic violence, have banned alcohol completely – but in most countries it's freely available. Many countries with their own breweries brew excellent beers. Australian, New Zealand and US beers are also available in most countries.

Before drinking mixed drinks, ask if the drink has been diluted with water. In many countries the tap water should not be drunk.

Traditional Highs

Drinks made from fermented coconut sap (called coconut wine, sour toddy, *kaleve*, *tuba* or *kaokioki*) are popular on many Pacific islands. Kava is even more widespread. Another nonalcoholic form of high is betel nut (see Food in the Solomon Islands chapter).

The Face of the Coconut

The importance of the coconut to Pacific islanders is highlighted by a widespread traditional story. Many Pacific cultures tell the tale of the man Tuna, the lover of Hina. When Tuna was killed by a jealous suitor (Maui in some tellings), he became the coconut, and his face is represented by the three black depressions at the top of the coconut's shell. Push your straw through Tuna's mouth, the only depression that pierces the shell, and you can drink the coconut's juice. It is also through Tuna's mouth that the shoot of a new coconut tree grows, providing food for the children of Hina.

South Pacific Diving

Dramatic drop-offs, pristine sheltered lagoons, ocean dives, magnificent reefs and caves, exceptional wrecks, an incredibly rich and colourful fauna and warm tropical waters – the South Pacific has just about everything a diver could hope for and provides memorable experiences for expert divers as well as for beginners.

Most dive sites in the South Pacific are largely uncrowded and untouched compared with overexploited areas in the Caribbean and Red Sea, providing an exclusiveness which can be exciting.

Lonely Planet's Pisces series includes the following in-depth diving and snorkelling guides to the South Pacific: *Diving & Snorkeling Fiji*, *Diving & Snorkeling Papua New Guinea*, *Diving & Snorkeling Tahiti & French Polynesia* and *Diving & Snorkeling Vanuatu*.

DIVING CONDITIONS & EQUIPMENT

Diving is possible year round although conditions vary according to the season and location. Visibility is reduced in the wet season as the water is muddied by sediments brought into the sea by the rivers, and areas that are exposed to currents might also become heavy with particles. On average, visibility ranges from 15m to 50m.

Responsible Diving

Please consider the following tips when you're diving in order to preserve the ecology and beauty of reefs:

- Do not use anchors on the reef or ground boats on coral
- Encourage dive operators and regulatory bodies to establish permanent moorings at popular dive sites
- Avoid touching marine organisms with your body or by dragging equipment across the reef. The most gentle contact causes damage.
- Never stand on coral, even if it looks solid and robust. If you must hold on to the reef, only touch exposed rock or dead coral.
- Be conscious of your fins. Even without contact the surge from heavy fin strokes can damage delicate reef organisms.
- Practice proper buoyancy control. Major damage can be done by divers descending too fast and colliding with the reef. Make sure you are correctly weighted and that your weight belt is positioned so that you stay horizontal. If you've not dived for a while, practice in a pool first.
- Take great care in underwater caves. Spend as little time within them as possible as your air bubbles may catch in ceiling cavities, leaving previously submerged organisms high and dry.
- Leave corals and shells in their natural environment. Aside from ecological damage, taking marine souvenirs depletes the beauty of a site and spoils the enjoyment of others. The same goes for shipwrecks; respect their integrity (some sites are protected from looting by law).
- Take out all your rubbish and any litter you may find as well. Plastics, in particular, are a serious threat to marine life. Turtles can mistake plastic for jellyfish and eat it.
- Don't feed fish. You may disturb their eating habits, encourage aggressive behaviour or feed them food that is detrimental to their health.
- Minimise your disturbance of marine animals. In particular, do not ride on the backs of turtles, as this causes them great anxiety.

Title page: Schooling jacks in the waters off the Solomon Islands (Photograph by Casey Mahaney)

Getting Started

The South Pacific provides ideal conditions for beginners with its shel-tered lagoons, crystalline, warm water and prolific marine life. If you've always fancied diving but never taken the plunge, now's your chance.

A preliminary snorkelling session before attempting diving for the first time will help you to get used to wearing a mask and breathing through your mouth.

Arrange an introductory dive with a reputable dive centre. It will begin on dry land, where the instructor will run through basic safety procedures (such as the use of sign language to indicate that everything is 'OK' or 'not OK', and ear-equilibration techniques) and show you the equipment. The dive itself takes place in a safe location and lasts between 20 and 40 minutes under the guidance of the instructor.

You'll practise breathing with the regulator above the water's surface before going under. The instructor will hold your hand under water if need be, and guide your movements to a depth between 3m and 10m. Many centres start the instruction in waist-high water in a hotel swim-ming pool or on the beach.

There is no formal procedure but you shouldn't dive if you have a medical condition such as acute ear, nose and throat problems, asthma, epilepsy or heart disease (such as infarction), if you have a cold or sinusi-tis, or if you are pregnant.

If you enjoy your introductory dive, you might want to follow it up with a three- to four-day course to obtain a first-level certification recognised around the world.

In most Pacific countries the water temperature peaks at a warm 29°C during the rainy season, but can drop to 20°C in some areas at certain periods of the year. Though it is possible to dive without a wetsuit, most divers wear at least a Lycra outsuit to protect themselves from abrasions. A 3mm tropical wetsuit is most appropriate. If you don't want to bring your own equipment it can usually be hired from the larger dive centres. Equipment hire is sometimes included in the price of the dive.

DIVE CENTRES & COURSES

On most tourist-oriented islands you'll find professional and reliable dive centres staffed with qualified instructors catering to divers of all levels. Choose a dive centre affiliated with an internationally rec-ognised dive organisation such as PADI, NAUI, SSI or CMAS. Each dive centre has its own personality and style so, where possible, visit several dive centres to get a feel of each operation. Word of mouth should also let you know which ones are good. See the Activities sec-tions in individual country chapters for further details.

Diving in the South Pacific is expensive in comparison to most destinations in Asia, the Caribbean or the Red Sea. Single dives cost between US$30 and US$50; set dive packages (eg, two dives or 10 dives) are usually cheaper. All types of courses are available, including introductory courses (US$30 to US$60) and three- or four-day open-water certification courses (US$280 to US$500).

Open-water diving certificates are recognised worldwide. If you're a certified diver, ensure that you have your dive certificate with you. Dive centres welcome divers regardless of their training background, provided they can produce a certificate from one of the agencies mentioned earlier.

There are decompression chambers in Suva (Fiji), Pape'ete (French Polynesia), Port Vila and Santo (Vanuatu). In practice, however, patients are usually transferred to New Zealand or Australia.

DIVE SITES

The South Pacific boasts hundreds of breathtaking dive sites. Our list is by no means exhaustive and should be considered as merely a sample of the most renowned sites.

Rarotonga & the Cook Islands

On Rarotonga, **Matavera Drop-Off** plunges down a wall to 35m, then on to a sandy bottom at 60m. The major attraction, apart from the drop-off, is the abundance and variety of coral formations and fish. White-tipped reef sharks, eagle rays and sometimes whale sharks can be sighted nearby.

Close by, **Ngatangiia School** is riddled with swim-throughs and crevices that offer an ideal habitat for moray eels, lobsters, urchins, clams, lionfish, stonefish and shellfish.

Papua Passage refers to a natural opening chiselled into the lagoon, and varying in depth from 5m to 30m. Several tunnels lead off the passage, and eagle rays and turtles are regularly seen. The **Pinnacles**, formed by a series of large rocks on the edge of the drop-off, teems with colourful marine life and is rated as one of the Cooks' best sites.

Pre-Dive Safety

Any diving trip should be a safe and enjoyable experience. Before embarking on a trip, you should:

• Possess a current diving certification card from a recognised scuba diving instructional agency, or take an introductory course
• Obtain reliable information about physical and environmental conditions at the dive site (eg, from a reputable local dive-operator)
• Be aware of local regulations and etiquette about marine life and the environment. Ask permission of customary owners of the reef or beach if appropriate.
• Dive only at sites that are within your own realm of experience; if available, engage the services of a competent, professionally-trained dive instructor
• Be aware that underwater conditions vary significantly from one region, or even site, to another. Seasonal changes can significantly alter site and dive conditions. These differences may influence the equipment required for a dive and what diving techniques to use.

CASEY MAHANEY

CASEY MAHANEY

PHIL WEYMOUTH

TONY WHEELER

Top left: Diving, Kadavu, Fiji

Top right: Lagoon snorkelling, Fiji

Middle left: Dive school, Mana, Fiji

Middle right: Bora Bora Diving Centre, French Polynesia

Bottom: Schooling jacks and diver, Solomon Islands

CASEY MAHANEY

Top left: Nudibranch

Top right: Anemonefish

Middle top: Harlequin Ghost Pipefish

Middle bottom left: Red lionfish

Middle bottom right: Spiny sea urchin

Bottom: Blue-spotted stingray

Tahiti & French Polynesia

Rangiroa Atoll in the Tuamotu archipelago is a mecca for divers. The tidal flows create exceptional diving conditions and attract numerous open-sea species. **Tiputa Pass** is a world-class drift dive. Divers immerse themselves at the edge of the reef drop-off and let themselves be sucked into the lagoon through the pass with the incoming current, accompanied by a procession of fish, including numerous grey sharks.

Off the northwestern coast of Moorea is the **Tiki**, another exceptional site, renowned not so much for the seascape as for its density of marine life. Spectacular shark-feeding sessions are regularly held in less than 25m, attracting a crowd of grey sharks, black-tipped sharks and even bigger lemon sharks.

Off Bora Bora, don't miss **Tupitipiti**, one of the archipelago's most magical dive sites. It features a steep drop-off tumbled with rocks, dotted with caves and swim-throughs, and frequented by sharks, eagle rays and turtles.

In the Marquesas, devoid of coral reefs and lagoons, the main attraction is the **Orques Pygmees**, east of Nuku Hiva Island. Here you can snorkel or dive with dozens of melon-headed whales.

Niue

Niue has no fringing lagoon, but does have several coastal caverns. The **Ana Mahaga** (or Twin Caves) is the most exciting dive site. It features two large caves connected by a horizontal tunnel, at a maximum depth of 30m. Another popular site is **Snake Gully**, famous for its incredible population of sea snakes. **The Fans** near Tepa Point is a deep dive (30m to 40m) where experienced divers will enjoy the sight of enormous gorgonian fans.

Tonga

On Tongatapu, the diving is at its best at **Beach Dive**, off Ha'atafu Beach, where a succession of drop-offs descend from 3m to 15m and from 15m to 30m. 'Eua has some of the best **sea caves** in the world. Around Vava'u, two of the best dive sites are **Split Rock**, a dramatic slab that looks like it's been sliced clean in two with an enormous knife, and **Sea Fans**, which is full of large gorgonians. In Ha'apai, the **Lolani cave** is a 50m-long cathedral-like limestone cavern with a narrow entrance, for experienced divers only, where you can see sharks and a 2m grouper.

Fiji

The Fijian islands are the world's capital of soft corals. Off Taveuni Island, the most remarkable dive zone is **Rainbow Reef**, in the Somosomo Strait, which gets its name from the unbelievable colours of its corals. Here, all divers covet the legendary Great White Wall – a sheer drop-off starting at a depth of about 15m and ornamented with a profusion of magnificent soft corals. Tunnels and a myriad of small tropical fish add to the wonders of the dive.

Wild Encounters

The thousands of square kilometres of reefs that dot the South Pacific harbour tropical fish of every shape, colour and size. But what makes the diving so distinctive is the density of pelagics. Sightings of sharks can be expected virtually anywhere. White-tipped, black-tipped, grey, lemon, nurse and hammerhead sharks are the most common species. In many countries, shark-feeding sessions are held by a dive instructor and allow amazed divers to watch sharks at close range in safety.

Various species of rays may also be encountered. Stingrays can be found on sandy floors everywhere and magnificent manta rays are the star attraction of some islands of French Polynesia.

The South Pacific may not equal the Indian Ocean for invertebrates and coral formations, but some islands, such as Fiji, boast fantastic hard and soft corals and superb gorgonian fans.

East of Viti Levu, along Malolo Reef off the Mamanuca islands, do not miss the **Supermarket**, a dive famous for its regular shark-feeding sessions. Between 10 and 30 grey, black-tipped and white-tipped sharks run the show.

South of Viti Levu, **Caesar's Rock**, in Beqa's lagoon, boasts several coral pinnacles carved with a few tunnels and covered with brightly coloured soft corals and sea fans. The pinnacles are a magnet for marine life.

At **Kadavu's** spectacular sites, expect to find caves, vertical walls and abundant corals and fish.

If you go through a live-aboard operation, you'll dive either **E6**, a seamount rising from 1000m between Vanua Levu and Viti Levu, renowned for its abundance of pelagics, or **Wakaya Passage**, off Wakaya Island in the Lomaiviti Islands, which offers a mix of large species (manta rays and hammerhead sharks) and the usual plethora of tropical fish.

New Caledonia

New Caledonia boasts one of the largest lagoons in the world. Off Noumea, the huge **Passe de Boulari** is the most popular site. Pelagics, including manta rays, big wrasses and horse-eye jacks, are plentiful, and there's a large population of sharks. Nearby, *La Dieppoise* is a famous wreck, deliberately scuttled in 1988, lying at a depth of 26m.

Off the southern tip of Grande Terre, the **Aiguille de Prony** (Prony Needle), in Baie de Prony, features a unique topography, with a pyramid-shaped mineral spike rising from the sea bed 40m below the surface, to within 2m of the surface.

The stunning **La Faille de Poé**, off Bourail, is a narrow channel into the reef that runs perpendicular to the coast; it's the remnant of a former river bed and home to numerous rays, sharks and gropers.

Poum reef, off northern Grande Terre, is also spectacular and divers will experience thrilling encounters with sharks and rays near **Passe de la Gazelle** or in **Fausse Passe**.

Off Lifou Island, **Gorgone Reef** is the most renowned site. As its name suggests, it offers an incredible diversity of brightly coloured gorgonians, sea fans and soft corals.

Try **Vallée des Gorgones**, off Île des Pins near N'Gié Islet, northwest of the main island. You'll see many gorgonians, a variety of reef life and some pelagics in less than 20m. There are also interesting arches and swim-throughs.

Solomon Islands

Guadalcanal Island is a wonderland for WWII buffs, with many shipwrecks from battles resting close to the shore. The most popular sites, with some 50 other ships and aircraft in Iron Bottom Sound off Honiara, include *Bonegi I*, a 172m Japanese transport ship, varying in depth from 3m to 55m, and *Bonegi II*, another Japanese transport ship, still partly above the water's surface, with its stern submerged to 27m. Both wrecks are adorned with excellent coral and attract masses of fish.

Seven kilometres northwest of the town of Gizo on Ghizo Island, is the *Toa Maru*, a huge Japanese freighter that sank during WWII. It's well-preserved at a depth ranging from 7m to 37m. Divers can explore the ship's holds, which contain tanks, ammunition, a motorbike and sake bottles. **Grand Central Station** (18m) is 6km northwest, near Varu Island. It's an exhilarating spot to watch rays, sharks and barracudas.

In Western Province, off New Georgia Island, near Munda, try **Shark Point**, a drop-off patrolled by sharks and huge schools of pelagics. Near Uepi Island, in the beautiful Marovo Lagoon, the **Elbow** features a breathtaking wall carpeted with magnificent corals and dropping to a depth of 600m. Sharks and barracudas are common.

Samoan Islands

The limpid water and prolific coral on the northern and western ends of American Samoa support walls of coral over 18m deep. **Tutuila** and the smaller outlying islands offer some good sites.

Many of the popular dive sites in independent Samoa are close to the villages of Ninoa and Si'uma on the south coast of 'Upolu. **Palolo Deep Marine Reserve**, in Apia, and **Aganoa** are accessible from the shore.

Dive into History

No other area in the world boasts as many wrecks as the western part of the South Pacific. Vanuatu and the Solomons offer a fantastic variety of wrecks, dating mostly from WWII. These are in good condition, are festooned with soft corals and sponges that provide an eerie home for many underwater creatures, and are a paradise for wreck-diving enthusiasts. SS *President Coolidge,* in Vanuatu, is a wreck-diver's wet dream.

Wrecks are a fascinating experience for divers. Most are accessible to novice divers with certification. However, entering a wreck requires specific skills and divers should always explore these war relics under the guidance of an experienced local dive master

SOUTH PACIFIC DIVING

Vanuatu

Vanuatu is also renowned for its numerous WWII wrecks. Off Espiritu Santo, the SS *President* Coolidge is one of the world's most fascinating wreck dives. An impressive 654ft luxury liner, it was used as a troop ship during WWII. It sank in 1942 after hitting two mines, but remained in perfect condition. Divers can swim through numerous decks to inspect the rooms and mechanical parts. Many fish have taken up residence. The depth range is 21m to 67m.

Another amazing site off Espiritu Santo is **Million Dollar Point**, where thousands of tonnes of military paraphernalia were dumped by the US navy after the war. Divers swim among a jumble of cranes, bulldozers, trucks and other construction hardware at a depth ranging from surface to 35m. This junkyard, covering more than half a hectare, teems with marine life.

On the nearby island of Tutuba, **Tutuba Point** has spectacular hard and soft corals and offers a combination of caves and swim-throughs at 10m to 40m. The countless varieties of fish are another attraction at this site.

Off Efate Island, enjoy diving at the *Star of Russia*, a ship built in the 1800s which sank in Port Vila's harbour 70 years ago and now rests at a depth of 36m. **Black Sand Reef and Caves**, also close to Port Vila, features a reef chiselled with caves and swim-throughs, with corals and reef fish in abundance. The site's sandy bottom is home to many rays.

Getting There & Away

AIR

The first part of your journey is reaching the South Pacific. For the most part, this can be an expensive exercise – the smaller number of travellers in the region means that air fares are generally high. The main gateways to the South Pacific are the US, Australia, New Zealand and Japan.

International airlines flying between Australasia, Asia and the US link a number of the South Pacific countries. There are also many small local airlines that only service the Pacific region. The countries covered by each airline, and contact details, are listed under Airlines later in this section. While island-hopping around the Pacific isn't difficult, some flights operate only once or twice per week from the smaller islands and you may be faced with a few scheduling problems on some routes.

Airlines

The following airlines serve the South Pacific region. This list will be useful both for getting to the Pacific and for getting around the region. Use the websites listed to check up on the most up-to-date routes, schedules and prices.

Many airlines also operate a domestic service around their own country. Details of domestic services are given in the individual country chapters.

Air Fiji (W www.airfiji.net) Offers mainly domestic services around Fiji and flies also to Tonga and Tuvalu
Australia (☎ 02-9221 9988) Sydney
Fiji (☎ 331 3666) Suva; (☎ 672 2521) Nadi
New Zealand (☎ 09-308 5206) Auckland
USA (☎ 1 888 234 5447)
Air France (W www.airfrance.com) Flies from Paris to New Caledonia and Tahiti (French Polynesia) and from Japan to New Caledonia
Australia (☎ 1300 361 4000)
France (☎ 0 820 820 820)
New Caledonia (☎ 25 88 88)
Tahiti (☎ 47 47 47)
UK (☎ 0845 0845 111)
USA (☎ 1 800 237 2747)
Air New Zealand (W www.airnz.co.nz) Flies to most Pacific countries
Australia (☎ 13 24 76)
Cook Islands (☎ 26300)
Fiji (☎ 330 1671) Suva; (☎ 672 0070) Nadi
Germany (☎ 800 181 77 78)

New Caledonia (☎ 28 66 77)
New Zealand (☎ 0800 737 000)
Samoa (☎ 20825)
Tahiti (☎ 54 07 40)
Tonga (☎ 23 192)
UK (☎ 0800 028 4149)
USA (☎ 1 800 262 1234)
Vanuatu (☎ 22666)
Air Niugini (W www.airniugini.com.pg) Connects PNG with the Solomon Islands and Australia
Australia (☎ 1300 361 380)
Papua New Guinea (☎ 327 3555)
Solomon Islands (☎ 22895)
Air Pacific (W www.airpacific.com) Flies between Fiji, Japan, Australia, New Zealand and mainland US. It also flies to Samoa, Tonga, Vanuatu and the Solomon Islands
Australia (☎ 1 800 230150)
Fiji (☎ 672 0888) Nadi
New Zealand (☎ 0800 800 178)
Samoa (☎ 22738)
Tahiti (☎ 43 06 65)
Tonga (☎ 23 422)
USA (☎ 1 800 227 4446)
Vanuatu (☎ 22836)
Air Tahiti Nui (W www.flyatn.com) Flies between Tahiti (French Polynesia), the US, France, New Zealand and Japan
France (☎ 01 56 81 13 30)
Japan (☎ 03-3475 1511) Tokyo
New Zealand (☎ 09-308 3360) Auckland
Tahiti (☎ 46 02 02)
USA (☎ 1 877 824 4846)
Air Vanuatu (W www.airvanuatu.com) Flies to Australia, New Zealand, New Caledonia and Fiji
Australia (☎ 02-9299 9737) Sydney
Fiji (☎ 672 2521) Nadi
New Caledonia (☎ 28 66 77)
New Zealand (☎ 09-373 3435) Auckland
Vanuatu (☎23848)
Aircalin (W www.aircalin.nc) Flies from New Caledonia to Australia, New Zealand, Japan, Vanuatu, Fiji and French Polynesia. It is the only airline that flies to Wallis & Futuna.
Australia (☎ 02-9244 2211) Sydney
Fiji (☎ 672 2145) Nadi
Futuna (☎ 72 32 04)
Japan (☎ 03-3475 1511) Tokyo
New Caledonia (☎ 26 55 00)
New Zealand (☎ 09-308 3363) Auckland
Tahiti (☎ 47 47 47)
Vanuatu (☎ 22739)
Wallis (☎ 72 28 80)

Aloha Airlines (W www.alohaairlines.com.au)
Flies from Hawaii to Rarotonga
Cook Islands (☎ 24040)
Hawaii (☎ 808-484 1111)
USA (mainland) & Canada (☎ 1 800 367 5250)
Corsair (W www.corsair.fr) Flies from Paris, Los
Angeles and San Francisco to Tahiti (French
Polynesia)
France (☎ 01-49 79 49 79) Paris
Tahiti (☎ 42 28 28)
USA (☎ 1 800 677 0720)
Hawaiian Airlines (W www.hawaiianair.com)
Flies to the US, American Samoa and Tahiti
(French Polynesia)
American Samoa (☎ 669 1875)
Hawaii (☎ 808-838 1555) Honolulu
Tahiti (☎ 42 15 00)
USA (mainland; ☎ 1 800 367 5320)
Japan Airlines (JAL; W www.jal.co.jp) Flies
from Tokyo to Hawaii and New Caledonia
Hawaii (☎ 1 800 525 3663)
Japan (☎ 0120 25 5931)
New Caledonia (☎ 25 88 09)
Korean Air (W www.koreanair.com) Flies from
South Korea to Fiji
Fiji (☎ 672 1043)
South Korea (☎ 02-554 6000)
LanChile (W www.lanchile.com) Flies between
Chile and French Polynesia, with stops at
Easter Island
Australia (☎ 1 300 361 400)
Chile (☎ 02-526 2000) Santiago
New Zealand (☎ 09-309 8673) Auckland
Tahiti (☎ 42 64 55)
Polynesian Airlines (W www.polynesianairlin
es.co.nz) Flies from Samoa to Australia, New
Zealand and the US. It flies to Hawaii, Ameri-
can Samoa, Fiji and Tonga.
American Samoa (☎ 699 9106)
Australia (☎ 1 300 653 737)
Fiji (☎ 672 2521) Nadi
Hawaii (☎ 1 800 264 0823)
New Zealand (☎ 0800 800 993)
Samoa (☎ 22 737)
Tahiti (☎ 43 06 65)
Tonga (☎ 24 566)
USA (mainland; ☎ 1 800 264 0823)
Qantas (W www.qantas.com.au) Code-shares
with some Pacific airlines, flying from Australia
to New Zealand, New Caledonia, Vanuatu,
Tahiti (French Polynesia), Hawaii and Fiji.
Australia (☎ 13 13 13)
Fiji (☎ 672 2880) Nadi
Germany (☎ 01 805 250 620)
New Caledonia (☎ 28 65 46)
New Zealand (☎ 09-357 8900) Auckland
Tahiti (☎ 43 06 65)
UK (☎ 0845 7 747 767)
USA (☎ 1 800 227 4500)
Vanuatu (☎ 23848)

Warning

The information in this chapter is particularly
vulnerable to change: Prices for international
travel are volatile, routes are introduced and
cancelled, schedules change, special deals
come and go, and rules and visa requirements
are amended. You should check directly with
the airline or a travel agent to make sure you
understand how a fare (and ticket you may
buy) works and be aware of the security requirements for international travel.

The upshot of this is that you should get
opinions, quotes and advice from as many
airlines and travel agents as possible before
you part with your hard-earned cash. The
details given in this chapter should be regarded as pointers and are not a substitute
for your own careful, up-to-date research.

Royal Tongan Airlines (W www.royaltonganair
lines.com) Flies from Tonga to Australia, New
Zealand, Hawaii and Fiji
Australia (☎ 02-9787 9222)
Fiji (☎ 672 4355) Nadi
Hawaii (☎ 1 800 486 6426)
New Zealand (☎ 09-624 1160) Auckland
Tonga (☎ 23 414)
Samoa Air (W www.samoaair.com) Flies be-
tween American Samoa and Samoa
American Samoa (☎ 699 9106)
Samoa (☎ 22 901)
Solomon Airlines (W www.solomonairlines
.com.au) Flies from Honiara on the Solomon
Islands to Australia, Vanuatu and Fiji
Australia (☎ 02-9244 2189) Sydney
Fiji (☎ 672 2831) Nadi
Solomon Islands (☎ 667 20031)
Vanuatu (☎ 23838)

Buying Tickets

Most destinations in the South Pacific are
relatively expensive transport-wise both to
get to and to get around. Unless you have
unlimited funds allowing for the luxury of
travelling when and where you feel like it,
most of your travel will need to be planned
in advance. As well as purchasing a ticket to
the region, consider purchasing an air pass
(see Air Passes later in this chapter) to ease
the cost of travel between countries.

Although it's not impossible to organise
your own travel in the South Pacific, a good
travel agent can be worth their weight in gold
when it comes to finding special fare deals
and giving advice on everything from air

passes to the best travel insurance to bundle with your ticket. In addition to the traditional travel operators, there are agencies that specialise in diving tours and other activity-based tours. Their packages typically include flights and accommodation, plus any activity fees and tours.

It is always worth putting aside a few hours to research the current state of the travel market, either with your travel agent or the Internet. Start early: some of the cheapest tickets have to be bought months in advance and some popular flights sell out quickly. For long-term travel there are plenty of discount tickets valid for 12 months, allowing multiple stopovers with open dates. When you're looking for bargain air fares, go to a travel agent rather than directly to the airline. From time to time, airlines do have promotional fares and special offers but generally they only sell fares at the official listed price. As well as the fare price, also consider the route, the duration of the journey and any restrictions on the ticket. Check your dates carefully before booking your ticket as there can be considerable low and high season price variations; going just a day or two earlier or later can make a big difference in cost.

If you purchase a ticket and later want to make changes to your route or get a refund, you need to contact the original travel agent. Airlines only issue refunds to the purchaser of a ticket – usually the travel agent who bought the ticket on your behalf. It's often desirable to change your route halfway through a trip, so think carefully before you buy a ticket that is not easily refunded.

Use the fares quoted in this book as a guide only. Although correct at the time of research, most are likely to have changed by the time you read this. Remember to reconfirm your onward or return bookings – at least 72 hours before departure is standard on international flights.

Under the different regions later in this section, we give prices to get to the main centres in the Pacific: Honolulu (Hawaii), Pape'ete (French Polynesia), Nadi (Fiji), Sydney (Australia) and Auckland (New Zealand). From these cities, you will be able to pick up connecting flights to most destinations elsewhere in the region.

Round-the-World Tickets Various airline alliances offer round-the-world (RTW) tickets, which give travellers an almost endless variety of possible airline and destination combinations. RTWs can be excellent value – expect to pay around US$2000, A$2790 or UK£1200. Star Alliance (a code-sharing group of airlines that includes Air New Zealand) offer some of the best RTWs for the region.

Fiji is the most popular destination for travellers on RTWs but Tonga, Samoa, Tahiti and the Cook Islands can all be visited as part of a RTW. Check with your travel agent for more information on these tickets.

Circle Pacific Tickets Circle Pacific tickets are similar to a RTW ticket but are used for travel between countries in the Pacific region only. On a Circle Pacific ticket you can travel between Australia, New Zealand, North America and Asia with stopover options in the South Pacific. There are advance-purchase restrictions and limits on how many stopovers you can make but these tickets are good value for travel in the region, especially for travellers from the US.

For an idea of price, you should expect to pay around US$2290 for a fare which includes: Los Angeles–Tahiti (Pape'ete)–Cook Islands (Rarotonga)–Fiji (Nadi)–Auckland–Brisbane–Singapore–Los Angeles.

Air Passes Inter-country flights in the Pacific can be prohibitively expensive. The only really workable way to travel to more than a handful of countries is by using an air pass. Fortunately, there are some excellent air passes taking in several South Pacific countries for a reduced price. Some passes are arranged by airlines, while others are put together by travel agents. There may be conditions attached to these passes, such as the number of days travelling, the travel termination date or minimum stays in each country. Seating availability for heavily discounted fares can be quite limited, so book early. Some passes can only be purchased when you buy your ticket; you won't be able to purchase them once you have arrived in the South Pacific.

If you think air-pass conditions are complex, you'll be happy to hear that they often confuse airline agents too. You have to communicate your desired itinerary carefully so that the agent gets everything right, but the complexity means that things are ultimately a bit flexible. Prices and conditions attached to air passes change often, so check the current situation with a travel agent or the airline. Contact details for the airlines listed are given earlier in this chapter.

Boomerang This Qantas pass can be used to travel between Australia, New Zealand, Fiji, Vanuatu, Tonga, Samoa, New Caledonia and the Solomon Islands. The pass is also valid on Air Pacific and Air Vanuatu flights. The pass starts from US$195/€200 for travel between two 'zones' and increases in price according to the number of zones you cross.

The pass is only available when you purchase a ticket to Australia, New Zealand, Fiji and Vanuatu and is not available to residents of Australia, New Zealand or the southwest Pacific countries listed above.

Circle South West Pacific This pass allows for travel to two or more islands in the southwest Pacific. Starting from A$780 (depending which countries you visit), this pass allows travel from Australia's east coast to Samoa, Tonga, New Zealand, Solomon Islands, Vanuatu, Fiji or New Caledonia. For an extra A$150 to A$400 (depending on the flight), you can add an extra country.

Travel must start and finish in Australia and must be completed within 28 days. Accommodation must be pre-booked for the full period.

Island Explorer Circle Fare With this Polynesian Airlines pass you can fly from New Zealand to Samoa, Tonga and Australia (Sydney) and either Fiji or Hawaii. The 45-day pass is only available for departures from New Zealand and costs NZ$1699.

Polypass This Polynesian Airlines pass allows for travel between Samoa, Tonga, Fiji, Australia and New Zealand. It costs US$1099 for (almost) 45 days of unlimited travel – except during the Christmas period – and you can start and end your trip in any of these countries. Travel to Honolulu, Los Angeles and Tahiti can also be included for an additional amount.

Visit the South Pacific With this pass you can travel on a number of airlines between Australia, New Zealand, PNG, the Solomon Islands, Vanuatu, New Caledonia, Fiji, Tonga, Niue, Samoa and French Polynesia.

The pass costs US$190 to US$340 per sector (depending on the sector) and you can purchase additional sectors at participating airline offices in the South Pacific. The pass is only available when you purchase your ticket to the South Pacific and isn't available to residents of Australia, New Zealand or any of the countries listed above.

Student & Youth Fares Full-time students and people under 26 have access to better deals than other travellers. The better deals may not always be cheaper fares but can include more flexibility to change flights and/or routes. You have to show a document proving your date of birth or a valid International Student Identity Card (ISIC) when buying your ticket and boarding the plane. There are plenty of places around the world where nonstudents can get fake student cards but if you get caught using a fake card, you could have your ticket confiscated.

Travellers with Special Needs

Airlines can often make special arrangements for travellers such as wheelchair assistance at airports or vegetarian meals on the flight. 'Skycots', baby food and nappies should be provided by the airline if requested in advance. Children aged between two and 12 can usually occupy a seat for around two-thirds of the full fare, and do get a baggage allowance.

North America

Los Angeles and Honolulu are the main gateway cities for travel between North America and the South Pacific. From Los Angeles there are direct flights to Honolulu, Pape'ete, Rarotonga, Nadi and Apia (Samoa) – as well as numerous flights to Sydney and Auckland – from where you can connect to other destinations in the Pacific. Air New Zealand flights from Los Angeles to Australia and Auckland often include one free stopover in the South Pacific. From Canada, most flights to the South Pacific will also travel via Los Angeles and/or Honolulu.

Many of the air passes mentioned (see Air Passes earlier in this chapter for prices and information) are excellent value for travellers from North America.

In general, June to August is the cheapest and November and December are the most expensive months to travel to the South Pacific.

The USA Discount travel agencies in the US and Canada are called consolidators, and can be found through the Yellow Pages or major newspapers. The *Los Angeles Times*, *New York Times*, *San Francisco Examiner*, *Chicago Tribune*, *Toronto Globe & Mail*, *Toronto Star*, *Montreal Gazette* and *Vancouver Sun* have weekly travel sections with ads and information.

For straightforward fares, there are plenty of good air fares to the South Pacific on sites like ⓦ www.orbitz.com, ⓦ www.cheaptickets.com and ⓦ www.expedia.com.

Travel agents in the US who specialise in the South Pacific region include:

Newmans Vacations (☎ 800-421-3326,
　ⓦ www.newmansvacations.com)
Pacific for Less (☎ 808-249-6490,
　ⓦ www.pacific-for-less.com)
South Seas Adventures (☎ 800-576-7327,
　ⓦ www.south-seas-adventures.com)

Year-round fares to Honolulu start from around US$560 from Los Angeles and US$1120 from New York. From Los Angeles low/high season fares start from US$880/1300 to Pape'ete and US$1290/1660 to Nadi. From New York and other east coast cities return low/high season fares start from US$1380/1760 to Pape'ete and US$1720/2125 to Nadi.

As well as the Air New Zealand stopover deal mentioned earlier, Air New Zealand also offers another excellent deal from Los Angeles which allows for four stopovers in the Pacific en route to Auckland. The stopover options are Honolulu, Nadi, Pape'ete and Rarotonga. In the low season, expect to pay around US$1350 for a return fare to Auckland, including one free stopover. Other stopovers cost US$150 each. Check with Air New Zealand or your travel agent for ticket options and restrictions.

Canada The *Globe & Mail*, *Toronto Star*, *Montreal Gazette* and *Vancouver Sun* are good places to start looking for cheap fares. For straightforward online bookings try ⓦ www.expedia.ca and ⓦ www.travelocity.ca. **Goway** (☎ 800-387-8850; ⓦ *www.goway.com*) is a Toronto-based travel agency specialising in trips to the Pacific.

Year round fares to Honolulu are around C$700 from Vancouver or C$1120 from Toronto. Fares from Vancouver to Nadi start from C$1650/2270 or C$1950/2440 to Pape'ete in the low/high season. From Toronto and Ottawa, return low season fares to Nadi start from C$2080 and C$2420 to Pape'ete.

Europe

There are flights from most major cities to Los Angeles, Honolulu, Sydney or Auckland from where there are connecting flights to South Pacific. Frankfurt and London have the most flight options but generally there is not much variation in fares between cities. There are cheaper and shorter flights via Tokyo (Japan) and Seoul (South Korea) but there are fewer and less convenient Pacific connections from these two cities.

Considering how far the South Pacific is from Europe, a RTW ticket could be the most economical way to get to the region and you get to more places, such as Asia and Africa as well as the Pacific. Low season for travel from Europe is from April to June and October to November. High season is July to September and during the Christmas and New Year period.

The UK Discount air travel is big business in London. Advertisements for many travel agencies appear in the travel pages of the weekend broadsheet newspapers, in *Time Out*, the *Evening Standard* and in the free magazine *TNT*.

Recommended travel agencies include:

All Ways Pacific (☎ 01494 432747,
　ⓦ www.all-ways.co.uk)
Bridge the World (☎ 0870 444 7474,
　ⓦ www.b-t-w.co.uk)
Flightbookers (☎ 0870 010 7000,
　ⓦ www.ebookers.com)
Trailfinders (☎ 020-7938 3939,
　ⓦ www.trailfinders.co.uk)

From the UK, flights via Los Angeles are generally the easiest – and often the cheapest – option for travel to the South Pacific. Air New Zealand flights from London to Australia or New Zealand often allow for stopovers in the South Pacific. Flights from London via Seoul and Tokyo are another possibility.

Return fares to Nadi start from £650/1050 in the low/high season; to Pape'ete, expect to pay around £890/1450 for a return in the low/high season. Return low-season fares to Honolulu start from £420; to Sydney and Auckland, fares start from £620.

Continental Europe In the Netherlands, try **My Travel** (☎ 1900 10 20 300; ⓦ *www.mytravel.nl*) for online fares and **Wereldcontact** (☎ 0343-530530, ⓦ *www.wereldcontact.nl*) for flight/accommodation deals.

In Germany, **Adventure Travel** (☎ 979 9555; ⓦ *www.adventure-holidays.com*) and **Art of Travel** (☎ 089-2110760; ⓦ *www.artoftravel.de*) specialise in South Pacific travel.

Recommended agencies for fares in France include **OTU Voyages** (☎ *0820 817 817;* W *www.otu.fr)* and **Nouvelles Frontières** (☎ *0825 000 747;* W *www.nouvelles-frontieres.fr).* Both **Iles Du Monde** (☎ *01 43 26 68 68;* W *www.ilesdumonde.com)* and **Ultramarina** (☎ *0 825 02 98 02;* W *www.ultramarina.com)* specialise in travel to the Pacific.

From Paris and Frankfurt low season return fares to Pape'ete start from €1350, while fares to Nadi start from €1050. From major cities expect to pay around €900 for a return fare to Honolulu.

Australasia

Despite its proximity to Australia and New Zealand, travel to the South Pacific from that region can be reasonably expensive. Generally there is not much variation between the low and high season fares except during Christmas holiday season when fares increase considerably.

The east coast of Australia has excellent connecting flights to Melanesia (Vanuatu, Fiji and New Caledonia) while Auckland or Wellington in New Zealand have good connections to Polynesia (Cook Islands, Samoa, Tonga and French Polynesia).

Australia's east coast and New Zealand are both included in the Polypass, which can be a good value option for visiting Fiji, Samoa and Tonga. The Circle South West Pacific air pass is handy for visiting the islands of Melanesia from Australia and the Island Explorer Circle Fare is a good choice for travellers departing from New Zealand.

Australia Quite a few travel offices specialise in discount air tickets. Some travel agents, particularly smaller ones, advertise cheap air fares in the travel sections of weekend newspapers, such as the *Age* (in Melbourne) and *Sydney Morning Herald.*

For online fares, try W www.travel.com.au or W www.webjet.com.au. **Hideaway Holidays** (☎ *02-9743 0253;* W *www.hideaway.com.au)* is a Pacific travel specialist and comes highly recommended. Other travel agencies specialising in the Pacific include **Talpacific Holidays** (☎ *02-9244 1850;* W *www.talpacific.com)* and **Pacific Holidays** (☎ *02-9080 1600;* W *www.pacificholidays.com.au).*

Return fares to Nadi from Sydney and Brisbane start from A$880/1020 in the low/high season. Fares from Melbourne are slightly more expensive – expect to pay around A$940/1070. From Sydney, return fares to Pape'ete start from A$1049/1299 in the low/high season and from Brisbane and Melbourne, fares start at around A$1099/1329. Fares to Port Vila (Vanuatu) from Brisbane start from A$580/680 in the low/high season, A$680/810 from Sydney and A$810/910 from Melbourne.

New Zealand The New Zealand Herald has a travel section in which travel agents advertise fares. **Travel Online** (W *www.travelonline.co.nz)* is good for online fares. Both **Talpacific Holidays** (☎ *09-914 8728;* W *www.travelarrange.co.nz)* and **Air New Zealand** (☎ *0800 737 000;* W *www.airnewzealand.co.nz)* offer a range of fares and packages from New Zealand to most South Pacific destinations.

From Auckland, return fares to Nadi start from NZ$935 in the low season to NZ$1075 in the high season. To Port Vila, return fares start from NZ$910/1270 in the low/high season and to Pape'ete, fares start from NZ$1310/1530 in the low/high season.

Asia

Flying from Japan there are direct flights to Pape'ete, Noumea and Nadi and there are also direct flights from South Korea to Nadi. From other destinations, the easiest option is to fly to Australia or to New Zealand and connect there with onward flights to the South Pacific. Most countries offer fairly competitive air-fare deals – Bangkok, Singapore and Hong Kong are some of the best places to shop around for discount tickets.

Japan & Korea Recommended agencies in Japan include **STA Travel** (☎ *5391 3205;* W *www.statravel.co.jp)* and **No 1 Travel** (☎ *3205 6073;* W *www.no1-travel.com).*

From Japan, return fares to Nadi are around ¥89,000 (US$730) and from South Korea about US$1250.

South America

LanChile operates flights between Santiago and Pape'ete; one flight a week has a stopover on Easter Island. For more information on fares and schedules contact LanChile or **Student Flight Centre** (☎ *02-335 0395)* in Santiago, an affiliate of STA Travel. From Santiago, return fares to Pape'ete cost around US$1500.

SEA

Within the South Pacific countries, inter-island shipping routes can be used to reach smaller islands that do not have an air service. Cruise ships provide an expensive way of reaching the major tourist destinations. Cargo vessels, some of which carry passengers, travel between island groups and the main Pacific-trading nations. Another option is to get to the South Pacific on your own yacht (or on someone else's). All of these options are discussed in more specific detail in the Getting Around the Region chapter.

ORGANISED TOURS

Travel agents and airlines have a range of flight/accommodation packages which are worth considering. There are many options, and prices depend on the season, type of accommodation and length of trip. Although not pushed by travel agents, it is possible to book a package and extend your stay with independent travel. Once your package of relative luxury ends, there's nothing stopping you from staying on in the Pacific a while longer (usually a maximum of one month). You will just have to make sure you return to your original destination for your flight home.

Getting Around the Region

AIR

In the South Pacific region, air travel is the primary way of getting around. As well as the major airlines, there are several airlines run by Pacific nations that can get you to the less-accessible parts of the Pacific. For the most part regional air travel is expensive, but there are a number of international and domestic air passes available which can make air travel more affordable. See the Getting There & Away chapter for more information on international air passes and the Getting There and Away sections in individual country chapters for information on domestic air passes.

SEA

There's a certain romance in the idea of doing at least some of your travel around the Pacific by sea. It's much slower than flying, and usually not any cheaper – but if you've got lots of books you want to read, or just a love of the ocean, this could be the route for you.

Cruise Ship

The cruise ship industry has experienced a renewal in recent years. They will never be the cheapest or the fastest way from A to Z but cruise ships are not just about getting there. The facilities on board usually range from luxurious to even more luxurious. This is not a form of travel with a budget option.

It is recommended you book cruises through a travel agent as they are always well informed and should be able to tell you what the options are. Contact your travel agent well in advance if you are planning on taking a South Pacific cruise.

Cruise-ship fares vary, but generally prices start at about US$200 per day. Major destinations are Noumea (New Caledonia), Port Vila (Vanuatu) and Pape'ete, Mo'orea and Bora Bora in French Polynesia. Melanesian cruises usually depart from Australia's east coast. Other cruises depart from the US east coast, and Honolulu is another hub.

An alternative to traditional cruises is offered by **Society Expeditions** (W *www.societyexpeditions.com*). These small-scale adventure-type cruises last from 18 to 25 days, visiting a number of countries in the South Pacific including Tonga, Fiji, Niue and French Polynesia. The cruises cost from US$5975 to US$8329 per person and all departures are from Los Angeles.

Cargo Ship

It's not cheap and the food can be less than excellent, but if you've got the time, travelling by cargo ship is a way to reach some of the less accessible Pacific islands. You can just do one or two legs of a cargo-ship journey, so you can combine cargo-ship travel with air travel and plan for substantial stopovers at your island of choice. The cost per day of cargo-ship travel (around US$100) is about half that of the cruise ship low-end options. The ship's number one concern is the cargo, which can result in sudden changes to your schedule as ports change their unloading timetable or strikes persuade your ship's captain to avoid a port altogether. Build flexibility into your plans and book well ahead.

Travel agents don't book cargo ship travel. You can either book through a freighter agent or directly with the shipping company. A round trip of about 30 days from the US taking in Fiji and Tahiti will cost around US$3950.

Some freighter agents are:

Freighter Travel (W www.freighter-travel.com)
Freighter World Cruises (W www.freighter world.com)
TravLtips (W www.travltips.com)

Yacht

Between May and October, the harbours of the South Pacific swarm with cruising yachts from around the world. If you have your own yacht, you've probably got the most flexible system of transport in the Pacific. Slightly less flexible options are chartering a yacht or joining the crew on someone else's yacht.

Almost invariably, yachts follow the favourable westerly winds from the Americas towards Asia, Australia or New Zealand.

Popular routes from the US west coast take in Hawaii and Palmyra Atoll before following the traditional path through Samoa and American Samoa, Tonga, Fiji and New Zealand. From the Atlantic and Caribbean, yachties access this area via Panama, the Galápagos Islands, the Marquesas, the Society Islands and the Tuamotus. Possible stops include Suwarrow (northern Cook Islands), Rarotonga or Niue.

Because of the cyclone season, which begins in November, most yachties try to clear

Fiji or Tonga and be on their way to New Zealand by the early part of that month.

The yachting community is quite friendly, especially toward those who display an interest in yachts and other things nautical. Yachties are a good source of information about world weather patterns, navigation and maritime geography. They're also worth approaching to ask about day charters, diving and sailing lessons.

Crewing Often yachties are looking for crew, and for those who'd like a bit of low-key adventure, this is a great opportunity. Most of the time, crew members will only be asked to take a turn on watch – that is, scan the horizon for cargo ships, stray containers and the odd reef – and possibly to cook or clean up the boat. In port, crew may be required to dive and scrape the bottom, paint or make repairs. In most cases, sailing experience is not necessary and crew members can learn as they go. Most yachties charge crew US$10 to US$15 per day for food and supplies.

If you're trying to find a berth on someone else's yacht (or trying to find crew for your own boat) ask at local yacht clubs and look at noticeboards at marinas and yacht clubs. The west coast of the US – San Francisco, Newport Beach and San Diego – is the place to start looking. Australia's northeastern seaboard is good and so is Auckland in New Zealand. In the Pacific, it shouldn't be too difficult to find crew or a yacht in Honolulu, Pape'ete, Pago Pago, Apia, Nuku'alofa, Noumea or Port Vila.

If you'd like to enjoy some relative freedom of movement on a yacht, try to find one that has wind-vane steering; the tedious job of standing at the wheel staring at a compass all day and all night is likely to go to the crew members of the lowest status (that's you). Comfort is also greatly increased on yachts that have a furling jib, a dodger to keep out the weather, a toilet and shower.

Yachts rigged for racing are usually more manageable than simple live-aboards. As a general rule, about 3m of length for each person aboard affords relatively uncrowded conditions.

Red Tape Even on your own yacht you're not completely free to do as you please (you are if you stick to the high seas, but if you want to take advantage of a country's facilities, you have to obey its laws). You must enter a country at an official 'port of entry'

Responsible Yachting

- Don't add to the unsightly (and ecologically hazardous) trash floating up on island beaches by allowing rubbish to fall into the sea, even if you are nowhere near an island. Rubbish can float a long way!
- Many harbours are fished for food. So unless you have holding tanks or on-board sewerage treatment, use on-shore toilet facilities when you are in harbour.
- Never anchor on coral, or allow your anchor to drag through live coral.
- When in public view, observe the local customs regarding dress. Don't lounge about the deck topless on Sunday, for example!

(usually the capital). If this means sailing past a dozen beautiful outlying islands on the way to an appointment with an official in a dull capital city, bad luck. Ports of entry are listed in the Getting There & Around sections of individual country chapters.

When you arrive, hoist your yellow quarantine flag (Q flag) and wait for the appropriate local official to contact you. Often, you are expected to alert them by VHF radio (usually on channel 16). Ask customs officials at the port of entry about requirements for visiting other islands in the country. Bear in mind that you are legally responsible for your crew's actions as well as your own.

Ferries

Within a country, ferries are often the only way to get to some of the outer islands. See Getting Around in the individual country chapters for details about inter-island travel within a country.

Organised Tours

Ocean Voyages (W www.oceanvoyages.com) organise yacht charters in the South Pacific. It's possible to charter the whole boat or book a single berth on a yacht sailing a particular route. In some cases a charter could be about the only way to get to remote islands or atolls if you don't have your own yacht.

Another possibility is aboard the tall ship **Søren Larsen** (W www.sorenlarsen.co.nz) which sails from Auckland and though the South Pacific between June to November each year. It's possible to join the *Søren Larsen* in Auckland or at any of the ports on the trip: Tonga, Fiji, Vanuatu and New Caledonia.

BUS

Large and populous islands will usually have some kind of bus service. However, Pacific island public transport is rarely described as ruthlessly efficient. Buses are often privately (or sometimes family) owned. It is not unusual for owner-drivers to set their own schedules, and if there aren't many people travelling on a particular day, the buses may just stop altogether. Build flexibility into your plans.

CAR & MOTORCYCLE

Larger islands and tourist destinations will usually have some car or motorcycle rental companies operating. Fares and rules vary enormously – see the individual country chapters for more details.

Most Pacific countries drive on the right-hand side of the road. The exceptions are the Solomon Islands, Fiji, Tonga, Cook Islands, Niue, Tuvalu, Kiribati and Nauru. Take extra care when you're driving on the 'wrong' side of the road – or when crossing the road on foot. The rules for getting a driving permit are explained in the individual country chapters.

In rural areas, roads may be no more than dirt tracks used mostly for foot traffic. Be wary of people or animals on the road; drive especially carefully near villages. Road conditions can be atrocious if there has been cyclone or flood damage recently (or even if there hasn't!).

Make sure you get the insurance rules and conditions explained when you rent a car, and ask about petrol availability if you're heading off the main routes. Check your own travel insurance policy too – some do not cover unsealed roads or riding a motorcycle (see Travel Insurance in the Regional Facts for the Visitor chapter).

BICYCLE

On flat Pacific islands, riding a bicycle can be an excellent way to get around. See Getting Around in the individual country chapters for details about renting a bike, or just ask around when you get there. Most bikes will not come with a safety helmet or a bike lock unless you ask for them.

Watch for other traffic and poor road surfaces, and check your travel insurance for disclaimers about hazardous activities. If you're bringing your own bike into the country, ask the airline about costs and rules regarding dismantling and packing the bike.

HITCHING

Although it has a lot going for it, hitching is never entirely safe and we cannot recommend it. Travellers who decide to hitch should understand that they are taking a small but potentially serious risk. People who do choose to hitch will be safer if they travel in pairs and let someone know where they plan to go.

In some Pacific countries hitching is an accepted way of getting where you're going, and is practised by locals and tourists alike. In others it's not the local custom and only tourists are seen trying it. It is possible anywhere, however, and can be quite fast.

The main difficulty on a Pacific island is that rides won't be very long, perhaps only from one village to the next, and it could take you a while to go a longer distance. Still, given the sorry state of the bus service in some regions, hitching is a way to see the area without renting a car. It's also a great way to meet the locals and is an option for getting home after the buses have stopped, which can happen at almost any time in some areas. You might be expected to pay a small fee for a ride, so offer what you think the ride is worth – although offers of payment will often be refused.

Easter Island

Tiny Easter Island is one of the most isolated places on earth – the nearest populated landmass is the even tinier Pitcairn Island, 1900km west, while the South American coast is 3700km east. World famous for its enigmatic stone statues, the island attracts a growing number of visitors, but remains unspoiled and sparsely populated. A Chilean territory since 1888, it's officially known by its Spanish name, Isla de Pascua, but it retains an essentially Polynesian character. Locally, it is called Rapa Nui and also Te Pito o Te Henua, 'The Navel of the World'.

Facts about Easter Island

HISTORY

It's generally accepted that the Pacific Islands were settled by people moving by sea south and east from Asia (see History in the Facts about the South Pacific chapter). But because Easter Island is the most south-easterly corner of Polynesia, some theories have linked the ancestral Easter Islanders to the South American mainland (a mere 3700km away). Local folklore has it that King Hotu Matua brought the original settlers, but that there was a period of rivalry between two different peoples, intriguingly called the Long Ears and the Short Ears.

Thor Heyerdahl's 1947 *Kon-Tiki* expedition proved it was possible to cross to the Pacific islands from South America on balsa-wood rafts, and Heyerdahl visited Easter Island in 1955 to seek more evidence of links to South America. He speculated that the oral tradition could be reconciled with separate migrations of the Short Ears from Polynesia and the 'more advanced' Long Ears from South America. Heyerdahl's adventures and ideas had great popular appeal, but modern linguistic and cultural studies conclude that the Rapa Nui people are of Polynesian ancestry, and that the first of them arrived from the Marquesas Islands around AD 400.

The Rapa Nui developed a unique civilisation, characterised by the construction of the stone platforms called *ahu* and the distinctive Easter Island statues called *moai* (see the Archaeology section later). Easter Island is also unique in the Pacific for the development

At a Glance

Capital City: Hanga Roa

Population: 4200

Time: Six hours behind GMT

Land Area: 117 sq km (45 sq miles)

Number of Islands: One (plus some small islets near the coast)

Telephone Code: ☎ 56-32

GDP/Capita: Not applicable

Currency: Chilean peso (US$ also accepted) (Ch$100 = US$0.14)

Languages: Spanish & Rapa Nui

Greeting: *Hola* (Spanish) or *'Iorana* (Rapa Nui)

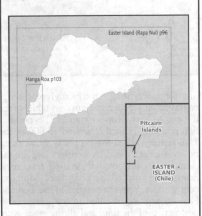

Highlights

- **Orongo Ceremonial Village** – where the birdman priest ruled, by the side of a witch's cauldron crater lake

- **Moai** – stern and serene, the mysterious guardians of the island

- **Hanga Roa** – relaxed town where horses rule the roads and island music streams out from every restaurant

- **Rapa Nui culture** – a smooth blend of Polynesian and Chilean culture, best experienced at the Iglesia Hanga Roa

EASTER ISLAND (RAPA NUI)

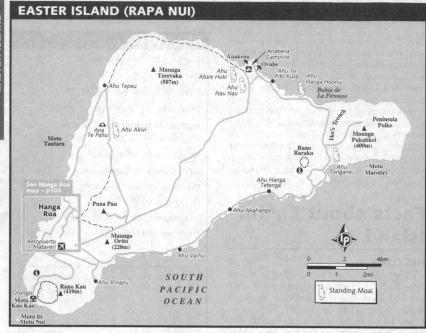

of a form of writing – the hieroglyphic script engraved on wooden *rongorongo* tablets (see the boxed text 'Rongorongo'). The population probably peaked at around 15,000 in the 17th century, when the people were working on ever-larger *moai*. A conflict late in the century, possibly over dwindling resources, nearly exterminated the Long Ears. More recent warfare, between peoples of the Tuu and Hotu-iti regions, resulted in the progressive destruction of the *ahu*, and all the *moai* were ultimately toppled.

European Arrival

When the Dutch admiral Jacob Roggeveen arrived on Easter Sunday 1722, the islanders were living a healthy subsistence from cultivated gardens of sugar cane, sweet potatoes, yams and taro. Many of the great *moai* were still standing, but there was no sign of any modern implements, suggesting the islanders did not trade with the outside world.

In 1774, the English navigator James Cook described the Rapa Nui people as poor, small, lean, timid and miserable, and noted that many *moai* had been damaged and many *pukao* (a separate stone topknot that sat atop many *moai*) had fallen – apparently as a result of

intertribal wars. Fourteen years later, the doomed French explorer La Pérouse found the people prosperous and calm, suggesting a quick recovery. In 1804, a Russian visitor reported more than 20 standing *moai*, but later accounts suggest further disruption.

Contact with outsiders nearly annihilated the Rapa Nui people. A raid by Peruvian blackbirders (slavers) in 1862 took a thousand islanders away to work the guano deposits of Peru's Chincha islands, where about 900 of them perished. After intense pressure from the Catholic Church, some survivors were returned to Easter Island, but many of them had contracted smallpox and died on the ship. Only 15 of the islanders made it back, and they carried smallpox with them. In a final tragedy, the resulting epidemic reduced the local population to just a few hundred.

A brief period of French-led missionary activity saw most of the surviving islanders converted in the 1860s. In 1870, Jean-Baptiste Dutroux-Bornier, established a sheep-farming operation and sent many islanders to work on plantations in Tahiti. Conflicts arose with the missionaries, who were at the same time deporting islanders to missions on Mangareva (in the Gambier Archipelago). Dutroux-Bornier was assassinated by an islander in 1877, and his estate was contested in litigation until the time of the Chilean takeover.

Chilean Rule

After its defeat of Bolivia and Peru in the War of the Pacific (1879–84), Chile entered an expansionist phase, and its navy annexed Easter Island in 1888, considering it a potentially strategic naval base. Chile soon leased the island to Williamson, Balfour & Company, a British-Chilean farming and grazing enterprise. This company managed the island through its Compañía Explotadora de la Isla de Pascua (CEDIP), which was the de facto government until the 1950s, though islander welfare was a low priority and there were several uprisings against the company.

In 1953, the Chilean government revoked CEDIP's lease and the navy took charge. After 1967, a civilian administration proved more benevolent and made improvements to water and electricity supply, medical care and education. In 1985, the airport was expanded and improved as an emergency landing site for the US space shuttle. Though there were some local objections, the larger runway enabled the establishment of a regular commercial air service, which strengthened links with the mainland and made tourism feasible for the first time.

ARCHAEOLOGY

The most common archaeological remains are the *ahu* – some 245 of these stone platforms surround the coast. *Ahu* were village burial sites and ceremonial centres and are thought to derive from altars in French Polynesia. The *ahu moai* supported massive carved figures, which probably represented clan ancestors. From 2m to 10m tall, these stony-faced statues stood with their backs to the Pacific Ocean, looking over villages of oval, boat-shaped houses. Some statues were even crowned with a large red *pukao*, or 'topknot'. Although this style of statue is unique in the Pacific, there are similarities with the stone *tiki* of the Marquesas Islands, and the *ahu* are similar to the carved backs of ceremonial seats found elsewhere in Polynesia.

How were the *moai* moved from where they were carved at Rano Raraku volcano to the *ahu* around the coast? Legend says that priests moved the *moai* by the power of their *mana* (personal spiritual power), with the statues themselves 'walking' a short distance each day.

US archaeologist William Mulloy proposed that a sledge was fitted to the *moai*, which was then lifted with a bipod and dragged forward a short distance at a time. Heyerdahl and 180 islanders managed to pull a 4m *moai* across a field at Anakena and he figured that they could have moved a larger one with wooden runners and more labour.

Many stone structures have been demolished, damaged, recycled or rebuilt, both during tribal conflicts and under CEDIP. For example, the pier at Caleta Hanga Roa is built on stones from dismantled *ahu*. Several *moai*, and numerous smaller artefacts, have been taken by collectors and museums. Some *moai* have been completely restored, while others have been re-erected but are eroded. Many more lie on the ground, toppled over – usually face down – near an *ahu*, or abandoned on the long drag from Rano Raraku.

GEOGRAPHY

Easter Island is roughly triangular in shape, with an extinct volcanic cone in each corner – Maunga (Mt) Terevaka, in the northwest corner, is the highest point at 507m. Much of the interior of Easter Island is grassland, with cultivable soil interspersed with rugged lava fields. Wave erosion has created steep cliffs around much of the coast, and Anakena, on the north shore, is the only sandy beach. The volcanic soil is quite fertile, but so porous that water quickly drains underground – there are no permanent streams.

CLIMATE

Just south of the Tropic of Capricorn, Easter Island has a mild climate with average daily temperatures around 20°C to 25°C. Annual average rainfall is about 1235mm. The island is hottest in January and February and coolest (but still warm) in July and August. May is the wettest month, but downpours can occur at any time.

ECOLOGY & ENVIRONMENT

The lack of trees on the island is usually attributed to the earlier use of timber for scaffolds and rollers to make and move the stone statues, though this is supposition – more recent agricultural activities may also be partly responsible. One consequence of the deforestation may have been islanders' isolation, because there were no trees big enough to make an ocean-going canoe. Parts of the island are being replanted, but mostly with eucalyptus trees.

Rongorongo

One of Easter Island's unsolved mysteries is the undeciphered script called *ko hau motu mo rongorongo* – literally 'lines of script for recitation'. Carefully inscribed on shaped wooden tablets, the script comprises rows of small figures or glyphs, about 1cm high, depicting people, animals, stylised plants and geometric shapes. Oral tradition has it that King Hotu Matua brought *rongorongo* tablets to the island with learned men who could read and recite the inscriptions. The recitations were said to be of three different types – hymns, criminal deeds and war stories. Missionary Eugene Eyraud saw many tablets on the island in the 1860s, but no-one could or would read the script. Within a few years, many of the tablets had disappeared, and attempts to have islanders read the script seemed to result in a mere description of the characters.

Only 21 original *rongorongo* tablets survive, including one made from a fragment of an oar from a British Navy ship. This indicates that the script was being written, or at least copied, as recently as the early 18th century. However, no *rongorongo*-literate islanders survived the 1862 slave raid and the epidemics that followed.

One fascinating feature of the tablets is the way they are written. Starting in the bottom left, the script reads across to the right, then the tablet is rotated 180° and the next line reads to the right again – every second line is upside down.

There have been many attempts to decipher the script, but the only consensus is that a small part of one tablet appears to be a lunar calendar, which corresponds to a modern lunar almanac. The number of different figures (some 200) is more than would be needed for a phonetic alphabet, so they may be ideographs, like Chinese characters.

Alternatively, the characters may be a series of prompts to assist in the recitation of a ritual chant or story.

Despite much speculation, the *rongorongo* script is not related to any form of writing from the Indus Valley, ancient Egypt or anywhere else – it is truly unique to Easter Island.

FLORA & FAUNA

Deforestation and grazing has seen the loss of nearly all the distinctive local vegetation, and most of the island is now covered in grassland. Lakes in some of the volcanic cones have thick growths of *tora* reeds – they are very similar to some South American types (eg, in Lake Titicaca), but their presence here predates any human arrivals. There are no endemic bird or animal species.

GOVERNMENT & POLITICS

Administratively, the island is part of Chile's fifth region, Region V, with its capital at Valparaíso on the mainland. The Chilean government owns most of the land and appoints Easter Island's governor. The mayor and locally elected council have very limited powers. Two competing Consejos de Ancianos (Councils of Elders) represent native rights.

ECONOMY

Cattle and sheep grazing, fishing and market gardens supply local needs, but tourism is the only activity that brings money to the island. That said, tourism is strong, but not booming – 24,000 visitors, including visitors from cruise ships, visit the island each year. Islanders have concerns that some tourist money goes off island (that is, profits from Hotel Hanga Roa are sent to its mainland owners). Easter Island receives substantial economic support from the mainland, and the thousand or so residents from mainland Chile *(continentales)*, mostly government employees, also bring some income to the island's economy.

POPULATION & PEOPLE

The population of 4200, includes one-third non–Rapa Nui people who are from the Chilean mainland and a substantial number of Rapa Nui who are actually living, permanently or temporarily, off the island.

ARTS

Apart from the famous *moai*, the island has a number of distinct art styles, notably the *moai kavakava*, or 'statues of ribs', said to represent ghosts. Some wood carvings have features similar to New Zealand tiki faces, while others are reminiscent of the petroglyphs found at sites around the island.

Rapa Nui music, which historically may be derivative of other South Pacific sounds, is distinctive and enjoyable. Compact discs and cassettes of local groups, such as Topantani, are available locally. The elaborately costumed and talented musical group Kari Kari performs regularly at Hotel Hanga Roa and Hotel Iorana.

SOCIETY

Despite its unique language and history, contemporary Rapa Nui does not appear a 'traditional' society – its continuity shattered by the near extinction of the population in the last century. Rapa Nui people identify more as Pacific Islanders than Latin Americans. Large extended families bind most of the islanders together with much respect to the elders.

RELIGION

Most Easter Islanders are still at least nominally Catholic. Sunday services at Iglesia Hanga Roa blend Polynesian and Catholic iconography and music.

LANGUAGE

Spanish is the official language, but the indigenous language is Rapa Nui, an Eastern Polynesian dialect closely related to the languages of French Polynesia and Hawaii. Some people in the tourist business speak English. Speaking some Rapa Nui impresses the locals, but Spanish is more useful.

Spanish Basics

Hello.	*Hola.*
Goodbye.	*Adiós.*
How are you?	*¿Cómo estás?*
I'm well (thanks).	*Bien (gracias).*
Please.	*Por* favor.
Thanks.	*Gracias.*
Yes.	*Sí.*
No.	*No.*

Rapa Nui Basics

Hello.	*'Iorana.*
Goodbye.	*'Iorana.*
How are you?	*Pehe koe?*
I'm well.	*Rivaria.*
Thank you.	*Maururu.*

Facts for the Visitor

SUGGESTED ITINERARIES

Allow a day for the sites near Hanga Roa, another day for a circuit of the northeast, and a third day to see the Rano Kau volcano, the birdman sites and Ahu Vinapu. The northeast circuit has the best sites, so do that first if the weather is fine. If you have the time, energy and equipment, consider circuiting the island on foot or by horse. Allow at least three days to see the major sites.

PLANNING
When to Go

The weather is mild at any time, but most visitors to the island come in late December to January (the South American summer holidays), in February for the Semana de Rapa Nui festival, and in August to September (the northern hemisphere summer holidays).

Maps

Free tourist maps, at Sernatur and tour agencies, show important archaeological sites, but lack adequate road information. The 1:30,000 *Isla de Pascua-Rapa Nui: Mapa Arqueológico-Turístico* and the 1:32,000 JLM *Isla de Pascua Trekking Map* are available at shops.

TOURIST OFFICES

Sernatur (☎ 100 255; @ sernatur_rapanui@ entelchile.net; Tu'u Maheke, Hanga Roa) provides some information on the island.

VISAS & EMBASSIES

Visa requirements are the same as for mainland Chile. Citizens of Canada, the UK, the US, Australia, NZ and most Western European countries need passports only. Upon arrival, visitors receive a tourist card and entry stamp that allows a stay of up to 90 days. Passports are obligatory and are essential for checking into hotels, cashing travellers cheques and for other activities. Check with a Chilean embassy for the latest information. There's no consulate on the island, but many countries have an embassy in Santiago.

To rent a car, you'll need an International Driving Permit (IDP).

CUSTOMS

There are no currency restrictions. Duty-free allowances include 400 cigarettes or 50 cigars or 500g of tobacco; 2.5L of alcoholic beverages; and perfume for personal use.

EASTER ISLAND

MONEY

Easter Island uses the Chilean *peso* but the US dollar is readily accepted. In Hanga Roa, the Banco del Estado changes US dollars at reasonable rates, but charges US$10 commission on travellers cheques; there's also an ATM. Exchange rates are better at the gas station on Hotu Matua. Some eateries and stores show prices in both dollars and pesos, but use a lower conversion rate, so using pesos saves money. Some *residenciales* (basically B&Bs), hotels and tour agencies take credit cards.

Exchange Rates

Approximate rates for the Chilean peso and the US dollar are listed below.

country	unit		peso
Australia	A$1	=	Ch$478
Canada	C$1	=	Ch$537
euro zone	€1	=	Ch$850
Fiji	F$1	=	Ch$381
Japan	¥100	=	Ch$609
New Zealand	NZ$1	=	Ch$415
Pacific franc	100 CFP	=	Ch$700
Samoa	ST1	=	Ch$236
Solomon Islands	S$1	=	Ch$97
Tonga	T$1	=	Ch$334
UK	£1	=	Ch$1197
USA	US$1	=	Ch$715
Vanuatu	100VT	=	Ch$596

country	unit		dollar
Australia	A$1	=	US$0.67
Canada	C$1	=	US$0.75
Chile	Ch$100	=	US$0.14
euro zone	€1	=	US$1.18
Fiji	F$1	=	US$0.53
Japan	¥100	=	US$0.85
New Zealand	NZ$1	=	US$0.58
Pacific franc	100 CFP	=	US$0.97
Samoa	ST1	=	US$0.33
Solomon Islands	S$1	=	US$0.14
Tonga	T$1	=	US$0.47
UK	£1	=	US$1.67
Vanuatu	100VT	=	US$0.83

Note: to check current exchange rates, see W www.oanda.com.

Costs

Budget approximately US$30 to US$40 a day for comfortable, but not opulent, lodging, plus US$15 to US$25 on meals. Cheaper lodging does exist, but is still costly at US$15 for basic services, while top-end spots jump to US$160. A day's car hire costs around US$50; a bicycle will cost closer to US$20. Full-day tours will put you back US$35. Note that bargaining is not a common practice on Easter Island, although in the low season it's fine to ask for discounted rates.

POST & COMMUNICATIONS

Easter Island's international telephone code is the same as Chile's (☎ 56), and the area code (☎ 32) covers the whole of the island. International calls (dial ☎ 00) are expensive: US$2 per minute minimum. Mobile phones do not work on Easter Island. See under Hanga Roa later for details of the post and telephone offices.

DIGITAL RESOURCES

The **Easter Island homepage** (W *www .netaxs.com/~trance/rapanui.html*), has background facts and comprehensive links to information on everything from local politics to archaeology and tour operators. For current information on Rapa Nui research and travel try the **Easter Island Foundation** (W *www .islandheritage.org*).

BOOKS

Thor Heyerdahl's *Kon-Tiki: Across the Pacific by Raft* and *Aku-Aku: The Secret of Easter Island* are both worthwhile books; the first is an account of his 1947 attempted voyage to Rapa Nui in a balsa raft, while *Aku-Aku* further expounds upon his theories of Polynesian migrations.

For a more humorous and contemporary story of a similar voyage, take a gander at *8 Men and a Duck: An Improbable Voyage by Reed Boat to Easter Island* by Scottish travel writer Nick Thorpe. *Trespassers on Easter Island,* by Hanns Ebensten, chronicles the impact of foreigners on the island since 1722.

Englishwoman Katherine Routledge led the first archaeological expedition in 1914, which she describes in *The Mystery of Easter Island*.

Bavarian priest Sebastián Englert spent 35 years on Rapa Nui, until his death in 1970; his *Island at the Center of the World* retells the island's history through oral tradition. Lonely Planet's *Chile & Easter Island* travel guide provides a more thorough description of the island.

RADIO & TV

Chilean programmes are beamed to the island via satellite.

TIME

Easter Island is two hours behind mainland Chile, six hours behind GMT, or five hours behind GMT in summer (daylight saving time).

HEALTH

There is no malaria, dengue fever or other health risks. The local water supply is OK, but short-term visitors would be wise to stick to bottled water. If you have travelled in a yellow-fever-infected country in the last 10 years, proof of yellow fever vaccine is now required to travel to Easter Island. For medical services see the Hanga Roa section. See the Health section in the Regional Facts for the Visitor chapter for further information on health.

SOCIAL GRACES

Climbing on stonework at most archaeological sites is forbidden. The *moai* in particular are made of quite soft stone, and can easily be damaged.

DANGERS & ANNOYANCES

The weather can be hot and there is little shade or fresh water available outside town. On excursions, take bottles of water, a long-sleeved shirt, sunglasses, a hat and sun block.

BUSINESS HOURS

Offices are open from 9am to 5pm, with some closing for an hour at lunch time. Restaurants tend to close early if business is slow.

PUBLIC HOLIDAYS & SPECIAL EVENTS

Chilean public holidays include New Year's Day, Semana Santa (Holy Week; the week before Easter), Asunción de la Virgen (the Assumption), Columbus Day, Todos los Santos (All Saints' Day) and Navidad (Christmas) – see the Regional Facts for the Visitor chapter for dates. In addition there is:

Día del Trabajo (Labor Day) 1 May
Glorias Navales (Naval Battle of Iquique) 21 May
Corpus Christi 30 May
Día San Pedro y San Pablo (St Peter's & St Paul's Day) 29 June
Día de la Independencia Nacional (Independence Day) 18 September
Día del Ejército (Armed Forces Day) 19 September
Inmaculada Concepción (Immaculate Conception) 8 December

For 10 days in late January and early February, the Semana de Rapa Nui (Tapati festival) presents cultural and sporting events traditional to Easter Island.

ACTIVITIES

Surfing

The main break is Motu Hava, a quick walk from Hanga Roa, with consistent swells best from May through to August. The shore is shallow with a lot of reef and rock. Plenty of locals body-surf at the beach right at the town. The shop **Hare Orca**, next to the Orca Diving Center, rents boogie boards (US$16/27 per half/full day) as well as surfboards (US$22/33).

Diving

Steep drop-offs, abundant marine life and clear water make for good diving. Visit **Orca Diving Center** (☎ 550 375; 🌐 *www .seemorca.co.cl; Caleta Hanga Roa*) and, next door, **Mike Rapu Dive Center** (☎ 551 055; 🌐 *www.mikerapudiving.cl*). Dives, with all gear provided, cost about US$55 each. Bring proof of certification. Both shops also offer snorkelling excursions for US$32 to US$50 per person.

Getting There & Away

AIR

The only airline serving Easter Island is **Lan-Chile** (☎/fax 100 279; 🌐 *www.lanchile.com; Atamu Tekena*), which has an office near Pont in Hanga Roa. It has three flights per week to/from Santiago and to/from Pape'ete (Tahiti) in high season and two in the low season. A standard economy round-trip fare from Santiago can range from Ch450,000 to Ch600,000. Flights are often overbooked, so it is essential to reconfirm your ticket two days before departure; LanChile claims that you don't need to reconfirm once you're on the island. From Pape'ete to Easter Island, flights costs around Ch33,330, good for a stay of seven to 21 days.

From Sydney and Auckland you can reach Easter Island on the Qantas/LanChile flights to Santiago, stopping in Pape'ete and Easter Island. A round-trip flight costs up to NZ$4320. Or take a round-trip ticket from Auckland to Easter Island, with a stopover in Pape'ete for NZ$5000. Easter Island can be included in round-the-world (RTW) or Circle Pacific tickets with One World Alliance, which includes LanChile. See the Getting There & Away chapter for RTW tickets, air passes and airline contact details. The airport departure tax is Ch18,000.

SEA
Few passenger services go to Easter Island, but see Cruise Ship in the Getting Around the Region chapter for more information. A few yachts stop here, mostly in January, February or March. Anchorages are not well sheltered, and coming ashore can be difficult.

ORGANISED TOURS
Organised tours of Easter Island are usually part of a South American package, arranged via Santiago. They are an expensive option – around US$2000 for a week – considering that it is easy to arrange accommodation and local tours on the island. Companies with Easter Island tours include:

Eldertreks (☎ 416-588 5000, 800-741 7956,
 W www.eldertreks.com)
Far Horizons Archaeological & Cultural Trips
 (☎ 505-343 9400, 800-552 4575, **W** www
 .farhorizon.com) Includes trips during the
 Tapati festival
Festival Tours (☎ 407-850 0680, 800-225
 0117, **W** www.festivaltours.com)
Nature Expeditions International (☎ 800-869
 0639, **W** www.naturexp.com)

Getting Around

It's possible to walk around the island in a few days, but be prepared for the summer heat, lack of shade and scattered water supply. While distances appear small on the map, visiting numerous archaeological sites can be tiring. With good transportation, it's possible to see all the major archaeological sites, at least superficially, in about three days, but many people take longer.

CAR & MOTORCYCLE
Established hotels and agencies rent Suzuki 4WDs for US$55 to US$65 per eight-hour day, US$60 to US$90 per day; locals may charge less – ask at *residenciales* or at Sernatur. Hotels and agencies generally accept credit cards, but private individuals expect US dollars. In Hanga Roa, **Comercial Insular**

(☎ 100 480; *Atamu Tekena)* provides the best service for rentals. Also look for signs in windows of businesses. Outside the high season, prices are negotiable. Insurance is not usually included and some cars are very far from perfect. Make sure the car has all the necessary fixings should a tyre go flat (not uncommon).

Motorcycles are rented for about US$30 per eight hours and US$55 per day. Given the occasional tropical downpours, a jeep is more convenient and more economical for two or more people.

BICYCLE
Mountain bikes are readily available from hotels and car rental agencies for about US$11 to US$16 per eight hours, US$16 to US$22 per day. Take the bike for a test spin and make sure that gears and brakes work and that the seat is at least bearable. Keep in mind that roads around the south part of the island are steep and winding. There's an air pump at the gas station near the airport.

LOCAL TRANSPORT
Taxi
Taxis cost a flat US$2 for most trips around town. Longer trips can be negotiated, with the cost depending mainly on the time – for example, a round trip to the beach at Anakena costs US$16.

Horse
For sites near Hanga Roa, horses can be hired for around US$13 to US$38 per eight hours, but many of the horses are either poorly maintained or unaccustomed to a strange mount. Horse gear is very basic and potentially hazardous for inexperienced riders. Wear long pants if you do ride anywhere.

ORGANISED TOURS
Tours of the sites will cost you around US$35 to US$40 per person per day; US$20 to US$25 per person per half-day. **Kia Koe Tour** (☎ 100 282; **W** *www.kiakoetour.co.cl; Atamu Tekena)* is one of the largest and most generalised tour company. **Haumaka Tours** (☎/fax 100 274; **W** *www.haumakatours.com)*, in the Aloha Nui Guest House (see Places to Stay later in this chapter), is run by guides Ramon Edmunds Pakomio and Josefina Nahoe Mulloy, who are both fluent English speakers; Josefina is the granddaughter of archaeologist William Mulloy.

Hanga Roa

pop 3800

The lone *moai* statue of Ahu Tautira stands guard over the soccer field, where school kids kick around a ball, avoiding the horses grazing at the goal posts. Fishing boats, with outboard engines buzzing, enter and leave the small bay, while locals greet each other on the main road, en route to buy their groceries – vegetables from local gardens, dry goods from Chile. They catch up on the town news as Latino pop and local music blare from the surrounding restaurants. Small, but brimming with life, and the only settlement on the island, Hanga Roa has all the basic services and offers a good deal of fun.

Orientation

There are a number of shops, an artisans' market and several eateries on Atamu Tekena. Old maps show this as Policarpo Toro, which is now the name of the road along the waterfront. The bank, tourist office, and other public buildings are in the blocks between Atamu Tekena and the small bay called Caleta Hanga Roa. Outside of this main area, the irregular dirt roads are rarely marked and actual street addresses nonexistent. Fortunately, locals kindly explain where places are, or escort you. The place is so small that you'll learn your way around in a day or so.

Information

Tourist Offices Near Caleta Hanga Roa, **Sernatur** (☎ 100 255; e *sernatur_rapanui@ent elchile.net; Tu'u Maheke; open 8.30am-1pm*

HANGA ROA

PLACES TO STAY
2 Residencial Mahina Taka Taka Georgia
3 Residencial Chez Goretti
10 Hotel O'Tai
17 Hotel Martin y Anita Prioriti
18 Residencial Vai Kapua
22 Hotel Orongo
31 Hotel Hanga Roa
35 Residencial Kona Tau (HI)
37 Aloha Nui Guest House; Haumaka Tours
38 Residencial Miru; Gringo's Pizza
40 Hotel Iorana

PLACES TO EAT
8 Avarei Pua
9 La Caleta
19 Aeropuerto
20 Café Tavake
26 Restaurant Pea
28 Supermercado Kai Nene
29 Ariki o Te Pana

OTHER
1 Museo Antropológico Sebastián Englert
4 Toroko
5 Orca Dive Center
6 Mike Rapu Dive Center
7 Hare Orca
11 Soccer Field
12 Post Office
13 Plaza Policarpo Toro
14 Mercado Artesanal
15 Iglesia Hanga Roa
16 Hospital Hanga Roa
21 Fruit & Vegetable Market
23 Feria Municipal
24 Banco del Estado; ATM
25 Sernatur
27 Entel
30 Aloha Pub
32 Comercial Insular
33 Kia Koe Tour
34 Cámara de Turismo
36 LanChile
39 Piditi

& 2.30pm-6pm Mon-Fri, also 9am-1pm Sat Jan-Feb) is at Policarpo Toro. The **Cámara de Turismo** *(☎ 550 055; ℮ camararapanui@ entelchile.net; Atamu Tekena; open 9am-1pm & 3pm-6pm Mon-Fri)*, near Pont, is an organisation of local businesses and has a useful orientation brochure.

Post & Communications There's a **post office** *(Te Pito o Te Henua; open 9am-5pm Mon-Fri, 9am-noon Sat)* and the **Entel telephone office** *(open 8am-6pm daily)* is in a cul-de-sac opposite Sernatur. A public pay phone across the street from Entel can be used to make a collect or card call overseas. Internet cafés spring up and quickly close down: enquire about the newest places at Sernatur. Rates can be as steep as US$4 per hour.

Laundry No laundry is currently available on the island. Most *residenciales* and hotels can do your laundry, but avoid per-piece charges.

Medical Services The **Hospital Hanga Roa** *(☎ 100 215)* is one long block east of the church.

Chilean National Forests Authority (Conaf) The national park that covers most of the island is managed by the Chilean National Forests Authority (Conaf). The **Conaf office** *(☎ 100 236)* is south of town on the road to Rano Kau. They may give suggestions on hiking and camping. See the Anakena section later for camping ground details.

Museo Antropológico Sebastián Englert
Located north of town, the museum *(admission US$2; open 9.30am-12.30pm & 2pm-5.30pm Tues-Fri, 9.30am-12.30pm Sat & Sun)* uses text and photographs to explain the Rapa Nui people's history. It also displays the *moai kavakava* and replica *rongorongo* tablets, skulls from bodies originally entombed in *ahu,* basalt fishhooks and other implements, obsidian spearheads and many other weapons.

Places to Stay
In Hanga Roa, *residenciales* provide decent lodging without breaking the budget. Many offer meals for about US$15 each, although it's easy to find cheaper food in town. Reservations are only necessary in the peak times of August and January to February, when

prices may be higher. Hotel or *residencial* proprietors with whom you've booked a room will meet you at the airport. If you don't have a reservation, you can check for availability with representatives who have booths by the baggage claim section.

Budget In a friendly family house, **Residencial Kona Tau** *(☎ 100 321; ℮ kona tau@entelchile.net; Avareipua; members/ nonmembers US$15/20)* is a pleasant HI affiliate, and serves large breakfasts. Members pay less but share the room, while nonmembers get their own rooms with private bathroom. Single rooms are hard to come by in the busy season. Rooms outside the main house are better.

Residencial Miru *(☎ 100 365; Atamu Tekena; per person with shared/private bathroom US$10/15)* is basic and offers kitchen use; breakfast is US$5.

Residencial Vai Kapua *(☎ 100 377; ℮ vai kapua@entelchile.net; singles/doubles US$25/ 40)*, in a cul-de-sac off Te Pito o Te Henua, is very good value. It's centrally located, friendly and quiet. It has plain but large, bright rooms with pretty gardens.

Mid-Range Brimming with the magic of the island, **Residencial Mahina Taka Taka Georgia** *(☎ 100 452, fax 100 105; ℮ riro roko@entelchile.net; cnr Atamu Tekena & Tahai; per person US$30)*, is run by the knowledgeable and gregarious Lucia Riroroko Tuki. Rooms are basic and a bit musty, but common areas are comfortable. The house is a 30-minute walk north of town.

Residencial Chez Goretti *(☎/fax 100 459; ℮ chezmariagoretti@entelchile.net; Atamu Tekena; per person with breakfast US$40)*, also a 30-minute walk north of town, is excellent value. Marvellous gardens are spread out over the spacious grounds. Rooms are large and sunny, and the superb gathering and dining area includes a bar.

Hotel Orongo *(☎/fax 100 294; Atamu Tekena; singles/doubles US$45/75)* is a friendly, intimate, five-room hotel, with pleasant gardens, large, bright rooms and an excellent restaurant.

Hotel Martín y Anita Prioriti *(☎/fax 100 593; ℮ hmanita@entelchile.net; Simón Paoa; singles/doubles US$50/80)* offers large rooms in a lush garden setting, some with air-con. Martín and Anita operate a second nearby house for overflow business, where they put mostly solo travellers.

Aloha Nui Guest House (☎/fax 100 274; e haumaka@entelchile.net; cnr Atamu Tekena & Hotu Matua; singles/doubles US$55/100) has decent, spacious rooms with private bath, set among attractive gardens. Both English and German are spoken.

Top End The traditional favourite, **Hotel O'Tai** (☎ 100 250, fax 100 482; e otaira panui@entelchile.net; Te Pito o Te Henua; singles/doubles US$70/95) is conveniently situated, pleasantly landscaped and has a swimming pool. Superior rooms (US$130) are larger and include air-con.

Hotel Iorana (☎/fax 100 312; e iorana hotel@entelchile.net; Policarpo Toro; singles/doubles US$89/121) has rooms in a quiet area (except during the infrequent landings at the airport) with coastal views and a pool.

Hotel Hanga Roa (☎/fax 100 299; e res hangaroa@panamericanahoteles.cl; singles/doubles from US$140/160) is near Caleta Hanga Piko in Pont. Standard rooms are large and bright, but older and unexciting; some have a view of the sea. Superior rooms (US$270) are in bungalows, all with an ocean view, ceiling fan, TV and a minibar; although some are near a noisy generator.

Places to Eat
Besides great fruit juices and fish, the island's cuisine is rather bland and moderately expensive. For self-catering options, there are **Supermercado Kai Nene** (Atamu Tekena) with the best selection of basic goods, the morning **market** where vendors sell fruit and veggies opposite the Feria Municipal, and **Aeropuerto** (Plaza Policarpo Toro) for fresh bread and cheeses.

Ariki o Te Pana (☎ 100 171; Atamu Tekena; lunches US$5-10), near the supermarket, has

scrumptious empanadas (turnover with veggies, ground beef or cheese, US$2 to US$3) that are a lunch in themselves, plus cold drinks and large lunches.

Café Tavake (☎ 100 300; Atamu Tekena; set menu US$5, sandwiches US$3) is good for cheap meals, sandwiches and late-night snacks and drinks.

Gringo's Pizza (☎ 100 365; Residencial Miru, on Atamu Tekena; small pizza US$6) serves up good pizzas, empanadas, vegetarian meals and great big juices.

La Caleta (☎ 100 607; Te Pito o Te Henua; sandwiches US$4, mains US$9) is a good bet for sandwiches and burgers, and it has a pleasant view of the harbour. Around the corner, **Avarei Pua** (☎ 100 431; cnr Policarpo Toro & Te Pito o Te Henua; mains US$9-10) serves filling, well-priced meals, including excellent ceviche (raw fish cooked with lime juice, US$6).

Restaurant Pea (☎ 100 382; Policarpo Toro; mains US$10), at Playa Pea, has fine tuna, steak and chicken dishes and friendly service. Sandwiches (US$4) are also available.

Entertainment
Aloha Pub (cnr Atamu Tekena & Englert) has a pleasant atmosphere and is good for a drink and pub food. Dancing through the night is a way of life here. **Toroko** (Policarpo Toro), best on Thursday and Friday, jams with a mix of modern tunes and island pop. **Piditi** (Hotu Matua) is slightly less frenetic and best on Saturday. The cover charge at both Toroko and Piditi is about US$4, drinks are expensive, and nothing gets going until after 1am.

The elaborately costumed and talented group **Kari Kari** (☎ 100 595) performs island legends through song and dance at the Hotel Hanga Roa. Performances include

When Hollywood Came to Town
The 1994 movie Rapa Nui, co-produced by Kevin Costner, is B-grade matinee material at best, but had a huge impact on Easter Island. Hundreds of the islanders worked as extras and the production brought an injection of cash to the economy. Locals were concerned that the filming would ruin many of the sacred sites, but the film company paid for a thorough clean-up and made a substantial donation to the national park.

The film stimulated local pride in the island's culture, but presents some inaccurate images, such as events that occurred over several centuries as happening in just a few years. On a positive note, the film's scenery has all the rugged and remote appeal of the island itself, which is good publicity for the local tourism industry. Locals are quick to mention if they or their friends appeared in the movie and nightclubs sometimes play the movie on TVs, while everyone dances to the island's contemporary beat.

the obligatory and hilarious 'let's watch the tourists dance this stuff' routine. Shows cost US$17; check postings at the hotel and at Sernatur for current showtimes.

Shopping

Hanga Roa has numerous souvenir shops. The best prices are found at the open-air **Feria Municipal** (cnr Atamu Tekena & Tu'u Maheke). The **Mercado Artesanal** (cnr Tuukoihu & Ara Roa Rakei), across from the church, has more choices. Both are open mornings and late afternoon Monday to Saturday. Look for replicas of standard *moai* and *moai kavakava*, replicas and cloth rubbings of *rongorongo* tablets, and fragments of obsidian from Maunga Orito. Discourage reef destruction by not purchasing *any* coral products.

Parque Nacional Rapa Nui

Since 1935, much of Easter Island's land and all the archaeological sites have been a national park (admission US$11; open daily). The park is administered by Conaf which charges admission at Orongo, valid for the length of your stay. The park has been a World Heritage Site since 1995. Although the government, in cooperation with foreign and Chilean archaeologists and locals, has done a remarkable job in restoring monuments, some islanders view the park as just another land grab on the part of colonialist invaders.

NEAR HANGA ROA

Sites of interest around town can be seen in a few hours by car or motorbike. By bicycle, the circuit would take a full day. Walking, you could get around everything in a long day, except the Puna Pau *pukao* quarry.

Ahu Tahai

A short hike north of town, this site contains three restored *ahu* and is a favourite sunset spot. Ahu Tahai proper is in the middle, with a solitary *moai*. Ahu Ko Te Riku is to the north, with a topknotted and eyeballed *moai*. Ahu Vai Uri has five eroded *moai* of varying sizes.

Ahu Akapu

A solitary *moai* stands here, on the coast just north of Ahu Tahai. It's another great sunset spot.

Ahu Tepeu

Four kilometres on a rough road north of Tahai, this large *ahu* has several fallen *moai* and a village site with foundations of *hare paenga* (elliptical houses) and the walls of several round houses.

Ana Te Pahu

Off the dirt road between Akivi and the west coast, Ana Te Pahu is a former cave dwelling with an overgrown garden of sweet potatoes, taro and bananas. The caves here are lava tubes, created when rock solidified around a flowing stream of molten lava.

Ahu Akivi

Unusual for its inland location, this *ahu* has seven restored *moai*. They are the only ones that face towards the sea, but like all *moai*, overlook the site of a village, traces of which can still be seen.

Puna Pau

The soft, red, stone of this volcanic hill was used to make the reddish, cylindrical *pukao* that were placed on many *moai*. Half-finished *pukao* have been rolled down the hill, and remain in a scattered line. Look for the partly hollow underside designed to slot onto a *moai* head. Puna Pau is only a couple of kilometres east of town, but it's only accessible via a rough and very roundabout road.

THE NORTHEAST CIRCUIT

This loop takes in the three finest sites on the island and can be done in a long day with motorised transport. It's good to go anticlockwise, because Rano Raraku is a magnificent highlight in the late afternoon. Heading northeast from the airport, a paved road runs 13km to the north coast.

Anakena

The legendary landing place of Hotu Matua, Anakena has several caves and is popular for swimming and sunbathing. The curving, white-sand beach is a perfect backdrop for **Ahu Nau Nau**, with its fine row of *moai*. A 1979 excavation and restoration revealed that the *moai* were not 'blind' but had inlaid coral and rock eyes – 'eyes that look to the sky', in a Rapa Nui phrase.

On a rise south of the beach stands **Ahu Ature Huki** and its lone *moai*. Heyerdahl and a dozen islanders took nine days to lever up this statue with wooden poles and ropes.

Conaf operates a free, barebones **camping ground** across the street from Anakena. Although a water tank provides drinking water, it has been known to run out; it's best to bring your own food and water.

Ahu Te Pito Kura

Here, beside Bahía de La Pérouse Bay, a massive 10m *moai* lies face down with its neck broken. It is the largest *moai* moved from Rano Raraku and erected on an *ahu*. Its resemblance to the incomplete figures at Rano Raraku suggests that it is also one of the most recent.

Poike Peninsula

The eastern corner is a peninsula formed by the extinct volcano Maunga Pukatikei. Legend says that the Long Ears retreated to Poike and built a 2km defensive trench that they filled with wood and set ablaze, though recent studies show no fire damage in the area.

Ahu Tongariki

In 1960, a tsunami demolished several *moai* and scattered *pukao* far inland from this, the largest *ahu* ever built. A Japanese project has restored the 15 imposing *moai* at this stunning oceanside location. The statues gaze over a large, level village site, with ruined remnants scattered about and some petroglyphs nearby.

Rano Raraku

This volcano, where *moai* were cut from the porous grey rock, is a wonderfully evocative place. Groups of *moai* are partly buried, their heads sticking out from the grassy slopes. Others are in the early stages of carving – the largest is a 21m giant, but most range from 5.5m to 7m. Most were carved face up, horizontal or slightly reclined. Over 600 of these figures stand and lie around Rano Raraku, and a number are scattered face-down in an irregular line to the southwest.

Be sure to walk up and around to the inside of the crater, which has a reedy lake and an amphitheatre of handsome heads. Climb right to the top for a fabulous 360° view.

Rano Raraku is a detour off the rugged south-coast road, about 18km from Hanga Roa. There are several ruined *ahu* along the way.

THE SOUTHWEST

The southwest corner of the island is dominated by the Rano Kau crater. On its seaward slopes, the low stone houses of **Orongo ceremonial village** were used during the rituals of the 'bird cult' in the 18th and 19th centuries.

The climax of the rituals was a competition to retrieve an egg of the sooty tern *(Sterna fuscata)*, which breeds on the small *motu* (islets) just offshore. Young men climbed down the steep cliffs and swam out to the islands to search for an egg. The egg was then tied to the forehead for the return swim and final climb. Whoever returned first with an intact egg won the favour of the god Makemake as well as great community status. Birdman petroglyphs are visible on a cluster of boulders between the cliff top and the crater's edge. Orongo is either a steepish 2km climb from town, or a short scenic drive.

Ahu Vinapu

Beyond the eastern end of the airport runway, a road heads south past some large oil tanks to Ahu Vinapu, with several toppled *moai*. Vinapu is most famous for its tight-fitting stonework, which some claim is similar to a style found at Inca sites on the South American mainland.

Fiji

Lapped by warm azure waters, fringed with vibrant coral reefs and cloaked in the emerald green of the tropics, Fiji is a paradise-seeker's dream come true. Amid its wealth of natural beauty, Fiji's true magic lies in its people and their fascinating blend of diverse cultures. Not surprisingly, it's one of the Pacific's most popular tourist destinations.

Fiji is also one of the most influential of the Pacific nations and home to both the South Pacific Forum and the University of the South Pacific. Despite not so distant political upheaval, Fiji's strong tourist infrastructure remains intact and has something to offer travellers on any budget. Take an adventure cruise, go hiking, rent a car or hop on a local bus, spend a day or spend two months. With over 300 islands in its archipelago, Fiji is yours to explore.

Facts about Fiji

HISTORY
Vitians
The word Fiji is actually the Tongan name for these islands – it was adopted and made prevalent by the Europeans. Before this, the inhabitants called their home Viti. Vitian culture was shaped by Polynesian, Melanesian and Micronesian peoples over 35 centuries of settlement. In about 1500 BC, the Lapita people arrived from Vanuatu and the eastern Solomon Islands. For about 1000 years, they lived along the coasts and fished to their hearts' (and stomachs') content. Around 500 BC, they became keen on agriculture, the population shot up, tribal feuding got nasty and cannibalism became common.

European Arrival
The archipelago's treacherous reefs and the Fijians' reputation as formidable warriors and ferocious cannibals deterred sailors from visiting the islands. During the 17th and 18th centuries the only Europeans to settle in Fiji were the odd deserting or shipwrecked sailor and an escaped convict or two. It wasn't until the early 19th century that European whalers, sandalwood and bêche-de-mer traders arrived. The introduction of firearms by the Europeans resulted in an increase in violent tribal warfare, with some chiefs selling their land and even villagers for

At a Glance

Capital City (& Island): Suva (Viti Levu)
Population: 840, 000
Time: 12 hours ahead of GMT
Land Area: 18,300 sq km (7140 sq miles)
Number of Islands: 300
International Telephone Code: ☎ 679
GDP/Capita: US$1260
Currency: Fijian dollar (F$1 = US$0.53)
Languages: English, Fijian & Hindi-Fijian
Greeting: *Bula* (Fijian) & *Kaise* (Hindi-Fijian)

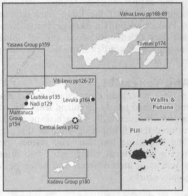

Highlights
- **Warm hospitality** – Fiji's multi-ethnic inhabitants are renowned for it
- **Snorkelling and diving** – Fiji's extraordinary coral reefs draw enthusiasts from around the world
- **Bouma National Heritage Park** – hike through this lush rainforest on the garden island of Taveuni
- **Yasawa and Mamanuca Islands** – a sun-seeker's tropical paradise
- **Suva Museum** – a window into the cannibalism and culture of Fiji's past
- **Namosi Highlands** – kayak and raft through the spectacular gorges
- **Navala** – picturesque highland village
- **Levuka** – the wild-west capital of the 19th century
- **Sigatoka Sand Dunes** – wander along this windswept coastline

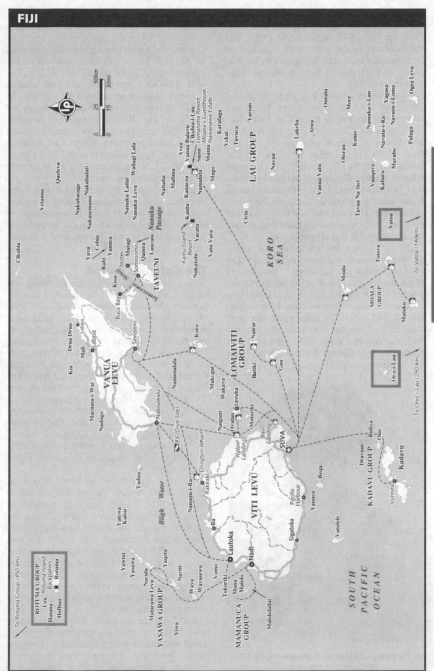

arms. War between the competing chiefs of the southeastern regions became the norm from the late 1840s to the early 1850s, and the eventual victor, Ratu Seru Cakobau of Bau, became known to foreigners as Tui Viti (King of Fiji), despite having no real claim over most of Fiji.

Missionaries entered Fiji from Tahiti and Tonga via the Lau group, where Tonga had become the controlling force. Cakobau reluctantly adopted Christianity on the threat of withdrawal of Tongan military support, and those under his influence followed. As Cakobau was not the king he claimed to be, some villages attempted to oppose his rule by rejecting Christianity. Nevertheless, missionaries and Fijian ministers gradually displaced the priests of the old religion and assumed their privileged positions. Their influence on traditional culture and everyday life was all-pervasive.

By the 1830s a small whaling and beachcomber settlement had been established at Levuka on Ovalau and this quickly became one of the main ports of call in the South Pacific. It was the centre of the notorious blackbirding trade which originally encouraged the emigration of, and eventually kidnapped, labourers from throughout the South Pacific (mainly the Solomons and Vanuatu) to work on Fijian plantations (see History in the Regional Facts for the Visitor chapter).

Portrait of a Fijian man (engraving by JD McDonald, 19th century)

In the 1860s Cakobau's responsibilities as 'King of Fiji' became more than he'd bargained for. When the home of the American Commercial Agent was accidentally destroyed by fire and locals helped themselves to his possessions, 'King' Cakobau was held responsible. This set a precedent and claims against Cakobau rose to an inflated US$45,000. In 1862 Cakobau proposed that, in exchange for cession of Fiji, Britain foot the bill to cover his debts. Rumours and spe culation caused a large influx of British settlers who bickered between themselves and disputed with Fijians over land. Levuka became a lawless, greedy outpost bordering on anarchy.

In 1871 Cakobau formed a Fiji-wide government but, unable to maintain peace, it quickly crumbled. Two years later, Britain agreed to annex Fiji, citing blackbirding as its principal justification. Fiji was pronounced a British crown colony on 10 October 1874.

The Colonial Period

With a slump in the cotton market at the end of the US Civil War, Fiji's economy was depressed. Unrest and epidemics followed, with measles wiping out a third of the indigenous population. Europeans were still greatly outnumbered by Fijians and the recent Maori–Pakeha wars in New Zealand prompted fears of racial war. Like the missionaries before it, the colonial government sought the support of the chiefs through which to control the masses. The existing Fijian hierarchy was incorporated into the colonial administration, reinforcing the chiefs' traditional influence. To curb quibbling and keep the chiefs happy, the sale of land to foreigners was forbidden. Today 83% of the land is still owned by indigenous Fijian communities.

Levuka's geography hindered expansion, so the administrative capital was moved to Suva in 1882. Under increasing pressure to make the Fijian economy self-sufficient, the colonial government turned to sugar plantations, which demanded large pools of cheap labour. Since blackbirding was under control, slavery was abolished and the employment of Fijians as plantation labourers was prohibited, an indentured-labour system was established using Indian workers. A total of 60,537 Indians were transported to Fiji from 1879 to 1916, under five-year contracts. While many came with hopes of escaping poverty, they were faced with heavy work allocations, low wages, unjust treatment, rationed food and overcrowded accommodation. Crime, suicide and disease were rife. People from all Indian backgrounds were crowded together, breaking down many cultural barriers and establishing the basis for today's Indo-Fijian society. At the end of their contracts, with few prospects in India, the vast majority of the labourers decided to stay in Fiji. They were prohibited from buying land and discouraged from interacting with Fijians. Instead, Indians moved into small business, trade and bureaucracy, or took out long-term leases as independent farmers.

By the mid-1930s, Australian dominance in the Fijian economy had extended from sugar to gold mining. Europeans maintained a monopoly on freehold land and power in the civil service and labour laws remained unfair. Movements for change fragmented along racial lines.

Independence
On 10 October 1970, Fiji regained its independence after 96 years of colonial administration. The new constitution followed the British model, however political seats and parties were racially divided.

In the first few years after independence, Fijians were optimistic about their future. But as the economy worsened, underlying racial tensions grew. The majority of Indo-Fijians and indigenous Fijians belonged to the poorer working classes and competition in business, education and employment tended to be seen in purely racial terms. In 1975 the nationalist movement's leader called for the repatriation of the entire Indo-Fijian community, most of whom were fourth-generation Fijians. The 1977 elections saw indigenous Fijian votes divided, giving the Indo-Fijian National Federation Party (NFP) the lead. Its victory was short-lived, however, as the governor general called for a new election and the indigenous Alliance Party regained its majority.

Military Coups of the 1980s
Greater unity among the working classes led to a shifting of loyalties and the formation of the multi-ethnic Fiji Labour Party (FLP). In 1987 an FLP–NFP coalition defeated the Alliance Party but, despite having a Fijian prime minister and majority indigenous-Fijian cabinet, the new government was labelled 'Indian dominated'. Racial tensions rose. The extremist Taukei movement, supported by eastern chiefs and the indigenous Fijian elite, launched a destabilisation campaign, playing on indigenous Fijians' fears of Indo-Fijian domination and loss of land

rights. Demonstrations were held, Indo-Fijian businesses suffered violent attacks and petrol bombs were thrown into the government offices in Suva. On 14 May 1987, only a month after elections, Lieutenant Colonel Sitiveni Rabuka invaded parliament with armed soldiers, arrested the new leader and his cabinet, and formed a civil interim government with himself as military member.

Talk of new elections led to more violent protests by Taukei extremists and, in September 1987, Rabuka again intervened with military force. The constitution of 1970 was turfed and Fiji declared a republic. Rabuka proclaimed himself head of state and appointed leaders of the Taukei movement and army officers as ministers. Arrests of community leaders and academics followed, a curfew was imposed in urban centres, newspapers were closed and all political activities were restricted. Fiji was dismissed from the Commonwealth.

Post-Coup Politics & Constitutional Changes
The economic consequences of the coups were drastic. Fiji experienced negative growth in gross domestic product, a devalued dollar, inflation and wage cuts. The economy's two main sources of income, sugar and tourism, were seriously affected and aid from overseas was suspended. The coups benefited only a minority of indigenous Fijians and tensions within the Fijian community itself were exposed. Large numbers of people, especially Indo-Fijians, emigrated.

The new 1990 constitution increased the political power of the Great Council of Chiefs and the army and reserved the position of prime minister and a majority of seats in the house of representatives for indigenous Fijians. Those involved in the coups were given immunity from legal prosecution and compulsory Sunday observance imposed Christian religious values on the whole population. Indo-Fijian political leaders denounced the new constitution as racist and undemocratic, claiming it condemned Indo-Fijians to perpetual minority status.

Before the 1992 general election, Rabuka exchanged his military career for leader of the Soqosoqo-ni-Vakavulewa-ni Taukei Party (SVT). The SVT won through false campaign promises and by seeking coalition partners in Indo-Fijian members.

In 1995 the National Bank of Fiji was confirmed bankrupt. The following year, a

Constitutional Review Commission (CRC) called for a return to a multi-ethnic democracy. A new constitution was declared in 1997 with the position of president reserved for an indigenous Fijian, but no provision of ethnicity for the prime minister.

History Replayed

In the May 1999 elections, Fijian voters rejected Rabuka and the SVT. The FLP won the majority of seats and formed a coalition with the Fijian Association Party. Indo-Fijian Mahendra Chaudhry became prime minister, but indigenous Fijians were far from pleased. Convinced that their traditional land rights were at stake, protests increased and many refused to renew century-old leases to Indo-Fijian farmers.

On 19 May 2000, armed men (mostly defectors of the Fijian army's Counter Revolutionary Warfare unit) entered Parliament in Suva and took 30 hostages, including Prime Minister Chaudhry. Failed businessman George Speight quickly became the face of the coup, claiming to represent indigenous Fijians. He demanded the resignation of both Chaudhry and President Ratu Sir Kamisese Mara and that the 1997 multi-ethnic constitution be abandoned.

Minor looting and razing followed in Suva. While the atmosphere was not particularly violent, support for Speight's group was widespread and Indo-Fijians suffered such harassment that many fled. Both Chaudhry and Mara eventually stepped down and the head of Fiji's military, Commander Frank Bainimarama, announced martial law.

After long negotiations between Speight's rebels and Bainimarama's military, it was agreed that the rebels would approve a president who would appoint an interim government to rule until elections could be held under a new constitution. If Speight's group released the hostages and returned all weapons, they'd receive amnesty. After eight weeks, the hostages were freed, the 1997 constitution was revoked and Ratu Josefa Iloilo was named president. When Iloilo appointed Qarase as prime minister rather than the candidate favoured by the rebels, Speight rang the president and allegedly threatened his life. This was exactly what Bainimarama was waiting for – the army moved quickly, arresting a bamboozled Speight and over 300 sympathisers. Speight and his gang were formally charged with treason and their amnesty erased.

The coup drew international disapproval and travellers were given sever warnings to steer clear of Fiji. The economy, particularly the tourism sector, collapsed.

To Be Continued...

In November 2000 the High Court ruled that the May coup had no legal standing and, therefore, that Ratu Sir Kaimisese Mara was still president of Fiji and that the 1997 multi-ethnic constitution was still in place. In 2001 Fiji was taken to the polls in order to restore democracy.

The election was rife with bullying and vote-buying. Ousted prime minister Chaudhry ran, as did George Speight. Both won seats but Speight was unable to take his up due to his inconvenient incarceration. Qarase, heading his Fijian People's Party (SLD), won the election but proceeded to violate the constitution by including no Indo-Fijians in his Cabinet. In the meantime, Speight pleaded guilty to treason. He was given a death sentence, which, within a day, was quickly commuted to life imprisonment – likely out of fear of further protests and rioting.

As was the case in the 1980s, the coup benefited only those indigenous Fijians at the top. Today, trade sanctions, farm closures, the tourism slump and government cuts have cost about 20,000 jobs and led much of the population into poverty. Indo-Fijians, many of them professionally trained, continue to leave the country in droves. As the economy slowly struggles to its feet and tourists return to Fiji, racial issues continue to simmer behind the scenes with no resolution in sight.

GEOGRAPHY

The Fiji archipelago has about 300 islands, varying from those a few metres in diameter to Viti Levu (Great Land), at 10,390 sq km. Only about one-third are inhabited. The smaller islands are generally of coral or limestone formation, while the larger ones are of volcanic origin; hot springs continue to boil on Vanua Levu. Fiji's highest peak is Viti Levu's majestic Mt Tomanivi (Mt Victoria) at 1323m.

Suva, the country's capital, largest city and main port, is on the eastern side of Viti Levu. The main international airport is in the western town of Nadi, near Lautoka, Fiji's second largest city and port. Nadi and Suva are linked by the fully sealed Queens Rd (221km), along the island's southern perimeter, and by the mostly sealed Kings Rd (265km), around the northern side of the island.

Independence Day celebrations, Rotuma, Fiji

TOM COCKREM

Navala village, Nausori Highlands, Viti Levu, Fiji

ROBYN JONES

Indian sweet shop, Suva, Fiji

LIZ THOMPSON

DAVID WALL

Coral Coast, Viti Levu, Fiji

DAVID WALL

Korolevu, Viti Levu, Fiji

ROBYN JONES

Guard at Government Buildings, Suva, Fiji

CLIMATE

Fiji has a mild, tropical maritime climate throughout the year, with average temperatures of around 25°C. Hot summer days can reach 31°C and, during the coolest months (July and August), the temperature can drop to between 18°C and 20°C. Humidity is high, with averages ranging from 60% to 80% in Suva and 60% to 70% in Lautoka. The wet season is November to April and the dry season from May to October, but rainfall occurs throughout the year. November to April is also the cyclone season. Fiji has been hit by an average of 10 to 12 cyclones per decade, with two or three of these being very severe. In early 2003 Cyclone Ami hit northwestern Fiji, leaving Labasa under 1.2m of water and wiping out much of the sugarcane industry.

The larger islands have mountain ranges lying across the path of the prevailing easterly wind and the southeast trade winds, resulting in frequent cloud and greater rainfall on the eastern sides and clearer skies on the western side. Most of the resorts are concentrated on the sunny southwestern side of Viti Levu and in the Mamanuca and Yasawa groups. Smaller islands tend to have dry and sunny microclimates.

ECOLOGY & ENVIRONMENT

While the logging industry has grown in Fiji, many villages are turning to ecotourism as an alternative means of income. Waste management is a national problem and marine pollution near Suva is severe. Over-fishing and destructive fishing techniques are commonly employed and global warming has contributed to extensive coral bleaching. Conservation groups based in Suva include the South Pacific Action Committee for Human Ecology and Environment (Spachee), the World Wildlife Fund (WWF) and Greenpeace.

FLORA & FAUNA

Most of Fiji is absolutely lush with bright, fragrant flowers and giant, leafy plants and trees. Fiji has over 3000 identified plant species, with one-third of these endemic. Much of the native flora is used for food, medicine, implements and building materials. The national flower, the *tagimoucia* or *Medinilla waterhousei*, only grows at high altitudes on the island of Taveuni and Vanua Levu.

Fiji's fauna is at its most colourful and diverse underwater where fish, mammals and coral abound. Above ground, bats are Fiji's only native mammals. You'll likely spot Fiji's most common wild animals, the Indian mongoose and the cane toad, both introduced to control pests in the sugar-cane plantations. The ancestors of Fiji's crested iguana are thought to have floated to Fiji on vegetation from South America.

Fiji has at least 25 species of endemic birds. Despite the relatively short distance between islands, some birds, such as the Kadavu Shining Parrot or the Taveuni Orange Dove, are found on one island only. Fiji has around 100 bird species, a number of which are extremely rare and heading towards extinction. These include the Fiji Petrel, the Long Legged Warbler, the Red Throated Lorikeet and Pink Billed Parrot Finch. Birds you're more likely to spot are the Silktail, Barking Pigeon, Whistling Dove, Giant Forest Honeyeater and the Wandering Whistling Duck. *Birds of the Fiji Bush*, by Fergus Clunie, is a good reference for bird-watchers. Also worth checking out is W www.pacificbirds.com. Taveuni, eastern Vanua Levu, Kadavu, and Colo-i-Suva Park are all good areas for bird-watching.

GOVERNMENT & POLITICS

The Republic of Fiji is presently governed by the Fijian People's Party (SLD), led by Laisenia Qarase. His largest opposition, the Fiji Labour Party, is led by Indo-Fijian Chaudhry and has been granted no seats in the Government's Cabinet, which is against the constitution. For more details, see the History section earlier.

Local government includes city, town and municipal councils. Chiefs make decisions at a local level and are extremely influential at a national level through the Great Council of Chiefs.

ECONOMY

Sugar has been the mainstay of the economy for most of the 20th century. Both it and tourism, Fiji's other main earner, were extremely hard hit by the May 2000 coup. A high proportion of Fiji's tourism revenue is diverted overseas to foreign investors. Fiji also exports molasses, gold, timber, fish, copra and coconut oil, clothing, forest wood chips, timber, leather products and furniture. Many villagers live a semisubsistence lifestyle. Fiji has long been reliant on aid from Australia and New Zealand.

POPULATION & PEOPLE

Fiji has a total population of 840,000 according to the UN's estimate for 2002 (Fiji last took a census in 1996). About 39% are urban dwellers and 75% live on Viti Levu, followed by 18% on Vanua Levu.

The population is the most multiracial in the South Pacific. Indigenous Fijians are predominantly of Melanesian origin, but there are Polynesian aspects in both their physical appearance and their culture. Most Indo-Fijians are descendants of indentured labourers; from the late 1940s until the military coups of 1987, Indo-Fijians accounted for over half of the national population. Following the coups of the past three decades, large numbers have emigrated and today about 45% of the population is Indo-Fijian while 50% is indigenous.

The term 'Fijian' is reserved for indigenous Fijians only. There are about 4500 Fiji-born 'Europeans' and over 10,000 'part Europeans', many of them descendants of 19th-century traders or planters. Among the Pacific islanders in Fiji are Tongans, Samoans, Banabans (Micronesians) and Tuvaluans. The 8600 people of Rotuma are of Polynesian origin and there are more than 8000 descendants of blackbirder labourers from the Solomon Islands. Officially, 0.7% of the population (5000 people) are of Chinese origin. However, over the past decade many Chinese have migrated to Fiji, often illegally. Some estimates place the Chinese population in Suva alone at 20,000.

Education is not officially segregated but ends up so as schools are run by the major religions. The literacy rate is high at 87%.

ARTS

Indigenous Fijian villagers still practise traditional arts and crafts, such as woodcarving and pottery, dance and music, and making *masi* (bark cloth, also known as tapa). Some arts remain an integral part of the culture, while others are practised solely to satisfy tourist demand. Visitors are often welcomed with an indigenous *meke*, a dance performance enacting stories and legends. Indo-Fijians, Chinese-Fijians and other cultural groups also retain many of their traditional arts.

Contemporary art includes fashion design, pottery and, though not common, painting and photography. The most likely place to see contemporary work displayed is Suva.

SOCIETY
Traditional Culture

Indigenous Fijians Many features of Viti's rich culture were suppressed by missionaries in the mid- to late 19th century. However, throughout the colonial era the chiefly system and village structure survived, and many aspects of the communal way of life remain today. Most indigenous Fijians live in villages in *mataqali* (extended family groups) and acknowledge a hereditary chief who is usually male. Each *mataqali* is allocated land for farming and also has communal obligations. Based on interdependence, village life is supportive but also conservative; being different or too ambitious is seen to threaten the village's stability.

Concepts such as *kerekere* (obligatory sharing) and *sevusevu* (a gift presented in exchange for an obligatory favour) are still strong, especially in remote areas. The consumption of *yaqona*, or kava, is still an important social ritual and clans gather on special occasions for traditional *lovo* feasts and *meke*.

Village life is now only semisubsistent; cash is needed for school fees, community projects and imported goods. Many young people travel to the cities for education, employment or to escape the restrictions of village life. Competition for urban jobs is tough and the cities' social structures are less supportive than those in villages.

Indo-Fijians Most of this group are fourth- or fifth-generation descendants of indentured labourers. The changes these labourers were forced to undergo, such as adapting to communal living of Indians from diverse backgrounds, created a relatively unrestricted, enterprising society distinct from the Indian cultures they left behind. This is the basis for the Indo-Fijian culture of today.

Extended families often live in the same house and, in rural areas, it's common for girls to have arranged marriages at a young age. Many women wear traditional dress, although dress codes are more cosmopolitan in Suva.

Indo-Fijians tend to be involved in commerce, transportation and farming on leasehold land. Recently, there has been a movement to maintain and preserve cultural values, particularly through Indo-Fijian cultural centres.

RELIGION

Religion is extremely influential and important in all aspects of Fijian society. Only 0.4% of the population are nonreligious. Christian denominations command the largest following (53% of the population), followed by Hindus (38%), Muslims (8%), Sikhs (0.7%) and other religions (0.1%).

LANGUAGE

Most local people you'll meet can speak English and all signs and official forms are in English. Nevertheless, this language is not the mother-tongue of almost all local people – the majority of indigenous Fijians speak Fijian at home while Indo-Fijians speak Fijian-Hindi.

In this guide a macron over a vowel (eg, ā) indicates that it has a long sound; a tilde (eg, ĩ) indicates that the vowel is nasalised.

Fijian Basics

Hello.	Bula!
Hello. (reply)	Io, bula.
Hello. (reply; more respectful)	Ia, bula.
Good morning.	Yadra.
Goodbye. (if you don't expect to see them again)	Moce.
See you later.	Au sā liu mada.
Yes.	Io.
No.	Sega.
Thank you (very much)	Vinaka (vakalevu)

Fijian-Hindi Basics

Hello. ('How are you?')	kaise.
Fine. (response)	tik.
Farewell.	fir milegā.
Yes.	hā.
No.	nahĩ.

There are no equivalents for 'please' and 'thank you' in Fijian-Hindi. To be polite in making requests, people use the word *thorā* ('a little') and a special form of the verb ending in *nā*, eg, 'Please pass the salt' (*thorā nimak denā*).

Facts for the Visitor

SUGGESTED ITINERARIES
One Week

For a beach holiday, visit the Yasawas or Mamanucas for a few days. Finish the week by visiting the picturesque village of Navala in the Nausori Highlands.

For those wanting to get off the well-trodden tourist track, hop on a flight for historic Levuka in the Lomaiviti Group. Spend a few days there, then relax for a day or two on the offshore island of Caqelai. En route back to Nadi, stop off in Suva to visit the museum.

A good way to pack a lot into a few days is to join an adventure cruise from Savusavu or Nadi.

Two Weeks

Do Yasawas/Mamanucas, the Highlands and the Lomaiviti Group, or spend the second week either exploring Viti Levu more thoroughly or visiting Taveuni.

One Month & Over

Combine some of the above, trying out the ferries as well as flights. Explore Vanua Levu by 4WD or visit the Kadavu Group.

PLANNING

The best time to visit is during the dry season, from May to October. Pack lightweight clothes, good walking sandals and perhaps walking boots.

A Brush with Culture

Before the practice was stamped out by the missionaries, Fijians decked themselves out in face and body paint on a daily basis. They worked from a palette of yellow from ginger root or turmeric; black from burnt candlenut, charcoal or fungus spores; and blue and vermilion introduced by the traders. A typical day saw Fijians made up in stripes, zigzags and spots. Ceremonies and war called for more specialised designs. Men mostly used red and black, associated with war and death, while women favoured yellow, saffron, pink and red, with fine black circles drawn around their eyes for beauty. Pregnant women were considered sexually *tabu* (taboo) and painted with turmeric; males found smudged with the yellow paint were ridiculed.

These days, there's not a stripe or a zigzag to be found among indigenous Fijians. However, in Indo-Fijian society, body painting still remains an important and commonly practiced art. A tradition brought from India, intricate *mehndi* (or henna) designs are most commonly painted on women's hands and feet for marriage ceremonies. Hidden in the design will often be the initials of the groom. If the husband can find them, he will be the dominant partner; if he fails, his wife will rule the roost. The henna lasts anywhere from a few days to three weeks; as long as it does, the new bride is exempt from all housework.

As in much of the world, henna tattoos are becoming trendy and you may spot young Indo-Fijian women painting them onto customers in Fijian markets.

If you are going directly to a remote budget place, it's best to bring your personal needs from home.

TOURIST OFFICES

The South Pacific Tourism Organisation has an office in Suva (see Information in the Suva section).

The **Fiji Visitors Bureau** (FVB; ☎ 0800 721 721) is the primary source of tourist information in Fiji, with a 24-hour, toll-free helpline for complaints or emergencies – ring from anywhere in Fiji. Local offices include:

Nadi (☎ 672 2433, fax 672 0141) Airport Concourse, Nadi International Airport
Suva (☎ 330 2433, fax 330 0970, W www.bula fiji.com) Thomas St

The FVB also has overseas offices and representatives:

Australia (☎ toll-free 1800 251 715, fax 612 9264 3060, W www.bulafiji-au.com) Level 12, St Martins Tower, 31 Market St, Sydney 2000
Canada (☎ toll-free 1800 932 3454, fax (604) 670 2318) 1275 West 6th Ave, Vancouver, BC V6H 1A6
France (☎ 47 670 0967, fax 670 0918) 13 rue d'Alembert, Grenoble F-38000
Germany (☎ 304 225 6026, W www.bulafiji.de) Petersburger Strasse 94, 10247 Berlin
Japan (☎ 03 3587 2038, fax 3587 2563, W www.bulafiji-jp.com) 14th floor, NOA Building, 3-5, 2 Chome Azabudai, Minato-Ku, Tokyo 106
New Zealand (☎ 09 373 2133, fax 309 4720, W www.bulafiji.co.nz) 5th floor, 48 High St, Auckland, PO Box 1179
UK (☎ 0208 741 6144, fax 0208 741 6107, e allisterbruce@aol.com) 48 Glentham Rd, Barnes London SW13 39J
USA (☎ toll-free 1800 932 3454, fax 310 670 2318) 5777 West Century Blvd, Suite 220, Los Angeles, CA 90045

VISAS

A free four-month tourist visa is granted on arrival to citizens of more than 100 countries, including most countries belonging to the Commonwealth, North America, Western Europe, India, Israel, and Japan. Check W www.bulafiji.com/about/visitor/visitor.shtml for the full list. You'll need to have an onward ticket and a passport valid for at least three months longer than your intended stay. Nationalities from countries excluded from the custom's list will have to apply for visas through a Fijian embassy prior to arrival.

Tourist visas can normally be extended for an extra two months provided you have an onward ticket, proof of sufficient funds and a passport valid for three months after your proposed departure. Apply at the Immigration Department at **Nadi International Airport** (☎ 772 2263); **Nausori International Airport** (☎ 347 8785); **Lautoka** (☎ 666 1706; Namoli Ave); or **Suva** (☎ 331 2672; Gohil Building, Toorak). Those wishing to work need to apply to a Fijian high commission prior to arrival.

EMBASSIES & CONSULATES
Fijian Embassies Abroad

Fiji has diplomatic representation in the following countries:

Australia (☎ 06-260 5115, fax 260 5105, e fhc@cyberone.com.au) 19 Beale Crescent, Canberra, ACT 2600
Belgium (☎ 02-736 9050, fax 736 1458, e info@fijiembassy.be) 92-94 Square Plasky, 1030 Brusseles
Japan (☎ 03-3587 2038, fax 3587 2563) 14th floor, Noa Bldg, 3-5, 2 Chome Azabudai, Minato-Ku, Tokyo 106
Malaysia (☎ 03-2732 3335, fax 2732 7555) Level 2, Menara Chan, 138 Jalan Ampang, 50450, Kuala Lumpur
New Zealand (☎ 04-473 5401, fax 499 1011) 31 Pipitea St, Thorndon, Wellington; PO Box 3940
Papua New Guinea (☎ 211 914, fax 217 220) 4th floor, Defense House, Champion Parade, Port Moresby, NCD; PO Box 6117
UK (☎ 020-7584 3661, fax 7584 2838, e fijirepuk@compuserve.com) 34 Hyde Park Gate, London SW7 5BN
USA (☎ 202-337 8320, fax 337 1996, e fijiemb@earthlink.net) 2233 Wisconsin Ave, NW, Suite 240, Washington, DC 20007

Embassies in Fiji

The following countries have diplomatic representation in Fiji:

Australia (☎ 338 2211, fax 338 2065, e austembassy@connect.com.fj) 37 Princes Rd, Tamavua, Suva
European Union (☎ 331 3633, fax 330 1084, e eudelfiji@eu.org.fj) 4th Floor, Fiji Development Bank Centre, Victoria Pde, Suva
Federated States of Micronesia (☎ 330 4566, fax 330 0842) 37 Loftus St, Suva
France (☎ 331 2233, fax 330 1894, e presse@ambafrance.org.fj) 1st floor, Dominion House, Thomson St, Suva
India (☎ 330 1125, fax 330 1032, e hicomind suva@connect.com.fj) Suite 270, Suva Central, PO Box 471, Suva

Japan (☎ 330 2122, fax 330 1452) 2nd floor, Dominion House, Thomson St, Suva
Malaysia (☎ 3312166, fax 330 3350) 5th floor, Air Pacific House, Butt St, Suva
Marshall Islands (☎ 338 7899, fax 338 7115) 41 Borron Rd, Samabula, Government Buildings, Suva
Nauru (☎ 331 3566, fax 330 2861) 7th floor, Ratu Sukuna House, Suva
New Zealand (☎ 331 1422, fax 330 0842, e nzhc@connect.com.fj) 10th floor, Reserve Bank Building, Pratt St, Suva
Tuvalu (☎ 330 1355, fax 330 1023) 16 Gorrie St, Suva
UK (☎ 331 1033, fax 330 1046, e ukinfo@bhc.org.fj) Victoria House, 47 Gladstone Rd, Suva
USA (☎ 314 466, fax 300 081, e usembsuva@connect.com.fj) 31 Loftus St, Suva

MONEY

Bank business hours are from 9.30am to 3pm Monday to Thursday (to 4pm on Friday). The ANZ at Nadi airport provides a 24-hour service. AmEx, Visa and Thomas Cook travellers cheques can be changed in most banks, exchange houses and larger hotels. Major credit cards are also readily accepted, although some resorts will charge you an additional 5%. ANZ banks in larger centres can often give cash advances on credit cards. Many budget places will accept cash only and remote islands often have limited (if any) banking facilities – check before heading out. The ANZ and Westpac have automatic teller machines (ATMs) in Suva, Nadi, Lautoka, Labasa and Savusavu.

Currency

The local currency is the Fiji dollar (F$), which is fairly stable relative to the Australian and NZ dollars. All prices quoted herein are in F$ and inclusive of VAT (or value added tax – a 12.5% sales tax on goods and services).

Exchange Rates

To check current exchange rates visit w www.oanda.com. At the time of writing exchange rates were as follows:

country	unit		conversion
Australia	A$1	=	F$1.25
Canada	C$1	=	F$1.40
euro zone	€1	=	F$2.22
India	R100	=	F$4.00
Japan	¥100	=	F$1.59
Malaysia	MYR1	=	F$0.49
New Zealand	NZ$1	=	F$1.09
UK	UK£1	=	F$3.14
USA	US$1	=	F$1.87

Costs

Travelling independently in Fiji is good value compared to many Pacific countries; if you're careful, you can get by on a pretty tight budget. Local restaurants, transport and shops can be extremely good value for money, particularly in more remote areas, but anything geared for tourists is far more pricey. On average, budget travellers can expect to pay about F$50 to F$75 per day for food, transport and clean accommodation. If you stay only in dorms and dine on corned beef, you can do it for cheaper. On a mid-range budget you can expect to spend around F$150 to F$200 per day on meals and accommodation. If you're looking to stay in top-end resorts, you can do it for around F$300 per day. If you're able to spend any more than that you can expect pure luxury.

Island hopping is generally fairly pricey; if you're planning to move around a lot, your expenses will go up so it's good to plan your route to avoid backtracking.

While tipping is not expected in Fiji, many resorts have a 'Staff Christmas Fund' jar for tips. Indigenous Fijians generally don't like to bargain but bargaining customary in most Indo-Fijian stores. Many Indo-Fijian shop owners and taxi drivers consider it bad luck to lose their first customer of the day; you can expect an especially hard sales pitch early in the morning as well as some good deals.

POST & COMMUNICATIONS

Post offices are open from 8am to 4.30pm weekdays. Most have fax services. Public telephones require a phonecard, available from post offices, some pharmacies and newsagents. A growing number of cybercafés means you can access email and the Internet in most tourist destinations.

As the only mobile phone company in Fiji, **Vodaphone** (w www.vodafone.com.fj) is huge. It operates a GSM digital mobile service and has roaming agreements with Australia, New Zealand and UK companies.

The international telephone code for Fiji is ☎ 679, followed by the local number. There are no area codes. To use IDD (International Direct Dial) dial ☎ 00 plus the country code.

DIGITAL RESOURCES

Internet sites worth visiting include:

Fiji Government (w www.fiji.gov.fj) Contains press releases, news and immigration updates
Fiji Post (w www.fijipost.com) Fiji's daily newspaper online

Fiji Village (W www.fijivillage.com) Geared for overseas Fijians, this site is updated with daily news and has excellent links to local events, including music, movies and sport. The only catch is the US$35 subscription fee.

Fiji Visitors Bureau (W www.bulafiji.com) Offers information on accommodation, activities and getting around, with links and an email directory

Fijilive (W www.fijilive.com) Live updates on Fijian news

BOOKS

If you're planning on spending much time underwater, Lonely Planet's *Diving & Snorkeling Guide to Fiji* is indispensable, with detailed information on over 70 of Fiji's best dive sites. The *Fijian phrasebook* will help you chat with locals. If you are going to wander around Fiji for a while, want a deeper look into the culture or are keen to get off the beaten track, travel with a copy of Lonely Planet's *Fiji*.

Exodus of the I Taukei, Lako Yani ni Kawa I Taukei (2002), by Andrew Thornley, looks at the lasting impact of Methodism in Fiji in light of Fiji's contemporary political arena. *The Inheritance of Hope: John Hunt, Apostle of Fiji* (2000), also by Andrew Thornley, details the life of an English missionary in Fiji from 1839–1948.

Journals of Baron Anatole von Hugel, by Roth & Hooper, is an interesting account of the baron's experiences in Fiji between 1875 and 1877. *Five Years Among the Cannibals* (1851), by A Lady (aka Mary Davis Wallis), is the memoirs of the wife of a Yankee trading captain. *My Twenty-One Years in the Fiji Islands*, by Totaram Sanadhya, is a first-hand account of the indenture system.

For insight into more recent history, check out *Broken Waves – A History of the Fiji Islands in the Twentieth Century* (1992), by Brij V Lal. *Changing Their Minds: Tradition & Politics in Contemporary Fiji & Tonga* (1998) is an intriguing look at how traditions have been created, altered and interwoven into the political scene. *Confronting Fiji's Future* (2000), an academic work that went to print as Speight stormed the government, gives a mainly Indo-Fijian perspective of society over the past couple of decades. *Government by the Gun: the unfinished business of Fiji's 2000 Coup* (2001) looks at the development of indigenous Fijian society.

Myths and Legends of Fiji and Rotuma (1967) by Reed & Hames, has lots of short stories with characters like the powerful shark-god Dakuwaqa and the great snake-god Degei.

Traditional Handicrafts of Fiji (1997) by Tabualevu, Uluinaceva & Raimua, discusses and gives directions in weaving, pottery and *masi*. For a look at traditional indigenous Fijian healing practices, read *The Straight Path of the Spirit: Ancestral Wisdom and Healing Traditions in Fiji* (1999) by Richard Katz.

Children of the Sun (1996), with photos by Glen Craig and poetry by Bryan McDonald, is Fiji's most popular coffee-table book. *Fiji, the Uncharted Sea*, by Frederico Busonero, has great underwater photography.

Fiji – Beneath the Surface (2000), by Professor Patrick Nunn, is an interesting compilation of environmental articles which appeared as weekly columns in the *Fiji Times*.

There is a small but strong community of poets, playwrights and other contemporary writers in Fiji. Works by Joseph Veramu include a short-story collection, *The Black Messiah (1989)*, and the novel *Moving Through the Streets (1994)*, portraying urban teenagers in Suva. The Fiji Writers Association has published *Trapped: A Collection of Writings From Fiji*. *Beyond Ceremony: An Anthology of Drama from Fiji*, edited by Ian Gaskel, is a collection of work by Fiji's foremost contemporary playwrights.

NEWSPAPERS & MAGAZINES

Fijians 'read all about it' in the *Fiji Times*, founded in Levuka in 1869, and the *Daily Post*. Australian newspapers (although not hot off the press) are available at some newsagents in Suva.

RADIO & TV

Radio stations on Fiji include the government-sponsored Radio Fiji 3 and FM 104, the commercial station FM 96 and Radio Pacific FM 88.8, run by the Student's Association of the University of the South Pacific. Fiji has one television station, first aired in 1993, and Sky satellite TV in some resorts and bars.

TIME

Fiji is 12 hours ahead of GMT, with the International Dateline doglegging east around the islands. Daylight saving was introduced in 1998.

HEALTH

While Fiji is malaria-free, there can be occasional outbreaks of dengue fever, a mosquito-transmitted disease; precautions should always be taken. When snorkelling or diving, take great care not to touch anything – some of the most beautiful sealife is also the most poisonous.

Health facilities aren't fantastic in Fiji; many are suffering staff shortages as trained Indo-Fijians hightail it out of the country. Suva and Lautoka have the best facilities; in smaller towns they can bandage you up and dole out antibiotics. If you're really ill, hop a flight for New Zealand or Australia.

It's usually safe to drink water at resorts but always ask first. Bottled water is readily available in towns but not in villages. See the Health section in the Regional Facts for the Visitor chapter for further information.

SOCIAL GRACES

Thanks to the missionaries, modest dress is the rule. Women shouldn't swim or sunbathe naked or topless, unless at exclusive resorts. When in a village don't wear hats, caps or sunglasses, and don't carry cameras or bags over your shoulder. Shoulders should be covered and women should wear knee-length *sulu* (skirts). Never touch an indigenous Fijian's head or hair – it's considered *tabu* (sacred).

Village Visits & Kava Ceremonies

Try not to show up to a village uninvited, or, if you do, ask the first person you meet to introduce you to the chief. Always take a *sevusevu* of about 500g (F$15 to F$20) of pounded kava or a bundle of roots. Almost all land is owned by villages, including beaches; always seek permission before wandering through the wilderness or lounging on the sand.

The chief will usually welcome you with a small kava ceremony (see the boxed text 'Kava' in the Regional Facts for the Visitor chapter).

DANGERS & ANNOYANCES

Fiji is a safe and friendly place to travel. However, crime increased significantly after the coup of 2000 and the economic slump. In Nadi and Suva, avoid walking around at night, even in a group, as muggings are common. Don't hitchhike – locals do it, but as a foreigner, you're a sitting duck for muggers.

As you exit customs at Nadi Airport, you'll likely be swarmed by hoteliers and representatives from local travel agents. We receive lots of letters from travellers who feel the tours and package deals they bought on arrival were rip-offs. Talk to other travellers about the current scene and keep your options open by not paying too much money up front.

Sword sellers have all but disappeared, with the FVB actively curtailing their 'business'. If anyone becomes overly friendly, wants to know your life story and begins carving your name on a long piece of wood, just walk away.

BUSINESS HOURS

Most businesses open weekdays from 8am to 5pm, and some from 8am to 1pm on Saturday. Government offices are open from 8am to 4.30pm weekdays (to 4pm on Friday). Many places close for lunch from 1pm to 2pm and practically nothing happens on Sunday.

PUBLIC HOLIDAYS & SPECIAL EVENTS

Fiji observes the standard Western holidays (New Year's Day, Easter and Christmas); see the Regional Facts for the Visitor chapter for dates. Other holidays in Fiji include:

National Youth Day Late March/early April
Prophet Mohammed's Birthday May
Ratu Sir Lala Sukuna Day First Monday in June
Queen's Birthday Mid-June
Constitution Day July
Birth of Lord Krishna August/September
Fiji Day (Independence Day) Early October
Diwali October/November

Fijian festivals include:

February/March
Hindu Holi (Festival of Colours) People squirt coloured water at each other, best seen in Lautoka.

March/April
Ram Naumi (Birth of Lord Rama) Hindu religious festival in Suva Bay. Worshippers wade into the water and throw flowers.

August
Hibiscus Festival Held in Suva, with lots of floats
Ritual Fire Walking Performed by Indo-Fijians in many Hindu temples (try the Maha Devi Temple, Howell Rd, Suva).

September
Sugar Festival Lautoka's streets come alive with parades and fun fairs.

October/November
Diwali Festival (Festival of Lights) Hindus worship Lakshmi, houses are decorated, business is settled, and candles and lanterns are set on doorsteps to light the way of the god. This is a great time to shop as there are lots of sales.
Ramlili (Play of Rama) Hindus celebrate through theatrical performances the life of god-king Rama and his return from exile.

FIJI

ACTIVITIES

Viti Levu and Taveuni are the best islands for hiking. Colo-i-Suva Forest Park on Viti Levu and the Lavena Coastal Walk and Tavoro Falls on Taveuni have marked trails that don't require guides or permission. Other good places for hiking are Mt Tomanivi on Viti Levu, and Koroyanitu National Heritage Park and Mt Koroyanitu near Lautoka.

Snorkelling is a definite highlight with great sites dotting most coasts. As many reefs are very close to the coast, it is a relatively inexpensive pastime but in many places you can only swim at high tide and channels can be dangerous.

Fiji is world famous as a diver's mecca with magnificent sites and dive resorts for every budget. See the 'South Pacific Diving' special section earlier in this book. Prices range from F$120 to F$180 for a two-tank dive and F$350 to F$600 for an open-water certification course. Most operators belong to the **Fiji Dive Operators Association** (FDOA; ☎ 885 0620, fax 885 0344; Ⓦ www.fijidive.com; Savusavu), which requires its members to abide by international diving standards. Some places have half-price dive specials from mid-January to the end of March.

Sea-kayaking tours are available during the drier months between May and November – refer to individual island sections for details.

Surfing usually requires boat trips as the majority of breaks are on offshore reefs. The best spots are in barrier-reef passages along southern Viti Levu (Frigate Passage) and in the southern Mamanucas (Malolo and Wilkes passages group). There are a few places along Queens Rd on Viti Levu's Coral Coast where you can paddle out to the surf, including the beach-break at the mouth of the Sigatoka River and in front of Hideaway Resort.

ACCOMMODATION

There is no shortage of accommodation options, ranging from dorm beds for F$12 to exclusive resorts charging up to F$2000 per night. Prices often vary (February and March are the low season) with 'walk-in' rates for a fraction of the advertised price. Mid-range amenities usually include a reasonably comfortable mattress, air-con, tea- and coffee-making facilities and a restaurant, bar and pool.

There are many budget and mid-range hotels on Viti Levu, especially in Nadi, Lautoka, Suva and along the Coral Coast. Some of the budget places allow camping, otherwise you'll need the permission of village landowners.

The term 'resort' is used very loosely in Fiji and can refer to any accommodation near the sea, ranging from backpacker-style to farmyards to luxury. Budget places usually offer *bure* (thatched dwellings) and rudimentary facilities. For those happy to spend a few hundred dollars per day for extra comfort, services and activities, there are countless options. Mainland resorts have more choices for tours, entertainment and dining, however offshore islands usually have better beaches. Many resorts offer pre-booked package deals.

FOOD

Fiji's food is a blend of Fijian, Polynesian, Indian, Chinese and Western styles. Traditional indigenous foods include *tavioka* (cassava), *dalo* (taro), seafood in *lolo* (coconut cream) and *kokoda* (raw fish marinated in coconut cream and lime juice). Every large town has supermarkets and a fruit-and-veggie market. Village shops have little more than corned beef as villagers grow their own produce.

Suva, Nadi and Lautoka all have a variety of restaurants ranging from cheap cafés to fine dining. It can be difficult to find indigenous Fijian food in restaurants, however resorts often have *lovo* nights. Indo-Fijian and Chinese-Fijian restaurants are much easier to come by. Most restaurants have some vegetarian options and you'll find strictly vegetarian Indo-Fijian restaurants in Suva and Lautoka.

DRINKS

Mineral water and long-life milk are readily available. Fresh fruit juices are great, though 'juice' on a menu often means super-sweet cordial. Fiji Bitter and Fiji Gold are locally brewed beers. Kava (or *yaqona*) is the national drink, and is an integral part of Fijian life. It is mildly narcotic and looks like muddy water – you won't escape trying it!

ENTERTAINMENT

Nadi has little nightlife, although the larger mainland resorts have discos, live bands, *meke*, *lovo* nights and fire-walking performances. Beachcomber Island Resort in the Mamanucas has a reputation as a party island for young backpackers. Suva, with its cosmopolitan and student population, is the nightlife capital (while it does have a few great bars and clubs, don't expect Rio).

In small towns and remote areas, the popular pastime is drinking kava. These sessions are often accompanied by singing and storytelling till the wee hours. You'll likely be invited to join in – this is a great way to meet locals. Every major town has at least one cinema; Suva and Lautoka have comfortable Village cinema complexes with recent, mainstream Western releases, Indian Bollywood films and great popcorn. Rugby is huge in Fiji and even the smallest village has a playing field.

Little happens on Sunday, so it's a good idea to organise activities in advance or attend a Fijian church service to hear some singing.

SHOPPING
Nadi, the Coral Coast and Suva have many souvenir shops. Savusavu is also a good place to pick up handicrafts and contemporary pieces and Kioa is known for its woven goods. Popular mementos include *bula* ('welcome') shirts in colourful prints; Indian saris and jewellery; traditional wood carvings such as w ar clubs, cannibal forks and *yaqona* bowls; *tapa* cloth; woven mats and baskets; and pottery and sandalwood or coconut soap.

Getting There & Away

AIR
Most international flights to Fiji arrive at Nadi International Airport, with a few flights landing at Nausori airport near Suva.

As you enter the arrivals area in Nadi, you will be greeted by guitar serenading and a sea of smiling faces, mostly representatives of local accommodation and the many travel agencies. It's worth ducking into the FVB office (see Tourist Offices earlier) to escape the crowd and get an update on available accommodation and activities. The arrivals area also has a board displaying the names and rates of hotels in the Nadi area that are members of the Fiji Hotels Association.

The Nadi airport has a 24-hour ANZ bank and currency exchange, many travel agencies, airline offices, car rentals, a post office, restaurants, duty-free shops and luggage storage. There are frequent local buses into Nadi (9km), departing from just outside the Queens Rd entrance.

From Nausori International Airport, 23km northeast of Suva, Air Fiji has flights to Tuvalu and Tonga, Royal Tongan Airlines has flights to Tonga, and Air Pacific has a direct route from Sydney. Otherwise the airport is mostly used for domestic purposes. The small premises have an ANZ bank.

Fiji is a popular stopover between North America and Australia or New Zealand, and for travellers on round-the-world tickets. Air Pacific, Qantas and Air New Zealand fly the Australia/Fiji route, and Air Pacific and Air New Zealand service Fiji/New Zealand. Air Pacific, Air Canada and Air New Zealand fly Fiji/Vancouver via Honolulu and Air New Zealand flies Fiji/LA and Santiago. Both Air Pacific and Air New Zealand fly to/from Japan; Air Pacific also has flights to Thailand and South Korea. Most flights to Southeast Asia go via Australia or New Zealand.

Return fares to Nadi from Canada are around C\$1860/2200 for low/high season; return fares from Sydney or Brisbane are typically around A\$750/990 for low/high season (add A\$50 to fares starting from Melbourne); and from Auckland expect to pay about NZ\$950/1140.

Many airlines provide connections between Fiji and other Pacific countries, including Air Nauru, Aircalin, Nadi–Papeete (Tahiti); Solomon Airlines and Royal Tongan Airlines. Air Pacific flies Nadi–Honiara, Nadi–Apia (Western Samoa), Nadi–Port Vila (Vanuatu), and Nadi–Fua'amotu. Air Fiji flies Suva–Funafuti (Tuvalu) and Suva–Tonga.

Fiji is included in a large number of air passes. See the introductory Getting There & Away chapter for more information.

The following international airlines have representatives in Fiji:

Air Fiji (Nadi ☎ 672 2521, Suva ☎ 331 3666, [W] www.airfiji.net) General sales agents for Air India
Air Nauru (Nadi ☎ 672 2795, Suva ☎ 331 3731 [W] www.pacificislands.com/airlines/Nauru.htm)
Air New Zealand (Nadi ☎ 672 0070, Suva ☎ 330 1671, [W] www.airnz.co.nz)
Air Pacific (Nadi ☎ 672 0888, Suva ☎ 330 4388, [W] www.airpacific.com) General sales agents for Air Canada, British Airways, Cathay Pacific Airways and Malaysia Airlines
Air Vanuatu (Nadi ☎ 672 2521, Suva ☎ 330 0771, [W] www.airvanuatu.com)
Aircalin (Nadi ☎ 672 2145, [W] www.aircalin.nc) General sales agents for Air France
Polynesian Airlines (Nadi ☎ 672 2521, Suva ☎ 331 5055, [W] www.polynesianairlines.co.nz)
Qantas Airways (Nadi ☎ 672 2880, Suva ☎ 331 1833, [W] www.qantas.com.au)
Royal Tongan Airlines (Nadi ☎ 672 4355, Suva ☎ 330 9877, [W] www.royaltonganairlines.com)
Solomon Airlines (Nadi ☎ 672 2831, Suva ☎ 331 5889, [W] www.solomonairlines.com.au)

FIJI

Departure Tax

An international departure tax of F$20 applies to all visitors over 12 years old.

SEA

Travelling to Fiji by sea is difficult unless you're on a cruise ship or yacht. See the Cargo Ship section in the introductory Getting Around the Region chapter for other options.

Visiting yachts must first call at a designated port of entry – Suva, Lautoka, Savusavu or Levuka – to be cleared by customs, immigration and quarantine. Present a certificate of clearance from the previous port of call, a crew list and passports. Before visiting the outer islands, you must seek approval from the **Ministry of Foreign Affairs** (☎ 321 1458; 61 Carnarvon St, Suva) or from the commissioner's office in Lautoka, Savusavu or Levuka. Departing Fiji, you'll need to complete clearance formalities and provide inbound clearance papers, your vessel's details, your next port of call, and have paid all port dues and health fees. The useful *Yacht Help Booklet, Fiji* is available from FVB.

ORGANISED TOURS

While travelling independently is easy in Fiji, many visitors prearrange some type of package tour. It may be the ideal option if you have limited time, prefer an all-inclusive upfront price, wish to stay in a particular resort or want to pursue special interests like diving. Many travel agents can organise this package trips and can often get cheap deals.

With many package deals it's possible to extend your stay in Fiji on either side of your tour, giving you a chance to experience Fiji independently as well as time to relax and be pampered in a resort. This is a great option for those looking to add a bit of adventure to their beach holiday.

Getting Around

Travelling around and between Fiji's islands is easy. For those on a budget or looking to mix with the Fijians, catch a local bus, carrier (small truck with tarpaulin-covered frame) or ferry. For those short on time but not on cash, there are express buses, rental vehicles, and small, zippy planes.

AIR

Air Fiji and Sun Air both have regular flights by light plane. It can be a rocky ride but the views are spectacular. The prices on shared routes are almost identical and are extremely reasonable.

Air Fiji (W www.airfiji.net)
Labasa (☎ 881 1188, fax 881 3819)
Levuka (☎ 344 0139, fax 344 0252)
Matei (☎ 888 0062)
Nadi (☎ 672 2521, fax 672 0555)
Nausori Airport (☎ 347 8077, fax 340 0437)
Savusavu (☎ 885 0173)
Suva (☎ 331 3666, fax 330 0771)
Sun Air (W www.fiji.to)
Labasa (☎ 881 1454, fax 881 2989)
Matei (☎ 888 0461)
Nadi Airport (☎ 672 3016, fax 672 3611)
Nausori Airport (☎ 347 7310, fax 347 7377)
Savusavu (☎ 885 0141)
Suva (☎ 330 8979, fax 330 2089)

Charter services and joy flights are available with:

Island Hoppers (☎ 672 0410, fax 672 0172, W www.helicopters.com.fj) Helicopter rides including hotel transfers to Mamanuca islands resorts
Turtle Airways (☎ 672 1888, fax 672 0095, W www.turtleairways.com) Float-planes for sightseeing and resort transfers

Air Passes

Air Fiji has a 30-day Discover Fiji Pass for F$540 (US$270). It's only sold outside Fiji in conjunction with an international airfare. Set itineraries include Nadi–Taveuni–Suva–Kadavu–Nadi, Nadi–Taveuni–Suva–Levuka–Suva–Nadi, as well as Nadi–Savusavu–Suva–Kadavu–Nadi–Malololailai–Nadi. It's best to book your seats, as the small planes can fill up. Children under 12 pay half price and infants are charged 10%. There is a US$60 predeparture cancellation fee, and reimbursement is minimal once in Fiji. If you are a student, a 25% discount applies to regular airfares, which may be more economical than the air pass.

BUS

Catching a local bus on Fiji's larger islands is an inexpensive and fun way of getting around. While they can be noisy, the open, unglazed windows are perfect for the tropics and offer excellent views of the passing countryside. Everyone on board helps pull the large tarpaulins over the windows when it starts raining. There are bus stops but you can generally just hail buses, especially in rural areas. See specific destinations for details.

FIJI

CAR & MOTORCYCLE

Ninety percent of Fiji's 5100km of roads are on Viti Levu and Vanua Levu (about one-fifth are sealed). Both islands are fun to explore by car. Driving is on the left-hand side of the road with a speed limit of 80km/h on the open road and 50km/h in town areas. As a rule, local drivers are maniacs, so take care, especially on gravel or pot-holed roads. Avoid driving at night as there are many pedestrians and wandering animals. In cane-cutting season sugar-trains have right of way. A current driving licence from any English-speaking country is valid here.

Rental

Renting 4WD vehicles is most economical if you can split the cost with a group. Consider support service, insurance, VAT, exclusions and the excess/excess waiver amount (they vary greatly) and whether you can take the vehicle on unpaved roads. Service stations are virtually unheard of once you leave main centres, so fill up before you go.

Reliable car-rental agencies include:

Avis Rent-A-Car
  Nadi Airport (☎ 672 2688, fax 672 0482,
  e aviscarsfj@connect.com.fj)
  Nausori Airport (☎ 347 8963)
  Suva (☎ 331 3833)
Budget Rent-A-Car
  Labasa (☎ 881 1999)
  Nadi Airport (☎ 672 2735, fax 672 2053)
  Nausori Airport (☎ 347 9299)
  Somosomo (☎ 888 0291, fax 888 0275)
Hertz
  Nadi (☎ 672 3466, fax 672 3650)
  Suva (☎ 338 0981)
Thrifty Car Rental
  Nadi Airport (☎ 672 2755, fax 672 2607,
  e rosiefiji@connect.com.fj)
  Suva (☎ 331 4436)

BICYCLE

Fiji's larger islands have good potential for cycling, although some areas are extremely hilly and rugged and Fijian drivers can be rather unaware of cyclists. The best time to bike is in the 'drier' season and good spots include the Coral Coast on Viti Levu, the unsealed Hibiscus Highway on Vanua Levu, and Ovalau's coastal road. Bicycles can be hired on the Coral Coast, Nadi, Taveuni and Ovalau; always test the brakes and gears beforehand.

HITCHING

The cost of transport in Fiji is so reasonable, it's really not worth hitching. Locals do it,

paying the equivalent of the bus fare to the driver, but you're far safer catching the bus.

BOAT

With the exception of the upmarket resort islands, often the only means of transport to and between islands is by small local boats, especially for the backpacker resorts. Life jackets are rarely provided; if the weather looks ominous or the boat is overcrowded, seriously consider postponing the trip!

Inter-island trips for sightseeing, catamaran transfers and sailing cruises are available in the Mamanuca group, the Yasawa group and from Savusavu – see these sections for more details.

Ferry

Regular ferry services link Viti Levu to Vanua Levu and Taveuni, and also Viti Levu to Ovalau. See the Fiji map at the beginning of this book for ferry routes. The Patterson Brothers, Beachcomber Cruises and Consort Shipping boats carry passengers, vehicles and cargo, although most car-rental agencies won't let you take their car on board. Irregular boats also take passengers from Suva to Lau, Rotuma and Kadavu. Ferry timetables are notorious for changing frequently and there is often a long wait at stopovers. Toilets can become filthy, so take your own toilet paper.

Useful ferry services include:

Beachcomber Cruises
  Lautoka (☎ 666 1500, fax 666 4496)
  Savusavu (☎ 885 0266, fax 885 0499)
  Suva (☎ 330 7889, fax 330 7359) Taina's
  Travel Service, Suite 8, Epworth Arcade
  Taveuni (☎ 888 0216, fax 888 0202)
Consort Shipping
  Suva (☎ 330 2877, fax 330 3389) Ground
  floor Dominion House Arcade, Thomson St
Grace Ferry Services
  Savusavu (☎ 885 0622)
  Taveuni (☎ 888 0134)
Kadavu Shipping
  Suva (☎ 331 2428, fax 331 2987) Office No 1,
  Old Millers Wharf, Walu Bay
Patterson Brothers Shipping
  Labasa (☎ 881 2444, fax 881 3460)
  Lautoka (☎ 666 1173, fax 666 7269)
  Levuka (☎ 344 0125)
  Suva (☎ 331 5644, fax 330 1652) Suites 1 & 2,
  Epworth Arcade, Nina St

Nadi to Mamanucas South Sea Cruises has a catamaran shuttling daily between Denarau Marina and the Mamanuca Islands, with a second connection to Musket Cove Marina on Malololailai. See the Mamanuca Group section.

Nadi to Yasawas South Seas Cruises has daily services between the Viti Levu mainland and the Yasawas (Waya, Naviti and Tavewa). See the Yasawa Group section.

Nadi to Vanua Levu Beachcomber Cruises' catamaran, *Lagilagi*, operates twice-weekly (Tuesday and Saturday) between the Viti Levu mainland and Vanua Levu. It stops at Beachcomber Island (Mamanucas) and on request, Nananu-i-Ra (off Northern Viti Levu). One-way from Viti Levu and Vanua Levu costs F$90.

Suva to Taveuni On a twice-weekly basis, Consort Shipping's *SOFE* travels Suva–Koro–Savusavu–Taveuni return, departing Suva on Wednesday morning and Saturday evening. The trip takes about 11 hours to Savusavu (seat/bunk F$40/75), and another six hours to Taveuni (seat/bunk F$45/85). The Suva–Taveuni trip involves a 13-hour stopover in Savusavu.

Beachcomber Cruises' *Adi Savusavu* has better facilities and has Suva–Savusavu–Taveuni voyages three times weekly. It departs Suva for Savusavu (F$45/65 economy/first class, 11 hours) on Tuesday mornings, Thursday midday and Saturday evenings, from where it continues to Taveuni (F$22/45 economy/first class Savusavu–Taveuni, 5 hours; F$50/70 economy/first class Suva–Taveuni, 5 hours).

Grace Ferry Services has a Savusavu–Buca Bay–Taveuni bus/ferry service (F$15) involving 1½ hours by bus to Natuvu, Buca Bay, and 1¾ hours by ferry to Waiyevo (Taveuni). The buses depart Savusavu and Naqara on Monday, Wednesday and Friday mornings.

Lautoka to Labasa Patterson Brothers plies this route four times weekly (F$50) with a bus (3½ hours) from Lautoka, a ferry (3¾ hours) to Vanua Levu, and another bus to Labasa (4 hours).

Suva to Labasa Patterson Brothers claims to run the bus/ferry route, from Suva to Labasa via Natovi and Nabouwalu, daily (F$43, 10 hours), except Sunday and public holidays – although it's notoriously unreliable.

Suva to Levuka This Patterson Brothers bus/ferry service runs from Suva to Levuka via Natovi and Buresala, (F$24, 4½ hours), daily except Sunday, departs Suva from the

Western Bus Terminal, Rodwell Rd. It's known to be somewhat unpredictable.

Suva to Levuka Daily services except Sunday leave Suva at midday for Leluvia (F$30 one way) and Levuka (F$50 one way) via Bau Landing. Contact Leluvia Island Resort for bookings.

Yacht
Yachting is a great way to explore the Fiji archipelago (see Getting There & Away earlier for more information). It is also possible to charter boats (although by law you must also hire a Fijian guide).

LOCAL TRANSPORT
Taxi
Main towns have plenty of taxis. Only in Suva do they use their meters, so always confirm the price in advance.

ORGANISED TOURS
Fiji has many companies providing tours within the country, including hiking, cycling, kayaking, diving, bus and 4WD tours. Cruises to the outer islands such as the Mamanucas and Yasawas are popular. Viti Levu has the majority of tours, although there are excellent options on Ovalau, Taveuni and Vanua Levu.

Viti Levu

pop 581,000 • area 10,400 sq km
As the largest island in the archipelago, Viti Levu (Great Island) undoubtedly attracts the most visitors. The diverse landscape offers great hiking, surfing and river outings. Its mountainous interior is scattered with remote villages and culminates in Tomanivi (Mt Victoria, 1323m), Fiji's highest peak. Viti Levu is also home to the country's vibrant capital and is the gateway to the sunny Yasawa and Mamanuca islands. Around 75% of the country's population lives on Viti Levu.

Getting There & Away
Most travellers arrive in Fiji at Nadi International Airport. See Getting Around near the beginning of the chapter for fares and details of airline offices. Nadi is also Fiji's main domestic transport hub – from here there are flights to many of the other larger islands and reliable boat services. See Getting There & Away near the beginning of this chapter for more information.

Domestic Air Services Fiji is also well serviced by internal airlines, which have frequent and generally reliable flights. Most of Air Fiji's services operate out of Nausori, while Sun Air base and major hub is Nadi; prices are reasonable and on shared routes are almost identical.

Getting Around

Express buses, tourist buses, minibuses and carriers zip around the island via the Queens and Kings Rds. Before heading to an isolated area, check that there is a return bus so that you don't get stranded – sometimes the last bus of the day stays at the final village.

For social bugs, Feejee Experience has recently begun bussing budget travellers between Viti Levu's most popular resorts and sites. The four-day travel pass (F$269) is packed full of activities and allows you to stop and start as you like. Contact **Sun Vacations** (☎ 672 4273, fax 672 5829; W www .sunvacationsfiji.com; Nadi International Airport concourse) or Tourist Transport Fiji (see following) for more information.

Bus Routes The following bus companies run services in Viti Levu:

Fiji Holiday Connections (☎ 672 0977) Suite 8, arrival concourse, Nadi airport. Operates a Nadi–Suva minibus shuttle (about 3½ hours, express 2½) along Queens Rd, with stops at hotels along the Coral Coast. Departs Nadi in the early morning and Suva in the afternoon. Book a day in advance.

Pacific Transport Limited (Nadi ☎ 670 0044, Lautoka ☎ 666 0499, Sigatoka ☎ 650 0088, Suva ☎ 330 4366) Operates a regular Lautoka–Suva bus service (F$12, six/five hours regular/express, about six express buses daily) via the Coral Coast on Queens Rd. The first express bus leaves Lautoka at 6.30am and the last about 6pm.

Sunbeam Transport Limited (Lautoka ☎ 666 2822, Suva ☎ 338 2122) Operates Lautoka–Suva express buses via Queens Rd (F$12, five hours), via Kings Rd (F$11, about six hours).

Tourist Transport Fiji (toll-free 0800 672 0455, W www.newzealand.com/fiji/greatsights) Offers coach tours and is Feejee Experience's agent

United Touring Fiji (Nadi airport ☎ 672 2811, Suva ☎ 331 2287) Has a daily Nadi–Suva express air-con coach service (F$30, 4½ hours) along Queens Rd, with stops at Nadi airport and larger hotels. Departs Nadi about midday and Suva around 7.30am. Nadi International Airport to Korolevu costs F$20.

NADI & AROUND

pop 30,900

As the country's main tourism hub, it's hard to avoid Nadi (pronounced **nan**-di), although you wouldn't be blamed for trying. While uninspiring, it's a convenient base to organise trips around Viti Levu or to offshore islands. There's heaps of accommodation and countless organised day-trips that pick up from Nadi hotels.

Nadi is Fiji's third-largest city and home to a large population of Indo-Fijian farmers whose sugar-cane crops thrive in the area's hot and relatively dry climate.

Orientation

Queens Rd heads south from Lautoka, passing Nadi airport, crossing the Nadi River and then becoming Nadi's main street, lined with shops and restaurants. This main street ends in a T-junction at the large Swami temple. From here Queens Rd continues right to Suva, while the Nadi Back Rd bypasses the busy centre and rejoins Queens Rd near the airport. The road to the Nausori Highlands leads off into the mountains from the Nadi Back Rd.

The market, bus station and post office are downtown, east of the main street.

Near the Nadi River bridge, just north of town, Narewa Rd leads 6km west to **Denarau Island**. This is the turf of Nadi's most upmarket resorts and **Denarau Marina**, from where most tours and boat services depart for the Mamanuca and Yasawa islands.

Wailoaloa Rd also turns west off the Queens Rd near Martintar, with Wailoaloa Beach about 1.75km from the highway.

FIJI

A Big Day Out

Looking for a day excursion from Nadi? Try one of these options:

• Cruise or fly to the Mamanucas for swimming, snorkelling or diving
• Hike the mountains of Koroyanitu National Heritage Park
• Explore the Sabeto region by mountain bike
• Hire a 4WD or take a tour to the Nausori Highlands
• Kayak or raft on the Navua River in the Namosi Highlands
• Visit the Sigatoka Sand Dunes
• Ride the Coral Coast Scenic Railway

FIJI

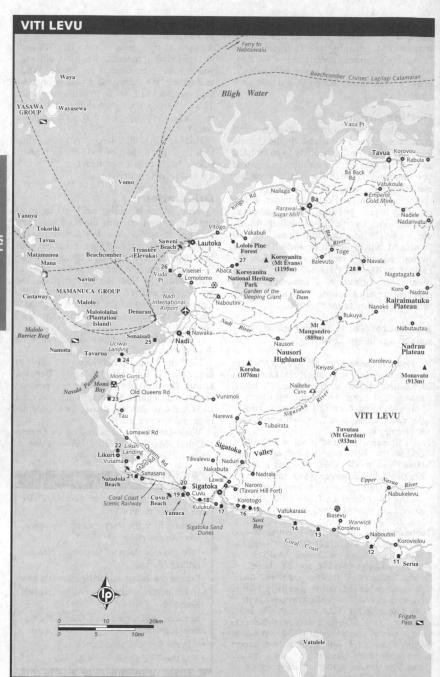

VITI LEVU

Ferry to
Nabouwalu

Beachcomber Cruises' Lagilagi Catamaran

Bligh Water

Waya

YASAWA
GROUP
Wayasewa

Vatia Pt

Tavua Korovou
Rabula

Ba Back
Rd
Vatukoula
Vomo
Nailaga Ba Emperor
Gold Mine
Nadele
Kings Rd Nadarivatu
Rarawai
Sugar Mill River
Vitogo Toge
Yanuya Vakabuli Navala
Tokoriki Lololo Pine Balevuto 28
Tavua Saweni Forest Nagatagata
Beach Lautoka Koroyanitu
Matamanoa Treasure 27 (Mt Evans) Koro Nadrau
Mana Beachcomber (Elevuka) 26 (1195m) Rairaimatuku
Viseisei Koroyanitu Nanoko Plateau
Vuda Abaca National Heritage
Navini Pt Lomolomo Park Vaturu
Castaway MAMANUCA GROUP Garden of the Dam Nubutautau
Malolo Sleeping Giant
Nadi Naboutini Bukuya
Malololailai International
(Plantation Denarau Airport Nadi River Nadrau
Malolo Island) Nawaka Plateau
Barrier Reef Nausori
Sonaisali 25 Nadi Mt Korolevu Monavatu
Namotu Uciwai Mangondro (913m)
Tavarua Landing (889m)
24 Nausori
Momi Guns Highlands Keiyasi
Navula Porose Momi Koroba Naihehe
Bay Old Queens Rd (1076m) Cave Sigatoka River
23
Tau Vunimoli VITI LEVU
Narewa
Tubairata Tuvutau
Lomawai Rd (Mt Gordon)
22 Likuri (933m)
Likuri Landing Upper Navua River
Vusama Tilivalevu Naduri Sigatoka Valley Nabukelevu
Natadola 21 Sanasana Nakabuta
Beach 20 Lawai Nadrala
Coral Coast 19 Sigatoka Naroro
Scenic Railway Cuvu (Tavuni Hill Fort)
Cuvu 18 Korotogo Biasevu
Beach 17 15 Warwick
Yanuca Kulukulu 16 Vatukarasa Korolevu
Sigatoka Sand Sovi 14 Naboutini
Dunes Bay 13
Coral Coast 12
Korovisilou
11 Serua

0   10   20km
0   5   10mi

Frigate
Pass

Vatulele

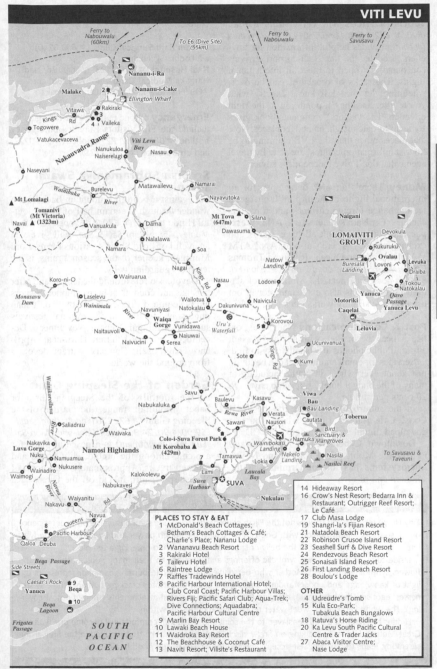

FIJI

PLACES TO STAY & EAT
1 McDonald's Beach Cottages;
  Betham's Beach Cottages & Café;
  Charlie's Place; Nanamu Lodge
2 Wananavu Beach Resort
3 Rakiraki Hotel
5 Taileu Hotel
6 Raintree Lodge
7 Raffles Tradewinds Hotel
8 Pacific Harbour International Hotel;
  Club Coral Coast; Pacific Harbour Villas;
  Rivers Fiji; Pacific Safari Club; Aqua-Trek;
  Dive Connections; Aquadabra;
  Pacific Harbour Cultural Centre
9 Marlin Bay Resort
10 Lawaki Beach House
11 Waidroka Bay Resort
12 The Beachhouse & Coconut Café
13 Naviti Resort; Vilisite's Restaurant

14 Hideaway Resort
16 Crow's Nest Resort; Bedarra Inn &
   Restaurant; Outrigger Reef Resort;
   Le Café
17 Club Masa Lodge
19 Shangri-la's Fijian Resort
21 Natadola Beach Resort
22 Robinson Crusoe Island Resort
23 Seashell Surf & Dive Resort
24 Rendezvous Beach Resort
25 Sonaisali Island Resort
26 First Landing Beach Resort
28 Boulou's Lodge

OTHER
4 Udreudre's Tomb
15 Kula Eco-Park;
   Tubakula Beach Bungalows
18 Ratuva's Horse Riding
20 Ka Levu South Pacific Cultural
   Centre & Trader Jacks
27 Abaca Visitor Centre;
   Nase Lodge

Information

Tourist Offices The **Fiji Visitors Bureau** *(FVB; ☎ 672 2433, fax 672 0141; W www.bula fiji.com)* provides helpful information for travellers. Located at the Nadi airport arrivals concourse, it's open to meet all international flights. The racks of brochures can be overwhelming; let the staff know exactly what you're after and they'll point you in the right direction. The visitors' comments book gives some up-to-date insight on budget places. Note that places other than the FVB claiming to be 'tourist information centres' are actually travel agents that don't give independent advice.

Money There's an **ANZ bank** open for all international flights at the airport. It charges a fee to change foreign currency and travellers cheques. On Nadi's main street, **ANZ**, **Westpac** and **National Bank** all have ATMs and exchange money. There's also an ANZ ATM at McDonald's on Queens Rd and a **Thomas Cook** *(Main St, Nadi; open 9am-5pm Mon-Fri, 8.30am-noon Sat)* near the Mobil petrol station. Larger hotels also exchange money but usually have slightly worse rates than banks.

Post & Communications Nadi's **post office** is near the market, with another at Nadi airport. Public phones are usually easy to find.

Services for email and Internet can be found just about everywhere in Nadi, including at many of the budget hotels. Expect to pay 10 to 20 cents per minute.

In the suburb of Martintar try the **West Coast Café** (closes 10pm) where you can download digital camera images onto CD.

Downtown, **Cybercafé** *(501 Main St, Nadi)* is near the Mobil petrol station and **Novex Microsystems** has lots of terminals at the southern end of town.

Medical Services For medical treatment, contact:

Dr Ram Raju Surgical Clinic (☎ 670 0240) 2 Lodhia St, Nadi
Nadi Hospital (☎ 670 1128) Market Rd, Nadi
Namaka Medical Centre (☎ 672 2288) cnr Queens Rd and Namaka Lane, Namaka

Emergency Phone numbers for emergencies include the Fiji Visitors Bureau's **emergency hotline** *(☎ 0800 6721 721)*, **police** *(☎ 670 0222)* and **ambulance** *(☎ 670 1128)*.

Sri Siva Subramaniya Swami Temple

Set against a beautiful mountain backdrop, a wander through the main hall of this colourful Hindu temple *(☎ 670 0016; open 5am-8pm Mon-Fri, 5am-8pm Sat & Sun)* will give you an eyeful of Lord Shiva's various forms. Lord Murugan, keeper of the seasonal rains, is the temple's guardian deity.

Devotees circle around the temple and offer bananas and coconut or burn camphor. Visitors are welcome if dressed modestly. Don't snap photos inside the temple. Annual festivals such as Karthingai Deepam (November or December), Panguni Uthiram Thiru-naal (April) and Thai Pusam (January) attract devotees from around the world.

Garden of the Sleeping Giant

At the foothills of the Sleeping Giant or Sabeto mountain range, the Garden of the Sleeping Giant *(☎ 672 2701; adult/child/family F$9.90/4.90/24.90; open 9am-5pm Mon-Sat, Sun by appointment)* is a peaceful place for a picnic among the orchids, lily ponds and forested tracks. Approximately 6km north of Nadi airport, turn inland off the Queens Rd

Hindu Symbolism

Tiny Hindu temples and shrines dot the Fijian countryside, each one symbolising the body or residence of the soul. For Hindus, union with God can be achieved through prayer and by ridding the body of impurities – hence, no meat in the belly or shoes on the feet when entering a temple.

Inside temples, Hindus give symbolic offerings and blessings to their many gods. Both water and flowers symbolise the Great Mother who personifies nature, while burning camphor represents the light of knowledge and understanding. Smashing a coconut denotes cracking humans' three weaknesses: egotism (the hard shell), delusion (the fibre) and material attachments (the outermost covering). The white kernel and sweet water represent the pure soul within.

Hindus believe that a body enslaved to the spirit and denied all comforts will become one with the Great Mother. Life is like walking on fire; a disciplined approach, like that required in the firewalking ceremony, leads to balance, self-acceptance and the ability to see good in all.

NADI

FIJI

PLACES TO STAY
1 Tokatoka Resort Hotel
2 Raffles Gateway Hotel
4 Tanoa International Hotel
5 Fiji Mocambo
8 Travellers Beach Resort
9 Tropic of Capricorn Resort
11 New Town Beach Motel
12 Club Fiji Resort
15 Beachside Resort
18 Sandalwood Lodge
19 The West's Motor Inn
20 Nadi Bay Hotel
22 White House Visitors Inn
25 Sunseekers Hotel
55 Nadi Hotel

PLACES TO EAT
6 Maharaj Restaurant
13 Colonial Plaza;
   Mama's Pizza Inn;
   Bakery; Supermarket
27 Continental Cakes & Pizza
28 Daikoku Restaurant
30 Mama's Pizza Inn
34 Chefs (The Corner)
35 Chefs, the Restaurant
40 Bakery
43 Sentai Seafood Restaurant
46 Food for Thought

OTHER
3 Nadi International Airport;
   Fiji Visitors Bureau;
   Post Office; ANZ Bank
7 Turtle Airways
10 Inner Space Adventures
16 Ed's Bar; West Coast Cafe;
   Viti Surf Legend
17 Self Service Laundry
21 McDonald's
23 Captain Cook Cruises

To Garden of the
Sleeping Giant (6km),
Stoney Creek
Resort (9km),
Vuda Point & First Landing
Beach Resort (12km)
& Lautoka (24km)

Nadi

Nadi Bay

Wailoaloa
Beach

Nadi Airport
Golf Club

New Town
Beach

Namaka

Martintar

Miegunyah

To Bukuya &
Nausori Highlands
(29km)

To Denarau Island,
Denarau Marina,
Denarau Golf &
Racquet Club &
Sheraton Resorts (5km)

Denarau
(Narewa Rd)

To Sonaisali Island
Resort (12km),
Redezvous Beach
Resort (20km) &
Suva (187km)

Nadi River
Bridge

Nadi

Nadi Back Rd

See Enlargement

Otana River

OTHER (continued)
24 Mosque
26 Air Fiji
29 Cybercafe
31 Aqua-Trek
32 West End Cinema
33 Thomas Cook
36 Jack's Handicrafts
37 Morris Hedstrom Supermarket
38 SPR Music;
   Brijal's Photo Services;
   Boom Box
39 ANZ Bank
41 National Bank
42 Surgical Clinic
44 Budget Pharmacy
45 Nadi Medical Clinic
47 Caines Photofast
48 Viti Surf Legend
49 Market
50 Telecom;
   Post Office
51 Novex Microsystems;
   South Pacific Islanders
   Handicrafts
52 Nadi Civic Centre
53 Westpac Bank
54 Handicraft Market
56 Police Station
57 Swami Temple
58 Bus Station
59 Nadi Hospital

To Bridge

River

Nadi

Ashram Rd

Sukuna St

Vunavau Rd

Koroivolu Ave

Nadi Back Rd

To Bus Station
(100m) &
Hospital
(400m)

Hospital Rd

Park St

Clay St

Main St

Sahu Khan

Naitavo La

Vunalolo St

Sagayam Rd

0   200m

0   0.25   0.5mi
0   0.5   1km

Enamanu Rd

Wailoaloa Rd

Nadi Bay Rd

Queens Rd

Kennedy Ave

Nadi River

Ragg St

Nadi Back Rd

Nawson Highlands Rd

Legalega Rd

Votualevu Rd

Yavusania

onto Wailoko Rd. A taxi from Nadi will cost around F$12.

Visiting the Highlands

If you're pressed for time, organised tours can be a good way to visit the interior and its villages. The highland village of Abaca in the Koroyanitu National Heritage Park is an easy day trip from Nadi or Lautoka; try **Mount Batilamu Trek** (☎ 0800 6720 455, 672 3311; e batilamutrek@compuserve.com). **Rivers Fiji** (Viti Levu map; ☎ 345 0147; w www.rivers fiji.com; Pacific Harbour) has both rafting and kayaking on the Upper Navua River and to the Namosi Highlands. **Rosie Tours** (☎ 672 2755, fax 672 2607; w www.rosiefiji.com; Nadi Airport) has daily (except Sunday) hikes to the Nausori Highlands for F$60, including lunch, as well as six-day highland tours. **Wacking Stick** (☎ 672 4673, 995 3003; w www .wackingstickadventures.com; Stoney Creek Resort) offers excellent mountain-bike tours to the Sabeto Valley.

Diving

Inner Space Adventures (☎/fax 672 3883; New Town Beach) offers good-value budget dive trips to the Mamanucas, charging F$110 for a two-tank dive including all gear, lunch and transfer from Nadi hotels. Open-water certification costs F$380.

Dive Tropex (☎ 6701 888; Sheraton Fiji Resort, Denarau Island) has better and faster boats and covers a wider range of dive sites in the Mamanucas. A two-tank dive trip costs F$150. Open-water certification costs F$620.

Aqua-Trek (☎ 6702 413; w www.aquatrek .com; 465 Main St, Nadi) sells diving and snorkelling gear, but has no excursions from Nadi.

Jet-Boat Trips

Shotover Jet Fiji (☎ 750 400, fax 750 666) has a noisy, hair-raising jet-boat trip (adult/child F$59/25, 30 minutes) through the Nadi River mangroves. It departs from Denarau Marina with a courtesy minibus for hotel transfers.

Golf & Tennis

The **Denarau Golf & Racquet Club** (☎ 675 9710) has an immaculately groomed 18-hole golf course with bunkers in the shape of sea creatures. Green fees are F$95/55 for 18/9 holes. The all-weather, grass tennis court fees are F$20 per hour with racket hire for F$10.

Nadi Airport Golf Club (☎ 672 2148; New Town Beach; F$15 for 18 holes), near Turtle Airways, is a much cheaper option.

Scenic Flights

On a clear day, most domestic flights offer gorgeous views of islands, coral reefs and blue-green waters. Easy day trips include Nadi to Malololailai and Mana in the Mamanucas (confirm in advance to use resort facilities). Joy flights are available by seaplane with Turtle Airways and by helicopter with Island Hoppers. (See the Getting Around section near the start of this chapter).

Cruises to the Mamanucas & Yasawas

Day trips and cruises to the stunning Mamanuca and Yasawa islands are understandably popular. Malololailai, Mana, Beachcomber and Castaway islands usually take day-trippers. South Seas Cruises also has a sailing trip to Monuriki in the Mamanucas, where Tom Hanks was deserted in the film *Castaway*. See Mamanucas Group for more information on tours and transport.

Places to Stay – Budget

Consider whether you want the convenience of staying close to downtown (where there are more places to eat), at the black-sand Wailoaloa and New Town beaches (fairly isolated but peaceful) or in Martintar, between the airport and downtown Nadi.

Martintar While slightly sleazy, the suburb of Martintar has a number of services close by and regular buses along Queens Rd.

Nadi Bay Hotel (☎ 672 3599; e nadibay@ connect.com.fj; Wailoaloa Rd; dorm beds without/with air-con F$18/22, singles/doubles with shared bathroom F$48/56, singles/ doubles/triples with private bathroom F$75/ 90/100, apartment F$85/110/130; all private rooms including breakfast) is clean and welcoming and one of Nadi's best budget places. Set next to cane fields, the small hotel has a pleasant outdoor **dining area** (breakfast from F$6, lunch F$7-9, dinner F$11-16). Room 21b, with views over the pool, is the best standard. The self-contained, air-con rooftop apartment has fantastic views to the bay and the mountains and can be a 6-bed dorm for F$25 per person. Credit cards are accepted.

White House Visitor's Inn (☎ 670 0022; 40 Kennedy Ave; dorm beds F$11, fan-cooled singles/doubles with private bathroom F$35/ 45, twins with shared bathroom F$30, air-con doubles F$45, all include basic breakfast) is fairly small and shabby, but reasonably clean and definitely friendly. There's a communal kitchen and adjacent **Chinese restaurant** (meals F$6- 15). It's 15-minutes by foot or F$3 by taxi from downtown.

Sandalwood Lodge (☎ 672 2044, fax 6720 103; Ragg St; e sandalwood@connect.com.fj; singles F$75-85 doubles F$80-90, children free, extra adult F$7), 200m off the Queens Rd, is good value and an excellent option for self-caterers and families. Self-contained rooms surround a grassy courtyard and palm-shaded swimming pool. The family room is spacious (for up to six people) and the 'orchid wing' has newer furnishings and fittings.

The budget rooms at **The West's Motor Inn** and **Raffles Gateway Hotel** can be good options (see Places to Stay – Mid-Range later in this section).

At the Beach Wailoaloa and New Town beaches, though far from pristine, are a peaceful alternative to town with good sunset views. Food options and transport are limited; infrequent local buses service Wailoaloa and most hotels offer free transfers from the airport.

Travellers Beach Resort (☎ 672 3322; e beach villa@connect.com.fj; dorm beds F$11, singles/ doubles with fan F$33/40, with air-con F$40/ 55, villas with fan/air-con F$66/77) has friendly staff and a poolside **bar and restaurant** (dinner around F$14) serving good food right on the beach. Rooms in the front building face the pool and beach. Upstairs, corner rooms in the rear building are bright and breezy. Self-contained jamboree-style villas are on a separate site.

Tropic of Capricorn Resort (☎ 672 3089; 11 Wasawasa Rd; air-con dorms F$15, apartment rooms with fan/air-con F$40/60) is a new place with clean, airy dorms, beach access and a pleasant pool. Two-bedroom apartments are back from the beach; you can rent the whole apartment (price negotiable) or a double room with shared kitchen and living areas. The upstairs units are brighter and have a veranda.

New Town Beach Motel (☎ 672 3339, 6723 420; 5 Wasawasa Rd; dorm beds/doubles/family F$13/40/50) is quiet, clean and homey with a fan-cooled, five-bed dorm. Meals are F$7/9 for lunch/dinner. There's a nice swimming pool and deck in the back garden.

Beachside Resort (☎ 670 3488, fax 670 3688; e beachsideresort@connect.com.fj; Wailoaloa Beach; studio/mountainview room F$45/ 55, air-con gardenview/oceanview doubles F$70/ 90, fan-cooled bure F$140, 2 children under 12 free), 80m back from the beach, has a cosy

atmosphere and the comforts of a mid-range hotel. The excellent, poolside **Coriander Café** (mains lunch/dinner F$10/16) has a creative menu featuring cassava wedges, fruit smoothies and good coffee.

Club Fiji Resort (☎ 670 2189; e reservations@ clubfiji-resort.com; Wailoaloa Beach; dorm beds F$14, garden/oceanview/beachfront bure F$55/ 90/121, hotel room doubles F$150) can be a good place for a Nadi stopover. The grounds are pleasant, on a stretch of dark-sand beach. Oceanview bure have better maintenance and newer furnishings. Air-con beachfront rooms in a hotel block have a balcony to the bay and can be interconnecting (F$200 for a family). There's a small pool and a large **bar-restaurant** (meals F$15-20) with so-so food and occasional live entertainment. A daily shuttle bus (F$2.50) heads to downtown Nadi, and a taxi costs F$6.

Downtown Nadi Near the post office downtown, **Nadi Hotel** (☎ 670 0000; Koroivolu Ave; dorm beds F$15, doubles/triples with fan F$50/ 70, with air-con in old bldg F$60/80, in new bldg F$70/90) is also close to the market and bus station and is frequented mostly by locals. The mixed 10-bed dorms are on opposite sides of the swimming pool and are not bad value. Standard fan-cooled rooms are a bit musty and air-con rooms in the old building are pretty dingy. Rooms in the newer building are better, though not noisy with the disco next door.

Sunseekers Hotel (☎ 670 0400; Narewa Rd; dorm beds F$8.80, singles/doubles with fan F$35/40) is a convenient spot, only a few minutes' walk from the northern end of downtown. The hotel is reasonably clean and an OK option for travellers on a tight budget. Some rooms have a private toilet and shower, and there's a deck, bar and (sometimes filled) swimming pool.

Other Areas On a rise in the cane fields, **Stoney Creek Resort** (☎ 672 2206; e stoney creek@connect.com.fj; Sabeto; dorms F$16, fan-cooled bure F$40-66) commands a 360-degree view of the mountains and Nadi Bay. Accommodation is simple and airy with a comfortable dorm and small bure with excellent views. The **restaurant** (breakfast/lunch/dinner around F$8/10/18, Sunday lovo lunch/buffet dinner $18/15) overlooks the pool. The resort is northeast of the airport in the Sabeto Foothills, an area great to explore on mountain bike. Head north along Queens Rd for 3km, then 6km east along Sabeto Rd. There's a free airport shuttle and 'Sabeto' buses from Nadi; a taxi is F$7/12 from the airport/town.

Rendezvous Beach Resort (☎ 651 0571; e rendezvous@infofiji.com; Uciwai Landing; dorm beds F$45, singles/doubles F$60/110, meals included) is a surf and dive camp run by a local surfer and his Japanese dive-instructor wife. Don't come for the beach but for quick access to the Mamanuca surf breaks and dive sites. Accommodation is simple but clean. Surfing boat fees are F$35/50 for half-/full-day trip. The resort is about 20km southwest of Nadi, along Uciwai Rd. Local buses depart from Nadi bus terminal at 8am and 1pm Monday to Saturday.

Places to Stay – Mid-Range

Raffles Gateway Hotel (☎ 672 2444, fax 672 0620; e rafflesresv@connect.com.fj; standard doubles with air-con F$55, deluxe doubles/quads F$125/150, suites F$170, 2 children under 16 free), opposite the airport, is good value with pleasant gardens and a waterslide into an enormous swimming pool. Standard rooms upstairs are generally better than those on the ground floor and deluxe rooms are more spacious. The poolside bar and **restaurant** (meals around F$18) isn't a bad spot to wait for a flight.

Tokatoka Resort Hotel (☎ 672 0222, fax 672 0400; e tokatokaresort@connect.com.fj; Queens Rd; studio doubles/triples F$145/165, villa doubles/quad F$160/210, one-bedroom villa doubles/quad F$205/255, two-bedroom villas F$325) is also just opposite the airport. Great for families, it has a swimming pool with waterslide, a nice garden, and good disabled and pram access. Most units have cooking facilities and there's a small supermarket. The **restaurant-bar** (lunch F$7-17, dinner F$16-25) serves meals by the pool. Child-minding is available for F$3.50 per hour.

The West's Motor Inn (☎ 672 0044, fax 672 0071; e westsmotorin@mail.is.com.fj; Queens Rd; standard singles or doubles/triples F$60/75, deluxe doubles/triples/family F$105/125/135) is good value and has happy staff. Rooms have fans and air-con, and the spacious deluxe rooms overlook the swimming pool and an enormous mango tree. Standard rooms in the building next door are generally lighter and better ventilated. The poolside bar and **restaurant** (dinner mains F$14-19) offers OK meals.

First Landing Beach Resort (☎ 666 6171, fax 666 8882; e firstlanding@connect.com.fj; Vuda Point; superior/deluxe/oceanview cottages F$121/143/176, including breakfast) is a nice spot on the water's edge with views to the Mamanuca islands. The air-con cottages (up to four people) are in a large garden and have mosquito-screened verandas. There's a lovely swimming pool and you can snorkel and swim off the sandy beach at high tide. The pleasant restaurant specialises in seafood (see Places to Eat following).

Places to Stay – Top End

Near the Airport There are two large, up-market hotels within a few minutes' drive of the airport. Both offer perfectly comfortable but pretty standard business-type rooms, fitness and convention centres, swimming pools and 24-hour cafés.

Fiji Mocambo (☎ 672 2000, fax 672 0324; W www.shangri-la.com; singles/doubles F$190/200) has rooms with mountain views, a nine-hole golf course and tennis courts. There are live bands Friday and Saturday nights.

Tanoa International Hotel (☎ 672 0277, fax 672 0191; e tanoahotels@connect.com.fj; doubles F$190, executive rooms F$200) is locally owned and has a sleepy, islander feel about it. The **restaurant** (all-day dining F$9-16, dinner F$19-30) serves OK fare.

Denarau Island The upmarket Denarau Island feels a world away, but is just 6km west of downtown Nadi on reclaimed mangrove. The beach has dark-grey sand but the Sheraton Resorts take day-trippers to a private offshore island with white-sand beaches. The resorts have heaps of facilities including restaurants, bars, boutiques, a golf and tennis club, lawn bowling, fitness centres and a spa. Snorkelling and fishing trips, windsurfing, sailing and cruises depart from the nearby marina. Young families are well catered for with a kids' programme and baby-sitting services.

Sheraton Royal Denarau Resort (☎ 675 0000, fax 675 0818; e sheratondenarau@sheraton.com; gardenview/beachfront rooms F$460/680), Fiji's first luxury hotel, has traditional rooms in luxuriant, tropical gardens.

Sheraton Fiji Resort (☎ 675 0777, fax 675 0818; W www.sheraton.com/fiji; singles or doubles F$520-803) has rooms with ocean views and a more modern Mediterranean style than the Royal.

Sheraton Denarau Villas (☎ 675 0777, fax 675 0818; W www.sheraton.com/denarauvillas; deluxe/seafront guestroom F$580/700, suites F$785/935, villas F$1070-1560) are an option if you are after resort facilities but prefer an apartment with cooking facilities. The stylish villas have two and three bedrooms.

Sonaisali Island Just 300m off the mainland Sonaisali Island Resort (☎ 670 6011, fax 670 6092; ☒ www.sonaisali.com; doubles F$335, oceanview/beachfront/family bure F$410/460/550, including breakfast) is about 12km southwest of Nadi. Located on a dark-sand beach with quick access and great views to the Mamanucas, it's well equipped with a swimming pool, sunken bar and beachfront restaurant. An optional meal package costs F$60/30 per adult/child. Free activities include windsurfing, catamaran sailing, canoeing and tennis. Rates at Dive Sonaisali are F$150 for a two-tank dive day trip and F$450 for 10 tanks over five days. Snorkelling trips cost F$22 per person. To reach the resort, head south on Queens Rd, turn at Nacobi Rd and drive for a couple of kilometres to the resort landing and taxi stand.

Places to Eat
Touristy Nadi caters well for a variety of tastes and budgets. Most places serve a mixture of Indian, Chinese and Western dishes, with a Fijian dish or two, and resorts often have traditional *lovo* nights. There are many cheap lunchtime eateries downtown that aren't squeaky clean but have good food and are popular with locals. Try around Nadi Civic Centre.

Cafés For good coffee and milkshakes try Surf Republic (Main Street, downtown Nadi).

Continental Cakes & Pizza (☎ 670 3595; Main Street, downtown Nadi; medium pizza F$9-18) serves pizza and supplies many of the hotels with cheesecakes, croissants and coconut tarts. Lamb shank rolls are F$4.50.

Chefs (The Corner) (Sagayam Rd; open 8am-9pm Mon-Sat) has good-value quality meals, including curries (F$7) and coconut pies.

Restaurants Those after international cuisine and candlelit dinners try Chefs, the Restaurant (☎ 670 3131; Sagayam Rd; open 10am-2pm & 6pm-10pm Mon-Sat), one of Nadi's more expensive restaurants.

Maharaj Restaurant (☎ 672 2962; Queens Rd, Namaka; dishes F$6-15) might not look special but has Nadi's best curry and also does takeaway. It's near the airport.

Food for Thought (open 8am to 6pm Mon-Sat), upstairs off the main street, has vegetarian *thali* for F$5 and Internet access.

Mama's Pizza Inn (☎ 670 0221; large pizza F$15-23), downtown or at the Colonial Plaza in Namaka (Queens Rd), is an inexpensive option for good pizza and pasta. Try the tasty vegetarian bolognaise spaghetti for F$6.50.

Sentai Seafood Restaurant is the best place for Chinese dishes and has good seafood.

Daikoku Restaurant (☎ 670 3622; à la carte meals F$18-29), downtown, has superb Japanese teppanyaki (F$22 to F$48) as well as miso soup, sushi (F$5 to F$7) and noodles (F$12 to F$18).

West Coast Café (Queens Rd, Martintar), next door to Ed's Bar, serves delicious and innovative snacks, pizzas and seafood in a relaxed, friendly atmosphere.

Stoney Creek Resort (☎ 672 2206; Sunday lovo lunch/buffet dinner $18/15) is a great spot north of town, surrounded by cane fields and cradled by the mountains. See Other Areas under Places to Stay – Budget earlier.

First Landing Seafood Restaurant (☎ 666 6171; Vuda Point; snacks F$10, mains from F$20) has decks on the beach for outdoor dining and views of the Mamanucas.

Self-Catering Nadi has a large produce market with lots of fresh fruit and vegetables. There are several large supermarkets and bakeries downtown.

Entertainment
Nadi isn't a hive of nightlife. Head to Ed's Bar (Queen's Rd, Martintar) or Mama's Pizza downtown if you're looking for a drink. Fiji Mocambo Hotel has live bands, karaoke and rave music on Friday and Saturday nights. The Sheraton Royal has a disco at the Planters Club Bar, Wednesday night fire-walking and Saturday night *meke* (F$50/25 per adult/child over 12, including a *lovo* dinner).

There are a few cinemas downtown that show Hollywood and Bollywood movies (admission is F$3). Try the West End Cinema (Ashram Rd) or check listings in the *Fiji Times*.

Shopping
Nadi's Main St is largely devoted to souvenir and duty-free shops. If you're looking for something for the mantelpiece back home, head to Jack's Handicrafts, or South Pacific Islanders Handicrafts, an artists' co-op. Practice your bargaining skills at the outdoor handicraft market near the Civic Centre. Surf Republic has a small art gallery with work by Fijian and Indo-Fijian artists.

SPR Music and the Boom-Box are good places to sample music by local bands.

Viti Surf Legend has boards for sale and hire, and Aqua-Trek has dive and snorkelling gear.

Getting There & Away
See the Getting There & Away and Getting Around sections near the start of this chapter for information on Nadi international airport, inter-island air and boat services, and car rental.

Getting Around
There are regular local and express buses that travel along Queens Rd and local Nadi buses to New Town Beach but not to Denarau Island. Taxis are plentiful in Nadi but they don't use meters, so agree on a price before getting in.

LAUTOKA
pop 43,274
The waterfront town of Lautoka, with the beautiful Koroyanitu Range as a backdrop, offers a slight respite from the tourist hype of Nadi. Lautoka is Fiji's second port and largest city after Suva. While not especially interesting, there's a small **botanical garden** in the south and a large **produce and handicraft market** near the bus station, from where buses travel to Suva via the northern Kings Rd and southern Queens Rd. The **Lautoka Sugar Mill** (1903) is at the heart of the community; in cutting season, sugar trains putt along the main street and in September the city crowns a Sugar Queen at the annual **Sugar Festival**.

In the mountains 10km east of Lautoka, **Koroyanitu National Heritage Park** is a fantastic place for hiking. Beautiful trails meander through native rainforest, past waterfalls, archaeological sites and natural swimming pools. (See Koroyanitu National Heritage Park later in this chapter).

Information
Several banks downtown will change money and travellers cheques. **ANZ** has ATMs on Naviti St and near the cinema on Namoli Ave. The **Cathay Hotel** also changes money at bank rates.

The **post office** (cnr Vitogo Pde & Tavewa Ave) has a few public telephones. **Compuland** (Vitogo Pde) has email and Internet services, as does the **Downtown Post Shop** (Yasawa St) and **SITA Travel** (Naviti St). For health emergencies, contact **Lautoka Hospital** (☎ 6660 399; Thomson Crescent) or **Vakabale St Medical Centre** (☎ 665 2955; 47 Drasa Avenue).

Places to Stay
Sea Breeze Hotel (☎ 666 0717, fax 666 6080; Bekana Lane; air-con & seaview singles/doubles/triples/family F$40/49/52/56, singles/

doubles with fan F$33/37, all with private bathroom) is at the end of a quiet cul-de-sac on the waterfront, close to the bus station. This is a good place for getting over jet lag before heading inland or to offshore islands. There's a breakfast room, a quiet bar and lounge, and a swimming pool. Fan-cooled rooms are often booked out.

Cathay Hotel (☎ 666 0566; e cathay@fiji4less.com; Tavewa Ave; dorm beds F$12, singles/doubles with fan F$33/44, self-contained with air-con F$46/55) is a good place to meet other budget travellers and has a swimming pool, bar and a restaurant that serves OK meals for F$4 to F$8. The fruit smoothies are fab. Check out the various dorms – some are less ventilated than others.

Lautoka Hotel (☎ 666 0388; e ltkhotel@connect.com.fj; 2-12 Naviti St; singles or doubles with air-con & private bathroom F$40, deluxe singles or doubles F$65) is popular with locals and tourists. Give the old wing a miss – it may have cheap beds but is grungy and a potential firetrap. The new wing has good air-con motel rooms (deluxe) around a small swimming pool.

Saweni Beach Apartment Hotel (☎ 666 1777; e saweni@fiji4less.com; camp sites per person F$7, dorm beds F$11, brown house doubles $40, oceanview/poolside one-bedroom apartments F$55/50) is a low-key place for budget self-caterers, about 6km southwest of Lautoka and 2km off Queens Rd. The beach isn't great but there's a small swimming pool and a bar. The fan-cooled apartments are clean and spacious and the 'brown house' (actually orange) is a good option closer to the beach.

Waterfront Hotel (☎ 666 4777, fax 666 5870; e waterfront@connect.com.fj; Marine Dr; rooms/suites F$115/135) is the only upmarket hotel in Lautoka, catering mainly to business travellers. Rooms are not bad value, suites are spacious and there's a modern lounge and bar, a pool and a good restaurant (Fins; see Places to Eat following).

Places to Eat
Lautoka is far from overflowing with good restaurants.

Ganga Vegetarian Restaurant (cnr Naviti & Yasawa Sts) is one of the town's best options. Prices range from under F$2 for simple dishes, soups and lassi, to F$5 for a thali food platter.

The Chilli Tree Café (☎ 665 1824; 3 Tukani St) is recommended for coffee, cake, quiche and sandwiches.

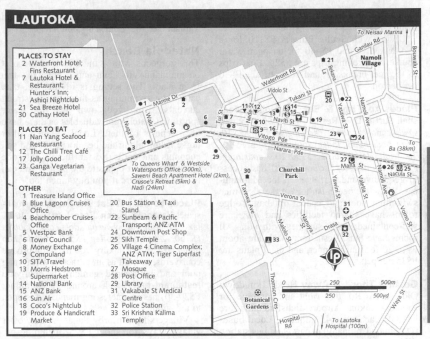

LAUTOKA

PLACES TO STAY
2 Waterfront Hotel;
   Fins Restaurant
7 Lautoka Hotel &
   Restaurant;
   Hunter's Inn;
   Ashiqi Nightclub
21 Sea Breeze Hotel
30 Cathay Hotel

PLACES TO EAT
11 Nan Yang Seafood
   Restaurant
12 The Chilli Tree Café
17 Jolly Good
23 Ganga Vegetarian
   Restaurant

OTHER
1 Treasure Island Office
3 Blue Lagoon Cruises
   Office
4 Beachcomber Cruises
   Office
5 Westpac Bank
6 Town Council
8 Money Exchange
9 Compuland
10 SITA Travel
13 Morris Hedstrom
   Supermarket
14 National Bank
15 ANZ Bank
16 Sun Air
18 Coco's Nightclub
19 Produce & Handicraft
   Market
20 Bus Station & Taxi
   Stand
22 Sunbeam & Pacific
   Transport; ANZ ATM
24 Downtown Post Shop
25 Sikh Temple
26 Village 4 Cinema Complex;
   ANZ ATM; Tiger Superfast
   Takeaway
27 Mosque
28 Post Office
29 Library
31 Vakabale St Medical
   Centre
32 Police Station
33 Sri Krishna Kalima
   Temple

Jolly Good (*cnr Naviti & Vakabale Sts; mains under $4*) is a popular outdoor venue with inexpensive Indian, Chinese and Fijian fast food.

Tigers Superfast Takeaway (*Namoli Ave*), near the cinema, is very popular with locals after a quick bite.

The Lautoka Hotel (*mains F$8-15*) serves reasonable pizza, Chinese, Indian and European meals.

Nan Yang Seafood Restaurant (☎ 665 2668; Nede St; soups F$9-15, seafood F$13-28) has good quality Chinese food.

Fins Restaurant (*Waterfront Hotel*) is the most upmarket restaurant and has pleasant harbour views.

Entertainment
Lautoka has a cushy **Village 4 Cinema Complex** (Namoli Ave). If you're game on Friday and Saturday nights, try **Coco's Night Club** (Naviti St) or head to the Lautoka Hotel for the **Ashiqi Nightclub** or **Hunter's Inn** (Tui St).

Getting There & Around
Lautoka is 33km north of Nadi and 24km north of Nadi airport. Local buses shuttle between Lautoka and Nadi every 15 minutes during the day and less frequently in the

evening. Taxis cost about F$7/20 to Lautoka/Nadi airport.

There are regular express buses along the Kings and Queens Rds (see Getting Around under Viti Levu earlier), and Viti minibuses head for Suva.

Lautoka is easy to get around on foot. Taxis are plentiful and short rides are cheap.

SOUTHERN VITI LEVU
The sealed and scenic Queens Rd follows the southern coast of Viti Levu, from Lautoka to Suva. It's dotted with accommodation options, particularly along the stretch of coastline known as the Coral Coast with its wide fringing reef offshore. Both Pacific and Sunbeam have regular buses along the Queens Rd (see Getting Around under Viti Levu earlier).

Momi Bay
South of Nadi, Queens Rd winds through cane fields. The first interesting detour is towards Momi Bay along the old unsealed Queens Rd. The turn-off is 18km from Nadi (46km from Lautoka).

En route you'll pass **Momi Guns**, a WWII battery on a hilltop overlooking the strategic Navula Passage. With restored bunkers and a photo display, history buffs will find it worth a quick look.

Diving with **Scuba Bula** is F$110 for a two-tank dive and F$440 for an open-water course. Snorkelling trips are F$20. Boat trips to the reef-breaks around Namotu are F$30 per person.

Places to Stay & Eat The isolated **Seashell Surf & Dive Resort** (☎ 670 6100; ℮ sea shell@connect.com.fj; camping per tent F$10, dorm beds F$55, lodge doubles/triples F$60/ 70, triples/family bure F$150/200, apartment F$500, dorms rates include meals) has access to good dive and surf sites in the Mamanucas. While the beach isn't great there's a nice swimming pool and beachfront bar. Lodge rooms have shared facilities and bure are self-contained; bring supplies with you. All rooms have fans. Restaurant meals are about F$10/20 for lunch/dinner, and meal plans are F$35 per person.

Getting There & Away Head 11km down Old Queens Rd, turn right and continue for another 1.5km. Airport transfers/taxis are F$15/45 each way (45 minutes). Local buses (Dominion Company) depart Nadi bus station (F$2, three times daily). There are also daily local buses and taxis from Sigatoka (20km).

Robinson Crusoe Island

This small coral island, also known as Likuri, is just offshore Natadola Beach.

Robinson Crusoe Island Resort (☎ 651 0100; ℮ robinsoncrusoe@connect.com.fj; dorm beds F$65, small double bure F$70, double bure island/beach F$75/80, all with shared facilities & meals) is a small-scale budget resort and one of Fiji's best party islands. It has a nice white-sand beachfront, spectacular sunsets and an intense entertainment programme. Accommodation is simple and comfortable with shared, bucket showers and buffet meals. Activities include windsurfing, snorkelling, kayaking and volleyball. Boat trips to Natadola beach (including snorkelling with turtles) are F$30 per person. **Aqua-Trek Robinson Crusoe** dive shop offers two-tank dive excursions for F$102, and open water dive courses for F$450.

Getting There & Away A free shuttle bus service from Nadi hotels takes you to the **boat landing** (Maro Rd), about 6km off Queens Rd on the road to Natadola Beach. The boat (F$45 return per person) takes 30 minutes. Day-trips visit from Nadi and Coral Coast

hotels and there's a cruise/railway trip from Yanuca (see the Yanuca section later).

Natadola Beach

This gorgeous white-sand beach is the best on mainland Viti Levu and a great day-trip from Nadi. The setting is idyllic, but take care when swimming as there can be strong currents. Bring your own gear for water sports and watch your valuables as there have been reports of theft. Local villagers offer horse riding along the beach (F$10) and sell coconuts and crafts. So far, there's only one up-market resort opposite the beach; you can have a drink there if you buy lunch too.

Places to Stay & Eat The charming, small-scale **Natadola Beach Resort** (☎ 672 1001, fax 6721 000; ℮ www.natadola.com; doubles F$350, 2-bedroom suites F$530; no children under 16) offers luxury rooms with private courtyards, as well as an attractive swimming pool and landscaped garden. Its courtyard **restaurant-bar** (lunch around F$15, dinner F$20-30) has an interesting menu and is open to the public.

Villagers from nearby Sanasana may offer **village stays** for about F$25, including accommodation and meals. Ask for **Ilami Nabiau** at the police post at the Queens Rd-Maro Rd turn-off, or contact **Save** (☎ 650 0800) or **Baravi** (☎ 650 0222) in Sanasana village.

Getting There & Away The Maro Rd turn-off heads south to Natadola off Queens Rd, 36km from Nadi. Watch for a temple with a life-size goddess on the corner. After 9.5km, turn left at a T-junction. There are no direct buses from Nadi. From Sigatoka there are six buses daily except Sunday (F$2, one hour). The Coral Coast Scenic Railway runs scenic tours to this beach. Keen walkers could follow the track between Yanuca and Natadola Beach (about 3½ hours) and then catch the train or bus back.

Yanuca & Around

Past the turn-off to Natadola, Queens Rd winds southeast through hills and down to the coast at Cuvu Bay and the island of Yanuca, linked to the mainland by a causeway.

The **Coral Coast Scenic Railway** (☎ 652 8731; Queens Rd) offers scenic rides on an old, diesel sugar-train, past villages, forests and sugar plantations, to the Natadola Beach. The 14km trip takes about 1¼ hours, leaving at 10am and returning at 4pm (F$75 including lunch). Better value is the rail-a-way-sail-a-way trip (F$99), combining a one-way train ride and a trip to Robinson Crusoe. Children travel for half-price if under 12 and for free if under six. You'll find the railway station at the causeway entry to the Fijian Resort.

Ka Levu South Pacific Cultural Centre (☎ 552 0200; Queens Rd; open 10.30am-3.30pm Tues-Sun; admission F$80), opposite Shangri-La's Fijian Resort, has kava ceremonies and Pacific legend enactments, a replica of a traditional village and contemporary Indian dancing on display.

Places to Stay & Eat Adjoining the Cultural Centre is **Trader Jacks and the Pig Hunters Bar** (dorm beds F$65, including all meals), offering budget accommodation, a daily *lovo* and free entry to the cultural centre tour (good value considering the price tag of the tour).

Shangri-La's Fijian Resort (☎ 652 0155, fax 650 0402; ⓦ www.shangri-la.com; lagoonview/oceanview doubles F$370/410, family room F$510; studios & suites F$680, beach bure F$950, all including breakfast & dinner) covers the entire 43-hectare island of Yanuca. The resort is extremely family-oriented; two children can share with parents for free and there is babysitting (F$15 three hours), a teenagers' club and 'little chiefs' club'. There are lots of land- and water-based sports to keep you busy and an adults-only swimming pool. Motorised sports cost extra and diving is with Coral Coast Scuba Ventures. A two-tank dive costs F$190, or F$620 for an open-water course.

Getting There & Away The Fijian Resort is about a 45-minute drive from Nadi and 11km west of Sigatoka. There are regular express buses, minibuses and carriers travelling along Queens Rd (see Getting Around under Viti Levu earlier). A taxi to Nadi airport is about F$65 while the Coral Sun coach is F$25.

Sigatoka & Around
pop 8000
Near the mouth of the large Sigatoka River, Sigatoka is predominantly a farming community, as well as a service town for tourists visiting the Coral Coast resorts. The town centre has a **produce market**, a few souvenir shops and is overlooked by a large, hilltop **mosque**.

Head to **Gerona Medical and Surgical Clinic** (☎ 652 0128, 652 0327 after hrs; Sigatoka Valley Rd) for medical assistance.

Sigatoka Sand Dunes While grey-brown rather than Sahara-golden, these windswept dunes (admission F$5, open 8am-6pm daily) are nonetheless spectacular and a great place for a walk. Located near the mouth of the Sigatoka River, the dunes are about 5km long, rising to about 60m at the western end. The dunes have been forming over millions of years. However, human skeletal remains and pottery shards discovered here suggest that there was once a prehistoric village near the eastern end of the dunes. The area was declared a national park in 1989 in an attempt to help preserve the site. Enter through the **Sigatoka Sand Dunes Visitor Centre**, 4.5km west of Sigatoka. Allow about one hour for the walking tour.

Tavuni Hill Fort On the eastern side of the river, this defensive hill fortification (Kavanagasau Rd; adult/child/family F$3/6/15; open 8am-5pm Mon-Sat) was used in times of tribal war. The steep limestone ridge, about 90m high at the edge of a bend in the Sigatoka River, was an obvious strategic location. As a means of income for villagers, the site has been restored and has an **information centre**, a number of grave sites, a *rara* (ceremonial grounds) and a *vatu ni bokola* (head-chopping stone). About 4km north, regular local buses pass Tavuni Hill seven times daily. Taxis are about F$5.

Activities For a gallop along the beach, contact **Ratuva's Horse Riding** (☎ 650 0860). On a hill about 5.5km west from Sigatoka, it charges F$20/15 per person per hour for individuals/groups of five or more.

Sigatoka has Fiji's only beach break, over a large, submerged rock platform covered in sand. Surfing is possible at the point break at the mouth of the Sigatoka River.

Places to Stay & Eat The surfers' hangout **Club Masa Lodge** (☎ 651 1347; camping per person F$18, dorm beds F$30, doubles F$40, all including breakfast & dinner) is near the river's mouth. Managed by a local family, it has ocean and river access for surfing, windsurfing and canoeing; bring your own gear. To reach the resort, turn off Queens Rd 2km southwest of Sigatoka; head 2km down the dusty Kulukulu Rd, turn left at the T-junction and continue for about 1km to Kulukulu village. Club Masa is a further 200m south. Sunbeam buses depart from Sigatoka for Kulukulu six times daily.

For nice lunches, try **Le Café** (lunch around F$10) on the main street near the larger bridge. There are **bakeries** and many cheap eateries near the market and bus station, serving Chinese, Indian and Fijian meals. Self-caterers can stock up at the **Morris Hedstrom supermarket**.

Korotogo & Korolevu

Beginning at the Sigatoka River, the Coral Coast is a 45km stretch of fringing reef dropping off dramatically into deep ocean. The majority of beach along here is only suitable for swimming and snorkelling at high tide. Queens Rd between Korotogo and Korolevu is gorgeous with scenic bays, beaches and mountains views, as well as many resorts.

East of Korolevu, **Baravi Handicrafts** (☎ 652 0364; open daily) sells local crafts, clothes and jewellery.

Organised Tours You can take tours with **Adventures in Paradise** (☎ 652 0833; e wfall@ connect.com.fj), which offers day-trips to Naihehe cave for F$100 (see Sigatoka Valley later in this chapter) and F$90 tours, including a village visit, kava ceremony, lunch and transport from Coral Coast and Nadi hotels; its office is just west of Outrigger Reef Resort. Rivers Fiji pick up from Coral Coast resorts (see the Pacific Harbour section later).

Places to Stay – Budget On top of its restaurant, **Crow's Nest Resort** (dorm beds F$15) has a nice six-bed dorm (no cooking facilities), overlooking the pool. (See Places to Stay – Mid-Range later for more details.)

Tubakula Beach Bungalows (☎ 650 0097; e tubakula@fiji4less.com; dorm beds F$15, 3-person self-contained bungalows poolside/ oceanview/beachfront F$60/70/80, for renovated bungalows add F$20, all fan-cooled) is a good budget place on a decent stretch of beach. Dorms have communal cooking facilities and there are spacious gardens, a swimming pool, restaurant and bar, and mini-market.

The Beachhouse (☎ 653 0500, toll free 0800 6530 0530; e info@fijibeachouse.com; camping per person F$12, five-/three-/two-bed dorms per person F$19/22/24, garden doubles F$55, shared facilities and kitchen) offers budget-chic accommodation and a friendly atmosphere. The beachfront has a grassy area under coconut trees and a nice little stretch of white-sand beach. The on-site **Coconut Café** (breakfast/lunch/dinner F$4/7/9) has good meals, plunger coffee, smoothies (F$4) and free afternoon tea. Activities include canoeing and snorkelling. This place is very popular, so try to book ahead.

Waidroka Bay Resort (☎ 330 4605; e waid rokaresort@suva.is.com.fj; dorm beds F$18, lodge rooms per person F$55, bure doubles/triples F$100/140) is on a beautifully secluded section of the coast and caters mainly to adventurous divers and surfers. Dorm and lodge accommodation is simple and the comfortable bure have oceanfront verandas. There are no self-catering facilities but there is an on-site **restaurant** (meal packages F$40 per day, lunch under F$10 dinner F$12-18). Diving is F$110 for a two-tank dive and offshore snorkel trips are F$20 per person. Six surf breaks are nearby (F$15 per person for a boat) and it's a half-hour boat trip to Frigate Passage (F$45 per person). The resort hires out reasonably good surfboards (F$25 per day). Fishing, kayaking, hiking and village visits are also offered. Transfers from Nadi airport or from the Queens Rd turn-off can be organised if you call ahead. Expect to pay F$80 to F$100 for a taxi from Nadi.

Places to Stay – Mid-Range Just west of the Outrigger Hotel, the **Bedarra Inn** (☎ 650 0476, fax 652 0116; e bedarra@connect.com.fj; doubles F$125 including breakfast, children under 16 free) is a small hotel with a swimming pool and pleasant gardens. This is a good mid-range option for those after an intimate atmosphere. There's a separate bure for maximum privacy as well as spacious family rooms. Bedarra has the best restaurant in the area which is open to nonguests. Transfers are F$30 from Nadi airport.

Crow's Nest Resort (☎ 650 0513, fax 652 0354; e crowsnest@connect.com.fj; Korotogo; 4-person self-contained unit F$88) is 7km east of Sigatoka, on a hill across the road from the beach. Units with balconies and seaviews are a bargain. It also has dorm accommodation (see Places to Stay – Budget earlier). The resort has a nice swimming pool and a sundeck adjacent the restaurant.

Waidroka Bay Resort (bure doubles/triples F$100/140) has comfortable, fan-cooled, oceanfront bure (see Places to Stay – Budget earlier in this section).

Crusoe's Retreat (☎ 650 0185, fax 652 0666; w www.crusoesretreat.com; triples seaview/ seaside bure F$150/180) is on a beautiful, hilly beachfront setting, well off the beaten track. The spacious fan-cooled bure are comfortable and good value. Three meals a day costs around F$100 per adult. A tennis court, saltwater swimming pool, glass-bottomed boat and snorkelling equipment will keep you busy. The resort's dive shop charges F$150 for a two-tank dive or F$15 per person for offshore snorkelling trips. The resort is 5km off Queens Rd; return transfers (adult/child F$100/50) to Nadi Airport are available.

Places to Stay – Top End The giant **Outrigger Reef Resort** (☎ 650 0044, fax 652 0074; W www.outrigger.com/fiji; doubles from F$410, bure from F$480), on the Korotogo hillside, commands superb views over the coral reef. Near the 70m swimming pool are more rooms in the old Reef Resort building, revamped beyond recognition. *Bure* decorated with hand-painted *tapa* are scattered throughout the resort's gardens and along the beachfront. With three restaurants, bars, shops, a sports club, a nightclub and evening entertainment, it's a resort-lover's resort.

Hideaway Resort (☎ 650 0177, fax 652 0025; W www.hideawayfiji.com; fan cooled/air-con bure triples F$240/260, beachfront bure doubles with air-con F$310, 2-bedroom bure F$410, all including breakfast) is a popular resort on a good stretch of beach. The two-bedroom *bure* are good value for families while the spacious beachfront *bure* will suit honeymooners. With lots of amenities, entertainment, a surf break just offshore, and an excellent swimming pool, the atmosphere here is enthusiastic. Non-motorised activities are included in the tariff and diving is with SPAD-South Pacific Adventure Divers. An optional meal plan (F$40 per person per day) includes lunch and two-course dinner.

The Naviti Resort (☎ 653 0444, fax 653 0099; W www.navitiresort.com.fj; mountainview/oceanview doubles F$190/220, including 2 children) is popular with families, with good wheelchair and pram access. A hilly backdrop protects the beach and the resort's small, private island. Meal packages are F$60 per adult. Lots of activities and non-motorised sports (including golf, tennis, horse riding and windsurfing) are included in the price. The Naviti is a few kilometres west of Korolevu.

Places to Eat For excellent dining and scrumptious meals, head to **Bedarra Inn Restaurant** (☎ 650 0476; mains F$14-30). The restaurant has pick-up and drop-off services for guests of local hotels.

Le Café (☎ 652 0877; Korotogo; dishes around F$10; open 4pm-10pm daily), just west of the shops, has a Swiss chef who whips up tasty pizzas and European-style food.

Coconut Café (☎ 653 0500; breakfast F$3-5.50, lunch/dinner F$7/9), at the Beachhouse

near Korolevu, is a popular spot with backpackers and a nice place for a break if you are travelling along the Coral Coast. It has good coffee and fresh-fruit smoothies. For dinner, place an order before 4pm.

Vilisite's Restaurant (☎ 653 0054), near the Naviti Hotel, serves à la carte and set-menu dishes on a veranda overlooking the water. Octopus and fish fillets are F$19.50, while a meal of king prawns is F$32.

Getting There & Away The Korotogo area is about 8km east of Sigatoka, while Korolevu village is 31km east of Sigatoka. See Getting Around under Viti Levu earlier.

Pacific Harbour

East of Korolevu, the vegetation turns greener and denser as Queens Rd hugs the coast to Pacific Harbour. A planned, upmarket housing development that never took off, Pacific Harbour has meandering drives, canals, a golf course, many, many vacant lots and plenty of rain. Most people come here for the awesome surf-break, the world-class diving at nearby Beqa Lagoon, or the spectacular Namosi Highlands in Pacific Harbour's backyard (see Namosi Highlands).

Things to See Take a sunset walk up to the hilltop for a lovely view of Beqa Lagoon. The **Fijian Cultural Centre & Marketplace** (☎ 345 0177), about 1km east of Pacific Harbour International Resort, has seen better days. Geared towards tour groups by the busload, it has a few gift shops and provides a quick caricature of Fijian history. Children may enjoy taking the **Lake Tour** in a *drua* (double-hulled canoe) around the small islands and mock village. There are also fire-walking and *meke* performances on Tuesdays, Thursdays and Saturdays.

Activities Pacific Harbour International Resort allows visitors to use its facilities and join tours. Dinghy sailing, windsurfing or glass-bottomed boat coral viewing costs F$15 and a one-hour horse ride is F$10/15 per child/adult. Cruises to offshore Yanuca are F$60 per person.

About 2km inland, you can practice your swing around the lakes and canals of the **Pacific Harbour Golf & Country Club** (☎ 345 0048). Green fees are F$20/25 for nine/18 holes.

Frigate Passage is a surfer's haven. There are also surf camps on Yanuca (see that section later).

Diving The well-established **Aqua-Trek** (☎ *345 0324, 670 2413 Nadi;* ⓔ *aquatrekbeqa@connect. com.fj),* at Pacific Harbour International, offers two-tank dives for F$160, with dive packages making it much cheaper. Open-water courses are F$600. **Aquacadabra** (☎ *3450 911;* ⓔ *info@ aquacadabradiving.com)* is quickly gaining a good reputation as a reliable operator, with new, fancy equipment. **Dive Connections** (☎ *345 0541;* ⓔ *diveconn@connect.com.fj; 16 River Dr)* offers two-tank dive (including lunch) for F$130 and the open-water course is F$395, though a number of readers have been very unimpressed with their safety standards.

River Tours Based at Pacific Harbour, **Rivers Fiji** (☎ *345 0147, mobile phone 999 2349;* ⓦ *www .riversfiji.com)* offers excellent kayaking and rafting trips to the Namosi Highlands. **Wilderness Ethnic Adventure Fiji** (☎ *338 7594, fax 330 0084)* takes tours to Navua River, picking up passengers from Pacific Harbour and Suva hotels (see Organised Tours under Suva). **Discover Fiji Tours** (☎ *345 0180, fax 345 0549;* ⓦ *www.dis coverfijitours.com)* based in Navua, has several tours to the Navua River area, included guided hikes across the Namosi Highlands.

Places to Stay Located conveniently on the canal, **Pacific Safari Club** (☎ *345 0498, toll free 0800 345 0498; dorm beds F$18, self-contained singles/doubles F$40/45)* has spacious and comfortable rooms and friendly, helpful management. Turn inland on River Dr, opposite Pacific Harbour International Resort, and take the first left.

Accommodation at **Dive Connections'** self-contained flat (☎ *345 0541;* ⓔ *diveconn@ connect.com.fj; singles/doubles F$30/40),* next to the office, is great value.

Club Coral Coast (☎ *345 0421;* ⓔ *clubcoral coast@connect.com.fj; budget doubles F$25, doubles/triples F$70/100)* has a nice swimming pool and tennis court. Family rooms can be good value but budget rooms are tight with shared facilities. Turn inland on River Dr, opposite Pacific Harbour International Resort, cross the canal and turn left at Belo Circle.

Pacific Harbour International Hotel (☎ *345 0022, fax 345 0262;* ⓔ *centrapacharb@connect .com.fj; doubles F$143 plus F$25 per extra adult, suites F$275)* dates from the early 70s and has spacious grounds, a swimming pool, fairly standard air-con rooms and lots of activities, including tennis, windsurfing, snorkelling and a kids' club. Most activities cost extra. The dark-sand beach is all right for swimming.

Pacific Harbour Villas (☎*/fax 345 0959;* ⓔ *hps@fijirealty.com; nightly/fortnightly villas F$100/600)* are spacious, modern houses on quiet streets around the golf course and can be a good option for families with their own transport.

Places to Eat Stop in at **Kumaran's Restaurant and Milk Bar** (☎ *345 0294; mains F$5-12),* across from Pacific Harbour International, for a tasty roti parcel or other cheap and simple Indian, Chinese and Fijian dishes. There are a couple of inexpensive **takeaways** in the Fijian Cultural Centre & Marketplace as well as the **Oasis Restaurant** (☎ *450 617; mains from F$15; open lunch & dinner)* which has burgers and sandwiches from F$4.50 to F$7.

Loraini's Restaurant (☎ *345 0544; Deuba Inn, Queens Rd, Deuba; mains under F$10)* has good value curries, Chinese and European dishes and very friendly service. It also has a bar with happy hour from 6pm to 7pm.

Nautilis Restaurant *(meals F$12.50-22.50),* at Pacific Harbour International Hotel, welcomes visitors.

There is a supermarket in the Cultural Centre, a good produce market in Navua, and roadside stalls selling fruit and vegetables.

Getting There & Away Pacific Harbour is 78km east of Sigatoka and 49km west of Suva. It's about an hour's express bus ride from Suva and three hours from Nadi. See Getting There & Away at the beginning of the Viti Levu section.

ISLANDS OFF SOUTHERN VITI LEVU

Offshore from Pacific Harbour, a 64km-long barrier reef encloses the large **Beqa Lagoon** and the islands of Beqa and Yanuca. The lagoon is popular with divers for world-famous sites like Side Streets and Caesar's Rocks, while surfers head for the huge left-hand waves at **Frigate Passage**.

Beqa
area 36 sq km
Volcanic and rugged, Beqa is known for its onshore villages that practice traditional firewalking, and for its fantastic offshore dive sites.

Lawaki Beach House (☎ *992 1621;* ⓔ *info@ lawakibeachhouse.com; Lawaki; dorm beds F$70, double bure per person F$80, including meals),* a new budget place on the southwestern side of the island, can accommodate a maximum of 10 people. There's good snorkelling off a secluded white-sand beach and the owners can arrange village trips for interested guests. Payments are by cash only. Transfers are by small, local boats from Navua (about F$100) or try to join a local village boat to Beqa for F$15 per person (see the Dangers & Annoyances section earlier).

On the western side of the island, **Marlin Bay Resort** (☎ 330 4042, fax 330 4028; ⓦ www.marlin bay.com; double bure F$400) caters mostly for divers on prebooked packages with luxury air-con *bure*, a large restaurant-lounge and a pool on a coconut-tree-fringed beach. Meal plans are F$110 per person per day. Rates include snorkelling, kayaking, unlimited shore diving, hiking to waterfalls and village visits. Two-tank dive trips cost F$160. Boat transfers from Pacific Harbour are F$100 per person return.

Yanuca

Not to be confused with Yanuca near Sigatoka (Shangri-La's Fijian Resort), this small island with beautiful beaches is 9km west of Beqa, with **Frigates Passage** surf break to the south.

Batiluva (☎ 343 1019, 992 0019; ⓔ batiluva@ pacific-harbour.com; dorm beds F$100, double bure F$220) is a surf camp offering fairly comfortable accommodation in a large 12-bed dorm *bure* or in the 'love shack' (minimum stay two nights). The beach here is pretty but for a good snorkel you need to go on a short boat trip. 'Gourmet jungle meals' and daily

boat trips to the surf break are included in the price.

Frigate Surfriders (☎ 345 0801, 925 3097; surfers/nonsurfers camping or dorm beds F$75/ 35, includes meals & daily surf trips), run by a local surfer, is a basic surf camp on a small white-sand beach. Sleep in a beach-hut dorm or pitch your own tent for the same price. Snorkelling, diving, canoeing and hiking can be arranged.

Transfers between Pacific Harbour and Yanuca are by small boat (F$40 return).

SUVA
pop 358 495

Nestled on the harbour with views to the surrounding mountains, Suva (pronounced s*oo*-va) is one of the most laid-back capitals you're likely to come across. Its wooden, colonial buildings, friendly population and nearly cosmopolitan air make it worth a day or two of your time. Take in the museum, lounge in the cafés, check out the nightlife or head out to the nearby Colo-i-Suva Park for a quiet escape into the lush rainforest.

Suva is Fiji's political and administrative capital and home to about half of the county's population. As the largest city in the South Pacific, Suva has become an important regional centre with the University of the South Pacific, the Forum Secretariat and many embassies to prove it. As with most cities, urbanisation has also brought new difficulties – crime and poverty have increased in recent years and around

---

Dining on the Dead

Fijians began feasting upon one another as far back as 2500 years ago. In traditional Fijian society, dining on the enemy was considered the ultimate revenge. A disrespectful death was a lasting insult to the enemy's family and the departed spirit. When missionaries brought cannibalism to a halt in the late 19th century, it had become an ordinary, ritualised part of life. Bodies were either consumed on the battlefield or brought back to the village spirit house, where they were butchered, baked and eaten on the local war god's behalf. In celebration of the event, men performed the *cibi* (death dance) and women the *dele* – a dance in which they sexually humiliated corpses. Captives were often forced to watch their own body parts being consumed or even to eat some themselves!

For cannibalistic feasts, men fed themselves with special long-pronged wooden forks. Considered sacred relics, these forks were kept in the spirit house away from women or children. Mementos were kept of the victims to prolong the victor's sense of vengeance. Necklaces, hairpins or earlobe ornaments were made from human bones and skulls were sometimes made into *tanoa* (kava drinking bowls). Flesh was smoked and preserved for snacks, and war clubs were inlaid with teeth. Viti Levu Highlanders placed the bones of victims in tree branches as trophies and rows of stones were used to tally the number of bodies eaten by the chief.

Early European visitors and settlers were understandably obsessed with cannibalism. Those who managed to keep their wits and limbs about them recorded gruesome, fascinating stories.

CENTRAL SUVA

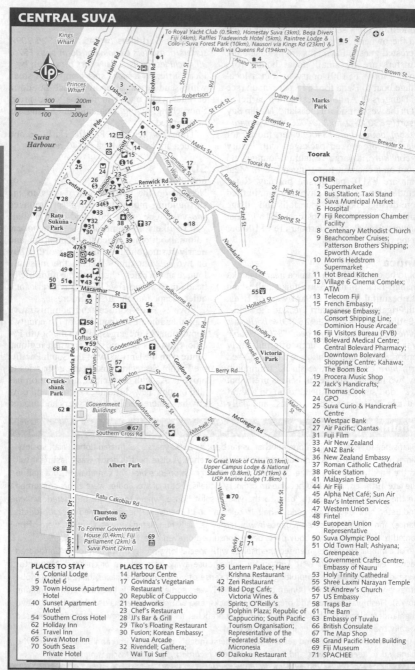

OTHER
1 Supermarket
2 Bus Station; Taxi Stand
3 Suva Municipal Market
6 Hospital
7 Fiji Recompression Chamber Facility
8 Centenary Methodist Church
9 Beachcomber Cruises; Patterson Brothers Shipping; Epworth Arcade
10 Morris Hedstrom Supermarket
11 Hot Bread Kitchen
12 Village 6 Cinema Complex; ATM
13 Telecom Fiji
15 French Embassy; Japanese Embassy; Consort Shipping Line; Dominion House Arcade
16 Fiji Visitors Bureau (FVB)
18 Bolevard Medical Centre; Central Bolevard Pharmacy; Downtown Bolevard Shopping Centre; Kahawa; The Boom Box
19 Procera Music Shop
22 Jack's Handicrafts; Thomas Cook
24 GPO
25 Suva Curio & Handicraft Centre
26 Westpac Bank
27 Air Pacific; Qantas
31 Fuji Film
33 Air New Zealand
34 ANZ Bank
36 New Zealand Embassy
37 Roman Catholic Cathedral
38 Police Station
41 Malaysian Embassy
44 Air Fiji
45 Alpha Net Café; Sun Air
46 Bav's Internet Services
47 Western Union
48 Fintel
49 European Union Representative
50 Suva Olympic Pool
51 Old Town Hall; Ashiyana; Greenpeace
52 Government Crafts Centre; Embassy of Nauru
53 Holy Trinity Cathedral
55 Shree Laxmi Narayan Temple
57 US Embassy
58 Traps Bar
61 The Barn
63 Embassy of Tuvalu
66 British Consulate
67 The Map Shop
68 Grand Pacific Hotel Building
69 Fiji Museum
71 SPACHEE

PLACES TO STAY
4 Colonial Lodge
5 Motel 6
39 Town House Apartment Hotel
40 Sunset Apartment Motel
54 Southern Cross Hotel
62 Holiday Inn
64 Travel Inn
65 Suva Motor Inn
70 South Seas Private Hotel

PLACES TO EAT
14 Harbour Centre
17 Govinda's Vegetarian Restaurant
20 Republic of Cuppuccino
21 Headworks
23 Chef's Restaurant
28 JJ's Bar & Grill
29 Tiko's Floating Restaurant
30 Fusion; Korean Embassy; Vanua Arcade
32 Rivendell; Gathera; Wai Tui Surf
35 Lantern Palace; Hare Krishna Restaurant
42 Zen Restaurant
43 Bad Dog Café; Victoria Wines & Spirits; O'Reilly's
59 Dolphin Plaza; Republic of Cappuccino; South Pacific Tourism Organisation; Representative of the Federated States of Micronesia
60 Daikoku Restaurant

half of Suva's inhabitants are crowded into settlements on land that has no title.

On a less serious but equally grey note, clouds tend to hover over Suva and frequently dump rain on the city (around 300mm each year) – often a welcome relief to the heat and humidity.

History
In the 1850s Chief Cakobau proclaimed himself Tui Viti (King of Fiji) and began to trade bits and pieces of Fiji with foreign settlers who began arriving in the country in the mid-1800s. The only Europeans in the Suva area hailed from Melbourne, seeking new sources of fortune after the decline of the Australian gold rushes. In 1868 the Australians agreed to pay off Cakobau's inflated debts with American immigrants in return for trade sanctions and a large chunk of land, 9000 hectares of which covered the Suva Peninsula.

The powerful Chief Cakobau forced Fijian villagers already living on the peninsula to relocate. New Australian settlers arrived in 1870 and tried growing cotton and sugar cane in what is now downtown Suva. While their farming attempts flopped, land value was increased by encouraging the government to relocate the capital from Levuka to Suva in 1882. By the 1920s Suva was a flourishing colonial centre.

The capital most recently hit international headlines in May 2000 when George Speight and his military entourage held the government hostage in Suva's Parliament Buildings (see the History section under Facts about Fiji).

Orientation
Suva is on a peninsula, with the downtown area facing the protected Suva Harbour to the west. Apart from the relatively flat downtown area, the peninsula is hilly. There are three major roads in and out of the city: Queens Rd via Lami to the west, Princes Rd along the Tamavua ridge to the north and Kings Rd heading northeast towards Nausori.

Suva's downtown area is along Victoria Pde, parallel to the waterfront. If you continue south, you'll pass the Government Buildings, Albert Park and Thurston Gardens, where Victoria Pde becomes Queen Elizabeth Dr. This then passes Government House and winds all the way around Suva Point at the tip of the peninsula. Queen Elizabeth Dr finishes on the eastern side of the peninsula at Laucala Bay, near the University of the South Pacific and the National Stadium.

Maps Around the back of the Government Buildings, **The Map Shop** (☎ 321 1395; Room 10, Department of Lands and Surveys; open 8am-1pm & 2pm-3.30 Mon-Fri, closes 3pm Fri) stocks a good map of Suva and its surrounding areas as well as large, detailed survey maps of the rest of Fiji.

Information
Tourist Offices The best source of information is the Fiji Visitors Bureau (☎ 330 2433, fax 330 0970; W www.bulafiji.com; cnr Thomson & Scott Sts; open 8am-4.30pm Mon-Thur, 8am-4pm Fri, 8am-noon Sat), where friendly staff stock countless brochures for Suva and the surrounding area.

The **South Pacific Tourism Organisation** (☎ 330 4177, fax 330 1995; W www.spto.org; 3rd floor, Dolphin Plaza, Victoria Pde) also has an office in Suva.

Money To change money or travellers cheques, head to **Westpac Bank** (☎ 330 0666; 1 Thomson St), **ANZ bank** (☎ 330 1755; 25 Victoria Pde) or **Thomas Cook** (☎ 330 1603; 21 Thomson St). Westpac has an ATM outside the Village 6 Cinema Complex and ANZ has ATMs and will also do credit card advances. Banking hours are 9.30am to 3pm Monday to Thursday (Friday to 4pm). Some hotels, including the budget South Seas Private Hotel and Travel Inn, will change travellers cheques for guests at bank rates. For money in a hurry, **Western Union** (☎ 331 4812; cnr Victoria Pde & Gordon St; 8am-4.45pm Mon-Fri, 8am-1.45pm Sat) does worldwide money transfers.

Post & Communications There are a number of cardphones, including outside the GPO. From **Fintel** (☎ 331 2933, fax 330 1025; 158 Victoria Pde; open 8am-8pm Mon-Sat) you can make international calls and send faxes and telegrams. You can also call home from **Telecom Fiji** (☎ 311 2233; Victoria Pde; open 8.30am-4.30pm Mon-Thur, 8.30am-4pm Fri).

Internet cafés will soon be as common as curries in Suva. **Bav's Internet Services** (Victoria Pde; per min/hr F$0.10/5; open 8am-10pm Mon-Thur, 8am-1am Fri & Sat, 9am-8pm Sun) has a fairly speedy connection. **Alpha Net Café** (☎ 330 0211; Victoria Pde; per min F$0.10; open 8am-8pm Mon-Thur, 8am-5pm Fri & Sat, 10am-4pm Sun) offers Internet access and also repairs laptops. **Fintel** (see earlier; per min F$0.15) has a number of well-connected computers; you purchase your time on-line via debit cards in denominations of 15/30/60/120 mins.

There's a number of laid-back coffee houses around Suva that offer Internet access. Try **Republic of Cappuccino** *(per min F$0.15, F$1 minimum charge)* or **Kahawa** *(per min F$0.20)*.

Bookshops The **USP Book Centre** *(☎ 321 2500, fax 330 3265; University of the South Pacific;* **W** *www.uspbookcentre.com)* is stocked with a fantastic selection of local and international novels, Lonely Planet guides and books covering everything from land rights to legends of the Pacific region (many published by USP's Institute of Pacific Studies). Other than a sale table of random novels, it's all a bit pricey but the pickings are superb. You can order books online from their website; they'll courier them to your doorstep overseas.

The gift shop at the Fiji Museum (see later) also has a fairly good selection of Fijian history and cultural books (many no longer in print outside of Fiji) as well as cookbooks and bird books from the area.

Medical Services The **Boulevard Medical Centre** *(☎ 331 3355, fax 330 2423; 33 Ellery St)* is open from 8.30am to 5pm weekdays and 8.30am to 11.30am Saturdays.

For prescriptions and other medical provisions try **Central Boulevard Pharmacy** *(☎ 330 3770; Shop 13, Downtown Boulevard Shopping Centre)*. Opening hours are 8.30am to 5.30pm Monday to Thursday, 8.30am to 6pm Friday and 8.30am to 1pm Saturdays.

The **Colonial War Memorial Hospital** *(☎ 331 3444)* is located on Waimanu Rd. If your illness is the result of ascending too quickly from a dive, contact **Fiji Recompression Chamber Facility** *(☎ 885 0630, fax 885 0344; Corner of Amy & Brewster Sts)*.

Emergency In the event of an emergency, some useful numbers are:

Ambulance	☎ 3301 439
Emergency	☎ 000
Fiji Recompression Chamber	☎ 3362 172
FVB Emergency Hotline	☎ 0800 721 721
Police	☎ 3311 222
Tourist Police	☎ 3302 433 + 215

Dangers & Annoyances Despite its small size, Suva suffers many of the same dangers as most urbanised centres. Pickpockets roam, so keep your valuables out of sight, particularly in crowded areas like the market or dance floors. As night descends, be sure to follow the locals' lead and take taxis everywhere; cab fares are cheap and muggings are common.

Things to See

Suva's downtown area has a number of colonial buildings, making it a pleasant place to stroll. It's also worth wandering along the seawall walk south of town for views of the mountains. The walk is lined with dramatic, old jungle-like trees, and at low-tide you'll see an abundance of crabs and fish in tidal pools.

The bustling **Suva Municipal Market** *(Rodwell Rd; open mornings Mon-Sat)* is definitely worth a gander and is a great place to buy kava for village visits. Vendors sell exotic fruit and vegetables, *nama* (seaweed), multi-coloured fish, bound crabs, pungent spices and neon Indian sweets.

The impressive **Government Buildings** (1939 and 1967), at the end of Carnarvon St, are set on heavy foundations atop reclaimed land. The Department of Lands & Survey was the scene of the 1987 coup. Some departments and the courts remain here, while the rest of government moved to the new **Parliament Buildings** *(☎ 330 5811; Battery Rd)* in 1992. Apparently, these premises are just as prone to coups, as proven by George Speight in 2000. If you'd like to visit, you must phone first; unexpected guests will be turned away.

Albert Park *(Victoria Pde)* is where the aviator Kingford Smith landed on the first plane journey across the Pacific. Opposite the park is the imposing and somewhat haunted looking **Grand Pacific Hotel** (1914). Built by the Union Steamship Company, its ship-style architecture is now dilapidated.

Thurston Gardens (1913) is a peaceful place to wander. The gardens were closed at the time of writing but due to reopen in the near future.

With beautiful lawns, the USP's main **Laucala Campus** *(☎ 331 3900; USP;* **W** *www.usp.ac.fj)* is also pleasant spot. Inside the northwestern entrance, on the right, is a small botanical garden with trails winding around Pacific trees and plants. Also on campus, the **USP Oceania Centre** has temporary local art exhibits; you may even catch an artist at work. The university's main entrance is off Laucala Bay Rd, about a 15-minute drive from downtown Suva. Hop on a Raiwaga bus from Victoria Pde.

Fiji Museum Full of excellent exhibits and well-maintained artefacts, the Fiji Museum *(☎ 3315 944;* **e** *fijimuseum@connect.com.fj; Ratu Cakobau Rd; adult/child F$3.30/free; open 9.30am-4pm Mon-Sat)* is well worth a few hours of your time. With excellent descriptions, the museum takes you through the history of Fiji's peoples, cultures, languages, animal life, pottery and more recent migration, as well as more gory accounts of warfare and cannibalism. Beyond the shop is a larger, two-storey wing that looks at early traders and settlers, blackbirding and Indian indenture. Upstairs is the small **Indo-Fijian Gallery** with local, contemporary artwork.

Colo-i-Suva Forest Park For a tranquil escape from the hustle and heat of the city, wander deep into the wilds of this lush rainforest – complete with clear pools of water, singing birds and gorgeous vistas. The 245 hectare Colo-i-Suva Forest Park (pronounced tholo-ee-**soo**-va) (☎ 332 0211; admission adult/ child F$5/0.50; open 8am-4pm Mon-Sun) has 6.5km of excellently maintained walking trails, complete with Indiana Jones-esque rope swings and stone steps across streams. There are three natural swimming holes, picnic tables, shelters and change rooms. Home to 14 different species, the park is a hotspot for bird watching; keep your eyes open for the scarlet robin, spotted fantail, golden dove and the barking pigeon.

The park is 11km north of Suva on Princes Rd. The Visitor Information Centre is on the left side of the road as you approach from Suva; buy your ticket here and then head over the road to the entrance booth. The park receives rain approximately four days each week; the trails can be extremely slippery so be sure to wear good footwear. To reach the park, catch the regular Sawani bus from Suva bus station (20 mins, F$0.65). If you drive out to the park, leave any valuables at the Visitor Information Centre, not in your car, as robberies are not unheard of.

Activities

Seldom crowded, the giant, outdoor **Suva Olympic Pool** (224 Victoria Pde; open 10am-6pm Mon-Fri & 8am-6pm Sat Apr-Sept; 9am-7pm Mon-Fri & 7am-7pm Sat Oct-Mar), is an oasis on a hot day. Entry is fantastically cheap – adults get in for F$1.65 and children (13 years and under) for F$0.80.

Beqa Divers Fiji (☎ 336 1088, fax 336 1047; 75 Marine Dr, Lami) run dive trips to Beqa Lagoon, rent out gear and run diving courses, including Open Water PADI (F$495), Rescue Diver (F$420) and PADI Dive Master (F$880). The Holiday Inn can organise dive trips to Beqa Lagoon with **Aqua-Trek**, based at Pacific Harbour (see that section earlier).

For surfers, there's a break near Suva lighthouse, accessible by boat; the **Fiji Surf Association** (☎ 336 1358) may be able to give some advice on how to get out there and local conditions.

Visiting yachties can get membership at the **Royal Suva Yacht Club** (☎ 331 2921, fax 330 4433; ℮ rsyc@connect.com.fj; office open 9am-1pm & 2pm-4pm Mon-Fri, 9am-1pm Sat). Mooring fees are F$50 for the first day and F$15 per day thereafter. Even without a yacht, overseas visitors are welcome. Its **bar** (open 8am-10pm Mon-Thur, 8am-midnight Fri & Sat) is a popular watering hole and has great views of the bay and surrounding mountains.

Organised Tours

Wilderness Ethnic Adventure Fiji (☎ 331 5730, fax 331 5450; ₩ www.wilderness.com.fj) does pick-ups from Suva hotels for rafting and canoeing tours (F$99/60 adult/child) on Navua River, half-day tours to Nasilai village (F$49/33 adult/child) and city tours of Suva (F$79/44 adult/child).

Adventure Fiji can organise four- to six-day highland hikes, following a route used by missionaries since 1849. Accommodation and meals are in villages along the route. The hike is run from May to October; visit the tour desk at the Holiday Inn for more information.

Places to Stay – Budget

On the edge of the rainforest **Raintree Lodge** (☎ 332 0562, fax 332 0113; ℮ raintreelodge@ connect.com.fj; Princes Rd, Colo-i-Suva; camping/ dorms/doubles F$10/18-20/50, all with shared facilities and kitchens) offers Suva's best budget accommodation. The wooden dorms are cosy and the surroundings are gorgeous, although camping can be a muddy ordeal in the rain. Once the site of a quarry, the pit has been transformed into a lake, complete with grass carp and telapia fish. Facilities include fishing, volleyball, canoeing, swimming, and mountain bikes (free with deposit). There's a lakeside lovo on Sundays, kava sessions many evenings and a bar with great cocktails and a pool table. Staff are fantastically friendly, the atmosphere is relaxed and the restaurant is superb (see Places to Eat later in this section). The lodge also offers upmarket bure (see Places to Stay – Top-End later in this section). Raintree Lodge is about 10km from Suva, next door to Colo-i-Suva Park. It's a cool retreat from the city but don't forget your bug repellent. Catch the Sawani bus from Suva's bus terminal (20 mins; F$0.65).

FIJI

Colonial Lodge (*☎/fax 330 0655; 19 Anand St; dorms/singles/doubles with shared facilities F$17/38/48, singles/doubles with private bathroom F$50/60, all including breakfast*) is the best option if you want to stay closer to town. Run by a friendly family, the restored colonial home has a large veranda where you can lounge in a hammock. Private rooms upstairs are much brighter than those downstairs (with the exception of the comfortable double with private bathroom). The lodge is a 20-minute walk from town but the area is notorious for muggings; make sure you get a taxi after dark. The lodge has two dogs to keep you safe; unfortunately they may also wake you up at night.

Sunset Apartment Motel (*☎ 330 1799, fax 330 3446; cnr Gordon and Murray Sts; dorms/singles/doubles F$9/42/48*) is a few minutes downtown. Dorms are clean and an excellent deal with shared facilities, a kitchen, 24-hour reception and individual lockers. Private rooms are basic but pleasant with a balcony, private bathroom, fridge and TV.

South Seas Private Hotel (*☎ 331 2296, fax 330 8646; e southseas@fiji4less.com; 6 Williamson Rd; dorms/singles/doubles F$12/19/28*) is somewhat reminiscent of a 1940s asylum building however, with a big garden and comfy lounge, it's an old standby in Suva. Dorms are basic but clean; private rooms are bare and a little rundown. Payment is in full on arrival, cash only, although the hotel exchanges travellers cheques at bank rates.

Travel Inn (*☎ 330 5254, fax 330 8646; e travel inn@fiji4less.com; singles/doubles/triples F$22/30/39, self-contained flats F$60*) is conveniently located on a quiet street, an easy walk to the city centre. The quaint, old u-shaped building looks like a 1950s motel. Rooms are fan-cooled and paired to share a bathroom and a small stoveless kitchen area. Payment is cash only on arrival.

Places to Stay - Mid-Range

USP Upper Campus Lodge (*☎ 321 2614, 321 2639, fax 331 4827; e usplodges@usp.ac.fj; singles/doubles with shared facilities F$39/45, self-contained singles/doubles F$54/64*) has fantastic bungalow-style units with balconies overlooking the botanical gardens. Comfortable and self-contained with kettles, toasters and microwaves (but no stoves), this is an excellent deal. As a guest, you also gain access to the university's sports facilities. Rooms inside the lodge with shared facilities are clean and spacious but lacking character. The lodge is on the right as you enter through the uni's

northwest entrance. The **USP Marine Lodge** (*same contact as above; singles/doubles F$44/59*) is further down the road. Rooms are bright and clean with views of the sea. Doubles have kitchens and all rooms have bathrooms. Reception is at the Upper Campus Lodge.

Town House Apartment Hotel (*☎ 330 0055, fax 330 3446; 3 Forster St; singles/doubles standard F$48/60, singles/doubles one-bedroom apartment F$60/70, extra adult F$12*) has clean apartments with kitchen facilities, a balcony with good views and cheery decor from the 50s. Standard rooms aren't quite as nice, with a wee balcony but no view.

Motel 6 (*☎ 330 7477, fax 330 7133; 1 Walu St; standard/deluxe F$44/55, family room F$77-88, all with private bathroom*), off Waimanu Rd, has new, clean rooms and helpful staff. What they're lacking in character, they make up for with balconies and views of the harbour. Reception is through an unmarked orange door.

Suva Motor Inn (*☎ 331 3973, fax 330 0381; e suvamotoinn@connect.com.fj; cnr Mitchell & Gorrie Sts; standard/2-bedroom flats F$90/155*) has spacious, tidy rooms with no frills but lots of light. Apartments have kitchen facilities and are built around a courtyard with a pool and waterslide. It's good value if you're travelling in a group as standard rooms sleep three and two-bedroom flats sleep six.

Places to Stay - Top End

Homestay Suva (*☎ 337 0395, fax 337 0947; e homestaysuva@connect.com.fj; 265 Princes Rd, Tamavua; doubles in house downstairs/upstairs F$150/160; singles/doubles in annex F$160/180, including breakfast*) is a fabulous place to rest travel-weary bones. This gorgeous colonial house is on Tamavua Ridge, with spectacular views over Suva Harbour. Rooms are beautiful, plush and extremely comfortable. Home-cooked dinners are available on request. Book in advance (no young children).

Raintree Lodge (*☎ 332 0562, fax 332 0113; e raintreelodge@connect.com.fj; Princes Rd, Colo-i-Suva; single & double bure/family bure F$110/165, extra person F$28*) has beautiful bure set in the rainforest. Each has a balcony with its own private view of the lake and the beds are as comfortable as clouds. The family bure sleeps a maximum of ten people with a loft for children. For a description of facilities see Places to Stay - Budget earlier in this section.

Southern Cross Hotel (*☎ 331 4233, fax 330 2901; 63 Gordon St; singles & doubles without/with breakfast F$120/135*) is being transformed into one of Suva's finest hotels.

Polished mahogany floors and panelled walls give rooms a warm, posh country-club feel. Each room has a balcony and there's a pool in the central courtyard.

Holiday Inn (☎ 330 1600, fax 330 0251; e reservations@holidayinnSuva.com.fj; standard/superior F$175/275) has a great location on the southern edge of town. Rooms are cool, spacious and clean but somewhat worn. The bar and garden are also showing a bit of wear and tear but have an excellent view of the sea.

Raffles Tradewinds Hotel (☎ 336 2450, fax 336 1464; Queens Rd, Lami; standard/deluxe F$80/120, 1 child under 16 free in standard, 2 in deluxe) has outlived its heyday – its glamour is somewhat frayed and its decor definitely tilts towards the 60s. Nevertheless, it's comfortable, has beautiful views of the sailboats in the harbour and staff are friendly. There's a small pool and bar next to the water. Deluxe rooms are bigger and brighter. The hotel operates a water taxi to Suva (F$44 per person), bay cruises and fishing trips.

Places to Eat

Restaurants While not known for its restaurant scene, dining options in Suva are definitely improving.

Raintree Lodge (☎ 332 0562, fax 332 0113; Princes Rd, Colo-i-Suva; breakfast/lunch or dinner F$10/15) has an excellent restaurant where you can dine amid the trees over the quarry-cum-lake. The service is stellar and the menu has Fijian dishes, mixed grills, curries and fresh fish with tasty marinades. There are good veggie options and the pancakes at breakfast are a must. There is also a kids' menu, unique (if pricey) cocktails and cheesecake for dessert. To get there, see Places to Stay earlier in this section.

JJ's Bar & Grill (☎ 330 5005; Stinson Pde; light meals from F$9, lunch/dinner under F$18), next to Ratu Sukuna Park, is very popular with Suva's upwardly mobile crowd and resident expats. The atmosphere is American casual-dining and the food is excellent, particularly the fresh seafood. Outside on the patio you can enjoy sea views and snacks.

Tiko's Floating Restaurant (☎ 331 3626; open noon-2pm & 5pm-10pm Mon-Sat; mains F$25) is one of Suva's most atmospheric dining options. The anchored cruising vessel rocks in time to the live local music. The menu includes lobster, prawns, curried or grilled fish, teriyaki steak, chicken and vegetarian dishes. Value isn't fantastic but the bar is well stocked and the sea breezes are worth the splurge.

Chef's Restaurant (☎ 330 8556; Victoria Pde; lunch/dinner F$16/32; open 11am-2pm & 6pm-9.30pm Mon-Sat) may be lacking atmosphere, but it's regarded as Suva's top restaurant by many Suvanese. The menu is certainly more exciting than the decor, with Tex Mex, Indian and pasta dishes for lunch and seafood dishes like slow-roasted snapper for dinner.

Indo-Fijian There are enough hole-in-the-wall curry houses in Suva to set your head spinning and your mouth watering. This is where those on tight budgets can eat like kings.

Ashiyana (☎ 331 3000; Old Town Hall Bldg, Victoria Pde; mains F$9; open 11.30am-2.30pm & 6pm-10pm Tues-Sat, 6pm-9.30pm Sun) feels like an Indian diner. From your booth you can feast on tandoori, veggie thali or the F$6 lunch special. Wash it all down with an excellent cup of chai.

Hare Krishna (☎ 331 4154; cnr Pratt and Joske Sts; mains F$2; open 9am-7.30pm Mon-Thur, 9am-9pm Fri, 9am-3.30pm Sat) is popular with local Indo-Fijians for its vegetarian curries and samosas and even more so for its homemade ice cream (F$1.25/2.60 small/large). Service is canteen-style.

Govinda's Vegetarian Restaurant (☎ 330 9587; 93 Cummings St; Thali Combo F$6.50; open 9am-7pm Mon-Fri, 9am-3pm Sat) is a friendly canteen serving up dosas (savoury crisp Indian crepes), curries and Indian sweets.

Chinese Suva's most stylish Chinese restaurant, the **Great Wok of China** (☎ 330 1285; cnr Bau St & Laucala Bay Rd, Flagstaff; dishes around F$25; open noon-2pm & 6.30pm-10pm Mon-Fri, 6.30pm-10pm Sat & Sun), serves a huge range of spicy Sichuanese dishes. Relax amongst the bamboo screens and, if you're brave, fill up on delicacies like bêche-de-mer.

Lantern Palace (☎ 331 4795; 10 Pratt St; mains F$10; open 11.30am-2.30pm & 5pm-10pm Mon-Sat, 5pm-10pm Sun) serves reliable, good-value dishes. It's a bit dark but extremely popular with customers who crowd around big, round tables to feast on seafood, chop suey and Mongolian sizzling grills. Set menus for four to eight people are around F$16 per person.

Japanese For excellent Japanese food, it is definitely worth splashing out at **Daikoku Restaurant** (☎ 330 8968; Victoria Pde; mains F$15). Sip Japanese beer (F$6.50) or sake (F$5.50) as professional teppanyaki chefs whip up a

FIJI

gourmet, sizzling feast at your table. Sushi, tempura and sashimi are all delicious. Bring your own wine for an F$8 corkage fee.

Zen Restaurant (☎ *330 6314; level 1, Pacific House, Butt St; mains around F$15, lunch special F$7; open 11.30am-2.30pm & 6pm-9pm Mon-Fri, 11.30am-2.30pm Sat)* offers casual dining on its covered deck. Specialities include smoked sashimi and Japanese curry. The lunch special is a serious bargain.

Cafés & Snack Bars With some of the best coffees in town, **Republic of Cappuccino** (☎ *330 0333; Renwick Rd; coffees F$3; open 7am-11pm Mon-Sat, 10am-7pm Sun)* is a popular hangout. Enjoy a latte, fresh juice or cake on a comfy couch while you read the café's newspapers and magazines. There's a smaller outlet in Dolphin Plaza on Victoria Pde.

Kahawa (☎ *330 9671; Plaza One, Downtown Blvd Shopping Centre, Ellery St; drinks F$3; open 7am-6pm Mon-Thur, 7am-4pm Fri & Sat, 7am-1pm Sun)* is another place to sink into a comfy couch or relax on the patio. Check out the book exchange and enjoy coffees, *chai*, smoothies, cakes and cinnamon buns.

Fusion (☎ *330 9117; Vanua Arcade, Victoria Pde; sandwiches F$4; open 8am-5pm Mon-Sat)* has fantastic, giant sandwiches, wraps, coffees, the best smoothies in town and lots of options for vegetarians.

Headworks (☎ *330 9449; upstairs, cnr of Renwick and Thomson Sts; dishes F$4; open 8am-7pm Mon-Sat)* serves smoothies, filled croissants, cakes, lasagne and sandwiches along with coffees and teas. Comfy chairs are on the balcony overlooking downtown Suva. When you tire of the view, you can get your hair done next door in the café's salon.

Bad Dog Café (☎ *330 4662; cnr Macarthur St & Victoria Pde; mains F$10; open 11am-11pm Mon-Wed, 11am-1am Thur-Sat)* has tasty soups, pasta, gourmet pizza and huge coffees. It has an extensive list of beers and cocktails or you can BYO from Victoria Wines next door (F$6 corkage fee).

Rivendell (☎ *330 4662; Queensland Insurance Bldg, Victoria Pde; lunch and breakfast F$4; open 7am-4.30pm Mon-Fri, 7am-2.30pm Sat)* serves sandwiches, quiche, burgers, smoothies and cake in an indoor courtyard. It's a good option for a quick lunch or for an early breakfast of muesli or French toast.

Fast Food Suva has a few **food courts**: one at Downtown Boulevard Shopping Centre (*Ellery St)*, another upstairs in Harbour Centre (*Scott St)* and one at Dolphin Plaza (*cnr Loftus St & Victoria Pde)*. All have a variety of takeaway-food outlets, including pizza, pasta, Chinese, curries and Fijian dishes for around F$5.

Self-Catering The **Suva Municipal Market** is the best place for fish, fruit and vegetables. There are a couple of supermarkets downtown on Rodwell Rd, facing the bus station. At the **Hot Bread Kitchen** (☎ *331 3919; open 5.30am-7pm Mon-Fri, 5.30am-1pm Sat)* you can pick up fresh cheese-and-onion loafs and coconut rolls.

Entertainment

Bars & Clubs While little ole' Suva doesn't rival London or Bangkok for nightlife, there are a couple of great clubs where you can shake your booty. You don't need to get completely dolled up but if you're wearing shorts or flip-flops you'll be turned away.

Traps Bar (☎ *331 2922; Victoria Pde; happy hour 6pm-8pm; open 6pm-1am daily)* is justifiably popular. The pub-like front room and snooker room are good places to grab a beer and socialise while the trendy back room has a vibrant dance floor, laser lights and a well-stocked bar. The music is a good mixture of current and older dance and pop.

O'Reillys (☎ *331 2968; cnr of Macarthur St & Victoria Pde; open 6pm-1am Mon-Sun)* has nothing Irish about it. Despite being more of a bar than a club, it gets packed out on weekends with people dancing with poles and on the tables. Music is an odd but fairly good mixture of dance and pop, and the crowd is an equally unusual mixture of students, expats and business folk.

The Barn (☎ *330 7845; Carnarvon St; open 6pm-1am daily)* is a rugged bar with live music every night but Sunday and Monday. Music is mainly country with a bit of pop and reggae thrown in for good measure. The cowboy crowd is a little older.

Cinemas The **Village 6 Cinema Complex** (☎ *331 1109; Scott St; admission F$5)* shows recently released Hollywood and Bollywood films. See the cinema section of the *Fiji Times* for what's screening.

Shopping

For a good selection of souvenirs, crafts and Fiji-made clothes at reasonable prices, head to **Jack's Handicrafts** (☎ *330 8893; cnr Renwick Rd & Pier St; open 9am-5.30 Mon-Fri, 9am-2pm Sat)*.

Moving to a Different Beat

Dancers pay homage to the steady beat of the drums, seemingly oblivious to the spectators. The poorly lit room is crowded with both tourists and locals, with the 'bulas' and singing barely audible above the din. But as a big, indigenous Fijian man – who should be playing the chief in this scene – approaches with a flower behind his ear and a pitcher of beer on his tray, you don't need any reminding that this is no *meke*. This is Saturday night in Suva, when the country's urban youth let down their hair and pole dance to pop music.

Fiji's urban youth face many of the same difficulties as young people around the globe: teenage parenting, crime, drugs and skyrocketing unemployment (only one in eight school leavers finds a job). However, these youths also find themselves straddling two opposing worlds – the traditional, conservative society of the villages many have left behind and the liberal, individualistic lifestyle of the modern and increasingly Westernised city. While many face the near impossibility of surviving unemployment in the city, returning 'home' to a village sporting dreadlocks and skin-tight jeans isn't much easier. Youth have little room to voice their own opinions and it's not entirely surprising that many look for routes out of the country.

The rising club and café culture is bringing together youths from indigenous and Indo-Fijian backgrounds, in the midst of a city filled with ethnic strife. This is not the Fiji of postcards, of grass skirts and beachside *lovo* but it's well worth grabbing a cappuccino or putting on your dancing shoes to check out Fiji's rising urban youth culture. It's an unexpected eye-opener.

The **Suva Curio & Handicraft Centre** *(Stinson Pde)* has endless stalls and is an interesting place to just wander around. It can offer up some fantastic buys but be prepared to bargain! The **Government Crafts Centre** *(☎ 331 5869; Macarthur St; open 8am-4.30pm Mon-Thur, 8am-4pm Fri, 8am-12.30pm Sat)* sells wares of a consistently high quality, but is generally more expensive than anywhere else.

Gathera *(☎ 330 5565; Queensland Insurance Bldg, Victoria Pde; open 9am-5pm Mon-Fri, 9am-1pm Sat)* has beautiful goods from throughout the South Pacific. Pick up handmade hammocks, soaps, candles, bedspreads, cards and carvings. It's not cheap but it is excellent quality.

Try **Procera Music Shop** *(☎ 331 4911; Greig St; open 9am-2pm & 2.30pm-5.30pm Mon-Fri, 9am-1pm Sat)* for top Fijian and Hindi releases. **The Boom Box** *(☎ 330 8265; Downtown Blvd Shopping Centre)* has newish Euro and US releases but is fairly pricey.

Fuji Film *(☎ 331 3911; Shop 11, Vanua House, Victoria Pde; open 9am-5pm Mon-Fri, 9am-1pm Sat)* has a good reputation for high-quality one-hour film processing.

If you're looking for beachwear, daypacks, snorkel gear or surfboards, **Wai Tui Surf** *(☎ 330 0287; Queensland Insurance Bldg, Victoria Pde; open 8.30am-5pm Mon-Fri, 8.30am-2pm Sat)* has lots of name-brand goods to keep you afloat.

Getting There & Away

Suva is well connected to the rest of the country by air and inter-island ferries, and to western Viti Levu by buses and carriers. Most international flights, however, arrive at Nadi International Airport.

Air Nausori International Airport is 23km northeast of central Suva. See the Nausori section for more details on the airport and how to reach the airport from Suva.

Bus & Carrier There are frequent local buses operating along Queens Rd and Kings Rd from Suva's main bus terminal. See 'Getting Around' under Viti Levu for further information. Small trucks or carriers will also take passengers along Queens Rd. If you happen to be travelling in a group, you'll find that you can often get a taxi for little more than the price of a bus.

Boat From Suva there are regular ferry services to both Vanua Levu and Taveuni (Beachcomber Cruises and Consort Shipping) and to Ovalau (Patterson Brothers Shipping). See the Getting Around section near the start of this chapter for further details. There are also irregular boats that take passengers from Suva to Kadavu, Lau and Rotuma (see Mamanuca Group, Lau Group and Rotuma later in this chapter for further information).

Getting Around

It is easy to get around central Suva on foot. Taxis are quite cheap for short trips and they actually use the meter! The busy local bus station is next to the market: ask bus drivers or locals about the ever-fluctuating timetables.

VITI LEVU'S KINGS ROAD

Heading along eastern and northern Viti Levu, Kings Rd ambles through farmland and up past remote highland villages. Connecting Suva and Lautoka, it's a beautiful trip by bus or 4WD. Korovou, Rakiraki, Tavua and Ba each have a simple hotel, and there's an upmarket resort near Rakiraki and several budget resorts offshore on Nananu-i-Ra.

Nausori

pop 22,000

On the eastern bank of the Rewa River, Nausori is a bustling service centre for the area's agricultural and industry workers. Its only draw for travellers is its airport – the country's second largest. There are a couple of banks and some inexpensive eateries near the bus station but you'll be better off staying in Suva, 19km southwest.

Information The airport is about 3km southeast of Nausori. Air Fiji, Air Pacific and Royal Tongan Airlines have international flights from here. It's also a hub for Air Fiji and Sun Air domestic flights. The airport premises are small and low-key with an **ANZ bank** open for international flights only. Taxi rides between the airport and Suva cost about F$17. **Nausori Taxi & Bus Service** (☎ 312 185, 304 178) has buses to/from the Holiday Inn Hotel in Suva (F$2.50). If you're not in a hurry, cover the 3km to Nausori's bus station by taxi (about F$3) and catch one of the frequent local buses to Suva bus station (F$1.50).

Korovou & Natovi Landing

At Korovou, about 50km north of Suva, Kings Rd continues northwest through dairy-farming country and into the hills. Another road follows the coast to Natovi Landing (about a 20-minute drive) from where there are bus/ferry services to Labasa (Vanua Levu) and Levuka (Ovalau) – see the Getting Around section near the start of this chapter.

If you do get stuck in Korovou, **Tailevu Hotel** (☎ 343 0028; camp sites F$5, dorm beds F$8, singles/doubles with private bathroom F$20/ 35) has budget accommodation.

Vaileka, Rakiraki & Ellington Wharf

Heading northwest from Korovou is a stunning journey: the mountain road winds along Wainibuka River, past small villages and Viti Levu Bay and down to Rakiraki. Against the skyline, the imposing **Nakauvadra Range** is believed to be the home of the great snake-god Degei, creator of all the islands.

Inland from Rakiraki, about 2km off Kings Rd past the sugar mill, is the township of **Vaileka**, with the bus station, taxi stands, banks, a market, supermarket and a few cafés (one with Internet access). Stick to bottled water while in this area – the tap water is unsafe.

The turnoff to **Ellington Wharf** is 5km east of Rakiraki; the wharf is a further 1.5km. Ferries leave here for Nabouwalu, Vanua Levu, Savusavu and Denarau (see the Getting Around near the start of this chapter for ferry details).

Heading out of Rakiraki towards Nadi, look out for **Udreudre's Tomb**, the resting place of Fiji's most notorious cannibal whose personal tally reached at least 872 corpses. It's about 100m west of the Vaileka turn-off, on the left.

Activities Head to **Ellington Wharf Adventure Water Sports** (☎ 669 3366, 942765; w www .sailboardingsafaris.com) for snorkelling trips (from F$25 per person plus F$20 gear hire), windsurfing (from $30 per hour), catamarans, diving and sea-kayaking trips around the islands and bays.

Places to Stay & Eat Budget travellers usually head straight out to Nananu-i-Ra, though Ellington Wharf now has a 10-bed **dorm bure** (☎ 693 333; F$20) with an outside toilet and cold shower – OK as a stopover.

Rakiraki Hotel (☎ 669 4101; Kings Rd; singles/ doubles with fan F$38/46, with air-con from F$50/66, air-con singles/doubles in newer bldg F$88/99), 1.8km east of the Vaileka turn-off, has musty but reasonably good-value rooms and a pool. The **restaurant-bar** (lunch F$10; dinner mains F$13-17) has standard fare like curries, roasts and fried fish.

Wananavu Beach Resort (☎ 669 4433, fax 669 4499; e wananavuresort@connect.com.fj; gardenview/oceanview/beachfront double bure F$185/215/245 plus F$25 per extra person, self-contained villas F$300, all air-con), east of Rakiraki, is a comfortable, good-value resort with beautiful views of Nananu-i-Ra island and the mountainous coastline. Ask about walk-in deals. Meal plans are an extra F$88 per person. Visitors are welcome at the **restaurant/bar** *(dinner mains around F$25)*, a great spot with good food. There is a marina nearby, a nice swimming pool, tennis and volleyball courts, diving and snorkelling. Airport transfers from Nadi are F$100 by taxi or F$15 per person by minivan.

Getting There & Away Sunbeam has regular express buses along the Kings Rd from Suva and Nadi (see the Getting Around section under Viti Levu earlier), which stop at Vaileka and the turn-off to Ellington Wharf. To avoid lugging groceries and gear 1.3km to the wharf, get off at Vaileka and catch a taxi (F$8). Sharing a taxi from Nadi is about F$80.

Nananu-i-Ra
area 3.5 sq km

Nananu-i-Ra is a beautiful, hilly island with scalloped bays, white-sand beaches and mangroves. It's a quick and inexpensive island getaway, handy to Nadi. There are no roads and no village and most residents are of European descent so there's little contact with indigenous culture.

Activities An abundance of sealife makes for great snorkelling offshore; head to the island's northern side for sea snakes. The island's exposure to the trade winds makes it popular for windsurfing, especially from June to August when winds are generally 10 knots and above. Basic windsurfing gear is available from Ellington Wharf Adventure Water Sports.

The surrounding reefs have some amazing dive sites, though the windy weather can make it somewhat tricky. **Ra Divers** (☎ 669 4511; **W** www.radivers.com; Nananu-i-Ra) charges F$140 for a two-tank dive and F$475 for an open-water course, although one reader complained about pushy instructors.

Crystal Divers (☎ 6694 747; **W** www.crystal divers.com; Nananu-i-Ra) has a good reputation, better boats, and takes divers to excellent advanced dive sites. They're not cheap (F$220 for a two-tank dive) but offer package deals through resorts.

Places to Stay & Eat It's a good idea to book accommodation ahead as the island can get busy. There's no bank and some budget places do not accept credit cards. All of the budget places have kitchens for guest use,

with basic supplies available at Betham's Beach Cottages shop. Both Betham's and McDonald's Nananu Beach Cottages have outdoor cafés. Power is by generator, so no lights or fans after 10pm.

McDonald's Beach Cottages (☎ 669 4633; *dorm beds F$17, doubles cottage F$70 plus F$9 per extra person, private house $100)* has the liveliest atmosphere. Dorm accommodation (maximum five people) is in a new building in the garden. Of the self-contained cottages, beachfront *bure* number five is the best. The private house (no kids) is also great with 24-hour electricity. Meal packages are F$25 per day and the outdoor restaurant/bar *(breakfast/lunch/dinner from F$8/10/20)* has a pleasant atmosphere. Snorkelling gear/kayaks are F$6/8 per half day. Visa and MasterCard accepted.

Betham's Beach Cottages (☎ 669 4132; **e** bethams@connect.com.fj; *dorm beds F$17, self-contained cottage doubles F$85 plus F$10 per extra person)* has two spacious dorms without fans. The beachfront cottages are clean and roomy. Discounts of 20% apply from October to mid-December. Betham's beachfront café offers sandwiches for lunch (under F$5) and dinner for F$11 to F$16.

Charlie's Place (☎ 669 4676; **e** charlies place@connect.com.fj; *dorm beds F$17, self-contained cottage doubles F$70 plus F$9 per extra person)* offers the most privacy. Of the two hillside cottages, one is used as a dorm, the other is good for families and both have beautiful bay views. There's also a cottage in the garden next door.

Nananu Lodge (☎ 669 4290; *camping per person F$10, dorm beds F$20, cottage doubles F$40)*, on the northwest point of the island, has a lovely beach and is far more remote, about a 1½-hour walk (at low tide) from the other budget places. There's a small basic shop but bring your own food. Beachfront cottages have two bedrooms and shared kitchen and bathroom. You can snorkel offshore (F$10 equipment hire) and there are excellent walks from here to secluded One Beach (about 45 minutes one way).

Getting There & Away Nananu-i-Ra is a 15-minute boat ride from Ellington Wharf with each resort running their own transfers (around F$18 per person return). Arrange your pick-up in advance (there is also a phone at Ellington Wharf). Boat transfers for the budget resorts are around F$18 per person return.

VITI LEVU HIGHLANDS
Nadarivatu & Navai

The forestry settlement of Nadarivatu is a beautiful highland area with fresh mountain air. Hike up to Mt Lomalagi for great views (3 hours return). The **Forestry Office** (☎ 668 9001) can arrange for camping, dorm accommodation or a homestay with a local family (bring provisions and give money/groceries to cover costs). Alternatively, seek permission from the manager at **Vatukoula's Emperor Gold Mining Company** (☎ 668 0630) to stay at the goldmine's spacious rest house.

About 8km south of Nadarivatu, **Navai** is at the foot of Fiji's highest peak, **Tomanivi** (Adam and Eve's place; 1323m), also known as Mt Victoria. Allow at least five hours return to hike from the village. Guides can be hired for F$10. The last half of the climb is akin to rock climbing and can be extremely slippery.

Getting There & Away The turnoff for Nadarivatu is about 3km east of Tavua – it's a steep, rough trip (30km, 1½ hours!). Local bus services from Tavua ceased operating due to poor road conditions. The road from Navai to Suva is barely passable and best avoided.

Koroyanitu National Heritage Park

For nature lovers, the Koroyanitu National Heritage Park is definitely worth a hike. The area has beautiful nature walks through native Dakua forests and grasslands, birdwatching, archaeological sites, waterfalls and swimming. Contact the **Abaca Visitor Centre** (☎ 666 6644, after the beep dial 1234, fax 6666 590; admission F$5) for more information. **Abaca** (pronounced am-**barth**-a) village is at the base of **Koroyanitu** (Mt Evans) and is one of six villages within the park benefiting from ecotourism.

Hiking From Nase Lodge, a climb to the summit of **Castle Rock** (1 hour) will reward you with panoramic views of the Mamanucas and Yasawas. You can hire local guides to take you there or on half or full-day hikes of the area.

Mount Batilamu Trek (☎ 0800 6720 455; 672 3311, ✉ batilamutrek@compuserve.co; tours run mid-April–mid-Nov) organises 2½-day tours up the Sabeto Valley, including village visits and transfers from Nadi/Lautoka hotels for F$355.

Places to Stay & Eat Experience highland village culture through **village stays** (F$30 per

night, including all meals, 3 night minimum stay). Contact Abaca Visitor Centre for details.

Nase Lodge (camp sites per person F$10, dorm beds F$15) is about 400m uphill from Abaca, with cooking facilities, a cold-water shower and toilet. Bring your own supplies. Breakfast/lunch/dinner in the village costs F$5/7/10-15 and there's local entertainment on Thursday nights (F$20 per person).

Getting There & Away Abaca village transport (☎ 666 6590) has a carrier to Lautoka (F$8, daily except Sunday). If driving from Lautoka (1 hour), turn inland off Queens Rd at Tavakubu Rd, then right at Abaca Rd. It's a further 10km of gravel road up to Abaca (4WD only).

Nausori Highlands

The Interior of Viti Levu is one of the best places to experience traditional Fijian culture in small villages and settlements scattered throughout the fantastic landscape. Sunday is a day of rest, so village visits may be disruptive and unappreciated.

Navala Nestled in the rugged grassy mountains and on the banks of the Ba River, Navala (population 800) is by far Fiji's most picturesque village. The houses here are all traditional *bure*, built with local materials. While it's a photographer's dream, you must ask permission to take pictures. The village welcomes visitors who present a *sevusevu* (a gift such as *yaqona*) and donation of F$15. If you arrive independently, ask the first person you meet to escort you to the chief. The village has a radio-telephone for emergencies.

Places to Stay & Eat On the river's edge a kilometre south of Navala, the friendly **Boulou's Lodge & Backpacker Hostel** (☎ 666 6644 after the beeps dial 2116; dorms/bure per person F$45/55, including meals) offers village trips, horse riding, swimming, and *bilibili* (bamboo raft) trips. There are cold-water showers and flush toilets but no electricity. Meals include plenty of homegrown fruit and vegetables and local dishes. It's best to ring in advance.

Getting There & Away There are local buses from Ba to Navala (1½ hours) daily, except Sunday. Aim for the midday one to avoid arriving late in the village. Carriers cost about F$25 for the vehicle. If driving from Ba, there are a couple of turns to watch out for: at the police post turn left, passing a shop on your right and at the next fork in the road, keep left. The road is rough and rocky, but usually passable – seek local advice before heading out.

SIGATOKA VALLEY
Naihehe Cave, about an hour's drive upriver from Sigatoka, was once used as a fortress by hill tribes and has the remains of a ritual platform and cannibal oven. **Adventures in Paradise** (☎ 652 0833; e wfall@connect.com.fj) offer guided tours departing Nadi/Coral Coast for F$120/100, including lunch and *bilibili* rafting.

NAMOSI HIGHLANDS
The steamy Namosi Highlands, north of Pacific Harbour, have Fiji's most spectacular scenery – complete with rainforests, steep ranges, deep river canyons and tall waterfalls. If you have your own wheels (preferably 4WD) take a detour inland from Nabukavesi.

Rivers Fiji (☎ 345 0147; W www.riversfiji.com; Pacific Harbour) offers well-organised trips with great equipment. The day trip to Wainikoroiluva (Luva Gorge) is highly recommended, including a village visit and kayaking (F$175/160 from Nadi/Suva or the Coral Coast).

Discover Fiji Tours (☎ 345 0180; Navua) has two-day guided hikes across Namosi Province as well as village visits and *bilibili* expeditions on the Navua River (see Visiting the Highlands under Southern Viti Levu earlier).

Mamanuca Group

Set in an azure lagoon, the sunny Mamanucas are undeniably enticing. With white-sand beaches, coconut palms and colourful offshore reefs, many of the twenty or so islands are popular day excursions from Nadi or Lautoka. You'll also find excellent diving (such as the famous Supermarket site), radical surf-breaks (off Tavarua and Namotu) and both budget and luxury accommodation. Most resorts barge in their water from the mainland and rely on generator power.

Getting There & Around
South Sea Cruises (☎ 675 0500, fax 675 0501; e southsea@connect.com.fj) runs a fast catamaran from Denarau Marina to most of the Mamanuca islands: Castaway, Malolo, Mana (F$60 one way), Treasure Island (F$50), Bounty Island (F$40) and South Sea Island (F$30). Hopping between islands costs F$40. Matamanoa and Tokoriki are linked by a smaller launch to

Mana (F$100). Coaches transfer guests to Denarau Marina from hotels and resorts in Nadi (free) and on the Coral Coast (F$20).

Malolo Cat (☎ 666 6215), a fast and comfortable catamaran, shuttles between Malololailai and Denarau Marina three times daily (F$40/20 adult/child one way, 50 minutes).

Prices for quick, scenic flights are comparable to catamaran prices. Sun Air and Air Fiji have daily flights (so long as there are enough passengers) from Nadi to Mana (about F$70 one way) and Malololailai (about F$60).

Turtle Airways and Island Hoppers can get you to the islands by seaplane or helicopter (see the Getting Around section near the start of this chapter). Yachts can be hired at Musket Cove Marina on Malololailai.

BOUNTY ISLAND
area 0.02 sq km
The interior of this coral island is home to endangered bird species and the rare Fiji crested iguana. Hawksbill Turtles nest on the island's white-sand beach while pristine coral is just offshore. Bounty Island, also known as Kadavu, is just 15km from Viti Levu.

Bounty Island Sanctuary Resort (☎ 672 2852; W www.fiji-bounty.com; dorm beds F$55, rooms or tents per person F$70, including meals) is a beautiful budget resort with good snorkelling, excellent food and friendly staff. Rooms are spacious with comfortable bunk beds, while two-room tents sleep four people. There are enough shared toilets and showers to keep everyone happy. Activities include canoeing, kayaking, sailboarding (F$5 per hour) and biking (F$10 per day). Diving and other motorised activities can be arranged with Subsurface on Beachcomber Island.

BEACHCOMBER ISLAND
area 0.2 sq km
Tiny Beachcomber Island, or Tai, has a great garden and is circled by a beautiful beach.

Beachcomber Island Resort (☎ 666 1500, fax 666 4496; W www.beachcomberfiji.com; dorms bunks F$75, lodge singles/doubles F$180/240, beachfront bure singles/doubles F$270/320, all include buffet meals) covers the entire island. With a party reputation, it attracts a young crowd and caters for up to 250 guests. While it's not a secluded oasis, you can opt out of the evening entertainment and have a very relaxing time here. Buildings and rooms are spread throughout a gorgeous garden, including the huge, 84-bunk dorm *bure* (with individual lockers provided). Fan-cooled

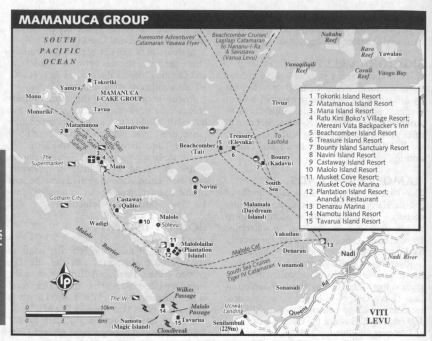

MAMANUCA GROUP

1 Tokoriki Island Resort
2 Matamanoa Island Resort
3 Mana Island Resort
4 Ratu Kini Boko's Village Resort;
   Mereani Vata Backpacker's Inn
5 Beachcomber Island Resort
6 Treasure Island Resort
7 Bounty Island Sanctuary Resort
8 Navini Island Resort
9 Castaway Island Resort
10 Malolo Island Resort
11 Musket Cove Resort;
   Musket Cove Marina
12 Plantation Island Resort;
   Ananda's Restaurant
13 Denarau Marina
14 Namotu Island Resort
15 Tavarua Island Resort

lodge rooms are good value and comfortable beachfront *bure* offer lots of privacy.

Activities include snorkelling (equipment free for house guests), waterskiing (F$30 per hour), parasailing (F$50), catamaran sailing (F$25 per hour), windsurfing (F$10 per hour), jet-skiing (F$80 per half hour), canoeing (F$14 per day) and fishing (F$200 for a maximum of four people). **Subsurface** (☎ 6666 738; W www.fijidiving.com) is an excellent diving operation based on the island, charging F$180/350/550 for a two-tank dive/six dives/unlimited dives. Open-water courses are taught in Japanese or English for F$615. Diving is half-price during February and March for guests staying at least five nights. Beachcomber offers speedboat transfers for late flight arrivals (F$30). Day-trippers are often accepted to the island.

TREASURE ISLAND
area 0.06 sq km
The coral Treasure Island (Elevuka) is covered in tropical gardens and ringed by a white-sand beach.

Treasure Island Resort (☎ 666 6999, fax 666 6955; W www.fiji-treasure.com; air-con *bure* F$395) caters really well for families and

honeymooners with around 70 comfortable beachfront *bure*. Optional meal packages cost F$55/62 for two/three meals daily; otherwise breakfast/lunch/dinner is about F$13/17/36.

Amenities include nightly entertainment, a freshwater pool, an excellent kids' club and babysitting services. Windsurfing, canoeing, snorkelling, volleyball, minigolf, coral viewing and fishing are all included. Diving trips are organised with Beachcombers' Subsurface.

NAVINI
Centrally located in the Mamanuca Group, Navini is another tiny coral island surrounded by a white-sand beach and offshore reef.

Navini Island Resort (☎ 666 2188, fax 666 5566; W www.navinifiji.com.fj; 1-bedroom/premier/5-person duplex/honeymoon bure F$450/480/520/590) is a pleasant family-run resort, great for families or couples who want a friendly, intimate atmosphere away from crowds of tourists. Service is excellent; the 30-strong staff outnumbers the guests. *Bure* are all within 10m of the beach. Honeymoon *bure* have a private courtyard and spa. All guests usually dine together at one table; a meal plan for adults costs F$85, for 6- to 12-year-olds costs F$49, and for 2- to

5-year-olds F$36. The food is good, especially the fresh fish.

Snorkelling is excellent just off the beach and kayaking, windsurfing, volleyball, coral-viewing boards, fishing and villages trips are all included. Diving can be arranged with **Subsurface** at Beachcomber Island.

Navini guests are picked up from Nadi or Lautoka hotels; return transfers cost F$180/90 (adult/child); children under five are free.

MALOLOLAILAI
area 2.4 sq km

The second-largest island in the Mamanucas, Malololailai has a bit more going on than many of its tiny neighbours, with two resorts, a marina, shops and a restaurant.

Musket Cove Marina

In September each year, the **Musket Cove Yacht Club** (☎ 666 2215, fax 666 2633; W www .musketcovefiji.com) hosts Fiji Regatta Week and the Musket Cove to Port Vila yacht race. Yachts can anchor at the marina year-round from F$46 a week, and stock up on fuel, water and provisions at the general store. The marina also offers a choice of charter yachts.

Activities

Subsurface at Musket Cove (☎ 662 2215; W www.fijidiving.com) is a well-equipped dive shop with quick access to great dive sites on the Malolo Barrier Reef. A two-tank dive costs F$180, a six-tank package F$350 and an open-water course F$615. **Plantation Divers** (Plantation Island Resort) offers two-tank dives (F$130), ten-tank packages (F$495) and open-water courses (F$570).

Malololailai is near to a number of surf-breaks but there's no official transport to reach them. If you're willing, **'Big Johnnie'** can get you there in his life jacket-less, radio-less, flare-less and insurance-less boat. Contact him at Plantation Island Resort's boatshed; for one person rates are F$40; for two to three people F$30 per person; for four to five people, F$25 per person.

Places to Stay & Eat

Plantation Island Resort (☎ 666 9333, fax 666 9423; W www.plantationisland.com; lodge per person F$44, hotel rooms F$190, beachfront/garden bure singles & doubles F$385/470, 6-person beachfront/garden bure F$490/570, studio bure doubles F$280), one of Fiji's first resorts, is family oriented with a fun and lively atmosphere. The two-bedroom bure

are popular and often booked out. The Dive Lodge is a new, budget option with shared facilities (no kitchen). Optional meal packages are F$55/36 for three/two meals a day or around F$12 to F$20 for lunch and F$17 to F$24 for dinner. The resort's many activities include snorkelling trips, canoeing, windsurfing, golf and tennis.

Musket Cove Resort (☎ 666 2215, fax 666 2633; W www.musketcovefiji.com; beachfront/lagoon/seaview bure doubles F$440/410/375, villa doubles from F$530, air-con hotel rooms F$240), adjacent to Musket Cove marina, best suits couples and families after a quiet holiday. Relax in the spacious gardens, large pool, or at the island bar. Hotel rooms are good value and newer Armstrong Island villas have overwater verandas and a private pool. The poolside restaurant, **Dick's Place** (mains F$12-30, 3-course set menu F$30), serves international cuisine, some Indian and Fijian dishes and the occasional pig on the spit. Activities such as windsurfing, canoeing, hand-line fishing and snorkelling are included. Game fishing, diving and use of catamarans costs extra.

Ananda's Restaurant (mains around F$20, kids' meals F$9), next to the general store, offers a change from the resort restaurants. Dine on tasty food and enjoy live music in the evenings.

MALOLO

The largest of the Mamanuca Islands, Malolo is home to two villages, mangroves and coastal forest. The island's highest point, **Uluisolo** (218m), was used by villagers as a hill fortification and later by the US forces as an observation point during WWII. A hike to the top will be rewarded with panoramic views of the Mamanuca islands and the southern Yasawas.

Malolo Island Resort (☎ 666 9192, fax 666 9197; W www.maloloisland.com; oceanview/beachfront bure F$440/500 for up to 2 adults and 2 children, including non-motorised activities), on the western side of the island, has simple but comfortable bure, a nice pool and a kids' club. There is a hillside **restaurant** (mains F$25) and a beachfront bar/restaurant. Optional meal packages cost F$30/60 per child/adult per day. Diving is with **Subsurface** at Musket Cove (see Malololailai earlier).

CASTAWAY ISLAND
area 0.7 sq km

Reef-fringed Castaway Island, also known as Qalito, is 27km west of Denarau.

FIJI

Castaway Island Resort (☎ 666 1233, fax 666 5753; W www.castawayfiji.com; fan-cooled garden/oceanview/beachfront bure F$510/550/610, up to 4 adults or family of 5, non-motorised activities included) has simple but spacious bure with intricate *masi* ceilings. Relax at the pool and dine at the open-air pizza bar or on the dining terrace (all-day casual meals F$10-14; dinner F$14-22), perched on the point overlooking the water. Alternatively pay F$50 per day for unrestricted selection from lunch and dinner menus.

The resort has a clinic, a crèche, a first-rate kids' club and lots of activities. **Castaway Dive Centre** is excellent and charges F$90 for a one-tank dive and F$450 for unlimited dives. Open-water courses are F$550 per person in a group, or F$695 for individual lessons. Several speciality diving courses are also offered. Day-trippers are often accepted to the island.

MANA

The beautiful island of Mana has grassy hills, lovely beaches and a wide coral reef. The southeastern end is home to a large luxury resort and two budget resorts, next to the island's village. The northern and western beaches are quite good for snorkelling with lots of tiny, colourful fish.

Places to Stay & Eat

Past animosity with the neighbouring budget resorts compelled Mana Island Resort to erect a fence, making it clear that its facilities, beach shelters and deck chairs are for its guests only. Nevertheless, relations between the resorts appear to be improving.

The two budget resorts are run by very competitive brothers. Politics aside, the staff at both places are usually friendly and the party atmosphere can be fun – this is *not* a quiet escape. Each year, we receive mixed reports about both resorts; avoid paying too much upfront so that you have the option to move if you're unhappy. You can use credit cards here but will need to bring some cash. Beware of theft on the beaches and in dorms. There is a shop next to Ratu Kini's reception desk selling basic goods, but bring mosquito repellent, snacks and kava.

Ratu Kini Boko's Village Resort (☎ 672 1959; e rtkinihostel@connect.com.fj; Nadi; camping per person F$30, dorm beds F$45, bure with shared bathroom singles/doubles F$60/80, bure with private bathroom singles/doubles F$75/95, including meals) has accommodation of various sizes and types, from a concrete house to traditional *bure*. Most of it is set back from the beach among breadfruit trees. Food quality is variable and activities include snorkelling trips (F$10 per person), kayaking (F$5 per hour), visits to Monuriki (F$50) – where Tom Hank's *Castaway* was shot – and island hopping (F$35). They also offer two-tank diving trips for F$150.

Mereani Vata Backpacker's Inn (☎ 666 3099, 6702 763; Nadi; dorm beds F$45, doubles F$80, including meals) has a 10-bed girls' dorm with bathroom, another 24-bed dorm and four double rooms. Activities include reef-fishing trips (F$5), four-island sightseeing (F$35), a 'Tom Hanks picnic' to Monuriki (F$50), snorkelling and a weekly kava ceremony.

Mana Island Resort (☎ 665 0423, fax 665 0788; W www.manafiji.com; garden bure F$300, oceanview bure or hotel room F$400, honeymoon bure F$900, including non-motorised activities, 2 children free) is one of Fiji's largest island resorts. Garden *bure* sleep up to four people and oceanview *bure* are spacious and elevated with a porch. The new honeymoon *bure* have open-air spas and decks just a few metres from the water. Meal plans are available and the south beach *restaurant* (mains from F$25).

Resort facilities include a pool, tennis courts, and a play centre for children. **Aqua-Trek** (☎ 670 2413; W www.aquatrek.com) offers one-tank boat dives for F$80 and open-water courses are F$600.

Getting There & Away

Flying is the quickest and most scenic way to get to Mana, but the airstrip is part of Mana Island Resort (for the use of its guests only).

Boat transfers to the budget resorts depart from New Town Beach (in front of Travellers Beach Resort), taking 45 minutes to 1½ hours and costing F$40/70 per person one-way/return. Avoid over-crowded boats and make sure there are life jackets on board.

MATAMANOA

Small and secluded, Matamanoa rises conically from the sea. Located just north of Mana, it's covered in dense vegetation, dotted with coconut palms and fringed by white-sand beaches.

Matamanoa Island Resort (☎ 666 0511, fax 666 1069; W www.matamanoa.bulafiji.com; double bure F$450, double unit F$270; minimum stay three days, includes breakfast and non-motorised activities) has 20 *bure* on a high point overlooking a lovely beach. Air-con units have either beach or garden views. Meal plans cost F$56/28 per adult/child. Activities include 'honeymoon island' picnics and trips to the nearby pottery village of Tavua (on Tavua island). Diving is with Aqua-Trek, based on Mana.

To reach Matamanoa by boat, take South Sea Cruises' catamaran to Mana and then the shuttle catamaran to Matamanoa.

TOKORIKI

The small, hilly island of Tokoriki has a beautiful, long white-sand beach facing west to the sunset. Near the northern end of the Mamanucas, it has a special, remote atmosphere.

Tokoriki Island Resort (☎ 666 1999, fax 666 5295; W www.tokoriki.com; deluxe bure up to 4 people F$570, including breakfast & non-motorised activities) has comfortable air-con bure just a few steps from the beach. Lunch (around F$15) is served on the pleasant terrace and pool area; gourmet candle-lit dinners (from F$25) are available in the restaurant. Activities include tennis, canoeing, sailing and snorkelling. The resort's well-equipped dive shop visits pristine local sites. A two-tank dive costs F$150.

To get to Tokoriki by boat, catch South Sea Cruises' catamaran to Mana and then the shuttle catamaran.

TAVARUA

area 0.12 sq km

This small coral island is at the southern edge of the Malolo Barrier Reef and is surrounded by beautiful white-sand beaches. There's great surfing to be had at nearby Cloudbreak and Restaurant Break.

Tavarua Island Resort (☎ 672 3513, fax 670 6395; e tavarua@connect.com.fj; bure singles/twins F$300/450, including meals, transfers and surf trips, minimum one-week stay) is popular with American surfers. Accommodation is in simple bure along the beach.

Bookings need to be made well in advance. Transfers are from Nadi.

NAMOTU

area 0.0015 sq km

Namotu is a tiny island that has been transformed from not much more than a sand bar into a nicely landscaped resort.

Namotu Island Resort (☎ 670 6439, fax 670 6039; shared bure per person F$240, double bure F$630, includes meals and unlimited surfing) is an intimate resort, idyllic for surfers, windsurfers, divers and honeymooners. The restaurant-bar and swimming pool area has great views to the surf break and out to the open ocean. Use of kayaks and snorkelling gear is included in the price and diving is arranged with Subsurface on Malololailai. Children under 12 years are not accepted at the resort.

Check in (and out) is on Saturday only. Guests usually book and pay in advance, but Namotu does occasionally take 'walk-ins'. The resort will arrange for a driver to pick up its guests from Nadi.

A Hairy Situation

For indigenous Fijians, the head is tabu. In reverence to this sanctity, Fijians once spent entire days with the hairdresser. Symbolising masculinity and social standing, men sported flamboyant, often massive hair-dos, ranging from the relatively conventional giant puffball (up to 30cm tall) to more original shaggy or geometric shapes. Styles were stiffened into place with burnt limejuice and dyed grey, blue, orange, yellow and white, sometimes striped or multicoloured. Women, on the other hand, wore far more conservative hair-dos – close-cropped with random tufts died rusty brown or yellow. A wife's hair could never outdo her husband's and a husband's could not outdo the chief's.

People slept on uncomfortable-looking wooden pillows to keep their coiffure from being spoilt. The head was specially dressed for festive occasions with accessories like hair scratchers (practical for lice), ornamental combs, scarlet feathers, flowers and grated sandalwood. Shaving one's head was a profound sacrifice for a man and often done as a symbol of mourning or to appease a wrathful ancestral spirit.

Early Europeans were astonished by the variety of elaborate styles. Soon after a missionary measured one hair-do at 5m in circumference, the custom was deliberately suppressed by Christians who regarded the practice as not suitable for the 'neat and industrious Christian convert'. These days, you're unlikely to see any hair-dos as fantastical as those around before the missionaries took their clippers to them. Nonetheless, it's interesting to notice the increasing amount of long, dyed and relatively big styles worn by younger indigenous Fijians, compared with the conservative crops sported by the older generations.

Yasawa Group

Famous for lovely white-sand beaches, crystal-blue lagoons and rugged volcanic landscapes, this 90km-long chain of 20 islands draws many paradise seekers. Due to great improvements in transportation to the islands, new budget resorts are appearing, offering the same access to superb beaches as upmarket resorts.

The sunny Yasawas are sparsely populated, with most people living in small, isolated villages. There are no shops, banks, postal or medical services and phones are not always reliable. In the local dialect, known as Vuda, *cola* (pronounced thola) often replaces *bula* and *vina du riki* is used instead of *vinaka*.

Dangers & Annoyances

Some budget resorts offer their own, cheaper boat transfers to the Yasawas. The long trip is across an exposed stretch of water and weather conditions can change quickly. In the past passengers have been stranded for hours due to engine failure and in 1999 an overcrowded boat sank. It's worth checking beforehand if boats have sufficient life jackets, a marine radio and are licensed by the Fijian government.

Activities

For divers, the spectacular reefs of the Yasawas offer brilliant corals, walls, underwater caves and many areas yet to be explored. There are dive operations based on Tavewa, Wayasewa and Waya.

Bring good boots or sandals, as the hilly islands of Wayasewa and Waya are great for hiking.

Organised Tours

Kayaking For kayaking trips, check out **Southern Sea Ventures** (☎ 02-9999-0541 *in Australia;* ⓦ *www.southernseaventures.com).* All-inclusive nine-day trips (May to October) cost F$1890 per person with snorkelling and village visits en route.

Sailing Safaris & Cruises Organised sailing safaris are a popular way to experience the Yasawas and a good option for budget travellers. **Captain Cook Cruises** (☎ 670 1823; ⓦ *www.captaincook.com.au; 15 Narewa Rd, Nadi*) has sailing trips to the southern Yasawas aboard a tall-ship. Swimming, snorkelling, fishing, hikes, village visits and *lovo* feasts are

all part of the deal. Accommodation is in simple *bure* ashore or on fold-up canvas beds aboard. Prices per person (twin share) are F$540/648 for a three-/four-day trip.

Cruises are an excellent mid- to top-range option for visiting the Yasawas. Take it easy aboard your luxury vessel, pop overboard for excellent snorkelling and diving, drop in on beautiful white-sand beaches and stop to visit local villagers. Captain Cook Cruises (see earlier) offer cruises through the Yasawas and Mamanucas aboard a 68m boat equipped with swimming pool, bars, lounges and air-con accommodation. Prices per person (twin share), including all meals and activities (except diving), are F$1270/1531 (three-night cruise) or F$2668/3214 (seven-night cruise) for cabin/stateroom. Children under two years are free; those up to 15 years pay F$300 to F$700 per night. Cruises depart from Denarau Marina.

Blue Lagoon Cruises (☎ 666 1662; ⓦ *www .bluelagooncruises.com; 183 Vitogo Pde, Lautoka)* tour the Yasawas in 56m motor yachts. Cruises cost from F$671/1006/1809 for two/three/six nights per person in twin-share cabins. Children are given substantial discounts. Transfers, cruise activities and food are included but drinks, snorkelling, diving and equipment hire is extra. Diving is with Westside Watersports (see the Diving section under Tavewa). See their website for info on super-luxury cruises. Boats depart from Lautoka's Queens Wharf.

Getting There & Around

Most people travelling to the Yasawas go by the comfortable *Yasawa Flyer* ('the yellow boat') operated by **South Sea Cruises & Awesome Adventures Fiji** (☎ 675 0499, fax 675 0501; ⓦ *www.awesomeadventures.co.nz),* departing 9.15am daily from Denarau Marina. It takes about 1½ hours to Kuata or Wayalailai (F$65), two hours to Waya (F$65), 2¾ hours to Naviti (F$75) and 3¾ hours to Tavewa (F$85). Inter-island fares are F$40 to F$50. The 'Bula Pass' (F$240) is a good deal if you want flexibility, allowing unlimited island hopping for 21 days but only one return to Denarau. Awesome Adventures' package deals can be worthwhile if you are short on time – visit up to four different islands for three/seven nights at F$200/495 per person including transport, meals, accommodation and activities.

Turtle Airways (☎ 672 1888; ⓔ *turtleair ways@connect.com.fj)* has seaplanes flying daily from Nadi to Tavewa Island (F$100, 30 minutes).

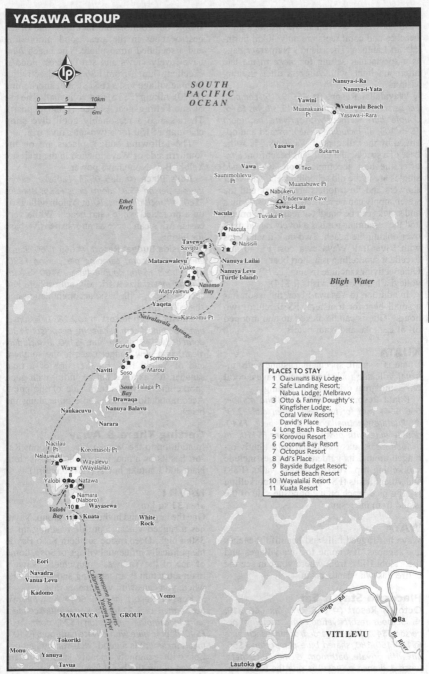

YASAWA GROUP

SOUTH
PACIFIC
OCEAN

Nanuya-i-Ra
Nanuya-i-Yata

Yawini
Muanakuasi
Pt
Vulawalu Beach
Yasawa-i-Rara

Yasawa
Bukama

Vawa
Saunimolilevu
Pt
Teci

Muanabuwe Pt
Nabukeru
Underwater Cave
Sawa-i-Lau

Nacula
Tuvaka Pt

Ethel
Reefs

Nacula
1
Naisisili
Tavewa
Savutu
Pt
3
2
Matacawalevu
Vuake
Nanuya Lailai
4
Nanuya Levu
(Turtle Island)
Matayalevu
Nasomo
Bay
Yaqeta
Katasomu Pt

Bligh Water

Naivalavala Passage

Gunu
5
6
Somosomo
Soso
Marou
Naviti
Soso
Bay
Talaga Pt
Drawaqa
Naukacuvu
Nanuya Balavu
Narara

Nacilau
Pt
Nalauwaki
Koromasoli Pt
7
Wayalevu
(Wayalailai)
Waya
8
Yalobi
9
Natawa
Namara
(Naboro)
10
Wayasewa
Yalobi
Bay
11
Kuata

White
Rock

Eori
Navadra
Vanua Levu
Kadomo

Vomo

Kings Rd

Ba

Ba River

MAMANUCA
GROUP

Awesome Adventures' Yasawa Flyer
Catamaran

VITI LEVU

Tokoriki
Monu
Yanuya
Tavua

Lautoka

FIJI

PLACES TO STAY
1 Oarsmans Bay Lodge
2 Safe Landing Resort;
  Nabua Lodge; Melbravo
3 Otto & Fanny Doughty's;
  Kingfisher Lodge;
  Coral View Resort;
  David's Place
4 Long Beach Backpackers
5 Korovou Resort
6 Coconut Bay Resort
7 Octopus Resort
8 Adi's Place
9 Bayside Budget Resort;
  Sunset Beach Resort
10 Wayalailai Resort
11 Kuata Resort

0   5   10km
0   3   6mi

WAYASEWA

Also known as Wayalailai, Wayasewa's good beaches and coral reefs are only 40km north-east of Lautoka. The island's **Namara** village is a spectacular setting for *meke* in the late afternoon light, with villagers often inviting visitors.

Wayalailai Resort (☎ 666 9715; camping per person F$30, dorm beds F$40, singles F$45, double bure without/with private bathroom F$85/105, all including meals), owned and operated by the villagers of Wayasewa, is at the base of a spectacular cliff. The beachfront *bure* offer the best accommodation, while basic singles are in the old schoolhouse. Cold-water showers and flush toilets are shared, and the water supply can be restricted at times. Drinks and snacks can be bought at reasonable prices, and the restaurant-bar has a lovely raised deck overlooking the beach. Two-tank diving trips with **Dive Trek Wayasewa** cost F$140 and excellent snorkelling is a short boat ride away. Other activities include fishing (F$10), hiking, volleyball and village visits (F$14).

In addition to Yasawa Flyer, the resort has a small boat for transfers (F$80 return, two hours). Guests can be picked up and dropped off at Lautoka and Nadi hotels.

KUATA

Kuata is a small, spectacular island with unusual volcanic rock formations, caves, coral cliffs and great offshore snorkelling.

Kuata Resort (☎ 666 9715, island number 666 6644 wait for two beeps then dial 3233; e kuatares@hotmail.com; dorm beds F$40, double bure with private bathroom F$110, all include meals) has traditional *bure* tightly arranged around its gardens. Activities include snorkelling trips (F$10), guided walks (F$8) and village visits (F$14). The best snorkelling is off a nice beach on the opposite side of the island from the resort.

WAYA

Waya has rugged hills and beautiful beaches and lagoons. It's home to four villages and the Yalobi Hills, from where you can see the entire Yasawa islands chain.

Places to Stay & Eat

Octopus Resort (☎ 666 337, fax 666 210; e octopus_resort@yahoo.com; camping per person F$40, doubles garden/ocean/beach bure F$130/150/180, shared bure per person F$55, all with private bathroom & mosquito nets, lunch & dinner included) is one of the most 'up-market' budget resorts in the Yasawas, with simple but comfortable facilities, one of the best beaches in the area, good snorkelling and a secluded atmosphere. The beach *bure* have lovely views and sea breezes. Food is excellent (lunch from F$6.50) and activities include village visits (F$18), reef snorkelling (F$20), hiking (F$15) and volleyball. The use of snorkelling gear is free (F$50 deposit). There's also a reasonably good **dive shop** charging F$150 for a two-tank dive trip.

The following budget places are on the southern side of Waya, tucked in the majestic Yalobi Bay. None have power.

Adi's Place (☎ 665 0573, Lautoka; camping per person F$20, dorm beds F$35, doubles F$80, all including meals) at Yalobi village is on a protected white-sand beach. While very basic, Adi's can serve as an inexpensive base for hiking.

Bayside Budget Resort (☎ 665 1460; e sos ene@connect.com; camping per person F$30, dorm beds F$40, double bure F$100, all including meals) has a friendly atmosphere and secluded feel, with basic accommodation and shared facilities.

Sunset Beach Resort (☎ 672 2832; e sunset beach@connect.com.fj; camping per person F$30, dorm beds F$45, double bure F$140, all including meals) is a new budget place at the southern end of Yalobi Bay, on the edge of a tidal sandbar. It's exposed but beautiful, with good snorkelling on the eastern side of the point. Accommodation is in simple *bure* along the beach.

Getting There & Away

In addition to the *Yasawa Flyer*, Octopus Resort has its own boat and fetches guests from Nadi and Lautoka hotels (F$120 return).

NAVITI

area 33 sq km

One of the largest and highest of the group, Naviti has a rugged volcanic profile reaching up to 380m high. Deep inside southern Soso Bay is the politically influential village of **Soso**, home of one of the Yasawas' high chiefs. Naviti's main attraction is an amazing snorkelling site where you can swim with manta rays.

Korovu Resort (☎ 666 6644 wait for two beeps then dial 2244; e Korovoultk@connect .com.fj; camping per person F$24, dorm beds F$40, double bure with private bathroom F$100, meals included) is a good, well-run budget option with genuinely friendly staff. *Bure* are spaced along the beachfront with bay views.

Offshore snorkelling is OK (gear hire F$5 per day, snorkelling trip F$15) and village visits (F$20 per person), guided hikes (F$15) and fish-trolling (F$35) are also available.

Coconut Bay Resort *(☎ 994 2429; dorm beds F$40, double bure with shared facilities F$100, double bure with shower F$110-150, including meals)* is just five minutes' walk south of Korovou, on the same beach and with similar facilities and activities to its neighbour. Staff are friendly and meals are simple but OK.

TAVEWA
area 3 sq km

Smack in the middle of the Yasawa Group, the small, low island of Tavewa has good beaches, swimming and snorkelling. The village-less island is freehold land with long-established budget resorts among the coconut trees of the old copra plantation. The best beach is at southern Savutu Point, with excellent snorkelling just offshore.

Good sea kayaks are available for hire (F$5 per hour) from Kingfisher Lodge. Diving with **Westside Watersports** *(☎ 666 1462; W www .fiji-dive.com)* costs F$145 for a two-tank dive and F$550 for an open-water course. The dive shop is on the beach in front of Otto & Fanny Doughty's.

Places to Stay & Eat

Otto & Fanny Doughty's *(☎/fax 666 1462 Lautoka, ☎ 665 2820 island; dorm beds F$70, double bure F$150)* has an excellent location just inland from the lovely Savutu Point. *Bure* are dotted around a pleasant garden with the large six-bed dorm *bure* set back from the beach. Meals are delicious but you can opt out of the meal package (less F$35 from rates per person per day) and pay for individual meals (breakfast/lunch/dinner F$7/15/20). Nonguests can have lunch or dinner here (phone in advance) and everyone is welcome for afternoon tea and cake (3pm to 5pm, F$2).

Kingfisher Lodge *(☎ 666 6644 wait for two beeps then dial 2288, ☎ 665 2820 contact through David's Place; e nacula@hotmail.com; single/double bure F$90/160)* is best suited for couples after a quiet time. On the beachfront just north of David's Place, it has just one comfortable, fan-cooled cottage in a jungle-like garden. The owner can provide meals, or you can head to Otto & Fanny's restaurant.

The two other budget resorts on Tavewa are fairly similar in feel and quality. Both have spacious grounds adjacent to the beach with

simple traditional *bure*. Standards can be a bit haphazard so keep your options open by not paying too much upfront. *Bure* at both have mosquito nets and concrete and are occasionally visited by crabs and mice. Both resorts offer volleyball, nightly music and kava sessions, fishing (F$10), beach trips to nearby islands (F$5 to F$10), village visits (F$25) and trips to Sawa-i-Lau caves.

Coral View Resort *(☎ 666 2648 island, ☎ 672 4199 Nadi; e coral@connect.com.fj; camping per person F$30, dorm beds F$40, standard/superior double bure F$85/95, including meals and 1 activity per day)* has a fairly ordinary beach with some OK coral about 30m offshore and Savutu Point a 20-minute walk away. Facilities are basic and shared.

David's Place *(☎ 665 2820, 672 1820 Nadi airport; e davidsplaceresort@yahoo.com; camping per person F$27, dorm beds F$40-45, double bure without/with private shower F$95/105, includes meals)* has received mixed reports from readers. The quality and quantity of meals and services are variable. BBQ and *lovo* nights are regularly hosted.

Getting There & Away

In addition to the *Yasawa Flyer*, Coral View has its own boat transfer from Lautoka (F$70/120, three hours, one way/return). Guests of other resorts can be included for a little extra.

NACULA

Nacula has beautiful beaches for swimming and snorkelling, rugged hills for hiking and four villages to visit.

Oarsmans Bay Lodge *(☎ 672 2921; e nacula@ hotmail.com; camping per person F$20, dorm beds F$35, double bure with private bathroom F$110, 6-person family bure F$270)* is near Nacula village, on an excellent white-sand beach with good swimming and snorkelling. There is a great view to the lagoon from the 20-bed dorm in the dining-bar's attic and the double *bure* are clean, timber-clad units with ceiling fans. Meal packages cost F$35 per person and paddleboats and snorkelling gear are free. There are boat trips to Sawa-i-Lau (F$30) or snorkelling trips to the Blue Lagoon (F$12). Diving can be arranged with Westside Watersports (see Tavewa).

Safe Landing Resort *(☎ 672 2780; e nacula@ hotmail.com; dorm beds F$55, double bure without/with bathroom F$100/160, including meals)*, near the southern village of Naisisili, is on a beautiful point and has great atmosphere and helpful staff. There's easy access to good snorkelling but the beach is tidal. Accommodation is in traditional *bure* or newer units. Enjoy free village visits, a couple of small paddleboats, snorkelling gear (F$5 per day), snorkel trips (F$10 per person), island hopping (F$10 per person each way) and Sawa-i-Lau trips (F$25).

Nabua Lodge (☎ *666 9173;* e *nacula@hot mail.com; dorm beds F$45, double bure without/ with private shower F$90/120, including meals)* is on a flat, grassy site with a tidal white-sand beach fringed by reefs. Managed by an amiable local family, it's a great place to switch to Fiji time and absorb the local lifestyle. Accommodation is in simple traditional *bure* and only one has electricity (otherwise, kerosene lamps are provided). Meals are basic, but normally sufficient. Snorkelling gear can be hired (F$2 per day) or there are boat trips to Blue Lagoon (F$10) or Sawa-i-Lau (F$25 per person).

Melbravo (☎ *666 9173;* e *nacula@hotmail .com; dorm beds F$45, double bure without/ with private shower F$90/120),* right next door to Nabua Lodge, has a similar standards and prices to its neighbour.

MATACAWALEVU
This hilly, volcanic island is protected by the large Nasomo Bay on its eastern side.

Long Beach Backpackers (☎ *666 6644 after beep dial 3032; dorm beds F$35, double bure F$77)* is on a lovely, long and curved beach with a protected lagoon. The site is stunningly beautiful and there is good snorkelling nearby, including an excellent reef drop. It has easy access to the small rocky island. There's a F$5 charge per person for pick-ups from the *Yasawa Flyer* or F$20 per person to meet the seaplane at Tavewa.

Teas & Tonics
It's hard to find a native tree or plant in Fiji that's *not* used by indigenous Fijians for its curative or preventative properties. Pounded into juices, strained into tonics, administered as teas or plasters, herbal medicine is not the alternative here, but the norm. Villagers possess an immense knowledge of the plants around them and their uses, accumulated over thousands of years and passed from generation to generation. If you fall or suffer a bit of indigestion on a village tour, you'll soon be offered a remedy. It might not be tasty, but chances are it'll work.

SAWA-I-LAU
At Sawa-i-Lau, underwater limestone rocks are thought to have formed a few hundred metres below the surface and then uplifted over time. Shafts of daylight enter the great dome-shaped cave (15m tall above the water surface) where you can swim in the natural pool. With a guide, a torch and a bit of courage, you can also swim through an underwater passage into an adjoining chamber. The limestone walls have mysterious, indecipherable carvings, paintings and inscriptions. Most Yasawa budget resorts offer trips to the caves and local cruise ships call here.

Rotuma

pop 3000 • area 30 sq km
Isolated some 470km north of the Yasawa Group, Rotuma has a skyline etched by extinct volcanic craters and is home to the Rotuman gecko and red-and-black Rotuman honeyeater. Colonies of seabirds squawk from small, offshore islands like Hofliua, also known as 'split island' for its spectacular rock formation.

Rotuma's indigenous Polynesian villagers have a distinct culture influenced more by invading Tongans of the 17th century than by Fijians. In the late 18th century, Rotuma became an important port and the local people were exposed to traders, runaway sailors and missionaries. Various versions of Christianity were introduced, leading to factious warring and prompting Rotuman chiefs to cede Rotuma to Britain. Rotuma joined the Fijian colony in 1881.

In 1988 Rotumans called for independence – a movement squashed by the Fijian government.

There are no banks or shops here, just a cooperative.

Places to Stay
For many years travellers were unwelcome. However, the Rotuman chiefs now allow small numbers of visitors. Bring cash and do not turn up unannounced. Ring the island's **district officer** (☎ 889 1011, 889 1089) for permission.

Rotuma Island Backpackers (☎ *889 1290; camping per double F$15)* in Motusa has village stays. Meals are available and you'll need to bring your own tent.

Getting There & Away
Sun Air has weekly flights on Saturdays from Nausori to Rotuma (3¼ hours). Contact

Kadavu Shipping (☎ 3312 428, Suva) for information on its irregular passenger service to Rotuma (F$90/130 for deck/cabin, 2 days). Yachts must obtain permission to anchor from the Ahau government station in Maka Bay, on the northern side of the island.

Ovalau & The Lomaiviti Group

area 484 sq km
Just off the coast of Viti Levu, the Lomaiviti Group feels worlds away. Rustic, peaceful and sunnier than Viti Levu's east coast, the islands' laidback pace is infectious.

Steeped in history, Ovalau is one of the largest islands of the group and home to picturesque Levuka, Fiji's earliest European settlement and the country's first capital. With plenty of accommodation, it's a fantastic place to spend a few days. South of Ovalau, the tiny coral islands of Leluvia and Caqelai have sandy beaches, good snorkelling and simple budget resorts.

Many of the Lomaiviti (or Central) islands are difficult to reach and have no facilities for tourists, including Gau, the largest in the group. Wedge-shaped Koro rises abruptly from deep water and has lush rainforest and great diving; the easiest way to visit it is by hopping on the Tui Tai (see the Savusavu section).

LEVUKA
pop 3750
Sandwiched between the sea and lush, green mountains, Levuka's colourful downtown looks like it's been lifted straight out of a Wild West film. Once the lawless centre of the blackbirding trade, its now slow paced, charming and extremely welcoming to visitors. You'll find good food, excellent accommodation and lots to do.

Traders began settling in Levuka in the 1830s and by the 1850s it had become increasingly rowdy, with a reputation for wild drunkenness and violence. In the 1870s a flood of planters and other settlers came to Fiji, and the booming town was home to about 3000 Europeans and 52 hotels. When Fiji was declared a British colony in 1874, Levuka was its capital until land constraints led the government to move to Suva in 1882. While the northern end of town was swept away in the hurricanes of 1888 and 1905, many of the boom-time buildings remain. Today, much of the population is

of mixed Fijian and European descent, with a scattering of Indo- and Chinese-Fijians and a small expat community. You'll soon catch wind of the island's main employer, the Pacific Fishing Company (Pafco) located just south of Levuka.

Information
Ovalau Tourist Information Centre *(Community Centre, Morris Hedstrom Bldg; open 8am-1pm & 2pm-4.30pm Mon-Fri)* has friendly staff who do their best to help track down any information you're after. Also check with the Whale's Tale restaurant or Ovalau Watersports – both have lots of tour notices and accommodation advertisements on display.

The **Westpac Bank** on Beach St exchanges travellers cheques and foreign currency and gives cash advances on Visa or MasterCard. **Colonial Bank**, also on Beach St, exchanges travellers cheques and currency.

There's a cardphone outside the **post office** *(Beach St)*. At **The Royal Hotel** you can get online for F$0.20 per minute.

In an emergency, contact **Levuka Hospital** (☎ 344 0152; Beach St) or the **police station** (☎ 344 0222; Totogo Lane).

Things to See
About 10 minutes' walk south of town is **Cession Site**, where the Deed of Cession was signed in 1874. Across the road is the traditional **Provincial Bure**, used by Prince Charles in 1970 – something locals are sure to tell you. Ask permission to visit in the building round back.

Downtown stands the former **Morris Hedstrom** trading store (1868), the first in Fiji. Behind its restored facade is a branch of the **Fiji Museum** *(admission F$2; open 8am-1pm & 2pm-4.30pm Mon-Fri)*, with an amazing array of artefacts and information packed into it.

Have a nose in at the timber interior of the **Sacred Heart Church** (1858) *(Beach Street)*. Other buildings to watch out for are Levuka's **original police station** (1874); the **Ovalau Club** (1904), Fiji's first private club; and the **former town hall** (1898). You'll also find the stone shell of the South Pacific's first **Masonic Lodge** (1875), burnt to the ground during the 19 May coup. Supposedly, a riotous group of villagers descended from Lovoni in rampant support of George Speight and fell upon the Lodge. Local Methodist leaders had long alleged that the secret Masonic society was in league with the devil and that tunnels led from beneath the lodge to Nasora House (the

LEVUKA

To Cawaci &
Bishops' Tomb
(5km)

Vakaviti

Levuka Creek

Levuka
Village

0   100   200m
0   100   200yd

Mission Hill

PLACES TO STAY
6 Mavida Guest House
8 Levuka Homestay
11 The Royal Hotel

PLACES TO EAT
20 Emily Café
23 Whale's Tale
24 Kim's Paak Kum Lounge; Inn's Boutique Fashion Wear
28 Coffee in the Garden

KORO SEA

Rd

Hill St
Chapel St
King St
Church St
Langham St
Beach St

Nasau Park

Totoga Creek
Garner Jones Rd
Hennings St
Totoga La
Beach St

OTHER
1 Methodist Church & Cemetery
2 Church of the Holy Redeemer
3 Levuka Hospital
4 Methodist School
5 199 Steps of Mission Hill
7 Navoka Methodist Church
9 Patterson Brothers Shipping
10 Produce Market
12 Ruins Masonic Lodge
13 Former town hall
14 Ovalau Club
15 Old Police Station
16 Police Station
17 Katudrau Trading Mini Market
18 Bakery
19 Sacred Heart Church
21 Marist Convent School
22 Taxi & Carrier Stand
25 Colonial Bank
26 Levuka Cinema; Cinema Café

To Nasova
(Cession Site) (300m),
Natokalau (6km) &
Airport (17km)

27 Morris Hedstrom Building; Ovalau Tourist Information Centre; Fiji Museum
29 Queen's Wharf
30 Post Office; Customs Office
31 Ovalau Watersports
32 Air Fiji Travel Centre
33 General Store
34 Westpac Bank
35 Pafco Cannery

local government building), the Royal Hotel, and through the centre of the world to Mason HQ in Scotland. Some say the church leaders egged the Lovoni mob on and watched in delight as the building went up in smoke.

The **199 Steps of Mission Hill** are worth climbing for the fantastic view. The **Navoka Methodist Church** (1860s), near the foot of the steps, is one of Fiji's oldest churches.

In **Cawaci**, located north of town, Fiji's first two Catholic bishops rest in the gothic style **Bishops' Tomb** (1922).

Activities

Cycling is a good way to explore Levuka and its surrounding area. Mountain bikes are available from **Inn's Boutique Fashion Wear** (☎ 344 0374; 1/4/8 hrs F$3/10/15) downstairs from Kim's Paak Kum Lounge, and from **Ovalau Watersports** (☎ 344 0166, fax 344 0633; W www .owlfiji.com; open 8.30am-4pm Mon-Sat; 1hr F$5, half/full day F$10/15). Both businesses are closed Sundays.

The Lomoviti waters offer some great dive sites where you can encounter manta rays, hammerheads, turtles and whitetip reef sharks. Colourful hard and soft coral also makes for good reef snorkelling. Ovalau Watersports offers two-tank dives with good gear for F$130 and open-water courses for F$460 (with instruction in English or German). Reef snorkelling trips cost F$30 per person.

Organised Tours

Epi's Tour (10am Mon-Sat) to Lovoni village, set in the crater of a lush, extinct volcano, is extremely popular. The charismatic Epi explains local customs and flora and brings to life the history of his people through fantastic storytelling. Depending on the weather conditions, the tour can be a varying combination of hiking and transport on local carrier. Once you've reached the village and presented your *sevusevu*, you can take a dip in the river and then feast on a delicious local lunch. The full day costs F$30/40/50 per person with a minimum of 4/3/2 people. Book through Ovalau Watersports.

Natokalau Village Tour (starts 9.45am Mon-Sat) is an excellent way to experience genuine village life and to meet Fijians going about their daily tasks: weaving mats, farming, preparing meals. After presently your *sevusevu*, hike up the hillside to Natokalau's original site and ancestral burial grounds. The guide, Kali, is extremely good-natured and will fetch fresh coconuts, tell local legends, and take you on a *bilibili* ride at sea. The tour includes lunch in the village and costs F$27.50 per person. Book in advance at Ovalau Watersports.

Henry Sahai *(☎ 344 0096; Mon-Sat)* will take you on a walking tour of Levuka, sharing his first-hand knowledge of 90 years of local history. The cost is F$8 per person; call Henry or book at Ovalau Watersports.

Places to Stay

Levuka Homestay *(☎/fax 344 0777; Church Street;* **W** *www.levukahomestay.com; singles/ doubles F$115/130 including breakfast, extra person F$40)* is pure comfort. Newly built and gorgeous, it has a gob-smacking view over the sea and a huge deck with hammocks to enjoy it from. Rooms are beautiful, the lounge has lots of books and videos to borrow and breakfast is sumptuous. The laid-back owners will go out of their way to ensure you enjoy your stay in Levuka. Prices are extremely reasonable for what's on offer.

The Royal Hotel *(☎ 344 0024, fax 344 0174;* **e** *royal@connect.com.fj; dorm beds/singles/ doubles/triples F$10/18/28/35, garden & self-contained cottages F$80, all with private bathroom except dorms, payment by cash only)* is the town's most unique option. The weatherboard building is Fiji's oldest hotel and oozes colonial atmosphere, although it's a bit worn at the edges. Some rooms (and beds) are better than others; try to get a seaview room. Dorms are in a colonial-style house with kitchen facilities. More recently built air-con cottages are in the front garden (maximum 3 people). The hotel has a lovely pool, bar and billiard room, and shows videos each night at 8pm sharp! All facilities are for guests only.

Mavida Guest House *(☎ 344 0477; dorm beds F$10-15, doubles F$20-30, all including breakfast & mosquito nets, all shared facilities)*, an excellent budget choice, is a rambling house that dates back to the 1860s. Staff are extremely friendly and shared facilities are clean. Four-bed dorm rooms are spread throughout the house; to reach some private rooms you have to go through a dorm or two.

Places to Eat

Whale's Tale *(☎ 344 0235; 3-course special F$14, mains F$9; open 11am-3pm & 5pm-9pm Mon-Sat)* has fantastic soups, salads, seafood and pasta dishes, all made from fresh ingredients. The vegetarian dishes are tasty, the three-course special is a steal and desserts are divine. This place is cosy and very popular – arrive early or book ahead.

Kim's Paak Kum Lounge *(☎ 344 0059; mains F$8; open 7am-2pm & 6pm-9pm Mon-Sat, Sun noon-2pm & 6pm-9pm)* is a great place to dine, especially on the balcony overlooking the water. With an epic menu of Asian and Fijian dishes, it will keep both vegetarians and carnivores happy. Stumped for choice? Try the Thai curry – it's superb. Staff are ultra-friendly.

Emily Café *(☎ 344 0382; pizza F$7; open 7am-2pm & 6pm-9pm Mon-Sat)* is a good place to stop for an egg bun in the morning. It's very basic but friendly, and in the evening serves good pizza.

Coffee in the Garden *(☎ 344 0471; drinks/ snacks/Sunday breakfast F$2.50/2/3.50; open 8am-6pm Mon-Sat, 9am-11.30am Sun)* is a secluded garden on the seafront where you can sip ice coffees and nibble on muffins, quiche or calamari. Enter through the large gate to the left of the Community Centre. Sunday's fry-up breakfast is very popular.

Cinema Café *(☎ 344 0666; drinks F$2; open 8am-4pm Mon-Sat)* is a funky, bright place for coffee or milkshake. It's also great for people-watching along Levuka's main drag.

On Saturdays, there's a **produce market** on the north side of Totoga Creek. You can get fresh bread at the **bakery** and most everything else at **Katudrau Trading Mini Market** and the **General Store**, both on Beach St.

Getting There & Away

Air Fiji *(☎ 344 0139, fax 344 0252; Beach St)* has twice-daily flights between Nausori airport and Bureta airstrip on the southwestern side of Ovalau, about 40-minutes' drive from Levuka (minibus/taxi F$3.60/$20). Minibuses meet all flights and return according to flight schedules – ask at Air Fiji.

Patterson Brothers Shipping *(☎ 344 0125; Beach St; open 8.30am-4.30pm Mon-Fri)* has bus/ferry services from Levuka to Suva, Labasa and Leluvia (Suva/Labasa F$22/55) – see Getting Around at the beginning of this chapter. You must book at least a day in advance, and on Friday for weekend sailings.

CAQELAI

The beautiful white-sand beaches of this tiny island are fringed with palms and other large trees and, if you're lucky, you may see some **dolphins** and **baby turtles** swimming past.

Caqelai Resort *(☎ 343 0366; camping with/ without meals F$24/12, dorm beds/bure F$28/ 60 including meals, all per person with shared bucket toilets & showers)* is a small and well

FIJI

What Lies Beneath

If you head out to the islands south from Ovalau, your boat will likely travel through Qavo Passage, a break in the reef. Many indigenous Fijians believe that beneath these waters lies a sunken village where ancestral spirits continue to reside. Stories of fishermen hooking newly woven mats are whispered around Levuka. When passing over this *tabu* site, Fijians remove their hats and sunglasses and talk in hushed, reverent tones as it is believed that the spirits are capable of doling out nasty punishments to those who upset them. Whether or not you choose to believe the story, avoid offending and upsetting your hosts – respect their beliefs and following suit. One tourist who refused to take off his baseball cap sent a Fijian woman into terrified hysterics.

kept place run by the Methodist Church of Moturiki. Those after a secluded paradise will love it here. Facilities are very basic but the small *bure* on the water's edge are lovely, the food is superb and the staff are extremely friendly. Dorm accommodation is located in weatherboard buildings. There is no alcohol for sale on the island but you can easily bring your own.

Lionfish and octopi make offshore snorkelling fantastic, and gear is available for F$6 per day. At low tide walk out to Snake Island (named after its many resident sea snakes) for even better snorkelling. Diving can be arranged with Leluvia's dive shop, and you can join village trips to Niubasaga on Moturiki for the Sunday church service or boat trips to tiny Honeymoon Island. Evenings see singing and dancing around a beach bonfire.

Getting There & Away

If you're coming from Levuka, book transport and accommodation from The Royal Hotel. One-way boat transfers cost F$15 per person in a group, F$30 for one person or F$40 for a return day trip (including meals).

From Suva, catch a bus heading down Kings Rd from the main bus terminal and get off at Waidalice. You need to call ahead for a boat from Caqelai to pick you up (F$25/40 per person group/solo).

LELUVIA

Just south of Caqelai, Leluvia is another palm-fringed coral island with golden-sand beaches.

You can swim, explore the tidal pools, do some OK snorkelling or some great diving.

Leluvia Island Resort (☎ 330 1584; dorms/bure/cabins with toilet $30/35/45 per person, including meals) has seen better days. Management wars have taken their toll and maintenance is beginning to wane. Meals are just OK but you can bring your own food and self-cater. The dorm is reminiscent of a bunker and cement cabins are gloomy. The simple *bure* are the best option. The office sells snacks and cold beer. We're keeping our fingers crossed that the new management gets this beautiful oasis back on its feet.

Nautilus Dive Fiji (☎ 330 1584) is run separately from the resort and has a good reputation for safe gear and excellent dives. Single/double dives cost F$75/120, multi-day dive packages are available and the open-water course costs F$390. You can rent snorkelling gear for F$10 per day and, for another F$10, you can be taken by boat to brighter coral offshore. The Dive Shop also has one of the best **book exchanges** we saw in Fiji.

To get to Leluvia, see the Getting Around section near the start of this chapter.

NAIGANI
area 1.5 sq km

Naigani, also known as Mystery Island, has a mountainous interior, white-sand beaches, lagoons and a fringing coral reef. It also holds the remains of a **precolonial hillside fortification** and 'cannibal caves', where, according to locals, 1800 villagers were slaughtered by marauding tribes. The place is *tabu* and locals keep away; out of respect, do the same.

Naigani Island Resort (☎ 330 0539, fax 330 0925; ✉ www.fijifvb.gov.fj/resorts/naigani.htm; studios/5-person villas F$120/150), on the grounds of an old copra plantation, caters to couples, families and small groups. The spacious garden and beachfront villas are great value. The bar and restaurant are in the restored plantation homestead – daily meal packages cost F$45/60 for two/three meals. Facilities include a kids' programme, golf course and pool. Snorkelling is excellent immediately offshore and there are good dive sites nearby via the resort's dive operation. Other activities include nature-trail walks, kayaking, windsurfing, fishing and day excursions to Levuka.

Return transfers to/from Suva, via Natovi Landing, are F$60/30 per adult/child. Return launch transfers to/from Taviya village, near Rukuruku on Ovalau, are F$45.

NAMENALALA
area 0.4 sq km

The volcanic island of Namenalala rests on the Namena Barrier Reef. A natural sailors' refuge, Namenalala has lovely beaches and an old **ring fortification** – the villages disappeared long ago.

Moody's Namena (☎ 881 3764, fax 881 2366; W www.fiji-islands.com/moodys.html; bure per person F$378, including meals, 5 night minimum, no children; closed November-March) has six timber and bamboo bure on a forested ridge. Nearby diving is excellent and costs F$85 per tank (divers must be certified). All other activities – windsurfing, fishing, snorkelling, barrier reef excursions and canoeing – are included in the rate. The island has a nature bird-watching reserve. Transfers are arranged by the resort.

Vanua Levu

pop 139,514 • area 5587 sq km

Dubbed Fiji's best-kept secret, Vanua Levu is making it onto more and more travellers' itineraries. While accessible from Viti Levu, it retains a feeling of remoteness and offers a window into traditional Fijian life. Volcanic in origin, Vanua Levu has few beaches but its nearby reefs offer some of Fiji's best snorkelling and diving. The island's many deep bays are great for kayaking and the rugged interior rainforest makes for good bird-watching.

Vanua Levu is Fiji's second-largest island. Brimming with stunning vistas and rainforest, the southeast coast is dotted with small indigenous-Fijian villages. Savusavu is the main tourist destination, where you'll find the majority of activities. Much of the western coast is remote and accessible only by boat while the north is home to Indo-Fijian sugarcane farmers.

The tourism infrastructure on Vanua Levu remains frail, making it an independent traveller's paradise. Hire a jeep and head off exploring down those wild, tropical roads. Just remember, villagers here are less used to tourists and you cannot wander on foot through the countryside without permission from the landowners.

Getting There & Away
Vanua Levu is easily reached by frequent flights and less-frequent ferries from Viti Levu. See the Getting Around section near the start of this chapter for more information.

SAVUSAVU & AROUND
pop 4970

Dusty little Savusavu sits on a peninsula, looking out across Savusavu Bay to the western mountain range. While the town itself isn't so picturesque, the views certainly are and the sunsets can be spectacular.

Savusavu is Vanua Levu's second largest town and home to a mixed population of indigenous Fijians, Indo-Fijians and expats. With profitability of copra production on the wane, Savusavu's economy is leaning more and more towards tourism and the town has nicknamed itself 'the hidden paradise'. The town is now well serviced by airlines and ferries and its sheltered bay and marinas make it a popular stop for cruising yachties who can carry out immigration formalities here.

Savusavu Bay once saw a great deal of volcanic activity and **hot springs** continue to bubble near the wharf and behind the playing field. Don't even think about bathing in them – they're literally boiling hot.

Information
ANZ bank and **Westpac** have branches on the main street opposite the bus station. Both change currency and travellers cheques and give cash advances on major credit cards. There is an ATM outside ANZ that accepts all major debit and credit cards.

The **post office** is at the eastern end of town near Buca Bay Rd. You'll find cardphones there, near the banks and outside the Copra Shed Marina. If you're looking to get online, try **Savusavu Real Estate & Internet Centre** (☎ 885 0929; Copra Shed Marina; per minute off-/on-line F$0.25/0.35; open 8am-5pm Mon-Fri, 8am-noon Sat) or **Plantation Real Estate & Internet** (☎ 8850 801; per minute F$0.35; open 9am-4pm Mon-Fri), where you'll also find a good **book exchange**.

Air Fiji (☎ 885 0173), **Sun Air** (☎ 885 0141) and **Beachcomber Cruises** (☎ 885 0266) have their offices at the Copra Shed Marina.

In an emergency call the **hospital or ambulance** (☎ 885 0444) or **police** (☎ 885 0222). There's a **private health centre** (☎ 885 0721) in the town centre.

Cruises & Marinas
Try **Tui Tai Adventure Cruises** (☎ 8853 032, 6661 500; fax 6664 496; W www.tuitai.com; Copra Shed), who pack in lots to see and do but not too many guests. Sailing between Vanua Levu, Taveuni, Kioa and Koro, you'll get to snorkel, kayak, bike, hike, swim, fish, dive or

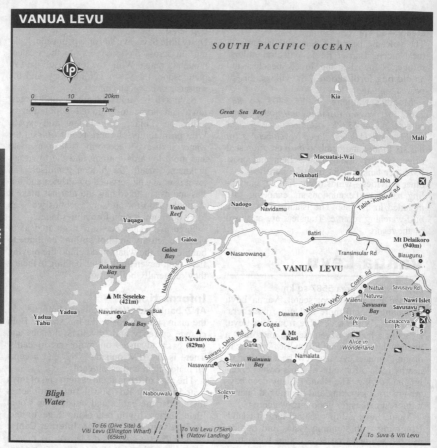

VANUA LEVU

SOUTH PACIFIC OCEAN

Kia

Mali

Macuata-i-Wai

Nukubati   Naduri   Tabia

Nadogo   Navidamu   Tabia-Korovuli Rd

Vatoa
Reef

Yaqaga

Galoa   Batiri   Mt Delaikoro
                                                                    (940m)
Galoa   Nasarowanqa   Transinsular Rd   Biaugunu
Bay   Rd

Rukuruku   VANUA LEVU
Bay
                                                    Coast Rd
▲ Mt Seseleke   Natua   Savusavu Rd
(421m)   Natuvu
Navunievu   Bua   Waileuv West Valeni Savusavu   Nawi Islet
Yadua Yadua   Bay   Savusavu
Tabu   Bua Bay   Dawara   Natovatu   3
                                              Cogea   Pt   4   5
            Mt Navatovotu   ▲ Mt   Alice in
            (829m)   Kasi   Wonderland
                        Sawani Daria Rd   Daria
            Nasawana   Sawani   Wainunu   Namalata
                              Bay
Bligh
Water   Nabouwalu   Solevu
                            Pt

To E6 (Dive Site) &   To Viti Levu (75km)   To Suva & Viti Levu
Viti Levu (Ellington Wharf) (Natovi Landing)
(65km)

just lounge on deck to your heart's content. Dolphins swimming alongside the boat, starlit dinners on deck and the warm villagers you meet en route all make it a blissful experience. The service and food is fantastic, the gear is tops and the snorkelling and diving sites are some of the world's best. Four-day cruises cost F$920/1700/2650 for dorm bunk/cabin/luxury cabin accommodation, including all meals and activities except bar bills and diving; there's also a three-day option. Cruises are geared for independent travellers but guides are available for all activities. For what you're getting, it's a real bargain.

For those looking to charter their own boat, **SeaHawk Yacht Charters** (☎/fax 885 0787; ℮ seahawk@connect.com.fj) rents out a sailboat staffed with captain and a cook/crew for around F$400 per person per day, including

meals. SeaHawk also offers full day and half-day cruises in the area.

Copra Shed Marina (☎ 885 0457, fax 885 0989; ℮ coprashed@connect.com.fj) has been rebuilt into Savusavu's service hub for tourists and expats. Moorings in the pretty harbour costs F$10/150 (day/month). A few doors west, the newly opened **Waitui Marina** (☎ 885 0122, fax 885 0344) offers mooring for F$7/42/150 per day/week/month.

Diving
With excellent underwater sites, Savusavu is a diver's mecca. **L'Aventure Jean-Michel Cousteau** (☎ 885 0188, fax 885 0340; W www .fiji-islands.com/cousteau; Jean-Michel Cousteau Resort), run by the son of the famous Jacques, runs excellent two-tank dives for F$160 and open-water courses for F$450.

VANUA LEVU

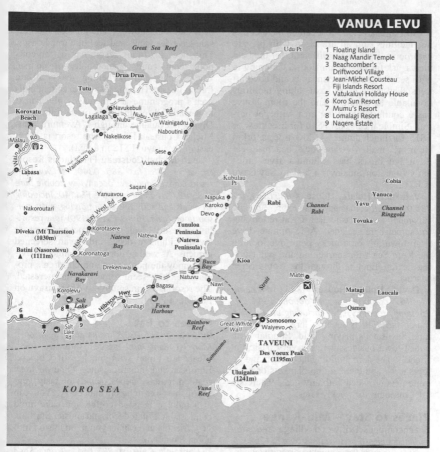

1 Floating Island
2 Naag Mandir Temple
3 Beachcomber's
  Driftwood Village
4 Jean-Michel Cousteau
  Fiji Islands Resort
5 Vatukaluvi Holiday House
6 Koro Sun Resort
7 Mumu's Resort
8 Lomalagi Resort
9 Naqere Estate

FIJI

Eco Divers-Tours (☎ 885 0122, fax 885 0344; ⓦ www.ecodivers-tours.com) also offers two-tank dives for F$130, night dives for F$90 and the PADI course for F$460.

Other Activities

You can ask at one of the marinas for a lift over to the little **beach** on Nawi Islet or rent a kayak from Eco Divers-Tours (see above) and paddle the 250m. Eco Divers-Tours also advertises a variety of **village, hiking and kayaking tours** in the area; ask which ones are available.

Places to Stay – Budget

Beachcomber's Driftwood Village (☎ 885 0046; fax 885 0334; ⓔ driftwood@connect. com.fj; dorm beds F$39, breakfast included) has an immaculate, cabin-style dorm with

private lockers, hot showers and a veranda with a fantastic sea view. The quiet resort has a beautiful pool, good restaurant and bar, and a jetty across the street for swimming or snorkelling. They also have equipment for biking, fishing, kayaking and volleyball. Staff are welcoming and helpful. A taxi from town is F$3.

Copra Shed Marina (☎ 885 0457, fax 885 0989; ⓔ coprashed@connect.com.fj; 2-bedroom flats F$90, double studio flats F$45) has clean and spacious self-contained flats with sunny sea views and good facilities. Staff are very friendly.

Mumu's Resort (☎ 885 0416, fax 885 0402; camping F$5, dorm beds F$17, singles & doubles F$35-75, 5-person Pool House F$150; 4-person Dream House F$80) sits on a ruggedly beautiful point about 17km east of Savusavu. Although somewhat run down, it's full of character. Most cabins have cooking facilities and all are clean with private bathrooms. Each one is different; for the best views, ask for the Dream House. Camping is with sea views, under pandanus and coconut trees. The basic dorm has cooking facilities (available to campers) and the main house has a comfortable sitting area with pet parrots. Simple meals cost F$10 for breakfast or F$15 for lunch/dinner. At low tide, snorkel from the small, volcanic-rock beach. Local Savusavu buses pass Mumu's five times daily (once on Sunday); a taxi to Savusavu is F$12.

Vatukaluvi Holiday House (☎ 885 0561, fax 885 0989; self-contained house F$55, 7 people maximum) is a fantastic deal if you're looking for somewhere secluded. A 15-minute drive from town, it's on a rocky point overlooking the Koro Sea with snorkelling and windsurfing nearby. Enquire through the Copra Shed Marina.

David's Holiday House (☎ 885 0149; camp sites F$7, dorm beds/singles/doubles F$11/20/25, family room F$30, all including breakfast & shared facilities) is set in a large garden behind Savusavu's playing field. Popular with out-of-town businessmen, it's very basic but friendly. The dorm building has no fan and no top sheets, and there are no blankets or mosquito nets provided with any beds. There's a 10% discount for weekly rates.

Places to Stay – Mid-Range

Beachcomber's Driftwood Village (see entry earlier; doubles/6-person family bure F$125/255, breakfast included) is a quiet resort with sweeping views of the sea, offering top-end rooms for mid-range prices. Bure are private and extremely comfortable. See Places to Stay – Budget in this section.

Hot Springs Hotel (☎ 885 0195, fax 885 0430; e hotspring@connect.com.fj; doubles with fan/air-con F$80/125, including breakfast, F$22 per extra person, up to 2 children free), smack in the middle of town, has that typical hotel feel. Rooms are cool and comfortable with tiled floors and water-view balconies. There's also a nice pool on a large, sunny deck and a pleasant restaurant and bar.

Places to Stay – Top End

Koro Sun Resort (☎/fax 885 0150; e res@korosunresort.com; single/double bure F$225/275, triples/quads/quins in 2-bedroom bure F$430/480/530, all meals included) has really

beautiful, plush bure with four-poster bamboo beds and rock showers. The bure on the hillside have sea views and feel like tree houses. This new, luxurious resort has a gorgeous pool, tennis courts, a nine-hole golf course, kayaks, bikes and snorkelling gear – all are free to guests. There is also an excellent children's programme and massages given next to a waterfall, on the edge of the rainforest. Diving is available through L'Aventure Jean-Michel Cousteau Diving. The resort is 13km east of Savusavu (F$12 in a taxi).

Jean-Michel Cousteau Fiji Islands Resort (☎ 885 0188, fax 885 0340; W www.fiji resort.com; gardenview/oceanview double bure F$850/970, 2-bedroom bure F$1140, including all meals and activities except diving, extra person under/over 16 yrs F$140/190) is a resort-lover's resort. Meals are gourmet and bure are lavish, with large decks and private screened gardens. As well as oodles of planned activities, enjoy the pool, gym and children's programme. Staff seem somewhat disinterested. The resort is 15km southwest of Savusavu on Lesiaceva Point.

Places to Eat

Bula Re (☎ 885 0307; mains about F$8; open Mon-Sat 8am-9pm) serves fantastic food. Meals are Fijian with touches of Chinese, European and Indian cuisines. Dine on fresh seafood, pastas, crepes, salads or tasty veggie dishes like tempeh and curry. You can also indulge in good coffee and cake amid comfortable Fijian decor and music. Staff are very friendly and can let you in on lots o f info about Savusavu.

Captain's Café (☎ 885 0511; Copra Shed Marina; small/medium/large pizza F$10/15/20, breakfast F$8; open 8.30am-8.30pm Mon-Fri, 9am-9pm Sat, 11am-8.30pm Sun) is well known for its pizzas but also has fish and chips, sandwiches and full breakfasts. The views of the yacht-dotted harbour from the deck make up for its average food.

Beachcomber's Driftwood Village (☎ 885 0334; lunch/dinner F$7/15) serves set meals in its poolside bure. The food is an imaginative mix of Fijian and Western. In the evening you can dine to the tune of local musicians.

Hot Springs Hotel (☎ 885 0195; breakfast F$6.50, Sunday lunch F$12.50; breakfast 7am-9am, dinner 7pm-9pm daily) is a great place for breakfast with a view, and the buffet will keep you going all day. Sunday lunch includes house wine or draft beer and is accompanied by a live string band.

Vidya Chand's Seaview Café *(main street; open 9am-6pm Mon-Fri, 9am-1pm Sat; meals F$5)* is bright and cheerful, serving good Indian curries, rice and roti.

Savusavu has an **MH Supermarket** and a **market** *(open Mon-Sat)* selling fruit, veggies and lots of kava. The **Hot Bread Kitchen** *(open Mon-Sun; main street)* bakes fresh loaves daily.

Entertainment
Try either of the marinas for a drink with local expats and visiting yachties. The **Planters Club**, on the western edge of town, is a popular hangout for local copra farmers.

Shopping
Located in the Copra Shed, **The Art Gallery** and **Tako Handicraft** sell paintings, cards, sculptures and handicrafts by local artists. Across the street from the Copra Shed is a shack where a local man sells wooden carvings and around back of the **market** is a room devoted to local handicrafts.

Getting There & Away
See the Getting Around section near the start of this chapter for more information about getting to and from Vanua Levu.

Buses to Labasa (F$5, three hours, four times daily) depart from 7.30am to 3.30pm Monday to Saturday and from 9.30am to 3.30pm on Sunday. Buses also take the scenic route from Savusavu to Labasa along Natewa Bay (9am, F$10, six hours). Buses from Savusavu to Napuca (F$5.40, 4½ hours), at the tip of the Tunuloa Peninsula, depart at 10.30am and 2.30pm daily. The afternoon bus stays there overnight and returns at 7am. For confirmation of bus timetables, ring **Vishnu Holdings** (☎ 885 0276).

Getting Around
Savusavu's bus station and taxi stand are in the centre of town, near the market. Hiring a small carriers from the bus station is reasonable if travelling in a group. There are local buses from Savusavu to Lesiaceva Point and to Savusavu airstrip, 3km south of town. A taxi between the airport and Savusavu is F$2.

Budget Rent a Car (☎ 881 1999) in Labasa will deliver and pick up 4WD jeeps in Savusavu.

TUNULOA PENINSULA
Lush and scenic Tunuloa Peninsula is an excellent area to explore by 4WD. If you can arrange a guide in Savusavu or from your resort, it also offers great bird-watching and hiking. The bumpy, rough Hibiscus Hwy passes copra plantations, old homesteads and waving villagers. The road becomes extremely slippery with the rain; if driving, double-check the tyres before you set out. There are no restaurants or shops along this route.

About 20km east of Savusavu, the Hibiscus Hwy turns south; the turn-off to the north skirts Natewa Bay to Labasa. At Buca Bay, the highway turns north (left) through the habitat of the rare **silktail bird**, sadly listed on the world's endangered-species list.

If you turn south (right) at Buca Bay, you'll head up over the mountain to the village of **Dakuniba**. The going is slow but you'll be rewarded with dazzling views. Just outside Dakuniba, mysterious **petroglyphs** are inscribed on large boulders; be sure to bring a *sevusevu* for the village chief.

Places to Stay
Naqere Estate (☎ 888 0022; e naqere@ connect.com.fj; singles/doubles F$110/150 including all meals, shared bathroom, minimum

3 nights, maximum 4 people) is a beautiful, spacious B&B set in a peaceful garden about 25km from Savusavu. Extremely comfortable with water views, this is a perfect place to get off the beaten track and relax. Snorkel, kayak or take a dip in the nearby swimming hole.

Lomalagi Resort *(☎ 881 6098, fax 881 6099; W www.lomalagi.com; self-contained villa doubles F$375 including all meals, no children)* is high on a hill overlooking beautiful Natewa Bay. The rubber ducky in the tub may not suit everyone, but views from villa decks are spectacular and utter privacy is guaranteed. The seawater pool is gorgeous and activities include kayaking, swimming, village trips, snorkelling and biking. The resort is about 20km east of Savusavu.

The **Rainbow Reef Resort** is southeast of Buca Bay and accessible by boat from Taveuni. See the Places to Stay section under Taveuni for more information.

LABASA & AROUND
pop 24,095
Labasa, Vanua Levu's largest town, is on the northwestern side of the island's mountain range, about 5km inland on the banks of the meandering Labasa River. In 2003, cyclone Ami left Labasa under 1.2m of water and all but obliterated the area's important sugarcane industry. Labasa's population is predominantly Indo-Fijian.

While Labasa is a bustling trade, service and administrative centre, it doesn't have a lot to offer tourists. Most shops and services can be found on Nasekula Rd, the main street. In an emergency, contact the **police** *(☎ 881 1222; Nadawa St)* or the **hospital** *(☎ 881 1444; Butinikama-Siberia Rd)*.

Cobra Rock
Brightly painted red, yellow and blue, **Naag Mandir Temple** is built around the sacred Cobra Rock. About 3m in height, the rock's natural curved formation resembles a cobra poised to strike. Covered in colourful flower and tinsel garlands, the rock is beseeched with offerings of fruit, fire and coconut milk. Devotees swear that the rock grows in size and that the roof has had to be raised several times over the years. Remove your shoes before entering and circle the rock clockwise three or five times. Buses from Labasa to Natewa Bay pass the temple; a taxi costs F$10. If you're driving, head east out of town and turn left onto Wainikoro Rd, just past the sugar mill. The temple is a further 10km.

Places to Stay
Labasa Riverview Private Hotel *(☎ 881 1367, fax 881 4337; Nadawa Street; dorm beds F$15, singles/doubles with shared facilities F$20/30, with private bathroom F$30/40, with private bathroom and air-con F$45/55)* is an excellent budget option. Rooms are cosy and comfortable and the five-bed dorm has a clean, well-equipped kitchen. A five-minute walk north of town, this place is relaxed and safe and has a very friendly proprietor.

Grand Eastern Hotel *(☎ 881 1022, fax 881 4011; W www.tokatoka.com.fj; Rosawa St; standard/deluxe rooms F$95/115)* is Labasa's most upmarket hotel, with a beautiful pool and decent restaurant. Rooms don't have much character but do have small porches, air con, private facilities and views of the river.

Places to Eat
Labasa's main street is teeming with hole-in-the-wall Indian and Chinese restaurants.

Oriental Bar & Restaurant *(☎ 881 7321; Nukusima St; meals F$5-10; open 10am-3pm & 6.30pm-10pm Mon-Sat, 6.30pm-10pm Sun)* feels rather upmarket but has extremely reasonable prices. The bar is fairly well stocked and the menu has a good variety of tasty Chinese dishes, with lots for vegetarians. No caps or vests allowed.

Grand Eastern Hotel *(F$10/12/15 breakfast/ lunch/dinner; open 7am-9.30am, 11.30am-2pm & 6.30pm-9pm daily)* serves Western-style food in its restaurant. It's decorated with historical photos of Labasa and spills out onto the deck, making it a pleasant place to dine.

Getting There & Around
See Getting Around at the start of the chapter for information on reaching Vanua Levu.

There are regular buses between Labasa and Savusavu (F$5.50, five times daily, four on Sunday) departing between 7am and 4.15pm. A 9am bus takes the scenic route to Savusavu along Natewa Bay.

Taxis are plentiful, with the main stand near the bus station. **Budget Rent a Car** *(☎ 881 1999; Vakamasisuasua)* is south of town and rents out 4WD vehicles. The airport is about 11km southwest of Labasa.

OFFSHORE ISLANDS
The island of **Kioa** is inhabited by Polynesians originally from the tiny coral reef island of Vaitupu in Tuvalu. The community purchased Kioa in 1947 to reduce population pressure on Vaitupu. The one village

is colourful and immaculately kept and the villagers are known throughout Fiji for their woven crafts. You cannot arrive without an invitation and there's no tourist accommodation. Tui Tai Adventure Cruises visits Kioa (see the Activities section under Savusavu).

East of Tunuloa peninsula, **Rabi** is populated by Micronesians originally from Banaba (Ocean Island) in Kiribati. If you're interested in visiting Rabi, request permission from the **Island Council** (☎ 881 2913).

Taveuni

Taveuni's stunning natural beauty makes it a haven for divers, bushwalkers and nature lovers. Nicknamed 'The Garden Island', it's a profusion of tropical plants and flowers, with world-class dive sites on its doorstep. Taveuni is easily accessible and relatively compact yet far from feeling overrun.

The small population is spread thinly across the island – there are villages and small towns but no urban centres. The population is mainly indigenous Fijian with a smaller crowd of Indo-Fijians and expats.

Taveuni is the third-largest Fijian island, with a largely rugged coastline set against some of Fiji's highest peaks. The cloud-shrouded Uluigalau (1241m) is the country's second-highest summit, and the volcanic soil and abundant rainfall make Taveuni one of Fiji's most fertile areas. The island's northeast is fringed by reefs, the eastern side has dramatic waterfalls and the southern coast is eroded by the sea, forming caves and blowholes.

Dangers & Annoyances
In recent years, theft has become an increasingly common problem on Taveuni and it's worth taking precautions. Always lock your door when sleeping and keep valuables out of sight. Don't wander around alone at night.

Diving
Beneath the indigo waters of the Somosomo Strait are a gazillion fish, sharks, turtles, fantastic coral and, in November, pilot whales. Sites include the infamous 32km-long Rainbow Reef, the Great White Wall, the Zoo and Vuna Reef. Water clarity is reduced in January and February due to plankton blooms and northerly winds from the equator.

There are a number of dive operations in Matei, as well as one in Waiyevo and another in the southern Dolphin Bay Divers' Retreat.

Bird-Watching
Taveuni is one of Fiji's best locations for bird-watching. Over 100 species of birds can be found, partly because the mongoose was never introduced here. Try Des Voeux Peak at dawn for a chance to see the rare orange dove and the silktail. Along Levena Coastal Walk, keep your eyes peeled for parrots, fantails, flame doves, Fiji goshawk and wattled honeyeater.

Snorkelling
The four small islands immediately offshore from Naselesele Point have some good snorkelling. Also try Prince Charles Beach or Beverly Beach. In Matei, Aquaventure rents out gear (F$20) and will take snorkellers (minimum 4) to Qamea (F$40 per person). Next door, Island Pizza will also take you out to nearby snorkelling sites (F$30) and Taveuni Estates Dive rents out snorkelling gear (F$15). Southern Taveuni's Dolphin Bay Divers' Retreat has excellent offshore snorkelling.

Getting There & Away
Matei airport is on the southern tip of Taveuni; both the Sun Air and Air Fiji offices are there. Ferries depart from the Government Wharf and the Korean Wharf, south of Waiyevo. For more information on reaching Taveuni, see Getting Around near the start of the chapter.

Getting Around
Getting around Taveuni involves a bit of planning, the main disadvantage being the length of time between buses. To get around cheaply and quickly you need to combine buses with walking, or share taxis with a group. You can rent 4WD jeeps in Naqara but it's far cheaper to hire a taxi for the day.

From Matei airport expect to pay about F$15 to Waiyevo and F$30 to Vuna (Dolphin Bay Divers' Retreat) in a taxi. Matei has many places to stay that are within an easy walk from the airport and most upmarket resorts provide transfers for guests.

Bus Taveuni's bus schedule is very lax, and buses may show an hour early or late. Be sure to double-check return bus times when you board, just to make sure there is one.

Pacific Buses (☎ 888 0278; Naqara) runs buses from Wairiki to Bouma at 8.30am, 11.30am and 5pm (Monday to Saturday). The last bus of the day continues to Levena where the first bus of each morning starts out at 5.45am. On Tuesday and Thursday, all buses go as far as Levena. On Sunday there is one

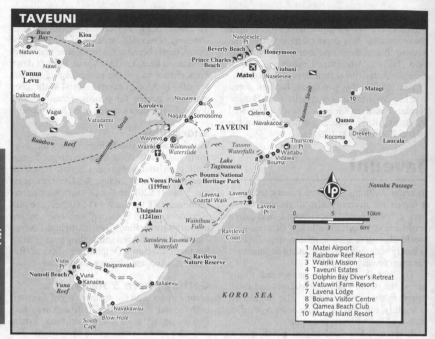

TAVEUNI

1 Matei Airport
2 Rainbow Reef Resort
3 Wairiki Mission
4 Taveuni Estates
5 Dolphin Bay Diver's Retreat
6 Vatuwiri Farm Resort
7 Lavena Lodge
8 Bouma Visitor Centre
9 Qamea Beach Club
10 Matagi Island Resort

bus at 3.30pm from Wairiki to Levena and one from Levena to Wairiki at 7.30am.

From Naqara, buses run to southern Taveuni at 8.30am, 11.30am and 4.30pm (Monday to Saturday). On Sunday the bus departs Naqara at 3.30pm and returns the following morning. From Matei, buses run to Wairiki at 7am, 11.30am and 3pm (Monday to Saturday).

Car Hire 4WDs for around F$145 per day at **Budget Rent a Car** (☎ 888 0291; *Garden State General Merchants, Naqara*). It's more economical and probably safer to hire a taxi for the day.

Taxi These are readily available in the Matei and Waiyevo areas – it may be wise to book ahead on Sunday. Hiring a taxi for a day to tour the island should cost under F$100; you'll inevitably get a better deal if you ask a local to negotiate for you. For destinations such as Lavena you can go by bus and return by taxi but you must arrange this before you go.

WAIYEVO, SOMOSOMO & AROUND

While not the most picturesque part of the island, this area has the majority of services and can be a good base. Somosomo is the largest village on the island and headquarters for its chiefly leadership. Somosomo runs directly into Naqara, the village with the largest downtown, including supermarkets, the island's one bank and transport links. A short taxi ride or a long, dusty walk away is Waiyevo, with the hospital, police station and more ferry links. Another 2km south of Waiyevo is Wairiki village, with a general store, a cinema and a beautiful old hilltop Mission.

Information

The **Colonial National Bank** (*Naqara*) exchanges currency and travellers cheques, but won't do cash advances and doesn't have an ATM. The larger supermarkets and top-end resorts may accept credit cards for a fee.

You'll find a cardphone outside the **post office** (*Waiyevo*) and outside Naqara's supermarket. **Garden State General Merchants** (☎ 888 0291; *Naqara*) has one computer with Internet access for F$0.50 per minute. **Ross Handicrafts** (☎ 3309 727; *Waiyevo*) also has an Internet connection for F$0.40 per minute.

On hand for emergencies are the **hospital** (☎ 888 0444; *Waiyevo*) and **police** (☎ 888 0222; *Waiyevo*).

Things to See & Do

Although the International Dateline officially doglegs Fiji, the **180-degree Meridian** cuts straight through Taveuni, about a 10-minute walk south of Waiyevo. A red survey beacon marks the spot along the water and there's an info board on the field above.

In the mid-17th century, Taveuni warriors defeated and dined on Tongan invaders. **Wairiki Catholic Mission** was built in 1907 in tribute to the French missionary who helped the local warriors with their fighting strategy (but, one can assume, not with their dinner plans). The grand mission looks out over the Somosomo Strait. Its beautiful stained glass reportedly hails from France. It's worth attending Mass on Sunday for the spirited singing.

Waitavala Waterslide is not for the faint of heart – a bruise or two is unavoidable as you fly down these natural rock chutes. It can be extremely dangerous, so ask about conditions first and watch a local before you attempt. Walking north from Waiyevo, take the first right, another right and head left downhill. This is private property so if you pass anyone, ask permission.

At 1195m, **Des Voeux Peak** is Taveuni's second-highest point. On a clear day, views are fantastic – it's possible to see Lake Tagimaucia and, if you're really lucky, the Lau Group. Allow three to four hours to walk the 6km up and at least two to return. From Waiyevo, take the inland track just before Wairiki Catholic Mission. On weekdays it's sometimes possible to hitch a ride with public workers.

In the mountains above Somosomo, **Lake Tagimaucia** rests in an old volcanic crater. Fiji's national flower, the rare *tagimaucia*, grows on the lake's shores and blooms from late September to late December. The hike is overgrown and muddy, starting from Somosomo where you need to present the chief with a *sevusevu* and ask permission. Take lunch, preferably a guide and allow eight hours for the round trip.

Aqua-Trek Taveuni *(Garden Island Resort Waiyevo)* is a well-equipped dive shop with two-tank dives for F$165 and multi-dive packages. Open-water courses cost F$660.

Places to Stay

Kool's Accommodation *(☎ 888 0395; Naqara; dorm beds/singles/doubles F$15/20/30)* is a friendly place with basic, clean rooms in a well-maintained building. Private rooms have attached bathrooms and there's a kitchen for guest use but no fridge. Rooms are fan-less. The reception doubles as S&J's Video Club.

First Light Inn *(☎ 888 0339; e firstlight@connect.com.fj; Waiyevo; doubles/triples with fan $50/60, doubles/triples with air con $60/70, all with private bathroom; kitchen available)* is a great mid-range option; nothing flashy but clean and great value. The deck has views over the strait and is a good place to catch the sunset if you can ignore the noise of the neighbouring resort's generator. The reception doubles as the office for Consort Shipping.

Garden Island Resort *(☎ 888 0286, fax 888 0288; e garden@connect.com.fj; Waiyevo; dorm beds/singles/doubles F$35/150/185, children under 12 free, meal plan per person F$80)* used to be a Travelodge and hasn't lost that average hotel feel, but rooms are clean and comfortable with air-con and sea views. There's no beach but you can swim at high tide. The lovely pool and restaurant-bar area looks across the strait. Two of the hotel rooms have been converted into good-value four-bed dorms.

Rainbow Reef Resort *(☎ 888 1000, fax 888 1001; W www.rainbowreefresort.com; double bure with/without spa F$860/770, family bure F$860, including meals, 3 night minimum)*, on Vanua Levu, is reached from Taveuni. The closest resort to the famous Rainbow Reef,

The Legend of the Tagimaucia

There once lived a young girl with a wild spirit and a tendency to be disobedient. One fateful day, her mother lost her patience and beat the girl with a bundle of coconut leaves, saying she never wanted to see her again. The distraught girl ran away until she was deep in the forest. She came upon a large vine-covered *ivi* (Polynesian chestnut) tree and decided to climb it. The higher she climbed, the more entangled she became in the vine and, unable to break free, she began to weep. As giant tears rolled down her face they turned to blood and, where they fell onto the vine, they became beautiful white and red *tagimaucia* flowers. Calmed by the sight of the flowers, the girl managed to escape the forest and returned home to an equally calm mother.

this small-scale, family-friendly place has a lovely white-sand beach and plush, beachfront cottages. Activities include hiking, kayaking and snorkelling. Diving and tours to Taveuni cost extra. Transfers are F$110 return, by boat from Taveuni.

Places to Eat

Garden Island Resort Restaurant *(Waiyevo; breakfast/lunch/dinner under F$10/10/20)* is a pleasant place to dine with live local music in the evenings. Meals are mainly Western and not overly inspired.

Wathi-po-ee Restaurant and Cannibal Café (☎ 888 0382; *Waiyevo; mains F$5; open 8am-7pm Mon-Fri, 8am-2pm Sat)* below the First Light Inn, is a basic, friendly place with an outdoor area overlooking the strait. Breakfast is omelettes and sausages, while lunch and dinner is mainly Chinese with some *dalo* thrown in for good measure.

Makuluva Restaurant (☎ 994 5394; *Waiyevo; breakfast/lunch F$3/4; open 8am-4pm Mon-Fri & Sun)* is in the old market building across from the Garden Island Resort. It's very basic but the cheerful owner whips up great pancakes and hot chocolate for breakfast, and Fijian, Indian and Chinese dishes for lunch. Vegetarians will find lots of options here.

Kumars Restaurant (☎ 888 0435; *Naqara; mains F$4; open 7am-5.30pm Mon-Sat)*, aka the Green Curry Hut, has Indian dishes as well as a few basic Fijian dishes and the prerequisite chop suey. It's basic and popular with locals.

If you're self-catering, **Kaba's Supermarket** *(Naqara)* is fully stocked. **Hot Bread Bakers** (☎ 888 0504; *Naqara; open daily)* sells fresh breads, buns, cupcakes and tasty pizza.

SOUTHERN TAVEUNI

The road south from Waiyevo winds along the rugged coast, through beautiful rainforest, *dalo* and coconut plantations to Vuna and Kanacea villages.

Activities

Diving and snorkelling on the Vuna Reef is excellent; go through **Dolphin Bay Divers** (☎/fax 888 0125; *Dolphin Bay Divers' Retreat;* W *www.dolphinbaydivers.com)* where a shore shore/night/two-tank dive costs F$50/75/130. They also offer multi-day dive packages and lots of courses including the open-water option for F$550. Divers taking a course get free dorm accommodation and transfers from Matei.

Vatuwiri Farm Resort (☎ 888 0316) offers fishing, catamaran trips, horse riding, hiking and bird-watching.

Places to Stay & Eat

Dolphin Bay Divers' Retreat (☎/fax 888 0125; *dorm beds F$10, main-house doubles with private/shared bathroom F$50/35, double/ triple/quad bure with private bathroom F$75/ 80/85)* is set in a peaceful location with gorgeous sea and sunset views. Once Susie's Plantation, it has undergone a change of ownership with dramatic improvements. Enjoy excellent diving and snorkelling, kava drinking in the evenings and a *meke* on Friday nights. Internet access and tours are available. The double with private bathroom in the main house is spacious and comfortable and the garden *bure* are pleasant. Dorms are basic but clean and slated for renovation. Breakfast and dinner are available for F$25. Airport transfers are free to guests staying in a *bure* for three nights. Major credit cards accepted.

Vatuwiri Farm Resort (☎ 888 0316, fax 888 0314; *cottage doubles $F110, homestead single room F$110, all with private bathroom; closed Oct-Jan)* is unlike any other resort you'll set foot in. With horses, cattle and honking geese, a visit here will give you a chance to experience life on a plantation. Stay with the friendly family in the homestead or in a small cottage perched on the water's edge. There are loads of activities, including swimming and snorkelling, or you can just enjoy the peace and quiet. Three meals a day are F$70.

Taveuni Estates (☎ 888 0044; e *taveunie states@connect.com.fj)* is a luxury home-development project. At the time of research, construction begun for fantastic-sounding dorms next to a black-sand beach with a tree-house bar. Prices are proposed at F$20 per night – it's worth checking out.

MATEI & AROUND

Matei is a residential area on Taveuni's northern point. Much of the freehold land has been bought by foreigners searching for a piece of tropical paradise. It's near the airport, and there are a number of places to stay, some of the island's best dining options, dive shops, a couple of beaches and nearby snorkelling.

Information

Matei doesn't have much in the way of services. There's a cardphone at the airport and another outside Bhula Bhai Supermarket. Swiss Divers offers Internet services.

Diving

Aquaventure (☎/fax 888 0381; W www.aqua venture.org), based at Beverly Beach, has a reputation for conducting safe and reliable dives. A two-tank dive with/without equipment costs F$150/130. They offer multi-dive packages and a number of courses, including the open-water certificate for F$550. Dive sites include Rainbow Reef and the Great White Wall.

Swiss Fiji Divers (☎/fax 888 0586; W www .swissfijidivers.com), next door, offers high-quality gear including computer consoles, masks with underwater communication and scooters. Two-tank dives cost F$190 for tanks and weights only and an open-water course including all gear costs F$760.

Taveuni Estates Dive (☎ 888 0653; W www .taveunidive.com) is new on the scene. An outpost of Taveuni Estates, it has that wet-behind-the-ears feel to it. A two-tank dive costs F$130 (F$20 for gear) and the open-water course is F$530. It's next to Bhula Bhai Supermarket.

Places to Stay – Budget

Beverly Beach Camping (☎ 888 0684; camping with/without own tent F$8/10) is about 15 minutes' walk west of the airport. The small site can accommodate a maximum of 12 people is set between the road and a white-sand beach, beneath huge, poison-fish trees. It's well maintained and a good place to relax. Basic facilities include flush toilets, a shower and a sheltered area for cooking and dining.

Bibi's Hideaway (☎ 888 0443; camping F$12, 2-bedroom family cottage 1/2 rooms F$50/90, cottage singles/doubles F$60/80; bure F$80, all with mosquito nets, all self-contained) has homey little cottages set in a huge, beautiful garden. A ten-minute walk west from the airport, it's extremely peaceful and the welcoming family will invite you to help yourself to luscious produce from the garden. Bring mosquito•coils. There's electricity in the evenings but no fans.

Karin's Garden (☎/fax 888 0511; doubles or twin F$95, minimum 2-night stay), with a bird's eye view of the reef, has a double bure with shared kitchen, sitting room and long veranda. Across from Bibi's, the wooden rooms are spacious, comfortable and very cosy. There's beach access at the end of the property and the owners are relaxed and affable. Rooms have fans and electricity in the evenings.

Little Dolphin Treehouse (☎ 888 0130; cottage doubles F$90, no children), southeast of the airport, is a fantastic place with a well-equipped kitchen downstairs and a comfortable double room upstairs. It has lots of privacy, fabulous sea views and friendly owners.

Tovutovu Resort (☎ 888 0560, fax 888 0722; dorm beds F$15, bure doubles/triples with kitchen F$75/85, double bure without kitchen F$65, all private rooms with bathroom) has no beach does have but comfortable bure, hot water, fans and electricity in the evening. The eight-bed dorm is a good option for backpackers, with a communal kitchen and deck. There's a good restaurant on site and activities include biking and snorkelling. The resort is a 20-minute walk southeast of Matei airport.

Places to Stay – Mid-Range

The very popular **Coconut Grove Beachfront Cottages** (☎/fax 888 0328; W www.coconut grovefiji.com; doubles in main house per person F$110, cottages doubles per person F$150-190, including breakfast & dinner, all with private bathroom) is small and well-maintained. All rooms are spacious and comfortable, and cottages all have private outdoor rock showers. There's access to a small, white-sand beach from where you can explore with the two-man kayak (hour/half-day/full-day F$15/35/55). The owner is affable and privacy is guaranteed. It's often full so book ahead. Walk-in rates may apply from January to March.

Audrey's by the Sea (☎ 888 0039; cottage F$175, no children) is a self-contained cottage in a peaceful garden. The lacy decor may not be everyone's cup of tea but it's comfortable and spacious with a small beach across the road. Audrey is very welcoming and lives a 10-minute walk southeast of the airport.

Places to Stay – Top End

Taveuni Island Resort (☎ 888 0441, fax 888 0466; W www.taveuniislandresort.com; standard/ luxury bungalows F$1044/1240 including meals, maximum 14 guests) is opulent. With the air of a millionaire's clifftop beach house, it's all polished wood and wicker and has a stunning pool, gorgeous views, and a nearby white-sand beach. Meals are a gourmet's delight.

Maravu Plantation Resort (☎ 888 0555, fax 888 0600; W www.maravu.net; duplex bure singles/doubles/triples F$420/640/780, deluxe bure singles/doubles/triples F$460/ 720/900, family duplex F$960, all including meals; children's accommodation free, kids' meal plan F$60 per day) has spacious, plush cottages dotted among the coconut groves. Meals are sumptuous, there's a lovely pool, lots of activities and a small white-sand beach across the road.

FIJI

Places to Eat

Island Pizza (☎ 888 8083; regular/large pizza F$15/18; open 10am-9.30pm daily) serves delicious, thin-crusted pizzas on a wooden deck over the water. Surrounded by a pretty patch of golden sand and leafy trees, it's a perfect place to relax. Prices are very reasonable and they'll also deliver if you pay the transport. You'll find it next to Aquaventure and Prince Charles' Beach.

Coconut Grove Café (☎ 888 0328; breakfast/lunch/dinner F$6/10/15; open Mar-Dec) has great food made from fresh ingredients. The menu includes homemade pasta, soups, salads, fish and delicious desserts. Meals are served on the veranda, overlooking the water and nearby islets. Place your dinner order before 4pm.

Karin's Garden (☎ 888 0511; set-menu dinner F$15) serves excellent European-style dinners from a cliff-top house. The menu is generally meat or fish with homemade bread and fresh vegetables. The property has spectacular views at sunset. Book before 3pm.

Tovutovu Resort (☎ 888 0560; mains F$10) has a restaurant with an outdoor deck and tasty, good-value meals. On Fridays there's a well-attended buffet and music night (F$15).

Lal's Curry Place (☎ 888 0705; meals $8; open Mon-Sat), southeast of the airport, serves heaps of great Indian food for a steal. A meal includes soup, curry, roti, rice and chutney.

Audrey's Sweet Something's has teas, brewed coffees and excellent cakes. Indulge in some fudge cake or homemade kaluha.

Bhula Bhai Supermarket (☎ 888 0462; open daily), a 15-minute walk southeast of the airport, sells groceries for self-caterers.

EASTERN TAVEUNI

Eastern Taveuni's beautiful, wild coast and lush rainforest is a magnet for nature lovers. Having rejected logging in favour of ecotourism, the locally managed Bouma Environmental Tourism Project is working fabulously.

Bouma National Heritage Park

This national park (admission F$5) protects over 80% of Taveuni's total area, with several kilometres of bush walks, the three beautiful **Tavoro Waterfalls** and natural swimming pools. The walking track begins opposite the reception bure, south of the river in Bouma.

The first waterfall is only 10 minutes' walk along a flat path and is a great place for a dip. The second waterfall, a further 30 or 40 minutes along, is smaller than the first but also has

a good swimming pool. The track is steep in places with a river crossing, but has steps and handrails and a spectacular view through the coconut trees. The 30-minute hike to the third and smallest fall is less maintained and often muddy. It has a great swimming pool and, if you bring your snorkelling gear, you'll be able to see the hundreds of prawns in the water.

If you are keen walker, try the **Vidawa Rainforest Hike**, a full-day guided hike taking in historic fortified village sites, rainforest and Tavoro Waterfalls. Book in advance. The fee of F$60/40 for adults/children includes pick-up and drop-off at your hotel, guides, lunch and afternoon tea.

Places to Stay & Eat A lovely spot to picnic or camp, **Tavoro Waterfalls Visitor Centre** (☎ 888 0390; camping F$10 per person, meals F$5-10; open 9am-4pm daily) offers simple meals and is equipped with a kitchen, toilets, an open shower and a covered eating area. The generator kicks in for the evening. Staff are friendly and will let you store your bags here while you hike up to the falls.

Waitabu Marine Park

This area offers excellent snorkelling off a white-sand beach. Recently opened to tourists, you can only visit the park with a guide. The village of Waitabu has set up a half-day tour including a guided snorkel, bilibili ride, morning and afternoon tea in the village and transport to and from Matei. The cost is F$50 for adults and F$25 for 12- to 17-year-olds (children under 12 not accepted). Book with **Aquaventure** (☎ 888 0381) in Matei.

Lavena Coastal Walk

The 5km Lavena Coastal Walk is well worth the effort. The trail follows the forest edge along the beach, passes peaceful villages and then climbs up through the tropical rainforest to a gushing waterfall. There's some good snorkelling and kayaking here, and Levena Point is good for swimming (as demonstrated by Milla Jovovich in Return to Blue Lagoon).

The path is clearly marked and well maintained. To see and reach the falls at the end of the trail, you have to walk over rocks and swim a short distance through two deep pools. Two cascades fall at different angles into a deep pool with sheer walls. If you're visiting in the rainy season, it can be difficult, if not dangerous, to reach the falls. Ask at Levena Lodge for current conditions. At any time of year (even if it hasn't been raining), violent flash floods can occur and readers have advised staying to the left of the pool, where you can make an easier getaway.

The park is managed through **Lavena Lodge**. Park entrance is F$5 or F$15 with a guide. Kayaks can be hired for F$40 per day and guided kayak tours are available.

Places to Stay & Eat Run by friendly, informative staff, **Lavena Lodge** (☎ 888 0116; twins per person F$15; maximum 8 people) has basic rooms with a shared kitchen and facilities. Rooms are clean and there's electricity in the evening. Next to a beach, this is a great place to relax under the trees after a hard day's hike. Meals are available from the lodge (F$7/10 breakfast/lunch or dinner). Bring your own supplies and definitely bring water.

OFFSHORE ISLANDS
Matagi
area 1 sq km
Stunning Matagi is 10km off Taveuni's coast, with steep rainforest sides rising 130m.

Matagi Island Resort (☎ 888 0260, fax 888 0274; W www.matangiisland; standard bure singles/doubles/triples F$364/610/720, deluxe bure singles/doubles/triples F$280/850/970, treehouses F$1070, all including meals and most activities) is built along a white-sand beach. Deluxe bure are spacious and the fantastic 'treehouses' have views to the beach. Activities include windsurfing, kayaking, waterskiing and saltwater fly-fishing. There's 30 dive spots within 10 to 30 minutes of the island; a two-tank dive costs F$180. Transfers to the island cost F$120 per adult.

Qamea
area 34 sq km
Only 2.5km east from Taveuni, Qamea is home to six villages. The island's coast has a number of bays with white-sand beaches and the interior is covered with steep green hills and valleys. Qamea is known for *lairo*, the annual migration of land crabs in late November.

Qamea Beach Club (☎ 888 0220, fax 888 0092; W www.qamea.com; bure singles/doubles/triples F$820/1100/1240, villa doubles F$1400, including meals and transfer, children under 13 not accepted), located along a lovely white-sand beach, has a fresh spring-water swimming pool and luxury bure with hammocks and views. There's excellent snorkelling, windsurfing, sailing, nature walks and village visits. The resort's dive shop has reasonable rates.

Kadavu

pop 12,000 • area 450 sq km
About 100km south of Viti Levu, these isolated islands have remained aloof from Fiji's major historical events, with a tourism industry only slowly creeping onto the scene. Most visitors are nature lovers, bird-watchers and divers, drawn to the island for its lush wildlife. The main island of Kadavu is virtually cut in three by deep bays, with the impressive **Nabukelevu** (Mt Washington) towering above at 838m. The prevailing southeasterly winds can batter the exposed southeastern side of the island. Expect rough weather from April to August.

On a narrow isthmus between Namalata Bay and North Bay, the small town of Vunisea has Kadavu's few services and an airstrip. Bring cash with you as the bank does not exchange travellers cheques or give cash advances. In the event of an emergency, dial the **police** (☎ 333 6007) or the **hospital** (☎ 333 6008).

Activities
The mountains have rainforest, numerous waterfalls and **hiking trails**. Ask locals about current conditions and request permission from local villagers before setting out.

Kadavu has excellent **diving** with the famous **Astrolabe Reef** skirting the eastern side of the group. Expect to see brilliantly coloured corals, vertical drop-offs and a really wonderful array of marine life. Unfortunately, the weather often dictates which sites are available and can diminish visibility. See the Places to Stay section later for dive operators.

The best **surfing** in Kadavu is found around **Cape Washington**, at the southernmost end of Kadavu.

For kayak tours of the islands, contact **Tamarillo Sea Kayaking** (☎ 04-801 7549 in New Zealand; W www.tamarillo.co.nz; May-Sept). An eight-day tour costs around F$2200 per person. **Dive Kadavu Resort**, **Matava** and **Jonas Paradise** have ocean kayaks for hire.

Dangers & Annoyances
The ferry trip to Kadavu from Suva can be rough and the timetable is erratic, so you should fly instead. The small boats used for transfers to/from the airstrip often don't have life jackets or radios.

Places to Stay – Budget
Jona's Paradise Resort (☎ 330 7058, 339 6538; e jonasparadise@connect.com.fj; camping per

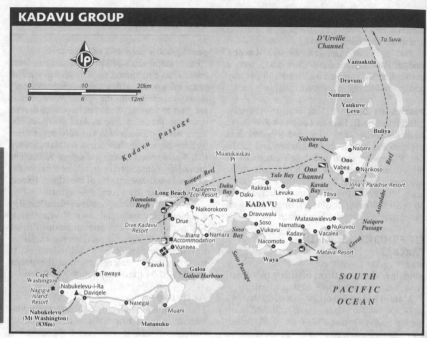

KADAVU GROUP

person F$50, dorm beds F$60, bure per person with/without shower F$100/80, all including meals, minimum 3 nights) is rustic and peaceful, with a great white-sand beach and offshore snorkelling. The beachfront *bure* and 4-bed dorm have toilets and hot-water showers. Meals are basic – bring extra snacks. At the time of research, the dive operation (F$145 for a two-tank dive) was without certified instructors. Jona has a good boat for return transfers from Vunisea airstrip (F$110 per person).

Matava Resort (☎ 330 5222; e matava@connect.com.fj; *dorm beds F$18, double bure with shared bathroom F$55, waterfront/oceanview bure doubles with private bathroom F$100/120, private house F$220*) is a picturesque place on the eastern side of the island with great snorkelling and kayaking. It can be windy, but is ruggedly beautiful. Rustic, comfortable *bure* with shared bathroom are good value. A meal package is F$50, served on the restaurant's veranda. The resort's dive operation has new gear and offers manta ray, cave and shark dives. A two-tank dive is F$115 and the open-water course is F$500. Other activities include hiking, village visits, windsurfing and surfing. The boat trip from Vunisea airstrip (F$30 one way, 50 mins) can be rough.

Places to Stay – Top End

Dive Kadavu Resort (☎ 331 1780, fax 330 3860; w www.divekadavu.com; *oceanview single/double bure F$320/560, quads per person F$220, all including meals and airport transfers*) caters mainly to divers. It's on the western side of Kadavu, sheltered from the prevailing winds, and has a lovely beach for swimming and snorkelling. The comfortable fan-cooled *bure* have insect screening, hot water and good ventilation. Meals are tasty and the restaurant is a nice spot to relax. Children under 10 are not accepted. **Dive Kadavu** has an excellent set-up and good equipment, with Namalata Reef 5km offshore. Two-tank dives cost F$180 and open-water courses are F$660. Activities include snorkelling trips, windsurfing, kayaking, forest walks and a weekly *lovo*. Airport transfers take 15 minutes by resort boat.

Papageno Eco-Resort (☎ 3303 355, fax 330 3533; w www.papagenoecoresort.com; *fancooled bungalow singles/doubles F$260/440, includes meals and transfers, minimum 3 nights*) is a quiet, family-friendly retreat 14.5km northeast of Vunisea. Bungalows are spacious and comfortable, and face a sandy beach. Activities include snorkelling, walks, village visits and diving through Dive Kadavu Resort.

Excellent meals, with plenty of homegrown fruit and veggies, are served in the plantation house with live, local music in the evenings.

Nagigia Island Resort (*☎ 331 5774;* e *sales@ fijisurf.com; cottage doubles per person per night less/more than seven nights F$200/150, cottage dorms per person less/more than seven nights F$90/110)* is a surf resort on a stunning site near Cape Washington, at the southwestern end of Kadavu. From your cottage perched over the water, enjoy fantastic views of the surf break and across imposing Nabukelevu. There are five nearby breaks producing rideable waves all year round with bigger swells mid-year. For F$24, you get unlimited boat service to all surf breaks, or you can also paddle out to the main break. Other activities include scenic walks and village/snorkelling trips. Diving can be arranged with Dive Kadavu. Good food is served in the restaurant-bar with meal plans available for F$50. Return boat transfers from Vunisea airstrip are F$120 per person.

Getting There & Around
Air Fiji and Sun Air have daily return flights to **Namalata airstrip** (*☎ 333 6042)* on Kadavu. Confirm flights the day before departure. See Getting Around at the start of the chapter.

The MV *Bulou-ni-ceva* ferries between Suva and Kadavu (F$42 per person one-way), mainly for cargo and local use. It's irregular and unreliable, taking anything from four hours to two days and ranging from bearable to terrible, depending on the weather. Contact **Kadavu Shipping** (*☎ 331 2428)* in Suva.

Kadavu has few roads, and small boats are the principal mode of transport. Book in advance to arrange transfers from Vunisea airstrip to resorts. Boat trips are expensive and most don't have life jackets or radios. In rough weather it can be tough.

The Lau Group

Lying halfway between Tonga and Fiji's main islands, the 57 islands of the Lau Group are scattered across over 400km and surrounded by great masses of reefs.

Lau islanders are known for their woodcarving and *masi* (bark cloth) crafts and have been greatly influenced by neighbouring Polynesian cultures. In 1947 a Tongan fleet under Enele Ma'afu invaded Lau and by the mid-19th century the region was dominated by Tongans. Ma'afu aimed to conquer all Fiji and convert the people to Christianity; he was one of the signatories to the deed of cession to Britain in 1874.

You'll find no banks, a scant tourism infrastructure and little rain in the Lau Group.

Diving
The remote Lau Group is still relatively unexplored by divers. Nai'a Cruises, a live-aboard operator, offers special charters to Lau. *Fiji Aggressor*, another live-aboard, also visits Lau. See Getting Around at the beginning of this chapter for ferry details.

VANUA BALAVU
area 53 sq km
This beautiful island, averaging about 2km wide, has lots of sandy beaches and rugged limestone hills. The Bay of Islands at the northwestern end is used as a cyclone shelter by yachts. Lomaloma, the largest village, was Fiji's first port, regularly visited by sailing ships trading in the Pacific. Today the people of Vanua Balavu largely rely on copra and bêche-de-mer for their income.

Moana's Guesthouse (*☎ 895 006; Sawana; rooms per person F$50, including meals)* is a perfect place for those after peace and solitude. With little to do but snorkelling, fishing and village visits, you can experience a bit of pristine Fiji. The guesthouse is built in traditional Tongan style, with two bedrooms and a living area. Two beachside *bure* are also available.

Getting There & Away
Vanua Balavu is 355km east of Nadi. Air Fiji has a weekly flight (Tuesdays) from Nausori. See the Getting Around section near the start of this chapter for airline details.

If you have plenty of time, you can also reach the island by cargo/passenger boat. Saliabasaga Shipping and Ika Corporation both have fortnightly trips from Suva to the Lau Group. A one-way fare with Saliabasaga Shipping is F$80, including meals. Expect to spend about a week on board.

FIJI

New Caledonia

To experience the Pacific with a taste of France there's no better place than New Caledonia, where Melanesian tradition blends with French sophistication. New Caledonia sits in the southwest of the Pacific surrounded by the world's second largest coral reef. Though governed by France, Nouvelle-Calédonie, to its French speaking inhabitants, or Kanaky to the pro-independence among them, is gradually gaining greater autonomy.

Noumea, with its mouth-watering *patisseries*, gourmet restaurants and fashionable shops, is often likened to the French Riviera. But the capital's flair is a stark contrast to the simplicity of the rest of the country.

New Caledonia's diverse landscapes of sunny beaches, rugged mountains, rolling plains, cool forests and lush tropical vegetation offer a fabulous mix of scenery. Activities include excellent diving and snorkelling, river canoeing and kayaking, and horse-trekking in the mountains.

Most visitors can find what they're looking for, whether it be the smiling crowds of a colourful Pacific town or the tranquillity of nature, the comfort of a luxury hotel or the conviviality of a humble tribal homestay.

Facts about New Caledonia

HISTORY
New Caledonia was first populated by hunter-gatherers, known as Lapita, who arrived from the islands of Vanuatu around 1500 BC. The Lapita were named after a site near Koné on Grande Terre where their elaborate, pin-hole pottery was discovered (see History in the Facts about the South Pacific chapter, and the boxed text 'Lapita' in the 'South Pacific Arts' special section).

From about the 11th century AD until the 18th century, New Caledonia saw another wave of migration, this time from western Polynesian islands.

European Explorers
The English explorer James Cook spotted Grande Terre in 1774, and named this new land New Caledonia because the terrain reminded him of the highlands of Scotland (which was called Caledonia by the Romans).

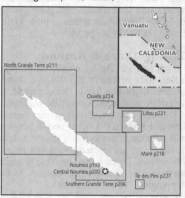

Highlights
- **Parc de la Rivière Bleue** – canoe down a silent river by the light of the moon, through a spooky drowned forest to a shimmering lake
- **Île des Pins** – skim over a sparkling bay on a traditional wooden sailing canoe
- **Ouvéa** – watch the sunset across a calm lagoon from anywhere along Ouvéa's endless, soft, white-sand beach
- **Eating** – place your order for a gourmet French meal or a traditional Kanak *bougna*
- **Jean-Marie Tjibaou Cultural Centre** – explore this architectural masterpiece and cultural sanctuary
- **Horse trekking** – discover the wild interior and isolated villages on horse back
- **Scuba diving** – observe the marine life around the world's second largest reef

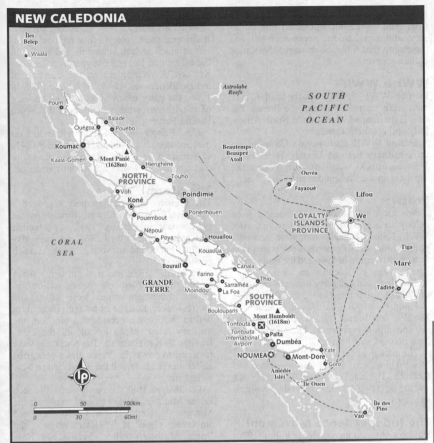

French interest in New Caledonia was sparked 14 years later when Louis XVI sent Comte de La Pérouse to explore its economic potential. La Pérouse and his crew disappeared during a violent cyclone in the Solomon Islands. A French search mission, led by Admiral Bruny d'Entrecasteaux, landed at Balade on 17 April 1793.

Hunters, Traders & Missionaries

In the 19th century, British and American whalers, followed by sandalwood traders, were the first commercial Westerners to land on the islands.

Later that century, many Kanaks were taken to work on foreign plantations as labourers by 'blackbirders' (essentially slavers – see History in the Facts about the South Pacific chapter).

Then came the men of God. Two Protestant Samoan missionaries from the London Missionary Society (LMS) were the first to arrive on Île des Pins in 1841. Meanwhile on Grande Terre, seven French Marists established missions at Pouébo and Balade on the northeastern coast in December 1843.

The French Colonial Order

In 1853, the new emperor, Napoleon III, ordered the annexation of New Caledonia, under the pretext of protecting France's floundering Catholic missions. The French flag was raised at Balade on 24 September 1853. New Caledonia was founded as a penal colony and the first shiploads of convicts arrived in May 1864 at Port-de-France (present-day Noumea).

When settlers started to encroach on tribal lands, hostilities between the French and

Kanaks began. The Revolt of 1878, led by Chef Ataï, broke out around La Foa on 25 June and went on for seven months. The repression that followed damaged the Kanak culture forever.

WWI & WWII
During WWI, 5500 Caldoche and Kanak men were recruited to form the French Pacific Battalion, which fought in North Africa, Italy and southern France.

During WWII, the colony's US allies set up a military base on Grande Terre. From Noumea attacks were launched against the Japanese in the Philippines and Coral Sea.

Postwar
New Caledonia's status was changed from colony to a French overseas territory after WWII. Kanaks began to formulate their own political and social demands. They were given French citizenship in 1946 and the more privileged became eligible to vote.

The first political party that was inclusive of Kanaks was formed in 1953. Called Union Calédonienne (UC), it was a coalition of Kanaks, small-scale landowners, missionaries and union supporters. Their motto was 'two colours, one people'.

The nickel boom of the 1950s and 1960s brought prosperity but it also harvested bitter fruits. The Kanaks wanted their land back and the next two decades saw violent political struggles.

The Independence Movement
Having witnessed independence in Fiji (1970) and Papua New Guinea (1975), new groups formed wanting more than the limited autonomy that the UC had aspired to. Several pro-independence parties decided to merge to form the Front de Libération Nationale Kanak et Socialiste (FLNKS; Kanak Socialist National Liberation Front). The UC president, Jean-Marie Tjibaou, was its first leader.

Between 1984 and 1986, Kanaks and whites violently provoked each other. This period of chaos is commonly referred to as Les Évènements (The Events). To calm the situation, a plan that included a referendum on independence and self-government 'in association' with France was proposed in 1985. But it was rejected by the independence movement.

The Calm before the Storm
After the French legislative elections in May 1986, an uneasy calm prevailed as the new

conservative minister in charge of the territory released his plan for New Caledonia's future. It stripped the territory's four regional councils of much of their autonomy and abolished the office that had been buying back land for Kanaks. A referendum on the question of independence was scheduled for late 1987. In 1986, the party received the official backing of the intergovernmental agency, the South Pacific Forum (SPF).

On 13 September 1987, the referendum on independence was held and boycotted by 84% of Kanaks. Of the 59% of eligible voters who cast a ballot, 98% were against independence.

The Storm
The French National Assembly approved a new plan for the territory put forward by the government in January 1987. An election was called for 24 April 1988, the same day as the first round of voting for the French presidency.

In April 1988, a group of militant Kanaks seized the *gendarmerie* (police station) on Ouvéa. Four gendarmes were killed and the rest taken hostage in a cave. Three days before the French presidential election, the military launched an assault on the cave, leaving 19 Kanaks dead. The Socialists were returned to power in France and a concerted effort was made to end the bloodshed in New Caledonia.

On 26 June 1988 the newly elected French Prime Minister, Michel Rocard, brokered the Matignon Accords. This was a historic peace agreement signed at the Hôtel Matignon, the Prime Minister's office, by the two New Caledonian leaders, the FLNKS's Jean-Marie Tjibaou, and Jacques Lafleur, the leader of the ruling party Rassemblement pour la Calédonie dans la République (RPCR; Rally for New Caledonia within the Republic).

Under the accords, it was agreed that New Caledonia would be divided into three regions – the Southern, Northern and Loyalty Islands provinces. The last two would both be likely to come under Kanak control in an election. The accords stated that a referendum on self-determination would be held in 1998, with all New Caledonians eligible to vote.

Towards Independence
On 4 May 1989, Jean-Marie Tjibaou and his second-in-command were shot on Ouvéa while attending a tribal gathering to mark the end of the mourning period for the 19 Kanaks killed during the hostage crisis a year earlier.

Their murderer was a local Kanak who believed that the FLNKS leaders had sold out by signing the Matignon Accords.

The assassinations ended the political violence in New Caledonia. As agreed in the accords, France poured money into education, construction and infrastructure in an attempt to 'rebalance' the territory's economy and give a greater share of resources to Kanaks.

A new step was taken in May 1998, when the RPCR, FLNKS and the French government signed the Noumea Accord. It focused on the gradual transfer of power from the French State to New Caledonia and on the recognition of Kanak culture. A referendum on full independence will be held 15 to 20 years from the signing of the accord.

CLIMATE

New Caledonia has a temperate, oceanic climate and seasons that alter little. From mid-November to mid-April it is warm and humid. Average maximum temperatures vary between 22°C and 28°C, and minimums range from 11°C to 17°C. February is the hottest month. The coolest period is July to August.

There is no real dry season, as rain is adequate all year and abundant from January to late April. The cyclone season is from January to March.

ECOLOGY & ENVIRONMENT

Traditionally, the Kanaks had a very sensible relationship with the environment, considering it their *garde-manger* (food safe). This contrasts greatly with modern-day attitudes and practices. Mining, smelting, urbanisation around Noumea, bushfires and feral cats and dogs are the predominant dangers to nature in New Caledonia.

FLORA & FAUNA

Despite its small size, New Caledonia's biodiversity is rich. The trees you'll see include araucaria pines, banyan, coconut, *houp*, *kauri* and *niaouli* trees. Mangrove and *niaouli* savannah are typical of Grande Terre's west coast. Of the 3200 flowering plant species in New Caledonia, 77% are endemic.

There are an estimated 73 species of indigenous terrestrial birds. The most renowned indigenous species is the endangered *cagou* (see the boxed text 'The Cagou' in this chapter). Of the few land mammals, only *roussettes* (members of the fruit bat family) are indigenous. Horses, cattle, deer, wild pigs and feral cats have been introduced.

New Caledonia's waters are rich with around 2000 species of fish. Reef sharks, stingrays, turtles, dugongs, dolphins, gorgonian coral, sponges, sea cucumbers, molluscs, cowrie and cone shells, giant clams, squid and the beautiful nautilus, all thrive in these waters. New Caledonia's 14 species of sea snakes are often sighted on the water's surface or on land. The most commonly seen is the amphibious *tricot rayé* or banded sea krait. It's highly venomous, but not aggressive and bites are extremely rare.

GOVERNMENT & POLITICS

There are two main political adversaries: the right wing RPCR and the pro-independence FLNKS.

Since the Noumea Accord in May 1998, New Caledonia is no longer a French Territoire d'Outre-Mer (TOM) or overseas territory, but a 'special territorial entity within the French republic'. Its inhabitants are currently French citizens. New Caledonians vote in national and presidential elections and elect three representatives to the French National Assembly in Paris.

The French government still controls many of the main sectors of society: the territory's defence and justice system, law and order, immigration, secondary and higher education, and currency.

Since the signing of the Matignon Accords in 1988, New Caledonia has been governed by a 54-member Territorial Congress. It is made up of three Provincial Assemblies – the Northern, Southern and Loyalty Islands – which act as local parliaments with independent budgets and administrations.

In 1999, the Congress elected New Caledonia's first government that holds executive power. It's a collegial government made up of both RPCR and FLNKS members. Interestingly, a minor pro-independence party, the Fédération du Comité de Coordination des Indépendantistes (FCCI), has formed a coalition with the RPCR giving it the government majority. The government continues on its rather shaky road but, so far, with no major upset.

ECONOMY

New Caledonia's economy centres around the mining and metallurgy industry. Grande Terre is the world's third-largest nickel producer after Russia and Canada. Tourism, agriculture, fishing and aquaculture contribute to a lesser degree. Two big nickel-processing projects are in the pipeline in the north and south.

France is its main trading partner and supplies half the imported consumer products: mainly food, machinery and transport equipment. On top of that, the trade balance gap is largely bridged by enormous French funding.

POPULATION & PEOPLE

New Caledonia has a population of 222,000 with a density of 12 people per sq km. Kanaks make up 44% of the population, Europeans 34%, with other Pacific Islanders, Asians and other races making up the rest. The population is largely confined to the Noumea area.

Kanaks are Melanesians, like their neighbours in Vanuatu and Fiji. The French are divided into two main groups – the Caldoches and the *Métros* (meaning from metropolitan France). The Caldoches are the descendants of French convicts and settlers. The French who come to New Caledonia to work for a few years with the benefit of high wages are called *Métros* or, usually more derogatorily, *Zoreilles*.

EDUCATION

A formal education is compulsory for all New Caledonians between the ages of six and 16. Primary education is in the hands of each province. Secondary schools are under state control and the teachers are mostly from France. There is also a university, Université de la Nouvelle-Calédonie (UNC), in Noumea.

ARTS

Kanak culture and arts have been going through a mini-renaissance in recent years, due largely to the efforts of the **Agence de Développement de la Culture Kanak** (*Agency for the Development of Kanak Culture*, ADCK; ☎ 41 45 55, fax 41 45 56; e adck@canl.nc) and to the impetus generated by the Jean-Marie Tjibaou Cultural Centre. Music, dance, theatre and art exhibitions are staged throughout the year. See the 'South Pacific Arts' special section for details on traditional Melanesian art forms, and the boxed text 'Jean-Marie Tjibaou Cultural Centre' in this chapter.

Contemporary music includes *kaneka*, a blend of modern instruments with ancestral harmonies and rhythms. Most songs are sung in Kanak languages and are immensely popular throughout New Caledonia.

Other Kanak cultural artistic outlets are dance, woodcarving and weaving.

SOCIETY
Traditional Culture

Kanak *La coutume*, the essential component of Kanak identity, is a code for living that encompasses rites, rituals and social interaction between and within the clans. The clan, not the individual, was *the* important element in traditional Kanak society. The clan's activity was centred around the largest hut, the *grande case*, where the *chef* (chief) lived (see the boxed text 'Kanak Grande Case').

The exchange of gifts is an important element of *la coutume*, as it creates a much-revered network of mutual obligations. The one who offers a gift receives prestige from this action while placing an obligation, which is never ignored, on the receiver to respond. In all the important stages in life, such as birth, marriage and mourning, a gift is given, symbolic offerings are made and discussions are held.

When Kanaks enter the home of a chief, they will offer a small token as a sign of respect and to introduce themselves. Food, textiles, money or a packet of cigarettes are the traditional and contemporary offerings.

Kanak Grande Case

The *grande case* (big hut) is one of the strongest symbols of the Kanak community. It is the widest and tallest *case* in each clan settlement and traditionally home to the chief. Today, the chiefs all have modern homes located close to the *grande case*, where tribal gatherings and discussions still take place.

Where possible, the hut is built on a knoll above the rest of the village. The central pillar, an immense trunk of a carefully chosen tree, is erected first. It will support the entire *case* and symbolises the chief. A stone hearth is laid between the central pillar and the door.

The entrance to the *grande case* is via a low doorway flanked by carved posts. Inside, the walls and ceiling are lined with wooden posts or beams, lashed to the frame with strong vines and all of which lean against the central pillar, symbolising the clan's close link to the chief. Finally, a *flèche faîtière*, a spear-like carving that becomes home to ancestral sprits, is erected on the roof.

Place Names

You'll come across many different spellings for Kanak place names. We have used the most commonly used spellings in this chapter.

Also note that in New Caledonia the French word *tribu* (tribe) is used to refer to a Kanak village.

❋❋❋❋❋❋❋❋❋❋❋

French The Caldoche are very much outdoors people, with fishing and hunting topping the list of favourite pastimes. Those who live in rural areas (ie, outside Noumea) are known as *Broussards*. Many *Broussards* are cattle breeders and have forged a culture of their own similar to that of outback Australia. In Noumea, the culture, cuisine, clothing and art of the urban Caldoche and *Métros* is similar to that of urban France.

RELIGION

Almost two-thirds of the population is Catholic. Of these, just over half are Europeans and the remainder are Kanaks and Wallisians. Protestants make up one-quarter of the population; Kanaks form the majority of followers. Other religious groups include Muslims, generally of Indonesian descent, Mormons and Buddhists.

LANGUAGE

French is the official language of New Caledonia. English is limited mostly to people in the tourist industry. In addition, Tahitian, Wallisian, Indonesian and Vietnamese are also spoken, but mainly in Noumea.

An estimated 27 distinctly different Kanak languages coexist in New Caledonia, but unlike neighbouring Vanuatu, Kanaks have no unifying indigenous language.

For useful phrases in the French language, see the appendix at the back of this book.

Facts for the Visitor

SUGGESTED ITINERARIES

Depending on the time and money you have to spend, the following itineraries could be considered:

Three Days
Spend one day sightseeing and shopping in and around Noumea. Next day, take a day trip to Amédée Islet (or go to a small islet closer to Noumea by taxi boat). On the final day, hire a car and drive to the Parc de la Rivière Bleue where you can go canoeing or walking.

One Week
You could spend two days in Noumea; two days on Île des Pins and do an outrigger sailing canoe trip; a day or two exploring around the southern tip of Grande Terre; and a day trip to Oua Tom, near La Foa, to experience life in a Kanak tribe.

Two Weeks
Spend two days in and around Noumea, and go hiking at Monts Koghis. One day exploring the southern tip of Grande Terre or canoeing at the Parc de la Rivière Bleu. Then take off for five days in a car around Grande Terre discovering the scenic east coast and the rolling plains of the west coast. Spend three or four days visiting a couple of the Loyalty Islands. Go to Ouvéa, the only atoll, with its endless beach, then choose between Lifou and Maré. The last two days can then be spent on Île des Pins.

PLANNING
When to Go
The best time to visit is from September to November when the days are not too hot or sticky and there's less likelihood of rain. June and July can also be pleasant.

Maps
The best map of New Caledonia is the IGN Nouvelle-Calédonie map (scale 1:500,000), which gives an overview of Grande Terre and the islands. For greater detail, IGN also publishes a four-map series of New Caledonia on a scale of 1:200,000. The Noumea tourist office has a detailed map of the capital for free.

Charts can be looked at in the **CNC** (☎ 26 27 27), or purchased in the **Marine Corail shop** (☎ 27 58 48). The Service Hydro-graphique et Océanographique de la Marine (SHOM) produces excellent mariners' maps covering all New Caledonia's territorial waters. They're available from Marine Corail for 3100 CFP each.

TOURIST OFFICES
Local Tourist Offices
The tourism offices for Noumea and the Southern, Northern and Loyalty Island provinces are all based in Noumea. See Information under Noumea later in this chapter.

Tourist Offices Abroad
Nouvelle-Calédonie Tourisme Point Sud (☎ 24 20 80; @ info@nouvellecaledonietourisme-sud.com; 20 rue Anatole France) deals with the overseas promotion of the destination. Some of its addresses overseas are:

Australia (☎ 02-9261 8688, ℮ info-syd@
newcaledoniatourism-south.com) Suite 402,
Level 4, 117 York St, Sydney, NSW 2000
France (☎ 01 42 73 69 80, ℮ info-par@nou
vellecaledonietourisme-sud.com) 7 rue due
Générale Bertrand, 75007 Paris
Japan (☎ 03-3583 3280, ℮ info-tyo@new
caledoniatourism-south.com) Landic Akasaka
No 2 Bldg 9F, 2-10-9 Akasaka, Minato-Ku,
Tokyo 107-0052
New Zealand (☎ 09-585 0257, ℮ info-akl@
newcaledoniatourism-south.com) PO Box
4300, Auckland

VISAS & DOCUMENTS
EU citizens, Swiss nationals and citizens of
Canada, Australia and NZ are allowed entry
into New Caledonia for three months without
a visa. Citizens of Japan and the US are allowed entry for one month without a visa.

Those travelling from New Caledonia to
other French territories – Tahiti or Wallis &
Futuna – for which they need a visa should
obtain it in their home country.

International Driving Permits are not required to drive in New Caledonia – a valid
licence from your country will suffice.

EMBASSIES & CONSULATES
French Embassies & Consulates Abroad
Diplomatic representation abroad includes:

Australia
  Consulate: (☎ 02-9261 5779) Level 26,
  St Martin's Tower, 31 Market St, Sydney,
  NSW 2000
  Consulate: (☎ 03-9602 5024) Suite 805, Level
  8, 150 Queen Street, Melbourne, Vic 3000
France
  Embassy: (☎ 01 43 17 53 53) Ministère des Af-
  faires Etrangères, 37 Quai d'Orsay, 75007 Paris
Japan
  Embassy: (☎ 03-5420 8800) 11-44 4 Chome,
  Minami-Azabu, Minato-Ku, Tokyo 106
New Zealand
  Consulate: (☎ 04-384 2555) 13th floor, Rural
  Bank Bldg, 34/42 Manners St, PO Box 1695,
  Wellington
UK
  Consulate: (☎ 020-7073 1200) 21 Cromwell
  Rd, London SW7 2EN
USA
  Embassy: (☎ 202-944 6000) 4101 Reservoir
  Rd NW, Washington, DC 20007
  Consulate: (☎ 310-235 3200) Suite 300,
  10990 Wilshire Boulevard, Los Angeles,
  CA 90024
  Consulate: (☎ 212-606 3680) 934 Fifth Ave,
  New York, NY 10021

Embassies in New Caledonia
The following are some of the nations that
are represented in New Caledonia (all offices
are in Noumea):

Australia (☎ 27 24 14) 7th floor, Immeuble
  Foch, 19-21 Av du Maréchal Foch
Germany (☎ 26 16 81, ℮ w.forster@lagoon.nc)
  19 rue de la Gazelle, Magenta
Indonesia (☎ 28 25 74) 2 rue Lamartine, Baie
  de l'Orphelinat
Japan (☎ 25 37 29) 45 rue du 5 Mai, Magenta
Netherlands (☎ 28 48 58) 33 rue de Sébastopol
New Zealand (☎ 27 25 43, ℮ nzcgnou@
  offratel.nc) 2nd floor, 4 Blvd Vauban
UK (☎ 28 21 53, ℮ gbconsul@offratel.nc) 14
  rue du Général Sarrail, Baie de l'Orphelinat
Vanuatu (☎ 27 76 21) 53 rue de Sébastopol

CUSTOMS
Travellers are allowed to bring in 200 cigarettes or 50 cigars or 250g of tobacco, 2L
of wine, one bottle of spirits or liqueur, and
50g of perfume. Up to 900,900 CFP (around
€7,600), or the equivalent in other currencies,
can be imported without being declared.

It is strictly forbidden to bring in firearms,
ammunition, drugs or animals. Animals will
be quarantined. Plants and seeds must be declared to customs.

When leaving, the export of anything that
appears on the Washington Convention list
(regarding the commerce of endangered flora
and fauna) is prohibited. Old objects of ethno-
graphic interest are also not to be taken out of
New Caledonia.

MONEY
Most foreign hard currencies, cash and travellers cheques can be readily changed. ATMs
are plentiful in Noumea, and away from the
capital you'll find ATMs in major towns. Some
post offices are also equipped with ATMs. The
ATMs accept MasterCard, Visa and Eurocard.

Credit cards are accepted by hotels, restaurants, big shops and airline offices in Noumea,
but not at budget places outside the capital.

Currency
The currency used in New Caledonia is the
CFP (Cours du Franc Pacifique), or Pacific
franc. The same currency is used in French
Polynesia and Wallis & Futuna – although the
money may have the mint mark of Noumea or
Pape'ete, the two are interchangeable.

CFP banknotes come in denominations of
500, 1000, 5000 and 10,000 CFP. Coins come
in units of 1, 2, 5, 10, 20, 50 and 100 CFP.

Exchange Rates

The CFP is tied to the euro (€) at a fixed rate, with €1 equal to 119.33 CFP.

country	unit		Pacific franc
Australia	A$1	=	68 CFP
Canada	C$1	=	76 CFP
Easter Island	Ch$100	=	14 CFP
euro zone	€1	=	119 CFP
Fiji	F$1	=	54 CFP
Japan	Ῡ100	=	86 CFP
New Zealand	NZ$1	=	59 CFP
PNG	K1	=	29 CFP
Samoa	ST1	=	34 CFP
Solomon Islands	S$1	=	14 CFP
Tonga	T$1	=	48 CFP
UK	£1	=	171 CFP
USA	US$1	=	102 CFP
Vanuatu	100VT	=	85 CFP

For current exchange rates, see W www.oanda.com.

All banks handle foreign exchange. With the exception of the American Express office in Noumea, the banks charge a 520 CFP commission on cash or travellers cheque transactions.

Most banks in Noumea are open Monday to Friday from 7.20am or 7.45am to 3.30pm or 3.45pm. Most are closed on weekends. In the countryside, many banks close for lunch.

Costs

New Caledonia is expensive. Most of the goods are imported and are therefore pricey. In Noumea, expect to go through about 2500 to 5000 CFP per day on a budget. Even camping is pricey, with most sites charging around 1000 CFP. You'll pay around 8500 CFP for a double room in a mid-range hotel. At top-end hotels doubles start around 14,000 CFP.

You don't have to tip in New Caledonia.

POST & COMMUNICATIONS

There are post offices throughout Grande Terre and the outlying islands. Look for the Office des Postes et Télécommunications (OPT) sign. Standard office hours are Monday to Friday from 7.45am to 3pm.

Airmail letters up to 20g cost 105 CFP to Australia and New Zealand, 135 CFP to North America and Asia and 155 CFP to Europe (100 CFP to France). Postcards cost 100 CFP to any destination.

Most post offices have a poste restante service where mail sent to you can be picked up for a 70 CFP-per-letter charge.

The phone service throughout New Caledonia is good. Mobile phone numbers begin with a 7 or 8. To make a phone call you can buy either a *télécarte* (telephone card) and use a public box or an *IZI* card and use a fixed phone. *Télécartes* cost 1000 CFP (25 units), 3000 CFP (80 units) or 5000 CFP (140 units), while *IZI* cards cost 1000 or 3000 CFP. Both cards are available from post offices and some tobacconists' shops in Noumea.

You can use either card to make an international phone call. The international access code is ☎ 00. To phone Australia and New Zealand you'll be looking at 60/72 CFP per minute in off-peak/peak time. To Canada and France it's 80/96 CFP and to the US and Europe it costs 100/130 CFP. Reverse charge calls can be made from the main post office in Noumea.

For directory assistance dial ☎ 1012. For emergency dial ☎ 17. New Caledonia's international telephone code is ☎ 687.

Faxes can be sent from post offices. A page costs between 500 and 1000 CFP depending on the destination.

DIGITAL RESOURCES

Nouvelle-Calédonie Tourisme Point Sud (W *www.newcaledoniatourism-south.com*) has pictures and information on the major attractions.

Another useful website is W www.kaori.nc which contains links to New Caledonian websites, news and upcoming events.

For further information see the Digital Resources section under Noumea.

BOOKS

Les Évènements of the 1980s have led to some very readable English-language analyses of New Caledonia's history and independence movement. Several books written by Kanaks on their culture have been published and translated into English.

Guidebooks

Let Me Guide You in Noumea, by Jacqueline Julien, takes readers on a tour of modern-day Noumea, situating the various suburbs in their historical context. It also contains an index of practical information.

Discover Isle of Pines, by Hilary Roots, is a small, but complete, booklet covering the island.

Lonely Planet's New Caledonia guidebook has more detailed information on travel in New Caledonia.

NEW CALEDONIA

History & Politics

There are two excellent books that trace New Caledonia's history from the original Kanaks to the 1980s. *The Totem and the Tricolour*, by Martyn Lyons, covers the history up to the 1984 crisis but not *Les Évènements* themselves. Alternatively, there's John Connell's *New Caledonia or Kanaky?*, which details events up to the French government's Fabius Plan.

Society & Culture

Produced just after the Melanesia 2000 festival, *Kanaké – the Melanesian Way*, by Jean-Marie Tjibaou was a landmark book to mark the festival. Tjibaou used colour photos, poems, legends and imagery to explain Kanak culture. The impact of modernism on his people is discussed and an outline for the future is drawn.

Horizons Pacifiques by Anne Pitoiset, a journalist working in New Caledonia, looks at how the social changes that have taken place in New Caledonia over the years have defined a new multi-ethnic society. The book contains black and white photos of New Caledonians from different ethnic backgrounds by Jean-François Marin.

NEWSPAPERS & MAGAZINES

Les Nouvelles Calédoniennes (120 CFP) is the only daily newspaper. It has a pro-French viewpoint. *Les Info* (150 CFP) is a weekly paper and *Le Chien Bleu* (200 CFP) is a monthly satirical paper. *Mwa Vee* is a quarterly publication devoted to Kanak culture. All major French newspapers and magazines are easily found in Noumea.

English-language publications include the *International Herald Tribune*, *Time*, *Newsweek* and various Australian women's magazines such as *Australian Women's Weekly*.

RADIO & TV

TV in New Caledonia operates through Télé Nouvelle-Calédonie, part of the French territories broadcasting service. Most TV programmes are dispatched directly from metropolitan France and all are in French or dubbed into French. There are also Canal+ and Canal Satellite, French-based pay TV channels.

Major radio stations include the French government-run Radio Nouvelle-Calédonie, the private and pro-RPCR Radio Rythme Bleu (RRB), and Radio Djiido, a pro-FLNKS private station.

HEALTH

New Caledonia has no tropical diseases and is malaria-free.

In Noumea, there are two public hospitals, various private clinics and many chemists. Each rural town has a *dispensaire* (community clinic), where you can receive emergency first-aid.

The water in New Caledonia is safe to drink. For more information see the Health section in the Regional Facts for the Visitor chapter.

SOCIAL GRACES

Do not walk around in swim wear or skimpy clothes away from beaches. Outside Noumea the dress code is conservative.

It's wise to ask permission of local people before wandering around any tribal areas – including cemeteries.

DANGERS & ANNOYANCES

Thefts and attacks on tourists are not commonplace but you should, nevertheless, exercise caution when walking alone at night in Noumea.

Ask reliable-looking locals whether it's safe to stay at free camping grounds as security is a problem at some.

On the roads, be wary of drunk drivers as New Caledonia has a high death toll from alcohol-related road accidents.

Along the coast or in the water, be aware of the various venomous sea creatures. Underwater, stay away from any sea snakes as their venom can be deadly.

When swimming or snorkelling, don't underestimate the sea's current.

Though it may be plentiful, possession of marijuana is illegal in New Caledonia.

BUSINESS HOURS

Government offices and most private businesses are open Monday to Friday from 7.30am or 8am to 4pm or 5pm but close between 11.30am and 1.30pm. The exceptions are the banks in Noumea and most post offices around New Caledonia, which remain open at lunch time.

In general, shops are open weekdays from 7.30am to 11am and 2pm to 6pm, and Saturday from 8am or 9am to noon. However, some supermarkets and small convenience stores often don't close for lunch and are open all day Saturday and Sunday morning.

Sunday is extremely quiet throughout New Caledonia.

PUBLIC HOLIDAYS & SPECIAL EVENTS

New Caledonia follows France in major public holidays, including New Year's Day, Easter, Ascension, Whit Monday, Labour Day, Bastille Day, Assumption Day, All Saints' Day, Veteran's Day and Christmas (see the Regional Facts for the Visitor chapter for dates). New Caledonia's national day is 24 September.

Other events include:

March
Festival of the Yam Kanak festival marking the beginning of the harvest. For more information see the boxed text 'Festival of the Yam' in this chapter.
Koneva Exhibition Tjibaou Cultural Centre Annual event featuring work of New Caledonia's leading contemporary Kanak artists

April/May
Triathlon Internationale de Noumea Attracts athletes from the Pacific, Europe and Japan

Mid- to late May
Avocado Festival Held in Nece, Maré. The island's biggest fair, to celebrate the end of harvest.
La Régate des Touques Held in Noumea. People build decorative floats from empty oil barrels and paddle furiously in a noisy, colourful race along Anse Vata.

July/August
Noumea Contemporary Art Biennale Held every two years, features the work of local and international artists

Marathon Internationale de Noumea Held annually, attracts top athletes from as far away as Kenya and Canada.

August/September
Live en Août Noumea annual music festival featuring foreign and local bands
Foire de Bourail Held in Bourail. Huge three-day country-style agricultural fair featuring a rodeo, cattle show, horseracing and a beauty pageant.

October
Équinoxe Held in Noumea. Biennial festival of contemporary theatre, dance and music featuring local and international artists.

ACTIVITIES
Sailing

The lagoon's calm water offers excellent sailing. Sheltered anchorages can be found in the many protected bays and, for the most part, are deserted, with the exception of Amédée Islet and Île des Pins, which are popular sailing destinations for locals on weekends. The only place in the country with full facilities for yachties is Noumea.

Canoeing & Kayaking

The Parc de la Rivière Bleue, east of Noumea, is a tranquil spot for canoeing and kayaking. Other popular spots are on the Dumbéa River, just north of Noumea, and the Tontouta River, which have faster currents. Night-time trips are organised on the Rivière Bleu and Dumbéa when there's a full moon. **Terra Incognita** (☎ 78 94 46, ☎/fax 41 61 19) organises trips on all these rivers.

NEW CALEDONIA

Festival of the Yam

The Festival of the Yam takes place at harvest time, generally in mid-March, about six months after the yams are planted. However, unlike harvest festivities in many other countries, this is not a huge public affair with singing and dancing. Instead it's a calm gathering of the clan and a sharing of the blessed yam, which is treated with the reverence normally reserved for a grandfather or ancestor. Many Kanaks living in Noumea return to their villages for this event.

The elders decide when it is time for the harvest, and traditionally watch nature for signs indicating that the yam is ready, including the appearance of certain stars, such as the Southern Cross, or the flowering of a particular tree. The official start of the harvest comes when the first yams are pulled from a sacred field and presented to the older clansmen and the chief. The next day, everyone gathers in the local church (this part, of course, has occurred only since the missionaries arrived) and the pile of yams is blessed by the priest. The roots are then carried in a procession to the *grande case*, from where they are distributed among the tribe. Out of respect, the yam is never cut, but is broken like bread.

Some tribes in the Yaté/Goro region have started welcoming visitors to this festival. You'll need to ask at the tourist office in Noumea to find out dates and arrangements.

Snorkelling

New Caledonia has the world's second-largest reef, so there's no shortage of snorkelling sites. The best are the reefs around the Loyalty Islands and Île des Pins. Preferably, bring your own equipment and watch out for strong currents.

In Noumea, take a taxi-boat to Île aux Canards (Duck Island) or Îlot Maître, both marine sanctuaries, or on a day trip to Amédée Islet. There's an interesting underwater circuit at Île aux Canards. Follow the numbered buoys.

Diving

New Caledonia has wonderful dive opportunities. There are internationally approved dive companies in Noumea, Bourail, Poum, Poindimié, Hienghène and Îlot Casy on Grande Terre, and on Lifou, Ouvéa and Île des Pins.

Enthusiastic divers can purchase a 10-dive package for 44,200 CFP at several affiliated clubs around the country including **Améedée Diving Club** and **Scubaventure** in Noumea (see Diving in the Noumea section). The package is valid for a year.

The sea temperature around New Caledonia peaks at a warm 29°C in February and drops to 20°C in August.

The standard price for a dive is around 6000 CFP, equipment included. CMAS and PADI diving certification courses are available. Most dive locations are at the outer reef and are reached by boat.

Other Watersports

Noumea's beaches catch strong sea winds – *planche à voile* (windsurfing) and kite surfing are enormously popular. Windsurfing equipment can be rented at the main beach, Anse Vata. Catamarans, jet skis, canoes and kayaks can also be hired.

Hiking

During the cooler mid-year months, hiking in New Caledonia is superb. Around Noumea, Monts Koghis and the Parc de la Rivière Bleue are popular hiking areas.

Along the northeast coast, many walking paths wind up to waterfalls or lead into the mountains from river valleys.

Serious hikers should visit the **Direction des Resources Naturelles** (☎ 24 32 55; 19 Av du Maréchal Foch) in Noumea. At this office you can pick up free brochures (mainly in French but sometimes also in English) detailing a selection of hikes on Grande Terre.

Horse Riding

Horse treks will let you get to know Broussard ways a little better and are quite popular along Grande Terre's west coast. A two- or three-day safari into the mountains can be arranged at Bourail, Koné and Pocquereux, near La Foa.

ACCOMMODATION

Accommodation in hotels is pricey in New Caledonia, except if you buy a package deal in your own country. Most hotels and resorts are in Noumea, but the west coast, Maré, Lifou and Île des Pins have some good options.

If you're on a budget, stick to homestays, gîtes and camping grounds. Camping is possible almost everywhere except in Noumea. Official campsites with running water and showers exist around Grande Terre and on the islands. Usually you'll be looking at about 1000 CFP to pitch your tent.

Tribal gîtes are an authentic form of accommodation that sees you staying in one of the traditional Melanesian *cases* (traditional Kanak house) belonging to a local family or in a bungalow. The facilities in *cases* are basic. Bedding is on foam mattresses placed on woven pandanus mats on the floor. Expect to pay about 1800 to 2000 CFP per night. Bungalows range from being Spartan to quite modern. The more expensive gîtes have private shower and toilet facilities in each bungalow. Prices range from 2000 to 6000 CFP for one person, to 3000 to 6500 CFP for two.

New Caledonia's sole HI hostel is in Noumea.

FOOD

New Caledonia has a wide variety of cuisines, but the most common restaurants are French, Vietnamese, Chinese and Indonesian. Outside the capital, restaurants are somewhat scarce and are usually attached to hotels. Restaurants are generally open from 11am to 2pm and from 7pm to 11pm. Few establishments are open on Sunday.

The best value for money is a *plat du jour* (dish of the day), which typically costs about 1000 CFP. Better still, a *menu du jour* (fixed-price three-course meal), usually referred to simply as a *menu*, costs about 1500 CFP. *Snacks* (cafés) are the cheapest type of restaurant, and serve simple dishes for about 850 CFP.

In *la brousse* (the rest of Grande Terre outside Noumea) and on the islands, you'll have the opportunity to taste venison (along the west coast), fish, lobster, coconut crab, *roussette* (a fruit-eating flying fox) and various traditional Kanak food sources, including *bougna* (see the boxed text 'Preparing a *Bougna*' following).

The morning market in Noumea sells fresh fish, fruit and vegetables. Supermarkets abound in Noumea. However, in village shops the supplies can be limited.

DRINKS
Throughout New Caledonia the water is safe to drink. But if in doubt, bottled water is widely available. Coffee is very popular and costs between 100 and 180 CFP.

The preferred alcoholic drinks are both *vin* (wine) and *bière* (beer). The favourite local beer is Number One. You'll find French, Italian, Australian, New Zealand and Californian wine available in Noumea supermarkets.

On Lifou and in Noumea, kava imported from Vanuatu is sold from private houses called *nakamal* – look for the red lanterns and hand-painted signs. See the boxed text 'Kava' in the Regional Facts for the Visitor chapter.

ENTERTAINMENT
The local live music arena features many Kanak bands, playing mainly reggae and *kaneka* (their own brand of contemporary music).

Kanak and Polynesian floor shows are staged in a few of the bigger hotels, or when cruise ships dock.

Preparing a Bougna

The main Melanesian dish in New Caledonia is the *bougna*. Meant for times of sharing – such as during tribal festivals, weddings or after Sunday mass – the *bougna* is a combination of delicious chunks of yam, taro, sweet potato and banana, with pieces of chicken, crab, lobster or other meat. All this is covered in coconut cream then wrapped in banana leaves, tied tightly with palm fronds and baked in an earth oven, for about two hours.

Most Melanesian-run gîtes or homestays can prepare a *bougna* but you usually have to give a day's notice. Expect to pay from 1500 CFP to 3000 CFP per person. Lobster *bougna* is the most expensive.

SPECTATOR SPORTS
Cricket has been the favourite sport of Kanak women since the missionaries introduced it to the Loyalty Islanders in the 1850s. *Pétanque*, sometimes called *boules* (bowls), is played mainly by men on a *boulodrome*, a rough but flat gravel pitch.

As in France, football (soccer) is the most popular sport. Volleyball is also popular and there's growing interest in rugby.

SHOPPING
You'll find woodcarvings by Kanak sculptors in several craft centres in Noumea and on roadside stalls along the northeast coast.

Also look for cassettes and CDs of local *kaneka* bands, sold in music shops and supermarkets in Noumea. Current favourites include Dick and Hnatr Bouama, Edou, OK Ryos, Tim Sameke and We Ce Ca.

There is a plethora of duty-free shops in Noumea selling imported French perfumes, jewellery and clothing.

Getting There & Away

AIR
Airports & Airlines
The major airlines flying into New Caledonia are Qantas, Air New Zealand and Air Vanuatu. Focusing more on connections with Pacific destinations is the territory's international carrier, Air Calédonie International (Aircalin). Air France flies code share with Aircalin.

All international flights land at Tontouta international airport, 45km northwest of Noumea. For details on travelling between Tontouta and Noumea, and contact details for local airline offices, see Getting There & Away in the Noumea section. Rates quoted below are all return fares. For further details on airlines see the Getting There & Away chapter.

These are rates if purchasing tickets in Noumea. Cheaper rates may be available elsewhere.

North America
The main gateway to New Caledonia from North America is Los Angeles. You can fly with Air France or Air Tahiti Nui (US$1060) to Tahiti where you can connect with an Aircalin flight to Noumea. Or with Air New Zealand via Auckland (US$995) or Qantas via Sydney (US$1190).

NEW CALEDONIA

Another option is to fly with Air Pacific from Los Angeles to Noumea via Nadi. The price is in the same range.

Europe

Air France code sharing with Aircalin are the major carriers between France and Noumea, with flights via Japan. See Getting There & Away in the Noumea section.

Australasia

Australia is a good jumping-off point to New Caledonia. Qantas and Aircalin flights leave from Brisbane (three flights a week) and Sydney (daily except Monday and Saturday). A return excursion fare from Sydney or Brisbane costs US$515/545 in low/high season.

There are three flights per week between Auckland and Noumea, either with Air New Zealand or Aircalin. The 90-day return excursion fare costs from US$380.

Asia

Osaka and Tokyo are the only Asian cities directly connected with New Caledonia. Aircalin flies there for US$995.

South America

Use an Aircalin flight to Tahiti and connect with a Lan Chile flight to Santiago, via Easter Island. A return ticket costs US$1200. Or fly with Qantas via Sydney (US$1218).

The Pacific

See Air Passes in the introductory Getting There & Away chapter for several air passes that include New Caledonia.

Vanuatu You can fly between Port Vila and Noumea several times a week (US$365 return, Aircalin weekend special deal US$270, one hour) with Aircalin or Air Vanuatu. Air Vanuatu is represented in Noumea by **Axxess Travel** (☎ 28 66 77).

Fiji Aircalin flies to Nadi once or twice a week (US$590 return; two hours).

Wallis & Futuna Twice a week, Aircalin flies to Hihifo on Wallis Island (3 to 4½ hours). Once a week, a flight then continues to Vele on Futuna (six hours). The return fare for either is US$480/550 in low/high season.

French Polynesia Aircalin flies to Pape'ete's Faa'a airport once a week (US$600 return; 5¾ hours).

SEA
Cruise Ship

All cruise ships dock in Baie de la Moselle, south of Noumea. They also drop anchor at various spots around New Caledonia and then shuttle their passengers ashore to spend a day on the beach.

Pacific Sky and *Pacific Princess* (departing Sydney) are the most regular visitors to these waters. Ask your travel agent for more information. In Noumea, contact **CMA-CGM** (☎ 27 01 83, e *nma.scristofoli@cma-cgm.com; 32 rue du Général Galliéni).*

Yacht

New Caledonia welcomes about a thousand yachties every year, mostly during the peak season between August and October. The only place in the country with full facilities for yachties is Noumea; the approach to the capital is well marked.

Noumea is the only official Port of Entry – you must arrive here first and go through immigration formalities before dropping anchor anywhere else. Ahead of arrival in Noumea, use VHF Channel 67 to contact the **capitainerie** *(harbour master's office; ☎ 27 71 97, fax 27 71 29; BP 2960, Noumea).*

The **Cercle Nautique Calédonien** *(CNC; ☎ 26 27 27, fax 26 28 38; VHF Channel 68; BP 235, Noumea; rue du Capitaine Desmier)* is a yacht club at Baie des Pêcheurs.

Cruising New Caledonia & Vanuatu, by Alan Lucas, gives details on many natural harbours and out-of-the-way anchorages. The *Cruising Guide to New Caledonia,* by Joël Marc, Ross Blackman and Marc Rambeau, is a general yachting guide that also provides an exhaustive list of possible anchorages around the islands. Also see Maps in the Facts for the Visitor section, earlier.

ORGANISED TOURS

Package deals to New Caledonia from Australia and various countries often work out to be cheaper than doing it on your own and are a good option for people whose holidays are limited to one or two weeks.

From Australia most deals include return economy air fares from Brisbane, Sydney or Melbourne, accommodation in high-class hotels and the possibility of many other incentives, such as free air tickets for children, airport transfers, breakfast, casino chips, watersports equipment and car hire.

In Australia **Air Calédonie Holidays** *(☎ 02-9299 8854, tollfree 1300 886 363,*

fax 9299 6330; W www.aircaledonieholidays
.com; level 12, HCF Bldg, 403 George St, Sydney, NSW 2000) has a variety of packages.

Getting Around

AIR
New Caledonia's only domestic airline, Air Calédonie, operates out of Magenta airport in Noumea and flies to the towns of Koné, Touho, and Koumac on Grande Terre, to Waala on Îles Belep, to each of the four Loyalty Islands and to Île des Pins.

The main office for **Air Calédonie** (☎ 28 78 88, fax 28 13 40; e commercial@air -caledonie.nc; W www.air-caledonie.nc; 39 rue de Verdun, Noumea; open 7.30am-5pm Mon-Fri, until 11am Sat) is in town. There's also a booking office at Magenta airport (☎ 25 21 77). Air Calédonie agencies exist at all flight destinations.

Note: Fares quoted above are standard fares and include a 700 CFP tax. Peak flights cost 8% more and off peak are 12% less. Children under 12 pay half price.

To save money on your domestic flights, enquire about special coupons available for non-residents at Air Calédonie. A four-flight coupon for travellers with an international flight ticket costs 26,220 CFP.

For schedules enquire at the Air Calédonie office.

BUS
There's a fairly good bus system on Grande Terre that connects most of the towns. Buses leave from the old **bus station** (36 rue d'Austerlitz) near the market. There is a small **kiosk** (☎ 24 90 26; open daily 7.30am-noon

& 1.30pm-4pm) where you can get bus schedules and buy tickets. There are plans to transfer the bus station. For an update enquire at the tourist information office.

On the other islands, aside from school buses, there are practically no buses and it's best to pre-arrange transport or hitchhike.

CAR & MOTORCYCLE
Grande Terre has one main road that runs the length of its west coast. Another runs two-thirds of the way down its east coast. The roads have various names, such as the RT1, RP4, RPN10. At the northern end the RPN7 connects the two coastal roads. Five other roads traverse the central mountain chain connecting its two coastlines.

New Caledonia's major roads are all in sealed and good condition, but most minor roads are unsealed. On the east coast between Canala and Thio (26km) is a 13km-stretch of single-lane dirt road. Traffic operates on a one-way system from 6am to 6pm. North-bound cars leave the Thio end at odd hours and southbound traffic sets off from Canala at even hours. It's impassable by conventional vehicles after heavy rain.

As in France, driving is on the right-hand side of the road. Each town will have one petrol station or at least a pump.

Rental
Car-rental companies abound in Noumea, but the larger ones also have desks at the airport. The tourist office in Noumea has a list of the rental companies.

Most companies charge about 1200 to 2500 CFP per day (on average) for a small sedan. In addition, there's a charge of 20 to 36 CFP per kilometre, plus daily insurance and petrol.

NEW CALEDONIA

Domestic Airfares

from	to	fare (CFP)	duration (mins)	frequency
Lifou	Mare	7080	30	3 days per week
Lifou	Ouvéa	4860	20	2 days per week
Lifou	Tiga	4800	20	2 per week
Mare	Ouvéa	10,010	80	1 per week
Mare	Tiga	3980	15	1 per week
Noumea	Belep	17,000	140	2 per week (via Koné & Koumac)
Noumea	Île des Pins	7080	20	daily
Noumea	Koné	11,170	40	daily except Saturday
Noumea	Koumac	12,370	90	2 per week
Noumea	Loyalty Islands	10,160	35	daily (except Tiga)
Noumea	Touho	11,170	40	4 days per week
Ouvéa	Tiga	7920	65	1 per week (via Lifou)

Busing Around Grande Terre

destination	fare (CFP)	duration (hrs)	frequency
Bourail	1100	2½	Mon-Sat
Canala	1100	3½	daily
Hienghène	1650	6½	Mon-Sat
Houaïlou	1250	4	daily
Koné	1300	4	daily
Kouaoua	1100	3½	Mon-Wed & Fri
Koumac	1650	5½	daily
La Foa	900	1¾	Mon-Sat
Poindimié	1450	5	daily
Pouébo	1850	6½	Wed & Fri
Sarraméa	950	2	daily
Thio	1000	2	daily
Yaté/Waho	600	2	Mon-Sat

Some companies offer good deals such as one/two weeks all-inclusive rental from 20,000 CFP plus petrol.

In the Loyalty Islands and Île des Pins transport arranged through gîtes and hotels is expensive. Although prices are much less competitive than in the capital, it might be worth hiring a car if you're in a group.

A valid driving licence from your own country is needed, and often a security deposit of 100,000 CFP.

Point Rouge (☎ 28 59 20, fax 24 99 94; 75 Av Maréchal Foch, Noumea) rents scooters for 1800 CFP a day.

Discount Location (☎ 24 10 42, 77 54 42; e discountloc@lagoon.nc; 135 Rte de l'Anse Vata) rents camping cars (2/5/7 person vehicles 45,000/65,000/95,000 CFP per week).

BOAT
Ferry
The *Betico*, a fast passenger ferry, sails regularly between Noumea and the Loyalty Islands and Île des Pins. The **ferry terminal** (☎ 26 01 00; 1 Av James Cook), opposite the Bingo, is open between 7.30am and 5.30pm weekdays, and from 6am to 10pm on Saturdays.

A one-way economy-class ticket from Noumea to the Loyalty Islands costs 5450 CFP and to Île des Pins 3650 CFP for adults. Going between islands costs 2750 CFP. An Île des Pins day trip costs 6300 CFP, otherwise return fares are double. Children pay around half price.

The **Havanah** (☎ 27 36 73) is a slow cargo ferry that also carries passengers. It sets sail for the Loyalty Islands from Noumea every Monday (adult/child 4500/3000 CFP), leaving from the southern end of rue Jules Ferry.

Yacht & Speedboat Charter
Yachts can be chartered from **Noumea Yacht Charter** (☎ 28 66 66, fax 28 74 82; Port Moselle, Noumea). **Pacific Charter** (☎/fax 26 10 55; Port Moselle, Noumea) has 200 HP speedboats available for hire from around 30,000 CFP per day. It also has a catamaran. Both of the offices are located in the blue-roofed wooden chalet right next to the market.

See Yachts under Getting There & Away and Sailing under Activities earlier in this chapter.

LOCAL TRANSPORT
Bus
Noumea is the only town in New Caledonia that operates an urban bus system (for more information see Noumea's Getting Around section later in this chapter).

Taxi
Taxis are confined to Noumea and the larger towns on Grande Terre. The taxis run on a meter.

ORGANISED TOURS
Tour operators in Noumea organise a host of trips to get visitors out of the capital and into *la brousse*. **Caltours** (☎ 41 10 92, 81 20 01; 7 rue Charles-de-Verneilh) organise tours throughout Grande Terre.

Outside Noumea, gîte and hotel owners on Île des Pins and the Loyalty Islands run tours of the islands. Some of their counterparts on Grande Terre also run day tours of their local areas. Weekend horse treks are organised at Koné, Bourail, and at Pocquereux, near La Foa.

Noumea

pop 85,000
Noumea is the nerve centre of New Caledonia
and 40% of the population have made it their
home. It is also the top tourist destination in
New Caledonia.

Sitting on a peninsula in the southwestern
region of the island of Grande Terre, Noumea is made up of hills and sloping valleys
that have gradually been integrated into the
growing metropolis. Bay after bay carves the
coastline, giving it the charm of a city that
opens out to the sea.

Noumea is home to the majority of New
Caledonia's Europeans and has all the facilities of a modern city. For tourists, it is an ideal
starting point for exploring New Caledonia.

History

In 1854, a French naval officer, Tardy de Montravel, wanting to seal France's recent possession of New Caledonia, chose Noumea as the
site for the colony's administrative centre.

In the early 1860s, the French chose Île
Nou (today the Nouville Peninsula) as the site
for a convict prison and in 1864 the first ship,
Iphigénie, arrived with 248 convicts from
France. Noumea was transformed in 1875,
when gold and nickel started to be mined.

The city was the US military headquarters
during its WWII Pacific operations. Soon
after it became the seat of the then South Pacific Commission (SPC) – see Government &
Politics in the Facts about the South Pacific
chapter. With the nickel boom of the late
1960s and early 1970s, Noumea's population
grew rapidly.

During *Les Évènements*, violent confron-
tations erupted in the city centre. Since the
signing of the Matignon Accords, peace has
returned to Noumea. In recent years, the city
has been going through a building spree un-
paralleled since the nickel boom era.

Orientation

The city centre is spread along Baie de la
Moselle. A grid of ruler-straight streets lines
the centre, the heart of which is Place des
Cocotiers.

The main tourist area is at Anse Vata and
Baie des Citrons, which are connected to
central Noumea by two main routes, namely
the inland road, Route de l'Anse Vata, and the
picturesque coastal route that hugs the three
large bays that carve the city's southwestern

edge: Baie de l'Orphelinat, Baie des Citrons
and Anse Vata.

Noumea's central district is bordered to the
south by Av de la Victoire/Henry Lafleur. Immediately south of this busy road is the city's
small Quartier Latin (Latin Quarter) where
many quaint old colonial houses still stand.
Further east is Vallée des Colons, also with
an old colonial atmosphere.

Information

Tourist Offices The **Office du Tourisme de Noumea et de la Province Sud**
(☎ 28 75 80, tollfree 05 75 80; ᴇ office
-tourisme@canl.nc; 14 rue Jean Jaurès, Place
des Cocotiers; open 8am-5.30pm Mon-Fri,
9am-noon Sat), located at the western end
of Place des Cocotiers, is the tourist office
for Noumea and the Southern Province. The
friendly staff speak English. A smaller **office**
(☎ 28 75 80; open 9am-5.30pm Mon-Sun) is
located in the beachfront *fare* (thatched-roof
building) on Promenade Roger Laroque at
Anse Vata. It hands out free city maps, and
Noumea and Southern Province pocket guides
with lots of useful information.

The **Office du Tourisme de la Province
Nord** (☎ 27 78 05; ᴇ infos.tourisme@province
-nord.nc; 35 Av du Maréchal Foch; open
9am-4pm Mon-Fri, 9am-noon Sat) is in Le
Village shopping centre.

Destination Îles Loyauté (☎ 28 93 60;
ᴇ destil@canl.nc; 113 Promenade Roger
Laroque; open 8am-6pm Mon-Fri, 8.30am-
11am & noon-5pm Sat), the Loyalty Islands
information office, is in front of the Lantana
Beach Hôtel at Anse Vata.

Money Most banks have their main branch
on Av de la Victoire/Henry Lafleur. **Banque
Calédonienne d'Investissement** (BCI; ☎ 24
20 60; cnr rue du Général Mangin & rue
Anatole France; open 7.50am-5pm Mon-Fri
& 7.30am-11.30am Sat) is very central and is
the only bank open until 5pm on weekdays.
Most banks have an ATM.

American Express (Amex; ☎ 28 47 37, fax
27 26 36; 29 Av du Maréchal Foch) is located
in Center Voyages. It does not charge commission on travellers cheques or cash.

Post & Communications There's the **main
post office** (☎ 26 84 00; 9 rue Eugène Porch-
eron; open 7.45am-3.30pm Mon-Fri, 7.30am-
11am Sat) near Commissariat Central.

Those needing an Internet fix can head to
Cyber Point NC (5 rue Auguste Brun; open

NOUMEA

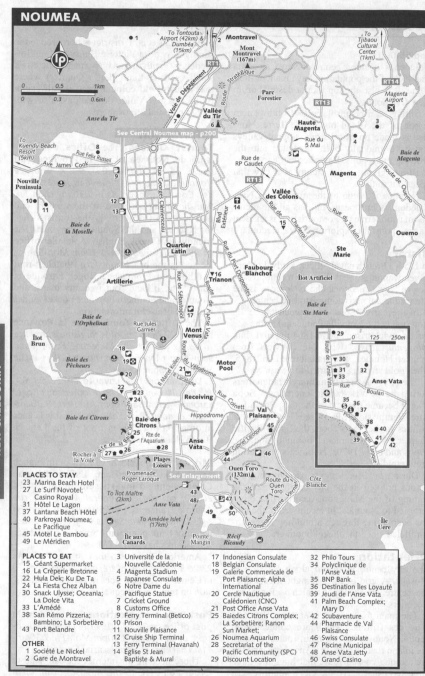

To Tontouta Airport (42km) & Dumbéa (15km)

Montravel
Mont Montravel (167m)

To Tjibaou Cultural Center (1km)

RT1

Route Stratégique

Parc Forestier

RT14

Magenta Airport

Voie de Dégagement

Anse du Tir

Vallée du Tir

Haute Magenta

Rue du 5 Mai

RT13

Baie de Magenta

See Central Noumea map - p200

To Kuendu Beach Resort (5km)

Rue Felix Russell

Rue Georges Clemenceau

Rue de RP Gaudet

RT13

Magenta

Route de Ouemo

Ave James Cook

Nouville Peninsula

Vallée des Colons

Rue du 18 Juin

Baie de la Moselle

Rue de Charleroi

Ouemo

Quartier Latin

Ste Marie

Artillerie

Rue de Sébastopol

Faubourg Blanchot

Îlot Artificiel

Baie de l'Orphelinat

Trianon

Rue Jules Garnier

Mont Venus

Baie de Ste Marie

Îlot Brun

Route de l'Anse Vata

Baie des Pêcheurs

R Marcel Kollen / R Lacabane

Motor Pool

Route du Vélodrome

Rue Colnett

29

Route de l'Anse Vata

125   250m

30
31
33

32

Anse Vata

Rue   Boulari

Receiving

34

35
36
37

BNP Bank

Baie des Citrons

Baie des Citrons

Hippodrome

Val Plaisance

Promenade Roger Laroque

38
40
39
41
42

R Gabriel Laroque

45

Rte de l'Aquarium

Anse Vata

28

43
44

46

Rocher à la Voile

27   26

25

Plages Loisirs

Promenade Roger Laroque

See Enlargement

Ouen Toro (132m)

Côte Blanche

To Îlot Maître (2km)

Anse Vata

47

Route du Ouen Toro

Île Uere

To Amédée Islet (17km)

48

49   50

Promenade Pierre Vernier

Île aux Canards

Pointe Mangin

Récif Ricaudy

NEW CALEDONIA

8am-8pm Mon-Sat, 8am-noon Sun) behind the Musée de Nouvelle-Calédonie. It costs 500 CFP per half-hour online.

At **Lagoon Micropolis** (☎ *28 18 18; 21 rue de l'Alma; open 8am-6pm Mon-Sat),* in the Micropolis shop next to TATI in the Galerie Alma, half an hour online costs 420 CFP.

Travel Agencies For domestic travel arrangements, try **Center Voyages** (☎ *28 40 40; 27 bis Av du Maréchal Foch)* or **Alpha International** (☎ *27 24 20; Galerie Commerciale de Port Plaisance).*

Bookshops & Libraries A good source for information on Kanak culture is the **médiathèque** (media library) in the Jean-Marie Tjibaou Cultural Centre, 10km north of Noumea.

Librairie Montaigne (☎ *27 34 88; 27 rue de Sébastopol)* and **Librairie Pentecost** (☎ *28 88 82; 34 rue de l'Alma)* have a small range of contemporary English-language novels, as well as international magazines and newspapers, maps, and regional travel guides.

Medical Services & Emergency The city's main hospital is **Hôpital Gaston Bourret** (☎ *25 66 66; 7 rue Paul Doumer).* Pharmacies are dotted all over Noumea. On Saturday afternoons and Sundays only one emergency pharmacy, on a rotating schedule, is open. In an emergency you can call the **police** (☎ *17)* or **SAMU** *(medical aid and ambulance;* ☎ *15).*

Place des Cocotiers

The natural starting point for exploring Noumea is Place des Cocotiers. Named after the coconut palms that fringe the area, the square was the army's vegetable garden in the 19th century. In the middle of Place des Cocotiers is the **Fontaine Céleste**, a fountain erected in 1892 that marks the starting point for determining road distances from the capital throughout the territory. To the east, in the top quadrant, is a **bandstand**, a famous Noumea landmark dating back to the late 1800s. On the western side, a **statue of Admiral Olry**, the colony's governor between 1878 and 1880, overlooks the **Hôtel de Ville** (Town Hall).

Bibliothèque Bernheim

This attractive, colonial-style public library *(cnr rue de la Somme & Av du Maréchal Foch; open 1pm-5.30pm Tues, Thurs & Fri, 9am-5.30pm Wed, 9am-4pm Sat)* has a lovely wooden interior.

Musée de la Ville de Noumea

The Noumea Museum (☎ *26 28 05; rue Jean Jaurès; admission free; open 9am-5pm Mon-Sat),* dwarfed by gigantic palm trees, is housed in the city's old town hall next to Place des Cocotiers. The building is a fine example of colonial architecture. Displays are changed every few months.

Musée de Nouvelle-Calédonie

The Museum of New Caledonia (☎ *27 23 42; 45 Av du Maréchal Foch; adult/student*

Jean-Marie Tjibaou Cultural Centre

The Jean-Marie Tjibaou Cultural Centre (☎ *41 45 55, fax 41 45 56;* W *www.adck.nc)* is an innovative and commanding piece of architecture. This Kanak and Oceanic cultural centre is dedicated to the man many remember as New Caledonia's peacemaker. It sits on a quiet promontory at Tina, about 10km from central Noumea, where it rises from the bush in a series of tall, curved wooden posts set in semi-circles. It was designed by famous Italian architect Renzo Piano (best known as one of the architects who designed the controversial Pompidou Centre in Paris), who incorporated aspects of traditional Kanak architecture in his contemporary design.

It's set in eight hectares of peaceful woodland and mangrove. Le Chemin Kanak (the Kanak Path), weaves through the grounds where a variety of trees and plants of cultural significance – such as yams, taro, *houp*, araucaria and *kaori* – are interspersed with sites representing Kanak myths and customs. There is also a customary area where three traditional Melanesian *cases* stand.

Inside the centre are items of Kanak heritage, monumental sculptures by artists throughout the Pacific, a performing arts arena, a multimedia library and exhibition rooms. There's also a shop and café.

The centre is open to the public from 9am to 5pm Tuesday to Sunday. Entrance costs 500 CFP and is free for students (add 1500 CFP if you want a guided tour in English).

NEW CALEDONIA

CENTRAL NOUMEA

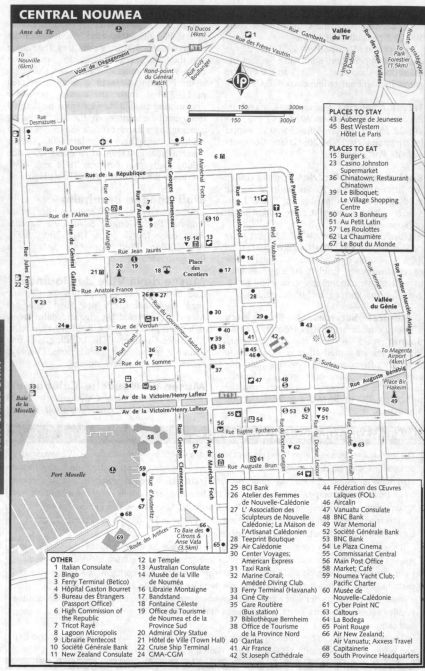

PLACES TO STAY
43 Auberge de Jeunesse
45 Best Western
   Hôtel Le Paris

PLACES TO EAT
15 Burger's
23 Casino Johnston
   Supermarket
36 Chinatown; Restaurant
   Chinatown
39 Le Bilboquet;
   Le Village Shopping
   Centre
50 Aux 3 Bonheurs
51 Au Petit Latin
57 Les Roulottes
62 La Chaumière
67 Le Bout du Monde

OTHER
1 Italian Consulate
2 Bingo
3 Ferry Terminal (Betico)
4 Hôpital Gaston Bourret
5 Bureau des Étrangers
  (Passport Office)
6 High Commission of
  the Republic
7 Tricot Rayé
8 Lagoon Micropolis
9 Librairie Pentecost
10 Société Générale Bank
11 New Zealand Consulate
12 Le Temple
13 Australian Consulate
14 Musée de la Ville
   de Nouméa
16 Librairie Montaigne
17 Bandstand
18 Fontaine Céleste
19 Office du Tourisme
   de Noumea et de la
   Province Sud
20 Admiral Olry Statue
21 Hôtel de Ville (Town Hall)
22 Cruise Ship Terminal
24 CMA-CGM

25 BCI Bank
26 Atelier des Femmes
   de Nouvelle-Calédonie
27 L' Association des
   Sculpteurs de Nouvelle
   Calédonie; La Maison de
   l'Artisanat Calédonien
28 Teeprint Boutique
29 Air Calédonie
30 Center Voyages;
   American Express
31 Taxi Rank
32 Marine Corail;
   Amédeé Diving Club
33 Ferry Terminal (Havanah)
34 Ciné City
35 Gare Routière
   (Bus station)
37 Bibliothèque Bernheim
38 Office de Tourisme
   de la Province Nord
40 Qantas
41 Air France
42 St Joseph Cathédrale

44 Fédération des Œuvres
   Laïques (FOL)
46 Aircalin
47 Vanuatu Consulate
48 BNC Bank
49 War Memorial
52 Société Générale Bank
53 BNC Bank
54 Le Plaza Cinema
55 Commissariat Central
56 Main Post Office
58 Market; Café
59 Noumea Yacht Club;
   Pacific Charter
60 Musée de
   Nouvelle-Calédonie
61 Cyber Point NC
63 Caltours
64 La Bodega
65 Point Rouge
66 Air New Zealand;
   Air Vanuatu; Axxess Travel
68 Capitainerie
69 South Province Headquarters

or child 200/50 CFP; open 9am-11.30am & 12.15pm-4.30pm Wed-Mon) is an excellent place to start exploring Kanak culture. Displays include a magnificent exhibition of sculptured wooden totems, elaborate masks, ceremonial axes and a variety of spectacular weapons. There's also an enormous *pirogue* (outrigger canoe) and a beautiful replica of a *grande case*.

Churches
One of Noumea's landmarks is **St Joseph's Cathedral**, which stands on a hill at the end of rue de Verdun. It overlooks the city and is easily spotted from the sea at Baie de la Moselle. The cathedral was built in 1888 by convict labour.

Parc Forestier
The Parc Forestier (☎ 27 89 51; Rte Stratégique; adult/child 300/100 CFP; open 10.15am-5.45pm Tues-Sun, 10.15am-5pm May-Aug) is just below the summit of Mont Montravel. It was established in 1972 and is a botanic garden and fauna park. You can see New Caledonia's endangered national emblem, the *cagou* (see the boxed text 'The Cagou' later in this chapter), as well as many other species of birds endemic to either New Caledonia or other Pacific nations. Also present are *roussettes* (flying foxes or fruit bats).

The park is about 4km northeast of the city centre; the *Petit Train* (see Organised Tours) and organised-tour buses stop at the gate but no public buses pass this way.

Noumea Aquarium
The small aquarium (☎ 26 27 31; Rte de l'Aquarium; adult/pensioner/student/child 650/300/210/115 CFP; open 10.30am-4.45pm Tues-Sun) at Anse Vata, created in 1956, is worth a visit. The display tanks contain rare and unusual species of marine life, including sea snakes, sharks and eels, all in a coral environment.

Nouville
The hilly peninsula of Nouville, where a few **convict buildings** still stand, rises to the west of central Noumea.

At the end of the peninsula is **Kuendu beach**. It's a relaxing place but the shallow, often-murky water is not great for swimming. There's a good place to **snorkel** just behind the point where there's also a nudist shingle beach.

Island Escapes
Amédée Islet This small coral islet, about 20km south of Noumea, is a marine reserve, noted for its clear water, its popularity as a day-trip destination and the 56m-high **lighthouse** that rises from its centre.

The only commercial operator is **Mary D** (☎ 26 31 31; Promenade Roger Laroque; adult/child 10,600/5950 CFP; open 7.30am-noon & 1pm-6pm Mon-Fri, 7.30am-noon Sat), which has an office in the Palm Beach complex at Anse Vata. Its plush vessel reaches the island in 40 minutes, leaving at 8.15am from Port Moselle or 8.45am from the Anse Vata jetty, and returning by about 5pm. It has fixed schedules on Wednesday, Friday, Saturday and Sunday, and otherwise operates according to demand. The tickets include a buffet lunch and shark feeding at the reef. Snorkelling equipment can be rented for 1000 CFP.

Other Islets Watertaxis from **Plages Loisirs** (☎ 26 90 00; 80 Promenade Roger Laroque; open 8am-5pm daily), in the beachfront *fare* at Anse Vata, ferry people to **Île aux Canards** (750 CFP return), just off Anse Vata beach, and to **Îlot Maître** (2200 CFP return).

Beaches
The two most popular tourist beaches are **Anse Vata** and **Baie des Citrons**. On a windy day at Anse Vata you can watch the colourful kite surfers and windsurfers whizzing up and down the bay.

Diving
Noumea has some excellent offshore dive spots, including the Passe de Boulari, Passe de Dumbéa and the wreck of *La Dieppoise*. There are several internationally recognised diving clubs based in the city, including **Amédée Diving Club** (☎ 26 40 29, fax 28 57 55; 28 rue du Général Mangin) and **Scubaventure** (☎ 79 26 79; 2 bis rue Gabrièle Laroque) which also operates from *Le Méridien* hotel.

Other Water Activities
Plages Loisirs (☎ 26 90 00; 80 Promenade Roger Laroque; Kayaks per hour/half-day/full day 1000/2600/5200 CFP, windsurfers 1250/3640/7280 CFP) rents water-sport equipment.

Organised Tours
Several English-speaking operators run minibus tours of Noumea (6950 CFP; three hours), with pick-ups from your hotel. These include

Center Voyages and Alpha International (see Travel Agencies earlier in this section).

Most tourists prefer **Le Petit Train** *(☎ 43 37 43; adult/child 1100/550 CFP return, 1½ hrs)* tours. These miniature trains chug cheerfully from Anse Vata to the city centre several times a day. They also go to the Jean-Marie Tjibaou Cultural Centre (adult/child 1300/700 CFP return, admission to the centre is extra, 4 hours) four times a week. You can buy tickets from the driver at the main stop at the Palm Beach complex at Anse Vata.

Places to Stay – Budget

The **Auberge de Jeunesse** *(HI Hostel; ☎ 27 58 79, fax 25 48 17; 51 Pasteur Marcel Ariège; 4-bunk rooms per person member/ nonmember 1300/1500 CFP, doubles or twins per member/nonmember 3100/3500 CFP; office open 7am-11am & 5pm-7.30pm Mon-Sat, 7am-10am & 6pm-7.30pm Sun)*, perched behind St Joseph's Cathedral, has a fantastic view overlooking the city and Baie de la Moselle. The large, four-storey building is very clean. Its dormitory-style rooms, with large, lockable metal wardrobes, sleep four people. Outside office hours you can drop off luggage but you can't check in unless you've made a reservation. There's a big kitchen with excellent cooking facilities. Luggage lockers cost 100/200 CFP per day/ week. Mail (BP 769, 98845 Noumea Cedex) and faxes can be sent here. Credit cards are accepted.

Motel Le Bambou *(☎ 26 12 90, fax 26 30 58; 44 rue Spahr, Val Plaisance; 1 or 2-person studios 6150 CFP)* is set in a residential area. It's quiet and clean. Each studio has a small balcony, fan and cooking facilities. The motel is 1km from Anse Vata beach.

Marina Beach Hotel *(☎ 28 76 33, fax 26 28 81; e marinab@canl.nc; 4 rue August Page, Baie des Citrons; 2-person rooms 6850 CFP)* has attractive studios with TV, air-con and kitchenettes. There's a small swimming pool out the back and a spa pool.

Places to Stay – Mid-Range

Best Western – Hôtel Le Paris *(☎ 28 17 00, fax 28 09 60; e leparis@canl.nc; 47 rue de Sébastopol; singles/doubles 7850/8850 CFP)*, recently affiliated to the international chain, is in the city centre. It has 48 newly renovated comfortable rooms. There is currently no restaurant so guests have to eat off premises but the hotel provides meal vouchers for nearby restaurants.

Lantana Beach Hôtel *(☎ 26 22 12, fax 26 16 12; e lantana@canl.nc; 133 Promenade Roger Laroque; singles/doubles/triples 7750/ 8750/9750 CFP)* is in the heart of Anse Vata, across the street from the beach. The hotel has all the necessary amenities but it is slightly drab. Rooms with a balcony and sea view cost 500 CFP extra. A continental/American breakfast costs 900/1400 CFP.

Le Pacifique *(rooms from 10,400 CFP)* is attached to the Parkroyal hotel at Anse Vata but offers cheaper accommodation (for details see the Parkroyal Noumea in Places to Stay – Top End).

Places to Stay – Top End

Anse Vata's waterfront has the pick of Noumea's top-end hotels. The following are just a few.

Hôtel Le Lagon *(☎ 26 12 55, fax 26 12 44; e lelagon@lagoon.nc; 143 Rte de l'Anse Vata; 2-person 'studio' rooms 10,350 CFP, 1-bedroom 4-person apartment 13,350 CFP)* is a serenely decorated five-storey hotel. The rooms all have kitchenettes. Breakfast costs an extra 900 CFP. The hotel has a bar and nice restaurant. It's a two-minute walk to the beach; bus No 7 stops out the front.

At the northern end of Promenade Roger Laroque in Anse Vata, across the street from the beach, is **Le Surf Novotel** *(☎ 28 66 88, fax 28 52 23; e novotelnc.resa@offratel.nc; 55 Promenade Roger Laroque, Anse Vata; 1/ 2 people rooms with/without view 16,800/ 14,000 CFP, suites 27,500-35,500 CFP)*. It offers a continental/American breakfast for 1400/1800 CFP. There is also a French restaurant and the Casino Royal.

Parkroyal Noumea *(☎ 26 22 00, fax 26 16 77; e resa.parkroyal@mls.nc; 123 Promenade Roger Laroque, Anse Vata; doubles with/without ocean view 20,000/16,000 CFP, luxury rooms from 20,000)* is right in the midst of the tourist atmosphere at Anse Vata but you have to cross the street to get to the beach. The hotel has all the facilities you'd expect, including a large swimming pool.

Le Méridien *(☎ 26 50 00, fax 26 51 00; e le.meridien@meridien.nc; garden/ocean view rooms 19,500/22,500 CFP, suites from 48,000 CFP)* is draped around Pointe Magnin at the far end of Anse Vata beach. Together with its sister establishment on Île des Pins, this five-star hotel is New Caledonia's top resort. The resort has everything that's needed for a splurge of this kind.

Out of town on the Nouville Peninsula is **Kuendu Beach Resort** (☎ 24 30 00, fax 27 60 33; ⓔ kuendubeach@lagoon.nc; 1/2-person garden/beach bungalows 12,150/ 18,150 CFP, over-water bungalows 32,150 CFP). It has air conditioned, garden and beachfront bungalows and thatched bungalows built on pillars over the water. Resort facilities include a swimming pool, two restaurants and water-sports equipment for hire. The resort provides free transport for its guests to and from central Noumea, several times a day.

Places to Eat

A multitude of restaurants compete for the appetites of tourists and locals alike, offering French, Vietnamese, Chinese and Japanese cuisines, among others. French and seafood restaurants are the most expensive. Many cafés and restaurants are closed on Sunday or Monday.

City Centre You'll find numerous, small and inexpensive **snacks/cafés** in Chinatown in the southern part of the city centre. **Restaurant Chinatown** (☎ 27 17 11; cnr rue de la Somme & rue d'Austerlitz; menu from 1250 CFP, plat du jour from 850 CFP; open lunch & dinner Mon-Sat), in the small Chinatown mall, is very good.

The **café** (Port Moselle; open from 5am to around 11am daily) inside the market serves croissants, coffee and freshly squeezed orange juice.

Burger's (☎ 24 99 89; 37 rue Jean Jaurès; open lunch and dinner Mon-Sat), next to Villa Vanille, is a popular sandwich bar that does great takeaways, including delicious kebabs (550 CFP), salads, paninis, quiche and sandwiches (from 350 CFP). You can eat across the street in the shady Place des Cocotiers.

Le Bilboquet (☎ 28 43 30; Av du Maréchal Foch; plat du jour 1050 CFP; open 9am-10pm Mon-Thur, 9am-11.30pm Fri & Sat), at Le Village shopping centre, serves a full breakfast for 1300 CFP. A pain-au-chocolat or croissant costs 150 CFP. At lunch time only it offers a plat du jour.

Le Bout du Monde (☎ 27 77 28; rue d'Austerlitz; all-you-can-eat cold-lunch buffet 1020 CFP, menu weekdays/weekends 2300/2500 CFP) is a relaxing bar and restaurant next to the marina at Port Moselle. It's open daily and has Internet access (520 CFP for 30 minutes).

Quartier Latin & Trianon You'll find a cosy Chinese atmosphere at **Aux 3 Bonheurs** (☎ 27 45 32; 58 Av de la Victoire/Henry Lafleur; mains 1100-1800 CFP) and tasty Chinese dishes.

La Chaumière (☎ 27 24 62; 13 rue du Docteur Guegan; lunch/dinner menu 1700/ 2600 CFP) serves good French food. It also has à la carte options.

Au Petit Latin (☎ 28 47 57; 7 bis rue du Docteur Lescour; meals from 850 CFP) is a wee place with very reasonable prices. Its speciality is a fish or beef bobotie, a South African dish, which costs 950 CFP.

La Crêperie Bretonne (☎ 27 37 14; 5 rue Ange Berlioz; crepes from 300 to 1200 CFP), with an atmosphere reminiscent of Brittany, specialises in galettes (savoury crepes) and crepes at reasonable prices.

Baie des Citrons The colourful French-Basque-Spanish restaurant **La Fiesta Chez Alban** (☎ 26 21 33; 5 Promenade Roger Laroque; meals from 990-3000 CFP) serves large helpings for reasonable prices.

Hula Dek (☎ 27 46 46; 27 rue Jules Garnier; open daily; 3-course lunch special 1150 CFP, à la carte from 1800 CFP) has a terrace restaurant right on the beach.

Baie des Citrons complex has a good choice of restaurants serving seafood, crepes, salads and various international cuisines.

Anse Vata Open daily, **San Rémo Pizzeria** (☎ 26 18 02; 119 Promenade Roger Laroque; small/large pizzas from 900/1350 CFP) serves spaghetti, meat dishes and salads.

L'Amédée (☎ 26 10 35; 153 Rte de l'Anse Vata; menu 1600 CFP), specialising in seafood, is good value. It's popular with locals. Except for dinner on Saturday, it's closed at the weekend.

Port Belandre (☎ 25 07 00; Promenade Roger Laroque; open 11.30am-2pm & 7pm-late Tues-Sun; meals from 1800-4000 CFP) is an attractive restaurant built over the water at the southern end of Anse Vata. It serves haute cuisine. There's also a snack, serving cheaper meals, open from 7am to 6pm.

Fast Food There are a few beachfront snacks along Baie des Citrons serving burgers, fries or rice and chicken-type meals. A half-baguette sandwich costs around 300 to 400 CFP.

Snack Ulysse (open 10am-9pm daily; baguette sandwiches from 350 CFP, dishes from

800 CFP), on Route de l'Anse Vata, close to Hôtel le Lagon, has tasty baguette sandwiches. A vegetarian burger costs 450 CFP.

Bambino (☎ 26 11 77) is at the Anse Vata shops near the Parkroyal hotel. It serves hamburgers for 500 CFP. Its speciality is Chinese soup (750 CFP).

La Sorbetière (☎ 26 28 03; open daily), near Bambino at Anse Vata and also at the Baie des Citrons complex, sells a mouthwatering range of ice creams from 200 CFP, and gaufres (waffles) and crepes from 250 CFP.

A popular takeaway source is **Les Roulottes** (rue Georges Clémenceau), minivans, that gather in the large carpark, opposite the market. These vehicles line up every evening, including Sunday, from about 6pm, and serve an array of cold salads, drinks, cakes and hot meals such as chicken or beef curry with rice and bread for 700 CFP. They operate until about 11pm.

Self-Catering Noumea's market (open around 5am-11am daily) is opposite the bus station and next to Port Moselle. On Saturday and Sunday there's a colourful multi-ethnic atmosphere.

In addition, you'll find several well-stocked supermarkets, including the **Casino Johnston** (cnr rue Anatole France & rue Jules Ferry), near the Gare Maritime where the big cruise ships dock.

At the Baie des Citrons complex there is a small grocery shop called **Sun Market** (open 6am-10pm daily).

Entertainment

Ciné City (Av de la Victoire/Henry Lafleur, opp the market; admission 850 CFP) and **Plaza cinema** (65 rue de Sébastopol; admission 850 CFP) screen current releases. Non-French movies are all dubbed in French.

La Bodega (☎ 27 45 74; 12 bis rue du Docteur Lescour) is a popular Spanish-style bar where a glass of sangria costs 400 CFP and a plate of tapas is 600 CFP. On Wednesday evenings it offers free salsa dance classes in its enclosed courtyard.

There are a number of nightclubs and bars in the **Baie des Citrons complex**. At the opposite end of Baie des Citrons, the Hula Dek becomes the **Ku De Ta** nightclub from 10.30pm to 3am nightly.

If you're into gambling, head for **Casino Royal**, in the Surf Novotel, or the **Grand Casino**, next to Le Méridien's at Anse Vata.

Jeudi de l'Anse Vata is an extremely popular street market that is held every Thursday from 5.30pm to 8.30pm on the waterfront directly in front of the Anse Vata shops. There is a different theme each week. Street performers, arts and crafts stalls and multi-ethnic local crowds create a lively atmosphere.

Shopping

Duty-free shops specialising in French goods – clothing, lingerie and shoes – are dotted along rue de Sébastopol and rue de l'Alma.

Two shops selling local clothing brands are **Teeprint Boutique** (48 rue Anatole France) and **Tricot Rayé** (27 rue de l'Alma).

Curio and Pacific artefact shops are also abundant, particularly along rue Anatole France and Av du Maréchal Foch. You can try **L'Atelier Artisanal des Femmes de Nouvelle-Calédonie** (cnr rue Gouverneur Sautot & rue Anatole France).

Getting There & Away

Air All international flights arrive at Tontouta airport, where passengers must pass through customs and immigration. For more information see the Getting There & Away section earlier in this chapter. For information on air travel within New Caledonia see the Getting Around section.

Major airlines in Noumea include:

Air Calédonie International (Aircalin) (☎ 26 55 00) 8 rue Frédéric Surleau
Air France (☎ 25 88 00) 41 rue de Sébastopol
Air New Zealand (☎ 28 66 77) Axxess Travel, 22 rue Duquesne
Qantas (☎ 28 65 46) 35 Av Maréchal Foch – access from rue de Verdun

Car & Motorcycle Cars, camper vans and motorcycles (see Getting Around earlier in this chapter) can be hired from the various rental companies in Noumea. The **Noumea tourism office** (☎ 28 75 80, fax 28 75 85) has a list of car rental companies.

Boat Most cruising yachts anchor at Port Moselle. A passenger ferry connects Noumea with Île des Pins and the Loyalty Islands – for more information see the Getting Around section earlier in this chapter.

Getting Around

To/from Tontouta Airport Tontouta international airport is 45km, or 40 minutes by car, north of Noumea. It is serviced by buses and minivan operators.

Agence ORIMA (☎ 28 28 42; 27 Av du Maréchal Foch) and **Philo Tours** (☎ 28 99 57; 10 rue Pasteur Benignus) operate minivans between Noumea and the airport, dropping-off and picking-up from where you're staying. It's 2500 CFP one way.

Carsud (☎ 25 16 15; 380 CFP; Mon-Fri 5am-5.40pm from Tontouta, 4am-7pm from Noumea, shorter hours Sat & Sun) blue-and-white buses are the cheapest way of getting to and from the airport. The main station is at Montravel just north of the city centre. At Tontouta buses stop outside the airport terminal. In Noumea you get on or off at the *Passeport* stop by the **passport office** (cnr rue Georges Clemenceau & rue Paul Doumer). Express buses take a more direct route via the Savexpress although the fare is the same as the slightly longer route via Dumbéa. The journey takes about 1¼ hours either way. There are several buses a day. You can pick up schedules at the Montravel station.

To/from Magenta Airport The domestic airport at Magenta is 4km east of the city centre and is easily reached by public transport. For more information see under Bus.

For information on domestic flights see under Air in the Getting Around section at the beginning of this chapter.

Bus The bus stops are marked by a white pillar with a blue bus sign. Red-and-white city buses operate from 6am to 7pm Monday to Friday, and 7am to 7pm at the weekend. During the week they run every 15 minutes and on Saturday and Sunday they run every 30 minutes.

In the city centre all of the buses depart from the bus stop on rue Clémenceau near the intersection with rue de la Somme in the Chinese Quarter. The exception to this is bus No 1 going to Kuendu Beach, which

Taxi Fares

from	to	fare (maximum four people)
Anse Vata	City centre	1100 CFP
Anse Vata	Magenta airport	1600 CFP
City centre	Magenta airport	1200 CFP
City centre	Tontouta airport	8000 CFP

you should catch from the old **Gare Routière** (rue d'Austerlitz).

The ticketing system that is described here was about to be introduced at the time of research. There's a **ticket office** (Place des Cocotiers; single adult/child 150/100 CFP, all-day 650 CFP; open 6am-6pm daily) located near the Noumea tourism office. You will need to purchase your ticket from a ticketing machine as it will cost you 50 CFP more to buy it directly from the driver. There are machines at Place des Cocotiers and next to a few bus stops. Away from the city centre, see if the nearest *magasin* (shop) has a machine. All-day tickets can only be purchased at the office in Place des Cocotiers. You'll need to validate your ticket as you get on the bus.

For more information on bus routes, pick up a brochure from the tourist office.

Taxi The main taxi rank (☎ 28 00 30) is in the car park on the corner of rue Austerlitz and rue de Verdun, though you can also hail a cab from virtually anywhere around Noumea. Taxis operate 24 hours a day, seven days a week.

Bicycle & Scooter In Noumea bicycles can be rented from **Plages Loisirs** (☎ 26 90 00; 80 Promenade Roger Laroque; open 8am-5pm) at Anse Vata (per hour/half/full-day 520/1040/1560 CFP). **Point Rouge** (☎ 28 59 20, fax 24 99 94; 75 Av Maréchal Foch, Noumea) rents scooters.

Useful Bus Routes From The City Centre

destination	bus No	colour	duration (mins)
Anse Vata	1/7	green/orange	25/30
Baie des Citrons	1	green	20
Kuendu Beach	1	green	15
Magenta airport	2	blue	15
Tjibaou Cultural Centre	2	blue	25

Grande Terre

pop 198,000 • area 18,580 sq km
Grande Terre is a mountainous island, 400km
long and 50km wide, encompassed by a barrier reef.

SOUTHERN GRANDE TERRE
Southern Grande Terre is made up of three distinct regions: the desert-like southern tip with
its bright-red earth and stunted vegetation;
the west-coast plains dotted with Caldoche
towns; and the lush east coast inhabited by
Kanak people.

The Southern Tip
As you head east from Noumea along the RP1
you'll come across the village of St Louis with

its red-roofed Catholic church in the distance.
St Louis was the site of ethnic unrest in 2002
so it's probably best to avoid entering the village. Soon after is the turn-off to Mont-Dore
Sud, Plum and Prony.

Pacific Free Ride (☎ *41 66 22, 79 22 02;
per person half-day kayak/quad 5000/10,000
CFP*) run adventure activities in the Plum area
(minimum two people). A full-day sea kayaking and quad biking package costs 7500 CFP
per person or you can abseil down a waterfall
for 8000 CFP. Pick-ups from Noumea are possible at no extra cost.

The 'real' southern tip around Baie de
Prony is accessible by conventional vehicles.
Initially, **Prony** was a convict settlement before becoming a mining village. It's a solitary
place where the bush silently invades old
ruins. This image may be about to change as

SOUTHERN GRANDE TERRE

PLACES TO STAY & EAT
1 Refuge de Farino
2 Hôtel Banu; La Fautaua;
  La Tavola Pizzeria
3 Naïna Park Hôtel
4 Pocquereux Randonnées
5 Gîte Ouroué
6 Chez Marie-Georgette
7 Conviva
8 Camping de Bouraké
9 Les Paillottes de la
  Ouenghi
10 Auberge du Mont Koghi;
   Koghi Parc Aventure
11 Site de Netcha
12 Gîte Iya
13 Gîte St Gabriel
14 Gîte Kanua

The Cagou

A stocky, flightless bird, the *cagou (Rhynocetos jubatus)* is New Caledonia's national bird. It is an endangered species, owing to dogs and feral cats hunting it, and wild pigs disturbing its habitat.

A successful breeding programme has been carried out at the **Parc de la Rivière Bleue**, east of Noumea, where numbers are slowly rising. This is the only place you're likely to see one in the wild. Keep a look out in the early evening. Otherwise you can see one at the **Parc Forestier** in Noumea.

Standing 0.5m tall, this plump nocturnal bird has soft, silky-grey plumage, red eyes and an orange beak. It is most noted for its cry, which is reminiscent of a dog's bark and is only made in the early morning. When startled or protecting its young, the cagou spreads out its wings, which are laced with dark-grey-and-white stripes, and raises its silky top-knot crest.

Living in isolated pairs in damp rainforest or at slightly higher altitudes, it feeds on worms, snails and insects. Once or twice a year, the female lays one egg. Typically, it takes a month to hatch, after which both parents raise the baby.

JACQUI SAUNDERS

the area is now the site of a multi-billion dollar nickel mining and processing project which has environmentalists worried about possible adverse effects on the fragile land and lagoon ecosystems. There are spectacular views of the surrounding reef and Baie de Prony with its sole islet, **Îlot Casy**, accessible by boat.

Following the RP3, you'll arrive at the western end of the vast, artificial **Lac de Yaté**, a hydroelectric dam, which offers wide panoramas and some superb areas for nature lovers, including the massive **Parc de la Rivière Bleue** (☎ 88 10 75; *entry per car 500 CFP plus per person per day 100 CFP; open 7am-5pm Tues-Sun*). This recreational park is a protected nature reserve that is home to many bird species, including New Caledonia's national bird, the *cagou*. One of its famous features is a drowned forest where skeletons of old trees protrude tragically from the water. The last cars are allowed in at 4pm. The entrance is 2.5km from the RP3 turn-off (it's signposted). There are several hikes detailed in the park's brochure. Bring food supplies as there are no shops. It's possible to camp at many points along the Rivière Bleue (daily entry fee includes camping) and there are two basic refuges in the park where you can stay overnight. Bring your own bedding.

Terra Incognita (☎ 78 94 46, ☎/fax 41 61 19), which has an English-speaking guide, hires canoes and kayaks (per hour/half/full day 1300/4350/8500 CFP) on the Rivière Bleue, the river that feeds the lake. When there's a full moon, it organises magical moonlight canoeing trips down the silent river through a spooky drowned forest to the shimmering lake. It does pick-ups from Noumea for an extra fee.

At Pernod Creek, 20km past the turn-off to the Parc de la Rivière Bleue, a dirt road (in the process of being sealed) leads off from the RP3 to the **Chutes de la Madeleine** (*entry 300 CFP; open 8am-5.30pm daily*). This small waterfall, about 11km from the turn-off, is the area's most famous sight. There's a botanical area by the waterfall that highlights the region's endemic plant species. About 2km downriver there's a camping ground.

From the Lac de Yaté, the RP3 winds up a mountain before dropping steeply to the sea on the other side. At the bottom of the escarpment, if you turn right and cross a small bridge, the road leads past Wao to tourist gîtes and camping grounds. If you continue, the road veers left to Yaté village, where there's a small shop and petrol pump. The long bridge across the Yaté river, before the village, ends at the small settlement of Unia.

South of Wao is Goro and the **Wadiana Falls** are a kilometre further on. The road passes right next to the falls, which cascade from a rocky cliff into a natural pool at the bottom where you can swim. From Goro, you can go to Port-Boisé and round past Prony back to Noumea.

NEW CALEDONIA

Places to Stay & Eat Just before the Chutes de la Madeleine, Site de Netcha (*☎ 79 81 25; camping per tent 1000 CFP, plus per car 700 CFP; mountain bike/canoe hire per half-day 520/1100 CFP; open 8am-5.30pm daily*) is a quiet riverside camp site. The river is deep and great for swimming. There are shady thatched shelters, barbecues and toilets. The camp site is always open so you can still get in if you arrive after the office has closed. Bring your own supplies (although if you get caught out, the office sells emergency supplies).

Gîte Iya (*☎ 46 90 80; camping per tent 1500 CFP, small/large bungalows with shower 5000/6000 CFP; menus 2000-3000 CFP*) is about 3km south of Wao. It's a bit run down these days but it's in a lovely sheltered spot overlooking a small beach squeezed between low coral cliffs.

Gîte St Gabriel (*☎/fax 46 42 77; camping per person 700 CFP, double traditional/ modern bungalows 5800/6800 CFP plus each extra person 900 CFP*) is 3km past Touaourou. It's set on the beachfront amid coconut palms. It's restaurant serves good food. A standard plat du jour will cost you 1800 CFP. A bougna/lobster meal costs 2500/3600 CFP but you'll have to ask for it a day in advance.

Gîte Kanua (*☎ 46 90 00; camping per person 800 CFP, bungalows per double 8000 CFP plus each extra person 900 CFP*), is at Port-Boisé. The restaurant serves meals from 2000 CFP (the Sunday buffet is extremely popular with Noumeans). Various tours can be organised and there are rental canoes.

Getting There & Away The bus to Yaté (550 CFP; 1¾ hours), Wao (550 CFP, 1¾ hours), Touaourou (650 CFP, two hours), and Gîte St Gabriel (700 CFP, two hours) leaves from the Montravel bus station, Monday to Saturday at 11.30am.

The Road North

Known as the Route Territoriale 1 (RT1), the road north traverses the island's western coast with its open expanses and cattle stations, all the way to Poum, a journey of 424km. En route it skirts the mountain range of the interior and in places you'll see a nickel mine.

Two northbound roads lead out of Noumea. The more direct is the Savexpress toll road (150 CFP per car), starting at Koutio. The other road north is the RT1, which winds past Monts Koghis, 14km north of Noumea. The area is popular for hiking, with trails ranging from 30 minutes to six hours.

Koghi Parc Aventure (*☎ 43 02 52; open 10am-5pm Sat & Sun*) operates a forest adventure circuit (2000 CFP) high in the tree tops with rope ladders, swinging bridges and flying foxes. There are four levels ranging from 2m to 18m high. The circuit takes 1½ hours so the latest you can start is at 3.30pm.

Continuing along the RT1, you pass Dumbéa where there's a golf course. The Dumbéa river is a popular weekend picnic spot. The next town is Païta. In October it organises the Fête du boeuf, an annual agricultural fair with a popular rodeo.

Past Tontouta, where New Caledonia's international airport is located, you'll find Boulouparis. About 1km north of this small town is the junction for the RP4 to Thio.

Places to Stay & Eat In the Mont Koghis, Auberge du Mont Koghi (*☎ 41 29 29, fax 41 96 22; @ koghiland@offratel.nc; forest refuges 6000-7500 CFP, chalets 7500 CFP*) sits 482m above sea level overlooking Noumea and the barrier reef on the horizon. Its accommodation options include timber refuges in the forest and chalets at the Auberge. The Auberge's restaurant serves specialities from the Savoy region in the French Alps for about 3200 CFP per person. It's open at any time of the day for a refreshment or snack.

Les Paillottes de la Ouenghi (*☎ 35 17 35, fax 35 17 44; bungalows per couple 9000 CFP*), in Boulouparis, is about 2.5km off the main road, 5km southeast of the village. It has an 18-hole golf course, individual bungalows, a spacious restaurant and a swimming pool. It organises horse riding and canoeing. The restaurant mainly serves à la carte meals, with most main courses priced around 1500 CFP. Menus, on Sundays only, cost between 2800 and 5000 CFP.

Camping de Bouraké (*☎ 35 17 06*), close to Boulouparis, has toilets and hot showers. It is also free.

Convivia (*☎ 46 90 90; camping per adult/child 900/600 CFP; breakfast from 750 CFP*), at Ouano Beach, between Boulouparis and La Foa, has immaculate camping facilities, including a laundry, and disabled toilets. Tent sites have thatched shelters, and there's a restaurant where the speciality is crab (950 CFP). The signposted turn-off from the RT1 is 22km northwest of Boulouparis. For pick ups you can call from the phone booth at the turn-off. It's a relaxing spot although the lagoon is shallow and not great for swimming.

Getting There & Away The Monts Koghis area is not easily reached without private transport. The turn-off to the auberge is 14km north of central Noumea on the road to Dumbéa. From here, it's another 5km up to the auberge.

Carsud (☎ 25 16 15) operates buses between Dumbéa and Noumea (260 CFP one way) which leave from the Montravel station in Noumea. Any bus heading from Noumea along the west coast or going up to the east coast will drop you in Boulouparis. The fare is around 800 CFP.

La Foa

At the entrance to **La Foa**, about 110km from Noumea, the old **Passerelle Marguerite** straddles the river next to the modern bridge used today. On the main street past the **Cinema Jean-Pierre Jeunet**, where an annual film festival is held around June, is the friendly tourist information office **La Foa Tourisme** (☎ 41 69 11; e lafoatourisme@canl.nc; w www.lafoa .com; open 8am-5.30pm Mon-Fri, 9am-5pm Sat & Sun). Behind the office there's an park with tall wooden sculptures.

Oua Tom is a delightful multi-ethnic Kanak village. Over the generations, the Kanak villagers have mixed with Polynesians, West Indians, Europeans and Arabs. You can go on a guided village and botanical tour through the forest (500 CFP, one hour), and eat *bougna* (2000 CFP). Longer walks are possible (1500 CFP, 3 to 6 hours). Contact **Chez Marie-Georgette** (☎ 44 38 17) where you can also pitch your tent for 500 CFP or hire one for 1000 CFP. The signposted turn-off is 13.5km south of La Foa from where it's another 5km.

Farino sits up in the cool highlands off the road to Sarraméa. It's known for its market held every second Sunday of the month. The real crowd puller is its **Vers de Bancoule** market day in September, which culminates in a contest to see who can eat the most fat, wriggling white grubs.

Petit Couli is a small tribal village famed for the beautiful, old *grande case*, standing at the end of a double row of araucarias, on the main road just past the Sarraméa turn-off.

Situated in a side valley off the RP5, **Sarraméa** is like a cool oasis after the open plains preceding it. The area is greened by forests and occasionally interrupted by meadows with tall trees. The **Syndicat d'initiative de Sarraméa** (☎ 44 39 55), a small information office, is signposted as you enter the village.

Horse trekking is available at **Pocquereux Randonnées** (☎ 77 32 54; half/full day 5000/8000 CFP, overnight trek 20,000 CFP), a ranch near La Foa. The signposted turn-off is 2km south of La Foa from where it's 10km. There is a rough dormitory at the ranch (1000 CFP per person) or you can camp (500 CFP per person). Meals can be prepared for 1800 CFP.

Places to Stay & Eat With attractive, shady garden bungalows, **Naïna Park Hôtel** (☎ 44 35 40, fax 44 39 35; bungalows per one/two persons 5650 CFP, per extra person 1200 CFP; breakfast 650 CFP, meals from 1100 CFP) is 1.5km south of La Foa and has a restaurant and a nice pool.

Hôtel Banu (☎ 44 31 19, fax 44 35 50; double rooms 4350 CFP, per extra person 800 CFP, bungalow doubles/triples 6350/7150 CFP; meals from 1950 CFP, seafood dishes from 3080 CFP), in La Foa, is opposite the post office on the RT1. The rooms have uncomfortable beds and are noisy, but the air-con bungalows further back from the main road are comfortable. It has a pool and restaurant, and there's an impressive collection of caps in the bar – at last count there were 4240.

In La Foa, you can also eat at **La Fautaua** (☎ 44 35 00; open lunch & dinner Mon-Sat, lunch only Sun; menu 1400 CFP), a thatched restaurant near the southern end of town, or **La Tavola Pizzeria** on the main road near the tourism office.

Refuge de Farino (☎ 44 37 61; 4/8 person bungalow 4500/6000 CFP weekdays, 6000/9500 CFP weekends), in a tranquil bush setting in Farino, has self-contained bungalows. It also offers quad biking (5000/6000 CFP, 30 minutes) and horse riding.

There is a supermarket in La Foa.

Getting There & Away For information on buses from Noumea see under Bus in the Getting Around section.

Mining Towns

Hidden by the central mountain chain, southern Grande Terre's east-coast mining region, which includes the towns of Thio, Canala, Kouaoua and Poro, tends to leave travellers in a mixed state of awe and unease. Most peoples' lives are dedicated to work in the opencast nickel mines. But aside from the ugly scarred mountains, the landscape is stunning, with waterfalls and deep bays.

The **Musée des Mines** (Mine Museum; ☎ 44 51 77; adult/child 200 CFP/free; open

8am-3pm Tues-Fri, 8am-noon Sat & Sun) in Thio, which was a nickel-mining centre for several decades, displays local photographs from the early 1900s as well as a collection of minerals. It closes early on Wednesdays.

West of Thio, Canala sits at the end of the long, wide Baie de Canala. The town and surrounding area is backed by steep, scrubby mountains from which the mighty **Ciu waterfalls** cascade. Situated in an inland valley, they offer wide views over the valley and the start of the deep bay. The falls can be reached along a small dirt road to the right, about 1.5km from Canala, on the road towards Thio. The turn-off is unmarked. From here it's about 4km to the top of the falls. A small path leads to the falls.

Places to Stay & Eat The most pleasant place to stay around Thio is **Gîte Ouroué** *(☎ 44 50 85; camping per tent 1000 CFP, bungalows 3000 CFP)*, located on the beachfront 4.5km from town, off the road to Canala. You can camp here or stay in one of four sparsely furnished bungalows, which have views of coconut palms and the water. The bungalows are for up to three people. A fish dinner costs 1800 CFP. The gîte is signposted; from the turn-off, it's 1.5km to the beach.

Getting There & Away For information on buses from Noumea see under Bus in the Getting Around section. There are no buses between Thio and Canala. By car, the Canala–Thio road includes a stretch of dirt road, open to traffic from either direction at alternate hours, which snakes up and around a steep hill eventually to cross Col de Petchécara (435m). For more information see Car & Motorcycle in the Getting Around section.

THE NORTHWEST COAST

Much of the northwest coast has been cattle country since the early colonial days, when settlers claimed the land and the Kanaks were forced to leave. The scenery is plain and rather monotonous; rounded hills stretch down to flat grasslands. The coast is lined with mangrove swamps and shallow bays, where the beaches are nothing to get excited about. Around Népoui and Koné the hills have been sliced open for nickel mining. In the far north, beyond Koumac, the scenery softens to quiet woodlands and gentle hills.

The RT1 is a good sealed road, skirting the mountains all the way from Noumea to Poum in the north.

Bourail
pop 4900
Bourail has a busy rural town atmosphere and a strong Caldoche community. It's the next biggest town after Noumea and sits on the plain 162km from the capital. It was founded in 1867 as a penitentiary.

About 9.5km south of Bourail on the RT1 is the **New Zealand War Cemetery**. It's the resting place for 212 soldiers killed in the Pacific during WWII. The majority of the New Zealand troops arrived in 1942 to prepare for the Pacific war. About 2.5km further south, also flanking the RT1, is the **Cimetière des Arabes** next to a mosque. The origins of those buried here date back to the 1871 Berber insurrection in the former French colony of Algeria. A number of rebels were deported to New Caledonia and at the end of their prison terms some chose to stay.

Travellers will find bank, supermarket and post office facilities in Bourail. About 800m south of the town centre, the stone **Bourail Museum** *(☎ 44 12 18; adult/child 250/100 CFP; open 8am-11am & 1pm-5pm Mon-Sat, 8am-3pm Sun)* focuses on the early settlers of Bourail and the presence of New Zealand troops during WWII. There's an eerie guillotine and, out the back, a more cheerful *case*. There are some English explanations.

The nearby coast has the renowned **La Roche Percée** (The Pierced Rock) landmark, an unusual rock formation 7km from the RT1 turn-off just south of Bourail. Further north of the rock is the **Plage de Poé**, a beautiful, long, white-sand beach. From the RT1 turn-off it's 15.5km to the beach. Off Bourail, **La Faille de Poé** is a popular dive. Another good dive is **La Fausse Pate de l'Île Verte** which has beautiful caves, canyons, fish, turtles and coral. Diving is offered at **Sub Loisirs** *(☎ 44 20 65; e butterfly.diving@lagoon.nc; two-dive package with/without equipment supplied 10,400/9,360 CFP)*, located at the Base Nautique de la Roche Percée.

If you are interested in horse trekking, contact **Marcel Velayoudon** *(☎ 44 14 90, 87 62 96; hourly outings 2000 CFP, overnight weekend trips including meals and accommodation 17,000 CFP)* – the signposted turn-off is about 3km north of town from where it's 150m.

Base Nautique de Poe *(☎ 44 23 27)*, on the beach near the camping ground, hires kayaks (1100 CFP per hour), windsurfs (2600 CFP per hour) and mountain bikes (1000 CFP per hour). Glass-bottom-boat tours cost 1800 CFP.

NORTHERN GRANDE TERRE

Îles Belep (18km)
Île Baaba
Récif de Cook
Boat-Pass
Tiabet
Île Balabio
Baie de Banaré
Poum
Baie d'Harcourt
Arama
Col d'Amoss (368m)
Balade
SOUTH PACIFIC OCEAN
0   25   50km
0   15   30mi
Baie de Nehoue
RPN1
Mine Pilou
RPN7
Ouégoa
Pouébo
Récif de Colnett
Tiébaghi
Cols de Crève-Cœur
Diahot
RPN10
Cascade de Tao
Récif de Koumac
Koumac
Mont Colnett (1505m)
Réserve du Mont Panié
Mont Panié (1629m)
Récif de Mengalia
Récif de Mathieu
Kaala-Gomen
Ouaième
Hienghène
Lindéralique Cliffs
NORTH PROVINCE
Tiendanite
Touho
Récif de Poindimié
RT1
Ouaco
Témala
Bopope
Tiwaka
Poindimié
Récif de Gatope
Voh
Massif de Koniambo
RPN2
Mont Aoupinié (1006m)
Nahoi
Ponérihouen
Foué
Koné
RPN7
Le Tamaon
Réserve de l'Aoupinié
Ba Falls
Récif de Koné
Pouembout
Forêt Plate
Gohapin
Grottes d'Adio
Houaïlou
RT1
Poya
Népoui
Col des Roussettes (381m)
CORAL SEA
Passe de Muéo
SOUTH PROVINCE
La Néra
Bourail
To Noumea (125km)
Plage de Poé
La Roche Percée

PLACES TO STAY & EAT
1 Relais de Poingam
2 Camping Golone
3 Malabou Beach Resort
4 Camping d'Amoss
5 Camping de Tao
6 Gîte Weouth; Camping Chez Maria
7 Koulnoué Village (Club Med)
8 Camping de Gatope
9 Foué
10 Gîte d'Atéou
11 Gîte Tamaon
12 Gîte Newe Jie
13 Camping de Tiakan
14 Poé Beach Resort; Camping de Poé

NEW CALEDONIA

Places to Stay & Eat A nice spot to camp on the beachfront with plenty of shade is at **Camping de Poé** (☎ 41 28 78; camping per tent beach front/garden 1500/1000 CFP; bungalows 2500 CFP, extra person 100 CFP) although the tiny, bare bungalows are overpriced. There's also a small shop. It's 15.5km from the RT1 turn-off.

Hôtel La Néra (☎ 44 16 44, fax 44 18 31; rooms per 1/2 people 5650/6650 CFP; meals from 1500 CFP) has a nice view overlooking the Néra River but is right beside the busy main road at the turn-off to Plage de Poé. It has eight rooms, all with TV, private facilities and air-con.

Poé Beach Resort (☎ 44 18 50, fax 44 10 70; e poebeach@lagoon.nc; rooms per person with fan/air-con 6803/7153 CFP; double air-con bungalows 7753 CFP) has a great beach-front setting at the end of Plage de Poé, 17km from the RT1 turn-off. Prices include half-board. Renovations are planned for 2004.

Le Relais Gourmand (☎ 44 23 23; menu 1900 CFP) is the best place to dine in Bourail. It's at the northern end of town.

Along the busy main road in town you'll also find several unpretentious **snacks**. Vietnamese dishes from 990 CFP are the speciality at **Le Motu**, sandwiches at **Snack Hibiscus** start at 300 CFP and at **Zam Zam** you'll pay 1300 CFP for a plate of steak and fries. There are also a couple of supermarkets.

Getting There & Away Buses from Noumea to Bourail usually continue on along the northwest coast or cross to the northeast coast. For more information on buses from Noumea see under Bus in the Getting Around section.

Pouembout
pop 1400

Pouembout is an administrative centre for the Northern Province. The Koné–Tiwaka road across the mountain range to the east coast is about 5km north of the town.

Hôtel Le Bougainville (☎ 47 20 60, fax 47 29 84; rooms 5720 CFP, extra person 1000 CFP, bungalows per double 6750 CFP, extra person 1000 CFP), the only accommodation in town, has a superb thatched *case* that serves as a restaurant and lounge. The hotel has eight bungalows and six basic but clean rooms, with TV and air-con. The restaurant serves a *menu du jour* for 1750 CFP. Breakfast is 950 CFP.

Gîte Tamaon (☎ 47 90 22, ☎/fax 47 27 26; camping per person 700 CFP, bungalows per 1/2 people 4000/5000 CFP) is 13km from Pouembout along the dirt road to Fôret Plate. It's well signposted. Horse excursions of the region can be arranged.

Getting Around All buses bound for Koné and Koumac leaving Noumea stop at Pouembout.

Koné
pop 4750

Koné is the capital of the Northern Province. It's surrounded by the rolling hills of the Massif de Koniambo and flat cattle pastures.

Koné is probably most noted for its excellent **horse trekking** opportunities. **Koné Rodéo** (☎ 47 21 51), run by Patrick Ardimani, organises various treks into the untamed regions around town. The signposted stables are 2km north of town, down a dirt road to the right.

Voh is a small place north of Koné. Unusual mangrove designs have saved it from fading into oblivion. The most notable of these natural art works is the heart-shaped **Coeur de Voh** which appears on the cover of the famous book of aerial photography, *Earth from Above*, by Yann Arthus-Bertrand. To see it you can climb to a viewpoint on the Kathépaï Massif. It's an hour's walk from Voh. It's not signposted but **Gladys Hervouet** (☎ 47 27 68) usually shows tourists the way. It's best seen from the air though and if you contact **Alain Nouard** (☎ 47 25 93) in Koné or **Pierre Couget** (☎ 47 32 87) in Pouembout, they can fly you there in a microlight (ULM in French) for around 5000 CFP.

Places to Stay & Eat The best place to eat is **Tumbala Café** (☎ 42 44 39; plat du jour 900 CFP, menu 1750 CFP; open Mon-Sat until late), a bright and colourful multi-ethnic café. The menu features a variety of meals including Moroccan dishes. Breakfast is 700 CFP. There's also Internet access (500 CFP per half hour). It's at the northern end of town.

Monitel L'Hibiscus (☎ 47 22 61, fax 47 25 35; rooms 5750 CFP, extra person 500 CFP, rooms by pool 7300-7800 CFP) is Koné's top-end accommodation option. It's a modern hotel at the southern entry to the town. It can organise excursions around Koné. A *menu* is 1900 CFP (Monday to Friday only).

Hôtel Koniambo (☎ 47 39 40, fax 47 39 41; rooms/bungalows per person 5500 CFP, extra person 500 CFP), another option, is opposite the airfield on the RT1 about 3km north of the centre. It has simple bungalows and a row of motel rooms. There's also a swimming pool. A plate of stuffed shellfish costs 1500 CFP.

Gîte d'Atéou (☎ 47 26 13; camping per tent with/without meals 600/1500 CFP, case per person 900; breakfast 500 CFP) is 12km northeast of Koné. It's cheaper to camp if you order meals from the gîte. A meals costs 1400 CFP. This tribal gîte also organises guided walks and horse treks from 1500 CFP. Ring in advance.

Camping de Gatope (☎ 47 62 46; camping per person 500 CFP) is on the nice Gatope beach near Voh. The turn-off, in Voh, is signposted.

There's a grocery store on the main road in Koné.

Getting There & Away Koné has an airfield. For flight information, see the Getting Around section at the beginning of this chapter.

For information on buses from Noumea see under Bus in the Getting Around section.

Koumac
pop 3000

Sitting on the edge of a sprawling plain 368km from Noumea is Koumac, an agricultural centre.

It's not really a tourist destination although there's a good rural atmosphere at the annual fair that takes place around September 24. Like every good rural fair involving stockmen in New Caledonia, the highlight is the rodeo.

In the town centre there's an eye-catching barrel-shaped church, **Église Ste Jeanne d'Arc**, constructed in 1950 out of an aircraft hangar. It has beautiful stained-glass windows and an impressive array of woodcarvings inspired by traditional Kanak art and incorporating Christian symbolism.

Ranch La Crinière (☎ 47 54 82, 47 90 20), close to town, offers **horse riding** (2500 CFP, one hour). A *Broussard* tour is a two-day trip with some cattle droving thrown in (17,000 CFP, all inclusive per person, minimum eight people).

Léonce Weiss (☎ 47 65 32, 83 16 31), a sculptor whose studio is in Koumac's industrial zone, on the main road 2.5km south of town, welcomes visitors.

Places to Stay & Eat Towards the marina, **Camping de Pandop** (☎ 47 62 46; *camping per person 500 CFP*) is a shady beachfront spot, 2km south of town.

Monitel Koumac (☎ 47 66 66, fax 47 62 85; *bungalows per 1/2 people 6800/7300 CFP*) is south of the roundabout. An assortment of well-kept bungalows, all with the necessary private facilities, have been built around a large swimming pool. The restaurant is large and serves a *menu du jour* for 1900 CFP.

Hôtel Le Grand Cerf (☎/fax 47 61 31; *bungalows per 1-person 5200 CFP, extra person 500 CFP*), the most central place, is just north of the roundabout. It has nine bungalows with TV and private facilities, a bar and a swimming pool. The restaurant only serves breakfast (600 CFP). The walls, built from different coloured stones, add some charm to this otherwise plain hotel.

There are also a couple of **snacks, boulangeries** (bakeries) and several well-stocked **supermarkets**. **Le Crow's Nest** (☎ 47 10 41; *meals around 1800 CFP; open lunch & dinner Tues-Sat, dinner only Mon*) is a nice restaurant by the waterfront next to the port, 2km west of the roundabout.

Getting There & Away Koumac has a small airport. For flight information, see the Getting Around section at the beginning of this chapter.

Koumac's bus station is 450m south of the roundabout. For information on buses from Noumea see under Bus in the Getting Around section.

Koumac to Boat-Pass

On leaving Koumac, Grande Terre tapers into a narrow peninsula that is carved by many bays. About 8km north of Koumac, the RPN7 turns eastwards off the RT1 and crosses the tip of Grande Terre, through beautiful hilly country

over the Cols de Crève-Cœur, to Ouégoa and on over Col d'Amoss to the east coast.

About 20km north of Koumac and easily visible from the main road, the **Tiébaghi mine** was once the largest and richest chromite mine in the world. The old mine is now defunct but you can take a guided tour of the **old mining village** (☎ 42 49 13; *adult/child 2000/500 CFP*) nearby.

Poum The northernmost village on Grande Terre is Poum, 56km north of Koumac. A road (5km before Poum) continues north, ending at Pointe Nahârian. Most of it is unsealed. This is the tip of Grande Terre and is also known as **Boat-Pass**, which is the name of the channel separating Île Baaba from the mainland. It's a hilly terrain that's exposed to the sea, with sandy beaches surrounded by stunted vegetation and grassland. The mosquitoes here are notorious. The road is rough and slippery when wet.

Malabou Manta Diving (☎ 47 60 60, fax 47 60 70; e malabeachotel@canl.nc; *2-dive package with/without equipment supplied 12,000/10,000 CFP*) organises dives in the area.

Places to Stay & Eat A luxurious place, **Malabou Beach Resort** (☎ 47 60 60, fax 47 60 70; e malabeachotel@canl.nc; *bungalows 2/3 people 9880/12,480 CFP, suites 19,240 CFP*) is built along Baie de Nehoue, about 15km south of Poum. A collection of square bungalows and luxury suites with all facilities dot the peaceful grounds. The suites can sleep up to five. A wide array of activities can be arranged through the resort including diving. The restaurant offers a *menu* for 2800 CFP and other à la carte specialities. Breakfast is 1300 CFP.

Camping Golone (☎ 47 90 78; *camping per person 600 CFP, bungalow per double small/large 4000/5000 CFP, extra person 500 CFP; menu 1650 CFP*) sits tranquil and isolated, on a small peninsula 5km from the main road. It has a nice beach in between the mangroves and a warm welcome. The restaurant serves a seafood platter for 2600 CFP. Breakfast is 600 CFP. The turn-off is to the left about 400m north of Malabou Beach.

Relais de Poingam (☎ 47 92 12; *camping per tent 500 CFP, bungalows per double 6800 CFP, extra person 1500 CFP*) sits on a long, open beach about 3km before Boat Pass. It has comfortable bungalows with attractive external bathrooms and plain weatherboard bungalows.

NEW CALEDONIA

The restaurant offers a number of mouthwatering dishes, including venison curry in coconut cream (980 CFP). The shallow lagoon is not great for swimming but the hotel has a nice salt-water swimming pool.

Getting There & Away There are infrequent bus connections on the little-travelled road between Koumac and Poum. It's best if you have your own transport.

Îles Belep
This remote archipelago is 50km northwest of the northern tip of Grande Terre.

The Belep Islands are home to around 1000 Kanaks. The islands are rarely visited by tourists as there are only a couple of flights and boats per week, and there is no tourist accommodation.

THE NORTHEAST COAST
The beautiful wild scenery of the northeast coast makes it Grande Terre's most impressive region. The area is characterised by lush forests, rivers, streams, waterfalls and coastal coconut groves. There are fascinating rock formations in the vicinity of Hienghène, as well as New Caledonia's highest peak, Mont Panié (1629m). The region's hub is Poindimié, an attractive town stretched out along the coast. Quaint roadside stalls with honesty boxes sell fruit, shells and carvings.

The northeast coast is home to numerous Kanak clans. Many Europeans left prior to or during Les Évènements, in the mid-1980s.

Houaïlou to Poindimié
Houaïlou, 68km northeast of Bourail, is the first coastal village you'll come to after descending from the mountains on the RT3. It's built along a river of the same name and is set in lush surroundings.

The **Ba Falls** are 13.5km north of the Houaïlou bridge. The track leading to the falls is on the left, directly after a large bridge. It is a ten-minute walk.

Ponérihouen is a small village 46km northwest of Houaïlou, a couple of kilometres inland on a bend in the Nabai River.

Places to Stay & Eat About 7km north of Ponérihouen, **Camping de Tiakan** (☎ 42 85 14; camping per person 500 CFP) has a lovely beachfront setting amid a large palm grove. It's on the right-hand side, down a dirt track leading off the RT3, and is well signposted. There is a small **épicerie** just 100m down the road.

Poindimié
pop 4340
About 308km from Noumea, Poindimié is the administrative centre of the northeast coast. It's a place with great atmosphere, stretched along a rocky coastline. It has all the necessary services, such as inexpensive accommodation, good restaurants, supermarkets, a hospital, a **post office** (☎ 42 71 00; open 7.45am-3pm Mon-Fri), **BCI bank** (☎ 42 71 13; open 7.35am-11.30am and 12.15pm-3.45pm Mon-Fri) and a **gendarmerie** (☎ 42 85 17).

Tiéti beach is in front of the municipal camping ground and is one of the finest sandy beaches in the area.

For **scuba diving**, contact **Tiéti Diving** (☎ 42 42 05; e tieti.diving@offratel.nc; 2-dive package with/without equipment supplied 11,500/10,000 CFP), based at the Monitel de Tiéti. You'll explore the outer reef, about 30 minutes away by boat.

Places to Stay & Eat The following places are listed from south to north.

Inland from Poindimié, **Gîte Newe Jïe** (☎ 42 70 74; case or bungalow per person 1950 CFP) is a nice place to stay. There's no restaurant but it serves breakfast for 600 CFP and there are cooking facilities. Turn off 2km south of Poindimié at the Vallée d'Ina signpost. The gîte is signposted.

Up on the hill before the swimming pool, **Restaurant Les 3A** (☎ 42 71 10; meals around 1800 CFP) is a spacious terrace restaurant with a spectacular view of the sea and distant islands. Chinese cuisine is the house speciality.

Hôtel Le Tapoundari (☎ 42 71 11; air-con rooms per person 6240 CFP, extra person 500 CFP; plat du jour or buffet 950 CFP) is set beside the Poindimié River, just below the main bridge. Its brightly decorated restaurant is open Monday to Saturday. At lunch time it serves a buffet or plat du jour and for dinner there's an à la carte menu. Book in advance as it's popular.

The **Monitel de Tiéti** (☎ 42 64 00, fax 42 64 01; bungalows per single 6500 CFP, extra person 1000 CFP; menu 1900 CFP, plat du jour 1200 CFP) is a fairly big beachfront complex with a restaurant, swimming pool, bar and dive centre.

The **Camping Municipal** at Tiéti beach, next to the Monitel de Tiéti, is free but not a safe place to stay. The beachfront at the Monitel is more secure; you can also camp for free.

Poindimié to Hienghène

About 5.5km north of central Poindimié the tall, red spire of the church at **Tié Mission** rises suddenly out of the quiet countryside. Around 8km past the mission you'll cross the wide Tiwaka River and immediately come across the turn-off for the scenic Koné–Tiwaka road. Continuing north, the road climbs and dips along the pretty coast towards **Touho**, a small village built on a picturesque bay.

About 9km before Hienghène, the scenery dramatically changes to black jagged cliffs towering over startling green water.

Hienghène

pop 2600

Hienghène is known throughout New Caledonia for two significant reasons. Firstly, its coastline is carved with the most fascinating rock formations that New Caledonia can offer.

In a more sober vein, Hienghène was also the scene (in 1984) of one of New Caledonia's most brutal modern-day massacres, when Caldoche gunmen ambushed a group of Kanaks killing 10 of them. The village was also home to former Hienghène mayor and assassinated FLNKS leader, Jean-Marie Tjibaou. His tribal community of **Tiendanite**, where he was buried, lies about 20km inland from Hienghène. Near Tjibaou's grave are the graves of the men killed in the ambush.

There is a post office, but no banks. A small **tourist office** (☎ 42 43 57; open 8am-noon & 1pm-5pm Mon-Fri, 8am-3pm Sat) is located opposite the signposted Gîte Ka Waboana in the village centre. It will move to the nearby marina (under construction at the time of research) once it's completed. It can organise various tours and accommodation in tribal gîtes. A bank and petrol station are also planned but at the time of writing the nearest petrol station was on the main road 18km south of Hienghène.

Goa Ma Bwarhat Cultural Centre (☎ 42 80 74; open daily 9am-4pm, except Mon 11am-4pm) is situated on the right just before the bridge into Hienghène. Some days it opens earlier and closes later. It contains a one-room **museum** (adult/child 100/free CFP) that exhibits various artefacts. Displays in its exhibition room change frequently. There are also sculpture and weaving workshops.

Lindéralique Cliffs are black limestone cliffs that start south of Hienghène, near Club Med, and continue to the bay of Hienghène. Rising abruptly out of nowhere, they stretch in places to 60m and are topped by jagged,

sharp edges. The most famous of the rock formations is **La Poule de Hienghène**, or the Brooding Hen – a high, rocky slab rising from the centre of Hienghène bay. Slightly northwest is the **Sphinx**, another of nature's masterpieces. The former is best viewed from the **lookout**, around 1.5km south of the cultural centre. A signpost marked 'Point de Vue' shows you the way.

The **Base Nautique** (☎ 42 80 74) is based temporarily at the cultural centre and rents kayaks, canoes and mountain bikes. One-hour canoe hire costs 500 CFP.

Koulnoué Village (see Places to Stay & Eat following) runs **motorised canoe** and **catamaran tours** up the Hienghène river and beneath the Lindéralique cliffs. The prices range from 1700 CFP to 3120 CFP per person depending on the size of the group.

For **scuba diving**, contact **Koulnoué Dive Centre** (☎ 42 83 59; e koulnoue.dive@lagoon.nc; two-dive package with/without equipment supplied 12,000/10,000 CFP), based at Club Med. You can discover the outer reef.

Places to Stay & Eat In the heart of Hienghène, **Gîte Ka Waboana** (☎/fax 42 47 03; bungalows/units 1-2 persons 6500/7000CFP, extra person 1000 CFP; menu 1800 CFP) is perched on a hill opposite the marina site. The view from the bar stretches out across the wide river. It has nice bungalows and self-contained units. Breakfast costs 600 CFP.

Koulnoué Village (☎ 42 81 66, fax 42 81 75; e clubmed.koulnoue@offratel.nc; bungalows 1-2 persons 9880 CFP, extra person 2600 CFP), a Club Med establishment with luxury bungalows, is stretched out along a coconut-palm-lined beach and overshadowed by the Lindéralique cliffs. There's a pool, tennis court, canoes, bar and restaurant. The reception has facilities for exchanging cash as well as travellers cheques. The village runs various tours and rents mountain bikes. Club Med's restaurant, which is open to nonguests, prepares a copious buffet lunch daily (cold/hot buffet from 1950 CFP) and dinner (2950 CFP). The turn-off to Club Med is 8.5km south of Hienghène from where it's another 1.25km.

Gîte Weouth (☎ 42 45 16; camping 800 CFP, rooms/bungalows per person 1300/1900 CFP; menu 1900 CFP) is about 7.5km north of Hienghène. It's just off the main road, to the right. The accommodation is very basic and set back from the waterfront behind some houses. The waterfront is pretty but there's no beach. You can order a *bougna* for 2100 CFP per person and boat trips can be organised.

Camping Chez Maria *(camping per tent 800 CFP)*, just 3km further north, is more secluded and has a lovely beach. You can pitch your tent in a peaceful coconut grove. You can contact Maria through the tourism office although you don't need to book. There's a carved wooded camping sign.

There's a **snack** *(menu around 1800 CFP)* near the tourist office. It's open daily although the hours are erratic. Next door is a **small shop** *(open 7am-noon & 3pm-5pm Mon-Fri, Sat & Sun 7am-noon)*.

Hienghène to Pouébo

Between Hienghène and Pouébo the scenery becomes more dramatic with lush, mountainous countryside. The road travels along beside the sea and there are numerous bridges across small rivers and creeks where they flow into the lagoon. Stalls dot the side of the road and powerful waterfalls tumble down the mountainsides.

Bac de la Ouaïème is New Caledonia's last surviving river ferry. It takes vehicles across the Ouaïème River, 17km northwest of Hienghène. The free ferry runs 24 hours a day. The sealed road ends 4km before the ferry and the dirt road continues to Pouébo for about 26km.

The **Cascade de Tao** plummets down from the Massif du Panié, which dominates this section of the coast. The path up to the falls starts about 7km north of the Ouaïème River ferry, at a cottage just after a bridge. The falls can easily be seen from the centre of this bridge. An entry fee of 200 CFP per person is levied on those walking up to the falls.

Mont Panié The highest peak in New Caledonia's is Mont Panié (1628m). It is possible to climb the mountain from a trail starting near Tao falls, but the return trip takes the best part of a day. There is a refuge on the mountain (at 900m) where hikers can stay overnight.

Places to Stay & Eat About 13km north of the Ouaïème River ferry is **Camping de Tao** (☎ 85 97 34; *camping per tent 1000 CFP*). It has a very pretty setting on the beachfront beside a little stream. Call between 7am and 8am or in the evening when the mobile phone is switched on – or simply turn up.

Pouébo
pop 2700

Pouébo is 63km northwest of Hienghène and is the last village settled close to the sea (about 2km inland) on the northeast coast. The first Europeans to arrive in Pouébo (in July 1847) were Catholic missionaries who had come down from Balade, a little further north.

Pouébo Mission Church still stands on the original mission site on a rise above the main road. It has an attractive facade and stained-glass windows portraying different saints.

Balade

Balade is 11km north of Pouébo's mission church and is more an historical site than a village or community. Set amid hills, coastal mangrove plains and *niaouli* trees, this was the first place that European explorers set foot on New Caledonian soil. Captain Cook landed here in September 1774. There's a chapel at Balade on a knoll beside the main road with beautiful stained-glass windows depicting scenes from the early missionary days.

Camping d'Amoss (☎ 47 90 24; *tents 500 CFP; bungalow 2000 CFP; meals 800 CFP*) is a delightful spot 10km northwest of Balade. It's on the beachfront at the foot of Col d'Amoss on a dirt road, 1km off the main road. You'll need to bring your own sheets if you plan to stay in the rustic bungalow.

Balade to Ouégoa

After leaving Balade, the lush, spectacular scenery changes to grasslands and wooded hills. About 9km from Balade, the main road turns southwest and inland winding up Col d'Amoss and down to Ouégoa.

Ouégoa is an outpost town and the only significant northeastern village that is not settled close to the sea.

Mr Armand Ogushiku, known locally as Bouli, organises **canoe and kayak tours** (☎ 47 91 58, 81 10 09; *per hour/day 500/3000 CFP*) on the Diahote River. He also runs a **camping ground** *(per tent 1000 CFP)* with hot showers. Coming from Balade, the signposted turnoff is on the left 100m after the bridge, from where it's another 4km.

Getting There & Away

Three main roads span the central mountain chain: the RT3 between Bourail and Houaïlou; the Koné–Tiwaka (RPN2) road, further north; and the RPN7 linking Koumac and Balade via Ouégoa. One main road connects the northeast coast towns. If you take the Koné–Tiwaka road, make a detour through the mountain village of Bopope with its *cases* perched prettily on the steep slopes.

Air Touho has the only regional airfield. For flight information, see the Getting Around section at the beginning of this chapter.

Bus The buses to this coastline are less frequent than to destinations along the northwest coast. For information on buses from Noumea see under Bus in the Getting Around section.

The Loyalty Islands

The Loyalty Islands consist of three raised coral platforms and one atoll, about 100km off the east coast of Grande Terre. From south to north they are Maré, Tiga, Lifou and Ouvéa. Totalling 1980 sq km, they are roughly 50km apart and have their highest point (138m) on Maré. There are no rivers, though fresh water is found in numerous deep caverns and *trous* (holes) in or under the coral platform. You must seek permission from locals before visiting any caves. While nature is not as diverse here as on Grande Terre, the Loyalty Islands' eroded limestone coastlines are very impressive. Towering araucarias look down on the most sublime beaches that New Caledonia can offer.

Traditional Kanak society has been best preserved in these islands. Ancient traditions remain strong and lifestyles centre around community concerns.

For those looking for an authentic taste of island life, tribal gîtes and *logements chez l'habitant* (homestays) are dotted around the islands. There's a clinic in the main centre of each island.

History
Melanesians have inhabited the Loyalty Islands for millennia, but hundreds of years ago seafaring Polynesians arrived, dominating and ultimately mingling with the Melanesians.

Bruny d'Entrecasteaux is supposedly the first European to have spotted Ouvéa before landing on Grande Terre in April 1793. In 1827, Dumont d'Urville was officially sent to chart the islands. Whalers and sandalwood traders were the next arrivals, followed by evangelist Tongan teachers from the London Missionary Society (LMS) as early as 1841.

The Catholic missionaries arrived in the Loyalty Islands in 1856, but were unable to

convert all of the islanders. Caught between the two factions, the social structures of the clans on the three islands broke down and wars broke out. The wars raged until 1864, when the colony's Governor Guillian officially took possession of Lifou and Maré. Ouvéa followed the next year.

In the second half of the 1800s, islanders from Maré and Ouvéa were taken by blackbirders (see History in the Facts about the South Pacific chapter) to Australian sugarcane plantations to work.

After blackbirding came to an end, the two world wars and the appeal of the lucrative mining industry saw many more islanders leave their homes. In more recent decades they have been followed by students needing to gain a secondary or tertiary education, and people in search of a job.

The population of the four Loyalty islands is 98% Kanak, with only a handful of French. A large proportion of the islands' population live or work in Noumea.

MARÉ
pop 8000 • area 650 sq km
Maré is a lush island with a magnificent, steep coastline dropping into the big blue of the Pacific. It's the second largest of the Loyalty Islands and its coral cliffs are the group's highest, rising abruptly to 138m. While only a few beaches interrupt the cliff-lines, those that do are intensely beautiful.

Maré's population encompasses about 20 clans divided into eight chiefdoms. The clans all speak Nengone.

Information
There's a **BCI bank** (☎ 45 40 62; open 7.15am-noon & 1.15pm-4pm Mon-Fri), **post office** (☎ 45 41 05; open 7.45am-11.15am & 12.15am-3pm Mon-Fri) and a **gendarmerie** (☎ 45 41 17); all located in Tadine.

Tadine & Western Maré
The west-coast town of Tadine is the island's administrative centre and port. This was the home town of Yeiwene Yeiwene, the second in command of the FLNKS, who was assassinated on Ouvéa in May 1989 (see History in Facts about New Caledonia). He is buried here, by the sea.

The village has no beach. At the T-junction, close to the sea, a monument is dedicated to the people who drowned on an inter-island trader, *Monique*, in 1953. The disaster remains a mystery as no trace of the ship, which disappeared between Maré and Lifou, was ever found. At least 126 people, including many Maréans, were on board. In some cases entire families disappeared.

Between Tadine and Cengeité is l'**aquarium naturel**, a round, naturally carved rock pool fed from underground. Its clear translucent water is home to a variety of fish. The aquarium is on the right-hand side, roughly 3km from the Tadine gendarmerie, just before a slight rise in the road and the start of small cliffs to the left.

Cengeité and **Wabao** in the southwest corner of Maré have an idyllic setting beside a long, white beach and sparkling lagoon. Cengeité, which boasts the island's only top-end hotel, Nengone Village, starts about 8km south of Tadine. Wabao is home to two gîtes that are on the small coastal road, which leads off to the right as you arrive from Cengeité before looping back to the main road.

From Nengone Village it's an easy 6km walk to **Baie de Pede**, on the northern side of **Cap Wabao**. A track starts at the hotel and runs parallel to the beach. Near Cap Wabao, the track veers inland and meanders through a forest beneath a small cliff. Turn left at the end of the cliff and follow the wide path straight ahead through a wooded paddock to Baie de Pede.

About 9km from Cengeité, the southwest coastal road passes through **Medu** next to **Eni**, where it ends. From Wabao it's a picturesque route along the coast. About 500m before Medu, on the road's final curve, is **La grotte de Pethoen**. A foot track winds its way inland over the limestone floor for 100m to a large cavern where stalactites drip into cool, saline water. However, the cave is often littered with rubbish.

There's a small beach at Eni. Past the beach there's a cemetery where a couple of tracks lead to the edge of the cliffs from where there are nice views.

Going north from Tadine, the road winds along a spectacular coastline of limestone rock until **Nece**, 8km north of Tadine. After Nece, the road continues close to the base of the limestone cliffs before climbing steeply up the plateau to the village of **Padawa**. A tranquil place, it's dominated by a white church and separate bell tower, which face the sea. From Padawa, it's about 10km to the fishing community of **Roh**, where there's a monument commemorating the arrival of the first Polynesian missionaries on the island in 1841.

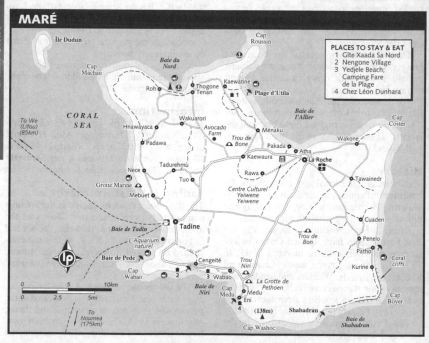

MARÉ

PLACES TO STAY & EAT
1 Gîte Xaada Sa Nord
2 Nengone Village
3 Yedjele Beach;
  Camping Fare
  de la Plage
4 Chez Léon Dunhara

About 3km off the La Roche–Tadine road, on the road to Thogone, the **Trou de Bone** is one of Maré's most impressive *trous* (sinkholes). The sheer sides of this enormous cavity drop to a lush tropical garden with a small waterhole. It's on the right-hand side of the road as you're heading to Thogone but isn't signposted.

La Roche & Eastern Maré

The spacious village of La Roche (The Rock) is built near the base of a limestone cliff, known locally as 'Titi'. La Roche's most noticeable structure, after the rock, is the impressive pink-toned Catholic church, which sits at its base. Founded in 1866, it boasts the only stained-glass windows on the island and is partly enclosed by thick stone walls. The **Yeiwene Yeiwene Cultural Centre** (☎ 45 44 79; *open 7.30am-11.30am & 1pm-5pm Mon-Fri*) is about 2km out of La Roche, on the road to Tadine. A large, traditional Melanesian-style complex completed in 1993, it now houses a large exhibition room and library.

Nine kilometres east of La Roche and 2km north of Wakone village is **le Saut du Guerrier** (the Warrior's Leap). It is a gap in the cliffs, 5m wide and 30m above the pounding surf. Here Hnor, from the Hnathege clan, escaped his enemies by leaping across the abyss. The entire area around Wakone is rugged, with splendid rock formations and crevasses.

The scenery at **Shabadran**, in the south of Maré, deserves an accolade of superlatives. There's a curved sandy beach cut off from the sea by a wide reef. Waves crashing on the reef send soft foaming water cascading gracefully over coral terraces into a tiny sparkling lagoon. To visit, you must pay **Damas Béaruné** (☎ 45 05 96; *day trip per person min 4 2000 CFP, overnight in rustic fare per person including meals 12,000 CFP*). He lives in Kurine, the last village on the road southeast, and will provide a guide. You need a moderate level of fitness for the three-hour walk and good footwear is imperative on the sharp coral cliffs. There is some easy cliff climbing involved.

Places to Stay & Eat

Wabao's accommodation options sit across the road from a blissful beach close to Cengeité village. They have splendid views of the water and reef.

Yedjele Beach (☎/fax 45 40 47; *singles/ doubles 6000/6500 CFP, extra person 7000 CFP*) has clean bungalows nestled in a shady forest setting. Each bungalow has a small

attic, TV, large terrace and a good kitchenette. On request, meals can be provided – a *menu* costs 1800 CFP and breakfast is 500 CFP. Credit cards are accepted.

Just down the road is **Camping Fare de la Plage** (☎/fax 45 42 24; *per tent 1100 CFP; meals 700-1600 CFP*). It serves meals in a thatched shack but a new restaurant was under construction at the time of research. A *bougna* is 1400 CFP per person. It rents bikes for 1200 CFP per day and canoes for 350 CFP per day.

Nengone Village (☎ 45 45 00, fax 45 44 64; W www.nengone-grands-hotels.cc; *bungalows 1-2 people 8500 CFP; menu 2500 CFP*), at Cengeité, is Maré's only top-end hotel. Its restaurant is by a swimming pool that overlooks a white-sand beach and blue lagoon. The hotel has attractive, square bungalows along the waterfront. All have air-con, TV and a small terrace. The hotel can arrange car rental and airport transfers. Bike hire costs 600 CFP (half day).

Chez Léon Dunhara (☎ 45 43 70; *per tent 1000 CFP, case per person 1500 CFP*), in Eni, sits tranquilly in well-kept grounds under a coconut grove overlooking the sea. Eni beach is 150m down the road. There's an attractive *fare* for relaxing and dining – breakfast is 500 CFP and a meal (they serve great seafood) costs 1500 CFP for guests or 2500 CFP if you're just dining. There are free bikes for guests. Airport and other transfers can be expensive.

Gîte Xaada Sa Nord (☎/fax 45 43 85; *per tent 1000 CFP, case per person 1500 CFP, rooms 5000 CFP*), in the northern Kaewatine community, is set in a large clearing. It's a family-run place with a row of rooms which can accommodate up to three people. Its restaurant serves a *plat du jour* for 800 CFP and breakfast for 400 CFP. From the gîte you can walk (45 minutes one way) through a cool forest to Plage de Utila. As the track is quite rough you'll need a guide – ask at the gîte. Airport/wharf return transfers cost 2000/3000 CFP.

Getting There & Away

The airport is at La Roche, a village 22km northeast of Tadine and 1km from the village itself. There's an **Air Calédonie desk** (☎ 45 55 10). The passenger ferry wharf is at Tadine.

For more information on flights and passenger ferry services see the Getting Around section at the beginning of this chapter.

NEW CALEDONIA

Getting Around

Maré has no public transport. Transfers to and from the airport or the ferry wharf are organised by most accommodation places. It's best to arrange it when you book your visit. You'll be looking at 2400/1000 CFP for a return transfer to the airport/wharf from Cengeité.

Cars are available for 7000 CFP per day (unlimited kilometres) from **Maré Île de Beauté** (☎ 45 43 75) in Nécé or at many of the Places to Stay. Cars will usually be delivered to your hotel or gîte, or you can pick them up at the airport on arrival.

Tours of the island are organised by **Tour of the Island** (☎ 45 42 36; per person 2500 CFP) or by most hotels and gîtes.

TIGA
pop 380 • area 10 sq km

The tiny island of Tiga, just 6km by 2km in size, sits midway between Maré and Lifou, roughly 30km from the closest point of both. Like its neighbours, Tiga is a raised coral platform, 76m at its highest point and encircled by a fringing reef.

The Tokanod clan inhabits the northwest corner, where Tiga is least exposed and the reef most accessible. There's a post office, church, clinic and small supply store.

Getting There & Away

There is only one direct flight a week between Noumea and Tiga (10,160 CFP, 40 minutes). For more information on domestic flights and passenger ferry services see the Getting Around section at the beginning of this chapter.

LIFOU
pop 11,500 • area 1196 sq km

Lifou is the largest of the Loyalty Islands and is bigger than Tahiti. This raised coral platform has wonderful limestone caves, bleached-white sand and rich sea-life amid the coral reefs.

Lifou is the most populated Loyalty Island. The island has three chiefdoms; Wetr, Gaïcha and Lössi. The local language, Drehu, is also the indigenous name for Lifou.

Information

The small tourist information office, **CEMAID** (☎ 45 00 32; e cemaid@lagoon.nc; open 7.30am-11.30am & 12.30pm-4.30pm Mon-Fri), next to the *mairie* (town hall), hands out informative island maps and brochures. It has a desk at the airport that's open at each arrival. You can change money at the **BCI bank** (☎ 45 13 32; open 7.20am-noon & 1pm-3.45pm Mon-Fri) on the main road opposite the Air Calédonie office. BCI has an ATM (DAB). The **post office** (☎ 45 11 00; open 7.45am-3pm Mon-Fri) is behind the provincial headquarters. **Sumaline** (☎ 45 02 94) is a cyber café and video club on the main road 300m south of the roundabout. Internet connection costs 500 CFP for half an hour.

We & Northern Lifou

We is Lifou's main centre and the island's only town. It's home to the provincial headquarters. It is curled around the wide, sandy Baie de Châteaubriand.

There are many worthwhile walks on the island. The **CEMAID** office provides information on guided walks.

Three kilometres southeast of the airport, **Hnathalo** is the home of the *chef* (chief) of Wetr. Behind the chief's concrete house, which is near the church, there's a *grande case* surrounded by a wooden palisade.

Northeast of the airport is **Tingeting** where you can visit the impressive **Grotte du Diable** (Devil's Cave). **Adrien Trohmae** (☎ 45 17 93; tour per adult/child 700/350 CFP, filming 500 CFP) runs guided tours. Photographs are free but you must pay to film the cave. Return transfers from We cost 4000 CFP per carload. Turn right after the church and follow the signposts to Adrien's house.

Jokin is Lifou's northernmost village. It sits atop the steep cliffs of Jokin. Its attractive *case* behind the church has a magnificent view over a wide bay. A footpath next to the *case* leads down to a little limestone cove where you can snorkel.

Easo sits peacefully on a cliff above the wide Baie du Santal. The road west of the church leads to the **Chapelle Notre Dame de Lourdes**, a small chapel topped by a large statue, perched high above the sea at the end of the Peninsula. About 250m before you reach the chapel car park, a track on the right leads down to **Baie de Jinek**. Here you can snorkel amongst a multitude of fish and coral in a wonderful natural aquarium.

Xepenehe is 4km east of Easo, overlooking Baie du Santal. It has a few more services than other villages which makes it the second most significant settlement after We.

Peng is a blissful, secluded sandy beach on Baie du Santal, 3.5km off the We–Drueulu road along a dirt road.

About 20km west of We, **Drueulu** lines the small Baie de Drueulu, part of the larger

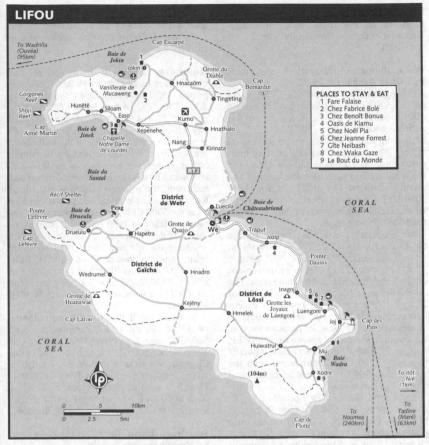

LIFOU

PLACES TO STAY & EAT
1 Fare Falaise
2 Chez Fabrice Bolé
3 Chez Benoît Bonua
4 Oasis de Kiamu
5 Chez Noël Pia
6 Chez Jeanne Forrest
7 Gîte Neibash
8 Chez Waka Gaze
9 Le Bout du Monde

Baie du Santal. There's a lovely beach. From Drueulu you can take the long southern road through several tribal communities to **Mu** and **Xodre** in the southeast of the island.

For **scuba diving**, contact **Lifou Fun Dive** (☎/fax 45 02 75; www.lifoufundive.com; 2-dive package with/without equipment supplied 11,960/10,400 CFP) in Easo. The dive sites have an abundance of soft corals, gorgonians and sharks. For more details see the 'South Pacific Diving' special section. The club also organises sailing trips.

Southern Lifou

Ten kilometres southeast of We is the village of **Jozip** where you can watch **Dick Emile Ukewed** (☎ 45 14 79) at work in his wooden sculpture workshop. Mr Ukewed has sculptures for sale and is open daily (closed at weekends).

Continuing south, 26km from We, **Luengoni** boasts one of the most beautiful beaches in New Caledonia. You'll often see turtles swimming in the calm turquoise lagoon. You can also swim in a beautiful underground cave at **Les Joyaux de Luengoni** (The Jewels of Luengoni). **Chez Noël Pia** (☎ 45 03 09) leads tours here for 1000 CFP per person.

Eleven kilometres south of Luengoni is **Mu** which is famous in New Caledonia for its resident crocodile. Poor Hector, the country's unique croc, once lived on a distant shore but lost his way in a storm several years ago and was washed up on the beach in Mu. He's been confined to a dingy shower ever since. To see him contact **Chez Waka Gaze** (☎ 45 15 14).

The southern road ends at **Xodre**, a small settlement with a rugged coastline.

Places to Stay & Eat

Lifou has quite a diverse range of accommodation options, conveniently spread over the island.

We A 10-minute stroll north of town you'll find **Chez Rachel** (☎ 45 12 43, fax 45 00 78; bungalows per person 6500 CFP, extra person 500 CFP; studio rooms 1/2/3 people 6000/6500/7000 CFP; camping per person with/without tent hire 1500/800 CFP), set back from the beach in a sheltered verdant setting. The motel's clean self-catering bungalows have refrigerators and hot water, and the small studio rooms have kitchenettes and private facilities. The motel charges 1900/1000 CFP for airport/wharf return transfers. Its restaurant currently serves only breakfast for 500 CFP per person.

We's upmarket abode is **Drehu Village** (☎ 45 02 70, fax 45 02 71; ⓦ www.drehu .grands-hotels.cc; bungalows 1-2 people 8500 CFP; menu 2500 CFP). It's a quiet place on the beachfront with a swimming pool. The hotel's design and decor are identical to that of Nengone Village at Cengeité on Maré, except here the bungalows are built in pairs. Guest facilities are also the same. Its restaurant serves various dishes including a *menu* for 2500 CFP. *bougna* is 1800 CFP and breakfast amounts to a hefty 1200 CFP. Return transfers to the airport cost 1700 CFP. It hires out canoes and bicycles to guests only.

Le Grand Banian (☎/fax 45 05 50; studios per person 6500 CFP, extra person 500 CFP; meals from 1200 CFP) is up on a plateau (about 1km from the main road; it is signposted) north of We and has a wonderful view over Baie de Châteaubriand. Its three adjoining studios have kitchenettes. At its small restaurant overlooking the bay, a plate of *tapas* costs 520 CFP. You can also order kangaroo. Return transfers to the airport/wharf are 2000/1000 CFP.

All of the above places accept credit cards. Their restaurants are open to non-guests but you would be wise to book. **Chez Hugo** (☎ 82 32 63; menu 1200 CFP; open 8.30am-6pm Tues-Sun) has a nice setting on the waterfront road near Chez Rachel. It serves burgers from 550 CFP. **Snack Madinina** (☎ 45 01 88; meals from 1000 CFP; open lunch and dinner Mon-Sat), close to the Protestant church on the main road, is a pleasant, waterfront eatery with an open-air *fare* and generous servings of West Indian food.

For self-caterers, **Korail** next to the Shell station and **Vival** by the roundabout on the main road are relatively well-stocked supermarkets.

Northern Lifou In Jokin, behind the church, **Fare Falaise** (☎/fax 45 02 01; case per person 1500 CFP, bungalows single/double 5000/5500 CFP, rooms 5000 CFP, camping per tent 1500 CFP; kayak/bike hire per half day 1500/1000 CFP; meals from 1000 CFP) is perched on the very edge of the cliff above the sea. From here the sunsets are breathtaking. Its bungalows have private facilities and rooms in a new house have shared kitchen and bathroom. It also offers boat trips and island tours at reasonable prices and guests can hire a car for 5000 CFP per day. Airport/wharf return transfers cost 1600/2000 CFP per person. Credit cards are accepted.

Along the winding forest road south of Jokin you can stay at **Chez Fabrice Bolé** (☎ 45 07 69; case/thatched bungalow per person 1500/2500 CFP; camping per tent 1000 CFP), a homestay on a vanilla farm in Mucaweng.

In Easo, you'll find **Chez Benoît Bonua** (☎ 45 90 08, 87 46 67; camping per tent 800 CFP, case per person 1500 CFP; canoe hire per hour 500 CFP). It's on the road to the Chapelle Notre Dame de Lourdes and has a scenic location overlooking Baie du Santal. There's a new amenities block. A *bougna* costs 6000 CFP (six servings) and a simple meal is 600 CFP. Guests can use the kitchen.

Southern Lifou The following places are listed heading south from We.

At Jozip, the comfortable **Oasis de Kiamu** (☎ 45 15 00, fax 45 16 00; ⓦ www.oasis-de -kiamu.com; doubles 7000 CFP, dorm rooms per person 1500 CFP) is set in a quiet garden beneath a cliff across the road from a pretty little sandy cove. The restaurant looks out onto a small swimming pool. Breakfast costs 850 CFP and a *menu* is 2000 CFP.

In Luengoni, the first place you'll come to is **Chez Noël Pia** (☎/fax 45 03 09; case per person 1500 CFP, camping per tent 1000 CFP, extra person 100 CFP). It's a humble but welcoming place on a small coral headland at one end of the magnificent Luengoni beach. In the early morning dozens of turtles swim beneath the headland. Meals can be ordered or guests can cook their own food in a *fare* equipped with cooking facilities. Breakfast is 500 CFP. A restaurant was under construction at the time of research. Noël arranges reputable snorkelling excursions to the nearby reefs for 1000 CFP per person, cave tours and three-hour guided bush walks for 1500 CFP per person.

Just 500m down the road still beside the beach, is the basic but acceptable **Chez Jeanne Forrest** (*☎/fax 45 16 56; case per person 1800 CFP, bungalow single/double 2000/3000 CFP, camping per tent 1000 CFP; meals from 1200 CFP*). It's not signposted. Grandfather Forrest was an English whaler who married a local Kanak woman. Jeanne's specialty is *bougna* which costs 1800 CFP per person. Breakfast is 400 CFP.

A little further on, a signpost on the left indicates the turnoff to the secluded **Gîte Neibash** (*☎/fax 45 15 68; paillottes 3500 CFP, extra person 1000 CFP, bungalows single/ double/triple 6000/6500/7500 CFP, camping per tent 1500 CFP, case 2500 CFP, extra person 500 CFP*) right on the beach. The bungalows are comfortable and have private bathrooms but the *paillottes* (straw huts) are very basic. Airport/wharf return transfers cost 2000/1000 CFP per person. The restaurant serves breakfast for 700 CFP and a *menu* costs 1800 CFP. Credit cards are accepted. A neighbour hires canoes and wind surfers. Enquire at the gîte.

In Mu, **Chez Waka Gaze** (*☎/fax 45 15 14; camping per tent 1000 CFP, case per person 1500 CFP, bungalow single/double 1500/2000 CFP; meals from 1200-2000 CFP*) sits on a long exposed beach. Airport/wharf return transfers cost 2500/2000 CFP. For 200 CFP you can visit Hector the crocodile (see Information earlier).

Near the end of the southern road you'll find the aptly named **Le Bout du Monde** (the back of beyond) (*☎/fax 45 02 46; camping per tent 1000 CFP; case per person 1250 CFP; seafood meals from 2000 CFP*) in Xodre. This lovely place has a thatched restaurant atop coral cliffs where the view stretches off across the ocean. Steps lead down to a small sandy beach. The speciality is coconut crab and sea food, and it's best to order 24 hours in advance. Airport/wharf return transfers cost 2000/1200 CFP.

You'll find groceries with limited supplies in each village.

Getting There & Away
Lifou's Wanaham airport terminal is 18km north of We, close to the village of Kumo. **Air Calédonie** has a desk *(open flight times)* at the airport and an **office** *(☎ 45 55 50; open Mon-Fri 7.30am-5.15pm, closed for lunch, 7.30am-noon Sat)* on the main road in We.

The passenger ferry docks at We. For more information on flights and passenger ferry services see the Getting Around section at the beginning of this chapter.

Getting Around
Most accommodation places will provide transfers to and from the wharf and the airport, but you'll need to book this when you reserve your accommodation.

There are a few 'school buses' on Lifou which leave various villages very early on weekdays for We but don't operate during school holidays. Aside from hitchhiking, which can involve very long waits depending on where you're going, it's the cheapest transport.

There's a bus in Xodre that does a daily run to We via the coastal road, departing at 6am. You can flag it down. It returns around 11am. The fare is around 400 CFP.

Cars can be hired from several private operators on the island, including **Loca V** (*☎/fax 45 03 20*) and **Aero Location** (*☎ 45 04 94, 81 31 21*). Prices range from 5000 CFP to 8000 CFP per day.

Island tours are organised by **Someltrans** (*☎ 45 14 78*). It costs 2300 CFP per person to tour the north or south and 4100 CFP per person for a full island tour. The company also does pick-ups and drop-offs.

OUVÉA
pop 4500 • area 160 sq km
A 35km-long atoll, Ouvéa comprises two large masses of limestone joined by a thin, natural causeway only 400m wide at its narrowest point. On one side of this sliver of land is a 25km-long perfect white beach lapped by the soft aquamarine waters of an enormous lagoon. On the other side, a fringing reef and coral cliffs break the Pacific's mighty swell.

Seventeen clans live on Ouvéa where the inhabitants are of Melanesian and Polynesian origin. The atoll's Melanesian name is Iaai which is also the name of the Melanesian language spoken here. The name Ouvéa comes from Uvea, the original name of Polynesian Wallis Island, and the Wallisian language Faga Uvea is also spoken on the island.

Ouvéa is also home to the horned parakeet, known locally as *la perruche d'Ouvéa*, an endangered green bird, native to the island, which makes a raucous chuckling sound.

The Pléiades Islands are a chain of 21 tiny, uninhabited coral islets surrounding Ouvéa to the west just like a necklace. The unspoilt Beautemps-Beaupré Atoll is 15km north of the Passe d'Anemata.

Information

The **gendarmerie** (☎ 45 71 17) and **post office** (☎ 45 71 00; open 7.45am-11.15am & 12.15pm-3pm Mon-Fri) are at Fayaoué. There's a **BCI bank** (☎ 45 71 31; open 7.20am-3pm Mon-Fri, closed for lunch) at Wadrilla.

Northern Ouvéa

The following places are listed from Fayaoué heading north.

At **Fayaoué**, stretching 3km along the lagoon, take a look at the Protestant church and its larger, twin-towered Catholic neighbour.

Approximately 5km east of Fayaoué, **Kong Houloup** is a cave near the airstrip. It's set in a cliff wall that obstructs the ocean view. **Lazard Jedyjah** (☎ 45 72 20), who lives in the house by the football field just east of the airport, takes guided tours (1000 CFP per person).

The memorial for the 19 Kanaks who died during the hostage crisis in 1988 (see History in Facts about New Caledonia) is by the roadside at **Wadrilla**. It's also the site where Jean-Marie Tjibaou and Yeiwene Yeiwene were killed.

The long thin neck of land joining Ouvéa's two land masses starts just after Wadrilla and continues for 15km, almost to St Joseph. Beside the road you'll see small furnaces for drying copra.

About 9km north of Wadrilla is the **Trou Bleu d'Anawa**, a deep hole with the most amazing blue water. Take the dirt track off to the left when the road curves abruptly to the right (ask permission from the people living in the house close by). Follow this track for 100m to a clearing. From here an overgrown footpath to the right leads to the hole.

Several tribes live in the vicinity of **St Joseph**, Ouvéa's northern hub where there's a *chefferie* (Kanak Chief's compound) surrounded by a wooden palisade.

From St Joseph, the road veers east through Weneki and Gossanah, the site of the 1988 Ouvéa massacre, to Ognat. Beside the road just before Ognat there's a pretty beach hidden by bush. From Weneki a road north takes you through coconut plantations to Ouvéa's northernmost settlement at Teouta.

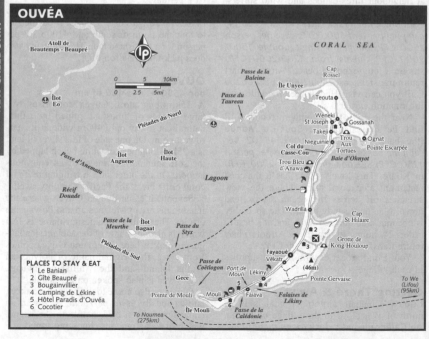

OUVÉA

PLACES TO STAY & EAT
1 Le Banian
2 Gîte Beaupré
3 Bougainvillier
4 Camping de Lékine
5 Hôtel Paradis d'Ouvéa
6 Cocotier

Southern Ouvéa

The following places are listed from Fayaoué heading south.

About 9km south is the village of Lékiny. To the east, the **Falaises de Lékiny** tower above a shallow inlet that forms part of the larger Baie de Lékiny. At low tide you can wade across to where a wooden ladder leads to a shelf in the cliffs. Along this shelf towards the open sea is a cave where worn stalactites hang dejectedly from the roof. Beyond the cave, a reef blocks off the sea from the bay. There's abundant coral here making it a great spot for snorkelling. Ask permission at the village or **Camping de Lékine** first.

The **Pont de Mouli**, Ouvéa's only bridge, is a local landmark. It joins Ouvéa to its southern tip where it's separated by a wide channel. From the bridge, the view is almost surreal, with the pure white sand contrasting sharply against the different shades of brilliant blue water. Stop here a while and watch sharks, rays, turtles and fish swim under the bridge.

Six kilometres southwest of the bridge is Ouvéa's southernmost village, **Mouli**, where an avenue of araucaria pines leads up from the beach to its Catholic church. Just north of Mouli is a **coconut fibre women's cooperative** (☎ 45 72 37) where strong hand-spun rope is made. Visitors are welcome.

In Mouli you'll also find a dive centre, **Ouvéa Plongée** (☎/fax 45 09 90, 2 dives 12,000 CFP). It organises dives in the Pléiades du Sud (the southern islets).

You can take a **boat trip** to the Pléiades du Nord or Sud with **Le Banian** or **Cocotier** (see Places To Stay & Eat following).

After Mouli, the beach gives way to coral rocks, while a road meanders along the peninsula's last 3km to the tip of the island. Here two rocky outcrops are separated by a small beach. Snorkelling is excellent, but beware of strong currents.

Places to Stay & Eat

Eateries are attached only to accommodation and you must let your host know half a day in advance if you want to dine. There is a grocery shop in each village. The following places are listed from north to south.

The only place to stay in the north is **Le Banian** (☎ 45 70 63, 84 79 48; camping per tent 1000 CFP, case per person 2500 CFP, extra person 500 CFP). It's in the Tribu de Heo near St Joseph. A bougna for two costs 3000 CFP. The owner also organises boat trips.

Gîte Beaupré (☎ 45 71 32; bungalows per double 6050 CFP, studio rooms per 1/2 people 3850/4400 CFP) is relatively modern and has three wooden bungalows with a shower. There are also basic studio rooms. Bikes are available for 1500 CFP per day. Gîte Beaupré prepares a simple but generous meal for 1980 CFP. Airport/wharf return transfers cost 1000/1600 CFP. Credit card is accepted.

Bougainvillier (☎/fax 45 72 20; camping per person 1000 CFP, bungalows with shared facilities per person 3000 CFP, extra person 500 CFP), in Ouassadieu community north of Fayaoué, is set back several hundred metres from the beach. It has Melanesian-style bungalows. Breakfast costs 500 CFP, while other meals cost 1500 CFP. Airport/wharf return transfers cost 800/1600 CFP.

Camping de Lékine (☎ 45 90 20; tent sites 1000 CFP, tent hire 1500 CFP; meals 1000 CFP) boasts a wonderful location beside the Baie de Lékiny. You can pitch your tent or rent one. Add 200 CFP if you want to use the cooking facilities. The restaurant serves simple meals. Airport/wharf return transfers cost 1200/1500 CFP.

Hôtel Paradis d'Ouvéa (☎ 45 54 00, fax 45 54 01; bungalows with garden/beach view 33,000/50,000 CFP; menus from 2000 CFP) is the island's only luxury hotel. It sits right on the beach just south of the Pont de Mouli. There's a restaurant and a pretty swimming pool with an artificial waterfall. Airport transfers cost 2000 CFP.

Cocotier (☎ 45 70 40; camping per tent 1000 CFP, case or fare with half/full board 4000/5000 CFP; meals 1800 CFP), in Mouli, is 500m north of the church on the main road. This tribal gîte-cum-snack has two cases and two fare that can sleep 10 people. Although comfort is minimal, it has a great setting. A lobster meal or bougna costs 3000 CFP. Airport/wharf return transfers cost 2000/2500 CFP. The owner also organises boat trips to the **Pléiades du Sud** (3000 CFP per person) with a picnic lunch provided for a minimum of three people.

Getting There & Away

Ouvéa's small airport at Houloup is 5km northeast of Fayaoué. It has an **Air Calédonie desk** (☎ 45 55 30) that opens according to flight times. Ouvéa's wharf is at the centre of the island and 6km north of Wadrilla.

For more information on domestic flights and passenger ferry services see the Getting Around section at the start of this chapter.

Getting Around

Although there is not much traffic on Ouvéa, hitchhiking is relatively easy as there's only one main road and drivers are willing to stop. Unless a flight is arriving or departing, the airport road is usually deserted. All gîtes will pick you up and take you back to the airport or the wharf at Wadrilla if you're arriving on the passenger ferry, but you should arrange this when you reserve your room.

The island's one bus does a run from St Joseph to Mouli and back once a day in the morning (not on Sunday). It leaves St Joseph at 7am, picking up passengers en route, and departs from Mouli at 9am. From Fayaoué to St Joseph it's 150 CFP, while it's 100 CFP to Mouli.

Ouvéa Location (☎ 45 73 77) at Fayaoué rents cars for 8000 CFP per day with fuel. Places to stay can also arrange car hire.

Gîte Beaupré rents bikes for 1500 CFP per day and **Le Banian** charges 1000 CFP per day.

Most places that offer accommodation can arrange a tour of the island for between 2000 CFP and 3000 CFP per person with a minimum of two to four people.

Île des Pins

pop 1900 • area 152 sq km
This beautiful island boasts sublime beaches and bays. It was given its contemporary name by English explorer Captain Cook, inspired by the araucaria pine that line the island's shore. To its indigenous inhabitants it is known as Kunie.

Fifty kilometres southeast of Grande Terre, Île des Pins extends 17km from north to south and is 14km wide. The island is more or less circular in shape, with a low tableland sweeping around the 60km coastal perimeter. Île des Pins' southwest region is dominated by Pic N'Ga (262m), the island's highest peak.

Eight main clans live on the island. In early times, the Kunies were the only people in New Caledonia who travelled by sea and could navigate by the stars. They sailed on *pirogues*, great double outrigger canoes that carried more than 40 people.

Administratively, Île des Pins is part of New Caledonia's Southern Province, governed from Noumea. The island's chief is locally elected as the mayor. The small island's economy is based largely on tourism and it also exports sandalwood oil.

History

The island's original settlers were the Kunies, people of Austro-Melanesian stock. In the early 17th century they were conquered by a warring tribe from Lifou.

In 1774, James Cook sighted and named the island, Isle of Pines. In the first half of the 1800s, traders rushed from Sydney to harvest the island's sandalwood.

In 1841, they were followed by missionaries from the London Missionary Society (LMS) who attempted unsuccessfully to establish themselves on the island's northern tip. The French annexed the island on 29 September 1853. By this time the Kunies' Catholic conversion was well underway due to the influence of French Marist missionaries.

Following the death of the Kunie leader Vendegou in 1855, tribal wars erupted. This was due in part to the succession of his daughter, Queen Hortense.

In 1872, Île des Pins became a convict settlement for Communards, political prisoners from the Paris Commune uprising in France. Also incarcerated were 750 Kanaks who had staged the great 1878 uprising against colonial settlers in the La Foa area. The Île des Pins prison finally closed in 1911 and the colonial administration handed the island back to the Kunies.

Information

Pick up brochures from the **Office du Tourisme de Noumea et de la Province Sud** (☎ 28 75 80, tollfree 05 75 80; ℮ office -tourisme@canl.nc; 14 rue Jean Jaurès, Place des Cocotiers; open 8am-5.30pm Mon-Fri, 9am-noon Sat). There is an **information desk** (☎ 46 14 00) at the Île des Pins airport which opens for flights. For another excellent source of information go to Ⓦ www.ile-des -pins.com.

Île des Pins' only **post office** (☎ 46 11 00; open 7.45am-11.15am & 12.15pm-3pm Mon-Fri) is in Vao. It also has a public telephone. Another is at the airport. In Kuto there's a phone at the army holiday camp across the road from Kuto beach. The **BCI bank** (☎ 46 10 45; open 8am-noon & 1.30pm-4pm Mon-Fri) is in Vao, 100m from the church. The **gendarmerie** (☎ 46 11 17) is near the wharf in Kuto.

Vao

Vao is located on the island's southernmost tip and is the only real village on Île des Pins. It is home to the *chef* and has most of the administrative facilities.

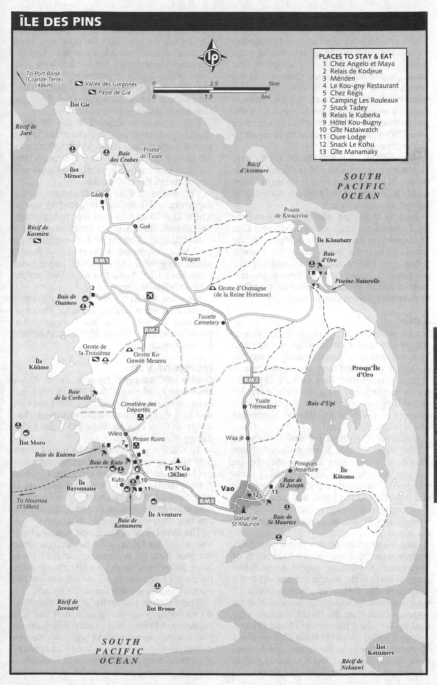

ÎLE DES PINS

PLACES TO STAY & EAT
1. Chez Angelo et Maya
2. Relais de Kodjeue
3. Mériden
4. Le Kou-gny Restaurant
5. Chez Régis
6. Camping Les Rouleaux
7. Snack Tadey
8. Relais le Kuberka
9. Hôtel Kou-Bugny
10. Gîte Nataiwatch
11. Oure Lodge
12. Snack Le Kohu
13. Gîte Manamaky

To Port Boisé
(Grande Terre)
(48km)

Vallée des Gorgones

Passe de Gié

Îlot Gié

Récif de
Jaré

Baie
des Crabes

Pointe
de Tuure

Récif
d'Aventure

SOUTH
PACIFIC
OCEAN

Îlot
Ménorë

Gadji

1

Gué

Pointe
de Kwacivita

Île Kônubutr

Récif de
Kasmira

Wapan

Baie
d'Oro

3 4

RM1

Grotte d'Oumâgne
(de la Reine Hortense)

5

Piscine Naturelle

Baie de
Ouameo

2

Touete
Cemetery

RM2

Grotte de
la Troisième

Grotte Ko
Gnwëë Meureu

Presqu'Île
d'Oro

Île
Kûûmo

RM3

Baie
de la Corbeille

Cimetière des
Déportés

Yuate
Trémwâtre

Baie d'Upi

Île
Kôtomo

Wèro

Prison Ruins

Waa jë

Pinogues
departure

Îlot Moro

6 7

8

Baie de Kutema

Baie de Kuto

9

Kuto

10

Pic N'Ga
(262m)

Vao

12

Baie de
St Joseph

13

Île
Bayonnaise

11

To Noumea
(118km)

Île Aventure

RM3

Statue de
St Maurice

Baie de
St Maurice

Baie de
Kanumera

Récif de
Jawaaré

Îlot Brosse

SOUTH
PACIFIC
OCEAN

Récif de
Nekaawi

Îlot
Kotumere

0   2.5   5km
0   1.5   3mi

NEW CALEDONIA

Vao's **Mission Church**, in the village centre, was built in 1860. It was established by the Marist priest Father Goujon, who managed to convert the entire island in just over 30 years from his arrival in 1848. The **sculptors** who made the beautiful wooden sculptures at the airport and at the Méridien Hotel live in Vao where you can watch them at work. William Paouro's workshop is opposite Snack Le Kohu and **Samuel Vendegou** (☎ 46 12 05) is based about 200m from the church at the intersection on the main road.

About 500m from Vao church, the **Baie de St Maurice** was the site of the first Catholic service held on Île des Pins. A statue of Christ stands high upon a coral platform encircled by carved wooden totems.

Baie de St Joseph, also referred to as Baie des Pirogues, about 2km east of Vao near Gîte Manamaky, is known for its outrigger sailing canoes. Along the beach under the coconut palms you can watch sailors building the *pirogues*. A trip on one of these crafts is a must if you're visiting Île des Pins (see Getting Around later in this section).

Kuto

Six kilometres west of Vao, this lovely area of silky white sand, calm aquamarine water and lush vegetation is breathtakingly beautiful. Although you'll find the bulk of gîtes here, it remains a quiet spot. **Baie de Kuto** is perfect for swimming and **Baie de Kanumera** for snorkelling; be warned that the large coral outcrop at the western side of Kanumera beach is strictly off limits.

Boutique Créations Île des Pins (☎ 46 12 68; open 9am-11.30am & 2pm-5.30pm Mon-Sun), a cute little souvenir shop beside the gendarmerie, sells hand-painted T-shirts and *pareo* (sarong-type garments), postcards and books about the island and local cuisine. The English-speaking owners, Albert and Cleo (Hilary Roots), are knowledgeable about the island.

The silent stone **prison ruins** where deportees were held are about 1.5km north of Kuto beach, towards the airport. About 700m north of these is the signposted turn-off to the **Cimetière des Déportés** which is 600m off the main road. It contains the remains of some 240 deportees from the Paris Commune who died on the island between 1871 and 1880.

You can also climb **Pic N'Ga** (262m). It is a 50-minute (steady) hike to the top, and the vista from the top is superb. The signposted path to the summit begins near Relais le Kuberka.

North of Kuto

Grotte de la Troisième, a freshwater cave, has a name carried over from the penal era, when the local district was known as the Third (*la Troisième*) commune. It's a cave, 8 to 10m deep, where highly experienced scuba divers can dive among stalactites and stalagmites. Take a torch to light your way down the steep, sometimes slippery, floor of the cave.

The signposted turn-off from the main road is just north of the intersection to the airport coming from Kuto. About 800m down the narrow dirt road there's a clearing where cars can turn around. A path to the right leads 30m through the bush to the cave.

The isolated **Baie de Ouameo** is the departure point for divers going to Gadji, which is a 20-minute boat ride to the north. The sunsets from here are beautiful.

Gadji, the northernmost community on the island, was formerly the capital of Kunie, where the *grands chefs* had their power base. From here, Chef Vendegou waged war on the tribes of Grande Terre.

Here too the first sandalwood traders and evangelists made landfall in New Caledonia, the latter in 1841. Gadji has a beautiful bay but near the shore it's muddy and not suitable for swimming.

North of Vao

Grotte d'Oumagne (*Grotte de la Reine Hortense; admission 200 CFP*) is Île des Pins' most famous and frequently visited cave. It was here that Queen Hortense supposedly hid for several months between 1855 and 1856, during the tribal wars.

To reach it you walk through a cool forest with tall tree ferns to where a statue of the Virgin Mary watches over the entrance. The mud floor is flat but slippery when wet and there is a high ceiling of large stalactites. A little stream runs through the interior, disappearing, like the few tiny bats, into the depths of the cave.

The cave is east of the airport. Coming from Vao, it's about 13km – continue straight along the road past the airport intersection. It's another 500m from the signposted turn-off. Julie, the cave's caretaker, hands out torches and can answer questions about the cave's history.

The **Piscine Naturelle** is near the Baie d'Oro halfway up the island's east coast. It is sheltered behind two islands, which create two natural causeways. At high tide, the sea rushes in and covers the sandy causeways with knee-deep water. Hours later, it empties, leaving just one pool of water, coloured the most exquisite turquoise imaginable. Towering over this are proud araucarias.

The turn-off to Baie d'Oro is opposite the small Touete cemetery, about 9km north of Vao, on the main road to the airport.

For more information about organised tours see Getting Around later in this section.

Diving

All diving on Île des Pins is arranged through **Kunie Scuba Centre** (*☎/fax 46 11 22; e kunie scuba@canl.nc; 2-dive package 12,480 CFP*), based at Relais de Kodjeue at Baie de Ouameo. There is a rich variety of sites at Gadji, especially Vallée des Gorgones. Divers will enjoy both the vision of soft and hard corals and a profusion of sea life, including eagle rays and leopard sharks.

Places to Stay & Eat

Vao Area Overlooking Baie des Pirogues, **Gîte Manamaky** (*☎/fax 46 11 11; self-catering bungalows per 2/3/4 people 6750/7650/ 8200 CFP; breakfast 800 CFP, seafood meals from 3100 CFP; boat trips with fish meal/ without fish meal/with lobster meal 6500/ 4250/8500 CFP*), about 1.5km from Vao's church (follow the main northbound road until you see the signpost), is the only place where you can sleep in the vicinity of Vao. It has four bungalows made from stone, wood, bark and thatch with giant mollusc-shell wash basins and coral floors in the bathrooms. You can order a fish dish in the gîte's thatched restaurant for 1200 CFP. The gîte also organises boat trips to **Atoll de Nokanhui**.

Snack Le Kohu (*☎ 46 10 23; open 6am-6pm Wed-Mon, 6am-7.30pm Sat & Sun*) serves snacks and meals including toasted sandwiches (220 CFP), chicken and fries (800 CFP) and ice cream (200 CFP). The local owner, Jean-Marc Vanho, is happy to talk to diners about local history and culture. The *snack*, with its blue A-frame roof, is beside the main road next to the empty field before the turn-off to Gîte Manamaky.

Kuto At the eastern end of Baie de Kanumera, **Oure Lodge** (*☎ 43 13 15, fax 43 13 44; W www.ourelodge.com; beach/lagoon view/ garden bungalow 37,000/33,600/28,600 CFP, one/two room bungalow 22,600/41,200 CFP; pizzas from 900 CFP, à la carte mains 2100-4500 CFP*) is ideally situated on the waterfront. This new lodge caters to an upmarket clientele. It has air-conditioned bungalows with a mini-bar, phone and internet connection. There's an

open-thatched beach bar and dining area, a swimming pool and restaurant. Activities for guests include deep sea fishing, picnic trips to islets, car, scooter and bike hire.

Gîte Nataiwatch (*☎ 46 11 13, fax 46 12 29; camping per tent 1500 CFP, self-catering bungalows per 1/2 people 6650 CFP, per extra person 500 CFP, twin bungalows per 1/2 people 6550 CFP, per extra person 500 CFP; breakfast 850 CFP; bike hire per half/ full day 1040/1560 CFP; car hire per day 7280 CFP*) sits in a nice wooded area about 100m from the water, towards the eastern end of Baie de Kanumera. Its twin bungalows don't have kitchen facilities but have private shower and toilet, while the self-catering bungalows use the same toilet and shower block as campers. In the restaurant, a plate of *escargots* costs 3120 CFP.

Hôtel Kou-Bugny (*☎ 24 92 80, fax 24 92 81; e resbugny@canl.nc; bungalows per 5 people 17,950 CFP, deluxe bungalows 21,050 CFP*) is just across the road from the beach in a forest-like setting. It has a small swimming pool. There's an all-you-can-eat 2600 CFP lunch buffet, as well as a lobster or snail menu for 3770 CFP. The hotel also sells takeaway sandwiches (390 CFP).

Relais Le Kuberka (*☎ 46 11 18, fax 46 11 58; rooms per 1/2/3 people 6150/6650/7150 CFP, bungalows per person 7150 CFP, extra person 500 CFP; meals from 835 CFP, menus from 1560-2080 CFP; car hire per day 7280 CFP plus per km 40 CFP*), away from the beach on the main (inland) road through Kuto, has clean rooms and bungalows with toilet/shower facilities and fridges. It's set in a garden and there's a pool. It's about 350m to the beach. A seafood meal costs 4680 CFP.

Camping Les Rouleaux (*☎ 46 11 16; camping per person 940 CFP; breakfast 600 CFP; airport/wharf return transfers 500 CFP*) has the same sandy beach and beautiful turquoise water as elsewhere on the island, but also has surf especially in the winter. It's 1km from the main road. Heading north, the turn-off is just before Snack Tadey.

Snack Tadey (*☎ 46 10 68; open 8am-5pm Mon-Sat, 9am-5pm Sun*), on the northern side of Kuto, is a small *snack*-cum-shop. It has cold drinks, sandwiches (310 CFP) and simple meals (850 CFP to 1000 CFP).

North of Kuto On the calm waterfront of Baie de Ouameo, **Relais de Kodjeue** (*☎ 46 11 42, fax 46 10 61; traditional/beach/suite bungalows per 1-2 people 7800/14,100/19,000*

CFP, extra person around 950 CFP; simple menu 2350 CFP) has wonderful sunsets. Its suite bungalows have terraces built out over the beach as well as a TV and fridge. The traditional bungalows have cooking facilities.

The hotel has a pool and a grocery store. There's a restaurant where salads cost 1500 CFP and a seafood *menu* is 4800 CFP. Car (6000/8000 CFP, half/full day), scooter (3000/4000 CFP, half/full day) and bicycle (1500/2000 CFP, half/full day) rental is available.

Chez Angelo et Maya *(☎ 88 19 74; case with beds per double/group 2000/3500 CFP, case with mats per double/group 2000/3000 CFP, camping per tent 500 CFP; menu around 700 CFP)* is a simple tribal homestay in remote Gadji. Comfort is minimal and there's no electricity but the welcome is extremely warm. When you call to book, let the phone ring for a long time as it's a public phone booth down the road from the homestay. A shuttle operates from Monday to Friday between Gadji and Vao. It leaves Gadji at 7am and arrives in Vao at 8am, and returns to Gadji shortly after. A one-way fare is around 500 CFP.

Baie d'Oro The most luxurious place to stay in New Caledonia, together with its counterpart in Noumea, is **Le Meridien** *(☎ 46 15 15, fax 46 15 16; ⓦ www.lemeridien-iledespins.com; deluxe rooms 46,176 CFP, garden/beach bungalows 53,176/57,176 CFP; lunch/dinner menu 3800/4680 FP).* Surrounded by coconut palms, the large swimming pool's design creates the illusion that it's part of the lagoon. The grounds are beautifully kept. The restaurant serves snacks from 400 CFP.

Restaurant Kou-gny *(☎ 46 10 65; camping per tent 1200 CFP)* is a modest place but has an excellent reputation for both its setting and lobster meals. Tables spread with seafood are set under the trees on the beach overlooking a dreamy lagoon. It's along from the Meridien but you have to walk through the forest to get there or, from the *Piscine Naturelle*, follow the right hand causeway then walk along the beach. A lobster meal costs 3700 CFP and a fish meal is 2000 CFP but you must book the day before. If you're camping, don't leave your belongings unattended. They make easy pickings as, other than at lunch times, the place is usually deserted.

Chez Regis *(☎/fax 43 45 55; camping per person 500 CFP; bungalows per double 7500 CFP, extra person 1000 CFP; plat du jour 1500 CFP),* famous for its *bougna*, offers accommodation in bungalows, tastefully decorated using local materials. The open-thatched restaurant overlooks one of the causeways leading to the *Piscine Naturelle*. It will cost you 2200/2500 CFP per person for a chicken/fish *bougna*. You must give a day's warning.

Île des Pins' *escargot* are a local culinary speciality served by most places. All restaurants attached to *gîtes* or hotels accept nonguests. Throughout Île des Pins, it is a good idea to place orders a few hours in advance to allow the staff time to plan the meal.

Getting There & Away

Île des Pins' airport is 9km north of Kuto. **Air Calédonie** has an **office** *(☎ 44 88 50; open 7.30am-11am & 2pm-5pm Mon-Fri, until 11am Sat)* at Kuto or the **airport** *(☎ 44 88 40).* Its ferry wharf is at Kuto.

For more information on flights and passenger ferry services see the Getting Around section at the beginning of this chapter.

Getting Around

There is no public transport on Île des Pins. The *gîtes* provide airport transfers if you have booked accommodation (1200 CFP to 1800 CFP both ways). The island's unique **taxi** *(☎ 78 49 84)* charges 1500 CFP return from the airport or wharf to your hotel.

Cars can be rented from Relais de Kodjeue, Gîte Nataiwatch, Relais Le Kuberka and Hôtel Kou-Bugny. You'll be looking at around 6000/8000 CFP for a half/full day. The price usually includes petrol. Relais de Kodjeue also hires scooters for 3000/4000 CFP per half/full day. Bike hire from Gîte Nataiwatch and Relais de Kodjeue costs around 1040/2000 CFP for a half/full day. It's cheaper from the former.

Most *gîtes* can arrange island tours. They cover the island's most important sights in a space of two or three hours. On average they charge from 1200 CFP to 1800 CFP per person. **Hikada** *(☎ 46 10 90)* organises 4WD tours across the interior plateau. A half day tour costs 3000 CFP.

Tours on an **outrigger sailing canoe** *(1500 CFP)* can be arranged through your hotel or *gîte* or simply turn up at the beach any day of the week before 8am. The most popular is the trip to the Baie d'Upi on the east coast, followed by a short walk across the narrow neck of the Presqu'Île d'Oro and a *bougna* lunch at Chez Regis. All the gîtes charge 2500 CFP per person for this trip including transfers but not the *bougna*.

For boat trips see Gîte Manamaky in Places to Stay & Eat.

Niue

Although the name actually means 'Behold the coconut', Niue (pronounced 'new-ay') is affectionately known as 'the Rock of Polynesia'. Standing alone and isolated midway between New Zealand (NZ) and French Polynesia, Niue is the smallest self-governing state in the world. Its closest neighbours are Tonga, about 600km southwest, and Rarotonga, 1000km southeast.

Niue is quiet, easy-going and very friendly, and its dramatic rocky coast, beautiful forest, amazing cave formations and superb scuba diving are unlike almost anywhere else in the South Pacific. With very few tourists and a population of less than 1800, Niue is the perfect place to be completely alone.

Facts about Niue

HISTORY

Niue's first settlers arrived about 1000 years ago. The Niuean language is based on both Samoan and Tongan, with traces from Pukapuka in the Cook Islands. But whether the Samoans or the Tongans arrived first is open to dispute – possibly the settlers came in waves from both directions.

James Cook stopped by in 1774 on his second Pacific voyage, but his attempts to land were repulsed three times. He dubbed Niue 'the Savage Island', in contrast to Tonga, which he had christened 'the Friendly Islands' (see the boxed text 'Cook's Friendly Islands' in the Tonga chapter). Niueans insist that Cook's unfriendly reception might simply have been a strong 'challenge' rather than outright hostility. Either way, it was enough to frighten off visitors for many years.

The pioneering missionary John Williams came by in 1830, but continued on his way. It was not until 1846 that Peniamina, a Niuean who had been converted to Christianity in Samoa, established the first Christian foothold on the island with the London Missionary Society (LMS). He was followed in 1849 by Paulo, a Samoan missionary.

Apart from visits by whalers and Peruvian slave ships, Niue's major problem in the later years of the 19th century was exactly the same as it is today: an unstoppable exodus of islanders looking for employment abroad. The missionaries had the island firmly under control when Niue briefly became a

At a Glance

Capital City: Alofi

Population: 1736

Time: 11 hours behind GMT

Land Area: 259 sq km

Number of Islands: One

International Telephone Code: ☎ 683

GDP/Capita: US$3600

Currency: New Zealand dollar (NZ$) (NZ$1 = US$0.59)

Languages: English & Niuean

Greeting: *Fakaalofa atu*

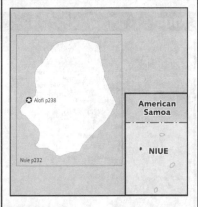

Highlights

- **Scuba diving** – discover the excellent sites at Ana Mahaga and Snake Gully
- **Snorkelling** – take in Snake Gully and the rock pool at Hio Beach
- **Exploring caves and chasms** – the Vaikona and Togo chasms are magnificent
- **Bushwalking** – dense forest and lonely sea tracks

British colony in 1900, before being handed over to NZ the next year. The Niueans were not consulted about this imperial handover, but they protested loudly when NZ proposed lumping their island in with the Cook Islands.

Niue remained a quiet backwater through the first half of the 20th century until after WWII, when pressure began for self-government.

231

However, Niueans, aware that their economy was heavily dependent upon NZ aid and remittances from relatives living in NZ, were in no hurry to go it alone. In 1974, Niue achieved self-government in 'free association' with NZ. Niueans hold NZ citizenship, which means Niue has enormous trouble stemming the flow of emigration that has seen the population figure tumble below 2000. There are now serious questions over whether Niue can remain a viable independent state and many believe it's only a matter of time before Niue places itself fully in the hands of New Zealand.

GEOGRAPHY

Niue is a *makatea* (raised coral island), like Rurutu in French Polynesia or 'Atiu in the Cook Islands. It's one of the largest upthrust coral atolls in the world, with two tiers, one rising 20m sheer from sea level and the second as high as 65m. There are few beaches and no rivers, but many caves, chasms, ravines and gullies around the coast. There's a fringing reef around much of the island, but no lagoon.

CLIMATE

During the December to March cyclone season the average temperature is 27°C, dropping to 24°C during the rest of the year when the southeast trade winds blow. Rainfall totals around 200cm a year, with the wettest time of year being between November and April.

ECOLOGY & ENVIRONMENT

The island limestone is extremely porous and rainfall simply disappears on contact. At various points around the island fresh water can be seen percolating into the sea. Although

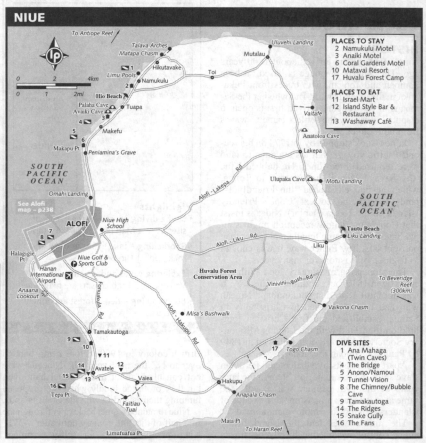

NIUE

To Antiope Reef

PLACES TO STAY
2 Namukulu Motel
3 Anaiki Motel
6 Coral Gardens Motel
10 Matavai Resort
17 Huvalu Forest Camp

PLACES TO EAT
11 Israel Mart
12 Island Style Bar & Restaurant
13 Washaway Café

Talava Arches
Matapa Chasm
Hikutavake
Limu Pools
Namukulu
Hio Beach
Palaha Cave Tuapa
Avaiki Cave
Makefu
Makapu Pt
Peniamina's Grave

Uluvehi Landing
Mutalau
Toi
Vaitafe
Anatoloa Cave
Lakepa

Alofi-Lakepa Rd

SOUTH PACIFIC OCEAN

Omahi Landing

See Alofi map – p238

ALOFI
Niue High School
Halagigie Pt
Hanan International Airport
Anaana Lookout
Niue Golf & Sports Club

Ulupaka Cave Motu Landing

SOUTH PACIFIC OCEAN

Tautu Beach
Liku Landing
Liku

Alofi-Liku Rd

Huvalu Forest Conservation Area

Vinivini-Bush Rd

To Beveridge Reef (300km)

Alofi-Hakupu Rd

Fonuakula Rd

Misa's Bushwalk

Vaikona Chasm

Tamakautoga

Avatele
Vaiea
Tepa Pt
Faitiau Tuai
Limufuafua Pt

Togo Chasm

Hakupu
Anapala Chasm
Mata Pt

To Haran Reef

DIVE SITES
1 Ana Mahaga (Twin Caves)
4 The Bridge
5 Anono/Namoui
7 Tunnel Vision
8 The Chimney/Bubble Cave
9 Tamakautoga
14 The Ridges
15 Snake Gully
16 The Fans

NIUE

there is no permanent surface water, the island has a huge water lens and there is usually an adequate supply.

FLORA & FAUNA

The Huvalu Forest Conservation Area in the island's east preserves a patch of dense tropical forest with spectacular trees and wildflowers. Niue's east coast is particularly untouched, with thickets of impenetrable coastal vegetation and shady woods. There are many birds – including *veka* (wood hens), swamp hens, parakeets and white-tailed terns – but the only native mammals are rats and fruit bats. Feral cats are a major problem, devastating native wildlife. Niue's enormous coconut crabs (*uga*; '**oong**-a'), are a popular delicacy.

In the clear waters around Niue you'll find lots of tropical fish, but the island is best known for its black-and-grey-striped *katuali* (sea kraits). Although these sea snakes have a strong venom, their mouths are too small to bite. They're not aggressive – you'd have to shove a finger down a sea snake's throat to provoke it to bite you – and they are often as curious about you as you are about them. Visitors soon become accustomed to swimming in what could be described as snake-infested waters.

Pods of small spinner dolphins are found along the island, including off the coast at Alofi; the name comes from the dolphin's practice of spinning around when it jumps clear of the water. Humpback whales migrate north from the Antarctic to breed in Niue's waters between June and November.

Niue's coastal waters are protected by legislation. Fishing with explosives or poisons is banned and no marine creatures can be taken using scuba equipment. Also, net fishing has never caught on in Niue. Tradition requires that the popular *ulihega* bait fish (round-eye scad) can only be caught with coconut bait or lures, and only from recognised bait-fishing areas, usually around canoe landing places down sea tracks (tracks leading from the road to the coast). From January to May, *kaloama* (juvenile goatfish) and *atule* (big-eye scad) seasons may close certain spots such as Avatele beach, Avaiki reef (off Tuapa) and Utuko Reef areas. Signs are posted.

GOVERNMENT & POLITICS

Niue elects a 20-member legislative assembly, led by a premier and three ministers, every three years. It boasts the perhaps dubious distinction of having the world's highest per capita number of politicians – one MP for every 86 people!

Young Vivian was elected premier in 2002, taking over from the colourful Sani Lakatani, who became renowned for his wildly ambitious (and unsuccessful) schemes to generate revenue for Niue, including a plan to make Niue the information technology hub of the Pacific. Recently, the government was considering a proposal from a Korean Christian sect to build a walled holy citadel on Niue in return for an undisclosed sum, an idea vehemently opposed by residents.

ECONOMY

Foreign aid, principally from NZ, and money sent back by Niueans living overseas are the twin pillars of the island's economy.

The old copra trade has long gone; cotton and bananas once had short spells as export products; and sewing footballs for the NZ market also died. Niuean honey is excellent, and after a brief lull is back in production under New Zealand ownership. A little taro

The Rat & the Octopus

One day, long before people arrived in Niue, a rat was foraging on the reef and became so preoccupied it failed to notice the incoming tide. Trapped on the reef edge, the rat squeaked for help and a kindly octopus popped up and offered to carry the rat to shore. Balanced on the octopus' head, the rat was soon back on dry land, but instead of thanking the octopus for its kindness the rodent defecated on its head as it jumped off. The octopus was outraged and promised that in future any rat that ventured on to the reef risked being hauled under and drowned.

Many years later, when the island was populated, someone heard the tale of the ungrateful rat and devised an unbeatable octopus lure. Take one tiger cowrie and one mourning cowrie shell and tie them back to back to look like a rat's body. Add a stick for the tail and some straw to form the head and whiskers. Tie the lure on a fishing line, lower it over the edge of the reef and it's certain death for any octopus.

NIUE

is exported and there are some pretty stamps for collectors. The tourist 'flow' is more of a trickle, thanks largely to Niue's enduring air-service problems.

There is some small-scale agriculture and fishing, and every night hordes of outrigger canoes head out to fish the fringing reefs.

POPULATION & PEOPLE

The vast majority of Niueans don't live on Niue. At the turn of the 20th century the population was around 4500, at independence in 1974 it was still around 4000. Now it's down to 1736 and falling. There are about 18,500 Niueans living in NZ and around 3000 in Australia, a fact reflected in the abandoned houses you'll see all over the island.

ARTS

There's a little woodcarving and pandanus weaving, but no large-scale production. The large, dramatic canvases of NZ artist Mark Cross, who is married to a Niuean, can be seen in the lobbies of the Hotel Niue and Matavai Resort and at Tahiono Arts in the Commercial Centre in Alofi.

SOCIETY

Niue is still a traditional Polynesian society in many respects and the people are very conservative. On Sunday, church and quiet are the order of the day and no boats are allowed to go to sea between 4am and 9pm – so there's no scuba diving or fishing. The radio station also shuts down on Sunday, swimming is only permitted at a couple of beaches and after church your choices are a long afternoon siesta or watching videos.

Traditional customs continue, such as the *kaloama* spawning season, when a number of beaches and swimming holes are closed. A *fono* (ban on fishing) is declared by a village council and signs are posted on the sea tracks and at beaches and canoe landings.

Teenage boys enter adulthood with a haircutting ceremony, and for girls there is a similar ear-piercing ceremony.

RELIGION

Churches of the Protestant Ekalesia Niue, related to the original LMS, are found in every village. Since WWII, Roman Catholic, Mormon, Seventh-Day Adventist, Baha'i and Jehovah's Witness churches have all set up on Niue. As elsewhere in the Pacific, church services are noted for their inspiring singing.

LANGUAGE

The Niuean language is similar to Tongan and also has Samoan influences. The letter 'g' is pronounced 'ng' as it is in Samoan. Most people speak English as a second language but a few words of Niuean will go down well.

Niuean Basics

Hello.	*Fakaalofa atu.*
Goodbye.	*Koe Kia.* (to one person), *Mutolu Kia.* (two or more people)
How are you?	*Malolo nakai a koe?*
I'm well (thanks).	*Malolo (fakaaue).*
Please.	*Fakamolemole.*
Thank you.	*Fakaaue lahi.*

Facts for the Visitor

SUGGESTED ITINERARIES

Niue doesn't offer a wealth of options, but a week's stay could include a day or two in Alofi, a one-day drive around the island, a day or two bushwalking through the centre of Niue and some snorkelling, scuba diving and fishing.

PLANNING
When to Go

The best time to visit Niue is between May and October, when temperatures are slightly lower and there is no danger of cyclones. Low season (though Niue doesn't really have a busy period) is November to June, when many guest houses offer discounts on room rates.

The Christmas/New Year period should be avoided, as flights get booked out by Niueans returning from New Zealand for the holidays and it's easy to get stranded on the island a lot longer than you planned.

TOURIST OFFICES

The friendly **Niue Tourism Office** (☎ 4224; W *www.niueisland.com*) is at the Commercial Centre in Alofi. Niue is represented abroad by the South Pacific Tourism Organisation (see the Regional Facts for the Visitor chapter).

VISAS & DOCUMENTS

A passport is required to enter Niue. There are no visa requirements for stays of less than 30 days, as long as you have an onward ticket and 'sufficient' funds.

CUSTOMS

Don't bring fresh food with you – there are strict quarantine regulations on the island.

MONEY

New Zealand dollars (see Exchange Rates in the Rarotonga & Cook Islands chapter) are used on Niue. There are NZ$5, 10, 20, 50 and 100 notes and 5c, 10c, 20c, 50c, NZ$1 and NZ$2 coins. The **Westpac bank** *(open 9am-3pm Mon-Fri)* changes travellers cheques and exchanges foreign currency, but charges NZ$10 for credit-card advances on Visa or MasterCard. You can use credit cards at the pricier hotels, car-rental agencies and the island's only dive shop, in Alofi.

Costs

Niue sits somewhere in the middle of the Pacific budget league table – more expensive than Tonga or Fiji, but cheaper than Tahiti or New Caledonia. The bare minimum would be around NZ$60 per day for the cheapest guest house and meals. A better-quality room plus some water activities or a rental car will set you back at least NZ$200 per day.

POST & COMMUNICATIONS

The **post office** and **numismatic office** is in the Commercial Centre and has some pretty stamps, but mail to or from Niue can be very slow.

Internet access is free (yes, *free*!) on Niue. The **Internet Users' Society** *(☎ 4603, 1157; open 9am-3pm Mon-Fri)* in Alofi has terminals for public use.

The **Telecom office** *(open 24 hrs)* is in the Commercial Centre. Peak rate charges are NZ$1.60 per minute for a call to NZ, NZ$2.30 to Australia or NZ$4.20 to North America or Europe. The international access code is ☎ 00.

DIGITAL RESOURCES

Most businesses have email addresses and websites. The **Internet Users' Society** (W *www .niue.nu)* website has useful information, links to other sites and weekly news. The **Niue Tourism** (W *www.niueisland.com)* website has a comprehensive guide to accommodation and activities on the island.

BOOKS

Terry Chapman's *Niue – A History of the Island* (1982) tells the full story of the island and can be bought in Niue; treat it with caution, as dates may be inaccurate. *Niue, The Island & Its People*, by S Percy Smith, is a reprint of a study of the island first published in 1902. Novels by Niuean John Pule include *The Shark that Ate the Sun* and *Burn My Head in Heaven*.

Niue of Polynesia: Savage Islands, by the First Latter-Day Saint Missionaries, is a portrait of the country from the viewpoint of those trying to re-convert it.

There's a **library** with a good Pacific section opposite the hospital.

RADIO & TV

Niue Radio broadcasts at 91MHz and 102MHz FM from 6am. Television broadcasts start at 6pm; both radio and TV shut down around 11pm. On Sunday both start broadcasting in the evening. The weekly *Niue Star* is the island's newspaper.

TIME

Niue is east of the International Date Line and 11 hours behind GMT. When it is noon in Niue it is 3pm in Los Angeles, 11pm in London and 11am the next day in Auckland.

HEALTH

There is no malaria on Niue and no dengue has been recorded here since the early 1990s. The tap water is safe to drink.

The **Lord Liverpool Hospital** *(☎ 4100)* is in south Alofi.

BUSINESS HOURS

Shops are generally open 8am to 4pm Monday to Friday, and in the morning and late afternoon on Saturday.

PUBLIC HOLIDAYS & SPECIAL EVENTS

Niue celebrates New Year's Day, Easter, Anzac Day and Christmas (see Public Holidays in the Regional Facts for the Visitor chapter for dates). Niue's independence is marked by the Constitution Celebrations around 19 October, with singing, dancing, sports events and handicraft displays. The Monday of these celebrations is Peniamina Day, celebrating the arrival of Christianity in 1846. Each village has its own show day during the year, and the island has a surprising number of golf tournaments.

ACTIVITIES

Niue's active **Hash House Harriers** *(☎ 4052)* run on Monday afternoon. Visitors are welcome at the Niue Golf & Sports Club's nine-hole golf course, across from the airport terminal. The club also has tennis courts.

NIUE

Niue is small enough, the traffic light enough and some of the sea tracks rough enough to make Niue a great place for mountain biking.

Snorkelling

Niue Dive (☎ 4311; Alofi) operates snorkelling trips and the Snake Gully site is equally interesting for snorkellers and divers. There's good snorkelling at the Limu Pools and Matapa Chasm, while just north of Hio Beach is an idyllic little rock pool, ideal for snorkelling at low tide. There are places around the island where snorkellers can swim outside the reef but you need to be a confident swimmer and should seek local advice about entry points and water conditions before venturing offshore. The Omahi sea track, just north of Alofi, is a good entry point, but the entry point off Avatele Beach is dangerous – there have been drownings here.

Diving

Niue Dive (☎ 4311, mobile 3483; W www.dive .nu) is the island's only dive shop. A two-dive boat trip with full gear costs NZ$160. This is a good operation: the equipment is top quality, moorings are used at the dive sites and there's no fish feeding.

Niue has no rivers running into the sea, so visibility is stunning, especially in the May to October dry season, when 40m visibility is the norm. The water is warm, peaking at 29°C in January and falling to only 25°C in August.

Caves and sea snakes are Niue's two prime dive attractions. Directly offshore from the Limu Pools is Ana Mahaga (Twin Caves), where two chimneys plummet down through the reef then turn through 90° to emerge as

huge caves on the reef edge. A horizontal tunnel joins the two caves to make this one of Niue's most spectacular dives. It's nearly 30m deep at the cave floors.

Off Makefu village in the northwest is The Bridge, which begins with a descent under a coral archway, emerging onto a hard coral wall where sharks and turtles are often seen.

South of The Bridge is the twin Namoui/Anono dive site, a protected marine reserve where turtles are a common sight.

There are three dive sites off Alofi. Tunnel Vision is a curved tunnel opening into a cavern system, where it's possible to surface through a hole and look out to sea. The Chimney drops more than 20m straight down before emerging as a reef cave. This site is often paired with the Bubble Cave, a shallow cave system where divers can surface in an air chamber filled with stalactites. Between the Chimney and the Bubble Cave are a series of swim-throughs and a wall with lots of marine life.

Farther south, off Tamakautoga, is a drift dive along a pristine hard coral reef featuring lots of gullies and numerous sharks.

Outside the pretty little bay at Avatele there are several popular dives, including The Ridges and Snake Gully, where divers will encounter all the sea snakes they might ever hope to meet in a lifetime. On the surface snakes are constantly popping up to grab a breath before heading down again. Down in the gully there are snakes winding along the bottom, snakes seemingly sleeping and snakes knotted up together.

A little further south The Fans features wonderful gorgonian fans below 30m, but this dive cannot be made if there is a current running around Tepa Point.

Fishing

Wahoo, tuna and mahimahi (dolphin fish) are abundant around Niue. Horizon Charters (☎ 4190, 4312; 4/8hr trip NZ$300/450) runs fishing trips on a well-equipped boat with a maximum of five people. You should contact Horizon Charters to book before you arrive on Niue.

Akau Charters (☎/fax 4025; e jeffwood@ niue.nu) charges NZ$160 for four hours for a maximum of three people. Additional hours are NZ$40.

SHOPPING

Some handicrafts and T-shirts are available from shops in the Commercial Centre, such as Taoke Prints and Hinapato Handicrafts.

Beaches & Swimming

Niue has none of those long sweeps of golden sand that you find on Pacific postcards. In fact even finding a place you can go for a swim can be difficult. Around most of the coast, waves beat straight onto the reef only a stone's throw from the towering cliffs. There are, however, a few tiny patches of beach and some delightful natural rock pools – ideal for a swim or snorkel, though often only accessible at low tide. On Sunday, swimming is only allowed at the Limu Pools and Matapa Chasm. Swimming may also be banned at some places during the January to May kaloama spawning season.

NIUE

Getting There & Away

AIR

Polynesian Airlines *(book through Peleni's Travel Agency* ☎ *4317;* ⓦ *www.polynesianair lines.com)* has direct flights to Niue, departing Auckland on Saturday, arriving in Niue on Friday afternoon. The return fare is about NZ$1190. From Samoa, the plane lands on Niue on Monday on its way to Auckland. The return fare from Samoa is around 645ST.

In Alofi you should reconfirm your tickets with Peleni's Travel Agency. The Christmas/New Year period gets very busy – in January 2003 dozens of passengers were stranded on Niue for weeks – so book well ahead.

Departure taxes are $25 per passenger 12 years and over.

For further details on airlines see the Getting There & Away chapter at the start of the book.

SEA

There are no passenger ships servicing Niue. Many yachts turn up between April and December, when there is no risk of cyclones. Visiting yachties should note that it's preferable to arrive on weekdays. There is no accessible pier or wharf at Niue but moorings are available at a cost of NZ$5/10 per day for a small/large yacht.

The **Niue Yacht Club** *(*☎ *4052;* ⓦ *www.niue island.com/yachting.html)* can give useful information to yachties.

Yachties are also subject to the NZ$25 departure tax.

Getting Around

AIR

Hanan International, Niue's airport, is about 2km southeast of the centre of Alofi. There are taxis at the airport for the twice-weekly flights; the fare to anywhere is around NZ$5. Most accommodation places on the island will collect you from the airport, many for free.

CAR & MOTORCYCLE

Niue has more than 100km of paved road but no public transport. A variety of vehicles can be rented from **Alofi Rentals** *(*☎*/fax 4017;* ⓔ *alofirentals@niue.nu)* and **Niue Rentals** *(*☎ *4216;* ⓔ *niuerentals@niue.nu).* Usually there are plenty of vehicles available but it may be wise to make advance reservations.

Car rental is around NZ$55 per day, motorcycles NZ$25 and mountain bikes NZ$10. Minibuses are also available, from NZ$65 per day. They're all cheaper by the week.

The roads are uncrowded and the driving is conservative. Driving is on the left-hand side of the road and the speed limit is 40km/h in town and 60km/h out of town. Visitors must present their driving licence to the police in Alofi to obtain a local licence for NZ$2.

HITCHING

Hitching is relatively easy, although traffic is light, particularly on the east coast.

LOCAL TRANSPORT
Taxi

There are a number of taxis around town, including **Mitaki Taxis** *(*☎ *4084)* and **Alofi Rentals** *(*☎ *4017, 1107).*

ORGANISED TOURS

Island Hopper Vacations Niue *(*☎ *4307, after hours 4162;* ⓔ *island.hopper.niue@niue .nu)* operates round-the-island tours, village visits, walking tours, canoe trips and the like. All tours are NZ$35 per person. **Tapeu Fisheries** *(*☎ *4106)* does glass-bottom-boat trips. **Herman Tagaloailuga** *(*☎ *3106)* is an expert on shells who leads reef walks, and **Tamafai Fuhiniu** *(*☎ *1193)* is a canoe maker who will tell you all about traditional Niuean *vaka* (canoes) and take you out on one.

The Ulupaka and Anatoloa Caves are on the family land of **Tali Magatogia** *(*☎ *4381)* and he does tours to either or both caves. Wear old clothes, as you will get pretty dirty. The Ulupaka Cave trip takes about 1½ hours and includes a squeeze through the 'keyhole'; the Anatoloa trip is slightly shorter. Both caves have spectacular stalagmites and stalactites. The tours cost around NZ$40/20 per adult/child under 15, including lunch and safety gear.

Misa, a friendly Niuean and well-known Pacific ecotourism identity, does **forest nature walks** *(*☎ *4381)* for NZ$35 for adults (children 16 and under pay one dollar per year of age). In a couple of hours' in the island's dense forests, you will learn to identify different plants and trees, see how to construct an *uga* (coconut crab) trap, hear about traditional ways of catching fruit doves and starlings (you need 15 to 20 for a square meal!) and find out about Misa's childhood in the forest. All tours require a minimum of two people.

NIUE

Around Niue

ALOFI
pop 582

Alofi consists of one street stretching for several kilometres along the coast. Right by the airport turn-off is the **Huanaki Cultural Centre & Museum** (admission by donation; open 9am-4pm Mon-Fri), with interesting displays on the island's history and traditional life.

The **Opaahi Landing**, in the middle of Alofi, is the best known place where James Cook tried, unsuccessfully, to come ashore in 1774. Alofi has several other traditional canoe landing spots; opposite the police station the **Utuko sea track** leads down to a handkerchief-sized beach. In north Alofi the **Omahi sea track** leads to a point where you can swim outside the reef if conditions are suitable.

Towards the northern end of town the **Ekalesia Church** is on Tomb Point, opposite the Commercial Centre, overlooking the island wharf. Headstones outside the church mark the graves of two island kings, Tuitoga (pronounced 'tui tonga'; r. 1876–87) and Fataaiki (r. 1888–96). These two kings were actually elected. Fataaiki was only a part-time king, reckoning his other job as a schoolteacher was more important.

The grave of NZ Resident Commissioner Hector Larsen is here. He was murdered in his bed by escaped prisoners in 1953 (there wasn't another murder on Niue until 2000), a time when the island was in turmoil over proposals to allow cargo ships to be unloaded on Sunday and other changes to long-held traditions.

Ships anchor offshore from the wharf and even containers are wrestled ashore by barge. Opposite the wharf area there's a **war memorial**, beside which are two vertical stone slabs that were the seats used for the coronations of Tuitoga and Fataaiki.

AROUND THE ISLAND

Almost all of the island's attractions are on the coast and getting to them may involve a bit of scrambling or walking. It's 60km right round the island on the coast road; the destinations and distances listed here are in a clockwise direction from the junction by the police station in the middle of Alofi. On the east coast, between Lakepa in the northeast and Vaiea in the southwest, there's about 15km of unsealed road. Cyclists intent on making the complete trip around the island should start early and carry plenty of fluids.

All around Niue you'll see signs to 'sea tracks' leading down to canoe landings on the coast. Some of the landings are floodlit at night, when much of the fishing takes place.

Avaiki Cave (7km) is clearly signposted from the road; a path leads down through a narrow gorge to an impressive coastal cavern sheltering a beautiful rock pool filled with crystal-clear water, just to the north of where

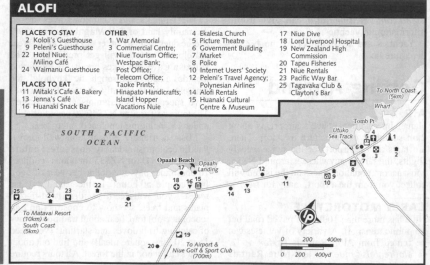

ALOFI

PLACES TO STAY
2 Kololi's Guesthouse
9 Peleni's Guesthouse
22 Hotel Niue;
   Milino Café
24 Waimanu Guesthouse

PLACES TO EAT
11 Mitaki's Cafe & Bakery
13 Jenna's Café
16 Huanaki Snack Bar

OTHER
1 War Memorial
3 Commercial Centre;
   Niue Tourism Office;
   Westpac Bank;
   Post Office;
   Telecom Office;
   Taoke Prints;
   Hinapato Handicrafts;
   Island Hopper
   Vacations Nuie

4 Ekalesia Church
5 Picture Theatre
6 Government Building
7 Market
8 Police
10 Internet Users' Society
12 Peleni's Travel Agency;
   Polynesian Airlines
14 Alofi Rentals
15 Huanaki Cultural
   Centre & Museum

17 Niue Dive
18 Lord Liverpool Hospital
19 New Zealand High
   Commission
20 Tapeu Fisheries
21 Niue Rentals
23 Pacific Way Bar
25 Tagavaka Club &
   Clayton's Bar

the trail emerges on the coast. Swimming in the pool is forbidden on Sunday and when the *kaloama* spawn. Legends relate that the first canoe bringing Niuean settlers to the island landed here. Only 200m further on is **Palaha Cave**, with stalagmites and stalactites.

Probably the finest (and longest) stretch of sand on the island, **Hio Beach** (9.9km), is reached by a wooden stairway down the cliffside. At low tide you can walk across the reef about 100m north to an idyllic snorkelling pool. The winding chasm is full of tropical fish, and is fringed with coral; it features not only small overhangs and caves but two swim-throughs. This is snorkelling at its finest.

At one of the island's most popular swimming and snorkelling spots, fresh water percolates into the **Limu Pools** (10.5km), creating an out-of-focus effect and making the water noticeably cooler than the sea, particularly at low tide. As well as colourful fish, you may also see black-and-grey-striped sea kraits in the pools. The second pool is just to the north, with a natural bridge between it and the sea. Just offshore is **Ana Mahaga**, one of the island's most spectacular scuba diving spots.

At 11.7km from Alofi, a turn-off in Hikutavake village leads to two attractions. Take the right fork first for the 15-minute walk (approximately 1km) to the **Talava Arches**, a series of huge arches and deep caves. You can only reach the main cavern at low tide, and a torch can be useful. Just five minutes down the left fork trail enjoy a refreshing dip in the **Matapa Chasm** (the favourite swimming spot of Niue's kings of yesteryear). This narrow channel, running straight out to the sea, is blocked off and almost sealed by a rock formation.

The sea track at **Mutalau** (18.6km) leads down to the **Uluvehi Landing**, passing a display panel recounting the dramatic events of Christianity's arrival on Niue.

The **Anatoloa Cave** (23.6km), just before the village of **Lakepa** (24.7km), and the **Ulupaka Cave** (25.9km), just after the village, are extensive limestone cave systems complete with stalactites and stalagmites. They're on private property and you can only visit them with Tali's Tours (see Organised Tours under Getting Around earlier).

From the seaward side of the village green in **Liku** (30km) a drivable sea track runs down to the sea, where there are several pretty little beaches but nowhere to swim, except some small rock pools at low tide.

The trail to the **Vaikona Chasm** (33.7km) is not always distinct, but it's marked with red trail arrows, so it's easy to follow, as long as you pay attention. A 20-minute walk (1km) through shady forest drops down through a maze of paths through dead coral pinnacles, suddenly bringing you up beside a huge hole in the ground. Way below is the chasm. The trail continues round to the other side of the chasm where a sign warns you, in no uncertain terms, that the cave leading to the chasm is unsafe and you enter at your own risk.

If you decide to take the risk it's a relatively easy clamber down through the sloping cave to orange ropes leading to the chasm floor. There's a small freshwater pool at this end of the chasm but a little further in is a much larger pool. Green ferns contrast with the brilliant blue of the water and high above there's an oval of sky fringed with green. It's a magical place and if you swim to the end of the long pool and dive under the wall you will come up in a large, dark cave. Making one dive into the dark is scary enough, but for the truly brave it's said that there's an ongoing series of caves beyond the first. A mask and snorkel and an underwater light are required.

After leaving the chasm you can walk on to the coast, but take care – the red arrows stop. It's advisable to mark where you emerge on the cliffs, as the scenery looks remarkably similar. The trail is difficult to find and clambering over razor-sharp, crumbling limestone rocks and beating your way through the tangled vegetation is seriously unpleasant. A local guide is recommended for this walk.

The **Togo Chasm** (36.5km; pronounced 'tong-oh') is easy to find. The trail is well kept and the 20-minute walk through the forest is followed by a sharp descent through a jagged forest of threatening pinnacles. A long ladder takes you down to a picturesque little oasis – a sandy-floored ravine with palm trees. Unfortunately, this postcard-perfect beach isn't on the sea. The far end of the ravine is cut off by a pool of stagnant water. If you make your way behind the boulders at the ladder end, a cave leads through to the sea, where waves crash onto the rocks at the entrance. Back at the top of the ladder, continue a few steps to the cliff edge, where you can look down into the chasm, the sea cave or along the dramatic coastline.

At the village of **Hakupu** (40.7km), the drivable sea track takes you to within a few minutes' walk of the **Anapala Chasm**. A long flight of steps descends between the narrow ravine walls to a long freshwater rock pool, traditionally used as a water source in times of drought.

NIUE

Turn towards the coast at **Vaiea** (45.6km) and take the marked Vaiea sea track to the site of the deserted village of **Fatiau Tuai**. After a short distance the road forks; take the right fork – the village was located at the next fork in the road. Take the left fork from the village site to reach the rugged coastline. The villagers were relocated to Vaiea in the 1950s and there are only scattered remains of the old settlement.

The road drops steeply to the village of **Avatele** (pronounced 'avasele'; 48.6km) where there's a pretty, but rocky, little beach on a sheltered bay. The new **Washaway Café** overlooking the beach is a great spot for a drink. You can also try out kayaking here. There are some popular dive sites just off-shore from the bay, including one of Niue's best, Snake Gully. Just beyond Avatele is the **Matavai Resort** (50.4km) and the village of **Tamakautoga** (51km), with a small beach at the end of the sea track and another dive site.

The final attraction before completing the circuit is the **Anaana Lookout** (54.3km), with stirring views back along the rocky and rugged coastline towards Tepa Point, just beyond Avatele.

NIUE'S REEFS

Niue is a single island, but there are also three reefs in its waters. **Beveridge Reef** is 300km southeast of Niue, and the huge horseshoe-shaped reef has a 5km sandpit on its northwest side. There's also a wreck of an old tuna-fishing boat, washed high and dry on the east side of the reef. There's scuba diving in the reef pass, which is wide enough to allow boats to sail into the deep and open lagoon.

The other reefs are **Antiope** and **Haran**.

PLACES TO STAY

Apart from the Hotel Niue and the Matavai Resort, accommodation generally includes kitchen facilities – shared in the cheaper places – and laundry facilities. They all have their own email addresses, though they may only be checked irregularly.

Huvalu Forest Camp is the only real back-packer accommodation on Niue. It's a long way from anywhere, on the remote eastern side of the island, just south of the trail to the Togo Beach. There are rather basic cooking and bathroom facilities. You can camp here or use the bunkroom; budget for NZ$10 to $15 a night. Book through the Niue Tourism Office (☎ 4224, W www.niueisland.com).

Waimanu Guesthouse (☎ 4366, fax 4225; e akipulu@niue.nu; singles/doubles NZ$40/ 55, larger room NZ$65, units NZ$80) is at the southern end of Alofi, perched on the cliff edge and close to the Amanau sea track, leading down to a natural pool inside the reef. There are four rooms with shared facilities. There's a larger room with an attached bathroom and two self-contained units with kitchen facilities.

Kololi's Guesthouse (☎ 4258, fax 4290; e rupina@niue.nu; standard/large doubles NZ$38/45, doubles with bathroom NZ$60, 2-bedroom unit NZ$95) is centrally located but set back from the main road. There are four rooms with shared bathroom. Three of them are twin rooms, one is a double room. Upstairs there's a room with a bathroom and an adjoining smaller bedroom. A new two-bedroom unit is also available. There's a communal kitchen, laundry and lounge room with TV.

Peleni's Guesthouse (☎ 4153, fax 4322; e tokes@niue.nu; singles/twins/triples NZ$30/ 40/54), in the centre, is slightly back from the road, opposite the gym. There are three rooms with shared bathroom, kitchen and laundry. Two rooms have two single beds and the third has a double and two singles.

Heading up the coast north from Alofi are three small places.

Coral Gardens Motel (☎ 4235, fax 4237; W www.coralgardens.nu; singles/doubles NZ$80) is 5km north of Alofi and has five pleasant separate fale (thatched-roof building) each with an attached bathroom, a small kitchen, ceiling fan, TV and veranda. There's a bar on the cliff edge. Right in the middle of the grounds is a spectacular sinkhole with a pool where you can swim (in the right conditions). Steps and a ladder lead down to the waterline. The resort also has a fine sunset-view-deck at the Makapu Point lookout.

Anaiki Motel (☎ 4321, fax 4224; e anaiki@ niue.nu; singles/doubles/triples/quads NZ$60/ 70/80/90), another 2km from Coral Gardens Resort and adjacent to Avaiki Cave, is a simpler place, with five self-contained units.

Namukulu Motel (☎ 4052, fax 3001; e namu kulu_motel@niue.nu; singles/doubles/triples/ quads NZ$90/125/145/165 high season), 10km from the centre of Alofi, is further up the coast from the Anaiki Motel. There are three very well-designed fale, each with a double room and a couple of single beds in the entrance lounge area. The huts also have a bathroom, kitchen, ceiling fan and veranda and there's an attractive swimming pool. Rates are NZ$20 to NZ$30 lower in the wet season (November to April). A two-bedroom house just down the road can accommodate six. Internet services and car rentals are available.

Top of the heap are Niue's two larger scale resorts.

Hotel Niue *(☎ 4091, fax 4372; e niuehotel@ niue.nu; singles from NZ$75, doubles from NZ$95, family rooms from NZ$140, honeymoon suite from NZ$145)* in Alofi's south seems to have emerged from a period of uncertainty and has recast itself as an upmarket resort offering a Niuean cultural experience. It has traditional *fale* along the cliff edge, a rock pool, Niuean Island Nights, 'make your own *umu*' days and traditional canoe trips. There's modern resort conveniences, like a licensed bar and the new Milino Café restaurant.

Matavai Resort *(☎ 4360, fax 4361; e mata vai@niue.nu; singles/doubles NZ$180/220, suites with air-con NZ$225/280)* is 10km south of Alofi between Tamakautoga and Avatele. The rooms all have a bathroom, fridge, TV, ceiling fan, veranda, ISD phone and access to the guest laundry. There's a restaurant, two bars and two swimming pools spectacularly perched on the cliff edge, with a path leading down to the reef. Use of mountain bikes, golf clubs and tennis rackets is free.

PLACES TO EAT

Self-caterers arriving on the Friday flight from Auckland can get basic supplies in grocery shops on Saturday. Don't bring fresh food, as it may be subject to quarantine regulations. The weekly market on Friday morning has decent produce if you get there very early. Around the island most villages have a small shop, although you may need to ask where it is.

If you're eating out, booking ahead is strongly recommended, though at lunch time, when various places open during the noon to 1.30pm peak period, there's no problem.

Huanaki Snack Bar *(☎ 4071)* is in the Huanaki Cultural Centre & Museum compound. It serves a variety of burgers at around NZ$4.50, sandwiches at NZ$2.50, and other light meals.

Mitaki's Cafe & Bakery features fish, pies, sausages and the like, all with chips. It is open late on Saturday and also bakes bread.

There are several fast food places in the stores at the Commercial Centre.

Jenna's Café *(☎ 4316; snacks, meals NZ$5-8; open 9am-2pm Tues-Fri)* offers good lunchtime alternatives to chips, with a range of food from filled rolls to focaccia, pasta and pizzas. On Tuesday night there's an all-you-can-eat buffet dinner with a mix of international and Niuean food for NZ$24.

At night the restaurants at the Matavai Resort and the Hotel Niue's Milino Café are the most reliable. The **Matavai Resort's restaurant** *(mains NZ$18-30; open 7pm-9pm)* does a popular Friday fish-and-chip night (6pm to 8pm, NZ$10) and Saturday Niuean barbecue buffet (from 7.30pm, NZ$18) and is open on Sunday. On other nights its menu features main courses, good food and very substantial serves. The Hotel Niue's **Milino Café** serves a range of Niuean and European food and is open daily; nonguests are welcome.

Located in the southeast, **Island Style Bar & Restaurant** *(☎ 4379, 1223; mains NZ$25-30)*, between Avatele and Vaiea, opens Friday and Saturday for Niuean buffet-style dinners.

Israel Mart *(☎ 3844)* is a general store and ice-cream parlour on the edge of Avatele village. It's a popular hang-out on Sunday, when it's open all day.

Hakupu village puts on a regular **fiafia (dance) night** *(☎ 4381 or contact Niue Tourism Office for information)*, usually on Wednesday, if a minimum of 10 people book. The cost per person is NZ$35 including transport. There's a delicious selection of Niuean dishes cooked *umu*-style (in an underground oven). A traditional welcome by the village women, music and dances accompany the food. *Ota* (raw fish marinated in coconut milk and lime juice) and *uga* are island specialities.

Washaway Café *(☎ 3822; meals NZ$8-15)* on Avatele Beach is a fantastic, friendly place and one of the world's few 'self-help' bars: at the end of the night, you tell the owner how much you've drunk and pay accordingly. The food's popular too – visitors can even do a turn as guest chef. It's open Thursday to Sunday and closes when the last person leaves.

ENTERTAINMENT

New Zealand beers are NZ$2 or $2.50 a can at island bars.

Pacific Way Bar, next to the Waimanu Guesthouse on the south side of Alofi, and the **Tagavaka Club & Clayton's Bar**, a stone's throw further south, are the popular local bars.

Top Club, at the Niue Golf & Sports Club golf course, welcomes visitors.

You can also get a beer at the **Hotel Niue** in Alofi, the **Coral Gardens** motel in the north and the **Matavai Resort**, **Washaway Café** and **Island Style Bar & Restaurant** to the south. Friday and Saturday nights are dance nights.

The cinema, opposite the Commercial Centre, shows fairly current films for NZ$5.

NIUE

Pitcairn Island

Tiny Pitcairn Island, beautifully green and lush with a population you could easily seat in a city bus, is most famous as the hideaway settlement for the notorious *Bounty* mutineers. Now, over 200 years later, it is one of the last remnants of the British Empire. The viability of the island's population is now in jeopardy following multiple charges against nine male islanders in Pitcairn's child-sex trials of 2003 (some charges date back 40 years). Included in the Pitcairn group of islands are two low-lying atolls, Oeno and Ducie, and the World Heritage–listed Henderson Island, a *makatea* (raised coral island) with a virtually untouched environment and endemic birdlife.

Facts about Pitcairn Island

HISTORY

The islands of the Pitcairn group have always had a close connection with Mangareva in the Gambier Archipelago (French Polynesia), and, at one time, a Polynesian trading triangle operated between Mangareva, Pitcairn and Henderson. Mangareva's lagoon had abundant supplies of black-lipped pearl oyster shells, which made fine scrapers or scoops and could be cut to make fish hooks. Pitcairn had the only quarry in this part of Polynesia where flakes could be taken off the sharp-edged stones to make adzes and other cutting tools. Inhospitable Henderson Island's small population supplied red tropicbird feathers, green turtles and other 'luxury' goods.

Overpopulation devastated Mangareva, deforestation removed the trees used for making the great seagoing canoes and, in a classic ecological disaster, the downfall of Mangareva led to the abandonment of both Henderson and Pitcairn.

In 1606, when the explorer Pedro Fernández de Quirós chanced upon Henderson Island, the island was uninhabited and presumably Pitcairn Island had also been evacuated.

The four Pitcairn Islands would probably have been annexed by the French along with the Tuamotu and Gambier islands were it not for the British settlement. Henderson, Oeno

At a Glance

Capital City (& Island): Adamstown (Pitcairn)

Population: 45

Time: 8½ hours behind GMT

Land Area: 43 sq km (17 sq miles)

Number of Islands: Four

Telephone No: ☎ 872-76233-7766

GDP/Capita: Not applicable

Currency: NZ dollar (NZ$1 = US$0.59)

Languages: English & Pitcairn English

Greeting: Hello

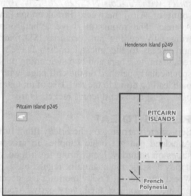

Highlights

• **Pitcairn Island** – reminders of the island's *Bounty* history and the *Bounty* models for sale, carved by a mutineer's descendant

• **Ducie Atoll** – a beautiful lagoon with an amazing collection of flotsam on the beach

• **Henderson Island** – the classic *makatea* geology of the island, and its four endemic bird species

• **Polynesian petroglyphs** – Pitcairn's pre-European history is carved into the rocks at Down Rope

and Ducie were annexed in 1902 and appropriate signs were erected on each of these uninhabited islands. For further information about Pitcairn's history see the History section later.

PITCAIRN ISLANDS

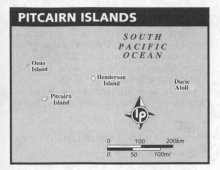

GEOGRAPHY & GEOLOGY

The four islands of the Pitcairn group, essentially outliers of the Tuamotu and Gambier islands of French Polynesia, comprise 43 sq km of land scattered over a vast tract of ocean; it's more than 500km from Oeno in the west to Ducie in the east. Tiny Pitcairn is a high island – the tip of a mountain rising out of the sea – with an intermittent fringing reef. Oeno and Ducie are classic atolls, a scatter of low-lying sandy islets on a coral reef fringing a central lagoon. Henderson, the largest island in the group, is a *makatea* island, an ancient coral reef pushed up above sea level by geological forces.

Pitcairn lies 2100km east of Easter Island, or some 5350km northwest of New Zealand. The nearest inhabited island is Mangareva in French Polynesia.

CLIMATE

Pitcairn's climate is mild and equable with mean monthly temperatures varying from 19°C in August to 24°C in February. The lowest temperature ever recorded is 10°C; the highest 34°C. Annual rainfall (around 1800mm) is spread fairly evenly, although July and August are usually the driest months and November the wettest.

ECONOMY

Although the islanders are essentially self-sufficient for food they have become used to many imported goods. Fuel is needed for their motorcycles, for outboard motors and for the island's electricity generator. Island homes are typically equipped with all the usual electrical gadgets.

Some islanders hold government jobs, though most income derives from selling the island's famous stamps to collectors, or selling curios to passing ships (sometimes by mail order). From time to time the British government funds major infrastructure projects such as apiculture (bee-keeping). Dehydrated fruits and honey are exported worldwide, and domain names ending in Pitcairn's '.pn' suffix are also for sale.

POPULATION & PEOPLE

The population of Pitcairn is around 50 although there are many more Pitcairners resident overseas. There are major concerns that the island cannot maintain a viable population and may eventually be deserted. The people of Pitcairn are descendants of the original *Bounty* mutineers and their Tahitian companions, plus other arrivals over the years. The *Bounty* family names, Adams, Young and Christian, are still common.

RELIGION

In 1887, a Seventh-Day Adventist missionary from the US converted the whole island, so Saturday is observed as the Sabbath, alcohol is ostensibly banned (that ban seems to be slipping) and the islanders are not supposed to eat pork (that ban can be a bit loose as well) or fish that do not have scales (the islands supply of lobsters are used for bait!). Interest in religion has been declining in recent years.

LANGUAGE

Pitcairners communicate quite happily in English but among themselves lapse into Pitkern (18th-century seafaring English spiced with Polynesian words). So when Pitcairners go out to shoot goats they do it with *muskets*, the goats end up as *wekle* (victuals) and houses have a *deck*.

Facts for the Visitor

VISAS

No visa is necessary for visitors while their ship is present. If you want to stay on Pitcairn after your ship leaves, however, your stay must be approved by the islanders and a six-month stay permit issued.

Visa applications are processed by the **Pitcairn Islands Administration** (☎ 64-9-366 0186, fax 366 0187; ✉ pitcairn@iconz.co.nz; postal address: Private Box 105 696, Auckland, NZ). Think up a good reason for your stay and allow six months for the application to be considered. The application fee is NZ$10, and the licence itself NZ$150 (NZ$75 for visitors under 18).

MONEY

New Zealand dollars (see Exchange Rates in the Rarotonga & Cook Islands chapter) are the official currency of Pitcairn Island although other major currencies will be happily accepted. Personal cheques and travellers cheques can be cashed at the Island Secretary's office.

Budget on at least NZ$300 per week.

POST & COMMUNICATIONS

You can phone or fax Pitcairn Island through Inmarsat, but the charges are based on satellite time so you get billed for dialling and connection times whether or not the phone is answered. Count on about NZ$15 a minute.

You can expect the **control room phone** (☎ 872-76233-7765) to be answered between 1730 and 0500 GMT, or use the answering machine. The public telephone number is ☎ 872-76233-7766; the fax number is 7767.

To write to anybody on Pitcairn Island, address mail to: the resident's name, Pitcairn Island, South Pacific Ocean (via NZ) – count on about three months each way. A number of Pitcairners are ham radio amateurs.

DIGITAL RESOURCES

For further information on Pitcairn, try the following websites:

Pitcairn Island (W www.lareau.org/pitc.html) With information, history, genealogy, virtual shopping, and links to articles
Pitcairn Islands Government (W www .government.pn) With Pitcairn's history, Philatelic Bureau and 'A Guide to Pitcairn' order form
Pitcairn Islands Study Centre (W http: //library.puc.edu/pitcairn) With shipping schedules and Pitcairn history

For information on World Heritage–listed Henderson Island, visit W www.winthrop.dk /hender.html and W whc.unesco.org/sites /487.htm.

BOOKS

The *Guide to Pitcairn* (2000) is the official government publication about the islands. It's available from the Pitcairn Islands Administration (see under Visas earlier) for NZ$22 or via the Pitcairn Islands Government website.

Dea Birkett's *Serpent in Paradise* (1997) is a contentious account of the author's three-month stay on Pitcairn in 1991. After its publication, a Fletcher Christian descendant

commented, 'It's not quite a fatwa, but she's not welcome (on Pitcairn)'.

The Pitcairn Miscellany is the island's monthly newsletter. Overseas subscriptions are available by writing to: the Editor, *Pitcairn Miscellany*, South Pacific (via NZ). Annual subscriptions are NZ$10.

Further titles are listed in the boxed text 'Mutiny on the Bounty' later in this chapter.

TIME

Pitcairn is 8½ hours behind GMT (9½ hours during daylight saving).

Getting There & Away

Cargo vessels stopping at Pitcairn usually do not anchor, but pause to transfer cargo or passengers to longboats. The standard fare from Auckland to Pitcairn is around US$800 to US$1000 one way per person, though there are no longer any regular carriers. For schedules of Panama Canal–Auckland cargo ships that will take passengers, contact the British Consulate-General in Auckland, New Zealand, or the shipping companies; schedules are posted on the Pitcairn Islands Study Centre website. Getting off the island requires waiting until a ship comes by – it can be a long wait.

Mangareva is the best place to try your luck for a Pitcairn-bound yacht. Visiting yachties should come equipped – Pitcairners are happy to sell fresh fruit, which they grow on the island, but other supplies generally have to be imported from New Zealand and may be in short supply. There is no sheltered anchorage at Pitcairn and boats must be moved when the winds change.

Landings on Pitcairn are notoriously difficult; it's not unknown to travel all the way to the island and then be unable to set foot on land due to rough seas.

Pitcairn Island

pop 50 • area 5 sq km
Pitcairn Island is so tied up with the *Bounty* story that it's easy to overlook the fact that although it was uninhabited when the *Bounty* mutineers showed up in January 1790 it had, in the past, been settled by Polynesians. The small, green and fertile island rises precipitously from the surrounding sea.

PITCAIRN ISLAND

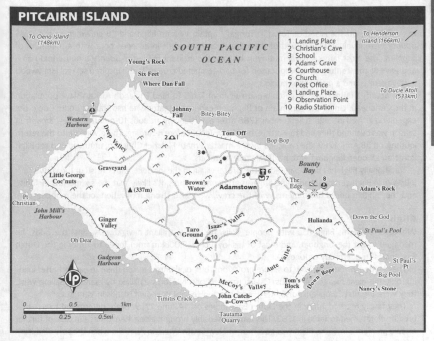

To Oeno Island (148km)

SOUTH PACIFIC OCEAN

To Henderson Island (166km)

1 Landing Place
2 Christian's Cave
3 School
4 Adams' Grave
5 Courthouse
6 Church
7 Post Office
8 Landing Place
9 Observation Point
10 Radio Station

To Ducie Atoll (533km)

Young's Rock
Six Feet
Where Dan Fall

Western Harbour

Deep Valley

Johnny Fall   Bitey-Bitey

Tom Off

Bop Bop

Graveyard

Little George Coc'nuts

▲ (337m)

Brown's Water

Adamstown

Bounty Bay

The Edge

Adam's Rock

Pt Christian

John Mill's Harbour

Ginger Valley

Oh Dear

Taro Ground

Isaac's Valley

Hulianda

Down the God

St Paul's Pool

Gudgeon Harbour

Aute Valley

Down Rope

St Paul's Pt

Big Pool

McCoy's Valley

Tom's Block

Nancy's Stone

Timitis Crack

John Catch-a-Cow

Tautama Quarry

0   0.5   1km
0   0.25   0.5mi

The island's curious array of place names confront the visitor immediately on arrival at the Bounty Bay landing. The accurately named Hill of Difficulty is the steep trail that leads up to Adamstown, perched 120m above the sea on the Edge. Houses in Adamstown are either 'upside' or 'downside' of the main road through the small settlement.

The island's power generator is turned on for nine hours per day. The island has a primary school but children move to NZ for secondary schooling.

HISTORY

It is believed there was a Polynesian settlement on the island between the 12th and 15th centuries, and perhaps an earlier settlement as long as 2000 years before. As the mutineers were to prove, small though it was, Pitcairn provided all the basic necessities of life.

In 1767, Philip Cartaret sailed by on HMS *Swallow* and named Pitcairn Island after Major Pitcairn of the marines. Finding it was one thing – they were unable to land and Cartaret's mischarting of the island by 300km made relocating it a problem.

In January 1790 the *Bounty* mutineers arrived at Pitcairn after a long search for a remote hideaway, far from the long arm of British naval justice. Led by Fletcher Christian the party was made up of eight other mutineers, six Tahitian men, 12 Tahitian women and a child. Once settled on the island the *Bounty* was burnt, both to prevent escape and to escape detection. The first years of the island's post-*Bounty* history saw a disastrous sequence of violence due to the English mutineers' condescending treatment of the Tahitians and the imbalance in male and female numbers. When a mutineer's partner died in a fall and he demanded that one of the Tahitians give up his wife, a cycle of murder and revenge commenced during which all six Tahitian men and five of the nine mutineers, including Fletcher Christian, were killed by 1794. Only Young, Adams, Quintal and McCoy survived.

A few peaceful years followed before McCoy discovered how to produce a killer spirit from the roots of the *ti* plant. By 1799, under the influence of the drink, McCoy had thrown himself into the sea with a rock tied around his neck and Quintal had become so crazed under the drink's influence that Adams and Young had killed him in self-defence. A year later Young died of asthma,

Mutiny on the Bounty

In April 1789, off the island of Tofua in Tonga, Captain William Bligh and 18 crewmen of the HMS *Bounty* were involuntarily relieved of their duties and set adrift in an open boat with a minimum of supplies. The most famous naval mutiny in history, the incident made the *Bounty* a household name and gave Bligh a centuries-long reputation for bad-tempered cruelty. It also inspired several Hollywood extravaganzas and a plethora of books.

The *Bounty's* mission was to fetch breadfruit from Tahiti to feed England's African slave population in the Caribbean. Under the command of Bligh, an expert navigator who had trained under Cook, the expedition arrived in Tahiti in September 1788 after a particularly arduous 10-month journey. Breadfruit season was over and they had to wait six months in Tahiti before returning. Three weeks into the return journey, on 28 April 1789, the crew, led by the master's mate Fletcher Christian, mutinied and set Bligh adrift on an open longboat with his loyal crew members.

Traditionally Bligh has been painted as the brutal villain in the incident, with Christian the crew's saviour. While Bligh certainly had some anger-management issues, it's likely that the six months in Tahiti, and the Tahitian brides taken by many of the crew, were also strong motivation for the mutineers.

Bligh

Whatever problems Bligh had with people skills, he was a brilliant navigator. Against the odds, he managed to get the longboat, and most of his loyal crew, 7000km from Tonga to Timor in the Dutch East Indies (modern-day Indonesia).

They landed in Tonga, hoping to secure provisions, but local unrest forced them to cast off after loading only the most meagre of rations. Quartermaster John Norton was killed by islanders. Sailing west, they were the first Europeans to sight Fiji, and charted several unknown islands in Vanuatu.

They finally reached Timor in the Dutch East Indies on 14 June 1789. Bligh, determined to get that breadfruit, returned to Tahiti in 1792. This time he sensibly brought along 19 marines – in case of further morale problems. In 1806, Bligh was governor of New South Wales in Australia when the so-called 'rum rebellion' overturned his government. Bligh was exonerated from blame – again.

The Mutineers

Under Christian's command the mutineers returned to Tahiti, then attempted to settle on Tubai in the Austral Islands. Meeting local resistance, they split into two groups: Fletcher taking a group of sailors and Tahitians off in search of Pitcairn Island, and a second group of 16 sailors staying behind on Tahiti.

leaving John Adams as the sole survivor of the 15 men who had arrived 10 years earlier.

This left Adams with 10 women, 23 children and his recent discovery of religion. Adamstown was a neat little settlement of God-fearing Christians when Captain Mayhew Folger of the American sealing ship *Topaz* rediscovered Pitcairn Island, solving the 19-year mystery of what had happened to Christian and the *Bounty* after the mutiny. By this time British attention was focused on the struggle with Napoleon and there was no interest in a mutineer, guilty of a crime that was now nearly 30 years old. The next visitors, the British ships HMS *Briton* and *Targus* in 1814, arrived unaware of Folger's earlier visit but also decided there was no point in taking any action against the lone mutineer.

Ship visits became more frequent, and by the time Adams died in 1829 there was

concern that the island would become over-populated.

In 1831 the British government relocated the islanders to Tahiti, but within months 10 of the Pitcairners, lacking immunity to a variety of diseases, had died – including Thursday October Christian, the son of Fletcher Christian and the first child to be born on Pitcairn. By the year's end the 65 survivors were all back on Pitcairn. The island became a British colony in 1838, but when the population grew beyond 150 there were fears of overpopulation. In 1856 the entire population, then numbering 194, was moved to Norfolk Island, an uninhabited former Australian prison-island between Australia and New Zealand. Not all the settlers were content with their well-equipped new home and, in 1858, 16 returned to Pitcairn, just in time to prevent the French annexing it to their

Mutiny on the Bounty

The Pursuit

After Bligh returned to England, Captain Edward Edwards (a tyrant who made Bligh look like a saint) was sent in the *Pandora* to search for the mutineers.

Edwards sailed past Ducie Island in the Pitcairn Islands group, but didn't see the larger island 470km to the west where Christian's small troupe had settled. However, Edwards did find and capture 14 of the 16 mutineers who had remained on Tahiti. He stuffed them into a cage on the *Pandora's* deck before heading back for England. Sadly Edward's sailing skills were not up to Bligh's standards. He ended up sinking the *Pandora* on the Great Barrier Reef off Australia. Of the surviving prisoners, three were ultimately hanged for the mutiny.

Books

The American duo of Nordhoff & Hall wrote three books on the *Bounty* mutiny and its aftermath in 1934. The first of the three, *Mutiny on the Bounty*, provided the plotline for the first two Hollywood versions of the story (see later). *Men against the Sea* follows Bligh's epic open-boat voyage, while *Pitcairn Island* follows Fletcher Christian and his band to Pitcairn.

Two other sources are Richard Hough's *Captain Bligh and Mr Christian* (1973) and Greg Dening's *Mr Bligh's Bad Language* (1992).

More recently, *Fragile Paradise*, by Glynn Christian (Fletcher's great-great-great-great-grandson), is a well-researched, if a little speculative, investigation of the mutiny and the story of the mutineers on Pitcairn.

Films

The first, and perhaps worst, film about the mutiny was *In the Wake of the Bounty* (1933) – a low-budget flick filmed in Pitcairn, Tahiti and Australia, memorable only for being Errol Flynn's first film (as a noble Fletcher Christian). Simultaneously, Hollywood was making *Mutiny on the Bounty* (1935) with Clark Gable in the same role – neither film was too concerned with historical accuracy.

The 1962 remake *Mutiny on the Bounty*, starring Marlon Brando as Christian and filmed in Tahiti, was slightly less inaccurate.

The Bounty (1984), based on Hough's book, is a surprisingly good re-enactment of the tale, with magnificent scenes of Moorea in French Polynesia. Anthony Hopkins plays a more likeable and complex Captain Bligh and Mel Gibson plays Fletcher Christian.

Polynesian colony. More families returned in 1864, raising the population to 43.

Right up to the mid-1870s, Pitcairners were followers of the Church of England. However, the arrival of a box of Seventh-Day Adventist literature from the US in 1876 saw the beginnings of change. A decade later, the arrival of a Seventh-Day Adventist missionary heralded real conversion from the teachings of Pastor Simon Young. A mission ship was sent out from the US in 1890 and the happy proselytes were baptised with a dousing in one of the island's rock pools, and its pigs were swiftly killed to remove the temptation of pork.

Although Pitcairn's population grew to 223 just before WWII, depopulation rather than overpopulation has become the major concern. In 1956 the figure was 161, in 1966 it was 96 and in 1976 Pitcairners numbered 74. Since then, the figure has wavered in the 40s and

50s. There are many empty homes and islanders fears that lack of opportunities will finally force the population below a viable level.

The most shattering event to have hit Pitcairn in 200 years started with an investigation in 1999 of allegations against 14 men (including a third of the island's adult population at the time plus several Pitcairn islanders who had moved offshore) on sexual-abuse counts dating back as far as 40 years ago. With Pitcairn's very small local population, the conviction of these men would have the potential to reduce the island's population to the point where the island is no longer viable. A veritable invasion of 12 lawyers and police officers from NZ and the UK arrived in early 2003 to charge the men. (Defence lawyers were welcomed warmly, with invitations to dinner coming thick and fast; prosecution lawyers and police found themselves a lot less popular.)

After the men were charged, proceedings shifted to a small courtroom in Auckland (NZ) which had been made legally part of Pitcairn Island for the purposes of the trial (four of the accused, who were living in Auckland at the time, had to be legally extradited to the Pitcairn courtroom for the trial!). At the time of writing the court case was ongoing.

Contact for the islanders is limited to visiting yachts, cargo ships that can be persuaded to stop and the occasional cruise ship.

THINGS TO SEE

There are many reminders of the island's *Bounty* origins, including Fletcher Christian's **Bounty bible**, kept in a glass case in the church. It was actually sold in 1839, but returned to the island in 1949. The **Bounty anchor**, salvaged by Irving Johnson in 1957, stands between the court house and post office, and there's a **Bounty cannon** further along the road. The anchor from the *Acadia*, wrecked on Ducie Atoll, is displayed on the Edge, overlooking Bounty Bay.

The only **mutineer's grave** is that of John Adams, who changed his name from Alexander Smith, perhaps hoping to avoid arrest if the feared naval squad ever turned up. **Fletcher Christian's cave**, overlooking the settlement, is where the leading mutineer is said to have hidden, either to watch for pursuing ships or to evade the killings that swept the island in the settlements' early years. On 23 January, the *Bounty*'s demise is commemorated by towing a burning model of the ship across Bounty Bay.

Petroglyphs on the rock face at the bottom of Down Rope are reminders of Pitcairn Island's pre-*Bounty* Polynesian habitation. The island's important Polynesian stone quarry is at Tautama, a kilometre west around the coast. When the mutineers arrived there were also *marae* platforms and stone images, which the devoutly Christian mutineers promptly tossed in the sea. The road to Down Rope continues to **St Paul's Point** and **Big Pool**, a beautiful natural pool fed and drained by the sea. Turpin or Mr T, the island's **Galapagos tortoise**, is the survivor of a pair left here by a visiting yacht in the 1940s.

PLACES TO STAY

There's no hotel on the island. **The Lodge**, a small, comfortable cottage, is available as long as it is not occupied by government officials. Visitors are also accommodated with islanders, typically paying about NZ$40/270 per night/week for room and board. The **Island Council** (☎ 872-7612-24115, fax 244116; postal address: Pitcairn Island, South Pacific Ocean, via NZ) will advise with whom accommodation has been arranged when they reply to you about your visitor-licence application.

SHOPPING

The islanders do a busy trade turning out curios for visiting ships. They include woven pandanus bags and a variety of sharks and dolphins carved out of *miro* wood as well as the famous models of the *Bounty*. Honey and Pitcairn Island stamps are also a specialty.

Limited food supplies are available in the Co-op Store, which opens three times a week for a few hours.

GETTING AROUND

Tin, *Tub* and *Moss* are longboats used for transport between Bounty Bay and boats anchored offshore, and for occasional trips to Oeno and Henderson. Three- and four-wheeled fat-tyred motorcycles, or ATVs, are the usual means of transport around the island; Pitcairners rarely walk. The island's six or so kilometres of dirt roads turn to sticky mud when it rains.

Reading the Land

There's a straightforward, down-to-earth approach to everything Pitcairnese and the island's place names are certainly simple, descriptive and rather worrying. Over the years islanders appear to have had a disturbing propensity for falling right off Pitcairn, many of them tumbling down a sheer cliff face while gathering bird eggs, chasing goats or fishing. Heathen idols were found and cast into the sea at Down the God, and the intriguingly named Little George Coc'nuts was a coconut grove owned by George Young, son of mutineer Ned Young. Right in Adamstown you find a spot with the dire name, Where Dick Fall. A little further to the west, below Christian's Cave, the cliffs must be particularly dangerous since the map lists: Where Dan Fall, Johnny Fall and the succinct Tom Off. It's no better on the west coast, Where Warren Fall, or the east coast, Where Freddie Fall. But the south coast has the most enigmatic and worrying warning of all – Oh Dear.

Other Islands

OENO ISLAND
pop 0 • area 1 sq km

Two narrow passages enter Oeno's central lagoon; the outer reef is about 4km across with one larger palm-covered island a few kilometres long on the western side. It points towards a smaller sandbank islet beside the narrow pass through the reef.

Captain James Henderson, who gave his name to Henderson Island, also came across Oeno Island in 1819, but it was an American whaling ship which gave Oeno its name in 1824.

After the *Bowden* was wrecked on Oeno in 1893, the captain and crew made their way to Pitcairn in the ship's boat. The Pitcairn islanders made four salvage trips to the *Bowden*, resulting in one of the islanders contracting typhoid fever from the filthy bilge water. Back on Pitcairn, the infection raced through the islanders, killing 13 people.

Pitcairners occasionally collect pandanus leaves here.

HENDERSON ISLAND
pop 0 • area 36 sq km

This classic example of a *makatea* island 168km east-northeast of Pitcairn is the largest island of the Pitcairn group. At 9.6km long by 5.1km wide, it is nearly eight times as big as Pitcairn itself. The island is believed to have been uplifted by three undersea volcanoes – Adams, Young and Bounty – to the southeast of Pitcairn.

A new fringing reef has grown up around two-thirds of the island's 26km coastline. The sheer 15m-high cliffs are the seaward face of the old coral reef. These run all the way around the island and are difficult to climb. The interior of the island rises to a 30m flatland with a central depression which was once the lagoon inside the old reef. The sharp, crumbling ground in the interior is carpeted with a dense thicket of waist-to-shoulder high *pisonia* brush, and stands of the fine *miro* wood, which Pitcairners occasionally harvest for woodcarving.

The island is populated by Polynesian rats, and four endemic land birds – the flightless Henderson rail, the colourful Stephen's lorikeet, the territorial Henderson fruit dove and the Henderson warbler. Nine seabird species and the occasional green sea turtle nest here.

HENDERSON ISLAND

North Beach • North East Pt
West End Cave
Lone Frigate Cave • Coconut Grove Shelter & Cave
Awahou Pt • Former Beacon
To Pitcairn Island (168km) • Tree area (30m above sea level) • SOUTH PACIFIC OCEAN
0 1.5 3km
0 1 2mi
South Pt

The usual landing spot is the long northeastern beach, which is littered with flotsam and jetsam. During certain tides there may be a freshwater spring in a cave at the north of the island.

Henderson is unusual for a raised atoll in that it has not been dramatically altered by exploitation for phosphate reserves. Because of this unique condition and its rare birdlife, the island was declared a Unesco World Heritage Site in 1988. Visitors require a licence to visit, which is dependent on approval by the Pitcairn Island Council.

History

Polynesians settled on Henderson between the 12th and 15th centuries and there may even have been earlier habitation between around 900 BC and 350 BC. Limited freshwater supplies, lack of soil for agriculture and difficult reef entries made Henderson a difficult place to live.

It was uninhabited when Portuguese explorer Quirós, sailing under the Spanish flag, visited in 1606. The island was rediscovered by the *Bounty* mutineers in 1790, en route to their new home on Pitcairn, and again in 1819 by Captain James Henderson of the British merchant ship *Hercules*.

The wrecking of the whaling ship *Essex* on the island in 1820 to 1821, after a charge by a sperm whale near the Marquesas, is believed to have provided the inspiration for Herman Melville's *Moby Dick*. During the crew's stay on the island, a cave was discovered containing six or eight skeletons. Six skeletons were found in a cave on the northeast coast by a visiting party from Pitcairn in 1958, though it's not known if they were the same skeletons.

A year earlier, Robert Tomarchin, an American, and his chimpanzee Moko made an unannounced six-week visit to the island. In the early 1980s another American, Arthur M 'Smiley' Ratcliffe (or Ratliff), had plans to buy or lease the island, flatten the vegetation, turn it into a cattle ranch and build a home and airstrip. This was a major factor in the island's subsequent World Heritage listing.

Over the years, various investigations into the island's natural history and archaeology have been conducted.

DUCIE ATOLL
pop 0 • area 1 sq km

This classic coral atoll consists of the 100m-wide main *motu* (island), Acadia Island, stretching for over 3km around the lagoon, and three smaller islands. The lagoon is inaccessible, but on its eastern side gentle whirlpools drain water straight out to the open sea. There are no palm trees and the vegetation is limited to just two hardy types. Polynesian rats, lizards and tens of thousands of seabirds inhabit the island.

In 1606, Ducie was discovered and named Encarnacion by Quirós. It was rediscovered by Edward Edwards on the *Pandora* in 1791, during his *Bounty* hunt, and named after his patron, Lord Ducie. After the British *Acadia* was shipwrecked here in 1881, the crew made a nightmare 13-day voyage to Pitcairn in the ship's boat. Two of them married Pitcairners and until recently, Coffin was a familiar Pitcairn family name (from one of those shipwrecked sailors, Phillip Coffin).

The usual landing point on Acadia Island is marked by a memorial, which notes the recovery of the *Acadia's* main anchor in 1990. The wreck of the ship is directly offshore from the **monument** in about 10m of water. A short distance to the west, a marked trail wanders across the island to the lagoon side. An alarming variety of flotsam litters the island, including countless glass bottles, plastic debris and hundreds of fishing-net floats.

Rarotonga & the Cook Islands

As a ukulele player croons welcome songs and a floral *'ei* (necklace) is wrapped around your neck at the airport, the beauty of the Cook Islands begins to reveal itself. The Cook Islands is an excellent destination for beach-potatoes and hardy adventurers alike. The beautiful main island of Rarotonga combines densely forested mountains and superb snorkelling reefs with excellent tourist infrastructure and a range of budget options. Aitutaki, the second-most populated island, rewards the effort required to reach it with one of the most beautiful lagoons in the Pacific. The isolated islands of the northern Cooks receive almost no visitors, except for the occasional delighted yachtie.

Facts about the Cook Islands

HISTORY
Cook Islanders are Polynesians, a Maori people related to the New Zealand (NZ) Maori and the Maohi of the Society Islands in French Polynesia. Historians believe that Polynesian migrations from the Society Islands to the Cook Islands began around the 5th century AD, and oral history traces Rarotongan ancestry back about 1400 years. A *marae* (religious meeting ground) on Motutapu, off the coast of Rarotonga, is estimated to be about 1500 years old. Rarotonga has always been the most influential of the Cooks, and it's assumed that the culture of its early inhabitants was largely duplicated on the other islands.

In the 14th century, canoes departed Rarotonga for Aotearoa (NZ); the settlers became the ancestors of the present-day NZ Maori tribes.

European Explorers
Pukapuka, in the Northern Group of the Cook Islands, was the first island to be sighted by a European (Don Alvaro de Mendaña y Neyra, on 20 August 1595). Eleven years later Pedro Fernández de Quirós stopped at Rakahanga, also in the Northern Group. There is no further record of European contact until 150 years later, when James Cook explored much of the group on his expeditions in 1773 and 1777.

In an atlas published in 1835, the Russian cartographer Admiral Johann von Krusenstern

At a Glance

Capital City (& Island): Avarua (Rarotonga)
Population: 14,000
Time: 10 hours behind GMT
Land Area: 241 sq km (94 sq mi)
Number of Islands: 15
International Telephone Code: ☎ 682
GDP/Capita: US$5060
Currency: New Zealand dollar (NZ$1 = US$0.59)
Languages: Cook Islands Maori & English
Greeting: *Kia orana*

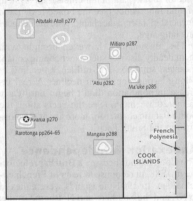

Highlights
- **Aitutaki's lagoon** – turquoise-coloured, with magnificent sand bars and coral ridges, ideal for snorkelling
- **Hiking** – Rarotonga's rugged interior of mountains, streams and valleys
- **Maungapu** – views over Aitutaki and its lagoon, from the island's highest peak
- **'Atiu's caves** – ancient burial sites and the Kopeka Cave, home to a rare species of swallow
- **Swimming** – freshwater pools in *makatea* caves on Ma'uke and Mitiaro
- **Northern Group islands** – gain a true sense of isolation and savour the wide horizon
- **Island nights** – indulge in island fare and watch the mesmerising dancers

251

named the Southern Group islands in honour of Cook. The Northern Group islands were called, among other names, the Penrhyn Islands and the Manihiki Islands.

Missionaries

Reverend John Williams of the London Missionary Society (LMS) first arrived on Aitutaki in 1821. Papeiha, a convert from Ra'iatea in the Society Islands, moved to Rarotonga in 1823, where he laboured for the rest of his life. In that period the missionaries established a religious control that holds strong to this day.

Government of the islands was left to the tribal chiefs and thus the individual islands remained independent political entities. The missionaries did not completely obliterate the island culture, as indicated by the endurance of *ariki* (paramount chiefs), the system of land inheritance (see the boxed text 'Land Ownership' later in the chapter) and the indigenous language.

The missionaries, however, brought with them deadly diseases such as whooping cough, measles, smallpox and influenza, leading to a long-lasting population decline. A real increase in population didn't begin until early in the 20th century. (See the Facts about the South Pacific chapter for more about missionaries in the South Pacific.)

Annexation & Independence

The Cook Islands became a British protectorate in 1888, in response to fears of French colonialism. In 1901 the islands were annexed to NZ and the Southern and Northern Groups together became known as the Cook Islands.

During WWII the USA built airstrips on Penrhyn and Aitutaki, but essentially the Cooks remained forgotten. In 1965 the Cook Islands became internally self-governing, although foreign policy and defence were left to NZ. The Cook Islands is precluded from taking a seat in the United Nations due to its close links with NZ. Islanders, however, gain automatic NZ citizenship.

GEOGRAPHY

The Cook Islands' small land mass (just 241 sq km) is scattered over about two million square kilometres of ocean about midway between American Samoa and Tahiti.

The 15 islands are conveniently divided into the Northern and Southern Groups. The islands in the Southern Group, constituting about 90% of the Cook Islands' total land area, are younger volcanic islands, while the Northern Group

islands are coral atolls that have formed on top of ancient sunken volcanoes (see the boxed text 'Coral Atolls' in the Facts about the South Pacific chapter). Only Rarotonga, the youngest island, is a straightforward volcanic, mountainous island.

Of the Southern Group, 'Atiu, Ma'uke, Mitiaro and Mangaia are 'raised islands'. They have *makatea* – rocky coastal areas made of uplifted coral reefs, surrounding higher central regions of volcanic soil. All the Northern Group islands are low coral atolls, with an outer reef encircling a lagoon.

CLIMATE

The Cook Islands has a pleasant, even climate year-round. Seasonal variations are slight, ranging from high/low temperatures of 29°C/23°C in February to 25°C/18°C from June to September. The wettest and hottest months are in the cyclone season between November and March. On average a mild cyclone will pass by two or three times per decade. Extremely severe cyclones average once every 20 years. Cyclone Martin struck Manihiki in November 1997 (see the Manihiki section later in the chapter for further information).

ECOLOGY & ENVIRONMENT

Waste management is a big issue in the Cook Islands. Glass, plastic and aluminium are collected in special bins for recycling, but there's still a huge amount of rubbish. Fertilisers, animal faeces and soil are washed into streams, causing algal blooms in the confined lagoons and contamination of town water supplies. Water supply is a major concern, especially since droughts have occurred in recent years.

Deforestation, agricultural chemicals and introduced species are all influences that native flora and fauna have had to contend with, and overfishing has affected marine life in some of the islands' lagoons. The Cook Islands Natural Heritage Project is cataloguing the hundreds of species of flora and fauna on the islands and promoting their conservation.

The biggest threat to the Cooks' northern coral atolls is global warming, which may render them uninhabitable within the next 100 years. See the boxed text 'Global Warming' in the Facts about the South Pacific chapter.

FLORA & FAUNA

The ubiquitous coconut palms, and gorgeous flowers that seem to grow with wild abandon almost everywhere, are the most noticeable natural features of the Cook Islands.

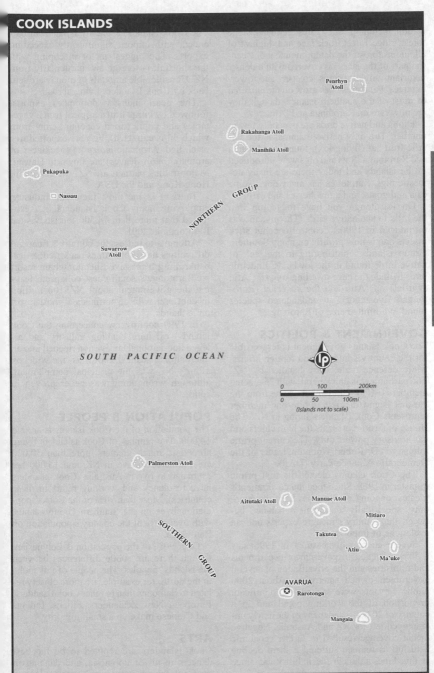

Rarotonga has a wide variety of native vegetation, including valley forest, fernland, slope forest, ridge forest, rock face and, highest of all, cloud forest; the damp, mountainous central part of the island is covered with a dense, luxuriant jungle of ferns, creepers and towering trees. Pandanus trees grow on the *makatea* of most of the southern islands, though they are now rare on Rarotonga and 'Atiu.

Fauna and native birds are generally few in number. The only native mammal is the Pacific fruit bat (flying fox), found on Mangaia and Rarotonga. Rats and pigs were introduced to the islands and today there are many domestic pigs. Rarotonga has many dogs, some cats and goats, and a few horses and cattle.

On Rarotonga you have to get up into the hills to see native birds. The mynah was introduced in 1906 to control coconut stick insects and is now prolific on many Southern Group islands, contributing to the lack of native birds found in the lowlands. Endemic birds include the cave-dwelling *kopeka* ('Atiu swiftlet) on 'Atiu and the *kakerori* (Rarotongan flycatcher), an endangered species found in a limited area of Rarotonga.

GOVERNMENT & POLITICS

The Cook Islands government is responsible for the country's internal and foreign affairs, while defence matters are handled by NZ. The parliament is unicameral, with 25 elected members (MPs): 24 members come from the various island districts, while one member represents Cook Islanders living in NZ. The House of Ariki represents the high chiefs and has advisory powers only. The current prime minister is Dr Robert Woonton, leader of the Democratic Alliance Party (DAP).

The Cook Islands elected its first prime minister in 1968. Since then the government's greatest ongoing problem has been the economy, specifically achieving a balance between the country's meagre exports and an avalanche of imports.

Severe economic measures in 1996 saw a 50% reduction in government departments and ministries and the privatisation of several government-owned enterprises. About 2000 public servants were sacked – a significant proportion of the working population in a country of 20,000 – and many of the newly unemployed left for NZ and Australia. Negative media coverage resulted in further economic hardship as tourism suffered a sharp decline at this time, although the industry has since gradually recovered.

ECONOMY

The Cook Islands' economy is far from balanced, with imports significantly exceeding exports. The biggest factor in coping with the shortfall is foreign aid, particularly from NZ. Considerable amounts of money are sent back by Cook Islanders living abroad.

The pearl industry dominates exports, followed by citrus fruits, tropical fruits, vegetables and copra (dried coconut kernel from which oil is extracted). Fish are exported live or chilled. Aromatic *maire 'ei* (necklaces of aromatic *maire* leaves) are flown to Hawaii. Major trading partners are NZ, Australia, Fiji, Hong Kong and the USA.

Tourism is the most important industry, employing many Cook Islanders; it's estimated that more than 74,500 tourists visited Rarotonga in 2001.

Attempts to redress the country's financial difficulties have sometimes backfired; a deal bankrolling a massive Sheraton-chain resort on Rarotonga's south coast collapsed, leaving the government about NZ$100 million in debt and with an unfinished ghost-resort on its hands.

In 1994 controversy concerning the Cook Islands' offshore banking industry and alleged international tax evasion ripened into an international scandal known as 'the winebox affair'; NZ was the principal complainant, although wrongdoing was never proven in court.

POPULATION & PEOPLE

The population of the Cook Islands is around 14,000. The number of Cook Islanders living abroad is much greater: more than 50,000 are estimated to live in NZ, and 15,000 are estimated to live in Australia (Cook Islanders have residency and working rights in these countries). More than 90% of the Cooks' population lives on the Southern Group islands, with over 60% of the country's population on Rarotonga.

Over 90% of the population is Polynesian, though there are subtle differences between the islands' peoples. The people of Pukapuka in the north, for example, are more closely related to Samoans than to other Cook Islanders. European New Zealanders, Fijians, Indians and Chinese make up a small minority.

ARTS

Cook Islanders are reputed to be the best dancers in all of Polynesia, and dancing in the Cook Islands is colourful, spectacular and very popular. Sample the wonderful music as well as the dancing at an 'island night' performance.

Traditional arts and crafts such as woven pandanus mats, baskets, purses, and fans are still in daily use. You'll see women going to church wearing finely woven white hats made of *rito*, an especially fine variety of pandanus; these hats are made on the Northern Group islands, but other islands also have distinct hat styles.

Beautifully crafted traditional ceremonial adzes and stone taro pounders are produced on Mangaia. Other arts you will see in the Cooks include the fine textile art known as *tivaevae*, an appliqué-and-embroidery creation made by women and used on bedspreads, cushion covers and for home decoration. You'll see people wearing an amazing variety of aromatic *'ei* and *'ei katu* (tiaras) made of flowers.

Jewellery is made from various materials, including shells. Nowadays, black pearls are the Cooks' largest industry, and black-pearl creations are a speciality. Other pearl-related arts include jewellery and carvings made of mother-of-pearl shell.

A few painters and writers live on Rarotonga. Their paintings are in local galleries and you'll find their books in local shops. Glass-blowing is also taking off on Rarotonga.

SOCIETY
Beneath a Western veneer, layers of Cook Islands culture survive. Every native Islander is part of a family clan, with each connected to the ancient system of chiefs. Rarotonga's six *ariki* clans are based on the land divisions from when the Maori first arrived on the island centuries ago. Even today, when an *ariki* is installed the ceremony takes place on an ancient family *marae*, and you will see ancestral graves beside modern houses.

Land Ownership
Land ownership in the Cook Islands is hereditary and land can only be leased, not sold, to outside parties. Because land is passed from generation to generation, people acquire curiously divided chunks of property; families might have a house by the coast, a citrus plantation somewhere else and the odd group of papaya trees dotted here and there. It can be a full-time job commuting from one farmlet to another.

RELIGION
Few people today know much about the traditional religion of the Cook Islands. The sophisticated system had 71 gods, each ruling a particular facet of reality, and 12 levels of heaven, some above the surface of the earth and some below. Today, the Protestant Cook Islands Christian Church (CICC) attracts about 70% of the faithful, with the remaining 30% Roman Catholic, Seventh-Day Adventist, Church of the Latter-day Saints (Mormons) and various other denominations.

LANGUAGE
Cook Islands Maori (Rarotongan), a Polynesian language most similar to New Zealand Maori and Marquesan (from French Polynesia), is the common language. There are some small dialectical differences between many islands and some northern islands have their own languages. English is spoken as a second (or third) language by virtually everyone.

See Language in the Facts about the South Pacific chapter for the pronunciation of the glottal stop. In Rarotongan, the glottal stop replaces the 'h' of similar Polynesian languages, eg, the Tahitian word for 'one', *tahi* (ta-hee), is *ta'i* (ta-ee) in Rarotongan.

Rarotongan Basics
Hello.	*Kia orana.*
Goodbye.	*Aere ra*
How are you?	*Pe'ea koe?*
I'm well.	*Meitaki.*
Please.	*Ine.*
Thanks (very much).	*Meitaki (ma'ata).*
Yes.	*Ae.*
No.	*Kare.*
Cheers.	*Kia manuia.*

Facts for the Visitor

SUGGESTED ITINERARIES
In one week you can visit the two principal islands, Rarotonga and Aitutaki. With a little more time, it's worth visiting other islands of the Southern Group: 'Atiu, Ma'uke, Mitiaro and/or Mangaia. Visiting the Northern Group islands requires more time, as they are right off the beaten track.

PLANNING
The moderate climate means you rarely need anything warmer than a short-sleeved shirt, but bring along a jumper (sweater) or jacket, especially during the cooler months from June to September. Bring wet-weather gear at

RAROTONGA & THE COOK ISLANDS

any time of year. You'll need a pair of sturdy shoes for climbing on Rarotonga or across the razor-sharp *makatea* of 'Atiu, Ma'uke, Mitiaro and Mangaia.

Most Western commodities are readily available but somewhat expensive. A torch (flashlight) is handy on the outer islands, where the power goes off at midnight, and for exploring caves.

When to Go

The Cook Islands offer warmth and sunshine year round. The drier months are between April and November. Book flights well in advance for December, when many Cook Islanders return home.

TOURIST OFFICES

The **Cook Islands Tourism Corporation** (*CITC*; ☎ 29435; ⓦ www.cook-islands.com; PO Box 14) is in the centre of Avarua on Rarotonga. Tourist information is also available from Cook Islands consulates. Overseas offices and representatives include:

Australia (☎ 02-9955 0446, ⓔ mareana -cookislands@bigpond.com.au) PO Box H95, Hurlstone Park, NSW 2193
Canada (☎ 888-994 2665, ⓔ cookislands@ earthlink.net) Suite 202, 280 Nelson St, Vancouver, BC V6B 2E2
Germany/Austria/Switzerland (☎ 030-929 2343) Zingster Strasse 72, D-13051, Berlin
New Zealand (☎ 09-366 1106, ⓔ albert -tourism@cookislands.co.nz) 1/127 Symonds St, PO Box 37391, Auckland
UK (☎ 020-8741 6082, ⓔ info@interface international.co.ck) 48 Glentham Rd, Barnes, London SW13 9JJ
USA (☎ 888-994 2665, ⓔ cookislands@earth link.net) Suite 200, 2250 E Imperial Hwy, El Segundo, CA 90245

The Cook Islands is also represented abroad by the South Pacific Tourism Organisation (see the Regional Facts for the Visitor chapter).

VISAS

No visa is required to visit the Cooks. A visitor permit, good for 31 days, is granted on arrival to people of all nationalities on presentation of a valid passport (with six months remaining validity), an onward or return airline ticket, and honour of the prior-booking arrangement (see Accommodation later in the chapter). Visitor permits can be extended for a maximum of five months at the **Ministry of Foreign Affairs & Immigration** (☎ 29347) in Avarua.

CONSULATES
Cook Islands Consulates

The Cook Islands has consulates or high commissions in various countries, including:

Australia (☎ 02-9907 6567, fax 9949 6664) Sir Ian Graham Turbott, 8/8 Lauderdale Ave, Fairlight, NSW 2094
New Zealand (☎ 09-366 1100, fax 309 1876) Laveta Short, 1st floor, 127 Symonds St, PO Box 37-391, Auckland
Wellington: (☎ 04-472 5126, fax 472 5121) 56 Mulgrave St, PO Box 12-242, Thorndon, Wellington
Norway (☎ 02-430 910, fax 22-444 611) Hallbjorn Hareide, Bydgoy Alle 64, 0265 Oslo 2
USA (☎ 805-987 0620, fax 383 2084) Metua Ngarupe, 1000 San Clemente Way, Camarillo 93010
Hawaii: (☎ 808-842 8999, fax 842 3520) Robert Worthington, c/o Kamehameha Schools, 144 Ke Ala Ola Rd, Honolulu 96817

Consulates in the Cook Islands

Foreign consulates and high commissions are all found on Rarotonga. They include the following:

France (☎ 22009) Mrs Marie Melvin, c/o Island Craft Ltd, PO Box 28, Avarua
Germany (☎ 23306) Dr Wolfgang Losacker, PO Box 125, Avarua
New Zealand (☎ 22201) Philatelic Bureau, PO Box 21, Avarua
UK (☎ 22000) Neil McKegg, Muri Beach

CUSTOMS

The following restrictions apply: 2L of spirits or wine or 4.5L of beer, plus 200 cigarettes or 50 cigars or 250g of tobacco. Bringing in plants or plant products and animals or animal products is restricted or prohibited. The importation of firearms, weapons and drugs is prohibited.

MONEY
Currency

New Zealand dollars (in denominations of NZ$5, NZ$10, NZ$20, NZ$50 and NZ$100) are used in the Cook Islands. You'll be lucky to receive Cook Islands coins (in denominations of 5c, 10c, 20c, 50c, $1, $2 and $5), but if you do, be sure to either spend them or exchange them before you leave the country (they have the same value as NZ currency), as Cook Islands money cannot be exchanged anywhere else in the world.

Exchange Rates

To check current exchange rates visit w www
.oanda.com. At the time of writing exchange
rates were as follows:

country	unit		NZ$
Australia	A$1	=	NZ$1.14
Canada	C$1	=	NZ$1.28
Easter Island	Ch$100	=	NZ$0.25
euro zone	€1	=	NZ$2.02
Fiji	F$1	=	NZ$0.93
PNG	K1	=	NZ$0.49
Samoa	ST1	=	NZ$0.57
Solomon Islands	S$1	=	NZ$0.23
Tonga	T$1	=	NZ$0.80
UK	£1	=	NZ$2.88
USA	US$1	=	NZ$1.71
Vanuatu	100VT	=	NZ$1.42

Exchanging Money

Cash & Travellers Cheques There are
ANZ bank ATMs at the airport on Rarotonga,
at the ANZ bank in Avarua and at Wigmore's
Superstore on the south side of Rarotonga;
many shops also have Eftpos facilities. You can
change money at the Westpac and ANZ banks
in Avarua, at the Administration Centre on Aitutaki, and at some hotels. You'll receive a better rate for travellers cheques than for cash; all
brands of travellers cheques are cashed at the
banks. Read up on the availability of exchange
facilities before heading to the outer islands
(see specific island sections for details).

Credit Cards Visa, MasterCard and Bankcard are readily accepted at most places on
Rarotonga. The Westpac and ANZ banks in
Avarua give cash advances on all three cards.
AmEx and Diners Club cards are accepted at
upmarket hotels and restaurants. Credit cards
are accepted at the larger hotels and resorts on
Aitutaki, and cash advances on credit cards
are available on Aitutaki and 'Atiu.

Costs

Accommodation costs the same all year
round. You could get by on NZ$30 per day
staying in budget accommodation, getting
around by bus or bicycle and preparing your
own food from non-imported ingredients;
budget on at least NZ$55 if you want to trade
the bicycle for a moped, eat out occasionally
and sink a couple of beers.

Package flight and accommodation deals
are a good way to bring your overall costs
down. Mid-range accommodation with a
restaurant meal each day and moped hire will
cost around NZ$140 per day, while adding
top-end accommodation to the equation will
mean a budget of at least NZ$200 per day.

Tipping & Bargaining

Tipping is not customary in the Cook Islands,
and haggling over prices is considered to be
very rude.

Taxes

There's a healthy slug on top of NZ prices
to cover shipping costs for imports. A 12.5%
VAT (value added tax) is factored into the
quoted price of most goods and services.

POST & COMMUNICATIONS

Poste-restante mail is held for 30 days at
post offices on most islands. To collect mail
at the post office in Avarua it should be addressed to you c/o Poste Restante, Avarua,
Rarotonga, Cook Islands.

All populated islands, with the exception of
Nassau, are connected to the country's modern
telephone system. Each island has a Telecom
office, which also provides fax, telegram and
telex services.

The country code for the Cook Islands is
☎ 682. There are no local area codes. Dial
☎ 00 for direct international calls or dial the
international operator on ☎ 015 for international and inter-island operator-assisted calls.
International information is ☎ 017; local information is ☎ 010.

Pre-paid 'Kiaorana' cards can be used for
local and international calls and are available in NZ$5, NZ$10, NZ$20 and NZ$50
denominations.

Analogue mobile phones can be connected
to the Kokanet service; contact **Telecom**
(☎ 29680; Rarotonga).

Email and Internet connections are available on Rarotonga and Aitutaki; see those
sections later for details.

DIGITAL RESOURCES

The following websites are useful sources of
information about the Cook Islands:

Cook Islands News (w www.cinews.co.ck)
Local daily newspaper site; updated weekly
Cook Islands Tourism Authority (w www
.cook-islands.com) Good introductory tourist
information
The Cook Islands Website (w www.ck) Local
business details, including tourist operations
Weather Online (w www.weatheronline
.co.uk/Pacific.htm) Weather reports

BOOKS

For a more in-depth travel guide to the Cook Islands, get a copy of Lonely Planet's *Rarotonga & the Cook Islands*.

How to Get Lost & Found in the Cook Islands by John & Bobbye McDermott concentrates on the Cook Islands many colourful characters.

Alphons MJ Kloosterman's *Discoverers of the Cook Islands & the Names They Gave* gives a brief history of each island, early legends and a record of European contact. *History of Rarotonga, up to 1853* by Taira Rere is a short, locally written history.

One of the best-known residents of the Cooks was the late Tom Neale. In *An Island to Oneself* he wrote of the periods during the 1950s, '60s and '70s he spent living as a hermit on the isolated northern atoll Suwarrow.

If you're interested in legends, look out for *Cook Islands Legends* and *The Ghost at Tokatarava and Other Stories from the Cook Islands* by notable Cook Islands author Jon Jonassen, and *Te Ata O Ikurangi: The Shadow of Ikurangi* by JJ MacCauley. Kauraka Kauraka has published several books of poems.

Good books on arts and crafts include Dale Idiens' *Cook Islands Art*, with black-and-white photos, and *Tivaevae – Portraits of Cook Islands Quilting* by Lynnsay Rongokea, which introduces 18 women and their colourful appliqué works.

The Cook Islands by Ewan Smith & Graeme Lay is a coffee-table book with magnificent photos. *Visions of the Pacific* by David Arnell & Lisette Wolk features exceptional photographs of the Pacific islanders who gathered on Rarotonga for the 1992 Maire Nui festival.

A useful guide to hiking and fauna and flora is *Rarotonga's Mountain Tracks and Plants* by Gerald McCormack & Judith Künzle. Also look for *Rarotonga's Cross-Island Walk* by the same authors. *Guide to Cook Islands Birds* by DT Holyoak has colour photos, and text for identifying local birds.

NEWSPAPERS & MAGAZINES

Rarotonga's *Cook Islands News*, published daily except Sunday, and the *Cook Islands Herald*, published on Wednesday, provide coverage of local events and a brief summary of international events. The daily *New Zealand Herald* is sold on Rarotonga the day after it's published. A small selection of foreign magazines is available in Avarua.

RADIO & TV

Radio Cook Islands (630 kHz AM) reaches all the islands and broadcasts local programmes, as well as Radio New Zealand news and Radio Australia's overseas world news service. The KC-FM (103.8 MHz FM) station is less powerful but can be received on most of Rarotonga.

Rarotonga has one television station, CITV. Tapes of its programmes are flown to some outer islands for rebroadcast. Marama is a cable channel available at upmarket hotels. There are numerous video-rental outlets on the islands.

PHOTOGRAPHY & VIDEO

Print and slide film, and video are available on Rarotonga. High-speed film is useful in the densely forested interior of Rarotonga, and in the *makatea* of 'Atiu and Ma'uke. Bring a flash for photographing inside caves.

TIME

The Cook Islands is east of the International Date Line, 10 hours behind Greenwich Mean Time (GMT). The country has no daylight-saving time. When it's noon in the Cooks it's 10pm in London, noon in Tahiti and Hawaii, 2pm in Los Angeles, 10am the next day in Fiji and NZ, and 8am the next day in Sydney.

HEALTH

The Cook Islands is generally a healthy place for visitors. Food is good, fresh, clean and readily available and there are few endemic diseases. There is no malaria risk in the Cook Islands, though there have been outbreaks of dengue fever in recent years. No vaccinations are required for travel here.

Although tap water is usually safe to drink on Rarotonga and on most of the outer islands, do ask about it. On Aitutaki, for example, there are some places where you should take your drinking water from a rainwater tank, rather than from the tap. If you have any doubts, boil your drinking water for five minutes or buy bottled water.

Every island has a basic medical clinic. Rarotonga has a hospital, an outpatient clinic and several private doctors. Patients on outer islands are often sent to Rarotonga for treatment.

Of the numerous souvenirs of your trip to the Cook Islands, most are less painful than a 'Rarotongan tattoo' (motorbike exhaust burn). To avoid this, get off on the other side.

SOCIAL GRACES

Friendliness and respect for others are highly valued in Cook Islands culture. Visitors are urged to dress modestly and refrain from topless bathing.

DANGERS & ANNOYANCES

Theft is a bit of a problem on Rarotonga. Avoid leaving money in your wallet on the beach while you're swimming, take clothes in from clotheslines at night and beware of leaving hotel rooms unlocked or easy to access.

Swimming is very safe in the sheltered lagoons but be very wary of the passages and breaks in the surrounding reef, where currents are especially strong. Rarotonga has several such passages, notably at Avana Harbour, Avaroa, Papua and Rutaki; they exist on other islands as well, often opposite streams.

Mosquitoes can be a real nuisance in the Cooks, particularly during the rainy season (around mid-December to mid-April). Use repellent; mosquito coils are available everywhere.

Women should be wary that consent to an invitation of a walk along the beach at night is seen by some as giving consent to sex.

BUSINESS HOURS

The usual business week is from 8am to 4pm Monday to Friday. Shops are also open until noon on Saturday and small local grocery stores are often open from 6am or 7am until 8pm or 9pm. Nearly everything is closed on Sunday, except some small grocery stores which open for a couple of hours very early in the morning and again in the evening.

PUBLIC HOLIDAYS & SPECIAL EVENTS

The Cook Islands has many public holidays, often accompanied by dancing and other activities. As well as New Year's Day, Easter, Christmas and Boxing Day, the public holidays are:

Anzac Day 25 April
Queen's Birthday First Monday in June
Gospel Day (Rarotonga) 26 July
Constitution Day (Independence) 4 August
National Gospel Day 26 October
Flag Raising Day 27 October

Gospel Day in particular is celebrated with much enthusiasm and takes place on different dates around the Cooks. Some of the more entertaining festivals are:

April
Island Dance Festival Week Held during the third week of April; has dance competitions

August
Constitution Celebration Beginning the Friday before 4 August; includes a 10-day sporting and dance festival

November
Tiare (Floral) Festival Held during the last week of November; has parades and more

ACTIVITIES

There's no better place to simply relax than the Cook Islands, but there are also plenty of activities to keep you busy.

Water Sports

The sheltered lagoons and beaches on all the islands are great for **swimming**, particularly on Rarotonga and Aitutaki. Lagoon cruise operators go out to some of the best **snorkelling** spots. **Diving** off these islands is especially attractive, with visibility of 30m to 60m and a great variety of both reef and pelagic sea life. Snorkelling gear is available for hire on Aitutaki and Rarotonga, where you'll also find sailing boats, windsurfers and other equipment.

Glass-bottomed boats operate from Muri Beach for viewing coral and tropical fish. Fully equipped boats for **deep-sea fishing** can be chartered on Rarotonga and Aitutaki. From July to October, **whale-watching** trips operate from several islands.

Visiting Marae

History and archaeology buffs will enjoy visiting the historic *marae* on many of the islands. These traditional religious meeting grounds are still very significant in some aspects of culture on Rarotonga and on other islands.

Other Activities

Rarotonga offers opportunities for rock climbing and challenging mountain hikes, as well as easy strolls through lush valleys, along beautiful white-sand beaches and along streams. Aitutaki, with its single small mountain, Maungapu (124m), and limitless beaches and trails, is also great for walking and exploring. 'Atiu, Ma'uke, Mitiaro and Mangaia all have interesting caves to explore.

ACCOMMODATION

Visitors are required to have booked accommodation before arriving in the Cook Islands.

Although enforcement of this requirement has become more relaxed and you can often choose a hotel when you arrive at the airport, the prior-booking rule is officially in place and it's best to have a booking, at least for the first night.

Rarotonga has a large variety of accommodation, including hostels, plenty of motel-style accommodation, and major resort hotels. Houses can be rented, fully furnished, for around NZ$250 to NZ$400 a week. There's organised accommodation on all the other Southern Group islands that have air services, particularly on Aitutaki.

Manihiki and Penrhyn are the only Northern Group islands with guesthouses. Elsewhere you may have to stay with local people; be sure to pay your way and bring food to share.

FOOD

Rarotonga has some great little restaurants and Aitutaki has a few, but elsewhere the choice and availability of places to eat is far more limited. Fortunately, most accommodation options have kitchen facilities; take supplies with you to the outer islands if possible. Gorge yourself on local fruit, vegetables and fish, which are inexpensive.

You won't find much local food on restaurant menus, so join an 'island night' buffet or barbecue to sample and savour local dishes. An *umukai* is a traditional feast cooked in an underground oven *(umu)*. *Ika mata* is raw fish marinated in lime juice and coconut milk.

DRINKS

Coconut water is the truly local drink and Cook Islands coconuts are especially tasty. Try also Atiu Island coffee, and fresh juices from the Frangi juice factory on Rarotonga. The quality of locally produced *nono* juice, lauded for its healing properties, is highly regarded. A wide variety of NZ and other international beers is available. Liqueurs (40% alcohol) are made from local products on Rarotonga.

For details on *tumunu* (bush-beer drinking sessions) see the boxed text 'Tumunu' in the 'Atiu, Ma'uke & Mitiaro section.

ENTERTAINMENT

The most typical Cook Islands entertainment is the 'island night', which starts with a buffet dinner of local food, followed by a floor show of dance, music and song. Cook Islanders love to dance and Friday is the big night. Organised pub crawls scour Rarotonga's venues. The Empire Theatre on Rarotonga screens recently released films.

SHOPPING
Traditional Handicrafts

The squat, ugly, but well-endowed figure of Tangaroa, the traditional god of the sea and fertility, has become the symbol of the Cook Islands. You can get Tangaroa figures in many different forms ranging from key-ring figurines 2cm high to huge ones standing 1m or more.

Ceremonial stone adzes with intricately carved wooden handles or stands and sennit binding, as well as stone taro pounders are made on Mangaia. *Rito* hats made of fine, bleached, woven pandanus leaves are a Cook Islands speciality; prices start at about NZ$90. Other pandanus products include mats, purses and fans.

Colourful and intricately sewn *tivaevae* (appliqué works) are traditionally made as burial shrouds, but they are also used as bedspreads and cushion covers. They take an enormous amount of time to make, so a full-size *tivaevae* will cost you several hundred dollars. Smaller wall hangings, cushion covers, and clothing using *tivaevae*-inspired patterns are cheaper.

Pearls, Shells & Jewellery

Pearls are farmed on Manihiki and Penrhyn and are sold on Rarotonga. Black pearls (which are very rare), golden pearls, white pearls, mother-of-pearl products and pearls embedded in their mother-of-pearl shells are all available, along with a lot of shell jewellery. *Pupu 'ei* – long necklaces made of tiny *pupu* shells collected on Mangaia – are a sought-after item.

Before you rush off to buy shells, remember that something has to be evicted to provide the shell, and conservationists fear that some species are being collected to the point of extinction.

Other Souvenirs

Pure coconut oils and coconut-oil-based soaps, liqueurs made from local fruits, and coffee from 'Atiu Island are all good souvenirs. Rarotonga has a couple of resident artists and their artworks are on sale. The local drumming can be intoxicating; CD's are available on Rarotonga.

There are also a fair number of souvenirs that don't originate from the Cooks at all, such as shell jewellery and wooden bowls made in the Philippines, and New Zealand Maori products masquerading as Cook Islands Maori items.

Getting There & Away

AIR
The Cook Islands can be included as a stopover between the USA and New Zealand, Australia or other Pacific islands. See the introductory Getting There & Away chapter for details on round-the-world tickets and Pacific air passes.

Low-season travel to the Cooks is from mid-April to late August, and the high season runs from December to February; other times are shoulder season. There's heavy demand from NZ to the Cooks in December, and in the other direction in January.

Airlines
Getting to the Cook Islands generally involves flying. **Air New Zealand** (W www.airnz .co.nz) and **Aloha Airlines** (☎ 808-486 7277 in Oahu, Hawaii, ☎ 800-432 7117 in Canada & Mainland USA; W www.alohaairlines.com) are the only regular international airlines servicing the Cooks, though it's still worth comparing prices and stopover options. Package deals (air fare plus accommodation) from travel agents can often cost the same or even less than the air fare alone.

Departure Tax
There's a NZ$25 departure tax (NZ$10/free for children aged two to 11/under two) when you fly out of Rarotonga.

North & South America
Air New Zealand flights to Rarotonga from the USA (departing Los Angeles), via Honolulu or Tahiti, cost US$895/985/1015 return in the low/shoulder/high season. Aloha Airlines' low-/high-season fares to Rarotonga from LA are US$995/1620. Both airlines fly between Rarotonga and Hawaii.

Flights to/from Canada (Vancouver) cost C$1610/2290 in the low/high season with Air New Zealand and C$1625/2200 with Aloha Airlines.

Combined LanChile and Air New Zealand flights to/from Santiago, via Tahiti, cost around US$1320.

Australasia
Air New Zealand has six direct flights weekly from Auckland to Rarotonga; return fares are NZ$995/1470 in the low/high season.

Flights between Australia and Rarotonga go via Auckland. A basic return fare to Rarotonga from Brisbane, Melbourne or Sydney costs A$995/1350 in the low/high season.

Asia
Air New Zealand's connections to/from Tokyo are either via Fiji or Auckland. The basic fare is around ¥240,000; cheaper fares may be available through some travel agencies – it's worth shopping around.

The Pacific
Apart from NZ, the only Pacific islands with direct flights to Rarotonga are Fiji (F$875 return), Tahiti (39,000CFP to 59,000CFP return) and Hawaii (see The Americas, earlier, for details). To visit any other Pacific island from the Cooks, you'll have to fly via one of these or NZ.

SEA
Various cruise ships stop in at Rarotonga and other islands but they don't take on passengers. They typically arrive in the morning and depart in the afternoon, after quick island tours.

Yacht
The other sea alternative is to come by yacht, except during the cyclone season from November to March. Once you arrive on Rarotonga, fly your Q flag and visit the **Harbour Master** (☎ 28814; Avatiu Harbour, Rarotonga). Other official ports of entry are Aitutaki, Penrhyn and Pukapuka, all of which have good anchorages. The virtually uninhabited Suwarrow Atoll, made famous by Tom Neale's book *An Island to Oneself*, is another favourite with yachties, but is not an official port of entry.

There's a remote chance of catching a yacht from the Cook Islands to Tonga, Samoa, Fiji, French Polynesia or NZ. Check the situation at Rarotonga's Ports Authority at Avatiu Harbour, and on its downstairs bulletin board, where yachties often leave messages if they are looking for crew.

Getting Around
Unless you've packed your yacht, inter-island travel is limited to passenger ships and Air Rarotonga flights. Flights to the Northern Group islands are expensive; only Manihiki, Penrhyn and Pukapuka have airstrips.

AIR

Air Rarotonga (☎ 22888; ☒ www.airraro.com) is the only commercial inter-island air service in the Cook Islands. There are several daily flights between Rarotonga and Aitutaki, several weekly flights between Rarotonga and the other Southern Group islands, and a weekly flight between Rarotonga and the Northern Group islands of Manihiki and Penrhyn. There are no flights on Sunday. See the individual island entries in this chapter for details of air fares and flight times.

BOAT

Most of the Northern Group islands are only accessible by ship. Shipping schedules are hard to pinpoint – weather, breakdowns, loading difficulties and unexpected demands can all put a kink in the plans. Ships usually stay at each island for just a few hours. Only Rarotonga and Penrhyn have wharves; at all the other islands you go ashore by lighter or barge. Trips from Rarotonga to the northern islands often take up to 10 days, as several islands may be visited.

Travel throughout the Southern Group islands usually involves setting off in the late afternoon or early evening and arriving at the next island early the next morning.

Taio Shipping (☎ 24905, 20535; ☒ risa@ taio.co.ck; Avatiu Harbour, Avarua, Rarotonga), downstairs in the Ports Authority building, can give information and schedules and make bookings on inter-island passenger and cargo services. To go anywhere in the Southern/Northern Groups costs NZ$65/200 one way; bring your own food. Boats to the Southern Group usually depart monthly, perhaps every two months to the Northern Group. Palmerston Atoll's boat, *Marster's Dream*, goes fortnightly to/from Rarotonga (NZ$300 return); contact the island's **mayor** (☎ 20893) or **secretary** (☎ 24005) for bookings.

LOCAL TRANSPORT

All the islands are good for cycling – the distances are short and the roads are quite flat. Rarotonga has a regular circle-island bus service, taxis, and plenty of bicycles, motorcycles, cars, Jeeps and minibuses for hire. Aitutaki has a taxi service and bicycles, motorcycles and cars for hire. 'Atiu has a taxi service, rental motorcycles and a Jeep. Ma'uke has rental bicycles and motorcycles.

Hitchhiking, though not the custom, is perfectly legal. You'll get some strange looks, but if you're cheeky enough to try, you'll probably get a lift fairly quickly.

ORGANISED TOURS

Circle-island tours on Rarotonga offer a good introduction to the island and its history, culture, people, agriculture and economy. Circle-island tours are also offered on Aitutaki, 'Atiu, Ma'uke and Mangaia. See the individual island entries for specific information.

Day tours from Rarotonga to Aitutaki are available. Rarotongan-based travel agencies can also help you organise single-island or multi-island package tours.

Rarotonga

pop 10,500 • area 67.2 sq km
Rarotonga is the main island and population centre of the Cook Islands. The interior is rugged, virtually unpopulated and untouched, while the coastal region is fertile and evenly populated. Fringing this is an almost continuous clean, white beach with clear, shallow lagoons and a protective outer reef.

History

Oral histories relate that Rarotonga was first discovered by Io Tangaroa (also known as Io Teitei), who came by canoe about 1400 years ago from Nuku Hiva in the Marquesas Islands (now part of French Polynesia). In the early 13th century, Tangi'ia, from Ra'iatea in the Society Islands, and Karika, from Samoa, arrived simultaneously at the head of two settlement expeditions. Tangi'ia and Karika fought each other at first, then ruled Rarotonga as joint kings.

Eventually the land was divided among six tribes, each headed by an *ariki* (tribal king). Due to frequent intertribal conflicts over land and other issues, people lived at higher elevations than they do today, for easier defence. They practised agriculture and raised livestock, including pigs.

Surprisingly, considering its historical importance, Rarotonga was one of the later islands to be found by Europeans. Philip Goodenough, captain of the *Cumberland*, showed up in 1814 and spent a bloody three months on Rarotonga unsuccessfully looking for sandalwood. In 1823 the missionaries John Williams and Papeiha set out to convert the Rarotongans, and in little more than a year Christianity had taken a firm hold.

Fearing French expansionism in the Pacific, Makea Takau, a Rarotongan *ariki*, requested British protection for the first time in 1865. In 1888, when a British protectorate was formally

Makea, king of Rarotonga, painted by the
Rev John Williams (watercolour 1830s)

declared over the Southern Group islands,
Rarotonga became the unofficial capital of
the group. The Cook Islands were annexed by
NZ in 1901, eventually becoming independent
in 1965.

Orientation
Finding your way around Rarotonga is easy –
there's a coastal road (the Ara Tapu), another
road about 500m inland (the Ara Metua),
and mountains in the middle. A number of
smaller roads connect the main roads and a
few others lead to inland valleys. The island
can only be crossed on foot.

The New Zealand Department of Lands
& Survey's excellent 1:25,000 topographical
map of Rarotonga (NZ$10) shows roads, a
number of walking trails, reefs and villages
and a separate enlargement of Avarua. Maps
are available at many shops in Avarua,
including the Bounty Bookshop and CITC
Shopping Centre (see Bookshops under Information for details).

Information
Tourist Offices CITC's helpful **Visitor
Information Centre** (☎ 29435; W www
.cook-islands.com; PO Box 14; open 8am-
4pm Mon-Fri, 8am-noon Sat) is in the centre
of Avarua. You can load up on brochures here
and pick up a free copy of the *What's On in*

the Cook Islands guide and *Cook Islands
Sun* map.

Money The two travellers banks on Raro-
tonga are **Westpac** (☎ 22014; Ara Maire
Nui), beside the Foodland supermarket, and
ANZ (☎ 21750; Ara Maire Nui), between the
CITC Shopping Centre and Banana Court.
Both are open 9am to 3pm Monday to Friday
and 9am to noon Saturday.

The **Westpac branch** at the airport is
open for all international flights; there are
ANZ ATMs in Avarua, at the airport and at
Wigmore's Superstore in the south. Travellers cheques and major currencies can be
changed at some of the larger hotels, and
some stores have Eftpos facilities.

Post & Communications The **post office**
(☎ 29940; open 8am-4pm Mon-Fri, 8am-
noon Sat) is just inland from the roundabout
in central Avarua. Postal depots operate at
several small shops around the island.

Telecom (☎ 29680; Tutakimoa Rd, Avarua; open 24hr) is a couple of blocks inland
from Cook's Corner Arcade. 'Kiaorana'
phonecards can be used for private telephones
and the public telephones dotted around the
island.

Internet and email connections are available at the post office, **Telepost** (☎ 29940;
Avarua; open 8am-4pm Mon-Fri, 8.30am-
noon Sat), and the following establishments:

Kavera Central (☎ 26144) Ara Tapu, Kavera.
Open 6.30am to 10pm Monday to Saturday,
6.30am to 9am and 4pm to 9pm Sunday.
NZ$0.25/minute.
Ronnie's Bar & Grill (☎ 20823) Ara Maire Nui,
Avarua. Open 11am to 11pm Monday to Thurs-
day, Saturday and Sunday, 11am to 2am Friday.
NZ$5/8 per 30 minutes/hour.
The Internet Cafe (☎ 27242) Muri Beach and
'Arorangi. Open from 8am to 6pm Monday
to Friday, 10am to 6pm Saturday and Sunday.
NZ$0.25/minute.

Travel Agencies Some useful travel agencies include:

Cook Islands Tours & Travel (☎ 28270, 20270
after hours, W www.cookislandtours.co.ck)
Rarotonga airport
Island Hopper Vacations (☎ 22576, fax
22036, W www.islandhoppervacations.com)
Banana Court, Ara Maire Nui, Avarua
Jetsave Travel (☎ 27707, fax 22036, W www
.jetsave.co.ck) Ara Maire Nui, Avarua

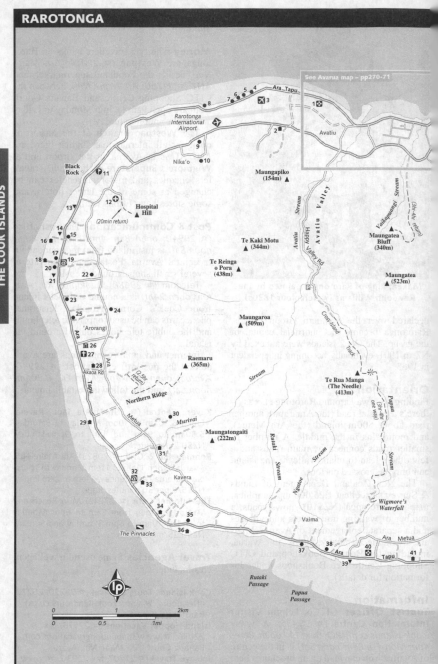

RAROTONGA

See Avarua map – pp270-71

Ara Tapu

Rarotonga International Airport

Nika'o

Black Rock

Hospital Hill
(20min return)

'Arorangi

Ara Tapu

Akaoa Rd

Northern Ridge
(2.5hr return)

Metua

Kavera

The Pinnacles

Avatiu

Maungapiko
(154m)

Avatiu Valley

Avatiu Stream

Happy Valley Rd

Vaikapuangi Stream
(3hr-4hr return)

Maungatea Bluff
(340m)

Maungatea
(523m)

Te Kaki Motu
(344m)

Te Reinga
o Pora
(438m)

Cross Island Track

Maungaroa
(509m)

Raemaru
(365m)

Te Rua Manga
(The Needle)
(413m)

Papua Stream
(3hr-4hr
one way)

Murivai

Maungatongaiti
(222m)

Ruaki Stream

Stream

Ngatangi Stream

Wigmore's
Waterfall

Vaima

Ara Metua

Ara Tapu

Rutaki
Passage

Papua
Passage

0   1   2km
0   0.5   1mi

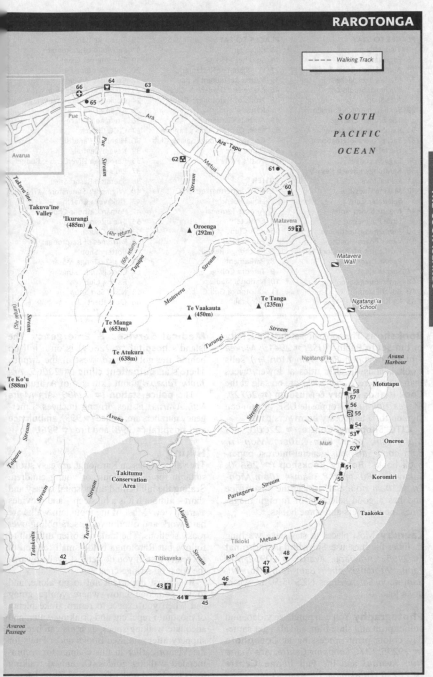

RAROTONGA

- - - - - Walking Track

SOUTH
PACIFIC
OCEAN

Avarua

Takuva'ine Valley

Takuva'ine Valley

'Ikurangi
(485m) ▲

(4hr return)

(6hr return)

Tupapa

Matavera

Oroenga
(292m) ▲

Stream

Te Vaakauta
(450m) ▲

Te Tanga
(235m) ▲

Matavera
Wall

Ngatangi'ia
School

Stream

Te Manga
(653m) ▲

Turangi

Stream

(5hr return)

Stream

Te Atukura
(638m) ▲

Ngatangi'ia

Avana
Harbour

Te Ko'u
(588m) ▲

Avana

Motutapu

Toiqara Stream

58
57
56
55
54
53
52
51
50

Oneroa

Mun

Totokoiu Stream

Tarua Stream

Takitumu
Conservation
Area

Akapuao Stream

Koromiri

Paringaru Stream

Taakoka

49

Tikioki

42

Metua

Titikaveka

Stream

Ara

48

47

46

43

44

45

Avaroa
Passage

RAROTONGA

PLACES TO STAY
2 Tiare Village
16 Edgewater Resort
18 Aunty Noo's Beach Lodge
28 Maria's Backpackers; Exham
    Wichman Studio &
    Arts Shop
29 Sunhaven Beach Bungalows;
    The Brunch Cottage
31 Rarotonga Backpackers
33 Backpackers International
    Hostel
34 Lagoon Lodges
36 Rarotongan Beach Resort
41 Palm Grove
42 Maiana Guesthouse;
    Saltwater Café
44 Moana Sands Hotel
45 Little Polynesian
50 Aremango Guesthouse
51 Vara's Beach House
54 Pacific Resort; Barefoot Bar;
    Pacific Divers
57 Sokala Villas
58 Aroko Bungalows
60 Royal Palms
63 Kii Kii Motel

PLACES TO EAT
13 Kikau Hut
14 Spaghetti House
21 Windjammer Restaurant
39 Vaima Restaurant & Bar
46 Maire Nui Gardens & Café
48 Fruits of Rarotonga; Tikioki
    Rentals
49 Ambala Gardens
52 Sails; Captain Tama's Lagoon
    Cruises; Rarotonga Sailing Club
53 Flame Tree
56 That's Pasta

OTHER
1 CITC Supermarket; CITC
   Liquor Centre
3 Airport Terminal
4 Cemetery
5 RSA Club
6 Fun Rentals
7 Rarotonga Rentals
8 Parliament
9 Tereora College
10 National Stadium
11 Rarotonga Golf Club
12 Hospital

15 Tipani Rentals
17 Snowbird Laundromat
19 The Internet Cafe
20 Dive Rarotonga
22 Cook Island Divers
23 Island Car & Bike Hire
24 Cook Islands Cultural Village
25 BT Bike Hire
26 Tinomana Palace
27 CICC Church
30 Highland Paradise
32 Kavera Central
35 Rarotonga Dive Centre; Budget
37 Piri's III
38 Sheraton Resort Site
40 Wigmore's Superstore; ATM
43 Titikaveka Church
47 Roman Catholic Church
55 The Internet Cafe
59 CICC Church
61 Perfumes of Rarotonga;
    Pottery Shop
62 Arai-Te-Tonga Marae
64 Cook Islands Game
    Fishing Club
65 Niki's Surf Shop
66 Outpatient Clinic

Bookshops The bookshop at the **University of the South Pacific** (USP; ☎ 29415; Makea Tinirau Rd; open 8am-4pm Mon-Fri) sells Cook Islands–specific titles at lower prices than elsewhere. Some books are on sale at the **Cook Islands Library & Museum** (☎ 20725; Makea Tinirau Rd), opposite USP, or you can sign up for a temporary borrowers card.

CITC Shopping Centre (☎ 22000; Ara Maire Nui; open 8am-4.30pm Mon-Fri, 8am-noon Sat) sells general-interest paperback books. **Bounty Bookshop** (☎ 26660; Takuva'ine Rd; open 8.30am-4.30pm Mon-Fri, 8.30am-noon Sat) is near the post office and has a good selection of foreign magazines, newspapers and some books.

Laundry Most places to stay have washing facilities for guest use. **Snowbird Laundromat** (☎ 21952; Ara Tapu, Avarua, ☎ 20952; Ara Tapu, 'Arorangi; open 8am-4pm Mon-Fri, 8am-noon Sat) charges NZ$4/5.50 to wash/dry a load.

Photography You can purchase video, and colour print and slide film, and also get same-day colour-print processing at **Cocophoto** (☎ 29295; CITC Shopping Centre, Ara Maire Nui, Avarua) and the **Fuji Image Centre** (☎ 26238; Tutakimoa Rd, Avarua).

Medical Services & Emergency The island's **hospital** (☎ 22664) is on a hill up behind the golf course, west of the airport. There's an **outpatient clinic** (☎ 20065; Ara Tapu, Tupapa) about 1km east of Avarua.

The **police station** (☎ 22499; Ara Maire Nui, Avarua) issues driving licences. Emergency numbers are: **police** (☎ 999), **ambulance and hospital** (☎ 998) and **fire** (☎ 996).

Hiking
The valley walks on Rarotonga are easy strolls suitable for older people or young children. Scaling the hill behind the hospital is easy and short – although it is a bit steep – and provides a great view. Most of the mountain walks are hard work and often involve scrambling over rocky sections. The trails are often difficult to follow, but Rarotonga is too small for you to get really lost. If you do get lost, walk towards the coast on a ridge crest.

It is most important not to go alone, and to let someone know where you're going and when you expect to return. Take plenty of mosquito repellent and drinking water, and adequate walking shoes, as trails can become slippery after rain. See Books under Facts for the Visitor earlier in this chapter for recommended walking guides. Organised walking tours are listed under Organised Tours later.

Snorkelling

Rarotonga's lagoon has some good snorkelling spots with plenty of marine life to watch. Titikaveka lagoon, opposite the Fruits of Rarotonga shop in Tikioki, is one of the best snorkelling spots; staff at the shop will look after your things while you're out in the water.

Tikioki Rentals (☎ 21509; Ara Tapu, Tikioki; open 10am-5pm Mon-Fri, noon-5pm Sat), near Fruits of Rarotonga, and **Captain Tama's Aquasports** (☎ 20810; Muri Beach; open 8am-6pm daily) rent snorkelling gear for around NZ$10 per day. Captain Tama's includes snorkelling in its all-day Captain Tama's Lagoon Cruizes.

Reef to See (☎ 22212) runs twice-daily, three-hour snorkelling trips (adult/child NZ$50/ 35) to the outer reef. All the diving operators will take snorkellers on trips outside the reef if there's room on the boat (NZ$20, equipment included).

To buy your own snorkelling gear, visit **Dive Shop Avarua** (☎ 24496; Mana Court, Avarua).

Surfing

Rarotonga doesn't offer the world's best surfing, but spots worth trying are in Avarua right in front of the traffic circle, Avana Harbour, Black Rock and Matavera. **Niki's Surf Shop** (☎ 26240; W www.cookislandsurf.co.ck; Ara Tapu), east of Avarua, sells surfing supplies (mostly après surf). You're unlikely to find surfboards for sale or rent on Rarotonga.

Diving

There are some great little sites outside the reef, with coral-encrusted canyons, caves and tunnels, and visibility of 30m to 60m (100ft to 200ft). The reef drop-off goes from 20m right down to 4000m, though most diving is done at 3m to 30m. See the special section 'South Pacific Diving' for some of the island's best dives. Diving operators include:

Cook Island Divers (☎ 22483, W www.cook pages.com/CookIslandDivers/) 'Arorangi
Dive Rarotonga (☎ 21873, W www.diveraro .com) 'Arorangi
Pacific Divers (☎/fax 22450, W www.pacific divers.co.ck) Muri Beach

All operators offer morning and afternoon trips outside the reef for certified divers (around NZ$75/130 for one/two dives). Cook Island Divers and Pacific Divers run PADI or NAUI certification courses (NZ$499) and introductory dives (NZ$50). Ask about night dives.

Sailing

Muri's lagoon is the best place for swimming, windsurfing, sailing and kayaking. Sailing races start at Muri Beach every Saturday at 1pm. Water-sports equipment can be hired on Muri Beach at Captain Tama's Aquasports; sailing and windsurfing lessons are available. **Rarotonga Sailing Club** (☎ 27349; Muri Beach) rents out small yachts (NZ$30/hour).

Deep-Sea Fishing

Right off the reef, deep-sea fishing is excellent, with catches of ma'i ma'i, tuna, wahoo, barracuda, sailfish and marlin in season. Compare charters and ask beforehand whether you can keep your fish – on some boats it's divided among the passengers but on others the boat operators keep the fish to sell to restaurants. Most fishing trips are from 4½ to five hours. The following operators have full safety gear:

Beco's Fishing Charters (☎ 21525, 24125) NZ$100 per trip
Fisher's Fishing Tours (☎ 23356) Polynesian-style catamaran, NZ$70 per trip
Manutea Fishing Charters (☎ 22560) Whale-watching in season, NZ$85 per trip
Pacific Marine Charters (☎ 21237) NZ$100 per trip
Seafari Charters (☎ 20328) NZ$100 per trip

Horse Riding

Near Rarotongan Beach Resort, **Aroa Pony Trek** (☎ 21415) offers two-hour horse rides through plantations to Wigmore's Waterfall and back along the beach. Rides (adult/child NZ$40/25) start at 10am and 3pm Monday to Friday; bookings are essential.

Other Sports

You can usually find a **volleyball** game on Muri Beach or at Rarotongan Beach Resort. **Tennis** courts and rental gear are available at Edgewater Resort and Rarotongan Beach Resort (phone for reservations; see Places to Stay – Top End under Around the Island later).

Lawn bowling is held at the **Rarotonga Bowling Club** (☎ 26277) in Avarua most Saturdays. The nine-hole **Rarotonga Golf Club** (☎ 20621) is just south of the airport; a round costs NZ$15.

Glass-Bottom Boat Tours

Located beside Rarotonga Sailing Club, **Captain Tama's Aquasports** (☎ 27350; Muri Beach) operates glass-bottom boat tours of the lagoon (NZ$60), including a stop at a small pearl farm, followed by an *umukai* and entertainment on Koromiri.

The semisubmersible **Reef Sub** (☎ 25837) takes two-hour cruises (adult/child NZ$45/30) from Avatiu Harbour twice daily Monday to Saturday.

Whale-Watching

Humpback whales visit the Cook Islands from July to October; you might see them just outside the reef. Pacific Divers (see Diving, earlier) and Reef Sub (see Glass-Bottom Boat Tours, following) offer whale-watching trips in season. The **Cook Islands Whale Education Centre** *(Ara Metua; open 10am-5pm Mon, Tues, Thur & Fri, noon-3pm Sat, 10am-3pm Sun)*, west of Avarua, has photos, videos and more of the world of dolphins and whales.

Scenic Flights

For a change of perspective, **Raro Scenic Flights** (☎ 22888) offers 20-minute flights for NZ$65. Or buzz over Rarotonga in a microlight with **Tandem Microflight** (☎ 55311) for NZ$95. Both are located at the airport.

Other Organised Tours

Circle-island tours provide a wonderful insight into aspects of Rarotongan history and culture. The **Cook Islands Cultural Village** (☎ 21314) circle-island tour (adult/child NZ$54/27) includes an island-style lunch and a show of traditional Cook Islands legends, song and dance. **Raro Tours** (☎ 25325) offers a 3½-hour circle-island tour (NZ$25). **Raro Mountain Safari Tours** (☎ 23629) runs three-hour inland 4WD expeditions (NZ$60/30).

Reservations are essential on all tours; tours only run when there are sufficient numbers.

You can take easy or strenuous walks into the **Takitumu Conservation Area** (TCA). Book at the **TCA office** (☎ 29906; e *kakerori@tca.co.ck; Ara Tapu, Avarua*). The five-hour tours (adult/child NZ$45/20) include the story of the kakerori, traditional uses of plants, a light lunch and transportation.

Pa Mountain Trekking (☎ 21079) offers a couple of tours, including the popular Cross-Island Walk (four hours, adult/child NZ$55/25), which includes an explanation of Rarotonga's fauna, flora and medicinal plants.

Bill's Mountain Treks (☎ 22244) runs a number of history-infused hikes.

Getting Around

To/From the Airport Most hotels, motels and hostels send vans to the airport to meet incoming international flights. **Raro Tours** (☎ 25325) operates an airport shuttle service (NZ$18 one way to anywhere on the island)

Bus Services run around the coast road in both directions, departing from the bus stop at Cook's Corner Arcade in Avarua. Clockwise buses depart hourly from 7am to 4pm Monday to Saturday, 8am to noon and 2pm to 4pm Sunday. Anticlockwise buses depart hourly from 8.25am to 4.30pm Monday to Friday and 8.30am to 12.30pm Saturday. Night buses operate on a more limited schedule. One-way/return fares are NZ$2.50/4, or NZ$17 for a 10-ride ticket. **Cook's Passenger Transport** (☎ 25512, 20349 after hours) has information and timetables. You can flag the bus down anywhere along its route.

Car, Moped & Bicycle To rent a motor vehicle you must obtain a local driving licence (NZ$10) from the police station in Avarua – a straightforward procedure. Your home driving licence or passport is needed for identification. Driving is on the left-hand side of the road.

Car-rental rates of around NZ$50 to NZ$70 per day become significantly cheaper for several days or a week; ring around for special deals. You can hire a moped for around NZ$27 per day, or get a good deal on weekly rates (around NZ$110). Mountain-bike rentals are around NZ$6/40 per day/week. Many of the companies listed here rent bicycles and mopeds, as do many hotels. Companies include:

Avis Rental Cars (☎ 22833, W www.avis.co.ck) Avarua
BT Bike Hire (☎ 23586) 'Arorangi
Budget Rent-A-Car & Polynesian Bike Hire (☎ 20895, W www.budget.co.ck) Avarua
Fun Rentals (☎ 26426, e funcars@funrentals.co.ck) opposite Rarotonga airport
Island Car & Bike Hire (☎ 22632, W www.islandcarhire.co.ck) 'Arorangi & Avarua
Rarotonga Rentals (☎ 22326) Avatiu
Tara's Rental Bikes (☎ 20757) Muri
Tipani Rentals (☎ 22328, 21617, fax 25611) 'Arorangi
Vaine's Rental Bikes (☎ 20331) Muri

Taxi Rates are about NZ$2.50 per kilometre; from Muri to the airport will cost NZ$40. Local taxi operators include:

BK Taxis (☎ 20019) Avarua
JP Taxis (☎ 26572) 'Arorangi
Muri Beach Taxis (☎ 21625) Muri
Ngatangi'ia Taxis (☎ 22238) Ngatangi'ia
Pokoinu Cab (☎ 20529) Pokoinu

AVARUA

The capital of the Cook Islands and Rarotonga's principal town, Avarua lies on the middle of the north coast, about 2km east of the airport. This relaxed town has all the basic services and some interesting places to visit. If you're looking for nightlife, Avarua is where you'll find it.

Orientation & Information

The main road, Ara Maire Nui, is part of Ara Tapu as it runs through town along the waterfront. An obvious orientation point is the traffic circle near the Takuva'ine stream and the Avarua Harbour entrance. West along the main road is Avatiu Harbour, where the inter-island passenger cargo ships are based. The airport is 1km or so further west.

See Information under Rarotonga, earlier, for details of services and facilities in Avarua.

Things to See

Just to the east of the traffic circle is the **seven-in-one coconut tree** – a group of seven tall coconut trees growing in a perfect circle.

Nearby the traffic circle, next door to the post office, is the Cook Islands **Philatelic Bureau** (☎ 29336; Takuva'ine Rd; open 8am-4pm Mon-Fri), where you can purchase uncirculated mint and proof sets of coins and notes, plus collector's editions of Cook Islands stamps.

Around 300m south is **Papeiha Stone** (Takuva'ine Rd), upon which Papeiha stood in 1823 when he preached the gospel on Rarotonga for the first time; the stone sits atop a raised traffic circle near its original site.

On the inland side of the main road, half a block east of the traffic circle, are the **Para O Tane Palace** and **Taputapuatea**, the palace area of Makea Takau who was the *ariki* of this district in 1888 when the British officially took control of the Cook Islands. The palace is the residence of Takau's descendant, Makea Nui Teremoana Ariki, and is not open to the public. Named after a temple in Ra'iatea in the Society Islands, Taputapuatea was one of the largest and most sacred *marae* on Rarotonga before it was destroyed by the missionaries.

A bit further east, on the waterfront side of the road, **Beachcomber Gallery** (☎ 21939; Ara Tapu; open 9.30am-4pm Mon-Fri, 9.30am-noon Sat) displays Cook Islander arts and crafts in a building constructed in 1845 by the LMS for its Sunday school. You can visit the workshop here to see black pearl jewellery and shell carvings being made.

On the opposite side of the road, to the south of Beachcomber Gallery, is the fine, white-painted **CICC** (Makea Tinirau Rd), which was built of coral in 1853. The **graveyard** around the church is worth a leisurely browse. At the front is a monument to Papeiha and just to the left (as you face the church) is the grave of Albert Henry, the first prime minister of the Cook Islands. The main church service is held at 10am on Sunday.

Inland behind the Para O Tane Palace, the **Cook Islands Library & Museum Society** (☎ 26468; Makea Tinirau Rd; museum admission NZ$2; open 9am-1pm Mon-Fri, also 4pm-8pm Tues, 9.30am-1pm Sat) houses a collection of rare books and literature on the Pacific. The small museum has an interesting collection of artefacts.

The **National Museum** (☎ 20725; Victoria Rd; admission by donation; open 8am-4pm Mon-Fri), around 600m east of the traffic circle, has a well-presented selection of Cook Islands and South Pacific artefacts.

Places to Stay

Central Motel (☎ 25735, fax 25740; e stop over@central.co.ck; Takuva'ine Rd; singles/doubles NZ$70/76), inland from the traffic circle, is not the most atmospheric place on the island, but the rooms are spotless and there's a spa pool.

Paradise Inn (☎ 20544, fax 22544; w www .cookpage.com/ParadiseInn/; Ara Tapu; budget singles NZ$52, single/double/triple/family units NZ$70/88/102/112), a short walk east of town, is a friendly spot with a beautiful view from the seafront patio. The amenities are great, but the beach isn't good for swimming.

Places to Eat

Rarotonga's main supermarkets, **CITC Wholesale Supermarket** (Ara Tapu; open 8am-5pm Mon-Wed, 8am-6pm Thur & Fri), near Avatiu Harbour, and **Foodland supermarket** (☎ 23 378; Ara Maire Nui; open 8am-6pm Mon-Fri, 8am-4pm Sat) have a wide selection.

T-Shayla Bakery (☎ 23559; Ara Tapu; open 7am-4pm Tues-Fri, 7am-2pm Sat), east of town near Paradise Inn, sells heavenly pastries and bread.

Mama's Cafe (☎ 23379; Ara Maire Nui), beside Foodland supermarket, serves good sandwiches, fast food, pastries and ice cream.

Palace Takeaways (☎ 21438; Avatiu Harbour; burgers NZ$5.50-7.50, hot meals NZ$10-13) is a favourite local haunt that's open late – try the legendary Palace Burger.

AVARUA

PLACES TO STAY	OTHER		
42 Paradise Inn	2 Snowbird Laundromat	14 Westpac Bank	24 Pearl Factory
49 Central Motel	3 Ports Authority;	15 Rarotonga Bowling Club	26 Ministry of Foreign
	Harbour Master;	17 Budget Rent-a-Car	Affairs & Immigration
PLACES TO EAT	Taio Shipping	Downtown Office	27 Post Office;
1 Palace Takeaways	4 Punanga Nui Market	18 Police Station	Philatelic Bureau;
16 Mama's Cafe;	5 Rarotonga Rentals	19 Bus Stop;	New Zealand High
Foodland Supermarket	6 Island Car & Bike Hire	Cook's Corner Arcade;	Commission;
25 Banana Court Bar & Nightclub;	7 Kenwall Gallery	Mae Jo's Takeaways;	Bounty Bookshop
Blue Note Cafe;	8 St Joseph's Catholic Church	Bergman & Sons	28 The Rock
Arasena Gallery;	9 Budget Rent-a-Car	Pearl Store	29 Seven-in-One Coconut Tree
Island Hopper Vacations;	Main Office	20 Fuji Image Centre	30 T's Tatts
Bergman & Sons	10 Ronnie's Bar & Grill	21 CITC Shopping Centre;	32 Ministry for Marine
31 Trader Jack's	11 Jetsave Travel;	Cocophoto; Telepost;	Resources
36 The Café	Vonnia's Store	Avis Rental Cars	33 Waterfront Arcade
37 Staircase Restaurant/Bar	12 Maui Pearls	22 ANZ Bank	34 Empire Theatre
41 T-Shayla Bakery	13 Island Craft Ltd	23 Visitor Information	35 Para O Tane Palace;
		Centre	Taputapuatea

Mae Jo's Takeaways (☎ 26621; Cook's Corner Arcade; burgers NZ$5, Chinese meals NZ$12-29) dishes up really enormous Chinese meals straight from the wok, as well as curries and burgers.

The Café (☎ 21283; Ara Tapu; breakfast NZ$4-11.50, lunch NZ$9.50-11.50, cakes NZ$4.50), across the road from Para O Tane Palace, is a groovy space with friendly service and delicious, healthy food. The coffee aficionados here serve up a great brew.

Blue Note Cafe (☎ 23236; Banana Court; breakfast NZ$8-15.50, mains NZ$11-15.50, cakes NZ$7.50-8.50) is a cruisy place serving tasty meals (with some island and vegetarian dishes) on the veranda in the Banana Court building.

Staircase Restaurant/Bar (☎ 22254; Ara Tapu; dinner NZ$12-15), east of the traffic

circle, is a family restaurant serving quality food at low prices. There's live music every night and a popular 'island night' on Thursday (NZ$20/5 with/without dinner).

Trader Jack's (☎ 26464; snacks from NZ$8, mains NZ$11-29.50), on the waterfront near the traffic circle, is popular with Rarotonga's genteel crowd; both indoor and deck tables have great sea views. The mainly seafood menu includes sashimi.

You can pick up fresh local produce on Saturday morning at **Punanga Nui Market**, near Avatiu Harbour. Whole fresh fish is often sold here early on any morning.

Entertainment
Empire Theatre (☎ 23189; Ara Maire Nui; adult/child NZ$5/3; open nightly), Rarotonga's only cinema, screens new films.

AVARUA

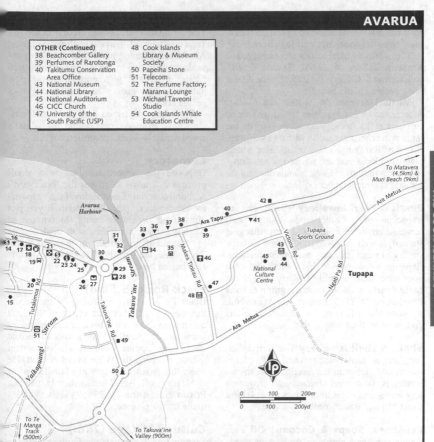

OTHER (Continued)
38 Beachcomber Gallery
39 Perfumes of Rarotonga
40 Takitumu Conservation
    Area Office
43 National Museum
44 National Library
45 National Auditorium
46 CICC Church
47 University of the
    South Pacific (USP)

48 Cook Islands
    Library & Museum
    Society
50 Papeiha Stone
51 Telecom
52 The Perfume Factory;
    Marama Lounge
53 Michael Taveoni
    Studio
54 Cook Islands Whale
    Education Centre

Friday night is the big party night. Many of the bars have live music and typically remain open until around midnight (2am on Friday night).

Trader Jack's (☎ 26464) plays live music nightly to an upmarket crowd.

Staircase Restaurant/Bar (☎ 22254; *Ara Tapu*) has live music from Tuesday to Friday and a melange of reggae, '70s hits and techno on Friday and Saturday; Thursday is 'island night'.

The Rock (☎ 27625; *Ara Tapu*), east of the traffic island, was *the* social spot at the time of writing.

Marama Lounge (☎ 29993; *Ara Metua*; *open daily*), beside the Perfume Factory, is huge on Wednesday and Thursday nights, when vanloads of backpackers pour in. Dive for free pearls in the swimming pool.

Ronnie's Bar & Grill (☎ 20823; *Ara Maire Nui*) has lots of local flavour – flex your vocal chords with karaoke here.

TJ's Nightclub (☎ 24722; *Ara Tapu*; *Fri & Sat cover charge NZ$2; open Wed-Sat*), is a *loud* dance spot popular with 18 to 25 year olds.

At night, Blue Note Cafe transforms into the **Banana Court Bar & Nightclub** (☎ 29061; *Ara Maire Nui; open Tues-Sat*), with live blues, reggae and rock, and dance parties.

Shopping
Arts & Crafts Traditional and modern arts and handicrafts are available throughout Rarotonga. **Island Craft** (☎ 22009; *Ara Maire Nui*) has an excellent selection of high-quality Cook Islands arts and crafts, including a collection of masks and spears.

Beachcomber Gallery (☎ 21939; Ara Maire Nui) has a wide selection of excellent weavings, *tivaevae*, paintings and jewellery.

The works of local artists are displayed at **Arasena Gallery** (☎ 23476; Banana Court), and **Kenwall Gallery** (☎ 25527; Ara Maire Nui), beside Pacific Supplies.

Michael Taveoni (☎ 24003; Ara Metua, Atupa) shows his excellent wood and stone carvings at his studio; stop when you see the large stone carvings. **Judith Künzle** (☎ 20959) is one of Rarotonga's best artists. Her watercolours of local land and seascapes, and drawings and paintings of Cook Islands dancers are for sale at Beachcomber Gallery.

Pearls & Pearl Jewellery Black pearls are a speciality of the Cook Islands. A single pearl can cost anything from NZ$5 (irregular and stunted) to well over NZ$1000. There's a large variety of pearl jewellery and other creations, so peruse a few shops to find something to suit your style. **Beachcomber Gallery** (☎ 21939), **Maui Pearls** (☎ 26066) and **Bergman & Sons Pearl Store** (☎ 21902), along Ara Maire Nui, are good places to start. A multitude of sellers operate from their homes also.

Shells & Shell Jewellery You'll find shell jewellery at many of the arts and crafts places mentioned earlier in this section. Necklaces, handbags, fans, wind chimes, statues, jewellery boxes and other items are sold at **Island Craft Ltd** and **Beachcomber Gallery**.

Perfumes, Soaps & Coconut Oil Pure coconut oil and perfumes and soaps made from pure coconut oil are sold at **The Perfume Factory** (☎ 22690; Ara Metua, Avarua) and **Perfumes of Rarotonga** (☎ 26238; Ara Tapu), among other places. Mango, banana and coffee liqueurs are also up for tasting and for sale.

Tattooing You're sure to remember your trip with this traditional Polynesian art as a souvenir. All-original Maori designs at **T's Tatts** (☎ 25157; Ara Maire Nui; open 10am-4pm Mon-Fri) start at NZ$40.

Pareu & Other Clothing Colourful tie-dyed and printed *pareu* (sarongs), souvenir T-shirts and Hawaiian-style shirts are sold in many shops around Avarua. You'll find a good selection at **Punanga Nui Market**, beside Avatiu Harbour. Both **Vonnia's Store** (☎ 20 927; Ara Maire Nui) and **Tuki's Pareu** (☎ 25 537; Ara Maire Nui) are also worth a look.

AROUND THE ISLAND

You'll find most attractions on or near the Ara Tapu coastal road. Travelling along the inland Ara Metua, running parallel to Ara Tapu, reveals another side to the island – swamp taro fields, goats and pigs grazing in pawpaw patches, citrus groves and ancestral graves beside houses.

The sights described here are listed anticlockwise from Avarua around the island's approximately 34km circumference.

Cemetery

Opposite the airport terminal is a small graveyard, known locally as the 'brickyard'. A controversial Czechoslovakian expatriate cancer-cure specialist, Milan Brych, set himself up here after being thrown out of Australia. Cancer patients who died despite his treatment are buried in the graveyard. Tom Neale, the hermit of Suwarrow Atoll, is also buried here.

Black Rock (6.5km)

Black Rock (Tuoro) is said to be the departure point from where the spirits of the dead commence the voyage back to the legendary homeland of 'Avaiki. This is also where the missionary Papeiha is supposed to have swum ashore, clasping the Bible over his head. He was actually rowed ashore in a small boat!

Nearby, off Ara Metua, the **Rarotonga Prison craft shop** (☎ 29457) sells ukuleles made by the prisoners.

Cultural Village (7km)

Visiting the Cook Islands Cultural Village (☎ 21314, fax 25557) on 'Arorangi's back road is a delightful experience; you'll probably learn more about traditional Cook Islands culture in one day here than during the entire rest of your stay. Guided tours feature demonstrations of many aspects of Cook Islands culture, visit traditional huts and include a feast of traditional foods and a rousing traditional music and dance show. Tours begin at 10am Monday to Friday and cost NZ$54/27 per adult/child; reservations are essential.

'Arorangi (8km)

On Rarotonga's west coast, 'Arorangi was the first missionary-built village, conceived of as a model for other villages on the island. Its main place of interest is the 1849 **CICC**; Papeiha is buried here. Rising up behind 'Arorangi is the flat-topped peak of Raemaru (365m). See the boxed text 'Aitutaki Gets a

Jean-Marie Tjibaou Cultural Centre, Noumea, New Caledonia

Kanak children, Lifou, New Caledonia

Petroglyphs, Down Rope, Pitcairn Island

Humpback whale, Niue

Aitutaki Lagoon, Cook Islands

Frangipani, Cook Islands

Woman with frangipani 'ei (necklace), Rarotonga

Traditional Polynesian dancing, Rarotonga

Mountain' in the Aitutaki Atoll section later in this chapter for the legend of its flat top.

Carver Exham Wichman's **arts shop** (☎ 21180; Maria's Backpackers) is behind his house in 'Arorangi. Artist Andi Merkens' vibrant oil paintings and prints are sold at **Pacific Arts** (☎ 20200; Ara Tapu).

Highland Paradise (9km)

High atop a slope behind 'Arorangi, Highland Paradise (☎ 24477, 20610; admission NZ$10; open 9.30am-4pm Mon-Fri) is on the site of the original Tinomana village before the introduction of Christianity. Members of the Pirangi family, descendants of Tinomana Ariki, take visitors on a two-hour tour of this tropical garden-lover's delight, telling stories of the old days. Tours commence at 10am and cost NZ$35, including lunch.

South Coast (12km to 20km)

On the eastern edge of the abandoned Sheraton site, a road leads inland to **Wigmore's Waterfall**, a lovely little waterfall dropping into a fresh, cool, natural swimming pool. The south coast of Rarotonga has good, sandy beaches; the reef is much further out here and the sea bottom is relatively free from rocks. **Fruits of Rarotonga** (☎ 21509), at Tikioki, makes delicious smoothies and jam, and the owners will mind your bags while you swim or snorkel.

Muri (22km to 25km)

Muri Beach, on Muri's lagoon on the southeast side of the island, is particularly beautiful. The shallow water has a sandy bottom dotted with countless sea cucumbers and some coral formations. Out towards the reef are four small *motu* (lagoon islets): Taakoka, Koromiri, Oneroa and Motutapu. Taakoka is volcanic; the others are sand cays.

Water-sports equipment and lagoon cruises are available from a couple of places here.

Matavera (27.5km)

The old CICC here is especially lovely at night when the outside is lit up. The scenery inland between Matavera and Avarua is beautiful. **Perfumes of Rarotonga** (☎ 26238; Ara Tapu; open 9.30am-4.30pm Mon-Fri) concocts perfumes, liqueurs and colognes. There's a pottery shop at the rear.

Arai-Te-Tonga (30km)

A small sign points off the road to the island's most important *marae* site, Arai-Te-Tonga.

When you meet Ara Metua there's a stone-marked *koutu* (ancient open-air royal court-yard) site in front of you. This whole area was a gathering place and the remains of the *marae*, the *koutu* and other meeting grounds are still here.

Cross-Island Hike

This three- to four-hour hike, from the north to south coasts via the 413m **Te Rua Manga** (the Needle), is the most popular walk on Rarotonga. It can also be done as a shorter walk from the northern end to the Needle and back again. It's important that you do the walk in a north–south direction, as the chances of taking a wrong turn are greater if you try it from the other direction. Be sure to wear adequate shoes and to take plenty of drinking water and mosquito repellent. Parts of the walk get extremely slippery in wet weather.

The road to the starting point runs south from Avatiu Harbour. The public bus will drop you at the harbour. See Organised Tours, earlier, for details of organised walks.

If you're driving, continue on the road up the valley by Avatiu Stream until you reach a prominent sign announcing the beginning of the walk and that vehicles cannot be taken past this point. A private vehicle road continues for about 1km.

A footpath takes off from the end of this vehicle road. After about 10 minutes it drops down and crosses a small stream. Avoid following the white plastic power-cable track up the valley; instead, pick up the track beside the massive boulder on the ridge to your left, after the stream crossing.

From here the track climbs steeply all the way to the Needle (about 45 minutes). At the first sight of the Needle there's a boulder in the middle of the path – a nice place for a rest. A little further on is a T-junction; the Needle is a 10-minute walk to the right. Up to now you've been ascending a ridge running in a north–south direction; at this junction it intersects with a ridge running in an east–west direction. This is an important junction and you will return to it after visiting the Needle.

Actually climbing the Needle is strictly for very serious rock climbers – it's high and sheer. You can, however, scramble around the northern side to a sheer drop and a breathtaking view from the northwestern corner. Take care on this climb: the ledge is very narrow and there's a long, unprotected drop which would be fatal if you slipped. Do *not* try to climb around to the southern side of the

Needle – it offers no view and is extremely dangerous.

Retrace your steps back to the T-junction, where the left fork heads east. Just before you reach the T-junction you'll come to a path along a white power-cable casing heading to the right (south). Some guides take this way, however, from the T-junction take the traditional track, which drops slightly and then climbs to a small peak that gives the best view of the Needle. From here the track leads down a long, slippery ridge for about half an hour. This descent can be treacherous in wet weather.

After about 30 minutes the track meets Papua Stream and follows it down the hill, zigzagging back and forth across the water. After another 45 minutes the track emerges in fernland. Here it veers away from the stream to the right, passing through the fernland. Be sure to stick to the main track; there are several places where newer, minor tracks seem to take off towards the stream but these end at dangerous spots upstream from the waterfall. Another 15 minutes further on, the main track turns back towards the stream, bringing you to the bottom of the beautiful **Wigmore's Waterfall** (take note, the mosquitoes here are particularly nasty). A rough dirt road leads from the south coast up to Wigmore's Waterfall. It's about a 15-minute walk down this road to the coast road, where you can flag down a bus.

Places to Stay

Rarotonga has a growing range of accommodation for every budget; most places have cooking and laundry facilities for guests and most provide free pick-up from the airport. The following places are listed anticlockwise around the island from Avarua's centre.

Renting a House A fully equipped two-bedroom house usually costs around NZ$250 to NZ$400 per week. Check the classified sections of the *Cook Islands News* and *Cook Islands Herald* or contact one of the following:

Cook Islands Tours & Travel (☎ 28270, fax 27270, ⓦ www.cookislandstours.co.ck)
Jetsave Travel (☎ 27707, fax 28807, ⓦ www.jetsave.co.ck)
Kii Kii Holiday Cottages (☎ 21937, fax 22937, ⓦ *www.kiikiimotel.co.ck*)

Places to Stay – Budget

Tiare Village (☎ 23466, ☎/fax 21874; ⓦ *www .tiarevillage.co.ck; Kaikaveka Dr, Nika'o; triples*

per person NZ$20, single/double chalets per person NZ$22/25, double units NZ$70), approximately 3km from the centre of Avarua, is a comfortable backpacker haven famous for its hospitality. There's a TV room, board games and a library. Ask about special weekly rates.

Aunty Noo's Beach Lodge (☎ 21253; *Ara Tapu, 'Arorangi; dorm beds/doubles per person NZ$10/13)*, close to the beach, is basic but friendly.

Maria's Backpackers (☎ 21180; *'Arorangi; dorm beds/units per person NZ$15/18)* is a pleasant duplex with self-contained units and dorm rooms.

Rarotonga Backpackers (☎ 21590; ⓦ *www .rarotongabackpackers.com; Ara Metua, Kavera; dorm beds NZ$20, doubles NZ$44-48)* clings to the hillside on the inland road. The rambling new structure has a kitchen/lounge area, swimming pool, great views and a communal feel.

Backpackers International Hostel (☎/fax 21847; ⓔ *annabill@backpackers.co.ck; Ara Tapu, Kavera; dorm beds NZ$15, triples/ doubles/singles per person NZ$15/16/26)* is a large concrete building with clean, friendly communal areas.

Maiana Guesthouse (☎/fax 20438; ⓦ *www .maianaguesthouse.co.ck; Ara Tapu, Titikaveka; dorm beds NZ$18, singles/doubles/ triples NZ$30/50/54)*, located on the south side of the island, is a popular, clean hostel with good cooking facilities and a lively lounge area.

Aremango Guesthouse (☎ 24362; ⓔ *arem ango@oyster.net.ck; Ara Tapu, Muri; rooms per person NZ$22)*, Muri's popular place, is clean and comfortable, with spacious rooms.

Vara's Beach House (☎ 23156, fax 22619; ⓦ *www.varas.co.ck; Ara Tapu, Muri; beds in 8-bed dorms NZ$20, singles/doubles NZ$36/ 48, doubles with bathroom NZ$60)* is a backpacker haven. The house right on Muri Beach can be noisy; the villas up the hill are more relaxed, with great views.

Places to Stay – Mid-Range

Lagoon Lodges (☎ 22020, fax 22021; ⓦ *www.cookpages.com/LagoonLodges/index .html; Ara Tapu, Kavera; bungalows NZ$140- 195, 2-bedroom villas from NZ$225)* is set back from the road, opposite the beach. Spacious bungalows are set around a garden, with a grass tennis court, trampoline and pool.

Palm Grove (☎ 20002, fax 21998; ⓔ *beach@ palmgrove.co.ck; Ara Tapu, Vaima; garden/*

beachfront bungalows NZ$190/290) has nicely appointed bungalows set among tropical gardens or overlooking a secluded beach. Rates include tropical breakfast.

Little Polynesian (☎ 24280, fax 21585; e littlepoly@beach.co.ck; Ara Tapu, Titikaveka; studio units NZ$250, cottages NZ$290), on a fine beach with great snorkelling, is private, secluded and intimate. The beachfront studio units and lagoon-side cottage are all self-contained; children aged 12 years and over are welcome.

Aroko Bungalows (☎ 23625, fax 24625; e aroko@bungalows.co.ck; Ara Tapu, Muri; garden/lagoon bungalows NZ$100/120) has comfortable units in a tranquil setting by Muri's lagoon.

Royal Palms (☎ 22838, fax 22836; w www .royalpalms.co.ck; Ara Tapu, Matavera; bungalows NZ$140) has three self-contained bungalows, tranquilly set among lush gardens inland of Muri Beach and Avarua. You'll need wheels.

Kii Kii Motel (☎ 21937, fax 22937; w www .kiikiimotel.co.ck; singles/doubles/triples/ quads from NZ$70/90/155/185, deluxe singles/doubles from NZ$120/150) is on the beach, about 2km east of Avarua. The beach is not good for swimming, but there's a decent pool. All rooms are self-contained; deluxe rooms overlook the ocean.

Places to Stay – Top End
Sunhaven Beach Bungalows (☎ 28465; w www.ck/sunhaven/; Ara Tapu, 'Arorangi; studios NZ$180, bungalows NZ$215-240) is a quiet spot with lovely, new bungalows fronting the beach. There's a pool, and hammocks slung between the trees.

Moana Sands Hotel (☎ 26189, fax 22189; w www.moanasandshotel.co.ck; Ara Tapu, Titikaveka; doubles/triples NZ$315/370, beachfront suites NZ$495) is in a peaceful spot on a good stretch of beach. Its 12 rooms, in a two-storey block, have verandas and small kitchens. Rates include complimentary tropical breakfast, canoes and snorkelling gear.

Pacific Resort (☎ 20427, fax 21427; w www .pacificresort.com; Ara Tapu, Muri; units from NZ$300, 2-bedroom villas from NZ$655), in a lovely position on Muri Beach, is Rarotonga's most attractive resort. The units are self-contained; rates include breakfast.

Sokala Villas (☎ 29200, fax 21222; e villas@ sokala.co.ck; PO Box 82; villas NZ$320-480) has excellently appointed self-contained villas right on Muri Beach. It's especially

popular with couples and honeymooners. Ask about 'early-bird' discounts.

Large Resorts The 'rack rates' at the two resorts are high; packaging your flights and accommodation will provide cheaper rates.

Rarotongan Beach Resort (☎ 25800, fax 25799; w www.rarotongan.co.ck; Ara Tapu, Kavera; garden/beachfront rooms from NZ$360/475, suites from NZ$780) is really colourful – in fact, the vibrant mega-flora at reception may just swallow you whole! The resort fronts a beautiful stretch of beach, offers plenty of activities, is kid-friendly and wheelchair-accessible, with rooms equipped for travellers with disabilities.

Edgewater Resort (☎ 25435, fax 25475; w www.edgewater.co.ck; Ara Tapu, 'Arorangi; garden/beachfront rooms NZ$210/340, deluxe suites NZ$550) has all the facilities you'd expect in a huge resort.

Places to Eat
Eateries are listed here anticlockwise from west to east around the island.

Cafés & Takeaways Numerous takeaway joints surround the island, serving burgers and fried foods.

The Brunch Cottage (Ara Tapu, 'Arorangi; breakfast & snacks NZ$3.50-12; open 8am-2.30pm daily) serves fresh and tasty food in a dainty, louvered shack.

Saltwater Café (☎ 20020; Ara Tapu, Titikaveka; breakfast NZ$7.50-15, burgers NZ$6.50-11) serves tasty breakfast and lunch, fabulous pure-fruit smoothies and espresso coffee. Wednesday is 'Wok Thai' night from 5pm to 8pm; on Sunday the café runs hot.

Maire Nui Gardens & Café (☎ 22796; Ara Tapu, Titikaveka; muffins & cakes NZ$2.50-5), on the south side of the island, has a beautiful, peaceful garden atmosphere and tasty snacks. Admission to the gardens is NZ$3.

Fruits of Rarotonga (☎ 21509; Ara Tapu, Tikioki; smoothies NZ$3.50, sandwiches from NZ$3.50, snacks from NZ$1), opposite the island's best snorkelling spot, sends the bubbling aroma of jams and relishes out like a siren's call. The food is good and cheap, and staff will look after your belongings while you swim.

Ambala Gardens (☎ 26486; Muri; meals NZ$10-12, cakes NZ$3-5; open 9am-3pm Thur-Sat) serves delicious food in its tranquil gardens high above Muri Beach.

Restaurants Most restaurants serve Australian and NZ wines; reservations are recommended.

Kikau Hut (☎ 26860; Ara Tapu, 'Arorangi; mains NZ$13.50-25) resembles a colourful fish…as long as that fish comes in the shape of a circular hut and in the form of delightful cuisine, such as seafood, Thai and vegetarian dishes. Kikau's *ika mata* is well regarded.

Spaghetti House (☎ 25441; mains NZ$17), fronting Edgewater Resort, serves all the usual suspects – hearty pastas, gourmet pizzas and grills.

Windjammer Restaurant (☎ 23950; Ara Tapu, 'Arorangi; mains NZ$22.50-29.50, 3-course special NZ$25), in a pleasant, cane-bedecked hut, serves sushi and sashimi, as well as meat and seafood dishes infused with European, Asian and Cajun flavours.

Vaima Restaurant & Bar (☎ 26123; Ara Tapu, Vaima; mains NZ$18.50-29.50) is an enchanting beachside restaurant, serving mainly seafood (but it does it so well!), including some of the best raw fish on the island.

Sails (☎ 27349; Muri Beach; lunch NZ$7-22, dinner mains NZ$18-26), perfectly positioned with beachside decking overlooking Muri's lagoon, whips up tasty fare for breakfast, lunch and dinner, as well as gourmet baguettes, vegetarian dishes and cakes.

Flame Tree (☎ 25123 after 3pm; Muri Lagoon; mains NZ$19-26) serves international cuisine in an intimate setting under a fiery flame tree.

That's Pasta (☎ 22232; Ara Tapu, Muri; dishes NZ$12-16.50) turns out authentic, freshly made pasta and Italian sauces, with lots of love. *Belissimo!*

Self-Catering You'll barely be more than walking distance from one of the small markets dotted around the island. **Wigmore's Superstore** (☎ 20206; Vaima'anga; open 6am-8pm daily) has a selection of fresh and packaged foods, a liquor shop, ATM and petrol.

Entertainment

Island Nights & Buffets Indulging in an 'island night', including an island buffet meal and show, is a *must* in the Cook Islands; there's one virtually every night of the week on Rarotonga. The most popular are at the **Edgewater Resort** (☎ 25435; 'Arorangi; dinner & show NZ$45, show only NZ$10) and **Staircase Restaurant/Bar** (☎ 22254; Ara Tapu, Avarua; dinner & show NZ$20, show only NZ$5).

Backpackers International Hostel (☎ 21 847; Ara Tapu, Kavera; guests/nonguests NZ$20/25) has an enormously popular island buffet on Saturday; book by 4pm Friday.

Piri Puruto III (☎ 20309) zips up coconut trees, demonstrates traditional firemaking and serves an *umukai* (NZ$45) on Sunday.

Bars The main bar action centres on Avarua. **Mama Josie's Nite Life Tours** (☎ 27242) provides the transport for Wednesday night's 'Chill Out' tour (three to four bars, NZ$12) and the 'Friday Night, Party Hard' tour (seven bars, karaoke and dancing, NZ$15).

The **RSA Club** (☎ 20590; Ara Tapu), opposite the airport, is a popular spot to while away the time between check-in and departure.

The larger resorts have attached bars; **Barefoot Bar** (☎ 20427; Pacific Resort, Muri Beach), opposite the beach, is a lovely spot for drinks.

Sails (☎ 27349; Muri Beach) has a wonderful view to wash down with beverages.

Cook Islands Game Fishing Club (☎ 21 419; Ara Tapu, Tupapa) is a friendly place with cheap beers and a pool table.

Aitutaki Atoll

pop 1800 • area 18.3 sq km
Nestled in a huge triangular lagoon, Aitutaki is one of the most beautiful coral islands in the Pacific. The hook-shaped atoll is the Cooks' second-most populated island and the second-most visited by tourists. The outer reef of the lagoon is dotted with beautiful *motu*.

History

Various legends tell of the first Polynesian settlers, led by Ru from 'Avaiki, arriving at Aitutaki by canoe. He arrived with his wives and family at the Akitua *motu* (now the Aitutaki Pearl Beach Resort). Aitutaki's original name was Ararau 'Enua O Ru Ki Te Moana (Ru in Search of Land over Sea) – the present name, *a'i tutaki*, means 'to keep the fire going'.

Aitutaki's European discoverer was Captain William Bligh, who arrived on the *Bounty* on 11 April 1789 (17 days before the famous mutiny). In 1821 John Williams left Papeiha and Vahapata here to convert the islanders to Christianity. The 1850s saw Aitutaki become a favourite port of call for whaling ships scouring the Pacific. During WWII the island went through great upheaval when a large US contingent built two long runways.

AITUTAKI ATOLL

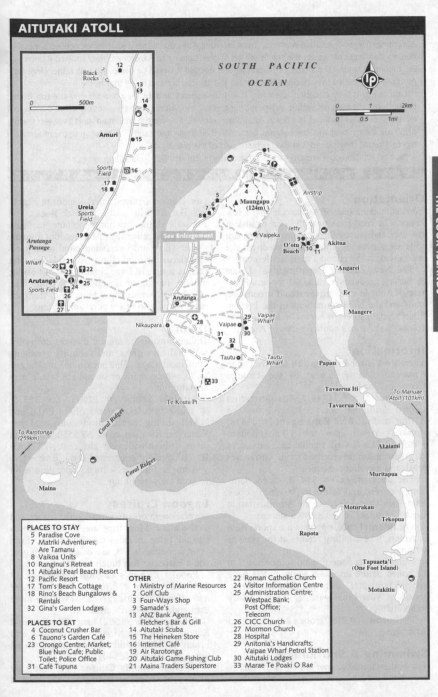

SOUTH PACIFIC OCEAN

Black Rocks

Amuri

Sports Field

Ureia Sports Field

Arutanga Passage

Wharf

Arutanga Sports Field

See Enlargement

Maungapu (124m)

Airstrip

Vaipeka

Jetty

O'otu Beach

Akitua

'Angarei

Ee

Mangere

Arutanga

Nikaupara

Vaipae

Vaipae Wharf

Tautu

Tautu Wharf

Papau

Tavaerua Iti

Tavaerua Nui

To Manuae Atoll (101km)

Te Koutu Pt

Coral Ridges

Coral Ridges

To Rarotonga (259km)

Akaiami

Muritapua

Maina

Moturakau

Tekopua

Rapota

Tapuaeta'i (One Foot Island)

Motukitiu

RAROTONGA & THE COOK ISLANDS

PLACES TO STAY
5 Paradise Cove
7 Matriki Adventures; Are Tamanu
8 Vaikoa Units
10 Ranginui's Retreat
11 Aitutaki Pearl Beach Resort
12 Pacific Resort
17 Tom's Beach Cottage
18 Rino's Beach Bungalows & Rentals
32 Gina's Garden Lodges

PLACES TO EAT
4 Coconut Crusher Bar
6 Tauono's Garden Café
23 Orongo Centre; Market; Blue Nun Cafe; Public Toilet; Police Office
31 Café Tupuna

OTHER
1 Ministry of Marine Resources
2 Golf Club
3 Four-Ways Shop
9 Samade's
13 ANZ Bank Agent; Fletcher's Bar & Grill
14 Aitutaki Scuba
15 The Heineken Store
16 Internet Café
19 Air Rarotonga
20 Aitutaki Game Fishing Club
21 Maina Traders Superstore
22 Roman Catholic Church
24 Visitor Information Centre
25 Administration Centre; Westpac Bank; Post Office; Telecom
26 CICC Church
27 Mormon Church
28 Hospital
29 Anitonia's Handicrafts; Vaipae Wharf Petrol Station
30 Aitutaki Lodges
33 Marae Te Poaki O Rae

Aitutaki Gets a Mountain

According to legend, Aitutaki was once just a low atoll. The inhabitants decided they needed a mountain, so they went off across the sea in search of one. Coming to Rarotonga, they spotted Raemaru, the mountain behind the village of 'Arorangi, and decided it would be perfect. It was rather large for Aitutaki, however, so they decided they'd take just the top off and bring that home.

Late at night, they encircled Raemaru, thrust their spears in until they had severed the top from the bottom, and took off with it. When morning came, the 'Arorangi villagers set off in hot pursuit to reclaim their mountain. But the fierce Aitutakian warriors, holding the mountain aloft between them with their spears, beat the Rarotongans back with their single free hands. After bringing the mountain top to Aitutaki they placed it in the northern part of the island.

Back on Rarotonga, Raemaru today has a distinctly cut-off, flat-topped appearance.

Orientation

You can make a tour of Aitutaki in just a few hours. The road runs near the coast most of the way and passes through several pleasant villages. Arutanga, about halfway down the west coast, is the island's main settlement.

The New Zealand Department of Lands & Survey produces a 1:25,000 topographical map of Aitutaki showing the island's roads and trails and the coral formations in the lagoon. Tourist publications *What's On in the Cook Islands* and *Jason's* contain maps of Aitutaki.

Information

There's a **Visitor Information Centre** *(open 8am-4pm Mon-Fri)* next to the Orongo Centre in Arutanga.

Westpac *(☎ 31714; Administration Centre, Arutanga; open 9.30am-3pm Mon & Thur)* and the **ANZ Bank agent** *(☎ 31418; Amuri; open 9am-3pm Mon-Fri)* next door to Fletcher's Bar & Grill handle cash advances on credit cards and change foreign currencies (cash and travellers cheques).

The **post office** *(☎ 31470; open 8am-3pm Mon-Fri)* and **Telecom** *(☎ 31680; open 8am-4pm Mon-Fri)* are in the Administration Centre. Aitutaki issues its own stamps.

The **Internet café**, opposite the sports field at Amuri, was awaiting repairs at the time of writing.

Water from an underground source needs to be boiled before drinking. Some hotels have special rainwater tanks for drinking water, so ask at your hotel whether it's necessary to boil it.

The **hospital** *(☎31002; open 24hr)* is behind Arutanga.

Swimming & Snorkelling

The best swimming, snorkelling and beaches are around the lagoon *motu*, accessible by boat (see Lagoon Cruises, later). Opposite Fletcher's Bar & Grill, south of Black Rocks, you can walk all the way out to the outer reef on a natural coral causeway that starts 50m from the shore. There are interesting coral rock pools and places for snorkelling just inside the outer reef. A couple of large coral heads, just off the airstrip, support an abundance of marine life; the channel separating Akitua *motu* from the main island also offers good snorkelling.

Diving

Diving outside the lagoon features drop-offs, wall and cave dives, and visibility averaging 40m most days. The occasional manta ray, turtle, whale shark or humpback whale may also drop in.

Aitutaki Scuba *(☎ 31103, fax 31310; @ scuba@aitutaki.net.ck)* offers PADI and NAUI diving certification courses; Open Water certification costs NZ$550. One-tank dives without/with gear hire cost NZ$75/85. If you're really concerned about dive safety you might find the Aitutaki operation a bit relaxed for your liking.

Lagoon Cruises

Several operators offer trips on the lagoon and to the *motu*. Most trips are six-hour cruises and the price includes transport to and from your accommodation, use of snorkelling gear and a barbecue fish lunch on the *motu*.

Popular **Bishop's Lagoon Cruises** *(☎ 31 009, fax 31493; @ bishopcruz@aitutaki.net .ck)* offers fun cruises (NZ$55) with no more than eight people to a craft.

Teking *(☎/fax 31582)* visits One Foot and Rapota Islands on Monday, Wednesday and Friday (NZ$35), and includes Maina on its Saturday cruise (NZ$40).

Paradise Islands Cruises *(☎ 31248, fax 31369; @ bookings@airraro.co.ck)* runs a stately cruise on a 21m catamaran, *Titi Ai Tonga*, with great food and plenty of room, for NZ$65.

Samade's (☎ *31526; O'otu Beach; open 7am-6pm daily*), directly opposite the Aitutaki Pearl Beach Resort, rents kayaks (one hour/half-day/full day NZ$10/15/20), and **Matriki Adventures** (☎ *31564*) rents dinghies for NZ$40 per day.

Fishing
Both **Aitutaki Sea Charters** (☎ *31695*) and **Clive Baxter** (☎ *31025*) take big-game fishing trips outside the reef for around NZ$110 per person, including all gear. **Barry Anderson** (☎ *31492*) offers full-day fishing trips inside the lagoon (NZ$150/180 for one/two people).

Aitutaki's fishermen congregate at the **Aitutaki Game Fishing Club** near the wharf; if you're keen to go fishing, stop by.

Other Organised Tours
You can visit the highest peak, Maungapu, and ancient *marae* with **Safari Inland Tours** (☎ *31426*); a three-hour tour costs NZ$35.

Aitutaki Walkabout (☎/fax *31757*; W www .aitutaki-walkabout.com.au) leads a walking introduction to island life. Tours start at 11am and 1pm Monday to Saturday and run for two hours (adult/child NZ$30/10).

AROUND THE ISLAND
Arutanga
Arutanga is a pleasant, sleepy little town. Built in 1828, the weathered CICC beside the harbour is the oldest church in the Cooks. There's beautiful carved wood painted red, yellow, green and white all around the ceiling, dark woodcarving over the doorways, simple stained-glass windows and an anchor placed on the ceiling.

Marae
Aitutaki's *marae* are notable for their large stones. Orongo *marae* used to sit where the Blue Nun Cafe is today, in Arutanga. The main road goes right through a big *marae* at the turn-off to Aitutaki Lodges; the stones are along both sides of the road. On the inland road between Nikaupara and Tautu, follow the 'Marae' sign to some of the most magnificent *marae* on the island: Tokangarangi, Taravao, Te Poaki O Rae and Paengariki. These *marae* may have been reclaimed by the jungle; check for information before you go looking for them.

Maungapu
The 30-minute hike to the top of Maungapu (124m), Aitutaki's highest peak, is worth the effort for the view over the entire atoll. The lush interior gives way to the turquoise lagoon, breaking surf and azure sea. The walk starts off gently, from a sign opposite the Paradise Cove motel, and gets steeper as you near the top.

Aitutaki Lagoon
Aitutaki's marvellous lagoon, dotted with sand bars, coral ridges and 21 uninhabited *motu*, is large, colourful and full of life.

Maina, a *motu* in the southwestern corner of the lagoon, offers the best snorkelling on the coral formations near its shore and around the large powder-white sand bars just to its north and east. **Tapuaeta'i** (One Foot Island) is the best-known *motu*, with its lovely white stretch of beach and brilliant, pale-turquoise water. You can get your passport stamped here and also send specially stamped postcards from the 'post office'.

Places to Stay – Budget
Paradise Cove (☎ *31218*; ℮ *mtl@aitutaki .net.ck; singles/doubles in house NZ$25/35, single/double huts NZ$35/50, bungalows NZ$150*) is on a beautiful stretch of beach with fine white sand and good snorkelling. Rooms in the house share a kitchen, bathroom and lounge; the bungalows are self-contained and comfortable. The traditional *kikau* (thatch-roofed) huts are basic but atmospheric.

Matriki Adventures (☎ *31564*; ℮ *matriki@ aitutaki.net.ck; single/double bungalows per person NZ$35/25*) has secluded bungalows with decks, cooking facilities and shared bathrooms, on a good stretch of beach.

Vaikoa Units (☎/fax *31145; Amuri; units per person NZ$40*) has six self-contained, colourful, island-style units on a lovely white beach good for swimming and snorkelling.

Tom's Beach Cottage (☎ *31051*, fax *31409*; ℮ *papatoms@aitutaki.net.ck; Amuri; singles/doubles/triples NZ$35/50/58, bungalow singles/doubles/triples NZ$84/94/110*) is a friendly beachfront place. The rooms share amenities, cooking facilities and a lounge.

Places to Stay – Mid-Range
Gina's Garden Lodges (☎/fax *31058*; ℮ *queen@aitutaki.net.ck; Tautu; singles/ doubles NZ$75/120, extra child/adult NZ$20/30*) is set back from the beach, but readers rave about its 'Garden of Eden'–like setting and friendly proprietors.

Rino's Beach Bungalows & Rentals (☎ 31 197, fax 31559; e rinos@aitutaki.net.ck; Ureia; garden/beachfront rooms NZ$111/ 169, deluxe beachfront doubles NZ$221), on the beach, has a variety of self-contained units sleeping up to six people; the deluxe beachfront rooms have great views.

Places to Stay – Top End
Are Tamanu (☎ 31810, fax 31816; w www .aretamanu.com; Amuri; doubles NZ$400- 451) has luxury, thatch-roofed units around a small garden, with a bar and pool overlooking the beach. Each self-contained unit has a king-size bed, air-con and fan. Use of bicycles and kayaks is free.

Aitutaki Pearl Beach Resort (☎ 31201, fax 31202; w www.aitutakipearlbeach.com; rooms NZ$335, bungalows NZ$595-975, over-water bungalows NZ$1195), on Akitua motu (joined to the main island by a footbridge), offers luxurious accommodation in a secluded spot.

Overlooking a sandy beach, **Pacific Resort** (☎ 31720, fax 31719; w www.pacificresort -aitutaki.com; lagoon-view bungalows NZ$615, beachfront bungalows/suites/villas NZ$710/930/1150) has simply stunning bungalows well positioned for privacy.

Places to Eat
Locally grown produce is sold at the **market** (Orongo Centre; open 7am-3pm Mon-Sat), where you might also find freshly caught fish. **Maina Traders Superstore** (Arutanga) and **The Heineken Store** (Amuri) are well stocked, though pricey; the latter sells hot takeaway food, fresh sandwiches and bread.

Tauono's Garden Café (☎ 31562; smoothies NZ$4, cakes NZ$5.50, meals from NZ$12), in the north, will whip up wholesome food with freshly picked items from its abundant garden. Organic fruit and vegetables, cakes, coffee and smoothies are also available.

Blue Nun Cafe (☎ 31604; Orongo Centre, Arutanga; burgers NZ$4-7, mains NZ$9-14) is a pleasant open-air café/bar serving burgers, curries and fish dishes.

Coconut Crusher Bar (☎ 31283; dinner NZ$12.50-26, island-night buffet NZ$25), in the north of the island, is a true island-style restaurant/bar, with a thatched roof, open-air dining and a popular 'island night' on Thursday (reservations essential). There's live music and dancing every night except Friday.

Café Tupuna (☎ 31678; mains NZ$25-28; open 6pm-9.30pm Mon-Sat), with its sandy floors and tropical garden setting, is a good place to spoil yourself. Delightful aromas waft from the kitchen, where Tupuna lovingly prepares her unique cuisine – Aitutaki land crabs may even be on the menu.

Entertainment
The 'island nights' on Aitutaki are some of the best in the Cook Islands. Bars here take it in turns to put on the show and the accompanying buffet, which cost from NZ$25 at local bars and restaurants to NZ$50 at the large resorts. You can also just watch the show for the price of a drink. **Coconut Crusher Bar** (☎ 31283), **Blue Nun Cafe** (☎ 31604; Orongo Centre) and **Fletcher's Bar & Grill** (☎ 31 418; Amuri) are popular spots. Ask where the action is for the night at your place of accommodation.

Samade's (☎ 31526; O'otu Beach) offers kayak hire, traditional food and a magnificent beach – it's particularly popular on Sunday afternoon.

Aitutaki Game Fishing Club (☎ 31379; usually open 4pm-late Mon-Sat), at the foot of the wharf in Arutanga, is a simple and friendly place to enjoy a cheap, cold beer and beautiful sunset views. Thursday and Friday nights are the best for socialising at the club.

Manuae Atoll
The tiny, unpopulated islets of Manuae (population zero, area 6.8 sq km) and Te Au O Tu, jointly known as Manuae, lie 101km from Aitutaki Atoll and belong to the people of Aitutaki. These islets are the only parts of a huge volcanic cone to break the ocean's surface. The cone measures 56km from east to west, 24km north to south. The other high point on the rim of this vast cone is the Astronomer Bank, 13km west of Manuae, which comes to within 300m of the ocean's surface.

Copra-cutting parties visit Manuae from Aitutaki occasionally, as they have done for a century or more. In 1823 the missionary John Williams visited the island and found about 60 inhabitants. There were only a dozen or so in the late 1820s, and missionaries took them to Aitutaki. Later, various Europeans made temporary homes on Manuae. The best known was William Marsters, who in 1863 was relocated to Palmerston with his three wives.

Shopping
Aitutakian crafts include woven pandanus purses, bags, mats and hats, shell-and-*rito* fans, white *rito* church hats, shell jewellery, wooden drums, ukuleles and colourful pareu. Island crafts are available at the **Orongo Centre** (*Arutanga*), by the wharf. **Anitonia's** (*Vaipae*) makes wooden drums, ukuleles and other handicrafts.

Getting There & Away
Air Rarotonga (☎ *31888 in Arutanga;* ☎ *22 888 on Rarotonga*) operates flights from Rarotonga to Aitutaki (NZ$154 one way, 50 minutes) at least three times daily from Monday to Saturday; there are no flights on Sunday. The Super Saver fare (NZ$127 one way) applies to certain flights. All the Rarotongan-based travel agencies offer package deals to Aitutaki. Flights depart Aitutaki for 'Atiu (NZ$138) on Tuesday and Friday, and 'Atiu for Aitutaki on Tuesday.

Air Rarotonga runs day trips to Aitutaki, including flights and a lagoon cruise on *Titi Ai Tonga*, for NZ$389/195 per adult/child. Flights depart from Rarotonga airport at 8am and return at 6.30pm Monday to Saturday.

See Boat in the Getting Around section earlier in this chapter for information on shipping services to Aitutaki. Trips between Rarotonga and the Northern Group islands often stop at Aitutaki.

Getting Around
Island Tours (☎ *31379*), an airport transfer service, connects with all arriving and departing flights and costs NZ$8 into town. **Pacific Taxi** (☎ *31220*) is an expensive service; inquire about transportation when making bookings at hotels or restaurants.

Various places rent vehicles – bicycles/mopeds/cars cost around NZ$5/25/85 per day. **Rino Beach Bungalows & Rentals** (☎ *31197, fax 31559; Ureia*) has the largest range, though you could also try **Ranginui's Retreat** (☎ *31657; O'otu Beach*) and **Vaipae Enterprises** (☎ *31489; Vaipae*).

Palmerston Atoll

pop 52 • area 2.0 sq km
Palmerston is far to the northwest of the other Southern Group islands and is sometimes treated as part of the Northern Group. The lagoon is 11km wide at its widest point, and 35 small islands dot the reef.

The island's most famous resident was the prolific breeder William Marsters (died 1899), who, along with his three wives, is an ancestor of many Cook Islanders here and on several other islands.

Palmerston is a quiet little place. There is no organised accommodation, although the mayor, George Marsters (☎ 20893, Avarua, Rarotonga) can arrange home-stay accommodation for around NZ$30 per day. There are no flights to Palmerston, though *Marsters Dream* makes fortnightly trips (NZ$300 return, 22 hours each way) between Palmerston and Rarotonga. You can arrange transport with the mayor.

'Atiu, Ma'uke & Mitiaro

'Atiu, Ma'uke and Mitiaro are often collectively referred to as Nga Pu Toru (The Three Roots), and the links between the people of the three islands have been strong for many centuries. The islands are similar geographically, characterised by a narrow lagoon, *makatea* around the outer edge, and a higher interior.

Modesty standards on these outer islands are more conservative than on Rarotonga; locals will be upset by anyone going shirtless or wearing swimming gear in town.

Electricity operates from 5am to midnight daily.

Getting There & Away
The three islands can easily be visited as a group. Rarotongan-based travel agents can organise package tours to 'Atiu, Ma'uke and Mitiaro, either individually or combined. See under the individual island headings for more details on air travel.

For details on travelling by inter-island cargo ship, see Boat in the Getting Around section earlier in this chapter.

'ATIU
pop 611 • area 26.9 sq km
The third-largest of the Cook Islands, 'Atiu is noted for its *makatea*. 'Atiu's five villages – Areora, Ngatiarua, Te'enui, Mapumai and Tengatangi – are all close together in the hilly centre of the island, radiating out on five roads from the administrative centre and the CICC.

'Atiu has some fine beaches, magnificent scenery, excellent walks, ancient *marae* and limestone caves. Many visitors stay only a couple of days, but the island is worth a longer visit.

History

'Atiu's traditional name is 'Enua Manu, which can be translated as 'Land of Birds' or 'Land of Insects'. 'Atiuans were the warriors of the Cook Islands and their colourful and bloody history includes many raids on neighbouring islands.

The European discovery of 'Atiu is credited to James Cook on 3 April 1777. Rongomatane, the leading 'Atiuan chief, was converted to Christianity after the missionaries passed his challenge of eating sugar cane from the sacred grove; he subsequently ordered all the idols on the island to be burnt. The arrival of the missionaries Williams and

Papeiha is still celebrated here on Gospel Day on 19 July.

Information

The **ADC Shop** (☎ 33028; Areora) offers cash advances on credit cards (Visa, Master-Card or Bankcard); travellers cheques (NZ dollars only) can be cashed at the **Centre Store** (☎ 33773; Te'enui). The **Telecom and post offices** (☎ 33680; Mapumai; open 8am-noon & 1pm-4pm Mon-Fri) are in the same building.

Caves

The *makatea* is riddled with limestone caves, complete with stalactites and stalagmites. You'll stumble across many small caves in any ramble through the *makatea*, so take a torch (flashlight). Wear good shoes – the

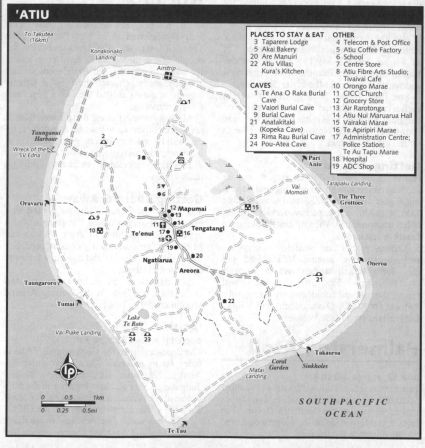

'ATIU

To Takutea (16km)

Konakonako Landing

Airstrip

Taunganui Harbour

Wreck of the SV Edna

Oravaru

Taungaroro

Tumai

Te'enui

Mapumai

Tengatangi

Ngatiarua

Areora

Lake Te Roto

Vai Piake Landing

Vai Momoiri

Tarapaku Landing

The Three Grottoes

Oneroa

Takauroa

Coral Garden

Sinkholes

Matai Landing

Te Tau

Pari Aniu

SOUTH PACIFIC OCEAN

0   0.5   1km
0   0.25   0.5mi

PLACES TO STAY & EAT
3   Taparere Lodge
5   Akai Bakery
20 Are Manuiri
22 Atiu Villas;
    Kura's Kitchen

CAVES
1   Te Ana O Raka Burial Cave
2   Vaiori Burial Cave
9   Burial Cave
21 Anatakitaki (Kopeka Cave)
23 Rima Rau Burial Cave
24 Pou-Atea Cave

OTHER
4   Telecom & Post Office
5   Atiu Coffee Factory
6   School
7   Centre Store
8   Atiu Fibre Arts Studio; Tivaivai Cafe
10 Orongo Marae
11 CICC Church
12 Grocery Store
13 Air Rarotonga
14 Atiu Nui Maruarua Hall
15 Vairakai Marae
16 Te Apiripiri Marae
17 Administration Centre; Police Station; Te Au Tapu Marae
18 Hospital
19 ADC Shop

coral is razor-sharp; a walking stick is a great help also.

You must go with a guide to visit the major caves, which are on private land and difficult to find (see Organised Tours, later, for details of guides). Many caves were used for burials – do not move or take any of the bones.

Anatakitaki, also known as the 'Kopeka Cave' is 'Atiu's most famous and frequently toured cave. A hauntingly large and beautiful cave, it is the home of the *kopeka*, a rare bird, similar to a swift, which lives only on 'Atiu. The cave can be reached by a longish walk from the plateau road.

Te Ana O Raka burial cave, south of the airstrip, is just off the road and very easy to find, but you must go with a guide.

In the southwest, **Rima Rau** burial cave is reached by a vertical pothole. There are many bones in this cave and nearby there's a very deep sinkhole with a cold pool at the bottom.

Lake Te Roto is noted for its eels, a popular island delicacy. On the western side of the lake, a cave leads right through the *makatea* to the sea. You can wade through it for a considerable distance if the water in the lake is low enough.

Beaches

'Atiu's reef is close to shore – the surrounding lagoon is rarely more than 50m wide and the water is generally quite shallow. You can swim and snorkel at **Taunganui Harbour**, where the water is clear and deep. Thatch-roofed shelters have been erected near several beaches, including Taungaroro, one of the islands most popular beaches, and Takauroa.

On the west coast, **Oravaru** beach is thought to be where Cook's party landed. On the southeast coast, **Oneroa** beach has beautiful shells. South of Oneroa is the turn-off to **Takauroa** beach. If you walk about 100m back along the rugged cliff face there are some sinkholes deep enough for good snorkelling. They're only safe at low tide or when the sea is calm.

At low tide the lagoon from Takauroa beach to Matai Landing drains out through the sinkholes and fish become trapped in a spot known as the **Coral Garden**, which becomes a fascinating natural aquarium.

Coffee Plantations

Coffee was first introduced to 'Atiu by early 19th-century traders and missionaries. After

---

Tumunu

When English whalers came to 'Atiu to provision their ships over 200 years ago there was no alcohol, only *kava* (see the boxed text 'Kava' in the Regional Facts for the Visitor chapter). 'Atiu was covered with oranges and it was not long before a wild brew was concocted with the help of the whalers. It is still drunk to this day.

The *tumunu* (bush-beer drinking sessions) came into existence during the period when missionaries attempted to stamp out *kava* drinking in the Cooks and men would retreat to the bush to drink home-brewed 'orange beer'. The *tumunu* is the hollowed-out coconut-palm stump traditionally used as a container for brewing the beer. Drinking *kava* was always a communal activity with ceremony involved – despite the change in the potion, the ceremony continued.

Tumunu are still held regularly on 'Atiu. All retain some of the ancient ceremonies associated with drinking *kava*, but the container is likely to be plastic nowadays. Technically, however, bush-beer drinking sessions are illegal.

Staff at the place where you're staying can arrange an invitation to visit the local *tumunu*. Traditionally it is for men only, and women rarely participate, but the rules relax somewhat for tourists and any visitor, male or female, is welcome. Just be wary of over-imbibing – bush beer is very strong.

---

a century of ups and downs, the industry was revitalised in the mid-1980s by German-born **Juergen Manske-Eimke**. He established the Atiu Coffee Factory, and the Atiu Coffee Growers Association was formed.

'Atiu produces two brands of coffee: **Atiu Island Coffee** (☎ 33088) and Juergen Manske-Eimke's **Atiu Coffee** (☎ 33031; W www.adc.co.ck/coffee), the larger operation, which offers tours of the coffee plantation and factory (NZ$10).

Atiu Fibre Arts Studio

The Atiu Fibre Arts Studio (☎ 33031, fax 33032; W www.adc.co.ck/art; Te'enui; admission free; open 8am-3pm Mon-Fri, 8am-1pm Sat) specialises in *tivaevae*. The cost of a machine-sewn double- to queen-size *tivaevae* is NZ$600 to NZ$1100; a hand-sewn one, requiring countless hours of work, costs NZ$1500 or more.

The studio also produces a variety of other textile arts. Products are exhibited in its gallery, workshop and café building.

Organised Tours

Atiu Tours (*☎/fax 33041; ✉ marshall@oyster .net.ck*) runs a circle-island tour (3½ hours, NZ$35) visiting the *marae*, historical spots and beaches, and an excellent *makatea*-and-cave tour (2½ hours, NZ$15) to Anatakitaki Cave, which features a subterranean candle-lit swim.

George Mateariki (*☎ 33047*) runs ecological bird-watching tours (two to three hours, NZ$20).

If you've got your own transport, **Aue Rakanui** (*☎ 33256*) will lead you to his family's cave, Te Ana O Rakanui, and will tell you the story of his ancestors (NZ$20).

Places to Stay

Are Manuiri (*☎ 33031, fax 33032; ✉ adc@adc .co.ck; Areora; shared rooms per person NZ$30, singles/doubles & triples NZ$60/ 75*) is a pleasant three-bedroom house with a shared kitchen, living room and thatched veranda. You'll feel like you're part of the village here.

Taparere Lodge (*☎/fax 33034; shared rooms per person NZ$30, twins & doubles NZ$70*), set in lovely grounds, has two self-contained units that can sleep up to four people.

About 1km out of Areora, **Atiu Villas** (*☎ 33777, fax 33775; single/double/triple standard bungalows NZ$90/100/110, family bungalows NZ$110/120/130*) has four delightful A-frame chalets each made from local materials. The chalets all have a kitchen with a fridge and a cupboard full of food; you're billed for what you use at the end of your stay.

Mata Arai (*☎ 33088; house per week NZ$150*) rents her house for a minimum of two weeks.

Places to Eat

'Atiu has two **grocery stores** and **Akai Bakery** (*☎ 33207; Mapumai*).

Tivaivai Cafe (*☎ 33031; Atiu Fibre Arts Studio, Te'enui; cakes NZ$2.50, breakfast NZ$8-10*) serves Atiu Island coffee, homemade cakes, breads and jams, good breakfasts and fresh fruit juice.

Kura's Kitchen (*☎ 33777; Atiu Villas; dinner NZ$25*) provides evening meals; book before 3pm.

Entertainment

On some Saturday nights, **Kura's Kitchen** turns into a thatched, open-air pavilion bar and features dances, a rousing local band and occasional floor shows. A disco is held at the **Atiu Nui Maruarua Hall**, opposite the CICC, on most Friday nights. See the boxed text 'Tumunu' earlier for information on bush-beer drinking sessions.

Shopping

Woodcarving is popular on the island and many carvers sell from their homes. You can see workshops along the road as you pass through the villages. Coffee produced on the island and goods from the Atiu Fibre Arts Studio are popular souvenirs.

Getting There & Away

Air Rarotonga (*☎ 33888*) flies between Rarotonga and 'Atiu daily except Sunday (NZ$138 one way, 40 minutes, four times weekly). Flights also connect 'Atiu with Ma'uke and Mitiaro (NZ$90) and Aitutaki (NZ$138). See Boat in the Getting Around section earlier in this chapter for information on inter-island shipping services.

Getting Around

You will need transport to get around 'Atiu. Accommodation places rent mopeds (NZ$25 per day). **Are Manuiri** (*☎ 33031*) also rents out a 4WD (NZ$65 per day). **Clara George** (*☎ 33255*) provides a taxi service.

MA'UKE

pop 440 • area 18.4 sq km

Ma'uke is the easternmost of the Cook Islands. It sees few visitors, but is easily reached on regular flights. Inland from its encircling fossil coral reef, a band of swampland surrounds the flat, fertile central land.

A couple of the island's highlights are **Kea's Grave** and the **Divided Church**, which was built by two villages, Areora and Ngatiarua, in 1882. When the outside was completed, there was disagreement between the villages about how the inside should be decorated, and the solution was to have a wall built down the middle and let each village have its own church within a church! The wall has since been removed, though the interior is decorated in different styles. Each village has its own entrance, sits in its respective end and takes turns singing the hymns. The minister is expected to straddle the dividing line down the middle of the pulpit.

MA'UKE

PLACES TO STAY	11	Telecom; Post Office
3 Cove Lodge	13	Paepae'a Marae
6 Tiare Holiday Cottages	17	Marae Rangimanuka
		(Uke's Marae)
OTHER	22	Kea's Grave
1 Hospital		
2 Sports Field	**CAVES**	
4 Air Rarotonga	7	Kopupooki
5 Government		(Stomach Rock)
Administration Centre;	12	Vai Tango
Marae O Rongo;	14	Vai Ou
Produce Market	15	Vai Moraro
8 Tura's Bar	16	Vai Tunamea
9 Puarakura Marae;	18	Vai Moti
Wendy's Store;	19	Vai Tukume
Ariki Store	20	Vai Ma'u
10 The Divided Church	21	Motuanga Cave
(CICC)		(Cave of 100 Rooms)

Information
The **Telecom and post offices** (Ngatiarua village; open 8am-noon & 1pm-3pm Mon-Fri) are in the centre of the island.

Wendy's Store (☎ 35102; Areora) is the ANZ bank agent.

Caves
Ma'uke has *makatea* riddled with limestone caves, many filled with cool water and wonderful for a swim. The easiest cave to reach, and one of the larger ones for swimming, is **Vai Tango**, a short walk from Ngatiarua village. You'll probably need someone to guide you there the first time.

Other interesting caves in the north of the island, a short walk off the main road, are **Vai Ou**, **Vai Tunamea** and **Vai Moraro**. The **Motuanga Cave** (or the 'Cave of 100 Rooms',

each room with its own pool) is Ma'uke's best-known cave. It is entered on land and extends out towards the sea and under the reef.

Beaches
An 18km-long road runs around the coast of the island. The fringing-reef platform is narrow, but Teoneroa beach is fairly good, as is the beach at Arapaea landing. Beaches on the southern side, such as Anaokae, are pleasantly secluded. Others such as Anaraura and Teoneroa have picnic areas with thatched shelters.

South of Tiare Holiday Cottages, the first turn-off towards the sea leads to **Kopupooki** (Stomach Rock) beach. Past the last outcrop visible from the beach is a lovely cave full of fish, good for swimming and snorkelling. It's accessible only at low tide. Many more little caves and beaches are dotted around the island.

Marae
Ma'uke's best-preserved *marae*, still used for stylised ceremonial functions, is the **Puarakura Marae**. There's a triangular area enclosed within a rectangle with seats for the *ariki*, *mataiapo* (heads of sub-tribes) and *rangatira* (nobility).

Near the reservoir is **Marae Rangimanuka**, the *marae* of Uke (Ma'uke's ancestor and namesake). It's completely overgrown but is not difficult to get to with a guide.

Organised Tours
Inquire at **Tiare Holiday Cottages** (☎ 35083) for a guided cave tour (NZ$20 to NZ$25) or fishing trips (NZ$75).

Places to Stay & Eat
Tiare Holiday Cottages (☎ 35083, fax 35 102; cottage singles/doubles NZ$30/45), on the coast near the village, has simple cottages. Each cottage contains a fridge, and there's an open-air kitchen and dining area, (cold) showers and shared toilets. Kura will cook some meals (breakfast NZ$6.50, dinner NZ$12.50).

Cove Lodge (☎ 35664, fax 35094; house per week NZ$50), on the northern edge of Kimiangatau village, is available for long-term rental. Ask around for other houses.

You can buy fresh fruit and vegetables, burgers (NZ$4) and hot meals (NZ$15) at the **produce market** (from 8.30am Friday), near the wharf. Freshly baked bread is available at **Ma'uke Trading** (☎ 35011; Kimiangatau).

RAROTONGA & THE COOK ISLANDS

RAROTONGA &
THE COOK ISLANDS

Liquid meals are available at **Tura's Bar** (☎ *35023; open Fri*), Ma'uke's only bar, opposite Ma'uke College.

Shopping
Ma'uke is noted for its pandanus mats, purses, hats and baskets. Bowls shaped like the leaves of the breadfruit tree and carved from miro wood are another craft. To buy handicrafts, ask at the place where you're staying.

Getting There & Around
Air Rarotonga (☎ *35888 in Kimiangatau; ☎ 35120 at the airport*) flies between Rarotonga and Ma'uke (NZ$154 one way, three times weekly). Flights also connect Ma'uke with Mitiaro and 'Atiu (NZ$90, twice weekly). See Boat in the Getting Around section earlier in this chapter for details of travelling by cargo ship to the island.

Tiare Holiday Cottages (☎ *35083*) rents out a motorbike, the *Night Rider* (NZ$20 per day), and bicycles (NZ$8.50 per day), and provides airport transfers (NZ$5 return).

MITIARO
pop 236 • area 22.3 sq km
Mitiaro is not one of the Cooks' most beautiful islands, but you can pass a pleasant few days here. The people are very friendly, and all live in one small village on the western side of the island. To see the sights, especially the caves and the *marae*, you'll need a local person to guide you. This can easily be arranged at the place where you're staying.

Mitiaro has a raised coral limestone outer plain. The interior of the island is very flat and much of it is swampland, with two sections deep enough to be called lakes: Te Rotonui (Big Lake) and Te Rotoiti (Small Lake).

Many handicrafts are still made on Mitiaro, and traditional customs are still practised. Women weave pandanus strips into floor mats, fans, handbags and other items. Big bowls are carved from solid wood and canoes are still made the traditional way. Fishing and planting are timed by the phases of the moon, and traditional arts are taught to both boys and girls.

Information
Ask for the **tourism officer** (☎ *26260*) at the Administration Centre near the wharf, which also houses the **Telecom and post offices** (*open 8am-4pm Mon-Fri*). You'll need to change money before you arrive on Mitiaro.

Mosquitoes are a real pest here. Bring repellent, sturdy shoes for walking across the *makatea*, and sunglasses, as the white road surfaces are extremely reflective.

Beaches, Caves & Pools
A 10-minute walk from the village on the Takaue road, **Vai Marere** is the only sulphur pool in the Cook Islands. All you can see from the road is a big hole in the ground but it opens up into a large cave with stalactites. The water is refreshingly cool.

Vai Tamaroa, on the eastern side of the island, is about a 15-minute walk across sharp *makatea* from the coast road. You may need a local guide, as the trail is faint. A road to **Vai Nauri**, also on the eastern side, has been cut so you can drive right up to it. Vai Nauri is a large, brilliantly clear pool in a big cave. The women hold gatherings known as *terevai* at both Vai Tamaroa and Vai Nauri, where they gather to swim and to sing the bawdy songs of their ancestors.

Marae & Te Pare Fort
There are *marae* in the inland areas where the villages used to be, although many are overgrown. **Takero** *marae* in the old Takaue village area has a huge stone seat of the *ariki* and several old graves near the *marae*. The **Karangarua** *marae* in the old Atai village area has also been excavated.

In the southeastern part of the island are the stone remains of the ancient **Te Pare Fort**, built as a defence against 'Atiuan raids. An underground shelter was large enough for the people to congregate in during times of danger, while above was a lookout tower from which approaching canoes could be seen.

To visit the Te Pare Fort and *marae*, you must first ask permission of Po Tetava Ariki, to whom the *marae* belongs. His speaker, the **tourism officer** (☎ *26260*), will take you to the fort for NZ$20.

Plantations
In the 1800s the islanders moved their houses to a seaside village, but continued to use the fertile, peat-laden plantation areas in the island's centre. There are roads across the *makatea* to the plantations, although many people still make the long trip on foot.

Cook Islands Christian Church (CICC)
The white-painted CICC with its blue trim, parquet ceiling decorated with black-and-white stars, and stained-glass windows is a fine sight, and the singing on Sunday is superb.

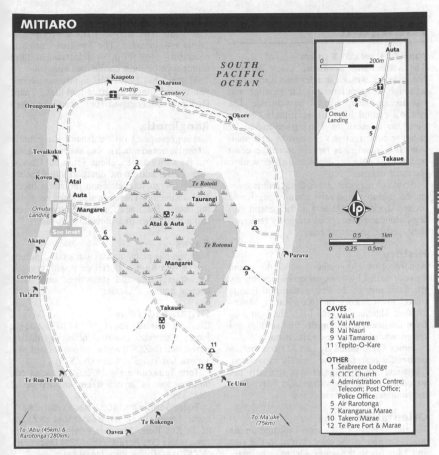

MITIARO

(map labels)

SOUTH PACIFIC OCEAN

Kaapoto
Okaraua
Airstrip
Cemetery
Orongomai
Okore
Tevaikuku
Kovea
Atai
Auta
Omutu Landing
Mangarei
See Inset
Akapa
Te Rotoiti
Taurangi
Atai & Auta
Te Rotonui
Mangarei
Parava
Cemetery
Tia'ara
Takaue
Te Rua Te Pui
Te Unu
Te Kokenga
Oavea
To 'Atiu (45km) & Rarotonga (280km)
To Ma'uke (75km)

Auta
Omutu Landing
Takaue

CAVES
2 Vaia'i
6 Vai Marere
8 Vai Nauri
9 Vai Tamaroa
11 Tepito-O-Kare

OTHER
1 Seabreeze Lodge
3 CICC Church
4 Administration Centre; Telecom; Post Office; Police Office
5 Air Rarotonga
7 Karangarua Marae
10 Takero Marae
12 Te Pare Fort & Marae

Cemetery
The cemetery on the island's northern side has a few modern-style tombs and older graves are marked simply by slabs of coral. At almost every grave, possessions of the deceased have been left at the headstone, along with eating utensils in case the spirit is hungry.

Lakes
Except in one spot, where there is a road leading to the shore of **Te Rotonui**, the lakes are hard to approach, as the surrounding area is exceedingly soggy. Where the road arrives at Te Rotonui the ground is firm, and there's a boat landing and a pleasant picnic spot.

Places to Stay & Eat
Three hearty meals and airport transfers are all included in the price at **Seabreeze Lodge**

(☎ 36153, fax 36683; Atai; rooms per person NZ$65). Bicycles (NZ$10 per day) and motorbikes (NZ$25 per day) are also available for rent.

Nukuroa Beach Lodge (☎ 36106, fax 36683; rooms per person NZ$31) has two rooms and offers full board.

Limited food supplies are sold at the small village **food shops**.

Getting There & Away
Air Rarotonga (☎ Mitiaro 36888) flies to Mitiaro from Rarotonga (NZ$154, 50 minutes, three times weekly); flights also connect Mitiaro with the islands of 'Atiu and Ma'uke (NZ$90). For more information on passenger-cargo ships to the surrounding islands, see Boat in the Getting Around section earlier in this chapter.

Mangaia

pop 780 • area 51.8 sq km
The second-largest of the Cook Islands,
Mangaia is not much smaller than Rarotonga,
although its population is far smaller and
has declined sharply in the past decade. The
island's central hills are surrounded by an
outer rim of *makatea*. The lagoon inside the
fringing coral reef is very narrow and shallow. The island rises rapidly from the coast
and in most places it drops as a sheer wall to
the inner region.

Scrub, ferns, vines and coconut palms grow
on the *makatea*, and *taro* swamps are found
around the inner edge and in the central valleys. Mangaian pineapples are justly famous –
they are big, sweet and juicy.

History
According to a Mangaian legend, the island
was not settled by voyagers on canoes, but by
the three sons of the Polynesian god Rongo
(also known as Lono or Ro'o). Rangi, Moko-
aro and Akatauira simply lifted the island up
from the deep, becoming its first settlers and
the ancestors of the Nga Ariki tribe.

James Cook sailed by in 1777 but met an
unfriendly reception and quickly moved on.
Missionary John Williams was similarly not
welcome in 1823 but subsequent Polynesian
missionaries had more success.

Orientation
The three main villages are all located on the
coast: Oneroa in the west, Ivirua in the east
and Tamarua in the south. Oneroa, the main
village, has three parts: Tava'enga and Kaumata on the northern and southern parts of the
coast respectively, and Temakatea is located
above. The airstrip is in Mangaia's north.

Information
Mangaia's **tourist office** (*☎ 34289; open
8am-4pm Mon-Fri*) is in the Administration
Centre at the bottom of the Temakatea road
cutting.

Pokino's Store (*☎ 34092; Oneroa*) is the
island's ANZ bank agent.

The **post office** (*☎ 34680; open 8am-
noon & 1pm-4pm Mon-Fri*) is in the government building opposite the tourist office. The
Telecom office (*open 7.30am-4pm Mon-Fri*)
is in Temakatea.

The electricity supply operates from 5am
to midnight daily.

Churches & Marae
There are typical, old CICCs in Oneroa,
Ivirua and Tamarua. The Tamarua church is
beautiful – look for the woodcarving and the
sennit-rope binding on the roof beams.

Mangaia has 24 pre-missionary *marae*, but
you'll need a local expert to find them. Tuare
George (see Organised Tours) can take you.

Rangimotia
The highest point on the island, Rangimotia
(169m) is not so much a peak as a high plateau,
but the views are excellent. From the Oneroa
side of the island, an old dirt road, suitable only
for 4WDs, motorcycles and mountain bikes,
leads to the top. There are also some easy hiking tracks. The track forks at the top and you
can follow either fork down to the coast.

Caves
Mangaia has many spectacular caves, including **Te Rua Rere**, a burial cave with crystalline stalagmites and stalactites, and some
ancient human skeletons.

Organised Tours
Clarke's Island Tours (*☎ 34303; Babe's
Place, Kaumata, Oneroa*) offers a full-day
island tour (NZ$50) and a canoe tour of Lake
Tiriara and Tangi'ia Cave (NZ$30).

Tere Tauakume (*☎ 34223*) offers an en-
thralling tour of several interconnected caves
(NZ$35).

Tuare George (*☎ 34092; Babe's Place, Kaumata, Oneroa*) runs a one-hour tour (NZ$20)
of Te Rua Rere, Mangaia's most impressive
cave, while **Ora Peraua** (*☎ 34280*) leads tours
(NZ$20) of Toru a Puru burial cave.

Places to Stay
All the places to stay on Mangaia make some
provision for food for their guests. Most accommodation is in Oneroa.

Mangaia Lodge (*☎ 34324, fax 34239; Oneroa; singles/doubles/triples NZ$25/40/60;
meals NZ$10*), near the hospital in Temakatea,
is a colonial-style lodge with a sunny, enclosed common terrace. Cooking facilities,
cold showers in basic amenities and breakfast
are included.

Babe's Place (*☎ 34092, fax 34078; Kaumata, Oneroa; rooms & full board per person
NZ$75*), beside the sea, has a large house and
four roomy motel-style units. Rates include
airport transfers. Self-catering is not possible
here. A dance competition is held here on Friday night; Saturday is straight-out dancing.

Ara Moana Hotel (☎ 34278, fax 34279; Ⓦ www.aramoana.com;Ivirua;singles/doubles NZ$35/55, single/double 1-room bungalows NZ$60/80; single/double/triple 2-room bungalows NZ$115/135/165; lunch NZ$10) is set in large grounds near the sea. Meals are available at the bar/restaurant on site; inform the owners in advance if you wish to self-cater.

Places to Eat

Limited supplies are available on the island, so consider bringing some with you.

You can get whatever fruits and vegetables might be around at the **market** (open from 8am Fri) beside the post office in Oneroa. **Pokino's Store** (☎ 34092; Tava'enga) is the best-stocked shop on the island but even its selection is limited. Freshly baked bread is available here and at **Auraka Bakery** (☎ 34281; Oneroa; meals NZ$8.50-15). Auraka's restaurant/bar is unfortunately only open when there are plenty of travellers on the island.

Ara Moana Hotel (☎ 34278) will prepare meals for casual diners – just ring ahead.

Shopping

Various arts and crafts are practised on Mangaia but there are no crafts shops or other organised outlets. Ask at the tourist office for information about local artisans. Look out for traditional woven reef sandals, stone pounders and Mangaia's famous carved stone axes.

Tuaiva Mautairi (☎ 34001) carves Mangaian ceremonial adzes, wooden drums and bowls, jewellery and stone taro-pounders. **Glenn Tuara** (☎ 34227) makes stone taro-pounders. Tivaevae is made on Mangaia but is generally not for sale.

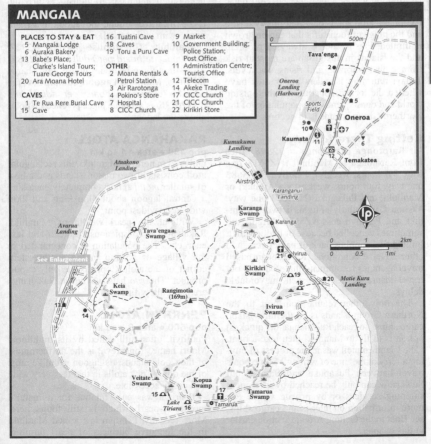

MANGAIA

PLACES TO STAY & EAT
5 Mangaia Lodge
6 Auraka Bakery
13 Babe's Place;
   Clarke's Island Tours;
   Tuare George Tours
20 Ara Moana Hotel

CAVES
1 Te Rua Rere Burial Cave
15 Cave

16 Tuatini Cave
18 Caves
19 Toru a Puru Cave

OTHER
2 Moana Rentals &
   Petrol Station
3 Air Rarotonga
4 Pokino's Store
7 Hospital
8 CICC Church

9 Market
10 Government Building;
   Police Station;
   Post Office
11 Administration Centre;
   Tourist Office
12 Telecom
14 Akeke Trading
17 CICC Church
21 CICC Church
22 Kirikiri Store

Getting There & Around

Air Rarotonga *(☎ 34888; Mangaia)* flies between Mangaia and Rarotonga (NZ$138 one way, 40 minutes, four times weekly).

See Boat in the Getting Around section earlier in this chapter for details on shipping services from Rarotonga to Mangaia.

Moana Rentals *(☎ 34307; Tava'enga)* rents new mopeds for NZ$30 per day; **Ara Moana Hotel** *(☎ 34278; Ivirua)* charges the same price for much older bikes.

The Northern Group

The Northern Group islands are low-lying coral atolls scattered in a vast expanse of sea. Despite the idyllic appearance, life on these atolls is hard. Fish may be abundant in the lagoon but atoll soil is only marginally fertile and the range of foodstuffs that can be grown is limited. Fresh water is always a problem and the islands in this group are most at risk from global warming and rising sea levels. Today, returning islanders and radios have whetted the locals' appetites for the outside world and consequently the population of the Northern Group islands is in decline.

Getting There & Away

Air Rarotonga *(Rarotonga ☎ 22888)* flies from Rarotonga to Manihiki (NZ$618 one way, 3½ hours, weekly), Penrhyn (NZ$683 one way, four hours, weekly) via Aitutaki or Manihiki, and Pukapuka (NZ$683 one way, 4½ hours, irregularly). Flights between Manihiki and Penrhyn cost NZ$180. Flights are sometimes cancelled because of bad weather, limited fuel supplies, lack of passengers, and other adverse conditions. Rarotongan-based travel agencies recommend that you take out travel insurance to cover such unavoidable delays.

The only other regular transport to the Northern Group islands is on the inter-island cargo ships. To reach Rakahanga, the quickest option is to fly to Manihiki then take a boat. (The island council was in the process of buying a ferry at the time of writing.) Some boats travel between Pukapuka and Samoa, but Suwarrow can only be reached by infrequent shipping services or by private yacht. For more information on inter-island cargo ships, see Boat in the Getting Around section earlier in this chapter.

MANIHIKI ATOLL
pop 660 • area 5.4 sq km

Manihiki is one of the most beautiful atolls in the South Pacific. Nearly 40 islands, some only tiny *motu*, encircle the 4km-wide, totally enclosed lagoon. Tauhunu is the main village, and there is a second village, Tukao. Manihiki has no safe anchorage for visiting ships, which consequently stay offshore.

The famous **Manihiki black pearls** are the economic mainstay of the island and are a significant export. The abilities of the island's pearl divers are legendary – they can dive to great depths and stay submerged for minutes at a time.

In November 1997 Cyclone Martin struck Manihiki with full force, causing major destruction and the loss of 19 lives. The island's buildings, completely destroyed, have since been rebuilt and the pearl industry is thriving. You can take a guided tour of a pearl farm (NZ$30), travel around the lagoon in a small boat, swim and snorkel.

Manihiki Guesthouse *(☎/fax 43307; Tauhunu; full board per adult/child NZ$82/45)* is in a three-bedroom house with shared facilities. **Manihiki Lagoon Lookout** *(☎/fax 43331; Tukao; full board per adult/child NZ$70/35)* is a unique place perched on poles above the lagoon.

RAKAHANGA ATOLL
pop 130 • area 4.1 sq km

Only 42km north of Manihiki, this rectangular atoll consists of two major islands and a host of smaller *motu*, almost completely enclosing a central lagoon about 4km long and 2km wide at its widest point.

Without the pearl wealth of Manihiki, Rakahanga is conspicuously quieter and less energetic. The population is concentrated in the village of Nivano in the southwestern corner of the atoll. Copra is the only export product. The *rito* hats woven on Rakahanga are particularly fine.

PENRHYN ATOLL
pop 600 • area 9.8 sq km

Penrhyn, often still called by its traditional Maori name, Tongareva, is the northernmost of the Cook Islands. Its lagoon is unlike most of the other Cook atolls in that it is very wide and easily accessible.

Penrhyn was once famous for its natural mother-of-pearl, which is still found here. More recently, Penrhyn has joined Manihiki in the lucrative business of pearl farming.

Some interesting shell jewellery is produced on the island. Penrhyn is also noted for its fine *rito* hats.

Soas Guesthouse (☎ *42019; Omoka Village; full board per adult/child NZ$82/45*) offers basic, clean accommodation with shared facilities. The Tini family, who operate the guesthouse, can assist with boat and fishing trips.

PUKAPUKA ATOLL
pop 530 • area 5.1 sq km
Shaped like a three-bladed fan, Pukapuka has an island at each 'blade end' and another in the middle. The only landing place is accessed via narrow and difficult passages through the reef on the western side of Wale, the northernmost island.

There are three villages – Ngake, Roto and Yato – all on Wale Island. *Puraka* (taro), copra and smaller quantities of coconuts, bananas and papayas are grown. Due to their relative proximity to Samoa, the islanders' customs and language are more closely related to those of Samoa than to the rest of the Cooks. There's a notably decorated Catholic **church** on the island and excellent **swimming** and **snorkelling**, particularly off the central island, Motu Kotawa. Pukapuka is noted for its finely woven mats.

During the 20th century, South Seas character Robert Dean Frisbie lived for some time on the island and wrote *The Book of Puka-Puka* and *The Island of Desire*.

Contact the **island council** (☎ *41711; Rota*) to arrange home-stay accommodation.

SUWARROW ATOLL
pop 2 • area 0.4 sq km
Suwarrow is one of the best-known atolls in the Cook Islands, due to a prolonged visit by New Zealander Tom Neale. Between 1952 and his death in 1977, Neale lived on the island for extended periods as a virtual hermit. His book *An Island to Oneself* is a South Seas classic.

Neale's memory lives on and yachties often call at the atoll, one of the few in the northern Cooks with an accessible lagoon. Neale's room, in a house badly in need of repair, is furnished just as it was when he lived here; visitors fill in a logbook left in the room.

Suwarrow has been declared a national park (the Cook Islands' only national park) to preserve its pristine natural character; it is inhabited by two caretakers.

Samoa

Samoa is the last place on earth to see the sun set. The arbitrariness of the International Date Line means many travellers arrive the day before they left. But these are not the only reasons why this is a place where you can rediscover yesterday. Samoa's way of life – the *fa'a Samoa* (Samoan way) – has been remarkably resilient to Western influences and for world-weary travellers that is perhaps its major attraction.

Geographically, Samoa consists of 13 stunningly beautiful tropical islands, created millions of years ago and still bearing the scars of volcanic activity. Politically, eight of those islands constitute the independent state of Samoa, while the five islands to the east are a US territory, known as American Samoa. The people all speak the same language and practise the same customs. Until 1900 their history, documented in this chapter, was the same.

The capital of independent Samoa, Apia, is an enchanting, if slightly ramshackle, port town, slowly adopting the trappings of the modern age but so far without losing its warmth and laid-back friendliness. Samoans are proud of their islands and their *fa'a Samoa*, and though they recognise the need to embrace the 21st century, they want to do it on their terms. They warmly welcome travellers, but they are committed to sustainable tourism, so that nobody loses in Paradise Found.

Facts about Samoa

HISTORY

The Samoan islands were initially settled by the 'Lapita' culture (see the boxed text 'Lapita' in the 'South Pacific Arts' special section), from Fiji and Tonga, in about 1500 BC. Many old Samoan legends made Fijian kings and princesses as their heroes.

In AD 950 warriors from nearby Tonga invaded and established rule on Savai'i, the nearest island to Tonga, then moved on to 'Upolu. They were eventually repelled by Malietoa Savea, the chief of the Samoas, whose title was derived from the shouted tributes of the retreating Tongans to this *malie toa* (brave warrior). A treaty of peace between the two countries was drawn up and the Samoans were left by the Tongans to pursue their own course.

At a Glance

Capital City (& Island): Apia ('Upolu)
Population: 176,848
Time: 11 hours behind GMT
Land Area: 2934 sq km (1145 sq miles)
Number of Islands: Eight
International Telephone Code: ☎ 685
GDP/Capita: US$3500
Currency: Samoan tala (ST1 = US$0.32)
Languages: Samoan & English
Greeting: *'Talofa,' 'Malo'* (informal)

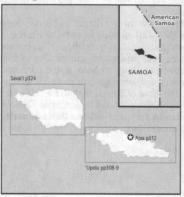

Highlights

- **Falealupo Peninsula, Savai'i** – lovely wild beaches with a beautiful rainforest reserve. Walk through the treetops to spend the night in a 225-year-old banyan tree

- **Kirikiti** – it's not cricket – well not as the Test teams know it. But this home-grown version is certainly a great spectator sport

- **Pulemelei Step Pyramid & Olemoe Falls, Savai'i** – Polynesia's largest and most mysterious ancient monument and Samoa's most beautiful waterfall and pool

- **Alofa'aga Blowholes** – one of the world's largest marine blowholes that will blow your mind and hurl your coconuts to the gods

- **Sale'aula Lava Field** – a vast expanse of black basalt formed by flowing lava, where you can see the remains of a buried village

- **Robert Louis Stevenson Museum** – visit the beautiful former home and last resting place of the famous Scottish writer

292

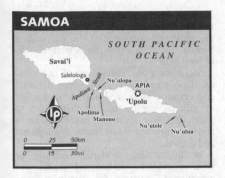

SAMOA

SOUTH PACIFIC
OCEAN

Savai'i

Salelologa

Nu'ulopa
APIA
'Upolu

Apolima
Manono

Nu'utele
Nu'ulua

0   25   50km
0   15   30mi

The earliest known evidence of human occupation in the islands is the Lapita village, partially submerged in the lagoon at Mulifanua on the island of 'Upolu; carbon tests have tentatively dated the site at 500 BC. Undecorated pottery – known as Polynesian plainware – of a comparable age has been found in American Samoa, at Aoa on the island of Tutuila and at To'aga on the island of Ofu.

At numerous other sites on 'Upolu, Savai'i and Tutuila (and to a lesser extent on Manono and Ta'u), archaeologists have discovered odd platforms, with stone protrusions radiating from their bases, which have been dubbed 'star mounds'. Information gathered from oral traditions and archaeological studies suggests that these structures were used in the ancient sport of pigeon-snaring (see the boxed text 'Star Mounds of Ancient Power' in the American Samoa chapter).

On Savai'i, near the village of Palauli, you'll find the mysterious Pulemelei Step Pyramid, the largest ancient structure in Polynesia.

European Arrival

Although whalers, pirates and escaped convicts had landed in the islands earlier, the first European on record to approach the Samoan islands was the Dutchman Jacob Roggeveen, in 1722. Louis-Antoine de Bougainville also passed through Samoan waters in 1768, bartering with the inhabitants of the Manu'a Islands. The ill-fated La Pérouse and the *Bounty*-mutineer-hunter Captain Edward Edwards both had skirmishes with locals in 1791.

By the 1820s quite a few Europeans, most of them escaped convicts and retired whalers, had settled in the islands. The European settlers established a society in Apia and a minimal code of law in order to govern their affairs, all with the consent of 'Upolu chiefs, who maintained sovereignty in their own villages.

Missionaries

Encouraged by the similarity of Christian creation beliefs to Samoan legend, and by a prophecy by Nafanua the war goddess that a new religion would take root in the islands, Samoans were quite well prepared to accept the message of Christian missionaries, who arrived in the early 19th century. The wondrous possessions of the *palagi* (Westerner) were also seen as evidence that their god was more generous than the old Samoan gods.

Squabbling Powers

There were (and still are) four 'paramount' families – equivalent to royal dynasties – in Samoa: the Malietoa, Tupua Tamasese, Mata'afa and Tu'imaleali'ifano. During the 1870s a civil dispute between two kings, one in the east and one in the west, divided Samoa. Much land was sold to Europeans by Samoans seeking to acquire armaments to settle the matter.

The British, Americans and Germans set about squabbling over Samoan territory. The compromise, the Tripartite Treaty signed in 1899, gave control of Western Samoa to the Germans and German Samoa (eastern Samoa) to the Americans.

Twentieth Century

In February 1900 Dr Wilhelm Solf was appointed governor. Although the Germans had agreed to rule 'according to Samoan custom', they hardly kept their word.

By 1908 many Samoans had decided they could take it no longer. An official resistance force, the Mau a Pule (Mau Movement), was organised on Savai'i by Namulau'ulu Lauaki Mamoe. Fearing violence, Germany sent warships, and in January 1909 Namulau'ulu and company were exiled to the island of Saipan in the Northern Mariana Islands (a German colony at the time).

At the outbreak of WWI Britain persuaded nearby New Zealand (NZ) to seize German Samoa. Preoccupation with affairs on the home front prevented Germany from resisting.

Under the NZ administration, Samoa suffered a devastating outbreak of influenza in 1919; 8500 people – almost a quarter of the population – died, and it was many years before NZ was forgiven for the administration's tragic mismanagement of the epidemic.

Discontent with the NZ administration, and an increasing call by the Mau Movement for independence, culminated in the authorities opening fire on a demonstration at the Court House in Apia in 1929. Eleven Samoans, including the Mau leader Tupua Tamasese Lealofi III, were killed.

Following a change of government (and policy) in NZ, Western Samoa's independence was acknowledged as inevitable and even desirable and in 1959 Prime Minister Fiame Mata'afa was appointed. The following year a formal constitution was adopted, and on 1 January 1962, independence was finally achieved.

Samoa Today
In June 2002 NZ's prime minister, Helen Clark, formally apologised to Samoa's prime minister, Tuilaepa Sailele Malielegaoi, for the part the former NZ administration had played in the influenza epidemic. The Samoan Prime Minister told his NZ counterpart that there was no longer any need for an apology, as Samoa had forgiven NZ long ago. Perhaps ironically, there are now nearly as many Samoans living in NZ as in their own islands.

GEOGRAPHY
Samoa, with a total land area of 2934 sq km, consists primarily of the two large islands of Savai'i (1700 sq km) and 'Upolu (1115 sq km), both of volcanic origin. Its highest peak, Mt Silisili on Savai'i, rises to 1866m.

Manono and Apolima lie in the 18km-wide Apolima Strait separating 'Upolu and Savai'i. A few other uninhabited rocky islets and outcrops are found to the southeast of 'Upolu.

CLIMATE
There is a distinct wet season (summer) between November and April and a so-called dry season (winter) from May to October. The most comfortable period to visit the Samoan islands is between May and October. The average temperatures range from 21°C to 32°C (70°F to 90°F). Year-round humidity averages about 80%. Cyclone season is between November and April.

ECOLOGY & ENVIRONMENT
Though the rainforests of the Samoan islands have sustained a culture for 3000 years, population pressures and the push for Western-style development threaten their existence.

Of all the environmental challenges facing the Samoan islands, deforestation is one of the most serious problems. In independent Samoa, forest accounts for less than 37% of land area.

Since the early 1990s, several key areas on 'Upolu and Savai'i have been declared conservation areas, and a growing number of villages are committing themselves to protecting their forests and marine resources and moving towards sustainable development and growth.

In 2002 a National Marine Sanctuary for whales, dolphins, turtles and sharks was established, covering the country's entire 128,000 sq km exclusive economic zone.

FLORA & FAUNA
On the heights of Savai'i and 'Upolu one finds temperate forest vegetation: tree ferns, grasses, wild coleus and epiphytic plants. The magnificent banyan tree dominates the landscape of the higher areas of these islands. Other parts of the Samoas are characterised by scrublands, marshes, pandanus forests and mangrove swamps. The rainforests of Samoa are a natural apothecary, home to some 75 medicinal plant species.

Because the Samoan islands are relatively remote, few animal species have managed to colonise them. The Lapita brought with them domestic pigs, dogs and chickens, as well as the ubiquitous Polynesian rat. But apart from two species of fruit bat and the small, sheath-tailed bat, mammals not introduced by humans are limited to the marine varieties. Whales, dolphins and porpoises migrate north and south through the Samoas, depending on the season.

Pili (skinks) and *mo'o* (geckos) can be seen everywhere and various types of turtles visit the islands. The harmless *gata* (Pacific boa) may occasionally be seen throughout independent Samoa.

Almost 900 species of fish and nearly 200 species of coral have been documented. There are also several shark species, which generally don't pose much of a risk to humans.

National Parks
One of only two fully fledged national parks in the Samoan islands, O Le Pupu-Pu'e National Park is on the southern shore of 'Upolu. An increasing number of villages in Samoa are establishing their own conservation areas.

GOVERNMENT & POLITICS

The national government of Samoa operates under a British-based parliamentary system, revised to accommodate local custom and Christian principles. (For more information see Traditional Culture under Society later in this section.)

Until recently, voting rights in the country were restricted to the 20,000 official *matai* (chiefs). After a referendum in 1990, universal suffrage was extended to all citizens 21 years of age and over, but only *matai* have the right to stand for election.

There are currently two major political parties represented in the Fono (Parliament): the ruling Human Rights Protection Party (HRPP) under Prime Minister Tuilaepa Sailele Malielegaoi, and the opposition Samoan National Development Party (SNDP), led by Lemamea Mualia Ropati. In 2002 two new political parties were formed, which so far have very few supporters.

ECONOMY

Since independence, Samoa has concentrated on developing a modern economy based on traditional village agriculture and primary products. Subsistence agriculture still supports around 75% of the population. The primary sector employs more than half the workforce and accounts for 50% of GDP and about 80% of export earnings. About 30% of the workforce is employed by the government. Despite huge investments in agriculture, fisheries and forestry, there has been a continuing decline in the export of primary products including copra, coconuts, taro, cocoa and *'ava* (kava). At the same time, there has been a rise in imports.

In recent years the government has promoted the development of light manufacturing industries but the economy continues to depend heavily on foreign aid.

The government's economic strategy for 2002 to 2004 identified tourism as a key strategic area for the future development of the Samoan economy. In 2002 the government outlined a vision for a more focused future for tourism that would support the further development of sustainable tourism and respect the *fa'a Samoa*.

POPULATION & PEOPLE

The 2001 census put the population of independent Samoa at 176,848 people, the huge majority of them ethnic Polynesians. The overwhelming majority – 134,020 – live on the island of 'Upolu or its tiny satellite islands,

and 38,836 of these people live in the urban area of Apia. In contrast, the population of the so-called big island of Savai'i has dropped to 42,824.

The Samoa 2000 Demographic Survey, reported that the average household size was 8.2 persons and women were giving birth to an average total of 4.3 children.

ARTS
Dance & Fiafia

Originally, the *fiafia* was a village play or musical presentation in which participants would dress in a variety of costumes and accept money or other donations. These days the term '*fiafia* night' may often refer to a lavish presentation of Samoan dancing and singing staged at the larger hotels, usually accompanied by a huge buffet dinner. But traditional *fiafia* are still performed during weddings, birthdays, title-conferring ceremonies or for the opening of new churches or schools and the like.

Most dance is performed by groups to the rhythm of a beating wooden mallet.

Music

Songs are written to tell stories or commemorate events, most of which are sad and stirring. Love songs are the most popular, followed by patriotic songs extolling the virtues of the Samoas.

Another highly respected institution is the brass band and musical competitions between villages are common.

Architecture

The most prevalent manifestation of traditional – and practical – Samoan architecture is the *fale*, an oval-shaped house of wooden posts and open walls to allow 'natural air-conditioning'. It's traditionally built on a stone or coral rock foundation and thatched with woven palm or sago leaves. Woven coconut-leaf blinds can be pulled down to protect against rain or prying eyes. Although *fale* are now built with more sturdy materials, incorporating such things as corrugated iron rooves and louvred windows, the traditional *fale* shape still influences modern buildings.

Siapo & le Toga

The bark cloth known as *siapo* in Samoa, made from the inner bark of the paper mulberry tree *(u'a)*, provides a medium for some of the loveliest artwork in the Samoas.

Woven from pandanus fibres split into widths of just a couple of millimetres, the precious cloth *(ie toga)* takes years of painstaking work and, when finished, has the look and feel of fine linen or silk. *Ie toga*, along with *siapo*, oils, and mats woven for sleeping or sitting on, make up 'the gifts of the women' that must be exchanged at every formal Samoan ceremony. Agricultural products comprise 'the gifts of the men'.

SOCIETY

The *fa'amatai* (*matai* system of government) is practised throughout the Samoas and has its roots in ancient Polynesian culture. Each *nu'u* (village) comprises a group of *'aiga* (extended families) that include as many relatives as can be claimed. The larger an *'aiga* the more powerful it is, and to be part of a powerful *'aiga* is the goal of all tradition-minded Samoans.

The *'aiga* is headed by a *matai*, who represents the family on the *fono* (governing council). *Matai*, who can be male or female, are normally elected by all adult members of the *'aiga*, but most candidates hold titles of some description and many inherit office automatically.

The *fono* consists of the *matai* of all of the *'aiga* associated with the village. The *ali'i* (high chief of the village) sits at the head of the *fono*. In addition, each village has one *pulenu'u* (a combination of mayor and police chief), and one or more *tulafale* (orator or talking chief). The *pulenu'u* is elected every three years and acts as an intermediary between the village and the national (or, in the case of American Samoa, territorial) government. The *tulafale* is an orator who liaises between the *ali'i* and outside entities, carries out ceremonial duties and engages in ritual debates.

Beneath the *matai*, members of a village are divided into four categories. The society of untitled men, the *aumaga*, are responsible for growing the village food; they were traditionally the warriors of the village. The *aualuma* is the society of unmarried, widowed or separated women. They are responsible for providing hospitality and producing *ie toga*, *siapo* and oils. Married women are called *faletua ma tausi*. Their role revolves around serving their husband and his family. The final group is the *tamaiti* (the children). Close social interaction is generally restricted to members of one's own group.

Sa

Sa, which means 'sacred', is the nightly vespers. It's not applied strictly, and not all villages enforce it. In central Apia on 'Upolu you'll seldom see it, but it does happen in the outlying villages and around Pago Pago in American Samoa. Sometime between 6pm and 7pm a village gong sounds (often a conch shell is blown), signifying that the village should prepare for *sa*. When the second gong is sounded, *sa* has begun. All activity should come to a halt. If you're caught in a village during *sa*, stop what you're doing, sit down and quietly wait for the third gong, about 10 or 15 minutes later, when it's over.

Traditional Medicine

Traditional healers are typically women, but may also be men, who learn their methods during a long apprenticeship. An apprentice must learn to recognise several hundred species of rainforest plants, each with its own medicinal value. Modern healers are taught to take notes and to keep a close and accurate record of each patient's symptoms, their diagnosis, treatment and response.

Fa'afafine

By traditional definition, a *fa'afafine* is a male who opts to dress and behave as a female, for whatever reason. The word means simply 'like a woman' and is similar to the Tahitian *mahu* or Tongan *fakaleiti* (see the boxed text 'Fakaleiti' in the Tonga chapter).

Tattooing

Samoa is the last of the Polynesian nations where traditional tattooing is still widely practised (against the wishes of many religious leaders).

The traditional tattoo *(pe'a)* normally covers the man's body from the waist to the knees. Women can also elect to be tattooed, but their designs cover only the thighs.

The skills and tools of the *tufuga pe'a* (tattoo artist) were traditionally passed down from father to son and sharpened sharks' teeth or boars' tusks were used to carve the intricate designs into the skin. It was believed that the man being tattooed must not be left alone in case the *aitu* (spirits) took him. In most cases the procedure takes at least a fortnight. Noncompletion would cause shame to the subject and his *'aiga*.

The Pain and Pride of the Pe'a

The full-bodied *pe'a*, which extends from the waist to just below the knees, is a prized sign of status in Samoa. It can take several weeks to complete and is a very painful process. Thus, anyone who undergoes the ritual is considered to be extremely brave. Any adult member can, in effect, receive a *pe'a* if the *'aiga* (extended family), *tufuga* (expert) and village leaders agree that it is suitable.

The *tufuga tatatau* (master tattooist) is considered an artist and the visual arts in Samoa have been represented by the designs of the *pe'a* and the *siapo*. The *tufuga* is usually paid with traditional gifts of *ie toga* and food.

Tattooing was discouraged when the missionaries came, but as young Pacific Islanders take pride in their cultural heritage, there has been a revival of interest in the traditional designs, but with a contemporary twist.

The contemporary tattoo sported by many young, more Westernised Samoans, comes without social and cultural restrictions. But the designs may signify a person's *'aiga*, ancestors, reference to nature or something very personal. The wrist and armband tattoos may have been originally developed for tourists, but they have developed into a popular Samoan fashion and many young Samoans sport a wrist, arm or ankle tattoo of their own design. They can be made with the modern machine or by the traditional comb.

There is a tattoo shop in Apia, near the Maketi Fou, but it involves modern machinery. *Tufuga tatatau* can be found at Faleasa village, near Apia and on Manono Island. If you are keen to observe the *tufuga tatatau* at work, contact the Samoa Tourism Authority Visitors Bureau in Apia (see Information under Apia in the 'Upolu section later in this chapter) for their names and addresses. On Savai'i, contact Moelagi Jackson at the Safua Hotel (see Places to Stay & Eat under Around the Island in the Savai'i section later in this chapter).

'Ava Ceremony

'Ava (kava) is a drink derived from the ground root of the pepper plant. See the boxed text 'Kava' in the Regional Facts for the Visitor chapter for further information. The *'ava* ceremony is a ritual in the Samoas, and every government and *matai* meeting is preceded by an *'ava* ceremony.

RELIGION

From 1830, when the Christian missionaries first arrived in the Samoas, the Samoan people have been ardent followers of the Christian faith, building so many temples to the Lord that they have earned a reputation as the 'Bible belt of the Pacific'. Freedom of religion is enshrined in independent Samoa's constitution. Still, there has been some discontent in recent years as the Mormon Church has increased the size of its congregations as well as its churches. Membership of the Congregational Church, derived from the London Missionary Society (LMS), has dropped somewhat to 38%, while about 22% are Catholics. Then come the Mormons at 14%, followed by the Methodists (11%) and the Assembly of God (5%). Numerous other, mainly Christian, faiths account for the remaining 10%.

LANGUAGE

Samoan is the main language spoken in both independent and American Samoa, although most people speak also English as a second language. Samoan is very similar to Tongan and is one of the oldest Polynesian languages.

In Samoan, the 's' replaces the 'h' of many other Polynesian languages, 'l' replaces 'r', and a glottal stop (see under Language in the Facts about the South Pacific chapter) replaces 'k'. Therefore, the Tahitian word for 'one', *tahi*, is *tasi* in Samoan, *rua* (two) is *lua*, and *ika* (Rarotongan for 'fish') is *i'a*. The soft 'ng' sound in Samoan is written as a 'g' (*palangi*, for example, is pronounced 'pah-lah-ngee').

Samoan Basics

Hello.	*Talofa* or *Malo*.
Goodbye.	*Tofa*.
How are you?	*O a mai 'oe?*
I'm well (thanks).	*Manuia (fa'afetai)*.
Please.	*Fa'amolemole*.
Thanks (very much).	*Fa'afetai (tele)*.
Yes.	*Ioe*.
No.	*Leai*.
Two beers please.	*E lua pia fa'amole mole*.

Facts for the Visitor

SUGGESTED ITINERARIES
Depending on the length of your stay and your particular *interests*, you might want to see and do the following things:

One week
Tour the 'Big Island of Savai'i': include an overnight stay in a tree house on Falealupo Peninsula, a couple of days on the beach at Manase or Satuiatua and a hike on the Tafua Peninsula.

Two weeks
Add to the above: a visit to Manono Island, an excursion into the Uafato Conservation Area on 'Upolu, a couple of days on the beach in the Aleipata district and a visit to the Sataoa & Sa'anapu Wetlands Conservation Area.

Three weeks
Extend the above and/or add: two or three days hiking in A'opo Conservation Area on Savai'i or O Le Pupu-Pu'e National Park on 'Upolu.

One month
Add to the above: a visit to the islands of Aunu'u and Ofu in American Samoa.

PLANNING
When to Go
Weatherwise, the most comfortable time to visit the Samoas is between May and October, during the dry season.

Maps
The Samoa Tourism Authority Visitors Bureau in Apia has free copies of a good map of Samoa published by **Jasons** (W *www.jasons.com*) in 2002. You can get the more detailed 1:195,000 map published by South Pacific Maps in 1999 (distributed worldwide through *Hema Maps*) for ST15 at the Department of Lands, Survey and Environment in Apia.

The University of Hawaii publishes a larger-scale map of Samoa. In Apia on 'Upolu, you might find it at Aggie's Gift Shop.

TOURIST OFFICES
Local Tourist Offices
The **Samoa Tourism Authority Visitors Bureau** (☎ *63500;* e *samoa@samoa.ws;* W *www .visitsamoa.ws; PO Box 2272, Apia; open 8am-4.30pm Mon-Fri, 8.30am-noon Sat)* is housed in a modern *fale* behind Beach Rd. The authority publishes a free visitor guide, updated each year, and it's an excellent source of information. The website is good, too.

Tourist Offices Abroad
The Samoan Tourism Authority has offices in the following countries:

Australia (☎ 02-9824 5050, e samoa@ ozemail.com.au) PO Box 361, Minto Mall, Minto, NSW 2566
New Zealand (☎ 09-379 6138, e samoa@ samoa.co.nz) Level 1, Samoa House, 283 Karangahape Rd, PO Box 68423, Newton, Auckland
USA (☎ 916-538 0152, e sdsi@compuserve .com) Lake Blvd 475, PO Box 7740, Tahoe City, CA 96145

Samoa is represented abroad by offices of the South Pacific Tourism Organisation (SPTO; see the Tourist Offices section in the Regional Facts for the Visitor chapter).

VISAS
Visitors entering Samoa require a valid passport and an onward ticket. You're also required to provide a contact address within the country. Visas may be extended by several weeks at a time by the immigration office in Apia.

EMBASSIES & CONSULATES
Samoan Embassies & Consulates
In countries without Samoan diplomatic posts, Samoa is represented by NZ and British diplomatic missions. Samoa has diplomatic representation in the following countries:

Australia (☎ 02-6286 5505) PO Box 3274, 13 Culgoa Circuit, O'Malley, ACT 2606
New Zealand (☎ 04-472 0953) 1A Wesley Rd, Kelburn, PO Box 1430, Wellington
UN (☎ 212-599 6196) 820 2nd Ave, Suite 800, New York, NY 10017, USA

Embassies & Consulates in Samoa
The following countries have diplomatic representation in Samoa:

Australia (☎ 23411) PO Box 704, Beach Rd, Apia (Canadian Consular services provided by Australian High Commission)
France (☎ 26940) Zita Sefo-Martel, Beach Rd, Apia
Germany (☎ 22634) Werner Schrekenberg, Beach Rd, Apia
New Zealand (☎ 21711) PO Box 1876, Beach Rd, Apia
UK (☎ 21758) Bob Barlow, Beach Rd, Apia
USA (☎ 21631) Loame Viliamu Bldg, PO Box 3430, Apia

CUSTOMS

Visitors can bring in a 1L bottle of spirits and up to 200 cigarettes duty-free. Plant material, vegetables and meat may not be imported without a permit from the quarantine section of the Department of Agriculture. Any sexually explicit material considered by officials to be objectionable will be confiscated.

MONEY
Currency

The Samoan tala (dollar), which is divided into 100 *sene* (cents), is the unit of currency in independent Samoa.

Exchange Rates

Approximate rates for the Samoan tala are listed below:

country	unit		tala
Australia	A$1	=	ST2.01
Canada	C$1	=	ST2.21
Easter Island	Ch$100	=	ST0.43
euro zone	€1	=	ST3.50
Fiji	F$1	=	ST1.64
New Zealand	NZ$1	=	ST1.77
PNG	K1	=	ST0.87
Solomon Islands	S$1	=	ST0.41
Tonga	T$1	=	ST1.41
UK	£1	=	ST5.01
USA	US$1	=	ST3.01
Vanuatu	100VT	=	ST2.55

To check current exchange rates, see W www.oanda.com.

Exchanging Money

Cash & Travellers Cheques The most acceptable foreign currencies for exchange are US, NZ and Australian dollars. The three main banks in independent Samoa and those that change travellers cheques and foreign currency are the ANZ Bank, Westpac and the National Bank of Samoa. All have their main branches in central Apia, with subsidiary offices in Salelologa on Savai'i. At Faleolo airport there are currency-exchange branches that open to coincide with incoming and outgoing flights; the ANZ Bank also has an ATM there, and in central Apia and Savai'i. All the banks charge a small commission for changing travellers cheques. Both ANZ and Westpac can do Visa and MasterCard cash advances.

Credit Cards In Apia, most mid- to upper-range hotels, car-rental agencies, upmarket restaurants and craft shops accept credit cards.

Costs

Samoa is one of the cheapest places to travel in the South Pacific. However, in many cases, accommodation is on the expensive side for what you get. In Apia, dormitory beds can be found for around ST30, and you can get a decent though pretty basic room with air-con and private bathroom for anything from ST100 per person. Local transport is cheap, but not always safe and seldom reliable. Car hire, however, is quite expensive. Food served in restaurants is also quite expensive. Many hotels have kitchens for guests, and food at the markets is cheap. Staying in beach *fale* is a good option – you'll usually pay around ST60 per night, including bedding and hearty meals. Costs of imported goods is high, so bring your own sunscreen and toiletries.

Tipping & Bargaining

Tipping and bargaining are not encouraged in Samoa.

Taxes

There is a 12.5% tax on goods and services, usually included in marked prices. Prices quoted in this chapter include tax.

POST & COMMUNICATIONS
Post

The **main post office** (Beach Rd, Apia; open Mon-Fri 8am-4.30pm), now run by Samoa Communications, is one block east of the clock tower. It sells postcards, souvenir envelopes and first-day covers as well as stamps and aerograms.

In Apia, poste restante is located in a separate office from the main post office, just down Post Office St, behind the main lobby. To receive poste-restante mail, have it addressed to you at: Poste Restante, Chief Post Office, Apia, Samoa.

Telephone & Fax

Samoa Communications (Beach Rd, Apia; open 8am-10pm daily), licensed since 1999 by the government to run the country's postal and communications network, offers telephone, telex and fax services. Fax services are available between 8am and 4.30pm Monday to Friday; telephone and telex services operate from 8am to 10pm daily. There are new touch-dial public phones in the Lotemau Centre and at several other places in central Apia. Buy phonecards from its office, from Telecom Samoa Cellular or selected shops near pay phones.

SAMOA

Samoa has its own mobile phone system, operated by **Telecom Samoa Cellular** (☎ 26 081; ✉ peter.connor@tnzi.com; Lotemau Centre, Beach Rd). The system is analogue and if your phone is the same you can contact Telecom Samoa, who will give you a separate phone number and charge the service and all calls to your credit card. Alternatively, you can rent a phone for the duration of your stay from **VIP Cellphone Rentals** (☎ 21415/ 24024; ✉ gary@samoalive.com).

Email & Internet Access
There are several places in central Apia where you can log on, and many hotels offer Internet connection as well. In Savai'i there are at least two public places in Salelologa where you can check your emails, and as new phone lines are extended to outlying areas, many beach resorts are planning to set up websites and offer email access to their guests too.

DIGITAL RESOURCES
The following websites provide useful information on independent Samoa:

Samoan Hotel Association (W www.samoahotels .ws) This is a good, current listing of places to stay, and includes photos of many of the properties.
Samoa Observer (W www.samoaobserver.ws) This site features news and opinions on current affairs in independent Samoa and the region.
Samoa Sensation (W www.samoa.co.uk) This terrific website has lots of useful links, including the Samoan telephone directory.
Samoa Visitors Bureau (W www.visitsamoa .ws) The most comprehensive site for independent Samoa, this includes an up-to-date events calendar, information on activities, and a directory of hotels, services and organisations useful for visitors.

BOOKS
Lonely Planet's *Samoan Islands* guidebook has more detailed information on travel in the Samoas.

For a brief, well-presented and accessible overview of modern and traditional life in the Samoas, with evocative colour pictures by Samoan photographer Evotia Tamua, *Samoa, Pacific Pride* by Graeme Lay, Tony Murrow & Malama Meleisea is a good place to start.

American ethnobotanist Paul Alan Cox travelled to a remote Samoan village on the edge of a rainforest to search for traditional remedies for modern diseases. *Nafanu:*

Saving the Samoan Rain Forest is his beautifully written account of how he became involved in a campaign to stop the logging that was threatening to destroy not only the wildlife and plants but a whole culture.

Lagaga – A Short History of Western Samoa, by Malama Meleisea and other contributors, is the definitive work and the best available source of information about the history of independent Samoa. The same author has also written *The Making of Modern Samoa*, a fascinating examination of the complex web of traditional authority in Samoa and the dilemma the government faces in balancing this with the Western legal system of authority.

Robert Louis Stevenson's novels *The Ebb-Tide* and *The Wrecker*, and his short story *The Beach of Falesaá*, were all written at the Vailima estate above Apia during the last four years of the author's life.

Coming of Age in Samoa by Margaret Mead is perhaps the most infamous work ever written about the Samoas. Written nearly 100 years ago after the 23-year-old anthropologist spent several months on the island of Ta'u, this small, and at times poetic book played a big role in the nature-versus-nurture debate and has always attracted controversy. In the 1980s, Australian anthropologist Derek Freeman's *The Fateful Hoaxing of Margaret Mead* methodically attempted to discredit Mead's research and writings on the subject of adolescent girls in Samoa.

The oral tradition of recounting myths, legends, histories and fables is still very much alive in Samoa. *Tala o le Vavau – The Myths, Legends and Customs of Old Samoa* is a good collection of Samoan legends, as is *Fagogo – Fables from Samoa in Samoan and English* by Richard Moyle.

Albert Wendt, now Professor of Literature in NZ, is Samoa's most renowned author. His novels include *Leaves of the Banyan Tree*, *Flying Fox in a Freedom Tree*, *Pouliuli*, *Birth and Death of the Miracle Man*, *Inside Us the Dead*, *Shaman of Visions* and *Sons for the Return Home*.

Samoan performance poet, teacher and writer Sia Figiel uses traditional storytelling in her work. Her powerful first novel *Where We Once Belonged* (1996) won the Commonwealth Writers Prize in 1997. Her second novel *We Who Do Not Grieve* was critically acclaimed. Another powerful novel is *Alms for Oblivion* by the founder of the *Samoa Observer*, Fata Sano Malifa (1993).

NEWSPAPERS & MAGAZINES

The outspoken *Samoa Observer* comes out daily except Monday. The *Sunday Newsline* is published weekly and the government-run paper *Savali* comes out twice a week. The local news magazine *Talamua* is published monthly.

RADIO & TV

Samoa has two radio stations. Magic 98FM, broadcasting 24 hours from 6am to midnight, plays popular music. The government-run AM station Radio 2AP operates on two channels: the English-language channel broadcasts from 5pm to 11pm weekdays, the Samoan channel from 6am to 11pm daily. TV Samoa mainly broadcasts overseas programmes.

LAUNDRY

Laundry prices are quite high relative to other costs. Most mid-range and top-end hotels offer same-day laundry services.

HEALTH

There is no malaria in the Samoan islands; the only infectious diseases you should be aware of are occasional cases of dengue fever and filariasis (see Health in the Regional Facts for the Visitor chapter).

The **National Hospital** (☎ 21212; *Ifiifi St*) in Apia is inland in the village of Leufisa (about five minutes by taxi from the centre of town). Health treatment is free to Samoan citizens and legal residents but visitors must pay a small fee.

If you can't spend a day waiting to see the hospital doctor, you'd do well to shell out a bit more money and visit the excellent, private **MedCen Hospital**, based at Vailima, where it costs ST55 for a visit; see Medical Services under Apia in the 'Upolu section later in this chapter for more details.

Prescription medicines are available at the National Hospital dispensary for a nominal fee. There are several **chemist shops** in Apia, mostly around Beach Rd. The well-stocked **Samoa Pharmacy** (☎ 20355), up past Hotel Kitano Tusitala on the Mulinu'u Peninsula, has extended opening hours.

Don't drink the water – and that includes ice. Bottled water is readily available.

SOCIAL GRACES

Although many visitors to the Samoas wish to see traditional villages, such visits can be extremely disruptive. It's best not to arrive in a village on a Sunday.

Shoes should be removed when entering a *fale* and never enter during prayers or meetings, or make noise or commotion.

Throughout the Samoas, women are best advised to wear knee-length skirts or *lava-lava* (sarongs) and should avoid wearing shorts or bathing gear away from the beach. Men should wear knee-length, baggy shorts (or a *lava-lava*) and a shirt while walking in the streets. Also see Social Graces in the Regional Facts for the Visitor chapter.

WOMEN TRAVELLERS

Samoa is very safe for women, but a lone foreign woman can still attract more attention than she might want. Just be firm, talk about your family, preferably mention a partner, and dress modestly. Men will invariably apologise if you make it clear that their attentions are misplaced.

DANGERS & ANNOYANCES

Theft isn't a huge problem, but remember that the concept of personal property is a recent introduction to Samoan society.

Beware of scams that involve unauthorised people asking for a custom fee to access a site. If you are in doubt, ask to see the *pulenu'u* before paying.

Be wary of aggressive dogs, particularly around Apia.

BUSINESS HOURS

Banks are open from 9am to 3pm weekdays; some stay open until 4pm on Thursday and Friday. Government offices open from 8am to noon and 1pm to 4.30pm.

Shops are open from 8am to 4.30pm, often with an hour's break for lunch. Restaurants and takeaway shops operate between 8am and 4pm if they serve breakfast and lunch or from 6pm to 10pm if they serve only an evening meal. Saturday shopping hours are from 8am to 12.30pm.

Markets open about 6am and generally close around 4pm. The Maketi Fou in Apia is active 24 hours a day. The big market day is Saturday.

On Sunday, most places are closed, but in Apia you can still have fun at the fish market and at Maketi Fou.

PUBLIC HOLIDAYS & SPECIAL EVENTS

Public holidays celebrated include New Year's Day, Good Friday, White Sunday (the second Sunday in October), and Christmas. In

SAMOA

Worms Rise at Midnight

Some time in October or November, on the seventh day after the full moon, the palolo reefworm or, more technically, a polychaete worm of the *Eunicidae* family (*Eunice viridis*) emerges from the coral reefs to mate. The blue-green vermicelli-shaped worms, rich in calcium, iron and protein, are a prized delicacy in much of the South Pacific. The worms are said to taste like creamy caviar and, according to some, are a great aphrodisiac. Parties and musical festivities take place on the beaches throughout Samoa while villagers anxiously anticipate the big event. When the worms finally appear at around midnight, crowds carrying nets and lanterns wade into the sea to scoop them up.

addition, independent Samoa celebrates the day after New Year's Day, Boxing Day and:

Flag Day 17 April
Anzac Day 25 April
Aso o Tina (Mothers' Day) May
Independence celebrations 1 to 3 June
Labor Day 4 August
White Monday October
Palolo Day October/November

Some of the more popular festivals are held towards the end of the year. The Teuila Festival, a well-attended, week-long annual event featuring sporting competitions, music and dance, takes place in early September in Apia. Another event to look out for is the Rise of Palolo celebrations in October (see the boxed text 'Worms Rise at Midnight').

ACTIVITIES

Whatever you do in Samoa, whether it's bushwalking, surfing, or snorkelling, be sure to ask the local owners before using their land, beach or lagoon.

Snorkelling

There is no shortage of snorkelling possibilities in Samoa, but not many places hire out gear. One of the best and easiest places to catch a glimpse of the underwater scene is at Palolo Deep National Marine Reserve near Apia (you can hire gear here).

The best areas for inexperienced snorkellers are along the Aleipata coast at the eastern end of 'Upolu and around the island of Manono. Just off the south coast, near Poutasi, is Nu'usafe'e Islet, which offers some of the most diverse corals and fish around 'Upolu. Strong swimmers and snorkellers can also tackle the turbulent waters en route to the excellent snorkelling around Nu'utele and between Malaela village and Namu'a Island, in the Aleipata district.

The dive centres mentioned here offer organised snorkelling trips to sites around 'Upolu:

Dive & Fly Samoa (☎ 54066, ⓦ www.diveandflysamoa.com) This place is located at Jane's Beach Fale at Manase Beach in northern Savai'i
Pacific Quest Divers (☎ 24728, ⓦ www.dive.ws) This outfit operates from Beach Rd, Apia, five minutes' walk east of Aggie Grey's Hotel
Snuba Samoa Tours (☎ 25726, 71156, ⓔ snuba samoa@lesamoa.net) PO Box 6247, Apia

Surfing

Shallow waters, sharp reefs, treacherous currents and inconsistent breaks make surf conditions in Samoa difficult and often dangerous for inexperienced or reckless surfers. It's best to go with an experienced operator.

There are two main surf resorts on 'Upolu and one on Savai'i. In 'Upolu, **Salani Surf Resort** (ⓦ *www.surfsamoa.com*) is based at Salani Beach and **Sa'Moana** (ⓦ *www.samoanaresort.com*) is at Salamumu Beach. To avoid crowded breaks, these operators take bookings through agents. Check their websites for details.

Savai'i Surfaris (☎ *58 248, fax 58 007*) offers some excellent packages; for further information see Organised Tours under Getting Around in the Savai'i section later in this chapter. Also check out the **Maninoa Surf Camp** (☎ *29 162*), a more affordable option between its upmarket neighbours the Sinalei Reef Resort and Coconuts Beach Club & Resort (see The South Coast under Around the Island in the 'Upolu section later in this chapter).

Kayaking & Canoeing

Sea kayaking is an excellent way to explore the islands and is one of the only ways to access some of the more remote parts of the coastline. Tours are available with **Ecotour Samoa** (see Organised Tours in the Getting Around section later in this chapter) and **Island Explorer** (☎ *22401*; ⓦ *www.islandexplorer.ws*).

A number of villages offer tours in traditional outrigger canoes. Sinalei Reef Resort and Coconuts Beach Club & Resort, on the south coast of 'Upolu, offer a variety of organised boat tours. In Apia, six-man outrigger canoe teams race across the harbour most evenings. Head down to the sea wall at around 5pm if you'd like to join in.

Fishing

The reefs and their fishing rights are owned by villages, so you can't just drop a line anywhere; if you'd like to fish with the locals, ask at your beach *fale* or speak to the *pulenu'u*.

Game fishing has become increasingly popular in the islands and independent Samoa has been rated one of the top 10 game-fishing destinations in the world. For information on the annual Samoa international game-fishing tournament, visit **W** www.fishing.ws.

Operators who offer game-fishing trips include:

Alfred's Fishing Charters (**☎** 24067,
  e t.alfred@pasifika.ws)
Boomerang Fishing Safaris (**☎** 40358,
  e boomerangcreek@yahoo.com)
Great White Charters (**☎** 74728,
  e rlee@samoa.ws)
Lady Saele Charters (**☎** 22790,
  e saele@mailcity.com)
Pacific Quest Divers (**☎** 24728,
  W www.dive.ws)
Samoa Marine (**☎** 22721,
  e pmeredith@samoa.ws)
Sau'la Fishing Charters (**☎** 70001,
  e pm@samoa.ws)

Hiking

Hiking possibilities on 'Upolu include the coastal and rainforest walks in O Le Pupu-Pu'e National Park; the coastal route from Falefa Falls to Fagaloa Bay; the rugged hike between the village of Uafato and Ti'avea; the short but steep walk to the summit of Mt Vaea (475m) to see the graves of Robert Louis and Fanny Stevenson; and the muddy but rewarding hike to Lake Lanoto'o in the central highlands. For guided bush and coastal walks, contact **SAMOAonFOOT** (**☎** 21529) or **Ecotour Samoa** (see Organised Tours in the Getting Around section later in this chapter).

On Savai'i, there's even more scope. Shorter possibilities include the hike to Olemoe Falls and the mysterious Pulemelei Step Pyramid; to the blowholes south of Salelologa; and into the rainforest at Sasina. Longer day hikes might include exploration of the Mt Matavanu area, the Tafua Rainforest Preserve or the Falealupo Rainforest Preserve.

For more of an expedition, you can hire a guide and climb up into the Cloud Forest Preserve on Mt Silisili, the highest point in the Samoas. Guided walks (among other activities) are offered on tiny, traditional Manono Island.

Squash & Tennis

If you thrive in heat and humidity, you could try a game of squash at the **Apia Squash Courts** (**☎** 20554) near the Apia wharf. There are also public tennis courts at Apia Park and some hotels have courts for guests.

Golf

If you prefer a more sedate game, visitors are welcome at the 18-hole, par-72 course at the **Royal Samoan Country Club** (**☎** 20120), near Fagali'i airport, just east of Apia. You can join in the official competition on Saturdays. Gear is available for hire and green fees are minimal. The newer **Faleata Golf Course** (**☎** 23964), a few kilometres south of the Apia suburb of Vaitele, also hires out gear to visitors.

ACCOMMODATION

Compared with more-developed Pacific islands such as Hawaii and Fiji, accommodation options in the Samoas are fairly limited, but there's a range to suit most budgets. The beach *fale*, with meals included, are a good, and rather romantic, option if you don't mind roughing it a bit. Though there are several expensive resorts to choose from, don't expect anything too sophisticated.

Budget

You can stay in a beachside *fale* on 'Upolu, Savai'i and Manono in Samoa for about ST60, including meals.

In Apia's guesthouses and cheaper hotels, decent singles/doubles start at about ST60 and dorm beds at around ST35. Most places only have cold-water facilities, but you're unlikely to be bothered by that in such a warm climate.

There are few opportunities for camping. More than 80% of Samoan land is under customary ownership and to camp anywhere, even on seemingly secluded beaches, you must ask permission from the traditional owners.

Mid-Range & Top End

In Samoa there are quite a few smaller hotels and bungalow-style resorts in the mid-range bracket, where prices for single/double rooms range between ST100 and ST110 and around ST160 and ST180.

SAMOA

You won't find any five-star hotels in Samoa but there are a couple of upmarket hotels in Apia, where prices range from ST200 for a standard double to more than ST300 for 'deluxe' rooms.

Village Stays

In Samoa, home and village stays can be organised through **Safua Tours** (see Organised Tours in the Getting Around section later in this chapter) in Lalomalava on the island of Savai'i.

See Social Graces earlier in this section for tips on how to behave in a traditional village.

FOOD

Traditional Samoan food is very good and some excellent dishes are made from tropical crops. Meals consist mostly of such items as root vegetables, coconut products *(niu* and *popo)*, taro *(talo)*, breadfruit *(fuata)*, fresh fruit, pork *(pua'a)*, chicken *(moa)*, fish *(i'a)* and corned beef *(pisupo)*. The best way to sample the local cuisine is to stay in a village, be invited into a Samoan home or take part in an *umu* feast. An *umu* is a traditional Polynesian earth oven (made above the ground in Samoa). The midday Sunday meal, *to'ona'i*, is almost always cooked in an *umu*.

Vegetarians are not well catered for.

Most restaurants in independent Samoa are in Apia. Cheap meals start at around ST10, and an upmarket feed starts at around ST25.

The cheapest food of all is to be found in the markets. Every village has a small grocery store where you can buy basic goods.

DRINKS

Despite the variety of fruit on hand, fresh juices aren't very popular – sugary cordial is easier to find. A delicious Samoan drink is *koko Samoa*, a chocolate drink made with locally grown roasted cocoa beans, sugar and water. An unusual hot drink you might come across is *vaisalo*, which is made from the milk and flesh of coconuts and thickened with starch. Some resorts and *fale* will serve you a coconut with a straw in the hole from which you can drink the delicious coconut juice.

Samoa's locally brewed lager, Vailima, is very good and is available almost everywhere.

ENTERTAINMENT

Bars and nightclubs are very popular with urbanised Samoans. See individual sections for further information.

SPECTATOR SPORTS

The most popular sports are netball and rugby (Samoa's national rugby team, Manu Samoa, qualified for the 2002 World Cup). Most afternoons, Samoans gather on *malae* (village greens) to play very energetic and exciting games of rugby, volleyball and a unique brand of cricket, *kirikiti* (see the boxed text 'The Civilising Influence of Cricket' below).

The Civilising Influence of Cricket

One of the primary requirements for any serious *kirikiti* player is the ability to dance and play cricket at the same time. This is, as Tapu Misa, columnist with the *Samoa Observer* has pointed out, something that few Test cricketers have been able to demonstrate. Nor can they whistle and handclap in chorus while attempting to catch a ball.

Kirikiti is a unique South Pacific version of the English game of cricket and is a great example of how an imported measure of civilisation has been adapted to suit Samoan needs and traditions. The willow bat became a three-sided club of a size that would make any warlord happy, and the ball was fashioned out of rubber – all the better to be catapulted into the local lagoon. This is a colourful game, too – Samoans keep their whites for church on Sunday; the runs are made in *lava-lava* and sandals.

And the rules? Well, it's just not cricket. There can be any number of players in a Samoan team. Which means a game can continue for days, sometimes weeks, at a time. But there's none of that 'stand and watch the grass grow' stuff about this game either. As the batsman swings at every ball, the leader of the opposite team jumps up and down and blows his whistle incessantly in a kind of syncopated rhythm. The rest of the team also gyrates, clapping hands in rhythmic harmony, at the same time watching for an opportunity to catch out the rival. Only when all the batsmen of the opposing team have been dismissed does the other team get its chance.

It's energetic, it's exuberant and it's lots of fun. From June to September you'll see it in every village just before the sun goes down.

Alofa'aga Blowholes, Savai'i, Samoa

Falealupo Rainforest Preserve, Samoa

Playing *kirikiti*, Samoa

Robert Louis Stevenson Museum, Apia, Samoa

PETER HENDRIE

Ofu, American Samoa

PETER HENDRIE

Panpipe players, Malaita, Solomon Islands

TONY WHEELER

Sausau Church, Sigave, Futuna

Getting There & Away

AIR
Airports
The majority of visitors to the Samoas arrive on scheduled flights at Faleolo airport 35km west of Apia on 'Upolu, or at Tafuna International Airport (Pago Pago airport) on Tutuila in American Samoa.

From NZ, Australia, Fiji, Tonga, Hawaii and Los Angeles (LA), access to Samoa is fairly straightforward. From anywhere else, however, travelling to the Samoan islands will entail first reaching one of these connecting points. Auckland and Nadi/Suva (Fiji) are the most convenient and best-served runs. See the Air section in the regional Getting There & Away chapter near the start of this book for further information.

Airlines
The major carriers to the Samoan islands are **Air New Zealand** (W www.airnz.co.nz) and **Polynesian Airways** (W www.polynesianairlines.com). Other options are **Hawaiian Airlines** (W www.hawaiianair.com) and **Samoa Air** (W www.samoair.com); the latter flies between the two Samoas as well as to the Vava'u group in Tonga. Several air passes that include Samoa are listed in the regional Getting There & Away chapter near the start of this book.

Airline offices in the Samoas are:

Air New Zealand
Samoa: (☎ 685-20825) Lotemau Centre, Apia, Samoa
Hawaiian Airlines
American Samoa: (☎ 684-699 1875) Tafuna Airport, Pago Pago
Polynesian Airlines
American Samoa: (☎ 684-699 9126) Tafuna Airport, Pago Pago
Samoa: (☎ 685-22737) NPF Bldg, Beach Rd, Apia
Samoa Air
American Samoa: (☎ 684-699 9106) Tafuna Airport, Pago Pago
Samoa: (☎ 685-22901) Beach Rd, Apia

Departure Tax
There is a departure tax of ST30 when flying out of Samoa, payable at the airport at the time of check-in. The American Samoa departure tax is US$4.50 but it's included in the price of airline tickets.

North America
Most flights from the US depart from LA or San Francisco. **Air New Zealand** offers direct flights between LA and Apia, and there are also flights via Honolulu, Fiji or Auckland. Return fares to Apia start from around US$1200 from San Francisco or LA and US$1425 from Seattle in the low season (December to April). Return flights to Pago Pago start from around US$1200 from LA or US$870 from Honolulu.

Europe
See the regional Getting There & Away chapter near the start of this book for information about getting to Samoa from Europe.

Australasia
As there is only one direct flight a week from Australia, most flights to the Samoas are via Auckland or Nadi in Fiji. From NZ there are a number of flight options with either **Air New Zealand** or **Polynesian Airlines**. Return fares from Auckland to Apia on either airline start at NZ$1270 in low season (December to April). Flight/accommodation packages from NZ can be excellent value; such packages can sometimes work out cheaper than the flight alone.

The Pacific
While island-hopping around the Pacific isn't difficult, some flights operate only once or twice per week from the Samoan islands and you may be faced with a few scheduling problems on some routes. There are regular direct flights to Fiji, Tonga and Hawaii, but if you are travelling on to other Pacific islands you'll need to either fly back to NZ to make connections, or travel via Tonga or Fiji. See the regional Getting There & Away chapter for details on air passes.

SEA
Cargo Ship
From Apia you can escape to the more remote Tokelau islands aboard the cargo ship that sails twice a month and is Tokelau's only passenger link with the rest of the world. For sailing dates and fares, contact the **Tokelau Apia Liaison Office** (TALO; ☎ 685-20822, 71805, fax 21761; e zak-p@lesamoa.net; PO Box 865, Apia) in Samoa.

Yacht
Often, yachts will anchor in Pago Pago Harbor in American Samoa to stock up on provisions at the local supermarkets. From there,

most of them stop at Apia and a few cruise around Savai'i before moving on to Tonga.

The only official ports of entry into the two countries are Apia and Pago Pago. If you're sailing out of independent Samoa from Savai'i, you'll need to check out of the country in Apia or you'll have to sail back against prevailing winds to do so.

Apia Harbour Visiting yachts need to contact the **Samoa Port Authority** (*SPA;* ☎ *23552*) at least two days before they arrive in Apia (via radio – Signal Side Band or VHF on Channel 16) to arrange immigration, customs, health and quarantine clearance. The SPA charges up to ST$75 for berth/mooring for one month. There are bathroom and shower facilities available and you can buy fresh water for 10 *sene* per gallon.

The friendly **Apia Yacht Club** (☎ *21313;* ⓔ *andreasmith@smithsystems.com.ws*) is near the end of Mulinu'u Peninsula.

Pago Pago Harbor The anchorage at Pago Pago Harbor is free for seven days. After that you are charged between US$7.50 and US$22.50 per month, depending on the length of your yacht.

Those arriving by yacht from Hawaii must present a US customs clearance document from Honolulu.

The Pago Pago Yacht Club, in Utulei, is a friendly place to gather information about local yachting conditions.

Getting Around

This section contains information relevant to both Samoas. See Getting Around in individual sections dealing with the islands of Samoa and American Samoa in the relevant chapters for more details.

AIR

The main inter-island transport in the Samoas is by **Samoa Air** and **Polynesian Airlines**. The former flies between Apia (from Fagali'i airport just east of town) and Pago Pago; between Pago Pago, Ofu and Ta'u and between Pago Pago and Savai'i. Polynesian Airlines flies between Pago Pago, Apia and Savai'i.

Samoa Air runs three to six daily flights between Apia and Pago Pago. Polynesian Airlines does the 20-minute hop from Apia's Fagali'i airport to Savai'i's Maota airport on the island's southeast side three times daily.

BUS

Travelling by public bus is the most common method of getting around. In Samoa, bus services operate at the whim of the drivers. If your driver feels like knocking off at 1pm, he does. Buses are scarce on Saturday afternoon and Sunday.

Buses are very inexpensive, though also not very comfortable. The most you'll pay in Samoa for a trip across one of the islands is around ST$5.60. Most local trips cost around ST$0.80 to ST$0.90. In American Samoa you'll pay less than 50c for most local buses and only a few dollars for further afield.

In American Samoa, the island of Tutuila is served by small *'aiga*-owned buses. The buses theoretically run until early evening. It's difficult to find transport after about 2pm on Saturday, and on Sunday the only buses running are those taking people to church.

To stop a bus in either Samoa, wave your hand palm down as the bus approaches. To signal that you'd like to get off the bus, either knock on the ceiling or clap loudly. Pay the fare to the driver or leave the money on the dashboard as you leave. Try to have the exact change.

CAR

Getting around by car in the Samoas is quite straightforward. You'll normally get by using your driving licence from home, but occasionally visitors to independent Samoa will be required to get their licence endorsed at the courthouse in Apia (ST10).

In independent Samoa, the speed limit within Apia and villages is 40km/h (25mph); outside populated areas, it's 55km/h (35mph). In American Samoa, the speed limit is 24km/h (15mph) through villages and 40km/h (25mph) outside populated areas. In both independent and American Samoa, vehicles drive on the right – most of the time.

You must be at least 21 years of age to hire a car in Samoa and tariffs on hire cars are regulated by the government.

BICYCLE

For fit, experienced cyclists, touring 'Upolu and Savai'i by bicycle can be great (but hot). The roads are generally in very good condition and traffic is minimal.

The island of Tutuila in American Samoa is much less suitable for cycling; Although smaller than 'Upolu or Savai'i, Tutuila is more mountainous, and the traffic is heavier.

BOAT
Ferry
Ferries and launches connect al l the main Samoan islands. The largest car ferry, the *Lady Naomi*, owned by the Samoa Shipping Corporation, runs between Apia and Pago Pago Harbor once a week. It leaves Apia for Pago Pago on Wednesday at 10pm and returns on Thursday at 4.30pm. The trip takes about eight hours each way. The fare from Apia to Pago Pago is ST40, but it's US$40 (about three times as much) in the opposite direction. Cars cost ST240/480 one way/return from Apia and US$261/522 from Pago Pago.

Buy tickets from the **Samoa Shipping Corporation** (☎ 20935; ℮ ssc@samoa.ws; *Beach Rd*), past Aggie Grey's Hotel, going towards the wharf, in Apia. In Pago Pago, tickets must be purchased at least one day in advance from **Polynesia Shipping** (☎ 633 1211), on the dock in Fagatogo.

Yacht
Private yacht owners who intend to cruise around Savai'i should apply for a cruising permit at the **Ministry of Foreign Affairs** (☎ 25313) located in the main government offices building on Beach Rd in Apia. The permit will be issued within one or two days.

TAXI
Taxis in the capital cities are plentiful and quite cheap. You can often hire a taxi for a day or half a day for less than you'd pay for a hire car.

Taxis charge a minimum of ST$2 and you can get to most places around central Apia for that price. A copy of taxi fares is available from the Samoan Visitors Bureau, but for longer trips you often just settle a price with the driver beforehand.

ORGANISED TOURS
There are several excellent organised tours in Samoa. Those in American Samoa are much more limited in scope and about twice the price. The following are just a few of the many companies offering different types of tours:

Adventure-Man Tours & Rentals (☎ 41067, 28172, 🗔 www.adventureman.ws) Based in the Aleipata area of 'Upolu, this outfit offers to help you bike, hike and 4WD around 'Upolu and Savai'i. Jump off waterfalls and swim with sea turtles. Expect to pay between ST75 and ST160 per person per day.

Ecotour Samoa (☎/fax 22144, 🗔 www.ecotour samoa.com) PO Box 4609 Mata'utu-uta, Samoa, Beach Rd, Apia. Ecotour Samoa offers an action-packed safari (US$167 per person per day) taking visitors (maximum of 15) to villages in 'Upolu, Namu'a, Manono and Savai'i. It also runs a seven-day tour (US$267 per day), with three nights in hotels and four in villages; sea-kayaking tours staying overnight in villages (US$167 per day); a seven-day American Samoa ecotour (US$267 per day); as well as bird-watching tours and a unique Samoan Survival experience on an uninhabited volcanic island for US$167 per day.

Oceania Travel & Tours (in Apia ☎ 24443, 22552, in Pago Pago ☎ 633 1172, 🗔 www.oceania -travel.ws, www.samoa-travel.com) Based at Hotel Kitano Tusitala on Beach Rd in Apia, and also in Pago Pago at the Rainmaker Hotel, Oceania offers full- and half-day tours to and from Samoa and American Samoa. Air fare and pick-up are included in the price.

Safua Tours (☎ 51271) Safua Hotel, Lalomalava, Savai'i, Samoa. Safua provides excellent cultural, educational and scenic tours, including a half-day tour to the Pulemelei Step Pyramid and an excellent cliff-top walk from Cape Paepaeoleia on the Tafua Peninsula. Home and village stays are also offered.

Samoa Scenic Tours (☎ 26981, after hours ☎ 70 446, 🗔 www.samoascenictours.com) Based at Aggie Grey's, Samoa Scenic Tours runs full- and half-day scenic, cultural and ecotours with experienced and helpful guides. Most half-day tours cost between ST44 and ST66 per person. Full-day tours to places like Manono Island, Lalomanu Beach and Matareva Beach cost around ST110 per person.

'Upolu

pop 134,024 • area 1115 sq km
'Upolu is the second-largest island of Samoa. About 40% of the island is characterised by relatively gentle volcanic slopes rising to crests of around 1000m. The highest peak is Mt Fito (1028m), which lies within the O Le Pupu-Pu'e National Park. The interior of the island is covered in indigenous rainforest, which accounts for about 20% of the total land area.

Around 30% of 'Upolu is customary land (ie, owned by extended families and unable to be sold), the bulk of which is cultivated for subsistence agriculture. Most villages lie along the coast.

A fairly good system of roads makes all parts of the island easily accessible from the national capital and hub of activity, Apia.

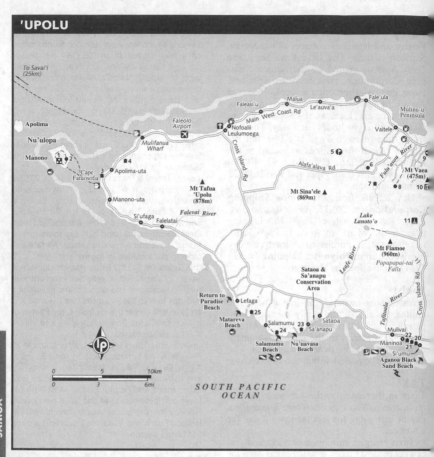

'UPOLU

To Savai'i (25km)

Apolima
Nu'ulopa
Manono
Faleolo Airport
Mulifanua Wharf
Cape Fatuosofia
Apolima-uta
Manono-uta
Si'ufaga
Falelatai
Falevai River
Mt Tafua 'Upolu (878m)

Faleasi'u
Malua
Le'auva'a
Fale'ula
Main West Coast Rd
Nofoalii
Leulumoega
Cross Island Rd
Alafa'alava Rd
Mt Sina'ele (869m)

Mulinu'u Peninsula
Vaitele
Fuluasou River
Mt Vaea (475m)
Lake Lanoto'o
Mt Fiamoe (960m)
Papapapai-tai Falls
Lefie River
Tofitoelia River
Cross Island Rd

Return to Paradise Beach
Lefaga
Matareva Beach
Salamumu
Salamumu Beach
Nu'uavasa Beach
Sataoa
Sa'anapu
Satoaa & Sa'anapu Conservation Area
Mulivai
Maninoa
Si'umu
Aganoa Black Sand Beach

0   5   10km
0   3   6mi

SOUTH PACIFIC OCEAN

Getting There & Away

All overseas flights arrive in Apia, which is the capital of 'Upolu. Flights for Savai'i and Pago Pago leave from Fagali'i airport, a few kilometres east of Apia. The bus fare between the airport and Apia is around ST1.50. Taxis between Fagali'i airport and central Apia cost around ST8.

Taxis between Apia and Faleolo airport cost between ST40 and ST45. **P&F Schuster Tours** (☎ 23014) runs an airport shuttle service (ST10), which visits all the major hotels.

Getting Around

Bus The buses connecting Apia with other parts of 'Upolu leave from the main bus station near the central market, Maketi Fou, off Fugalei St, and from the bus area behind the flea market.

From Apia, fares to the western end of 'Upolu (Mulifanua and Manono-uta) or Mulivai are ST2. To Si'umu costs ST3.30, to Lefaga it's ST2.10 and to Aleipata, ST3. For an up-to-date list of bus fares and routes contact the Samoa Tourism Authority Visitors Bureau.

The buses are colourful and fun, but they are also very hot and uncomfortable, often unsafe and there's no room for any luggage. If you'd prefer to get around the island in air-conditioned comfort, the **Green Turtle bus** (bookings through 5 Star Travel in Apia ☎ 22144, 29629; **w** www.greenturtletours. com) is a good, reliable option. The bus circumnavigates the island every day, including Sunday, picking up visitors from their hotels, stopping at sites of interest and allowing time for swimming, photography as well as

SAMOA

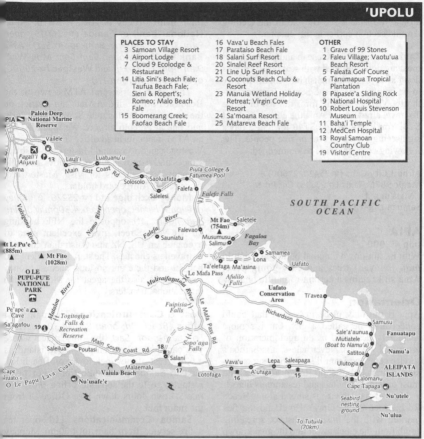

'UPOLU

PLACES TO STAY		OTHER
3 Samoan Village Resort	16 Vava'u Beach Fales	1 Grave of 99 Stones
4 Airport Lodge	17 Parataiso Beach Fale	2 Faleu Village; Vaotu'ua Beach Resort
7 Cloud 9 Ecolodge & Restaurant	18 Salani Surf Resort	5 Faleata Golf Course
14 Litia Sini's Beach Fale; Taufua Beach Fale; Sieni & Ropert's; Romeo; Malo Beach Fale	20 Sinalei Reef Resort	6 Tanumapua Tropical Plantation
	21 Line Up Surf Resort	8 Papasee'a Sliding Rock
	22 Coconuts Beach Club & Resort	9 National Hospital
	23 Manuia Wetland Holiday Retreat; Virgin Cove Resort	10 Robert Louis Stevenson Museum
15 Boomerang Creek; Faofao Beach Fale	24 Sa'moana Resort	11 Baha'i Temple
	25 Matareva Beach Fale	12 MedCen Hospital
		13 Royal Samoan Country Club
		19 Visitor Centre

SAMOA

demonstrations. If you'd like to stay somewhere overnight and be picked up a few days later that can be arranged too. The one-day trip costs ST90; the jump-on/jump-off option is ST168.40. Prices include GST.

Car Three good cross-island roads pass over the east–west central ridge and divide the island roughly into quarters. The central one begins in Apia at Falealili St before becoming the Cross Island Rd.

The northeastern section of 'Upolu is the most rugged; you'll need a 4WD to negotiate the track to Fagaloa Bay. If you're planning to take your vehicle on the ferry to Savai'i you'll need a jeep; a normal vehicle doesn't have enough clearance. Some rental agencies, like Avis, don't allow their vehicles to be transported on ferries.

Prices start at around ST150 per day for a Suzuki 4WD jeep. Discounts are offered for longer-term rental. There are plenty of agencies, so ring around for the best deal. The following are recommended:

Apia Rentals (☎ 24244, fax 26193, e apiarentals@ipasifika.net)
Avis Car Rentals (☎ 20486, fax 26069)
Blue Pacific Car Hire (☎ 22668, fax 25668, e bluepacificsale@lesamoa.net)
Budget Car Hire (☎ 20561, fax 22284, e budget@ipasifika.net)
Funway Rentals (☎ 22045, fax 25008, e funwayrentals@samoa.ws)

Bicycle Several beach resorts and hotels hire out bicycles. In Apia, **Seaside Inn** (☎ 22578; Beach Rd) hires bicycles from around ST24 per day. **Holiday Rentals** (☎ 22578, fax 22918) is another option. For information on cycling around the islands see Bicycle in the Getting Around section earlier in this chapter.

Taxi Samoan taxis are cheap and plentiful and most are now equipped with seat belts. Drivers don't always speak English but will always try to be helpful. Ask at the Samoa Tourism Authority Visitors Bureau for a full list of fares. To travel anywhere in Apia the charge is about ST3. You'll pay around ST40 for half a day's sightseeing for up to four or five people. The following companies are recommended:

Airport City Cabs (☎ 25420, 21600)
Magic 98FM Taxis (☎ 25215) Cnr Rd & Mata'utu St
Samoan Lager Taxis (☎ 25909)

APIA
pop 40,000
With its run-down colonial buildings, big old *pulu* (banyan) trees and easy-going pace, Apia still retains a certain romantic charm.

Orientation
Apia is the only place in Samoa that could conceivably be called a city, but it's more accurately described as an agglomeration of urbanised villages. Nevertheless, it is Samoa's service centre and you'll find shops, supermarkets, tourist information, travel agencies and most of Samoa's hotels and restaurants here.

Most of the activity is spread along Beach Rd between Aggie Grey's Hotel and the flea market, with the business district spreading south from the clock tower into the area known as Chinatown. The central market, Maketi Fou, and the main bus station are a couple of blocks south of the clock tower, between Fugalei and Saleufi Sts. The wharf lies at the eastern end of the harbour. The marine reserve, Palolo Deep, is just beyond the wharf.

Information
Tourist Offices The **Samoa Tourism Authority Visitors Bureau** (☎ 63500; e sam oa@samoa.ws; open 8am-4.30pm Mon-Fri, 8.30am-noon Sat), is in a traditional-style *fale* on Beach Rd, not far from the clock tower. This should be your first port of call, as the information is excellent and the staff are helpful. The free booklet *Samoa What's On* is updated regularly. The Visitors Bureau can also give you up-to-date information on bus and taxi rates, bus timetables and a free copy of the Jasons map of Samoa.

Money Samoa's three main banks all have their main offices on Beach Rd in Apia. **National Bank of Samoa** (☎ 26019; open 9am-3pm Mon-Fri, 9am-noon Sat), **ANZ Bank** (☎ 69999; open 9am-3pm Mon-Wed, 9am-4pm Thurs-Fri) and **Westpac** (☎ 20000, open 9am-3pm Mon-Fri).

The ANZ has several ATMs: two at the Beach Rd office; one in Mata'utu district; or the corner of Matafagatele St near Apia Park; and one at Faleolo airport. Westpac also has an ATM inside its head office. Both ANZ and Westpac can do Visa and MasterCard cash advances and Eftpos facilities are now available at many retail outlets for Visa, MasterCard, Access and AmEx card holders.

Money Exchange Ltd (☎ 23276; e money ex@ipasifika.net; open 8am-4.30pm Mon-Fri, 8am-noon Sat), opposite the NPF building on Mt Vaea Street, gives excellent rates of exchange on US, NZ and Australian currency or travellers cheques. The staff are efficient and helpful and there are no long queues. Money Exchange is also the agent for Money Gram international transfers.

Post & Communications The **main post office** (Beach Rd; open 8am-4.30pm Mon-Fri, 8am-noon Sat), the only place where you can buy stamps on the whole island, is a block east of the clock tower on Beach Rd, next to Samoa Communications. For poste restante, go to the separate **office** (Post Office St) two doors down Post Office St from the main lobby.

Samoa Communications Ltd operates a fax service from 8am to 4.30pm Monday to Friday, and a telephone and telex service from 8am to 10pm daily. There are also pay phones in the Lotemau Centre, in the arcade beside the Air New Zealand office, at Fugalei Market, at Hotel Kitano Tusitala and at the airports. Shops around these points sell phonecards (ST5, ST10, ST20 and ST50), and you can buy them at **Telecom Samoa Cellular** (☎ 26081) right next to the post office.

You can rent a mobile phone from Telecom Samoa or from **VIP Cellphone Rentals** (☎ 21 415, e gary@samoalive.com), but it won't be much use in many places outside of Apia. Communications may improve when Samoa switches from analogue to digital phones.

Internet access is now relatively easy and connections are good. Most Internet cafés charge around ST3 for 15 minutes, ST10 or so for an hour. **Computer Services Ltd** and **Le Samoa.net**, both in the Lotemau Centre, have everal computers and are very popular, so you may need to wait. They're open business hours only. If you'd prefer to surf the Internet over an espresso, **Cappuccino Vineyard**, behind ACB House, has a couple of computers and you'll usually find one free. If you need to check your emails on the weekend or after hours, **2u.Services** opposite Pasefika Inn on Apia Park Rd offers Internet access every day between 8am and 8pm, or later if you need to.

Travel Agencies Two recommended local agencies are **Island Hopper Vacations** (☎ 26 940, fax 26941; e samoa.sales@islandhopper com.ws), in the Lotemau Centre, and **Oceania Travel & Tours** (☎ 24443, fax 22255), at the Hotel Kitano Tusitala.

Bookshops Books are a rare commodity in Samoa, perhaps because it has a such a strong oral tradition. There are only two bookshops in Apia, both with a very limited range of titles of interest to foreign travellers. The **Wesley Bookshop** in the Wesley Arcade off Beach Rd, not far from the Samoa Tourism Authority Visitors Bureau, and **Ia Malamalama** also on Beach Rd, close to Aggie Grey's, mostly sell religious books and a small stock of educational books about Pacific history, politics and culture. You may find some books about Samoan culture at **Aggie's Gift Shop** (Beach Rd). If you want pulp fiction or even the odd classic, you can pick up second-hand books upstairs at the **CCK store** in Convent St.

Libraries The **Nelson Public Library** (Beach Rd; open 9am-4.30pm Mon-Thur, 8am-4pm Fri, 8.30am-12.30pm Sat), just by the clock tower, allows travellers to borrow books for ST5 plus a ST15 refundable deposit. The Pacific Room has a good collection of books and journals about Samoa, but it closes for lunch hour at noon.

Universities The **National University of Samoa** (☎ 20072) has its lovely campus at Vaivase, just southeast of the town centre. The University of the South Pacific, which is based in Suva, Fiji, has its **Agriculture Department** (☎ 21671) in Alafua, on the outskirts of Apia.

Laundry One of the most convenient of the several laundrettes in Apia is **Cleanmaid Laundromat** (Mata'utu St; open 7am-6pm Mon-Sat), opposite Pasefika Inn. Other laundrettes about town include the **Three Corners**

Laundromat, at the top of Mt Vaea St, and **Faupepa's Laundromat**, near the National Hospital.

Medical Services The best option for medical assistance is the private **MedCen Hospital** (☎ 26519, 26323; e medcen@ipasifika.net; open 24hr), based at Vailima, a few hundred metres past the Robert Louis Stevenson Museum. It costs ST55 to see a doctor, on site from 8am to 10pm. By all accounts, this place is very professionally run. For a list of other private doctors and dentists around Apia, contact the Samoa Tourism Authority Visitors Bureau or consult the authority's free booklet.

Emergency In an emergency, the following numbers are used: **ambulance** (☎ 999), **fire** (☎ 994), **police** (☎ 995) and **National Hospital** (☎ 996).

Maketi Fou
The main market, between Fugalei and Saleufi Sts a couple of blocks south of Beach Rd, is the centre of activity in Apia and has the biggest and best selection of fresh produce, as well as the lowest prices in the South Pacific. It's right next to the central bus terminal and is busy, crowded and lively at just about any time of day or night, Sundays and public holidays included.

Flea Market
Apia's flea market (Beach Rd; open 8am-4pm Mon-Fri, 8am-noon Sat) is housed in the old central market building down on Beach Rd, west of the clock tower. Here you'll find cheap clothing and craft stalls selling everything from siapo and 'ava bowls to coconut shell jewellery. Tucked beyond the craft stalls, on the northern side of the market, is a row of cheap food stalls.

Fish Market
The fish market (open daily) is just east of the flea market. It's open every day, but Sunday morning is the busiest time, as people rush in before going off to church to buy fresh fish for the traditional Sunday umu lunch.

Churches
Nobody seems to be quite sure how many churches there are in Apia and the surrounding area but it's obvious from their prominence as well as their predominance that

SAMOA

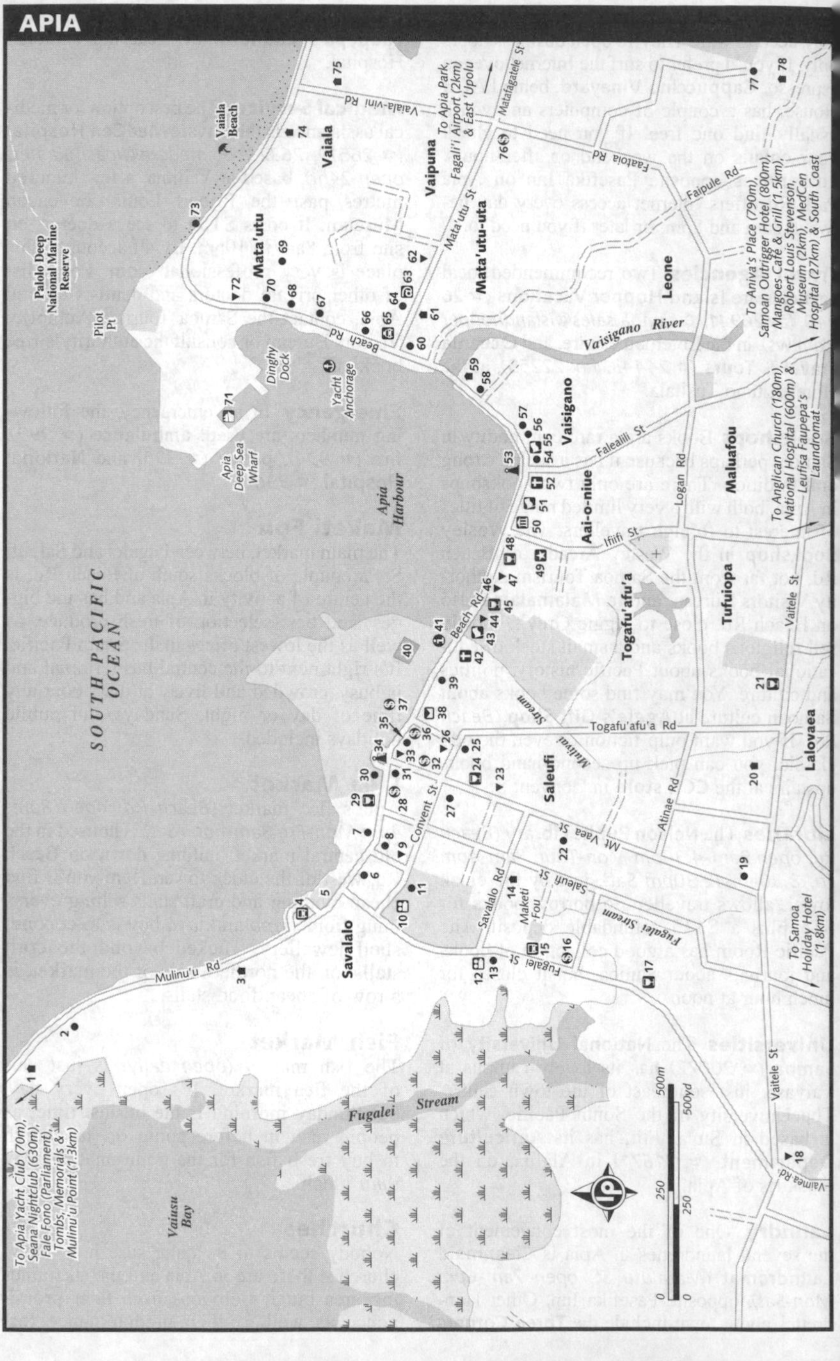

APIA

SAMOA

SOUTH PACIFIC OCEAN

Palolo Deep National Marine Reserve

Pilot Pt

Vaiala Beach

Vaiala

Mata'utu

Vaipuna

Mata'utu-uta

Leone

Vaisigano River

Vaisigano

Maluafou

Aai-o-niue

Togafu'afu'a

Tufuiopa

Apia Deep Sea Wharf

Yacht Anchorage

Dinghy Dock

Apia Harbour

Saleufi

Lalovaea

Savalalo

Maketi Fou

Vaiusu Bay

Fugalei Stream

Beach Rd

Convent St

Mt Vaea St

Saleufi St

Fugalei St

Savalalo Rd

Mulinu'u Rd

Matafagatele St

Vaiala-vini Rd

Faatoia Rd

Faipule Rd

Falealili St

Logan Rd

Ifiifi St

Togafu'afu'a Rd

Atinae Rd

Valtele St

Valtele Rd

Vaimea Rd

Mulivai Stream

Fugalei Stream

To Apia Park,
Fagali'i Airport (2km)
& East 'Upolu

To Anivá's Place (790m);
Samoan Outrigger Hotel (800m);
Mangoes Café & Grill (1.5km);
Robert Louis Stevenson
Museum (2km), MedCen
Hospital (27km) & South Coast

To Anglican Church (180m);
National Hospital (600m);
Leufisa Faupepa's
Laundromat

To Samoa
Holiday Hotel
(1.8km)

To Apia Yacht Club (70m),
Seana Nightclub (630m),
Fale Fono (Parliament),
Tombs, Memorials &
Mulinu'u Point (1.3km)

0   250   500m
0   250   500yd

APIA

PLACES TO STAY
1 Hotel Millenia
3 Hotel Kitano Tusitala; Oceania Travel & Tours; Seaview Brasserie & Bar
14 Apia Central Hotel
20 Seipepa
59 Aggie Grey's Hotel; Samoa Scenic Tours; Old Fale Restaurant; Le Tamarina
61 Pasefika Inn
74 1848 Princess Tui
75 Vaiala Beach Cottages
78 Hidden Garden Stay

PLACES TO EAT
9 Cappuccino Vineyard & Internet
18 Le Culinaire's Bistro
23 Leaves of the Banyan
26 Gourmet Seafood & Grill
33 Chan Mow Supermarket
44 Rainforest Café & Restaurant
46 Sails Restaurant & Bar; Tauese Theatre
47 The Coast Bar & Grill; Bad Billy's
62 Steak-House Restaurant
72 MD's Big Fresh

OTHER
2 Samoa Pharmacy
4 Bus Station
5 Flea Market
6 Samoa Air; Molesi Supermarket
7 Fish Market

8 National Bank of Samoa; ACB House
10 Magik 2 Cinema
11 Immigration Office
12 Myna's Cinema
13 Tokelau Apia Liaison Office
15 Main Bus Station
16 National Bank of Samoa
17 JT's Sports Bar & Café
19 Three Corners Laundromat
21 Mt Vaea Nightclub
22 Apia Rentals
24 Eye Spy
25 CCK Store
27 Lotemau Centre; Air New Zealand; Island Hopper Vacations; Public Telephones; AQM Fine Foods; Computer Services Ltd; Le Samoa.net
28 Westpac Bank & ATM
29 RSA Club
30 Nelson Public Library
31 NPF Building: Polynesian Airlines; Budget Car Rentals
32 Money Exchange Ltd
34 Clock Tower
35 Molesi Store
36 ANZ Bank & ATMs
37 Samoa Central Bank
38 Post Office
39 Wesley Bookshop
40 Government Offices Building; Ministry of Foreign Affairs
41 Samoa Tourism Authority Visitors Bureau

42 Catholic Cathedral
43 Australian High Commission
45 On the Rocks
48 Otto's Reef
49 Police Station
50 Museum of Samoa; Supreme Court
51 New Zealand High Commission; Department of Lands, Surveys & Environment
52 Congregational Christian Church
53 John Williams Memorial
54 Moana Divers
55 US Embassy
56 Ecotours; Green Turtle Tours; Molesi Supermarket
57 Ia Malamalama Bookshop
58 Aggie's Gift Shop
60 Avis Rent-a-carls
63 2U.Services
64 Cleanmaid Laundromat
65 Magic 98FM Taxis
66 Samoa Shipping Corporation
67 Samoa Mariner; Pacific Quest Divers
68 Seaside Inn
69 Apia Squash Courts
70 Funway Rentals
71 Harbour Master & Ferry Landing
73 Palolo Deep Marine Reserve Entrance
76 ANZ ATM
77 Tennis Court

Christianity is big business in Samoa. With the church central to Samoan life, villages compete to build the biggest as well as the best, and most have at least two, and sometimes even three churches. The landmark on the waterfront is the **Catholic cathedral**, recognisable by its roof-top Madonna. The **Wesleyan church** nearby is also an imposing structure.

The missionary John Williams, who brought Christianity to Samoa in 1830, was killed and eaten in Vanuatu nine years later but his bones were recovered and laid to rest on the site of what is now the **Congregational Christian Church** on the corner of Beach Rd and Falealili St. If you want to hear some great singing, dress as the locals do on a Sunday – in tight white – and join them in church. Don't forget to carry a fan – the gospel is hot in those missionary-influenced weatherboard *palangi* buildings.

The **Anglican church**, located on Ifiifi St, not far away from the National Hospital, is a lovely, unassuming building with some really impressive glasswork in the stained-glass windows.

In recent years, the Mormon Church has been giving the more traditional Samoan churches a run for their money (literally) and its popularity, and number of churches, has grown considerably.

The **Protestant church** in Beach Rd, just up from Aggie Grey's, has services in English every Sunday at 9.30am and 7pm, and visitors are welcome.

Clock Tower
Though you may find street names on maps of Apia, you won't often find them on the streets themselves and Samoans almost never refer to them. The clock tower – constructed in memory of those killed in WWI – in the centre of town is a very useful landmark for giving directions, though not for telling the time, which is different according to which clock face you look at.

Government Buildings

Upstaging the churches, the most imposing feature of the modern Apia skyline is the seven-storey **government offices building**, which towers above the area reclaimed from the sea, behind the Samoa Tourism Authority Visitors Bureau.

The **Supreme Court** (*cnr Beach Rd & Ifiifi St*) is in a two-storey knocked-about colonial building, near the site where the bloody clash between the Mau (Samoan for Samoans) Movement and the NZ police resulted in the deaths of 11 Samoans, including the Mau leader Tupua Tamasese Lealofi III, on 28 December 1929.

The **police station** (*Ifiifi St*) is just around the corner and at 7.45am every weekday the Police Band marches from here to the government building to commemorate Samoa's independence. Vehicle and pedestrian traffic is stopped and the national anthem is played while the flag is raised.

Samoa's modern parliament building, opened in 1972, is a traditionally shaped **Fale Fono**, down towards the end of the Mulinu'u Peninsula.

Museum of Samoa

There's a good, although small, display of Samoan history and culture at this museum (☎ 63444; Beach Rd; admission free; open noon-3.30pm Mon-Fri). It's upstairs in the same building as the Supreme Court.

Memorials

The Mulinu'u Peninsula seems to serve as a repository for political monuments and memorials. Past Hotel Millenia there is a cluster of monuments, including the German Flag Memorial, erected in 1913 just one year before the NZ takeover of Western Samoa. It commemorates the raising of the German flag over the islands on 1 March 1900.

On the east side of Mulinu'u Peninsula, near the observatory, are the **tombs of Malietoa Tanumafili I** and **Malietoa Laupepa**, the father and grandfather, respectively, of the present ceremonial head of state. At the very end of the peninsula are the **mausoleum of Tupua Tamasese** and the magnificent seven-tiered **tomb of the Tu'imaleali'ifano dynasty**.

Palolo Deep National Marine Reserve

Past the wharf is Palolo Deep National Marine Reserve (*Beach Rd, Va; adult/child ST2/1;*

open 8am-6pm daily). There's a magnificent snorkelling here, as well as several shady comfortable spots for picnicking and relaxing. But always be aware of currents.

It's the perfect spot to spend a Sunday when visitors aren't welcome on many other beaches, and snorkelling gear can be rented for ST10.

Places to Stay – Budget

Samoan Outrigger Hotel (☎/fax 20042; e outrigger@samoa.ws; PO Box 4074, Moto'utua; garden fale per person ST35; singles/doubles with shared facilities ST70/80, with private facilities ST80/100, with air-con ST100/120; family rooms ST120) used to occupy a prime position down on Beach Rd, but had to move inland after its lease expired. It is now located about 10 minutes' walk up the Cross Island Rd from the centre of town. The new premises are in a well-renovated 110-year-old colonial building with high ceilings and the managers have maintained the charm and atmosphere that have made the Outrigger a longtime favourite with travellers. In addition to a 12m swimming pool, there's a fully equipped kitchen, pool table, laundry (ST6 for a load of washing, ST5 for the dryer), telephone/fax/Internet service, a BBQ, and cold Vailimas for sale. It's an excellent budget choice and is often booked out, so reservations are advisable. Rates include continental breakfast.

1848 Princess Tui (☎ 23342; W www.princesstui.ws; 1 Vaiala Beach Rd; singles/doubles/triples/quads ST66/77/110/135, with air-con & bathroom ST89/99/125/129) styles itself as a 'bed and breakfast by the sea'. It occupies the old colonial house where the Outrigger used to be, set in lovely gardens looking out over Vaiala Beach. The staff are helpful with travel advice and organisation when asked. Continental breakfast is included and there are kitchen and laundry facilities for guests. It's clean, charming and airy, and budget-priced if you don't mind sharing. There are, however, a few extra costs, including key deposit, luggage storage (one day free, ST3 per bag per day thereafter), air-conditioning and sea views.

Seipepa (☎/fax 25447; W www.samoa-experience.com; off Vaitele St, Lalovaea), south of the centre and tucked away among village houses, is a popular, lush 'travel home' about 15 minutes' walk from the centre of town. There are no set accommodation rates – guests pay what they feel to be fair – but generally ST35 to ST60 is appreciated; Both Visa and MasterCard are accepted here.

Guests can sleep either inside the house (in twin and double rooms with lockers and 'natural' air-conditioning supplemented by fans) or in a *fale*, including possibly the only double-storey *fale* in all of Samoa. There are spotless communal (cold-water) showers and toilets. Continental breakfast is also provided. Seipepa is a great place to sample traditional food (eaten whilst sitting on the floor), especially on Sunday, when a midday *umu* is prepared. Guests can also learn how to open coconuts, weave a basket and make Samoan coconut oil.

Cloud Nine Ecolodge (☎ 28899; *Silver Streams, Tapatapao, Aleisa East, PO Box 3456 Apia; singles & doubles ST70*) is ideal if you want to escape the hot hustle and bustle of central Apia and be at one with nature. This unique mountain-top lodge is only 15 minutes and several degrees away from the heat of the city, and its name is well chosen. Watch the swooping birds and feel the cooling breezes as you sip cool drinks on the balcony, with the rainforest at your feet. In the evening you can watch the sun set over the island of Savai'i beyond the sweep of Apia's lights as you enjoy a quiet meal at the restaurant or a drink from the bar.

Hidden Garden Stay (☎ 25416; *Vini Rd; fale per person ST15*), out near Apia Park, is definitely one of the best options for budget travellers, despite the fact that it's not the closest place to the centre of town. There are four charming, breezy *fale* on stilts set in lovely gardens. Rates include breakfast, shared kitchen and toilet, and an outdoor (cold) shower.

Places to Stay – Mid-Range
Pasefika Inn (☎ 20971, fax 23303; W www.pasefikainn.ws; *Mata'utu St; singles/doubles with fridge, air-con & bathroom with hot water ST100/120, with air-con & spa bath ST198/237*) is well positioned just off Beach Rd, opposite the 2U.Services Internet café. This three-storey hotel is popular with Samoan expatriates and people on work trips. The rooms are spacious and clean and the service is efficient and friendly. The nicest rooms have balcony views of the harbour, but they cost a little extra. There's a fully equipped communal kitchen, TV and video room, bar, and same-day laundry service. You can choose to go without the air-conditioning, but you'd be mad to miss it. Breakfast, included in the room rate, features all-you-can-eat fruit, fresh coconut, toast and hot Samoan pancakes with jam.

Aniva's Place (☎ 20501, ☎/fax 23431; e anivas@samoa.net; *PO Box 1604; singles/doubles/triples with shared facilities ST95/115/135*) is up near the National Hospital. Friendly and super-clean, it's a good option in this price range, even if it is a bit of a hike to town (about 15 minutes). Rooms in this spacious home are a bit dark and pokey, though comfortable, and have fans and phones; four have air-con (ST20 extra). Bathroom and toilets are communal. There's a large lounge with TV and video and kitchen upstairs for guests, a swimming pool and bar, as well as same-day laundry service and Internet access (free at the time of research). Rates include breakfast and dinner can be provided on request. Prices quoted here are for cash; rates are a little extra if you pay by credit card.

Apia Central Hotel (☎ 20782, fax 26206; W www.samoahotels.ws/ahkams.htm; *Savalalo Rd; singles/doubles/triples with bathroom & fan ST105/145/180, with air-con ST145/180/215*) is just a short walk from Maketi Fou and the town centre. The best thing about this hotel is its central location. It has a nice bar and restaurant and a very pleasant courtyard. Rooms are nicely decorated with traditional Samoan *siapo*; they have phones, and some have fridges, but the ground-floor rooms are a bit dark and damp-smelling, and may be noisy.

Places to Stay – Top End
Aggie Grey's Hotel (☎ 22880, fax 23626; W www.aggiegreys.com; *Beach Rd; standard singles/doubles/triples ST346.50/363/382, fale-style bungalows ST418/440/456.50, suites ST781/803/819.50*) is a member of the Austrian-based 'The Most Famous Hotels in the World' association. It's certainly famous, at least in the Pacific, and its rates reflect this. But the fame, one suspects, is more due to the fact that for a long time it was the only hotel in Apia, and indeed Samoa, and current management has certainly not discouraged the tradition of Aggie-ography. The hotel foyer is full of memorabilia to remind 21st-century guests of the life and times of its founder – feted as one of last century's *grand dames* and reputedly the inspiration for James Michener's character Bloody Mary, made infamous in the film of the book *Tales from the South Pacific*. The hotel certainly isn't the Ritz. The standard rooms are better value than the dreary bungalows, although neither have much Pacific flavour. The gardens, however, are lush and tropical, and there's a pool for guests.

Hotel Kitano Tusitala (☎ 21122, fax 23652; W www.kitano.ws; Mulinu'u Rd; standard singles & doubles with air-con ST310, triples ST355; superior singles & doubles ST432, triples ST468; singles & doubles with balcony & pool view ST540, triples ST575; family/ executive suites ST432/772), Apia's other big hotel, is situated on the Mulinu'u Peninsula. It's how you'd imagine a resort in the Pacific to be: central pools and bars shaded by palms and surrounded with traditional fale, all in an atmosphere of calm (if not sedation). The only thing missing is the beachfront. If you're travelling with kids and after something more upmarket, this is a good option; children under 14 stay for free and there's a children's playground on the premises. There are also tennis courts and two restaurants, including the excellent Seaview Brasserie & Bar (see Places to Eat). There's a discount of 25% for stays of more than three nights.

Hotel Millenia (☎ 28284, fax 28285; W www.hotelmilleniasamoa.com; Mulinu'u Rd; singles & doubles ST192-464), more like a large family home than a hotel, stands out because of its lovely staff. Rooms have air-con, bathroom and TV. It charges in US dollars but we've tried to give the current Samoan tala equivalent. The hotel is in a terrific location on the Mulinu'u Peninsula, with refreshing sea breezes, but the Seana nightclub is next door, so you might want to ask for a room away from the action. Internet access (ST5 for 15 minutes) and laundry services are available. There's a restaurant and a very popular bar. Rates include a cooked breakfast.

Vaiala Beach Cottages (☎ 22202, fax 22008; e vaialabeach@samoa.ws; Vaiala-vini Rd; singles/doubles/triples/quads ST158/183/ 207/244, upmarket singles/doubles/triples ST220/253/286), close to Vaiala Beach, is pleasant and is a good option for families. Set in spacious gardens close to the sea, the cottages have a bathroom, ceiling fan and gas stove, and sleep up to three adults and two children.

Places to Eat

Apia has a huge selection of restaurants and cafés. The Samoa Tourism Authority Visitors Bureau can provide a full and detailed list. Most restaurants and cafés are closed on Sunday.

Snacks & Cheap Meals One of the best places for a cheap meal, particularly breakfast, is the **Maketi Fou** or the **food stalls** behind the flea market. Look out for delicious palusami and drinking coconuts. Try a few Samoan pancakes washed down with a cup of yummy koko Samoa.

Gourmet Seafood & Grill (☎ 24625; cnr Convent & Post Office Sts; mains ST10-15), popular with both locals and travellers, has a pleasant, relaxed feel and offers a good range of simple dishes such as veggie burgers, fish and chips, steak teriyaki, sushi, and a great seafood platter with salad (ST10.50).

Cappuccino Vineyard (☎ 22049; light meals ST6-15) is a Western-influenced, modern, Internet café and one of the best places in town for an espresso. By night it's a wine bar and serves snacks such as spicy meatballs and chicken satay sticks (both ST8). It's in a mall that extends from ACB House on Beach Rd.

Leaves of the Banyan (☎ 22876; Mt Vaea St; meals ST8-13) is a tiny, very cute café. Meals are served outdoors under umbrellas in a tropical setting – a great spot to relax with a fresh juice (ST3). Beautifully presented and healthy, the menu includes things like sushi and pasta salad.

The Coast Bar & Grill (☎ 26669; Beach Rd; meals ST7-15) is one of the best-value places to eat in town. Great food (such as delicious lemon-grilled fish steak), excellent service and a relaxed atmosphere are topped off with balcony dining overlooking the harbour on Beach Rd. It's a popular nightclub in the evening.

Apia Yacht Club (☎ 21313; Mulinu'u Rd), a welcoming place at the top of the Mulinu'u Peninsula, offers meals such as fish and chips (ST10) and sashimi (ST8).

Restaurants Open late from Monday to Friday, **Rainforest Cafe & Restaurant** (☎ 25 030; Beach Rd; breakfast ST5.50-16.50, lunch ST10-16.50, dinner ST20-24) is recommended. The fare, especially the curry, is excellent, as is the service. Vegetarian food can be prepared on request. You'll need to bring your own alcohol.

Mangoes Café Bar & Grill (☎ 73467; Cross Island Rd; 3-course set meals ST50-60) is located near the Robert Louis Stevenson Museum at Papaloloa. There's a wide selection of salads and meats, which you grill yourself, a full bar service and you can dine in, or out on the deck, which has a terrific view of the valley down to the ocean.

Steak-House Restaurant (☎ 22962; Mata'utu St; meals ST18-28), another good option that won't completely break the bank, is a popular spot next door to a gym; it serves 'Fitness Plates'. Half-serves and cheaper lunch specials (ST10) are also available.

Sails Restaurant & Bar (☎ 20628; *Beach Rd; all-day breakfast ST15.50, lunch ST15-27, dinner mains around ST32*) is housed upstairs in a slightly dishevelled but charming 140-year-old colonial building that was the first Samoan home of Robert Louis Stevenson. It's very popular, but some travellers think it's overpriced. From its balcony you can look out over the harbour and listen to the evening cacophony of birds in the stately old banyan trees. Lunch dishes include sashimi (ST15), *nasi goreng* (ST16) and beef stroganoff (ST17). The more extensive dinner menu is international and eclectic. Vegetarians can be catered for and there are special children's meals. Best of all, it's open for dinner on Sunday.

Le Culinaire's Bistro (☎ 24804; *Vaitele St; dinner mains ST26-45*), tucked away and understated, is a very stylish establishment with an enchanting outdoor eating area and a cosmopolitan menu.

Seaview Brasserie & Bar (☎ 21122; *Hotel Kitano Tusitala; mains ST27-46, children's meals including main & dessert ST15*) is the best restaurant at Hotel Kitano Tusitala and definitely one of the finest in town. It has atmosphere, sea breezes and its sophisticated menu has a heavy Japanese influence. The international wine list is extensive.

Old Fale Restaurant (☎ 22880; *Aggie Grey's Hotel; breakfast & lunch ST15-25, dinner buffet ST44*) offers an excellent dinner buffet following the Wednesday evening *fiafia*. Sunday is barbecue night (ST35) and there's live Polynesian music nightly.

Le Tamarina (☎ 22880; *Aggie Grey's Hotel*) is Aggie's more formal restaurant. It features a huge seafood spread on Saturday for ST60 per person.

One of the best places for a traditional Sunday lunch, **Pasefika Inn** (☎ 20971; *Mata'utu St; lunch ST40*) is excellent value.

Cloud 9 (☎ 28899), high up in the hills above Apia, offers Sunday lunch in the clouds, overlooking the rainforest.

Self-Catering For fresh produce, the best place to head is **Maketi Fou**, or the **Fish Market**. You'll find a reasonable selection of groceries at **Chan Mow supermarket**, near the clock tower and the two branches of **Molesi Store** (*Beach Rd*), farther west and near the clock tower. Other good options include **MD's Big Fresh** (*Beach Rd*), up near

the wharf, and **AQM Fine Foods**, a smaller shop in the Lotemau Centre.

Entertainment
Bars & Clubs Apia has a huge number of bars and nightclubs, but what's hip today may not be cool tomorrow. **RSA Club** (☎ 20171; *Beach Rd*), near the clock tower, is one of the stayers. In the evening it turns from a big rattling pool hall and bar into a popular nightclub. While this is an excellent place to see some real Samoan nightlife, things can get rough here at times; females should not go alone.

Otto's Reef (☎ 22691; *Beach Rd*) is a beer garden with pool tables and darts. It may not always be packed to the rafters, but it's been around for a while.

The Coast Bar & Grill (☎ 26669; *Beach Rd*), next door to Otto's, was one of the current happening places at the time of research. This could be due to its DJ's taste in music, the yummy cocktails or maybe it's the karaoke.

On the Rocks (☎ 20736; *Beach Rd*), a couple of doors down from The Coast Bar & Grill, is an air-conditioned bar that serves huge cocktails for very reasonable prices. The bar staff will mix anything on request and there's always an interesting mix of locals and *palagi*. Happy hour is from 4pm to 6pm and a live band plays on Tuesday and Thursday. Cocktails cost ST8, jugs ST20.

JT's Sports Bar & Café (☎ 22221; *Fugalei St*), about 10 minutes' walk from Beach Rd, is an airy bar brimming with sports paraphernalia. It's also a popular spot for Saturday breakfast.

Mt Vaea Nightclub (☎ 21627; *Vaitele St*) is a low-roofed nightclub that has a similar vibe to the RSA and is just as popular. It's one of the few places where you might be able to keep dancing past midnight.

Eye Spy (☎ 20805; *Mt Vaea St*) is a bit better behaved than either the RSA or Mt Vaea. It's also close to town and attracts a good mix of locals and *palagi*.

Bad Billy's (☎ 30258; *Beach Rd*) is a restaurant by day and bar/nightclub by dusk. It's downstairs from The Coast Bar & Grill.

Seana (☎ 24971; *Mulinu'u Rd*) has a pleasant atmosphere and attracts an older crowd. There's a live, local band from Wednesday to Saturday.

Cinemas A double cinema complex, **Magik 2 Cinema** (☎ 28127; *Convent St; tickets before/after 5pm ST7/9*) shows popular mainstream flicks.

SAMOA

There are also a couple of more character-filled options for nightly movie shows: the old **Tauese Theatre** *(Beach Rd)*, downstairs from Sails Restaurant, and **Myna's Cinema** *(☎ 21806; Fugalei St)*.

Fiafia Spectacular Samoan dance performances *(fiafia)* are staged regularly at various hotel venues; they're all good. A buffet dinner usually accompanies the performance, although you can choose to see the show only. The *fiafia* at **Aggie Grey's Hotel** *(show ST11, dinner & show ST44)* is staged on Wednesday evening. **Hotel Kitano Tusitala** *(show ST10, dinner & show ST55)* has its *fiafia* on Friday.

AROUND THE ISLAND
Every beach on 'Upolu could be described as idyllic. A few days of languorous swimming off white sandy beaches, exploring reefs, rainforests, mountains and quiet villages and you'll wonder why the rest of the world ever seemed attractive.

Northeastern 'Upolu
Uafato Conservation Area The northeastern coastal region of 'Upolu is the wildest and least visited part of the island, containing some of the best scenery. A 4WD track follows the rugged coastline as far as the picturesque village of Uafato, where 14 sq km of the surrounding rainforest and coastal waters have been declared a conservation area. This is believed to be one of the few areas left in Samoa where there is an intact band of rainforest stretching from the sea to the interior uplands. The area also contains one of the largest remaining stands of *ifilele*, the tree used for carving *'ava* bowls, as well as a range of bat and bird species, including the rare *manumea* or tooth-billed pigeon.

A number of traditional carvers live in Uafato and are more than happy to demonstrate their art to visitors. Although there is no formal accommodation here, it is possible to stay overnight. Ask to speak to the *pulenu'u* when you arrive.

The best way to get to Uafato is along a road (4WD only, about 10km) signposted off Le Mafa Pass Rd to the village of Ta'elefaga. From Apia, this route is occasionally served by buses marked 'Fagaloa'.

Piula College & Fatumea Pool Usually known simply as 'Piula Cave Pool', Fatumea Pool *(admission ST2; open 8am-4.30pm Mon-*

Sat) lies beneath Piula Methodist Theological College, 18km east of Apia. It's a wonderful spot to spend a few hours picnicking, swimming in the clean, clear springs and exploring the water-filled caves.

Central 'Upolu
Robert Louis Stevenson Museum & Mt Vaea Just 4km inland from Beach Rd, off the Cross Island Rd, is the beautifully restored **home** *(☎ 20798, fax 25428; adult/ child under 12 ST15/5; open 9am-3.30pm Mon-Fri, 8am-noon Sat)* of Robert Louis Stevenson, the famous Scottish author who spent the last four years of his life in Samoa. Stevenson and his wife, Fanny, are buried on top of nearby Mt Vaea (475m), with a marvellous view over Apia.

Visitors to the museum are obliged to take a tour, the price of which is included in the entrance fee. If you'd also like to walk up to the Stevensons' tomb (a relatively short but very steep climb), or spend some time wandering around the botanic gardens and rainforest, allow at least half a day.

A taxi from Apia to Vailima should cost around ST17. To go by bus, take the Mulivai or Salani bus from the Maketi Fou.

Baha'i Temple From near the highest point of the Cross Island Rd, the 28m Niue limestone dome of the Baha'i House of Worship *(☎ 24192)* points skyward. This imposing and very beautiful structure is one of only seven Baha'i houses of worship in the world. Visitors are welcome and attendants at the information centre will happily answer your questions.

Lake Lanoto'o Known also as Goldfish Lake, Lake Lanoto'o is an eerie, pea-green crater lake in the central highlands of 'Upolu full of wild goldfish (and also leeches). It's a great place for a swim, but a little spooky because of alternating warm and cold currents, and the fact that the bottom of the lake has never been found. Very few visitors ever see this lovely and unusual spot.

The walk to the lake can take three to four hours and it's challenging, so not recommended for anyone unused to physical exertion. If you're not very adventurous and don't fancy the possibility of getting lost, call ☎ 21529 to organise an excellent guide (ST35 per person).

Papapapai-tai Falls About 2.5km south of the Baha'i temple, look for the Papapapai-tai waterfall sign on your right. It's only a few steps to the lookout for this spectacular 100m waterfall that plunges into a dramatic, forested gorge. Don't venture near the unstable cliff edge.

Papasee'a Sliding Rock A trip to the Papasee'a Sliding Rock *(admission ST2)* is obligatory for every visitor to Samoa, although, once there, many can't seem to muster the nerve to enjoy the star attraction, a 5m slide down a waterfall into a jungle pool. The best time to visit is between December and June; at other times the water levels may be low and the slide not as fun (or safe).

Take the Se'ese'e bus from the Maketi Fou and ask to be dropped off at the turnoff for Papasee'a. Walk 2km up the hill to the entrance; pay your admission only to the women at the entrance. The climb down is via 200-odd very steep and slippery steps.

Tanumapua Tropical Plantation A few kilometres inland from Vaitele, just west of Apia, this is a pleasant rural retreat from town, where you can stroll amid tropical flower gardens and crops such as coffee, bananas, papayas, pineapples, kava and cacao.

From town, take the first left turning west of the old site of the Mormon temple and it's about 8km along Alafa'alava Rd on the right-hand side. A taxi from Apia costs about ST18.

Western 'Upolu
Leulumoega You only need to drive along the stretch of road between Apia and Faleolo airport to see how literally the Samoans have taken the official motto 'Samoa is Founded on God'. There are reputedly more than 90 multicoloured churches representing numerous denominations in this area alone. One of the most interesting is the Congregational church at Leulumoega, 5km east of the airport. While you're in the area, visit the **School of Fine Arts** *(☎ 42536)*, beside the Maloa Theological College. You'll see some wonderful woodcarvings and other artwork by students.

Places to Stay & Eat At Cape Fatuosofia on the western tip of 'Upolu, **Samoan Village Resort** *(☎ 46028, fax 46098; W www.samoa villageresorts.com; Main West Coast Rd; fale ST460)* offers 10 deluxe self-contained *fale* in a lovely palm garden, all with excellent sea views. The beach is picturesque, but not great for snorkelling or swimming. There's a small restaurant and bar, swimming pool

and hot tub. A taxi from the airport will cost about ST20.

Airport Lodge *(☎ 45583, fax 45584; W www.samoahotels.ws/airportlodge.htm; Main Coast Rd; standard singles/doubles/ triples ST110/125/140, with air-con ST140/ 168/190)*, 6km west of Faleolo airport and a few minutes from the ferries for Savai'i and Manono islands, has airy and light-filled bungalows in a garden setting, with a safe jetty for swimming. All rooms have hot showers and fridges. Airport transfers can be arranged.

Southern 'Upolu
Beaches Along with the Aleipata Islands area and Manono Island, the south coast of 'Upolu offers plenty of beautiful palm-fringed beaches. Custom fees may vary slightly but, in general, access to beaches costs ST5 to ST10 for cars, ST3 for motorcycles and bicycles, and ST2 for pedestrians. Some beaches offer basic *fale* accommodation.

In the Lefaga district is the idyllic **Return to Paradise Beach** *(open Mon-Sat)*, where the film of the same name was shot in 1951. The beach is indeed paradise, but swimming in the sea can be somewhat hellish, with shallow reefs, volcanic boulders and heavy surf. To get there by public transport, catch the brightly painted Return to Paradise Beach bus at the Maketi Fou in Apia.

The next beach heading east is **Matareva**, a series of delightful coves with safe, shallow **snorkelling** and lots of rock pools. There are a couple of basic overnight *fale*, showers and a shop. Access from the main road is down a 2.5km dirt track.

A couple of kilometres east is another good spot, **Salamumu Beach** *(open Mon-Sat)*, about 5km off the main road. About 15km farther east is **Aganoa Black Sand Beach**; the water here is deep enough for **swimming** (it's sheltered and safe) and there's good **snorkelling** at the far end of the bay. There's also a popular **surf break** here, called Boulders, but the 4km track down to Aganoa is pretty rough in any vehicle.

Sataoa & Sa'anapu Conservation Area
In an effort to preserve one of 'Upolu's most important coastal wetland areas, the mangrove forests around the villages of Sataoa and Sa'anapu on the south coast have been declared a conservation area. The local conservation committee maintains the nature trail that winds through the mangroves for a couple of kilometres and offers excellent

SAMOA

outrigger canoe tours for ST20. Guided trips to nearby Anaseao Cave can be arranged and there are good opportunities for **bird-watching**. Sa'anapu village provides basic *fale* accommodation. Sataoa and Sa'anapu are signposted off the Main Coast Rd about 12km to the west of the Cross Island Rd.

O Le Pupu-Pu'e National Park

O Le Pupu-Pu'e is Samoa's only fully fledged national park. The northern boundary of the 29-sq-km park is formed by a ridge between volcanic Mt Le Pu'e (885m) and Mt Fito (1028m). In the south is the rugged O Le Pupu Lava Coast. The park entrance is near Togitogiga Scenic Reserve.

There are three **hiking** trails. The main inland trail, which begins at the first car park near the information sign, goes past the ranger's house and up through thick rainforest to Pe'ape'a Cave – actually a lava tube – which is full of circling white-rumped swiftlets *(pe'ape'a)*. Be careful climbing down into the pit on the mossy, slippery rocks. The return walk will take about four hours and is only recommended for people with hiking experience. It pays to drop in at the ranger's house for information or to organise a guide. Pe'ape'a Cave is closed in bad weather.

Another six hours' or so hike will bring you up to Ofa Waterfall. It's advisable to take a guide with you; contact the **Department of Environment & Conservation** (☎ 23800) in Apia.

At the far-western boundary of the park, a 3.5km track (open 6am to 6pm daily) leads south to the magnificently rugged O Le Pupu Lava Coast.

Togitogiga Falls & Recreation Reserve

The falls are just to the east of O Le Pupu-Pu'e National Park. The entrance is the same as for the park – just drive on to the second parking area. There are several pools, all great for swimming, and you can jump from the cliffs into the churning water below the largest one. Camping is permitted (no charge, but there's a two-day minimum stay) and there are toilets and changing rooms on site.

Sopo'aga Falls

On Le Mafa Pass Rd, just south of the turn-off to the southern Main Coast Rd, is a lovely garden and picnic site that overlooks the 50m Sopo'aga Falls and its immense gorge. The custom fee is ST6 per car; ST2 if you're on foot.

Places to Stay & Eat Whether you want to stay in a simple village *fale* or an upmarket beach resort with all the trimmings, you have an abundance of choice in this part of Samoa. For a full list of options, check the Samoa Tourism Authority's free booklet or its website ⓦ www.visitsamoa.ws.

Matareva Beach Fale *(fale per person around ST20)*, set in well-kept gardens, is 2.5km down a rough dirt track at lovely Matareva Beach. You'll need to bring your own food. This is a popular spot with locals on the weekend.

Sa'moana Resort *(☎/fax 71460; ⓔ samoana@samoanaresort.com for local inquiries; bungalows per person ST350)*, one of the two big surf resorts in Samoa, is gorgeous. Nestled among coconut palms at lovely Salamumu Beach (5km down an unsealed road), it's primarily a surf resort, but caters to anyone wanting an idyllic beach holiday. There's a great lounge area with pool and Ping-Pong tables, a TV, video, bar and library. There's also a superb saltwater pool on the edge of the ocean. Because the surf in Samoa is all on coral, it's for advanced surfers only. If that's you, see Water Sports under Activities in the Regional Facts for the Visitor chapter. For bookings, contact **World Surfaris** *(☎ 07-5444 4011, fax 5444 4911; ⓦ www.worldsurfaris.com)* in Australia. Rates include all transport to surf spots, activities and three meals daily.

Manuia Wetland Holiday Retreat *(☎ 26 225; PO Box 900, Apia; beachside fale per person ST20, single/double/triple bungalows ST60/120/150)*, close to the village of Sa'anapu, has seven beachside *fale* and three basic self-contained bungalows, each with a double and single bed, fridge, small electric stove and cold-water shower. You'll need to bring your own food, although you can buy fresh fish from the locals. There are three barbecue areas.

The villages of **Sataoa** and **Sa'anapu** are making a concerted effort to preserve their **mangrove forests**, so if you'd like to stay in a traditional village in this conservation area, the small fees you are charged for accommodation or activities such as guided walks and canoe tours, will help to maintain and protect the mangroves. Ask to speak to a member of the village conservation committee. There are no big waves or sharp coral at Sa'anapu Beach, so it's a good spot for kids.

If you arrive by the Green Turtle bus and walk along Sa'anapu Beach and through the

rainforest to **Virgin Cove Resort** (☎ 75000;
W www.virgin-cove.ws; PO Box 2291, Apia;
single/shared fale ST75/55; single/shared
honeymoon fale ST95/65; single/double
bungalows ST160/190) you may think you
have died and gone to heaven. This is such
a romantic spot, especially if you're lucky
enough to stay in the sought-after honeymoon *fale* with the best sea view on the
coconut block. The resort is now being
managed in accordance with the principles
of sustainable ecotourism, by Mats and Sia,
who also run the popular Seipepa in Apia.
It's perfect for those who want to escape the
conveniences of modern Western life. Dine
on delicious fresh fish and a wonderful
mixture of European and Samoan dishes by
the flickering light of solar-powered coconut
shells. If you're planning to drive yourself,
you'll need a 4WD.

Coconuts Beach Club & Resort (☎ 24849,
fax 20071; W www.coconutsbeachclub.com;
PO Box 3684, Apia; standard singles/
doubles with air-con ST250/313, 'treehouse'
singles/doubles ST408/472, deluxe beach
bungalows from ST567/630, over-water fale
ST884/948), further east at Maninoa village,
is a relaxed and inviting resort set up by a
couple of escaped LA lawyers. The riches-
to-rags tradition has been faithfully upheld by
the urbane manager Ned and his laconic side-
kick Mika, the 10-star chef from New York
and Hawaii who abandoned fame and fortune
to bring joy to the plates of the many faithful
Coco Nuts (they even have their own newsletter) who return here each year. There's a
three-night minimum stay. There's a range of
accommodation here, from the over-the-top,
over-water *fale* at the end of the resort's own
jetty, to the standard rooms in a pleasant
courtyard. In addition to the gecko-shaped
swimming pool with its swim-up bar, guests
can use kayaks, *paopao* and snorkelling
gear, and also rent bikes, windsurfers and
jeeps. The restaurant is open every day
and nonguests are welcome. It serves up
breakfast (ST15 to ST28), lunch (around
ST25) and dinner (mains around ST35) and
has a good vegetarian menu. Then there's
Sieni's Three-Star-Bar, a good place to
get tiddly on Pacific-themed cocktails (all
around ST15). Mika has got married again,
so he no longer sleeps on the bar. If he's not
entertaining enough for you, there's a *fiafia*
every Saturday night.

Line Up Surf Resort (☎ 73085; fale
per surfer/nonsurfer ST70/50), sandwiched

between its two glamorous neighbours, is a
friendly little place that has five beach *fale*
and a bar with a pool table. It's a good
option for cheap accommodation on this
stretch of coast. Rates include breakfast,
dinner and transport to surf spots.

Sinalei Reef Resort (☎ 25191, fax 20285;
W www.sinalei.com; PO Box 1510, Apia;
garden-view singles & doubles ST650, fale
suites ST820, beachside fale ST1090) is elegant and luxurious. It's set in 13 hectares of
landscaped grounds, with a gorgeous central
pool, bar and restaurant area, tennis courts,
and golf course. The resort was so warmly
recommended by its obviously rather well-
heeled guests that it was taken over for a
year by a small group of mysterious people
variously described as artists or religious
fanatics. The closure of the resort attracted
so much local concern that the paid-up group
moved out early. Though the gates were still
closed when we passed through, management promises it will soon be business as
usual again.

Salani Surf Resort (☎/fax 41069; W www
.surfsamoa.com; full surf package ST390,
nonsurfer ST310, B&B doubles per person
ST75), at the mouth of the Fuipisia River on
the edge of Salani village, is mainly about
surfing but it also has a good emphasis on
Samoan culture. The surf package includes
transfers, accommodation, all meals, a wide
range of daily tours, *fiafia*, activities (eg,
sea kayaking, fishing, biking, volleyball,
table tennis and snorkelling), and, most
importantly, surf guides and boat transport to the best breaks. Nonsurfers get
all of the above without the surfing bits,
and the B&B package includes the use
of resort amenities. Accommodation is in
cute, individual bungalows with decks and
shared bathrooms. As the surf in Samoa is
challenging, Salani generally only takes
experienced surfers, and only 12 at a time.
For bookings, contact **Waterways Travel**
(☎ 818-376 0341, fax 376 0353; e water
ways@waterwaystravel.com) in California,
or **Atoll Travel** (☎ 03-5682 1088, fax 5682
1202; W www.atolltravel.com) in Australia.

Parataiso 2000 Fale (e parataisobeachfa
les@ecotoursamoa.com; fale per person with
all meals ST60) is on the other side of the
river from Salani. Access is off Le Mafa Pass
Rd. This place has eight *fale*, a real village
feel (no phone here yet) and a lovely stretch
of beach. Nella can arrange demonstrations
of basket and *ie toga* weaving.

Vava'u Beach Fale (☎ 26940; fale ST170) is further east, at the village of Vava'u. There's a rough road down, but once you get to this idyllic, secluded spot, you may never want to leave. Each *fale* has its own bathroom and kitchenette and all have recently been refurbished. You can prepare your own food or order from the restaurant. Make sure you ask for a *fale* at the western end of the property, where the beach is quite magical, protected by an islet only about 100m offshore; this must be the original Treasure Island. Explore the caves with a kayak, swim and snorkel in the deep turquoise lagoon, but stay away from the treacherous currents just beyond the islet. And don't get your kayak grounded on the reef unless you are wearing reef shoes. Bookings through **Island Hopper Vacations** (☎ 26940; e samoa.sales@island hopper.com.ws) or **Ecotour Samoa** (☎/fax 22144; e tours@ecotoursamoa.com) only.

Aleipata District

The **reefs** in the Aleipata district at the easternmost end of the island are 50m or so offshore and the water is a remarkable turquoise blue, making for the loveliest beaches and the best **swimming** on 'Upolu. The **snorkelling** is excellent, but beware of the numerous cone shells: some are just mildly poisonous, but the most beautiful can be the most deadly.

The uninhabited islands of **Nu'utele** and **Nu'ulua**, part of the Aleipata Islands Conservation Area, are important sea-bird nesting grounds and are great to snorkel around also.

Places to Stay & Eat At Lalomanu village in the Aleipata district, **Litia Sini's Beach Fale** (☎ 4105; e talofalava65@yahoo.com) is the most popular, with a restaurant and bar. It can organise transport directly from the airport or ferry if you like. **Taufua Beach Fale** (☎ 26 451; e taufuabeach@lesamoa.net), with a small store and snorkelling gear for hire, has 13 *fale* and plans to open an Internet café. There are at least half a dozen more places around Lalomanu, including **Sieni & Ropert's**, and **Romeo**. Most charge between ST50 and ST60 per person, including meals, and supply sleeping mats and mosquito nets.

West of Lalomanu, near the villages of Saleapaga and Lepa, although the beach isn't quite as good, the accommodation is much the same. **Boomerang Creek** (☎ 40358; e bo omerangcreek@yahoo.com; singles/doubles ST50/80), set back off the road on the hillside at Saleapaga, has four lockable *fale*. As its name implies, this place is run by an Australian (with a penchant for adventure) and you'll usually find plenty of his compatriots snorkelling, kayaking, cycling and deep-sea fishing nearby or just drinking beer at the bar or eating lobster in the excellent and fully licensed restaurant (also open to nonguests). There's a *fiafia* night (ST30 for show and buffet meal) on Saturday, starting at 7pm.

Faofao Beach Fale (☎ 41067; fale per person ST20, with 3 meals ST60), a kilometre or so west of Boomerang, has 15 *fale*, a small store (selling cold Vailima, of course), cooking facilities and free tropical fruit, tea and coffee. The owners take very good care of guests and can organise hiking trips (ST20) or even a massage. There's a *fiafia* in the **restaurant** on Saturday night, which showcases the talent of the local youngsters (free for guests, ST30 including dinner and show for nonguests) and a *to'ona'i* (traditional *umu*-cooked lunch) on Sunday.

Manono

pop 960 • area 3 sq km

The tiny, traditional island of Manono harks back to an earlier Polynesia. With no vehicles, no roads, no dogs, no noise and little evidence of the 20th century anywhere, it's a magical and extremely relaxing spot to spend a few days. You can walk all the way around it in 1½ hours.

The Manono villagers, most of whom live in thatched *fale* and have a semi-subsistence lifestyle, have pledged to work towards creating a totally sustainable island and are looking at ways to protect their fragile island ecosystem. Tourism is community based, with activities designed to contribute to the conservation of the environment and the traditional way of life.

Things to See & Do Early in the morning is the best time to stroll around the island. Wending its way between the sea and the bottoms of people's gardens, the track is less a road than a path edged with distinctive yellow *lautalotalo*, banana palms and hibiscus.

At Lepuia'i village is the **Grave of 99 Stones**, which dates back to the late 19th century. High chief Vaovasa, who reportedly had 99 wives, was allegedly killed by villagers as he tried to escape from 'Upolu with his 100th wife. His body was brought back to Manono, where a grave was to be built with 100 stones; you can see a large gap where the final stone has yet to be placed.

At Faleu village near Matasiva Point, there's a **monument** commemorating the landing of the Methodist missionary Reverend Peter Turner on Manono in 1835.

On top of Mt Tulimanuiva (110m) is a large, 12-pointed **star mound**, thought to have been used in the ancient competitive sport of pigeon-snaring. Nearby is the grave of Afutiti, who was buried standing up to keep watch over the island.

You can take a **guided tour** around the island, including a visit to the star mound, for ST20 per person (plus ST15 for lunch). Outrigger-canoe **fishing trips** and **canoe tours** to uninhabited Nu'ulopa Island can be arranged from ST40 per person. For ST10 you can join village women in traditional **weaving**, **cooking** and **craft making**. For any of these activities, contact the **Vaotu'ua Beach Resort** (☎ 46077). **Ecotour Samoa** (☎/fax 22144, 71414) offers **sea-kayaking trips** to Manono. A portion of the income from all of these activities goes into an environment-conservation fund. The island is well protected by coral reef, with excellent **snorkelling** opportunities and lovely **beaches**, but you'll need to bring your own gear. Each of the four villages has declared its waters to be marine reserves.

Places to Stay & Eat Not far from the launch landing, **Vaotu'ua Beach Resort** (☎ 46077; e vaotuuabeachresort@ecotour samoa.com; fale per person ST60) is a laid-back place. Its eight open-sided *fale*, shaded by enormous *talie* trees, sit by the water's edge. One large *fale* sleeps groups and has a rustic dining room attached. The other seven *fale* sleep one or two people. Rates include dinner and breakfast, and lunch is an additional ST15; once you've tried the excellent food here you may want to ask about the discount rates offered for longer stays.

There are kiosk-type **shops** in Faleu where you can buy basic supplies and bottled water.

Getting There & Away To visit Manono, take the Falelatai bus from Apia and get off just south of the Samoan Village Resort at the western end of 'Upolu – look for the Manono Boat Access sign. From there, small **launches** leave for Manono; departure times are generally determined by passenger interest. You'll pay about ST2 each way if there are several people waiting, or a bit more if there are only a couple of passengers. If you miss the regular morning runs, special charters will cost as much as ST20 for the entire boat.

Apolima

pop 88 • area 1 sq km

Samoa's fourth island, Apolima, lies in the Apolima Strait, outside the reef that encircles 'Upolu and Manono. The remnant of a volcanic crater, it meets the sea in high, steep cliffs, and there's only a tiny and difficult entrance from the sea through to the single, hardly touched village. There are sea-bird rookeries on the cliffs.

Getting There & Away Arranging a visit to Apolima will be tricky, but if you're keen, seek out **Mr Sa'u Samoa** (☎ 46017) at the village of Apolima-uta on 'Upolu.

Savai'i

pop 42,824 • area 1700 sq km

Much of Savai'i – the largest island in Polynesia outside NZ and Hawaii – still remains uninhabited and pristine and it has retained its traditional ways even more than 'Upolu. Savai'i is also notable because it has the highest concentration of volcanic cones – 450 – anywhere in the world. Scattered across the island are numerous archaeological sites, many of which figure in ancient myths and legends. There are fortifications, star mounds and ancient platforms, some almost swallowed up by the nearly impenetrable jungle.

Orientation & Information

The Samoas' largest island is also its wildest. A string of volcanic craters, some active, extend along the central ridge of the island from the east coast at Tuasivi to within 5km of Samoa's westernmost tip at Cape Mulinu'u. Mt Silisili (1866m) is the highest point in the Samoan islands. The north coast of Savai'i is punctuated by lava fields.

Getting There & Away

Air Flying between 'Upolu and Savai'i is highly recommended – the flight isn't very expensive and the bird's-eye view of the islands is wonderful.

From Fagali'i airport, just east of Apia, **Polynesian Airlines** (in Apia ☎ 22737) flies to Ma'ota airport on the southeast coast of Savai'i, 5km west of Salelologa, twice a day; the fare is ST66/92 one way/return. Both Polynesian and **Samoa Air** (in Apia ☎ 51387) fly between Pago Pago in American Samoa and Ma'ota airport (US$110/150) several times weekly.

SAMOA

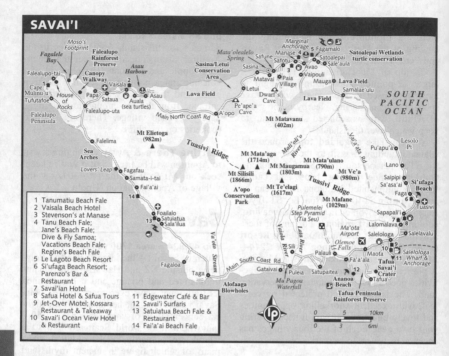

SAVAI'I

1 Tanumatiu Beach Fale
2 Vaisala Beach Hotel
3 Stevenson's at Manase
4 Tanu Beach Fale;
   Jane's Beach Fale;
   Dive & Fly Samoa;
   Vacations Beach Fale;
   Regine's Beach Fale
5 Le Lagoto Beach Resort
6 Si'ufaga Beach Resort;
   Parenzo's Bar &
   Restaurant
7 Savai'ian Hotel
8 Safua Hotel & Safua Tours
9 Jet-Over Motel; Kossara
   Restaurant & Takeaway
10 Savai'i Ocean View Hotel
   & Restaurant

11 Edgewater Café & Bar
12 Savai'i Surfaris
13 Satuiatua Beach Fale &
   Restaurant
14 Fai'a'ai Beach Fale

Boat The **Samoa Shipping Corporation** (*in Salelologa ☎ 51477, in 'Upolu ☎ 20935/6; Beach Rd, Apia; e ssc@samoa.ws*) operates a vehicle and passenger ferry, *Lady Samoa II*, between Mulifanua Wharf on the western end of 'Upolu and Salelologa on Savai'i. It sails from Salelologa on Monday and from Wednesday to Saturday at 6am, 10am and 2pm, and from Mulifanua at 8am, noon and 4pm on the same days. On Sunday, the ferry leaves Savai'i at 10am and 2pm, and 'Upolu at noon and 4pm. The *Lady Samoa II* is serviced on Tuesday, when the smaller *Samoa Express* steps in to transport people from Salelologa at 10am and 2pm, and from Mulifanua at 8am and noon.

If you're planning to take a car across (ST55 one way for a medium-sized vehicle), it's advisable to book a couple of days in advance at the Samoa Shipping Corporation office on Beach Rd in Apia, not far from the Apia Deep Sea Wharf. Passenger tickets (ST7 each way) can also be bought here, although it's not really necessary – they're easily purchased at either dock. You need to arrive at Mulifanua Wharf at least an hour prior to departure. The 22km crossing takes about 1½ hours.

For those travelling without vehicles, **Tausala Cedar** (*☎/fax 51413, ☎ 71395*) runs an express boat service (subject to weather conditions), which takes about 30 minutes. Tickets cost around ST12, less for children, and can be bought at the wharf. The express leaves from Salelologa from Monday to Thursday at 6.15am, 9.15am and 1.15pm, and from Mulifanua at 7.15am, 11.15am and 3.15pm. On Friday the times are the same, but the last trip from Mulifanua is at 3pm and from Salelologa there's an extra trip at 4pm. On Saturday there are boats from Mulifanua at 7.15am and 11.15am and from Salelologa at 9.15am and 1.15pm. On Sunday a boat leaves Salelologa at 1.30pm and Mulifanua at 3.30pm.

Getting Around

To/From the Airport Whenever a plane arrives at Ma'ota airport, nearly every taxi on Savai'i is waiting for it, but they are relatively expensive: to Salelologa the fare is ST7.80 and ST22 to Tuasivi (about 13km). Public buses are very convenient for getting to Salelologa from the airport (ST1 to ST1.50), but if you're travelling to Tuasivi or further north, you'll have to change buses

SAMOA

at Salelologa. Airport transfers can be arranged with most hotels, provided you book in advance. Buses and taxis also greet every ferry arrival.

Bus The buses of Savai'i are crowded, vibrantly coloured and blast Samoan-style pop music (a charming mix of rap, reggae and the odd hint of country and western). The market near the Salelologa wharf is the main terminal for regular buses to Lalomalava, Tuasivi, Palauli and Gataivai. The Lava Fields Express trundles regularly between Salelologa and Fagamalo. Less frequently, buses go to Safotu or Sasina on the north coast and Asau in the northwest.

Way out on the northwestern end, buses run regularly between Asau and Falelima. The only bus going to Falealupo from the wharf in Salelologa is marked 'Tufutafoe'. It leaves the wharf at around 9.15am, goes along the south coast up to Asau on the north coast, then doubles back to Falealupo from there. The return bus leaves at the ungodly hour of 4am.

Ferry passengers will have the most luck connecting with buses to out-of-the-way destinations – that is, beyond the cluster of villages along the southeast coast. Buses bound for the north and west coasts depart as soon as the ferry comes in. The fare from the Salelologa wharf to Lalomalava is only 80 *sene*. About the most you'll pay for a bus from the wharf is ST5.60 (to Asau). The trip to the blowholes at Taga costs ST2.30.

A **Green Turtle** bus, similar to the one operating in 'Upolu, will soon be circumnavigating Savai'i daily. Contact Green Turtle at **5 Star Travel** (☎ 22144, 29629; ⬚ *www.greenturtle.ws; Apia*) for more up-to-date information.

Car The roads are quiet, but keep an eye out for kids, stray pigs and *kirikiti* games. Where possible, avoid driving in the evening, when whole villages (including animals) appear to take to the road, seemingly oblivious of possible danger from four-wheeled fellow travellers.

Petrol is available at Salelologa, Lalomalava, Manase in the northeast and Vaisala in the northwest. The **Savai'i Travel Centre** (☎ 51206) and **Big Island Rentals** (☎ 51499, 51552), part of Sina World Travel located in the same arcade as the National Bank of Samoa in Salelologa, both have Suzuki jeeps to rent from around ST150 per day. A car-rental agency is also being established at Manase. Contact **Vacations Beach Fale** (☎ 54 024; ⬚ *leota@samcom.com.ws*) for more information. You can also bring hire cars on the ferry from 'Upolu.

Boat Yachties wanting to cruise around Savai'i must first obtain a cruising permit from the **Ministry of Foreign Affairs** (☎ 25 313; Apia). There are anchorages at Fagamalo, Salelologa Wharf and Asau Harbour.

Organised Tours For organised sightseeing and cultural tours around Savai'i, you can't beat **Safua Tours**, operating from the **Safua Hotel** (☎ 51271). The knowledge and generosity of tour organiser and guide Warren Jopling, a 'retired' Australian geologist, is legendary; he has lived on Savai'i for over 20 years and knows more than nearly anyone about its geology, flora and fauna. Half-day tours cost ST60 per person; full-day trips are ST100 (including a light lunch and custom fees). Concessions are available for students and volunteers, and rates are negotiable for groups. The tours focus on natural history, archaeology and cultural experiences. There are set day tours, but these can be altered according to individual interests.

Another option is **Big Island Tours & Adventures** (☎ 51552, 51499), part of Sina World Travel in Salelologa, which offers everything from laid-back beach tours to hikes up Mt Silisili. Half-/full-day tours cost ST70/140.

The Ancient Homeland, Havaiki

As they expanded to new islands, all Polynesians remembered the name of their homeland – often naming new islands in its honour. Depending on the local dialect the homeland was remembered as Havai'i (in the Society Islands), 'Avaiki (Cook Islands), Hawaiki (Aotearoa) and, of course, Hawai'i (in the Hawai'ian islands). For many, the name 'Havaiki' represents not only a physical location, the homeland, but also a mythical promised land to which souls return after death. In Samoa, where 'h' is pronounced as 's' and 'k' is dropped, the original island's name became Savai'i.

If you're considering going to Savai'i to surf, there's an excellent tour operator on the island, **Savai'i Surfaris** (☎ 58248, fax 58007 for local inquiries); bookings are through **Atoll Travel** (☎ 03-5682 1088, fax 5682 1202; W www.atolltravel.com) in Australia. Seven-night packages, excluding air fares, cost around ST1600 per person twin share in a hotel room, or from ST1730 per person staying in a beach fale, with two daily meals included (less for nonsurfers). Both rates include all transfers and surf transportation. The outfit has moved camp to Ananoa Beach, 15 minutes from Salelologa, just after the Tafua rainforest.

The ubiquitous **Ecotour Samoa** (☎ 22144, 25993 after hours) can also organise tours of Savai'i to suit your particular requirements.

SOUTHEASTERN SAVAI'I
Information
You can change money at any of the three banks in Salelologa: **National Bank of Samoa** (open 9am-3pm Mon-Fri, 8.30am-11.30am Sat); **ANZ Bank** (open 9am-3pm Mon-Fri); and **Westpac Bank** (open 8.30am-3pm Mon-Wed, 8.30am-4pm Thur & Fri). The ANZ Bank has an ATM, and there is another branch of **Westpac** (open 12.30pm-3pm Mon & Wed) in Vaisala.

The **main post and telephone office** (Main South Coast Rd; post office open 8am-noon & 1pm-4.30pm Mon-Fri; telephone office open 8am-noon & 1pm-4.30pm daily) is a bit out of the way: it's on the left-hand side about 1km from the turn-off to Ma'ota airport from Salelologa. International calls can be made at the telephone office. There are also post offices at Tuasivi, Asau, Fagamalo and Sala'ilua (not open weekends).

If you need to check your emails, you can log on at **Savai'i Computer Training Centre** (☎ 51038) in Salelologa, in the arcade opposite the market, where you'll also find **Samoa World Travel** and **Samoa Air** (☎ 51002) offices; they're open 9am to 5pm weekdays. There's an **Internet café** (open Mon-Fri 9am-4pm, Sat 8am-noon) in Salelologa, opposite Westpac; it's a bit pricey at ST8 for 15 minutes, but connections are good.

For travel arrangements to and from 'Upolu, or transport around the island, try the **Savai'i Travel Centre** (☎ 51206, fax 51291), which is also an agent for Polynesian Airlines, or **Sina World Travel** (☎ 51499), both in Salelologa. The Internet café is also an agent for Polynesian Airlines.

Salelologa
Besides the market, the only real points of interest in the Salelologa area are **blowholes** on the lava coast south of the wharf. There are two ancient **star mounds** just north of the Main Coast Rd, about 200m west of its intersection with the wharf road, and across the street there are two **platform mounds**. They're overgrown and difficult to find, so you may need directions from locals.

Tuasivi Ridge
The Tuasivi ridge begins near the village of Tuasivi and rises in a series of craters that form the spine of Savai'i, ending just inland of the village of Falealupo. The Samoans named it 'the enchanted ridge' because they believed it possessed supernatural powers.

Beaches
All along the east coast between Salelologa and Pu'apu'a, there are nice beaches and good **snorkelling**. Most of the villages will charge custom fees of about ST5/2 per car/person to use their beaches. The best are at Faga and Lano. The area also has numerous freshwater pools and springs.

Pu'apu'a
In the village of Pu'apu'a are two freshwater bathing **pools** maintained by the local women's committee. The pool on the eastern side of the road is for women and the one on the western side for men. Ask villagers' permission before jumping in. Just south of Pu'apu'a are several other springs, including Vaimanuia ('Healthy Waters').

Tafua Peninsula Rainforest Preserve
The Tafua Peninsula Rainforest Preserve is one of Samoa's most accessible and beautiful stands of rainforest, with rugged stretches of lava coast, studded with cliffs, sea arches and blowholes. On the western coast a track leads south to the lovely white, coral-sand **Ananoa Beach** (open 8am-6pm daily), where there are several picnic fale. There are strong currents here, so ask locals about conditions and swim with care. Don't forget your mosquito repellent. Custom fees are ST10/5 per bus/car and ST2 for cyclists and pedestrians.

A highlight is the extinct, forest-choked Tafua Savai'i crater, above the village of Tafua, where the relatively rare Samoan flying fox can sometimes be seen.

Places to Stay & Eat

In Salelologa, **Savai'i Ocean View Hotel and Restaurant** (☎ 51409, fax 58249; singles/doubles per person ST110), only about 100m from the wharf, is a small hotel with a great restaurant and bar. The bungalow rooms, surrounded by a garden courtyard, have a kitchenette, fan, mosquito nets and separate bathroom, but no air-conditioning. The light and airy restaurant (open 7pm to 10pm) looks out onto the sea and is a great place for cocktails. Mains cost around ST35 and specialities are lobster and pan-fried fish. MasterCard, Visa and Eftpos cards are accepted.

Jet-Over Motel (☎ 51565; singles & doubles with fan/air-con ST80/150), located at the back of the arcade opposite the market, has spacious, clean rooms; the bright air-con rooms come with microwaves, telephones and balconies with ocean views.

For a cheap snack, the **general store** opposite the Ocean View Hotel serves up oka (ST2), good fish and chips (ST6.50), curry and rice, and other basic dishes.

Inside the market are a number of **food stalls** serving local dishes for rock-bottom prices.

Kossara Restaurant & Takeaway (☎ 51 216; breakfast ST4-7, lunch ST9-18), opposite the Big Island CCK store, is popular with local workers. Breakfast costs ST4 to ST5 and a cup of delicious Samoan cocoa costs ST1.30. Pan-fried fish and chips will set you back about ST15 to ST18; fish chowder and toast costs ST8.50.

Edgewater Café & Bar (☎ 51497) is a terrific, split-level complex, built right on the water and blessed with cooling sea breezes. To get there turn left from the wharf and travel about 1km. It's perfect for a quiet lunch as you contemplate the turquoise sea and the boat you are about to miss at the wharf. At night, it's very popular with locals and American Peace Corps alike. Enjoy a beer among floodlit mangroves, a game of pool or just site back and listen to the music (there's a DJ every night). Seafood costs around ST30 and you can get nibbles for around ST15. Saturday is the big night, and you can drink and dance until midnight, when the police come to make sure patrons go home to make it for the early-morning church services on Sunday.

Safua Hotel (☎ 51271, fax 51272; ℮ safua hotel@lesamoa.net, safuahotel@yahoo.com; single/double/family fale-style bungalows with toilet & cold-water shower ST88/99/ 130, village stays per person ST50) is 6km northeast of Salelologa at Lalomalava. It's an excellent place for those wanting to immerse themselves in Samoan culture rather than idle on a beach. You'll rarely find such an excellent chance to gain an insight into Samoan ways, history and geology. The proprietor, Vaasili Moelagi Jackson, holder of several chiefly titles and undisputed Queen of Savai'i, is as interesting as any of the sites on the island. She and Warren Jopling, the manager of Safua Tours, know Savai'i and Samoan culture inside out. In addition to its huge evening meals (often accompanied by a live band of local musicians), the hotel stages a *fiafia* whenever there are plenty of guests, and an *umu* feast after church on Sunday. Village-stay rates include meals, tent space as well as use of facilities. Rates are negotiable for students, groups and for stays of more than five days. Breakfast costs ST15, light lunch ST15 and the sumptuous dinner ST20 to ST35.

Savai'ian Hotel (☎ 51206, fax 51291; ⊠ www.lesamoa.net/savaiian; PO Box 5082, Lalomalava; singles/doubles/triples with air-con, cooking facilities & hot shower ST110/ 135/160, single/double fale with shower & toilet ST44/66), across the road from and about 200m south of the Safua Hotel, has more of a resort feel. Meals are served in a large, open-air building; breakfast costs from ST5.50 to ST15 and dinner between ST25 and ST35. Prices include transfers to/from the wharf or airport.

Si'ufaga Beach Resort (☎ 53518, fax 53535; ℮ siufaga@lesamoa.net; PO Box 8002, Tuasivi; camping per person ST15, standard singles/doubles/triples ST110/120/ 130, superior singles/doubles/triples ST190/ 210/230) is a friendly resort in the village of Faga, immediately north of Tuasivi. Standard rooms have a ceiling fan, fridge and toilet, and some have a hot shower. The *fale* are set on a large grassy lawn facing lovely Si'ufaga Beach, which is safe for swimming and great for snorkelling (provided the tide's in).

Another good reason to stop off at Si'ufaga Beach Resort is **Parenzo's Bar & Restaurant**, a taste of the Mediterranean in the Pacific. It boasts the only espresso machine on the island, hand-carried from Rome! Eat pasta dishes (around ST21) and seafood (about ST25) on the balcony overlooking the palm-fringed sea.

SAMOA

NORTHEASTERN SAVAI'I

Lava Field

The Mt Matavanu eruption from 1905 to 1911 created a moonscape in the northeastern corner of Savai'i, as hot lava 10m to 150m thick flowed across plantations and villages, destroying everything in its path. Between Samalae'ulu and Sale'aula, the Main Coast Rd crosses the lava field and passes a couple of interesting sites. Just east of the road is the village of **Mauga**, which means 'hill', built in a circular pattern around a nearly perfect crater. After the eruptions, the intense heat and porous rock caused a scarcity of fresh water in the area. An enormous Catholic church has been built here to replace the first Catholic church in Savai'i, destroyed by the lava in 1906.

About 3km north of Mauga, the road passes the **Sale'aula lava ruins** and the remains of the old **LMS, Catholic and Methodist churches**. The most interesting and best preserved is the LMS church, where 2m of lava flowed through the front door and the corrugated iron roof collapsed on top of the then plastic lava.

The old Sale'aula village was near the northernmost limit of the lava flow. Parts of the original ground surface weren't touched by lava, including sections of an old cemetery behind the LMS church.

A short walk north of the LMS church is another 'divinely protected' site, the **Virgin's Grave**. It's really not much more than an ill-defined strip of lime cement with some colourful plants around it, but for many it's a site of veneration.

There's a custom fee of ST2 per person. To get up this way by bus, take the Lava Fields Express, or the Manase bus, which runs regularly between Salelologa and Fagamalo.

Satoalepai Wetlands

The village of Satoalepai, 5km northwest of the lava fields, is one of a growing number of Samoan villages committed to the sustainable development of their local resources. It runs a turtle-conservation project and offers visitors village accommodation, local guides and **canoe tours** through the wetlands (ST4 per person). Ask to speak to the *pulenu'u* or one of the local conservation officers.

Fagamalo

Immediately west of Satoalepai is Fagamalo, which is known as an excellent spot for **surfing**, though the swells are not always constant, and **windsurfing**. There's a marginal anchorage here, too. You'll find comfortable bungalow accommodation on the beach just west of the village.

Manase

This pretty little village has won Samoa's best-kept village prize three times in a row.

Safotu

The long, strung-out village of Safotu has three large and prominent churches in a row in its centre. The almost medieval-looking one is the Sacred Heart Catholic church. Next door is the LMS church and further along, the Methodist church. To the west of the churches, near the sea, is a series of **freshwater pools** for bathing or swimming; some are for men, some for women, so ask first. Just to the east of Safotu are pleasant beaches, an upmarket resort and the most popular budget accommodation on the island.

Mt Matavanu Crater Walk

One of the most dramatic natural features of Savai'i is Mt Matavanu (402m), the volcanic cone that spewed destruction over the northeast coast of the island. It's possible to do this walk in a day from Paia village (about 16km return), but it's a very hard slog and not advisable without a guide (ST5 to ST10 per person). Speak to the *pulenu'u* in Paia. It's possible to drive almost to the turn-off to the crater, but only in a 4WD; again, take a guide. Once you get to Paia, you may want to stop and have a look at the ancient fort and mound on top of the hill.

Mata'olealelo Spring

This ample freshwater spring in the village of Safune bubbles up through a pool into the sea – perfect for a refreshing swim. Be sure to ask permission and pay your fee of ST5 per person before plunging in.

Sasina & Letui Conservation Area

The villages of Sasina and Letui are part of a large coastal rainforest conservation area that extends from the coast up to the inland village of A'opo. Fiu Sefau of Letui can take people to visit the nearby **Pe'ape'a Cave** (ST3 per person). It's well signposted and only a 10m walk from the road. It's a great place to spot hundreds of white-rumped Polynesian swiftlets, which nest there. You can find basic village **accommodation** in both Sasina and Letui for ST20 per person (ST50 including meals).

Places to Stay & Eat

There are now several good accommodation options in northeast Savai'i, as well as those in the conservation villages of Satoalepai, Sasina and Letui.

Le Lagoto Beach Resort (☎ 58189, fax 58249; PO Box 34, Fagamalo; bungalows ST320, small beach house ST320, large beach house ST460), hugging a beautiful beach, is expensive compared with its neighbours. However, it would be a good option for small groups, especially the large beach house (for up to seven people). Bungalows (up to five people) have hot shower, kitchenette, TV and fan. There's also an elegant restaurant and bar, where breakfast costs ST12, lunch ST15 and main meals at dinner around ST40.

Tanu's Beach Fale (☎ 54050; fale per person ST50) has for some time been the most popular place in Savai'i. Just west of Manase, Taito Muese Tanu and his vast family have created a relaxing and welcoming environment. Of the 30 fale, 16 are scattered along the beach – there's nothing quite like waking up to the ocean lapping at your doorstep. Rates include breakfast and dinner, and meals are eaten communally at a long table. The (cold) shower (a charming pipe sticking out of the wall) and toilets are communal. There are outrigger canoes for guests' use, a small shop and a fiafia every Saturday night. Tanu's bus meets the noon ferry at Salelologa, arriving back at the fale at about 2pm.

Jane's Beach Fale (☎ 54066; e janes@westsamoa.org; standard/waterfront fale per person ST50/70), recommended by quite a few travellers, is already giving Tanu's a run for your money, though it's a bit quieter. The fale are enclosed, each with its own delightful balcony, and are set in a grassed area under palms. There's also a bar, and kayaks for guests to use. Rates include breakfast and dinner. **Dive & Fly Samoa** (☎ 54066; w www.diveandflysamoa.com), a PADI dive centre that promises 'your dreams come true', is based here and offers a 10% discount for Jane's guests; check the website for more details.

Stevenson's at Manase (☎/fax 58219, fax 24166; e snm@lesamoa.net; PO Box 210, Apia; hotel-style singles/doubles with air-con ST40/100, beachfront villas with 2 double beds & air-con ST220), a more upmarket place, is split down the middle by the road. The resort's basic fale and the more cushy villas are on the beach. Reception and the hotel rooms – a bit impersonal, but set in lovely grounds – are on the other side of the road. The hotel has a pleasant restaurant, two bars, paddle boats and outrigger canoes, and fiafia nights on Friday and Saturday (provided there are enough guests). Tours can be arranged. Airport and ferry transfers cost ST30 per person one way.

Vacations Beach Fale (☎/fax 54024; w www.savaiivacations.com; PO Box 3526, Apia; fale per person ST60, child age 1-6/6-11 free/half-price) is a family enterprise. Surrounded by lush green trees and white sandy beaches, it pretty much lives up to its claim of being a heaven on earth. The family-run fale are aimed more at the locals than at palangi, though they, of course are very welcome. You can sit on the little wooden jetty sipping an ice cold beer or glass of wine from the well stocked bar, as the sun slips down into the water. The restaurant serves delicious local food as well as European dishes, except on Sunday, when the traditional to'ona'i is available. The fale are the traditional, palm-thatched open kind, but this place accepts AmEx, MasterCard, Visa, Access and Eftpos cards.

Opposite, there's a small store, **Elaine's Handy-Mart** (where you can buy delicious, warm and stodgy coconut buns on Sunday afternoon) and a petrol station (which doesn't always have petrol). Watch for the Internet café that is due to open next door and the car-hire agency that is setting up beside it.

Regine's Beach Fale, just before Vacations Beach Fale travelling north from Salelologa, is a relative newcomer to the Manase beach fale scene. It charges ST55 person for a fale, including breakfast and dinner. Lunch costs ST5. This is a simple place, on an idyllic beach. There's no phone, but the staff are friendly and the enclosed showers and toilets are clean and well maintained.

NORTHERN & WESTERN SAVAI'I
A'opo Conservation Area & Mt Silisili

The two-day return trip up Mt Silisili (1866m) takes you through rarely visited **rainforest**. It is possible for experienced hikers to do this walk in one day – if you leave around 3am you'll get back about 8pm. If you're interested, speak to the pulenu'u of A'opo (the mayor's house is by the big mango tree in the centre of the village), who will arrange a guide for ST30 per person per day. You'll need to carry food and water for two days and provide supplies for the guide. It can get cool in the evening, so take warm clothing, a sleeping bag and tent and wear sturdy boots.

Asau & Vaisala

Asau, 9km west of A'opo, is the main anchorage on Savai'i and is the service centre for the western end of the island. Asau airport, which was completely destroyed by Cyclone Ofa in 1990, has been rebuilt but is seldom used. There's a **store** here selling groceries and crafts, and a **post office**. At Vaisala, 5km farther west, there's a **petrol station** and a branch of the **Westpac bank**. In the village of Auala, between Asau and Vaisala, the local women's committee looks after a large pond full of protected **sea turtles**.

Falealupo Peninsula

At the far northwestern end of Savai'i is the wild and beautiful Falealupo Peninsula, where you'll find **rock pools**, **caves**, and ancient **star mounds**. Cape Mulinu'u is the most westerly land point on earth – and the spectacular sunsets are the last in the world. Take great care swimming here; there's a strong rip and you could end up in the Solomon Islands. Beach fees are ST20/5/2 per bus/car/pedestrian. If you're not driving, you'll have to walk or take a taxi the 7km from the main road at Falealupo-uta.

Falealupo Rainforest Preserve Considered sacred by the villagers of Falealupo, the 12,000-hectare area of lowland rainforest on the northern side of the peninsula became the first customary-owned conservation area in Samoa in 1989. American ethnobotanist Dr Paul Alan Cox was working with indigenous healers in Falealupo when he discovered that the local *matai* had reluctantly signed a contract with a Japanese logging firm in order to pay for construction of a primary school. As the whole village wept over the loss of the rainforest, Dr Cox decided to personally guarantee the money for the school. On learning of this, Chief Fuiono Senio ran 9km through the forest to stop the bulldozers. Unfortunately, the reserve suffered serious damage during the cyclones of the early '90s (60% of the trees were destroyed, and bird and bat numbers dropped significantly), but it is slowly recovering.

Canopy Walkway This walkway was opened in May 1997 as a foreign-funded ecotourism project designed to help support Falealupo village and its rainforest. Some travellers have complained of being 'ripped off'; the actual walkway was closed for some time in 2002 while it was being completely reconstructed, and there wasn't much to see for the requested ST20. However the 24m-long swing bridge hoisted 9m above the rainforest floor and the 20m stairway that ends in the uppermost reaches of a 225-year-old banyan tree are now fully operational here. The **tree house** here is really just a platform (no roof), but it's a magical place to spend the night; book through the Vaisala Beach Hotel, or just turn up. The fee charged for access to the walkway should cover entrance to the House of Rocks and the rock enclosure called **Moso's Footprint**, allegedly made by the giant as he stepped from Fiji to Samoa.

Rock House About 300m inland from the village of Falealupo are two closely associated lava tubes known as the Rock House. Inside is a very crude stone armchair and stone benches around the sides. There's a custom fee of ST5 per person, and you may have to wade through a swamp to get here.

Sea Arches

A couple of kilometres southeast of Falelima are two impressive natural sea arches, caused by the pounding waves. About 300m east of the large arch at Falelima is an old **blowhole** that shoots blasts of warm air, known locally as Moso's Toilet.

Beaches

There are pleasant beaches at Fai'a'ai, about 16km southeast of the Falealupo Peninsula, and nearby at Foailalo and Satuiatua. Fai'a'ai and Satuiatua both offer basic beachside

Gateway to the Underworld

Falealupo Peninsula figures prominently in local legend. The natural beauty of the area belies the dark significance it holds for Samoans, who believe that the gateway to the underworld of the *aitu* (spirits) is found at the place where the sun sets in the sea. During the night, these spirits wander abroad, but at daybreak they must return to their hellish home or suffer the unpleasant consequences of being caught out by daylight.

According to tradition, there are two entrances to the underworld, one for chiefs and another for commoners. One entrance is through a cave near Cape Mulinu'u and the other – repeating a theme found in ancient cultures from the Pacific to Britain – is over the sea towards the setting sun.

accommodation; Foailalo has several picnic *fale*. Satuiatua, about one hour by bus (ST3) from Salelologa, has some of the best **surf** in Samoa. The custom fee for day use for any of these beaches is ST10 per person.

Places to Stay & Eat

Clinging to a slope above a lovely white-sand beach, **Vaisala Beach Hotel** (☎ *58016, fax 58017;* e *vaisala@ipasifika.net; singles/doubles/triples ST88/99/110),* a 31-room hotel in Vaisala on the northwest coast, resembles a seaside boarding house. Rooms are basic but pleasant and come with showers (warm water) and terrific balcony views; some have air-conditioning (no extra charge). The formal bar/restaurant is open from 7pm to 11pm. Breakfast is available (from ST10), toasted sandwiches cost ST5 and set-menu dinners are ST33.

The Canopy Walkway in the Falealupo Rainforest Preserve offers accommodation in the top of a **banyan tree** for ST50 per person, plus ST20 for two meals. You can book through the Vaisala Beach Hotel, or just turn up at the tree. Don't drink too much before you bed down – it's a long, dark way down to the bottom if you suddenly find you need to answer the call of nature.

Tanumatiu Beach Fale *(fale per person ST40)* is on the edge of the Falealupo Peninsula and on one of the most idyllic beaches in Samoa. Comfortable mattresses, bedding, mosquito nets and oil lamps are provided. There's a toilet and outside shower on the site. Beyond the family house is an ancient star mound. *Fale* rates include two meals. The custom fee for beach use is ST5 per car.

Fai'a'ai Beach Fale (☎ *56023; fale per person ST30)* is about 16km southeast of the Falealupo Peninsula, perched on the clifftop just off the Main South Coast Rd and down a very steep path. The two large *fale* sleep up to about six people and there's another smaller one. Rates include breakfast and dinner.

Satuiatua Beach Fales *(☎/fax 56026;* e *satuiatuabeachresort@ecotoursamoa.com; PO Box 5623, Sala'ilua; fale & 2 meals per person ST55, honeymoon fale per person ST100),* about 7km further down the coast from Fai'a'ai Beach Fale, is a spot that travellers (especially surfing types) return to time and again. Satuiatua has four large beachside *fale* (which sleep six to eight people) and six small *fale* on a lovely beach shaded by massive *pulu* trees. The beach is good for snorkelling and has some of the best surf on the island.

Fishing trips with the locals as well as hikes to a nearby cave can be arranged. There's also a restaurant here serving some of the best food on Savai'i, and a shop selling basic supplies and beer. Satuiatua is about one hour by bus (ST3) from Salelologa. Rates drop to ST44 for stays of longer than one week.

SOUTHERN SAVAI'I
Olemoe Falls

Olemoe Falls is a lovely jungle waterfall that plunges into the crystalline waters of a deep blue **pool**, which is marvellous for swimming and diving.

Take the bus west from Salelologa to just past the bridge across the river near Palauli, where a track leads around to the western side of the pool. Fees are ST2 for those on foot, ST5 for jeeps, ST10 for vans.

Pulemelei Step Pyramid

Polynesia's largest ancient structure is the Pulemelei Step Pyramid (marked on the Jasons and Hema maps as Tia Seu Ancient Mound). This large pyramid, the ancient purpose of which is a mystery, measures 61m by 50m at the base and rises in two tiers to a height of more than 12m. The main approach to the summit is up a sunken rampway on the eastern and western slopes. Smaller mounds and platforms are found in four directions away from the main structure. There is a relatively large platform about 40m north of the main pyramid, connected by a stone walkway. It's sometimes difficult to find because of fast-growing vegetation.

Gataivai

This village sits beside a veritable water garden of cascades as the Vaiola River rushes to its climax at **Mu Pagoa Waterfall**, where it plunges 5m into the sea. The approach to the falls is from the village of Puleia, beside the Main South Coast Rd on the opposite (left) bank of the river.

Alofa'aga Blowholes

This is not just another set of blowholes. There's little to equal them anywhere else in the world. At the village of Taga, pay the custom fee (ST2/7 per person/car) and walk down the hill and west along the coast for about 10 minutes. You'll emerge from the coconut plantation with a clear view across the black lava coast and before the blowholes. Don't forget to take coconut shells to test the ejectory power of the blowhole gods.

American Samoa

The US territory of American Samoa shares a language, culture and pre-1900 history with independent Samoa. Though increasingly it looks to the US mainland for its popular culture, as well as for its finance, you will still find traditional open-hearted Samoan hospitality here, and some of the most breathtaking scenery in the Pacific, seldom visited by tourists.

In Pago Pago there's fast-food, American football and cable TV, and, when the wind blows the wrong way over the beautiful harbor, the potent smell of tuna processing. Since Somerset Maugham immortalised the town in his story of the notorious Sadie Thompson, the American Dream has tended to predominate over the novelist's. But there are still plenty of the dark and dangerous fishermen's bars where a cast of curious characters from around the world have been meeting for almost a century. And *fa'a Samoa* (the Samoan way) hasn't entirely disappeared either. The vigorous young men who play *kirikiti* (Samoan cricket) on the reserve may wear baseball caps but they bat and bowl (as they dance and clap) with floral *lava-lava* (sarongs) tied over their shorts.

Facts about American Samoa

HISTORY
For details of pre-1900 Samoan history, see History in the Facts about Samoa section in the Samoa chapter.

US Military Rule
The islands of eastern Samoa were formally annexed to the USA in 1900 by a deed of cession signed by all the local chiefs and became a naval station under the jurisdiction of the US Department of the Navy. The USA agreed to protect the traditional rights of the indigenous Samoans in exchange for the military base and coaling station. The inhabitants acquired the status of US nationals but are still denied a vote or representation in Washington.

In 1905, the military commander of Tutuila was given the title of governor and the territory officially became known as American Samoa.

At a Glance

Capital City (& Island): Pago Pago (Tutuila)
Population: 63,000
Time: 11 hours behind GMT
Land Area: 197 sq km (77 sq miles)
Number of Islands: Seven
International Telephone Code: ☎ 684
GDP/Capita: US$8000
Currency: US dollar
Languages: Samoan & English
Greeting: *'Talofa,' 'Malo'* (informal)

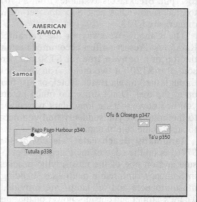

Highlights
- **Aunu'u Island** – a beautiful island just minutes by boat from Tutuila. Don't miss the lake of red quicksand, the crater lake full of eels and Ma'ama'a Cove, a wild cauldron of surf.

- **Ofu Beach** – part of the national park, South Ofu offers the finest snorkelling in the territory. A contender for the most beautiful beach in the South Pacific.

- **Bushwalking on Tutuila** – a pristine rainforest just hours away from Pago Pago Harbor.

- **Saua** – Samoans claim their islands to be the birthplace of Polynesia, the Manu'a Islands to be the birthplace of Samoa, and quiet Saua on Ta'u to be the birthplace of Manu'a. A sacred site by any measure!

AMERICAN SAMOA

Moves for More Democracy

Between 1967 and 1975, dissatisfied by lack of sufficient funds from Washington to maintain amenities, American Samoans voted, in a series of referenda, for direction by appointed governors. A subsequent referendum determined that they were ready for democratically elected leadership and some measure of autonomy.

GEOGRAPHY

American Samoa comprises five islands and a few rocky outcrops, giving a total land area of 197 sq km. The main island, Tutuila, where 95% of the territory's population lives, is 30km long and up to 6km wide.

The Manu'a group, about 100km east of Tutuila, consists of the three main islands of Ta'u, Ofu and Olosega, all wildly steep and beautiful examples of volcanic remnants.

The easternmost island of the Samoas is tiny Rose Atoll.

ECOLOGY & ENVIRONMENT

The biggest issues affecting the environment in American Samoa are its population growth rate of 3.8% per year, the increased preference for Western goods and equipment, increased generation of waste and greater pressure on treated-water supplies.

FLORA & FAUNA

On Ofu, Olosega and Ta'u one finds temperate forest vegetation: tree ferns, grasses, wild coleus and epiphytic plants. The harmless *gata* (Pacific boa) may occasionally be seen on Ta'u Island in American Samoa. Fifty-nine bird species have been recorded in American Samoa.

See Flora & Fauna in the Facts about Samoa section in the Samoa chapter for more information about plants and animals in the Samoan islands.

National Parks

The 4000-hectare National Park of American Samoa (NPS) consists of three distinct areas on three separate islands. Other protected areas in American Samoa are Fagatele Bay National Marine Sanctuary on Tutuila Island, and Rose Atoll, which is a wildlife refuge for nesting sea turtles and sea birds.

GOVERNMENT & POLITICS

American Samoa is an unincorporated and unorganised territory of the United States. Not all provisions of the US Constitution apply and it is the only territory whose residents are nationals, rather than citizens, of the USA and who are not governed by an act of the US Congress. Instead, it has its own constitution, supervised by the US federal government, which established three branches of government: executive, legislative, and judicial.

Although American Samoans are not automatically granted US citizenship, they may freely apply for it. Their status as US nationals allows them freedom of entry into the USA.

In 1977 American Samoans were allowed to elect their own governor and lieutenant-governor for four-year terms. In 1980 they were also allowed to elect a nonvoting delegate to serve a two-year term in the US House of Representatives.

In 2000 Tauese Pita Sina was elected as governor and Togiola Talalelei Tulafono as the lieutenant-governor.

ECONOMY

About one third of American Samoa's workforce is employed by the government. The two tuna canneries on Tutuila employ another third, with the rest employed in retail and service enterprises.

American Samoa's territorial status allows all businesses based there, such as the tuna canneries and textile manufacturers, to export their goods duty-free to the USA. This is an important consideration, as American Samoa is not required to adhere to US minimum-wage standards.

The US Department of Interior provides operating and capital improvement projects (CIP) grants to the American Samoan government. The annual operations grant is generally around US$23 million and the CIP grant around US$10 million. There is also a technical assistance grant of about US$1 million for education-related programmes.

AMERICAN SAMOA

See the Samoa Chapter

American Samoa is similar to independent Samoa in many ways. For further information on arts, books, climate, dangers and annoyances, language, religion, social graces, traditional culture and women travellers, see the relevant sections in the Samoa chapter.

POPULATION & PEOPLE

The population of American Samoa is around 63,000, with 95% living on the main island of Tutuila, which has an annual population growth rate of 3.8%, one of the highest in the world.

Facts for the Visitor

PLANNING

For information about the best time to travel in the Samoas, see Planning in the Facts for the Visitor section of the Samoa chapter.

Maps

The University of Hawaii publishes a larger-scale map of American Samoa. In Pago Pago on Tutuila, you can usually find it at the bookshop at the National Park Visitor Information Center (see Tourist Offices following).

If you're planning to hike or drive around American Samoa you can buy a copy of the US government's topographical map for around US$15 from Friendly Car Rental in Tafuna on Tutuila (see Getting Around near the start of the Tutuila section).

TOURIST OFFICES

The **American Samoa Office of Tourism** (☎ 633 1092; W www.amsamoa.com; PO Box 1147, Pago Pago, American Samoa 96799, USA) is hidden away in an unimpressive weatherboard building next to the yacht club in Utulei. If you manage to find it, you can get a rudimentary map of Tutuila and the harbor area, a few brochures and the excellent free booklet A Walking Tour of Historic Fagatogo. Ask for details of the homestay programme, which gives visitors a chance to stay with Samoan families for between US$25 and US$100 per night.

The **National Park Visitor Information Center** (☎ 633 7082; W www.nps.gov/npsa; Pago Plaza, Pago Pago), at the western end of the harbor, has some great brochures and maps, and a small bookshop. If you want to stay in a traditional village, ask about the excellent homestay programme.

American Samoa is represented abroad by offices of the South Pacific Tourism Organisation (SPTO; see Tourist Offices in the Regional Facts for the Visitor chapter).

VISAS & DOCUMENTS

No visas are required of visitors to American Samoa but US citizens need proof of citizenship and everyone else must have a valid passport (citizens of independent Samoa require an entry permit). Everyone, including US citizens, must have an onward ticket.

Applications for visa extensions, work permits and long-stay permits must be organised through the immigration office in the Executive Office building in Utulei.

EMBASSIES & CONSULATES

All American Samoan diplomatic affairs are handled by the USA. There are no consulates or embassies in American Samoa and no places able to issue visas for the USA.

CUSTOMS

Customs and immigration are handled at the airport and at the port in Fagatogo. If you're arriving by yacht, raise the quarantine flag as you enter Pago Pago Harbor and anchor. Visitors can bring in one gallon (3.8L) of liquor and up to 200 cigarettes duty-free.

MONEY
Currency

The US dollar is the currency used in American Samoa.

Exchange Rates

To check current exchange rates visit W www.oanda.com. At the time of writing exchange rates were as follows:

country	unit		US$
Australia	A$1	=	US$0.67
Canada	C$1	=	US$0.74
Easter Island	Ch$100	=	US$0.15
euro zone	€1	=	US$1.18
Fiji	F$1	=	US$0.54
New Zealand	NZ$1	=	US$0.58
PNG	K1	=	US$0.29
Samoa	ST$	=	US$0.33
Solomon Islands	S$1	=	US$0.14
Tonga	T$1	=	US$0.47
UK	£1	=	US$1.68
Vanuatu	100VT	=	US$0.83

Exchanging Money

The **Bank of Hawaii** and the **ANZ Amerika Samoa Bank** in Pago Pago both have ATMs and can give cash advances on major credit cards. The latter charges a US$5 commission on travellers cheques. There's also an ATM and branch of the Bank of Hawaii in Pava'ia'i, and in Tafuna. The ANZ also has a branch in Tafuna. Banks are open from 9am to 3pm Monday to Friday, with a service window open until 4.30pm on Friday. The Tafuna branch of the Amerika Samoa Bank is open from 9am to noon on Saturday.

There is no currency-exchange office at the airport.

Credit Cards Visa, AmEx and MasterCard are accepted at the bigger hotels, as well as by most tourist-oriented shops and restaurants on Tutuila. Both banks give credit-card cash advances.

Costs

Costs in American Samoa are quite a bit higher than in independent Samoa. There's not a lot of choice of accommodation and what is available is relatively expensive. Although B&B or village accommodation may cost around US$50 per person per night, most of the decent motel rooms with shared facilities will cost around US$85 for single or double occupancy. Expect to pay around US$7 for a cheap breakfast or lunch and anywhere from US$8 to US$25 for a main at dinner. Public transport is cheap and you're unlikely to pay more than US$2 for a bus fare on Tutuila.

Tipping & Bargaining

Tipping and bargaining are not customary in American Samoa.

POST & COMMUNICATIONS
Post

US stamps are used and US postal rates apply. The zip (postal) code for all of American Samoa is 96799.

The **main post office** (open 7.30am-4.30pm Mon & Fri, 7.30am-3.30pm Tues-Thur, 7.30am-1pm Sat) is near the *malae* (village green) in Fagatogo, in the same building as the Bank of Hawaii.

Have mail addressed to yourself care of General Delivery, Pago Pago, American Samoa 96799. If you're arriving by yacht, include the name of the vessel, under which mail is usually filed.

Telephone & Fax

The **American Samoa Telecommunications Authority office** (open 24hr daily), to the west of the *malae* in Fagatogo, is open for local and international calls. Telex and fax services are also available here. Local calls cost just US$0.10 each. **Blue Pacific Communications** (☎ 699 2759; ✉ sales@bluesky.as) has an office in Pago Plaza where you can buy phonecards that can be used for long-distance calls from any touch phone. You can also arrange to rent a cell (mobile) phone from Blue Pacific as well, a better option than bringing your own.

Email & Internet Access

There are a few places in Pago Pago where you can receive emails – see Information under Pago Pago in the Tutuila section later in this chapter. There's not much Internet availability outside Pago Pago.

DIGITAL RESOURCES

The following websites feature useful information about American Samoa:

American Samoa Historic Preservation Office (W www.ashpo.org) This site includes information about the office and its aims, along with a good walking tour

American Samoa Telecommunications Office (W www.samoatelco.com) This site is a good source of information for those wanting to get connected

National Park of American Samoa (W www.nps.gov/npsa) This excellent site features information on the park's homestay programme, maps, beautiful photos and information on wildlife

Office of Tourism (W www.amsamoa.com) This is quite a good site, with information on history, language and customs, a calendar of events and an up-to-date listing of places to stay and eat

Samoa News (W www.samoanews.com) For the latest in American Samoan news and views

NEWSPAPERS & MAGAZINES

The **Samoa News** (☎ 633 5599) is published Monday to Friday. The *Samoa Post* is published Tuesday, Thursday and Sunday. They cover local and sports news in detail.

RADIO & TV

Radio KHJ (93FM) plays a variety of music 24 hours a day, along with local news reports. Radio KSBS (92.1FM) plays a similar selection of popular music from 6am to midnight.

The government-owned TV station, KVZK, broadcasts on two channels: Channel 2 shows local and noncommercial programmes from the USA, while Channel 4 broadcasts commercial US programmes. There's also US cable TV for subscribers.

HEALTH
The **LBJ Tropical Medical Center** (☎ 633 1222; open 8am-4pm Mon-Fri) in Faga'alu can provide basic medical services, but anyone suffering serious medical problems is advised to go to Hawaii or New Zealand (NZ). Emergency doctors are on duty at all hours. There is a good pharmacy close to the hospital.

The main water supply in Pago Pago is OK to drink. Untreated village water, however, should be avoided.

BUSINESS HOURS
Banks are open from 9am to 3pm Monday to Friday; some stay open until 4pm on Thursday and Friday. Government offices open at 9am and close at 5pm.

Shops are open from 8am to 4.30pm, often with an hour's break for lunch. Restaurants and takeaway shops operate between 8am and 4pm if they serve breakfast and lunch or from 6pm to 10pm if they serve only the evening meal. Saturday shopping hours are from 8am to 12.30pm.

Markets open about 6am and close at about 3pm. The big market day is Saturday.

Most places are closed on Sunday.

PUBLIC HOLIDAYS & SPECIAL EVENTS
Public holidays celebrated in both American and independent Samoa include New Year's Day, Good Friday, White Sunday (the second Sunday in October), and Christmas. In addition, American Samoa celebrates Martin Luther King Day, US Independence Day, Columbus Day, Veterans Day (for these holiday dates, see the Regional Facts for the Visitor chapter), Tourism Week in early July, and the following extra holidays:

President's Day Third Monday in February
Flag Day 17 April
Memorial Day Last Monday in May
Arbor Day November

ACTIVITIES
Swimming & Snorkelling
Some of the best snorkelling is to be found in the National Park of American Samoa (NPS)

on the rugged little island of Ofu. The best spots for swimming and snorkelling on Tutuila are along the south coast near the western and eastern ends of the island, and along the north coast. Always ask permission from local villagers before using their beach, and bring your own snorkelling gear.

Diving
On the northern and western ends of Tutuila, corals are prolific and visibility is excellent. John Harrison (Divemaster), who runs the **Tutuila Dive Shop** (☎ 699 2842, 258 2842; ℮ scuba@blueskynet.as; PO Box 5137 Pago Pago), can organise dives for those interested. Or contact the **Pago Pago Dive Club** (🆆 www .geocities.com/pagopagodivers).

Surfing & Windsurfing
Some of the best surfing is found just beyond the reef near Faganeanea, but it's risky. If the trade winds are blowing and the tides aren't right, surfing is impossible.

Hiking
There are limited opportunities for hiking in American Samoa, though the US National Parks Service is planning a series of walking trails in the Tutuila and Ta'u sections. Check with the **National Park Visitor Information Center** (☎ 633 7082) in Pago Pago.

The well-established 5km (3.1 mile) trail to the top of Mt Alava (491m) above Pago Pago Harbor is easily accessible and offers excellent views. The remote island of Ta'u has some very wild and untouched scenery. Sections of the coast are accessible and inland walks to Judds Crater (six hours return) is possible. You'll need to take a local guide.

Golf
The **Ili'ili Golf Course** (☎ 699 2995), south of Tafuna International Airport, is very scenic and quite cheap.

ACCOMMODATION
Accommodation options are still quite limited in American Samoa but there have been some recent attempts to undo the bad reputation the country has suffered, mainly because of the continued sad decline of the once-grand Rainmaker Hotel. A new upmarket hotel is being built near the Tafuna airport and there are a quite a few decent motels and privately run B&B options; these are not particularly cheap, however. There's not a great tradition in the US territory of *fale* (traditional thatch-

roofed huts), but local villagers living close to the national park are being encouraged to provide inexpensive lodging for visitors. The tourist office runs a homestay programme and the **National Park Visitor Information Center** (☎ 633 7082) can organise overnight stays in traditional villages.

Decent 'budget' accommodation starts at US$50 for a single room. Most places have hot water. There are only three or four hotels in the mid-range category, with singles and doubles starting at around US$60.

FOOD
Most restaurants in American Samoa are in Pago Pago. You'll pay US$5 for a cheap meal and US$30 for a splurge. Self-caterers can get supplies at markets and village grocery stores.

See Food in the Facts for the Visitor section in the Samoa chapter for information about traditional Samoan food.

ENTERTAINMENT
Pago Pago has one or two nightclubs and a couple of modern cinemas showing current mainstream movies.

SHOPPING
You can pick up some cheap clothing and consumer items in American Samoa because there's no sales tax, but there's nothing inspiring, even among the few souvenirs at the airport and the Rainmaker Hotel. The Jean P Haydon Museum sometimes has some interesting locally made items. Local identity 'Louie the Fish' carves beautiful jewellery out of bone – traditional fish hooks, sea turtles, fish and the like; ask at the Pago Pago Yacht Club.

Getting There & Around

See the Getting There & Away and Getting Around sections in the Samoa chapter for information about getting to and around American Samoa.

Tutuila

pop 52,250 • area 148 sq km (57 sq miles)
Tutuila is by far the largest of the islands of American Samoa. The dramatic landscape is dominated by steep, rugged and lush forested mountains that branch out from the central

ridge, confining most of the development to a narrow strip along the south coast. Pago Pago Harbor is all that remains of the volcanic crater. The north coast is so wildly eroded that only a few tributary roads connect it with the long highway that snakes around the south coast.

Matafao Peak, just west of Pago Pago Harbor, above Fagatogo, is the highest point, at 653m. Immediately to the east of the harbor is Mt Pioa (523m), more commonly known as Rainmaker Mountain.

History
Archaeological finds near the villages of Tula and Aoa on the far eastern tip of Tutuila, and at To'aga on the island of Ofu, reveal that the islands have been inhabited for more than 3000 years.

Getting Around
Bus Riding the squat, colourful 'aiga buses (family-owned trucks, converted to carry passengers) is a real highlight of a visit to America Samoa. They leave every couple of minutes from the main bus terminal at Fagatogo market between early morning and about 6pm – eastbound for Tula (US$1.25), and westbound for Tafuna and the airport (US$0.75) and Leone (US$1). Less frequently, buses go to Fagasa (US$0.75), A'oloaufou on the central ridge (US$1), Amanave (US$1.25), and Fagamalo in the far northwest (US$1.50). The most expensive fare is the US$1.75 trip over Rainmaker Pass to Vatia.

Car Tutuila's one main road (signposted Route 1) follows the twisty coastline from Fagamalo in the west of the island to Onenoa in the northeast, for about 50km (31 miles). The rental agencies listed here charge about US$75 per day plus insurance. Petrol costs about US$1.70 per gallon (36c per litre). The following are a list of car rental agencies:

Avis Car Rental (☎ 699 2746/4408, ⓔ res@avissamoa.com) Airport; Nu'uuli
Friendly Car Rental (☎ 699 7186) Tafuna
Pavitt's U-Drive (☎ 699 1456) Airport
Sir Amos Car Rental (☎ 633 4545) Fagatogo

Taxi Expect to pay about 16 times the bus fare, or just over US$1 per mile. This works out to around US$11 from the harbor area to Pago Pago airport at Tafuna, US$16 to Leone, US$4 to the tuna canneries and US$18 to Au'asi.

TUTUILA

PLACES TO STAY
1 Barry's B&B
3 Turtle & Shark Lodge
4 Tessarea's Vaitogi Inn
5 Ta'alolo Lodge & Golf Resort
10 Pago Airport Inn
11 Tradewinds West Hotel
22 Fale Pule
23 Lautu Simona's
24 Tisa's Barefoot Bar

PLACES TO EAT
9 Jeffrey's; Cost-U-Less
14 A & A Pizza
15 Nu'uuli Shopping Centre; Good Food Bakery; Rubble's Tavern

17 Deluxe Café
18 Hong Kong House

OTHER
2 John Williams Church
6 'Ili'ili Golf Course & Country Club
7 Malu Mai Beach Resort
12 Tia Seu Lupe (Star Mound); Catholic Cathedral
13 American Samoa Community College
16 Laufou Shopping Center
19 Wallace Theatres
20 Q Laundromat
21 LBJ Tropical Medical Center
25 Aunu'u Ferry Landing

PAGO PAGO

pop 3520

Pago Pago (pa-ngo pa-ngo) is an alluring mixture of the seedy and the dramatically beautiful. The picturesque harbor is surrounded by high, almost wicked-looking mountains that plunge straight into the sea. With its belching tuna factories and pollution in the harbor, it's too much like a working town for many travellers looking for palm-fringed Pacific paradise, but it's fascinating all the same.

Information

Tourist Offices The American Samoa Office of Tourism (☎ 633 1092; ⓦ www.am samoa.com; open 7.30am-4pm Mon-Fri) in Pago Pago is next to the yacht club at Utulei, just south of the Rainmaker Hotel. There's a faded sign outside, but it's easy to miss and not very sophisticated.

In Pago Plaza at the western end of the harbor you'll find the informative **National Park Visitor Information Center** (☎ 633 7082; ⓦ www.nps.gov/npsa; open 8am-4.30pm Mon-Fri, until noon Sat).

Money The **Bank of Hawaii** (☎ 633 4226; open around 9am-3pm Mon-Fri) and the **ANZ Amerika Samoa Bank** (☎ 633 1151; open around 9am-3pm Mon-Fri), both near the *malae* in Fagatogo, have currency-exchange facilities. They charge around 2% commission on travellers cheques. The ANZ also has a service window open until 4.30pm Monday to Friday and from 9am to noon Saturday. Both banks have ATMs and can give cash advances on MasterCard and Visa.

Post & Communications The post office (open 7.30am-4.30pm Mon & Fri, 7.30am-3.30 Tues-Thur, to noon Sat) is by the *malae* in the same building as the Bank of Hawaii. The American Samoa Telecommunication Authority, also next to the *malae*, near the courthouse, is open 24 hours for local and international telephone calls. Fax services are also available.

There are a few options for the **Internet**. The cheapest is at the **Feleti Barstow Public Library** (see Libraries, later), where you pay a US$25 refundable deposit for an ID card that gives you free Internet access. Another good option is the **Island Business Center** (☎ 633 1444), slightly west of the telephone office. It only has one computer, but it's pretty fast and costs US$5 an hour. Or if you'd like a coffee

while you cyberchat, the **DDW Internet Café** (see Places to Eat, later) is the place to head, although it's more expensive: US$5 for 30 minutes. However, Internet connections in American Samoa can be very slow – it might take you longer to log off than to order your toasted-cheese sandwich!

Bookshops Good bookshops are hard (well, impossible) to find in American Samoa. The **gift shop** at the airport, the **Wesley Bookshop** in Fagatogo, the **Rainmaker Hotel gift shop** and the **Transpac Store** at the Nu'uuli Shopping Center stock a handful of Samoan and Pacific titles.

Libraries The excellent **Feleti Barstow Public Library** (☎ 633 5816; ⓔ barstow@ya hoo.com; open 9am-5pm Mon, Wed & Fri, 9am-7pm Tues & Thur, 10am-2pm Sat), across from the Office of Tourism in Utulei, has a good Pacific collection, a children's room and a computer room from where email can be sent (see Post & Communications, earlier). Library cards are available for nonresidents for US$25 (refundable).

There's also an extensive Pacific collection at the **American Samoa Community College** (☎ 699 9155), southwest of Nu'uuli, but research must be done on site. The **Pago Pago Yacht Club**, next to the Office of Tourism, runs a casual library exchange.

Laundry There are dozens of laundrettes, most of which are open long hours, daily. At the southern entrance to the harbor is **IBM Laundromat & Store**, which charges US$0.75 to wash and the same to dry. **Q Laundromat** (open 24 hrs daily), in Nu'uuli, charges US$0.75/1 to wash/dry.

Emergency In an emergency you should call (☎ 911).

Mt Alava

Towering above Pago Pago Harbor is Mt Alava (491m). The National Park Service maintains the excellent 5km (3.1 mile) trail that follows the ridge to the top, where there are spectacular views. The trail begins at Fagasa Pass about 1km southwest of the park's visitor information centre.

Jean P Haydon Museum

Located across the road from the post office in Fagatogo is the Jean P Haydon Museum (☎ 633 4347; admission free; open 10am-3pm

PAGO PAGO HARBOR

PLACES TO STAY
6 Motu-o-Fiafiaga
Motel (Evie's Place);
Evie's Cantina;
Evalani's Cabaret
9 Sadie Thompson's;
Sadie's Restaurant
14 Scanlan's
26 Rainmaker Hotel;
Oceania Travel & Tours

PLACES TO EAT
2 Food Stalls
5 DDW Internet Café
22 Mom's Place
28 Pago Pago Yacht Club

OTHER
1 Chinese & Korean Bars;
Pool Halls & Night Club
3 Super K Supermarket
4 National Park Visitor
Information Center;
Pago Plaza; Blue Pacific
Communications
7 Pila Patu Store

8 Dinghy Dock
10 Fagatogo Market &
Bus Station
11 Courthouse
12 Island Business Center
13 Forsgren's
15 Office Communications
16 Fono (Parliament House)
17 Malae o Le Talu
(Town Square)
18 ANZ Amerika Samoa Bank
& ATM
19 Police
20 Main Post Office;
Bank of Hawai'i & ATM
21 Jean P Haydon Museum
23 Wesley Bookshop
24 Air Disaster Memorial
25 Governor's House
27 American Samoa Office
of Tourism
29 Feleti Barstow Public
Library

Mon-Fri), with early Samoan artefacts, including the *va'a* (bonito canoes) and *alia* (war canoes) that inspired the old name for Samoa, the Navigator Islands. **Kava ceremonies**, **weaving** and **woodcarving** demonstrations sometimes take place in the *fale* outside.

Fono

The large and impressive group of buildings beside the museum are known as the Fono (Parliament).

Market

The market and *'aiga* bus station are near the western end of Fagatogo village. Here, local growers come to sell their bananas, coconuts, breadfruit and other fresh produce. The big market day is Saturday.

Tuna Canneries

The two tuna canneries are in the mile-long industrial complex on the north coast of the harbor. Nearest to Pago Pago is **Starkist**. The other is **COS Samoa Packing**.

Flowerpot Rocks

The Flowerpot Rocks, or Fatumafuti, are found along the highway, near the village of Faga'alu. The legend says that Fatu and Futi were lovers living on the Manu'a Islands. They wanted to marry but were forbidden to do so because tradition prevents members of the same *'aiga* marrying. Both their boats were destroyed as they approached Tutuila and the two lovers were stranded on the reef, where they remain to this day. The area around Fatumafuti is a nice place to have a picnic.

AMERICAN SAMOA

Places to Stay

Fale Pule (☎ 633 5264; e lefalepule@samoa
telco.com; Shimasaki Turner Rd; regular
singles/doubles US$85/105, intermediate
singles/doubles US$95/115, single/double
suites US$130/150), in the village of Faga'alu,
is one of the most beautiful B&Bs you could
hope to find in the Pacific. At the top of a very
steep track, it has stunning views of Pago Pago
Harbor. Rooms have all mod cons (air-con,
bathroom and phone) but there's a lovely
homely atmosphere here and a superb common
lounge area – with cable TV and entertainment
system – that leads to a balcony with breathtaking views. An excellent breakfast is included
in the room rates. Other meals can be arranged
on request.

Motu-o-Fiafiaga Hotel (Evie's Place; ☎ 633
7777, fax 633 4767; e evalani_1@yahoo.com;
PO Box 1554; singles & doubles US$60) is
clean, comfortable, friendly and there's always
coffee brewing. Rooms have air-con, TV and
shared bathroom. Just try not to let the mir-
rored hallway and red and black decor dazzle
you. The motel also has a small workout room
and, amazingly for such a humid country, a
sauna. Next door, Evie (who was a big star in
Las Vegas in its Mafia days) runs a Mexican
restaurant and nightclub (see Places to Eat and
Entertainment, later). Rates drop to US$50 for
stays of two nights or more.

Sadie Thompson's (☎ 633 5981; e sadies@
samoatelco.com; PO Box 3222; singles/
doubles US$135/185) is a bit of a disappoint-
ment if you were expecting to find the sort of
establishment the infamous woman is supposed to have frequented. Accommodation is
pretty deluxe, and though this hotel has been
built within the weatherboard bungalow
where Sadie was supposed to have enter-
tained her 'guests', inside, you could be at
any motel almost anywhere in the world. If
you want US-style comfort and dinner with
tuna packing company executives, this is the
place to be.

If you want a taste of the seamy side of
Samoa, stay at **Scanlan's** (singles/doubles
US$25-50). Spasmodically run by Goony, a
German eccentric who came and never left,
this run-down little establishment offers the
most basic of 'motel-style' rooms for cash-
strapped blow-ins.

Rainmaker Hotel (☎ 633 4241, fax 633
5959; PO Box 996; standard singles & doubles
with air-con & bathroom from US$60, beach-
front deluxe rooms US$85, VIP fale US$90,
executive suites & fale US$150 plus US$15 per

extra bed), known by locals as the 'Painmaker'
and other epithets, was grand when it was built
in the 1960s. But the 181-room government-
run hotel has been seriously neglected and its
standards definitely don't live up its prices. But
if you want to experience first-hand what's
been described as the 'worst hotel in the South
Pacific', the best-value rooms are the beachside ones on the 2nd floor.

Tradewinds West Hotel (☎ 688 1922;
e hei@samoatelco.com; PO Box 670, Pago
Pago AM 96799), a new 105-room hotel in
Tafuna not far from the airport, is a valiant attempt to provide an alternative to the notorious
Rainmaker. When it opens late in 2003 there
will be Internet access from every room, a
swimming pool, and suites and double rooms
with hot water and TV.

Ta'alolo Lodge & Golf Resort (☎ 699 7201,
fax 699 7200; e taalolo@samoetelco.com;
PO Box 1266, Pago Pago; singles & doubles
with cable TV US$75-135) is an elegant
home-cum-guesthouse, just two minutes'
walk from the Ili'ili Golf Course. It's very
homely and welcoming, with a lovely swimming pool and gazebo. Most rooms have
air-con. The kitchen is available for guests'
use and Internet service can also be provided.
Rates include breakfast.

Turtle & Shark Lodge (☎ 688 1212 during
the day, 699 1212 at night & on weekends, fax 699 1212; e juanitalhall@turtle
andshark.com; PO Box 2506, Pago Pago;
singles/doubles with shared bathroom &
air-con US$85/100, with private bathroom
US$125/140), a lovely, secluded nine-room
guesthouse, is spectacularly located southwest of Vaitogi, overlooking Fogama'a Cove.
The trick is finding it – there are no signs,
so ring for directions. Guests have access to
two kitchens, Internet (free), a tennis court
and swimming pool. Rates include a light
breakfast.

Tessarea's Vaitogi Inn (☎ 699 7793, fax
699 7790; e tessa@samoatelco.com; PO Box
2551, Pago Pago; singles/doubles with TV
US$90/155), another pretty flash place, just
off the road down to the Turtle & Shark Site,
is tucked in Vaitogi village. It has a swimming
pool, and can also be tricky to find.

Lauti Simona's (☎ 644 2028, 258 1468)
is where the self-sufficient can reside in rustic splendour at beachside fale at beautiful
Amalau Bay. Mosquito nets, mattresses and
a barbecue grill are provided, but BYO food,
water and snorkel gear. There's no set fee, but
it's around US$10 per person.

Tisa's Barefoot Bar (☎ 622 7447; *fale per person US$25*) is a superb, enviro-friendly place on Alega Beach, with two sleeping *fale*. With its terrific view over the beach, this is definitely one of the best places to stay on Tutuila. Cooking facilities are available and reservations are advisable. Rates include breakfast.

Places to Eat

Most of the restaurants (and shops) on Tutuila are concentrated in Fagatogo and Pago Pago and along the stretch of highway between Pava'ia'i and Nu'uuli.

Snacks There are a few places near the market in Fagatogo that serve decent, cheap meals, with some Samoan food on the menu.

Mom's Place (☎ 633 5174; *meals US$3-5*), up past the main post office heading east, dishes up good pancakes and omelettes.

DDW Internet Café (*Don't Drink the Water;* ☎ 633 5297; *breakfast US$2.50-5, lunch US$3-9*) is a clean, inviting place in Pago Plaza at the western end of the harbor.

Evie's Cantina (☎ 633 4776; *mains US$6-9*), a good Mexican restaurant, also at the western end of the bay, adjoins the Motu-o-Fiafiaga Motel.

Pago Pago Yacht Club (☎ 633 2465; *mains around US$4*), right on the harbor in Utulei, is a terrific spot for a burger.

Jeffrey's (☎ 699 6560; *mains US$4-6*), out near the airport, opposite Cost-U-Less, is clean and pleasant, with good breakfast and children's menus.

A & A Pizza (☎ 699 9428), with a children's playground, is another popular place out near the Nu'uuli Shopping Center.

Restaurants With its period decor and atmosphere, **Sadie's Restaurant** (☎ 633 5981; *mains US$18-30*) is the most elegant and expensive restaurant in the territory. It's very popular with expats, yachties and business people. The menu has lots of seafood, including scallops, lobster tails and sashimi. There's a good selection of Californian and Australian wines starting at around US$20 per bottle (US$3.25 by the glass).

The dining room at **Rainmaker Hotel** (☎ 633 4241; *mains US$9-23*) offers burgers, steaks, seafood and Chinese. Every Friday it puts on a buffet, including some Samoan specialities, for US$15 per person.

If you'd like to eat lunch or a gourmet dinner and sip fine wine with friends on a balcony overlooking spectacular Pago Pago Harbor, Dean and Isabelle Steffany-Hudson can produce whatever you want, with a little notice. Contact **Le Fale Pule Lodge & Fine Dining** (☎ 633 5264, fax 633 5648; e *lefalepule@samoatelco.com*).

Self-Catering The central **market** in Fagatogo is a bit sad-looking but you should be able to pick up some fresh fruit and vegetables most days, except Sunday. There are plenty of well-stocked **supermarkets** and small Korean-run stores on Tutuila, such as **Super K Supermarket** at the top of Pago Pago Harbor, which usually has fresh fish.

Good Food Bakery (☎ 699 6233), in the Nu'uuli Shopping Center, has a great range. **Pila Patu Store** (☎ 633 4912; *open 24hr*), towards the western end of the harbor, is handy for late-night supplies. **Cost-U-Less** (☎ 699 5975), near the airport, sells imported groceries and household goods.

Entertainment

Bars & Clubs A must-visit place, **Tisa's Barefoot Bar** (☎ 622 7447; *open 11am-7pm daily, by reservation after 7pm*) is on lovely Alega Beach, about 10km (6.2 miles) east of Pago Pago (US$0.75 by bus). You can also stay the night here in a *fale* (see Places to Stay, earlier) and eat excellent organic food. There are kava nights, jazz nights, 'Nude Friday' and full-moon parties. Call to see what's coming up.

Maliu Mai Beach Resort (☎ 699 7232; PO Box 3263, Pago Pago; *open 8am-midnight Mon-Thur, 8am-2am Fri & Sat, 11am-9pm Sun*) is in a gorgeous position by the sea, not far from the airport. There's some sort of live entertainment every Friday from 8.30pm. You can also dine here: lunch meals cost around US$5 and dinner between US$10 and US$19.

Rubble's Tavern (☎ 699 4403) is in the Nu'uuli Shopping Center. If you fancy a good, cold beer, perch yourself on one of the coconut-tree-stump bar stools here. Happy hour is from 4.30pm to 6.30pm, but only from Monday to Friday (see also Places to Eat under Around the Island later in this section).

Pago Pago Yacht Club (☎ 633 2465; *open 11.30am-5pm Mon-Thur & Sun, until 8pm Fri & Sat*) is the place to go to meet yachties. During the cruising season it can get packed.

Evalani's Cabaret (☎ 633 4776; *open 5pm-11pm daily*), adjoining the Motu-o-Fiafiaga

Motel in Pago Pago, is the place for karaoke fans, especially if you like dancing to big-screen music videos.

On the northern bank of the harbor is the 'seedy side', with a rag-tag collection of Chinese- and Korean-run bars, pool halls and 'nightclubs' with names such as Red Door, gathered above the tuna canneries.

Cinemas At the **Wallace Theatres** (☎ 699 9334; adult/child US$6.50/4; open daily), a two-screen cinema on the main road in Nu'uuli, you can see the latest-release commercial movies. Cheaper tickets are available before 6pm.

EASTERN TUTUILA
National Park of American Samoa
Bounded by the Maugaloa Ridge to the south, this section of the park covers 1000 hectares of land (most covered in lowland and montane rainforest), as well as 480 hectares of offshore waters.

The 5km trail from Fagasa Pass to Mt Alava is the only official hiking trail here and anyone wanting to explore the national park should contact the Visitor Information Center (see Tourist Offices in the Facts for the Visitor section earlier in this chapter).

Amalau Valley Between Afono and Vatia is the secluded Amalau Valley, which is home to many forest bird species and the Samoan islands' two rare species of fruit bat.

Vatia Situated on the edge of a wide, coral-fringed bay, Vatia is a charming and friendly village that seems a million miles away from the big smoke over the ridge. There's a tiny uninhabited island, Pola, just offshore. Its magnificent sheer cliffs rise more than 120m straight out of the ocean and are home to numerous **sea birds** including frigate birds, boobies, white terns, tropicbirds and noddy terns. To get there, go to the end of the road through the village and then walk a quarter of a mile along the coral rubble beach.

For basic village accommodation contact the National Park Visitor Information Center in Pago Pago about the homestay programme. 'Aiga buses go to Vatia (US$1.50) several times a day.

Rainmaker Mountain (Mt Pioa)
This 523m mountain is the culprit that traps rain clouds and gives Pago Pago Harbor more

than its fair share of wet weather. It is also Tutuila's best example of a volcanic plug associated with the major fissure zone that created the island. Although it appears as one peak from below, the summit is actually three-pronged. Rainmaker Mountain and its base area are designated a national landmark site due to the pristine nature of the tropical vegetation on the slopes.

Alega Beach
One of Tutuila's finest beaches, Alega Beach is just 10km east of Pago Pago (US$0.75 by 'aiga bus). It's a great place to **swim** and **snorkel** (but check currents and conditions with locals first), and with Tisa's Barefoot Bar (see Bars & Clubs under Entertainment earlier in this section) right on the beach, it's the perfect spot for a cold beer. There's a small charge to use the beach.

Masefau & Sa'ilele
Near the village of Faga'itua, another cross-island road goes over to the north coast. The left fork leads down to the beautiful bay and village of Masefau. The right fork goes to the tiny settlement of Masa'usi and then through dense forest to Sa'ilele, which has one of the loveliest **beaches** on the entire island.

Au'asi Falls
Above the village of Au'asi is a pleasant waterfall, a nice place to cool off on a hot day. It can be reached by walking up the stream for about half an hour.

Aoa
Although the road between Amouli and Aoa is scenically rather uninteresting, more than 40 ancient **star mounds** have been found, but not yet excavated, in the bush near the spine of the island. In addition to the star mounds, Polynesian plainware (a type of undecorated pottery) has been found in the Aoa area. Some estimates date the pot shards found here from as early as 1000 BC, but the figure currently accepted by the scientific community is 500 BC.

Tula
Tula, the easternmost village on Tutuila, is a quiet and laid-back place with a pleasant white **beach**. It is the end of the bus line east, but if you have a reliable vehicle or feel like a nice walk, you can continue around the end of the island to Cape Mata'ula and Onenoa, a beautiful area of high cliffs, small plantations

Star Mounds of Ancient Power

More than 140 distinctive earthen, and sometimes stone, mounds, dating back to late prehistoric times, are scattered across the Samoan archipelago. Dubbed 'star mounds', the structures range from 6m (20 ft) to 30m (100 ft) in length, are up to 2½m (9 ft) high and have from one to 11 ray-like projections radiating from their base.

It is highly probable that these mounds were used for catching the revered Pacific pigeon (*lupe*), which isn't as pedestrian as it may sound. An extremely important sport of *matai* (chiefs), it had a five-month season, from June until the end of September, and involved nearly the entire population of the islands. The people would follow their *matai* into the forest to observe and support competitions.

Archaeologists have found strong evidence to suggest that though the structures were used primarily for pigeon-catching, they also served a much more complex function in Samoan society as sites for rituals related to marriage, healing and warfare. The star mounds also reflected the status of the *matai*, and pigeon hunting was the field in which personal ability and *mana* (personal spiritual power) could be expressed. Star mounds (sometimes called *tia seu lupe*) were therefore places of immense power.

In 1983, a Samoan *ali'i* (high chief) commented:

Do you know the star mounds? Well, they had to do with the *taulasea* (traditional healer) and energy and with special powers. The ancient Samoans did not build those just to catch pigeons. No Sir! They were part of our ancient religion, and so were the *taulasea* and the *taulaitu* (spirit medium)… The energy is still so strong on those mounds that it raises the hair on your body to visit them.

and forested slopes. The area between the villages has plenty of places to picnic, especially above the cliffs.

WESTERN TUTUILA
Matafao Peak
At 653m, Matafao Peak is the highest point on Tutuila. Above the 350m level, the mountain is designated a national landmark site.

Nu'uuli
Nu'uuli is primarily a loosely defined shopping area along the main road between Coconut Point and the airport turn-offs. There are quite a few restaurants along here (see Places to Stay & Eat later), as well as the Nu'uuli Shopping Center, the Laufou Shopping Center and the cinema complex, Wallace Theatres.

Tia Seu Lupe
American Samoa's Historic Preservation Office maintains a particularly well-preserved ancient Polynesian **star mound**, *tia seu lupe* (literally, 'earthen mound to catch pigeons'), near the Catholic cathedral at Tafuna. The mound has a unique connecting platform and views across to Matafao Peak. Call the **Historic Preservation Office** (☎ 633 2384) for an excellent personalised tour of the site. Adjoining the site is a small **rainforest reserve**. The nearby **cathedral** contains some

beautiful woodcarving and a fabulous photo-realist painting of a traditional Samoan family by Duffy Sheridan.

Fagatele Bay National Marine Sanctuary
Fagatele Bay is a submerged volcanic crater surrounded by steep cliffs. The area contains the last remaining stretch of coastal rainforest on the island.

The sanctuary is also home to several marine mammal species. Southern humpback **whales** winter here from August to November, several varieties of **porpoise** occasionally visit the sanctuary and sperm whales have been seen in the bay. Threatened and endangered species of **marine turtles**, such as hawksbill and green turtles, also use the bay. Other less frequent turtle visitors include the leatherback, the loggerhead and the olive Ridley.

The rocky cliffs surrounding the bay are home to numerous **sea birds**. All but traditional fishing methods are prohibited in the inner bay, the taking of invertebrates is prohibited and historical artefacts found in the bay are protected. It is possible to **dive**, **snorkel** and **swim** in the bay, but access is difficult. Contact the **Marine and Wildlife Resources Office** (☎ 633 7354), down by the market in Fagatogo, to arrange transport.

Leone

The village of Leone is the second-largest settlement on Tutuila and served as the Polynesian capital of the island. It was also the landing site of the first missionary, John Williams, who arrived on 18 October 1832 after spending two years in independent Samoa. A monument to Williams' efforts is in front of the church – the first church in American Samoa.

'*Aiga* buses direct to Leone leave every couple of minutes from the main terminal in Fagatogo (US$1); Leone is the turnaround point.

Leone Falls & Ancient Quarry

The small waterfall and ancient stone quarry complex behind Leone village is close to Barry's B&B. To get to the waterfall go up the road past the white Catholic church near the town centre to the end of the pavement, then follow the short walking track to the head of the valley, where a ribbon-like waterfall plunges into a moss-covered basin. An artificial catchment barrier creates a freshwater pool at the bottom. It's a cool and pleasant spot, but wear strong footwear, as the track can be extremely muddy.

The basalt quarry, known as Tataga Matau, above Leone is one of the most important archaeological sites in the South Pacific. Surveys carried out during the past 10 years have identified 10 quarry sites on Tutuila and archaeologists believe the island was the centre of a large trade network that stretched across the South Pacific. Artefacts made of stone from the Tutuila quarries have turned up as far away as the Solomon Islands.

There's also a **star mound** at the Leone quarry similar to those found at Aoa.

Massacre Bay

The hiking trail down to A'asu at Massacre Bay leaves from the village of A'oloaufou, high on the spine of Tutuila, above Pava'ia'i on the main road. Massacre Bay is the site where, on 11 December 1787, 12 men from La Pérouse's ships *La Boussole* and *Astrolabe*, as well as 39 Samoans, were killed in a skirmish. An obscure **monument** in A'asu commemorates the European crew members who died there.

To get to A'oloaufou, take a Leone-bound bus from the market in Fagatogo to Pava'ia'i (US$0.75) and wait on the corner there for one headed up the hill.

Across from the large park in A'oloaufou is a colourful garden. The trail to A'asu takes off downhill just east of that garden and continues for about 4km (2.5 miles) to the beach.

There is only one family living in the old deserted village of A'asu. On arrival, it's best to introduce yourself and ask for permission to use their beach.

For this trip, experienced hikers should plan on one hour to walk down and half as long again for the climb back up. There is no road outlet from A'asu.

Cape Taputapu

The village of Amanave lies at the end of the beaten path. A short distance beyond the village on Loa inlet is a lovely white-sand beach, generally known as **Palagi Beach**. It's just east of Cape Taputapu, which is Tutuila's westernmost point and a national natural landmark site.

You can walk to the beach via the track above the shoreline; allow about 10 to 15 minutes. You can paddle and **snorkel** in the small pool by the offshore island but be mindful of strong currents.

Places to Stay & Eat

The places listed here are all in western Tutuila.

Barry's B&B (☎ 688 2488, fax 633 9111; PO Box 5572, Pago Pago; singles/doubles with fan & shared bathroom US$40/50), a comfortable home full of character, is in a quiet and leafy setting near Leone Falls. Barry can provide evening meals (US$5 each), a laundry service and free island tours that range from gentle outings to strenuous five-hour hikes. If necessary, he will pick up guests from the airport or town. Rates include breakfast.

Pago Airport Inn (☎ 699 6333, fax 699 6336; ⓔ pagoinn@blueskynet.as; PO Box 783, Pago Pago; singles/doubles US$75/85) is a stone's throw from the airport. This double-storey hotel in Tafuna village has 20 rooms, with more on the way. Rooms have air-con, private bathroom, TV and fridge. There's an airport shuttle service (free, provided you tip).

Deluxe Café (☎ 699 4000; meals US$6-12; open 7am-2pm Tues-Sat, 9am-2pm Sun), close to the cinema in Nu'uuli, is clean and pleasant. Meals include fresh local fish, salads and steaks and the extensive breakfast menu includes a bottomless cup of coffee.

Rubble's Tavern (☎ 699 4403; mains US$8-20; open 11am-midnight daily) is an inviting restaurant/bar with an interesting Polynesian-American decor. Rubble's lunch

AMERICAN SAMOA

and dinner specials include oriental chicken with teriyaki sauce (US$8), home-made meat loaf (US$8), New York steak (US$20 for 8oz, or US$24 for the '*matai* cut') and possibly the best spaghetti Bolognese (US$8) in the South Pacific. It also has cheaper burgers and sandwiches. Rubble's sometimes closes early on Sunday.

Hong Kong House (☎ 699 8983; mains US$8-13; open 10am-10pm Mon-Sat, from around 4pm Sun) is very popular. This bustling restaurant in Nu'uuli offers an extensive menu with carefully prepared Chinese favourites and a good selection for its vegetarian diners.

AUNU'U

pop 500 • area 3.1 sq km (1.2 sq miles)
Tiny Aunu'u Island, off the southeastern end of Tutuila, is a treasure house of natural phenomena and is a tranquil and pristine place, with no vehicles. The waters around the island are clear and blue and the village is spacious and unspoilt.

Pala Lake

Heading north from the village, you will arrive at Pala Lake after walking about 700m. This beautiful and deadly-looking expanse is a sea of fiery-red quicksand. During the rainy season, the sand thins out and is inhabited by grey ducks.

Red Lake

Red Lake, surrounded by Fa'imulivai Marsh, in the middle of Aunu'u's volcanic crater, is filled with **eels** and **tilapia fish**. The water is the colour of weak tea. You can walk out to the edge by following the track past Pala Lake and up the hill to the crater. Access to the lake is a little tricky. If you'd like a local guide, ask in the village.

Ma'ama'a Cove

This bowl in the rocks is a cauldron of surf that boils, pounds and sprays dramatically. The wave action here seems to be completely random. Don't venture too close to the edge.

Pisaga

The Pisaga is a region just inside the crater, below Fogatia Hill, where people are forbidden to call out or make loud noises lest they disturb the *aitu* (spirits) that inhabit this place. For a superb view over Red Lake, as well as Aunu'u village, climb up past the water tank on the slopes of Fogatia Hill.

Places to Stay & Eat

There is no formal accommodation available on Aunu'u but the Office of Tourism in Pago Pago can help arrange someone on Tutuila who can sponsor you. There's a **bush store** in the village where you can buy soft drinks and basic supplies.

Getting There & Away

Take the bus to the harbor at Au'asi (US$1 from Pago Pago). From here, a ferry travels frequently to and from Aunu'u Harbor for US$2 per person, though not on Sunday. If you can't be bothered waiting for the ferry, you can charter a boat from the bush store at Au'asi for US$10 each way for as many people as will fit. The trip takes about 15 minutes and can get a bit hairy through the strait, especially if the wind is blowing.

SWAINS ISLAND

pop 15 • area 3.2 sq km (1.3 sq miles)
It is not possible to visit Swains Island without permission from the Jennings family, who lives there. If you're interested, contact the **Marine and Wildlife Resources Office** (☎ 633 7354), near Fagatogo market.

Manu'a Islands

The three small islands of the Manu'a group (Ofu, Olosega and Ta'u) lie only 100km (62 miles) east of Tutuila but in many ways they are hundreds of years away. These are the most traditional and unspoilt islands of American Samoa and here you'll encounter the most stunning scenery in all of the Samoas – sparkling white beaches, soaring cliffs, crystal lagoons and mountain peaks.

Almost touching, Ofu and Olosega Islands arc a complex of volcanic cones that have been buried by lava from two merging shield flows. Deep valleys were carved out, leaving very high, sheer cliffs around the islands.

Remote Ta'u Island's sea cliffs are some of the highest in the world, rising 966m to Mt Lata. More than 2000 hectares of the dense rainforest of Ta'u is national park, and the island is dotted with inactive volcanic cones and craters.

History

Many Samoans believe Manu'a was the first land to be created by the god Tagaloa. Thus, the Tu'i Manu'a – the paramount chief of these islands – was held in high esteem and

OFU & OLOSEGA

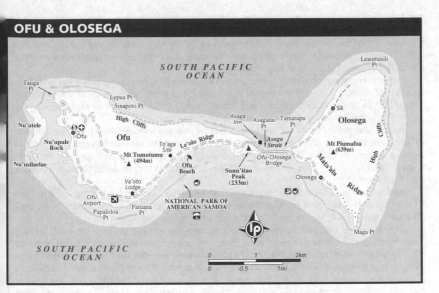

many supernatural powers were ascribed to holders of the title. All, of course, had exceptional prowess at war. The last Tu'i Manu'a ceded the islands in 1904, and in his will he stipulated that his title would die with him.

In 1993 the Ofu and Ta'u sections of the National Park of American Samoa were officially established after the signing of a 50-year lease with the traditional owners.

Orientation & Information

Manu'a is worth a stay of two days or two months. Although the lack of transport will slow you down, that's the charm. Bring your own snorkelling equipment, reading material and any particular foods you may need. There are no restaurants on the islands. Ofu village has an **ANZ Bank** *(open 8.30am-12.30pm Mon-Fri)* near the wharf, and a basic medical clinic. There's also an excellent baker at the Ofu post office.

Getting There & Around

Air Ofu airport is at Va'oto on the south coast at Fiti'uta – a flash new facility that replaces the old nightmare airstrip, which had a cliff on one end, a mountain at the other and lots of quirky air currents in between.

Samoa Air *(in Pago Pago ☎ 699 9106, in Ofu ☎ 655 1186, in Ta'u ☎ 677 3569)* flies twice a day between Tutuila and the Manu'a Islands, winds (or the gods?) willing. The planes stop at both Ta'u and Ofu whenever

there are passengers. Between Pago Pago and either of the Manu'a airstrips, the fare is US$55 each way or US$105 return. Phone and make a **reservation** *(in Pago Pago ☎ 699 9106, in Ofu ☎ 655 1103, in Ta'u ☎ 677 3569)* then reconfirm the return flight upon arrival. The trip between Ofu and Ta'u is US$28 each way.

Boat Water transport to the Manu'a Islands is at present limited to private yachts, which, if arriving from the east must check into Pago Pago before they're permitted to embark on the fierce beat into the wind that would get them back to Manu'a. Few bother.

American Samoa Inter-Island Shipping Company *(☎ 258 7333, 699 9951)* operates a weekly cargo ship, the *Manu'a Tele*, to the Manu'a Islands, which can take about 15 passengers (US$30 each way). It leaves Pago Pago at 10pm every Wednesday.

OFU
pop 400 • area 5.2 sq km (2 sq miles)
Ofu is the most dramatic and beautiful of the Manu'a Islands. It's the easiest to visit, and the one most often seen by outsiders.

Ofu Beach
Ofu's crown jewel is the beach along the south coast – 4km (2.5 miles) of palm-fringed white sand. The only footprints to be seen other than your own are those of birds and crabs.

And God Created Samoa

Samoans accept the scientific theory that Polynesians originally migrated to the islands from Southeast Asia by way of Indonesia. However, they believe this applies to all Polynesians except themselves. Their land, they claim, is the 'cradle of Polynesia'.

Samoa, they say, was created by the Polynesian sky god Tagaloa (Tangaroa). Before the sea, earth, sky, plants or people existed, Tagaloa lived in the expanse of empty space. He created a rock, commanding it to split into clay, coral, cliffs and stones. As the rock broke apart, the earth, sea and sky came into being. From a bit of the rock emerged a spring of fresh water.

Next, at Saua in the Manu'a Islands, Tagaloa created man and woman, whom he named Fatu and 'Ele'ele ('Heart' and 'Earth'). He sent them to the region of fresh water and commanded them to people the area. He ordered the sky, which was called Tu'ite'elagi, to prop itself up above the earth. Using starch and *teve*, a bitter-root plant and the only vegetation then available, he made a post for it to rest upon.

Tagaloa then created Po and Ao (Night and Day), which bore the 'eyes of the sky' – the sun and the moon. At the same time he made the nine regions of heaven, inhabited by various gods, most famously Rongo (or Ro'o), the god of agriculture, and Oro, the god of war.

In the meantime, Fatu and 'Ele'ele were doing as they were told and 'peopling the area'. Tagaloa, reckoning that all these people needed some form of government, sent Manu'a, another son of Po and Ao, to be the chief of the people. The Manu'a Islands were named after this chief, and from that time on, Samoan kings were called Tu'i Manu'a tele ma Samoa 'atoa (King of Manu'a and all of Samoa).

Next, the countries were divided into islands or groups of islands. The world now consisted of Manu'a, Viti (Fiji), Tonga and Savai'i. Tagaloa then went to Manu'a and noticed that a void existed between it and Savai'i. Up popped 'Upolu and then Tutuila.

Tagaloa's final command, before he returned to the expanse, was: 'Always respect Manu'a; anyone who fails to do so will be overtaken by catastrophe'. Thus, Manu'a became the spiritual centre of the Samoan islands and, to some extent, of all Polynesia.

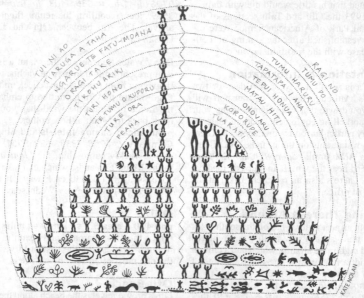

This diagram (first drawn in 1869) shows nine regions of heaven above the Earth – although most Polynesian cultures named only eight

The strip of beach stretching from Va'oto Lodge to the beginning of the Ofu-Olosega bridge plus 140 hectares of offshore waters comprise the Ofu section of the national park. With your own snorkelling equipment, parts of the stretch offshore are deep enough for some excellent viewing of **coral** and **tropical fish**. Almost 300 species of fish have been identified and the reef is believed to contain about 150 species of coral. Go out at low tide (at high tide, waves break over the reef and wash into the lagoon) and watch out for stinging flame coral.

The narrow strip of land that comprises the Ofu section of the national park is an important source of medicinal plants for the villages of Ofu and Olosega.

To'aga Site
About 1km (0.6 miles) northeast of Va'oto Lodge, behind Ofu Beach, is the To'aga site, where in 1987 archaeologists found artefacts from the earliest times of Samoan prehistory (500 BC) to modern times.

The site also has legendary and spiritual significance for Samoans. In fact, the entire area of bush between the road and Ofu Beach is believed to be infested with devilish *aitu*.

Ofu Village
Just 2km (1.2 miles) north of the airstrip is Ofu village. There is a calm **lagoon** for swimming (ask permission), but avoid the pass between Ofu and Nu'utele Island just offshore, as the currents are dangerous.

Mt Tumutumu
The track to the summit of Mt Tumutumu (494m) begins near the wharf and twists and climbs up to the TV relay tower atop the mountain. It's a hot and sweaty 5.5km (3.4 mile) climb, but the vegetation and views make it well worthwhile. If it's hot, allow a full day and don't forget to carry all the food and water you'll need.

Places to Stay & Eat
Va'oto Lodge (☎ 655 1120; e *vaoto@hotmail .com; singles/doubles US$35/40, plus US$15 for 3 meals*), a friendly place, is conveniently located beside the airstrip and a few steps from the beach. There are 10 basic but clean rooms, all with electric fan, hot shower and toilet. You'll find cold beer, books, TV and video in the large dining/common room. Guests can send email for free and hire a vehicle for US$35 per day. You're likely to share

the breakfast table with marine biologists and academics. Book ahead.

Asaga Inn (☎ 633 1164, fax 655 1164; *singles/doubles US$45 per person, extra person US$10*), right next to the Ofu-Olosega bridge, has huge air-con bedrooms, a good lounge area and a big, modern kitchen if you want to self-cater. There's a well-stocked shop next door; otherwise, three meals a day cost US$17 per person.

OLOSEGA
pop 400 • area 3 sq km (1.9 sq miles)
Olosega lies just 137m from Ofu and is joined to it by a cyclone-proof bridge. They are both encircled by the same reef. Olosega has a very nice beach along its southwest coast between the pass and the village. Ask permission if you want to swim or snorkel there. There's another small settlement at Sili on the northwestern side of the island.

Places to Stay & Eat
There is no official tourist accommodation on Olosega; however, excellent village stays can be arranged through the National Park of American Samoa's homestay programme. Contact the **Visitor Information Center** in Pago Pago. Basic, albeit expensive, supplies are available at the store in the village.

Getting There & Away
Since there is no harbor or airstrip, access to Olosega is on foot or by vehicle from Ofu. To walk from Ofu village to Olosega village will take about two hours.

TA'U
pop 3500 • area 39 sq km (15 sq miles)
At 966m, Mt Lata, the sacred mountain of Ta'u, is the highest point in American Samoa.

Ta'u feels seriously remote; it sees very few visitors and isn't really set up for tourists. If you'd like to spend a couple of days exploring the few parts of the island that are accessible, bring food supplies. It's fairly easy to hitch a ride between the eastern and western ends of the island.

It was in Luma that the young Margaret Mead researched and wrote her classic work *Coming of Age in Samoa* in 1925.

Fiti'uta Village
At the northeastern corner of Ta'u is the tiny, sleepy village of Fiti'uta. The **airstrip** is here, along with a **guest lodge** (see Places to Stay

AMERICAN SAMOA

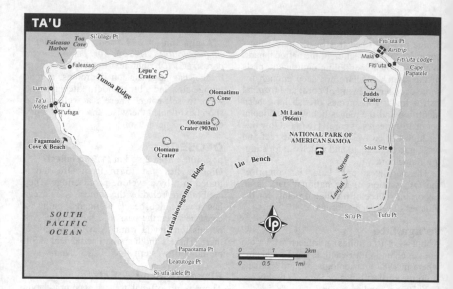

TA'U

Faleasao Harbor · Toa Cove · Si'ulagi Pt · Fiti'uta Pt · Airstrip · Maia · Fiti'uta Lodge · Fiti'uta · Cape Papatele · Faleasao · Lepu'e Crater · Tunoa Ridge · Luma · Ta'u Motel · Ta'u · Si'ufaga · Olomatimu Cone · Judds Crater · Fagamalo Cove & Beach · Olotania Crater (903m) · Mt Lata (966m) · NATIONAL PARK OF AMERICAN SAMOA · Olomanu Crater · Liu Bench · Saua Site · Mataalaosagamai Ridge · Laufuti Stream · SOUTH PACIFIC OCEAN · Si'u Pt · Tufu Pt · Papaotama Pt · Leatutoga Pt · Si'ufa'alele Pt · 0 · 1 · 2km · 0 · 0.5 · 1mi

& Eat, later), three **stores** selling basic supplies, a **post office** (at Mele's Store) and a **bank** (next to the airstrip).

National Park of American Samoa

The Ta'u section of the national park occupies 2160 hectares of land and takes in some of American Samoa's most dramatic scenery. There is a spectacular escarpment along the southern side of the national park and cliffs as high as 900m.

Ta'u's protected lowland and montane rainforest provide excellent habitats for fruit bats and many native birds. Other native wildlife includes the Pacific boa, which lives only on Ta'u and in only in very small numbers; 13 species of amphibians and reptiles; and 20 species of land snail. Endangered sea turtles are believed to nest along the remote shorelines.

Saua Site Halfway down the east coast of the island is the place where, according to Samoan legend, the god Tagaloa created the first humans before sending them out to Polynesia. This is also where the first Tu'i Manu'a was crowned. Only volcanic boulders, wild surf and a windswept beach mark this sacred place, but archaeologists have located the remains of an **ancient village** near Saua, and numerous grave sites between Saua and Si'u Point.

Laufuti Stream A rough plantation track follows the east coast as far as Tufu Point, and from here it's possible to hike 2km (1.2 miles) along the shoreline to Laufuti Stream where there's a **waterfall** and a nearby spring.

The southern coastline of Ta'u is so wild and pristine that it's worth a look even if you don't want to walk all the way to the stream. Anyone going beyond Si'u Point should take a guide.

Judds Crater The three-hour climb to the crater is possible with a local guide, but must be organised through the National Park Visitor Information Center in Pago Pago.

Ta'u Village

The main settlement on Ta'u consists of the twin villages of Luma and Si'ufaga at the northwestern corner of the island. In Luma are the **tombs** of the last Tu'i Manu'a and several other early politicians.

There are basic **stores**, including a bakery, in Ta'u. The waters off the northwest coast are treacherous. There are three ancient **star mounds** on the ridges above Faleasao.

Fagamalo Cove

From Ta'u village, the walk south to the **beach** at secluded Fagamalo Cove is a pleasant way to pass a couple of hours. The track along the west coast can be muddy, but it offers some nice views of the cliffs above and pounding surf below. Don't forget mosquito repellent.

Places to Stay & Eat

There are two motels on Ta'u, but by all accounts both of them are a bit grim. A better option for overnight visitors to Ta'u might be the National Park of American Samoa's excellent homestay programme.

Fiti'uta Lodge *(☎ 677 3155/3501; rooms per person US$40)*, the main official guest accommodation, is a Western-style house near the airport. Rooms are basic and share a (hot-water) bathroom. There's a kitchen and next door a shop that sells basic supplies. This place is under new management, so hopefully it'll lose its grim reputation. Rates include dinner.

Ta'u Motel *(☎ 677 3504/3155; singles/doubles with fan & hot water per person US$25/40)* doesn't provide meals and there are no restaurants. However, as with Fiti'uta Lodge, there's a guest kitchen and a store next door.

ROSE ATOLL

pop 0 • area 8 hectares

Rose Atoll is composed of tiny specks of land and the surrounding reef. Rose Islet, only 3m above sea level at its highest point, is a US national wildlife refuge, primarily to protect the green turtle. Permission to visit is very difficult to obtain.

Solomon Islands

Some of the islands of the Solomons are large with densely forested mountain interiors and fast-flowing rivers, while others are tiny, low-lying coral atolls that encircle stunning lagoons. The archipelago is the South Pacific's third largest. Most of its people live in small villages, where they cling to a subsistence lifestyle that has barely changed for centuries.

It's hard to believe that, until the 1930s, the ancestors of today's friendly, easy-going islanders were considered to be among the world's most violent and dangerous people. Head-hunting, cannibalism and skull worship were central elements of traditional culture. Sacred skull shrines remain as macabre and fascinating reminders of the old days.

The Solomons is a famous dive destination thanks to its wealth of colourful coral reefs, exciting underwater topography and hundreds of sunken WWII wrecks. It's a wonderful spot for snorkellers, too, and anglers will find the waters to be full of opportunity for sport and game fishing.

Little tourism infrastructure exists around the country and there are few restaurants or high-class hotels. But there is plenty of basic accommodation in the main tourist areas. If you don't need glitz or glamour, you'll find that the simplicity of life in the Solomons is an attraction in itself.

On the down side, the Solomons has developed a dangerous reputation following a period of ethnic conflict in 1999 and 2000. This is unfortunate as, while Guadalcanal and – to a lesser extent – Malaita continue to experience a breakdown in law and order, the rest of the country has not been involved in the violence. Check official travel advisories for the current situation.

Facts about the Solomon Islands

HISTORY

About 25 million years ago the first of the volcanic Solomon Islands rose from the ocean depths. By 25,000 BC, Papuan-speaking hunter-gatherers from New Guinea were settling the southern and eastern Solomon Islands. These were the first people to settle the Pacific, and the only inhabitants for many thousands of years. Austronesian-speaking

At a Glance

Capital City (& Island): Honiara (Guadalcanal)

Population: 410,000

Time: 11 hours ahead of GMT

Land Area: 27,540 sq km (10,740 sq mi)

Number of Islands: 992 (347 inhabited)

International Telephone Code: ☎ 677

GDP/Capita: US$605

Currency: Solomon Islands dollar (S$1 = US$0.14)

Languages: About 90 indigenous languages, plus Pijin

Greeting: *Halo* (Pijin)

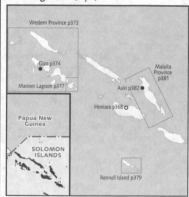

Highlights

- **Honiara** – take a guided tour of blood-soaked battlefields that claimed thousands of US and Japanese lives during WWII

- **Marovo Lagoon** – explore a myriad of idyllic tropical islands and meet friendly villagers on a tour by kayak or motor canoe

- **Diving** – marvel at the underwater world and its wealth of colourful fish, exquisite corals and WWII shipwrecks

- **Rennell** – visit beautiful Lake Te'Nggano and discover why it is one of the South Pacific's few world heritage sites

- **Russell Islands** – be inspired by the emerald islets surrounded by white beaches and turquoise shallows on an ultramarine sea as you fly over en route to Western Province

proto-Melanesians began arriving in the archipelago around 4000 BC. Lapita people (see the boxed text 'Lapita' in the 'South Pacific Arts' special section) appeared between 2000 and 1600 BC.

Most people lived in small villages on tribal lands. They practised shifting cultivation, fishing, hunting, carving, weaving and canoe building. Rule was by *kastom* (custom) as recalled by clan elders. Ancestors were worshipped and blood feuds, head-hunting and cannibalism were common.

Polynesians from the east settled the outer islands such as Rennell, Bellona and Ontong Java between 1200 and 1600 AD. Their settlements suffered raids from Tongans between the 14th and 18th centuries.

Spanish Exploration

Don Alvaro de Mendaña y Neyra left Peru with two ships in November 1567. On 7 February 1568 he saw and named Santa Isabel, and settled there. On 11 August, after six months of conflict, the voyagers set sail for Peru.

Mendaña returned in 1595 with four ships and 450 would-be colonists. He came upon and named Santa Cruz, and established a settlement there. Mendaña died of malaria. After two months the settlement was abandoned and the survivors limped back to Peru.

Mendaña's chief pilot from 1595 was the Portuguese Pedro Fernández de Quirós, who left Peru with three small ships on 21 December 1605 and reached the Duff Islands early in 1606.

Further Exploration & Early Trading

There was almost no further contact until the late 18th century. Captain Philip Cartaret, a Briton, came upon Santa Cruz in 1767 and then Malaita. British, French and American explorers followed.

Whalers started arriving in 1798. Sandalwood traders followed between the 1840s and late 1860s, buying pigs, turtle shell, pearl shell and bêche-de-mer. The sandalwood traders were cruel to the islanders and brought European diseases that caused them to die in their thousands. Resentment towards European treachery and diseases led to the murder of a number of missionaries.

The Solomons was the most dangerous place in the Pacific. Although they were very active elsewhere in the region, churches moved cautiously in the Solomons. From the 1860s, firearms traded with sailors produced an explosive growth in head-hunting and slave raids.

Blackbirders (slavers; see History in the Facts about the South Pacific chapter) took over 29,000 Solomon Islanders to work on sugar-cane plantations in Australia and Fiji.

The Protectorate

In the 1890s about 50 British traders and missionaries were in the Solomons, and Germany was active in New Guinea, the Shortlands, Choiseul, Santa Isabel and Ontong Java. On 6 October 1893 Britain proclaimed a protectorate over the archipelago's southern islands, which was extended in 1897 and again in 1898. In 1899 Britain relinquished claims to Western Samoa, and Germany ceded the Shortlands, Choiseul, Ontong Java and Santa Isabel to Britain.

Charles Morris Woodford became the first resident commissioner in 1896. Missionaries sought to eradicate local culture, declaring customs and ceremonies to be evil. Sorcery and head-hunting diminished, but natives died in huge numbers from European diseases.

The Kwaio Rebellion on Malaita in 1927 was a rejection of European values (see the boxed text 'The Kwaio Rebellion'). In 1928 several Kwaio rebels were hanged in the then-capital, Tulagi. Basiana, the defiant rebel leader, declared before his death, 'Tulagi will be torn apart, and scattered to the winds', and 14 years later it was.

The Kwaio Rebellion

On 4 October 1927, District Officer William Bell was in Kwaio territory (Malaita) to collect tax and confiscate rifles. With him were 14 Malaitan constables. A Kwaio called Basiana killed Bell, and in the ensuing melee all but one of the constables were killed.

The reaction in Tulagi, the capital, was immediate – and excessive. The cruiser HMAS *Adelaide*, which had been dispatched from Sydney, shelled all the villages it could find. As well, gardens were poisoned and sacred objects were destroyed. The Kwaio claimed that over a thousand people were killed.

Six Kwaio (including Basiana) were hanged in Tulagi and 30 others died in jail. This ruthless action subdued the Kwaio but left a long legacy of ill feeling towards government and Europeans.

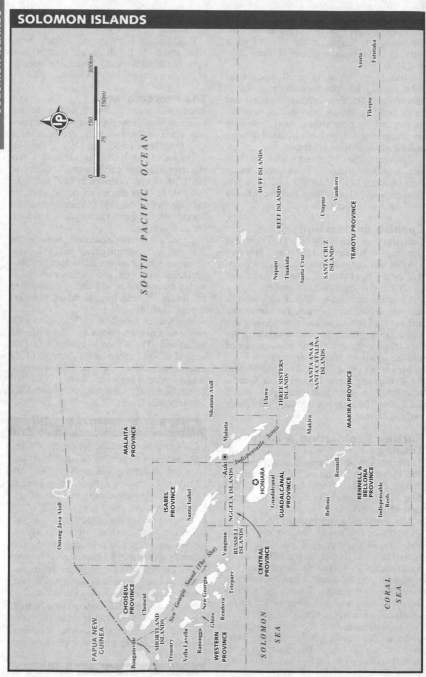

WWII

In April 1942 the Japanese seized the Shortland Islands. Three weeks later Tulagi was taken and the Japanese began building an airstrip on Guadalcanal.

US troops landed on Guadalcanal in August 1942. In the early hours of 9 August, while landings were in progress, a Japanese naval force left Rabaul in New Guinea to attack the US transports at Red Beach before they unloaded. This, the Battle of Savo, was one of the US navy's heaviest defeats – 1270 Allied sailors were lost.

The US forces gradually gained the upper hand, but at a tremendous cost of life on both sides. After six months the Japanese withdrew to New Georgia. During the Guadalcanal campaign, six naval battles were fought and 67 warships and transports sunk – so many ships were sunk off Savo, the Florida Islands and the northern coast of Guadalcanal that this area is now called Iron Bottom Sound. Around 7000 American and 30,000 Japanese lives were lost on land and at sea, many of them to diseases such as malaria.

As 1943 progressed, more islands were recovered by the Allies and by the year's end only Choiseul and the Shortlands remained in Japanese hands. The Allies recovered them after the Japanese surrender in 1945.

Postwar

Tulagi was gutted during the war and the Quonset-hut township of Honiara replaced it as the capital. The economy was in ruins.

A nationalist movement sprang up in Malaita. Called Marching Rule, it was a self-reliant movement opposed to any cooperation with the British authorities, which had been restored after WWII. Its members were regimented into coastal villages dependent on community-based agriculture. Marching Rule was also cargo-cultist, believing that US goods would be delivered to islanders by those US forces remaining behind in the Solomons after WWII. Mass arrests of followers by British authorities in 1947 and 1948 caused the movement to wane, and it died out after the last of the US forces left in 1950. Britain began to see the need for local government, and regional assemblies were introduced.

There was a governing council elected in 1970. The British Solomon Islands Protectorate was renamed the Solomon Islands five years later and independence was granted on 7 July 1978.

In the late 1990s long-simmering ethnic tension between the Gwalese people of Guadalcanal and immigrants from Malaita escalated into violence (see the boxed text 'Ethnic Tension' in the later section on Honiara). Hundreds of people died, thousands were displaced and the national government was overthrown prior to the signing of a peace agreement in Townsville, Queensland, in October 2000.

By this time, however, the country's economy – never robust – was a shambles. Major income earners such as fish canneries and the country's only gold mine had closed, tourism had virtually ground to a halt and the country was surviving on aid donations. A national election held in December 2001 saw Sir Allan Kemakesa elected prime minister, with a brief to address law and order, and corruption. Eighteen months later these issues remain significant obstacles to recovery.

GEOGRAPHY

The islands of the Solomons form a scattered double chain that extends 1667km southeast from Bougainville in Papua New Guinea (PNG). The third largest archipelago in the South Pacific, the Solomons cover over 1.35 million sq km of sea. The total land area is 27,540 sq km.

Of the 992 islands, 347 are populated. The largest islands are Guadalcanal (5302 sq km), Malaita (3840 sq km), Santa Isabel (3380 sq km), Choiseul (3200 sq km), Makira (3188 sq km) and New Georgia (2145 sq km). The country's highest peak, Mt Makarakombu (2447m), is on Guadalcanal. There are active volcanoes, and earthquakes are common.

Most islands are fringed with coral reefs and sheltered lagoons; many have formed around volcanic cones, while others are former reefs that have been uplifted by volcanic activity. Rennell is the South Pacific's most striking example of a raised coral atoll.

CLIMATE

From late May to early December (the dry season) southeasterly winds produce pleasantly mild weather. Rainfall is light and rain periods are usually several days apart.

From mid-December to mid-May, monsoon winds come from the west or northwest and bring the wet season. This is a time of higher temperatures, humidity and rainfall. Short, sharp, torrential rains are followed by bright sunshine. Honiara's annual rainfall is about 21.5cm, which is drier than most of the rest of the country. Some parts, like Guadalcanal's south coast, receive as much as 12.5m of rain!

Cyclones can blow up between January and April. Daytime coastal temperatures vary through the year from 21°C to 32°C. At night the temperature falls to around 19°C. The humidity can be oppressive and is highest in the morning, regularly reaching 90%.

FLORA & FAUNA

The Solomons has over 4500 plant species, including 230 varieties of orchid. Tropical rainforest covers the islands, although logging operations have degraded much of this, and there are also mangrove forests. Many plants are traditionally utilised for building materials, food and medicine.

The spectacular marine environment is home to a bewildering variety of fish, corals, anemones and many other creatures, including eight species of venomous sea snakes. Several islands are breeding grounds for green and hawksbill turtles.

The Solomons is home to 173 bird species, 40 of which are endemic. Some species, such as the Rennell fantail and the slaty flycatcher of Vanikoro, are found only on one island.

There are four rat species that are larger than domestic cats! Other land mammals include the cuscus and flying fox (fruit bat).

Compared with islands further east, the Solomons harbour a huge variety of reptiles. As well as sea snakes there are seven land species, three of which are nonvenomous. The latter includes two species of boa. Among the lizards are the 1.5m-long monitor lizard and the dangerous saltwater crocodile, which can exceed 5m. The latter are common in the mangrove inlets of Vella Lavella. There's also a harmless freshwater variety.

More than 130 butterfly species are found locally, and 35 are endemic. The two largest forms, the Queen Victoria birdwing and the blue mountain birdwing, have wing spans over 25cm.

JANE HART

A male frigate bird in a courtship display. Frigate birds are important in island folklore.

GOVERNMENT & POLITICS

The Solomon Islands is a parliamentary democracy with a single legislative assembly. The 50-seat parliament is in Honiara. Elections are held every four years and all citizens over 18 years may vote.

The British Crown, as leader of the Commonwealth, is head of state; the governor general, chosen by parliament, acts as the monarch's representative.

The judicial system is British: the Solomons has a high court, court of appeal and magistrates' court. Village elders conduct local courts and there's a customary land appeal court.

ECONOMY

The country's main natural resources are its trees and fish; the export of logs is by far the highest earner for the islands, but the industry is not sustainable at the present rate of extraction. Other important exports are copra, cocoa and palm oil. There are economic deposits of bauxite, phosphates, gold, silver, copper, manganese and nickel, but none are being mined. The economy has gone into a downward spiral since the country was torn apart by ethnic strife in 1999 and 2000 (see the boxed text 'Ethnic Tension' in the Honiara section of this chapter). In 2003 the Solomons was close to bankruptcy and was almost totally dependent on foreign aid for its survival.

Agriculture

About 30% of the land is cultivable, but only in small parcels. The only extensive area of good agricultural soil is the Guadalcanal plains. Gardening, coconuts and fishing satisfy basic village needs, and earn a modest cash income.

Fishing

The waters of the Solomons are rich in tuna, and there is a cannery located in the Western Province. The sale of fishing licences to overseas interests is the Solomons' second-biggest earner.

Tourism

The tourism industry has collapsed along with the rest of the economy since the ethnic troubles of 1999. Less than 5000 tourists, most of them from Australia, arrived in the Solomons in 2002.

Only the Western Province and the capital, Honiara, have any real tourism industry.

POPULATION & PEOPLE
The Solomons' population at the time of the 1999 census was 410,000. Melanesians represented 94% and Polynesians 4%, while Micronesian settlers from Kiribati – still called Gilbertese – accounted for 1.4%. The remainder was made up of Asians and expats, mainly Aussies, Kiwis, Brits and Yanks.

The Solomons' population density of 14.5 people per sq km is one of the Pacific's lowest. From the early 1970s until recent times the population increased annually by 3.5%; the rate has now dropped to 2.8%, still among the world's highest. Death rates and infant-mortality rates are falling, and life expectancy is now over 70 years (having risen from only 54 in the late 1980s).

About 86% of the population lives in rural villages. Urban drift caused Honiara's population to grow by 7% per year until the ethnic tension on Guadalcanal halted this trend.

ARTS
Literature
Ples Blong Iumi – The Solomon Islands, the Past Four Thousand Years, by Sam Alasia and others, contains contributions by 14 Solomon Islanders. *Zoleveke – A Man from Choiseul*, by Gideon Zoleveke, recounts the story of a Choiseul man who became a cabinet minister.

From Pig-Theft to Parliament – My Life Between Two Worlds, by Jonathan Fifi'i, tells of the author's childhood in Malaita, the Marching Rule movement and parliamentary life. *Kanaka Boy*, by Sir Frederick Osifelo, is the autobiography of the first Solomon Islander to be knighted.

Carving
There are strong carving and artefact-making traditions in the Solomons. Once more widespread, pottery is now only produced in north-western Choiseul.

Carvings incorporate human, bird, fish and other animal motifs, often in combination, and they frequently represent deities and spirits. Wooden carvings are often inlaid with nautilus or trochus shell. Carvings of *nguzunguzu* (canoe figureheads, also carved in miniature) and animals are produced from kerosene wood and ebony (ebony is now rare and very expensive – beware of inferior timbers blackened with stain). Decorated bowls are widely available, as are stone replicas of traditional shell money. The best wooden carvings come from Marovo and Roviana Lagoons.

Nguzunguzu
Carvings called *nguzunguzu* (pronounced 'noo-zoo-noo-zoo') once adorned the prows of canoes, where they warded off water spirits, guided the craft through jagged reefs and protected the warriors aboard. The figurehead rests its chin either on two clenched fists (for war), a human head (head-hunting) or on a dove (peace). The best carvings are made of ebony and inlaid with pieces of pearly nautilus shell, making a striking contrast with the smooth, jet-black timber.

Although native to Western Province, the *nguzunguzu* has been taken up as a kind of national symbol and embossed on the one dollar coin.

Weaving
Bukaware baskets, trays, table mats and coasters are made in many parts of the Solomons and are woven from the very tough *asa* vine. Gilbertese make sturdy, brown sleeping mats out of the pandanus leaf. Finely woven shoulder bags are produced on Rennell and Bellona.

Tattoos
Many tattoo patterns are traditional markings that confirm a person's age and social position. Tattooing is more common among fairer-skinned peoples.

Facial engraving is practised on Malaita; a grooved, unpigmented design is made using a scraper bone against the skin. In northern Malaita, men are tattooed below the eye and women decorate their breasts.

Chests are tattooed on the islands of Rennell and Bellona.

Currency
Kastom mani is used for paying bride price and other special transactions. Shell money is used in Malaita, while in the Temotu Islands red-feather coils are still used.

SOCIETY
Solomon Islanders' obligations to their clan and village chief bigman are eternal and enduring, no matter whether they live in the same village or have moved to another country entirely. The *wantok* system is observed here like in most Melanesian cultures (for more information see the boxed text 'The Wantok System' later).

The Wantok System

Fundamental to the Solomons' culture and common to many Melanesian societies is the idea of *wantok*. In Pijin, *wantok* simply means 'one talk', and your *wantok* are those who speak your language – your clan and family. All islanders are born with a set of obligations to their *wantok*, but they're also endowed with privileges that only *wantok* receive.

Within the village, each person is entitled to land and food, and to share in the community assets. And any clans people, whether in Honiara or Hanoi, are expected to accommodate and feed their *wantok* until they can make more permanent arrangements.

For most Melanesian villagers it's an egalitarian way of sharing the community assets. There's no social security system, and very few people are in paid employment, but the clan provides economic support and a strong sense of identity.

The *wantok* system affects everything – if you are tendering out a construction project and a *wantok* bids, you give the contract to the *wantok*. If your bus driver is a *wantok* you won't have to pay. And if you have a *wantok* in the judiciary maybe you won't go to jail.

In the political and public-affairs arenas, however, the *wantok* system translates as nepotism and corruption. In the Solomons it has undermined democratic institutions and hampered the country's development.

Traditional Culture

There are about 90 indigenous languages and dialects in the Solomon Islands. Beliefs, ceremonies, authority systems and proclamations of status often differ from island to island.

Kastom Villagers refer to their traditional ways, beliefs and land ownership as *kastom* (custom); it's bound up in the Melanesian systems of lore and culture (see Society in the Facts about the South Pacific chapter).

Dances, songs and stories celebrate war, hunting and the harvesting of crops. Many islanders believe in magic and devils. In Malaita the spirit of a dead person can live in a shark; the shark is offered gifts and is worshipped.

Village Life Most Solomon Islanders live in coastal villages close to freshwater springs. Each family has a small coconut plantation for copra production and cash income, and a few scattered vegetable plots.

The nearby bush provides foods (including nuts, ferns and fruits); materials for leaf-house and canoe construction, rope and basket making; and firewood.

RELIGION

About 96% of the population are Christians. Of these, 35% are members of the Anglican-affiliated Church of Melanesia and 20% are Roman Catholics.

Islanders still practise pre-Christian religions in a few remote areas, particularly on Malaita, and in other places traditional beliefs are observed alongside Christianity.

LANGUAGE

It's quite common for people from villages only a few kilometres apart to speak mutually unintelligible languages, so islanders who aren't *wantok* communicate in Pijin. People who have received some education generally speak English so you can get by in the Solomons without learning any Pijin. However, English is perceived to be a 'serious' language – if you're able to converse in Pijin, people lose their shyness and really open up to you.

Lonely Planet's *Pidgin* phrasebook has a large section on Solomon Islands Pijin.

Facts for the Visitor

PLANNING
When to Go
The most comfortable time to visit is between June and September; humidity levels are lowest from October to December.

Maps
Ordnance Survey maps are available at Ministry of Lands & Housing offices in each provincial centre. The **Honiara branch** (☎ 21 511) has all of the Solomons' survey maps. Hema produces a map (1:1.2 million) of the Solomons that is widely available.

What to Bring
Light summer clothing is suitable for day and night all year round; the style for men and women is casual.

Lightweight poncho-style rainwear that will cover your backpack and double as a groundsheet is recommended.

You will need sandals, sneakers or diving boots for walking over coral reefs. Sturdy shoes are best for walking through the bush and light trousers will protect your legs from scratches.

Beachwear should be conservative. A mosquito net, sleeping mat and light cotton sheet are essential if you are staying in villages; a flashlight (torch) is essential wherever you're staying.

Other useful items you might like to bring include candles, matches, water bottles and a Swiss army knife.

Tampons, sanitary pads, nappies and condoms can be purchased in Honiara and other main towns.

TOURIST OFFICES
Local Tourist Offices
The Solomon Islands Visitors Bureau (SIVB) is in Honiara. See that section for contact details.

Tourist Offices Abroad
See Tourist Offices in the Regional Facts for the Visitor chapter for offices of the South Pacific Tourism Organisation (SPTO), which represents the Solomon Islands abroad.

VISAS
Every visitor must have a valid passport, onward ticket and adequate funds.

In theory, entry visas are not required as a visitors permit for a stay of up to three months is granted upon arrival. However, the guidelines are ambiguous for nationals from former or continuing communist countries, the Indian subcontinent, Nauru and Kiribati. Nationals from these places should seek advice from a Solomon Islands embassy before travelling.

Visitors permits can be extended for a further three months at the **Immigration Office** (☎ 22585) in Honiara. The extension costs S$33 for each month.

Applications for US visas can be routed through **Keithie Saunders** (☎ 22393, fax 24 027) of BJS Agencies.

EMBASSIES & CONSULATES
Solomon Islands' Embassies & Consulates
The Solomon Islands' diplomatic representation abroad includes:

Australia
High Commission: (☎ 02-6282 7030, fax 6282 7040, e info@solomon.emb.gov.au) PO Box 256, 1st floor, JAA Bldg, Unit 4/19 Napier Close, Deakin, NSW 2600
Consulate: (☎ 02-9361 5866, fax 9361 5066) Level 5, 376 Victoria St, Darlinghurst, NSW 2010
Consulate: (☎ 03-8531 1000, fax 8531 1955) 1 Southbank Blvd, Melbourne, Victoria 3006
European Union
Embassy: (☎ 02-732 7085, fax 732 6885, e 106255.2155@compuserve.com) Ave Edourd 17, 1040 Brussels, Belgium
Japan
Honorary Consulate: (☎ 03-5275 0515, fax 222 5959 5960) 16-15 Kirakawa-cho, Z-Chome, Shiyoda-ku, Tokyo
Papua New Guinea
Honorary Consulate: (☎ 323 4333, fax 323 4334, e sihicomm@daltron.com.pg) PO Box 94, Unit 2, GB House, Port Moresby

Embassies & Consulates in the Solomon Islands
All foreign embassies and consulates are in Honiara.

Australia (☎ 21561, fax 23691) Mud Alley St
European Union (☎ 22765, fax 23318; e ec sol@solomon.com.sb) City Centre Building
France (☎ 22588, fax 23887) Tradco office, City Centre Building
Germany (☎ 22588, fax 23887) Tradco office, City Centre Building
Japan (☎ 22953, fax 21006) NPF building
New Zealand (☎ 21561, fax 23691) City Centre Building
Papua New Guinea (☎ 20561, fax 20562) Anthony Saru building
UK (☎ 21705, fax 21549) Telekom House

CUSTOMS
Visitors over 18 years may bring 2L of spirits and either 200 cigarettes, 250g of tobacco or 50 cigars into the country.

MONEY
Currency
The local currency is the Solomon Islands' dollar (S$); at the time of writing it seemed headed for another significant devaluation.

A supply of coins and small-denomination notes will come in handy in rural areas, at markets, and for bus and boat rides.

Exchange Rates
Approximate rates for the Solomon Islands' dollar are listed below:

country	unit		S$
Australia	A$1	=	S$4.88
euro zone	€1	=	S$8.46
Fiji	F$1	=	S$3.99
Japan	¥100	=	S$6.23
New Zealand	NZ$1	=	S$4.31
Pacific franc	100 CFP	=	S$7.07
PNG	K1	=	S$2.12
UK	£1	=	S$12.23
USA	US$1	=	S$7.35
Vanuatu	100VT	=	S$6.10

To check current exchange rates, see W www
.oanda.com.

Exchanging Money
The National Bank of the Solomon Islands
(NBSI), Westpac and ANZ will change
money in most major currencies. NBSI has a
network of branches and agencies around the
country; only the branches will change travellers cheques.

Travellers Cheques Stick to the name
brands: Visa, American Express and Thomas
Cook.

ATMs There's only one ATM in the country;
it's at the ANZ bank in Honiara.

Credit Cards The main tourist-oriented
businesses accept credit cards, but elsewhere
it's strictly cash. ANZ and Westpac give cash
advances on credit cards, NBSI does not.

Costs
It's possible to travel cheaply in the Solomons.
In the main towns you can get by on about
S$100 a day provided you take minibuses, stay
in budget accommodation and self-cater with
local fruit, vegetables, chicken and fish. An
accommodation and meal package in a village-
based lodge costs about the same, but of course
activities and transport will be extra. Small
cargo or passenger boats offer an inexpensive,
if unreliable, means of getting around.

Honiara, Gizo and Munda offer higher-
priced accommodation, restaurants and resorts.
Diving, tours and car hire will also push costs
up considerably.

Mid-range accommodation is available in
a few places, particularly Honiara, Auki and
Gizo. You can expect to pay from S$190 for
a fan-cooled room with private facilities in
Honiara, less on the outer islands. A typical
dinner in the country's better eateries costs
around S$40 for a main course.

There are several small dive resorts in the
Central and Western Provinces; the cheaper
places charge from S$350 per person for
accommodation and meal packages, with
transport and activities extra.

The country has three top-end hotels – two
in Honiara and one in Gizo. Expect to pay
from S$450 for a deluxe twin room at these
places.

Tipping & Bargaining
Tipping and bargaining are not part of
Melanesian culture and visitors are asked to
refrain from these practices. In the event that
a handicraft seems overpriced it is quite acceptable to ask for a 'second price'. Haggling
is considered rude.

Taxes
There's a 10% government tax on hotel and
restaurant prices, but more basic places often
don't charge it. All prices given in this book
are *inclusive* of tax.

POST & COMMUNICATIONS
Post
The only postal delivery is to post office
boxes or to poste restante.

Telephone
Solomon Telekom (☎ 21576) operates the
country's telephone system; a teleradio (radio
telephone) network connects isolated communities. Public phones are reasonably common
in most of the larger centres and phonecards
are widely available – Solomon Telekom is
the most reliable supplier.

The cheapest way to make an international
call is from a public phone with a phonecard.

The Solomons' international telephone
code is ☎ 677; there are no area codes.

Fax
Faxes can be sent internationally via Telekom offices for S$27 per page (minimum
two pages). Your hotel might do it cheaper.
Telekom will also receive faxes (S$4.15
per page), but they must be collected by the
customer.

Email & Internet Access
Telekom has public email facilities in Honiara, Gizo and Munda – these services are
to be extended to other centres. Honiara has
internet cafés. See Post & Communications
under Information in the Honiara section for
further information.

DIGITAL RESOURCES

The country's official website (**w** www
.commerce.gov.sb) has a number of useful links.
Most of the resorts and dive operators have
websites or at least an advertising presence on the web; SIVB has a new site at
w www.visitsolomons.com.sb.

BOOKS
Guidebooks & Travel

Dirk Seiling's self-published *Solomon Islands
Cruising Guide* is the definitive yachties
guide – contact Dirk at Dive Solomon Charters in Gizo.

The annual *Solomon Islands Trade Directory* has a lot of interesting background
information. It's published by **BJS Agencies**
(☎ 22393, fax 21017) in Honiara.

History & Politics

*The Search for the Islands of Solomon, 1567–
1838*, by Colin Jack-Hinton, records the history
of the European exploration of the Solomons.
Judith Bennett's *Wealth of the Solomons* is a
history of the archipelago from 1800 to 1978.

Passage, Port and Plantation by Peter
Corris recounts the blackbirding days. Hector
Hothouse's *White Headhunter – The Extraordinary True Story of a White Man's Life
among Headhunters of the Solomon Islands*
tells the story of Scotsman John Renton, who
lived in Malaita from 1868 to 1875.

*Lightning Meets the West Wind – The
Malaita Massacre*, by Roger Keesing &
Peter Corris, is the story of William Bell, a
district officer killed by Kwaio tribesmen in
1927. *The Maasina Rule Movement*, edited
by Hugh Laracy, is about a noncooperation
movement in Malaita after WWII.

WWII There are many books about the Guadalcanal campaign and coast-watch activities.
The Coast Watchers were a little-known force
of men who, operating from coastal vantage
points between New Guinea and Vanuatu, kept
the Allies informed about Japanese movements in the area. Their work was so effective that capture by the enemy meant instant
execution. Books on the subject include Eric
Felot's *The Coast Watchers*, H Macquarie's
Vouza and the Solomon Islands, Richard F
Newcomb's *Savo*, and *Guadalcanal Diary*,
by war correspondent Richard Tregaskis.

*The Big Death – Solomon Islanders Re-
member WWII*, by Geoffrey M White and
others, is a collection of stories told by islanders who took part in WWII.

James Jones' *The Thin Red Line* has been
made into a film. This grim WWII story is
fictional but set in Guadalcanal.

Arts & Crafts

*Grass Roots Art of the Solomons – Images
and Islands*, edited by John and Sue Chick,
is a good book on Solomons art.

NEWSPAPERS & MAGAZINES

The country's only newspaper is the daily
Solomons Star (S$2.50).

RADIO & TV

Local radio (SIBC) broadcasts programmes
in English and Pijin on MW (1035kHz) and
SW (5020kHz), with local and overseas features and news. The Australian Broadcasting
Corporation (ABC) is at 630kHz MW.

There's no local TV. Hotels with satellite
TV can pick up CNN, BBC World and Australian programmes.

PHOTOGRAPHY

The best times for photography are before
9.30am and after 4pm. If your camera is
automatic, it may overcompensate for the
Solomons' strong light, causing dark-skinned
faces to come out shadowy. Manual settings
are better for such pictures.

Most people are happy to be photographed
and won't expect money in return. Get permission before photographing *kastom* sites
(which may incur a fee).

Bring enough film for your entire trip.
Film prices are high and print film is only
available in a few towns; slide film is not
available *anywhere*.

TIME

Clocks are set to GMT plus 11 hours, one
hour ahead of Australia's Eastern Standard
Time. Local time is the same as in Vanuatu,
but one hour behind Fiji and New Zealand.
There is no daylight saving.

HEALTH

Malaria is the Solomons' major health risk.
Regardless of where you are, take care against
being bitten by mosquitoes, particularly
around dusk and dawn.

Unless you're reliably informed otherwise,
all drinking water should be regarded with
suspicion. Treat it either by boiling or by
adding purification tablets.

See the Health section in the Regional Facts
for the Visitor chapter for further information.

SOCIAL GRACES
Dos & Don'ts
Solomon Islanders are very tolerant of outsiders' unintentional errors, but they do expect their rules to be observed. If you accidentally breach a rule, apologies are usually sufficient. Land ownership and food growing are extremely delicate matters, however, so stick to the road when passing through a village. Don't pick fruit or flowers growing by the road – they belong to someone.

In remote areas people may wear few or no clothes. Despite this, foreigners exposing lots of skin can cause a negative reaction. Nude bathing and skimpy swimwear should be avoided, by both sexes. Women should keep their thighs covered at all times (wear a sarong or long shorts).

Men often hold hands with their male friends, and female friends do likewise. But local men will not touch women in public. It's OK for Western couples to do this, with restraint.

Tabu
Village life is beset with *tabu* (literally, taboo) and rural women's lives are particularly fraught with it. They may not stand higher than a male, nor can they step over a fire, as its smoke may rise higher than a man.

Men may not deliberately place themselves below women. So, walking under a woman's clothesline or swimming under her canoe is forbidden.

Villages have areas set aside for menstruating women and childbirth that are *tabu* for men. Women must enter confinement during their pregnancy and cannot cook or work in the garden.

Women are barred from going near men's *tabu* places, such as skull shrines; boys may only visit such sites once they're initiated.

Kastom Fees
Villagers charge *kastom* fees for access to some sites. Visiting a skull shrine or a cavern, onshore reef, thermal area, WWII site or deserted island may incur a *kastom* fee. Prices as high as S$50 may be asked, but S$10 is more common. Suggest what you're prepared to pay if the price is too high. Commissioning a local guide may help.

WOMEN TRAVELLERS
It's not usual for local young women to be out at night by themselves. Exercise normal caution in Honiara – after dark take a taxi and stay in busy areas. Female tourists swimming or sunbathing alone at isolated beaches might attract unwanted attention.

Foreign women travelling solo around remote villages are very rare. In villages male travellers are sometimes accommodated in structures that are *tabu* for women, so it might not be possible for couples to sleep together. There may be other areas that women are not allowed to see, and these should be respected.

It is *tabu* for females to show their thighs in public, so shorts should be knee-length and swimwear should be modest.

DANGERS & ANNOYANCES
Generally speaking, the Solomons is a very safe country to travel through, and violence or hostility towards expats or tourists is rare.

In 1999 and 2000 Honiara was the scene of bloody fighting between the Guadalcanal Islanders and Malaitans (see the boxed text 'Ethnic Tension' in the Honiara section for more information). In 2003 travel on Guadalcanal was not recommended outside Honiara, although the capital itself was quite safe. Seek advice from SIVB before venturing beyond the airport (11km east) and White River (4km west).

BUSINESS HOURS
Banking hours in Honiara are from 8.30am to 3pm Monday to Friday (ANZ and Westpac open at 9am). Government offices are open from 8am to noon and 1pm to 4pm Monday to Friday. Private businesses close half an hour later and operate on Saturday until noon.

Most shops in town open from 8.30am to 5pm Monday to Friday and until noon Saturday – some open longer, including on Sunday. Chinese shops often open at 7am and there are a few 24-hour stores.

PUBLIC HOLIDAYS & SPECIAL EVENTS
Independence Day is the Solomons' most important annual festival, with celebrations all around the country.

As well as New Year's Day, Easter, Whit Monday and Christmas, annual holidays in the Solomons include:

Queen's Birthday June
Independence Day 7 July
National Thanksgiving Day 26 December

ACTIVITIES

The Solomon Islands offers a range of outdoor activities, including bushwalking, kayaking, scuba diving, snorkelling, swimming, surfing, fishing, bird-watching and caving. There are also numerous archaeological and WWII sites to visit.

Golf, squash and tennis are played in Honiara and almost every village has a soccer field.

Snorkelling

Snorkelling in the Solomons is excellent. The warm, usually clear water of the lagoons and the countless colourful fish and corals make it a real treat. It's a good idea to bring your own gear, although most dive shops have rental equipment. Dive operators typically charge around A\$35 for snorkelling trips.

Diving

The Solomons is among the world's top diving destinations. The extensive coral and fish life alone are superb, but there are also hundreds of sunken WWII ships and aircraft. Many of these are accessible and, having been undisturbed for 60 years, have a wealth of objects *in situ*. (See the 'South Pacific Diving' special section.)

There are registered scuba operators in Honiara and the Western and Central Provinces. Due to the parlous state of the local currency they quote in Australian dollars – typical charges are A\$60 for one dive, A\$125 for a resort dive course and A\$450 for a PADI course. The dive operators rent all equipment.

Water temperatures in the Solomons are quite comfortable without a wet suit, but wear at least a T-shirt to protect your skin against grazes.

While underwater visibility is usually good to around 30m, it can be significantly less depending on conditions.

Scuba Trips In Honiara, **Bilikiki Cruises** (☎ 20412, fax 23897; W www.bilikiki.com) does extended scuba trips through the Russell and Florida Islands, and Marovo Lagoon. The charge per person is US\$445/592 a day for single/twin occupancy on the MV *Bilikiki*, and from US\$296/598 on the MV *Spirit of Solomons*. The company also has a **Canadian office** (☎ 250-383 7253, toll free US/Canada 1 800 663 5363).

Prearranged Dive Holidays Many divers pre-arrange their stay in the Solomons. Australian-based specialist companies offering package dive tours include **Always Dive Expeditions** (☎ 03-9885 8863, toll free 1 800 338 239) and **Dive Adventures** (☎ 02-9299 4633, 03-9646 5945, toll free 1 800 222 234).

Surfing

A number of places have good breaks, including Pailongge on Ghizo, Poro on Santa Isabel and Tawarogha on Makira; the Zipolo Habu Resort in the Western Province offers surf charters. Surfers should seek permission at the nearest village before entering the water.

Fishing

Most resorts and lodges can arrange fishing trips, and it's best if you bring your own gear. Sailfish, marlin, shark, tuna, kingfish, Spanish mackerel, barracuda and wahoo are common; several tour operators specialise in game and sport fishing. Always ask permission before casting off the shore into the sea or a river.

Hiking

The cooler mid-year months are most suitable for bushwalking. Most of the resorts and lodges offer walks of one description or another; the tour operators in Gizo and Munda can take you up the Western Province's dormant volcanoes. Climbing either Rendova or Kolombangara involves a two-day hike, but their summits offer magnificent views over Western Province.

ACCOMMODATION

Honiara, Gizo and Auki provide a range of options; elsewhere most of the tourist accommodation comprises small, traditional-style lodges. Booking your accommodation ahead will enable your host to meet you at the airfield or port – useful where there's no public transport.

Camping

Bush camping flies in the face of traditional Melanesian hospitality, and villagers may not be pleased if you insist on sleeping in a tent. A chief may give permission if you want to camp on a lonely beach or unpopulated island.

Village Stays

Most villages have a leaf house set aside for visitors' use. The charge is usually nominal. If there isn't a leaf house, you may be able to bed down in the local school or clinic.

Villages rarely have electricity and the water supply often comes from a stream or communal tap. The toilet is a hole in the ground, or a reserved place in the bush or over the reef. Bring enough food to share around – tinned meat or tuna, tea, coffee and sugar are useful.

Village stays can be pre-arranged with locals who have an idea of what tourists want and expect. Visiting on this basis is highly recommended – it is a wonderful experience for the traveller and it puts money into local communities.

The World Heritage Committee and the WWF have helped villagers set up several 'village-based' lodges around Marovo Lagoon (see Marovo Lagoon in the Western Province section of this chapter).

Contact the SIVB in Honiara if you want to stay in a village or a lodge. Staff can make suggestions and organise bookings.

Resthouses & Hostels

These comprise church hostels, provincial government resthouses and private resthouses. Most have ceiling fans, shared washing facilities and a communal kitchen. They generally charge around S$50 per person per night. Most of your fellow guests will be islanders. Alcohol and smoking are often forbidden.

Hotels & Resorts

Tourist-class hotels are confined to Honiara, Gizo, Munda and Auki. Although basic by international standards, they generally have rooms with or without private shower and air-con, depending on how much you're prepared to pay. A telephone, TV and tea-and-coffee-making facilities may be provided. Most have restaurants and bars.

Resorts are found away from towns, usually in idyllic locations on islands. Their accommodation is often in leaf huts – basic but picturesque.

FOOD

Only a few towns have restaurants, and imported foods are expensive. If self-catering, the best idea is to visit the local market where villagers gather on a daily basis to sell their produce. Prices here are very reasonable – S$2 for a hand of bananas and S$4 for an average-sized pineapple.

Chewing betel nut gives a mild high and is a popular pastime. It produces mouthfuls of bright orange saliva, which explains the splashes of what looks like orange paint everywhere. Tiny stalls selling betel nut line Honiara's main street.

DRINKS
Nonalcoholic Drinks

Coconut milk is a good substitute for untreated water. The Solomons Brewery produces bottled soft drinks.

Alcoholic Drinks

The Solomons produces its own beers – a German-style lager called Solbrew is most popular. Australian beers are also available.

The only bars in the Solomon Islands are those attached to clubs and hotels. Most of the country's more upmarket restaurants are licensed to sell alcohol.

ENTERTAINMENT

There is little worthwhile entertainment in Honiara and even less elsewhere. Pack some good books and your favourite indoor games.

SHOPPING

The only specialised handicraft shops are in Honiara and Gizo. Crafts (see Arts in the Facts about the Solomon Islands section earlier) can often be purchased directly from the makers.

Getting There & Away

AIR
Airports

The Solomons' only international airport is Henderson airport (air code HIR), 11km east of Honiara.

There are few direct flights to the Solomons. Only eastern Australia and a couple of South Pacific neighbours offer direct connections, and flights from there are expensive. See Air Passes in the regional Getting There & Away chapter earlier for information on combining the Solomons with other Pacific destinations.

Departure Tax

An airport tax of S$40 is charged on international flights leaving Honiara.

North America

Air Promotions Inc (see North America under Air in the Getting There & Away chapter) is the US agent for Pacific-based airlines, including Solomon Airlines. The best route between the USA and the Solomons is via Fiji using a regional air pass (see the Fiji chapter and Air Passes in the Getting There & Away chapter).

Europe

See the regional Getting There & Away chapter for details about reaching the Pacific from Europe.

The cheapest return fares are via Australia. A charter flight from London to Melbourne, Sydney or Brisbane could cost as little as £500 return, but there may be lots of restrictions. Scheduled flights start at around £600 in the low season.

Travelling west via the USA and Fiji is also a possibility. London–Los Angeles flights cost about £300 return, then you can pick up Air Pacific's flight to Nadi.

A round-the-world (RTW) airline ticket may work out cheaper than a return ticket. In the low season, a RTW fare including Brisbane could cost under £700, onto which you could add Honiara as a side trip.

Solomon Airlines has an office in Kent, England (☎ 019-5954 0737) that sells Air Pacific tickets.

Australasia

Solomon Airlines (ⓦ www.solomonairlines .com.au) flies direct from Brisbane to Honiara every Tuesday and Thursday, with the return flight leaving the following day. The average economy fare is A$950/1220 one way/return. Solomon Airlines' offices are in Brisbane (☎ 07-3407 7266), Sydney (☎ 02-9244 2189) and Melbourne (☎ 03-9920 3872).

Flights between Honiara and Auckland go via Brisbane. Typical fares between Auckland and Brisbane are NZ$420/770 one way/return with Qantas or Air New Zealand.

Asia

The most direct route to/from Asia is via Port Moresby in PNG, though, depending on your starting point, connections may be more frequent and cheaper going via Brisbane. Garuda connects Indonesia to Australia's east coast (Brisbane, Sydney or Melbourne). The low season, one-way fare to Sydney is A$765 from Jakarta and A$646 from Denpasar, with a free stopover allowed.

Qantas can get you from eastern Australia to Singapore during the low season for A$839/1129 one way/return; it sometimes has cheaper one-off deals.

For tickets purchased in Honiara, Solomon Airlines charges S$4766 to Manila, S$6387 to Hong Kong, S$5939 to Singapore and S$5578

to Seoul and four Japanese airports, including Tokyo. These destinations involve connecting flights with other airlines and all flights are routed via Brisbane.

The Pacific

Solomon Airlines has offices in Nadi, Fiji (☎ 722 831) and Port Moresby, PNG (☎ 325 5724). It also has sales agents in Suva, Fiji (☎ 315 889); Noumea, New Caledonia (☎ 286 677); and Port Vila, Vanuatu (☎ 23838).

Fiji Air Vanuatu and Solomon Airlines share a service on Thursday between Honiara and Nadi, routed via Port Vila. The one-way/ return fare is F$969/1939.

Papua New Guinea Air Niugini flies from Port Moresby to Honiara on Monday and Friday. The economy fare is K1360/1860 one way/return.

Vanuatu Services to Honiara from Fiji are routed through Vanuatu's capital, Port Vila. From there to Honiara costs 43,500VT (46,450VT return).

SEA
Cruise Ship

Honiara is occasionally visited by cruise ships; check with your travel agent for details.

Yacht

The Solomons is a favourite destination for yachties, with many taking refuge in the country's lagoons during cyclone season. Along with Honiara, Korovou (Shortland Islands), Gizo, Ringgi, Yandina, Tulagi Island and Graciosa Bay are official ports of entry into the country.

In Honiara, yacht owners leave 'crew wanted' notices at the **Point Cruz Yacht Club** (☎ 22500) behind the SIVB. See the Yacht section in the Getting Around the Region chapter for more pointers about travelling the Pacific by yacht. Also see the *Solomon Islands Cruising Guide* under Books in the earlier Facts for the Visitor section of this chapter.

Customs, Immigration & Fees Yachts should clear customs and immigration at an official port of entry. Officials will want to know your planned port of departure from the country. There's a S$100 fee (plus 10c a tonne) for yachts sailing in Solomons' waters.

Getting Around

Getting around the Solomons can be a challenge if time is important. Flights often leave earlier or later than scheduled, while boat and truck services are notoriously casual. Make a generous time allowance for unexpected delays in getting back if you venture away from the main towns.

AIR

The only domestic flier is Solomon Airlines, which services over 20 airfields around the country with its small fleet of Twin Otters. The baggage allowance is the standard 20kg per person.

Try to keep abreast of daily changes in scheduled departures (rural airport terminals can be reached either by radio or telephone) and make sure to confirm your onward ticket at least 72 hours before the scheduled time of departure – otherwise it may be given to someone else.

Try to get a window seat as the lagoons and islands look fantastic from the air.

BUS

Public minibuses are only found in Honiara. The flat S$2 fare will take you anywhere on the route, which is written on a placard behind the windscreen of the bus. Elsewhere, people pile into open-backed trucks or tractor-drawn trailers.

CAR & MOTORCYCLE

The country has around 1300km of public roads, most of which are generally in dreadful condition – travelling around in wet weather can be a real experience, even in the towns. International driving permits are accepted, as are most driving licences. People drive on the left-hand side.

Rental cars are only available in Honiara.

BICYCLE

Bikes are a popular form of transport and parts of the Solomons are very suitable for mountain biking. Dive Solomon Charters in Gizo and Go West Tours in Munda rent bikes (see the Gizo and Munda sections later for more information).

HITCHING

If you want a ride through the countryside, flag down a passing vehicle and ask the driver the cost of a lift. Many will give you a free ride, while others charge a small fee. In rural areas most vehicles double as public transport.

BOAT

The mostly small cargo and passenger boats that connect the various islands tend to be slow and prone to delays – the passenger services are generally the most reliable. Details of shipping movements are posted in company offices at main ports and announced over the radio.

Wharves are uncommon and motor-canoes are generally used to ferry cargo and people to shore.

Inter-Island Ships

Most shipping companies have offices near Honiara's main wharf.

For longer trips hire a cabin if you can, preferably one on the upper deck. No-one will enter your cabin uninvited, but an open door at night is an invitation for others to sleep on the floor. Cabins have mattresses, but you'll need a sleeping sheet and mat if you're going deck class.

There's usually drinking water and a kitchen with water on the boil. You'll need cutlery, a cup, a plate and a cooking pot. Bring a fishing line and enough food for the entire trip. If you have too much, give some away. The crew trail lines astern and when a large fish is caught everyone gets some.

Malaita Shipping (☎ 23501, fax 23503) services Malaita, **Wings Shipping** (☎ 22811) services the Western Province and Malaita, **Trans West Shipping** (☎ 60240 in Gizo, fax 60421) goes to the Western Province and Choiseul, and the **Isabel Development Company** (☎ 22126, fax 22009) goes to Santa Isabel.

Motor-Canoes

Motor-canoes (fibreglass or aluminium-hulled work boats fitted with an outboard motor) are the most common means of transport on the water. These little boats supply goods to stores all over the Solomons and locals pay a fare to travel aboard. There's a dry area in the bow for cargo, but everything else gets wet.

Safety is a consideration, especially outside the lagoons in foul weather – Solomon Islanders are skilled mariners, but they can be casual about safety. Flares, life jackets and fire extinguishers are conspicuously absent – don't get into a motor-canoe that doesn't at least have a paddle.

Canoe charters cost up to S$500 per day shared. This will include the canoe and driver, but probably not fuel (S$5 a litre in remote areas).

TAXI
Taxis are plentiful in Honiara and there are small fleets in Gizo and Auki. They don't have meters, so agree on the price before you set off.

ORGANISED TOURS
Tour operators usually have a set programme of excursions, but it's often possible to arrange a tailor-made tour based on your own special interests. From Honiara, tours of WWII battlefields are popular. In the Western Province operators combine diving with land-based attractions.

Guadalcanal

pop 100,000 • area 5302 sq km
Guadalcanal is the largest island in the Solomons group and has the national capital, Honiara.

Honiara began life as the huge US supply depot that was developed between Kukum and Point Cruz in 1943. Since then the capital has spread inland over nearby ridges, many of which were WWII battlefields.

HONIARA
pop 40,000
Honiara is the unprepossessing centre of government and commerce, and is the hub for tourism. Dive and charter boats are based here and there are hotels, restaurants, cafés, bars, markets and handicraft shops. However, travel outside Honiara is restricted (see the boxed text 'Ethnic Tension') and there is little of interest in the town itself. Many visitors find it preferable to spend less time here and more on the outer islands.

Orientation
The central area from the Solomon Kitano Mendana Hotel (usually shortened to Mendana Hotel) to Chinatown can be covered in a 30-minute stroll along Mendana Ave, the town's main strip. In this area are the central market, the port complex, shops, embassies, banks, hotels and restaurants. The 11km urban sprawl along the coast has the settlements of Rove and White River to the west, while eastwards are Chinatown and

Ethnic Tension

For many years the Gwale people of Guadalcanal had resented the fact that their traditional land was being gobbled up by outsiders attracted to the economic opportunities in Honiara. Much of their resentment was directed at recent migrants from Malaita. Not only were the Malaitans seen as the main land stealers, they seemed to get all the good jobs as well.

Finally the resentment and jealousy boiled over. Early in 1999 a group of young Gwalese formed the Guadalcanal Revolutionary Army (GRA). They began to terrorise rural Malaitans, thousands of whom were forced to flee to the capital or back to their home island. The Malaitan Eagle Force (MEF) was formed to protect the interests of Malaitans.

The Honiara Peace Accord was brokered in July, but this soon fell apart and fighting resumed. The MEF gained the upper hand in weaponry and eventually took control of the capital, which effectively became a Malaitan enclave. Hundreds of people were killed during the hostilities. The MEF ousted the prime minister in June 2000, and soon after a cabinet minister was assassinated by the GRA (now called the Isatabu Freedom Fighters).

Following mediation by Australia and New Zealand, the Townsville Peace Agreement was signed in October 2000. A general amnesty was declared and many (but by no means all) heavy weapons were handed in. Since then the agreement has generally been adhered to and conflict has ceased. However, in 2003 the presence of armed gangs in rural Guadalcanal made travel inadvisable outside Honiara.

Mataniko Village. Beyond them are Kukum and industrial Ranadi.

Information
Tourist Offices The Solomon Islands Visitors Bureau (SIVB; ☎ 22442, fax 23986; Mendana Ave; e info@sivb.com.sb) is beside the Mendana Hotel. It opens normal business hours and Saturday morning. There is little printed material, but the friendly staff can provide all local travel advice. SIVB can radio isolated lodges and villages to make bookings.

Money The NBSI, ANZ and Westpac banks have branches on Mendana Ave, and there's an NBSI branch in Chinatown.

SOLOMON ISLANDS

HONIARA

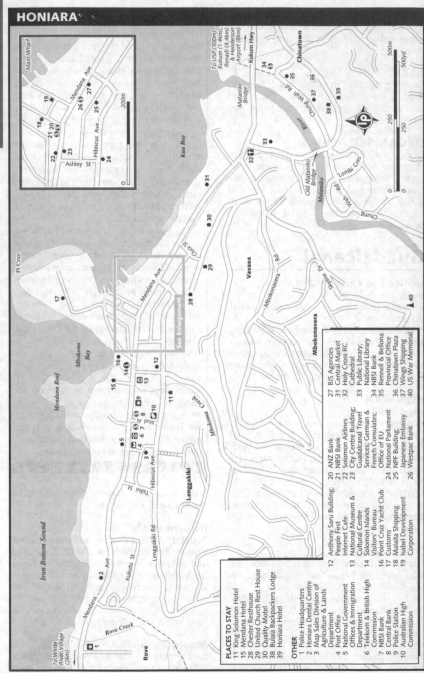

PLACES TO STAY
11 King Solomon Hotel
15 Mendana Hotel
28 Chester Resthouse
29 United Church Rest House
30 Quality Motel
38 Bulaia Backpackers Lodge
39 Honiara Hotel

OTHER
1 Police Headquarters
2 Honiara Dental Centre
3 Map Sales Division of
   Agriculture & Lands
   Department
4 Post Office
5 National Government
   Offices & Immigration
   Department
6 Telekom & British High
   Commission
7 NBSI Bank
8 Central Bank
9 Police Station
10 Australian High
   Commission

12 Anthony Saru Building;
   People First
   Internet Cafe
13 National Museum &
   Cultural Centre
14 Solomon Islands
   Visitors' Bureau
16 Point Cruz Yacht Club
17 Customs
18 Malaita Shipping
19 Isabel Development
   Corporation

20 ANZ Bank
21 NBSI Bank
22 Solomon Airlines
23 City Centre Building;
   Guadalcanal Travel
   Services; German &
   French Consulates;
   Office of EU
24 National Parliament
25 NPF Building;
   Japanese Embassy
26 Westpac Bank

27 BJS Agencies
31 Central Market
32 Holy Cross RC
   Cathedral
33 Public Library;
   National Library
34 NBSI Bank
35 Rennell & Bellona
   Provincial Office
36 Chinatown Plaza
37 Wings Shipping
40 US War Memorial

Post & Communications The main post office, on Mendana Ave, opens normal business hours and Saturday morning. A few steps away, Solomon Telekom has public email access (S$0.60 per minute), fax and telex services, as well as card and coin telephones. It opens similar hours.

The **People First Internet Café** (☎ 26358) in the Anthony Saru Building is open normal business hours. It charges S$13.50 per hour and there's a minimum fee of S$5.

Travel Agencies The country has one international travel agency. **Guadalcanal Travel Services** (GTS; ☎ 22587, fax 26184; e gts@solomon.com.sb; Mendana Ave), in the City Centre Building, offers hotel and flight bookings, plus tours and itineraries.

Libraries & Reading Rooms The public library, near Mataniko Bridge, is open daily except Wednesday. Behind it, the **National Library** (☎ 27412) has a large Pacific reference section, including many out-of-print titles on the Solomons. The University of the South Pacific's (USP) library has material from all over Oceania.

The embassies and high commissions in Honiara have reference materials on the Solomons as well as foreign newspapers.

Medical Services The **Central Hospital** (☎ 23600) is in Kukum. The **Honiara Dental Centre** (☎ 22746) is on Mendana Ave and the **Bartimaeus Vision Care Centre** (☎ 24040) is on Chinatown Ave.

Emergency The emergency numbers are: **ambulance** (☎ 911), **fire** (☎ 988 Honiara only) and **police** (☎ 999).

Dangers & Annoyances Honiara is where you're most likely to encounter crime in the Solomons. However, it's not a dangerous place and travellers needn't take any more precautions here than they would in any other city. Seek advice before travelling around Guadalcanal outside Honiara (see the earlier boxed text 'Ethnic Tension').

Raw sewage is pumped into the sea off Honiara and swimming is not recommended.

Things to See
The circular-shaped **National Parliament**, on the hill above Ashley St, opened in 1993. There's a public gallery and the sergeant-at-arms will give you a free tour.

In the town centre, the **National Museum & Cultural Centre** (☎ 22098; Mendana Ave; admission S$2; open 8am-4.30pm Mon-Fri, 8am-noon Sat) houses displays on dance, body ornamentation, currency, weaponry and archaeology. Behind it are eight traditionally constructed houses, each from a different province.

The **Central Bank** (☎ 21791; Mendana Ave) displays woodcarvings from Rennell and Makira, and traditional currencies, including Santa Cruz red-feather money, Malaitan dolphin-teeth and shell money, *mbarava* (white clam-shell carvings) from New Georgia, and Choiseul clam-shell money.

Skyline Drive provides commanding views over the town. The impressive **US War Memorial** is a hot 20-minute walk up from Mendana Ave.

Chinatown's main street, **Chung Wah Rd**, is one of Honiara's most interesting sights – it's lined by small stores and has a Wild West flavour.

Organised Tours
Battlefield tours around Honiara can be arranged through SIVB and GTS. The tours take about three hours and cost S$120 per person.

Lalae Charters (☎ 38888; e info@lalae.com.sb) offers game and reef fishing and general charters. The boat is usually moored at the Point Cruz Yacht Club.

Places to Stay – Budget
There are a number of budget accommodation options, but only those located close to the town centre are listed. All have communal kitchens, fan-cooled twin rooms and share facilities.

Bulaia Backpackers Lodge (☎ 28819; Chinatown; twins S$120) is of a very good standard. There's also a mini-mart on the premises.

United Church Resthouse (☎ 20028; Lower Vayvaya Rd; bed per person S$50) has a good view from the terrace. Alcohol and smoking are not permitted.

Chester Resthouse (☎ 26355, fax 23079; Lower Vayvaya Rd; twins S$100) is a five-minute walk from the centre of town. A laundering service is available; alcohol and smoking are not permitted here.

Places to Stay – Mid-Range
There are only a couple of mid-range places close to the town centre.

SOLOMON ISLANDS

Quality Motel (☎ 25150, fax 25277; e qml@ solomon.com.sb; Lower Vayvaya Rd; twins from S$190) overlooks Iron Bottom Sound. All of the motels rooms are self-contained and some also have air-conditioning, TV and telephone.

Honiara Hotel (☎ 21737, fax 20376; e hon hotel@solomon.com.sb; Chinatown; fan-cooled twins with share facilities S$220, air-con self-contained twins S$320) has a swimming pool, bar and restaurant. It's a few steps from Chinatown's colourful main street.

Places to Stay – Top End
Solomon Kitano Mendana Hotel (☎ 20071, fax 23942; e kitano@mendana.com.sb; Mendana Ave; singles/twins from S$484/528) is on the waterfront and has the best restaurant in town. It's usually referred to as the Mendana Hotel.

King Solomon Hotel (☎ 21205, fax 21771; e kingsol@solomon.com.sb; Hibiscus Ave; doubles from S$431) has TV and air-con in all rooms.

Entertainment
The Point Cruz Yacht Club (☎ 22500), next to the Mendana Hotel, has happy hour on Friday evening. Frequented by expats, yachties and well-heeled islanders, it's a pleasant place to enjoy a local beer and the sea breeze.

The bars at Honiara's two top-end hotels are always popular.

Shopping
There are several craft shops on Mendana Ave. Carvers sell their wares outside the Mendana Hotel, and the shop in the National Museum has some good artefacts.

Getting There & Away
Air Nearly all flights to the provinces originate at Henderson airport. See the main Getting There & Away section earlier for details about international flights. GTS is the agent for Air Niugini, Air Pacific and Qantas. The Solomon Airlines (☎ 20031) head office is on Mendana Ave in the centre of town.

Boat Shipping operators are listed in the Getting Around section and routes are covered in the regional sections. The best place to find motor-canoes travelling to neighbouring islands is beside the Point Cruz Yacht Club.

Getting Around
To/From the Airport The standard taxi fare into town is S$50. Major hotels do airport transfers for around S$25 per person.

Minibus Honiara's minibuses are cheap, frequent (in daylight hours) and an interesting way to rub shoulders with the locals. The flat-rate fare around town is S$2.

Car Renting a car is expensive. Economy Car Rentals (☎ 27100, fax 23593; e solmot@ solomon.com.sb; Mendana Ave) has cars from S$228 per day including insurance and kilometres. The office is next door to the SIVB.

Taxi There are taxis everywhere in Honiara. They don't have meters, so agree on a fare before hopping in – S$4 per kilometre is reasonable.

EAST OF HONIARA
Mataniko Falls
The waterfall thunders down a cliff straight into a cave; this cavern and others nearby were hide-outs for Japanese soldiers. It's a two-hour walk from Honiara. At Tuvaruhu, cross the river and follow it south. Find a guide after Tuvaruhu and expect to pay kastom fees.

Mt Austen Road
At Mt Austen you'll find a vandalised Japanese war memorial and an expansive view over Iron Bottom Sound towards Savo and the Florida Islands.

Betikama
About 6km from Honiara is the turn-off south to the Betikama SDA Mission, about 1.5km away. There's a large carving shop with a collection of WWII debris, and a saltwater crocodile in a pen behind the shop.

Henderson Airport
A memorial at the airport honours US forces and their Pacific Islander allies. About 100m to the west of the terminal is the US WWII control tower.

WEST OF HONIARA
Travel is not recommended beyond White River, a Gilbertese village about 4km west of the town centre. Law and order is a problem beyond here (see the Dangers & Annoyances section earlier for further information).

SOLOMON ISLANDS

Central Province

Central Province is made up of the Nggela (or Florida) group, Savo and the Russell Islands. There are dive operators and resorts in the Nggelas and the Russells.

NGGELA ISLANDS
pop 10,500 • area 391 sq km
Widely known as the Florida Islands, the rugged silhouette of the Nggela group is clearly visible on the northern horizon from Honiara.

Getting There & Away There are no operational airfields in the Nggelas. Motor-canoes link Tulaghi and Maravagi with Honiara. Small cargo boats ply between Tulagi and the capital, charging about S$50 one way.

Mana
This small island is near the northern end of the Nggela group. Canoe transfers per person are S$90 from Honiara and S$45 from Tulaghi.

Dive Maravagi (*☎/fax 29065; e scuba crew@yahoo.com.au*), based at the Maravagi Resort, offers shore and boat dives on WWII wrecks, coral gardens and a variety of underwater topography.

Maravagi Resort (*☎ 29065; full board per person S$300*) boasts an idyllic setting among large shady trees beside a sheltered cove; it's a relaxing place and a popular retreat for Honiara's expats. The resort has leaf-style rooms with ceiling fans, and a shower and toilet.

There's safe swimming and snorkelling right by the resort, which can arrange village tours and demonstrations of traditional women's dancing.

Tulaghi
Roughly central in the Nggela group, this small island is where Tulagi (the former capital) is located. It was a Japanese base during WWII. Today, Tulaghi has provincial government offices, a post office, NBSI branch, library, hospital and Telekom office.

There are numerous relics of WWII and the colonial era to explore. A two-hour walk takes you around the island.

Based at Vanita Accommodation, **Dive Tulagi** (*☎ 32052, fax 32131; e tulagidive@ solomon.com.sb*) caters for the serious wreck diver. Major attractions include the destroyer USS *Aaron Ward*, the oil tanker USS *Kanawha* and the corvette HMNZS *Moa*. All were sunk during the battle for Guadalcanal.

Vanita Accommodation (*☎ 32074, fax 32 186; twins S$120*) has eight twin-bed rooms, a bar and restaurant. The standard is very basic.

Offshore Islands
The Japanese made a last-ditch stand at **Ghavutu** and its tiny neighbour **Tanambogo**, to which it is joined by a narrow causeway. Once US forces began using Ghavutu as a seaplane base, the Japanese bombed it repeatedly. Wrecked US warplanes litter the wharf.

SAVO
pop 2300 • area 31 sq km
Savo, which is about halfway between the Russells and the Nggela group, is clearly visible to the northwest from Honiara. This rugged island has some spectacular hot springs, mud pools and geysers. SIVB can arrange a tour to see the thermal activity and the megapode birds that lay their eggs in the hot sand.

Megapodes
Known in Pijin as *skrab dak* or *scrab faol*, megapodes are chicken-sized birds that are widespread in the Solomons and Vanuatu. Megapodes usually build large mounds of dirt and leaves in which the eggs are incubated by the heat from the sun and rotting vegetation. In volcanic areas such as Savo, however, the birds just lay their eggs in holes scratched into the hot sand.

After eight or nine weeks the young hatch, fully developed. They peck their way out of their shells and scratch up to the surface through the soft sand. They can run immediately and fly shortly after.

Megapode eggs are considered a delicacy by islanders, and Savo's megapode-breeding area is divided into family plots. Care is taken not to over-harvest the eggs – there is a closed season each year when eggs may not be taken.

RUSSELL ISLANDS
pop 5000 • area 210 sq km

The mainly small islands of the Russell group are a spectacular sight as you fly over them en route from Honiara to the Western Province. Beef and copra-producers Russell Islands Plantation Estates Ltd (RIPEL) own much of the Russell Islands.

Live-aboard dive boats such as the MV *Bilikiki* do trips around the Russell Islands. The area has submarine caverns, prolific reef growth and many sunken war wrecks. The two inlets either side of Lever Point are excellent dive sites, with a vast number of war relics lying in 24m of water.

Mbanika
Separating Mbanika from Pavuvu (the two largest islands) is the deep Sunlight Channel. Yandina, on Mbanika's east coast, is the Russell Islands' subprovincial headquarters and RIPEL's company town.

The **dive resort** near Yandina was closed at the time of writing, but was expected to reopen soon. Accommodation is in air-con rooms with private facilities, and there's a bar. SIVB can provide contact details.

Solomon Airlines flies to Yandina twice a week from Honiara (S$205). Yandina is the first stop from Honiara for Gizo-bound boats.

Western Province

Pristine lagoons, tropical islets, spectacular diving and snorkelling, and skull shrines are just part of what makes the New Georgia region of the Western Province an essential place to visit on your trip. The many lagoons look exquisite from the air: the lush, forested islands, white-sand bars and beaches, turquoise coral shallows and inky-blue seas come together in a breathtaking vista as you fly overhead.

Gizo, Munda and Marovo Lagoon make up the backbone of the country's tourist industry. The province has a range of accommodation options (the resorts on Lola and Uepi offer an excellent standard) and is relatively well serviced by air and sea transport. Travelling here is not nearly the challenge that it is elsewhere.

Getting There & Away
Air Daily flights link the province's main airports to Honiara.

Boat Weekly return journeys from Honiara to Gizo are run by both **Trans West Shipping** (☎ 60240 in Gizo) and **Wings Shipping** (☎ 22811). Ports visited are Mbili Passage, Marovo Lagoon, Viru Harbour, Rendova, Munda and Ringgi. The trip takes 28 hours or more.

GHIZO
pop 6000 • area 37 sq km

Diving and snorkelling enthusiasts will be inspired by some of the underwater attractions on offer in this area. Its war wrecks and coral gardens provide some of the Solomons' best dive sites.

Gizo
pop 4500

Gizo was a Japanese seaplane base during WWII. Sprawled along the waterfront with steep hills behind, it is an interesting place and full of character. The initial impression is of a frontier town that has seen its heyday and is now quietly rusting away under the tropical sun.

There are ANZ and NBSI bank branches (you can get a cash advance on your credit card at the ANZ) as well as a hospital, police station, immigration and customs offices, and a busy central market. There are plenty of accommodation options and a variety of activities and excursions are offered by tour operators.

Organised Tours Friendly Danny and Kerrie Kennedy run **Dive Gizo** (☎ 60253, fax 60297; w www.divegizo.com; Middenway Rd) at the western end of town. They've been in business here since 1985, so they really know their way around.

Dive Solomon Charters (☎ 60324, fax 60137; w www.solomoncharters.com; Middenway Rd) is in the Gizo Hotel, and specialises in fishing.

Both companies can arrange sport-fishing charters and bushwalks, including a two-day climb of the dormant volcano located on Kolombangara.

Places to Stay – Budget There are a number of good, clean, friendly, budget options in Gizo. Unless otherwise stated, all have share facilities, ceiling fans and a communal kitchen.

Paradise Lodge (☎ 60024, fax 60200; e plodge@solomon.com.sb; twins with/without private facilities S$145/90) has a

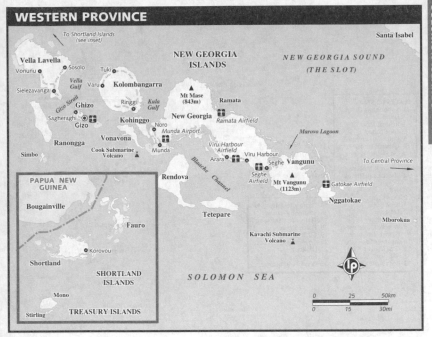

WESTERN PROVINCE

self-catering and full-board option. There's a bar on the premises and the ocean view is inspiring. It's a 15-minute walk to the town centre, or the owner will drive you down.

Naqua Resthouse (☎ 60012, fax 60278; *standard rooms per person S$50, self-contained air-con singles/doubles S$150*) is very comfortable. Its dining and lounge area is spacious and there are good views.

Phoebe's Resthouse (☎ 60336, fax 60035; *per person S$45*) is nearby and has nice views.

Gelvinas Motel (☎ 60276, fax 60323; *Middenway Rd; twins S$150*) is very central to the action – what there is of it! The rooms are all self-contained and quite comfortable, but there are no cooking facilities. Each room has a small balcony.

Kopik Guesthouse (☎ 60374, fax 60128; *Middenway Rd; per person S$50*) is also central. It is an older place, but it's clean and friendly.

Rekona Moa Moa Lodge (☎ 60368, fax 60021; *standard rooms per person S$50, self-contained singles/doubles S$66/110*) is spick and span throughout.

Koburutavia Divers Lodge (☎ 60257; *Middenway Rd; twins S$88*) is popular with divers; bookings can be made through Dive Gizo. The PT 109 Restaurant out the back is a good eatery.

Places to Stay – Top End Gizo has just the one top-end hotel.

Gizo Hotel (☎ 60199, fax 60137; e gizohtl@ solomon.com.sb; *Middenway Rd; budget rooms per person S$100; standard twins S$300, deluxe air-con twins from S$400*) has a good standard and one of the town's best restaurants. Its standard rooms, which sleep three people, have cooking facilities.

Shopping Carvers display their work at the Gizo Hotel. Another place to check is Dive Gizo, which has a good crafts shop.

Getting There & Away You can get to Gizo by plane or boat.

Air Gizo's airfield is on Nusatupe Island. A motor-canoe ride between the airfield and town costs S$20.

From Gizo, Solomon Airlines flies daily to Honiara (S$495), calling at Munda (S$193) and Seghe (S$240). Other flights go to Choiseul (S$280), Ballalae (S$280) and Ramata

SOLOMON ISLANDS

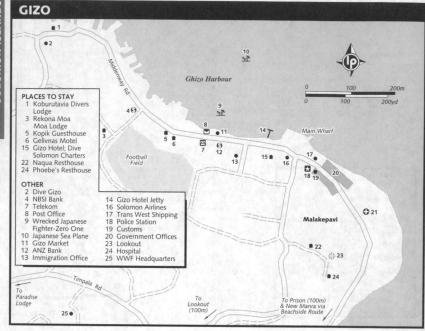

GIZO

Ghizo Harbour

Middenway Rd

0   100   200m
0   100   200yd

PLACES TO STAY
1 Koburutavia Divers Lodge
3 Rekona Moa Moa Lodge
5 Kopik Guesthouse
6 Gelivnas Motel
15 Gizo Hotel; Dive Solomon Charters
22 Naqua Resthouse
24 Phoebe's Resthouse

OTHER
2 Dive Gizo
4 NBSI Bank
7 Telekom
8 Post Office
9 Wrecked Japanese Fighter-Zero One
10 Japanese Sea Plane
11 Gizo Market
12 ANZ Bank
13 Immigration Office
14 Gizo Hotel Jetty
16 Solomon Airlines
17 Trans West Shipping
18 Police Station
19 Customs
20 Government Offices
23 Lookout
24 Hospital
25 WWF Headquarters

Football Field

Main Wharf

Malakepavi

Timpala Rd

To Paradise Lodge

To Lookout (100m)

To Prison (100m) & New Manra via Beachside Route

(S$195); the more remote strips, such as Gatokae, are serviced weekly.

Boat Trans West and Wings travel between Honiara and Gizo twice a week. Trans West charges S$153/207/623 for economy/1st class/cabin. Gizo's daily market generates regular motor-canoe traffic between the neighbouring islands.

Around the Island
Pailongge, 6km from Gizo, is a neat village with good surf breaks. **Saeraghi**, 11km from Gizo, has one of the Solomons' most beautiful beaches. It's about 500m before the village.

Nusatupe This island is just big enough for the airstrip. The World Fish Centre's **clam farm and research centre** (☎ 60022) is also here – for S$40 staff will show you around. Snorkelling over the giant clams in the ocean is fantastic – some are as big as armchairs.

Kennedy Island Seven kilometres southeast of Gizo, Kennedy Island is where John F Kennedy and 10 shipmates swam ashore after their PT-109 patrol boat was sunk by the Japanese destroyer *Amagiri* in August 1943.

Dive Gizo does BBQs for S$35 on this and nearby islands.

ISLANDS AROUND GHIZO
Kolombangara
Also known as Nduke, Kolombangara features a classic cone-shaped **volcano** that rises to 1770m. **Vila Point** was an important WWII Japanese base and you can still see guns in the bush.

The **KFPL Guest House** (☎ 60230) at Ringgi caters mainly for forestry workers. Most rooms have private facilities.

Simbo
This island has two active volcanic cones in the south. A **skull site** at Pa Na Ghundu contains 12 coral-stone reliquaries containing skulls and clam-shell money. Others are found at Pa Na Ulu and Gurava. Righuru has two **petroglyph sites**, and there's another at Vareviri Point.

Both the tour operators in Gizo do day trips to Simbo.

Ranongga
Ranongga's high west coast falls into deep water, while the east coast is lower, with terraces

and onshore reefs. For visitors, butterflies and birds are the main attractions.

Vella Lavella

This mountainous island is dominated by the dormant volcano Mt Tambisala – it is 790m high, yet its crater floor is close to sea level. There are **megapodes** in the Ulo River area, where there's a large **thermal area**, and parrots and butterflies are everywhere. Snakes and crocodiles are also plentiful.

In 1965 a WWII Japanese soldier was found still hiding in the bush, and there are said to have been other sightings since, including one in 1989.

Getting There & Away Vella Lavella has two airfields. Barakoma has weekly connections to Gizo (S$190) and Choiseul Bay (S$225). Geva is serviced weekly from Gizo (S$200).

Cargo boats and motor-canoes ply between Gizo and Vella Lavella, but boat services are irregular.

NEW GEORGIA ISLAND

pop 19,000 • area 2145 sq km

The area around New Georgia includes the islands of Vonavona, Kohinggo, Rendova and Tetepare. Munda, on New Georgia itself, makes a suitable base for exploring this part of the province.

Munda

New Georgia's largest settlement is a collection of villages strung 6km along the shore from Ilangana to Kindu. This was an important Japanese base during WWII, and many relics remain from those times.

The centrally located, nondescript village of Lambete has the airport terminal, government offices, an NBSI branch, a police station, hospital and Telekom office.

East of Lambete There are freshwater pools at **Ndunde** containing turtles and fish, and a small crocodile farm (admission S$10).

Kiambe Island is 100m from the shore, near Kia. Behind it is a US dump where landing craft carrying Jeeps were scuttled in the water at the end of WWII. More accessible is a huge pile of war material rotting in the bush behind Kia. It's a 20-minute walk from Agnes Lodge and worth the S$20 *kastom* fee.

Organised Tours Operating from Agnes Lodge, **Dive Munda** (☎ 61107; W *www.dive munda.com*) offers diving over numerous wall, wreck and reef sites.

Also based at Agnes Lodge, **Go West Tours** (☎ 61080) offers excursions to Roviana Lagoon, Mt Bau and WWII sites. It can also arrange sport-fishing trips.

Places to Stay On the waterfront, **Agnes Lodge** (☎ 61133, fax 61230; W *www.agnes lodge.com; backpacker rooms per person S$45, self-contained singles/doubles from S$195/220, single/double cottages S$330/ 360)* is a short walk from the airport terminal. All rooms are fan cooled, and there's a bar and restaurant.

Getting There & Away Travel by plane or boat to get to Munda.

Air The airport terminal has a customs and immigration office and a **Solomon Airlines counter** (☎ 61152).

Solomon Airlines connects Munda with Honiara (S$440), Gizo (S$190) and Seghe (S$190) daily. Twice a week, flights go to Ramata (S$190) and Viru Harbour (S$190).

Boat Trans West and Wings both visit Munda en route between Honiara and Gizo. Trans West charges S$144/201/591 for economy/ 1st class/cabin from Honiara and S$95/145/ 423 from Gizo.

Getting Around There are a few roads on New Georgia, but traffic is light. Elsewhere, transport is by motor-canoe, small copra launches or on foot.

Around Munda

Holupuru Falls This 10m waterfall is just north of the bridge over the Mburape River. Below the waterfall is a deep swimming hole.

Mt Bau Stones and pillars stand on raised platforms deep in the bush atop Mt Bau, representing ancestral spirits. The site is about 9km inland from the coast at Ilangana on an overgrown bush trail towards Enoghae Point. You will need a guide and should expect to pay a *kastom* fee.

Noro Sixteen kilometres northwest of Munda, Noro has a large fish cannery as well as a NBSI branch and a police station.

Noro Lodge (☎ 61238; *twins with share facilities per person S$35, twins with private*

SOLOMON ISLANDS

facilities from S$125) is mainly for fishery workers. There's a licensed restaurant.

Roviana Lagoon The notorious head-hunter Ingava ruled from a coral-walled fortress on **Nusa Roviana** until it was destroyed in 1892. His tribe had a dog, Tiola, as its totem, and people worshipped at a rock carved in its likeness before going head-hunting. Remains of the **Stone Dog** are still here. The fortress is up to 30m wide, and 500m of coral walls still remain. There's a giant's cave nearby. *Kastom* fees are charged at both sites. Nusa Roviana is 4km east of Munda.

Roviana Lagoon extends 52km eastwards from Munda to Kalena Bay, and has many small islets. Nusa Hope Island has a **crocodile farm** *(admission S$10)*.

Viru Harbour, 30km southeast, was an important WWII Japanese base and is now a saw-milling centre. In the 19th century, five coral-stone fortresses protected the sea entrance from head-hunters. Stone monoliths and coral-rock platforms stand on nearby ridge tops.

Vonavona Lagoon
This beautiful lagoon extends for 28km between the Blackett Strait islets and Nusaghele. There's a resort on Lola.

Skull Island This islet at the tip of Kundu Point (Vonavona) has a skull house, or reliquary, containing the skulls of many chiefs and warriors, and clam-shell valuables. The *kastom* owners, who live at Kumbonitu on Vonavona, charge S$10 to see the skulls. Skull Island is visited on tours from Munda and Lola.

Lola The Zipolo Habu Resort offers a range of activities, including scuba diving, village tours, bushwalks, sport-fishing charters and surf charters.

Zipolo Habu Resort *(☎ 61178, fax 61179; ℮ zipolo@solomon.com.sb; singles/doubles/ triples S$210/300/345)* has a white-sand beach and a stunning view across the lagoon to the volcano on Kolombangara. The rooms are leaf-house style; self-cater or take the meals package (S$245).

The 30-minute motor-canoe ride from Munda costs S$270 return.

Rendova
Due south of Roviana Lagoon, Rendova is home to 3000 people. Rendovan islanders perform war dances at cultural festivals.

The Japanese had more than 20 large anti-aircraft guns at Rendova Harbour. US marines captured the harbour in June 1943 and used it as a base for PT boats; these included PT-109, which was skippered by John F Kennedy.

Also called Mt Longguoreke, **Rendova Peak** (1063m) dominates the island. Climbing it takes two days return and requires a guide – you can do it on a tour from Lola. **Egholo Cove** is a large inlet with a rusting war wreck on the shore at its southern entrance.

Tetepare
At 120 sq km, this is reputed to be the South Pacific's largest uninhabited island. It is one of the Solomons' conservation jewels, with rainforest as yet untouched by logging companies. The island has important breeding grounds for leatherback and green turtles, dugongs and other rare wildlife. There is a research station, trained guides, canopy platforms for bird-watching, and accommodation huts.

Visits to Tetepare must be pre-arranged through **WWF** *(☎ 60191, fax 60294; ℮ wwf@ solomon.com.sb)* in Gizo. A S$50 *kastom* fee applies regardless of the length of visit.

MAROVO LAGOON
On New Georgia's eastern side, Marovo Lagoon is the world's finest example of a double barrier–enclosed lagoon. The lagoon is enclosed by land on one side and a double line of long, narrow islands on the other. It contains hundreds of beautiful small islands, most of which are covered by coconut palms and rainforest and surrounded by coral. World Heritage listing for the lagoon was being pursued until recently, when increased logging on New Georgia Island and Vangunu discouraged the proponents.

Information
Bookings for the resorts and lodges in the Marovo and adjoining Noro Lagoons can be made through SIVB and Dive Gizo. Unless stated otherwise, the lodges listed here are leaf-house style with twin rooms, share facilities and attractive waterfront settings. Most have no electricity.

EU funding has been granted for the development of a Marovo Lagoon–specific website that will include email connections. The website will be ready in 2003.

Seghe
This subprovincial headquarters on southeast New Georgia's coast has grown up around

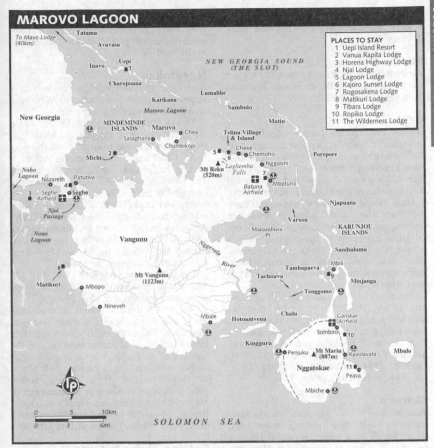

MAROVO LAGOON

PLACES TO STAY
1 Uepi Island Resort
2 Vanua Rapita Lodge
3 Horena Highway Lodge
4 Njai Lodge
5 Lagoon Lodge
6 Kajoro Sunset Lodge
7 Rogosakena Lodge
8 Matikuri Lodge
9 Tibara Lodge
10 Ropiko Lodge
11 The Wilderness Lodge

the US-built WWII airfield. The area's largest settlement is strung out along the Njai Passage, which links Noro Lagoon to Marovo Lagoon. There are no public telephones here.

Njai Lodge *(twins S$75)* is a short boat ride from the airport terminal. It has shared kitchen, toilet and shower facilities. Contact Jack Forest at **Gelvinas Motel** (☎ *60276, fax 60323*) in Gizo.

Benjamin Kaniotoku, owner of the Matikuri Lodge, is building a transit lodge near the airport terminal. The lodge will open in 2003.

Pavasa

This island is a short boat ride from Seghe.

Activities including fishing and snorkelling are available at **Horena Hideaway Lodge** *(with meals S$70)*. Transfers from Seghe cost S$50, shared.

Matikuri

The lodge on this small island offers several guided walks (including full-day walks) from Mbopo village on Vangunu. It can also arrange a trip to Bareho, a Seventh Day Adventist carving centre.

Matikuri Lodge *(with meals S$110)* is a very friendly place. Transfers from Seghe are S$25 per person each way.

Ramata

Mavo Lodge *(with meals S$85)* is at the Marovo Lagoon's northern end. It specialises in fishing trips, but there is also excellent snorkelling, village tours, skull shrines and bushwalks. **Go Tours Travel** (☎ *07-5591 2199, fax 5532 1854;* W *www.gotours.com.au*) in Queensland offers fishing packages to Ramata.

Solomon Airlines flies to Ramata twice a week from Honiara (S$420) and Gizo (S$190).

Michi

Vanua Rapita Lodge *(with meals S$110)* is a short boat ride from the mainland. Transfers from Seghe are S$30 each way.

Uepi

One of the lagoon's barrier islands, Uepi (pronounced 'oo-py') is a prime diving centre, and the nearby reefs offer superb snorkelling. From knee-deep water at Uepi's jetty, you can look down a spectacular 30m-deep drop-off with a garden of giant clams near the top.

Uepi Island Resort (**w** *www.uepi.com; full board from A$146*) quotes in Australian dollars, and has accommodation in self-contained, European-style bungalows. There's a bar and a library of books and magazines, plus a great view down the lagoon. Motor-canoe transfers from Seghe airstrip cost A$60 per person return.

The resort has a full dive shop. It can also arrange kayaking trips of up to 10 nights around the lagoon, as well as village tours, sport fishing and visits to carving centres.

In Australia, bookings are taken through **Tropical Paradise Pty Ltd** (**☎** *03-9787 7904, fax 9787 5904; PO Box 149, Mt Eliza, Victoria 3930)*. In Honiara contact SIVB.

Marovo

Sasaghana, on Marovo's western side, is a carving centre. On its eastern shore is Chumbikopi, where there's a war canoe on display (*kastom* fee S$10). Chea is where the Honiara–Gizo boats stop.

Vangunu

There are three lodges on the northeastern shore of this rugged volcanic island. All offer guided walks on **Mt Reku**, village tours, visits to *kastom* sites and fishing trips.

Lagoon Lodge *(S$100 full board)* is a great spot for bird-watching – 65 species have been recorded here. Romelus Paon, the owner, is keen to preserve the forest and his tours tend to have an ecological bias. Transfers from Seghe cost S$200, shared.

Kajoro Sunset Lodge *(S$90 full board)*, just across the bay, is owned by local legend and master carver John Wein. John's narratives on tribal history and excursions to *tabu* sites are fascinating. Transfers from Seghe cost S$200, shared.

Rogosakena Lodge *(S$100 full board)* is 6km west, near Lolovuro village, and just south of the airstrip at Mbatuna. It specialises in fishing trips.

Nggatokae

Nggatokae (pronounced 'gat-oh-kye') is a large volcanic cone that reaches its 887m peak on **Mt Mariu's** narrow crater rim.

Tibara Lodge *(full board S$100)* is on the island's northern tip near the Mbili Passage, which is on the Honiara–Gizo shipping route. Chief Luton offers various activities, such as bushwalks, fishing and snorkelling. The wreck of a USAAF B24D bomber lies crumpled in the nearby bush.

Ropiko Lodge *(S$100 full board)* is a short motor-canoe ride from the Gatokae airstrip. Activities include a visit to Mbiche village and its fascinating *kastom* sites, lagoon tours, fishing and snorkelling. A wrecked Zero fighter lies just beyond the resort.

The Wilderness Lodge (**☎** *0061 145 125 948 within the Solomons satellite;* **w** *www .thewildernesslodge.org; full board US$45)* quotes in US dollars, and is a large leafhouse with two bedrooms sleeping four persons each. The daily rate includes transfers from Gatokae or Mbatuna airstrips and the services of an English-speaking guide. Activities include a hike to the top of Mt Mariu for fantastic views of the lagoon; another good walk is the climb up to the crater rim of Mt Vangunu, on Vangunu. There's also sport fishing, a boat ride to see **Kavachi** (an active underwater volcano), and a visit to Mbiche.

Getting There & Away

Air Solomon Airlines flies daily to Seghe from Honiara (S$370) and continues on to Munda (S$190) and Gizo (S$240).

Boat Trans West and Wings pass through Marovo Lagoon weekly. Trans West charges S$132/189/555 for economy/1st class/cabin from Honiara to all Marovo ports; it's slightly cheaper coming from Gizo.

Rennell & Bellona Province

The Polynesian outliers of Rennell and Bellona are uplifted-coral atolls and extremely rocky. Eastern Rennell has been a World Heritage Site since 1998.

Flora & Fauna

The Rennellese orchid is particularly striking, with multiple mauve veins on a white flower and a pale-yellow undersurface.

A number of bird species are endemic to Rennell, including the Rennell fantail and the rare Rennell white spoonbill. At least eight subspecies that have evolved distinctive features have been identified.

Dawn and dusk see great flocks of frigate birds, cormorants and boobies circling over Lake Te'Nggano.

Getting There & Away

From Honiara, Solomon Airlines flies to Rennell (S$345) via Bellona (S$325) twice a week. The Bellona–Rennell sector costs S$190. Rennell airfield is known locally as Tinggoa.

Getting Around

To/From the Airport A tractor meets planes landing at Tinggoa airport. The 50km tractor ride between the airport and Lake Te'Nggano runs through rainforest and takes at least four hours. The one-way charge is S$50. Tractors are available for charter costing S$500 per day.

RENNELL ISLAND

pop 1500 • area 629 sq km

Surrounded by high cliffs, Rennell is a fine example of a raised coral atoll. At 130 sq km, **Lake Te'Nggano**, in the southeast, is the South Pacific's largest expanse of fresh water. The lake is the old lagoon floor, and the tall cliffs that surround it are the old reef. Its western end has 200-odd coral islets and swamps. Four large villages hug the shore, including Te'Nggano, the subprovincial headquarters. The fact that the lake and its surroundings are still largely undisturbed helped gain it World Heritage status.

Motor-canoe charters for lake trips are available, while guided rainforest walks cost S$10 per person per hour. **Octopus Cave** on the northern shore is a popular excursion.

Places to Stay

The island has several basic resthouses, which can be booked through SIVB.

Moreno Guesthouse *(S$50 per person)* is clean and has kitchen facilities. It's near Tinggoa airport.

Tahamatangi Resthouse *(S$50 per person)* is on the western shore of Lake Te'Nggano. There are basic kitchen facilities

and meals are available. Canoe transfers from Tebaitahe cost S$40.

Kiakoe Lakeside Lodge *(S$50 per person)* is on the northern shore. Canoe transfers are S$10 per person.

BELLONA
pop 1000 • area 15 sq km
Bellona is densely populated, with a fertile interior. The island is surrounded by forest-covered cliffs rising 30m to 70m – they're often easy to climb, unlike Rennell's cliffs.

Since the 1970s, Bellonese people have reacted against the dominance of fundamentalist Christianity. Many have deserted the large church-dominated villages and returned to their traditional lands.

Western Bellona
Bellona Island's most sacred ancient rituals took place at the Nggabengga site in **Matahenua**. Around here are caves where early Bellonese settlers lived; they were occupied right up to the 1930s.

Eastern Bellona
The **Tapuna** and **Saamoa Caves** are 1km to the north of Matangi. Tradition says the Hiti people, said to have been the island's first human residents, lived in stone buildings inside them. Stone remains can still be seen in Tapuna Cave.

The Hiti Walls at **Ou'taha** are a weathered line of coral rocks – the remains of an uplifted reef. The Hiti people are said to have built these huge coral structures before the first Polynesians arrived.

Places to Stay & Eat
Suani Resthouse *(per person S$50)* at Tangakitonga has a kitchen, and meals are available. Bicycle hire and bushwalking and snorkelling trips with lunch included can be arranged.

Aotaha Cave Resort *(per person S$70)* on the east coast enjoys cool sea breezes. This place is beautifully situated and some of the beds are actually in a cave. Meals are available on request.

Getting Around
A tractor trail runs from Potuhenua in the northwest, Bellona's only anchorage, and continues to the southeastern tip at Ana'otanggo. The island's only tractor meets every flight and ship, and shuttles passengers anywhere along its route for S$1.

Malaita Province

The Malaita Province's 96,000 people make it the most densely populated part of the country. The population is all Melanesian except for approximately 2000 Polynesians who live on the atolls of Ontong Java and Sikaiana.

MALAITA ISLAND
pop 89,000 • area 3840 sq km
Malaita's rugged highland interior rises to 1303m at Mt Kolovrat. Deep valleys, sharp ridges and fast-flowing rivers have obstructed cross-island movement and Malaitans speak many different languages.

The most interesting attractions for tourists on Malaita are cultural ones. Many people from central and southeastern parts of the island still worship ancestral spirits. The crowded artificial islands in Langa Langa and Lau Lagoons present a fascinating glimpse of an entirely different way of life (see the boxed text 'Artificial Islands' later for more details).

Getting There & Away Solomon Airlines flies daily from Honiara to Auki for S$225. Malaita Shipping plies twice weekly between Honiara and Auki, charging S$70/94/118 for economy/1st class/cabin.

Getting Around The airfield is 10km from Auki. A ride into town costs S$10 by truck or the Solomon Airlines bus.

Trucks are infrequent on Malaita's pot-holed rural roads. The best place to get a ride in Auki is at the wharf or nearby market when a ship calls in. If the roads are closed you'll have to walk or go by boat.

Auki
Auki has a population of 4000 and is the Solomons' third-largest town. It has branches of the ANZ and NBSI banks, a hospital, central market, provincial government offices, Telekom and Solomon Airlines.

There are wonderful views over Auki and its harbour from the lookout behind the prison.

Auki Island This 80m-wide artificial island is located 1km from town and is home to two families. It was, at one time, the home of shark worshippers and there are *kastom* areas containing ancestral skulls. Men can

MALAITA PROVINCE

visit these sites with permission from locals, but they are *tabu* for women. Local people have been known to ask S$50 landing fees from those wishing to see their island. It's not worth that much money.

Canoes go to or past the island from the Auki Wharf, Lilisiana and Ambu.

Lilisiana This very friendly village is a 1.2km walk from the wharf. Women can be seen making traditional shell money and necklaces here.

Places to Stay & Eat There are several accommodation options in Auki.

Auki Lodge (☎ 40131; Batabu Rd; fan-cooled singles/doubles S$120/160, air-con singles/doubles from S$165/195) is Lilisi-ana's top hotel. All rooms are self-contained

and there's a bar, restaurant and lounge with satellite TV.

Auki Motel (☎ 40014, fax 40220; Loboi Ave; rooms per person S$50) is basic but clean; rooms are air-cooled and have share facilities, and there's a kitchen and spacious lounge. It's above the Solomon Airlines office.

Golden Dragon Motel (☎ 40113; Loboi Ave; rooms with/without share facilities per person S$80/50) has a basic kitchen. If no-one is there, inquire at the Auki Store opposite.

Island Travellers Lodge (☎ 40320, fax 40155; Maasina Rulu Parade; per person S$60) has fan-cooled rooms and share facili-ties and a dining room.

Around Auki
Riba Cave This interesting, large cavern is a tough hour's walk east from Auki. The

AUKI

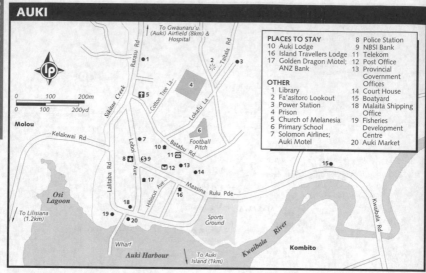

PLACES TO STAY
10 Auki Lodge
16 Island Travellers Lodge
17 Golden Dragon Motel;
   ANZ Bank

OTHER
1 Library
2 Fa'asitoro Lookout
3 Power Station
4 Prison
5 Church of Melanesia
6 Primary School
7 Solomon Airlines;
   Auki Motel

8 Police Station
9 NBSI Bank
11 Telekom
12 Post Office
13 Provincial
   Government
   Offices
14 Court House
15 Boatyard
18 Malaita Shipping
   Office
19 Fisheries
   Development
   Centre
20 Auki Market

kastom fee is around S$20 and you'll need a guide and a torch (flashlight).

Langa Langa Lagoon South of Auki, Langa Langa is famous for its artificial islands. One of these, Laulasi, is 400 years old. Tours can be arranged in Auki; ask at your hotel.

Onebulu Beach At the mouth of the Fiu River, 9km north of Auki, Onebulu is the best beach in the Auki area.

Northern Malaita Island

The 'north road' from Auki to Lau Lagoon follows the coast from Sisifiu to Silolo, providing

---

Artificial Islands

One of Malaita's features is the large number of artificial islands, particularly in Langa Langa and Lau Lagoons. Some of these date from the 1550s and new ones are built each year.

Stones from the lagoon floor are collected and piled on a sandbar or reef until they reach around 2m above the high-tide mark. Sand is spread around, houses are built and coconuts palms are planted.

The largest islands exceed 1 sq km in size and tend to be very crowded; some are surrounded by a coral wall. Most, however, are very small and only have room for a few houses.

---

sea views. Long stretches of white-sand beach line the shore.

Mbita'ama Shell money is made at Mbita' ama, 65km from Auki. Mana Ruuakwa, a **marine cave** at nearby Kwaiorua Point, penetrates inland, terminating in a deep hole. Islanders say sharks come here to sleep.

Mbasakana Beautiful Mbasakana Island is surrounded by coral reefs and white-sand beaches. The friendly villagers can show you an interesting cave nearby.

Malu'u This friendly subprovincial headquarters is a good stop on the 'north road' between Auki (five hours over 82km of dreadful road) and Lau Lagoon at the 'head road' two hours away. There's a good beach here, and another round the point to the east. The village has stores, electricity and piped water.

A 4km hilltop trail behind Malu'u leads to **A'ama**, where there's a *biu* (treehouse for initiated boys). **Uala**, which has a skull house, is a kilometre further on.

Malu'u Lodge *(per person S$50)* has some fan-cooled rooms, a kitchen and share facilities. Make bookings through SIVB or the **provincial government headquarters** (☎ 40253) in Auki.

Lau Lagoon This 35km-long lagoon contains more than 60 artificial islands (see the boxed text 'Artificial Islands' earlier). It stretches from the shallows between **Uruuru** and **Maana'omba** down to **Lolowai**.

Central & Eastern Malaita Island

There's a road across the mountaino us interior to the east coast around Atori that is washed out in the mid-year wet season. The route begins near Dala, and its most scenic spot is at Nunulafa, where it crosses over the Auluta Gorge.

It may be possible to visit some of the full-*kostom* Kwaio people who inhabit the rugged east-central part of Malaita. Their stronghold is between Uru Harbour and Olumburi. Check the current situation with the SIVB, who can give advice on guides and other matters.

Tahiti & French Polynesia

Better known by the name of its main island of Tahiti, French Polynesia and its islands have come to epitomise the Pacific dream. Here you'll find beautiful reef-fringed islands, palm trees and vividly blue lagoons, stunning diving, sensuous hip-swinging dancers and outrigger canoes propelled by powerful tattooed men. The islands comprise five distinctly different groups, scattered over an area as big as Europe.

French Polynesia is well known for the beauty of the islands, whether it's mountainous islands like Bora Bora or low-lying coral atolls like Rangiroa. Unfortunately it's equally well known for hitting visitors with some of the highest prices in the Pacific. Fortunately the beauty is real and the high prices are not always as bad as they seem. Visitors looking for island luxury and fine food – and equipped with industrial-strength credit cards – may decide that French Polynesia is worth the expenditure. Travellers on a tighter budget will be pleasantly surprised to find that there are backpacker resorts and low-key local *pensions* (guesthouses), moderately priced places to eat and excellent shipping services between the most popular islands of the Society Islands.

Facts about Tahiti & French Polynesia

HISTORY

It was almost a millennium after people reached Samoa and Tonga before the next great migration wave in 200 BC (some believe it may have been as late as 300 AD), east to the Society and Marquesas Islands of modern-day French Polynesia.

Here the new settlers called themselves the Maohi and their culture bloomed. The island of Ra'iatea (then known as Havaiki) became the cultural and religious centre of the vast region of Polynesia. This was the hub for the next great wave of migrations, which began in about 300 AD; legend has it that a stone from Ra'iatea was built into every temple on each new island.

These last voyages went southeast to Rarotonga and the southern Cook Islands, north to Hawaii, southeast to Rapa Nui (Easter Island) and via Rarotonga to Aotearoa (New Zealand) around 900 AD.

At a Glance

Capital City (& Island): Pape'ete (Tahiti)

Population: 245,405

Time: 10 hours behind GMT (Tahiti)

Land Area: 3500 sq km

Number of Islands: 118

International Telephone Code: ☎ 689

GDP/Capita: US$18,800

Currency: Cour de Franc Pacifique (CFP) (100 CFP = US$0.97)

Languages: Tahitian, French & English

Greeting: *'Ia ora na'* (Tahitian) or *'Bonjour'* (French)

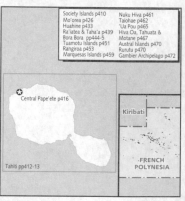

Society Islands p410	Nuku Hiva p461
Mo'orea p426	Taiohae p462
Huahine p433	'Ua Pou p465
Ra'iatea & Taha'a p439	Hiva Oa, Tahuata &
Bora Bora p444-5	Motane p467
Tuamotu Islands p451	Austral Islands p470
Rangiroa p453	Rurutu p470
Marquesas Islands p459	Gambier Archipelago p472

Central Pape'ete p416

Tahiti pp412-13

Kiribati

FRENCH POLYNESIA

Highlights

- **Arriving by sea** – approaching the beautiful, rugged coast of the Marquesas

- **Shopping for handicrafts** – admiring finely carved sculptures and gathering a fun collection of woven hats and bright pareu

- **Hiva Oa** – exploring the amazing *tiki* and other archaeological artefacts at the significant lipona site in the Marquesas

- **Bora Bora** – superb snorkelling with lagoon marine life

- **Pape'ete after dark** – eating alfresco from *les roulottes* and taking in the nightlife of colourful waterfront Blvd Pomare

- **Mo'orea** – the place daydreams are made of... and it's accessible to travellers on any budget

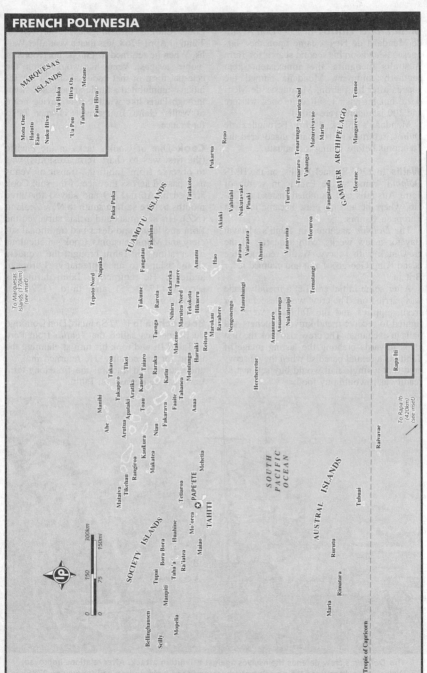

FRENCH POLYNESIA

TAHITI & FRENCH POLYNESIA

MARQUESAS ISLANDS

Motu One
Hatutu
Eiao
Nuku Hiva
'Ua Huka
'Ua Pou
Hiva Oa
Tahuata
Motane
Fatu Hiva

GAMBIER ARCHIPELAGO

TUAMOTU ISLANDS

To Marquesas
Islands (170km)
(see inset)

Pukarua
Reao

Tenararo Tenarunga Marutea Sud
Vahanga Matureivavao
Fangataufa
Morane
Mangareva
Temoe

Vahitahi
Nukutavake
Pinaki
Maria

Tatakoto

Akiaki
Turcia
Vairaatea

Tepoto Nord
Napuka

Takoto

Takume
Raroia

Paraoa
Ahunui

Vanavana

Tematangi

Morotiri

Fangatau
Fakahina

Poka Poka

Nihiru
Rekareka
Taenga
Tauere
Makemo
Marutea Nord
Tekokota
Katiu
Hikueru

Amanu

Hao

Nengonengo
Manuhangi

Manihi
Takaroa
Takapoto
Tikei
Aratika
Arutua Apataki
Kaukura Toau Kauehi Taiaro
Niau Raraka
Fakarava Faaite
Tahanea
Motutunga
Anaa
Haraiki
Reitoru
Marokau
Ravahere

Ahe

Mataiva
Tikehau
Rangiroa
Makatea

Anaanuraro
Anaanurunga
Nukutepipi

Rapa Iti

Hereheretue

SOCIETY ISLANDS

Bellinghausen
Scilly
Mopelia
Maupiti
Tupai
Bora Bora
Taha'a
Huahine
Ra'iatea
Mo'orea
Maiao

To Rapa Iti
(420km)
(see inset)

Tetiaroa
Mehetia

PAPEETE
TAHITI

SOUTH
PACIFIC
OCEAN

Raivavae

AUSTRAL ISLANDS

Tubuai

Rurutu

Maria
Rimatara

Tropic of Capricorn

300km

150mi

150
75

0
0

European Arrival

Mendaña & Quirós In 1595 Don Alvaro de Mendaña de Neyra came upon the Marquesas Islands on his second search for Terra Australis Incognita, the nonexistent great southern continent. Mendaña named the islands after his patron, Marquesas de Mendoza, but his visit resulted in open warfare and 200 islanders were killed.

Mendaña's pilot, Pedro Fernández de Quirós, returned in 1606 and discovered the Tuamotus before sailing to Vanuatu.

Wallis In 1767 Samuel Wallis, on the HMS *Dolphin*, came to the Pacific in search of Terra Australis and stumbled instead on Tahiti, where he and his crew became the first European visitors.

The *Dolphin* anchored in Tahiti's Matavai Bay for a few weeks, with a quarter of the crew sick with scurvy. Wallis renamed the island King George's Land and claimed it for Britain.

After some initial conflict a friendly trade was carried on. The crew were desperate for fresh supplies and the Tahitians were delighted to receive metal knives, hatchets and nails in exchange. The crew also took the first steps towards creating the lasting image of Tahiti as a sexual paradise when they discovered that a single nail would buy sex just as readily as it would buy food.

Bougainville The great French explorer Louis-Antoine de Bougainville arrived at Tahiti in April 1768, less than a year after Wallis. When he returned to Europe his reports of 'noble savages', Venus-like women with 'the celestial form of that goddess' and of the Tahitians' uninhibited attitude towards sex swept through Paris like wildfire. Not having heard of Wallis' claim, Bougainville claimed Tahiti for France.

Cook One of Cook's tasks in the Pacific (the first was to chart Terra Australis) was to observe from Tahiti the transit of Venus as it passed across the face of the sun. Cook arrived in April 1769 and stayed for three months before sailing south to New Zealand (NZ). His scientists and artists surveyed the flora and fauna and described traditional society and Maohi customs. Cook's meticulous observations of Tahiti brought the wonders of the island to an appreciative European audience. He returned to Tahiti during his second (1772–75) and third (1776–80) expeditions.

Boenechea In 1772 Spaniard Don Domingo de Boenechea sailed the *Aguilla* from Peru to Tahiti Iti and took his turn at claiming the island for his country. He returned in 1774 and established Tautira, the first long-term European settlement on Tahiti.

BY PERMISSION OF THE NATIONAL LIBRARY OF AUSTRALIA: NK1860

The *Dolphin*'s crew defends themselves against a Tahitian attack. After relations improved, Wallis' crew discovered the amazing purchase power of a single iron nail (engraving 1786).

However, the Spanish missionaries failed to convert the heathens and returned to Peru in 1775, ending Spain's role in Tahiti. When Cook visited again in 1777 he found a Spanish cross outside the abandoned mission house, carved with the year the mission was established. Cook added the dates of his own and Wallis' visit.

Bounty Mutineers

In 1789 the infamous mutiny on the *Bounty* occurred after Bligh's crew had spent six long comfortable months in Tahiti. See the boxed text 'Mutiny on the Bounty' in the Pitcairn Island chapter for more about the *Bounty*.

The mutineers returned to Tahiti and Tubuai in the Australs after the mutiny, then sailed to a more remote hideaway on Pitcairn Island. Sixteen stayed behind in Tahiti, a move that changed the course of history.

Before the Europeans arrived power had been a local affair. No ruler was strong enough to control more than their patch, and Tahiti was divided into a number of squabbling groups. However, once they realised the persuasive power of European weaponry, Tahitians pressed the *Bounty* mutineers to take sides in local conflicts. The mutineers became mercenaries to the highest bidder, the Pomare family.

That deal was the beginning of the Pomares' metamorphosis into a ruling dynasty. Pomare I, known as Tu, controlled most of Tahiti by the time he died in 1803 – his son Pomare II took over.

Whalers, Missionaries & Depopulation

The London Missionary Society (LMS) landed at Tahiti's Point Vénus in March 1797 and did its best to rid the islanders of their wicked ways. Dancing, 'indecent' songs, tattoos, nudity, indiscriminate sex and even wearing flowers in hair were banned once the missionaries had got their patron, Pomare II, on side.

Whalers and traders arrived in Polynesia in the 1790s, spreading diseases, encouraging prostitution and introducing alcohol and more weapons.

Plagued by diseases against which they had no natural immunity, the population plummeted. When Cook first visited, Tahiti's population was about 40,000. In 1800 it was less than 20,000 and by the 1820s it was down to around 6000. In the Marquesas the situation was even worse – the population dropped from 80,000 to only 2000 in one century.

Pomares & the Missionaries

After 1815 the Pomares ruled Tahiti, with Protestant missionaries advising them on government and laws and trying to keep whalers and Australian traders at arm's length. Pomare II died in 1821 and his son, Pomare III, who died in 1827, was succeeded by the young Queen Pomare IV.

The queen's missionary advisers, seeing her only as an interim ruler until the next king arrived, turned a blind eye to some of her youthful excesses. She was not averse to a little singing and dancing, and even visited passing ships. Queen Pomare IV made the most of her leeway and ruled Tahiti for 50 years.

English Protestant missionaries were the major advisers to chiefs in the Society, Austral and Tuamotu Islands. But in the Gambier Archipelago and the Marquesas Islands French Catholic missionaries were in control. In 1836 two French missionaries, Laval and Caret, visiting Pape'ete from the Gambier Archipelago were caught up in this rivalry when the British promptly arrested and deported them.

French Takeover

The French saw the deportation of Laval and Caret as a national insult. Demands, claims, counterclaims, payments and apologies shuttled back and forth. In 1842 Admiral Dupetit-Thouars settled matters by turning up in *La Reine Blanche* and pointing the ship's guns at Pape'ete, forcing Queen Pomare to yield. French soldiers promptly landed, along with Catholic missionaries.

The French arrested and deported George Pritchard, the British missionary who was the queen's consul and unofficial chief adviser. Queen Pomare, still hoping for British intervention, fled to Ra'iatea in 1844 and a guerrilla rebellion broke out on several islands. The rebels were subdued and by 1846 France controlled Tahiti and Mo'orea. The queen returned to Tahiti in 1847 as a mere figurehead.

Queen Pomare died in 1877; her son, Pomare V, had little interest in the position and abdicated in 1881. French power extended to include most of the other Society Islands in 1888, although rebellions rumbled on in Ra'iatea until almost the end of the century. The Gambier Archipelago was annexed in 1881 and the Austral Islands in 1900/01.

Twentieth Century

Soon after the turn of the century an economic boom attracted colonists, mostly French. By

1911 there were about 3500 Europeans in the islands, adding to Chinese immigration, which had begun in 1864 with cotton production at Atimaono on Tahiti. The foundations of a multiethnic society were in place.

French Polynesia was directly involved in both world wars. In WWI almost 1000 Tahitian soldiers fought in Europe and on 22 September 1914 two German cruisers patrolling the Pacific sank the French cruiser *Zélée* and shelled the Pape'ete market. In WWII 5000 US soldiers were based in Bora Bora, and a 2km runway was built in 1943. Tahitian volunteers in the Pacific Battalion fought in North Africa and Europe.

In 1946 the islands became an overseas territory within the French Republic, sparking agitation for independence. A political party, the Rassemblement Démocratique des Populations Tahitiennes (RDPT; Democratic Assembly of Tahitian Populations), took centre stage on the political scene for about 10 years.

On 22 July 1957 the territory officially became French Polynesia. The 1960s were a real turning point. In 1961 Faa'a airport was built, opening French Polynesia to the world. Shortly after, the filming of *Mutiny on the Bounty* on Tahiti poured millions of dollars into the economy. In 1963, the nuclear-testing Centre Expérimentation du Pacifique (CEP; Pacific Experimentation Centre) was established at Moruroa and Fangataufa.

From 1977 to 1996 French Polynesia took over internal management and autonomy. The nuclear testing of the era shook Polynesia physically, socially and economically – violent protests rocked Pape'ete in 1987 and 1995 and the CEP made French Polynesia economically dependent on France. The end to nuclear testing in 1996 also meant the end for the prosperity of the previous 30 years, even though France will continue aid until the end of 2005.

French Polynesia Today

Over the last few decades French Polynesia has been given more control over internal management (see Government & Politics later in this section). Independence remains a possibility, but French Polynesia would find it hard to cut the economic apron strings to France, as the islands have few natural resources to offset their high imports.

To a large extent even French Polynesia's physical future rests in the hands of larger, more powerful nations: the islands' vulnerability to the forces of nature were brought home during 2000/01, when they bore the brunt of El Niño. The islands, with their largely coastal populations, have a lot to lose with the rising sea levels of global warming but, unlike heavily industrialised nations, have very little control over their predicament. See the boxed text 'Global Warming' in the Facts about the South Pacific chapter.

GEOGRAPHY & GEOLOGY

French Polynesia is a vast, scattered collection of 118 islands and atolls that stretch across five million sq km of ocean. However, most of these volcanic blips are small and the five archipelagos have a total land area of barely 3500 sq km.

The Society Islands, the westernmost archipelago, have high mountains and lagoons protected by barrier reefs, sometimes dotted with small fringing islets known as *motu*. Subdivided into the Windward and Leeward Islands, the Societies are home to more than three-quarters of French Polynesia's population. Polynesia's administrative capital, Pape'ete, is on Tahiti.

The Tuamotus, east of the Society Islands, are classic low-lying coral atolls. The remote Marquesas, north of the Tuamotus and not far from the equator, are rugged high islands but lack barrier reefs or lagoons. Finally, there are the even more remote and scattered Australs, also high islands, and the tiny Gambier Archipelago.

CLIMATE

French Polynesia is well and truly in the tropics – its position between the Tropic of Capricorn and the Equator means it has a hot and humid climate. The summer (very) wet season runs from November to April, with the hottest days in February and March; the archipelago gets three quarters of its rain in this season. The winter dry season runs from May to October and the air is less humid then. However, it's not much cooler – temperatures vary by only a degree or two or two all year – the average is 27°C.

French Polynesia's trade winds blow from the northeast: the occasional *maraamu* (southeast trade winds) can bring lower temperatures and rain in the dry season; the occasional *toerau* (north-northeast wind) often precedes rain in the wet season. On the high islands, the morning *hupe* cools the hot coastal plain.

Cyclones are an ever-present threat: French Polynesia is generally spared, but on rare occasions has suffered major damage. For local weather reports phone ☎ 36 65 08.

ECOLOGY & ENVIRONMENT

The environmental repercussions of French nuclear testing are still hotly debated. The view that Moruroa and Fangataufa were fissured by tests and that radioactivity has escaped was confirmed in 1999 when the French government admitted for the first time that cracks existed in the atolls' coral cones.

Atolls are ecologically fragile places, but French Polynesia has been slow to do much to protect them. It's a catch-22: the islands' mainstay, tourism, depends on the idyll of an unspoilt natural environment, but increased development is tarnishing that image.

Rubbish is perhaps the most visible environmental problem. The Pacific islands don't have remote landfills to send their rubbish to, so it's not unusual to see garbage dumps spoiling the natural setting. The garbage pollutes the watercourses, which pollute the lagoons.

Only Bora Bora has a state-of-the-art sewerage plant. On other islands, private septic tanks and small sewerage stations are often badly maintained and unreliable, and inevitably the poorly treated outflow ends up in the lagoon, threatening the fragile reefs.

Scilly Atoll, in the Leeward Society Islands, is the only reserve, although several species of marine life are protected, notably rays and turtles.

FLORA

The luxuriant flora of French Polynesia, particularly on the high islands, is recent and introduced. Ancient Polynesian navigators brought plants and fruits that flourished. In the 19th century missionaries and settlers imported other ornamental and commercial plants.

Vegetation varies significantly from one archipelago to another. On the atolls, where the soil is poor and winds constant, bushy vegetation and coconut palms predominate. On the high islands, plant cover is more diverse and changes according to the altitude.

Tiare, Scent of Tahiti

The *tiare*, the Tahitian gardenia, is the emblem of French Polynesia. This delicate, snow-white flower is omnipresent on the islands. *Tiare* trees line the streets, and the flower is woven into garlands, tucked into hair and given to guests. Its distinctive, subtle fragrance seems to accompany you everywhere and is one of the lasting memories of a tropical holiday.

FAUNA

Like the flora, French Polynesia's fauna is limited compared with that of the west Pacific.

The first Polynesians tucked the first domestic animals – pigs, chickens and dogs – into their canoes. You're likely to share your room with one of their stowaways, the gecko, a small, harmless translucent lizard that is often seen clinging to walls. Horses have bred on the Marquesas, where goats also roam unchecked.

There are no snakes but plenty of insects. Mosquitoes are annoying, as are the Marquesan *nono* (sandflies): see the boxed text 'Oh No, It's the Nono!' in the Marquesas Islands section later in this chapter.

French Polynesia boasts about 100 species of *manu* (birds). On the low islands many nest on the ground or in bushes. The feathers of certain birds were once much sought after for headdresses and chieftains' belts. Sea birds include terns, petrels, noddies, frigate birds, boobies and tropicbirds. It's thought that up to one million *kaveka* (sooty terns) nest on 'Ua Huka in the Marquesas, while the Tuamotus have numerous islands inhabited only by birds.

The coral reefs provide a rich environment for marine life. Sea creatures include *rori* (sea cucumber), sharks, *ono* (barracuda), manta rays, moray eels, dolphins and the endangered *honu* (turtle). In Nuku Hiva, in the Marquesas, electra dolphins, also known as pygmy orcas or melon-headed whales, gather in their hundreds in a unique phenomenon; in the Australs whales are the attraction, and it's possible to swim with them.

On the islands, the waterways are home to eels and freshwater shrimps – highly valued in local cuisine.

Coconut crabs live on land and, as they are considered a delicacy, are extremely rare. They can live for up to 40 years and grow almost a metre long, albeit slowly; this slow growth rate has contributed to their decline.

GOVERNMENT & POLITICS

French Polynesia is a Territoire d'Outre-Mer (TOM; French Overseas Territory). The territory looks after local administration, education, taxation and foreign trade. France controls defence, law and order, foreign affairs, immigration and justice and is represented in French Polynesia by a high commissioner, appointed by France.

The Assemblée de Polynésie Française (Assembly of French Polynesia) is composed of 41 councillors elected from the five archipelagos every five years. The councillors elect

TAHITI & FRENCH POLYNESIA

the president of the Government of French Polynesia, the head of the territorial administration, who in turn appoints a council of ministers. French Polynesians participate in all French national elections, and elect two deputies and a senator to the French parliament. Proposed constitutional changes giving French Polynesia more autonomy are awaiting final ratification.

On one side of local politics is the Tahoeraa Huiraatira (Gathering of the People) party, which is currently in power. On the other side is Tavini Huiraatira (To Serve the People), the pro-independence party that wants to break all ties with France and return to Polynesian principles. Cronyism is rife in local politics, sometimes drifting towards corruption.

ECONOMY

Far from the myths of a carefree paradise, French Polynesia faces many economic challenges. The region became financially dependent upon France during the nuclear-testing era, when many people abandoned their traditional livelihoods for the promise of a better life in Pape'ete, some finding urban poverty instead.

With the end of nuclear testing, economic reality is hitting home, although France is continuing economic support until the end of 2005.

The territory government has its work cut out for it in increasing exports. Agricultural production declined with the urban migration of the CEP era and is slowly being built up: harvests of vanilla – said to be the world's best – are increasing; copra is an important source of income in the Tuamotus and the Marquesas; and an export fishing fleet is being developed. Mo'orea's intensively grown pineapples are the only fruit export. Beautiful black pearls are a key export, and recently the wonders of age-defying *noni* juice have become another important moneymaker.

However, tourism is the foundation of the government's plans for economic independence. The industry is being nurtured with tax breaks for luxury hotel development, more small operators in remote areas, and increased promotion.

POPULATION & PEOPLE

Of the population of 239,500, half is aged under 25 and the bulk – 86% – lives in the Society Islands (nearly half in Pape'ete). The remaining 14% is split between the Tuamotus, Marquesas, Australs and the Gambier Archipelago.

Ethnic Polynesians make up the bulk of society (65%); part-Polynesians (known as *demis* – literally, 'halves') account for 16% of the population; *popaa* (Westerner), 12%; and Chinese, 5%. Polynesians tend to make up the least privileged part of society and mostly live in outlying districts and islands.

ARTS

For a detailed description of individual handicrafts, see the 'South Pacific Arts' special section.

Dance

Early European explorers – fresh from strait-laced 18th- and 19th-century Europe – commented on the erotic explicitness of Tahitian dancing, so of course it was one of the first things the missionaries banned. It continued clandestinely and since the 1950s has been revived to become one of the best ambassadors for Polynesian culture.

Music

Traditional music can still be heard reverberating throughout the islands; its hypnotic and often complex drumbeat often accompanies dance performances, with guitars, ukuleles and percussion instruments playing a large part. Song, either secular or religious, is also important, and Sunday *himene* (hymns) feature wonderful harmonies. Modern Polynesian music blares out of *le trucks* (public buses), cafés and radios.

Architecture

Traditional Polynesian architecture blurs the line between indoors and outdoors, and buildings are rarely entirely closed from the elements. The *fare* (house) is the traditional dwelling, built in natural materials, with a framework of coconut wood and a roof of either woven coconut palms or pandanus leaves. It sits directly on the ground, without foundations.

Modern *fare* are often built with modern materials which, though less picturesque, better withstand cyclones. These days you're most likely to find traditional-style architecture at luxury hotels.

Painting

Think of painting and French Polynesia and Paul Gauguin is likely to come to mind. His vivid images helped shape Europe's exotic view of Polynesia (see the boxed text) and inspired a number of predominantly European artists to seek inspiration on the islands. After

Paul Gauguin

If one thing is responsible for Polynesia's enduring reputation as a paradise lost, it is the evocative paintings of Paul Gauguin (1848–1903).

Gauguin began to paint his first landscapes while working as a stockbroker in Paris. One of these was shown at the Salon Art Exhibition in 1876, and he exhibited with the Impressionists in 1879. The stock-market collapse in 1882 ended Gauguin's business career and, leaving his wife and children, he devoted himself exclusively to painting. The following years were particularly difficult, and he lived for a long while in virtual poverty.

In 1890 Gauguin left France to cultivate his art in Tahiti. In Mataiea, where the Gauguin Museum now stands, he captured images of daily life, and exuberant settings and flamboyant colours increasingly pervaded his painting.

But he sold few canvases, and to escape poverty he sailed for France in 1893. In November that year he held a large solo exhibition in Paris. He took up ceramics and began writing *Noa Noa* to help the public understand his work. Disappointed with the results, he returned to the South Seas in 1895.

His most powerful compositions, *Te Arii Vahine* (The Royal Woman; 1896), *Nevermore* (1897) and *Where Do We Come From? What Are We? Where Are We Going?* (1897) date from this final stay in French Polynesia, which was marked by illness and distress. After a failed suicide attempt, he took refuge on the island of Hiva Oa in the Marquesas, where he is fondly remembered. He continued writing, drawing, sculpting and painting until his death. It was during this period that he produced one of his most beautiful nudes, *Barbaric Tales* (1902).

Matisse, who stayed briefly in Tahiti, the best known is Frenchman Jacques Boullaire, who visited in the 1930s. Christian Deloffre, François Ravello, Michèle Dallet, Bobby André Marere (also known as a singer and musician), Jean Masson, Yrondi, Noguier and Erhart Lux also helped shaped the region's characteristic representational painting style.

Sculpture

Traditionally, the best sculpture and wood-carvings have come from the Marquesas, where fine *tiki* (carved human figures), *umete* (wooden dishes), mortars and pestles, spears and clubs, hair pins and other personal adornments are carved from rosewood, *tou* wood or in stone. The best-known contemporary sculptor is potter Peter Owen, who lives on Huahine in the Society Islands; Woody, on Mo'orea, is well known for his carving.

Clothing & Decoration

Dress in French Polynesia is an odd combination of the very dowdy, inspired by the missionaries; the very sexy, inspired by the tropical weather; and Western fashion.

The former is embodied in the Mother Hubbard or mission dress, a long floral dress often trimmed with lace, which is today really only worn by older women. These women also wear woven hats, often decorated with flowers or shells, particularly at Sunday church services.

Younger Polynesians tend to wear Western dress or the pareu, a cool, comfortable single piece of fabric decorated in bright designs.

Tifaifai These large, brilliantly coloured patchwork blankets are produced on a number of islands, including Rurutu in the Australs. Usually decorated with stylised flowers or fruit designs and used as tablecloths, bedspreads and curtains, *tifaifai* (colourful intricately sewn appliqué works) also have ceremonial uses. Wrapping a guest in one is a sign of welcome and it's an important traditional wedding gift.

Tapa The Marquesas is one of the last places to produce tapa cloth using traditional methods. It's made from the bark of the paper mulberry tree by women on the island of Fatu Hiva for ceremonies and collectors.

Plaiting & Basketwork Women make baskets, hats and panels used for roofing and walls. Coconut palm leaves are used for rough-woven work such as the walls of a *fare*, but for finer work, such as hats and mats, pandanus leaves are used. Some of the finest work comes from Rurutu in the Australs.

Shells, Flowers & Monoi Flowers are displayed, offered and worn throughout Polynesia, where even the night air carries the soft floral scents. *Tiare*, jasmine, hibiscus and frangipani are the blossoms most often used for necklaces and crowns.

Shells are used to make necklaces, traditionally used to garland people arriving at and departing the islands.

Wonderful *monoi* is coconut oil perfumed with crushed flowers (*tiare*, jasmine, sandalwood and the like). It's used for hair oil, ointment, sunscreen and even mosquito repellent.

Tattoos Traditionally this form of bodily decoration signified social status, with more tattoos added over a lifetime. Paradoxically, tattoos increased an individual's desirability while also being seen as a way of intimidating the enemy.

RELIGION

The arrival of Protestant missionaries at the end of the 18th century, followed soon after by the Catholics, marked the suppression of traditional religious beliefs and practices in French Polynesia. Their influence remains today, and about half of the population follows the Église Évangélique de Polynésie (Evangelical Church of Polynesia), which is Protestant; around 30% is Catholic; and Mormons, various other Christian sects, Judaism, Buddhism and Confucianism constitute the rest.

Missionaries did their best to obliterate the pre-European religion and culture, destroying stone *tiki*, demolishing *marae* (traditional temples), banning dancing and even dictating what people could wear. The churches still wield strong financial power and play a major role in the social life, politics and culture of the islands. Curiously, today the churches actively promote Polynesian tradition: Tahitian and Marquesan are the language of church services.

Archaeologists have repaired much of the damage to religious sites and some pre-Christian rituals and superstitions survive. Ancient tapu (sacred, prohibited, taboo) sites are respected and feared. Few Polynesians would dare to move a *tiki* or *marae* stone and on occasion they will consult a *tahua* (a traditional healer).

LANGUAGE

Tahitian and French are the official languages of French Polynesia, although Tahitian is spoken much more than it is written. Much of the tourist industry uses English, but if you venture to the more remote and less touristy islands it's useful to know some French. On all islands, at least trying a few words in French

will win you friends – fortunately, bad French is readily accepted. See the French Language appendix for some useful phrases.

Tahitian, known as Maohi, is a Polynesian language very similar to Hawaiian and Cook Islands Maori. Other languages in the islands include Austral, Marquesan and Tuamotuan.

In Tahitian, a glottal stop (see Language in the Facts about the South Pacific chapter) replaces the consonants 'k' and 'ng'. The Polynesian word *vaka* (canoe) is *va'a* in Tahitian. It's important to use the glottal stop, as the break can change the meaning of the word. For example, the Tahitian word *hoe* means 'paddle or row, but *ho'e* is the word for one.

Tahitian Basics

Hello.	*Ia ora na, nana.*
Goodbye.	*Parahi, nana.*
Welcome.	*Maeva, manava.*
How are you?	*E aha te huru?*
Thanks.	*Mauruuru roa.*
Yes.	*E, 'oia.*
No.	*Aita.*
My name is…	*To'u i'oa 'o…*
I don't understand.	*Aita i ta'a ia'u.*

Facts for the Visitor

SUGGESTED ITINERARIES

You're going for a holiday, so don't try to see everything – French Polynesia's five archipelagos cover an expanse of ocean as big as Europe and getting around can take time and planning. However, try to visit a few different islands to get a taste of the different cultures and landscapes.

In one week you could taste Tahiti, then head to Mo'orea and Bora Bora; if you're intent on the whirlwind visit you could also squeeze in one of the Tuamotus (flying direct from Bora Bora to Rangiroa).

Two weeks is the minimum time to have a decent look around the Society Islands (allow about two days on each island) and visit one of the Tuamotus.

In three weeks you could explore several islands in depth. You could visit all the main islands of the Society group, by air or sea, and continue to the Tuamotus (Rangiroa, Tikehau and Manihi) or the Australs (Rurutu and Tubuai) by air. Or else allow a week for the Society Islands, then take a 10- to 12-day cruise on the *Aranui* to the Marquesas.

A whole month would give you time to see the Society Islands, two or three atolls in the

Tuamotus and several islands in the Marquesas. Fly from Bora Bora to Rangiroa in the Tuamotus and Rangiroa to Nuku Hiva (Marquesas).

Then again, after a few days in French Polynesia, you might just decide to ditch your itinerary and unwind into the island-paced lifestyle.

PLANNING
When to Go
From May to October, when it's less humid and marginally cooler, is the best time to visit, although the intermittent *maraamu* trade winds can bring blustery weather and rain between June and August: in those months stick to the more sheltered northern sides of the high islands. It rains *a lot* between November and April.

During the busiest times you'll need to book air fares and accommodation well in advance. July's activities and festivals make it the busiest tourist month. School holidays, the same as in France, are also busy, especially at Easter and July/August. Christmas and New Year are even busier because they coincide with the start of the southern hemisphere holiday break.

Diving and surfing are popular year-round, but sailing is best if you avoid the tropical depressions from November to March. Walking is also better in the dry season – some trails are impassable when wet.

Maps
The 1:100,000 map *Tahiti Archipel de la Société* (IGN No 3615) is readily available in Pape'ete and from map specialists abroad. It covers the Society Islands and is the one really useful map for tourists. IGN also publishes maps at 1:50,000 for every island of the archipelago. For the Tuamotus the SHOM navy maps are the best available. For the Marquesas you can get SHOM or IGN 1:50,000 maps for Hiva Oa, Nuku Hiva and 'Ua Pou.

In Pape'ete these maps are sold at the **Prince Hinoi Centre** (Av du Prince Hinoi) and in the **Librairie du Vaima** (Vaima Centre).

TOURIST OFFICES
Local Tourist Offices
For information before you leave home contact **Tahiti Tourisme** (GIE; ☎ 50 57 00, W www.tahiti-tourisme.com; Immeuble Paofai, Bâtiment D, Blvd Pomare), which is based in Pape'ete. It has details of accommodation and local tourist operators, but only supplies information to people overseas.

Once you're in Tahiti, go to the Manava Visitors Bureau (see Information under Pape'ete in the Tahiti section later in this chapter).

Tourist Offices Abroad
Offices of Tahiti Tourisme include:

Australia (☎ 02-9281 6020, W www.traveltotahiti.com.au) 12 Ann St, Surry Hills, NSW 2010
France (☎ 01 55 42 64 34, W www.voyagea tahiti.com) 28 Blvd Saint-Germain, 75005 Paris
Germany (☎ 69-9714 84, W www.tahititourisme.de) Bockenheimer Landstr 45, 60325 Frankfurt/Main
New Zealand (☎ 09-368 5362, W www.tahiti-tourisme.co.nz) Level 1, Studio 2A, 200 Victoria St West, Auckland
USA (☎ 310-414 8484, W www.gototahiti.com) 300 Continental Blvd, Suite 160, El Segundo, CA 90245

French Polynesia is also represented overseas by the South Pacific Tourism Organisation (SPTO); see Tourist Offices in the Regional Facts for the Visitor chapter for details.

VISAS & DOCUMENTS
Everyone visiting French Polynesia needs a passport, and if you need a visa to visit France then you'll need one to visit French Polynesia; the general information section on W www.tahiti-tourisme.com lists who needs visas, or check with a French diplomatic office or travel agent. Some nationalities can stay three months without a visa; others are allowed only one month. Everyone except EU and French citizens must have an onwards or return ticket.

To extend a one-month visa contact the **Police aux Frontières** (Frontier Police; ☎/fax 42 40 74; e pafport@mail.pf), at Faa'a airport and next to the Manava Visitors Bureau in Pape'ete, at least one week before the visa or exemption expires. Extensions cost 3000 CFP and are for a maximum of two months.

Foreign visitors can't stay longer than three months; to stay longer you need to apply to the French consular authorities in your own country for a residence permit.

Car-rental agencies in French Polynesia only ask to see your national driving licence, so you don't need an international driving licence.

Formalities for Yachts
Sailors must present the certificate of ownership of the vessel, and are subject to the same passport and visa requirements as other

travellers. You need a return air ticket or a banking guarantee of repatriation equivalent to the price of an airline ticket to your country of origin.

Yachties must advise the Police aux Frontières of their final departure. If your first port of call is not Pape'ete, it must be a port with a *gendarmerie* (police station). Ports with *gendarmerie*: Afareaitu (Mo'orea, Society Islands), Uturoa (Ra'iatea, Society Islands), Fare (Huahine, Society Islands), Vaitape (Bora Bora, Society Islands), Taiohae (Nuku Hiva, Marquesas), Hakahau ('Ua Pou, Marquesas), Atuona (Hiva Oa, Marquesas), Mataura (Tubuai, Australs), Moerai (Rurutu, Australs), Rairua (Raivavae, Australs), Avatoru (Rangiroa, Tuamotus) or Rikitea (Mangareva, Gambier Archipelago). The *gendarmerie* must be advised of each arrival and departure, and of any change of crew.

Before arriving in Pape'ete announce your arrival on Channel 12. Report to the *capitainerie* (harbour master's office), in the same building as the Police aux Frontières, to complete an arrival declaration.

EMBASSIES & CONSULATES
French Embassies & Consulates
You'll find French diplomatic representation in:

Australia (☎ 02-6216 0100, W www.ambafrance -au.org) 6 Perth Ave, Yarralumla, ACT 2600
Canada (☎ 613-789 1795, W www.ambafrance -ca.org) 42 Sussex Dr, Ottawa, Ontario K1M 2C9
Fiji (☎ 331 22 33) Dominion House, Scott St, Suva
Germany (☎ 30-590 039 000, W www .botschaft-frankreich.com) An der Kochstrasse 6/7, D-10969 Berlin
New Zealand (☎ 04-384 2555, W www .ambafrance-nz.org) Rural Bank Bldg, 13th floor, 34-42 Manners St, PO Box 11-343, Wellington
UK (☎ 020-7073 1000, W www.ambafrance- uk.org) 58 Knightsbridge, London SW1X 7JT
USA (☎ 202-944 6000, W www.ambafrance- us.org) 4101 Reservoir Rd NW, Washington, DC 20007

Consulates in French Polynesia
As French Polynesia isn't an independent country it only has foreign consulates rather than embassies; many countries only have honorary consuls in Pape'ete, while Canada, the USA and Japan have no diplomatic representation. If you need a US visa the nearest place to inquire is Fiji. If you're Canadian and you lose your passport try the Australian consulate. These honorary consulates are all on Tahiti:

Australia (☎ 43 88 38) c/- Qantas, Vaima Centre, BP 1695, Pape'ete
Germany (☎ 42 99 94) rue Tihoni Tefaatau, BP 452, Pape'ete
New Zealand (☎ 54 07 47, e alan.roman@airnz .co.nz) c/- Air NZ, Vaima Centre, BP 73, Pape'ete

CUSTOMS
The duty-free allowance is 200 cigarettes (or 100 cigarillos, 50 cigars or 250g of tobacco), 50g of perfume, 2L of spirits or wine, two cameras and 10 rolls of unexposed film and one video camera. You can't import live animals (any on a yacht must stay on board) and certification is required for plants.

MONEY
Currency & Exchange Rates
The unit of currency is the Cour de Franc Pacifique (CFP), the French Pacific Franc, referred to simply as 'the franc' and used in New Caledonia and Wallis & Futuna as well as French Polynesia. Coins come in 1 CFP, 2 CFP, 5 CFP, 10 CFP, 20 CFP, 50 CFP and 100 CFP and notes are 500 CFP, 1000 CFP, 5000 CFP and 10,000 CFP. The CFP is pegged to the euro.

country	unit		pacific franc
Australia	A$1	=	68 CFP
Canada	C$1	=	76 CFP
Easter Island	Ch$100	=	14 CFP
euro zone	€1	=	119 CFP
Fiji	F$1	=	54 CFP
Japan	¥100	=	86 CFP
New Zealand	NZ$1	=	59 CFP
PNG	K1	=	29 CFP
Samoa	ST1	=	34 CFP
Solomon Islands	S$1	=	14 CFP
Tonga	T$1	=	48 CFP
UK	£1	=	171 CFP
USA	US$1	=	102 CFP
Vanuatu	100VT	=	85 CFP

To check current exchange rates, see W www .oanda.com.

Exchanging Money
The most common bank is the Banque Socredo. Most banks are concentrated in Pape'ete and the more populous islands of Mo'orea, Ra'iatea and Bora Bora. All the

TAHITI & FRENCH POLYNESIA

main islands in the Society group have at least a banking agency, though Maupiti's is rarely ever open. In the Tuamotus, only Rangiroa has a permanent banking service. In the Marquesas there are Socredo agencies on Nuku Hiva, 'Ua Pou and Hiva Oa. In the Australs, both Rurutu and Tubuai have Socredo branches.

Unless you're changing French francs there are hefty bank charges for changing money or travellers cheques. Typically it's at least 450 CFP. Rates on Tahiti tend to be better than those on other islands. Top-end and mid-range hotels, restaurants on the tourist islands, souvenir and jewellery shops, dive centres, major supermarkets and Air Tahiti accept credit cards, preferably Visa or MasterCard. You might find that many shops won't accept credit cards for amounts less than about 2000 CFP.

In theory you can withdraw money on your Visa card or MasterCard at an ATM; usually the exchange rate's better and the fee your bank charges will be less than what a bank in French Polynesia will. However, this seems to usually work with European cards only; have a backup plan just in case. ATMs are dotted around Tahiti, but are less common on other islands. Mo'orea, Huahine, Ra'iatea, Bora Bora and Rangiroa have ATMs (Rangiroa has the only ATM in the Tuamotus). On Nuku Hiva and Hiva Oa in the Marquesas and on Rurutu and Tubuai in the Australs there are ATMs inside the Socredo agencies.

Costs

French Polynesia is expensive by anyone's standards. It costs a lot to get there and once you've landed food and accommodation costs rack up quickly. Taxes hit the hip pocket: a TVA (*taxe sur la valeur ajoutée*; value-added tax) adds 6% to your hotel bill (on top of the 5% government tax and the *taxe de séjour* – accommodation tax or daily tax). See the boxed text 'Cheap Thrills' for tips about saving money.

All accommodation prices in this chapter include the TVA and *taxe de séjour* – it's the usual practice for hotels to quote without them, so make sure you clarify what little additions you should expect on your bill.

However, on the upside, you're not expected to tip. Bargaining's another thing that's not done in French Polynesia – except perhaps when buying black pearls, or craftwork directly from an artist.

You would not get by with much less than around 5000 CFP a day, and that would be staying in very basic accommodation as well as cooking for yourself. As a guide, expect to pay:

item	cost (CFP)
baguette	50
local beer	350
coffee	250–300
French-bread sandwich	500
café meal	1500
restaurant main	2500–3600
three-hour island tour per person	3500–5000
one scuba dive	5500–6500
guided walk per person	3000–15,000
camping/dorm bed per person	1000/2000
pension single/double per night	4500/6500
mid-range bungalow per night	10,000–40,000

POST & COMMUNICATIONS
Post

Mail to Europe, the USA and Australia takes about a week and the postal system is generally quite efficient. All the main islands have modern post offices. Postcards or letters weighing up to 20g cost 85 CFP to France, 120 CFP to anywhere else. There is no door-to-door mail delivery, so mail is usually addressed to a BP (*boîte postale*; post-office box) number.

To collect mail at the post office it should be addressed to you care of poste restante at the post office you'll be visiting, eg, Paul Gauguin, Poste Restante, Pape'ete, Tahiti, French Polynesia.

Telephone

The telephone system in French Polynesia is modern and widespread but is expensive for international calls. Public phone boxes are found in surprisingly remote locations. Most require phonecards rather than coins. Phonecards can be bought from post offices, newsagencies, shops and vending machines at Faa'a airport.

There are no area codes in Tahiti. Local phone calls cost 33 CFP for four minutes, while inter-archipelago calls cost 33 CFP per minute. The number for directory information is ☎ 3612.

French Polynesia's international telephone code is ☎ 689.

If you want to call overseas from French Polynesia dial ☎ 00. In order to make a reverse-charge call, ask for '*un appel payable à l'arrivée*'.

Cheap Thrills

You can do French Polynesia on a shoestring, but it's a real challenge. The cost of activities, accommodation and food can quickly add up, and if you're surrounded by travellers who appear to have fatter wallets than you do, it can all feel a bit disheartening.

Do not despair! A fresh baguette (around 50 CFP) is never far away, the cheapest dish on almost any menu is the wonderful and filling *poisson cru* (raw marinated fish; 1000 CFP), and the warm weather means camping or rudimentary accommodation is far from unpleasant.

The best thing you can do for your bottom line is get out of Tahiti. Close by, Mo'orea has camping grounds and better cheap accommodation. All over the archipelago families are opening up their homes as quaint and affordable little *pensions* (guesthouses; singles/doubles from 4500/6500 CFP per night), helping you meet your budget while you meet some locals. Many places have kitchens where you can cook your own meals; when eating out consider just ordering an appetiser – they're usually substantial and reasonably priced (800 to 1500 CFP) and fresh French bread will magically appear with every meal. In resorts you can often ask for filling french fries with your meal for no extra charge.

It's generally not far to anywhere on the island and riding a bike gets you chatting with the locals and gives more excuses to munch on tropical fruit; many *pensions* rent bicycles or have one for guest use, though they're likely to be old clunkers. If you bring a mask and snorkel, the joys of pottering about the aqua shallows of a lagoon are priceless.

Mere mortals can afford French Polynesia; it just takes creativity.

Email & Internet Access

Internet cafés are still fairly few and far between in French Polynesia, although most top-end hotels offer Internet access to their guests, and logging on is fairly straightforward on Tahiti, Mo'orea, Bora Bora, Rangiroa and Ra'iatea. You will generally pay around 500 CFP per half-hour.

DIGITAL RESOURCES

Many of the websites with information about Tahiti and French Polynesia are now in both French and English. Websites on specific topics are listed throughout this chapter; useful generalist English-language sites include the following:

Tahiti Communications (W www.tahiti.com) A travel agent's creation, this very ugly site includes links to news, events, daily weather and travel packages.

Tahiti Explorer (W www.tahiti-explorer.com) This agent's site includes background information, FAQs and a travel forum.

Tahiti Nui Travel (W www.tahiti-nui.com) This travel agent's site has the latest on airline prices and flight schedules into and around French Polynesia, plus useful background information on cruises and hotels.

Tahiti Tourisme (W www.tahiti-tourisme.com) The official Tahiti tourism website, this has lots of practical information and provides a general overview.

BOOKS

There is a wide range of literature on French Polynesia and a number of excellent bookshops in Pape'ete. Some of the most interesting titles are only readily available in French Polynesia and some, only in French.

Guidebooks

If you want more in-depth detail on French Polynesia, look for Lonely Planet's *Tahiti & French Polynesia* guidebook. The extensively illustrated Lonely Planet Pisces guide *Diving & Snorkeling Tahiti & French Polynesia* covers 40 popular dive sites in the Society Islands, the Tuamotus and the Marquesas.

Travel

In *Blue Latitudes: Boldly Going Where Captain Cook has Gone Before* (2002), Pulitzer-winning writer Tony Horwitz follows the voyages of Captain Cook with his beer-swilling friend Williamson. It's a brilliantly funny and insightful read. *Sultry Climates: Travel and Sex Since the Grand Tour*, by Ian Littlewood (2001), takes an unabashed look at the history of travel and sex, a pertinent topic given the attitude of many of the early explorers towards Tahitian women.

Paul Theroux was at his most sour when he visited *The Happy Isles of Oceania* (1992), describing Tahiti as 'a paradise of fruit trees, brown tits and kiddie porn', but the insights are up to his usual high standards.

Much more upbeat is Gavin Bell's award-winning *In Search of Tusitala* (1994), which traces the Pacific wanderings of Robert Louis Stevenson.

For classics, look to Herman Melville, Pierre Loti, Robert Louis Stevenson, Jack London and Somerset Maugham. Melville's tales of his travels whilst on whaling hellships are recorded in *Typee* (1846) and *Omoo* (1847).

French literature's primary contribution to Tahiti's bookshelves was Loti's 1876 novel *The Marriage of Loti*, which contributed to the romantic Tahitian myth.

History

One of the few Polynesian accounts of pre-European religion is Teuira Henry's *Ancient Tahiti* (1928). David Howarth's *Tahiti – A Paradise Lost*, which is now out of print, records the cultural collision between Europe and Polynesia.

In *The Word, the Pen, and the Pistol* (2000), Robert Nicole examines in detail the mythical values attributed to the Polynesians, as well as looking at the more recent history of French control and nuclear testing.

Tahiti, by George Calderon, who travelled around the Pacific in 1906, was reprinted in 2002. Calderon's drawings and elegant prose are captivating.

Natural History

The small *Birds of Tahiti*, by Jean-Claude Thibault & Claude Rivers, and *Sharks of Polynesia*, by RH Johnson, are worth a look.

Art & Culture

The Art of Tahiti, by Terence Barrow, is a succinct introduction to the art of the Society, Austral and Cook Islands (but it's out of print).

There's a whole paintbox of books on Gauguin and his works. Some of the most recent include John Borthwick's *Chasing Gauguin's Ghost: Tales of a Professional Tourist* (2002) and Eckhard Hollmann's *Paul Gauguin: Images from the South Seas* (2002). *Noa Noa – The Tahiti Journal of Paul Gauguin* is the artist's autobiographical account of life in Tahiti.

If painting on skin's more your thing, turn to *Tatau – Maohi Tattoo* by Dominique Morvan, a fascinating account of the resurgence of traditional tattooing in French Polynesia.

Hiva Oa – Glimpses of an Oceanic Memory, by Pierre Ottino & Marie-Noëlle de Bergh-Ottino (1991), is a locally produced book on the archaeology and art of the Marquesan island of Hiva Oa.

Breadfruit by Cëlestine Hitura Vaite provides a humorous look at love, life, family and tradition in Tahiti.

FILMS

Tahiti's role as a movie backdrop is almost exclusively tied up with the *Bounty*. Three times Hollywood has dispatched Bligh, Christian and the *Bounty* to Tahiti to relive the mutiny (see the boxed text 'Mutiny on the Bounty' in the Pitcairn Island chapter).

Tabu (1931) is the only decent film shot in Polynesia that has nothing to do with the *Bounty*. Shot on Bora Bora, the film explored the notion of tapu.

NEWSPAPERS & MAGAZINES

Most newspapers and magazines available in French Polynesia are in French, although you can usually find a pricey, dated English-language newspaper. In Pape'ete, **La Maison de la Presse** *(Blvd Pomare)* has a good selection, as does **Le Kiosque** *(Blvd Pomare)*, **Librairie du Vaima** *(Vaima Centre)*, the bookshop in the **Prince Hinoi Centre** *(Av du Prince Hinoi)* and **Librairie Archipels** *(68 rue des Remparts)*. On other islands TV is probably the best way to keep up to date with world events.

Tahiti Beach Press is a free English-language weekly tourist paper with some local news.

RADIO & TV

About 10 independent radio stations broadcast music, a few interviews and news in French and Tahitian. Broadcasting is mainly from Tahiti and Mo'orea. Radio France Outre-Mer (RFO) broadcasts many local programmes in Tahitian, as well as hourly news in French.

RFO also has two television channels: Télépolynésie and Tempo. The local news (Vea Tahiti) is broadcast in Tahitian at 6.45pm and in French at 7.05pm. The major islands get Canal+, while Tahiti and Mo'orea have Téléfenua, a cable package including CNN. The Australs, Tuamotus and Marquesas make do with Télépolynésie.

PHOTOGRAPHY

Film is expensive in French Polynesia and gets more difficult to find and even more expensive as you get further from Pape'ete. For 36-exposure film in Pape'ete, budget on 1700 CFP for slide film and 1000 CFP for print film. Fast developing and printing is easy to find on Tahiti and the other touristed islands but is costly. You will pay anywhere from 3400 to 4300 CFP to develop a 36-exposure print film.

Just for fun, throw in a disposable waterproof camera for underwater snorkelling or swimming shots in the clear water.

The tropical light is intense in French Polynesia, so it's better to take photographs in the early morning or late afternoon. No cultural restrictions apply to photography, but as a courtesy you should always ask permission when photographing people.

TIME

Tahiti (and neighbouring islands) is 10 hours behind GMT. The Marquesas are half an hour ahead of the rest of French Polynesia (noon in Tahiti is 12.30pm in the Marquesas) but check flight schedules carefully: Air Tahiti departures and arrivals for the Marquesas may run to Tahiti time.

LAUNDRY

You can get your clothes washed in French Polynesia – at a price. Big hotels charge through the nose for the service and laundrettes are expensive, charging around 1600 CFP to wash and dry a load, in Pape'ete and are unheard of elsewhere. Get used to hand washing and go out to dinner instead.

HEALTH

French Polynesia is an outdoorsy, healthy place and, apart from sunburn if you forget to cover up, you're unlikely to get ill. Food and water are good and there are few endemic diseases. Malaria does not exist here, but there have been outbreaks of dengue fever. Ciguatera also occurs. See Health in the Regional Facts for the Visitor chapter for more information.

Medical facilities are generally of a high standard and although the number of medical practitioners is limited on the outer islands there are hospitals or dispensaries.

Pape'ete has one public hospital, two private clinics and a number of pharmacies. All tourist islands have at least a medical cabinet with one or more physicians, and Mo'orea, Ra'iatea, Bora Bora, Nuku Hiva and Hiva Oa all have small medical centres. A doctor's consultation will cost you approximately 3000 CFP; French visitors can have this refunded when they return home, and EU citizens should obtain an E-111 form before leaving home.

Water

Tap water is only completely safe in Pape'ete, on Bora Bora and on Tubuai. On some islands, particularly low-lying atolls, rainwater is collected and stored separately from well water, which can be tainted by sea water. Bottled spring water and mineral water are readily available.

Bites & Stings

Take care on some walking routes – wasp nests sometimes overhang the path. Large centipedes can give a painful or irritating bite but are no more dangerous than a bee or wasp sting. In the Marquesas cover up against the irritating *nono* (see the boxed text 'Oh No, It's the Nono!' in the Marquesas Islands section later in this chapter).

SOCIAL GRACES

French Polynesia is generally very easy-going and there are few pitfalls for the unwary visitor; *'Aita pe'a pe'a'* ('No problems') is a common expression.

Religion permeates everyday life and, contrary to popular myth, Polynesian women are very chaste. Local women usually wear shorts and T-shirts in the water and nudity on the beach is only permissible on isolated *motu* (island). Bikini tops are not required at big hotel beaches and swimming pools but elsewhere going topless is inappropriate. The French air kiss is widely practised, but public displays of intimacy are seldom seen.

Respect archaeological sites; for many Polynesians these are living places and these people will be deeply offended if you move stones or *tiki* around on tapu sites.

Tipping is not expected and bargaining (except for pearls) is not practised. Respect private-property signs, which often indicate that entry is tapu. Most waterfront land is privately owned, so ask permission before making your way down to the water; ditto for *motu*. Fruit trees are almost always private property, so never pick fruit without asking first.

See Society & Conduct in the Facts about the South Pacific chapter for information about Polynesian tradition. See Accommodation in the Regional Facts for the Visitor chapter for advice about staying in Polynesian homes.

WOMEN TRAVELLERS

French Polynesia is a great place for solo women to explore. Local women are very much a part of public life in the region, and it's not unusual to see Polynesian women out drinking beer together, or walking alone, so you'll probably feel pretty comfortable following suit.

Exercise the same care you would anywhere in the world when walking alone or at night. 'Peeping Toms' can be a problem, so be cautious if you're staying in a place where you can be easily seen from the outside, particularly in the shower, and make sure your room is securely locked.

Bring tampons and pads from home; they're available in the bigger supermarkets around French Polynesia, but are remarkably expensive (800 CFP for 16 tampons; 400 CFP for 16 pads).

GAY & LESBIAN TRAVELLERS

French law prevails in French Polynesia, so there is no legal discrimination against homosexuals. Homophobia is uncommon; in fact, a fine old Polynesian transgender tradition is still alive and well here. *Mahu* are men who dress and act as women from childhood. They are similar to the *fakaleiti* of Tonga (see the boxed text 'Fakaleiti' in that country's chapter). Most, but not all, *mahu* are homosexual and many are *rae rae* (transvestites). The Tiki Soft C@fé in Pape'ete is a popular and hip spot for *popaa* (Westerner) gays.

Te Anuanua o Te Fenua *(Gay, Lesbian & Bisexual Association of French Polynesia; ☎ 77 31 11)* is based on Tahiti.

DISABLED TRAVELLERS

As elsewhere in the Pacific, travellers with restricted mobility will find very little in the way of helpful infrastructure. With narrow flights of steps on boats, high steps on *le trucks* (public buses) and difficult boarding on Air Tahiti aircraft, the itinerary for mobility-impaired travellers in French Polynesia resembles an obstacle course. However, all new hotels and public buildings must conform to certain standards, so expect a gradual change.

Those who are not put off by these obstacles should contact Te Nui o Te Huma, La Fédération des Handicapés de Polynésie *(Polynesian Association of War Invalids & Military Pensioners; ☎ 43 17 89)* for advice and assistance.

SENIOR TRAVELLERS

Older travellers will have no problems in French Polynesia. Air Tahiti gives reductions to those aged over 60 with a Carte Marama

(Third Age Card; see Reduced-Fare Cards under Air in the Getting Around section later in this chapter for details).

TRAVEL WITH CHILDREN

For a child-friendly holiday destination you can't go past French Polynesia. There are no major health concerns, the climate is good and you can find things kids will eat. Most locals have a number of children themselves and will not be troubled by a child having a tantrum at the next table. Children are very much a part of public life in Polynesia.

However, nappies (diapers) and block-out sunscreen are very expensive (1700 CFP for 38 nappies), so bring your own.

Medical facilities are widespread and Mamao Hospital in Pape'ete has a modern paediatric department.

You will have priority when boarding Air Tahiti aircraft. A Carte Famille (Family Card) entitles you to significant reductions on some flights (see Reduced-Fare Cards under Air in the Getting Around section later in this chapter for details). At hotels and guesthouses children under 12 generally pay only half the adult rate; very young children usually stay for free.

Some dive centres, such as Tahiti Plongée *(☎ 41 00 62)*, on Tahiti, take children aged eight and over on dives.

USEFUL ORGANISATIONS

Te Fare Tahiti Nui *(☎ 54 45 44/40; 646 Blvd Pomare, Pape'ete; open 8am-noon & 1pm-5pm Mon-Thur & 1pm-4pm Fri)*, the Maison de la Culture (Cultural Centre), is at the western exit from the city. It is devoted to promoting cultural events. Cultural weeks or gatherings are held there regularly. Tahitian language courses are available and the centre has a library.

DANGERS & ANNOYANCES

French Polynesia is not a particularly dangerous or annoying destination: all the more reason to go there.

You're unlikely to be kept awake by late-night revelry anywhere except in the heart of Pape'ete, but the roosters are another matter. Dogs can also be annoying, and although they're generally too lethargic to be bothered with travellers, a few travellers have been bitten, particularly in the Tuamotus – use common sense and steer clear of them.

French Polynesia may not have malaria, but the mosquitoes are still brutal. They are tolerable during the cooler season from May to October but can be a bother in the hotter, wetter months. For some reason, *marae* seem to attract them in swarms. The Marquesas' tiny *nono* are worse; see the boxed text 'Oh No, It's the Nono!' in the Marquesas Islands section later in this chapter.

Swimming in French Polynesia usually means staying within the protected waters of a lagoon, but swimmers should still be aware of tides and currents, and particularly of the swift movement of water out of a lagoon through a pass into the open sea.

Theft isn't a big problem, though don't expect your valuables to still be on the park bench if you leave them there. Even busy Pape'ete is relatively safe compared with cities in the USA and Europe, although occasional robberies and pickpocketings do occur. More-expensive hotels have a central safe. Don't leave anything of value in a rental car.

Yacht crews should take care in popular yachting centres like Bora Bora or in the Marquesas, where theft from yachts does happen.

Violence is also rarely a problem. Intoxicated youths are the most likely troublemakers – they might address you as a *titoi* (wanker), but this is unlikely to ruin your holiday!

BUSINESS HOURS

Like France, French Polynesia is the land of the long lunch. Do as the locals do and eat or take a siesta instead of trying to do business between noon and about 2pm.

Shops and offices open from 7.30am or 8am to 5.30pm Monday to Friday, although many places close an hour earlier on Friday. A long, leisurely lunch break is not uncommon. Tourist offices keep similar hours and also open at least on Saturday morning; in smaller places they may shut at about 4pm, and tiny offices open only on weekday mornings.

Food shops and supermarkets generally stay open late in the evening. Shops open until noon on Saturday, often until 5pm in Pape'ete, and almost all close on Sunday. Food shops and supermarkets are the exception: even on the smaller islands they tend to stay open every day.

Banks are typically open during business hours Monday to Friday, with a break for lunch.

Post offices in the islands usually open weekdays from 7am to 3.30pm, though the central office in Pape'ete opens longer and the post office at Faa'a airport is also open from 6.30am to 10am Saturday and Sunday.

PUBLIC HOLIDAYS & SPECIAL EVENTS

French Polynesia has the same major public holidays as France. It has a day off for New Year's Day, Easter, Ascension Day, Labour Day, Pentecost, Bastille Day, Assumption Day, All Saints' Day, Armistice Day and Christmas (see the Regional Facts for the Visitor chapter for dates), plus:

Arrival of the first Missionaries 5 March
May Day 1 May
VE Day 8 May
Autonomy Day 29 June

Other major events include:

January
Chinese New Year Usually falling between late January and mid-February, the new year is ushered in with dancing, martial arts displays and fireworks.

February
Tahiti Nui Marathon One thousand runners gather in Mo'orea for this long-established fund-raising event along a flat course past spectacular scenery.

March
Arrival of the First Missionaries On 5 March the landing of the first LMS missionaries is re-enacted at Point Vénus on Tahiti Nui. Celebrations are held at Protestant churches on Tahiti and Mo'orea and in Tipaerui and Afareaitu.

April/May
Beauty Contests Many contests are held ahead of the Miss Tahiti and Miss Heiva i Tahiti contests in June (Mr Tahiti contests are also held).

May
Billabong Tahiti Pro Surfing Tournament Three days of international-level surfing in the big waves of Puna'auia (Tahiti).

June
Miss Tahiti & Miss Heiva i Tahiti contests Winners of beauty contests around the archipelago in the last 12 months gather in Pape'ete to vie for the chance to represent French Polynesia around the world. Miss Heiva reigns for the month-long Heiva celebrations.
Tahiti International Golf Open This four-day event is held on Tahiti in late June or early July.

July/August
Heiva i Tahiti This major Polynesian festival, held in Pape'ete, includes traditional demonstrations throughout July. Mini-Heiva events take place on other islands in August.

September

Annual Flower Show In Bougainville Park, Pape'ete.

October

Stone-Fishing Contest Traditional stone-fishing celebrations take place in Bora Bora.

Carnival Late in the month there are parades with floats decked with flowers.

November

Hawaiki Nui Canoe Race The major sporting event of the year.

All Saints' Day Graves are cleaned and decorated in an explosion of flowers; families sing hymns in candle-lit cemeteries on 1 November.

December

Tiare Tahiti Days The national flower is celebrated on 1 and 2 December.

The Marquesas Festival A major arts festival at 'Ua Pou, celebrating Marquesan identity.

ACTIVITIES

For details on equipment hire or activity operators contact the **Manava Visitors Bureau** (☎ 50 57 12; e tahiti-manava@mail.microtech.pf) in Pape'ete.

Snorkelling

Snorkelling is a delightful and (usually) free way to experience the amazing underwater world of the territory. The coral reefs and numerous outcrops that dot the lagoons are perfect for snorkelling. You can often explore right out the front of your hotel, or you can go further afield on a lagoon tour by pirogue (dugout canoe) or by renting a boat with an outboard motor. It's a good idea to bring your own mask and snorkel.

Diving

Diving with rays and sharks, whale-watching, drift diving – French Polynesia provides superb dive sites and close encounters that will seduce even the most blasé diver. Conditions are close to perfect: visibility often reaches 40m and the water's a bath-like 29°C in summer and 26°C in winter, with only 1°C of variation down to 45m. You don't need a wetsuit; unencumbered by neoprene, diving in Tahiti is like sex without a condom. Most dives are only a five- to 15-minute boat trip from the shore.

Some of the territory's most spectacular dives, in the Tuamotu, Society and Marquesas islands, are spotlighted in this book's special section 'South Pacific Diving'. For more information look for Lonely Planet's *Diving & Snorkeling Tahiti & French Polynesia*.

There are about 25 professional dive centres in French Polynesia. They open year-round, usually daily. All are at least level 1 on the French CMAS scale and most have at least one PADI instructor. There are almost always staff who speak English. Operators are listed under Activities in island sections later in this chapter. A single dive typically costs 5500 to 6500 CFP (more for beginners), usually including equipment rental but not necessarily the 8% VAT.

An excellent website to drool over is W www.diving-tahiti.com.

Surfing

Polynesia was the birthplace of *horue* (surfing), and the sport is seeing a local revival. Tahiti, in particular, has surf shops, board shapers and a local surfing scene, and hosts an annual surfing contest (see Public Holidays & Special Events earlier in this section). Tahiti, Mo'orea and Huahine are the three main islands for surfing, but Rangiroa and Tikehau in the Tuamotus also have good surfing spots. Take a look at W www.surfingtahiti.pf for photos and contact details of local surfing groups.

Boating

Ra'iatea is the main yachting base in French Polynesia. There are a number of yacht-charter operations with a flotilla of modern monohulls and catamarans. You can rent small boats with outboards to explore the lagoons on some islands. Game-fishing boats are available for charter. For a list of operators, look up charter boats on W www.tahiti-tourisme.com.

Hiking

Get out of the towns and resorts and onto a walking track to see, smell, hear and meet the real French Polynesia. The high islands of French Polynesia offer some superb walks, from a few hours to a few days. For longer walks the tracks are sometimes hard to follow and a guide may be necessary. Tahiti and Mo'orea are the main islands for walking but there are also possibilities on Ra'iatea, Bora Bora and Maupiti. The Marquesas have huge untapped potential, as the only popular walks are on Nuku Hiva and 'Ua Huka.

Cycling

Hire a bicycle and explore French Polynesia at island pace. You'll get more opportunities

TAHITI & FRENCH POLYNESIA

to chat to locals and will see things you don't notice from behind a bus window. Many resorts will hire bicycles. Bring your own mountain bike and head into the interior for some gnarly trail riding; bring all spares, as repairs are fairly limited outside Pape'ete.

Horse Riding

To ride along the beach into a tropical sunset, head to equestrian centres on the larger Society Islands. They offer jaunts of a few hours or longer excursions to explore the island interiors. On the Marquesas horses are part of the landscape and there are various places to rent horses, with or without a guide.

Other Sports

You'll find squash and tennis courts on Tahiti. On other islands the larger hotels have tennis courts. Tahiti has the only golf course in French Polynesia and hosts a mid-year tournament; there are controversial plans to build another course on Mo'orea. Tahiti's soaring mountains promise interesting hang-gliding and there are facilities for this sport. Windsurfing and kite surfing are also practised. Noisy, horrible jet skis are also popular on some islands.

ACCOMMODATION

Although the travel brochures invariably show exotic over-water bungalows, French Polynesia actually has everything from camping and hostel dormitories to five-star luxury accommodation options. However, in all categories the balance between price and quality can be discouraging. Just expect it to be expensive, don't necessarily expect to get what you've paid for, and enjoy the other aspects of French Polynesia.

Air-con's often not supplied, even in some quite expensive places, but the night breeze means you can usually live without it. Many cheaper places don't supply towels or soap.

Credit cards are welcome at luxury resorts, but many mid-range places take cash only; budget places rarely take credit cards. The prices quoted in this book include taxes, but many places will quote you pre-tax prices and the add-ons might horrify you. We have rounded prices to the nearest 100 CFP, so use quoted prices as a guide only and be ready for an increase in taxes (which seems to happen every few years). The *taxe de séjour* (accommodation tax) is charged per person per night and can really add up for families.

Camping & Hostels

More camping grounds are springing up around French Polynesia, but more usually you'll find guesthouses with a spot where you can pitch a tent and use the facilities. Count on 1000 to 2500 CFP per person. Camping is possible on Tahiti, Mo'orea, Huahine, Ra'iatea, Bora Bora, Maupiti, Rangiroa, Tikehau and Mataiva. Make sure your tent is mosquito-proof and waterproof.

There are no youth hostels, but the larger of the Society Islands have guesthouses with dorm beds from 1500 to 3500 CFP per person.

Pensions

Pensions (guesthouses) are generally family affairs and are a great way to meet locals and other travellers, as well as to save money. You either stay in a room in the family house or an independent bungalow.

What they lack in comfort and facilities they usually make up in charm, both of the host, and the little home-made touches. The cheapest bungalows are equipped with shower, toilet, a bed with a screen to keep the mosquitoes at bay and a ceiling fan. Hot water is rarely available. Guesthouses often offer picnics, island tours, fishing trips and pearl-farm visits, or can put you in touch with local operators.

Many *pensions* offer (and sometimes insist upon) *demi-pension* (half-board), which usually means breakfast and dinner. It can cost from 4500 to 9000 CFP per person per day: prices vary widely from island to island. Young children are often allowed to stay for free, and children up to about 12 usually pay half-price. Credit cards are rarely accepted.

You can now book many *pensions* online via W www.haere-mai.pf.

Hotels

There is a glut of mid-range hotels on the more touristy islands, but on the more remote islands it's sometimes all (five-star glamour) or nothing (rudimentary *pensions*). Most mid-range places are well situated and more comfortable than the *pensions*, and there's usually a restaurant on site. You'll typically pay from around 10,000 to 40,000 CFP per night for a bungalow; almost all places in this category accept credit cards.

If you are ever going to pamper yourself, French Polynesia is a great place to do it. The sumptuous luxury hotels often manage to blend their opulent bungalows into the natural setting. Some of the top hotels are on isolated *motu* and can only be reached by boat. Four- and five-star hotels are found on Tahiti, Mo'orea, Bora Bora, Huahine, Ra'iatea, Taha'a, Rangiroa, Manihi, Hiva Oa and Nuku Hiva. You can expect restaurants, bars, a swimming pool, a shop or two and a well-organised activities desk. Most of the bigger hotels put on a Polynesian dance performance, often with buffet meal, a few times a week. You'll often have a choice of garden, beach or over-water bungalows (in ascending order of price). Glass-bottomed coffee tables looking into the water have become standard features of over-water bungalows, giving you a constantly changing fish tank in the floor. The prices are just as dazzling: expect to pay between 35,000 and 100,000 CFP per night, not including meals.

These complexes are not isolated fortresses. If you buy a drink at the bar or a meal in the restaurant you will be welcome to use the beach or watch a dance performance.

FOOD

If a good holiday for you is all about trying delicious food from other cultures then you'll be rapt with French Polynesia. The cuisine is multiethnic: from classic pasta to chow mein to *mahimahi* (dolphin fish) in coconut milk, the repertoire is varied. Nevertheless, Western favourites such as hamburgers and soft drinks are increasingly popular. Rice is found everywhere and pizza and pasta are common on the tourist islands, as is French cuisine. French bread, croissants and snacks are available everywhere.

Traditional cuisine, based on fresh produce, is called *maaa Tahiti* in the Society Islands and Tuamotus and *kaikai enana* in the Marquesas; it's traditionally eaten with the fingers and baked in an underground oven known as an *umu* or *ahimaa*. See the boxed text 'Local Food' for explanations of individual dishes.

Food prices mentioned in this section apply to Pape'ete; transport costs can push prices up on other islands.

Snacks

A *snack* in French Polynesia is actually a little snack-bar-cum-café. These places are usually pretty simple and cheap, and serve everything from sandwiches, known locally as *casse-croûte*, and salads to *poisson cru* (raw fish) and burgers. *Les roulottes* (food caravans – see the boxed text 'Les Roulottes' under Pape'ete in the Tahiti section later) also offer bargain dining.

Local Food

Try to go to a traditional feast at one of the big restaurants or, better still, a family *pension* (guesthouse).

Fish is likely to feature prominently. *Poisson cru*, raw fish in coconut milk, is the most-eaten local dish. Fish is also eaten grilled or poached, accompanied by lime, coconut milk or vanilla sauce. Lobsters, crayfish, sea urchins and freshwater shrimps are highly prized, usually served in curry. *Pua* (suckling pig) is the preferred meat for baking in an *ahimaa*.

Tropical fruit, in season, is eaten fresh or cooked; baked papaya is succulent. *Uru* or *maiore* (breadfruit) is eaten cooked.

To Western tastes, taro and other local staples can be rather bland and tasteless. They are usually boiled but additional flavouring can make them more palatable. *Fei* (a sort of plantain banana) is only eaten cooked and has a bittersweet taste. Taro root is eaten cooked, as are sweet potato and manioc (cassava).

For dessert, *faraoa coco* (coconut bread) is a tasty cake; *firifiri* are doughnuts and *ipo* is heavy Tuamotu bread made of flour, coconut juice, sugar and grated coconut.

Restaurants

Most restaurants are in Pape'ete and on the most touristy islands. They serve French, Polynesian and Chinese specialities and prices vary considerably. Count on 1500 to 2500 CFP for a main.

Try to have at least one meal in the sumptuous setting of a luxury hotel. Surprisingly, the prices are no higher than regular restaurants. Most of the hotel restaurants host superb buffet and dance performances a few times a week, which usually cost around 6000 CFP.

Self-Catering

Cooking for yourself can save you a lot of money in French Polynesia. Consider stocking up at the Marché de Pape'ete (Pape'ete Market), which is laden with vegetables, fruit, meat and fish from all the archipelagos. The Pira'e market, east of Pape'ete, also warrants a detour.

Supermarkets of varying sizes are dotted around the islands. Those on Tahiti, Mo'orea and Ra'iatea are very well equipped.

Most islands have at least one bakery. A French baguette costs less than 50 CFP and a *pain au chocolat*, about 120 CFP. Small food stalls along the road, particularly on Tahiti, sell fruit and vegetables.

European imports are heavily taxed (at 1000 CFP for a camembert, you'd have to be desperate for cheese!).

Fruit
In the right season French Polynesia is dripping with tropical fruit, including mangoes, grapefruit, green lemons, watermelons, pineapples and bananas. *Pamplemousse* (grapefruit) is the large, thick-skinned Southeast Asian variety, rather than the grapefruit that is common in Europe or North America. The rambutan, another Southeast Asian introduction, is a delicious red spiny-skinned cousin to the lychee. In the cooler months fresh fruit and vegetables will be hard to find outside Pape'ete.

DRINKS
Some delicious bottled fruit juices, coconut juice and mineral water are available to quench your thirst. Coffee (surprisingly, usually of the instant variety) costs 200 to 300 CFP.

The local Hinano brand of *pia* (beer) is sold in glass 500mL bottles, 330mL and 500mL cans and on tap. Allow at least 350 CFP in a bar or restaurant.

Pape'ete's supermarkets sell French wine from around 800 CFP. Restaurants sell wine for 1500 to 3000 CFP per bottle. *Maitai* is a local cocktail made with brown rum, white rum, pineapple, grenadine and lime juice, coconut liqueur and sometimes Grand Marnier or Cointreau.

ENTERTAINMENT
Come to French Polynesia to catch up on sleep. Pape'ete is the only place with a really active weekend nightlife. On other islands a drink in a bar and Polynesian dance performance in a big hotel is about as active as it gets. Jump at any chance to go to a *bringue*, a family event with friends.

SPECTATOR SPORTS
Polynesian kids are a sporting bunch and you may catch a volleyball or football event. The national sport is pirogue racing, especially on Tahiti. You will certainly have the opportunity to admire the pirogue teams training on the lagoon. Tahiti hosts an annual international surf competition. See Public Holidays & Special Events earlier in this section for major competition dates.

SHOPPING
Leave some room in your suitcase: French Polynesia has some excellent local crafts, many of which can be found on Tahiti, especially at the Pape'ete Market. For an explanation of local specialities see Art in the Facts about Tahiti & French Polynesia section earlier in this chapter. Beware of imported 'local' souvenirs – colourful woodcarvings probably come from Bali or Colombia.

Handicrafts include woven hats and mats, brilliantly coloured *tifaifai* and tapa. The Marquesas is the place to buy sculpture and woodcarving, although Pape'ete galleries sell this work at higher prices. Marquesan sculptors have a twice-yearly exhibition and sale in the Territorial Assembly building, usually in June and November.

Black pearls, cultivated in the Tuamotus, are sold in jewellery shops in Pape'ete and on other islands.

If your country allows you to import it, deliciously aromatic dried vanilla pods are good value and fresh off the farm. For a waft of Tahiti whenever you have a massage, pick up a bottle of *tiare*-scented *monoi* oil.

There are duty-free shops in Pape'ete and at Faa'a airport. Stamp collectors will love the interesting and colourful stamps; Pape'ete post office has a philately section.

Getting There & Away

AIR
Although you can't beat the romance of arriving by sea, most visitors to French Polynesia arrive by air.

Airports
Faa'a airport (☎ 82 60 61), about 5km west of Pape'ete, on Tahiti, is the only international airport.

Airlines
Airlines serving French Polynesia include Aircalin (Air Calédonie International); Air France; Air New Zealand; Air Tahiti Nui (French Polynesia's international airline, not to be confused with domestic airline Air Tahiti); AOM (Air Outre-Mer); Corsair; Hawaiian Airlines; LanChile; and Polynesian Airlines, in conjunction with Qantas.

For airline websites, see the regional Getting There & Away chapter near the start of this book. International airline offices in Pape'ete include:

Air France (☎ 47 47 47) rue Largarde
Air New Zealand (☎ 54 07 47) Vaima Centre, Blvd Pomare
Air Tahiti Nui (☎ 45 55 55) Immeuble Dexter, Pont de l'Est
Aircalin (☎ 85 09 04) Faa'a airport
Corsair (☎ 42 28 28) cnr Blvd Pomare & rue Clappier
Hawaiian Airlines (☎ 42 15 00) Vaima Centre, Blvd Pomare
LanChile (☎ 42 64 55) Vaima Centre, Blvd Pomare
Qantas Airways (☎ 43 06 65) Vaima Centre, Blvd Pomare

Flights go to Tahiti direct from Los Angeles (LA), Honolulu and Auckland (with onwards connections to Australia) and to a number of other Pacific islands. Tahiti is a popular stop on round-the-world (RTW) tickets and is included in several air passes; see the regional Getting There & Away chapter near the start of this book for details. There is no departure tax in French Polynesia.

North America
Fares to Tahiti from the USA are seasonal; late December to mid-June is the low season. All flights go via Hawaii or LA.

Hawaiian Airlines flies every week from Honolulu to Pape'ete with connections to/from LA (direct), San Francisco, Seattle and Las Vegas. Honolulu to Pape'ete return costs US$690/880 in low/high season.

From LA you can get direct flights to Pape'ete with **Air France** (three times weekly), **Air Lib** (three times weekly), **Corsair** (once weekly; also flies from San Francisco), **Air New Zealand** (four times weekly), and the Tahitian carrier **Air Tahiti Nui** (three times weekly). Los Angeles to Pape'ete return costs about US$700. Return fares from Los Angeles to Pape'ete range between US$850 and US$990.

From Canada you have to connect on the west coast or in Hawaii. Return fares from Vancouver via LA start from C$2017.

Europe
The three direct routes from Europe to Tahiti are from Paris, Frankfurt and London – RTW tickets or connections from the USA are another option. All airlines stop briefly in LA.

Corsair, **AOM** and **Air France** fly from Paris to Pape'ete (Air France three times a week,

Corsair once per week). **Air New Zealand** leaves from Frankfurt or London; it continues on to Auckland and Australia and has the option of stopovers in the Cook Islands and Fiji. Return fares from Paris and Frankfurt start at around €1450; Air New Zealand's low-season fare from London starts at £1120.

Australasia
All flights from Australia to Pape'ete are via Auckland. In Auckland, the twice-weekly **Qantas Airways** flights from Sydney connect with either **Air Tahiti Nui** or **Polynesian Airlines** for the Auckland to Pape'ete leg.

Fares increase considerably in high season for both Australia and New Zealand (July to September and over Christmas). From Sydney expect to pay around A$1100/1530 for a return trip in low/high season with **Qantas Airways** or **Air New Zealand**. From Auckland, return fares start at NZ$900/1280 in low/high season. Both **Air New Zealand** and **Qantas Airways/ Air Tahiti Nui** offer connecting flights from Pape'ete to LA.

Asia
Air Tahiti Nui flies between Tokyo, Osaka and Pape'ete. Return flights from Tokyo start at ¥177,516. From other parts of Asia the simplest connection is via Australia or New Zealand.

The Pacific
Hopping around the Pacific isn't difficult, but does require planning to fit in with infrequent flight schedules. Regular flights connect French Polynesia and New Zealand, Fiji, New Caledonia, the Cook Islands, Wallis & Fortuna and Hawaii.

Contact a travel agent with a good knowledge of the vagaries of travel in the region, such as **Hideaway Holidays** *(in Australia ☎ 02-9743 0253, fax 02-9743 3568; W www .hideawayholidays.com.au; in the USA ☎ 530-352 4069)*.

South America
LanChile has two flights a week between Santiago and Pape'ete, with one via Easter Island. Return fares are around US$1500.

SEA
Travelling to French Polynesia by yacht is entirely feasible; you can often pick up crewing positions from North America, Australia or New Zealand, or in the islands; ask at yacht clubs in San Diego, Los Angeles, San

Francisco, Honolulu, Sydney, Cairns or Auckland. See Formalities for Yachts under Visas & Documents in the Facts for the Visitor section earlier in this chapter for information about bringing your own boat into French Polynesian waters.

It takes about a month to sail from the US West Coast to Hawaii and another month south from there to the Marquesas; with stops, another month takes you west to Tahiti and the Society Islands. Then it's another long leg southwest to Australia or New Zealand.

ORGANISED TOURS

Package tours can be financial godsends in French Polynesia. Travel agents in all Western countries offer tours, including diving tours.

Tahiti specialists include:

Australia Hideaway Holidays (☎ 02-9743 0253, Ⓦ www.hideawayholidays.com.au)
Tahiti Vacations (☎ 800-553-3477, Ⓦ www.tahitivacation.com)
UK Sunset Faraway Holidays (☎ 020 7498 9922, Ⓦ www.sunsetfaraway.com)
USA: Tahiti Legends (☎ 800-200-1213, Ⓦ www.tahitilegends.com)

Getting Around

Getting around French Polynesia is half the fun. Travelling between islands involves flights or boat travel and, thanks to French government financial support, travel to the larger and more densely populated islands is relatively easy and reasonably priced, though getting to the remote islands can be harder. Some islands have paved roads, others just have rough tracks; only Pape'ete and its suburbs have reasonably comprehensive public transport. Renting a car or bicycle may be the best bet for exploring other places.

AIR

Apart from smaller charter-style operations, flying in French Polynesia means travelling with **Air Tahiti** and **Air Moorea**. Air Tahiti flies to 38 islands in all five major island groups; Air Moorea operates smaller aircraft between Tahiti, Mo'orea and Tetiaroa.

Most flights pass through Pape'ete; see the relevant island sections for details of frequency. For a bargain, buy an air pass that allows you to visit a number of islands for one fare. Another cost-saving option is a flight and accommodation package. For some islands there are even weekend packages. Contact Air Tahiti's travel arm **Séjours dans les Îles** (☎ 86 43 43, fax 86 40 99; Ⓦ www.sejoursdanslesiles.pf).

Domestic Air Services

Air Tahiti (☎ 86 42 42, 86 40 99 Sat afternoon & Sun; ℮ reservation@airtahiti.pf; Ⓦ www.air tahiti.pf; rue du Maréchal Foch; open Mon-Fri & Sat morning) has its headquarters in Pape'ete and also has an office (open 5am-5.30pm daily) in the domestic area in Faa'a airport. See the sections on the relevant islands for local Air Tahiti phone numbers or contact the head office.

Charter and helicopter services are available on Tahiti, Bora Bora and the Marquesas; see Getting There & Away under Pape'ete and Getting Around under Bora Bora and in the Marquesas Islands section for details.

Information You can take up to 32kg of luggage on board (Faa'a airport has a left-luggage facility). You're not officially required to reconfirm, but it's a good idea. Leave your contact details with the local agent; in remote locations schedules sometimes change. No-shows are penalised 25% of the fare.

Air Tahiti's flight schedule booklet is essential reading if you're planning a complex trip around the islands. At most Air Tahiti offices or agencies you can pay for flights by credit card. Flights are classified in ascending order of demand as blue, white or red.

Air Passes

Several passes allow you to save on visiting multiple islands – all require that you begin your trip in Pape'ete and limit the number of transits through Pape'ete. You are only allowed one stopover on each island but you can transit an island as long as the flight number does not change. Stopping at an island to change flights counts as a stopover.

Passes are valid for 28 days and all flights (except between Pape'ete and Mo'orea) must be booked at the beginning. You can fly either Air Tahiti or Air Moorea on the Pape'ete to Mo'orea sector. Once you've taken the first flight the routing cannot be changed and the fare is non-refundable. There may be restrictions on which 'colour' flights you can use.

The passes include *Passe Découverte* (Discovery Pass: four Society Islands; 23,000/13,000 CFP adults/children); *Passe Bora Bora* (all six Society Islands; 32,500/17,800 CFP); *Passe Bora Tuamotu* (add three islands in the Tuamotus; 47,500/25,300 CFP);

DOMESTIC AIR FARES

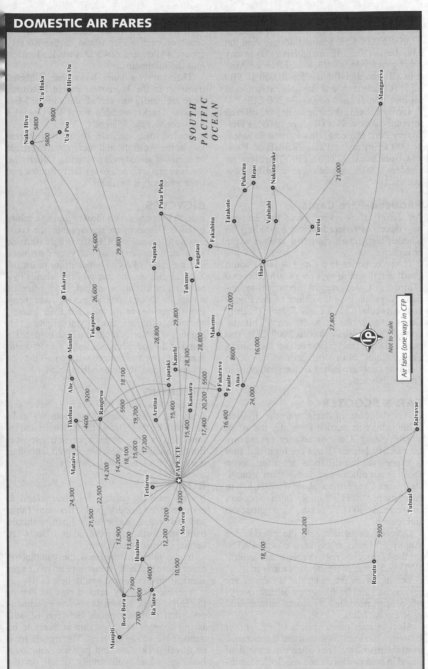

Air fares (one way) in CFP

Not to Scale

SOUTH PACIFIC OCEAN

and *Passe Lagons* (Lagoons Pass: Mo'orea, Rangiroa, Tikehau, Manihi and Fakarava; 37,000/20,000 CFP adults/children). Add the Marquesas (Nuku Hiva and Hiva Oa) to any other pass for 45,000/23,400 CFP or the Australs (Rurutu and Tubuai) for 20,000/10,900 CFP. A Marquesas and Australs extension to all four islands costs 65,000/34,300 CFP.

Limited flights (blue or white) are offered through a *Passe Bleu Découverte* (Blue Discovery Pass: Mo'orea, Huahine and Ra'iatea; 16,000 CFP) and a *Passe Bleu* (Blue Pass: add Bora Bora; 22,000 CFP). There are no children's fares and Mo'orea must be your last visit.

Reduced-Fare Cards

Air Tahiti offers several cards that let you buy tickets at reduced prices, depending on whether the flight is classified as blue, white or red.

If you're under 25 a *Carte Jeunes* (Youth Card) and if you're over 60 a *Carte Marama* (Third Age Card) gives you up to 50% reductions (depending on the colour of the flight) and costs 1000 CFP. A *Carte Famille* (Family Card) gives adults up to 50% and children up to 75% discount and costs 2000 CFP. You need a passport and photos and for the Family Card the kids' birth certificates.

These cards are issued on the spot, only in French Polynesia.

CAR & SCOOTER

Given the cost of taxis and the limited public transport outside Pape'ete, it's often worth renting a car or scooter to explore the Society Islands. Rates are high and fuel is expensive, but distances are short: even Tahiti is not much more than 100km around. Daily rates vary from about 7500 CFP in Pape'ete to 9000 CFP on Ra'iatea. Scooters cost around 6000 CFP per day throughout the archipelago.

Off-road excursions into the interior are usually off limits to anything except 4WDs. On the Marquesas, rental vehicles are mainly 4WD and come complete with a driver.

Driving is on the right, the standards are not too bad and traffic is light almost everywhere apart from the busy coastal strip around Pape'ete on Tahiti.

Most islands use a system of PK *(point kilométrique)* markers to indicate the distance from the main city. They often run around an island in both clockwise and anticlockwise directions, meeting at a roughly central point.

Roads

Well-maintained roads trace much of the coast of each major island in the Society group, while rougher 4WD roads lead inland into the mountains.

There are far more boats than wheeled transport in the Tuamotus. Except in towns, there are hardly any sealed roads in the Marquesas. Tracks, suitable for 4WD vehicles only, connect the villages.

Sealed roads encircle Tubuai and Raivavae in the Australs, and there are reasonable stretches of sealed road on Rurutu. Otherwise, roads in this archipelago are fairly limited and little transport is available.

BICYCLES

French Polynesia is an ideal region to explore by bike. Distances are manageable, the coast roads are generally flat, traffic is light (outside Pape'ete), you can travel at your own pace and are more likely to get chatting to locals. You can ride around many of the islands in a morning or afternoon. Bicycles can often be rented for about 1500 CFP per day, and many guesthouses have bicycles for their guests, sometimes for free, though you might be riding an old rattler. A mountain bike is ideal for some of the rougher roads and it's even worth bringing your trusty steed with you – they're accepted on all the inter-island ships.

HITCHING

Hitching (*auto-stop* in French) is never entirely safe in any country and women should never hitch alone. But on the less-touristed islands and on islands where public transport is limited hitching is widely accepted, although it might be a long wait between rides.

BOAT

It's no problem getting from one island to another in the Society group. Between Tahiti and Mo'orea, a number of companies shuttle back and forth daily; the other islands are served at least twice a week.

In the other archipelagos the situation is much more difficult, as there are no passenger ships; if time is limited you're best to fly.

You can generally catch a ride on one of the cargo ships, known as *goélettes* (schooners), that transport goods between islands. Island hopping by cargo ship is likely to be memorable, to say the least. You mostly have to travel deck class and provide your own bedding, which you simply unroll on the deck. You're likely to get wet and cold, and possibly seasick. Plus, the ships run to uncertain schedules. But then again, if you wanted to get off the beaten track, you were looking for adventure anyway!

Bonitiers (whaleboats) do many of the runs around islands or to nearby islands in the Tuamotus and the Marquesas.

Ferry

It takes between half an hour and an hour to travel between Tahiti and Mo'orea, depending on which company you go with. The car ferries, such as those run by Moorea Ferry, are slower than the high-speed ferries, which take only passengers, motorcycles and bicycles. The **Ono-Ono** *(in Pape'ete ☎ 45 35 35; one way/return 1050/2200 CFP)* has at least four crossings daily and docks at Cook's Bay rather than Vaiare, which is handy if you are staying nearby. See the Mo'orea section for more information about ferries to/from Mo'orea.

The **Maupiti Express** *(☎ 67 66 69 on Bora Bora; one way/return 2500/3500 CFP)* runs a high-speed service between Bora Bora, Taha'a, Ra'iatea and Maupiti.

Cargo Ship

Cargo ships have offices in the Motu Uta port area in Pape'ete (take *le truck* No 3 from the *mairie* (town hall)); offices open at 7.30am Monday to Friday, then usually break for lunch and close at 3pm or 4pm.

The **Vaeanu** *(☎ 41 25 35; per person deck/berth/cabin class 1956/5989/11,978 CFP)* has regular services through the Society group and is popular with shoestring travellers. For the Pape'ete–Huahine–Ra'iatea–Taha'a–Bora Bora round trip it leaves Pape'ete on Monday, Wednesday and Friday at 5pm (the Wednesday trip does not stop at Taha'a). The Huahine and Ra'iatea arrivals are in the middle of the night. The *Vaeanu* sets out from Bora Bora on Tuesday, Thursday and Sunday.

Hawaiki Nui *(☎ 45 23 24)* does the Society Islands circuit twice a week (Tuesday and Thursday at 4pm; per person deck class 1700/4950 CFP); **Aremiti 3** *(☎ 74 39 40/41)* leaves Pape'ete on Monday and Friday for Huahine and Ra'iatea (one way/return 5500/11,000 CFP; between the islands 1500 CFP). The **Taporo VI** *(☎ 42 63 93)* also does the Society Islands circuit three times a week.

The small **Maupiti To'u Aia** *(☎ 50 66 71)* goes to Maupiti from Pape'ete (2400 CFP one way) once a week, leaving on Wednesday evening and arriving at Maupiti the following morning. It returns to Pape'ete two days later.

About 10 ships operate through the Tuamotus; routes and fares vary, so it's best to check with the offices for the individual ships, they include the **Dory** *(☎ 42 30 55)*, **Cobia I** *(☎ 43 36 43)*, **Rairoa Nui** *(☎ 48 35 78)*, **Saint Xavier Maris Stella** *(☎ 42 23 58)*, **Nuku Hau** *(☎ 45 23 24)*, **Mareva Nui** *(☎ 42 25 53)*, **Vai-Aito** *(☎ 43 99 96)* and the **Kura Ora** *(☎ 45 55 45)*.

The *Aranui* and the *Taporo IV* go to the Marquesas, stopping in the Tuamotus en route. The **Aranui** *(☎ 42 62 40; ⓦ www.aranui.com)*, a veritable institution in French Polynesia, does 16 trips a year (see the boxed text 'The Aranui' in the Marquesas Islands section later in this chapter). The **Taporo IV** *(☎ 42 63 93)* runs every 15 days.

Services to the Australs are limited; the **Tuhaa Pae II** *(☎ 50 96 09/06; ⓔ snathp@ mail.pf)* goes three times a month, stopping at Rurutu and Tubuai on every trip and other islands less regularly. From Pape'ete to Rurutu, Rimatara or Tubuai costs 4046/5664/7789 CFP deck/berth/air-con cabin; to Raivavae costs 5832/8164/11,226 CFP. Add another 2800 CFP per day for three meals a day.

All the ships listed as going to the Tuamotus, bar the *Dory*, go to the Gambier Archipelago. The **Nuku Hau** *(☎ 45 23 24)* sails to the Gambier Archipelago via the Tuamotus (7900 CFP per person deck class, plus 1950 CFP for three meals a day). The **Taporo V** *(☎ 42 63 93)* sails through the eastern Tuamotus and the Gambier Archipelago once or twice a month.

Cruise Ship

At the other end of the spectrum from rudimentary cargo ships are the luxury cruise ships that operate in the Society Islands.

The magnificent *Haumana*, a 36m catamaran, takes up to 60 passengers on three- and four-day cruises between Ra'iatea, Taha'a and Bora Bora; contact **Bora Bora Pearl Cruises** *(☎ 43 43 03; ⓦ www.boraborapearl cruises.com)*. The *Tia Moana* and *Tu Moana*, also managed by Bora Bora cruises, offer seven-day cruises in the Society Islands.

The 320-passenger *Paul-Gauguin* departs Pape'ete weekly for a seven-day cruise around the Society group. Contact **Tahiti Nui Travel** *(☎ 54 02 00, fax 42 74 35; ⓦ www .tahitinuitravel.pf)* for information.

Contact Tahiti Tourisme (see Tourist Offices in the Facts for the Visitor section earlier in this chapter for contact details) to find out if Renaissance cruise ships *R3* and *R4* are operating again.

Yacht

French Polynesia is an enormously popular yachting destination. If you don't have the luxury of your own boat you can still set sail with a bareboat charter (you provision and crew it yourself) or a cabin on a crewed yacht. **Stardust Marine** (☎ 60 04 85) and **Moorings** (☎ 66 35 93; ⓦ *www.moorings.com*) in Ra'iatea are two of the most popular operations.

To pick up a crewing position check notice boards in popular restaurants and at the yacht clubs on Tahiti, Bora Bora, Ra'iatea and other major yachting stops.

LOCAL TRANSPORT
Taxi

Tahiti, Mo'orea, Huahine, Ra'iatea and Bora Bora have taxis, but they are prohibitively expensive (though you don't need to tip drivers). For example, you pay US$15 to US$20 for the 6km trip between Faa'a airport and Pape'ete! If you've booked accommodation at a hotel or *pension* you'll generally be collected from the airport – even if you have to pay, it's likely to work out much cheaper than a cab.

Le Truck

On Tahiti and the other Society Islands the traditional local form of transport is known as *le truck*. These public buses are cheap, convenient and very much a part of the Polynesian experience. Services on Tahiti are comprehensive and well organised, and *le trucks* have their route number and the final destination posted on the front. Official stops have blue signs and sometimes canopies and seats, but *le trucks* will generally stop for anybody who hails them. Fares start at around 130 CFP and rarely go above 400 CFP.

Sadly, *le trucks* are gradually being replaced by 'real' air-con buses that in theory will only stop at designated stops and will run to a timetable, though many locals doubt that such a sterile policy will stick. If *le trucks* are still running when you visit, catch one before it's too late.

Boat

A small boat with an outboard motor can be a great way to explore lagoons, and you can hire them in Mo'orea, Bora Bora and Ra'iatea without a permit. Standard charges are about 8000/11,500 CFP for a half-/full day.

Lagoon tours by pirogue are good value for two or more people. If you need to get across a lagoon, there will always be someone available with the appropriate boat – just ask around.

ORGANISED TOURS

Even if you have vowed never ever to go on an organised tour you might find yourself relenting in French Polynesia. They can be a really excellent way to get to difficult places, particularly if you are on your own. Tours vary from a half-day minibus island excursion to picnics on remote *motu* or even rugged 4WD trips to the interior; you should book through your accommodation or the tourist office.

Society Islands

The Society Islands, subdivided into the Windward (eastern) and Leeward (western) islands, are home to more than 80% of French Polynesia's population and are the destination for most visitors – most people arrive into and depart from Tahiti. Most of the Societies are high islands, and in some cases very high indeed. Bora Bora and Mo'orea, in particular, are spectacular.

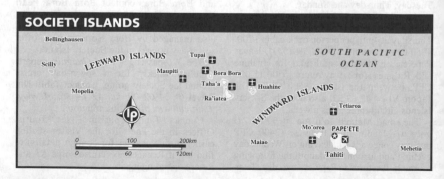

Tahiti

pop 169,674 • area 1045 sq km
It's common to speak of Tahiti as if it were the whole colony; in fact it is merely the largest island, the site of the capital (Pape'ete) and the only international airport (Faa'a). Tahiti doesn't match its reputation; the beautiful beaches on local postcards are on *motu* out from other islands, the glamorous over-water bungalows are on Bora Bora, the underwater glimpses of sharks cruising past colourful reefs are in the Tuamotus. Even Gauguin's paintings are mostly of the Marquesas, not Tahiti.

Tahiti deserves more than a cursory glance. The flipside to Tahiti's crowds, traffic jams, few beaches and often mediocre – and expensive – accommodation is the joys of the lagoon, the wild and uninhabited interior, the ancient *marae*, historic landmarks, small museums and the untouched wilderness of Tahiti Iti (Small Tahiti). Plus, there's Pape'ete, with a bustling waterfront, fine restaurants, good shopping and great dance performances. Tahiti warrants more than a quick stopover.

History
Like other islands in the Society group, Tahiti was created by volcanic eruptions. Larger Tahiti Nui (Big Tahiti) probably came into existence around 2½ to three million years ago, while smaller Tahiti Iti was created less than two million, perhaps less than a million, years ago.

Tahiti's rise to importance started in 1767 when Samuel Wallis made the European 'discovery' of the island. He was soon followed by Bougainville, then by Cook, who made Tahiti the favoured base of European visitors. It was this European presence that led to Tahiti's rise to Polynesian power. It was a fleeting moment, for soon Tahiti became a minor pawn in the European colonial quest and only a generation separated Tahiti's takeover by Pomare II (in 1815) to its annexation by France (1842).

Today Tahiti is home to about 70% of French Polynesia's population. Recent growth has been dramatic and Pape'ete has become the region's 'big city' – the place of bright lights and fragile prospects that sucks in the hopeful and helpless from other islands.

Orientation
Tahiti is a lopsided figure eight: the larger and most settled Tahiti Nui is connected by a narrow isthmus to small Tahiti Iti. From the narrow coastal fringe, where the majority of people live, the land sweeps rapidly upwards to a jumble of soaring, green-clad mountain peaks.

The centre of Tahiti Nui is effectively a single huge crater, with the highest peaks arrayed around the rim; the highest, Mt Orohena (2241m), is on the western side. The ridge continues to the spectacular rocky Diadème (1321m) and Mt Marau (1493m). Several valleys run down to the coast from the mountains, the most impressive being the wide Papenoo Valley to the north, which cuts through the ancient crater rim. Tahiti Iti's highest point is Mt Ronui (1332m), and its eastern end finishes with steep cliff faces in the Te Pari district.

A fringing reef encloses a narrow lagoon around much of the island, but parts of the coast, particularly the north coast from Mahina to Tiarei, are unprotected. Of the 33 passes through the reef the most important is the Pape'ete Pass into Pape'ete's fine harbour.

Swimming
You don't go to Tahiti for the beaches. However, if you want a dip, you're best to head out of town. The beach by the Hotel Sofitel Maeva is 8km from Pape'ete and right by the Outumaoro *le truck* stop. Along Tahiti Nui's north coast, **Point Vénus**, 10km out of town, is popular. There are short stretches of black-sand beach further along, such as the small bay just past the **Arahoho Blowhole** (22km from Pape'ete). On the south coast, there are white-sand beaches between 10km and 15km from Pape'ete, at Puna'auia.

Diving
Tahiti offers excellent diving for both experienced and beginner divers. Sites include **Les Failles d'Arue** (Cliffs of Arue) in Matavai Bay; the **Aquarium**, a delight for beginners, in the lagoon near Faa'a airport; and **La Source** (The Spring) in front of Fisherman's Point at Pun'aauia. Tahiti Iti has superb sites, such as **Le Trou du Lagon** (Hole in the Lagoon) and the **Grotte de Tetopa** (Tetopa Cave).

Tahiti's scuba centres include:

Aquatica Dive Center (☎ 53 34 96, W www .aquatica-dive.com) Beachcomber Intercontinental Resort
Eleuthera Plongée (☎ 42 49 29) Taina Marina, Puna'auia
Iti Diving International (☎ 57 77 93) PK6, Puunui Marina, Vairao, Tahiti Iti
Scuba Tek Tahiti (☎ 42 23 55) PK4, Arue Marina)
Tahiti Plongée (☎ 41 00 62) PK7.5

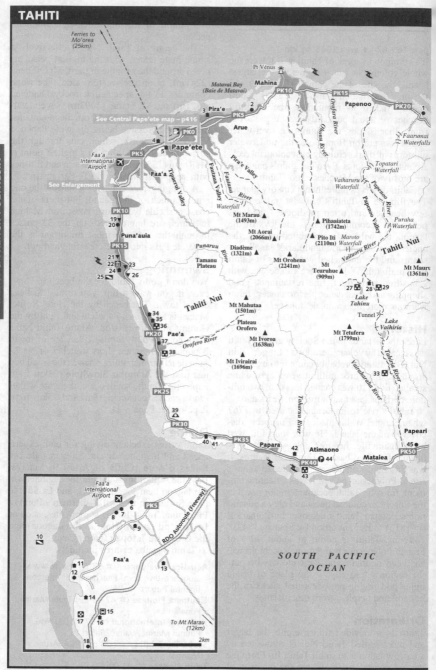

TAHITI

Ferries to
Mo'orea
(25km)

Matavai Bay
(Baie de Matavai)

Mahina

Pt Vénus

PK10

PK15

Papenoo

PK20

1

3 Pira'e

2

PK5

Arue

Faarumai
Waterfalls

See Central Pape'ete map – p416

PK0

4

5

Pape'ete

PK5

Oropara River

Topatari
Waterfall

Faa'a
International
Airport

Faa'a

Pira'e Valley

Fautaua Valley

Fautaua
River

Waterfall

Vaiharuru
Waterfall

Papenoo River

Puraha
Waterfall

See Enlargement

PK10

19
20

Puna'auia

PK15

Mt Marau
(1493m)

Mt Aorai
(2066m)

Tipaerui Valley

Punaruu
River

Tamanu
Plateau

Diadème
(1321m)

Pihaaiateta
(1742m)

Pito Iti
(2110m)

Papenoo Valley

Tahiti Nui

Maroto
Waterfall

Vaituoru River

21
22
24
23

25

26

Tahiti Nui

Mt Orohena
(2241m)

Mt
Teuruhue ▲
(909m)

Lake
Tahinu

Mt Maure
(1361m)

27
28
29

34
35
36

Mt Mahutaa
(1501m)

Tunnel

Lake
Vaihiria

PK20

Pae'a

37

Orofero River

38

Plateau
Orofero

Mt Ivoroa
(1638m)

Mt Tetufera
(1799m)

Taharuu River

Vaitaihauriha River

Tahiria River

33

PK25

Mt Ivirairai
(1696m)

39

PK30

Papeari

40 41

PK35

Papara

42

Atimaono

44

Mataiea

45

PK50

PK40

43

Faa'a
International
Airport

PK5

8 7 6

9

10

Faa'a

RDO Autoroute (Freeway)

11
12

13

14

15

16

SOUTH   PACIFIC
OCEAN

17

18

To Mt Marau
(12km)

0   2km

TAHITI

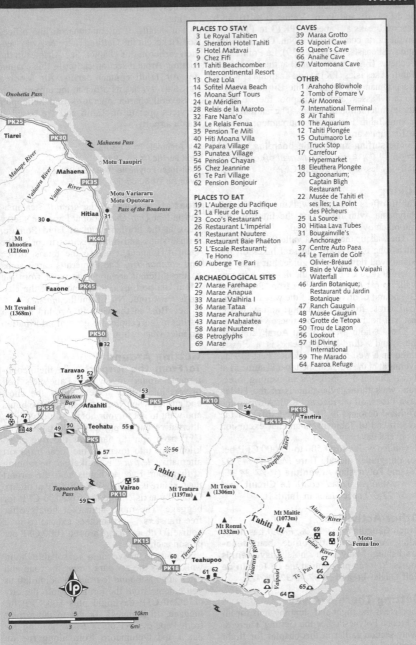

PLACES TO STAY
3 Le Royal Tahitien
4 Sheraton Hotel Tahiti
5 Hotel Matavai
9 Chez Fifi
11 Tahiti Beachcomber Intercontinental Resort
13 Chez Lola
14 Sofitel Maeva Beach
16 Moana Surf Tours
24 Le Méridien
28 Relais de la Maroto
32 Fare Nana'o
34 Le Relais Fenua
35 Pension Te Miti
40 Hiti Moana Villa
42 Papara Village
53 Punatea Village
54 Pension Chayan
55 Chez Jeannine
61 Te Pari Village
62 Pension Bonjouir

PLACES TO EAT
19 L'Auberge du Pacifique
21 La Fleur de Lotus
23 Coco's Restaurant
26 Restaurant L'Impérial
41 Restaurant Nuutere
51 Restaurant Baie Phaéton
52 L'Escale Restaurant; Te Hono
60 Auberge Te Pari

ARCHAEOLOGICAL SITES
27 Marae Farehape
29 Marae Anapua
33 Marae Vaihiria I
36 Marae Tataa
38 Marae Arahurahu
43 Marae Mahaiatea
58 Marae Nuutere
68 Petroglyphs
69 Marae

CAVES
39 Maraa Grotto
63 Vaipoiri Cave
65 Queen's Cave
66 Anaihe Cave
67 Vaitomoana Cave

OTHER
1 Arahoho Blowhole
2 Tomb of Pomare V
6 Air Moorea
7 International Terminal
8 Air Tahiti
10 The Aquarium
12 Tahiti Plongée
15 Outumaoro Le Truck Stop
17 Carrefour Hypermarket
18 Eleuthera Plongée
20 Lagoonarium; Captain Bligh Restaurant
22 Musée de Tahiti et ses Îles; La Point des Pêcheurs
25 La Source
30 Hitiaa Lava Tubes
31 Bougainville's Anchorage
37 Centre Auto Paea
44 Le Terrain de Golf Olivier-Bréaud
45 Bain de Vaima & Vaipahi Waterfall
46 Jardin Botanique; Restaurant du Jardin Botanique
47 Ranch Gauguin
48 Musée Gauguin
49 Grotte de Tetopa
56 Lookout
57 Iti Diving International
59 The Marado
64 Faaroa Refuge

Surfing

Classic surf spots include Matavai Bay (Baie de Matavai) and Point Vénus (PK10) and several breaks at Papenoo (PK13 to PK15.5) on the north coast of Tahiti Nui. On the south and west coasts, Papara (PK39), La Pointe des Pêcheurs (Fisherman's Point) at the Musée de Tahiti et ses Îsles (PK15) and Taapuna (PK12) are popular. On Tahiti Iti the Big and Small Vairao Passes and Teahupoo reef breaks attract international surfers. The annual Billabong Tahiti Pro surfing tournament is held at Teahupoo around May.

The **surfing and boogie-boarding school** *(☎ 45 44 00; ⓔ surfschool@mail.pf)* offers 10 half-day lessons for 26,500 CFP.

Hiking

Tahiti offers the best walking in French Polynesia, with hikes into the interior that can reach over 2000m altitude.

The walk up the Fautaua Valley to the waterfall is one of the most pleasant hikes on the island; you don't need a guide, but must get a permit (600 CFP) from the *mairie*. You can walk up **Mt Marau** (1493m) from Puna'auia (3½ hours) or drive most of the way up on the road across from Fa'aa airport and walk the last half-hour to the top for superb views.

The 4½-hour ascent of **Mt Aorai** (2066m), the island's third-highest peak, is a classic climb up a well-marked track. It's best to stay overnight at the hut near the top and summit at dawn. During dry spells it's an exciting three-hour walk through the tunnels of the **Hitiaa Lava Tubes**, off the road at PK40. A trip to the wild and desolate **Te Pari** (The Cliffs), at the eastern end of Tahiti Iti, is another excursion of several days.

Guided walks cost 6500 to 15,000 CFP per person; guides include **Tiare Mato** *(☎ 43 92 76)* and **Polynesian Adventure** *(☎ 77 24 37; ⓦ www.polynesianadv.com)*. **Le Circuit Vert** *(☎ 57 22 67)* specialises in Tahiti Iti.

Other Activities

Ranch Gauguin *(☎ 57 51 00; PK53)* has horse riding. Ask at the tourist office about **deep-sea fishing**. Many luxury hotels have **tennis courts**. You can play **golf** at the **Le Terrain de Golf Olivier-Bréaud** *(☎ 57 40 32; PK42)*.

Getting There & Away

Pape'ete is the flight and shipping hub for all of French Polynesia. See the Getting There & Away section earlier in this chapter for flight details.

Air Pape'ete's **Faa'a airport** *(☎ 82 60 61)* handles both domestic and international flights.

For details of international airline offices see Tickets in the Getting There & Away section earlier in this chapter. See Airlines in the Getting Around section earlier in this chapter for **Air Tahiti** contact details. **Air Moorea** *(☎ 86 41 41)* has its office at the airport.

Several charter operators and helicopter services operate on Tahiti and are based at Faa'a airport:

Air Archipels (☎ 81 30 30)
Héli Pacific (☎ 85 68 00)
Héli-Inter Polynésie (☎ 81 99 00)
Wan Air (☎ 80 05 59)

Boat Mo'orea ferries, the *Aremiti 3* catamaran and the *Ono-Ono* moor at Pape'ete's ferry quay at the northern end of Blvd Pomare. Cruise ships and other visitors moor at the Quai d'Honneur, close to the tourist office and *capitainerie*. The numerous cargo ships to the different archipelagos work from the Motu Uta port area, to the north of the city, on *le truck* route No 3 from the *mairie*.

See Boat in the Getting Around section earlier in this chapter for general information on inter-island ships.

Getting Around

To/From the Airport Like their counterparts around the world, Pape'ete's taxi drivers know they have you by the short and curlies when you arrive in the wee hours and want to get to your hotel. You have little alternative but to pay the 1600 CFP (2500 CFP from 8pm to 6am) for the five or so kilometres into town, as the local transport alternative, *le truck*, is unlikely to be running at that hour. Even to hotels near the airport the taxi fare is 1000 CFP (1500 CFP at night). Officially taxis charge an extra 100 CFP for baggage. The more upmarket hotels offer free transfers – just another excuse to treat yourself. Others charge around 1000 CFP per person each way.

If you do arrive at a reasonable hour, walk across the car park, cross the road and catch any eastbound *le truck* (heading left as you emerge from the terminal) into the city (130/250 CFP day/night plus 100 CFP for luggage, 15 minutes). To get to the airport from Pape'ete get on *le truck* heading for Faa'a and Outumaoro from along rue du Général de Gaulle.

Car Out of Pape'ete traffic is light and the driving isn't too scary. Rental agencies have desks at the big hotels, but offices include:

Avis (☎ 54 10 10) cnr rue des Remparts & Av Georges Clémenceau, Pape'ete; (☎ 43 88 99) Quai des Ferries, Pape'ete; (☎ 57 70 70) Taravao; (☎ 85 02 84) Faa'a airport
Centre Auto Paea (☎ 53 33 33) PK20.2, Pa'ea
Daniel Rent-a-Car (☎ 82 30 04, 81 96 32) Faa'a airport
Europcar (☎ 45 24 24) cnr Av du Prince Hinoi & rue des Remparts, Pape'ete; (☎ 86 60 61) Faa'a airport
Hertz (☎ 42 04 71) Tipaerui, Pape'ete; (☎ 82 55 86) Faa'a airport
Robert Rent-a-Car (☎ 42 97 20) rue du Commandant Destremeau
Tahiti Rent-a-Car (☎ 81 94 00) Faa'a airport

Taxi Taxis are so expensive that most people ignore them. They are metered, but any trip of a reasonable length will approximate a day's car hire. All the big hotels have taxi ranks, and there are plenty of taxis in central Pape'ete. To order a taxi, phone **Faa'a airport** (☎ 86 60 66), the **Vaima Centre** (☎ 42 60 77) or **Marché de Pape'ete** (☎ 43 19 62).

Le Truck On weekdays le trucks – and the new air-con buses – operate from dawn until about 5.30pm, except for the Pape'ete–Faa'a–Outumaoro line, which operates 24 hours (infrequently after 10pm). On weekends, particularly on Sunday, the service is less frequent. Fares for the shortest trips around Pape'ete, cost 130 CFP; this rises to 250 CFP after 6pm. About 20km from Pape'ete the fare increases in stages to around 200 CFP. Getting to the other side of the island might cost 450 CFP. Fares might well rise with the new buses.

The blue-signed le truck stops are often hard to spot, but you can just wave them down. There are basically three routes: greater Pape'ete, which is very useful for the Pape'ete–Faa'a airport trip (catch this along rue du Général de Gaulle); the east coast (also handy for Tahiti Iti; get on along Blvd Pomare); and the west coast (head to rue du Maréchal Foch and rue du Général de Gaulle).

PAPE'ETE
pop 26,181
Tahiti's busy metropolis has a reputation as being an ugly and overpriced port town, blighted by tasteless concrete development and heavy traffic. However, it's really not that bad. Amble along the waterfront watching boats come and go, join the locals for a meal at the mobile restaurants known as roulottes, soak up the Polynesian atmosphere in busy Pape'ete Market, and people-watch while you sip a coffee or glass of wine in a sidewalk café. Approached this way, Pape'ete can be very enjoyable.

History
The capital and largest city of French Polynesia, Pape'ete was a European creation. In 1769, when Cook anchored 10km east in Matavai Bay, there was no settlement in Pape'ete. The arrival of the LMS missionaries and the role of the young Queen Pomare made it a religious and political centre, and visiting whaling ships made it an increasingly important port. It became the administrative headquarters for the new French protectorate in 1842. By 1860 the town had already taken its present form, with a straggling European settlement between the waterfront and the street, then known as 'the Broom' and now as rue du Commandant Destremeau, rue du Général de Gaulle and rue du Maréchal Foch.

Chinese merchants and shopkeepers trickled in, but Pape'ete's population was still less than 5000 at the beginning of the 20th century. A disastrous cyclone in 1906 and a German naval bombardment in 1914, which destroyed the central market, took their toll, but during WWII the population reached 10,000 and by the early 1960s it was over 20,000. The city's growth and change accelerated in the 1960s with the opening of Faa'a airport, but it was nuclear-testing operations that really encouraged the flood of people from remote islands.

Orientation
Central Pape'ete curves around an almost-enclosed bay and the compact downtown district is easily covered on foot. Blvd Pomare follows the waterfront and most of the central businesses, banks, hotels and restaurants are concentrated along this busy street or in the few blocks back from the water's edge. The Vaima Centre marks the centre of the city, but it's the busy waterfront that is the city's true heart. The port zone, Fare Ute and Motu Uta, is visible across the harbour to the north.

Greater Pape'ete forms a long strip squeezed between the mountains and the lagoon for 30km along the north coast. The Route de Dégagement Ouest (RDO), French Polynesia's autoroute (freeway), runs slightly inland from the western edge of central Pape'ete to just beyond Faa'a airport, where it rejoins the

CENTRAL PAPE'ETE

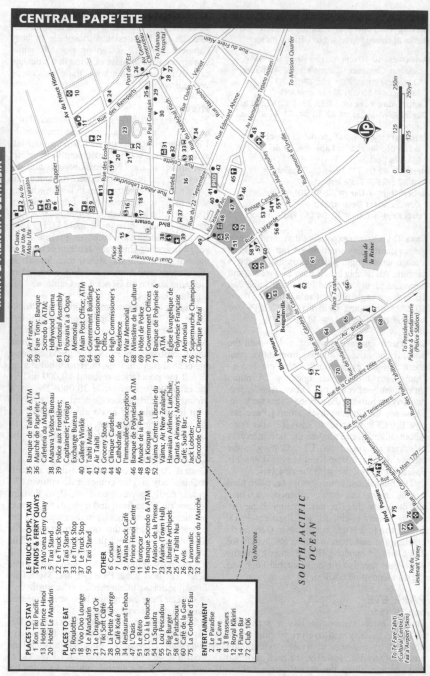

PLACES TO STAY
1 Kon Tiki Pacific
13 Hotel Prince Hinoi
20 Hotel Le Mandarin

PLACES TO EAT
15 Roulottes
18 Voo Doo Lounge
19 Le Mandarin
21 Le Dragon d'Or
27 Tiki Soft Café
28 La Petite Auberge
30 Café Koké
34 Restaurant Tehoa
47 L'Oasis
51 Le Rétro
53 L'O à la Bouche
54 La Squadra
55 Lou Pescadou
57 Big Burger
58 Le Patachoux
60 Café de la Gare
75 La Corbeille d'Eau

ENTERTAINMENT
2 Le Paradise
4 La Cave
8 3 Brasseurs
12 Royal Kikiriri
14 Piano Bar
72 Club 106

LE TRUCK STOPS, TAXI STANDS & FERRY QUAYS
5 Mo'orea Ferry Quay
22 Taxi Stand
31 Taxi Stand
33 Le Truck Stop
37 Le Truck Stop
50 Taxi Stand

OTHER
6 Corsair
7 Lavex
9 Mana Rock Café
10 Prince Hinoi Centre
11 Europcar
16 Banque Socredo & ATM
17 Maison de la Presse
23 Mairie (Town Hall)
24 Librairie Archipels
25 Air Tahiti Nui
26 Avis
29 Lavomatic
32 Pharmacie du Marché
35 Banque de Tahiti & ATM
36 Marché de Pape'ete; La Cafeteria du Marché
38 Manava Visitors Bureau
39 Police aux Frontières; Capitainerie; Foreign Exchange Bureau
40 Gallerie Winkle
41 Tahiti Music
42 Air Tahiti
43 Grocery Store
44 Clinique Cardella
45 Cathédrale de l'Immaculée Conception
46 Banque de Polynésie & ATM
48 Musée de la Perle
49 Le Kiosque
52 Vaima Centre: Librairie du Vaima; Air New Zealand; Hawaiian Airlines; LanChile; Qantas Airways; Morrison's Café; Sushi Bar; Jack Lobster; Concorde Cinema
56 Air France
59 Fare Tony; Banque Socredo & ATM; Hollywood Cinema
61 Territorial Assembly
62 Pouvana'a a Oopa Memorial
63 Main Post Office; ATM
64 Government Buildings
65 High Commissioner's Office
66 High Commissioner's Residence
67 War Memorial
68 Ministere de la Culture
69 Hôtel de Police
70 Government Offices
71 Banque de Polynésie & ATM
73 Église Évangelique de Polynésie Française
74 Memorial
76 Supermarché Champion
77 Clinique Paofai

coastal road. On the other side of Pape'ete, Av du Prince Hinoi and Av Georges Clémenceau, run east through the suburb of Pira'e before joining at Arue.

Information

Tourist Offices The main tourist office is the **Manava Visitors Bureau** (☎ 50 57 12; ⓦ www.tahiti-manava.pf; Fare Manihini, Blvd Pomare; closed Sat afternoon & Sun), in the centre of Pape'ete. It has helpful staff and information about the whole of French Polynesia. Although Mo'orea and Bora Bora have helpful tourist offices, the more remote islands don't, so if you have any queries make the most of this tourist office while you are in Pape'ete.

There is also an information desk at the airport.

Money Branches of **Banque Socredo**, **Banque de Tahiti** and **Banque de Polynésie** and ATMs are scattered around Pape'ete. Banque Socredo and Banque de Polynésie have branches at Faa'a airport, where there's an ATM.

Most Pape'ete banks change cash and travellers cheques. One **Banque Socredo** (Fare Tony, Blvd Pomare) has a machine that changes foreign bills. In the same building as the capitainerie there's a **foreign exchange bureau** (Quai d'Honneur; closed Sun afternoon).

Post & Communications Pape'ete's main post office (Blvd Pomare) faces the waterfront, next to Parc Bougainville. For normal postal services go upstairs from the Blvd Pomare entrance. To collect poste-restante mail go downstairs. The post office also offers phone, fax and telegram services, and opens Saturday morning.

Other post offices are in the surrounding suburbs and at Faa'a airport.

Email & Internet Access You won't be tripping over Internet cafés in Pape'ete. **Tiki Soft C@fé** (☎ 88 93 98; Pont de l'Est; 1000 CFP/hr) is a funky place frequented by a chic clientele. Upstairs in **La Maison de la Presse** (Blvd Pomare; 1000 CFP/1¼ hr) you can check your email to the accompaniment of local music, or try the **Mana Rock Café** (cnr Blvd Pomare & Av du Prince Hinoi; 1000 CFP/hr).

Bookshops Pape'ete has a few good bookshops, but the range in English is always the poor cousin to the French texts and newspapers on offer.

The best bookshop is the **Librairie du Vaima** (☎ 45 57 57; Vaima Centre). **La Maison de la Presse** (Blvd Pomare) has a good selection of newspapers and magazines, as does **Le Kiosque** (Blvd Pomare) at the front of the Vaima Centre.

Laundry Getting clothes washed on Tahiti is mighty pricey, although at least it's possible. **Lavomatic** (☎ 43 71 59; rue Paul Gauguin; open 6.30am-noon & 1.30pm-5.30pm Mon-Sat) charges 1600 CFP for a load to be washed and dried. **Lavex** (Blvd Pomare; open Mon-Sat) charges 1650 CFP to wash and dry a 7kg load.

Medical Services & Emergency The **Mamao Hospital** (☎ 46 62 62, 24-hr emergencies ☎ 42 01 01; Av Georges Clémenceau) is the biggest hospital in French Polynesia.

The two 24-hour private clinics – **Clinique Cardella** (☎ 42 81 90; rue Anne-Marie Javouhey), behind the cathedral, and **Clinique Paofai** (☎ 46 18 18; cnr Blvd Pomare & rue du Lieutenant Varney) – are more expensive than the public hospital.

In case of emergency call the following numbers: **police** (☎ 17) and for an **ambulance** (☎ 15). You can also call **SOS Médecins** (☎ 42 34 56) or **SOS Infirmières** (☎ 43 56 00).

Pape'ete Waterfront

Pape'ete's bustling waterfront is the capital's big attraction. Spend a while watching the yachts, cargo ships and inter-island ferries toing and froing with their cargos of people and goods; in the afternoon, fishing boats unload their glistening catch. Head back at night when the quay becomes a throng of people eating and socialising at les roulottes (see the boxed text 'Les Roulottes' later in this section). The eastern end is the entertainment district, with bars, clubs and, at night, rae rae.

Marché de Pape'ete

Pape'ete Market, between rue du 22 Septembre and rue F Cardella, is colourful, appetising and very Polynesian. It's bursting with flowers, food, tropical fruit, patisseries, art and souvenirs; the food is downstairs and the rest, upstairs. Try to visit early on a Sunday morning, the big day; all of Tahiti seems to flock here from 5am.

TAHITI & FRENCH POLYNESIA

City Walking Tour

Take an early-morning or early-evening city stroll, starting at the western end of busy Blvd Pomare with its overhanging trees and bright hibiscus. Close to the metal footbridge on the lagoon side of the road is the imposing **Te Fare Tahiti building**, the Polynesian-style cultural centre; try to catch an event there.

If you're passing the imposing pink-and-white **Église Évangélique de Polynésie Française** on Sunday you'll be treated to rousing Polynesian hymns and a flotilla of white hats as the congregation comes and goes. This is effectively Pape'ete's birthplace, as the first Protestant church (built here in 1818) signalled the town's creation.

Across the road is a **memorial** to the great double-canoe *Hokule'a*, which sailed from Hawaii to Tahiti in 1967 in a recreation of the journeys of legendary Polynesian navigators. As you walk east you might see local teams training in their racing pirogue, especially on Saturday morning.

Past Av Bruat, on the inland side of the road, **Parc Bougainville** is a shady green haven. Not surprisingly, it's fronted by a 1909 bust of the great French navigator. Behind the park the **Territorial Assembly** and other government buildings occupy the former site of the Pomare palace.

The useful, but rather drab, **Vaima Centre** is next on the inland side; with shops, a few restaurants and most of the airline offices. On the rue Jeanne d'Arc side, the **Musée de la Perle** *(Pearl Museum; ☎ 45 21 22; admission 600 CFP; open daily)* has everything you need to know about pearl cultivation.

Head down rue Jeanne d'Arc to the 1875 **Cathédrale de l'Immaculée Conception**, a lovely cool spot for a quiet moment. From the cathedral, Av Monseigneur Tepano Jaussen leads into the **Mission Quarter**, the site of Catholic colleges and Protestant schools, and the fine **bishop's palace** (1875) across the Papeava River.

Backtrack to rue du Général de Gaulle and turn left into rue du 22 Septembre to explore the **Marché de Pape'ete**.

Stroll back towards Blvd Pomare and pass the **Manava Visitors Bureau**, on the harbour side. The quay area here has had a facelift and is a good place to watch the world go by from a park bench.

On Blvd Pomare the sometimes-seedy but always-energetic entertainment district starts south of Av du Prince Hinoi and extends north past Av du Chef Vairaatoa.

Tourism and entertainment fade out as the road continues through the docks and industrial zone of **Fare Ute** (which becomes Motu Uta after the bridge). This is the sweaty working part of the harbour, where the copra boats unload their cargo and the sweetish smell of coconut hangs in the air.

Bain Loti

Loti's Bath, 2.5km inland, was where the beautiful maiden Rarahu met her hero in Pierre Loti's 1880 novel *The Marriage of Loti*. The pool is no longer the same pleasantly rural scene, but it remains a favourite local meeting place and swimming hole, and a bust of Loti overlooks the scene. From north of the centre, the Route de Fautaua runs inland through lower-income dormitory suburbs to the pool. A walking path leads inland: see Walking under Activities earlier in this section.

Places to Stay

Don't use Pape'ete as your yardstick for the rest of Polynesia; the choice is pretty basic and convenience is their sole advantage. For budget places you're best to take one of the *pensions* near the airport.

The luxury beachside hotels are outside the city, mostly beyond the airport (see Places to Stay under Tahiti Nui later). In all categories bargains are rare and the balance between price and quality is not good. Be sure to make reservations during the Heiva festivities in July, when many hotels are booked out.

In Central Pape'ete the mid-range places are standard business hotels; rooms with TV and bathroom; credit cards are accepted.

Hotel Le Mandarin *(☎ 50 33 50, fax 42 16 32; e chris@beaumont.pf; rue Colette; singles/doubles from 14,000/16,250 CFP)* is central, clean and quiet, and is possibly the best of the bunch. The rooms have great wooden furniture and good bathrooms. It's only a short stroll to Marché Pape'ete.

Kon Tiki Pacific *(☎ 54 16 16, fax 42 11 66; 271 Blvd Pomare; singles/doubles 11,250/13,700 CFP)* has a certain seedy charm and is unremarkable except for the fabulous water views from the front rooms.

Most places on the city fringes are on the west coast between Faa'a (the airport district) and Maeva Beach. Frequent Pape'ete–Faa'a–Outumaoro *le trucks* travel this stretch during the day and, usually, into the night. If you want a beach or pool you'll have to head to one of the big hotels. Places beyond PK8 are covered under Tahiti Nui later in this section.

Places to Stay – Budget These places don't accept credit cards and have shared bathrooms unless detailed otherwise; rates include breakfast.

Chez Fifi (☎ *82 63 30; dorm beds 2000 CFP, singles/doubles 3500/6000 CFP*) is a good, cheap option if you're arriving late or early. Follow the sign and take the small, steep road beside the Mea Ma laundry across from the airport car park; the guesthouse is 150m on the left. The *pension* is impeccably clean; there's a communal kitchen and meals are available for 2000 CFP.

Chez Lola (☎ *81 91 75; singles/doubles/triples 5000/6700/7000 CFP*) is quiet and near the airport, but on the inland side of the RDO, high up in the Saint-Hilaire district. Rates include daytime airport transfers. The Saint-Hilaire *le truck* passes close by about every hour during the week but it's easier to ask the owners to take you down to the main road.

Places to Stay – Mid-Range If you surf, head to **Moana Surf Tours** (☎/*fax 43 70 70; PK8.3; 12,000 CFP per person*). The tariff includes airport transfers, dorm accommodation, half-board and transport to whatever surf spot is pumping. This place is popular, so book well in advance.

Le Royal Tahitien (☎ *42 81 13, fax 41 05 35; rooms 10,800 CFP*) is on a reasonable black-sand beach in Pira'e. It has clean, motel-like rooms, a waterfront restaurant and local music performances on weekends; a *le truck* stops less than 100m from the hotel.

Hotel Matavai (☎ *42 67 67, fax 42 36 90; Route de Tipaerui; singles/doubles 12,000/16,000 CFP*) is handy to the airport, and has a swimming pool, spacious rooms and free airport transfers.

Sofitel Maeva Beach (☎ *42 80 42, fax 43 84 70; Maeva Beach; doubles from 14,100, suites 25,400 CFP*) is on one of the best beaches in the area, but is in dire need of a facelift, however, it closed for renovations for much of 2003 and should be open again by early 2004. The Outumaoro *le truck* stop is immediately beyond the roundabout, on the inland side of the road.

Places to Stay – Top End Prepare to be pampered. These hotels are where you go to get the best beaches (even if they are artificial), the best Polynesian dance troupes, weekend *tamaaraa* (traditional-style feasts) and beautiful views of Mo'orea.

Sheraton Hotel Tahiti (☎ *86 48 48, fax 86 48 00; ℮ reservations.tahiti@sheraton.pf; doubles/suites from 17,900/30,700 CFP*) is a lovely new hotel.

Tahiti Beachcomber Intercontinental Resort (☎ *86 51 10, fax 86 51 30; ℮ tahiti@intercinti.com; doubles/over-water bungalows from 33,800/52,900 CFP*), just west of the airport, is luxury incarnate.

Places to Eat

You won't be disappointed with Pape'ete's food, which spans cuisines from around the globe. If you can't find something you like you shouldn't be travelling.

However, on Sunday you're likely to have to stick to your hotel restaurant or cook for yourself, as most eating places close; exceptions are noted here. For breakfast you'll be able to find a snack bar in the centre where you can get an early coffee, baguette or pastry.

Be prepared to throw caution to the wind and spend more on dinner than you'd planned. It's sometimes only a small difference between a cheap (by Tahitian standards) restaurant and a truly fine one. Charge your meal to your credit card and save the baked feeds for when you get home.

Polynesian & French One of the best restaurants in town, **L'O à la Bouche** (☎ *45 29 76; Passage Cardella; mains 1700-2900 CFP; closed Sat lunch*) is unpretentious but treats its guests like royalty – even vegetarians (which is rare).

Morrison's Café (☎ *42 78 61; appetisers 900-2300 CFP, mains 1700-2700 CFP; closed Sat lunch*), atop the Vaima Centre, takes its name from Jim (not Van) – you'll work it out. It's cheesy, but popular, with rooftop and open-air sections.

La Petit Auberge (☎ *42 86 13; appetisers 1250-1950 CFP, mains 2650-3650 CFP; closed Sat lunch*), close to the Pont de l'Est roundabout, is one of Pape'ete's oldest restaurants. This intimate little place indulges French-cuisine enthusiasts with very fine cooking.

La Corbeille d'Eau (☎ *43 77 14; Blvd Pomare; appetisers 1700-3400 CFP, mains 2500-4600 CFP; closed Sat lunch*) is stylish and a favourite of Pape'ete businesspeople and politicians, though it's a bit out of the way.

Café Koké (☎ *50 22 44; rue Paul Gauguin; appetisers 550-2450 CFP, mains 1250-2600 CFP; open lunch Mon-Fri, dinner Fri & Sat*) is a sleek, modern restaurant with fabulous food.

Voo Doo Lounge (☎ 48 08 48; rue du Commandant Jean Gilbert; tapas 700-10,000 CFP, appetisers from 900 CFP, mains from 1900 CFP; open Tues-Sat) is a stylish, intimate spot to drink or enjoy great food.

Italian Pape'ete institution **Lou Pescadou** (☎ 43 74 26; rue Anne-Marie Javouhey; dishes 600-2700 CFP; open late) serves hearty pizzas and pasta dishes.

La Squadra (☎ 41 32 14; Passage Cardella; pasta dishes 1400-1600 CFP; open lunch Mon-Sat, dinner Wed-Sun) has an interesting menu.

Asian The long-established **Le Mandarin** (☎ 50 33 90; rue des Écoles; mains 1500-3600 CFP; closed Sat lunch), with its ornate Chinese interior, makes for a visual and culinary feast. **Le Dragon d'Or** (☎ 42 96 12; rue Colette; appetisers 900-2200 CFP, mains 1300-2300 CFP; open Tues-Sun) is another classic Chinese restaurant.

Restaurant Tehoa (☎ 42 99 27; rue du Maréchal Foch; mains 1060-1920 CFP; open lunch Mon-Sat, dinner Wed-Sat) is a rough-and-ready local favourite with large servings, fresh food and low prices.

Sushi Bar (Vaima Centre; plates 300-500 CFP; open lunch Mon-Sat, dinner Fri & Sat) is a stylish Japanese 'rotating sushi bar'.

Cafés On the Pont de l'Est roundabout **Tiki Soft C@fé** (☎ 88 93 98, 77 44 34) is a hip spot for a quick coffee or snack, and you can also check your emails; at night it's a bar with weekend DJs.

Big Burger (Au Rendez-Vous des Amis; ☎ 43 01 98; rue Largarde; meals 600-2300 CFP) is always jumping; meals are generous. Nearby **Le Patachoux** (rue Largarde) is a lovely little place with sandwiches (600 CFP) and good pastries (200 CFP).

Café de la Gare (☎ 42 75 95; rue du Général de Gaulle; dishes 1400-2300 CFP; open lunch only) is chic and trés français, but a little pricey.

In the middle of town, the Vaima Centre has a number of excellent cafés and cheap eats, including **Le Rétro** (☎ 42 86 83; open daily), which always seems to be open; **L'Oasis** (☎ 45 45 01; mains from 1400 CFP), especially in the morning; and **Jack Lobster** (☎ 42 50 58; closed dinner Sat), which has a Tex-Mex and steak menu.

The **Marché de Pape'ete** has a few **stalls** where you can buy cake, pizza and Chinese food.

Les Roulottes

Good food, good fun and the best prices in town: that's *les roulottes*, the bustling little food caravans that rock quayside Pape'ete every evening. Eating at a *roulotte* is part of the Pape'ete experience; at the very least stroll past to take in the atmosphere and the smells as all sorts of food sizzles and bakes and fries from inside these tiny vans. The action starts at about 6pm as flaps are lowered on each side to become counters – stools are set up for the customers while the staff inside the van prepare the food. The action continues into the early hours.

Roulottes turn out pretty much everything you'll find at regular restaurants but at lower prices, typically around 1000 CFP.

Hong Kong is one of the most popular *roulottes*; squeeze in for steak and chips or excellent chow mein; **Pizza Napoli** has good thin-crust pizzas; **Crêperie du Port** manages to serve everything from hamburgers to crepes; and **Glacier du Port** whips up outrageous combinations such as Nutella-and-banana waffles.

Self-Catering You can easily cook for yourself in Pape'ete; the **market** has wonderful fresh fish, fruit and vegies (make the most of this before you hit the islands), and there are a few large, well-stocked supermarkets. If you are staying in the centre, the most handy supermarket is **Supermarché Champion** (rue du Commandant Destremeau), close to the Paofai Church. There are a few **Carrefour supermarkets** (at PK4.5 in Arue and in the Moana Nui Commercial Centre at PK8.3 towards Puna'auia); there's **Hyper U** in Pira'e; and **Cash & Carry** at PK3 in Faa'a.

Entertainment

After a stay on other islands where nightlife is nonexistent, Pape'ete could almost pass for a wild and abandoned city – although actually it only gets busy on weekends.

Pubs On a balmy tropical evening the first question is where to go for a cold Hinano or a well-poured *maitai*. Many of the places along Blvd Pomare, the noisy nightlife strip, look pretty seedy, but they are frequented by local women and families, and are generally safe for single female travellers.

Many of Pape'ete's cafés are a great place for drinking, socialising and people-watching. Some of the best (listed under Cafés & Snack Bars earlier) include **Le Rétro**, **Café de la Gare** and **Tiki Soft C@fé**.

Voo Doo Lounge has great low-key music and a languid atmosphere. **Morrison's Café** is a popular drinking hole and has rock and blues groups playing several times a week. See Polynesian & French Restaurants under Places to Eat earlier in this section for details.

Several places along Blvd Pomare are good spots for a contemplative beer at any time, particularly the popular **3 Brasseurs** *(open daily)*, which has excellent boutique-brewery beer on tap and weekend cover bands.

Of course, the snazzy top-end hotels have bars where you can enjoy the ocean breeze and nibble the free peanuts.

Clubs Blvd Pomare is the main club strip. Some places open only on weekends, when you need to elbow your way in (although women tend to be more than welcome). At all but Le Paradise the weekend admission charge includes a drink.

Piano Bar *(rue des Écoles; admission 1500 CFP Fri & Sat; open Mon-Sat)* has a reputation that precedes it: it isn't a place for prudes. There's a drag show on Friday and Saturday at around 1am.

Le Paradise *(Blvd Pomare; admission men 2000 CFP Fri & Sat; open 10pm-3am daily)* attracts a slightly older crowd, predominantly Westerners.

La Cave *(Blvd Pomare; admission men 1500 CFP; open Fri & Sat)* is the place to head if you want a more *kaina* (local) atmosphere and dance music.

Royal Kikiriri *(rue Colette; admission 1000 CFP Fri & Sat; open Wed-Sun)* is home to the Trio Kikiriri, who ensure that you won't hear any techno here.

Club 106 *(admission men 2000 CFP; open Thur-Sat)*, on the waterfront, attracts an older crowd.

Cinemas Pape'ete has a few small cinemas, including **Concorde** *(☎ 42 63 60; Vaima Centre, rue du Général de Gaulle)*, **Hollywood** *(☎ 42 65 79; Fare Tony, rue Largarde)* and **Liberty** *(☎ 42 08 20; rue du Maréchal Foch)*. They screen average Hollywood blockbusters and the occasional French film. 'Version Originale' (VO; Original Version) indicates that the film will be shown in its original language, with subtitles; mainly it's 'Version

Française' (VF; French Version), with French voices dubbed over your favourite Hollywood actor. Admission costs 950 CFP.

Dance Performances Superb, colourful Polynesian dance performances are held several times a week in the big hotels. Brush aside images of cheesy tourist performances – these groups are professional and are enjoyed every bit as much by locals as by wide-eyed visitors. The 45-minute performances generally start at about 8pm. They're often accompanied by a sumptuous buffet (around 6000 CFP), although a drink at the bar will sometimes get you in.

Shopping

As well as pearls, pearls and more pearls, you can buy handicrafts from all over French Polynesia here: Marquesan woodcarvings, hats and baskets woven in the Australs, and colourful pareu.

For reasonably priced gifts for friends back home, start at the **Marché de Pape'ete**, where wooden salad servers, bright fabric, the wonderful *monoi* oil, pareu, jewellery and even mother-of-pearl love-heart key rings! Think carefully before getting that permanent souvenir, a tattoo.

The **Carrefour Hypermarket** near the airport sells the standard souvenirs – Tahitian soaps, preserves, chocolates, calendars and the like – for much less than most tourist outlets. It's across the road from the Outumaoro *le truck* stop.

Cruise Blvd Pomare, rue du Général de Gaulle, Fare Tony and the Vaima Centre for heaps of craft and souvenir shops of varying quality.

Several art galleries show the work of Polynesian artists, including **Galerie des Tropiques** *(☎ 41 05 00; cnr Blvd Pomare & rue Cook)*; **Olivier Creations** *(☎ 48 29 36; rue Paul Gauguin)*; and **Gallerie Winkle** *(☎ 42 81 77; rue Jeanne d'Arc)*.

You practically trip over Pape'ete's jewellery shops and pearl specialists. A single pearl costs around 15,000 CFP (cheaper if you don't mind imperfections); a decent-quality ring can cost anything from an almighty 140,000 CFP. If you want to shop around, there are numerous pearl shops and pearl farms on the outer islands.

Local music CDs are sold in city music shops and hypermarkets. **Tahiti Music**, diagonally opposite the cathedral, has a decent selection.

TAHITI & FRENCH POLYNESIA

AROUND THE ISLAND

Try to do a day trip around Tahiti Nui (Big Tahiti) if you possibly can. It's a great way to get a feel for life outside Pape'ete and to enjoy the island's lush vegetation. There are pockets of poverty, particularly in the valleys, where the water is not drinkable and unemployment is high, but you'll be hard-pressed to find a long face. You will find plenty of churches, kids on bikes and little stalls along the way.

Coast Road

We've described a clockwise circuit around Tahiti Nui; it's 114km and can be done in a day, but could be extended by staying overnight at an interesting little *pension* then taking in Tahiti Iti as well – accommodation and a Tahiti Iti excursion are described later in this section. Bring the mosquito repellent to make garden and forest walks more pleasant.

On Point Outuaiai in Arue, the **Tomb of Pomare V** (PK4.7) is the final resting place of the last of the Pomare dynasty. It was actually built for Queen Pomare IV, but her ungrateful son Pomare V had her remains evicted and when he died in 1891 it became his tomb.

The **Baie de Matavai** (Matavai Bay) was the favourite locale of early European explorers. On its western boundary, **Taharaa Point** (PK8.1) offers fine views towards Pape'ete. Point Vénus (PK10), the promontory that marks the bay's eastern end, was the site of Cook's observatory, built to record the transit of Venus across the face of the sun to try to calculate the distance between the sun and the earth. There's also a memorial to the first LMS Protestant missionaries, who made their Tahitian landfall here. Today it's a popular, shaded black-sand beach overlooked by an impressive lighthouse. It's unsigned; just turn off when you see shops and activity at PK10.

An often-crowded **surf break** just before the headland signals the start of the small village of **Papenoo** (PK17). The 4WD route up the Papenoo Valley starts here.

In the right swell the **Arahoho Blowhole** (PK22), just before Tiarei, puts on a good show. The fine sliver of black-sand **beach** just beyond makes a good picnic stop.

Near the blowhole a road turns off to the three **Faarumai Waterfalls** (PK22.1). It's a few hundred metres through forest to the first fall and, if the path's clear, 20 minutes further to the other two.

A plaque on the bridge at **Hitiaa** (PK38) commemorates the visit to Tahiti in 1768 by Louis-Antoine de Bougainville.

Once you reach **Taravao** (PK54) you're at the narrow isthmus where Tahiti Nui joins Tahiti Iti. Always a strategic spot, the town has been a military base on and off since 1844. It's a good place for lunch and is the place to turn off to Tahiti Iti.

In the **Jardin Botanique** *(Botanic Gardens; PK51.2; admission 500 CFP; open 9am-5pm daily)* walking paths wend their way through 137 hectares of ponds, palms and a superb thicket of bamboo. Nearby, the quietly decaying setting of the interesting **Musée Gauguin** *(Gauguin Museum; admission 600 CFP; open 9am-5pm daily)* is appropriate given the artist's troubled life. Don't expect too many original works but do wander the gardens, which feature three superb towering *tiki* from Raivavae in the Australs. You can get to both attractions from Pape'ete by *le truck*, but the last trip back leaves early in the afternoon.

From the **Bain de Vaima** (Vaima Pool; PK49) walk a few minutes inland to **Vaipahi Waterfall**, which drops from pool to pool through a stand of stately *mape* trees to a great viewpoint. A number of short walks continue – a one-hour walk brings you back to the road at PK50.2.

The turn-off for the rough track to the Tahiti Nui highlands is at PK47.5; a few kilometres later you pass through **Mataiea**, Gauguin 's happy home for a few years.

On the outskirts of Papara village, **Marae Mahaiatea** (PK39.2) was the most magnificent in Tahiti when Cook first visited; he wrote that it measured 80m by 27m at its base, rising in 11 great steps to a height of 13m. Today the densely vegetated crumbling remains are still impressive for their size. The site is unmarked – take the first turn towards the sea past the PK39 sign.

At PK28.5 wander the manicured path that runs beside the road and through **Maraa Grotto**, a series of overhung, ferny caverns with crystal-clear pools.

In the Pa'ea district tranquil **Marae Arahurahu** (PK22.5) is the best-looking *marae* on the island, and is beautifully maintained. The **Orofero River** (PK20) is a popular surfing break.

The excellent **Musée de Tahiti et ses Îles** *(Museum of Tahiti and its Islands; PK15.1; ☎ 58 34 76; admission 600 CFP; open 9.30am-5.30pm Tues-Sun)* in Puna'auia has one of the best collections in the Pacific. This is a great place to get your head around the geology, history, culture and art of the area. Outside is one of Tahiti's most popular surf breaks.

You can catch a Puna'auia *le truck* close to the museum.

Stop for a swim and a laze at any of the good **beaches** between PK15 and PK10 through **Puna'auia**, which has some fine restaurants (see Places to Eat later in this section).

Well into Pape'ete's urban sprawl, the pleasant, touristy **Lagoonarium** (☎ 43 62 90; *PK11; adult/child 500/300 CFP; open 9am-6pm daily*) has an underwater viewing room – if you can, you're better off going snorkelling to see the real thing.

Organised Tours

It seems that almost every hotel and travel agency offers an island-circuit tour by minibus. To go at your own pace hire a car or cycle (you'll probably need to bring your own bike). See Car under Getting Around earlier in this section for details of car-rental agencies.

Places to Stay

East Coast Head straight to **Fare Nana'o** (☎ 57 18 14, fax 57 76 10; e farenanao@mail .pf; PK52; bungalows with/without kitchen 11,000/7500 CFP), which is unlike anywhere else you'll stay in French Polynesia. The bungalows border on the Gaudi-esque and are simply stunning. Accommodation ranges from the famous tree house to two-storey, four-person bungalows.

South Coast On the lagoon side in Papara, **Hiti Moana Villa** (☎ 57 93 33, fax 57 94 44; e hitimoanavilla@mail.pf; PK32; bungalows with/without kitchen from 9500/8500 CFP) has a swimming pontoon, a pool and impeccable garden bungalows. There's a supermarket and restaurant nearby.

Papara Village (☎ 57 41 41, fax 57 45 74; PK38; bungalows 10,000 CFP), perched on the hillside 800m off the coast road, has well-equipped bungalows and fantastic views. The small Marae Tetaumatai is on site.

West Coast These quiet places are close to black-sand beaches. Regular *le truck* services run during the day but dry up towards 4pm or 5pm.

Le Méridien (☎ 47 07 07, fax 47 07 28; e reservations@lemeridien-tahiti.pf; doubles 39,000 CFP, over-water bungalows 53,400 CFP, suites 53,400-111,200 CFP), in Puna'auia, rivals the Tahiti Beachcomber Intercontinental Resort for luxury; its over-water bungalows are equally divine and are definitely bigger than their Beachcomber counterparts.

Le Relais Fenua (☎/fax 45 01 98; w www .relais-fenua.pf; PK18.25; singles/doubles/quads 7000/8400/14,000 CFP), in Pa'ea, is a great place to stay. Clean, spacious rooms with TV, bathroom and air-con are set around a swimming pool. Children under 12 years of age stay for free.

Pension Te Miti (☎/fax 58 48 61; PK18.6; dorm beds 2500 CFP, doubles 5500-7000 CFP), a friendly and popular place, is on the mountain side of the main road in Pa'ea, about 200m from the shore. Rates include breakfast; there's also an equipped kitchen, and meals are available.

Places to Eat

Lots of little **stalls** are set up along the road around Tahiti Nui, and restaurants dot the coastal road, particularly around Taravao. The places mentioned here are described clockwise around the coast.

Endearing **Fare Nana'o** (*see East Coast under Places to Stay, earlier; meals 3000 CFP*) allows nonguests to dine if they book. In Taravao, **L'Escale Restaurant** (☎ 57 07 16; mains 1500-2700 CFP; open Tues-Sat) serves fine French cuisine and Moroccan specialities in a classic setting, while **Te Hono** (☎ 57 21 84; mains 800-1300 CFP; open lunch Tues-Sun, dinner Tues-Sat) serves very good Chinese food but is a little sterile.

The choice of restaurants increases along the south coast. **Restaurant Baie Phaéton** (☎ 57 08 96; PK59; meals 900-1600 CFP; open lunch Tues-Sun, dinner Tues-Sat) has a superb view across Phaéton Bay from its terrace, and a mainly Chinese menu. **Restaurant du Jardin Botanique** (*Botanic Gardens entrance; appetisers 600-1950 CFP, mains 1700-3200 CFP*) is a good place for a light meal. **Restaurant Nuutere** (☎ 57 41 15; PK32.5; appetisers 1600-2400 CFP, mains 2300-3500 CFP; open Wed-Mon), in Papara, is a great little French restaurant.

Chic Puna'auia has many restaurants. **Restaurant L'Impérial** (☎ 45 18 19; PK15; appetisers 1000-1200 CFP, mains 1300-3300 CFP; open lunch & dinner Tues-Sun) is a good Chinese restaurant. **Coco's Restaurant** (☎ 58 21 08; PK13; appetisers 1800-3800 CFP, mains 2400-4100 CFP; open daily) has a magnificent seaside setting and fine food. **La Fleur de Lotus** (☎ 41 97 20; PK13; appetisers 1300-2300 CFP, mains 1300-4100 CFP) is a Chinese restaurant popular with locals. **Captain Bligh Restaurant** (☎ 43 62 90; PK11.4; appetisers 1300-2000 CFP, mains 1800-3400 CFP; open lunch Tues-Sun), at the Lagoonarium, is touristy and cavernous but not at all unpleasant. It puts on a Friday and Saturday evening buffet and dance performance by one of Tahiti's best island dance groups. **L'Auberge du Pacifique** (☎ 43 98 30; PK11.2; appetisers 2000-3400 CFP, mains 2600-3800 CFP), beside the lagoon, has become a Tahiti institution for its French-Polynesian menu.

INLAND TAHITI NUI

Although several roads and tracks climb a little way into the central highlands, only one route extends right across Tahiti. It's a wonderful, but quite rugged 39km road from Papenoo in the north to Mataiea in the south, via the Relais de la Maroto and Lake Vaihiria. Do this excursion for a completely different look at Tahiti: mountains, waterfalls, a lake and mysterious archaeological sites.

From Papenoo the track follows the wide **Papenoo Valley**, the only valley to cut right through the ancient crater, passing the **Topatari**, **Vaiharuru** and **Puraha Waterfalls**. The track passes the **Bassin Vaituoru** (Vaituoru Pool) and finally reaches the Relais de la Maroto.

From here tracks fan out to several hydro dams and the *marae* that were restored during the dam's construction. The extensive **Marae Farehape** site is almost directly below the ridge on which the Relais de la Maroto perches. The beautifully restored **Marae Anapua** perches above Vainavenave Dam. There are some fine natural swimming pools and striking waterfalls nearby.

If you're starting the route from the south coast, turn at PK47.5, between the Seventh-Day Adventist church and the Tahiria bridge. The track then turns left and follows the river upstream to a small catchment lake and the extensive remains of **Marae Vaihiria I**. The road climbs quickly to **Lake Vaihiria**, then descends steeply to a road junction; turn left to the Relais de la Maroto.

Organised Tours

A few companies specialise in cross-country 4WD tours. **Tahiti Safari Expedition** (☎ 42 14 15), **Patrick Adventure** (☎ 83 29 29, 72 08 09) and **Natura Exploration** (☎ 43 03 83) charge approximately 5000/7500 CFP for a half-/full day.

Places to Stay & Eat

The original accommodation quarters for workers on the hydroelectricity project, **Relais**

de la Maroto (☎ 57 90 29, fax 57 90 30; e maroto@mail.pf; 1-2-person rooms/bungalows 6500/9500 CFP), has very popular renovated motel-style rooms and a few lovely bungalows. The wine cellar at the restaurant here is exceptional.

Getting There & Away

You can either take an organised tour (see Organised Tours, earlier), mountain bike across (you'll probably need your own bike), walk the route in two days, or hire a 4WD, though check track conditions, as some parts are perilous.

TAHITI ITI

Tahiti Iti (Small Tahiti), also known as the Presqu'île (Peninsula), is where you get into the wild country; it has some superb walking trails. You cannot drive right around: the road only goes as far as Teahupoo to the south and Tautira in the north. Although walking trails extend around the coast from both ends the sheer Te Pari cliffs at the southeastern corner cut the trails in some places, which makes walking right around quite difficult.

The north coast road from Taravao runs through Pueu, past steep hills and numerous waterfalls, to Tautira. This stretch of coast has the highest rainfall on Tahiti. It's easy to walk beyond Tautira for a further 12km. Near the Vaiote River are some **petroglyphs** on boulders near the coast and a series of **marae** inland.

Two roads lead into the centre to a **lookout** that has views across the isthmus of Taravao to the towering bulk of Tahiti Nui. It's possible to walk for about an hour towards Mt Teatara (1197m). The two roads can be combined to form a loop: the first (7km) starts in Afaahiti, at PK0.6; the other turns off the north-coast road at PK2.5 and is rougher and more potholed.

The south-coast road runs past beaches and bays to Vairao and the small settlement of Teahupoo, passing a turn-off at PK9.5 which leads a short distance inland to the **Marae Nuutere**. The size of the waves at **Teahupoo** has earned the site the name 'Jaws of Water'. The road stops abruptly at the **Tirahi River** at PK18; from here it is an easy two-hour walk to **Vaipoiri Cave**.

Places to Stay & Eat

Punatea Village (☎/fax 57 71 00; e punatea _village@hotmail.com; PK4.7; doubles/bungalows 6100/9500 CFP), by the sea, has five small rooms with a shared bathroom or four spacious bungalows with private bathroom; breakfast (600 CFP) and dinner (2500 CFP) are available.

Pension Chayan *(☎ 72 28 40; PK14; bungalows 10,800 CFP)*, on the mountain side of the road, is a fairly new place, with four very comfortable bungalows.

Pension Bonjouir *(☎ 77 89 69; ⓔ bonjouir@ mail.pf; tent site 1200 CFP, doubles 5000-6500 CFP, 2-person/family bungalows 8000/ 15,000 CFP)*, popular with surfers for the nearby reef break and laid-back feel, is a little beyond Te Pari Village and is only accessible by boat. It has tent sites (the only camp site on Tahiti) and simple bungalows.

Te Pari Village *(☎/fax 42 59 12; bungalows with full board per person 9500 CFP)* is 10 minutes by boat from the Teahupoo pier, in the middle of a magnificent coconut grove beside the lagoon. The four traditional-style bungalows have bathrooms; rates include transfers from the pier.

Chez Jeannine *(☎/fax 57 07 49; doubles 5000 CFP, large bungalows 7900 CFP)* is an isolated place on the plateau road with beautiful views of the isthmus. The bungalows and rooms are well kept and the setting is pleasant.

Auberge Te Pari *(☎ 57 13 44; mains 1800-3300 CFP; open lunch Sat-Thur, dinner on demand)*, in Teahupoo on the beach at the end of the road, has a pleasant seaside terrace and specialises in crustaceans.

Restaurant Eurasienne *(open Fri-Wed)*, at Chez Jeannine, turns out Vietnamese, Chinese and French food.

Other Society Islands

MO'OREA
pop 14,226 • area 132 sq km
This is the place that daydreams are made of: mountains that leap out of the lagoon; fine beaches; restaurants dripping with fresh fish; stylish accommodation; terrific scuba diving and excellent walks; interesting *marae*; and a pleasantly unhurried pace of life. Even budget travellers can find reasonably priced places to stay, supermarkets and good-value snorkelling trips. Access to Mo'orea from Tahiti is absurdly easy; spend a day or two in Pape'ete then head straight over to this magical isle.

History
The island's ancient name was Aimeho; some speculate that Mo'orea ('yellow lizard') was the name of one of the ruling families of the island. Before Europeans arrived on the island Mo'orea was heavily populated.

Mo'orea had long been a refuge for Tahitians on the losing side of power struggles. In 1808 Pomare II retreated to Mo'orea, settled at Papetoai, befriended the LMS missionaries here and, when he mounted his return to power in 1815, took Christianity with him. Copra and vanilla have been important crops in the past but today Mo'orea is the pineapple-growing capital of French Polynesia; tourism is the island's other major business. Although development is an unstoppable beast here, the island has managed to maintain a tranquillity lacking in its more developed neighbours.

Orientation
A road runs around the coast and two roads leading from the two bays run into the interior; they meet and climb to the *belvédère* (lookout). The mountainous, untouched interior is covered in dense forests of *mape*, the gigantic Polynesian chestnut tree.

Most people live in coastal villages; with its frenetic quay, Vaiare is the busiest centre, but Afareaitu is the administrative centre. Tourist development is concentrated in two strips: from Maharepa down the east side of Cook's Bay (Baie de Cook) to Paopao, and around Hauru Point on the northeast corner of the island. The airport is at the northeast corner.

Beaches are rare; good ones are at Hauru Point and at Temae, near the airport.

The pointe kilométrique (PK) markers start at zero at the airport and meet at Haapiti, which is at PK24 in a clockwise direction and PK35 anticlockwise.

Information
The **Moorea Tourist Bureau** *(☎ 56 29 09, 56 38 53 on Mon; Hauru Point; closed Sun & Mon)* is at Le Petit Village shopping centre.

The **Banque Socredo** across from the quay at Vaiare has an ATM. Other banks (Banque Socredo, Banque de Tahiti and Banque de Polynésie) with ATMs are clustered around the small shopping centre at Maharepa at PK6.3. The rates are generally not as good here as on Tahiti.

There are **post offices** at Maharepa and Papetoai. Internet access is available at **Maria@Tapas** *(☎ 55 01 70; PK5; 500 CFP/30 min; open mornings Mon-Sat)*, in the Centre

MO'OREA

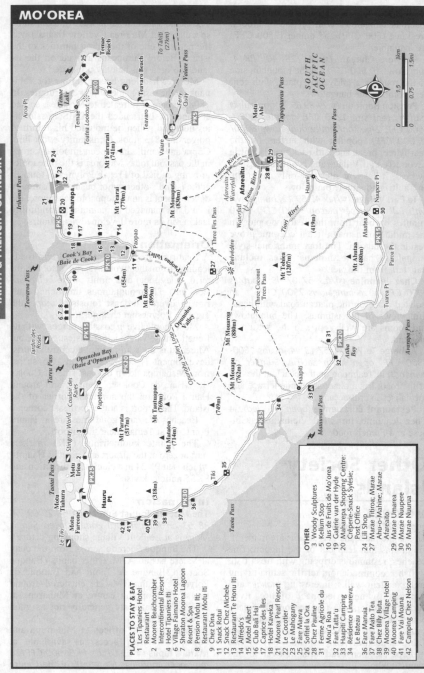

PLACES TO STAY & EAT
1 Les Tipaniers Hotel Restaurant
2 Moorea Beachcomber Intercontinental Resort
4 Hotel Tipaniers Iti
6 Village Faimano Hotel
7 Sheraton Moorea Lagoon Resort & Spa
8 Pension Motu Iti; Restaurant Motu Iti
9 Chez Dina
11 Snack Rotui
12 Snack Chez Michele
13 Restaurant Te Honu Iti
14 Alfredo's
15 Motel Albert
16 Club Bali Hai
17 Caprice des Iles
18 Hotel Kaveka
21 Moorea Pearl Resort
22 Le Cocotier
23 Le Mahogany
25 Fare Maeva
26 Sofitel Ia Ora
28 Chez Pauline
31 Ferme Agricole du Mou'a Roa
32 Fare Tatta'u
33 Haapiti Camping
34 Résidence Linareva; Le Bateau
36 Fare Manuia
37 Fare Mato Tea
38 Chez Billy Buta
39 Moorea Village Hotel
40 Moorea Camping
41 Fare Vai Moana
42 Camping Chez Nelson

OTHER
3 Woody Sculptures
5 Kellum Stop
10 Jus de Fruits de Mo'orea
19 Galerie van der Hyde
20 Maharepa Shopping Centre; Créperie-Snack Sylésie; Post Office
24 Lili Shop
27 Marae Titiroa; Marae Ahu-o-Mahine; Marae Afareaito
29 Marae Umarea
30 Marae Nuupere
35 Marae Nuurua

Kikipa; a small **tabac** *(café; 500 CFP/30 min; open Mon-Sat until 5pm)* in Paopao; and two places at Le Petit Village in Hauru Point – **Tiki@Net** *(☎ 56 39 42; open to 6pm daily)* and **Restaurant Iguane Rock Café** *(☎ 56 17 16; open to midnight daily)*.

In medical emergencies your hotel should be your first port of call. The **Moorea Hospital** *(☎ 56 23 23)* is in Afareaitu. There's a **pharmacy** *(☎ 56 10 51; PK6.5; open daily)* in Maharepa and another shortly after Tiki Village at PK31.

Mo'orea's Coastal Road

If you have the energy you can cycle around this 60km island circuit in a day (it's mostly flat), starting at the airport and going anticlockwise.

Technicolour pareu floating in the breeze at the Lili Shop announce **Maharepa village** (PK4 to PK5). The early-20th century **Maison Blanche** (PK5) is a fine example of a *fare vanira*, a plantation house from Mo'orea's vanilla-boom era.

Spectacular **Cook's Bay** (Baie de Cook) is somewhat misnamed – Cook actually anchored in Opunohu Bay (Baie Opunohu). With Mt Rotui (899m) as a backdrop, it's a lovely stretch of water. The road passes **Galerie van der Heyde**, which has a collection of Oceanic art. At the base of Cook's Bay the village of **Paopao** (PK9) has an interesting mural in its former fish market. A road leads inland from Paopao to meet the Opunohu Valley road.

Stop for a drink at **Jus de Fruits de Moorea** *(Fruit Juices of Moorea; ☎ 56 11 33; PK11; admission free; closed Sun)*, about 300m inland from the coastal road.

Opunohu Bay (Baie d'Opunohu) still feels wonderfully fresh and isolated. Almost at the top of the bay, **Kellum Stop** *(☎ 56 18 52; PK17.5; garden tours 500 CFP)* was the home of the wealthy Medford Kellum, who in 1925 brought six scientists to the region and kickstarted some of the pioneering Polynesian archaeological studies; call ahead for tours.

At PK18 a road turns inland along the Opunohu Valley to several *marae*, the *belvédère* and the walking route to Three Coconut Trees Pass (see Activities, later).

The coast road rounds **Hauru Point** (PK25 to PK30), the northwest corner of the island. The tourist strip starts with the Moorea Beachcomber Intercontinental Resort and ends at around PK31. Hauru Point has a 5km sandy **beach**, one of Mo'orea's best; you have to

walk through the grounds of a hotel to reach it. You can easily swim or snorkel to pretty little **Motu Tiahura** and **Motu Fareone**, though remember the *motu* are private (although the littoral areas aren't).

The evocative **Marae Nuurua** (PK31.5), on the water's edge at the end of a football field, marks the start of the less developed side of Mo'orea. **Haapiti** (PK37) and **Atiha Bay** (PK18) are popular with surfers.

Marae Nuupere (PK14) is on Nuupere Point immediately south of **Maatea** village, but it's on private property and visitors are discouraged. You can explore **Marae Umarea** (PK10), about 100m south of Chez Pauline in Afareaitu; this long wall of coral boulders along the waterfront is thought to date from about 900 AD and is the oldest on Mo'orea. Afareaitu's two **waterfalls** are a major attraction.

Vaiare (PK4) has a bustling port and is the start of the walk across the ridge to Paopao and Cook's Bay. Nearby, the best beaches on the east coast stretch from Teavaro to the airport. **Teavaro Beach** has good snorkelling.

The island road climbs away from the coast to the **Toatea Lookout**, with great views to Tahiti. A road on the lagoon side of the runway extends around **Temae Lake**, one of the rare breeding grounds for the only species of duck found in French Polynesia.

Paopao & Opunohu Valleys

Settlements are creeping up the Paopao Valley but the main activity is still farming, mostly pineapples. In the pre-European era the valleys were densely populated and the Opunohu Valley was dotted with *marae* – the largest number in French Polynesia – some of which have been restored and maintained.

The oldest structures date from the 13th century. From the car park beside the huge **Marae Titiroa** a walking track leads through dense forest to **Marae Ahu-o-Mahine**, with an imposing three-stepped *ahu* (altar). A short way up the road from Marae Titiroa is **Marae Afareaito** and an adjacent **archery platform**.

Beyond Marae Afareaito the road continues to climb steeply, winding up to the excellent **belvédère** on the slopes of Mt Tohiea (1207m).

Activities

It's wise to book activities as soon as you arrive on Mo'orea. Many of the bigger hotels have activities desks.

You'll probably spend as much time in the water as out of it. For the best **snorkelling** join a lagoon tour. **Hauru Point** has white-sand beaches and good snorkelling.

For **diving**, contact **Bathy's Club** (☎ *56 31 44)*, in the Moorea Beachcomber International Resort; **Moorea Fun Dive** (☎ *56 40 38*; W *www.divemoorea.com)*, at the Moorea Beach Club; **Scubapiti** (☎ *56 20 38;* W *www .scubapiti.com)*, the one centre that doesn't believe in fish feeding, at Les Tipaniers; and **Topdive – MUST** (☎ *56 17 32)*, on Cook's Bay. Most dive sites are along the north shore. They include **Le Tiki**, a popular shark-feeding centre; **Stingray World** (Bathy's Club only), where you can frolic with stingrays; the 20m-deep **Couloir des Raies** (Ray Passage); and, for more experienced divers, the 50m dive to the **Jardin des Roses** (Rose Garden).

Aqua Blue (☎ *56 53 53)*, in the Moorea Beachcomber Intercontinental Resort, does 'diving helmet' excursions on the lagoon bottom. **Dolphin & Whale Watching Expeditions** (☎ *56 14 70)* does trips to observe and research dolphins and whales around Mo'orea; **Mahana Tours** (☎ *56 20 44)* offers boat tours to see dolphins and, in season, whales.

Cycling is a great way to see Mo'orea's sights. **Rando Cycles** (☎ *56 51 99;* e *randocycles@ mail.pf; 1-day bike hire 1500 CFP, guided ride 5000 CFP)* rents mountain bikes and runs guided rides (minimum of five participants).

If **walking** is more your thing you're also in luck. Good hikes include the two-hour stretch from the ferry quay at Vaiare, over the crater ridge into the central valley, emerging at Cook's Bay. The climb from near the agricultural school in the Opunohu Valley to Three Coconut Trees Pass is spectacular but the trail can be hard to follow – consider a guide. **Tiare Mato** (☎ *43 92 76)*, **Polynesian Adventure** (☎/fax *43 25 95)* and Derek Grell of **Chez Tefaarahi Safari Tours** (☎/fax *56 41 24)* organise guided walks and climbs.

Horse rides are offered by **Tiahura Ranch** (☎ *56 28 55; 2 hrs per person 4500 CFP)*, at Hauru Point, and **Moorea Beachcomber Intercontinental Resort** (☎ *55 19 55, ext 1903; 2 hrs per person 5800 CFP)*.

Your guesthouse can suggest a **lagoon tour** operator; a six-hour tour visiting the two bays, feeding the sharks, swimming with the rays and having a *motu* picnic will cost around 6000 CFP.

Lots of operators offer three-hour **island 4WD tours** for about 5000 CFP, including **What to do on Moorea** (☎ *56 57 64)*, **Torea Nui Safari** (☎ *56 12 48)*, **Inner Island Safari Tours** (☎ *56 20 09)* and **Ron's Adventure** (☎ *56 42 43)*.

Other activities include fishing, parasailing, jet-skiing, water-skiing and helicopter flights.

Places to Stay

Most accommodation is concentrated on the east side of Cook's Bay and around Hauru Point. Mo'orea has superb over-water bungalows, but it also has the best selection (by local standards!) of budget *pensions* in French Polynesia.

Cook's Bay This magnificent bay doesn't have a beach but is quieter than Hauru Point.

Motel Albert (☎ *56 12 76; PK7; 3-/4-person units from 4300/8600 CFP)* is one of the island's best budget places. It has spacious units with kitchen and bathroom; there's a 1000 CFP one-night supplement but reductions for multiple nights.

Club Bali Hai (☎ *56 13 68, fax 56 13 27;* W *www.clubbalihai.com; doubles 15,700-17,900 CFP, bungalows 24,6000-32,300 CFP)*, across from Motel Albert, is a stylish, breezy spot with views of Mt Rotui.

Hotel Kaveka (☎ *56 50 50, fax 56 52 63;* W *www.hotelkaveka.com; bungalows 9800-22,000 CFP)* has nice dark-wood bungalows in a well-tended garden; half-board is available.

Shark Feeding – Captivating or Crazy?

Shark feeding is a popular activity at Mo'orea, Ra'iatea and sometimes at Bora Bora and Manihi. It's a spectacular activity: the dive master drops to the bottom at around 15m to 20m, signals to the divers to form a semicircle, and produces a hunk of fish from a feed bag. A cloud of fish closes in, and soon black-tip reef sharks, grey sharks and even lemon sharks appear. After 15 minutes of intense activity, the remains are tossed aside and the dive continues at a calmer pace.

However, feeding any fish, let alone sharks, disrupts natural behaviour patterns. Encouraging sharks to associate divers with a free feed can't be a good idea. Some dive centres refuse to indulge in the practice.

Moorea Pearl Resort (☎ *50 84 52; doubles 26,800-31,200 CFP, bungalows 36,800-65,600 CFP)* has replaced the old Bali Hai Moorea; it's quite spectacular. The bungalows are worth the extra money.

Cook's Bay to Hauru Point Excellent **Pension Motu Iti** (☎ *55 05 20, fax 55 05 21;* e *pensionmotuiti@mail.pf; garden/beach bungalows 10,500/12,000 CFP)* has a wonderful atmosphere and lovely restaurant.

Chez Dina (☎ *56 10 39; PK12.5; 2-/4-/5-person bungalows 6400/7100/8500 CFP)* is a delightful, homey place.

Village Faimano Hotel (☎ *56 10 20, fax 56 36 47; PK14.5; bungalows from 7500 CFP)* has seven bungalows beside the lagoon.

Sheraton Moorea Lagoon Resort & Spa (☎ *55 11 11, reservations 86 48 49; bungalows 42,300-80,100 CFP)* is deluxe and has one of the few bits of beach along this strip.

Hotel Tipaniers Iti (☎ *56 12 67, fax 56 29 25; bungalows 9100 CFP)* is associated with the popular Les Tipaniers at Hauru Point; it's impeccably clean and quiet and the bungalows have kitchen, sitting area, bathroom and veranda. Guests can join the main hotel's activities and a free shuttle bus runs to the restaurant.

Hauru Point This sector has a pleasant beach, and easily accessible *motu* directly offshore. Backpackers will find a place to stay here, but don't expect a warm welcome at either the very basic **Camping Chez Nelson** (☎ *56 15 18; * w *www.camping-nelson.pf; PK27; camping per person 1100 CFP, dorm beds/doubles 1600/4300 CFP, bungalows 3400-4500 CFP)* or **Moorea Camping** (☎ *56 14 47; PK27.5; camping per person 1000 CFP, dorm beds 1200 CFP, bungalows 4500-6000 CFP)*, which has crammed tent sites and bathrooms of dubious cleanliness.

Chez Billy Ruta (☎ *56 12 54; PK28; bungalows with/without kitchen 6800/5700 CFP)* has rudimentary waterside bungalows with excellent views.

Les Tipaniers Hotel Restaurant (☎ *56 12 67, fax 56 29 25;* e *tipaniersresa@mail.pf; bungalows with/without kitchen from 15,000/9000 CFP)*, on the outskirts of Hauru Point, has thatch-roofed bungalows with a veranda, small lounge area and bathroom; some have kitchen. This place has a beachside restaurant and bar.

Moorea Village Hotel *(Fare Gendron;* ☎ *56 10 02, fax 56 22 11;* e *mooreavillage@mail.pf;*

PK28; bungalows with/without kitchen from 20,300/10,700 CFP) is ideal for families, with functional, if crammed, bungalows with bathroom, fan and refrigerator. It offers lots of activities and has friendly staff.

Fare Mato Tea (☎ *54 14 36, fax 56 32 54;* e *mtt@mail.pf; PK28.7; 4-/6-person bungalows 9100/10,700 CFP, minimum 2 nights)* feels wonderfully tranquil and has spotlessly clean cabins.

Fare Manuia (☎ *56 26 17, fax 56 10 30; PK30; 4-/6-person bungalows 10,200/13,000 CFP)* has a sunny stretch of beach and well-equipped family bungalows. You'll find a washing machine, a pirogue for free use and a kayak that can be rented. There is a two-night minimum stay.

Moorea Beachcomber Intercontinental Resort (☎ *55 19 19, fax 55 18 88;* e *moorea@interconti.com; doubles 35,400 CFP, bungalows 39,800-65,600 CFP)* is one of the most luxurious spots on Mo'orea.

Club Med is closed while it's being completely rebuilt, but should reopen in late 2004 or early 2005.

Haapiti to Afareaitu Just north of Haapiti village, intimate **Résidence Linareva** (☎ *55 05 65, fax 55 05 67;* w *www.linareva.com; PK34.5; 1-/2-/4-person bungalows from 8700/10,500/22,500 CFP)* has very pleasant and well-furnished bungalows in a garden by the beach. Bicycles, pirogues and snorkelling equipment are provided free of charge and the restaurant, Le Bateau, has a good reputation.

Fare Tatta'u (☎/fax *56 35 83; PK21.3; dorm beds/bungalows 2700/6400 CFP)* is quiet and friendly, and popular with surfers because it's near Matauvau Pass. Prices quoted are for more than one night.

Ferme Agricole du Mou'a Roa (☎ *56 58 62, fax 56 40 47;* e *ferme.mouaroa@mail.pf; PK 21; dorm beds 2500 CFP)* is a great, ecofriendly place. A clean and simple colonial-style house has eight rooms with four to six beds in each. Camping is possible. Call to be picked up, as it's 4WD access only.

Haapiti Camping (☎/fax *56 43 02;* e *table saw@mail.pf; PK23.5; sites per person with/without tent 1050/1550 CFP)*, next to the Catholic church, is in a lush, remote valley with great views; it's close to the Haapiti surf break. Meals are available or guests can use the communal kitchen and eat from fruit trees on the property. Bungalows are also planned for the site.

Chez Pauline (☎ 56 11 26; doubles 6000 CFP), at Afareaitu, has a historic but decidedly spartan charm, and a restaurant that specialises in Tahitian cuisine.

Temae Looking across to Tahiti from Temae Beach, luxurious **Sofitel Ia Ora** (☎ 55 03 55, fax 56 12 91; beach/garden/over-water bungalows from 18,200/20,700/42,200 CFP) is on one of the island's best beaches.

Fare Maeva (☎/fax 56 18 10; bungalows 8100 CFP) is a charming, isolated place; its bungalows have kitchen and bathroom.

Places to Eat

You will eat well here, though plan to dine early – most places close towards 9pm and on Sunday the choice can be restricted. Some restaurants offer a transport service.

Maharepa & Cook's Bay In the Maharepa shopping centre, **Crêperie-Snack Sylésie** (open 6am-6pm) is an ideal place for breakfast or a snack but has a bland setting.

L'Ananas Bleu (open breakfast & lunch daily), in the Club Bali Hai, has great snacks and light lunches. The fishburger (1100 CFP) is delicious.

Le Mahogany (☎ 56 39 73; PK4, Maharepa; appetisers 600-1200 CFP, mains 1550-2450 CFP) is a pleasant little place with a French and Chinese menu.

Le Cocotier (☎ 56 12 10; Maharepa; daily specials 2050 CFP; open daily) is a popular French restaurant.

Caprice des Îles (☎ 56 44 24; open Wed-Mon), located just before Club Bali Hai, looks like an enormous Polynesian fare and has a menu varying from French to Chinese to Tahitian.

Alfredo's (☎ 56 17 71; mains 1450-2950 CFP; open daily) is a very popular Italian restaurant.

Restaurant Te Honu Iti (☎ 56 19 84; appetisers around 1300 CFP, mains around 2600 CFP; open daily) has excellent French food served on an over-water terrace.

Paopao has several small snack bars, including **Snack Chez Michèle** (salads 1350 CFP, mains from 1600 CFP; open daily) and **Snack Rotui**.

Papetoai & Hauru Point Expect to pay reasonable prices and to be greeted with a friendly welcome at **Chez Serge** (☎ 56 13 17; PK25, Papetoai; open daily), which serves delicious local dishes.

Les Tipaniers Restaurant (☎ 56 12 67), at the hotel of the same name, combines French–Italian food with a Tahitian flavour and has a great reputation. It's a movable feast, with breakfast and lunch at the beach while at dinner time it shifts to the main road.

Fare Vai Moana (☎ 56 17 14; mains 1100-2300 CFP), in the Hotel Fare Vai Moana, has a great beachside setting and occasional live music.

Moorea Village Hotel (☎ 56 10 02) has a restaurant in a local-style room facing the motu. On Saturday night there's a barbecue and on Sunday afternoon, a traditional Polynesian feast. Prices are very reasonable and there's often music with dinner.

Coco d'Îsle (☎ 56 59 07; daily specials 1200 CFP; open 6.30am-10pm daily) is a great little place with good tucker, although it's located in a dusty spot. It's cheaper for takeaway.

Chez Capo (☎ 56 54 89; appetisers 1300 CFP, mains 1500 CFP; open lunch Sun-Fri, dinner Sat-Thur) is set back from the road, and is an agreeable, shady place for a light Polynesian lunch.

Motu Tiahura The fairly new **Motu Moea – Restaurant la Plage** (☎ 74 96 96) has an idyllic setting on Motu Tiahura (also known as Motu Moea). The food is simple, fresh and reasonably priced. Catch a boat from Les Tipaniers Hotel Restaurant (500 CFP).

Haapiti In Résidence Linareva, **Le Bateau** (☎ 55 05 65; 1650-3750 CFP; open daily) is an excellent floating French restaurant; reservations are recommended. The waitresses sometimes put on a Polynesian dance between courses. Transport from Hauru Point costs 500 CFP.

Entertainment

The big hotels have bars where all are welcome to enjoy a predinner drink, and many of the restaurants listed earlier, such as **Le Cocotier**, **Les Tipaniers** and **Le Bateau** are good spots for a sunset tipple.

Maria@Tapas (☎ 55 01 70; PK5), in the Centre Kikipa, is a great, hip place for a drink at night; you can also eat here. Staff will collect you if you are eating there as well.

A couple of times a week (usually Wednesday and Saturday evening) the bigger hotels organise excellent **Polynesian music and dance performances** by local groups.

Shopping

The coastal road is littered with souvenir places. For pareu, T-shirts and other curios, try the **Lili Shop**, **Maison Blanche** and **Vaimiti**, between the airport and Cook's Bay. At Cook's Bay, stop at **Honu Iti Boutique** and the **boutique** in the Club Bali Hai. In Le Petit Village, the **Maison du Tiki** offers sculptures and Polynesian art.

Mo'orea has a number of art galleries, such as **Galerie van der Hyde** at Cook's Bay and **La Poterie de L'Aquarium – Teva Yrondy** close to the Kaveka Hotel. **Woody Sculptures** (☎ 56 37 00; Papetoai), just before the Hauru Point enclave, has woodcarvings by well-respected Woody.

The major black-pearl specialists have outlets in Mo'orea.

Getting There & Away

Crossing the 20km that separates Mo'orea from Tahiti is dead easy. It takes less than 10 minutes by plane, or half an hour by high-speed ferry.

Air Conveniently, **Air Moorea** (on Tahiti ☎ 86 41 41, on Mo'orea ☎ 56 10 34) flies from Faa'a airport on Tahiti to Mo'orea (3100 CFP) at least every half-hour. There's no need to book – just turn up and the airline will put on more flights if needed. At Faa'a airport, Air Moorea is in a separate small terminal, a short stroll east of the main terminal.

Air Tahiti (on Tahiti ☎ 86 42 42) also flies to Mo'orea, but chiefly for passengers connecting to other islands in the Society group. There's usually only one to three flights a day.

Sea Competition is fierce across the 'Sea of the Moon' between Tahiti and Mo'orea. First departures in the morning are usually around 6am; the last trips are in the afternoon around 4.30pm or 5.30pm.

The **Aremiti 4** (in Pape'ete ☎ 42 88 88, on Mo'orea ☎ 56 31 10) has at least four crossings daily (one way/return 1060/2120 CFP); the **Aremiti Ferry** (in Pape'ete ☎ 42 85 85, on Mo'orea ☎ 56 31 10) follows a similar timetable. **Moorea Ferry** (☎ 45 00 30) runs daily (one way 850 CFP). The **Ono-Ono** (in Pape'ete ☎ 45 35 35, on Mo'orea ☎ 56 12 60) has at least four crossings daily (one way/return 1050/2200 CFP); it docks at Cook's Bay rather than Vaiare.

You can buy your tickets at the ticket counter on the quay just a few minutes before departure.

Getting Around

Getting around Mo'orea without a car or bicycle is not all that easy. Distances are not great, but are often just a bit too great to walk. Many of the restaurants and quite a few pearl shops will pick you up for free or for a nominal fee.

The Cook's Bay hotels and *pensions* are 5km to 9km from the airport; the Hauru Point establishments are 25km to 30km away. It's a further 5km from the Vaiare quay. Air Moorea offers a 500 CFP minibus service to any of the island's hotels after each flight. Most hotels, even budget places, offer airport transfers.

Mo'orea **taxis** (☎ 56 10 18) are horribly expensive: from the airport to the Beach-comber Intercontinental, at the very start of Hauru Point, will cost approximately 3500 CFP. However, you may be able to find a shared taxi willing to take you from the quay to Cook's Bay, for example, for around 2000 CFP.

A shuttle bus meets some of the boat arrivals (200 CFP) and runs to or from any of the Cook's Bay or Hauru Point hotels.

Car-rental operators can be found at the Vaiare boat quay, the airport, some of the major hotels as well as dotted around Cook's Bay and Hauru Point. The main operators include **Europcar** (☎ 56 34 00), **Avis** (☎ 56 32 61) and **Albert Transport & Activities** (☎ 56 19 28), which generally has the lowest prices.

Tehotu Location (☎ 56 52 96), at the Vaiare ferry quay, rents scooters, as does Europcar.

Rando Cycles rents mountain bikes (see Activities, earlier) and many hotels also rent bikes for guest use.

Moorea Loca Boat (☎ 78 13 39; 2-/8-hr rental 6000/1000 CFP), at Tipanier Hotel, rents boats, an ideal way to explore the lagoon and small *motu*.

OTHER WINDWARD ISLANDS

Tahiti and Mo'orea are the only major islands in the Windward group; there are also two small high islands, Maiao and Mehetia, and a single atoll, Tetiaroa, which is owned by Marlon Brando. Tiny Tetiaro is picture perfect, with beautiful beaches, clear-blue water and a population comprised mainly of a variety of birds. However, the only place to stay on the island, **Hotel Tetiaroa Village** (☎ 82 63 02), is quite run down. Air Moorea flies here.

HUAHINE
pop 5411 • area 75 sq km

The easternmost of the Leeward Islands are Huahine's two islands which are Huahine Nui (Big Huahine) to the north and Huahine Iti (Little Huahine) to the south. The islands are only barely separated and at low tide you can wade from one to the other; a road bridge spans the narrow gap. Polynesian legend holds that the islands split when the god Hiro ploughed his mighty canoe into the island, creating deep, majestic Bourayne Bay to the west and Maroe Bay to the east.

Huahine is green, lush and beautiful and its easy-going atmosphere entices visitors to kick back and relax. It has some fine beaches to the south, excellent and easily accessible *motu*, great snorkelling and diving, popular surfing breaks and, in the village of Maeva, the most extensive complex of pre-European *marae* in French Polynesia. Each year in October or November, Huahine is the starting point for the annual Hawaiki Nui pirogue race; see the boxed text 'Hawaiki Nui Canoe Race'.

Orientation
A 60km, mostly sealed, road follows the coast most of the way around both islands. A series of *motu* stretches along the east coast of the two islands, while around the north coast is Lake Fauna Nui. It almost cuts off the northern peninsula, where the airport is, from the rest of Huahine Nui. There are only a few beaches.

Fare, the principal town, is on the west coast of Huahine Nui. Faie and Maeva, on the east coast, and Fitii, on the west, are the other main settlements on Huahine Nui. Huahine Iti has four villages: Haapu, Parea, Tefarerii and Maroe.

Information
Most services are in Fare. The **tourist office** (*☎/fax 68 78 81; open 7.30am-11.30am Mon-Sat*) is on the main street. **Banque de Tahiti** is opposite the quay and **Banque Socredo** is on the bypass road; both have ATMs.

The **post office** is to the north of town. Internet access is available at **Ao Api New World** (*☎ 68 70 99; 30 CFP per minute*) upstairs from the tourist office, or at **Pension Mauarii** (*see Huahine Iti under Places to Stay, later; 40 CFP per minute*) in Huahine Iti.

The two private **medical centres** (*☎ 68 82 20, 68 84 93*) are in Fare on the bypass road; there's also a **clinic** and **pharmacy** across from the quay.

Around Huahine Nui
This 60km clockwise circuit of the larger island starts at **Fare**, a sleepy South Seas port where people sit on the quay waiting for boats to arrive while children splash in the water. It has a colourful little waterside **market**, *roulottes*, shops and pleasant places to stay and eat. Fare looks over Haamene Bay, which has two passes to the sea.

A few minutes' walk north of Fare is the old Hotel Bali Hai, where a fascinating **archaeological site** was revealed during construction in 1972.

Lake Fauna Nui (also known as Lake Maeva), actually an inlet from the sea, has a number of ancient coral **fish traps** which are still being used; they are towards the seaward end, beside the bridge.

Maeva village was the seat of royal power on the island and nearly 30 *marae* are still scattered along the shoreline among the modern buildings of the village, and up the slopes of Matairea (Pleasant Wind) Hill; this area is well worth exploring – see under Maeva Marae Walk later in this section. On the water's edge on the Fare side of Maeva, the *fare potee* (chief's house or community meeting place) houses a small **archaeological museum** (*admission 300 CFP; open 9am-4pm Mon-Fri*).

The walking path emerges just south of **Marae Te Ava**. A short walk east leads to **Marae Fare Miro**, which has some particularly neat stonework and a fine setting. The massive **Marae Manunu** stands on the *motu*, across the bridge from the main Maeva complex. Manunu means 'eye of the north' and this was the community *marae* of Huahine Nui.

The coast road turns inland beside narrow Faie Bay to the village of **Faie**. Don't miss a visit to **Huahine Nui Pearls & Pottery**. Peter Owen, the owner, is a potter as well as a pearl farmer, and his work is shown in Pape'ete galleries. His studio is on his pearl farm on the lagoon; a ferry operates from Faie (1000 CFP) at 10am and 3pm daily except Sunday.

Huahine's famous blue-eyed eels can be seen in the river immediately downstream of the bridge. It's a steep climb to the **belvédère** on the slopes of Mt Turi. The road weaves through farms to return to Fare.

Maeva Marae Walk
It takes about two hours to explore the many *marae* around Maeva village.

Start at the defence wall on the Fare side of Maeva; it's thought to have been built by Polynesian resistance forces in their struggle

HUAHINE

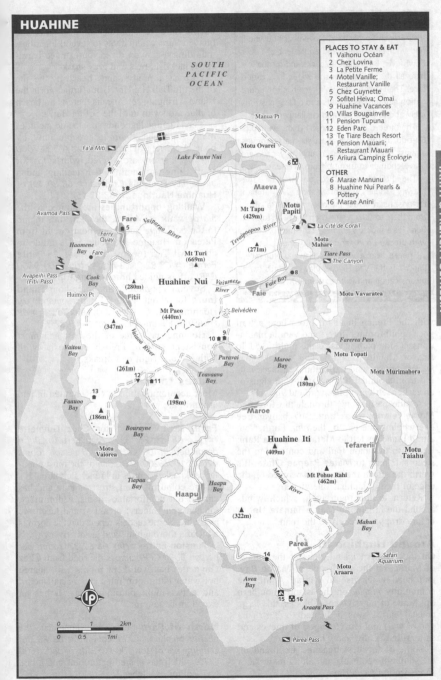

PLACES TO STAY & EAT
1 Vaihonu Océan
2 Chez Lovina
3 La Petite Ferme
4 Motel Vanille;
   Restaurant Vanille
5 Chez Guynette
7 Sofitel Heiva; Omai
9 Huahine Vacances
10 Villas Bougainville
11 Pension Tupuna
12 Eden Parc
13 Te Tiare Beach Resort
14 Pension Mauarii;
   Restaurant Mauarii
15 Ariiura Camping Écologie

OTHER
6 Marae Manunu
8 Huahine Nui Pearls &
   Pottery
16 Marae Anini

TAHITI & FRENCH POLYNESIA

SOUTH
PACIFIC
OCEAN

Manua Pt

Fa'a Miti

Lake Fauna Nui

Motu Ovarei

Avamoa Pass

Maeva

Fare

Vaiporao River

Mt Tapu
(429m)

Motu
Papiti

Ferry
Quay

Haamene
Bay   Fare

Tevaipoopoo River

(271m)

La Cité de Corail

Motu
Mahare

Avapeihi Pass
(Fitii Pass)

Cook
Bay

Mt Turi
(669m)

Tiare Pass

The Canyon

Huimoo Pt

Huahine Nui

Vaiumete
River

(280m)

Fitii

Faie

Fate Bay

Motu
Papiti

Motu Vavaratea

Mt Paeo
(440m)

Belvédère

(347m)

Vaitou
Bay

Vaiuaa River

(261m)

Farerea Pass

Motu Topati

Puravai
Bay

Maroe
Bay

Motu Murimahora

12

11

Teavaava
Bay

(180m)

13

Faauoo
Bay

(198m)

(186m)

Maroe

Bourayne
Bay

Huahine Iti
(409m)

Tefarerii

Motu
Vaiorea

Motu
Taiahu

Tiapaa
Bay

Haapu
Bay

Mt Pohue Rahi
(462m)

Mahuti River

Haapu

(322m)

Mahuti
Bay

Parea

Safari
Aquarium

14

Motu
Araara

Avea
Bay

15   16

Araara Pass

Parea Pass

0   1   2km
0   0.5   1mi

Hawaiki Nui Canoe Race

Visit French Polynesia in November and you'll find yourself in the island equivalent of Super Bowl fever. But forget fullbacks and footballs – here all the action's on the water, in a canoe race. The Hawaiki Nui Va'a race has the entire nation glued to its TV sets and talking passionately about favourites and challengers.

The three-day, four-island, 116km event pits 60-odd of the islands' best six-man pirogues against each other and against any paddlers brave enough to turn up from overseas.

The 116km race starts on Huahine. The brawny paddlers, who often sport vivid Tahitian tattoos, head across the open sea to Ra'iatea, from there to Taha'a, and then finally on to Bora Bora. It's a superb sight to see the men paddling with precise timing and lightning speed.

There's also a women's Hawaiki Nui race, known as the Vaa Hine, a play on words (va'a means canoe and vahine, woman).

with the French in 1846. From here a trail goes uphill through forest and vanilla plantations; a side path leads to the multitiered **Te Ana** or Matairea Huiarii. This complex has *marae*, houses and agricultural terraces dating from around 1300 to 1800, with signs of an earlier settlement from around 900 AD.

A side path winds through the forest to **Marae Tefano**, where a massive banyan tree overwhelms one end of the *ahu*. Further on, a trail branches left to **Marae Matairea Rahi**. Return to the main trail and continue to the steep side path to **Marae Paepae Ofata**. It's worth the effort: the *marae* is perched on the edge of the hill and has fine views.

Return to the main path, which winds around the hillside to **Marae Tamata Uporu** before dropping steeply to the road.

Around Huahine Iti

On the southern island, start at the village of Maroe, on the south side of **Maroe Bay**, and head clockwise to **Marae Anini**, the community *marae* on the island's southern tip. Made of massive coral blocks, this large coastal *marae* was dedicated to 'Oro (the god of war) and Hiro (the god of thieves and sailors) but is now sadly neglected.

Some of the best **beaches** are found on the southern peninsula and along its western shore around Auea Bay.

Activities

Pacific Blue Adventure (☎ 68 87 21), on the quay at Fare, offers **dives** to several locations, including a canyon dive; you can see barracuda, jackfish, rays and grey sharks.

Fare has a pretty, sandy **beach** by the site of the old Bali Hai Hotel, but further north the island's fringing reef means there is no beach or place to swim until the Sofitel Heiva.

The Huahine lagoon is superb and includes many untouched *motu* accessible only by boat. A variety of **lagoon tours** (6500-7500 CFP per person) are offered, with stops for snorkelling, swimming, fish feeding and a *motu*. Try **Poetania Cruises** (☎ 68 89 49) or **Huahine Nautique** (☎ 68 83 15).

Walking opportunities are limited to the *marae* walk at Maeva, the 3km trail inland to the *belvédère* and a one-hour circuit from Parea on Huahine Iti; you need a guide to climb Mt Turi (669m) from Fare. **La Petite Ferme** (☎ 68 82 98; 2-hr/day trip 4500/9800 CFP) offers guided **horse-riding** trips.

Several operators offer three-hour **island tours** for about 4000 CFP per person; try **Huahine Land** (☎ 68 89 21), **Felix Tours** (☎ 68 81 69) or **Huahine Explorer** (☎ 69 87 33).

Huahine has some of the best and most consistent **surf** in French Polynesia, with both left and right reef breaks.

Places to Stay

Most accommodation is concentrated in and around Fare.

Fare Reserve ahead for **Chez Guynette** (☎/fax 68 83 75; e chezguynette@mail.pf; dorm beds 1400 CFP, 1-/2-/3-person rooms 4200/5100/6200 CFP), one of the most popular backpacker centres in French Polynesia. It's on the colourful main street of Fare and has simple but comfortable rooms, a dormitory, kitchen and laundry; breakfast and lunch are available. Some readers report that the dorm is a bit of a thoroughfare and lacks privacy.

Pension Enite (☎/fax 68 82 37; rooms per person 8000 CFP), across the road from Chez Guynette, has well-kept rooms with shared hot-water bathroom; rates are for half-board and a two-night minimum stay. It has an excellent restaurant.

North of Fare Surfers will appreciate the nearby breaks at **Chez Lovina** (☎ 68 88 06; camping per person 1000 CFP, dorm beds 1600 CFP), which has shared bathrooms and a big, well-equipped kitchen.

La Petite Ferme (☎ 68 82 98; ⓔ lapetite
ferme@mail.pf; dorm beds/singles/doubles
1900/3300/4500 CFP, single/double bungalows 5300/8000 CFP), a popular horse-riding
centre, has simple dorm beds and a small
double room and bungalow. Rates include
breakfast and airport or quay transfers.

Vaihonu Océan (☎ 68 87 33; ⓔ vaihonu@
mail.pf; camping per person 1000 CFP, dorm
beds 1600 CFP, single/double cabins 3000/
4300 CFP, fare 6700 CFP), by the water, provides a good balance between price and quality. The dorm is clean, the fare well equipped,
and cabins have a shared bathroom. Bicycles
are available free for guests' use and airport
transfers are included.

Motel Vanille (☎/fax 68 71 77; ⓔ yvesmotel
vani@hotmail.com; rooms 5000 CFP, 1-2-per-
son bungalows 9500 CFP) is off the airport
road, 50m from the intersection with the
coast road. Pretty local-style bungalows with
hot-water bathroom and small veranda are set
around a swimming pool. Bicycles are available for guests' use. The restaurant here is
good; half-board is available.

Southern Huahine Nui Isolated **Pension
Tupuna** (☎ 68 70 21; 2-person bungalows
6100 CFP) is near Bourayne Bay, in a coconut
plantation by the lagoon. It has three simple
local-style bungalows with shared bathroom.
Meals (2000 CFP) are served in a fare potee
and airport transfers are free.

For furnished, fully equipped villas try
neighbouring **Villas Bougainville** (☎/fax 68
81 59; 2-3-/5-6-person villas 16,600/23,600
CFP) or **Huahine Vacances** (☎/fax 68 73 63;
ⓔ huahinevacances@hotmail.com; 5-7-person
villas 23,600-26,000 CFP). The former are in
a verdant setting on the north shore of Maroe
Bay; the latter are in a garden and overlooking the bay. Rates for both include the use of
a car and a boat, and airport transfers.

For a complete getaway head to **Te Tiare
Beach Resort** (☎ 60 60 50, fax 60 60 51;
ⓔ tetiarebeach@mail.pf; bungalows 35,700-
77,900 CFP), at the southwestern corner of
Huahine Nui. Accessible only by sea, this
appealing complex has traditional but luxurious bungalows. The restaurant has fine food
at reasonable prices. Airport transfers cost
5500 CFP return.

Maeva Area The biggest hotel on the island, **Sofitel Heiva** (☎ 60 61 60, fax 68 85 25;
1-2-person bungalows 33,100-65,000 CFP) is
in a beautiful spot with a sandy beach at the

southern tip of Motu Papiti, 8km from Fare.
It has a restaurant, bar and pool.

Huahine Iti Excellent **Pension Mauarii**
(☎/fax 68 86 49; ⓔ vetea@mail.pf; singles/
doubles 6900/8100 CFP, 1-2-person bungalows 10,600-16,000 CFP), about 3km from
Parea, has impeccable bungalows in a beautiful seafront garden. The adjoining lagoon-
side restaurant is well known; half-board is
available.

Ariiura Camping Écologie (☎ 68 85 20;
camping per person 1300 CFP, singles/doubles
in camping fare 2900/3900 CFP), on the beach
almost at the southern point of Huahine Iti, is
an excellent budget place with a relaxed atmosphere and lovely Polynesian setting. It's
close to prime surfing. The 'camping fare'
are small, simple cabins on the sand with a
bed and mosquito net – they don't lock and
the toilets are local style! You can use the
communal kitchen or buy meals at a small
thatched fare beside the beach.

Places to Eat
If you want to eat cheap or late in Fare head
to the quayside **roulottes** (dishes 800-1200
CFP; open early-late). Otherwise, most places
shut by about 9pm. For contact details for
most other places listed here, see Places to
Stay earlier.

On the main street of Fare, **Chez Guynette**
(breakfast 850 CFP, lunch 1000-1500 CFP;
open daily) is good for breakfast or a light
lunch in the open air.

Pension Enite (meals 2800 CFP; open Mon-
Sat dinner only) has a charming restaurant in
a waterside fare; it has an excellent reputation and serves local specialities. Bookings
are essential.

Tiare Tipanier (☎ 68 80 52; dishes 1100-
2000 CFP; closed Sun & Mon lunch) is very
popular, offering an excellent blend of price
and quality with fish, pizza and meat dishes.

Snack-Restaurant Hiti Ura (dishes 1000-
1500 CFP; open Tues-Fri lunch & dinner, Sat &
Sun dinner), in central Fare opposite the quay,
is a snack bar serving simple dishes.

Around the rest of the island the hotels are
the main places to eat.

Restaurant Mauarii (dishes 1500-4300
CFP; open lunch & dinner daily), at Pension
Mauarii on Huahine Iti, has some of the best
food on the island. For a real feast try a traditional Polynesian meal (2650 CFP).

Restaurant Vanille (dishes 1200-2200
CFP; closed Mon), at Motel Vanille, is a good

choice, while pleasant **Omai**, at the Sofitel Heiva, has a varied menu.

Eden Parc (*☎ 68 86 58; set menus 1000-2500 CFP; open lunch only Mon-Sat*), in the southeast corner of Huahine Nui, is a fruit farm and orchard with delicious cool fruit juices and set meals.

If you're preparing your own meals, fruit, vegetables, fish and other fresh supplies are available from Fare's impromptu quayside **marketplace**; food shops include **Super Fare Nui**, opposite the waterfront, and **Taahitini**, immediately south of the town centre. Other small **food shops** (with variable opening hours) are at Maeva and Fitii on Huahine Nui, and at Haapu and Parea on Huahine Iti.

Entertainment
Sofitel Heiva has twice-weekly buffet dinners with good **traditional dance performances** for 5000 to 6000 CFP.

Getting There & Away
Air Tahiti connects with Pape'ete (9800 CFP, 35 minutes) three to five times daily, with onward flights to Ra'iatea (5100 CFP, another 15 minutes) and/or Bora Bora (7300 CFP). For Maupiti (7700 CFP) you have to change aircraft at Ra'iatea. The **Air Tahiti office** (*☎ 68 77 02*) is on the main street in Fare, opposite the quay.

The *Aremiti 3* links Pape'ete, Huahine and Ra'iatea twice a week, on Monday and Wednesday. From Pape'ete to Huahine costs 5500 CFP; from Huahine to Ra'iatea costs 1760 CFP. The **office** (*☎ 74 39 40; open 9am-12.30pm & 1.30pm-3pm daily*) is on the quay in the centre of Fare.

The cargo ships *Vaeanu*, *Taporo VI* and *Hawaiki Nui* stop at Huahine.

Getting Around
The airport is 2.5km from Fare. Your accommodation will arrange taxi transfers (sometimes included in the tariff). It costs 600 CFP into Fare and 1100 CFP to the south of the island.

Huahine has little public transport. *Le truck* from each district shuttles in to Fare early each morning and returns to the various villages late in the morning (300 CFP). **Pension Enite** (*☎ 68 82 37*) and **Félix Tours** (*☎ 68 81 69*) can organise taxis.

Avis-Pacificar (*☎ 68 73 34*), **Europcar** (*☎ 68 82 59*) and **Huahine Location** (*☎/fax 68 78 85*) hire cars.

To hire an excellent mountain bike go to **Chez Huahine Lagoon** (*☎ 68 70 00; 1500*

CFP per day), on the waterfront at the north end of the main street of Fare. Some guesthouses and hotels have bicycles for guests.

For scooters, check with Europcar or Huahine Location.

Huahine Location hires boats with outboard motors.

RA'IATEA
pop 10,057 • area 170 sq km
Ra'iatea and its twin island Taha'a offer visitors an opportunity to enjoy a relaxed Polynesian lifestyle. Ra'iatea, the largest Leeward Island, has no beaches on the mainland, which might account for its less touristy flavour. However, its many *motu* have fine beaches, and its yachting marinas make it the sailing hub of French Polynesia. The lagoon is ideal for diving and pirogue tours, while the mountainous interior is great for walking and horse riding.

The island had a central role in ancient Polynesian religious beliefs. Marae Taputapuatea is the largest and most important in French Polynesia.

Only 3km separates Ra'iatea from Taha'a and the islands share a common lagoon. Visitors usually come to Ra'iatea first as the airport is there, and most inter-island ships dock at Uturoa.

History
Ra'iatea, known as Havai'i in ancient times (see the boxed text 'The Ancient Homeland, Havaiki' in the Samoa chapter), was the religious centre of the Society Islands and it was from here that the great Polynesian navigators are said to have continued the voyages to colonise other islands in the Pacific. Legend has it that Ra'iatea and Taha'a were the first islands to be settled, by people from Samoa, far to the northwest.

Missionary John Williams came to Ra'iatea in 1818 and the island remained under British missionary influence long after Tahiti came under French control. It was not until 1888 that the French attempted a real takeover and not until 1897 that French troops were sent to quell the final Polynesian rebellion.

Orientation
Ra'iatea's road hugs the coast. The mountainous interior includes the 800m-high Temehani Plateau and Mt Tefatua (Toomaru; 1017m).

The airport is at the northern tip of the island. Uturoa extends southeast of the airport. Small villages are scattered across the rest of the island.

Ra'iatea's Emblem – The Tiare Apetahi

Ra'iatea has one of the world's rarest flowers, the *tiare apetahi*. This endemic species is found only on Mt Temehani. The white flower is shaped like a half-corolla and opens dramatically at dawn. You should be able to see it while hiking on the mountain – it's strictly protected, so no picking.

Information

The **tourist office** (☎ 66 07 77; *open daily*) is in the *gare maritime* (dock terminal) in Uturoa.

The three French Polynesian **banks** have branches with ATMs in Uturoa. The **post office** is just north of the centre towards the airport.

For Internet access go to **Le Phénix** (☎ 66 20 66; *900 CFP per hr*), in an isolated building between the marina and the airport (look for the parrot on the window), or **Techniîles** (☎ 66 12 00), between the Champion Supermarket and the Moemoea snack bar.

Ra'iatea has good health facilities, including a **hospital** (☎ 60 02 91), opposite the post office, several doctors and a **pharmacy** (*open daily*) on the main street.

The **Bleu des Îles laundry** (*open Mon-Fri*), in the Tahina Shopping Centre, charges 1500 CFP a load for washing and drying. **Laverie Jacqueline** (☎ 66 28 36; *open Mon-Fri*) at the Apooiti Marina clubhouse, charges 300 CFP per kilogram for washing and drying.

Around the Island

This 98km clockwise circuit provides an opportunity to enjoy the island's relaxed atmosphere and splendid views of mountains and *motu*. Take a picnic, as there's nowhere to buy lunch. You can turn the route into a figure eight by taking the mountain road that travels between Faaroa and Faatemu Bays, passing an excellent lookout.

Uturoa, Ra'iatea's busy port, is the second-largest town in French Polynesia and is the administrative centre for the Leeward Islands. It's busy but not very pretty. The Protestant church on the north side of the town centre has a memorial stone to pioneer missionary John Williams. Mt Tapioi (294m) overlooks Uturoa.

Uturoa blends seamlessly into **Avera**, site of the final battle between the French and local rebels in 1897. Soon after the **Stardust Marina** (12.5km) a turn-off heads to the south coast. Turn right here to climb to a **belvédère** with great views of Faaroa Bay.

Turn left to reach **Marae Taputapuatea** (42km), which had immense importance to the ancient Polynesians. Any *marae* built on another island had to incorporate one of Taputapuatea's stones as a symbol of allegiance – even one in the Cook Islands or Hawaii! At the very end of the cape is the smaller **Marae Tauraa**, a tapu enclosure with the tall 'stone of investiture' where young *ari'i* (chiefs) were enthroned.

At Tevaitoa village massive stone slabs stand in the 50m-long wall of **Marae Tainuu** (95km), behind the church (the church was built on the *marae*). Turn-offs lead to the Temehani Plateau on the stretch to the **Apooiti Marina** (107km), then the road passes the airport and returns to Uturoa.

Activities

Hémisphère Sub (☎ 66 12 49), at the Apooiti Marina, and **Te Mara Nui** (☎ 66 11 88), at the marina at Uturoa, are the dive centres. The wreck of the **Nordby**, one of French Polynesia's few shipwrecks, and the superb **Teavapiti Pass** are popular **dives**.

Some of the reef *motu* have splendid **swimming** and **snorkelling**. Ask at your accommodation about renting a boat or joining a lagoon tour (about 5000 CFP per person).

Kaoha Nui Ranch (☎ 66 25 46; *1-hr/half-day rides per person 3700/5300 CFP*) offers guided **horse-riding** excursions.

Good **walking** opportunities include the walk up to the **Temehani Plateau** (you need a guide); the short climb up **Mt Tapioi**; the **Three Waterfalls walk** behind Kaoha Nui Ranch; and Hotopu, Opoa and Faeratai Valleys in the southwest.

Game-fishing trips aboard the **Sakario** (☎ 66 35 54) or the **Tevaite** (☎ 66 20 10) cost 70,000 to 80,000 CFP per day for up to four people.

If you don't want to hire a car or are on your own a **4WD tour** (*4000-5000 CFP*) can be a good option. Try **Raiatea Discovery** (☎ 66 24 16), **Rauvine Safari Tour** (☎ 66 25 50), **Jeep Safari Raiatea** (☎ 66 15 73) or **Hinerani Tours** (☎ 66 25 75). Book early.

Ra'iatea is the principal nautical centre in the Leeward Islands; it's the main place for **yacht charters** (see Yacht under Boat in the

Places to Stay

Most accommodation is in or close to Uturoa. Ra'iatea has several places where you can camp.

Uturoa Spacious **Raiatea Pearl Resort Hawaiki Nui** (☎ 60 05 00, fax 66 20 20; ⓦ www
.pearlresorts.com; PK2; rooms 16,700 CFP, bungalows 24,500-46,700 CFP) has comfortable accommodation.

Pension Tepua (☎ 66 33 00, fax 66 32 00; ⓔ pension-tepua@mail.pf; PK 2.5; dorm beds/singles/doubles 1600 CFP, 3800/6000 CFP, bungalows from 9100 CFP), beside the lagoon, has clean rooms for all budgets: dorm beds, simple rooms and comfortable and well-equipped bungalows.

Raiatea Bellevue Bed & Breakfast (☎/fax 66 15 15; singles/doubles 7100/8000 CFP), a quiet and relaxing place perched high above the north side of Uturoa, has extraordinary views. Rates include breakfast.

East Coast Equestrian **Kaoha Nui Ranch** (☎ 66 25 46; ⓔ kaohanui@mail.pf; PK6; singles/doubles 1900/3500 CFP, bungalow double 6400 CFP) is a large, green and pleasant property with impeccably neat rooms with shared facilities. There's a better-equipped room and a bungalow. Airport or dock transfers are free; meals are available.

Pension Manava (☎ 66 28 26; ⓔ manava@free.pf; PK6; rooms/bungalows 4200/5600 CFP) is a friendly place. The rooms have shared bathroom; the bungalow is tidy and spacious. Transfers are free.

Peter's Place (☎ 66 0 01; PK6.5; camping/rooms per person 900/1400 CFP), very spartan and rustic, with shared bathrooms, is cheap and simple but has lovely Polynesian ambience.

Pension Rauvine (☎ 66 25 50; ⓔ pension rauvine@mail.pf; PK 8.5; bungalows 5000 CFP) has simple bungalows with bathroom and kitchenette. Rates include transfers.

Pension La Croix du Sud (☎/fax 66 27 55; singles/doubles 7300/8000 CFP), opposite Stardust Marina, 12km from Uturoa, has a fine hillside setting and good food. Rates include breakfast and bicycle use.

Pension Te Maeva (☎/fax 66 37 28; ⓔ te maeva@mail.pf; PK24.7; camping 1/2 people 1700/2300 CFP, single/double bungalows 6100/7300 CFP) has comfortable bungalows with hot-water bathroom. Breakfast and transfers are included.

Hôtel Atiapiti (☎/fax 66 16 65; ⓔ atiapiti@mail.pf; bungalows from 9690 CFP), next to Marae Taputapuatea, is a tranquil place beside the lagoon and a small beach; it has spacious, comfortable bungalows.

West Coast On the waterfront in a coconut plantation. **Sunset Beach Motel** (☎ 66 33 47, fax 66 33 08; ⓔ sunsetbeach@mail.pf; PK5; camping per person 1100 CFP; bungalows from 7700 CFP) has large, comfortable bungalows and excellent kitchen facilities and bathrooms for campers.

Hôtel Tenape (☎ 60 01 00, fax 60 01 01; ⓔ hoteltenape@mail.pf; PK8.8; rooms/suites 20,700/29,600 CFP), 4km from the airport, is a pleasant colonial-style place with great views from its mountainside location. It has comfortable rooms, a good restaurant, bar and swimming pool.

Places to Eat

Uturoa has several well-stocked **supermarkets**, including **Champion** on the seafront.

Snack Moemoea (dishes 800-2800 CFP; open 6am-5pm Mon-Sat), located on the Uturoa waterfront, is a pleasant, busy little café with an open terrace and straightforward dishes.

Restaurant Chez Michèle (☎ 66 14 66; dishes 800-2000 CFP; open Mon-Fri & Sat lunch), in the Hôtel Hinano, offers Chinese, Tahitian and French dishes.

For good Chinese go to **Jade Garden** (☎ 66 34 40; dishes 1400-3000 CFP; open Wed-Fri, dinner only Sat), on the main street, or **Sea Horse** (☎ 66 16 34; dishes 900-1800 CFP; closed Sun night), in the gare maritime.

Napoli (☎ 66 10 77; dishes 900-1600 CFP, set menu 1800 CFP; closed Sat & Sun lunch & Mon) is a pizzeria near the Europcar agency.

East-coast options are limited: your best bet is **Pension La Croix du Sud** (set menu 2900 CFP; open daily), which has good, inventive food and an unbeatable view; bookings are required. Near Marae Taputapuatea, the restaurant at **Hôtel Atiapiti** (☎ 66 16 65; dishes 1000-2000 CFP; open daily lunch) is in a calm and pleasant lagoonside setting.

For reasonably priced French specialities in a formal setting head to **Hôtel Tenape** (dishes 1600-2900 CFP; open daily lunch & dinner) on the west coast.

Getting Around section earlier in this chapter for charter companies) and the departure point for numerous **cruises**.

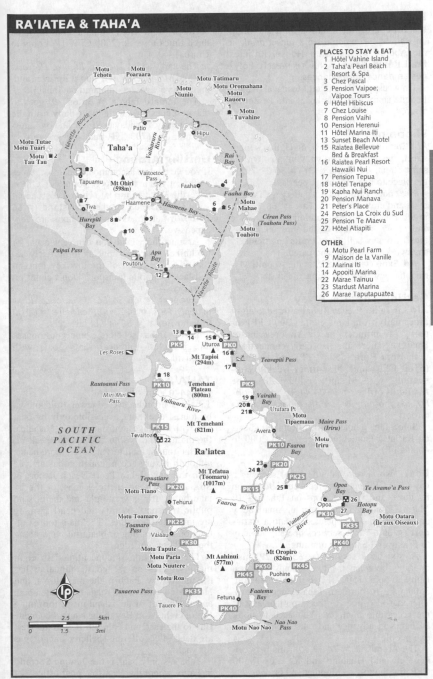

Entertainment

It's difficult to find a reason for a late night on Ra'iatea. You could sip a sunset drink at the Apooiti Marina **Club House**. Ra'iatea Pearl Resort Hawaiki Nui has weekly **Polynesian dance performances**.

On weekends Restaurant Moana, above the Leogite store, metamorphoses into **Le Zénith disco**.

Shopping

Arii Création (☎ 66 33 53), on Uturoa's main street, specialises in Polynesian tapa. On the same street, **La Palme d'Or** (☎ 66 23 79) is the place to head for black pearls.

Next door, **Anuanua** is a gallery with works by island craftspeople. **Te Fare** (☎ 66 17 17), in the Banque Socredo building, sells fabric and craftwork. Next to the *gare maritime*, local women sell their crafts, particularly shellwork, woodwork and pareu.

Art-Expo (☎ 66 11 83), at the Apooiti Marina, has jewellery, clothing and crafts.

Getting There & Away

Air Air Tahiti flies to Ra'iatea three to eight times daily from Pape'ete (11,200 CFP) directly (40 minutes) or via Mo'orea and/or Huahine. There are also daily connections with Bora Bora (5800 CFP) and Huahine (5100 CFP) and three-times-weekly connections with Maupiti (6400 CFP). The **Air Tahiti office** (☎ 60 04 4450; open Mon-Fri, Sat morning & Sun afternoon) is at the airport.

Some Taha'a hotels will collect their guests on Ra'iatea (sometimes free, or for 2000 to 4000 CFP).

Boat Two *navette* (shuttle boat) services a day (850 CFP one way) between Uturoa, on Ra'iatea, and various stops on Taha'a – Iti Marina, Poutoru, Tiva, Tapuamu, Amaru quay and Haamene – are operated by **Enota Transport** (☎ 65 67 10). Services operate Monday to Friday and Saturday morning.

A **taxi-boat service** (☎ 65 65 29) also operates between the two islands between 6am and 6pm (1500 CFP to southern Taha'a, 3500 CFP to northern Taha'a, per person). The boat also goes to the airport or any of the accessible pontoons. You need to book 24 hours in advance and must have at least two people.

The **Aremiti 3** (☎ 74 39 40) sails between Pape'ete and Huahine and Ra'iatea (5500 CFP, five hours) on Monday and Friday.

The **Maupiti Express** (☎ 67 66 69) travels between Bora Bora, Taha'a and Ra'iatea three times a week (2500 CFP, 1¾ hours to Uturoa).

The cargo ships *Vaeanu*, *Taporo*, *Hawaiki Nui* and *Maupiti Tou Ai'a* stop at Ra'iatea and, on most voyages, at Tapuamu on Taha'a.

The **Tamarii Taha'a** (☎ 65 65 29) goes to the west coast of Taha'a twice daily from the Uturoa quay, Monday to Friday and on Saturday morning (700 CFP, one hour to Patio).

Getting Around

If you've booked accommodation, most places will meet you at the airport (for a fee). Otherwise, the 3km taxi trip into Uturoa costs about 1000 CFP. There's another **taxi stand** (☎ 66 20 60) by the market but the taxis are very expensive.

Around the island you can rent a car or hitchhike – hitching appears to be fairly acceptable as a result of the low-key tourism and lack of public transport. Don't count on *le trucks*.

Europcar (☎ 66 34 06; e europcar-loc@ mail.pf), **Avis** (☎ 66 20 00), **Te Maire** (☎ 60 00 95) and **Hertz** (☎ 66 44 88) hire cars.

Europcar has scooters; some guesthouses hire bicycles. Europcar rents boats with outboards.

TAHA'A
pop 4470 • area 90 sq km

Taha'a is an undiscovered jewel, little known by tourist operators, accessible only by boat and with a village atmosphere. Like Ra'iatea, the main island has no beaches to speak of, and the tourist facilities are even more basic, although luxury accommodation has arrived with the new Tahaa Pearl Beach Resort & Spa. A coast road encircles most of the island but traffic is very light and there is no public transport. Vanilla and pearl farming are important activities. The main tourist attraction is the string of beautiful *motu* along the northern reef edge.

The population is concentrated in eight main villages on the coast. Tapuamu has the main quay, Patio is the main town, and Haamene is where the roads round the south and north part of the island meet, forming a figure eight. Apu Bay to the south, Haamene Bay to the east, and Hurepiti Bay to the west are deep inlets offering sheltered anchorages for yachts.

Taha'a's only bank is the **Banque Socredo** in Patio, where there's also a **post office**.

Around the Island

The 70km circuit of the island is quite possible as a bicycle day trip, although most of the route is unsealed crushed coral and there are some steep sections. Starting from the Marina Iti, the first *navette* stop from Ra'iatea and the best place to hire bicycles, the road hugs the coast around Apu Bay. At the top of the bay the route leaves the coast and climbs up and over to **Haamene** village. The **Maison de la Vanille** (☎ 65 67 27) and **Alfred** (☎ 65 61 16) are vanilla producers you can visit here (see the boxed text 'Taha'a – The Vanilla Island').

From **Tapuamu** the chain of *motu* that fringe the northern coast of the island come into view. Beyond **Patio** more of the 60-odd *motu* come into view. The road passes copra plantations to **Faaha** and Faaha Bay. On the north side of the bay you can visit **Motu Pearl Farm** (☎ 65 66 67).

The road climbs over a headland and drops into Haamene Bay. Turn east to Hôtel Hibiscus, where the Hibiscus Foundation is dedicated to saving turtles that have become entangled in local fishers' nets. The turtles are transferred to remote Scilly Atoll.

The coast road continues to Haamene, passing the pearl farms of **Pension Vaipoe** (☎ 65 60 83; admission 100 CFP) and **Rooverta Ebbs' Poerani** (☎ 65 60 25; admission 100 CFP), where you can watch pearl grafting, then winds around seemingly endless small bays before returning to the Marina Iti.

Activities

The only **dive** centre is at Tahaa Pearl Beach Resort & Spa. The Ra'iatea dive centres regularly dive east of the island by the Céran Pass (Toahotu Pass) and will collect you from hotels at the south of the island. You have to go to the *motu* for **swimming** and **snorkelling**.

You can **walk** the little-used 7km track across the centre of the island from Patio to Haamene but otherwise there's very few trails into the Taha'a interior. There are dazzling views of Haamene Bay from **Vaitoetoe Pass**.

Vanilla Tours (☎ 65 62 46) and **Tahaa Tour Excursion** (☎ 65 62 18) have good reputations for their island tours (3500 to 5000 CFP per person). Ask at your accommodation about **lagoon tours** (5500-8000 CFP per person).

Places to Stay

It's wise to make reservations so that you're collected from the appropriate village quay or even the airport on Ra'iatea.

The Island On Toamaro Point **Hôtel Marina Iti** (☎ 65 61 01, fax 65 63 87; e marinaiti@mail.pf; bungalows from 12,300 CFP), on the waterfront with a tiny beach, is the busiest place on the island. It has pleasant bungalows and a good restaurant. Half-board is available.

Pension Herenui (☎ 65 62 60, fax 65 64 17; bungalows with bathroom from 8100 CFP) has charming bungalows. Half-board is available. There is a swimming pool and the lagoon is across the road.

Pension Vaihi (☎ 65 62 02; bungalows with bathroom 6400 CFP) offers isolation and tranquillity beside the lagoon. Half- and full board are available. Ask the *navette* to drop you at the quay at Tiva, where the owners will pick you up.

Chez Louise (☎ 65 66 88; dorm beds 1500 CFP) might have a dormitory bed available if you are really penniless. Rates include breakfast.

Chez Pascal (☎ 65 60 42; bungalows per person 2600 CFP) has the island's cheapest bungalows, with shared toilet and shower. It's spartan, but clean, and has a Polynesian family atmosphere.

There are two places on the north shore of Haamene Bay.

Hôtel Hibiscus (☎ 65 61 06, fax 65 65 65; e hibiscus@tahaa-tahiti.com; bungalows from 9500 CFP) has well-equipped bungalows or other simpler ones. The hotel has a Saturday-night dance performance.

Pension Vaipoe (Chez Patricia & Daniel; ☎/fax 65 60 83; e v.p@mail.pf; bungalows

Taha'a – The Vanilla Island

Taha'a produces three quarters of French Polynesia's vanilla (about 25 tons annually). Several small family-run farms are open to the public; you can buy vanilla pods at reasonable prices (about 1000 CFP a dozen) and can find out about the delicate technique of hand fertilisation, known as 'marrying' the vanilla. Nine months later the pods are put out to dry; they turn brown over four to five months. They are then sorted and packaged before being sold in Pape'ete or exported.

8100 CFP) is a popular place with bungalows with bathroom, kitchenette and terrace. Half-board is available.

The Motu On a *motu* on the outer reef to the north of Taha'a, **Hotel Vahine Island** (☎ 65 67 38, fax 65 67 70; VHF 70; ⓔ *vahine .island@usa.net; beach/over-water bungalows 32,400/48,600 CFP*) is luxurious and has a load of activities. Airport transfers cost 5000 CFP per person return.

Tahaa Pearl Beach Resort & Spa (☎ 50 84 52, fax 43 17 86; ⓦ *www.pearlresorts.com; bungalows from 77,900 CFP*) is sumptuous. The setting on Motu Tau Tau, to the west of the island, is exceptional, but the service needs ironing out.

Places to Eat
Each village has **shops** but few restaurants.

Hôtel Marina Iti (*dishes 950-2400 CFP; open daily*) has a well-known restaurant that features French specialities, while the **Hôtel Hibiscus** (*dishes 1200-3100 CFP; open daily*) restaurant is also good.

Chez Louise, at Tiva, has an excellent reputation for local food.

Getting There & Away
See Getting There & Away under Ra'iatea earlier in this section.

Getting Around
There is no public transport and traffic is very light. Renting a car or a mountain bike are the only ways to see the island independently.

Hôtel Marina Iti (☎ 65 61 01) and **Monique Location** (☎/fax 65 62 48) rent small cars and bicycles. **Europcar** (☎ 65 67 00) also has cars, while the Hôtel Hibiscus has bicycles for its customers only. If you want a scooter you could rent one on Ra'iatea and bring it across on the shuttle.

BORA BORA
pop 7295 • area 38 sq km
The postcard views of Bora Bora are the stuff of South Pacific dreams – sandy, palm-fringed *motu* around a deep blue lagoon with a central island of mountains and peaks. Bora Bora is where the rich and famous come to play, and hotel chains come to open resorts. Despite the development, the lagoon is simply superb; there are several small archaeological sites and some reminders of WWII; and the Polynesian dance performances at the luxury hotels will have you wiggling your hips in delight.

Environmental awareness on the island has risen in recent years and bigger efforts are being made to contain the rubbish that can take the tropical shine off the island; it's a constant struggle to prevent overdevelopment while still maintaining the economic lifeline of tourism.

History
Not much of Bora Bora is flat, and land pressures helped create a warlike population that campaigned against other islands in the Society group. Only Huahine managed to resist the warriors of Bora Bora at their most expansive. Cook sighted Bora Bora in 1769, and an LMS missionary station was established on the island in 1820. WWII had a huge effect on Bora Bora, when a major US supply base was established on the island. Until Faa'a airport opened in Tahiti in 1961, the airport the Americans left was French Polynesia's main connection with the outside world.

In 2001 Bora Bora, with only one pass into its lagoon, was hit hard by the effects of El Niño, which discoloured the lagoon and bleached coral. The water is once again a sparkling aqua, but the damage to the coral is irreversible.

Orientation
A road circles the island, which is about 9km north to south and 4km across. Vaitape, on the western side, is the main settlement, looking directly out to Teavanui Pass, the only entry to the lagoon.

Information
The **Bora Bora Visitors Bureau** (☎/fax 67 76 36; *open 7.30am-4pm Mon-Fri*) has an office on the quay at Vaitape. There are branches of **Banque de Tahiti**, **Banque Socredo** and **Banque de Polynésie** in Vaitape; they each have ATMs. The **post office** is in the centre of Vaitape. **L'Appetisserie** (see Places to Eat later) offers Internet access for 2500 CFP an hour.

There's a craft centre, the **Centre Artisanal de Bora Bora**, which is in the same building as the tourist office. In Vaitape, **Cathina** (☎ 67 65 27) will do a load of laundry for 1800 CFP.

If you need medical assistance, inquire at your hotel. There is a **medical centre** (☎ 67 70 77) in Vaitape or you can contact **Dr Juen** (☎ 67 70 62). Vaitape has a **pharmacy** (*open daily, only briefly on Sunday*).

Stone-Fishing Festival

Bora Bora's annual stone-fishing festival takes place in the last week of October. It's not about catching rocks – rather, flower-bedecked pirogues fan out across the lagoon and beat the surface of the water with stones to herd the fish into an enclosure.

Events include singing and dancing, agricultural and craft displays, sporting events (including fruit-carrying races!), fishing contests, canoe races and a fire-walking ceremony.

Around the Island

Bora Bora's 32km coast road hugs the shoreline almost all the way around the island and is dotted with *marae* and WWII remnants. We describe an anticlockwise tour that starts in Vaitape; as it's flat except for the decent hill around Fitiiu Point it makes a good bicycle ride.

At 6km, Hotel Bora Bora at Raititi Point marks the start of the pleasant sandy stretch of **Matira Beach**. From the eastern edge of the Hotel Matira property a walking trail (10 minutes) runs up the hill to a battery of WWII **coastal defence guns**.

The Bora Bora Beachcomber Intercontinental Resort is on a side road that runs out to **Matira Point** and a great public beach. The annual Hawaiki Nui inter-island canoe race ends on this beach. Club Med (9km) has its own **belvédère** atop the ridge above the bay.

At Fitiiu Point (15km) the road climbs briefly away from the coast. Just as the road starts to climb, a track peels off to **Marae Aehua-tai** at the water's edge. The middle-of-nowhere **L'Espandon Restaurant** on Taimoo Bay (see Places to Eat, later) is a good place for a lunch or drink stop.

The small, private **Museé de la Marine** (*Marine Museum;* ☎ 67 75 24; *admission by donation*) has an interesting collection of model ships. The opening hours are haphazard, so make sure to call ahead. Just after **Taihi Point** a steep and often-muddy track climbs to a WWII radar station atop Popotei Ridge and on to a lookout above the village of Faanui.

At the end of Tereia Point a rectangular concrete water tank marks the position of another coastal gun. There's no path: just clamber straight up the hill for a couple of minutes. **Marae Fare-Opu** is squeezed

between the road and water's edge. Two of the slabs are clearly marked with turtle petroglyphs.

Faanui Bay was the site of the main US military base during WWII and there is still much evidence of the wartime operations there. From the picturesque **church** at the head of the bay an often-muddy road runs directly inland and over the ridge to drop into Vairau Bay just south of Fitiiu Point. **Marae Taianapa** (28km) is a fairly large *marae* on the inland side of the road located past Faanui village.

Marae Marotetini, a fine 50m-long royal *marae*, is just beyond the quay.

Activities

The most popular activity is probably diving; sharks, rays and other marine life abound: contact **Bora Bora Diving Centre** (☎ 67 71 84), **Nemo World** (☎ 67 63 00), **Topdive Bora Bora** (☎ 60 50 50; W *www.topdive.com*), **Bora Bora Blue Nui** (☎ 67 79 07; W *www.blue nui.com*) and **Diveasy** (☎ 67 69 36). **Anau**, with its visits by black-tip reef sharks and manta rays, is one of the most popular lagoon sites. **Toopua** and **Toopua Iti** are magnificent lagoon dives. Outside the reef, **Muri Muri** (La Vallée Blanche) is known for sharks.

Matira Point is the best stretch of **beach** on the main island; many *motu* have superb sand but ask permission before exploring them. The marine reserve off Hotel Bora Bora has excellent **snorkelling**.

Out of the water, Bora Bora offers plenty of good **walking**; a guide is recommended. Allow at least five hours (return) for the tough but rewarding ascent of **Mt Pahia** (661m).

Tupuna Mountain Safari (☎ 67 75 06; *half-day tour 5500 CFP*) runs 4WD guided tours to American WWII sites and archaeological sites. For scenic helicopter flights, contact **Héli-Inter Polynésie** (☎ 67 62 59; *15-min tour 15,000 CFP*).

Many of the hotels and guesthouses offer **lagoon tours** that include snorkelling, reef walking, a *motu* barbecue and both swimming and snorkelling stops; they cost approximately 5000/7500 CFP for a half-/full day. Several companies offer **deep-sea fishing** trips.

For horse riding on Motu Piti Aau, contact **Ranch Reva Reva** (☎ 67 63 63; *1-hr ride 6500 CFP*). Parasailing is offered by **Parasail** (☎ 67 70 34, *1/2 people per ride 10,000/17,000 CFP*).

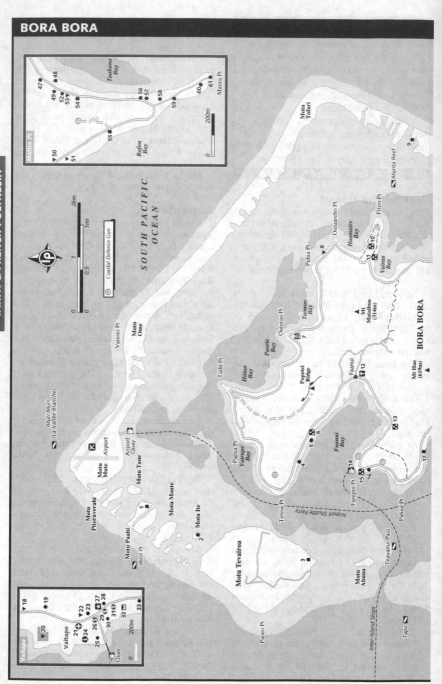

BORA BORA

TAHITI & FRENCH POLYNESIA

Matira Pt

47
48
49
52
53
54
56
57
58
59
60
61
Matira Pt

Tauhana Bay

Rofau Bay

50
51
55

200m
0

SOUTH PACIFIC OCEAN

2km
1mi

1
0.5
0

Coastal Defence Gun

Motu Todari

Manta Reef

9

Outuareho Pt
Haamaire Bay
10
11
Vairau Bay
Fitiiu Pt

Pahia Pt
8

Taimoo Bay

Mt Mataihua (314m)

BORA BORA

Outurau Pt
7
Paorie Bay

Popotei Ridge

Mt Hue (619m)

Hitiaa Bay

Tahiti Pt

Faanui
12

13

Vaitoto Pt
Motu Ome

Muri Muri (La Vallée Blanche)

Airport
Airport Quay

Papua Pt
Vairape Bay
4

5 6

Faanui Bay
14
15
16

17

Motu Pitiaverahi

Motu Mute

Motu Tane

Motu Moute

Farepiti Pt

Airport Shuttle Ferry
Tereia Pt

Pahua Pt

Motu Paahi
West Pt

1

Motu Ite
2

Motu Tevairoa

3

Motu Ahuna

Teavanui Pass

Inter-Island Ships

Tapu

Paeoo Pt

Vaitape

18
19
20
21
22
23
24
25 26
27
28
29
30 31
32
33

Vaitape

Quay
0   200m

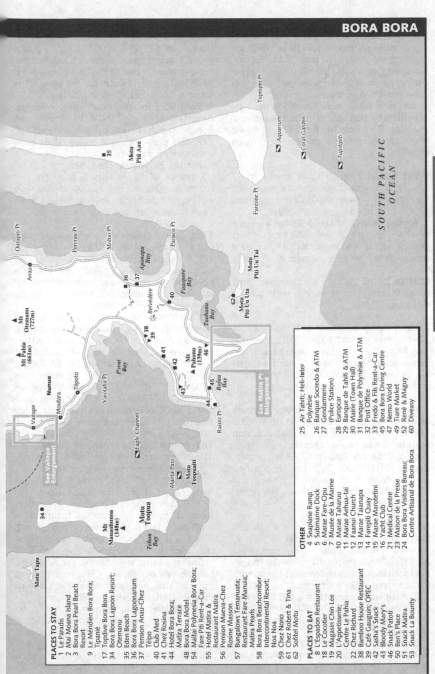

BORA BORA

SOUTH PACIFIC OCEAN

Tupitipi Pt

Motu Piti Aau

Aquarium

Coral Garden

Tupitipi

Outupiiu Pt

Percrau Pt

Mohio Pt

Faroone Pt

Anau

Aponapu Bay

Paaoa Pt

Motu Piti Uu Tai

Faanui Bay

Taahana Bay

Motu Piti Uu Uta

Mt Otemanu (727m)

Belvédère

Mt Pahia (661m)

Mt Pahonu (139m)

Nunue

Tiipoto

Moutara

Povai Bay

Vaitape

Vaiotaha Pt

Rofau Bay

Raititi Pt

See Matira Pt Enlargement

Eagle Channel

Matira Pass

Motu Toopuaiti

See Vaitape Enlargement

Tehou Bay

Mt Mauaohnnoa (148m)

Motu Toopua

Motu Tapu

PLACES TO STAY
1 Le Paradis
2 Mai Moana Island
3 Bora Bora Pearl Beach Resort
9 Le Méridien Bora Bora; Tipanié
17 Topdive Bora Bora
34 Bora Bora Lagoon Resort; Otemanu
35 Eden Beach
36 Bora Bora Lagoonarium
37 Pension Anau-Chez Téipo
40 Club Med
41 Chez Rosina
44 Hotel Bora Bora; Matira Terrace
48 Bora Bora Motel
54 Maitai Polynesia Bora Bora; Fare Piti Rent-a-Car
55 Hotel Matira & Restaurant Matira
56 Pension Maeva-Chez Rosine Masson
57 Bungalows Temanuata; Restaurant Fare Manuia; Matira Pearls
58 Bora Bora Beachcomber Intercontinental Resort; Noa Noa
59 Chez Nono
61 Chez Robert & Tina
62 Sofitel Motu

PLACES TO EAT
8 L'Espadon Restaurant
18 Le Cocotier
19 Magasin Chin Lee
20 L'Appetisserie; Centre Le Pahia
22 Chez Richard
38 Bamboo House Restaurant
39 Café Gauguin; OPEC
42 Sasha's Snack
43 Bloody Mary's
46 Snack Patoti
50 Ben's Place
51 Snack Matira
53 Snack La Bounty

OTHER
4 Seaplane Ramp
5 Submarine Dock
6 Marae Fare-Opu
7 Musée de la Marine
10 Marae Taharuu
11 Marae Aehua-tai
12 Faanui Church
13 Marae Taianapa
14 Farepiti Quay
15 Marae Marotetini
16 Yacht Club
21 Medical Centre
23 Maison de la Presse
24 Bora Bora Visitors Bureau; Centre Artisanal de Bora Bora
25 Air Tahiti; Heli-Inter Polynésie
26 Banque Socredo & ATM
27 Gendarmerie (Police Station)
28 Europcar
29 Banque de Tahiti & ATM
30 Mairie (Town Hall)
31 Banque de Polynésie & ATM
32 Post Office
33 Fredo & Fils Rent-a-Car
45 Bora Bora Diving Centre
47 Nemo World
49 Tiare Market
52 René & Maguy
60 Diveasy

Places to Stay

You could easily whittle away your life savings on deluxe hotels on Bora Bora, which are as sumptuous as the hype leads you to believe. However, you can also benefit from staying at cheaper *pensions* and even camping. Most accommodation is on the southern coast.

Two new hotels were planned at the time of writing: a **Paladien** was under construction, and **Hotel Bora Bora Nui Resort** (☎ 86 48 48; ⓦ *www.sheratonsintahiti.com)* was due to open in 2003.

West Coast Friendly **Chez Rosina** (☎ 67 70 91; ⓔ *adesaintpierre@mail.pf; singles/ doubles from 5400/6500 CFP, bungalows 13,800 CFP)* has a warm atmosphere.

Topdive (☎ 605050, fax 605051; ⓦ www.top dive.com; bungalows from 28,500 CFP)* is popular with divers; its restaurant has a good reputation and the price includes breakfast.

Matira Point With the best beach on Bora Bora, Matira Point is packed with accommodation.

Budget On the beach, **Chez Nono** (☎ 67 71 38; singles/doubles 5900/7000 CFP, bungalows from 9100 CFP)* has a large kitchen and lounge area. The rooms are quite comfortable, although the walls are paper-thin. There's a choice of small or family bungalows, all with bathroom.

Pension Maeva – Chez Rosine Masson (☎ 67 72 04; dorm beds/doubles 3500/6900 CFP)* has loads of charm and character; thin walls but the lagoon-side setting is a delight.

Chez Robert & Tina (☎ 67 63 55; singles/ doubles 5400/6600 CFP)* has simple fan-cooled rooms with shared bathroom and kitchen. Rates drop dramatically on subsequent nights.

Mid-Range Right on Matira Beach, **Hotel Matira** (☎ 67 78 58, fax 67 77 02; ⓦ www.hotelmatira.com; bungalows from 21,300 CFP)* has simple thatch-roofed bungalows with bathrooms and terraces (some with kitchenettes); it has a restaurant.

Bungalows Temanuata (☎ 67 75 61, fax 67 62 48; bungalows from 12,800 CFP)*, behind the Restaurant Fare Manuia, is a great choice and is often heavily booked.

Bora Bora Motel (☎ 67 78 21, fax 67 77 57; ⓦ www.boraboramotel.pf; single/double bungalows 14,600/21,100 CFP)* is on a cramped site right on the beach.

Top End With the best location on the island, **Hotel Bora Bora** (☎ 67 44 60, fax 60 44 66; bungalows 67,000-107,000 CFP)*, on Raititi Point, is the domain of the rich and famous. Its restaurant is one of the best places to eat on the island. The water out the front offers some of the island's best snorkelling.

Bora Bora Beachcomber Intercontinental Resort (☎ 60 49 00, fax 60 49 99; ⓦ www.bora bora.interconti.com; bungalows from 65,600 CFP)* has glass-bottomed coffee tables in its over-water bungalows.

Maitai Polynesia Bora Bora (☎ 60 30 00, fax 67 66 03; ⓦ www.hotelmaitai.com; rooms/bungalows from 28,000/45,700 CFP)* just beyond the Matira Point turn-off, offers a good balance between luxury and price.

East Coast One of the island's best budget places, **Pension Anau – Chez Téipo** (☎ 67 78 17; ⓔ teipo@tahiti.net; single/double/quad bungalows 7000/8000/11,000 CFP)* has well-equipped bungalows and includes breakfast in the price. It offers free transfers from the Vaitape quay and has bicycles.

Club Med (☎ 60 46 04, fax 60 46 10; ⓔ cm bora@mail.pf; singles/doubles per person from 31,000/25,800 CFP)* is a steal by Bora Bora standards but is getting a bit faded.

Bora Bora Lagoonarium (☎ 67 71 34; camping per person 1600 CFP, dorm beds 2500 CFP, doubles/2-person bungalows 6400/8600 CFP)* is seemingly made of cardboard, but it's clean and in a quiet area. It has a communal kitchen and rental bicycles.

The Motu Staying on one of the *motu*, the islands around the outer reef, ensures tranquillity, a complete escape and great views.

Eden Beach (☎ 74 24 62, fax 67 69 76; ⓔ info@ spmhotels.pf; Motu Piti Aau bungalows from 27,900 CFP)* is the best place to stay on Bora Bora. Although not quite as luxurious as some *motu* hotels, this intimate place is still divine and very stylish, and is environmentally friendly – it's largely solar-powered.

Sofitel Motu (☎ 60 56 00, fax 60 56 66; bungalows from 66,800 CFP)*, on tiny Motu Piti Uu Uta, has bungalows that combine Polynesian design with modern technology.

Le Méridien Bora Bora (☎ 60 51 51, fax 60 51 52; ⓔ sales@lemeridien-tahiti.com; bungalows from 66,800 CFP)* has fantastic architecture including glass floors in its over-water bungalows. The hotel is involved in sea-turtle protection work, and guests can watch rehabilitating turtles pottering about.

Bora Bora Pearl Beach Resort (☎ 60 52 00, fax 60 52 22; e info@SPMhotels.pf; *Motu Tevairoa; bungalows 53,400-80,100 CFP*) has luxurious bungalows, a magnificent swimming pool and over-water restaurant.

Bora Bora Lagoon Resort (☎ 60 40 00, fax 60 40 01; e bblr@mail.pf; *bungalows 55,100-91,700 CFP*) is on Motu Toopua, looking across the lagoon to Vaitape and across the Teavanui Pass. It's one of the most luxurious resorts on the island.

Mai Moana Island (☎ 67 62 45, fax 67 62 39; *Motu Ite; bungalows 27,000 CFP*) has three big bungalows in a dream-like setting; you can hire the entire *motu* for 45,000 CFP.

Le Paradis (☎/fax 67 75 53; *Motu Paahi; single/double/triple bungalows 10,700/ 16,000/18,200 CFP*) is an affordable *motu* resort with five local-style bungalows, in a lagoon-side coconut plantation; two have private bathrooms. Airport transfers are free. Credit cards are not accepted.

Places to Eat

Eat early – Bora Bora's restaurants shut at around 9pm. Some places offer a free transfer service to/from your hotel. All the luxury hotels have dance performances with buffet dinners several times a week. Expect to pay around 6500 to 7000 CFP.

West Coast Vaitape has good places for breakfast, a snack or a cheap meal. A string of **stalls** *(open daily)* along the main road sell sandwiches and cool drinks. At night several **roulottes** *(simple dishes around 1000 CFP)* set up along the main road.

L'Appetisserie (☎ 67 78 88; *pastries 130-400 CFP, toasted sandwiches 480-880 CFP*) is a pleasant little open-air snack bar and patisserie in Centre Le Pahia near the quay.

Chez Richard (☎ 67 69 69; *meals 1000-1500 CFP*) is a simple place that specialises in Chinese takeaway meals.

Café Gauguin (*sandwiches 1200 CFP; open 8am-4pm Mon-Sat*) is a special little spot for lunch or a cool drink.

Sasha's Snack (☎ 67 72 16), in Village Pauline, is a very Polynesian restaurant with great, simple food. Try to go to one of Sasha's buffet nights; locals and expats swear by them.

Le Cocotier (*appetisers 550-1500 CFP, mains 1200-2100 CFP; open 6.30am-8.30pm Mon-Sat*) is a very basic but good Chinese restaurant.

Bloody Mary's (☎ 67 72 86; *appetisers 1200-1500 CFP, mains 2500-2800 CFP; open*

Mon-Sat) is very pricey and inordinately proud of the list of celebrities who have dined there. Free transport is provided from anywhere between Vaitape and Club Med.

North of Vaitape, **Topdive Bora Bora** (☎ 60 50 50; *see Places to Stay earlier; appetisers 1900-2000 CFP, mains 3300-3600 CFP; open breakfast, lunch & dinner daily*) has a restaurant with fabulous cathedral ceilings and stylish decor.

Matira Point & Around Near the last Sofitel bungalows, **Snack Patoti** *(open lunch & dinner Mon-Sat)*, on the inland side of the road, has a small but interesting menu.

Ben's Place is a popular little café with a straightforward menu and variable hours.

Snack Matira (*Chez Julie; open 10am-6pm Tues-Sun*) is just beyond Ben's Place and is beside the lagoon. It's simple, but the prices are low and it's just a few steps from the beach.

Matira Terrace (☎ 60 44 60), at Hotel Bora Bora, offers excellent food in a romantic open-air setting looking out over the point; the prices are fairly reasonable.

Restaurant Matira (☎ 67 70 51; *appetisers 1050-1250 CFP, mains 1250-1550 CFP*), part of Hotel Matira, has a magnificent beachfront site and reasonably priced Chinese food.

Noa Noa (☎ 60 49 00), at the Bora Bora Beachcomber Intercontinental Resort, has an especially attractive beachside setting and specialises in fish.

Restaurant Fare Manuia (☎ 67 68 06; *appetisers 1500-2600 CFP, 3-course set menu 3950 CFP*), part of Bungalows Temanuata, is an intimate restaurant offering free transport.

Snack La Bounty (☎ 67 70 43; *mains 1100-2100 CFP; closed Mon*) is a basic, popular place with great fish dishes and interesting pizzas.

East Coast This relatively undeveloped strip often has roadside **stalls** selling cheap snacks. The only other choice is **L'Espadon Restaurant** (☎ 67 71 67; *appetisers 1200-2480 CFP, mains 1500-2690 CFP*), with very good food and a cheaper lunch-time menu (snacks 500-1500 CFP). Transport can be arranged.

The Motu Free shuttles, which generally operate until midnight, allow you to enjoy the restaurants at the luxury *motu* hotels. It's best to reserve.

Tipanié (☎ 60 51 51), in Le Méridien Bora Bora, is a superb surfboard-shaped restaurant by the lagoon. There's a smaller **restaurant** beside the pool. The shuttle operates from the Anau quay.

Otemanu (☎ 60 40 02), in the Bora Bora Lagoon Resort, defies superlatives. Perched over the lagoon, it's a great place for a candlelit dinner. The prices are as heady as the atmosphere! Shuttles operate from the Vaitape quay.

Bora Bora Pearl Beach Resort has two lagoon-side restaurants: one serves daytime snacks; the other is more formal *(Polynesia/seafood buffets 6200/6900 CFP)*.

Self-Catering All the *pensions* and many of the bungalows allow guests to use the kitchen, making self-catering easy and appealing. Fresh baguettes, cheese, cereal, pasta and the like (and, depending on the season, fresh fruit) are always available.

Tiare Market *(open Mon-Sat & Sun morning)* is well stocked with all the necessities. **Magasin Chin Lee** is a supermarket in Vaitape. There are a number of smaller **grocery shops** around the island, as well as a few bigger **supermarkets** just north of Vaitape.

Entertainment

Dinner and a show in one of the big hotels is about the limit of nightlife on Bora Bora; make the most of the daytime activities and have an early night.

Any of the luxury hotels will provide a cold beer or cocktail and a pleasant snack by the lagoon. The *motu* hotels run free shuttles until about midnight. The bar at **Bloody Mary's** is popular.

Don't miss a traditional dance performance by a local group in one of the luxury hotels. Some places allow you in for the price of a drink at the bar; others charge up to 2000 CFP entry; for 6000 to 7000 CFP you can combine the performance with a sumptuous buffet dinner. Performances take place two or three times weekly.

Shopping

Centre Artisanal de Bora Bora in the tourist office by the Vaitape quay has pareu, basketwork and other crafts produced by island women.

Artists galleries and pearl shops are scattered around the island. **Office Polynésien d'Expertise et de Commercialisation** *(OPEC; ☎ 67 61 62)*, an impeccably run rare-pearl company, is the place to come if you're serious about buying pearls.

Getting There & Away

Air The **Air Tahiti** office (☎ 67 70 35) is on the quay at Vaitape. There are at least six daily flights connecting Bora Bora with Pape'ete (13,600 CFP), sometimes direct (45 minutes), other times via Mo'orea (17,500 CFP), Huahine (7300 CFP) or Ra'iatea (5800 CFP). Air Tahiti also flies direct to the Tuamotus, going to Rangiroa (22,500 CFP, one hour 20 minutes) with an onward connection to Manihi (25,400 CFP).

Boat Inter-island boats dock at the Farepiti quay, 3km from Vaitape.

The cargo ship **Vaeanu** (☎ 41 25 35) makes three trips a week between Pape'ete and the Leeward Islands.

The **Maupiti Express** (☎ 67 66 69) makes regular trips between Bora Bora, Maupiti, Taha'a and Ra'iatea (2500/3500 CFP one way/return, one hour).

Hawaiki Nui (☎ 45 23 24) also does the Society Islands circuit.

Getting Around

Arriving on Bora Bora is quite dramatic. The airport is on Motu Mute at the northern edge of the lagoon; two large catamaran ferries then transfer you to the Vaitape quay (free). A regular bus service from the quay goes to the hotels at Matira Point (500 CFP).

You need to be at the quay at least 1¼ hours before your flight leaves. The top hotels transfer their guests directly to/from the airport, other places collect you at the quay.

Officially there's no *le truck* service on Bora Bora. Nevertheless, there often seems to be one going somewhere at the appropriate time, particularly for flight and boat departures.

Car-hire agencies are: **Europcar** (☎ 67 70 15), with an agency opposite the quay in central Vaitape plus desks in several hotels; **Fredo & Fils Rent-a-Car** (☎ 67 70 31), in Vaitape and at several hotels; and **Fare Piti Rent-a-Car** (☎ 67 65 28), in the Maitai Polynesia Bora Bora.

Bora Bora's back roads cry out for a mountain bike but you're unlikely to be able to hire one. You will find basic bikes for rent at Europcar, Fredo and Fare Piti, and at many hotels. Fare Piti rents scooters.

Renting a boat is a heavenly way to explore the lagoon. **René & Maguy** (☎ 67 60 61), next to Snack La Bounty, rents outboard-powered boats. **Village Pauline** has sea kayaks for rental.

MAUPITI
pop 1127 • area 11 sq km

The smallest and most isolated of the Society high islands, sweet Maupiti has impressive soaring, rocky peaks with slopes tumbling down to the lagoon. Like Bora Bora, Maupiti has a shimmering, shallow lagoon edged by a string of *motu* flaunting white-sand beaches. The difference is size (it's 32km around Bora Bora's coastal road, just 10km around Maupiti's) and the pace of life (Maupiti is very low-key and has little tourist infrastructure). After cyclone Oséa ravaged the island in 1997 many houses were replaced by less-interesting (but sturdier) modern buildings.

Maupiti is flanked by two large *motu*: Auira to the west, and Tuanai to the northeast, separated by little Motu Paeao. Small Motu Pitihahei and Motu Tiapaa are southeast of the island.

History

Sites on Motu Paeao, at the northern end of the lagoon, are some of the oldest in the Society Islands. The European 'discovery' of Maupiti is credited to the Dutch explorer Jacob Roggeveen in 1722. The French arrived late in the last century, but missionaries and local chiefs continued to wield power until after WWII. Maupiti has remained remarkably untouched by mass tourism and islanders rely on farming watermelon, copra and, recently, pearl oysters.

Orientation & Information

A 10km road circles the island and the string of buildings along the southeast coast technically constitutes two villages, Farauru and Vaiea, though they're difficult to separate. The church in the middle of the village strip is the most notable landmark. The *mairie*, **post office**, Air Tahiti office and **Banque Socredo** are in one neat little group immediately north. The bank is rarely open.

Things to See & Do

You can walk around the island in just a few hours. To reach some **petroglyphs** head north from the villages and turn inland just before the sign for Tahiti Yacht Charter; at a small water pumping station follow the stream for 100m and the boulders will be on the left. Follow the rocky riverbed further inland for a few hundred metres to a ruined **marae**.

The west coast, from Pohiva Point to Puoroo and Tereia Points, is dotted with **coastal marae**. On this coast, **Tereia Beach** is the finest on the island for white sand and swimming. It's easy to walk across the lagoon to **Motu Auira**, particularly at low tide.

In Atipiti Bay on the south side of the island, just northeast of the main quay, is the area known as Tefarearii, the 'House of Kings'. The island's nobility once lived here and **Marae Vaiahu** is a large coastal site.

Many *pensions* will organise **motu picnic trips**. **Motu Paeao** was the site for the important archaeological discovery of a series of 1000-year-old burial sites. Motu Tiapaa and Motu Auira have *marae* sites.

Snorkelling is particularly good around the southern Onoiau Pass. The *pensions* will organise lagoon tours with snorkelling stops (2000 to 5000 CFP).

Maupiti has some good **walking**, including the one-hour clamber up **Mt Hotu Paraoa** (250m), which looms high above the villages; the track is unmarked, so take a guide (about 2000 CFP per person; ask at your *pension*). It's a superb climb to the summit of **Mt Teurafaatiu** (380m), the island's highest point. Allow three hours for the round trip. The walk starts from the high point where the road crosses the ridge above Tereia Point and generally sticks to the ridgeline.

Places to Stay

Everything is family-style, although the *motu* resorts are a little more sophisticated. Most visitors opt for half- or full board. Hot water is not available and credit cards haven't arrived yet. Rates quoted are per person.

The Island None of the guesthouses has identifying signs, but anyone from the village will point them out. They're all either right on the lagoon or very close to it.

Pension Mareta (Chez Manu; ☎ 67 82 32; rooms with breakfast 2600 CFP), south of the church, is very basic and cheap.

Chez Floriette (☎ 67 80 85; bungalows with half-/full board 6100/7000 CFP), close by, has basic bungalows with shared bathroom. Rates include airport transfers.

Pension Eri (☎ 67 81 29; rooms with half-board 4500 CFP), 200m south and also on the lagoon side of the road, is a well-run place. The rooms have a shared bathroom.

Maupiti Loisirs (☎ 67 80 95; camping 2000 CFP, rooms with half-board 5100 CFP), a pleasant place, is on the western side of the island close to Tereia Beach and has clean but cramped rooms with shared bathroom. The food here is very good.

TAHITI & FRENCH POLYNESIA

The Motu Exchange the low-key bustle of village life for the pleasures of isolated white-sand beaches on the *motu*, but remember that the facilities and activities offered here are basic.

Pension Auira (*Chez Edna; ☎/fax 67 80 26; camping 1500 CFP, garden/beach bungalows with half-board 9100/10,100 CFP*) is on the eastern side of Motu Auira. The beach bungalows are a better option than the basic garden bungalows. Campers have bathroom and kitchen facilities and can buy meals.

Pension Papahani (*Chez Vilna; ☎ 67 81 58; bungalows with full board 9600-11,700 CFP*), at the northern end of Motu Tiapaa, is on a pretty beach. Its new, well-equipped bungalows are preferable to its older ones.

Maupiti Village (*☎/fax 67 80 08; dorm beds/rooms/bungalows with full board 5600/ 6600/8100 CFP*), a beautiful property on the ocean side of Motu Tiapaa, is a good option for budget travellers.

Kuriri Village (*☎/fax 67 82 23; e kuriru@ bigfoot.com; bungalows with half-/full board 11,500/14,100 CFP*), on the ocean side of Motu Tiapaa, is the only place offering much above budget-style accommodation. The food here has an excellent reputation.

Places to Eat

Most people opt for half- or full board at their accommodation. Several small **shops** sell basic supplies. **Snack Tarona** (*☎ 67 82 46; dishes 900-1200 CFP*), to the north of the village, serves simple dishes such as raw fish, tuna sashimi, pork with taro, and braised beef.

Getting There & Away

Air Tahiti (*☎ 67 80 20; closed afternoons*) flies three to five times a week to Pape'ete (14,000 CFP), mostly via Ra'iatea (6400 CFP).

Narrow Onoiau Pass, at the southern end of the lagoon, is the only entry point to the Maupiti lagoon; only smaller ships can get through. **Maupiti Express** (*☎ 67 66 69*) travels to Maupiti from Bora Bora on Tuesday, Thursday and Saturday (2000/3000 CFP one way/return). It leaves Vaitape (Bora Bora) at 8.30am and arrives in Maupiti at 10am, then returns at 4pm, allowing enough time to look around Maupiti; the crossing can be rough.

The small *Maupiti To'u Aia* makes a weekly trip to Maupiti from Pape'ete, also via Ra'iatea on alternate weeks (2400 CFP one way).

Getting Around

If you have booked accommodation you will probably be met at the airport; the return trip typically costs 1000 to 2000 CFP. Otherwise, a boat takes the Air Tahiti staff and any hangers-on back to the main island (400 CFP, 15 minutes).

Motu transfers cost between 500 and 1000 CFP return.

Guesthouses rent bicycles.

OTHER LEEWARD ISLANDS

There are four other Leeward Islands in the Society group: Tupai, Mopelia, Scilly Atoll and Bellinghausen Atoll (also known as Motu One). Mopelia is the only one with a pass that allows ships to enter its lagoon. They're important breeding grounds for green turtles.

Tuamotu Islands

The Tuamotus form the heart of French Polynesia: 77 atolls stretching 1500km northeast to southeast and 500km east to west. The total land area is only about 700 sq km, but the narrow chains of low-lying *motu* making up the islands encircle around 6000 sq km of sheltered lagoons – more than 1000 sq km in the vast Rangiroa lagoon alone.

The atolls are fragile and vulnerable: they have no protection against cyclones and their poor soil and lack of fresh water makes agriculture difficult. Named the 'Dangerous Islands' by Bougainville because of the difficulty of navigating around them, they've long remained in the shadow of the Society Islands. However, black-pearl cultivation and tourism are changing that, and the population is now steadily growing.

Even so, life in the idyllic Tuamotus remains simple and distractions are rare.

History

The history of the archipelago is a mystery: stories from early navigators, archaeological vestiges and fragments of ancient traditions give only clues. Ferdinand Magellan was the first European to chance upon the Tuamotus, at Puka Puka in 1521. Later European explorers were less than complimentary about the group – Le Marie and Schouten in 1616 spoke of the 'Islands of Dogs', the 'Islands without End' or simply the 'Islands of Flies'.

At the time of the first explorers' visits, the central and western areas of the Tuamotus were being torn apart by intense wars. Towards the

TUAMOTU ISLANDS

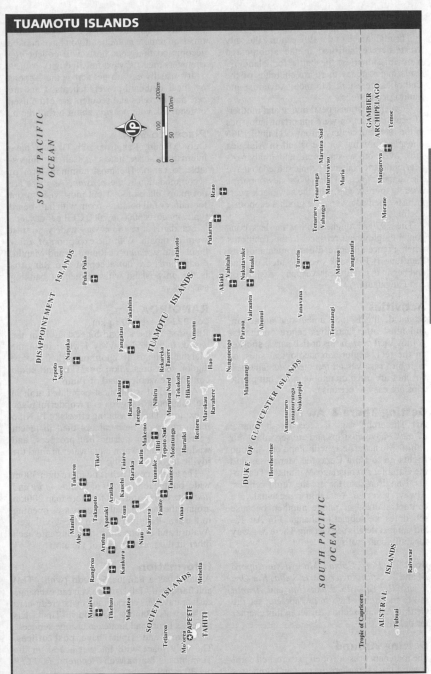

SOUTH PACIFIC OCEAN

GAMBIER ARCHIPELAGO

Temoe

Mangareva

Morane

Maria

Matureivavao

Marutea Sud

Vahanga

Tenararo

Tenaruga

Moruroa

Fangataufa

Reao

Pukarua

Tatakoto

Tureia

Vanavana

Nukutavake

Pinaki

Vairaatea

Akiaki

Vahitahi

Ahunui

DISAPPOINTMENT ISLANDS

Puka Puka

Fakahina

Fangatau

Napuka

Tepoto Nord

Amanu

Paraoa

Nengonengo

Manuhangi

Tematangi

Hao

TUAMOTU ISLANDS

Rekareka

Fauere

Tekokota

Hikueru

Marokau

Ravahere

Reitoru

Takume

Raroia

Taenga

Nihiru

Marutea Nord

DUKE OF GLOUCESTER ISLANDS

Anuanuraro

Anuanurunga

Nukutepipi

Hereheretue

Tikei

Takaroa

Manihi

Ahe

Takapoto

Apataki

Aratika

Kauehi

Taiaro

Toau

Raraka

Katiu

Makemo

Tuanake

Hiti

Tepoto Sud

Motutunga

Arutua

Rangiroa

Kaukura

Niau

Fakarava

Faaite

Tahanea

Anaa

Mataiva

Tikehau

Makatea

Mehetia

SOCIETY ISLANDS

Tetiaroa

Mo'orea

PAPEETE

TAHITI

SOUTH PACIFIC OCEAN

Tropic of Capricorn

AUSTRAL ISLANDS

Tubuai

Raivavae

200km
100mi

0   50   100
0   100   200

TAHITI & FRENCH POLYNESIA

end of the 18th century the ferocious warriors of Anaa Atoll spread terror across the region.

Through much of the 19th century the only Westerners established in the archipelago were missionaries; the battle for islanders' souls means today there are churches of the Catholic, Protestant, Mormon, Adventist and Sanito persuasions.

Copra plantations, pearl diving and mother-of-pearl production were important industries in the late 18th century. From 1911 until 1966 phosphate mining on the island of Makatea took over, but as the copra and mother-of-pearl industries faltered people started to leave the islands. Then, in the 1970s, new airstrips brought tourists who, with the new black-pearl industry, helped reverse the group's economic decline.

The 1970s brought another far less congenial employment prospect to the Tuamotus when France's Centre d'Expérimentation du Pacifique (CEP) took over the atoll of Hao and began to test nuclear weapons on Moruroa and Fangataufa.

Activities
Scuba diving is the number-one attraction, and most other activities centre on the lagoons. Visit pearl farms or fish parks, **snorkel** on the reef, explore archaeological sites, or visit bird reserves on remote *motu*. The best beaches are often on remote *motu*, but picnic trips are easy to organise.

Getting There & Away
Air The archipelago is accessible by plane: 27 atolls have airstrips and are served by Air Tahiti. Most traffic is with Pape'ete, though flights go to Bora Bora, the Marquesas and the Gambier Archipelago. Within the Tuamotus, Rangiroa and Hao are the flight centres. Always give the Air Tahiti representative a contact address or phone number, because schedules are subject to change. For Air Tahiti contact details see Getting There & Away for individual atolls.

Boat The *Dory, Cobia I, Mareva Nui, Taporo IV* and *V, Saint Xavier Maris Stella, Kia Ora II* and *III, Vai-Aito, Nuku Hau* and *Aranui* sail to the archipelago from Pape'ete; see the Getting Around section earlier in this chapter for details.

Getting Around
The road networks are often just crushed coral or sand tracks, perhaps just a few kilometres

long. There is very little public transport. Airports are sometimes near the villages, sometimes on remote *motu*, but if you have booked accommodation your hosts will collect you (transfers aren't always free, though).

It's usually easy to get across the lagoons by local outboard-powered boats. Cars are rare and bicycles and scooters are often used instead; ask your *pension* about hiring them.

Places to Stay
Only Manihi, Rangiroa and Tikehau have international-class hotels. It's all but impossible to camp. The most common form of accommodation is the *pension*. As there are not many places to eat out most visitors opt for half- or full board. A room with half-board typically costs 6000 to 7000 CFP per day.

Standards at *pensions* vary widely, so trust word of mouth. With the exception of a few hotels and *pensions* in Rangiroa and Manihi, credit cards are not accepted and Rangiroa is the only island with permanent banking services.

RANGIROA
pop 2334 • area 40 sq km
Rangiroa is the second-biggest atoll in the world, outranked only by Kwajalein in the Marshall Islands. Its enormous (1640 sq km) lagoon measures 75km by 25km and could contain the whole island of Tahiti.

Although it is the most-populated atoll in the Tuamotus, Rangiroa is a wonderful place to explore. The devastating effects of El Niño mean much of the coral has died in recent years, but other marine life prospers, and wading through warm aqua water around the idyllic lagoon is lovely.

The atoll's coral belt is no more than 300m wide, but the long circuit of islands, *motu* and *hoa* (channels) stretches for more than 200km around the lagoon, with three passes opening to the sea. Rangiroa has two sleepy villages: Avatoru and Tiputa, almost running into each other in the northern part of the atoll.

Information
Avatoru has a **Banque Socredo** (with ATM) and **Banque de Tahiti** where you can exchange cash or travellers cheques and make credit-card withdrawals. **Banque Socredo** in Tiputa has hopeless hours and limited exchange services.

Avatoru and Tiputa have **post offices**. The only place with Internet access in the Tuamotus is **Taaroa Web** (*Reporepo; 500 CFP per 30 mins*).

RANGIROA

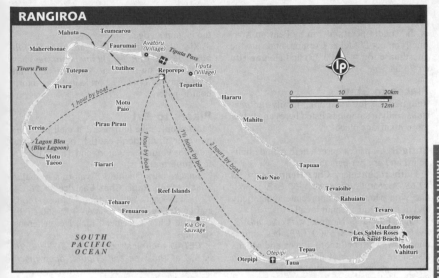

The **Centre Médical Avatoru** (☎ 96 03 75) is 2km east of Avatoru. The **Centre Médical Rai Roa** (☎ 96 04 44), about 1.5km east of Avatoru, has a private clinic.

Avatoru & Tiputa

Very quiet Avatoru is to the west of a string of islets that are separated by a number of *hoa* which are usually dry. It has a supermarket, a few little places to eat, two churches and a fishing and research centre specialising in cultured pearl research.

Even-quieter, charming little Tiputa is less touristy. It's at the eastern end, beyond the Tiputa Pass, and is actually the administrative centre for Rangiroa as well as Makatea, Tikehau and Mataiva. After leaving the village a track continues through coconut plantations until it stops at the next pass.

Most places to stay and eat are dotted along the string of islets east of Avatoru. The islet of Vaimate is immediately east of Avatoru, followed by Tevaiohie, Ariatea, Taamoi and, just across the pass from Tiputa, Reporepo.

Around the Island

Lagon Bleu (Blue Lagoon) is one hour away by boat on the western edge of the atoll, close to Motu Taeoo. A string of *motu* and coral reefs have formed a beautiful natural pool on the edge of the main reef, a lagoon within a lagoon. Less touristy **Lagon Vert** (Green Lagoon) is only five minutes from Avatoru by boat.

The magnificent **Les Sables Roses** (Pink Sand Beach) is on the southeastern edge of Rangiroa's lagoon near Motu Vahituri, 1½ to two hours from Avatoru by boat. Trips are expensive but worth it.

On the south side of the atoll, an hour by boat from Avatoru, **Île aux Récifs** (Reef Island), also known as Motu Ai Ai, lies in water dotted with *feo* (coral outcrops) that have weathered into strange petrified silhouettes; it's a great day trip.

Organised tours tend to be the best way to see the sights, though they rely on the weather and the number of takers. Lagoon and *motu* trips typically cost 7500 to 10,000 CFP. Try **Atoll Excursion** (☎ 96 02 88), **Tane Excursion** (☎ 96 84 68), **Ariitini Excursions** (☎ 96 04 41) and **Punua Excursions** (☎ 96 84 73). **Matahi Excursions** (☎ 96 84 48) has a glass-bottom boat.

Activities

Rangiroa is one of the best-known **dive sites** in the Pacific because of its sharks. Divers enter on the ocean side and drift with the strong current into the lagoon. Contact **Paradive** (☎ 96 05 55), the **Raie Manta Club** (☎ 96 84 80; **w** *www.raiemantaclub.free.fr*), **Six Passengers** (☎ 96 02 60), **Dream Dive** (☎ 96 03 72), **Topdive** (☎ 96 05 60; **w** *www.topdive.com*) or **Blue Dolphins** (☎ 96 03 01).

Guided **snorkelling** (*3-hr tour 4500 CFP*) through the passes is also popular.

To visit a **pearl farm**, try **Gauguin's Pearl** (☎ 96 05 39), about 1km west of the airport, or the small operations run by Pension Martine (contact L'Atelier Corinne, opposite the guesthouse, on ☎ 96 03 13) and **Heipoe Ura** (☎ 96 04 35).

Places to Stay

Rangiroa has lots of simple, family-run *pensions* (only a sample is listed here) and a few more luxurious places.

Budget All prices quoted here include half-board and are per person.

Fairly rudimentary **Chez Henriette** (☎ 96 84 68; Avatoru; bungalows 5400 CFP) is popular with people who appreciate authenticity and home-made coconut bread.

Chez Punua & Moana (☎/fax 96 84 73; Avatoru; bungalows 5900 CFP) has simple bungalows with bathroom. Punua and Moana also have a *pension* at the Lagon Vert, with three bungalows with communal facilities and the possibility of camping.

Pension Loyna (☎/fax 96 82 09; Avatoru; rooms 5900-7000 CFP) is a lovely, clean *pension*, oozing homeliness. It has rooms with/without bathroom, and a bungalow.

Chez Nanua (☎ 96 83 88; Avatoru; bungalows 4500-5100 CFP) is very cheap, relaxed and basic; simple meals are taken with the family.

Chez Cécile (☎ 96 05 06; Vaimate; single/double bungalows 6900/8500 CFP) is famous for Cécile's simple but wonderful cooking. Its newer spacious bungalows have bathrooms.

Chez Glorine (☎ 96 04 05; Reporepo; bungalows 7500 CFP) has particularly good food and well-maintained bungalows.

In Tiputa, **Chez Lucien** (☎ 96 73 55; bungalows 6000 CFP) has spacious, pleasant bungalows.

Mid-Range & Top End Rates here are per person.

Miki Miki Village (☎ 96 83 83, fax 96 82 90; Avatoru; single/double bungalows with half-board 11,700/19,200 CFP) has charming bungalows.

Les Relais de Josephine (☎/fax 96 02 00; Reporepo; bungalows with half-board 14,000 CFP) is immaculate, luxurious and great value.

Hotel Kia Ora (☎ 96 03 84, fax 96 04 93; **w** www.hotelkiaora.com; Reporepo; garden/over-water bungalows 31,200/64,500 CFP)

has extremely luxurious bungalows dotted around a magnificent coconut plantation on the lagoon's edge.

Kia Ora Sauvage (bungalows with full board 46,300 CFP, 2-night minimum stay) has a lovely setting on Motu Avearahi, about an hour away by boat. The price includes return boat transfers.

Places to Eat

Most people take half-board at their *pension*; however, if you don't eat fish, be prepared to cater for yourself. Avatoru and Tiputa have a few **supermarkets**.

Snack bars include Avatoru's popular **Snack Manu Ragi**; **Chez Béatrice** (☎ 96 04 12), 5km east, which does Chinese food; and **Le Relley Ohutu** (burgers 400-800 CFP), opposite Chez Glorine, which has generous servings.

CETAD technical school (☎ 96 72 96, 96 02 68 at the weekend; Tiputa; open lunch Tues & Thur) has a restaurant where students prepare lunch.

Several *pensions* allow nonguests to dine: a set menu of fish, rice, bread and a light dessert costs 2500 CFP. Try **Chez Glorine, Pension Teina & Marie, Pension Tuanake, Miki Miki Village** and **Chez Lucien**.

Les Relais de Josephine (set lunch/dinner 1200/3500 CFP), a cut above the rest, has an idyllic setting and divine food.

Hotel Kia Ora (appetisers 850-1400 CFP, mains 2500-4000 CFP) is very upmarket; on Wednesday and Sunday it has a buffet and Polynesian dance performance (5000 CFP).

Shopping

A few shops around Avatoru sell souvenirs, postcards, hand-painted pareu, film and local handicrafts. Try **Pareo Carole**, 1.5km east of Avatoru centre, **Ocean Passion**, across the road from the airport and the **shops** in the Hotel Kia Ora. For places to buy pearls see Activities earlier in this section.

Getting There & Away

Rangiroa is an important link for air and sea communication, as it's midway between the Society Islands and the Marquesas.

The airport is between Avatoru and Tiputa. **Air Tahiti** (☎ 96 03 41) is inside the air terminal building. Flights go to Pape'ete (15,000 CFP, one hour, several daily); Bora Bora (22,500 CFP); Nuku Hiva (the Marquesas, one a week); and, in the Tuamotus, Tikehau (5100 CFP) and Manihi (9800 CFP).

The *Dory, Mareva Nui, Vai-Aito, Saint Xavier Maris Stella* and *Rairoa Nui* stop in Rangiroa. The *Aranui* stops at Rangiroa on its return from the Marquesas.

Getting Around
If you have booked accommodation your hosts will meet you at the airport; however, transfers aren't automatically included in the price.

A sealed road runs the 10km from Avatoru village to the Tiputa Pass, but there's no public transport. Hire a bike or a scooter.

Boats regularly cross the pass separating the Avatoru islets from Tiputa village (1000 CFP return, 500 CFP extra for a bicycle).

Rangi Location (*☎ 96 03 28*) rents cars, curious three-wheeler fun cars and scooters.

Chez Hélène *(Avatoru)* rents bicycles; **Paréo Carole** (*☎ 96 82 45; Avatoru*) hires cars, scooters and bicycles; and **Hotel Kia Ora** has bicycles and scooters.

TIKEHAU
pop 400 • area 15 sq km

This enchanting, oval-shaped atoll is becoming popular with visitors looking for a quieter alternative to Rangiroa. Stretching over 26km, it has a lagoon dotted with *motu* that provide nesting grounds for birds. Most people live in the peaceful village of Tuherahera, on the southwest of the atoll.

There is no bank in Tikehau but there is a **post office**.

Scuba diving in the magnificent **Tuheiava Pass** is excellent; you're likely to see manta rays and sharks. Rangiroa's Raie Manta Club has an offshoot at **Tikehau Village** (*☎ 96 22 86*); other dive centres are in the village and at Hôtel Tikehau.

Lagoon excursions go to see the nesting birds on **Motu Puarua** *(Île aux Oiseaux or Bird Island; per person 4000-7000 CFP)* or to fish at **Tuheiava Pass** *(per person 3000-4000 CFP)*; pensions also offer **motu picnic trips**.

You can rent **kayaks** *(per day 1000-1500 CFP)* from **Aito Motel Colette** and **Pension Tematie**.

Places to Stay & Eat
The *pensions* in the village aren't on the lagoon, unlike those near the airport.

Aito Motel Colette (*☎ 96 22 47; rooms 3800, bungalows with half-/full board per person 8300/10,200 CFP*) is in an enchanting spot between the village and the airport; the rooms have an equipped kitchen, or you can choose beachside bungalows.

Pension Tematie (*☎/fax 96 22 65; bungalows with half-/full board 7500/9100 CFP*), nearby, has popular lagoon-side bungalows and a warm welcome; airport transfers are included.

Chez Justine (*☎ 96 22 87; camping per person with breakfast 1300 CFP, bungalows with half-/full board 6400/8000 CFP*) is 500m west of the airport on the edge of the lagoon; campers can order meals for 1500 to 2000 CFP.

Kahaia Beach (*☎ 96 22 77; bungalows with half-/full board 6100/7600 CFP*), the most remote option, is on a *motu* northeast of the airport. It has basic, lagoon-side bungalows.

Tikehau Pearl Beach Resort (*☎ 96 23 00, fax 96 23 01; W www.pearlresorts.com; bungalows 42,200-66,700 CFP*) is on Motu Aua a few kilometres northeast of the airport, a perfect place for a luxury version of Robinson Crusoe.

Chez Maui and **Chez Rosita**, in Tuherahera, sell general supplies and you can buy coconut bread on some days from the **bakery**.

The restaurant at **Tikehau Village** sometimes accepts nonguests; you must book.

Getting There & Away
The airport is about 1km east of the village entrance. **Air Tahiti** (*☎ 96 22 66*) flies 10 times a week between Pape'ete and Tikehau (15,000 CFP), direct or via Rangiroa (5100 CFP); several flights a week go to Bora Bora (21,500 CFP).

The *Mareva Nui, Saint Xavier Maris Stella, Dory* and *Vai Ato* stop at Tikehau.

Getting Around
The 10km track around the *motu* on which Tuherahera is situated passes the airport. Bicycles can be borrowed or hired from your hosts.

MATAIVA
pop 227 • lagoon area 25 sq km

This atoll looks unusual because the coral creates walls that divide the lagoon into about 70 basins of 10m depth. However, this may change dramatically if plans to mine the lagoon for phosphate go ahead. It's estimated that 12 million tonnes of phosphate lies below the surface, enough to support 10 to 15 years of mining; the damage of such large-scale industrial activity could mean disaster for the island. The islanders are hoping that increased tourism could stop the project.

The village of Pahua is divided by a pass just a few metres wide and no deeper than

1.5m. A bridge spanning the pass links the two parts of the village. Nine channels link the lagoon and the ocean. Mataiva (literally 'Nine Eyes') is named after these channels. Mataiva has superb beaches, numerous snorkelling spots and one of the few noteworthy archaeological sites in the Tuamotus. There's no bank, but Pahua has a post office.

Things to See & Do
Ofai Tau Noa (Le Rocher de la Tortue, or Turtle Rock) is a mushroom-shaped remnant of a former uplifted coral reef *feo* (coral outcrop). Take the track that starts at the bridge on the northern side of the pass for 4.7km, then take the side track on the left and cross the coconut plantation to the ocean.

Well-kept Marae Papiro has the legendary throne of the giant god Tu. It's about 14km from the village, southeast of the atoll at the end of the track.

The south of the atoll has many fine beaches.

Île aux Oiseaux (Bird Island) is a nesting place for *oio*, *tara* and red-footed boobies.

Don't miss the chance to accompany the fishers on their way to trap fish in one of the numerous fish parks around the lagoon and the pass.

Places to Stay & Eat
The guesthouses are similar; prices include airport transfers.

Mataiva Village (☎ 96 32 33; camping 1000 CFP; bungalows with half-/full board per person 5600/7100 CFP), the only guesthouse north of the pass, is clean and comfortable. Crayfish are a speciality.

Super Mataiva Cool (☎ 96 32 53; single/double bungalows with full board 10,100/13,100 CFP), south of the bridge and on the edge of the pass, has basic but decent units.

The *pensions* are really the only place to eat, although several small shops have basic food supplies.

Getting There & Away
The Air Tahiti (☎ 96 32 48) representative is the proprietor of the Mataiva Village. Two flights a week go to Pape'ete (15,000 CFP).

The *Mareva Nui* and *Saint Xavier Maris Stella* stop in.

Getting Around
A good-quality track goes almost all the way around the island. To the north, it finishes at Marae Papiro, about 14km away. To the

south, it's about 10km to the end. Cycling is an excellent way to get around. The *pensions* have bicycles for rent.

The *pensions* organise trips to the various sites by motorboat and by car, including a picnic (about 3000 CFP).

MANIHI
pop 770 • lagoon area 192 sq km
Manihi is world-famous for its pearl production and its lagoon is scattered with large-scale family and industrial pearl farms. The ellipse-shaped atoll is 28km long and 8km wide, with only one opening, the Tairapa Pass in the southwest. The exhilarating beauty of the lagoon and the riches of its underwater world were quickly recognised and an international hotel was built in 1977.

There is no bank on the atoll, though the Manihi Pearl Beach Resort may be able to change money in emergencies. The post office is in Paeua village, opposite the marina. Paeua has a hospital.

Things to See & Do
Head out of charmless Paeua to the pearl farms. From the first farm set up in Manihi in 1968 the industry has flourished into the South Pacific's main black-pearl centre. Try to visit a small family farm and a larger industrial farm, but avoid holiday periods, particularly Christmas, when the workers may be away. Prices tend to be lower than in Pape'ete or abroad.

The Manihi Pearl Beach Resort is the main organiser of pearl-farm visits, usually combined with a picnic and village excursion for 2544 CFP. You can also contact the small farms directly.

You can dive with Manihi Blue Nui (☎ 96 42 17; W www.bluenui.com); there's a great wall dive with excellent marine life.

Places to Stay
Reasonably priced accommodation is difficult to find and the facilities are scattered all over the atoll.

Motel Chez Jeanne (☎ 96 42 90, fax 96 42 91; beach/over-water bungalows per person 9600/13,900 CFP), on the lagoon side on Motu Taugaraufara, about 9km northeast of the airport, has well-equipped bungalows with bathroom. Meals are not provided.

Vainui Pearls (☎ 96 42 89, fax 96 43 30; rooms with full board per person 8900 CFP), on Motu Marakorako, east of the village and about a half-hour by boat from the airport, has eight rooms with shared bathrooms (which some readers say compromises privacy here). The owners have a small pearl farm.

Manihi Pearl Beach Resort (☎ *96 42 73, in Pape'ete ☎ 43 16 10, fax 96 42 72; beach/over-water bungalows 30,300/49,700 CFP*), two minutes from the airport, at the southwestern end of the lagoon, is a luxury resort in an idyllic setting of coconut groves and white-sand beaches.

Places to Eat
Apart from the guesthouses and hotels there are hardly any places to eat. In Paeua, there is a good **shop** near the marina. At the Manihi Pearl Beach Resort the **Poe Rava restaurant** (*appetisers 800-2000 CFP, mains 1300-2500 CFP*) has reasonable prices, especially for lunch.

Getting There & Away
The **Air Tahiti office** (☎ *96 43 34, 96 42 71 on flight days*) is in Paeua and, on flight days, at the airport. Flights go most days to Pape'ete (18,000 CFP), direct or via Ahe or Rangiroa (9800 CFP). Flights also go between Manihi and Bora Bora, via Rangiroa; flights go four times weekly to Bora Bora and twice weekly to Manihi (23,400 CFP).

The *Mareva Nui, Saint Xavier Maris Stella, Dory* and *Vai-Aito* stop at Manihi.

Getting Around
The only track links Taugaraufara to the airport and is about 9km long. Getting around the atoll requires ingenuity! The Manihi Pearl Beach Resort rents bicycles.

The airport is at the southwestern end of the atoll. You have to hitch a boat ride from the quay next to the airport *fare*.

To get to the dive centre from the village take the Manihi Pearl Beach Resort staff shuttle, which generally leaves the Paeua marina at about 6am and returns around 4pm; it'll take you for free. For other points around the atoll, talk to boat owners in the village.

AHE
Those who want to go off the beaten track will appreciate this atoll's quietness, idyllic scenery and gentle pace of life. The atoll was really only well known to yachties until an upmarket *pension* and dive centre opened in the last few years. Ahe's large lagoon is 20km long by 10km wide and is entered by the Tiareroa (or Reianui) Pass in the west. The village of Tenukupara is on the southeast side.

Coco Perles (☎/*fax 96 44 08; bungalows singles/doubles with full board from 12,100/ 22,100 CFP*), on a *motu*, has charming, well-designed bungalows in a coconut plantation. At the *pension*, **Ahe Plongée** (☎ *96 44 08*) does dives in the pass.

TAKAROA & TAKAPOTO
The atolls of Takaroa (Long Chin) and Takapoto (Short Chin) are labelled the King George Islands on marine maps.

Rectangular Takaroa Atoll (population 490) is 27km long by 6km wide and has only one pass, in the southeast, into the lagoon. Ninety percent of the 488 residents are Mormons and alcohol is prohibited. There is no bank but there is a **post office**, a **shop** and two *pensions*. Takaroa's lagoon has numerous **coral formations**, which are wonderful for snorkelling. At least four flights a week go to Pape'ete (1½ hours, 18,000 CFP) and Takapoto (4400 CFP), and frequent flights go to Manihi.

Takapoto (population 612) is 9km south. It is 20km long and 6km across at its widest point and doesn't have a pass. With its pearl farms, white-sand beaches and archaeological remains, Takapoto could one day become a popular tourist destination. The atoll has no bank but there is a **post office**.

The interesting **Marae Takai** archaeological site is well hidden, a long walk northeast of Fakatopatere. Follow the track that goes past the cemetery at the village exit for 15km. You will see a channel spanned by a stone bridge. Cross this bridge and immediately on the right, walk 60m along the channel towards the lagoon. Turn left and clear your way through bush for about 30m to reach the three *marae* in a little clearing.

Takapoto Village (☎ *98 65 44; bungalows with half-/full board per person 6800/8300 CFP*), on a small yellow-sand beach beside the lagoon, southeast of the village, has a comfortable bungalow and a room.

The airport is a stone's throw southeast of the village. **Air Tahiti** flies three times a week to Pape'ete (17,200 CFP, 1½ hours) and Takaroa.

The *Saint Xavier Maris Stella* and *Mareva Nui* serve Takapoto. *Taporo IV* and *Aranui*, en route to the Marquesas Islands, also stop there.

Bicycle is the best way to discover the atoll's few short tracks. Most guesthouses organise picnics on deserted *motu*, reached by speedboat (about 2000 CFP per person).

FAKARAVA

pop 467 • lagoon area 1121 sq km

Magnificent Fakarava is the second-largest atoll in the Tuamotu archipelago. The pass through the reef offers amazing diving and several dive cruise operators visit the atoll. Most people live in Rotoava village at the northeastern end, 4km east of the airport.

Relais Marama (☎ *98 42 51; camping 1400 CFP, single/double rooms 3600/4600 CFP, single/double bungalows 4400/5400 CFP*), on the ocean side of the *motu* at Rotoava, has functional rooms and new bungalows with shared bathroom; prices include breakfast and airport transfers. Half-board is available or you can use the kitchen. Mountain bikes are free.

Pension Havaiki (☎*/fax 98 42 16;* ⓔ *havaiki@mail.pf; bungalows with breakfast/full board per person 5000/9000 CFP*), 1km from the village centre on a magnificent beach, has charming bungalows and tasty, plentiful food.

At the other end of the atoll, **Motu Aito Paradise** (☎ *41 29 00;* Ⓦ *www.fakarava.org; full board per person 10,000 CFP*), on a superb *motu*, has six pretty bungalows.

The airport is about 4km from the village, west towards the pass. **Air Tahiti** (☎ *67 70 35*) flies to Pape'ete (17,400 CFP) daily except Thursday, and to Rangiroa and Kauehi (both 5500 CFP) once a week.

The *Saint Xavier Maris Stella*, *Vai-Aito* and *Mareva Nui* stop at Fakarava.

From Rotoava a track goes to the southwest of the atoll for about 40km. The guesthouses arrange boat excursions.

MORUROA

Moruroa (Mururoa) Atoll, 1250km southeast of Tahiti, will be forever synonymous with nuclear testing.

During the tests it was equipped with ultramodern electricity production installations, a desalinisation plant and an airport which handled large transport planes. Restaurants, cinemas, sports grounds and an internal radio and TV channel were there for the military staff. Today there's just a small contingent of French legionnaires. (For more background see Ecology & Environment in the Facts about the South Pacific chapter.)

OTHER TUAMOTUS

The only high island in the Tuamotus is Makatea, which was the centre of French Polynesia's booming phosphate-mining industry until the deposits were exhausted in 1966; today only 84 people live on the island.

Other Tuamotu atolls with airports and *pensions* include Arutua, Kaukura, Anaa, Nukutavake and Hao, the air traffic centre for the southern Tuamotus. Puka Puka has an airport, but Raroia doesn't.

Marquesas Islands

Te Henua Enana (The Land of Men) is the Marquesans' name for their archipelago. These bewitching islands of legend boast a wealth of archaeological remains, many of which are still to be catalogued.

The most northerly archipelago of French Polynesia, the Marquesas stretch over 350km and are divided into northern and southern groups. Only six of the 15 islands are inhabited (total population 8000) and travelling within the archipelago can be difficult.

The Marquesas' dramatic coastline of cliffs, needles and peaks towering to more than 1000m is the result of waves smashing against the rock, unmitigated by any sheltering reefs or lagoons. This rugged landscape is ridged with deep valleys draped in luxuriant tropical vegetation.

The small numbers of visitors who do come here are privileged to experience the mysterious ambience and warm welcome of a place that has to be experienced to be understood.

The archipelago is half an hour ahead of Tahiti time.

Marquesan Handicrafts

The Marquesas are famous for their excellent handicrafts, particularly their sculpture. *Tiki*, pestles, *umete* (bowls), adzes, spears, clubs, fishhooks and other work is done in *miro* (rosewood), *tou* (a dark, hard-grained wood), bone or volcanic stone. You will also find necklaces, Marquesan *umu hei* (a local potpourri) and the famous tapa cloth of Fatu Hiva, made from beaten bark and decorated with traditional designs.

Most villages have small *fare artisanal* (craft centre) with items for exhibition and sale but they may only be open when requested or when the *Aranui* is in port. Order early in case your piece has to be made; prices are cheaper here than in Pape'ete but you cannot pay with credit card.

History

The Marquesas were among the first islands in this region to be settled; from these groups people dispersed to the rest of Polynesia. Numerous archaeological remains have survived, including *tohua* (meeting places), *me'ae* (the Marquesan equivalent of *marae*), *pae pae* (paved floors or platforms) and *tiki*.

The Marquesas' isolation was broken in 1595, when Mendaña sighted Fatu Hiva and christened the island group in honour of the viceroy of Peru.

The French took possession of Tahuata in 1842 but the Marquesas were quickly marginalised in favour of Pape'ete for geographic, economic and strategic reasons. Upon contact with Western influences, the foundations of Marquesan society collapsed. Whalers brought alcohol, firearms and syphilis, while the colonial administration and missionaries paid little attention to the Marquesans' ancestral values. The population fell from an estimated 18,000 in 1842 to 2100 in 1926.

This century, the experiences of the painter Paul Gauguin drew world attention to the Marquesas. More recently, new transport and telecommunications infrastructures have decreased the archipelago's isolation, while archaeological discoveries have underlined the significance of Marquesan civilisation.

Getting There & Away

Air Air Tahiti flies direct between Pape'ete and the Marquesas (three hours) and, once weekly, from Rangiroa, in the Tuamotus, to Nuku Hiva. Nuku Hiva, Hiva Oa, 'Ua Huka and 'Ua Pou have airports. Three flights a week go from Nuku Hiva to 'Ua Pou, and one to 'Ua Huka.

Boat The *Taporo IV* and *Aranui* (see the boxed text) serve the Marquesas, travelling from Pape'ete via the Tuamotus (Rangiroa and/or Takapoto). Taiohae, Hakahau and Atuona are the only places with quays where the ships can dock; at other ports unloading is done with *bonitiers*.

Getting Around

Getting around the Marquesas is difficult. The valleys are isolated, making it virtually impossible to tour by road, and only the main settlements have sealed roads. Some settlements have no landing stage and

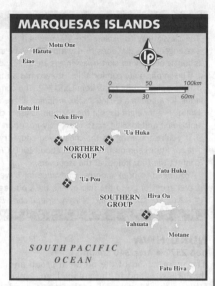

rough seas make landings challenging to say the least. The introduction of helicopter shuttles within the northern and southern groups has improved inter-island transport. **Héli Inter Marquises** (☎ 92 02 17; **e** *helico -nuku@mail.pf; Taiohae, Nuku Hiva*) does convenient but costly charters on Nuku Hiva and flies three times a week to 'Ua Pou, and to 'Ua Huka on demand.

Inter-island travel is via Air Tahiti, helicopters, *bonitiers* and the cargo ships *Taporo IV* and *Aranui*. Nuku Hiva and Hiva Oa are the hub islands; travel between the two is regular and reliable, but further afield can be more difficult. Don't expect things to go to schedule.

Land transport requires a 4WD (hired 4WD will come with a driver) because the roads are rough and the terrain is spectacularly steep. There is no public transport and helicopters are the main means of getting around islands. Travelling by sea, *bonitiers* and speedboats usually link the villages much more rapidly than 4WDs. You might also be able to hitch a ride on a passing boat or yacht.

Places to Stay

Nuku Hiva and Hiva Oa have several good hotels, particularly in Taiohae and Atuona. 'Ua Huka, 'Ua Pou, Tahuata and Fatu Hiva have family *pensions* and, sometimes, independent bungalows.

The Aranui

The classic way to explore the Marquesas is by sea, aboard the *Aranui* (Great Path), a cargo-and-passenger vessel that does 16-day trips from Pape'ete through the archipelago and the Tuamotus. Cargo is still its primary mission – passengers are a secondary consideration – but that's half the fun.

The ship is quite comfortable – it even has a mini-swimming pool, good food and plenty of wine. The complete cruise costs from US$1762. The complete 15- or 16-day cruise costs from US$1995 per adult for a bed in a C-class cabin, including all meals and taxes. It is also possible to join the ship from Nuku Hiva for eight days in the Marquesas (deck class costs US$1390). At each stop, while the ship is unloading and loading, passengers may go ashore to explore (excursions are included in the tariff).

If you're travelling on the cheap, you could try going deck class with local islanders, though the *Aranui*'s not keen on this. It costs about 3000 CFP to travel deck class from one island to another; contact the tour guides at the stopovers.

You need to book months in advance for travel during July/August and December. Contact your travel agent or go to the ship owner, the **Compagnie Polynésienne de Transport Maritime** (*CPTM*; ☎ 42 62 40; fax 43 48 89; W www.aranui.com; BP 220, Pape'ete).

NUKU HIVA
pop 2372 • area 340 sq km
The main island of the northern group and the largest island in the archipelago, Nuku Hiva is the Marquesas' administrative and economic capital. Most of the population are located in Taiohae on the south coast, Hatiheu on the north coast and Taipivai in the southeast.

Nuku Hiva was formed from two volcanoes, stacked one on top of the other to form two concentric calderas. The top of the main caldera forms a jagged framework that surrounds the Toovii plateau. The highest point on Nuka Hiva is Mt Tekao (1224m). To the south of this plateau the broken-mouthed caldera of the secondary volcano reaches its highest point at Mt Muake (864m) and outlines a huge natural amphitheatre. At its foot is a vast natural harbour, around which curls Taiohae, the island's main town. There are deep bays that cut right into the south and east coasts and on the north coast erosion has shaped impressive basalt *aiguilles* (needles). One of the *Survivor* television shows plonked its contestants in the wilds of Nuku Hiva.

Information
The **tourist office** (☎ 92 03 73; e marquises@mail.pf; open 7.30am-11.30am Mon-Fri) is in the *mairie* in Taiohae. **Banque Socredo**, on the seafront, handles exchange and credit-card withdrawals and has an ATM. The **post office** is on the eastern side of the bay. Several doctors, surgeons and dentists are based at the **hospital** (☎ 91 20 00), 100m from the post office.

Around the Island
Taiohae, the main centre, hugs Taiohae Bay for nearly 3.5km. Climb the Meau Valley for less than 1km to reach a restored **me'ae**, with a small contemporary *tiki*. The **Herman Melville memorial** is west of the town; the *Moby Dick* author made nearby Taipivai famous in his book *Typee*. Seven hundred metres closer to the centre is the **Piki Vehine Pae Pae**, also known as Temehea, an open-air museum in the form of a *ha'e* (traditional house). The restored **Tohua Koueva**, a sacred place venerated by the ancient Marquesans, is 1.5km up the Pakiu Valley on the road to Taipivai.

Walk or drive along a picturesque track to the summit of **Mt Muake** (864m). The cool **Toovii Plateau**, crossed by the Taiohae-Terre Déserte (airport) track and nestled among mountains, looks surprisingly like the mountains of Bavaria.

About 8km west of Taiohae, the **Hakaui Valley** is one of the island's most imposing sights. The river has cut vertical walls of nearly 800m into the basalt and after rain the **Vaipo Waterfall**, at 350m one of the world's highest, thunders into a basin. Almost uninhabited today, a paved road, once an **ancient royal way**, goes up the valley following the river past *pae pae*, *tohua* and *tiki* hidden behind a tangle of vegetation. From Taiohae, the valley can be reached by speedboat (about 20 minutes), on foot (two hours) or on horseback by a 12km bridleway. When you return to Hakaui Bay walk 100m east to the magnificent **Hakatea Bay**.

Scottish writer Robert Louis Stevenson succumbed to the charm of **Hatiheu** in the north of the island, 12km from Taipivai and 28km from Taiohae. The town's focal point is the wooden **church**, and the tiny seafront *mairie* houses a small **museum** with a collection of traditional Marquesan artefacts. From Taipivai, follow the main road inland and west. The track deteriorates as it climbs to the **Teavaitapuhiva Pass** (490m), with magnificent views. Shortly before Hatiheu is the **Hikokua archaeological site**, where modern *tiki* have been added to the old ones and the vast **Kamuihei & Tahakia archaeological site**.

Taipivai carpets the floor of a river valley. Allow 1½ hours by 4WD to travel the 16km northeast from Taiohae. From the village take the road towards Hatiheu for 1.5km to the turn-off where a steep 20- to 30-minute walk takes you straight to the **Paeke archaeological site**.

Charming **Hooumi**, surrounded by luxuriant vegetation, is about 4km east of Taipivai. The hamlet has a picturesque small timber church and a stunning, but *nono*-plagued, white-sand beach.

Peaceful **Anaho** can be reached by speedboat from Hatiheu (10 minutes) or on foot (45 minutes) along a picturesque track. The descent from Teavaimaoaoa Pass (218m), through a huge coconut plantation, is quite steep. A long white-sand beach runs beside one of the Marquesas best, sheltered anchorages. On the north coast, **Aakapa** is in a superb setting below high peaks; it can be reached on foot from Hatiheu or by speedboat.

Activities

Centre Plongée Marquises (☎ 92 00 88), in Taiohae, is the Marquesas' dive centre. Encounters with dolphins, hammerhead sharks and many other species make up for less-than-amazing visibility (only about 20m): popular sites include **Orques Pygmées (Pygmy Orcas)**, **Tikapo**, **Sentry of the Hammers**, **Grotte Ekamako (Ekamako Cave)**, **Motumano Point** and **Matateiko Point**. It's usually a 30- to 40-minute boat trip to the site.

Good **walking** tracks crisscross the island, including the hikes to the Hakaui waterfall, Colette Bay and to Anaho from Hatiheu.

For guided **horse rides** ask at your *pension* or contact **Le Ranch** (☎ 92 06 35; 1-hr/ 1-day ride 2000/8000 CFP) or **Chez Yvonne** (☎ 92 02 97; 1-day ride 5000 CFP).

Experienced parasailers might want to have a go on this magnificently mountainous island – there's a **parapente club** (☎ 92 05 30), but no instructors, in Taiohae. **Héli Inter Marquises** operates scenic 20-minute flights for a minimum of four people at 16,500 CFP each.

Pua Excursions (☎ 92 02 94; 42,000 CFP for 2 people) offers three-day tours; the price includes meals and accommodation.

TAHITI & FRENCH POLYNESIA

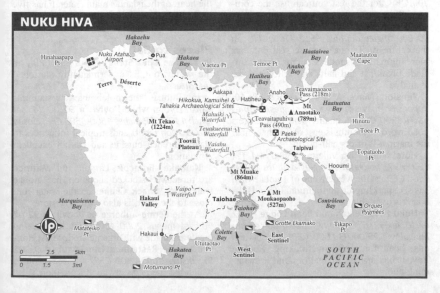

NUKU HIVA

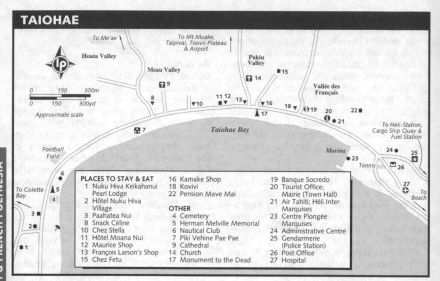

TAIOHAE

To Me'ae
To Mt Muake, Taipivai, Toovii Plateau & Airport
Hoata Valley
Pakiu Valley
Meau Valley
Vallée des Français
Approximate scale
Taiohae Bay
Football Field
Marina
Tennis
To Colette Bay
To Heli-Station, Cargo Ship Quay & Fuel Station
To Beach

PLACES TO STAY & EAT
1 Nuku Hiva Keikahanui Pearl Lodge
2 Hôtel Nuku Hiva Village
3 Paahatea Nui
8 Snack Céline
10 Chez Stella
11 Hôtel Moana Nui
12 Maurice Shop
13 François Larson's Shop
15 Chez Fetu
16 Kamake Shop
18 Kovivi
22 Pension Mave Mai

OTHER
4 Cemetery
5 Herman Melville Memorial
6 Nautical Club
7 Piki Vehine Pae Pae
9 Cathedral
14 Church
17 Monument to the Dead
19 Banque Socredo
20 Tourist Office; Mairie (Town Hall)
21 Air Tahiti; Héli Inter Marquises
23 Centre Plongée
24 Administrative Centre
25 Gendarmerie (Police Station)
26 Post Office
27 Hospital

Places to Stay

Taiohae The cheapest place is **Chez Fetu** (☎ 92 03 66; *rooms per person 2050 CFP*), which is simple and homely.

Paahatea Nui (*Chez Justin et Julienne;* ☎ 92 00 97, fax 92 00 97; *rooms/bungalows per person 2550/4050 CFP*) has six *pension* rooms with shared bathroom, as well as two bungalows with bathroom. Breakfast costs 700 CFP; for the rest you can use the communal kitchen.

Hôtel Moana Nui (☎ 92 03 30, fax 92 00 02; *singles/doubles 6650/7150 CFP*), in the centre of Taiohae on the seafront, has more upmarket, spotless rooms. Rates include breakfast and half- and full board are available.

Pension Mave Mai (☎/fax 92 08 10; e pension-mavemai@mail.pf; *singles/doubles 5850/6900 CFP*), a quality *pension* that gets good word of mouth, is east of Taiohae, near the marina. It offers half-board.

Hôtel Nuku Hiva Village (☎ 92 01 94, fax 92 05 97; *bungalows singles/doubles 6650/7800 CFP*), at the western end of Taiohae Bay, has six sparkling-clean traditional *fare*. Half-board is available.

Nuku Hiva Keikahanui Pearl Lodge (☎ 92 07 10, fax 92 07 11; w www.pearlresorts.com; *bungalows 29,000-39,000 CFP*) is a luxurious, beautiful place overlooking Taiohae Bay. It has air-con bungalows and a swimming pool.

Around the Island The excellent **Chez Yvonne** (☎ 92 02 97, fax 92 01 28; e hinakonui@ mail.pf; *bungalows per person with breakfast 4550 CFP*), in Hatiheu, has small local-style bungalows; half- and full board are available.

For something out of the ordinary try **Ferme-auberge de Toovii** (*Farm-inn;* ☎ 92 07 50, fax 92 00 04; e ferme-auberge@mail.pf; *single/double rooms 5050/7100 CFP*) in the heart of the island's main crater. It has five clean bungalows with bathroom and terrace. Half- and full board are available.

Places to Eat

In Taiohae **Chez Stella** (*dishes 850 CFP*), on the waterfront, is a permanently stationed *roulotte*.

In Taiohae the hotels have restaurants worth trying, while **Kovivi** (☎ 92 00 14; *set lunch 1400 CFP, dishes 1500-3500 CFP; closed Sun & Mon night*) adds tropical influences to classic French cuisine and has an excellent reputation.

Kamake, **François Larson** and **Maurice** are three well-stocked shops on the Taiohae waterfront. **Snack Céline**, on the waterfront close to the river, is also a grocery store.

At the **Ferme-auberge de Toovii** (☎ 92 07 50; *set menus 2000-4000 CFP; open daily*) meals are made with organic produce. At Hatiheu try the **Restaurant Hinakonui** (☎ 92 02 97; *dishes 1600-2500 CFP*) at Chez Yvonne, which has a deservedly good reputation.

TAHITI & FRENCH POLYNESIA

Getting There & Away

Air Nuku Hiva is the flight hub of the Marquesas. **Air Tahiti's office** (☎ 92 03 41), on the seafront in Taiohae, shifts to the **airport** (☎ 92 01 45) on flight days. There are six to seven flights a week between Pape'ete and Nuku Hiva (26,600 CFP, three hours), one of which stops at Rangiroa (Tuamotus).

Within the Marquesas, flights go from Nuku Hiva to Atuona (Hiva Oa; 9800 CFP), 'Ua Huka (5800 CFP) and 'Ua Pou (5800 CFP). Frequencies vary, but all of these flights connect to/from Pape'ete.

Héli Inter Marquises (☎/fax 92 02 17, at the heli-station ☎ 92 00 54, at the airport ☎ 92 04 40), located right next to the Air Tahiti office, has regular shuttle services to Hakahau ('Ua Pou, 12,500 CFP per person, 15 minutes) on Wednesday, Friday and Saturday.

Boat You can charter a *bonitier* to go to 'Ua Pou or 'Ua Huka (about 50,000 CFP). Contact **Laurent (Teiki) Falchetto** (☎ 92 05 78) or **Xavier Curvat** (☎ 92 00 88), the dive centre director.

The *Aranui* and the *Taporo IV* serve Nuku Hiva. The *Aranui* goes to Taipivai and Hatiheu as well as Taiohae.

Getting Around

A network of tracks links the airport, Taiohae, Taipivai, Hooumi, Hatiheu and Aakapa.

It's only 18km from Taiohae to Nuku Ataha airport at Terre Déserte but it takes at least two hours along the bumping, winding track. Approved 4WD taxis generally wait for each flight. It is nevertheless wise to book, either through your hotel or *pension*, or directly by contacting the taxi drivers: **Nuku Hiva Transports** (☎ 92 06 08), **Rose Marie Tours** (☎ 92 05 96) or **Huku Tours** (☎ 92 04 89). It's also possible to hitch.

You also have the option of taking the helicopter (7000 CFP per person, eight minutes).

You can rent 4WDs with or without a driver. From Taiohae for the vehicle alone (four passengers) count on 3000 to 5000 CFP to Muake, 15,000 CFP to Taipivai, 20,000 CFP to Hatiheu, and 25,000 CFP to Aakapa. Book through your accommodation or call the airport drivers. Count on 6000 CFP between Hatiheu and Aakapa. **Charles Monbaerts** at the Hôtel Moana Nui has a four-seat Suzuki for 11,000 CFP a day – good value if you're solo.

'UA HUKA

pop 571 • area 83 sq km

'Ua Huka lies 50km east of Nuku Hiva and 56km northeast of 'Ua Pou, and for some reason it is rarely visited. It's the driest island in all of French Polynesia and its wonderfully desolate scenery is accentuated by the free-ranging herds of semi-wild horses, hence the nickname 'Island of Horses'. The island boasts archaeological treasures and the Marquesas' first museum devoted entirely to archaeology. Thousands of birds nest on several offshore *motu*.

The densely vegetated Vaikivi Plateau occupies the northern edge of the island, while the island's villages – Vaipaee, Hane and Hokatu – all nestle around the edges of steep-sided valleys on the south coast. Mt Hitikau (855m) is the highest point on the island.

Vaipaee

The island's main town is at the end of the very narrow, deep and aptly named Invisible Bay. When the *Aranui* comes in, it manoeuvres in a space the size of a handkerchief and ties up to the rock face. The **museum** (admission free, donations appreciated) in the town centre has great symbolic value for the heritage-proud Marquesans and displays pestles, *tiki*, sculptures, *pahu* (drums), jewellery and period photos as well as a *ha'e*. The **arboretum**, halfway between Vaipaee and Hane, offers a striking contrast between the wealth of plants and the relative aridity of the island.

Oh No, It's the Nono!

A downside to travel in the Marquesas is the insidious *nono* (sandfly), which can turn an idyllic beach – the *nono*'s favourite haunt – into hell. In his book *In Search of Tusitala* Gavin Bell describes the problem with these creatures: while mosquitoes are 'like flying hypodermic needles, inserting suckers and withdrawing blood with surgical precision, the latter chew and tear at flesh to drink the blood, leaving ragged wounds susceptible to infection'.

Mosquitoes and *nono* are at their most ferocious during the wet season from November to March. You can do a lot to avoid being bitten (they're a good excuse for scuba diving!); see the boxed text 'Avoiding Mosquito Bites' in the Regional Facts for the Visitor chapter.

Around the Island

Each village has a *fare artisanal* (craft centre).

Hane was said to be the first Polynesian settlement in the Marquesas and has a small marine museum. Less than 30 minutes' walk from the village, the **Meiaute archaeological site** is one of 'Ua Huka's major attractions, with *tiki, pae pae* and *me'ae.*

Peaceful **Hokatu** is about 3km east of Hane in a sheltered bay. *Tupapau* (ghosts) are said to haunt **Grotte aux Pas** (Footstep Cave), slightly west of Point Tekeho, between Vaipaee and Haavei Bay. Thousands of *kaveka* (sooty terns) have taken up residence on the *motu* of **Hemeni** and **Teuaua**, near the southwestern point of 'Ua Huka.

'Ua Huka has the Marquesas' most beautiful beaches, albeit with *nono*. Accessible by speedboat or 4WD, **Manihina Beach**, between Vaipaee and the airport, is fringed with fine white sand. **Hatuana Beach** is in the west of the island; there are petroglyphs nearby. **Haavei Beach** is a beautiful inlet that belongs to the Lichtlé family; ask them (they live on the coconut plantation), for permission before plunging in. **Motu Papa**, a popular picnic and snorkelling spot, is just offshore from the airport, between Vaipaee and Hane. A speedboat drops you about 50m offshore and you have to swim ashore.

The little-visited **Vaikivi petroglyphs** site on the Vaikivi Plateau is worth the walk; the well-restored petroglyphs are engraved on a grey stone.

Activities

It's a beautiful three-hour **walk** inland from Vaipaee or Hane to the **Vaikivi petroglyphs**. The path climbs the long face of the ancient volcano caldera. Take a guide (3000 to 5000 CFP), as it's a long way and the trail isn't marked; ask about guides at your *pension.* The coastal route between Haavei and Hokatu offers spectacular views and is worth doing.

The most popular **horse ride** is from Vaipaee to Hane, passing the arboretum, airport and windswept arid plateaus before reaching the cliff road, which plunges towards Hane. A ride typically costs 6000 CFP, with guide (ask at your accommodation).

Places to Stay & Eat

'Ua Huka has a surprising number of guesthouses; all offer half-board, with good food and Marquesan specialities.

Chez Alexis Scallamera (☎ 92 60 19; *Vaipaee; rooms per person 2050 CFP*) is quiet and well kept; guests can use the kitchen. Rates include airport transfers.

Chez Christelle (☎ 92 60 85; *rooms per person 2050 CFP*) has sparkling clean rooms. Rates include airport transfers.

Mana Tupuna Village (☎/fax 92 60 08; *bungalows with half-board 6550 CFP*), at the exit from the village towards Hane, has three local-style bungalows with beautiful views.

Auberge Hitikau (☎ 92 61 74; *rooms per person 2050 CFP*), in Hane, has simple but clean rooms and a very good restaurant.

Chez Maurice & Delphine (☎/fax 92 60 55; *rooms/bungalows per person 2050/3050 CFP*) in Hokatu has excellent rooms and bungalows perched above the edge of town. Maurice is one of the best sculptors on the island.

Auberge Hitikau (*set meal 2000 CFP*) is the only real restaurant.

Getting There & Away

A weekly flight goes between 'Ua Huka and Nuku Hiva (5800 CFP), where it connects with Pape'ete (29,500 CFP). **Air Tahiti** has an office in Vaipaee (☎ 92 60 85).

In Hokatu, **Maurice Rootuehine** (92 60 50) and **Paul Teatiu** (☎ 92 60 88) can take you via speedboat to 'Ua Pou (50,000 CFP) or Nuku Hiva (60,000 CFP). The *Aranui* and the *Taporo IV* serve 'Ua Huka.

Getting Around

A 13km track links Vaipaee to Hokatu via Hane; the stretch from Vaipaee to Hane is surfaced. Haavei is also accessible by the track from Vaipaee. The airport is midway between Vaipaee and Hane. Transfers are usually included in *pension* prices.

The *pension* owners can take you by 4WD to visit the villages (10,000 CFP per day).

'UA POU

pop 2013 • area 125 sq km

'Ua Pou's sharp contours and 12 pointed pinnacles, like obelisks or columns of basalt, are often shrouded by cloud cover. Geologically the youngest in the archipelago, 'Ua Pou was the site of an ancient settlement, estimated to have been established around 150 BC, and fascinating archaeological remains can be seen in the Hakamoui and Hohoi valleys. 'Ua Pou is also noted for its culture and arts.

Most people live in Hakahau. A few villages are nestled in the steep-sided valleys along the east and west coasts.

Baie des Vierges (Bay of Virgins), French Polynesia

Tiki statues, Marquesas Islands, French Polynesia

Traditional dancer, Bora Bora, French Polynesia

Bora Bora, French Polynesia

Huahine, French Polynesia

Rangiroa lagoon, French Polynesia

Tahitian man, French Polynesia

Information

For tourist information contact **Rosita Teiki-tutoua** (☎ *92 53 36*), the head of the tourism committee, or the **tourist office** (☎ *92 54 20*). The **Banque Socredo**, in the *mairie* at Hakahau, changes notes and travellers cheques or does credit-card cash advances. The **post office** is to the west of the bay. **Restaurant-Pension Pukuéé** (☎ *92 50 83; 1500 CFP per load*) does laundry. A small **medical centre** is in the south of Hakahau.

Around the Island

The admirably restored **Tenei pae pae** in the middle of Hakahau is a platform of massive stone blocks supporting a shelter of plant material. The stone-and-timber **Catholic Church** in the south of town displays noteworthy sculptures by local artisans.

In the Hakamoui Valley the **Mataautea archaeological site** includes *pae pae*, bas reliefs and *tiki*. From Hakahau take the road to Hohoi for about 3km, take the left fork descending eastwards towards the ocean and 1km further on, on the right and set back from the track, is a *pae pae*.

Time seems to have stood still in picturesque little **Hohoi** in the southeast of the island, 13km from Hakahau. It has two *pae pae* and a curious pagoda-shaped church. The famous flowering pebbles of Hohoi, pieces of phonolite which have crystallised to form amber-coloured flower shapes, can be found on the beach. The **Hakaohoka Valley archaeological site** stretches back 2km from Hohoi Bay. There's a map of the site on Hohoi's pebbly beach, where you should pay 1000 CFP to the site custodian.

Charming **Hakahetau** in the island's northwest is noted for its red church tower near the waterfront. A 15km track snakes between the bare plateaus of the island's northeast, and along the section between Hakahau and Aneou airport you will see wild horses and goats on either side of the road.

Minute **Hakatao** is the most remote place on the island and is accessible by boat or by the track from Hohoi. **Hakamaii**, with its one street and pretty, bright stone church, is only accessible by boat. The tiny end-of-the-world village of **Haakuti** is at the end of the 22km track from Hakahau.

'Ua Pou has some good beaches (and *nono*). White-sand **Anahoa Beach** is a 25-minute scenic walk east of Hakahau. **Hakanai Bay** is a popular picnic spot; it's known as Plage aux Requins (Shark Beach). The black-sand

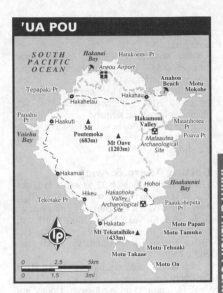

'UA POU

Puamau Beach is popular with young surfers. South of the island, **Motu Oa** is home to thousands of sea birds.

There are many hiking possibilities, including simply following the tracks from one village to another. If you intend to go off-track it's best to take a guide. You can rent horses from **Tony Tereino** (☎ *92 51 68; 6000 CFP per day*) at Pension Leydj in Hakahetau.

Places to Stay & Eat

All places to stay and eat are in Hakahau.

Restaurant-Pension Pukuéé (☎/*fax 92 50 83; singles/doubles 3050/5600 CFP*), on the eastern edge of town, has fine views; its **restaurant** (*meals 2500 CFP*) looks over the seafront and does great Marquesan cuisine.

Pension Vehine (☎ *92 50 63; singles/ doubles 2050/3100 CFP*), 500m from the seafront and around the corner from Air Tahiti, has two functional rooms. For a meal you only have a 20m walk to Snack Vehine.

Chez Dora (☎ *92 53 69; rooms with breakfast per person 3050 CFP*), in the centre, about 1km from the quay, offers half- and full board.

Pension Leydj (☎ *92 51 68; rooms with breakfast/half-board per person 3550/5550 CFP*), near the quay, is the home of sculptor Tony Tereino. The four rooms have shared bathrooms.

Hakahau has a couple of **snack bars** and **shops**. **Snack-Pâtisserie Vaitiare** (☎ *92 50*

TAHITI & FRENCH POLYNESIA

95; dishes 1200 CFP), on the western edge of town, opens daily and serves pastries and light meals.

Chez Rosalie (☎ 92 51 77; *Marquesan meal 2500 CFP*) only opens when the *Aranui* is in port, but is worth trying.

Vehine (☎ 92 53 21; *dishes from 750 CFP, set menu 2000 CFP; open lunch Mon-Sat*) opens for dinner on demand.

In the other villages you can go to a guest-house or make do with a few provisions from the **shops**.

Getting There & Away

The **Air Tahiti office** (☎ 92 53 41) is in Haka-hau, or at Aneou airport (☎ 92 51 08) on flight days. On Wednesday, Thursday and Friday a flight goes to Nuku Hiva (5800 CFP) with connections to Pape'ete (29,800 CFP). Two flights a week go to Atuona via Nuku Hiva (9800 CFP).

Héli Inter Marquises, based in Nuku Hiva, flies between Taiohae and Hakahau (12,500 CFP, 15 minutes) on Wednesday, Friday and Sunday.

The *Aranui* and *Taporo IV* serve 'Ua Pou; the *Aranui* stops at Hakahau and Hakahetau.

Getting Around

On the east coast, a track connects Haka-hau with Hohoi (13km) and continues to Hakatao on the west coast. On the west coast, Hakahau is connected to Hakahetau (15km), Haakuti (22km) and Hakamaii. The track doesn't make a complete circuit. Aneou airport is about 10km west of Hakahau, and if you've booked accommodation your hosts will collect you. Transfers cost about 2000 CFP per person return.

Ask at your *pension* about transport by car. Expect to pay 10,000 CFP to go to Hakamoui and Hohoi, and 15,000 CFP to go to Hakahe-tau and Haakuti.

HIVA OA

pop 1829 • area 320 sq km

Hiva Oa is the most important island in the southern group. The slopes of Mt Temetiu (1276m) and Mt Feani (1126m) form a vast amphitheatre, at the base of which is Atuona, the island's capital. This is where French painter Paul Gauguin and Belgian singer-poet Jacques Brel ended their wanderings. On the northeast coast, Puamau has the most important archaeological remains discovered to date in the Marquesas Islands. A site at Taaoa, in the southeast, is another archaeological treasure.

Information

Most services are in Autuona. In the centre, the **Atuona Tourist Committee** is in the *fare artisanal* (craft centre) behind the museum. The **Banque Socredo**, which changes notes and travellers cheques and allows credit-card withdrawals, is a block east, next to the Air Tahiti office. The **post office** is on the main road next to the *mairie*; the **hospital** (☎ 92 73 75) is behind the *mairie*. Puamau also has a **post office**.

Atuona

This trim, tidy town has the antiquated air of a tropical subprefecture. It is a place of pilgrim-age for fans of Gauguin, who lived here from 1901 to 1903, and Jacques Brel, who was a resident until 1978. At the north of Taaoa Bay, at the mouth of the Vaioa River, the town stretches up the valley for about 1.5km.

To one side of the small, sparse **museum** (☎ 92 75 10; *admission 400 CFP; open 7.30am-11.30am Mon-Fri*) is a faithful, but empty, rep-lica of Gauguin's home, the **Maison du Jouir** (House of Pleasure). Gauguin and Brel are buried in the small **Calvaire Cemetery** which dominates Atuona Bay.

Tohua Pepeu, in the town centre, includes a reconstructed *ha'e* (traditional house). The **Jacques Brel Memorial** is up a rough track near the airport; ask for directions.

It's a pleasant walk into the Faakua Val-ley to see the **Tehueto petroglyphs**, where stylised, horizontal human figures have been carved into an enormous basalt block. Near the village of Taaoa, 7km southwest of At-uona, another site, **Tohua Upeke**, has more than 1000 *pae pae*, some restored.

Around the Island

The village of **Puamau**, a 2½-hour drive east from Atuona, has an elegant seafront with a black-sand beach and is close to the most beautiful archaeological site in the Marquesas. In the village, **Tohua Pehe Kua** is the tomb of the valley's last chief. About 1.5km away, **Iipona** (*admission 200 CFP*) is an exceptional *me'ae* featuring five monumental *tiki*. The site is one of the most important testimonies to precontact Marquesan civilisation.

Tiny **Hanapaaoa** is in an area of wild beauty two hours' drive northeast from Atuona. Walk 15 minutes southeast to the strange **Tiki Moe One** adorned with a carved crown of flowers – you'll probably need a guide to find it.

There are **beaches** at Atuona, Puamau, Hanamenu and Hanatekuua.

HIVA OA, TAHUATA & MOTANE

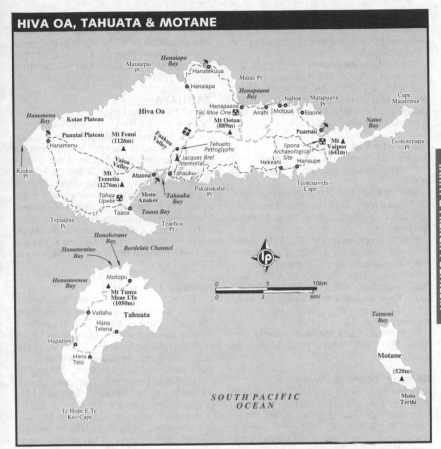

Activities

The 4WD tracks are good for **walking** but don't venture off them without a guide. Around Atuona there's an easy walk to the Tehueto petroglyphs. Ask at your *pension* about **horse riding**, or contact **Maui Ranch Tahauku** (☎ 92 74 92). **Deep-sea fishing** is also available.

Places to Stay

Accommodation is concentrated in Atuona and its surrounding area.

Bungalows Communaux d'Atuona (*at the mairie* ☎ 92 73 32; *bungalows 2550 CFP, 550 CFP per extra person*) has seven fully equipped *fares*. Booking is recommended.

Pension Ozanne (☎/fax 92 73 51; *single/double bungalows 4050/5100 CFP*), in the Atuona hills, has three well-equipped bungalows with superb views.

Pension Gauguin (☎/fax 92 73 51; e gauguin@mail.pf; *singles/doubles with half-board 6550/12,100 CFP*), in the east of Atuona Bay, is elegant, spotless and very popular. The food here is great.

Pension Moehau (☎ 92 72 69, fax 92 77 62; e moehaupension@mail.pf; *half-board per person 9500 CFP*), on a hillside near the outskirts of Atuona going towards Tahauku Bay, has eight modern, functional rooms of a superior standard with views.

Temetiu Village (*Chez Gaby;* ☎ 91 70 60, fax 91 70 61; e heitaagabyfeli@mail.pf; *single/double bungalows 5350/6500 CFP*), 20 minutes' walk from Atuona on the Tahauku Bay side, has six pleasant, well-designed bungalows with bathroom and is popular.

Hanakéé Pearl Lodge (☎ 92 75 87, fax 92 75 95; e hiva.oa.pearl@mail.pf; *1-2-person* bungalows 29,050-35,4150 CFP), perched on the hillside in Tahauku Bay, is the only luxury accommodation. It has air-con bungalows and a swimming pool.

Chez Marie-Antoinette (☎ 92 72 27; rooms with half-/full board per person 5800/ 7050 CFP), in Puamau, has two bare but clean double rooms with shared bathroom. An archaeological site with several *tiki* and tombs is on the guesthouse land.

Places to Eat

Atuona and Puamau have **food shops**, and **roulottes** sometimes appear near Tohua Pepeu in Atuona.

Snack Kaupe (☎ 92 70 62; dishes from 1000 CFP; closed Mon), in the centre of Atuona, offers lunch of pizza, fish or some Réunion specialties.

Hoa Nui restaurant (☎ 92 73 63; meals 2500 CFP) specialises in Marquesan cuisine and puts on a feast when the *Aranui* is in port. **Temetiu Village** (meals 2600 CFP) offers Marquesan meals with a view of Tahauku and Taaoa Bays. **Hanakéé Pearl Lodge** (set menu 2000 CFP), overlooking Tahauku Bay, is tasty but more expensive.

In Puamau, **Chez Marie-Antoinette** (set menu 2000 CFP) offers good Marquesan lunches.

Getting There & Away

Air Tahiti (in Atuona ☎ 92 73 41, at the airport ☎ 92 72 31) has connections to Pape'ete, Nuku Hiva and 'Ua Pou. Pape'ete–Nuku Hiva–Atuona flights (28,800 CFP) go five to six times a week. Five flights a week go to Nuku Hiva (9800 CFP). There are one or two Atuona–'Ua Pou–Atuona flights a week (9800 CFP) and one 'Ua Huka–Atuona–'Ua Huka flight per week (9800 CFP).

The *Aranui* and *Taporo IV* stop at Hiva Oa. **Ozanne Rohi** and **Médéric Kaimuko** (☎ 92 74 48) charter *bonitiers* for 15,000 CFP to Motopu (Tahuata), and 55,000 CFP to Fatu Hiva. The communal *bonitier* connects Fatu Hiva with Atuona (4000 CFP) once a week, usually on Monday.

Getting Around

The airport is 13km from Atuona. If you have booked accommodation your host will collect you. It's also possible to hitch a ride.

Excursions by 4WD cost 10,000 CFP to Taaoa; 12,000 CFP to Hanaiapa; between 15,000 and 20,000 CFP to Hanapaaoa; and 15,000 to 21,000 CFP to Puamau. Contact the

pension owners or **Ida Clark** (☎ 92 71 33). In Puamau, ask for **Étienne Heitaa** (☎ 92 75 28). **David Location** (☎ 92 72 87), in a small street a stone's throw from the Chanson, Ah You and Naiki shops, has a Suzuki you can drive yourself (12,000 CFP a day).

TAHUATA

pop 637 • area 70 sq km

Separated from Hiva Oa by the 4km-wide Bordelais Channel, Tahuata is the smallest inhabited island in the archipelago. Oriented along a north–south ridgeline, it has numerous inlets, two of which shelter the island's main villages, Hapatoni and Vaitahu. Tahuata's high-quality arts and crafts are a major contributor to the island economy; the dreamlike scenery is another great reason to visit.

For tourist information, contact the Vaitahu **mairie** (☎ 92 92 19) on the seafront. There is no bank. The **post office** and **infirmary** are in Vaitahu.

Around the Island

On the hill that dominates tiny **Vaitahu** village are a few remains of the **French Fort**. The seafront stone **Catholic church** includes a wooden statue which is a masterpiece of modern Marquesan art. A small Polynesian art and history **museum** is in the *mairie*. Copra-drying sheds are dotted here and there, and brightly coloured traditional *vaka* (outrigger canoes) are lined up on the shore. Some top-rate Marquesan sculptors work in Vaitahu.

Hapatoni curves around a wide bay several kilometres south of Vaitahu by boat (15 minutes) or bridleway. It has a 19th-century royal road and a magnificent **me'ae**.

Motopu, to the north, has a few dozen inhabitants and is accessible by 4WD by the track that crosses the island's interior.

Hanamoenoa Bay is a favourite anchorage for yachts between March and August.

The 17km track that joins Vaitahu and Motopu is ideal for **horse riding**; ask the locals about hiring horses.

Places to Stay & Eat

Pension Amatea (☎ 92 92 84; rooms per person 3550 CFP), in Vaitahu, has five rooms (shared bathroom) and offers half-board.

Every village has one or two small **shops**.

Getting There & Away

Tahuata doesn't have a landing strip. The **Te Pua O Mioi** (☎ 92 92 19) communal *bonitier* runs a Vaitahu–Atuona–Vaitahu ferry service on Tuesday and Thursday (1000 CFP per passenger return, one hour).

In Vaitahu **Yves-Bertrand Barsinas** (☎ 92 92 40) and **Louis Timau** (☎ 92 92 71) have *bonitiers* (20,000 to 25,000 CFP to Vaitahu or Hapatoni to Atuona). For Atuona see Getting There & Away under Hiva Oa.

The *Aranui* and *Taporo IV* serve Tahuata.

Getting Around

A 17km 4WD track crosses the island's interior to link Vaitahu with Motopu. It costs 15,000 CFP for one day's 4WD hire with driver.

Hapatoni is less than 15 minutes from Vaitahu by speedboat. It costs about 6000 CFP to hire a boat between Vaitahu and Hapatoni return, and 7000 to 10,000 CFP between Vaitahu and Hanahevane.

FATU HIVA

pop 631 • area 80 sq km

Fatu Hiva is the island of superlatives: the most remote, the farthest south, the wettest, the lushest and the most traditional. It was also the first island in the archipelago to be seen by the Spanish navigator Mendaña, on 21 July 1595.

About 75km south of Hiva Oa, Fatu Hiva consists of two craters forming arcs open to the west. Between the flanks of the calderas are two valleys in which nestle the island's only villages: Hanavave in the north and Omoa in the south. The phallic protuberances of Hanavave Bay caused it to be named Baie des Verges (Bay of Penises). Outraged, the missionaries hastened to add a redeeming 'i' to make it Baie des Vierges (Bay of Virgins).

Fatu Hiva prides itself on its top-quality art and crafts (it's the only island in French Polynesia where tapa is still made using ancestral methods). With no landing strip and with only occasional *bonitier* services, Fatu Hiva's gentle atmosphere of untouched paradise remains intact.

There is a **post office** in Omoa and an **infirmary** or **first-aid post** in both villages. There is no bank.

Around the Island

The red-roofed, white church with its slender spire dominates **Omoa**. Ask someone to take you to the giant **petroglyph** at the edge of the village: it's an enormous fish carved on a block of rock.

Hanavave is on the seashore, at the mouth of a steep-sided valley leading onto the **Baie des Vierges**, a favourite of passing yachties.

You can walk (four hours) or ride to the bay from Omoa along the island's only track. It's not particularly difficult except for the climb to the pass separating the two valleys.

Places to Stay & Eat

All *pensions* are in Omoa.

Pension Heimata (☎ 92 80 58; half-/full board per person 4050/5550 CFP) has two well-kept rooms with shared bathroom.

Chez Norma (☎ 92 80 13; doubles with half-/full board per person 3550/5050 CFP), near the beach, has six double rooms with shared bathroom.

Chez Lionel Cantois (☎/fax 92 80 80; bungalows singles/doubles 3050/5100) is the last house in the village, beside the river and in the middle of a beautiful tropical garden; it offers half-board.

Apart from the *pensions*, eating options are limited to a few small **grocers' shops**.

Getting There & Away

Fatu Hiva is the most difficult island to get to in the entire archipelago. Theoretically a communal *bonitier* goes between Omoa and Atuona on Tuesday (4000 CFP per trip). If it's not running you're left with the *Aranui* and the *Taporo IV* or a chartered private *bonitier*.

Getting Around

A 17km road links Hanavave with Omoa. It's impassable in wet weather, so journeys are often undertaken by motorised pirogue. Ask at your accommodation for advice on renting a 4WD (10,000 CFP a day with driver). Traditional outrigger canoes go between Omoa and Hanavave (5000 to 6000 CFP).

Austral Islands

Quite different in appearance and climate from the Society Islands, the spartan, scattered islands of the Austral group are an extension of the range of submerged peaks making up the southern Cook Islands. This 1300km chain includes five inhabited and two uninhabited islands, with a population of just over 6000. It's worth the effort of getting here to see humpback whales (in season) on Rurutu; to go hiking and explore ancient *marae*, hilltop fortresses and caverns; and for the chance to visit French Polynesia's most remote island. And, with the new airport on Raivavae, you can now visit one of the South Pacific's most precious gems; go before everyone else does.

TAHITI & FRENCH POLYNESIA

AUSTRAL ISLANDS

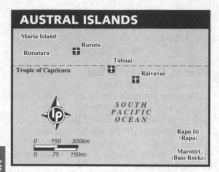

History

The Australs were the last in French Polynesia to be settled; it's believed the first arrivals came from Tahiti between 1000 and 1300 AD. James Cook was the first European visitor, sighting Rururu in 1769, but it was not until 1811 that the whole chain had been 'discovered'. The French did not take over the last of the Australs until 1901.

Getting There & Away

Air Tahiti flies to Rururu and Tubuai about four times weekly in low season, and five days weekly in high season. One flight travels Tahiti–Rururu–Tubuai–Tahiti, the other goes Tahiti-Tubuai-Rururu-Tahiti. A one-way Tahiti to Rururu fare costs 18,100 CFP; Tahiti to Tubuai, 20,200 CFP; and Rururu to Tubuai, 9300 CFP. **Air Tahiti** has offices at the airports on Rururu (☎ 94 03 57) and Tubuai (☎ 94 03 57).

The *Tuhaa Pae II* stops in the Australs.

RURURU

pop 2015 • area 36 sq km

Rururu has a high plateau, coastal limestone caverns and ancient *marae*. A continuous reef is rarely more than a stone's throw from the shoreline, so there's no lagoon as such. There are some good beaches, particularly south of Arei Point and at the southern end of the island. A network of minor tracks winds into the island's dense patchwork of plantations and ascend to the highpoint, Mt Taatioe (389m). Rururu's dance troupe regularly wins inter-island dance competitions. This is also the centre for stone-lifting competitions; the men's stone weighs a back-breaking 130kg.

Orientation & Information

Of the three main villages, Moerai is the largest. It is 4km south of the airport and has the cargo-ship dock, a **post office** with an

Internet connection (220 CFP for 15 minutes), a **Banque Socredo** and a few small **shops**. About one third of the scenic 36km road around the island is sealed.

Things to See & Do

Moerai has a picturesque little **Protestant church** dating from between 1865 and 1872. French Administrator Éric de Bisschop, the island's most famous resident, who dedicated himself to perilous voyages in unsuitable craft, is remembered by a simple **gravestone** in the cemetery.

Migrating whales come close to shore between July and October. Watch from the roadside observation platforms or swim with the whales on a diving trip with the **Raie Manta Club** (☎ 96 84 80; half-day per person 10,000 CFP).

Drive or cycle (it's *very* hilly) around the island to see many signs that Rururu began life as an upthrust reef. Going clockwise, pass the whale-watching tower near **Arei Point**, which has one of Rururu's impressive elevated reef cliffs then climbs inland and drop back to the coast at the village of **Hauti**. The road then runs along what was once the ancient lagoon bottom; the range of hills to the west is the

RURURU

old barrier reef. Near **Toataratara Point**, the southern tip of the island, are some lovely **beaches** and the small **Poreopi Marae**.

After climbing north then dropping into pretty **Avera** village the road passes the remnants of once-extensive **Marae Vitaria**. About 1km later, the huge **Ana Aeo Cave** has abundant stalactites and stalagmites. The road passes **Are Taofe**, a coffee house where you can taste and buy the local distinctive coffee. A **whale-watching tower** is on the outskirts of Moerai.

The gentle slopes of the island interior are perfect for **walking**; it's easy to climb the three highest peaks, Taatioe (389m), Manureva (385m) and Teape (359m).

Places to Stay & Eat
All of the accommodation places listed here provide free airport transfers and have options for half- and full board.

Friendly **Pension Ariana** (☎ 94 06 69; singles/doubles 4050/5100 CFP, single/double bungalows 4550/5600 CFP) has two rooms with shared bathroom and several simple, colourful bungalows with private bathroom.

Pension Temarama (☎/fax 94 02 17; e pensiontemarama@mail.pf; singles/doubles 3550/4600 CFP) offers spotless rooms, a warm welcome and good food.

Pension Teautamatea (☎/fax 94 02 42; e pension.teautamatea@free.fr; singles/doubles 4550/6600 CFP) is excellent, with clean rooms and an enchanting setting. Room rates include breakfast.

Manôtel (☎/fax 94 06 99; e manotel@mail.pf; 1-2-person bungalows 6100 CFP) has four new, clean, well-designed bungalows, with bathroom, close to the sea.

Getting Around
Most pensions offer 4WD island tours for about 4000 to 4500 CFP per person, and have bicycles for hire. Pension Temarama also hires out cars (a whopping 11,000 CFP per day) and scooters.

RAIVAVAE
pop 1049 • area 16 sq km
Proclaimed as one of the most beautiful islands in the Pacific, Raivavae is encircled by a motu-dotted reef. The new airport, built in 2002, is certain to mean tourism will take off here. Rairua is the site of the island's main shipping quay but Mahanatoa is the largest village.

At the time of contact with Europeans, Raivavae had a population of around 3000

people with a reputation as excellent seafarers (regularly visiting the Society Islands). In 1826 the same European fever that devastated Tubuai reduced the population to just over 100.

Tranquil Raivavae will attract visitors looking for a beautiful, different holiday destination. The island was once noted for the many massive stone *tiki*. The one 2m-high **tiki** remaining emanates great *mana* (supernatural power); it's at the site of the principal *marae*, near Rairua, while its relations stand in the gardens of the Gauguin Museum on Tahiti. At the other end of the island is **Marae Maunauto**.

Pension Ataha (☎ 95 43 69; 3050 CFP per person), by the sea at Rairua, has two rooms with shared bathroom, while **Pension Rau'uru** (☎ 95 42 88; singles/doubles 2550/4100 CFP), in Mahanatoa, is an equipped house with bathroom; both offer half- and full board.

Tuhaa Pae II sails by about twice a month.

OTHER AUSTRALS
Tubuai (population 2049), the largest of the Austral Islands, and the administration centre, doesn't have much to see. It has an airport, a bank and *pensions*.

The other Austral isles are accessible only by sea. At the far northwest of the chain, uninhabited **Maria Island** has abundant birdlife, while at the other end **Marotiri**, also known as Bass Rocks, are nine uninhabited rocky spires. Tiny **Rimatara** is the most densely populated island. **Rapa Iti** (Rapa) is the most remote and isolated island in French Polynesia.

Gambier Archipelago

pop 1087 • area 27 sq km
The most remote of the French Polynesian island groups, the Gambier Archipelago lies at the extreme southeast end of the long arc of the Tuamotus. Unlike the Tuamotu atolls, these are high islands and *motu* within an encircling reef. Mangareva (Floating Mountain), the largest within the group, is the only populated island.

History
The Gambier Archipelago was populated in three waves between the 10th and 13th centuries. A Catholic mission established on Mangareva in 1834 quickly converted the population. Over the next 40 years Father Honoré Laval and his assistant François Caret

TAHITI & FRENCH POLYNESIA

GAMBIER ARCHIPELAGO

SOUTH
PACIFIC
OCEAN

Maison Nucléaire
(Fallout Shelter)   Totegegie

Mangareva
          Rikitea   Tarauru Roa
Taravai   Rouru
                 Convent
                         Aukena

Agakauitai   Akamaru

          Makaroa
                    Manui
          Kamaka

0   5   10km
0   3   6mi   To Temoe
                       (50km)

It can accommodate 1200 people – several times today's population! Built on the site of Mangareva's greatest *marae*, the cathedral has twin blue-trimmed towers and an altar decorated with mother-of-pearl.

Other Laval constructions include the coastal **watchtowers and turret**, all that remain of the 'palace' he built for the island's last king. **Rouru Convent** once housed 60 Mangarevan nuns, although it's said Laval would hide every woman on the island in the convent whenever a whaling ship docked. An overgrown path leads uphill to the convent, passing a hollowed-out rock pool known as the **Queen's Bath**.

On the north coast is the rusting ruin of the **maison nucléaire**, a fallout shelter from the 1966–74 atmospheric testing period at Moruroa, 400km away. Islanders were squeezed into this windowless tomb for up to three days at a time; it's no wonder '*faaore te atomi*', 'no nuclear testing', is painted on Mangarevan walls.

Places to Stay & Eat

Chez Pierre & Mariette (☎ 97 82 87; *rooms with half-/full board per person 6550/8050 CFP*), 100m from the docks in Rikitea, has three rooms, a cold-water bathroom and kitchen.

Chez Bianca & Benoît (☎/fax 97 83 76; *half-/full board per person 6650/9400 CFP*), 1km from the quay, offers fine views across the bay to Aukena. Its three rooms share a hot-water bathroom.

Chez Jojo (☎/fax 97 82 61; *half-/full board 7900/8000 CFP*) is by the water, 5km from the quay. Its three rooms share a hot-water bathroom.

The village has some modest **food shops**.

Getting There & Away

Air Tahiti flies from Tahiti to Mangareva, sometimes via Hao once a week (55,600 CFP return, three hours 40 minutes).

The *Nuku Hau* and *Taporo V* sail via the eastern Tuamotus to the Gambier Archipelago about every three weeks.

Getting Around

The airport is on the largest *motu*, Totegegie, on the northeastern side of the lagoon. Local boats meet every flight; the journey takes 45 minutes.

The *pension* owners can organise island and boat tours. Mangareva has a few walking tracks.

transformed the islands, obsessively building wide roads, a massive cathedral, nine churches and chapels, monuments, lookout towers, wharves and a prison. The population of up to 6000 plummeted to below 500 within five decades. Laval and Caret's attempt to take Catholicism to the strongly Protestant Tahiti led to their being booted out of Pape'ete, a political act that triggered France's takeover of Tahiti.

Although France established a protectorate over the archipelago in 1844, it continued as a semi-independent entity until being annexed in 1881.

Orientation & Information

The wide lagoon is protected by a 90km coral barrier; 25 *motu* are dotted along its northern edge and three passes lead into the lagoon. Ten volcanic high islands are scattered in the lagoon but all but a handful of people live on Mangareva, the largest island.

The islands have a relatively mild climate and in winter it can actually get cool. The Gambier Islands are one hour ahead of Tahiti. Rikitea, the town on Mangareva, has **shops** and a **post office**.

Things to See & Do

At the upper part of Rikitea, on the slopes of Mt Duff (441m), the **Cathedral of St Michael**, built between 1839 and 1848, is the ultimate symbol of Laval's single-minded obsession.

Tokelau

The three small atolls of Tokelau (the name is a Polynesian word for the north wind) lie in a rough line 480km north of their nearest neighbour, Samoa. The three atolls are separated not only from the rest of the world but from each other; it is 92km between Nukunonu and Atafu, and 64km between Nukunonu and Fakaofo.

Each of the atolls is a ribbon of tiny *motu* (islands) surrounding a lagoon. Tokelau's people, about 500 per atoll, crowd into one small village perched on the main *motu* of each atoll – although Fakaofo Atoll has a smaller cluster of homes on a second island. These three atolls house a small population of hardy souls living what amounts to a subsistence lifestyle.

Facts about Tokelau

HISTORY
The atolls of Tokelau have been populated by Polynesians for about 1000 years. Traditional tales link the original settlers with Samoa, the Cook Islands and Tuvalu.

There was no 'Tokelau' until a series of wars in the 18th century united these previously fiercely independent atolls. At the end of the wars, Fakaofo had conquered Atafu and Nukunonu, bringing them under the rule of the god Tui Tokelau and creating the first united entity of Tokelau.

Soon afterwards, Tokelau came to the attention of those sailing by on various English and US ships. Whalers frequented the group in the 1820s, and in the middle of the 19th century missionary groups started paying attention to the spiritual wellbeing of the Tokelauans. First Catholic, then Protestant, Samoan missionaries converted the people of the three atolls to Christianity from the 1840s to the 1860s.

Conversion was a mixed blessing. The French missionary Pierre Bataillon transported 500 reluctant Tokelauans to Wallis Island in the 1850s because he feared they would otherwise die of starvation. Then Peruvian slave traders seized about 250 of the atolls' population in the 1860s. Together, missionaries, slaving and disease reduced Tokelau's population from about 1000 to only 200. Desperate to save the remaining people, Tokelauans pleaded with the UK for protection as a British

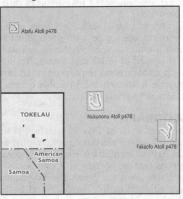

Atafu Atoll p478

TOKELAU

Nukunonu Atoll p478

Fakaofo Atoll p478

American Samoa

Samoa

Highlights
- **Tokelau** – just getting to Tokelau is a major achievement; the voyage by cargo ship from Samoa will be an adventure in itself

- **Kilikiti** – attending a match of this famous Polynesian game, a variation of cricket, will blow your mind (choose your side carefully)

- **Culture** – because of its isolation, Tokelauan society remains strong and intact; this is Polynesian culture at its most untouched

TOKELAU

colony, and was annexed into the Gilbert & Ellice Islands Colony (see History in the Tuvalu chapter) in 1889.

Emigration continued: in the early 20th century, large numbers of Tokelauans left their homes to work the phosphate mines of Banaba (Ocean Island) in the Gilbert & Ellice Islands. After New Zealand (NZ) took over responsibility for Tokelau in 1925, the

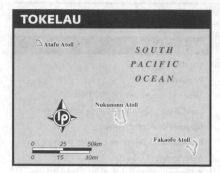

TOKELAU

Atafu Atoll

SOUTH PACIFIC OCEAN

Nukunonu Atoll

Fakaofo Atoll

0 ... 25 ... 50km
0 ... 15 ... 30mi

flow of emigration shifted to Western Samoa (then also a NZ territory). Samoa's independence in 1962 prompted Tokelauans to shift to NZ instead.

In recent years Tokelau has been moving towards independence, with government and administration increasingly based in Tokelau itself instead of in NZ and Samoa. To make this possible, recent improvements in infrastructure have included a reliable telephone system and an inter-atoll ferry.

GEOGRAPHY
The three atolls of Tokelau (Atafu, Fakaofo and Nukunonu) are classic coral atolls: thin necklaces of small islets surrounding central lagoons (see the boxed text 'Coral Atolls' in the Facts about the South Pacific chapter). Like all coral atolls, Tokelau's soil is thin, infertile and holds water poorly.

The low-lying islands have a maximum elevation of only 5m above sea level, and the land area is tiny: only 12.2 sq km over all of the three atolls. No islets are more than 200m wide.

CLIMATE
Tokelau's climate is tropical, with an average temperature of 28°C (82.4°F) and heavy but irregular rainfall. Tokelau is at the northern

The End?
Consisting only of low-lying coral atolls, Tokelau faces great risk from global warming. It is predicted that all three atolls will be uninhabitable by the end of the 21st century, and Tokelau's thousand-year-long history will be finished. See the boxed text 'Global Warming' in the Facts about the South Pacific chapter.

limit of the South Pacific cyclone zone, so tropical storms are rare. However, cyclones have caused extensive damage. See the Tokelau climate chart in the appendix of this book.

GOVERNMENT
The local government of Tokelau is composed of the three village councils – one on each atoll – called the *taupulega*, comprising the *matai* (male heads) of each family group. Each atoll elects a *pulenuku* (village mayor) as well as one *faipule* (atoll representative). A number of delegates from each atoll serve with the *pulenuku* and the *faipule* on Tokelau's legislative council, the General Fono. The three *faipule* form the cabinet, and one of their number becomes Tokelau's *Ulu o Tokelau* (head of government) on a rotating basis.

Tokelau is a non-selfgoverning territory under NZ administration. The United Nations (UN) has long been pushing the Tokelauans towards full independence; however, with substantial financial assistance, easy access to NZ schools and free emigration to relieve the pressure of overcrowding, many Tokelauans prefer their current status. Negotiations with NZ and the UN continue towards increasing autonomy.

ECONOMY
Foreign aid from NZ forms the bulk of Tokelau's economy: NZ$4 million per year, or NZ$2700 per head, which swamps the gross domestic product of NZ$1.2 million. Exports are minimal: stamps, coins and some handicrafts bring in a meagre income. Revenue is also raised by selling licences to fish in Tokelau's Exclusive Economic Zone (EEZ). Tokelau's isolation adds to the country's financial woes – telecommunications and transport cost 25% of the yearly budget. All medical supplies, equipment and many foodstuffs are imported.

The public service is the main source of regular income for Tokelauans; these jobs are rotated among villagers and a village tax is imposed on wages. The other major source of income is from the *aumaga*, or village workforce (see Society & Conduct). Payment for *aumaga* work, which was traditionally unpaid, provides an income for young Tokelauans who would otherwise have to look overseas for work. Remittances from Tokelauan relatives living overseas is another source of income.

TOKELAU

Population & Area

atoll	pop	land	lagoon
Atafu	588	3.5 sq km	17 sq km
Fakaofo	479	4.0 sq km	50 sq km
Nukunonu	361	4.7 sq km	98 sq km

POPULATION & PEOPLE

There are approximately 500 people on each of Tokelau's three atolls. Tokelauans are Polynesian, closely related to Tuvaluans, Samoans and Cook Islanders. A liberal sprinkling of European surnames in the islands is the legacy of some enthusiastic whalers and beachcombers of the late 19th century.

Land shortages have long forced emigrations from Tokelau, and many now live in Samoa and NZ. In fact there are almost 5000 Tokelauans in NZ – three times as many as in Tokelau itself!

EDUCATION

Three schools (one on each atoll) provide primary and secondary education, and many youngsters receive government scholarships to study in NZ, Fiji, Samoa, Tonga or Niue. Adult-education programs are conducted to improve awareness of health, environmental and dietary issues.

SOCIETY

Tokelau's isolation from the rest of the world, as well as NZ's 'hands-off' approach to its administration, has resulted in *faka Tokelau* (the Tokelauan way) being preserved to a far greater degree than indigenous culture has been elsewhere in the Pacific. However, the large numbers of Tokelauans living abroad has resulted in an ever-increasing awareness of the benefits of modern *palagi* (Western) culture among the Tokelauan people – whether perceived or real.

Partly because of the difficulty of travel between the atolls, Tokelau society is still compartmentalised into the three atolls and their single village. The one name describes both the atoll and the village: for example, Atafu Atoll/Atafu village. *Maopoopo* (village unity) is paramount in Tokelau. Beyond that, each village is divided into two *faitu* – or sides – on a roughly territorial basis. The two sides compete enthusiastically in fishing, action songs, dancing, sports and, most importantly, in *kilikiti* (see Spectator Sports later in this chapter). Each *kau kaiga* (family group) is led by the *matai*.

The elderly are awarded enormous respect in Tokelau, with the three *taupulega* (village councils of elders and *matai*) ordering daily life. Elders are still expected to contribute to the community; both through attendance at the *taupulega* and by encouraging the younger workers at their tasks.

Each village *taupulega* administers the *aumaga* (workforce), which gathers fish, harvests crops and maintains village buildings. Almost all males over school age, except for public servants, join the *aumaga*. The female equivalent is the *komiti a fafine* (women's committee), whose responsibilities include inspections to ensure village cleanliness and health.

Under Tokelau's almost-socialist system of *inati* (sharing), resources are divided between families according to need. *Inati* still operates – each day the village's catch of fish is laid out on the beach and apportioned by the *taupulega* – but it is under increasing pressure from the cash economy. Steps have been taken to ensure that employed Tokelauans, mainly public servants, do not receive unfair benefits though this principle of sharing.

The *inati* system developed over the centuries out of necessity: in an environment where resources are so scarce, community cooperation is extremely vital. Individualism is not a virtue in these circumstances, nor is it really an option.

And neither is privacy – Tokelau's islands are cramped beyond belief, even with emigration to NZ relieving some of the population pressure. On Fakaofo Atoll, there are still some 400 people living on tiny (4-hectare) Fale Island. In fact, Fale's population density, one of the highest in the Pacific, is such that the island's numerous *puaka* (domestic pigs) are 'squeezed out' to live on the beach and reef rather than on land.

There are only nine police officers in all of Tokelau, and no imprisonment system. In Tokelau's closely knit society, punishment takes the form of public rebukes, fines or labour.

RELIGION

Prior to the arrival of Christianity, Tokelauans worshipped a god called Tui Tokelau – personified in a slab of coral that's still standing in Fakaofo's village. The usual pantheon of Polynesian gods was acknowledged here, too.

Tokelau's modern religious distribution reflects the arrival of Samoan missionaries of different denominations during the 19th

TOKELAU

century: Atafu is almost completely Protestant, Nukunonu is largely Catholic, and Fakaofo, where Catholic and Protestant missionaries arrived almost simultaneously, is split between the two faiths. Even on Fakaofo, though, inter-denominational tension is all but unknown, as it would run contrary to the supreme concept of *maopoopo*.

LANGUAGE

Tokelauan is a Polynesian language, closely related to Tuvaluan and Samoan. Because of frequent contact with NZ, most Tokelauans speak some English – and some 3000 New Zealanders speak Tokelauan.

Tokelauan pronunciation is similar to other Polynesian languages, except that 'f' is pronounced as a soft 'wh', and 'g' is pronounced 'ng' (a soft sound) as in Samoan.

Tokelauan Basics

Hello.	*Malo ni* or *taloha*.
Goodbye.	*Tofaa*.
How are you?	*Ea mai koe?*
I'm well.	*Ko au e lelei*.
Please.	*Faka molemole*.
Thank you.	*Faka fetai*.
Yes.	*Io*.
No.	*Heai*.

The Tokelauan Fale

The traditional Tokelauan *fale* (house) has all but disappeared. Following damage from cyclones Ofa and Val, new housing was built with sturdy concrete in the hope that modern materials would withstand future cyclones more successfully than the traditional coral pebbles and wood. With rain run-off from roofs being the major source of fresh drinking water, pandanus-leaf-thatching have given way to corrugated iron as a roofing material.

More traditional Atafu still has a number of traditional *fale*, partly because that atoll has a better supply of the excellent building wood, *kanava*.

The largest and most ornate building on each atoll is the church, or three churches in Fakaofo's case. Other community focal points are the village cricket pitch and the *fale fono* (village hall). Tokelau's three *fale fono* are radically different from each other, ranging from Fakaofo's traditional open-sided *fale* to Nukunonu's pragmatic cargo shed.

Facts for the Visitor

PLANNING

The best months to travel to Tokelau are from April to October. Between November and January ships are usually full of scholarship students and other Tokelauans living abroad, returning to spend Christmas with their families. December to March is cyclone season, when the trip from Samoa could be rough.

Visitor Permits

The **Tokelau Apia Liaison Office** *(TALO;* ☎ *685-20822, 71805, fax 21761;* e *zak-p@lesamoa.net; PO Box 865, Apia)*, in Samoa, issues visitor permits. Accommodation must be arranged prior to departure (either at a hotel or with a local family) and a return ticket to Samoa must be booked. Also, consent must be given by the village *taupulega*. A visitor permit for a one-month stay in Tokelau costs NZ$20.

MONEY

Tokelauan coinage is largely aimed at the collector market. The NZ dollar (see Exchange Rates in the Rarotonga & the Cook Islands chapter) and the Samoan tala (see the Samoa chapter) are used instead. There are no banks in Tokelau.

COMMUNICATIONS

As part of the improved infrastructure necessary for independence, Tokelau was connected with the international phone system in 1994. The telephone code is ☎ 690.

DIGITAL RESOURCES

Apart from Lonely Planet's own Tokelau profile (w www.lonelyplanet.com/destinations /pacific/tokelau/) the most useful Tokelau website is **The Modern House of Tokelau** (w *www.tokelau.org.nz).*

BOOKS

Judith Huntsman and Antony Hooper's enormous *Tokelau – A Historical Ethnography* is *the* definitive text about Tokelau, telling you all you ever wanted to know about Tokelau and its people. With Allan Thomas and Ineleo Tuia, Huntsman has also compiled an interesting collection of tales called *Songs and Stories of Tokelau – An Introduction to the Cultural Heritage*. More easily found than either of these books is Neville Peat's short *Tokelau – Atoll Associate of New Zealand*.

Tokelau Telephones

While septic tanks are becoming more common in Tokelau, most people still make use of small huts perched above the lagoon. Such huts serve more than one purpose; they are a common meeting venue, and several men (or women) will gather in the one hut to swap gossip and discuss the busy day's events. This is why they're called 'Tokelau telephones'.

The Tokelau telephones have an obvious drawback. The atolls' lagoons are already under ecological pressure: garbage disposal directly into the lagoon is common (despite education programs encouraging composting and recycling) and the toilet huts add to this waste. Tokelau's telephones will eventually be phased out, their two functions replaced by sewerage tanks and modern telecommunications.

HEALTH

There is a hospital on each atoll, but a fact of life for Tokelauans is that any serious health problems out here can easily become life threatening – medical supplies are difficult to come by and specialist care is days away in Apia.

SOCIAL GRACES

Tokelau is a staunchly Christian country – the percentage of the population that does not belong to one of the two main churches is tiny – so criticising Christianity will not win you any friends among Tokelauans. Sunday is devoted almost entirely to church activities, with some time off for a large meal and a midday snooze. If you attend church yourself, you'll be better accepted by the community – and it will give you something to do on Sunday. Work and many activities are forbidden on Atafu and Fakaofo on Sunday; Nukunonu is less strict.

A conservative dress code is appropriate in all of the villages. Wearing bikinis or other skimpy swimwear is considered rude and should be reserved for the outer islets only.

Resources are scarce in Tokelau, so don't help yourself to things like coconuts. Tokelauan society is very similar to that of Samoa; see the Society and Social Graces sections in that chapter for more pointers.

USEFUL ORGANISATIONS

In Samoa, the **Tokelau Apia Liaison Office** (TALO; ☎ 685-20822, 71805, fax 21761; e zak-p@lesamoa.net; PO Box 865, Apia) should be the first port of call for all inquiries. It handles bookings on the monthly cargo ship (see Getting There & Away later in this chapter) and visitor permits.

In NZ, the **Tokelau Office** (☎ 64-4-494 8514, fax 494 8521, e talia.pereira@mfat.govt .nz; Private Bag 18-901, Wellington) is at the Ministry of Foreign Affairs & Trade.

ACTIVITIES

Diving inside the atolls' lagoons is fantastic. There is almost nothing in the way of search and rescue facilities though, so diving outside the reef should be undertaken with maximum caution. Talk to the locals to find out where the safest diving spots can be found. The nearest decompression chamber is so far away (Fiji) that it might as well be on Mars.

Ask the local men whether you can accompany them on fishing trips, but be aware that they are working and won't always be able to accommodate your wishes.

ACCOMMODATION

All accommodation must be arranged before travelling to Tokelau. Contact TALO in Samoa for help. There are a limited number of official places to stay in Tokelau. You may be able to arrange accommodation in a private home but it won't be easy without contacts on the appropriate atoll.

Nukunonu Atoll is a relative goldmine of options, with two places to stay. **Luana Liki Hotel** (☎ 4140), managed by Hete Perez, is a family-run hotel with six rooms for guests. **Fale Fa Resort** (☎ 4139) is run by the Nukunonu village. Inquiries should be directed to Iosefa Aselemo, the village clerk.

Meanwhile, on Atafu Atoll, master fisherman Feleti Lopa runs a small **accommodation house** (☎ 2146, fax 2108). There are no organised accommodation options on Fakaofo Atoll but speak to the people at TALO if, for some reason, you are dying to stay on Fakaofo.

Confirm the rates with TALO in Apia. Despite the optimistic names, these are not flash tourist resorts. Facilities are basic – all that is provided is a bed, meals and a bar.

Only one island (or two in the case of Fakaofo) is occupied at each atoll. Some of the more remote islets are quiet retreats where, if you have a tent, the days can be passed camping out or just sitting under the

ATAFU ATOLL

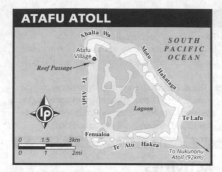

trees contemplating life. This is an option you could consider if claustrophobic village life is getting you down. Note that every single island in Tokelau, big or small, is owned by either a family or a village, and it's important to get permission to visit.

FOOD
The traditional method of cooking in Tokelau, most popular on Fakaofo, is the *umu* (earth oven), which will be familiar to anyone who has spent some time in the Pacific. Most households, however, cook on kerosene stoves. The traditional diet of fish, *kumala* (sweet potato), breadfruit, taro, pigs and fowl is supplemented by processed foods brought in on the monthly cargo ship to the village-owned co-op stores. Canned meat, which will also be familiar to any Pacific traveller, is in plentiful supply.

If you're staying with one of the establishments listed above, or with a local family, your food needs will be looked after. Processed food (and other supplies) can be bought from the small co-op stores on each atoll. Supplies of fresh fish, vegetables and drinking coconuts should be negotiated with someone from the *taupulega*.

DRINK
As on all coral atolls, fresh water is scarce. The porous coral soil drains quickly, so despite the heavy rainfall there are few groundwater reserves except on Fakaofo. Instead, rainwater is collected from roofs into rain-water tanks. Tank water tends to taste somewhat brackish, perhaps explaining the preference for 'cold stuff' (beer). Coconuts are plentiful, but make sure you have permission before grabbing one to drink from – such resources are limited in Tokelau.

Beer, when available, is sold at the co-op stores on Fakaofo and Nukunonu. (Its sale is strictly rationed on more-traditional Atafu Atoll.) Tokelau's isolation means that supplies of *hostuff* ('hot stuff'; spirits) and beer can be unreliable. *Kaleve*, made from fermented coconut sap, is also drunk.

ENTERTAINMENT
There is not much in the way of a nightclub culture in Tokelau. In fact, as any young Tokelauan who has spent some time in NZ will tell you, life in Tokelau can be downright dull! However, community discos are popular on all three atolls, involving cold stuff, loud music and dancing.

Although gambling for money is illegal, weekly bingo games are extremely popular with women. Prizes include boxes of washing powder and bottles of shampoo.

SPECTATOR SPORTS
Tokelauans play similar sports to Samoa and NZ. Rugby and netball are popular. In the Polynesian form of village cricket (called *kilikiti* in Tokelau; see the boxed text 'The Civilising Influence of Cricket' in the Samoa chapter), each side fields as many players as are available – 50 per side is not uncommon. A shot into the ocean or lagoon is a confirmed 'six'.

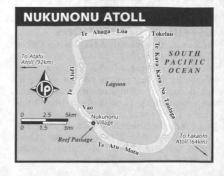

Getting There & Away

This is one of the most isolated spots on Earth and getting there can be difficult. Tokelau has no airstrip, so the only way to get there is by sea. A fortnightly cargo ship from Apia in Samoa is the only way travellers can get to Tokelau without a yacht. In fact, because of the hazards of anchoring, yachting to Tokelau is not much easier!

CARGO SHIP

Bookings on the fortnightly *MV Tokelau* are made through **Tokelau Apia Liaison Office** *(TALO;* ☎ *685-20822, 71805, fax 21761;* e *zak-p@lesamoa.net; PO Box 865, Apia)* in Samoa. Allow plenty of time to process your booking, and be aware that tourists are a lower priority than locals.

The trip to Fakaofo (the closest atoll to Samoa) takes about 28 hours, and travellers have a choice between cabin fare (NZ$528 return) and deck fare (NZ$286). In either case there will be plenty of company on the voyage – you'll be travelling with a boatload of Tokelauans from Samoa and NZ returning to Tokelau to see their families.

There is no harbour on any of the atolls. The ship waits offshore while passengers and cargo are transferred via small boats and dinghies – a hair-raising experience if seas are heavy.

YACHT
Seek advice about the voyage to Tokelau from someone who has been there, and see the introductory Getting Around the Region chapter for more information about sailing in the Pacific.

Tokelau's atolls are low-lying and make difficult visual targets. There are no harbours and anchoring offshore is difficult, especially in an offshore wind. The sea floor drops off sharply outside the coral reef and the water is too deep for most anchor chains. There is one anchorage beyond the reefs at each atoll, but leave a crew member aboard in case the anchor doesn't hold. The channels blasted through the coral are shallow and are intended for dinghies only.

If you're heading to Tokelau on your own yacht you still need to apply for a visitor permit (see Getting There & Away in the Samoa chapter) in Apia.

Getting Around

Inter-island travel is by the fortnightly *MV Tokelau* cargo ship (see earlier). Travel between the small islands on an atoll is usually accomplished with a small aluminium dinghy, or by wading if the tide is low enough.

Tonga

From Captain Cook to Paul Theroux, Tonga has beguiled, charmed and frustrated travellers who have tried to get under the skin of this enigmatic kingdom. Sometimes warmly friendly, sometimes reserved and insular, it defies sweeping description despite being one of the Pacific's most homogeneous societies. The modern world has made its mark, and traditional waist mats now compete with LA gang gear on Tonga's urban streets, but it is still a very conservative country, though one wrestling uneasily with inevitable change. Only its outstanding natural beauty remains constant – from the rainforests of 'Eua, the beaches of Ha'apai and the waterways of Vava'u to the magnificent diving throughout the country's waters. Yet despite this rich endowment, Tonga receives – and perhaps only wants – a relatively small number of visitors.

Facts about Tonga

HISTORY
One legend tells that the Tongan islands were fished out of the sea by the mighty Polynesian god Tangaloa. Another story has Tonga plucked from the ocean by the demigod Maui, a temperamental hero well known throughout the Pacific.

The date of the initial settlement of the Tongan group is around 1100 BC. It is believed that the Lapita people, who arrived in Tonga between 3300 and 3500 years ago, had their first capital at Toloa.

The first king of Tonga, known as the Tu'i Tonga, was 'Aho'eitu. He came to power some time in the middle of the 10th century and was the first of a line of almost 40 men to hold the title.

During the 400 years after the first Tu'i Tonga, the Tongans were often aggressive colonisers, extending their empire over eastern Fiji, Niue and northward as far as the Samoas and Tokelau. Tongan warriors occasionally raided as far east as the Solomon Islands – 2700km away.

European Arrival
Among the first Europeans to visit Tonga were Jacob Lemaire, Abel Tasman and James Cook. Other European explorers to pass through the islands included Englishman Captain Samuel

At a Glance

Capital City (& Island): Nuku'alofa (Tongatapu)

Population: 101,000

Time: 13 hours ahead of GMT

Land Area: 718 sq km (280 sq miles)

Number of Islands: 171

International Telephone Code: ☎ 676

GDP/Capita: US$2200

Currency: Tongan pa'anga (T$1 = US$0.47)

Languages: Tongan & English

Greeting: *Malo e lelei*

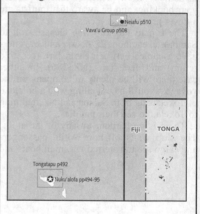

Highlights
- **Tongan feasts** – traditional music and dance, kava ceremonies and enormous meals, especially on Tongatapu and Vava'u
- **Mapu'a 'a Vaca Blowholes, Tongatapu** – a 5km stretch of geyser-like blowholes with fountains of seawater up to 30m high
- **'Eua** – an island of virgin tropical rainforests, limestone caves and dramatic cliffs
- **Ha'apai & Vava'u** – watching the humpback whales that come to breed every year
- **Tofua & Kao** – climbing eerie, uninhabited volcanoes that rise dramatically out of the ocean

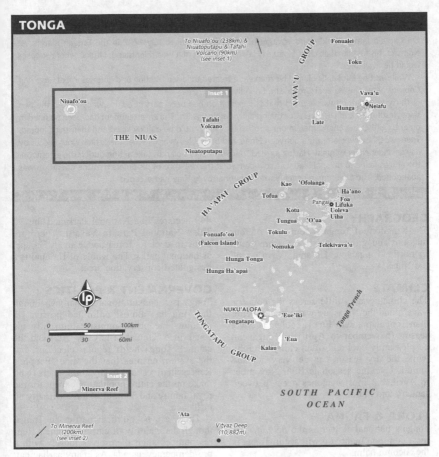

TONGA

To Niuafo'ou (238km) &
Niuatoputapu & Tafahi
Volcano (90km)
(see inset 1)

Fonualei

Toku

VAVA'U GROUP

Vava'u

Hunga ● Neiafu

Late

Inset 1

Niuafo'ou

Tafahi
Volcano

THE NIUAS

Niuatoputapu

HA'APAI GROUP

Kao   'Ofolanga

Tofua

Ha'ano

Foa

Pangai ● Lifuka

Kotu   Uoleva

Uiha

Tungua   'O'ua

Fonuafo'ou   Tokulu
(Falcon Island)

Nomuka   Telekivava'u

Hunga Tonga

Hunga Ha'apai

TONGATAPU GROUP

NUKU'ALOFA ✪

Tongatapu   'Eue'iki

'Eua

Kalau

Tonga Trench

0   50   100km

0   30   60mi

Inset 2

Minerva Reef

SOUTH PACIFIC
OCEAN

To Minerva Reef
(200km)
(see inset 2)

'Ata

Vityaz Deep
(10,882m)

Wallis and Frenchmen Jean-François de Galaup, comte de la Pérouse and Antoine d'Entrecasteaux.

House of Tupou

In 1831, missionaries baptised the ruling Tu'i Tonga, who took the Christian name George, then took over the title of Tu'i Kanokupolu as well. As King George Tupou I, he united Tonga and with the help of the first prime minister, Reverend Shirley Baker, came up with a national flag, a state seal and national anthem, and then began drafting a constitution, passed in 1875. It included a bill of rights, a format for legislative and judicial procedures, laws for succession to the throne and a section on land tenure. It is also responsible for Tonga's heavily Christian laws today.

The second king, George Tupou II, died at the age of 45 in 1918, and his 18-year-old daughter Salote became queen of Tonga. Queen Salote's primary concerns for her country were medicine and education. With intelligence and compassion, she made friends for Tonga throughout the world and was greatly loved by her subjects and foreigners alike.

Queen Salote's son, King Taufa'ahau Tupou IV, is the current ruler of Tonga. He has brought about a number of notable accomplishments, including the re-establishment of full sovereignty for Tonga on 4 June 1970 and admission to the Commonwealth of Nations and to the UN, although some of his economic decisions have been questionable (see the 'We Are Not Amused' boxed text later in this chapter for more information).

Cook's 'Friendly Islands'

On Captain James Cook's third voyage, he spent from April to July 1777 in the Tongan islands. At Nomuka, his first landfall, chief Finau of Ha'apai told him of a wealthier island, Lifuka, where supplies would be available.

While visiting Lifuka, Cook and his men were treated to lavish feasting and entertainment, inspiring Cook to name the Ha'apai Group 'the Friendly Islands'.

Thirty years later it was learned that the exhibition had been part of a conspiracy to raid the two ships *Resolution* and *Discovery* for their plainly visible wealth. The entertainment had been planned in order to gather the Englishmen in one spot so that they could be quickly killed and their ships looted. There was, however, a dispute between Finau and his nobles over whether the attack would occur by day or under cover of night. Having agreed to follow Finau's plan to take action during the afternoon, the nobles failed to do so. Finau was so incensed at the defiance of his orders that the operation was abandoned. The Englishmen never learned how narrowly they had escaped.

GEOGRAPHY

The Kingdom of Tonga is composed of four major island groups which are, from south to north: Tongatapu, Ha'apai, Vava'u and the Niuas.

CLIMATE

The climate varies little across the country. Vava'u and the Niuas are warmer and wetter than Tongatapu, and 'Eua is cooler. The wet season (November to April) in Tonga can be pleasantly cool and often chilly at night, while the dry season can get very hot and humid. Cyclone season is from November to April, but most cyclones occur between January and March.

FLORA & FAUNA

Tonga's national flower is the *heilala*. The most common plant you will see in Tonga is the coconut palm.

Dolphins and migrating humpback whales swim in the waters around Tonga. The humpbacks come from June to November and can often be seen offshore from the major islands.

The only land mammal native to Tonga is the flying fox, or fruit bat.

Tonga has surprisingly few birds, but of interest are the *henga* (blue-crowned lorikeet), the *koki* (red shining parrot) of 'Eua, and the *malau* (megapode or incubator bird), found only on the island of Niuafo'ou, but also being introduced to Late island in Vava'u.

National Parks

Tonga has eight officially protected areas, including five national marine parks and reserves, one national historic park (the 23-hectare Ha'amonga Trilithon Reserve), the 449-hectare 'Eua National Park and the Mt Talau National Park in Vava'u. There are plans to declare Tofua and Kao in Ha'apai as national parks. The whole of Ha'apai is a designated conservation area.

GOVERNMENT & POLITICS

Tonga is a constitutional monarchy, though the king has almost unlimited power. He appoints the prime minister (currently his son Prince 'Ulukalala Lavaka 'Ata) and the cabinet. Tonga holds regular elections, but the system ensures that the nine 'People's Representatives' elected by commoners (who make up the entire population except for the royal family and 33 nobles) have virtually no influence.

There are no political parties in Tonga, though the majority of current People's Representatives align themselves loosely with a pro-democracy agenda. As in any parliament, there are debates and votes, but in reality it is simply a rubber stamp for legislation driven by the royal family.

Tongans are broadly divided in their opinions on the system of government. Many see no need for change, while many others privately express frustration at the nepotism and the series of wasteful follies that have characterised many of the country's recent attempts at development.

Current Situation

Politically, Tonga is very stable (or static!). In the 2002 general election, seven of the nine elected People's Representatives declared themselves pro-democracy, an indication that while most Tongans would never want to abolish the Royal Family, many would like more say in the affairs of the country.

TONGA

ECONOMY

Tonga is highly dependent on remittances sent by Tongans living overseas, which amount to around T$80 million every year. However, the figure is dropping as the next generation of expat Tongans become more detached from their homeland.

Tonga's biggest export is squash pumpkin to Japan, followed by coconut products, vanilla, fish – and rugby players!

Tourism is also a significant source of income, but Tonga only gets around 36,500 tourists per year compared to neighbouring Fiji, which gets around 400,000.

POPULATION & PEOPLE

Tongans make up the vast majority of people in Tonga. There are a few *palangi* (Westerners) expats and a small but significant population of Chinese immigrants.

Tonga's average annual population growth rate is just 0.4% and the total population is estimated to be around 101,000. Tongatapu has more than 65% of the total population and Nuku'alofa (the island's capital) more than 20%.

Despite steady emigration (you'd be hard-pressed to find a Tongan who doesn't have relatives overseas), only Ha'apai and the Niuas suffer from falling populations.

Estimates state there are 50% to 100% more Tongans living abroad than there are in Tonga.

ARTS

Woodcarving is a popular Tongan art form and many excellent examples can be bought in stores or from the roadside. The Tongan gods Tangaloa and Hikuleo are popular subjects. See the 'South Pacific Arts' special section for more about Pacific carving.

The enormous Ha'amonga 'a Maui trilithon on Tongatapu is one of the most impressive carved stone structures in Polynesia.

Dance

The most frequently performed traditional dance in Tonga is called the *lakalaka*. A female solo dance, the most beautiful and graceful of all Tongan dances, is called the *tau'olunga*. The most popular male dance is the *kailao* – the war dance.

We Are Not Amused

While the king of Tonga probably has the best interests of the country at heart, his economic judgment has at times left room for improvement. In fact, the monarch's association with a series of ill-advised schemes has generated much private grumbling among Tongans and a lot of unkind attention from the world's press, who have widely and a little unfairly portrayed him as an autocratic buffoon.

Among the least plausible schemes were a plan to import and refine crude oil from Iran for shipment around the Pacific, an environmentally worrying scheme to burn used American car tyres to generate energy, designs for a floating city on Minerva Reef and, most unusual of all, the king's involvement with Korean Christian cultists who convinced him they had a machine that could convert seawater into natural gas. Even the apparently astute-sounding plan to construct an airport hotel in time for Tonga's much-hyped millennium celebrations failed, leaving a large concrete shell that now gapes at every new arrival.

There was even once rumoured to be oil under Tongatapu and drilling took place behind the Centennial Church in Nuku'alofa. But the king managed to alienate many Tongans at the time, first by decreeing that all land below six feet belonged to the state (to stop commoners staking claims on any oil) and then by allowing drilling to take place on Sunday.

But the most damaging dent to the king's reputation actually grew from one of his more financially successful ventures: the selling of Tongan citizenship to Chinese, which raised T$30 million. In the now infamous 'court jester' episode, he was persuaded to invest T$20 million of this Tonga Trust Fund money in some very questionable US companies by Bank of America 'financial advisor' Jesse Bogdonoff, who moved to Tonga and convinced the king to appoint him Tonga's official Court Jester. The money vanished, and Tonga stopped laughing.

Bogdonoff, whose previous occupations included selling magnets for back pain, was either an opportunistic swindler or a mid-level bank employee way out of his depth, depending on who you speak to. He protests his innocence. The government says he's a thief. Either way, Tonga has lost the money, with little hope of recovering it.

Tapa

Tapa is Tonga's most renowned craft. Along with pandanus weavings, tapa is considered part of the *koloa*, or wealth, of Tongan families. See the 'South Pacific Arts' special section for further information.

RELIGION

Tonga is, on the surface at least, a very religious country. The Free Wesleyan Church (the Royal Family's church of choice) claims the largest number of adherents, followed by the (Methodist) Free Church of Tonga, the Church of England, the Roman Catholics, Seventh Day Adventists and the wealthy and increasingly prominent Mormons.

Many Tongans still believe in the spirits, taboos, superstitions, medical charms and gods of pre-Christian Polynesia.

LANGUAGE

Tongan is a Polynesian language similar to Samoan. Because of the conquering exploits of ancient Tongans, similar languages are spoken on Wallis island and Niue. In Nuku'alofa at least, almost everyone can speak English.

Tongan Basics

Hello.	*Malo e lelei.*
Goodbye.	*'Alu a.*
How are you?	*Fefe hake?*
I'm well. (thanks)	*Sai pe. (malo)*
Please.	*Faka molemole.*
Thank you. (very much)	*Malo. (aupito)*
Yes.	*'Io.*
No.	*Ikai.*

Facts for the Visitor

SUGGESTED ITINERARIES

If you have only a few days in Tonga, it might be better to choose one island group (Tongatapu, Ha'apai or Vava'u) and concentrate your holiday there. For a quick hop around the country, allow at least three days per island group. Visitors hoping to see the Niuas should have very flexible itineraries.

PLANNING

May to October is the best time to visit. The wet season, from November to April, can be humid and wet; it's also cyclone season, but it is quieter and low season discounts are often available. Flights over the Christmas/New Year period can get very full with returning Tongans.

TOURIST OFFICES

Nuku'alofa, Ha'apai and Vava'u have offices of the **Tonga Visitors' Bureau** *(TVB; ☎ 25334, fax 23507;* W *www.vacations.tvb.gov.to).*

VISAS

Visas are not required by citizens of Australia and New Zealand, or Western European (plus Turkey, Russia and Ukraine), North American or Pacific Island countries. Citizens of Eastern European, African, Asian (except Japan, Singapore, Malaysia and Brunei), Middle Eastern and Central/South American (except Brazil) countries now need visas to enter Tonga. Upon arrival you must present a valid passport and an onward ticket to be granted a stay of 30 days. One-month visa extensions are granted at the Immigration Departments in Nuku'alofa, Ha'apai and Vava'u for stays up to six months, costing T$40 per extension.

EMBASSIES & CONSULATES
Tongan Embassies & Consulates

Tonga has diplomatic representatives in the following countries:

Australia (☎ 02-9929 8794, fax 9929 6778, W www.raedler.waterhouse@bigpond.com) 158 Pacific Hwy, North Sydney, NSW 2059
UK (☎ 020-7724 5828, fax 7723 9074) 36 Molyneux St, London W1H 6AB
USA (☎ 415-781 0365, fax 781 3964, e tania@sfconsulate.gov.to) 360 Post St, Suite 604, CA 94108
Office in Hawaii (☎ 808-953 2449, fax 955 1447) Suite 306B, 738 Kaheka St, Honolulu, HI 96814

Embassies & Consulates in Tonga

The following foreign diplomatic representatives can be found in Nuku'alofa:

Australia (☎ 23244, fax 23243, e ahc@kalianet.to) High Commission, Salote Rd
Canada Limited consular services available through Australian High Commission
European Union (☎ 23820, fax 23869) Commission office, Taufa'ahau Rd
Germany (☎ 23477, fax 23154) Consulate, Taufa'ahau Rd
New Zealand (☎ 23122, fax 23487, e nzhcnuk@kalianet.to) High Commission, Taufa'ahau Rd
UK (☎ 24395, fax 24109, e britcomt@kalianet.to) High Commission, Vuna Rd
USA (Peace Corps ☎ 25466, Ministry of Foreign Affairs ☎ 23600) National Reserve Bank

CUSTOMS

Travellers aged 18 or older may import up to 200 cigarettes and 2L of spirits duty free. Animals, fruit and other plant products require a quarantine certificate.

MONEY
Currency

Notes come in denominations of one, two, five, 10, 20 and 50 *pa'anga* (T$). Coins come in denominations of one, two, five, 10, 20 and 50 seniti.

US, New Zealand, Australian and Fijian dollars plus British sterling are the currencies that are most easily exchanged, but yen and euro are also widely accepted on Tonga. All major brands of travellers cheques are acceptable.

Credit cards are accepted at many tourist facilities, with Visa and MasterCard the most common. There are ATMs with Visa, MasterCard and Cirrus facilities in Tongatapu and Vava'u. Western Union has offices throughout Tonga, and MoneyGram is represented by the Westpac Bank of Tonga.

Exchange Rates

Approximate rates for the Tongan pa'anga are listed below:

country	unit		pa'anga
Australia	A$1	=	T$1.45
Canada	C$1	=	T$1.60
Easter Island	Ch$100	=	T$0.31
euro zone	€1	=	T$2.45
Fiji	F$1	=	T$1.16
Japan	¥100	=	T$1.80
New Caledonia	100CFP	=	T$2.05
New Zealand	NZ$1	=	T$1.24
PNG	K1	=	T$0.61
Samoa	ST1	=	T$0.71
Solomon Islands	S$1	=	T$0.29
UK	£1	=	T$3.53
USA	US$1	=	T$2.12
Vanuatu	100VT	=	T$1.77

To check current exchange rates, see Ⓦ www .oanda.com.

Costs

Prices have risen alarmingly in Tonga in recent years, but it's still one of the least expensive Pacific destinations. Strict budgeters could get by on T$35 a day. Around T$90 a day is the minimum if you're staying in mid-range accommodation and enjoying a few activities. Top-end travellers should budget for a daily minimum of around T$200.

Taxes

All prices in Tonga include 5% VAT. Hotel prices are subject to an additional 2.5% room tax. Taxes are not refunded to tourists.

POST & COMMUNICATIONS
Post

Postage rates for letters sent from Tonga are 60 seniti to the South Pacific region, Australia and New Zealand, 80 seniti to the rest of the world. Postcards cost 45 seniti to anywhere in the world.

Telephone & Fax

The **Tonga Telecommunications Corporation** has offices in all main centres, offering international calls, telegrams and faxes. Pre-paid telecards, which can be used anywhere, are also available.

Mobile phone users can get simcards in Tongatapu through **UCall** (☎ *0800 222; simcard T$55 including T$20 credit*) or **Tonfōn** (☎ *875 1000; simcard T$25 without credit*). Tonfōn's rates are cheaper, but UCall has the more reliable service. Coverage for both is limited.

Tonga's emergency phone number is ☎ 911. The international operator is ☎ 913. Directory assistance is ☎ 910.

Tonga's international telephone code is ☎ 676. There are no local area codes.

Email & Internet Access

In Nuku'alofa there are several Internet cafés and places to stay that offer services at around T$2 for 15 minutes. Vava'u has an Internet server, but it's very slow and rates are around 50 seniti per minute. Ha'apai has an email server, but no Internet.

BOOKS

Tonga Islands – William Mariner's Account, by Dr John Martin, is the best work available on pre-Christian Tonga.

Queen Salote of Tonga, written by Elizabeth Wood-Ellem, is a warm account of the queen's life.

Tales of the Tikongs, by Epeli Hau'ofa, is a must-read collection of wry, satirical vignettes on life in 'Tiko' (Tonga). It's very short, but it will give the visitor as much insight into the modern Tongan way of life as a dozen earnest cultural tomes.

TONGA

The New Friendly Islanders, by Kenneth Bain, deals with recent social changes and how they relate to Tongan tradition and world trends. It's an absorbing and entertaining read.

Island Kingdom Strikes Back, by Kalafi Moala, is a revealing account of intrigue, corruption, skulduggery and illegal arrest in the kingdom, as experienced by the author through the development of his newspaper *Taimi o' Tonga*, which the government has made efforts to ban. The book is only available outside Tonga.

The best bookshops in Tonga is the Friendly Islands Bookshop in Nuku'alofa (see the Nuku'alofa section), with a wide selection of literature, travel books, newspapers and magazines. The branches elsewhere in the country are not well stocked.

The office of **Vava'u Press** (☎ 25779, fax 24749; ℮ vapress@kalianet.to; PO Box 958, Nuku'alofa, Tonga) in Nuku'alofa sells excellent books on Tonga.

Lonely Planet's *Tonga* provides a lot more details on the country and is, of course, the most comprehensive guide available!

NEWSPAPERS & MAGAZINES

The *Tonga Chronicle*, the official newspaper published by the Tongan government, comes out weekly in Tongan and English editions.

Taimi o' Tonga is an independent weekly newspaper that offers a little more criticism and has frequently found itself in trouble with the government.

Matangi Tonga, a news magazine with analysis of Tongan current affairs, comes with an insert magazine, *Eva*, which has articles aimed at visitors, including a guided historical tour of an obscure Tongan village in every issue.

RADIO & TV

The government-owned Radio Tonga, A3Z (90FM), broadcasts a mix of traditional Tongan music, rock music and local and world

William Mariner

Thanks to a series of serendipitous incidents, the world has an extensive account of the customs, language, religion and politics of pre-Christian Tonga.

In February 1805, 15-year-old William Charles Mariner went to sea on the privateer *Port-au-Prince*. The voyage took the ship across the Atlantic, around Cape Horn, up the west coast of South America, to the Sandwich (Hawaiian) Islands and finally into Tonga's Ha'apai Group. The crew anchored at the northern end of Lifuka and was immediately welcomed with yams and barbecued pork. Their reception seemed friendly enough, but the following day the crew members became suspicious that some sort of plot was afoot. The ship's captain chose to ignore their fears.

On 1 December 1806, an attack was launched while 300 Tongans were aboard the ship. The British, sorely outnumbered, decided to destroy the ship, its crew and its attackers rather than allow it to be taken. Young Mariner was captured and escorted ashore.

Mariner was persecuted by the Tongans until he was summoned by Finau 'Ulukalala I, the reigning chief of Ha'apai. The king assumed that Mariner was the captain's son and ordered the young man's life to be spared.

Meanwhile, the *Port-au-Prince*, which hadn't been destroyed, was dragged ashore, raided and burned. The conflagration heated the cannons sufficiently to cause them to fire, creating panic among the Tongans. Mariner pantomimed an explanation of the phenomenon, initiating a rapport with the Tongans that would carry him through the next four years.

Mariner was taken under the wing of Finau and became privy to most of the goings-on in Tongan politics. He learned the language well and travelled with the chief, observing and absorbing the finer points of Tongan ceremony and protocol. He was given the name *Toki 'Ukamea* (Iron Axe) and Finau appointed one of his royal wives, Mafi Hape, to be Mariner's adoptive mother.

After the death of Finau, the king's son permitted young William to leave Tonga on a passing English vessel. Back in England, Mariner married, fathered 12 children and became an unsuccessful stockbroker. Were it not for a chance meeting with an amateur anthropologist, Dr John Martin, his unique Tongan experiences might have been lost. Martin, fascinated with Mariner's tale, suggested collaboration on a book and the result, *An Account of the Natives of the Tonga Islands*, is a masterpiece of Pacific literature.

William Mariner drowned in a canal in southern England in 1853.

Fakaleiti

Fakaleiti, men who dress and behave as women, are one of the most distinctive (and for many visitors surprising) features of Tongan culture. These men, known in other areas of the Pacific as *fa'afafine* (Samoa) and *mahu* or *rae rae* (French Polynesia), are a modern continuation of an ancient Polynesian tradition.

Most *fakaleiti* are probably gay. While many consider themselves ladies and wouldn't think of relating sexually to anyone but a masculine man, this is not true of all. Some are married to women and some – as many who have seen *fakaleiti* in a fight can testify – are not entirely ladylike. *Fakaleiti*, however, get away with promiscuity forbidden to biological females.

Many *fakaleiti* openly flaunt their sexuality and they are accepted as part of Polynesian society, so it might seem that there is no social stigma attached. This is partly true, partly not. Although adult *fakaleiti* are accepted, growing up as one is not easy. Many are tormented by other children and teenagers, and most Polynesian fathers do not feel a great pride if their sons turn out to be effeminate.

On Tongatapu, the Tonga Leitis' Association – who prefer to simply call themselves *leiti* (ladies) – sponsors several popular, well-attended annual events, including the international Miss Galaxy competition each June, which attracts *fakaleiti* and transvestites from several countries. Similarly popular contests are held in Samoa and American Samoa from October onwards.

news. Radio Millennium (89.1FM) and Radio Nuku'alofa (88.6 FM) also have mixed playlists, but are aimed more at young listeners.

Tonga has three TV stations – government-owned TV Tonga, the US Trinity Broadcasting Network and the Oceania Broadcasting Network – which are all heavily religious.

DIGITAL RESOURCES

Tonga Tourism's website (Ⓦ www.tongaholiday.com) is a good starting point for travel information, as is the Visitors' Bureau site (Ⓦ www.vacations.tvb.gov.to). Tonga on the Net (Ⓦ www.tongatapu.net.to) has general information about the country.

HEALTH

Tonga is free of malaria, but there are intermittent outbreaks of dengue fever. See the Health section in the Regional Facts for the Visitor chapter.

Water in Nuku'alofa is generally OK to drink, but it's probably wise to treat tap water elsewhere with suspicion.

Likewise, the only place with reasonable medical facilities is Tongatapu, where there are a number of decent clinics and a hospital with well-trained staff but often minimal equipment. Elsewhere in the country, hospitals are badly under-equipped and under-staffed and should not be relied upon to treat anything other than minor complaints.

SOCIAL GRACES

Foreigners are expected to provide amusement with their odd behaviour, but there are a few significant points to remember to ensure your peculiarities do not offend anyone.

Respectful dress is considered important in Tonga. Tongans are required by law to dress modestly in public, and though this code is more relaxed in Nuku'alofa and to a lesser extent Neiafu, it is advisable to follow it elsewhere. Tops covering the chest and shoulders and skirts reaching below the knees are the norm for women, though respectable sleeveless dresses are okay. Men must wear a shirt in public, except on beaches. Skimpy shorts, even on men, are considered inappropriate and swimsuits should only be worn in resorts or on very isolated beaches.

The concept of 'face' is also very strong in Tonga. Causing someone to lose face is a serious social transgression, so if a Tongan makes an innocent mistake, do not start waving and shouting about it, or you will likely cause them far greater anguish then they have caused you.

Dress

You'll often see Tongans wearing distinctive pandanus mats called *ta'ovala*. In place of a *ta'ovala*, women often wear a *kiekie*, a decorative waistband from which dangle woven strips of pandanus. Men often wear a wraparound skirt known as a *tupenu* and women an ankle-length *vala*, or skirt, and *kofu*, or tunic.

GAY & LESBIAN TRAVELLERS

Surprisingly in such a Christian country, male homosexuality is an accepted fact of life in Tonga and you'll see plenty of gay men around, including those following the fine

TONGA

old Polynesian tradition of *fakaleiti* (see the boxed text earlier). Lesbians are not generally accepted and keep themselves under cover.

DANGERS & ANNOYANCES

Tonga is a very safe country to visit. However, there has been a small but notable rise in attacks on *palangi* in Tongatapu and Vava'u, which usually go hand in hand with late nights and alcohol. Brawls are very common in bars – keep tuned for trouble.

In Nuku'alofa, cases of taxi drivers taking new arrivals to the wrong guesthouses are becoming regular, so make sure you get dropped where you asked to be dropped.

BUSINESS HOURS

Business hours are 8.30am to 5pm Monday to Friday, and Saturday mornings. Bank hours vary slightly, but are broadly from 9am to 4pm. In Nuku'alofa and Neiafu (Vava'u) banks also open for a few hours on Saturday morning. Government offices are open Monday to Friday from 8.30am to 12.30pm and 1.30pm to 4pm. Post offices are open Monday to Friday from around 8.30am to 4pm.

Café-style eateries open early and restaurants are typically open from lunchtime until around 10.30pm, but those that double as bars can stay open until 2am. Everything closes at midnight on Saturday and only those restaurants/bars that have accommodation are officially allowed to open on Sunday, though there are exceptions.

PUBLIC HOLIDAYS & SPECIAL EVENTS

In addition to New Year's Day, Easter, Anzac Day, Christmas Day and Boxing Day (see the Regional Facts for the Visitor chapter for dates), public holidays in Tonga include:

Prince Tupouto'a's Birthday 4 May
Emancipation Day 4 June
King Taufa'ahau's Birthday 4 July
Constitution Day 4 November
King George I's Birthday 4 December

King Taufa'ahau's birthday is celebrated with the week-long Heilala Festival featuring parades, dance and sporting competitions, arts and music.

ACTIVITIES
Snorkelling & Diving

Great visibility, comfortable water temperatures and sheltered waters create magnificent conditions for diving and snorkelling. Recent cyclones and coral bleaching have damaged sites all over Tonga, particularly in Vava'u and Ha'apai. See the special section 'South Pacific Diving' for a spotlight on some Tongan dive sites.

Sailing & Fishing

Vava'u has some of the best gamefishing in the Pacific. It is also a major yachting destination, with three large yacht-charter companies. In Tongatapu, there are also fishing and yacht charters at Royal Sunset Island Resort, while Sea-Taxi's power cruiser runs custom-made trips to virtually anywhere in Tonga (see Sailing in the Tongatapu section).

Whale Watching

Tonga is one the world's top whale-watching destinations between June and November, when humpback whales come to mate and bear their young. Vava'u is the main centre for whale watching, but there are also operators in Tongatapu, Ha'apai and 'Eua. See the boxed text 'The Whale Debates' in this chapter for more information.

Cycling

Flat terrain and generally slow driving make Tongatapu and Lifuka (Ha'apai) ideal for cycling. Bicycles can be rented on Tongatapu, 'Eua, Ha'apai and Vava'u.

Hiking

'Eua offers the best and most accessible bushwalking in Tonga. Other good hiking venues include the Niuas and many of the Ha'apai islands.

Caving

'Eua has the most dramatic caves in Tonga. 'Anahulu Cave on Tongatapu has a freshwater pool that is good for swimming.

Other Activities

Tongatapu's western waters offer world-class surfing, and there's excellent kayaking opportunities in Vava'u and Ha'apai.

ACCOMMODATION
Camping

Camping is generally discouraged in Tonga, and is illegal in Ha'apai and Vava'u unless it's part of a guided trip. But camping trips to deserted islands in Ha'apai and Vava'u are easily arranged and thoroughly recommended. A few places to stay allow camping.

Guesthouses

In Tongatapu and Vava'u it is easy to find clean, well-run guesthouses, many of which will have cooking facilities. In Ha'apai, cooking facilities are the norm, but the room standard is on the whole a lot lower. The average budget price is between T$15 and T$30 for a bed, a little more for a private bathroom.

Hotels & Resorts

There are a few upmarket resorts in Tonga, but nothing that could be called luxury accommodation.

FOOD

The Tongan diet consists mostly of root vegetables, coconut products, taro, fresh fruit, pork, chicken and fish, with little seasoning. However, the widespread preference for imported fatty meat and fast foods has contributed to a spiralling diabetes rate in Tonga and is a serious concern.

Traditional Tongan cuisine is available at some guesthouses, as well as at a few (mostly daytime) restaurants. Higher-priced restaurants in Tongatapu and Vava'u featuring foreign cuisines are of a uniformly high standard.

DRINK

Fruit juices are widely available as are, of course, the ubiquitous drinking coconuts. Kava is Tonga's most famous drink. See Food and Drinks in the Regional Facts for the Visitor chapter for more information on coconuts and kava.

Tongans are very fond of alcohol, particularly on Tongatapu and Vava'u. The most popular local bottled beer is Ikale.

The illegal island homebrew, known as *hopi*, often appearing as innocent-looking soft-drink flavours, is widely made to no fixed recipe and should be approached with caution.

ENTERTAINMENT

Make sure you don't miss a traditional feast while you're in Tonga. Feasts usually include kava ceremonies, stringband music, traditional Tongan singing and dancing and lots of food.

SHOPPING

Tongan handicrafts are usually good quality and reasonably cheap. There's refreshingly little cheap rubbish aimed at tourists.

Getting There & Away

AIR

From Fiji, Samoa, Los Angeles, Australia and New Zealand, access to Tonga is straightforward. Auckland (New Zealand) and Nadi/Suva (Fiji) are the most convenient connecting points. The major carriers are **Royal Tongan Airlines** (☎ 23414; W *www.royaltonganairlines .com*), **Air New Zealand** (☎ 23192; W *www.air nz.co.nz*), **Air Pacific** (*EM Jones Travel;* ☎ 23 422; e *jonestvl@kalianet.to*), **Polynesian Airlines** (☎ 24566; e *polyair@kalianet.to*) and **Air Fiji** (*Teta Tours;* ☎ 23690; e *tetatour@kalia net.to*). Overseas contact details for airlines are listed in the Regional Getting There & Away chapter.

Departure Tax

Departure tax is T$25, payable at the airport.

USA

Los Angeles and Honolulu are the two major gateway cities for travel between the USA (and Canada) and the South Pacific. The following are low-season fares.

From Los Angeles you can fly to Tonga once a week via Honolulu and Apia on Polynesian (around US$1290 return), or once a week on Air New Zealand via Apia (around NZ$1300 return). The fastest way into the southwest Pacific is to take the Air Pacific/Qantas or Air New Zealand flights direct from Los Angeles to Nadi. Both fly three times a week.

Royal Tongan Airlines is planning a Tonga–Apia–Honolulu service.

Australasia

Air New Zealand (around NZ$920 return), Royal Tongan Airlines (around NZ$950 return) and Polynesian Airlines (around NZ$880 return) operate direct flights between Auckland and Tonga.

From Australia, Polynesian has one direct flight per week between Sydney and Tonga, but you have to return via Auckland. Air New Zealand flights to Tonga from Australia are routed through Auckland. You can also fly to Tonga via Fiji from Brisbane (around A$1190 return), Sydney (around A$1150 return) and Melbourne (around A$1325 return).

Fiji's Air Pacific operates direct flights connecting Fiji with Auckland (NZ$935 return), with Qantas connections to other New Zealand cities.

TONGA

Europe

Europeans usually fly to the South Pacific via Los Angeles, Sydney or Auckland. Air New Zealand has cheap fares from London or Frankfurt to Los Angeles, with connections from Los Angeles to the rest of the South Pacific. A return fare to Fiji from London costs around £640 return. Korean Air also has cheap flights from London to Fiji, via Seoul, for around £630.

Asia

Air Pacific operates direct flights connecting Tokyo with Nadi three times a week (¥89,000 return); Korean Airlines flies twice weekly between Seoul and Nadi (1.1 million won return), with connections to London. In Nadi you can connect to a direct flight to Tonga three times a week with Air Pacific/Royal Tongan Airlines.

The Pacific

Nadi and Auckland are the region's two major air transport hubs. Nadi is a 1¼-hour hop from Tonga, and Auckland is a 2½-hour flight. The following fares are valid for either 28 or 30 days.

Direct Air Pacific/Royal Tongan Airlines flights between Tongatapu and Nadi operate three times weekly (F$450 return).

Air Fiji flies between Suva and Tongatapu three times weekly (FJ$528 return).

Polynesian Airlines has three weekly flights between Tongatapu and Apia (Samoa) for T$400 return. Air New Zealand flies to and from Apia once a week (820 tala return).

Various air passes connect Tonga with the other Pacific islands – see Air Passes in the regional Getting There & Away chapter near the start of the book.

SEA

Most yachts come to Tonga on the westerly trade winds from the Samoan Islands. Ports of entry for yachts are Nuku'alofa (Tongatapu), Neiafu (Vava'u), Pangai, Lifuka (Ha'apai), Falehau (Niuatoputapu) and Futu (Niuafo'ou).

In Nuku'alofa, raise your yellow quarantine flag and anchor in the restricted anchorage area, or pull up alongside Queen Salote Wharf or the yacht harbour (2.6m deep at the entrance and dredged to 3m inside) and summon **customs and immigration officials** (☎ 23651; VHF Channel 69). Instructions will be given on VHF Channel 12 or 13. Immigration officials are on duty-government hours.

In Vava'u, pull your yacht up at the southern end of Neiafu Wharf and contact the **boarding officers** (☎ 70053), **immigration** (☎ 71124), **customs** (☎ 70928) or the **harbour master** (VHF Channel 12), who all work from 8.30am to 4.30pm Monday to Friday.

In Ha'apai, check in with the customs officer inside the passenger shelter on Taufa'ahau Wharf upon arrival.

The customs clearance fee in Tonga is T$40 (an extra T$4 if outside working hours). Quarantine fees are T$20 for boats less than 25m and T$50 for longer boats. The immigration fee is free for the first month, T$30 for the second and T$40 for the third and subsequent months.

Getting Around

AIR

Flying is by far the easiest and fastest way to get around Tonga. Royal Tongan Airlines has two planes servicing domestic routes. There are no flights on Sunday and schedules are subject to change at short notice. It's important to tell the airline in advance if you have a connecting international flight so that you get your 20kg baggage allowance and don't get bumped off the flight (which often happens).

Direct return flights between Tongatapu and Vava'u operate at least once daily. Direct return flights between Tongatapu and Ha'apai also operate daily.

Flights between Tongatapu and the Niuas, via Vava'u, are scheduled to operate once a week, but often don't. Ha'apai and Vava'u are connected three times a week. The 10-minute flight between Tongatapu and 'Eua runs five days a week.

Air Passes

Royal Tongan Airlines' Kingdom Pass allows you to travel between Tongatapu, Ha'apai, Vava'u and 'Eua for T$287. The pass is sold only to travellers who have arrived from the northern hemisphere, but it can be bought inside Tonga as long as you present your ticket as proof.

CAR & MOTORCYCLE

Rental cars are available on Tongatapu, Ha'apai and Vava'u. Hiring a car or van with a driver is another option; this can be done on all of these islands, and on 'Eua. You must organise a Tongan driving licence from the police.

People drive very slowly in Tonga. The speed limit is 40km/h in villages and 65km/h elsewhere and, except for a few budding organ donors on Tongatapu, it is faithfully observed.

BOAT
Inter-Island Ferry
Several passenger freighters travel between the main island groups – if the weather is calm it can be a memorable way to travel. If seas are rough it will still be memorable, but for different reasons.

The main carrier is the *MV 'Olovaha*, run by the **Shipping Corporation of Polynesia** (☎ 24413), though the ship drifted onto the reef outside Tongatapu during Cyclone Ami in January 2003 and its future is uncertain. It does weekly runs from Tongatapu (Nuku'alofa) to Ha'apai (Lifuka and Ha'afeva, T$34, 12 hours) and Vava'u (Neiafu, T$48, 21 hours). Every couple of months it goes to the Niuas, but it is rarely able to land at Niuafo'ou. The *MV 'Otu Tonga* cargo vessel also takes passengers. It's a bit cheaper, but very slow (Ha'apai, T$33, 15 hours; Vava'u, T$44, 26 hours).

MV Pulupaki, run by **'Uliti 'Uata (Walter Line) Shipping** (☎ 23855), is a lot quicker (Ha'apai, T$34, 6½ hours; Vava'u, T$48, 11 hours), but offers only deck-class travel.

Between Tongatapu and 'Eua, Walter Line's *MV Ikale* is the quickest boat (T$12, 1½ hours), but had been out of action for several months at the time of writing. **Tofa Shipping** (☎ 21326) operates the *MV Alaimoana*, which does the crossing daily in 2½ hours for T$12. The trip is notoriously rough.

Other Vessels
Smaller islands off the main ferry routes can be reached by smaller boats in all island groups.

LOCAL TRANSPORT
To/From the Airport
Buses meet incoming flights on Tongatapu and Vava'u. A taxi ride between Fua'amotu airport and Nuku'alofa is T$15.

Bus
Local buses run on the islands of Tongatapu, 'Eua, Vava'u, and on Lifuka and Foa in the Ha'apai Group. Fares range from 40 seniti to T$1.20 depending upon the island and the distance travelled. Passengers usually pay when they get off.

Taxi
Taxis can be recognised by a 'T' in front of the numbers on the licence plate. There are plenty of taxis on Tongatapu and Vava'u, and a few on Lifuka and 'Eua.

ORGANISED TOURS
Commercial island tours operate on Tongatapu and Vava'u and less formally on 'Eua and Ha'apai. The Tonga Visitors' Bureau (TVB) will give good advice on the current operators. See the individual island sections for details.

Tongatapu

pop 69,000 (est) • area 260 sq km
Tongatapu (Sacred South) island, along with Nuku'alofa (Abode of Love), is the hub of all activity in Tonga. The majority of the island's population lives in Nuku'alofa and its adjoining villages.

History
Tongatapu's first European visitor was Dutchman Abel Tasman, who spent a few days trading with islanders and named the island Amsterdam. The next European contact came with James Cook, who became close friends with the 30th Tu'i Tonga, Fatafehi Paulaho.

BY PERMISSION OF THE NATIONAL LIBRARY OF AUSTRALIA, NK1426

Poulaho, king of the Friendly Islands (engraving by John Hall, 1784)

TONGA

TONGATAPU

NUKU'ALOFA
pop 23,000

In most countries, Nuku'alofa would be considered quite an attractive town. But Pacific towns often get a bad rap from visitors, who are perhaps disappointed to find bustle and concrete where they expected beachy serenity, and Nuku'alofa is no exception. It deserves much better. With its long stretch of well-kept waterfront, calm lagoon, historic weatherboard mansions, excellent bars and restaurants and compact modern(ish) facilities, Nuku'alofa is one of the Pacific's best capitals in which to spend a few days.

Information

Tourist Offices The **Tonga Visitors' Bureau** *(TVB; Vuna Rd;* W *www.vacations.tvb.gov.au; open 8.30am-4.30pm Mon-Fri, 9am-noon Sat & holidays)* is just west of the International Dateline Hotel.

Money Nuku'alofa has three banks – the **Westpac Bank of Tonga, ANZ** and **MBF** – all of which cash notes and travellers cheques and give advances on Visa and MasterCard. The Bank of Tonga and ANZ have 24-hour ATM machines with Visa, MasterCard and Cirrus facilities. All three open Saturday mornings.

Post The main **post office** *(cnr Salote & Taufa'ahau Rds; open 8.30am-4pm Mon-Fri)* has a poste restante window next to the main entrance – address to Post Restante, GPO, Nuku'alofa, Kingdom of Tonga.

Telephone & Fax Offering international telephone and fax services is the **Tonga Communications Corporation** *(☎ 26700; Salote Rd; open 7am-midnight Mon-Sat, 4pm-midnight Sun).* Telecards can be purchased for use anywhere.

Email & Internet Access The best places for Internet access are the **Pacific Royale Hotel Business Centre** *(☎ 23344; Taufa'ahau Rd; open 8.30am-1am Mon-Fri, 8.30am-midnight Sat)* and **Cyber Central** *(☎ 26885; Taufa'ahau Rd; open 8am-8pm Mon-Fri, 10am-2pm Sat).* Both charge T$2 per 15 minutes. Many places to stay offer Internet facilities.

Bookshops The best place to buy books is the **Friendly Islands Bookshop** *(☎ 23787; Taufa'ahau Rd),* with a good selection of newspapers and magazines, paperback books, travel titles and books about Tonga.

Laundry Virtually every hotel and guesthouse handles guests' laundry.

Medical Services You can call on the **Nuku'alofa Pharmacy** *(☎ 21007; cnr Mateialona & Siulikutapu Rds; open 10am-5pm Mon-Sat)* after hours.

The **Village Mission Clinic** *(☎ 29052; Ha'ateiho Village; open 2pm-4.30pm Mon, 8.30am-12.30pm Tues-Fri),* 5km south of Nuku'alofa, has a good reputation. Appointments are essential.

The **Fasi Mo e Afi Pharmacy** *(☎ 22955; Salote Rd; open 9am-5pm Mon-Fri, 10am-noon Sat)* is more conveniently located.

The **Vaiola Hospital** *(☎ 23200)* is recommended only for emergencies.

Zen Shiatsu massage centre *(☎ 878 1036; cnr Taufa'ahau & Wellington Rds; open 9am-5pm Mon-Sat),* at T$30 per hour, is worth every seniti. It's above the TCF Supermarket.

Royal Palace

The Royal Palace, a white, Victorian timber structure surrounded by large lawns and Norfolk pines, is a symbol of Tonga to the rest of the world. The palace grounds are not open to visitors but you can get a good view from the waterfront area on the west side.

Royal Tombs

The Mala'ekula, the large park-like area opposite the basilica, has been the resting place of the royals since 1893. It's off-limits to the public but you get a reasonable view from the perimeter fence.

Churches

Nuku'alofa's most distinctive structure is the **Basilica of St Anthony of Padua** *(Taufa'ahau Rd),* opposite the Royal Tombs. It has a beautiful interior of stained glass, wooden beams and hand-crafted furnishings.

The other Catholic church in town is **St Mary's Cathedral** *(Vuna Rd),* near Faua jetty. It's worth visiting for its beautiful rose gardens, stained glass and vaulted ceiling.

The **Centenary Chapel** *(Wellington Rd)* behind Mt Zion is the best place to sneak a look at the royal family, who worship here on Sunday. Dress well.

Market

Nuku'alofa's **Talamahu Market** is not only Tonga's best for produce, but it has some excellent Tongan handicrafts, tapa and woven mats that are worth checking out.

TONGA

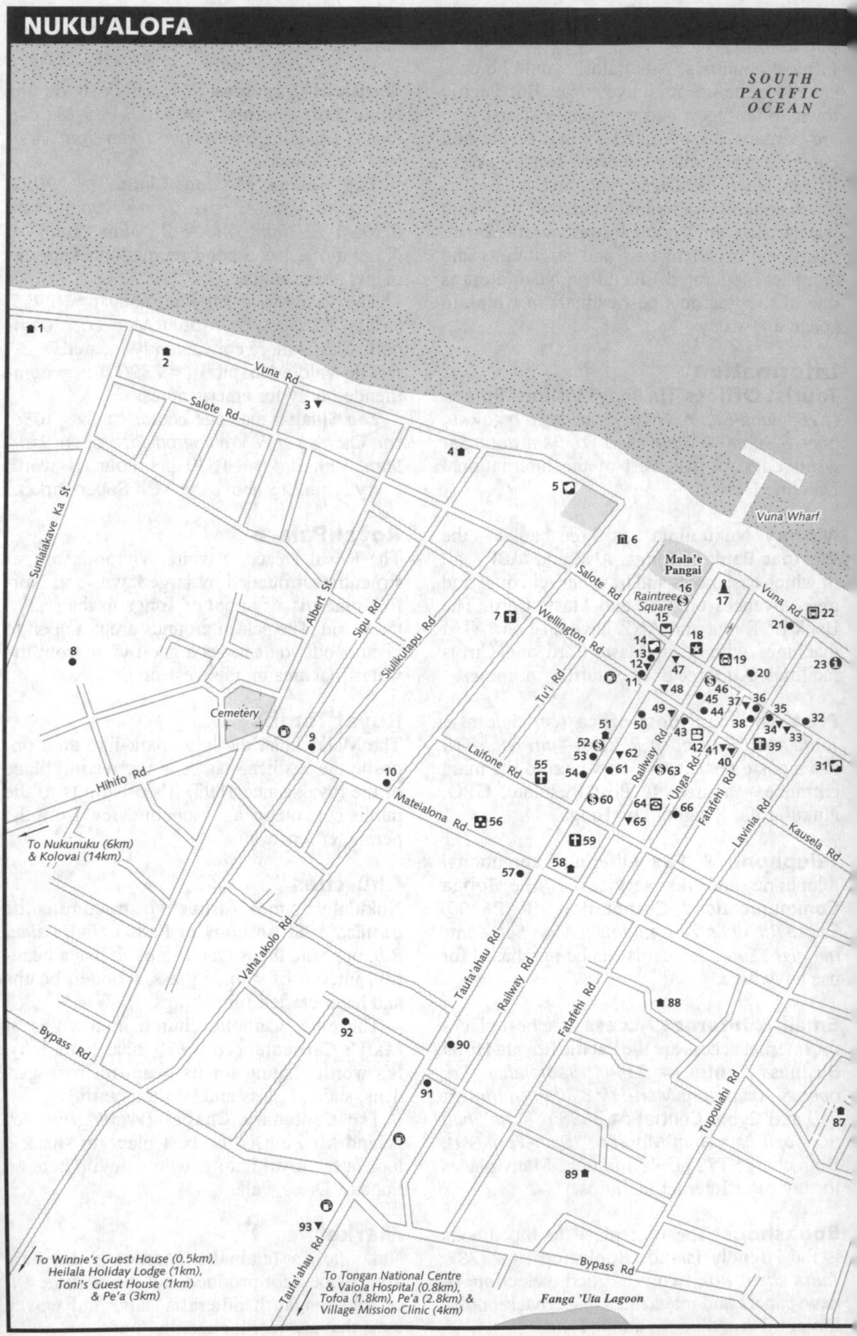
NUKU'ALOFA
SOUTH PACIFIC OCEAN
Vuna Wharf
Mala'e Pangai
Raintree Square
Vuna Rd
Salote Rd
Wellington Rd
Suniaiakave Ka St
Albert St
Sipu Rd
Siulikutapu Rd
Tu'i Rd
Cemetery
Hihifo Rd
Laifone Rd
Railway Rd
'Unga Rd
Fatafehi Rd
Lavinia Rd
Kausela Rd
Mateialona Rd
To Nukunuku (6km) & Kolovai (14km)
Vaha'akolo Rd
Taufa'ahau Rd
Tupoulahi Rd
Bypass Rd
To Winnie's Guest House (0.5km), Heilala Holiday Lodge (1km), Toni's Guest House (1km) & Pe'a (3km)
To Tongan National Centre & Vaiola Hospital (0.8km), Tofoa (1.8km), Pe'a (2.8km) & Village Mission Clinic (4km)
Fanga 'Uta Lagoon
1
2
3
4
5
6
7
8
9
10
11
12
13
14
15
16
17
18
19
20
21
22
23
31
32
33
34
35
36
37
38
39
40
41
42
43
44
45
46
47
48
49
50
51
52
53
54
55
56
57
58
59
60
61
62
63
64
65
66
87
88
89
90
91
92
93

TONGA

NUKU'ALOFA

PLACES TO STAY
1 Moana Beach House
2 The Captain Cook
   Apartments
4 Seaview Restaurant &
   Lodge
28 International Dateline
   Hotel
51 Pacific Royale Hotel;
   Business Centre;
   Wanda's
58 Misa's Guest House
67 Kaliloa Guest House
69 Villa McKenzie
81 Harbour View Motel
85 Tom's Bed & Breakfast
87 Diver's Lodge
88 Nerima Lodge
89 Sela's Guest House

PLACES TO EAT
3 Little Italy Pizzeria
12 Sia Leka's Takeaway
25 Emerald; Garden Bar
26 Hua Hua
33 Cowley's Bread Bin
34 Tasty Café

37 Molisi Tonga Limited
   Supermarket
40 Little Tokyo Restaurant
41 Coco's Deli Café
47 Friends Café;
   Pacific Fashions;
   Langafonua'ae Fefine
   Handicrafts
48 Suliana's;
   TCF Supermarket;
   Zen Shiatsu
49 Fakalato Restaurant;
   Snack & Milk Bar
62 Lunarossa Restaurant;
   TCF Supermarket
65 Sama Restaurant;
   Noble Restaurant
70 Fung Shing Restaurant
74 The Waterfront Café
84 Pot Luck Lunches
93 Masala

OTHER
5 British High Commission
6 Royal Palace
7 Centenary Chapel
8 'Atenisi Institute

9 Nuku'alofa Pharmacy
10 Queen Salote College
11 EM Jones Travel and Tours;
   Air Pacific
13 Friends Tours;
   Cyber Central
14 New Zealand High Commission
15 Main Post Office (GPO)
16 Westpac Bank of Tonga (ATM)
17 Town Common &
   War Memorial
18 Police Station
19 Talamahu Market Taxi
20 Talamahu Market
21 Ministry of Lands, Survey
   & Natural Resources
22 Western Bus Terminal
23 Tonga Visitors' Bureau
24 Eastern Bus Terminal
27 Niko's Bicycle Rental
29 National Reserve Bank;
   Ministry of Foreign Affairs
30 Australian High Commission
31 Swedish Consulate;
   Fasi Mo e Afi Pharmacy
32 Immigration
35 Polynesian Airlines
36 UCall; Palm Travel & Tours;
   Western Union
38 Royal Tongan Airlines;
   Vava'u Press
39 St Paul's Anglican Church
42 Loni's Cinema; DHL
43 Teta Tours;
   Air Fiji
44 Dateline Bookshop
45 Fung Shing Fast Photo
46 ANZ Bank (ATM)
50 Blue Pacific Music Store;
   Foto-Fix; Look Sharp Tonga
52 Western Union
53 Air New Zealand;
   Avis Car Rental

54 Friendly Islands Boookshop
55 Centennial Church of the Free
   Church of Tonga
56 Royal Tombs
57 Queen Salote Memorial Hall
59 Basilica of St Anthony of Padua;
   Public Library; Akiko's
60 MBF Bank
61 FIMCO Handicrafts Shop
63 Westpac Bank of Tonga &
   MoneyGram
64 Tonga Commmunications
   Corporation (local)
66 Tofa Shipping
68 Chinese Embassy
71 Tonga Communications
   Corporation
   (international)
72 Kinikinilau Shopping Centre;
   Super-Kava Market
73 Deep Blue Diving Centre
75 Tuimatamoana Harbour;
   'Eua Ferry; Fish Market;
   Fuel Station
76 Sea Star Fishing Co
77 Inter-island Ferry Terminal;
   'Uliti 'Uata Shipping
   (Walter Line)
78 Shipping Corporation of
   Polynesia
79 Ports Authority, Customs &
   Immigration
80 Fakafonua Shippping;
   Westpac Bank of Tonga;
   Royal Tongan Airlines
   Cargo
82 Billfish Bar & Restaurant
83 St Mary's Cathedral
86 First Wesleyan Church
90 Si'i Kae Ola Supermarket;
   Westpac Bank of Tonga
91 Tonfōn; ANZ Bank (ATM)
92 Teufaiva Outdoor Stadium

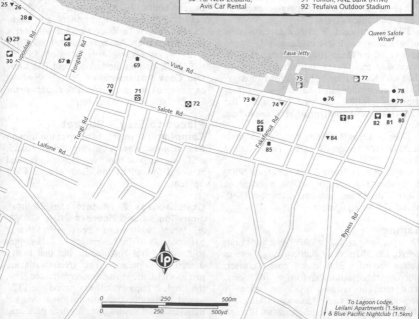

Yellow Pier

Queen Salote Wharf

Faua Jetty

Vuna Rd

Salote Rd

Tupoulahi Rd

Fongaloe Rd

Tungi Rd

Laifone Rd

Fakafanua Rd

Bypass Rd

To Lagoon Lodge,
Leilani Apartments (1.5km)
& Blue Pacific Nightclub (1.5km)

0   250   500m
0   250   500yd

TONGA

Tongan National Centre

The centre (☎ 23022; Taufa'ahau Rd, Vaiola; open 8.30am-4.30pm Mon-Fri) has seen better days, but the museum has enough interesting artefacts to make it worth an hour or two. The centre's **Cultural Tours** (T$8; 2pm Mon-Fri) are good value and include demonstrations of cooking, weaving, tapa-making and dancing. The **Tongan Evening** (T$20, dancing only T$6; 7.30pm Thur, book in advance) has one of the best traditional dancing shows in Tonga, though the feast attracts mixed reports. Dancing, weaving, tapa-making and Tongan language classes were set to begin in mid-2003, and the prices of all activities are 'under review'.

To get there, take the Vaiola bus from the eastern terminal on Vuna Rd (50 seniti), or take a taxi for T$4.

Diving & Snorkelling

See the 'South Pacific Diving' special section for some dive sites around Tongatapu and the rest of Tonga.

Deep Blue Diving Centre (☎/fax 23576; W www.deep-blue-diving.to; Vuna Rd; VHF Channel 14) offers two dives for T$120, including lunch, snacks and all gear. Five/10-dive packages cost T$540/1060. Open water courses are T$500, but the operators prefer to take prequalified divers.

The magnificent 'Eua sea caves – said to be among the finest in the world – were discovered by Deep Blue, who run two- to seven-day trips, with unlimited diving, to 'Eua and Kalau Island (T$380 for two days, T$190 each additional day). It also offers trips to beautiful, deserted Tau island for T$65/100 for non-divers/divers, including barbecue.

Deep Blue also has budget accommodation at its **Diver's Lodge** (☎ 23379; Fasi; singles/doubles T$34/68).

Royal Sunset Scuba Diving (☎/fax 21254; e royalsun@kalianet.to) on 'Ataha is close to a host of dive sites. Two-tank dives cost T$80, plus T$24 for equipment.

Sailing

The speedy **Sea-Taxi** (☎ 2975; e sugar@kalia net.to) has charters available to anywhere in Tonga aboard a 31ft luxury power cruiser, sleeping three adults and up to four kids, with rates at around US$5 per mile. A one-day return trip to 'Eua costs US$250. Deserted island snorkelling trips to Tau and Nuku cost US$175 for the whole boat.

The **Royal Sunset Island Resort** (☎/fax 21254; e royalsun@kalianet.to) operates the 15m luxury yacht *Impetuous* for visiting all of Tonga's island groups. Scuba equipment is available and the daily rate is T$503 to T$208 per person for two to six people. Add T$250 for yacht relocation.

Fishing

The Royal Sunset Island Resort has a 7m sportfishing boat costing T$280/560 (half/full day) for a maximum of three people.

Precision Charters (☎ 24700; e dwarner@kalianet.to) has a fully game-rigged 7.2m Buccaneer Billfisher for US$350 per day, including lunch, for a maximum of four people.

Sea-Taxi also does gamefishing charters for US$250/300 per half/full day, including all gear.

Whale Watching

Many gamefishing boats, as well as the Deep Blue Diving Centre, run whale-watching charters between June and November.

Places to Stay

As well as hostel, hotel and guesthouse options, there's lots of apartment accommodation in Nuku'alofa. Among the best are **The Lagoon Lodge** (26515; e lagoon.lodge@kalia net.to; 2-/4-person apartments per night T$146/250), with discounts for long-term bookings; **Leilani Apartments** (☎/fax 23910; 1-/2-/3-person apartments per month T$375/425/564), also on the lagoon; and **The Captain Cook Apartments** (☎ 25600; e phil@captaincook.to; singles/doubles per night T$125/140) on the waterfront.

Places to Stay – Budget

Camping It's possible to camp at the **Tongan Beachcomber Resort** on Pangaimotu island, a 20-minute boat trip from Nuku'alofa, and at **Good Samaritan Inn**. Both charge T$10 per tent.

Guesthouses & Motels The colourful, grotty **Toni's Guest House** (☎ 21049, 27068; e tonigh@kalianet.to; beds with shared bathroom T$10.75) has moved to Tofua, 4km south of central Nuku'alofa, but that hasn't dented its popularity. The green walls are just as vivid, the kava sessions just as regular, the English humour still as dry and the T$25 island tours still the best in town. Airport transfers are T$6 and there are free pick-ups/drop-offs into town.

Church feast, Tonga

MATT FLETCHER

Fatele (traditional music and dance perfomance), Nui Atoll, Tuvalu

PETER BENNETTS

Tepuka Vilivili Islet, Funafuti Atoll, Tepuka, Tuvalu

PETER BENNETTS

Land-dive tower, Salap, Vanuatu

Nambas villagers, Malekula, Vanuatu

Mt Marum volcano, Ambrym, Vanuatu

Moana Beach House (☎ 27406; Vuna Rd; singles/doubles with shared bathroom T$15/35, doubles with private bathroom T$60) is a budget guesthouse in a five-star waterfront location 1km west of the Royal Palace, and is thoroughly recommended. The rooms are plain but clean and there's a small kitchen, a games room and an enclosed veranda. Breakfast/dinner can be arranged for T$7/15.

Kaliloa Guest House (☎ 22314; Fongaloa Rd; beds in 4-person dorm T$20; singles/doubles with bathroom T$45/60; two-floor family room T$100) is a very pleasant, quiet little place just behind the Chinese Embassy, a short walk from town. The rooms, looking out onto a shady garden, are large, clean and basic. Breakfast costs T$5. This is a good choice for larger groups (the two-floor 'family room' sleeps up to seven).

Winnie's Guest House (☎ 25215; e winnies@kalianet.to; per person with breakfast T$30, students T$20) is a comfortable, homely place located 2km south of Nuku'alofa. It's very popular with visiting medical students (of which there are many), so book well in advance.

Sela's Guest House (☎ 25040; e mettonga@kalianet.to; off Fatafehi Rd; dorm beds T$10, singles/doubles with shared bathroom T$20/30, rooms with private bathroom T$50) is another old favourite in a sprawling wooden house, a 15-minute walk from town. The owners are friendly and helpful and provide lavish breakfasts for T$6. The rooms are OK, but mosquitoes can be a problem.

Misa's Guest House (☎ 27635; e Misa@MisasGuestHouse.com; cnr Railway & Mateialona Rds; singles/doubles T$20/40) in the old Toni's Guest House, is conveniently located, and has a homely living area and kitchen, though rooms are dark and a little depressing.

Places to Stay – Mid-Range
Nerima Lodge (☎ 25533, fax 25577; e naoko@maca.to; off Fatafehi Rd; singles/doubles/triples with shared bathroom T$43/68/96, singles/doubles with private bathroom T$55/80), clean and welcoming, is run by a knowledgeable, 'Tonganised' Japanese woman. The rooms and bathrooms are spotless and the price includes Western or Japanese breakfast. Excellent set-menu Japanese dinners can be arranged for T$30 a head (a minimum of four people) with plenty of advance notice. The royal family often orders takeaway.

Tom's Bed & Breakfast (☎ 22885, fax 23161; e kw@kalianet.to; singles/doubles with shared bathroom T$40/60, doubles with private bathroom T$80) is on a par with Nerima Lodge (it's even built by the same builder!) for cleanliness and friendliness. It feels a lot more like a home than a guesthouse, and prices include breakfast.

Heilala Holiday Lodge (☎ 29910, fax 29410; e info@heilala-holiday-lodge.com; PO Box 1698; singles/doubles T$55/48; fale singles/doubles T$55/68), around 4km south of Nuku'alofa, close to Toni's Guest House, is an excellent place to stay, with a cosy house and private tapa-lined fale (thatched-roof house) set in a neat garden with a shaded swimming pool. The price includes breakfast and there's a good garden restaurant, open with advance reservation to outside guests. Bicycle, scooter and car hire are available, and the owners can organise beach trips and island tours. One-night stays cost 50% extra.

Harbour View Motel (☎ 25488, fax 25490; e harbvmtl@kalianet.to; Vuna Rd; budget singles/doubles $40/60, standard rooms T$65/85, deluxe rooms T$105/115, family room T$125, executive suite T$160/170), opposite Queen Salote wharf, is a clean, bright and modern 12-room motel. The upper range rooms, if you can get one, are a much better bet than either the International Dateline or the Pacific Royale, supposedly Nuku'alofa's top-end hotels. Budget rooms have fan and shared bathroom. Standard rooms have fridge, air-con and shared bathroom. Deluxe rooms have air-con, TV/video, private bathroom and telephone. All prices include continental breakfast, and cars can be rented for T$50 per day.

Places to Stay – Top End
Seaview Lodge (☎ 23709; e seaview@kalianet.to; Vuna Rd; singles T$90, doubles T$110-155), 300m west of the Royal Palace, is one of the best places to stay in town, with modern, flawless rooms, all of which have air-con, phone, Internet port, TV, video and fridge. The top-end rooms have sea views.

Villa McKenzie (☎ 24998; Vuna Rd; singles/doubles T$105/125) is an immaculate old house with four elegant guest rooms, each with air-con and private bathroom, and an enormous living room with views of the sea. Rates include a full breakfast, and other meals are available by arrangement. There's a pleasant garden out the back.

International Dateline Hotel (☎ 23411, fax 23410; PO Box 39, Vuna Rd; standard singles/doubles T$99/115, superior singles/doubles/triples T$109/120/130, suites T$170) gets

TONGA

almost nothing but bad reports. At the time of writing it was undergoing an ambitious Chinese-funded renovation that promises to transform it into a quality hotel, but meanwhile the old rooms are average and the service patchy. Non-guests can use the pool and bar but the toilets are, by any standard, disgusting.

Places to Eat

From cold chips in a metal tray to lobster on fine china, Nuku'alofa has an extraordinary range of food for such a small town. Much of it is excellent, too, though it often comes at a price.

Restaurants & Cafés The excellent eatery **Friends Café** (☎ 22390; Taufa'ahau Rd; breakfast T$3.50-15, lunch T$4-15) looks like it came on holiday from Sydney and decided to stay. It's easily the best café in town, unrivalled for its good coffee, cakes, contemporary menu and friendly staff. It's often packed out at lunchtime, for good reason, and stays open until 10pm Monday to Friday.

Little Italy Pizzeria (☎ 25053; Vuna Rd; pizza & pasta T$9.50-15), west of the Royal Palace, has good food (particularly the pizzas) and a relaxed, cosy atmosphere. A great place to end up after an evening stroll along the waterfront.

Masala (☎ 26800; Taufa'ahau Rd; mains T$7.50-14) has mixed-origin Indian dishes of equally mixed quality, but is nonetheless very popular. Avoid the tandoori chicken and you won't go far wrong. The breads are very good. The restaurant is BYO and corkage is T$4.

Waterfront Café (☎ 24692; Vuna Rd; mains T$10-27) has a jovial atmosphere and a superb breezy waterfront location, which accounts for its popularity, but the European-style food is variable (you don't expect frozen veggies with a T$20 meal). It's also, deservedly, one of Nuku'alofa's most popular drinking venues. On Sunday it's open from 6pm to 9pm.

Little Tokyo (☎ 22474; Wellington Rd; mains T$6-16) is an authentic Japanese izakaya (drinking restaurant), where the décor is simple and the emphasis is as much on alcohol as it is on food. The don (meat/fish on rice) dishes are good value, but expect a long wait for any food.

Coco's Deli Café (☎ 26615; Wellington Rd; breakfast T$3-8, lunch T$6-8.50, dinner T$12-18) is worth a visit for its breakfast pancakes and homemade bagels, weighty rye-bread

sandwiches and cheap (T$1) plunger coffee. It's open from 7.30am.

Suliana's (☎ 22384; above TCF Supermarket, Wellington Rd; snacks & mains T$4-25; open until 9pm Mon-Fri), on a first-floor balcony, is a great spot to watch Nuku'alofa from above. It has excellent German food, as well as pancakes.

Of Nuku'alofa's many Chinese restaurants, **Emerald** (☎ 24619; Vuna Rd), **Fakalato** (☎ 24 101; Wellington Rd) and **Hua Hua** (☎ 27312; Vuna Rd) are all reasonable. **Fung Shing** (☎ 27881; Salote Rd) is notable for its frantic Sunday yum cha sessions, from 8.30am to 3pm, when most of Nuku'alofa's sizable Chinese community seems to turn up for a feed.

Two places share top prize for best budget lunch. **Akiko's** (☎ 25339; Taufa'ahau Rd, below the basilica; lunch T$3-5) serves a variety of Chinese dishes, teppanyaki, tempura and hamburgers. During school terms, **Pot Luck Lunches** (☎ 25091; off Salote Rd; lunch T$3-5) offers set-menu lunches cooked by students of the 'Ahopanilolo Technical College. You eat what you're given, like it or lump it (most will like it).

For Tongan staples like ota ika (raw fish) lu pulu (stuffed taro leaves in coconut cream) and fried fish/chicken/root crop combos, try the **Sama Restaurant** (lunch T$3-4) or **Noble Restaurant** (lunch T$3-4) next to each other on Railway Rd, or the 24-hour takeaway **Sia Leka's** (Taufa'ahau Rd; mains T$3.50-6; open until 2am except Saturday), opposite the Friends Café, which is always crowded and offers Western-style fast food and curries.

Fine Dining On the waterfront, the **Seaview Restaurant and Lodge** (☎ 23709; Vuna Rd; mains T$27-48) has a reputation for fine food and elegant surroundings, and is open evenings Monday to Friday. It's the first name on many residents' lips for special occasions, so book ahead.

Lunarossa Restaurant (☎ 26297; Taufa'ahau Rd, above TCF Supermarket; mains T$15-25) has excellent Italian food – including homemade pasta – and a good wine cellar.

Self-Catering The **Talamahu Market** has a good selection of fresh produce.

There are several decent bakeries around town, and **Cowley's Bread Bin** (Salote Rd) is one of the best.

Get your fish at the **fish market** on Tuimatamoana wharf (if you can get there for 5am) or at the **Sea Star Fishing Co** nearby.

Molisi Tonga Limited *(Salote Rd, opposite Talamahu Market)* is the best and most convenient supermarket in town, along with the **Super-Kava Market** *(Salote Rd)* in the Kinikinilau Shopping Centre. The trusty **Tonga Cooperative Federation** supermarket has two reasonable branches close together on Taufa'ahau Rd.

Entertainment
Island Buffets & Traditional Dance
The most popular places for dance and buffet evenings are the **Tongan National Centre** *(☎ 23022; T$20; Thur evening)*, the **Good Samaritan Inn** *(☎ 41022; T$20; Wed & Fri evening)* or, closer to town, the **Kahana Lagoon Resort** *(☎ 24239; T$20; Wed & Fri evening)*.

Pubs & Clubs Tongans drink with enthusiasm (just count the bouncers) and Nuku'alofa has a spirited bar scene, ranging from upmarket to unashamedly seedy. Friday is the big night, as everywhere closes at midnight on Saturday.

Along the waterfront on Vuna Rd are three popular venues. **Billfish Bar and Restaurant** *(☎ 24084)* is a large, relaxed open-air bar (with decent food) and one of the best and most popular drinking spots in town, especially later in the evening. There's live music Wednesday and Friday. **Waterfront Café** *(☎ 24692; Vuna Rd)* is equally popular and also has live music, while the **Garden Bar** *(☎ 22101; behind Emerald Restaurant)* has cheaper drinks and a more free-spirited atmosphere.

Wanda's *(☎ 23344; Taufa'ahau Rd)* next to the Pacific Royale Hotel is a small, Wild West Saloon-style bar and a favourite spot for Tongan boozers to end their evenings.

Nuku'alofa's intemperate youth converge on the **Blue Pacific Nightclub** *(☎ 25994; cover Fri T$6, Sat T$3)* for late-night Friday debauchery. It's 3km southeast of central Nuku'alofa and is open until 4am (until midnight on Saturday).

Cinemas The very basic **Loni's Cinema** *(☎ 23617; admission for 2 movies T$4)* shows Hollywood staples Thursday to Saturday, and midnight Sunday.

Shopping
A variety of good quality arts and crafts, tapa and pandanus mats can be found upstairs at the **Talamahu Market**.

Langafouna'ae Fefine Handicrafts *(Taufa 'ahau Rd)* is next door to Friends Café.

Popular local T-shirts are printed by **Blue Banana** *(☎ 41575)*, next to the grim Nawai Ali'i Beach Resort, and **Look Sharp Tonga** *(☎ 26056)*.

The Saturday-morning **flea market** *(Taufa 'ahau Rd)*, 3km south of Nuku'alofa, is good for second-hand clothes and even better for people-watching.

Getting There & Away
See the Tonga Getting There & Away section for information on transport between Tongatapu and other countries.

Getting Around
To/From the Airport Taxis meet all incoming flights, charging T$15 between the airport and Nuku'alofa. Many places to stay arrange transfers from the airport, or there's a **Teta Tours bus** *(☎ 23690)* that does the trip for T$10.

Bus Nuku'alofa's two bus terminals are close together on Vuna Rd. Buses to outlying areas of Tongatapu leave from the western terminal (close to Vuna Wharf), while Nuku'alofa buses leave from the eastern terminal (opposite the TVB). Fares range from 20 seniti to T$1. The bus service starts around 6am, with last buses running at around 4.30pm.

In urban areas of Tongatapu, bus stops are marked with a small sign reading 'Pasi'. Elsewhere, flag down a bus by waving. Passengers normally pay as they get off.

Car & Scooter Car rental companies in Nuku'alofa include **Avis** *(☎ 21179)*, with cars from T$88 to $108 per day with a T$250 deposit; **EM Jones Rental Cars** *(☎ 29917)*, T$50 to T$70 per day; **JR Rental** *(☎ 23344)*, T$60 per day, and **Challenge** from T$45 per day.

All rates include unlimited kilometres and special rates are usually available for weekends or long-term rentals. You must get a Tongan driving licence from the police before heading out.

Scooters are available from the **BP petrol station** next to the Masala Restaurant for T$10 per day.

Taxi Within Nuku'alofa, taxis charge a standard T$2 fare within town, or T$4 to T$5 to the outskirts. Long-term rates are about T$10 per hour. Taxis have a 'T' on the licence plate and are not permitted to operate on Sunday, but some guesthouses know secret Sunday taxi suppliers.

TONGA

Bicycle A bicycle stand on the waterfront, **Niko's Bicycle Rental** *(open 8am-5pm Mon-Sat)*, rents out bicycles in varying states for T$8 per day. Some guesthouses also have bicycles.

Boat The offshore island resorts all provide boat transport. Boat trips can also be arranged with the **Royal Sunset Island Resort** *(☎/fax 21254)* and **Sea-Taxi** *(☎ 22795)*.

AROUND THE ISLAND
Tongatapu features beaches, caves, blowholes and coral reefs, as well as some of the most extensive excavated archaeological sites in the Pacific.

Eastern Tongatapu
Mu'a & Lapaha In AD 1200, the 11th Tu'i Tonga, Tu'itatui, moved the royal capital from Heketa (near present-day Niutoua) to Lapaha, now known as Mu'a. The Mu'a area contains the richest concentration of archaeological remnants in Tonga. The *langi*, or pyramidal stone tombs, were traditionally used for the burial of royalty. In the vicinity of Mu'a there are 28 royal stone tombs, built with enormous limestone slabs carried by canoes either from nearby Pangaimotu, Motutapu and other parts of Tongatapu, or possibly from as far away as Ha'apai or even Futuna.

If you turn down the dirt road towards the sea, just north of the Catholic church, you reach a grassy area with two monumental mounds. This is Tonga's most imposing ancient burial site.

The structure closest to the main road is the **Paepae 'o Tele'a** (Platform of Tele'a), a monumental, pyramid-like stone memorial. Tele'a was a Tu'i Tonga who reigned during the 16th century, though his body is probably not inside.

The other structure, the **Langi Namoala** tomb, has a fine example of a *fonualoto* (vault for a corpse) on top – thought to be the burial site of a female chief – but it is also empty.

To the northeast of the two principal mounds is the **'Esi'aikona**, an elevated platform used as a rest area by the chief and his family. Also nearby is the **Hehea Mound**, built during an enormous ancient land-reclamation project.

Ha'amonga 'a Maui Trilithon Near Niutoua, at the eastern end of Tongatapu, is one of ancient Polynesia's most intriguing monuments. Archaeologists and oral history credit its construction to Tu'itatui, the 11th Tu'i Tonga. The structure consists of three large coralline stones, each weighing about 40 tonnes, arranged into a trilithic gate.

The Ha'amonga Trilithon is now preserved in the 23-hectare National Historic Reserve. From the entrance, a walking track winds northward past several *langi* (known as the *Langi Heketa*) and *'esi* (resting mounds), where interpretative signs make sense of the remaining mounds of stones.

It is now widely accepted that the trilithon had a similar function to Britain's Stonehenge: to track the changing seasons. Vegetation in line with the arms of the double-V design between the trilithon and the sea was cleared in 1967 and on the winter solstice the sun was seen to rise and set in perfect alignment with the clearings. On the summer solstice, the sun rose and set along the two other arms.

For the ancient Tongans, the significance of the summer solstice may have been related to the yam harvest, which was marked by the biggest festival of the year.

Seaward of the trilithon is a large stone called the **'Esi Makafakinanga**, supposedly Tu'itatui's backrest. Such chiefly backrests were common in Polynesia and apparently Tu'itatui used this one as a shield against attack from behind while he watched construction.

Take the infrequent Niutoua bus (T$1) and get off about 1km before Niutoua – the driver can indicate the spot. Head out early and return to Nuku'alofa in the early afternoon.

'Anahulu Cave Tongatapu's most famous cave is an eerie, otherworldly place full of stalactites and stalagmites and only marginally spoiled by vandalism. There's a very cool, refreshing pool to swim in. Bring a torch.

Buses run to Haveluliku (or to Fatumu just to the south) once or twice a day (T$1), but it's easier just to walk the 3km from Mu'a. From Haveluliku, take the dirt road southeast to a parking area and a set of steps leading to the cave.

Western Tongatapu
Tongan Wildlife Centre Bird Park The park *(☎ 29449; e birdpark@kalianet.to; Liku Rd, Veitongo; adult/child T$3/free; open 9am-5pm daily)* was established in 1990 to promote conservation awareness, collect data, carry out captive breeding, establish reserves and relocate rare and endangered indigenous bird species. The park also has a tropical garden containing examples of many medicinal

and food crops grown in Tonga. The park takes about 1½ hours to see and there are free guided tours.

Take the Vaini or Mu'a bus to Veitongo village (50 seniti) and get off at the Bird Park sign. From there, continue south for just over 2km to Liku Rd – the entrance is just south of the intersection.

Keleti Beach The clean and lovely Keleti Beach near the Wildlife Centre is actually a series of beaches divided by rocky outcrops. They slope gently into clear pools that are excellent for swimming in at high tide and lazing in at low tide. The outer reef consists of a line of terraces and blowholes that shoot like Yellowstone geysers when the waves hit them at high tide. Do not swim too close to the blowholes – there's a powerful vortex that can suck you under. Taxis from town cost T$8 each way.

Mapu'a 'a Vaca Blowholes These blowholes ('Mapu'a 'a Vaca' means 'Chief's Whistles') stretch for 5km along the south shore of Tongatapu, near the village of Houma. They are best viewed on a windy day at high (but not *too* high) tide, when the maximum amount of water is forced up through natural vents in the coral limestone, forming geyser-like fountains of seawater up to 30m high.

To get there by public transport, take a bus from Nuku'alofa to Houma and walk 1km south to the parking area above the blowholes.

Ha'atafu Beach Reserve The Ha'atafu Beach Reserve encompasses 8.4 hectares of shallow reef and an area of deep water just outside the breakers where some of the best surfing in Tonga can be found. The area inside the barrier reef has reasonable snorkelling and safe swimming. The reef breaks are only suitable for more experienced surfers.

The Hihifo bus passes all of Western Tongatapu's resorts and costs 80 seniti to T$1. A taxi from Nuku'alofa costs T$12.

Places to Stay & Eat The laid-back Ha'atafu Beach Resort (☎ 41088, fax 22970; e steve@surfingtonga.com; singles/doubles A$80/150, beds in 6-person dorm A$60) is an attractive resort specialising in surf holidays. Prices for the clean beachfront bungalows with shared facilities seem a little high, but they include breakfast, dinner and all watersports gear, and there's a 20% discount for

walk-in guests. Airport transfers cost T$40, shared between up to four people. The resort can arrange surfing safaris, boat trips and deep-sea fishing trips.

'Otuhaka Beach Resort (☎ 41599; e otuhaka@kalianet.to; fale doubles with shared bathroom T$35, bungalow with shared/private bathroom T$45/65, suite with 2 doubles, kitchen & bathroom T$170) has traditional fale and modern bungalows in a well-kept garden, right on magnificent Ha'atafu Beach. Non-guests can use the resort for a beach fee of T$2. Airport transfers are T$25.

After successive devastating cyclones in 2003, the **Good Samaritan Inn** (☎ 41022; e gsi@kalianet.to; camping T$10) is rebuilding once again. Bungalow accommodation was being repaired at the time of writing, but the T$20 Friday night Tongan buffet/entertainment evenings are back in action and still regarded as the best in Tongatapu. Taxis from Nuku'alofa cost around T$12; the Kolovai bus is 80 seniti. Guests get free pick up and daily shuttles into town.

Organised Tours

All-day taxi tours of Tongatapu, including all the traditional tourist sites, cost around T$60 to T$80 for up to four people. This can be an economical option if you're in a group.

Tony Matthias at **Toni's Guest House** (☎ 21 049, 27068; e tonigh@kalianet.to) runs exceptional island tours every day, including Sunday, for T$25 per person (minimum three people). Bring swimming gear, lunch and torch.

Teta Tours (☎ 23690; e tetatour@kalianet .to) offers half-island tours for T$20 and whole-island tours for T$35.

EM Jones Travel and Tours (☎ 23422; e jonestvl@kalianet.to) also offer whole-island trips, including lunch, for T$56 per person.

OFFSHORE ISLANDS & REEFS
Pangaimotu

The closest and cheapest island resort to Nuku'alofa is **Tongan Beachcomber Resort** (☎/fax 23759, 15762; fale singles/doubles with bathroom T$30/50, beds in 8-person dorm T$15, camping T$10). It's popular with weekend day-trippers escaping the activity taboo on Sunday, when mainland Tongan Christian society takes a very dim view of frivolity and fun. It has an excellent beach and the clear azure water offers better swimming than anywhere on Tongatapu. A bonus for snorkellers is the prow of the *My Lady Lata II* shipwreck poking eerily out of the water just offshore.

Sunday trips to Pangaimotu leave from Faua Jetty at 10am, 11am, noon and 1pm, returning at 3pm, 4pm, 5pm and 6pm. From Monday to Saturday the boat leaves at 10am and 11am, returning at 4pm and 5pm. The trip takes about 15 minutes and costs T$12 return.

Fafá Island Resort

Elegant and exclusive, **Fafá Island Resort** (☎ 22800, fax 23592; e fafa@kalianet.to; *fale singles/doubles T$120/135, superior fale T$240; half/full board T$75/90*) is set on a magnificent beach. The 18 *fale* are beautifully constructed from local materials, with the standard *fale* grouped inland and the superior *fale* looking out onto the beach. Airport to island transfers cost T$56 and the return boat trip from Nuku'alofa's Tuimatamoana Harbour costs T$28.

Day trips to Fafá leave at 11am every day and return at 4.30pm. The cost, including lunch, is T$35.

Royal Sunset Island Resort

On 'Atata Island, **Royal Sunset Island Resort** (☎ 21254; e royalsun@kalianet.to; *singles/doubles bungalows T$120/150, minisuites T$180, full board T$50*) has 16 excellent beachfront bungalows facing the sunset, each with fridge, ceiling fan, tea and coffee facilities and private bathroom. The restaurant/bar *fale* is impressive, and there's a saltwater pool and a billiard table. Airport to island transfers cost T$44. The resort is also a centre for sailing and gamefishing and arranges diving trips (see Activities in the Nuku'alofa section).

Day trips to the island, including barbecue lunch, snorkelling and boat transfer, cost T$35 and run only on Sunday. The boat leaves Tuimatamoana Harbour at 10am and returns at 4pm.

'Eua

With its rugged, untouched natural beauty and proximity to Tongatapu, 'Eua is growing in popularity as an alternative to the sea-and-sand holiday.

Information All basic services are in the small main town of 'Ohonua.

MAF (☎ 50122) is a good source of information about the 'Eua Plantation Forest, 'Eua National Park and other areas in the bush.

Friendly Islands Bookshop (☎ 50167) has an excellent colour A3 map of 'Eua for T$3.

Royal Tongan Airlines (☎ 50188) is at Kaufana Airport in Fata'ulua.

Northern 'Eua 'Eua's northern tip is relatively inaccessible, but has some impressive features. Popular sites are **Kahana Spring** and the nearby dramatic clifftop **viewpoints**, from where you can scramble down to isolated **Fangutave Beach**. From there it's possible to hike through the rainforest to some spectacular hidden **caves**.

Tracks can be difficult to find, so seek local advice, or better still, go with a local guide (see the Organised Tours section later).

Central 'Eua The eastern part of central 'Eua is covered with Tonga's greatest extent of natural rainforest, with dense jungle-like growth, giant tree ferns and vines and a couple of enormous, ancient banyan trees. The **'Eua National Park** and **'Eua Plantation Forest** cover much of the area, which is underlaid with eroded limestone, causing a Swiss-cheese landscape of caves and sinkholes. Only limited trails and routes penetrate the forest through the caves area, so it's best viewed with a guide. See the Organised Tours section later.

Central 'Eua's highlights are the **Hafu Pool**, the dramatic **Lauua and Lokupo lookouts** overlooking the park, beach and pounding ocean, and the **'Ana Kuma** (Rat's Cave), where those who brave the unnerving drop into it are rewarded by spectacular views.

Southern 'Eua Southern 'Eua's **Lakufa'anga** area contains the island's finest geological features, though you're faced with a long walk to reach them. The area's most prominent site is the **Rock Garden**, a collection of bizarrely shaped eroded coral slabs, surrounded by a grassy meadow with wild horses. Close by is the **Liangahu'o 'a Maui**, a giant limestone arch. Across the arch is the **Bowl of Cliffs**, an impressive half-circle of cliffs between which the seas churns like a flushing toilet bowl.

Places to Stay All accommodation on 'Eua is of the budget variety.

The Hideaway (☎ 50255; e hideaway@ kalianet.to; *Tufuvai village; singles/doubles/ triples/quads with private bathroom T$40/ 50/60/70, camping T$10*) is in a fantastic spot on a rocky shore facing the sunset – at the right time of year, you can see humpback whales from the rooms! Prices include breakfast and free airport/wharf transfers. The guided bushwalking tours are recommended (see Organised Tours later).

Taina's Guest House (☎ 50186; *Telefoni Rd; camping T$12, singles/doubles/triples T$20/*

25/30), otherwise known as the Maxi Scandic Hotel, is a very friendly, popular place with basic detached rooms, spacious grounds, a communal area and a guest kitchen which can be used for T$3. Breakfast/dinner is T$7/15 and pick-ups from the airport or wharf cost T$3. There's also bike/horse hire for T$10/15. It's a good base for exploring the National Park and the owners run tours for T$25 to T$30.

The Highlight (☎ 50143; singles/doubles T$20/35) is a new guesthouse out near the airport, with four clean rooms sharing two bathrooms with hot water. Rates include breakfast and the owners run island tours.

Places to Eat The Ta'anga Supermarket and Tonga Cooperative Federation in 'Ohonua have limited stocks, but it's advisable to bring some supplies from Nuku'alofa. Guesthouses all do decent food.

Entertainment The Hideaway has a bar open to guests and non-guests. The Haukinima Bar is a roughhouse joint in 'Esia, with cheap beer and pool tables. The Maxi Disco Hall opposite the Haukinima Bar is alcohol-free, but visitors – especially women – are advised to avoid it as the risk of harassment is very high.

Organised Tours The Hideaway runs a series of recommended bushwalking tours to 'Eua's prime sites. Walks are graded for difficulty, and cost T$40 including lunch. It also runs a vehicle tour of the island, also for T$40.

Taina's Guest House runs a National Park tour for T$25.

Whale-watching boat trips can be organised at The Hideaway for T$80/70/60 for one/two/three or more people (it's more expensive if only one person goes).

Getting There & Away There are flights five days a week from Tongatapu (single/return T$29/56; 10 minutes). The ferry trip from Tongatapu (single/return T$12/20) takes 1½ to 2½ hours (depending on the boat) and can be extremely rough.

Getting Around There is no bus service. Call for taxis (☎ 50039, 50152) or hitch.

Minerva Reef

This reef, awash most of the time, is Tonga's southernmost extremity. It lies 350km southwest of Tongatapu and serves as a rest point for yachts travelling from Tonga to New Zealand.

Ha'apai Group

pop 8400 • area 110 sq km
With a better infrastructure and marketing dollars, Ha'apai could easily be a major tourist destination. As it is, in return for sacrificing a few conveniences, Ha'apai's few visitors get perfect beaches, reefs, deserted islands and two spectacular volcanoes virtually to themselves. It's a sleepy, seductive place, well off the beaten track – and you get the feeling the people would prefer to keep it that way.

History
Archaeological excavations show the Ha'apai Group has been settled for at least 3000 years. Lapita pottery, carbon dated at 3000 years old, has been unearthed in the village of Hihifo.

The first European to visit the group was Abel Tasman in 1643. It was in these islands that James Cook and his men narrowly escaped attack (see the earlier boxed text 'Cook's 'Friendly Islands'').

LIFUKA GROUP
Most visitors stay within the Lifuka Group, where most accommodation is located. Lifuka island, with its capital Pangai, is the centre of Ha'apai's limited activity.

Lifuka & Pangai
Pangai is a small, tidy place with a pleasantly soporific atmosphere. There's not much to do except allow the pace of Ha'apai life to sedate you, but there's some good snorkelling off the sheltered western beaches.

Information The Tonga Visitors' Bureau (TVB; ☎ 60733; W www.vacations.tvb.gov.to; open 8.30am-12.30pm & 1.30pm-4.30pm Mon-Fri) has maps of town and useful information on things to do, and can arrange bookings for all Ha'apai guesthouses.

The Westpac Bank of Tonga (Holopeka Rd) does the usual transactions and MoneyGram transfers, but closes lunchtimes. The post office (Holopeka Rd) is next to Royal Tongan Airlines. The 24-hour Tonga Communications Corporation, on the road parallel to Holopeka Rd behind TVB, is open for domestic and international calls.

Royal Tongan Airlines (☎ 60566; open 8.30am-5pm Mon-Fri, 8.30am-noon Sat) is in the block of buildings opposite the TVB. Friendly Islands Bookshop (Holopeka Rd) has limited stocks and is at the north end of town.

Niu'ui Hospital (☎ 60201) is in the village of Hihifo, on the southern side of Pangai, but is very poorly equipped.

The water supply in Ha'apai should be used only for washing and bathing. Only drink water collected in rainwater cisterns.

Afa Eli Historical Museum This museum, between Palace and Haufolau Rds and close to the Langilangi Guesthouse, is a tiny shed with some 3000-year-old Lapita pottery excavated in Pangai. The 'research library' across the road looks more like a gift shop, but has a few specialist books.

Olovehi Tomb This tomb (*Loto Kolo Rd*) is in Hihifo, and its modern extension is the burial ground for people holding the noble title of Tuita.

Velata Mound Fortress About 1.2km south of Pangai, a turning towards the east leads you to a large sign describing the circular Velata Mound Fortress, a ring-ditch fortification of a type widely found throughout Tonga, Fiji and Samoa.

Shirley Baker Monument & European Cemetery About 800m north of Pangai, in the European cemetery, lies the grave and monument of Shirley Baker, Tonga's first prime minister. The TVB has a pamphlet with some interesting information about the characters buried in the cemetery. The Tongan cemetery is directly opposite.

Southern Lifuka On the south side of Pangai is the village of Hihifo. From here you can continue south along the dirt road all the way to Lifuka's south tip, where there's a fine beach.

Along the way, note **Hulu'ipaongo Tomb**, the large ancient mound on the west side of the road. The highest tomb on Lifuka, this is the burial site of the Mata'uvave line of chiefs.

Activities Ha'apai has good underwater visibility and amazing diving. There's also good snorkelling around Lifuka. Grab a copy of 'Snorkelling in Ha'apai' from the TVB for a map and descriptions of snorkelling sites.

Places to Stay Camping is prohibited throughout the Ha'apai Group, but it's possible to arrange deserted island trips to the idyllic Nukupule or Meama islands through the TVB. Legally, you must be accompanied by a guide or on an organised trip.

Pangai All of Pangai's accommodation is basic: don't expect rigorous cleanliness or energetic service.

Fifita Guest House (☎ 60213; *Fau Rd; singles/doubles T$20/35*) is ideally located in the centre of town and above Pangai's only restaurant, the Mariner's Café. The rooms here are very simple and don't have fans (though you may get one if you ask sweetly). There's a reasonable kitchen for guests and a cool, shady balcony. The price includes a good breakfast (see Places to Eat later).

Lindsay Guesthouse (☎ 60107; *Loto Kolo Rd; singles/doubles T$20/30, rooms with private bathroom T$45*) can be a hot hike from town, but it's a popular place. The rooms are, of course, basic, and the bathrooms don't exactly sparkle, but there's a great veranda and a café, grocery shop and bakery on the grounds (see Places to Eat later).

Langilangi Guesthouse (☎ 60038; *Palace Rd; singles/doubles T$15/25, family room T$35*) is set back from the road, about 300m up from Holopeka Rd. The rooms are unexceptional, but many visitors have commented on the friendliness of the place. Meals must be preordered and cost T$7/15 for breakfast/dinner, or there's a well-equipped kitchen for T$2 per day.

Evaloni's Guesthouse (☎ 60029; *Loto Kolo Rd; singles/doubles T$15/25, family room with bathroom T$60*) is a little gloomy, but adequate. The upstairs family rooms are a lot nicer, with couches, a fridge and a breezy balcony, but are overpriced. Meals can be prearranged at T$10/15 for breakfast/dinner, or you can use the large kitchen for T$2.

Around Lifuka All beachside accommodation is located outside Pangai. The east side of the island has big waves and the west is generally sheltered and placid.

Billy's Place (☎ 60336; *bungalow singles/doubles with bathroom T$45/55*) is planning a major upgrade (to be completed in late 2003) that will feature *fale* with electricity, fridges and other little luxuries, with correspondingly higher prices (the owners say they will keep some budget bungalows). There's a great beach and excellent snorkelling, but be prepared to cater for yourself in the evenings or do the run into town every night. No children under 12 are allowed. The price includes breakfast and a bicycle.

Mele Tonga Guesthouse (☎ 60042; *singles/doubles T$20/30; beach bungalows T$30*) has a pretty beachside location that manages to feel isolated even though it's not far from the main road. The simple rooms and bungalows are a hop and a skip away from the beach and there's an adequate kitchen for T$5 per day. Breakfast/lunch/dinner costs T$8/10/12.

Places to Eat The relaxed outdoor hangout, **Mariner's Café** (☎ 60374; VHF Channel 16; Fau Rd; snacks & mains T$3.50-15), is popular with visitors and the small, amiable band of resident Peace Corps volunteers. The food is pretty good and the pizzas are a local legend. It's a good place to pick up information during the day, or a hangover in the evening. On Sunday it's open from 6pm to 8pm.

Lindsay Café (☎ 60107; Loto Kolo Rd; breakfast T$4-10, dinner T$8-20), in the garden of the Lindsay Guesthouse (see Places to Stay earlier), is a reasonable alternative to the Mariner's Café. The food from a small menu is good and it's a relaxing place to sit with a few beers, though it's not exactly the most congenial of places.

Pangai's **produce market** is just north of the Tonga Development Bank, at the northern end of Pangai. Pickings range from slim to very slim.

Tonga Cooperative Federation, on Holopeka Road, is Ha'apai's only supermarket, stocking a small, unpredictable range of imported goods. The *fale koloa* (general stores) around town stock most basic necessities.

The **Matuku-e-tau Bakery** is at the Lindsay Guesthouse, and the **Foueti 'Ofa Bakery** is one block north. Both open around 5pm on Sunday, when there's a mad rush for bread.

Shopping In Pangai, the **Women's Island Development Handicraft Shop** (☎ 60478) sells good handicrafts.

Getting There & Away Ha'apai is well serviced by air and sea.

Air Ha'apai's Salote Pilolevu Airport is 3km north of Pangai. Royal Tongan Airlines operates flights daily (except Sunday) between Ha'apai and Tongatapu (T$89/167 single/return), and three times a week between Ha'apai and Vava'u (T$73/135 single/return).

Boat The MV 'Olovaha (if it's operating; see the Getting There & Away section under Niuatoputapu later), MV 'Otu Tonga and MV Pulupaki call in twice weekly at Pangai, on both their northbound and southbound runs between Tongatapu and Vava'u.

There are marginally protected anchorages along the lee shores of Lifuka, Foa, Ha'ano, Uoleva, Ha'afeva, Nomuka and Nomuka'iki.

Getting Around Some places to stay offer free transfers to/from the airport and wharf.

To/From the Airport Taxis charge T$3 to T$5 between the airport and Pangai. The bus between Pangai and the airport turn-off costs around 60 seniti, but you may be in for a long wait.

Bicycle Lifuka and Foa are flat. Some guesthouses can arrange rental, or get bikes from the Mariner's Café (see Places to Eat earlier). Costs are around T$5 to T$10 per day.

Bus Two buses run between Hihifo, at the southern end of Pangai, and Faleloa, the northernmost village, a 25-minute walk south of the Sandy Beach Resort on Foa Island. They run irregularly between 8am and 4pm Monday to Friday and until noon on Saturday. The trip from Pangai to Faleloa costs 60/80 seniti (small/large bus).

Taxi Several people in Pangai operate taxis. Try **Siaosi** (☎ 60072) or **Ioane** (☎ 60509), or ask your guesthouse to call one.

Foa

Heavily wooded and sparsely populated, Foa is north of Lifuka and connected to it by a causeway. At its northern tip is the best beach in 'mainland' Ha'apai – Houmale'eia – where there are great views, irresistible water and some good snorkelling.

Activities Based at Sandy Beach Resort on Foa, **Happy Ha'apai Divers** (☎ 60639; e herbert@kalianet.to) is a professional outfit focused on guests. Diving tends to concentrate on the north Lifuka Group; it's a good option for the freshly qualified. Open from 1 April to 30 November, it offers two-tank dives with gear for T$105. CMAS diving instruction costs T$510, and English and German are spoken.

Places to Stay One of Tonga's best resorts, **Sandy Beach Resort** (☎ 60600; e sandybch@kalianet.to; PO Box 61, Pangai; bungalows US$112; breakfast/dinner US$9/29) is on Houmale'eia Beach and it's open from 1 February to 30 November every year. The 12 bungalows are a little plain but the beach and range of activities more than make up for that. Prices include airport transfers, snorkelling gear, kayaks, canoes, bicycles, guided bushwalks, kayak tours, Tongan cultural shows and shuttles to Pangai. Children under 16 can stay by prior arrangement only. Happy Ha'apai Divers (see the Activities section earlier) runs dives and courses between April and November.

Getting There & Around The bus from Pangai stops at Faleloa, a 25-minute walk from the resort. A taxi to Houmale'eia should cost T$10 to T$12 – you may want to ask the driver to return to pick you up if you're day-tripping, or else face a long walk back.

By bicycle from Pangai takes around 45 minutes.

Nukunamo

The small uninhabited island of Nukunamo, immediately north of Foa, is surrounded by a shining white beach covered with beautiful shells.

At low tide, Nukunamo is accessible by snorkelling from the northern end of Foa. Only confident swimmers should attempt this, and only with local advice, as the currents through the pass can be powerful.

Ha'ano

The strikingly clean island of Ha'ano has lovely beaches. To get there, take the bus to Faleloa on Foa Island and catch one of the water taxis that leave for Ha'ano whenever the bus arrives. The fare between the islands is T$2 per person.

Uoleva

Uoleva, 1.5km south of Lifuka, is one of Tonga's most beautiful spots, with endless stretches of pristine beaches, superb snorkelling and almost complete seclusion.

Places to Stay Situated on a perfect white-sand beach, Daiana Resort (☎ 60290 or book through TVB; singles/doubles T$18/25; breakfast/dinner T$5/12) has become a popular place to spend a long time doing very little. The tapa-lined *fale* are very basic, with mattresses on the floor and mosquito nets, and there's a kitchen area where you can cook for T$2 per day. Meals must be prearranged and transfers cost T$10 each way.

Captain Cook Resort (☎ 60014 or book through the TVB; singles/doubles T$15/20; family fale T$25; breakfast/dinner T$4/10) a few minutes' walk down the beach from

Daiana Resort, has a shadier location, more comfortable *fale*, more appealing showers and an equally pristine beach. Sadly, it has also suffered from bad reports advising single women (or any women not accompanied by men) to stay away. This advice still holds true, but there's no reason for couples or families to avoid it and many visitors have recommended the place. Transfers are also T$10 one way.

Getting There & Around It's possible to walk between the southern tip of Lifuka and the northern tip of Uoleva at low tide, but get local advice (and a copy of the tide tables from the TVB) before you attempt it.

Both resorts will do the return trip to Pangai for day trips for T$20 per person. The TVB can also arrange boats for the day for around T$50.

'Uiha

The clean, friendly island of 'Uiha has two villages: 'Uiha, with the main wharf, and Felemea, about 1.5km south, where there's accommodation.

In the centre of 'Uiha village is a large, elevated burial ground containing several ancient **royal tombs**. At the village church are two **cannons** taken from a Peruvian blackbirding (slaving) ship – attacked and destroyed by the locals in 1863.

'Esi-'o-Ma'afu Homestay (☎ 60128; VHF Channel 16 or book through TVB; singles/ doubles T$20/25; breakfast T$6, dinner T$10-18), on the beach at Felemea village, is friendly with traditional, but rather dark, *fale*. You can do your own cooking or meals can be prepared if you book ahead. There's a family *'umu* (traditional Tongan feast cooked in an earth oven) most Sundays and guests can participate in village activities.

The TVB in Pangai can arrange boat transport for around T$10 each way.

Tofua

Tofua has the most active of Tonga's volcanoes. The island is mostly covered in virgin tropical forest, though kava (and, recently, less legal crops) is grown on the fertile slopes. In the centre is a circular crater, at the bottom of which is a beautiful, crystal-clear lake. Just offshore is where the infamous mutiny on the *Bounty* occurred (see the boxed text 'Mutiny on the Bounty' in the Pitcairn Island chapter).

To visit Tofua's crater, follow a track from the shore that leads up through a virgin forest full of birds, tree ferns and ironwood, and over fields of pumice and scoria to the rim of the gaping volcanic vent, where you can perch at the edge of the steaming inferno. The walk is 1¼ hours up and 30 minutes back down.

Trips to Tofua can be arranged through the **Mariner's Café** (see Places to Eat under Lifuka & Pangai earlier) or the TVB, costing T$250 per person (minimum three days and four people). Guides are an extra T$50 per day. From Nuku'alofa, **Sea-Taxi** (☎ 22975; e sugar@ kalianet.to) operates one- to three-day trips to Tofua and Kao for US$800 for the whole boat. Passengers must be prepared to swim to the shore.

Kao
On clear days, the immense volcanic cone of Kao, Tonga's highest mountain at 1109m, is visible from Lifuka. Trips can be arranged through **Sea-Taxi** and it's wise to take a guide.

OTHER HA'APAI GROUP ISLANDS
The deserted islands of **Nukupule** and **Meama** are perfect spots for a Robinson Crusoe experience, with stirring views of Tofua and Kao. Watersports Ha'apai can take you out there.

The twin volcanic islands of **Hunga Tonga** and **Hunga Ha'apai** are in the far southwestern corner of the Ha'apai Group. Both volcanoes have been dormant for several hundred years. The **Sea-Taxi** (☎ 22975; e sugar@kalianet.to) power cruiser can be chartered for day trips from Nuku'alofa, costing US$360 for the whole boat.

Vava'u Group

pop 16,200 • area 119 sq km
The Vava'u Group boasts picturesque islands, channels and waterways and scores of lovely, secluded anchorages, making it one of the world's top yachting destinations.

Beyond lush hills and islands, white-sand beaches and coral reefs teeming with tropical fish are quiet villages, hidden caves and windswept cliffs.

It's also a major whale-watching and diving destination, but be warned: Vava'u's watery wonders do not come cheap.

History
Islands of the Vava'u Group have been settled for around 2000 years.

When 'Ulukalala III died, King George Tupou I was entrusted to look after the throne

of Vava'u for 'Ulukalala IV, who was just a boy. But George seized the opportunity to add Vava'u to his own realm, eventually forming a united Tonga in 1845.

Geography
The Vava'u Group is actually a single block of limestone tilted toward Ha'apai. The northern extremity ends in high cliffs that plunge straight into the surf, while in the submerged southern part of the group, summits of numerous small islands and islets peek above the surface of the water, surrounded by coral reefs.

Climate
The Vava'u Group has the wettest climate in Tonga. Most of the rain falls from late November to April, which is also cyclone season.

NEIAFU
pop 5900
Prior to European contact, Neiafu was a sacred burial ground, and political unrest and tribal skirmishes were forbidden. Nowadays, with its peeling weatherboard facades and roaming pigs, Neiafu can look like a fading frontier town. In fact it's the closest thing Tonga has to a tourist centre, with bars, restaurants and marine activity operators lining the picturesque waterfront, and a boisterous nightlife when the ban on skirmishes is often overlooked.

Information
Maps The TVB has decent maps of Neiafu and the Vava'u Group. Yachties can pick up a beautifully drawn sea chart, showing all anchorages, from Sailing Safaris for T$10 (see the Sailing section later).

Tourist Offices The **Tonga Visitors' Bureau** (TVB; ☎ 70115, fax 70666; w www.vacations .tvb.gov.to; VHF Channel 16; Fatafehi Rd; open 8.30am-4.30pm Mon-Fri) are a friendly bunch and will assist with anything from car rentals to activity and accommodation bookings.

Money The **Westpac Bank of Tonga**, **ANZ** and **MBF** banks, all on Fatafehi Road, change cash and travellers cheques. The ANZ has a 24-hour ATM machine with Visa, MasterCard and Cirrus facilities. The Bank of Tonga and MBF open Saturday mornings until 11am.

TONGA

VAVA'U GROUP

Key (numbered locations):

1. Bayview Apartments
2. The Tongan Beach Resort
3. Hakula Lodge; Friendly Islands Kayak Company
4. Wreck of the *Clan MacWilliam*
5. Marcella Resort
6. Hinakauea Beach Feast
7. Ika Lahi Lodge
8. Blue Lagoon
9. Popao Resort
10. La Paella, Ark Gallery

TONGA

Post & Communications
The post office (open 8.30am-4pm Mon-Fri) is on Fatafehi Rd, north of the 'Utukalongalu market. Poste restante (c/o Return or Delivery, Post Office, Neiafu, Vava'u) is available, though yachties might find Sailing Safaris' service more convenient (c/o Sailing Safaris, Private Bag 56, Neiafu, Vava'u).

Behind the post office, the 24-hour **Tonga Communications Corporation** offers international calls, telecards and a fax service (during normal office hours).

Internet services are now available in Vava'u, but connection speeds are often excruciatingly slow. Beluga Diving, Sailing Safaris and many places to stay have Internet and email services. Expect to pay around 50 seniti per minute.

Vava'u has its own radio station: FM1, at 89.3 on the FM dial. A yachties' information net is on VHF Channel 6 at 8.30am Monday to Friday.

Bookshops The **Friendly Islands Bookshop** (☎ 70505; Fatafehi Rd) meets most stationery (but few reading) needs, and has photocopying. The **Dateline Bookshop** (Fatafehi Rd) has similar stock.

Laundry Most places to stay offer laundry services.

Medical Services Dr Alfredo Carafa's **Italian Clinic and Pharmacy** (☎ 70607, after hours ☎ 12045; Fatafehi Rd; open 9am-2pm Mon-Fri, 9am-10.30am Sat) is your best bet for minor complaints. It charges T$35 for consultations and T$20 for dive-health certificates.

More serious health troubles should be directed to the **Prince Wellington Ngu Hospital** (☎ 70201).

Emergency The **police station** is on Tu'i Rd. The emergency telephone numbers are: **police** (☎ 922, 70233), **fire** (☎ 933, 70089) and **hospital** (☎ 933).

Old Harbour (Neiafu Tahi)
Near the entrance to the sunken Hala Tafengatoto pathway in eastern Neiafu are several freshwater springs bubbling into the Old Harbour. The most reliable is Matalave, which lies around the harbour to the east. Nearby is the rocky outcrop said to have been the primary Vava'u landing site of the *kalia*, the double-hulled canoes used in ancient times.

St Joseph's Cathedral
A classic example of colonial architecture, this imposing Catholic cathedral is Neiafu's most impressive structure. Completed in the mid-20th century, its grand facade has survived successive cyclones and thousands of twilight photographs. The interior is splendid too, but dress respectfully before going in.

Mo'unga Talau
The protected Mo'unga Talau (Mount Talau) park, overlooking the Port of Refuge, is easily climbed in an afternoon. Continue west past the rugby field along Tapueluelu Rd and up through a residential area, until the road narrows into a bush track. When it begins to descend, a side track turns off to the right and leads steeply up over slippery rock surfaces to the summit, where you get a great view. There's a marked walking tour linking four viewpoints.

Diving
Vava'u's two operators have good reputations. **Beluga Diving** (☎/fax 70087; ⓦ www.belugadivingvavau.com; VHF Channel 16; Fatafehi Rd) charges T$110 for two-tank dives at separate sites. PADI open water courses cost T$400 for individuals, and T$350 for two or more people.

Dolphin Pacific Diving (☎/fax 70292; ⓦ www.academydivers.co.nz; VHF Channel 71) has a purpose-built dive facility next to the Puatakanave Nightclub. Two-tank dives cost T$90, PADI open water courses T$400 and IDEA courses T$350.

Snorkelling
Snorkelling trips are one of the most popular and cheapest ways to experience Vavau's underwater attractions. Most diving/fishing/whale-watching operators will run snorkelling trips whenever demand is there. Expect to pay a minimum of T$30 per person. **Sailing Safaris** (☎/fax 70650; ⓔ sailingsafaris@kalianet.to; VHF Channel 68) is a friendly outfit that runs special weekend trips, including barbecue, for T$70 per person.

Sailing
At the time of writing, **Sailing Safaris** was planning to shift its offices into the Mermaid Bar. It has a range of small boats from 7.8m at T$200 per day (add T$100 for a skipper). It also offers sailing training from 'Discover Sailing' one-day courses (T$300, up to four people) to five-day courses from T$1750.

TONGA

NEIAFU

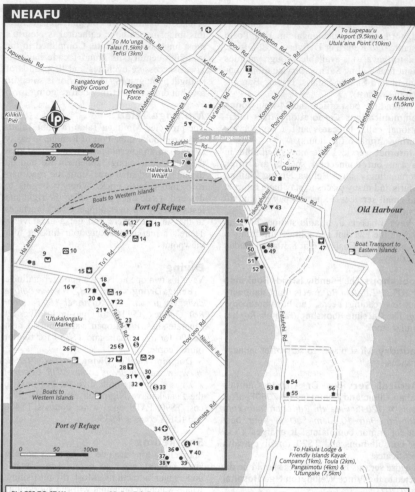

PLACES TO STAY
4 Port Wine Guest House
17 Adventure Backpackers;
    Royal Tongan Airlines
42 Hill Top Hotel; Sunset
    Restaurant & Pizzeria
53 Paradise International
    Hotel
55 Vava'u Guest House;
    Kiwi Magic
56 Twin View Motel

PLACES TO EAT
3 Mangele Bakery
5 George's Bakery
   (Siaosi Fainga'a Bakery)
16 'Alatini Fisheries
21 Vava'u Trading
    Centre
22 Kalia II Takeaway
23 TCF Supermarket
31 Royal Beer Shop

38 Pua Tale Fusi
40 Caffe Italiano
43 Lighthouse Café
44 Dancing Rooster
51 'Ana's Café;
    The Moorings

OTHER
1 Prince Wellington Ngu
   Hospital
2 Free Church of Tonga
6 Shipping Corporation of
   Polynesia & 'Uliti 'Uata
   Shipping (Walter Line) Offices
7 Customs Department
8 Vava'u Library
9 Post Office
10 Tonga Communications
    Corporation;
    Vava'u Handicrafts
11 Immigration
12 Sailoame Market & Bus Stop

13 Free Wesleyan Church
14 Lopaukamea Taxi
15 Police Station;
    Fire Station
18 EM Jones
19 JV Taxis
20 Ikapuna Store
24 MBF Bank
25 ANZ Bank (ATM);
    Western Union
26 Bus Stop
27 Ifo Ifo Bar
28 Bounty Bar; Teta Tours;
    Whale Watch Vava'u
29 Liviela Taxi
30 Angela Handicrafts
32 Friendly Islands Bookshop
33 Westpac Bank of Tonga
34 Italian Clinic & Pharmacy
35 Tropical Tease Clothing
36 Dateline Bookshop
37 Dolphin Pacific Diving

39 Nightclub, SF Paea &
    Sons Supermarket; Pua
    Café & Photo Developers
41 Tonga Visitors Bureau;
    Langafonua Handicrafts
    Shop; Leiola Duty
    Free Shop
45 Nasaleti House
46 St Joseph's Cathedral &
    Convent
47 Motele Nightclub
48 Leiola Duty Free Shop
49 Vava'u Laundry
50 Sailing Safaris;
    The Mermaid Bar &
    Restaurant;
    SS Marine Centre
52 Fangafoa Marina;
    Beluga Diving; Sunsail;
    Melinda Sea Adventures
54 Whales Alive; Look Sharp
    Vava'u; Fa Sea Jewellery

The Moorings (☎ 70016, fax 70428; W www
.moorings.com; VHF Channel 72), the world's
largest yacht charter company, has five catamarans and eight monohulls ranging from 12m
to 15m, sleeping up to 10 passengers. Prices
vary according to the season, but range from
around US$350 to US$900 per day for bareboat charters. The company has agents across
the world.

Sunsail (☎ 70646; W www.sunsail.co.nz;
VHF Channel 71), adjacent to Beluga Diving,
is a multinational charter operation with six
yachts and two catamarans in Vava'u. Bareboat
rates range from NZ$335 to NZ$795 per day in
the low season (January to March), to NZ$425
to NZ$975 in the high season for yachts.
Catamarans range from NZ$860 to NZ$920
low season, to NZ$1040 to NZ$1095 high
season. Skippers (NZ$140), cooks (NZ$130)
and guides (NZ$130) cost extra.

Melinda Sea Adventures (☎ 70975, in the
US ☎ 415-235 1464; W www.sailtonga.com;
VHF Channel 16), located below Beluga Diving, operates fully-crewed charters on the
13m traditionally rigged gaff ketch Melinda
(US$180 per person per night). It is also li-
censed for whale watching.

Sea Kayaking
From May to early December the Friendly
Islands Kayak Company (☎/fax 70173;
W www.fikco.com; VHF Channel 71) operates and runs camping and paddling expeditions around the Vava'u and Ha'apai groups
(US$578/1465 for five/12 days). No experi-
ence is required. It also runs whale-watching
tours, mountain-biking tours and shorter
guided kayak tours of Vava'u, and rents out
kayaks by the day for paddling in the harbour. From January to April, contact owners
Doug and Sharon Spence (☎ 03-482 1202)
in New Zealand or through the website.

Beluga Diving (see the Diving section earlier) also rents out single/double sea kayaks
for T$30/50 per day.

Fishing
Vava'u is regarded as one of the best game-
fishing destinations in the Pacific and a prime
site for catching marlin.

Dora Malia (☎ 70698, fax 70174; e ikap
una@kalianet.to), run by Pacific fishing vet-
cran Paul Mead, has charters at T$400 per day
for two people. The Dora Malia is run out of
the Ikapuna Store on Fatafehi Road, which
has a comprehensive range of fishing gear
(except for fly fishing).

MV Hakula and Maris King (☎ 70872, fax
70875; W www.fishtonga.com) can be chartered for A$600 per day. Both have a weigh
station at the Hakula Lodge base.

Target One (☎/fax 70955; e target1@
kalianet.to) is a fast, 8m gamefishing and
sportfishing boat that charters for T$600 per
day for the whole boat, including all gear, for
up to three people.

The Ika Lahi Lodge (☎ 70611; e ikalahi@
kalianet.to; VHF Channel 61) on Hunga Island
has three sport boats, one 24-footer at T$715
per day and two 31-footers at T$1100 per day.
See Hunga & Fofoa under Southern Vava'u
Islands later.

Whale Watching
Vava'u has fast become one of the world's top
whale-watching destinations and the number of
operators has expanded accordingly. Concern
over appropriate standards in the industry,
particularly over swimming with whales, has
also grown (see the boxed text 'The Whale Debates'). Whales Alive (☎ 70303) is an organisation in Vava'u devoted to whale protection.

Vavau's whale-watching operators have
formed an association, ostensibly to regulate
standards but also, it seems, to fix prices.
Some trips allow you to swim with the whales,
some don't – check when you book. All now
charge a standard T$95 per person per trip.

Whale Watch Vava'u (☎ 70493; W www
.whalewatch.to; VHF Channel 77) has two
boats, operating trips for a minimum of six
people. Lunch is US$5 per person.

Sailing Safaris (see the Snorkelling section
earlier) runs trips on the Whale Song (which
is equipped with hydrophones), and two other
speedboats.

Dolphin Pacific Diving (see the Diving
section earlier) runs trips, while Melinda Sea
Adventures (see Sailing) specialises in trips
for underwater photographers.

Whales in the Wild (☎ 70872, fax 70875;
e fishvavau@kalianet.to) operates out of the
Hakula Lodge (see Places to Stay later) and
offers swimming-with-whales trips, as well
as all-inclusive airfare, accommodation and
whale-watching packages.

Other Activities
Beluga Diving (see the Diving section earlier) offers parasailing (inquire about prices)
and windsurfers (T$30/50 per half/full day).

Powerboats with a skipper can be rented
from Sailing Safaris (see the Snorkelling section) for T$150 per day.

TONGA

The Whale Debates

Tonga is an important breeding ground for humpback whales and one of the best places in the world to see them.

Whales can be seen in Tongatapu and Ha'apai from June to November and in Vava'u from July to November, bearing young, caring for new calves and engaging in elaborate mating rituals.

Humpbacks are dubbed 'singing whales' because the males sing during courtship routines. The low notes of their 'songs' can reach 185 decibels and carry 100km through the open ocean. Humpbacks are also known for their dramatic antics in the water. They 'breach' (throw themselves completely out of the water), 'spyhop' (stand vertically upright above the water's surface), 'barrel roll' (splash the water with their long pectoral fins), and perform other remarkable acrobatic feats.

Humpback populations around the world have declined rapidly over the past 200 years, from 150,000 in the early 1800s to an estimated 12,000 today. The same predictable migration habits that once made the giants easy prey for whalers nowadays make them easy finds for whale watchers.

As Tonga's whale-watching industry has grown, so has concern over its possible impact. At the centre of the debate is the practice of swimming with whales. Some say the regular presence of boats and humans in the water disturbs the mothers and calves just when they are most vulnerable – and may force them to abandon the area before they are ready. But many people who have swum with whales say they experience a sense of mutual curiosity, rather than alarm or distress. Whale-watching operators should take their cue from the whales. If they seem disturbed and want to get away from the boat, then they should not be pursued.

The Ministry of Fisheries has a useful, detailed leaflet, *Whale Watching in Tonga*, which lays down strict guidelines for whale-watching boats, planes and swimmers.

Another major debate concerns whaling. Subsistence whaling was practised for centuries in Tonga, where about 10 whales were taken every year by primitive methods. It continued until 1979, when the king banned it.

In 2002, the Tongan Parliament passed a Bill to reintroduce whaling to the country. The king, under pressure (as whaling advocates claim) from Australia and New Zealand, quashed it.

Tonga's whaling lobby maintains that the reintroduction of subsistence whaling would give local people a crucial dietary option besides the cheap, fatty imported meats and fast foods that contribute to Tonga's alarming rate of diabetes. Since most of the best fish from Tongan waters is exported and doesn't end up in local hands, they say Tongans are currently left with little choice.

Conservationists – and Tonga's whale-watching operators (most of who, it must be said, are not Tongan) – say humpback populations are still too fragile and that the reintroduction of whaling would severely damage Tonga's tourism industry.

ANN JEFFREE

Bird-watching trips to Taula and Maninita islands – with reputedly one of the richest concentrations of birds in the Pacific – are run from December to April by Mounu Island Resort (see the Mounu & 'Ovalau section later).

Camping excursions can be booked through Adventure Backpackers (see Places to Stay later) or the Friendly Islands Kayak Company (see Sea Kayaking earlier).

Organised Tours

Island Tours Among local tour operators, only **Teta Tours** (*☎/fax 70488; Fatafehi Rd*) seems to be a long-term survivor, and its tours fluctuate in quality. Vava'u's terrestrial attractions don't need expert knowledge to explore – a local taxi can do the job, as can your own two pedalling feet.

Boat Tours Typically including Swallows' and Mariner's caves, picnicking on uninhabited islands and snorkelling at offshore reefs, boat tours also cater to individual whims. The presence of humpback whales is a special bonus from July to November.

Day tours are offered by Sailing Safaris and Melinda Sea Adventures, or ask the TVB which local boat owners are operating.

Places to Stay

There are all sorts of accommodation options in Neiafu, including a couple of apartments. **Bayview Apartments** (*☎ 70724; Vaipua; singles/doubles T$35/45*), just beyond the Vaipua Inlet causeway, has two well-furnished, attractive one-bedroom apartments with great views of Mount Talou and a good swimming area down the hill.

Sailing Safaris (see the Sailing section earlier) has a one-bedroom apartment for T$30 per night and a three-bedroom apartment sleeping up to six for T$300 per week.

Places to Stay – Budget

There is plenty of accommodation in Neiafu, but it's advisable to book ahead during peak months.

Adventure Backpackers (*☎/fax 70955; e backpackers@kalianet.to; Fatafehi Rd; dorm beds per person T$18, singles/doubles T$48/58, doubles with bathroom T$68*) has quickly eclipsed competitors in Neiafu with its central location and modern, service-oriented approach to the budget travel experience. It's well run and friendly, with hostel-style communal areas and a guest kitchen. The staff can arrange all kinds of activities.

Vava'u Guest House (*☎ 70300; Fatafehi Rd; 'Ranch House' singles/doubles with shared bathroom T$10/15, fale singles/doubles with private bathroom T$30/50*), at the quiet end of town, is Neiafu's original budget guesthouse. It's faded but friendly, and much more 'Tongan' than Adventure Backpackers, though it's not a good place to overcome your creepy-crawly phobias.

Port Wine Guest House (*☎ 70479; Ha'amea Rd; singles/doubles with shared bathroom T$15/25*) is another Neiafu stalwart, a basic, comfortable weatherboard homestead a few minutes' walk from town, run with charm by a local family. The rooms are spartan, but the kitchen, living area and veranda make up for it.

Places to Stay – Mid-Range

Hill Top Hotel (*☎/fax 70209; e sunset@ kalianet.to; VHF Channel 16; Holopeka Hill; garden/harbour view rooms T$70/100*) was severely damaged by Cyclone Waka in 2002, but has been renovated (again) with eight attractive, Mediterranean-style rooms – four have balconies with superb sweeping views over the Port of Refuge and Old Harbour. The adjacent Sunset Restaurant is another drawcard. You may need to arm yourself with anti-dog missiles for the night time walk up the hill.

Twin View Motel (*☎ 70597, fax 70622; off Fatafehi Rd; singles/doubles with bathroom T$70-120*) is probably the most attractive option for self-caterers. Perched on the hill behind the Vava'u Guest House, the units are spacious and immaculate, with large kitchens and dreamy views of the Port and Harbour.

Places to Stay – Top End

Hakula Lodge (*☎ 70872, fax 70875; e fish vavau@kalianet.to; Fatafehi Rd; singles/ doubles with bathroom A$135/175*) has two very homely units and a wide veranda looking out over a particularly beautiful turquoise stretch of the Port of Refuge. It's amiable and professionally run, and popular with game fishermen (as demonstrated by the weigh station at the jetty below). The owners run whale-watching trips and can arrange inclusive airfare, accommodation and activity packages. There are bicycles, kayaks and snorkelling gear for guests.

Paradise International Hotel (*☎ 70377, fax 70184; e tongaparadise@aol.com; Fatafehi Rd; singles/doubles from US$49/109*) is still the fanciest place to stay in Neiafu, but it's

TONGA

under new management and seems in danger of pricing itself out of the market.

Places to Stay – Around Neiafu

The Tongan Beach Resort (☎ 70380; e holidays@thetongan.com; VHF Channel 71; singles/doubles T$159) on one of mainland Vavau's prime spots on beautiful Hikutamole Beach, emerged from Cyclone Waka minus two luxury bungalows, but otherwise looks untouched. The surviving units are bright and attractive and the place has a laid-back atmosphere, with great food and a range of activities. Meal plans are T$65/80 for half/full board. A bonus is the treehouse, where amorous couples and lonely mystics can be served dinner over the water.

Marcella Resort (☎/fax 70687; e marcella@ kalianet.to; singles/doubles T$48/70) is neither on the water or close to town, but is nevertheless an appealing, low-key retreat. The private *fale* in the pleasant garden are ample, with tapa designs on the walls. There's also a decent bar and restaurant, which in the low season transforms into a Friday night venue popular with Vavau's young groovers. The resort no longer has bicycles, which might make getting in and out of town inconvenient.

Places to Eat

Restaurants Vava'u now closely rivals Tongatapu for its good food. It's usually not that cheap, but even budget travellers should unzip their money belts at least once to enjoy one of Neiafu's top restaurants.

Dancing Rooster (☎ 70886; Fatefehi Rd; mains T$19-25) is a very popular newcomer, serving up top-notch European-themed food in a cosy garden overlooking the Port of Refuge. The bar down the steps from the restaurant is an excellent hang-out and can stay open until 2am.

Sunset Restaurant (☎ 70209; VHF Channel 16; Holopeka Hill; mains T$15-30, pizza T$9-15), next to the Hill Top Hotel, has the best view in Neiafu, so good you could easily forget to eat. The food also has a fine reputation, with authentic pizza and pasta and a good wine list. It's open Sunday.

'Ana's Café (☎ 70664; VHF Channel 16; off Fatafehi Rd; snacks & mains T$5-16) is deservedly popular, with good food and drink, friendly staff and the memorable Friday yacht race, when the happy hour at the bar runs from 7pm to 9pm. It opens all day Sunday.

Caffe Italiano (☎ 71268; Fatafehi Rd; pizza & pasta T$10-18, mains T$20-30) doesn't have wonderful views or appetising decor, but it's a worthy and more conveniently located competitor to the Sunset Restaurant. It serves excellent Italian food, very good coffee and homemade Italian cream puffs for breakfast.

La Paella (☎ 16310; VHF Channel 10; dinner & entertainment T$40), out on Tapana island, is the place to go for an indulgent evening. Locals, yachties and visitors all rave about the Spanish food and entertainment evenings. Book through the owner's mobile (if it's working) or the radio. To get there, take a T$7 taxi from Neiafu to 'Ano Beach, where a boat will pick you up.

The **Lighthouse Café** (☎ 70524; VHF Channel 16; Tokongahahau Rd; breakfasts from T$4.50) has all the European breakfast staples, some excellent baguette sandwiches, and what is widely regarded as the best bread in town.

Pua Tale Fusi (☎ 70704; VHF Channel 16; off Fatafehi Rd; lunch T$8.50-11.50, dinner T$16.50-28.50) is run by the former owner of the hugely popular Mermaid. However, its future at the time of writing seemed dependent on the promised closure of the adjacent Puatakanave Nightclub. It's open Sunday.

Fast Food Next to SF Paea & Sons Supermarket, **Pua Café** (Fatefehi Rd; dishes T$1.50-4.50) is Neifau's first attempt at a Western-style fast-food (and photo-developing!) joint, with fish, chicken and chip assortments, some nice pastries and buns – and the worst coffee on the planet. **Kalia II Takeaway** (Fatafehi Rd; dishes T$3) serves up greasy, adequate staples from a yellow and green shed. Both places stay open until very late.

Tongan Feasts Feasts come and go, but at the time of writing two were operating, both offering sand, sea, good times and very full stomachs. The **Hinakauea Beach** feast is held on Thursday and costs T$25, while on Saturday there's a feast at **Barnacle Beach** for a minimum of six people, also for T$25. Book through the TVB.

Self-Catering Your supermarket needs are adequately met by the **Tonga Cooperative Federation** and the **Vava'u Trading Centre**, both of which open until noon on Saturday. The **Lighthouse Café** does the best breads, but basic loaves and buns are also available at **George's Bakery**, opposite the Church of Tonga, and the **Mangele Bakery** on T'ui Road. Good fruit and vegetables are abundant at the

'Utakalongalu Market on the waterfront, and you can either compete for fish at the Halaevalu Wharf or shop in expensive comfort among the imported goodies at 'Alatini Fisheries next to the market. For domestic alcohol needs, go to the Royal Beer Shop on Fatafehi Road. The Bounty Bar was also planning to open a more sophisticated bottle shop.

Entertainment
Pubs Neiafu has a lively bar scene, which frequently extends through the night on Friday. Neifau's main booze venues also serve food.

The Mermaid (☎ 70730; VHF Channel 16; Fatafehi Rd) is one of the best spots in town for a drink (the food's pretty good too). It's good-natured and boozy, with a fantastic deck on top of the water, and it's the only place in town to get draught Ikale. It closes when the last drinker leaves. If you choose to pass out there, the restaurant's open for a reviving greasy breakfast. There's a live band on Friday.

Bounty Bar (☎ 70576; VHF Channel 16; Fatafehi Rd) is also an eating establishment in its own right during the day, with appetising breakfasts and lunches. In the evenings, the Tongan and *palangi* patrons get down to some dedicated drinking into the early hours. It's closed Saturday and Sunday.

Ifo Ifo Bar (☎ 70285; One-Way Rd) is probably best left for drinks rather than food. It's relaxed and mostly friendly during the day, though it can get a little seedy at night.

Clubs The deafening Puatakanave Nightclub was earmarked for closure at the time of writing to make way for a new hotel. It's a rowdy, drunken affair.

The Marcella Resort runs an excellent, groovy Friday nightspot during low season, but its future may be uncertain after it was trashed and nearly burned down by drunks in New Year 2003.

The Motele Nightclub next to the former Garden Bay Village Resort (which was closed down by the TVB) runs regular Friday and Saturday clubs equal in noise and debauchery to the Puatakanave Nightclub.

Shopping
Excellent T-shirts and wrap skirts by local designers can be bought at the Tropical Tease (☎ 71271) workshop off Fatafehi Road, or at Sailing Safaris. It also makes custom screenprinting for cruisers. Good handicraft shops can be found all along Fatafehi Road and at Fa Sea Jewellery in the small shopping centre opposite the Paradise International Hotel. Look Sharp (☎ 70757) has a shop in the same centre, selling popular local T-shirts.

Getting There & Away
Air On the north side of the island, about a 15-minute drive from Neiafu, is Lupepau'u airport. Royal Tongan Airlines (☎ 70149; Fatafehi Rd) operates daily flights between Vava'u and Tongatapu (T$141/271 one-way/return) and three flights a week between Vava'u and Ha'apai (T$73/135 single/return).

Boat See the Activities section earlier for more information. The ferry offices are at Neiafu's main wharf.

Getting Around
To/From the Airport The Paradise International Hotel bus meets all incoming flights and provides free transport for hotel guests (T$4 per person for others). Several places to stay will provide airport transport on request. The TVB has set the taxi fare between the airport and town at T$7, though you may be asked for more.

Bus The buses run from the Sailoame Market and 'Utakalongalu Markets to most parts of Vava'u and connected islands, leaving when full. They usually make the run into town in the mornings and go out again in the afternoons, so they are not convenient for day trips from the town.

Car & Motorcycle There are self-drive cars for hire at JV Taxis (☎ 70136) for T$85 daily, or T$70 daily for three or more days. TVB says it can arrange cars for less. Other taxi companies will give you a car and driver for the day for around T$80. Ask around – it's easy to find someone with a car to drive you for around T$60.

Taxi In addition to JV Taxis, there is Liviela (☎ 70240) and Lopaukamea (☎ 70153). The maximum fare around Neiafu town is T$2.

Bicycle Vava'u is hilly, though manageable by bicycle. Several places to stay have bicycles for guests. Adventure Backpackers rents some eccentric machines for T$15 per day, or T$20 for brand new ones.

Boat See the Activities section earlier.

TONGA

AROUND VAVA'U
Sia Ko Kafoa
On the western shore of the Vaipua Inlet, connected to the Neiafu side by a causeway, are the twin hills of Lei'ulu (109m) and Sia Ko Kafoa (128m).

From Neiafu, follow the road north past the Prince Wellington Ngu hospital, and cross over the causeway spanning Vaipua Islet. The road then turns right and climbs up to the village of Taoa.

Lei'ulu, the hill behind Taoa, is used as a burial ground. Walk downhill along the coral road behind Lei'ulu hill; when the road begins to angle right on an uphill slope, about 10 minutes from the village, you'll see the track to the summit of Sia Ko Kafoa, turning uphill to the left.

On the summit is an 'esi – a rest-area mound for chiefs and nobles. Young virgins were sometimes presented to amorous chiefs here.

'Utula'aina Point
'Utula'aina Point provides perhaps the most spectacular views on Vava'u Island, though the track there is very overgrown. To get there, head north from Holonga village until you see a track that forms a fork. Head straight ahead from the intersection. It curves around to the left a bit and emerges into a grassy open area after 10 or 15 minutes. Bear right through the bushes, climb the short grassy knoll and you'll emerge on 'Utula'aina Point. There's also a steep track leading to a secluded **beach** 50m before the trailhead.

Makave
One of the most interesting beaches on Vava'u Island, Makave is easily accessed on foot from Neiafu along the shore of the Old Harbour. Walk past the entrance to Hala Tafengatoto and follow the shore east towards Makave village, the legendary home of a mysterious dark, giant people.

After an hour's walk from Neiafu, you'll reach the beach below Makave village where you'll find an ancient canoe-mooring site beside an impressive rock and cave. Farther east are the **freshwater springs** of Matalave.

Toula & Veimumuni Cave
Near the southern point of Vava'u Island is Toula village. When you reach Toula turn left (east) following the path uphill past a cemetery. As you begin to descend to the beach, you'll see Veimumuni Cave in the bluff. Inside is a nice freshwater spring and swimming hole.

Eme'io & Keitahi Beaches
Seldom visited, these two beaches are a dramatic, rugged alternative to the placid western waters. Eme'io Beach is well signposted all the way from Neiafu and has an idyllic, shaded grassy area. Though swimming conditions are not ideal, the pounding offshore surf, high cliffs and seclusion make up for it. Cars are charged T$2 to park here. Keitahi Beach is not as pristine, but the views are more dramatic and there are good swimming holes at low tide. There may be an entry fee of T$5, if anyone is around to collect it. To get there, turn left at an unmarked dirt road about 750m before Tu'anekivale village.

'Ano, Hinakauea & Talihau Beaches
'Ano and Hinakauea Beaches, near the southern end of Pangaimotu, are beautiful and very quiet (even the guesthouse has closed down), with sheltered turquoise water, abundant vegetation, good snorkelling and a safe anchorage. A taxi from Neiafu costs T$7.

Talihau Beach, 2 km past the turn-off for The Tongan Beach Resort, is also lovely for swimming. It's in Talihau village, so expect inquisitive youthful company.

SOUTHERN VAVA'U ISLANDS
Hunga & Fofoa
A large, sheltered lagoon formed by Hunga, Kalau and Fofoa offers excellent **anchorage** and impressive **snorkelling**.

Ika Lahi Lodge (☎ 70611; e ikalahi@ kalianet.to; VHF Channel 71; twin share with fans & air-con T$185, doubles T$200; meals per person T$75) is on the Hunga shore of the beautiful lagoon and specialises in fishing (see Activities under the earlier Neiafu section). Catamarans, lasers (small sailing boats), snorkelling gear and sea kayaks are available. Transfers cost T$100 per person.

Foe'ata & Foelifuka
The island of Foe'ata, immediately south of Hunga, offers glorious white **beaches** and good **snorkelling**. There is an anchorage on the north side of Foelifuka, beside Foe'ata.

Blue Lagoon (☎ 70976, 71300; e blagoon@ kalianet.to; VHF Channel 16; fale T$180, half/full board T$55/75) has six large fale on an idyllic beach on Foe'ata, each constructed from local materials and distinct from the other. It's part eco-lodge, part eccentric dream resort and the food is excellent. Transfers are T$110 per person.

Nuapapu

Nuapapu is best known for **Mariner's Cave**, a hidden cave at its northern end. An interesting phenomenon of this cave, caused by the swelling sea, is the fog that forms every few seconds, only to disappear again just as fast. Most boat tours stop here, but on windy days access can be difficult.

Vaka'eitu

Vaka'eitu is a small, hilly island, with secluded beaches on each side, a secure overnight anchorage and some of Vavau's best snorkelling in the close-by **Coral Gardens**.

Popao Resort (☎ 70308; ⓦ www.popao.net; VHF Channel 16; fale singles/doubles with private bathroom T$104-119; meals per day T$36) has been transformed into an attractive, breezy hilltop resort with stunning views east and west across the Vava'u Group. The four *fale* are well designed, with tiled floors and clean, bright bathrooms. There's a good bar and restaurant, which takes full advantage of the views. Camping is free as long as you pay the T$62 return transfers and buy the daily meal package.

Kapa

Kapa Island's main attraction is **Swallows' Cave** ('Anapekepeka), which cuts in to a cliff on the west side of the island. The cave is actually inhabited by hundreds of swiftlets, and the exceptional underwater visibility makes it great for snorkelling. Access by boat is dependent on relatively calm seas. It's also possible to swim into the cave in good conditions.

Taunga, Ngau & Pau

These sporadically inhabited islands have idyllic beaches, good snorkelling and four anchorages. At low tide, Ngau and Ta'unga are connected by a fine sandy beach. Ngau is in turn connected to the uninhabited island of Pau by a slender ribbon of sand that is exposed except at the turn of high tide. There's a superb anchorage in the bight of Ngau on the eastern shore.

'Eue'iki

'Eue'iki has easy boat access and the finest, brightest white sand in Tonga. At the time of research, the owner of the **Marcella Resort** (see Places to Stay under the earlier Neiafu section) was in the process of building five beach bungalows here, due to be completed in early 2004.

Mounu & 'Ovalau

A short distance southeast of Vaka'eitu are Mounu and 'Ovalau, two more of those perfect places Vava'u has in abundance.

Mounu Island Resort (☎ 70747; ⓔ mounu@ kalianet.to; VHF Channel 77; fale with private bathroom high/low season US$120/100; meals per day US$40) is another top-notch resort, though you must stay here for at least three nights unless agreed beforehand. Children under 12 are not accepted.

Maninita

Maninita, in the extreme south of the Vava'u Group, is very secluded. The terraced coral reef on the approach forms lovely tidepools, and the pristine forests in the island's centre are home to a profusion of birds almost unique to the Pacific islands. Mounu Island Resort runs **bird-watching** trips to here and to neighbouring Taula from December to April. There's an anchorage on the west side of the island.

EASTERN VAVA'U ISLANDS

Transport to the eastern islands is much shorter and easier if you start from Neiafu's Old Harbour.

'Ofu, Kenutu & Lolo

The waters around 'Ofu are the primary habitat of the prized but endangered *'ofu* shell – do not encourage their collection by buying them. The island is friendly and well worth a day's exploration.

The small uninhabited island of Kenutu, just east of 'Ofu, has superb beaches, and coral patches south of the island offer good snorkelling and diving. There's an anchorage on the western side. The reef between Kenutu and Lolo islands, immediately south, is very dramatic.

The Niuas

The remote Niuas ('Niua' means 'Rich in Coconuts') consist of three small volcanic islands in the extreme northern reaches of Tonga, where tradition is very much alive.

NIUATOPUTAPU

pop 1400 • area 18 sq km

The island of Niuatoputapu (Very Sacred Coconut) is 240km north of Vava'u. The north coast is bound by a series of reefs, but there is a passage through to Falehau wharf. Yachts anchor just northwest of the wharf.

Niuatoputapu is great for walking – most
of its interesting sights can be covered in two
days. All three villages – Falehau, Vaipoa and
the administrative capital, Hihifo – lie in a
5.5km line along the northern coast.

There are 14 churches on the island and
dress standards are very conservative, so it's
very important to dress appropriately.

There's good diving outside the reef, but no
diving equipment is available on the island.

Information

The 'capital' of the Niuas, the sleepy village of Hihifo (which only got telephones in
1998), on the northwestern corner of Niuatoputapu, boasts the **police station**, the **post
office** and a small **co-op store**. Money can
be changed at the **Treasury**.

Niutoua Spring

The cool, sparkling pool of Niutoua Spring
flows through a crack in the rock just west
of Hihifo; it's full of friendly fish and great
for a swim. If you intend to bathe at Niutoua,
bear in mind that the spectacle of *palangi* will
quickly draw an audience. Swim in baggy
clothes with a minimum of exposed skin.

Beaches

You could walk around the island along its
11km stretch of beach in about seven or eight
hours. The most beautiful beaches are on the
northwest side of the main island and on
Hunganga, the offshore islet, especially bor-
dering the channel between the two. The reef
is close in, making swimming difficult.

Western Waterways

Near Hihifo, a maze of shallow waterways
wind between the intermittent islets of Nuku-
seilala, Tafuna, Tavili and Hunganga. At low
tide you can walk anywhere in the area by
wading through a few centimetres of water.
At high tide, the passages (especially between
Niuatoputapu and Hunganga) are excellent
for swimming.

Places to Stay & Eat

You'll find lots of excellent **campsites** around
the convoluted waterways near Hihifo and on
the beach along the south coast. You need to
get permission first.

Palm Tree Island Resort (☎ 85090, fax 85
123; ✉ palmtreeislandtonga@yahoo.it; singles/
doubles T$120/160), a small resort on Hun-
ganga, is a peaceful retreat. The four *fale* have
hot water and electricity, and there's a dinghy

shuttle to Hihifo (or you can walk across at
low tide). Snorkelling, fishing and walking
trips can be arranged.

Kalolaine's Guest House (☎ 85021; singles/
doubles T$18/22) is the only other place to
stay. It's pretty basic, but remains friendly,
clean and homely and can be found at the
southeast end of Hihifo – there's no sign, but
everyone knows where it is. Meals must be
booked in advance.

It's a good idea to bring your own food to
the Niuas. There are only limited groceries
available at several small shops.

Getting There & Away

Air Flights are scheduled to land at Niuatop-
utapu once a week, but are often cancelled.
Tickets are T$250/477 single/return from
Tongatapu via Vava'u, or T$129/246 from
Vava'u.

Boat The *MV 'Olovaha* is supposed to call in
once a month, but the schedule is very unpredictable and the ship's status was uncertain at
the time of writing. Inquire at the TVB.

Most visitors to Niuatoputapu arrive on
private yachts. A note of caution for arriving
at the port: there is only one marker and two
range sites (which are inaccurate by about
5m). If you get the range sites to line up
you'll run aground!

NIUAFO'OU
pop 735 • area 50.3 sq km

Niuafo'ou, also known as Tin Can Island, is
the most remote island in Tonga, lying 640km
north and slightly west of Tongatapu; it's also
the only one with a notably different dialect
(the language is close to Samoan). A third of
the doughnut-shaped island, which is a collapsed volcanic cone, consists of barren and
impassable lava flows. Most of the water supply is contained in its large crater lakes and in
a sulphur spring. During the past 150 years,
Niuafo'ou has experienced 10 major volcanic
eruptions, though there hasn't been any major
activity since 1946.

Not surprisingly, the fiercely loyal residents
of Niuafo'ou have a reputation for toughness.

Information

Telephone service to Niuafo'ou commenced
in 1998. Mail usually comes by plane once
every three weeks. Money can be changed at
the Treasury.

Very little English is spoken on Niuafo'ou,
but the government workers speak it.

Things to See & Do

There's a track leading right around the island, which you can walk in about six hours.

One Niuafo'ou sight that must be seen is the splendid lake, **Vai Lahi**, which nearly fills the island's large crater. Along the southern and western shores is a vast, barren moonscape of **lava flows**. On the northern shore, mounds of volcanic slag, lava tubes, vents and craters are accessible from the main road. Beneath this flow is the buried village of **'Angaha**.

Keep an eye out for Niuafo'ou's most unusual inhabitants – the **megapode birds**, which use the warm volcanic soil to incubate their eggs (see the boxed text 'Megapodes' in the Solomon Islands chapter).

Places to Stay

There are numerous excellent **campsites** on the crater (especially on the lake shores), where drinking water is available, although camping will draw a lot of attention and curiosity. Some travellers have stayed at (and have given good reports about) the **Catholic Mission**.

It's wise to bring all your food with you.

Getting There & Away

Due to its volcanic nature, Niuafo'ou lacks a decent anchorage or landing site, leaving access reliant on the mercy of the wind and waves.

Air A one-way/return ticket from Tongatapu is T$284/545, or T$163/315 from Vava'u. Flight schedules are very prone to change.

Boat Getting to Niuafo'ou by boat is a gruelling ride and the landing is difficult. See the Niuatoputapu's Boat section for more information – these are the same boats that come to Niuafo'ou.

Tuvalu

Time moves at its own pace on the five atolls and four islands of this tiny Pacific nation. If hustle and bustle don't appeal, Tuvalu might just be the place.

The enormous changes in Tuvalu over recent years are nowhere more evident than on its capital, Funafuti Atoll. An increasing population density and a move away from subsistence traditions have brought serious problems, although the dangers of rising sea levels due to global warming could present even bigger ones in the future. Meanwhile, you can join the locals and float in Funafuti lagoon, race along the airstrip and take a nap in the afternoon. And if time is *really* no object, venture to the outer islands and atolls, where life is even more laid back.

Facts about Tuvalu

HISTORY
Tuvaluan mythology explains the formation of the islands by the battle between Te Pusi the Eel and Te Ali the Flounder (see the boxed text 'How the Islands Formed' later). Tuvalu (pronounced 'too-**vah**-loo') means 'Cluster of Eight'. The *ninth* island, Niulakita, has been inhabited only in recent times. A proposal to rename the country Tuiva, 'Cluster of Nine', met a cool reception.

Polynesians settled Tuvalu around 2000 years ago, mostly from Samoa via Tokelau, but also from Tonga and Uvea (Wallis Island). The northern islands, especially Nui, were also settled by Micronesians from Kiribati. These people adapted their style of living to the infertile atoll environment. A system of *te ano* (stockpiling) was adopted to guard against drought and famine.

Each hundred people or so were commanded by an *aliki* (a powerful chief). Under each *aliki* was his assistant, then elders, builders, priests and traditional healers, followed by ordinary people, new settlers and slaves at the bottom. As part of the traditional Polynesian religion, people were sometimes sacrificed to honour the gods and ancestor spirits. Each *sologa* (family) had a particular specialty or community responsibility, such as building, fishing and farming, healing, dancing and singing, or defence. Knowledge and skills were passed down by word of mouth and it was *tapu* (taboo) to leak this information to other families.

At a Glance

Capital: Funafuti Atoll
Population: 11,000
Time: 12 hours ahead of GMT
Land Area: 26 sq km (10 sq miles)
Number of Islands: Nine
International Telephone Code: ☎ 688
GDP/Capita: US$825
Currency: Australian dollar (A$1 = US$0.68)
Languages: Tuvaluan, Gilbertese & English
Greeting: *Talofa* (Tuvaluan)

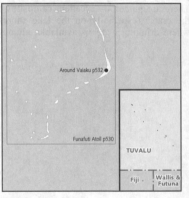

Around Vaiaku p532
Funafuti Atoll p530
TUVALU
Fiji · Wallis & Futuna

Highlights

- **Funafuti Conservation Area** – uninhabited islets, dolphins, manta rays and great snorkelling
- **Remote Funafala Islet** – laid-back village lifestyle
- **Funafuti Atoll** – a classic coral atoll with a stunning aerial view
- **Fatele** – Tuvalu's unique and very exciting music and dance performances
- **Funafuti Lagoon** – floating on the crystal-clear lagoon and gazing at the sky is a great way to kill time
- **Ano** – Tuvalu's unique ball game

Land was considered a family's most valuable asset and was passed down through the male side of the family. Communal lands were set aside to support and maintain those

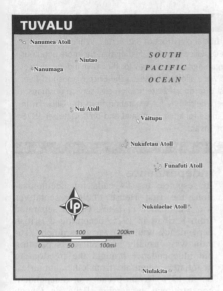

TUVALU

SOUTH
PACIFIC
OCEAN

Nanumea Atoll
Niutao
Nanumaga
Nui Atoll
Vaitupu
Nukufetau Atoll
Funafuti Atoll
Nukulaelae Atoll
Niulakita

0   100   200km
0   50   100mi

in need. Once married, a woman became part of her husband's family. As long as he could maintain his family, a man could marry as many women as he liked.

Outside Influences

The Spanish explorer Alvaro de Mendaña sighted the islands in 1568, but the first European contact wasn't until 1781, with another Spaniard, Francisco Antonio Mourelle, at Niutao. In 1819 an American explorer, De Peyster, named Funafuti 'Ellice's Island', after an English politician friend. By the 1830s all the islands had been charted.

In the 1820s, whalers and other traders began to visit the islands and traditional Tuvaluan society began to change with the introduction of alcohol, money and new tools and goods. The *aliki* were seen to lose their *mana* (power) as people lost respect for their leaders' often drunk and disorderly behaviour. While most *palagi* ('pah-lung-ee'; white people) lived peacefully with the islanders, many earned a reputation of being dishonest and possessive. This opinion worsened in 1863 when 'blackbirders' (slavers) raided the southern islands for labourers for the Peruvian guano mines. They were aided by a resident American beachcomber, who coaxed the islanders on to the ship by promising knowledge of Christianity. The blackbirders succeeded in taking 250 people from Nukulaelae and 171 from Funafuti.

The Samoan missionaries from the London Missionary Society (LMS), who arrived in 1865, had an even greater impact on Tuvaluan culture. They managed to oust the traditional religion while building on its influence. The new pastors began to dominate the *aliki* and take over their positions of authority and privilege. The Tuvaluan language was represented with Samoan orthography and sermons were delivered in Samoan. Ancestral shrines were replaced by churches, new laws were introduced and polygamy and sacrifices were forbidden. Use of the men's narrow, woven pandanus loincloth was suppressed. The quick, rhythmic dancing of the *fakanau* was banned by pastors who regarded it as sexually stimulating and 'evil' dancing. The custom of 'night creeping' (nocturnal visits by courting males to young women's houses) was discouraged.

In 1886 the imperial powers of Britain and Germany divided up most of the western and central Pacific, each claiming a 'sphere of influence'. Tuvalu fell within British 'influence', along with Kiribati and the southern Solomon Islands.

On Funafuti, in September 1892, the British representative, Captain Gibson, met with the elders and the resident missionary, who agreed to Tuvalu becoming a British protectorate. By this time the traditional power structure had lost most of its influence but not all were happy with Britain claiming their islands. Tuvalu was incorporated into the Gilbert & Ellice Islands Protectorate, partly to deter US influence in the area. Thus Tuvalu and Kiribati (and later Tokelau), although ethnically and culturally different, were arbitrarily joined. See the 'Independence for Tuvalu' boxed text in this chapter for more about the Gilbert & Ellice union.

Colonialism

Due to the wealth generated by phosphate mining on Banaba (Ocean Island in modern-day Kiribati), in 1916 Britain raised the status of the Gilbert & Ellice Island to Crown colony. Between 1900 and 1979 an average of 200 Tuvaluans were employed on Banaba at any given time, on two-year work contracts. Phosphate mining was hard work and in 1926 the entire Tuvaluan labour force went on strike for higher wages: everyone was repatriated.

Despite little direct *palagi* influence, laws imposed on the colony became increasingly strict and paternalistic. Authoritarian boarding

Independence for Tuvalu

The Gilbert & Ellice islands' union was largely an artificial construct of British rule. While Tarawa's independence movement was growing in the mid-1960s, Ellice Islanders, fearing that the more populous Gilbert Islands would have greater political clout, began agitating strongly for their own independence. In the 1967 House of Representatives the Gilberts were allotted 18 seats, the Ellice islands just five, but the Gilbertese also resented the Ellice Islanders' disproportionate hold on civil service positions.

In a 1974 referendum, Ellice Islanders voted overwhelmingly for separation from the Gilberts, in 1975 to 1976 Ellice Islanders departed Tarawa en mass for their homeland and on 1 October 1978 the Ellice Islands became the independent nation of Tuvalu.

schools were established by DG Kennedy, a New Zealand (NZ) schoolteacher who arrived in 1923. He also introduced the *fusi* (cooperative stores) and radio, and served as district officer until 1939. In 1894 sour toddy (the local coconut brew) and working on Sunday had been banned. In 1930 regulatio ns were imposed on dancing, feasting, domestic animals and night fishing – even sleeping in an eating house attracted a fine.

WWII

During WWII, Tuvaluan workers were trapped on Banaba when the Japanese invaded. From Kiribati, the Japanese planned to move south to Tuvalu but US forces set up base on Funafuti and built airfields at Nukufetau and Nanumea in the north. More than 6000 Americans were based in Tuvalu, from where they were able to bomb Japanese bases in Kiribati, Nauru and the Marshall Islands.

The locals of Fongafale were shifted to Funafala and Papaelise islets for the duration of the war, and contact between camp and village was controlled. Funafuti was attacked nine times during 1943, although few people were killed. On 23 April 1943, hundreds of people hid in the Funafuti church until an American soldier persuaded them to shelter in the dugouts. Ten minutes later the church was blasted. Generally, islanders gained material benefits from the occupation and saw the war as an exciting time.

Postwar

Postwar changes were significant. Some islanders chose to leave their overcrowded islands and use their war compensation money to migrate. Some of the people of Nanumaga shifted to Tonga and the Carolines. Others moved from Vaitupu to Kioa in Fiji. The colony headquarters was set up at Tarawa in the Gilberts (Kiribati) and many Tuvaluans went there for work or study.

Independence

In response to UN calls for decolonisation, the first House of Representatives was established in 1967. Tuvalu separated from Kiribati in 1975, becoming a British dependency with its own government. Tuvalu was virtually bankrupt on separation but independence brought the freedom to negotiate foreign aid from other countries. So in 1978 Tuvalu became an independent constitutional monarchy; Britain's Queen Elizabeth II is the head of state, represented by a governor general.

Aid money came flowing in. The Funafuti hospital was built in 1978 with aid from NZ, and in 1981 the deep-water wharf and cargo storage facilities were built with Australian money. In 1987, Australia, NZ and the UK together contributed A$24.7 million for a Tuvalu Trust Fund. Earnings from this fund have averaged over A$2 million annually. Taiwan financed the new Vaiaku Lagi Hotel in 1993 and there are other ongoing aid projects. Surprisingly, Tuvalu has proven adept at balancing the books despite its meagre economic resources (see the boxed text 'Dot tv' later in this chapter for more information).

GEOGRAPHY

Tuvalu is an archipelago of five coral atolls and four islands spread over 800km of ocean. Funafuti, the capital, is about 1100km north of Fiji, and the northern islands are about 250km south of Kiribati. Funafuti, Nukufetau, Nanumea, Nui and Nukulaelae are classic atolls with a continuous rim of reef surrounding a lagoon. The others are single coral islands with only landlocked lagoons or swamp. With a total land area of only 26 sq km, Tuvalu is one of the world's smallest countries. The highest land is a mere 5m above sea level.

CLIMATE

Tuvalu has a tropical maritime climate – the temperature rarely ranges outside 28°C to 31°C. Rainfall is high, up to 3500mm in the south (including Funafuti), and is usually brief and heavy. The wettest season is November to February. From May to October winds are light and from the southeast (the trade winds), changing to west–northwest during the 'cyclone season' (November to April). While Tuvalu is considered just outside the tropical cyclone belt, there were severe cyclones in 1894, 1972 and 1990. Three bad cyclones (Gavin, Hina and Keli) hit Tuvalu during the last El Niño period (March 1997 to April 1998) with heavy rains and strong winds. The increased frequency of cyclones has been inconclusively linked with global warming.

ECOLOGY & ENVIRONMENT

As an atoll nation, the major long-term ecological threat to Tuvalu comes from global warming (see the boxed text 'Global Warming' in the Facts about the South Pacific chapter) and rising sea levels. Population pressures and changing lifestyles are more immediate problems. Nearly half the population is squeezed on to narrow Fongafale Islet of Funafuti Atoll. An increasing population and lifestyle changes have brought environmental degradation (see the boxed text 'Funafuti's Fragile Environment' later). Changes in eating habits and a dependence on packaged imports, have led to severe garbage disposal problems on all the inhabited atolls and islands.

FLORA & FAUNA

Tuvalu's infertile atoll soils support coconut palms, pandanus, salt-tolerant ferns and some atoll scrub. Mangrove areas are rare. There are about 50 endemic plant species. Cultivated plants include banana, cassava, taro and breadfruit. Vegetation has an important role in foreshore protection but degradation is quite severe. Large tree species traditionally used for canoes and building are becoming rare.

Marine life is diverse, with dolphins and manta rays commonly seen in Funafuti lagoon. Turtles born in Tuvalu migrate to other Pacific countries and return to lay eggs. There are some indigenous birds, insects, lizards, frogs and land crabs, but no native land mammals. Rats, dogs, cats and pigs have been introduced. Many protected bird species are still commonly eaten on the outer islands. Wildlife within the Funafuti Conservation Area is protected.

How the Islands Formed

The Traditional Version

Tuvalu's islands were created by the mythological beings Te Pusi (The Eel) and Te Ali (The Flounder). Carrying home a heavy rock, a friendly competition of strength turned into a fight and Te Pusi used his magic powers to turn Te Ali flat, like the islands of Tuvalu, and made himself round like the coconut trees. Te Pusi threw the black, white and blue rock into the air – and there it stayed. With a magic spell it fell down but a blue part remained above to form the sky. Te Pusi threw it up again, and its black side faced down, forming night. With another spell the rock fell down on its white side and formed day. Te Pusi broke the rest of the rock into eight pieces, forming the eight islands of Tuvalu. With a final spell he threw the remaining pieces of blue stone and formed the sea.

The Scientific Version

After his Pacific voyages in 1835 to 1836, Charles Darwin proposed that coral atolls were built on slowly sinking volcanic rock, which at the same time was being built up by new deposits of coral. The subsidence theory explained why coral rock was found at depths far greater than the 40m at which coral polyps can survive. (See the boxed text 'Coral Atolls' in the Facts about the South Pacific chapter.) Darwin's theory was controversial at the time – others believed that reefs grew on underwater platforms raised by volcanic action.

Darwin proposed that a coral atoll be drilled for samples, and Tuvalu achieved scientific fame when the Royal Society of London sent expeditions to Funafuti. After three 'boring' expeditions, in 1898 scientists managed to obtain atoll core samples from 340m below the surface. When analysed back in London, they showed traces of shallow water organisms, thus supporting Darwin's hypothesis. Not until 1952, on Eniwetok in Micronesia, was it possible to drill to a depth of 1290m (right through the coral structure) and actually reach volcanic rock.

GOVERNMENT & POLITICS

Tuvalu has a Westminster-style parliamentary democracy with a 12-member elected parliament and a four-year term. The position of prime minister has been a musical chairs affair following the death in December 2000 of Ionatana Ionatana; the current incumbent is Saufatu Sopoanga. Each island is represented in the parliament and has its own *falekaupule* (island council).

ECONOMY

Most of the population relies on subsistence farming and fishing, and each island has a *fusi* (cooperative store). Apart from coconuts and pandanus, there are limited crops. Money is increasingly important as people become more reliant on imported food, petroleum, building materials and manufactured goods, mostly from Australia and Fiji. Most paid jobs are with the government.

Four big contributors to the islands' economy are remittances, licences, investments and 'dot tv' (see the boxed text). There's a large contingent of Tuvaluans working as seamen on international cargo ships and remitting most of their salaries back home. Licence fees from foreign ships fishing in Tuvalu's extensive territorial waters brings in another large chunk of income. The Tuvalu Trust Fund's careful investments are another important source.

Postage-stamp sales still bring in a little money, but copra production income is almost non-existent. Apart from seamen, smaller numbers of Tuvaluans also work in first-world countries and as phosphate miners on Nauru. Despite its idyllic atolls, Tuvalu is remote and air fares are expensive, so there is very little tourism. Most of the 1000 or so annual overseas visitors are aid workers, consultants and government employees.

External aid, mainly from Australia, NZ, the European Union, Taiwan and Japan, is a major source of income. Australian aid of A$2.5 to A$3 million is mostly in education and training. Taiwan is intending to fund the proposed A$7 million, multi-storey government buildings in Vaiaku (Fongafale).

POPULATION & PEOPLE

Over 90% of the 11,000 Tuvaluans are of Polynesian origin, although most of Nui's 600 people have Micronesian ancestors. Over 40% of Tuvaluans live on Funafuti; overseas there are about 750 contract workers on Nauru in the phosphate-mining industry, a couple of hundred students and about 500 seamen.

Tuvalu has a very high population density, currently averaging 419 people per sq km over its tiny land area. The population is mostly concentrated in the capital, Funafuti, which has a density of about 1600 people per sq km! At the current growth rate of 1.7% per year, the population is expected to double in 40 years. When the phosphate runs out on Nauru and the workers return, the problem will only worsen.

Tuvalu has one of the highest infant mortality rates of the region: 41 babies in 1000 die before their first birthdays.

EDUCATION

After separation from Kiribati, students started to go to Fiji for higher education, and there are now extension courses available through the University of the South Pacific (USP) on Funafuti. Education is free and compulsory; literacy is 93%. All islands have primary schools, but high school children have to board on Vaitupu.

ARTS

Traditional time-consuming handicrafts make imaginative use of limited materials. It can take two women a day to painstakingly prepare a handful of fine white *taa* (the youngest coconut leaves), so expect to pay a bit more for intricately woven items. Dyes of red, yellow, black and brown are obtained from natural materials.

Pandanus mats (sleeping, floor and ceremonial) are highly valued. The creation of ceremonial mats is often competitive, producing imaginative, brightly coloured applied designs. Sitting mats take up to a week to make, while sleeping mats can take five to 10 weeks.

Handicrafts include ornamental stars, woven pandanus balls, model *fale* and canoes, shell necklaces, hairclasps, brightly coloured dancing skirts and woven fans of varied design. Utilitarian items include baskets and trays, carved fish hooks and coconut-fibre rope. Wooden articles, such as drums made from hollow trunks (similar to the Fijian *lali*) and *toluma*, fishermen's round tight-topped boxes, are now fairly rare.

Fatele (traditional song and dance) are practised on festive occasions in the *maneapa* (open-air meeting-house). The dancers wear pandanus-strip skirts and flower garlands and use familiar Polynesian hand movements, but the young prefer international music and 'twists' (discos) at the nightclubs.

Fatele

Describing a *fatele* as a session of community music, singing and dancing omits the most important element – its competitiveness. At opposite ends of the *maneapa*, each village 'side' encircles a square wooden 'drum' on which the men pound a background beat backed by drumming on a metal cabin cracker tin.

Singers, male and female, sit cross-legged around the drummers, who start gently and build, the tempo getting faster and faster, louder and louder until it peaks in a thumping, crashing crescendo. The singing follows suit, starting softly and harmoniously and building to a full throated melange of harmonies and counter-harmonies. *Fatele* means 'to multiply', hinting at that steadily increasing speed.

To one side of the musicians and singers are the dancers, often a group of very substantial dames with flower *fous* wreathing their heads and brown grass skirts patently failing to circle their 'Mother Hubbard' shrouded bulk. An occasional male dancer jumps up to do a little warrior-like, bent-leg knee-knocking, but essentially it's left to the women to sway statuesquely, only varying their dance with a graceful little 'so beat that' swirl at the end.

The other side tries to.

SOCIETY

Tuvaluans traditionally live in *fale*, which have coral floors or raised wooden platforms. On Funafuti, however, most homes are built in the Western-style thate are inappropriately designed for the climate. People usually have little furniture and very few possessions apart from woven mats. *Maneapa* are the meeting places where all special events are held. Parliament sits at the large *maneapa* near the airport.

Women spend much of their time on handicrafts, especially weaving mats. When a *fale* is being built in the village it is common for many women to contribute by preparing thatching material. Both men and women enjoy wearing headdresses of flowers, shells and coconut leaves, not just for adornment but also for the perfume.

While much traditional culture has been retained, the family unit is being broken down as people are attracted to the cash economy on Funafuti. National independence and the accompanying dependence on foreign aid has brought an increasing number of *palagi*, mostly aid workers and volunteers. It is becoming more difficult to live by traditional subsistence fishing and agriculture in the high-density areas.

There are no longer chiefs in Tuvalu, but certain families are privileged and influential and have greater access to money and further education. There is an increasing economic divide between the relatively few wage-earning indigenous people (mostly government workers) and the grass-root villagers. The remote outer islands see little of the overseas aid.

RELIGION

Traditional Tuvaluan religious beliefs were ousted by the Samoan missionaries who arrived in the 1860s. Church is the main event on Sunday, which is a day of rest. Most people (97% of the population) belong to the Protestant Church of Tuvalu (Ekalesia Kelisiano o Tuvalu), which is derived from the LMS. Seventh-Day Adventists account for another 1.4% of the population, followed by Baha'i at 1%.

Religion is especially influential on the outer islands. In the past every *mataniu* (family estate) had to supply goods and support for community projects. The old men and people in the *maneapa* would assess how much each was to contribute. The church has incorporated this tradition and now demands money from parishioners for its projects.

LANGUAGE

English is widely spoken. Tuvaluan is a Polynesian language related to Tokelauan. Tuvaluan uses 'l' where some Polynesian languages use 'r' – so the name for a chief (*ariki* in the Cook Islands) is *aliki* in Tuvalu. When missionaries put the language into written form they used Samoan orthography, so as in Samoa, the letter 'g' is usually used for the soft 'ng' sound.

Tuvaluan Basics

Hello.	*Talofa.*
Goodbye.	*Tofa.*
How are you?	*E a koe?*
I'm well.	*Malosi.*
Please.	*Fakamolemole.*
Thank you.	*Fakafetai.*
Yes.	*Io* or *Ao.*
No.	*Ikai.*

Facts for the Visitor

SUGGESTED ITINERARIES

If you have plenty of time and feel adventurous, tackle the outer islands. While on Funafuti be sure to visit the conservation area, and consider a couple of days on Funafala Islet.

PLANNING

It takes a few days to accept Funafuti for what it is, to start enjoying the laid-back pace and appreciate the culture. You need plenty of time and flexible plans to visit the outer islands. The boat timetable is notoriously unreliable, so you can easily get stranded for weeks – or even months!

Tuvalu is relatively expensive compared to neighbouring Fiji, and air fares are high.

Maps

Excellent maps of the atolls may be available at the **Lands & Survey Department** (☎ *20 170*) on Funafuti. Alternatively, you could try **South Pacific Applied Geoscience Commission** (SOPAC; ☎ *381 139, fax 370 040*) in Suva, Fiji.

What to Bring

Bring toiletries and medical supplies as availability is limited. Nappies (diapers) and sanitary pads are generally stocked, but not tampons. Photographers should take film and snorkellers their own gear.

TOURIST OFFICES

Tuvalu has little tourist infrastructure. It's represented abroad by the South Pacific Tourism Organisation (SPTO). See the Regional Facts for the Visitor chapter for SPTO offices.

VISAS & EMBASSIES

Visitors do not require a visa and are granted a one-month entry permit on arrival. You need a valid passport and a return ticket – and a valid yellow-fever certificate if you have come from an infected area. Visa extensions, available at **immigration** (☎ *20 706*), are granted for a maximum of three months.

Tuvaluan Embassies & Consulates

Tuvalu's diplomatic representation abroad consists of one embassy:

Fiji (☎ 330 1355, fax 330 1023) 16 Gorrie St, PO Box 14449, Suva

Embassies & Consulates in Tuvalu

The only overseas consulate in Tuvalu is that of the Republic of China (Taiwan). Other major nations that have a South Pacific interest handle Tuvalu from their embassy in Suva in Fiji (see the Fiji chapter for further information).

MONEY

Australian currency is the legal tender, but there are also Tuvaluan 5c, 10c, 20c, 50c and $1 coins. The National Bank on Funafuti is the country's only bank (see Money in the Funafuti section). A 10% government tax on accommodation is included in prices listed in this chapter. Tipping isn't expected. Tuvalu is not cheap; Funafuti has the only regular hotels (rooms from A$30 per person) and restaurants (meals from A$5 to A$10). On the outer islands there's generally a guest house but visitors are so infrequent that there are unlikely to be any set prices.

Exchange Rates

Tuvalu uses the Australian dollar. To check current exchange rates visit Ⓦ www.oanda .com. At the time of writing exchange rates were as follows:

country	unit		A$
Canada	C$1	=	A$1.10
Easter Island	Ch$100	=	A$0.22
euro zone	€1	=	A$1.70
Fiji	F$1	=	A$0.80
New Zealand	NZ$	=	A$0.87
PNG	K1	=	A$0.43
Samoa	ST1	=	A$0.51
Solomon Islands	S$1	=	A$0.20
Tonga	T$1	=	A$0.69
UK	£1	=	A$2.45
USA	US$1	=	A$1.47
Vanuatu	100VT	=	A$1.23

POST & COMMUNICATIONS

The capital, Funafuti, has a post office and the Tuvalu Philatelic Bureau. Postal rates are 60c to Australia and 90c to the US, Europe and South America.

Tuvalu's international telephone code is ☎ 688.

The rather anonymous Funafuti Telecom office has a public fax (☎ 20 800) and telex (☎ 1800). International calls are sometimes difficult to connect. Calls per minute cost: Australia A$1.50; North America and Europe A$4; Fiji A$2; elsewhere in the Pacific

A$2.50. Local calls are 10c while calls to the outer islands are 60c per minute. Faxes cost $4, plus the regular per-minute telephone charge. There is no minimum charge using the direct dial international access code of ☎ 00. For operator calls dial ☎ 012 for international and ☎ 010 for local. The capital has cardphones although only the one in the Telecom office may be working; phonecards come in A$2, A$5, A$10 and A$20 value. The outer islands have phone operators from 8am to 11.30am; 12.30pm to 4pm and 7pm to 10pm Monday to Friday, 11am to 2pm Saturday and Sunday. You can dial direct anytime.

Email & Internet Access
For A$10 you can get a temporary .tv internet address for one month and log on to the internet by dialling the local server on ☎ 20 025.

DIGITAL RESOURCES
Tuvalu Online (Ⓦ www.tuvaluislands.com) is an excellent site with interesting links. It is produced by a Canadian/Tuvaluan family, and has photos, news headlines and general information about the country.

Dot tv

Tuvalu has a surprisingly solid economy for a scattering of tiny dots in the ocean. The country's trust fund has invested its nest egg wisely ('we don't want to be like Nauru', is a frequently heard warning), while hard-working seamen send their pay cheques home, and licences issued to the big Asian fishing fleets brings in another healthy stream of cash. And then there's dot tv.

Every country has a 'top level domain', the two letters which identifies it on the internet. Even the US has one, although it's not generally used – a dot com is assumed to be in the US while a com.au is in Australia, a co.uk in the UK and so on. Lucky Tuvalu didn't get tu (Tunisia and Turkey were both in line ahead of it) – it got tv. In the late 1990s, when it was realised how much TV companies would pay for an address like CNN.tv or BBC.tv, the .tv Corp was set up and in 2002 it was sold to VeriSign for US$45 million. Want to find out about Lonely Planet's television plans? It's on Ⓦ www.lonelyplanet.tv.

BOOKS
There are a few books about Tuvalu available at the **USP** (☎ 20 811, fax 20 704) on Funafuti. *Tuvalu, A History* (1983) was written by a team of Tuvaluans with the assistance of the Institute of Pacific Studies, USP. *The Material Culture of Tuvalu* (1961), by Gerd Koch, concentrates on the islands of Niutao and Nanumaga. *Strategic Atolls, Tuvalu and the Second World War* (1994), by Peter McQuarrie, is the book for the islands in WWII. *The People's Lawyer* (2000), by Philip Ells, is an amusing account of a young Voluntary Service Overseas (VSO) lawyer's spell in Tuvalu.

Time & Tide: The Islands of Tuvalu is a Lonely Planet photographic book about the islands.

NEWSPAPERS & MAGAZINES
The **Broadcasting and Information Office** (☎ 20 731, fax 20 732) on Funafuti publishes a monthly national newspaper in English and Tuvaluan – the *Tuvalu Echoes*.

TIME
Tuvalu is 12 hours ahead of Greenwich Mean Time (GMT). When it's noon in Tuvalu, it's noon the same day in Fiji, 10am the same day in Sydney, Australia, and 2pm the previous day in Hawaii.

RADIO & TV
Radio Tuvalu has programs in both English and Tuvaluan. Local TV is broadcast on Monday evenings each week, and from time to time an Australian channel can be picked up by satellite. Of course, videos are popular.

HEALTH
Tuvalu is malaria-free. Common health problems include staphylococcal skin infections, tuberculosis (TB), filariasis, scabies and infected cuts. Always boil your drinking water, or use bottled water. Groundwater is generally brackish and rainwater is stored in individual tanks. There is no organised sewerage disposal.

Tuvalu's only hospital is on Funafuti. The outer islands have trained nurses, but very limited facilities and drug supplies. Often patients have to wait months for transport to Funafuti hospital, and complicated cases are referred to Fijian hospitals. See the Health section in the Regional Facts for the Visitor chapter for further information.

SOCIAL GRACES

Traditionally men are allowed to do pretty much anything, but there are lots of rules for women. Women should cover up to below the knee or risk negative vibes from the old people. Unmarried girls usually bathe fully clothed or in shorts under a *sulu* (sarong-type garment).

Be very aware of when visiting a *maneapa*. No-one should walk in the inner circle – traditionally women weren't allowed to enter or speak. The poles of a *maneapa* have symbolic meaning and the place at either pole is reserved for important people. Sit down cross-legged, but never show the bottom of your feet or flash your thigh; avoid walking in front of people.

If visiting a home leave your shoes at the door and avoid walking over pandanus mats, especially the small ones used for sleeping.

When visiting an outer island it is customary to give presents to your hosts. Useful things such as groceries, clothing and toys are sure to be appreciated.

DANGERS & ANNOYANCES

Be careful with your feet, both in and out of the water! On Funafuti you'll come across broken glass and open cans – and some people use the beach as a public loo. The rough ocean side of the atoll is very risky for swimming. The recent resurfacing of all 19km of road on Funafuti has made traffic a lot more dangerous, the huge numbers of potholes used to slow everything down. Take care when the drink is flowing in Funafuti – Tuvaluans tend to be big so a bad drunk is not a pretty sight. Alcohol is banned on many of the outer islands.

See the Boat section under Getting Around for a warning on inter-island ship transfers.

BUSINESS HOURS

Government offices are open weekdays 8am to 4.15pm (to 1pm on Friday).

PUBLIC HOLIDAYS & SPECIAL EVENTS

In addition to New Year's, Easter, Christmas and Boxing Day (see the Regional Facts for the Visitor chapter), Tuvalu celebrates:

Funafuti Youth Day 11 February
Commonwealth Day March
Bomb Day (Japanese bombing Funafuti) 23 April
Gospel Day 2nd Monday in May
Queen's Birthday early June
Children's Day early August
Independence Day early October
Hurricane Day (1972 Cyclone Bebe) 21 October
Prince Charles' Birthday early November

ACTIVITIES

Once in Tuvalu, you have no option but to get into the slow swing of things since there is not much to do, and no reason to hurry! See Things to See & Do in the Funafuti section.

ACCOMMODATION

Funafuti has one fairly ordinary hotel and some less expensive guesthouses. Most of the outer islands have council guesthouses; make sure you give advance warning of your arrival.

FOOD

Staple foods include coconut, pandanus, bananas and fish, mostly tuna. Breadfruit is boiled, or fried as chips, and *pulaka* (swamp taro) is eaten boiled or roasted. Eating habits are changing as locals become dependent on tinned corned beef and other imports. There's a corresponding increase in diet-related disease.

On Funafuti restaurant meals are limited in variety. Fresh fruit and vegetables are a bit of a treat, but you may find some at the *fusi*.

DRINKS

Coconut milk and coconut toddy (fermented coconut-tree sap) are traditional drinks. Cans of mango and pineapple juice, soft drinks and beer are imported. Powdered and long-life milk are also available, although you may have to search several shops to find either.

ENTERTAINMENT

Feasts and dancing are held at the *maneapa* on special occasions, such as weddings and VIP visits. There are both volleyball and soccer

Ano: The Ball Game

To play *ano* you need two round balls, about 12cm in diameter and woven from dried pandanus leaves. (Similar cubic 'balls' are used for other ball games). The two opposing teams face each other about 7m apart in five or six parallel rows of about six people, and nominate their *alovaka* (captain) and *tino pukepuke* (catcher), who stand in front of each team.

Team members hit the ball to each other with the aim of eventually reaching the catcher. Only the catcher can throw the ball back to the captain to hit back to the other team. To keep the game lively, two balls are used simultaneously. When either ball falls to the ground the other team scores a point and the first to 10 points wins the game.

competitions, and cricket plus the local ball game of *ano* are played on special occasions – you might be able to join in. See Things to See & Do and Entertainment under Funafuti.

SHOPPING

Each island has a *fusi*, and Funafuti has a few stores with a limited supply of imported goods. Handicrafts can be purchased at the **Women's Handicraft Centre** and at the **craftswomen's stalls** at Funafuti airport.

Getting There & Away

AIR

Tuvalu's International Airport is on Funafuti. **Air Fiji** *(in Fiji ☎ 679-3313 666, fax 3300 771; *w* www.airfiji.net)* flies from Suva to Funafuti (F$650 one-way; Monday and Thursday). Make sure you reconfirm, as seats are in high demand and you could get stranded. There has been talk for years about extending the service north to Kiribati. For more details about airlines see the Getting There & Away chapter.

Departure Tax

An international departure tax of A$20 applies to all visitors over 12 years old.

SEA

The MV *Nivaga II*, a government-owned cargo/passenger ship, travels to Suva, Fiji, every three months or so (the trip takes five days). Fares are A$57.40/172.20 for deck/double cabin, without meals. You have to pay the return fare regardless. The ship also does very rare charter trips to Tokelau via Samoa. **Pacific Forum Line** *(in Fiji ☎ 679-315 444)* is the agent for the MV *Nivaga II* in Suva.

The cargo boat *Nei Matagare* makes irregular trips between Tuvalu, Tarawa (Kiribati) and Fiji. Suva–Funafuti deck class, including meals, is A$99 one-way. **Williams & Goslings** *(in Fiji ☎ 679-312 633)* are the Suva agents for the *Nei Matagare*.

Irregular cargo boats also link Funafuti with NZ, Australia and Wallis & Futuna.

Getting Around

CAR & MOTORCYCLE

Motorcycles and mopeds are the most popular means of land transport, and are available for rent on Funafuti. The capital has a minibus and taxi service. Driving is on the left side of the road.

BOAT

All inter-island transport is by boat. Only Funafuti and Nukufetau have reef passages large enough for ships to enter their lagoons and only Funafuti has a real dock. This means ships must load and unload into a small boat which can be hazardous in rough seas – not for those who aren't confident swimmers. The MV *Nivaga II* typically visits each of the outer islands once every three or four weeks. The southern trip takes three or four days, and the northern trips about a week. Don't expect too much comfort: it's often crowded with chickens and pigs as well as people, while toilets overflow and passengers are often seasick. A trip to the northern islands costs about A$100 for 1st class, including food, and A$17 deck class without food.

For bookings and schedule confirmation contact the **Marine Travel Office** *(☎ 20 744)* on Funafuti or the Telecom representative on the outer islands. Printed schedules are unreliable as the boat is often off for maintenance, or detouring to pick up VIPs.

It is also possible to visit the outer islands by chartering the government fishing boat (about A$1000 per day, including food). Make arrangements with the **Fisheries Department** *(☎ 20 344)* on Funafuti.

Visiting yachts have to check in at Funafuti for immigration and customs clearance on arrival, and before leaving Tuvalu. Therefore few yachts visit the outer islands.

Funafuti Atoll

pop 4500 • area 2.8 sq km
Funafuti (pronounced 'foo-**nah**-foo-ti') Atoll is the country's capital, with the administrative centre and airport. The vast lagoon, about 24km long and 18km wide, has four reef passages. Funafala Islet at the southern end of the atoll has simple accommodation, and the Marine Conservation Area on the western side is well worth a visit.

FONGAFALE ISLET

Fongafale (also spelt Fogafale or Fagafale) is the largest of Funafuti's islets. It's a long snake-like slither of land, 12km long and between 10 and 400m wide, with the South Pacific Ocean on the east and the protected

TUVALU

FUNAFUTI ATOLL

Money The **National Bank** (☎ 20 803, fax 20 802; open 9.30am-1pm Mon-Thur & 8.30am-noon Fri), just opposite the airport building, changes travellers cheques (A$1 commission for up to 10 cheques) and does cash advances on Visa and MasterCard (A$10 for up to A$200, A$25 for more than A$200); otherwise credit cards aren't accepted in Tuvalu.

Post & Communications The post office (open 8am-12.30pm & 1.30pm-3pm Mon-Fri) and **Telecom office** are both near the airport building in Vaiaku.

You can make calls from the **Telecom office** (fax 20 800) or by public phone outside. The town has a few other cardphones, some probably not working. The Telecom office and the **Vaiaku Lagi Hotel** sell phonecards. See the Facts for the Visitor section earlier for postal and telephone rates.

The **Tuvalu Philatelic Bureau** (☎ 20 223, fax 20 712), at the southern end of town, sells stamps to international collectors. The themes are Tuvaluan, but they are designed and printed overseas.

Travel Agencies See the **Travel Office** (☎ 20 737, fax 20 757) at the airport for ticketing and reconfirmation of flights. **Manu Travel Services** (☎ 20 649, fax 20 648) is also near the airport. Contact the **Marine Travel Office** (☎ 20 744) at the deep-sea wharf for information on boat services.

Libraries The **Library and Archives Office** (open 8.30am-noon & 1pm-5pm Mon-Thur, 8.30am-1pm Fri, 10am-noon Sat) is near the Philatelic Bureau at the southern end of town. The USP Extension Centre also has a library.

University of the South Pacific The USP Extension Centre (☎ 20 811, fax 20 704) is just south of the hospital at the northern end of town. It caters for about 250 extension students and specialises in accounting, economics and management. They have a few books about Tuvalu for sale.

Emergency & Medical Services The **Princess Margaret Hospital** (☎ 20 750) has about 30 beds, but is understaffed and the pharmacy often runs out of some drugs weeks or months before the next supply ship arrives. It has an ambulance service and there are visiting specialists from time to time.

The **Police Station** (☎ 911) is opposite the Vaiaku Lagi Hotel.

lagoon on the west. The airstrip runs from northeast to southwest on the widest part of the island with the village and administrative centre of Vaiaku on the lagoon side. The deep-sea wharf is 1.7km north of the hospital; the main road continues north and at times is almost half the islet's width!

During WWII, Fongafale was the main base for the American bombers in Tuvalu. Most of the population was relocated to Funafala Islet for the duration of the war. Fongafale has many small, garbage-filled, man-made lagoons known as 'borrow pits', where coral material was extracted for the construction of the airstrip.

Information
Tourist Offices Tuvalu receives few tourists. The **Conservation Area Department** (☎ 20 754, 20 489, fax 20 664) in Funafuti Town Council, north of the *fusi*, manages and arranges transport to the conservation area. **Radio Tuvalu** (☎ 20 731, fax 20 732), opposite the Vaiaku Lagi Hotel, has friendly helpful staff and is a good place to get the latest on what is happening. Otherwise, try the hotel and guesthouses.

Also worth a try is the **Ministry of Tourism, Trade & Commerce** (☎ 20 182, 20 191, fax 20 829), between the church and the *fusi*. Excellent maps of the atoll are usually available from the **Lands & Survey Department** (☎ 20 170) for A$10.

Things to See & Do

Wander around town or hire a moped to explore the islet. Every few blocks there is a *maneapa*; **parliament** meets at the one adjacent to the airport. Most of the houses are concrete-block hotboxes, or *palagi houses,* but people escape to their outdoor *fale umu* (kitchen huts) for some breeze, and even watch videos from outside!

Housing is fairly dense and boundary disputes are becoming common. As more people need to squeeze on less land, there are **communal plots** where banana plantations and crops are planted. The airfield takes up about 20 hectares of previously productive land. About 2800 coconut palms were felled and *pulaka* and taro-growing land was covered up. Between planes the airfield is used as the town's sporting ground.

At midday the streets are fairly deserted – it's the time for inaction – lying down in the *fale umu* or some other shaded spot. Early morning is the best time for a walk, when the motorcycles are zipping around, people are out sweeping the breadfruit leaves from their yards and the roads, and children are heading off to school in their brightly coloured uniforms. Locals enjoy hanging out at the *fusi*.

The vast Funafuti **lagoon** is stunning; ask someone for a paddle in their outrigger canoe. Initially visitors don't find swimming here particularly inviting after seeing the tins, glass, plastic and assorted rubbish littering the beach, which is also used as a toilet. Nevertheless, joining the locals and floating in the lagoon's turquoise waters is lovely at the end of a scorching day – just avoid touching the bottom! The concrete pier just south of Vaiaku Lagi hotel is a good spot to enter.

Late in the 19th century, coral-drilling expeditions from England came to Funafuti to investigate Darwin's theory of atoll formation (see the boxed text 'How the Islands Formed' earlier). The site, known as **David's Drill**, isn't particularly exciting: just a concrete base with a small hole in it. It is at the northern end of the town, not far from the hospital.

Take a trip to the far northern end of the island to feel just how narrow the islet is and witness the problems of rubbish disposal on such a tiny place. WWII reminders include the **borrow pits** (now used as dumping grounds or for pigsty drainage), and a corroded old **tank** near the deep-water wharf. There is also an underground **bunker** near the far-northern end of Fongafale. On the way you'll see a rusting Japanese fishing boat, wrecked during Cyclone Bebe in 1972.

Fongafale's beaches are nothing special – for cute islets with lovely beaches take a trip to the **conservation area** or **Funafala Islet**.

Places to Stay

Hotels About 100m northwest of the airport on the edge of the lagoon, you'll find **Vaiaku Lagi Hotel** (☎ *20 733, fax 20 504; singles/ doubles/triples A$88/99/109),* Tuvalu's only hotel. It has 16 air-con rooms, the upstairs ones with stunning sunset views over the lagoon. Upkeep and facilities are pretty ordinary for the price, but the staff are friendly

Funafuti's Fragile Environment

About 4500 people (nearly half of Tuvalu's population) are squeezed onto Funafuti's long, skinny 2.8 sq km Fongafale Islet. Only about a third of the islet is habitable – large areas are taken up by the airfield and by 'borrow pits', where material was excavated for its construction. With a growing population, and the change from subsistence agriculture to a cash economy, pressure on Funafuti's meagre resources is mounting.

The most obvious environmental problem is the lack of garbage disposal. While traditional throwaway attitudes remain, there is an increasing dependence on imported packaged food. On a place this tiny it is obvious where every tin can and piece of plastic ends up.

High-density living is also causing pollution and depletion of the ground water, and there is coastal erosion as sand and aggregate is extracted for construction, as well as contamination from household chemicals, pesticides and petroleum products. Industrial and commercial waste from the hospital, airport, port, power house, and fuel terminal is also a threat. The lack of water and sewage treatment and waste-disposal facilities led to outbreaks of disease in 1985 and 1990.

With these constraints on sustainable development, tourism could just contribute to the problem. Hopefully the many studies, reports and committee meetings – and negotiations for aid money – could lead to a more sustainable environment.

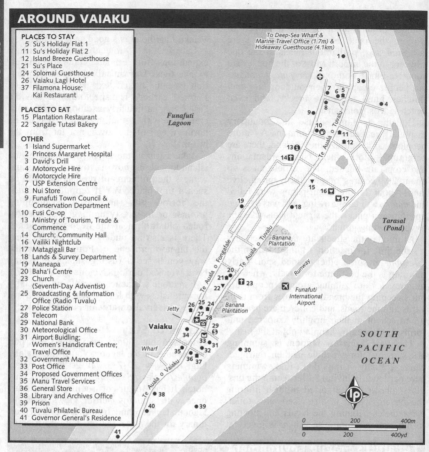

AROUND VAIAKU

PLACES TO STAY
5   Su's Holiday Flat 1
11 Su's Holiday Flat 2
12 Island Breeze Guesthouse
21 Su's Place
24 Solomai Guesthouse
26 Vaiaku Lagi Hotel
37 Filamona House;
    Kai Restaurant

PLACES TO EAT
15 Plantation Restaurant
22 Sangale Tutasi Bakery

OTHER
1   Island Supermarket
2   Princess Margaret Hospital
3   David's Drill
4   Motorcycle Hire
6   Motorcycle Hire
7   USP Extension Centre
8   Nui Store
9   Funafuti Town Council &
    Conservation Department
10 Fusi Co-op
13 Ministry of Tourism, Trade &
    Commence
14 Church; Community Hall
16 Vailiki Nightclub
17 Matagigali Bar
18 Lands & Survey Department
19 Maneapa
20 Baha'i Centre
23 Church
    (Seventh-Day Adventist)
25 Broadcasting & Information
    Office (Radio Tuvalu)
27 Police Station
28 Telecom
29 National Bank
30 Meteorological Office
31 Airport Buidling;
    Women's Handicraft Centre;
    Travel Office
32 Government Maneapa
33 Post Office
34 Proposed Government Offices
35 Manu Travel Services
36 General Store
38 Library and Archives Office
39 Prison
40 Tuvalu Philatelic Bureau
41 Governor General's Residence

To Deep-Sea Wharf &
Marine Travel Office (1.7m) &
Hideaway Guesthouse (4.1km)

Funafuti
Lagoon

Tarasal
(Pond)

Banana
Plantation

Runway

Funafuti
International
Airport

SOUTH
PACIFIC
OCEAN

Jetty

Vaiaku

Wharf

Banana
Plantation

0   200   400m
0   200   400yd

and travellers cheques are accepted. Most guests are on official business. Friday and Saturday are 'twist' nights, with loud music until midnight.

Guesthouses Generally guesthouses are a more economical option although sometimes room availability depends on whether family are visiting.

Filamona House (☎ 20 983; rooms with fan/upstairs with fan/air-con A$30/35/40) is conveniently located across from the Vaiaku *maneapa* by the airport. There are two rooms downstairs and three upstairs, a good communal lounge and kitchen, and a veranda upstairs. The associated restaurant is very popular (see Places to Eat following).

Solomai Guesthouse (☎ 20 572; room/flat A$38/76) may not always be open, but when

it is there are two simple rooms with shared bathroom and a self-contained flat upstairs with a lounge, two bedrooms and verandah.

Su's Place (☎/fax 20 611, 20 612; room with fan & shared bathroom/air-con A$33/40) is about 300m north of the airport building. The red-and-white building has three simple singles (two can be interconnected and house up to five people) and one air-con room. There is a communal area with a fridge and guests can cook for themselves, although Sue is a good cook. She can also arrange activities, such as motorcycle picnics to the end of the islet (A$15 per person) and fishing trips (A$150 for six hours).

Su's Holiday Flats (☎/fax 20 612; room with shared bathroom/air-con unit A$33/66) is a good option for self-caterers. The smaller, clean air-con unit has a well-equipped kitchen –

it's 1.2km north of the airport near the *fusi*. The other unit is 150m further south on the same road.

Island Breeze Guesthouse (☎ *20 606, 20 674, fax 20 675; dorm beds A$15, singles/ doubles A$25-30/30-35, with bathroom A$35/ 40*) is one kilometre north of the airport. There are three small, twin-bedded fan-cooled rooms but the low ceilings are a bit claustrophobic. Meals can be arranged for under A$7 and boat trips are available to Tepuka Islet for A$80 for up to five people.

Hideaway Guesthouse (☎/*fax 20 365; singles/doubles with fan A$33/44, apartment A$44-55*) is probably the nicest place to stay on the islet. Run by Rolf, a German ex-pat, and his Tuvaluan wife Emily, it's out of town, 2.5km north of the wharf. The stretch of the lagoon opposite is a good spot for swimming. The apartment is bright, mosquito-screened and has a kitchen and pleasant lounge. There are also two good, fan-cooled rooms with en suites. There are regular minibuses to the deep-sea wharf, from where it's about a half-hour walk. On weekdays there is a morning and afternoon bus to the door (60c).

Places to Eat
Vaiaku Lagi Hotel (☎ *20 733; lunch/dinner A$4.50/12*) also offers breakfast and sandwiches. Usually there's a choice of fish, chicken – sometimes lobster – and vegetables, but while the lunches are good value, dinner is much pricier.

Kai Restaurant (☎ *20 983; lunch/dinner A$4/5-7*) is part of the Filamona Guesthouse, by the airport. The restaurant is very popular and has a variety of dishes, including fresh fish.

Plantation Restaurant (*lunch/dinner around A$5*) is north of the airport and serves large Chinese-style dishes.

Su's Place (☎ *20 612; dinner around A$9*) caters for visitors as well as guests but book in advance.

The airport **kiosk** has sandwiches (usually canned corned beef) and soft drinks. Some of the places to stay will prepare picnic lunches to take on excursions to the islets. A good option is to self-cater if you can find enough fresh ingredients from the **fusi**. Watch out for the women pushing wheelbarrows of fresh tuna. There is another **supermarket**, a few other **grocery shops**, and the small **Sangale Tutasi Bakery** just north of the airport. Food can be pretty scarce if the supply boat has been delayed.

Entertainment
Special occasions, such as weddings, are held at many of the *maneapa*, and involve feasts and traditional dancing. Visitors may be invited along. The hotel organises traditional dancing for VIPs.

If you stay here too long you'll probably develop the curious habit of waiting for planes. The local paper warns:

Civil servants...tend to make a habit of going to the Terminal to see who is coming in by plane, thus leaving their offices empty and customers waiting to be served...

Tuvalu Echoes

Most bars have billiard tables, and weekend 'twists' (discos). **Vaiaku Lagi Hotel** is the mellowest, followed by **Vailiki Nightclub** and the raucous **Matagigali Bar**. The latter two are near the northern end of the airstrip; it's probably best to go with locals.

Shopping
Fongafale has few shops. The island **fusi** and the **supermarket**, both at the northern end of town, have a limited range of imported goods (see Planning in the Facts for the Visitor section earlier). The **post office** and the **Philatelic Bureau** have a few postcards and the **Nui store** opposite the USP Extension Centre sometimes sells regional magazines.

The **Women's Handicraft Centre** (☎ *20 852, fax 20 643; open 8am-noon & 1.30pm-4pm Mon-Fri & for flights*) is at the airport. They may only have shell necklaces and cane baskets but other times there are good-quality items of traditional design in natural materials. It sometimes has crafts from the outer islands. *The Handicrafts of Tuvalu* booklet may be available here.

Local craftswomen also have **stalls** set up near the Funafuti airport and sell brightly coloured, less labour-intensive items made especially for Tuvalu's small number of travellers; these are made with bright plastic yarn and shells. Departing loved ones or important guests are laden with farewell necklaces. See the earlier Arts section for more on handicrafts.

Getting There & Away
Air Funafuti International Airport's small wooden terminal was built in 1993 with Australian and European Union aid. Air Fiji has regular flights between Suva and Funafuti (see Getting There & Away earlier).

TUVALU

Boat Funafuti lagoon has two reef passages large enough for ships to enter, and a deep-water wharf north of Vaiaku. The cargo/passenger ship MV *Nivaga II* makes occasional voyages to Fiji (see the Getting There & Away section earlier). For bookings and schedule contact the **Marine Travel Office** (☎ 20 744) at the deep-sea wharf.

Getting Around

Bus Fongafale's minibus service (40c for the length of the town) is more like a mobile disco! The service runs from about 6.30am to 7pm (on Sundays only for church). There are weekday buses to the northern end of the island (60c), early in the morning and at about 4pm.

Car & Motorcycle Vehicles are in short supply. Motorcycles and mopeds are the most popular transport and are available for rent (A$10 to A$15 per day). The hotel pick-up and driver can be hired outside flight arrival/departure time (A$10 to end of the island).

Taxi The taxi costs A$4 from the hotel to the deep-water wharf, and A$2 from the hotel to the southern end of the islet near the governor general's residence. The taxi is based at the **Island Breeze Guesthouse** (☎ 20 606).

Bicycle The motorcycle rental places have the odd bicycle for hire. It's a nice pace for exploring the islet but avoid the midday heat.

Boat The easiest way to see the lagoon and some of the smaller islets is with the **Funafuti Town Council** (☎ 20 754, 20 489). The Council's boat costs A$80, including driver and guide, for a maximum of four passengers. You may be lucky enough to score a free ride if the conservation park workers are doing a survey. The hotel can arrange a boat for A$100 or you can negotiate with locals yourself. Don't expect lifejackets or safety gear!

FUNAFALA ISLET

This beautiful islet at the southern end of the atoll has a sandy beach and is good for a day-trip escape or a few days relaxation. When the Americans took over Fongafale in WWII the villagers were relocated here. Most moved back after the war, but there is still a very small community here. It is a lovely, remote place and the more traditional village lifestyle gives a taste of what the outer islands are like.

Funafala is about one hour by boat from Vaiaku (see Getting Around at the start of

the chapter). The tiny fibro **guesthouse** *(bed A$15)* has two beds, louvre windows and solar electricity, but no mosquito screens. It's next to a *maneapa* on the water's edge and has a toilet block and water tank. Take your own food as there are no shops. Book through the **Funafuti Town Council** (☎ 20 754, 20 489).

FUNAFUTI CONSERVATION AREA

The Funafuti Conservation Area project began in 1996, and is funded by the South Pacific Regional Environment Program (SPREP). It covers 33 sq km of lagoon, reef, channel, ocean and island habitats, on the western side of Funafuti Atoll. There are six islets: Tepuka Vilivili, Fualopa, Fuafatu, Vasafua, Fuagea and Tefala. It is home to seabirds and provides nesting sites for **green turtles**. There are many species of fish, hard coral, algae and invertebrates and the islets have 40% of the atoll's remaining native **broadleaf forest**. The objective of the project is to conserve marine and land-based biodiversity and allow for sustainable use of the atoll's natural resources.

The project is administered by **Funafuti Conservation Area Department** (☎ 20 489) and is open to visitors for **sightseeing, picnicking** and **swimming**. It's also a great place for **snorkelling**, with excellent visibility. Bring your own gear. You may see manta rays or groups of dolphins racing the boat.

AMATUKU ISLET

Amatuku Islet is about 10km north of Vaiaku. A boys' mission school was started here in the late 1890s, before being transferred to Vaitupu. The Tuvalu Maritime School was established here in 1979 with Australian government assistance. The training facilities are isolated to simulate ship operations. Tuvaluan seamen have a good reputation and easily find work with international shipping companies. Most send their wages back to their families, and their contribution is an important part of Tuvalu's economy.

Outer Islands

Tuvalu's remote outer islands and atolls are beautiful and pristine, but have very little infrastructure for visitors and are only accessible by irregular cargo boat (see Getting Around earlier). Give advance warning of your arrival and come prepared to be pretty much self-sufficient.

NUKUFETAU ATOLL
pop 750 • area 3 sq km

This atoll is the closest to Funafuti, about 100km to the northwest. During WWII large cargo ships and warships anchored in the lagoon, and two runways were built on Motulalo Islet. The shattered remnants of a B24 Liberator bomber can be found amongst the palm trees some distance north of the main runway. The island started the first primary school in Tuvalu and the annual Founding Day on 11 February is celebrated with gusto.

The **Council Guesthouse** (☎ *36 005; room A$20*) is right beside the primary school and has two bedrooms.

VAITUPU
pop 1200 • area 5.6 sq km

Vaitupu Island has the largest land area in Tuvalu. In 1947 some families migrated from the overcrowded island to the island of Kioa in Fiji. Motufoua is Tuvalu's only secondary school and over 500 students between the ages of 13 and 21 board here. In March 2000 a dormitory fire killed 18 teenage girls and their warden (the dormitory doors were locked and windows barred).

You can walk almost all the way around the densely vegetated island, wading across the shallow entrances to the two lagoons at low tide. Just south of the harbour in the village are the foundations of early trader Heinrich Nitz's house. His gravestone (the actual grave is further along the road) reveals that he was born in Stralsund, Germany, in 1839 and died on Vaitupu in 1906. Many islanders are descendants of Nitz. Continue around the southern end of the island, past the school – a small track directly opposite Te Motu Olepa islet leads a short way inland to a large horizontal slab just to the right (north) of the path. It was probably part of a pre-Christian site with good sunrise views but it's hard to find without local help. Continue along the coast past Elisifou agricultural station and the entrance to the larger lagoon to reach a shipwreck at the entrance to the smaller, northern lagoon. The Solomon Islands ship *Sisco* ran onto the reef in 1981 and sat there relatively intact until the late '90s when it crumbled apart.

The **Council Guesthouse** (☎ *30 005; bed A$10; meals A$8.50-15.50*) is behind the church and *maneapa*, close to the harbour. You can get meals here and the quantities are huge. The **fusi** is right by the harbour.

The Funafuti–Vaitupu trip on the MV *Nivaga II* takes eight or nine hours. Passengers are transferred to a small boat and shuttled into the harbour which is too small for larger boats.

NUI ATOLL
pop 600 • area 2.8 sq km

Nui Atoll has 11 main islets along the eastern side of its lagoon. There are several coconut-fringed, white-sand **beaches** and at low tide it is possible to walk between islets. Gilbertese is also spoken here as some of the people are of Micronesian descent. Contact the **local island council** (☎ *23 005*) if you want to stay at the **guesthouse**.

NANUMAGA ATOLL
pop 650 • area 2.8 sq km

Nanumaga (nah-noo-mah-nga) Atoll is oval-shaped with two landlocked lagoons and a narrow fringing reef. The northern lagoon has a legendary giant's footprint while the southern one has some impressively fearless fish; catching them is not allowed. The two island sides, Tonga and Tokelau, reflect the islanders' origins and are further subdivided into five clans. Respect for the elders suffered in 1979 when they spent almost all of the atoll's funds purchasing poor land in Texas! Contact the **island council** (☎ *33 005*) about their **guesthouse** (*bed A$40*), which is pricey at A$40 a night.

NIUTAO ATOLL
pop 750 • area 2.5 sq km

In 1949 Niutao acquired Niulakita and families were settled there to relieve overpopulation on the home atoll. The people, known for their traditional **handicrafts**, retain some traditional beliefs, and until 1982 they had among them a woman who had inherited the power to make rain. Niutao has a council **guesthouse** (☎ *28 005*).

NANUMEA ATOLL
pop 820 • area 3.9 sq km

Nanumea is Tuvalu's northernmost atoll and the closest to Kiribati. It is also one of the most beautiful, with a **fresh-water pond** (unusual for atolls) and a large **church** with a tall steeple and stained-glass windows. It suffered several Japanese attacks during WWII. Plane **wrecks** and a wrecked cargo ship near the main settlement serve as reminders. The old runway took up one-sixth of the land area and its construction involved felling almost half of the existing coconut trees. The Americans also blasted a passage in the reef and the lagoon is now a sheltered **anchorage** for yachts. Contact the **island council** (☎ *26 000*) about the **guesthouse**.

NUKULAELAE ATOLL
pop 360 • area 1.8 sq km

This atoll has two main islets, Niuoku and Tumuiloto, on the eastern side of the lagoon, but the population is all on Fangaua on the western side. Nukulaelae is about 120km southeast of Funafuti and is Tuvalu's easternmost atoll. In 1863 two-thirds of its population were kidnapped by blackbirders and forced to work as slaves in Peruvian mines. Today, the people from Nukulaelae have a reputation for their **dancing** and **singing**.

There is a pre-Christian **archaeological site** about half way along Niuoku bearing similarities to Polynesian *maraes* (although the islanders have interesting legends about it). Near the southern end of Tumuiloto, a memorial and a small chapel marks the shipwreck arrival site of Elekana, the Cook Islander credited with introducing Christianity to Tuvalu.

Visitors can stay at the island council **guesthouse** (☎ *35 005; bed A$10*). There are no passes into the lagoon and transfers ashore from larger ships can be tricky.

NIULAKITA
pop 40 • area 0.4 sq km

Tuvalu's ninth and most southern landmass is the tiny coral island of Niulakita. It is at a little higher elevation than the other islands, with fertile soils and lush vegetation. It has white-sand **beaches** within a close ring reef. Niulakita was not considered part of the eight islands of old Tuvalu, as it never had a permanent population. It had various foreign 'owners' and in the late 19th century was exploited for its guano; later, it was a copra plantation. In 1949, it was taken over by the people of Niutao.

There is no guesthouse but you could try to arrange to stay with one of the local families – contact the **island council** (☎ *21 022*).

Vanuatu

It's a rare traveller who doesn't like Vanuatu. There's something to suit all tastes: from honeymooners looking for a romantic, lazy time to adventurers keen to visit remote islands where villagers live as they have done for centuries.

While good beaches are not as numerous as you'd expect, the rest of the tourist-brochure hype is not far off the mark. There are several volcanoes, including the very accessible and active Mt Yasur, on Tanna; numerous cultural ceremonies, including the renowned Pentecost *naghol* (land diving); jungle waterfalls; and great opportunities for sailing, fishing, hiking and kayaking.

It's also a snorkellers' and divers' mecca: apart from countless coral reefs, the wreck diving here is terrific. Espiritu Santo – called Santo by just about everyone – boasts the world's largest diveable WWII shipwreck: the SS *President Coolidge*.

Pronounced 'van-**wah**-too', Vanuatu means 'Our Land'. The country's people are called Ni-Vanuatu, meaning 'Of Vanuatu'. Prior to independence from the UK and France in 1980, this long archipelago (1176km north–south) of 83 islands was known as the New Hebrides. James Cook gave it this name during his explorations in 1774 – the dark, rugged islands reminded him of the Hebrides group, off Scotland's western coast.

The national capital, Port Vila, or Vila as it is more commonly called, is the attractive hub of the country's tourist trade, on the island of Efate. Many people visit Vanuatu on seven-day packages and spend most of their time in Vila, often not realising they can stay on in the country after the package deal is up. If you *can* stay longer than a week and are interested in visiting islands other than Efate, it's well worth it.

While flying between the islands can get expensive, there are new village-based enterprises such as tours and bungalows springing up all the time on the outer islands. The bungalows are usually pretty rudimentary – think bucket shower, no electricity and roosters at 4am – but they're also very charming. Worth it, too, to visit some beautiful natural sites and to discover Vanuatu's fascinating, diverse culture.

The following pages concentrate on the places we think most travellers circling the Pacific would want to see in Vanuatu. While all the islands have unique offerings, several of them have been omitted due to space constraints. If you're after more in-depth information,

At a Glance

Capital City (& Island): Port Vila (Efate)

Population: 200,000

Time: 11 hours ahead of GMT

Land Area: 12,336 sq km

Number of Islands: 83

International Telephone Code: ☎ 678

GDP/Capita: US$1085

Currency: Vatu (100Vt = US$0.84)

Languages: Bislama, English, French & over 100 Melanesian languages

Greeting: *Alo* (Bislama)

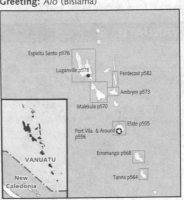

Highlights

- **Tanna** – Marvel at nature's fireworks display on a night visit to Mt Yasur volcano
- **Efate** – Quaff kava in a *nakamal*, then do your own gastronomic tour of Vila's culinary delights
- **Espiritu Santo** – Dive the mind-blowing SS *President Coolidge*, the world's largest, accessible WWII wreck
- **Pentecost** – Witness the remarkable *naghol* ceremony
- **Malekula** – Admire the *kastom* dances of the island's diverse cultural groups

try Lonely Planet's *Vanuatu*, or contact Vanuatu's National Tourism Office, provincial government offices or inbound tour operators (see Tourist Offices, Useful Organisations and Organised Tours, respectively).

Facts about Vanuatu

HISTORY

The first humans to reach Vanuatu crossed the sea from the Solomon Islands to Vanuatu's northern islands in about 1500 BC. People of the Lapita culture (see the boxed text 'Lapita' in the 'South Pacific Arts' special section for more information) are some of the ancestors of Vanuatu's modern Melanesian population.

Between the 11th and 15th centuries AD, a wave of Polynesian settlers sailed in from the central Pacific. A number of Vanuatu's traditions tell of cultural heroes arriving around this time from islands to the east.

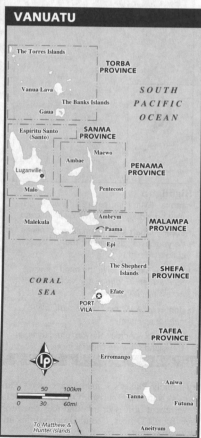

VANUATU

The Torres Islands

TORBA PROVINCE

Vanua Lava

The Banks Islands

Gaua

SOUTH PACIFIC OCEAN

Espiritu Santo (Santo)

SANMA PROVINCE

Maewo

Ambae

Luganville

PENAMA PROVINCE

Malo

Pentecost

Malekula

Ambrym

Paama

MALAMPA PROVINCE

Epi

The Shepherd Islands

SHEFA PROVINCE

CORAL SEA

Efate

PORT VILA

TAFEA PROVINCE

Erromango

Aniwa

0   50   100km
0   30   60mi

Tanna

Futuna

To Matthew & Hunter Islands

Aneityum

Ancient Vanuatu

As is the case today, Ni-Vanuatu lived in mainly small, clan-based villages. The archipelago's rich cultural diversity reflects the fact that these villages were often separated by significant physical barriers, such as difficult mountain terrain.

Everyone lived in the shadow of their ancestors' spirits. Some spirits were benevolent, but others were often hostile – famines, cyclones, enemy attack and other misfortunes could result if they became seriously displeased. Magic was the main defence against angry spirits.

Inter-island trade networks were well established, with large sailing canoes venturing as far afield as New Caledonia. Otherwise the different villages tended to regard their neighbours with deep suspicion, particularly if they spoke a different language. Interclan wars, which were commonplace, usually arose over such matters as the theft of crops, trespassing and suspected sorcery.

Sometimes, however, the attackers' aim was simply to kill or capture one or two males, whom they would carry off to eat. Generally, only men of certain rank were allowed to consume human flesh. (In cannibal areas it was considered a friendly gesture to present a neighbouring village with an arm or leg ready for cooking!) Naturally the victim's relatives would mount a reprisal raid. Such hostilities, once started, often continued indefinitely.

European Explorers

The first Europeans to visit Vanuatu, in May 1606, were members of the Spanish expedition led by Pedro Fernández de Quirós, who was convinced that in Santo he had found the fabled *Terra Australis Incognita*. It was not until May 1768 that Louis-Antoine de Bougainville sailed between Malekula and Santo, thereby proving that Vanuatu's largest island was not *Terra Australis* after all.

James Cook arrived in Vanuatu on 16 July 1774, on his second Pacific expedition. He drew the first charts of the region and gave his own names to the places he visited. Many of these names are still in use today, including Tanna, Erromango, Ambrym and the Shepherd Islands.

In 1789, shortly after the famous mutiny on the *Bounty,* William Bligh sailed through the northern Banks group in his longboat. He sighted several previously unrecorded islands, and returned three years later to confirm his discoveries.

Missionaries

The first Christian missionary on the scene was the Reverend John Williams, from the London Missionary Society (LMS). In 1839 he stepped ashore on Erromango, and was promptly killed and eaten. After this inauspicious beginning the Church decided to send Polynesian teachers from Samoa, hoping they would be more acceptable than Europeans. However, a number of them were also killed, or died of malaria.

In 1848 the Reverend John Geddie arrived on Aneityum and made it the headquarters for the Presbyterian mission in Vanuatu. Presbyterianism eventually became the major Christian denomination, particularly on the islands from Efate south. The Anglican Diocese of Melanesia followed in 1860 and became influential in the northern islands, while Catholicism arrived in 1887.

Although a steady stream of converts emerged, Ni-Vanuatu often mingled this new doctrine with their traditional beliefs. Many rejected Christianity altogether, preferring to stick with their age-old customs. Today around 90% of the population is at least nominally Christian. Most of the remainder are Jon Frum cultists (see the boxed text 'The Jon Frum Movement' later in this chapter) or adherents to indigenous religions.

European Settlement

Although a trading post was established on Aneityum in 1844, the first true European settler was a cattle rancher who arrived 10 years later. Others followed – particularly in the 1860s when the high price of cotton during the American Civil War lured settlers from Australia.

Neglected by the British government, which didn't want to be involved in the archipelago, most of the new settlers were soon near bankruptcy. Many sold their land to French interests, who were also busy buying up land from Ni-Vanuatu. By the mid-1880s, French settlers outnumbered the British by three to one.

Intense rivalry existed between the two groups and, thanks to the absence of law and order, brawls were commonplace. At the same time there were frequent clashes between settlers and Ni-Vanuatu, who resented the loss of their land.

As was the case elsewhere in the Pacific, the Ni-Vanuatu were decimated by the diseases Europeans brought with them. Some estimates put Vanuatu's population at about one million in the early 19th century. By 1870 the number was down to 650,000, and in the next 20 years it fell to around 100,000. This gloomy trend continued until 1935, when only 41,000 Ni-Vanuatu remained.

Condominium

In 1906 the Anglo–French Condominium of the New Hebrides was created as a response to German expansionism in the region. The agreement established Vanuatu as an area of equal influence for the two colonial powers, with neither having exclusive sovereignty. British and French nationals had equal rights, and retained their home country's citizenship, but Ni-Vanuatu were officially stateless.

Cynics called the Condominium the Pandemonium, as the dual administration produced a bizarre duplication of authorities that were seldom effective. For example, there were two education systems, two police forces and two currencies. Traditional Anglo–French rivalry reached new depths of farce in Vanuatu.

WWII

Japan's advance through the Pacific had reached the Solomon Islands by early 1942, when US forces arrived in Vanuatu. They began to construct bases, first at Havannah Harbour and Vila on Efate, then a much larger one in southeastern Santo.

With Japan's defeat in 1945, the US Forces withdrew leaving behind huge quantities of surplus equipment. Some of this was sold at bargain-basement prices and the remainder was dumped into the sea near Luganville on Santo.

Cargo cults appeared on several islands as villagers sought to secure the kind of wealth they'd seen being so wantonly discarded – they believed that if they acted like Europeans then 'cargo' would automatically come their way. Most of these movements waned when the riches failed to materialise.

Independence

Land ownership had become Vanuatu's major political issue by the mid-1960s. It was the spark that spurred the country to take the path to independence.

At this time white settlers 'owned' about 30% of the country's land area. A *kastom*-oriented movement called the Nagriamel (*kastom* ownership is the traditionally acknowledged ownership of a piece of land – see the glossary at the back of this book for more information) sprang up under the leadership of the charismatic Jimmy Stevens. Operating from Santo, its aims were to protect Ni-Vanuatu claims to their traditional land. By the late 1960s, Nagriamel had expanded to other islands in northern Vanuatu.

In 1971 the New Hebrides National Party, later called the Vanua'aku Party, was formed by an Anglican minister, Father Walter Lini. As Vanuatu became more politicised the Condominium authorities agreed to hold the country's first general election. This took place in November 1979, with the Vanua'aku Party being clear winners. Independence was fixed for mid-1980.

Serious threats of secession were being made on Santo and Tanna in early 1980; late in May matters came to a head. An insurrection on Tanna split the island between government supporters and rebels. On Santo, secessionists seized Luganville and hoisted the flag of the Independent Republic of Vemarana.

Several other northern islands proclaimed their own secessions during June. They merged and announced a Provisional Government of the Northern Islands, under Jimmy Stevens.

Order was not restored until the new government brought in soldiers from Papua New Guinea following independence on 30 July, after which the secessionist ringleaders were arrested and the rebellion collapsed.

New Nation

Since independence, the Vanuatuan government has established diplomatic relations with over 70 countries, signed the General Agreement on Tariffs & Trade (GATT), and declared the country a nuclear-free zone. Its desire has been for development that benefits everyone equally, while preserving customs and traditions.

Potentially serious cracks have begun to show over the past decade, however, with ongoing internal instability (see Government & Politics later in this chapter). Of major significance was the police mutiny trial in 2002 (still being heard at the time of writing), where eight high-ranking police and Vanuatu Mobile Force (VMF) officers stood trial for the unlawful arrests of 15 public officials, including the attorney-general and police commissioner.

GEOGRAPHY & GEOLOGY

Vanuatu lies squarely on the Pacific Ring of Fire, where the action of the Pacific tectonic plate being forced up and over the Indo-Australian plate causes frequent earth tremors. Much of the country experiences continual uplift (2cm per year in some areas), while other parts are subsiding. There are nine active volcanoes (seven on land), and fumaroles and thermal springs are found throughout the archipelago.

CLIMATE

Vanuatu's climate varies from wet tropical in the north to subtropical in the south. The dry season – from May to October inclusive – is dominated by fine, warm days and pleasantly cool evenings. November to April is the wet season, when higher temperatures, heavy rains and occasional cyclones are experienced.

Mean maximum temperatures in Luganville and Port Vila range from 27°C in July to 30°C in January. Lenakel (on Tanna) is a degree or two cooler. Mean minimum temperatures are eight or nine degrees below these maximums. Winter nights in Vila can drop below 12°C.

January to March are the wettest months; March averages 21 days of rain, contrasting with 13 in August (the driest month).

An average of 2.5 cyclones strike Vanuatu each year. Cyclones can occur any time between November and May, but the usual season is December to March inclusive.

FLORA

About 75% of the country is covered by natural vegetation, including rainforest and rain-shadow grasslands. Most of the forest has been heavily disturbed by cyclones, logging and subsistence farming, but the more pristine areas are botanical wonderlands.

The lord of most forests is the banyan tree, a huge fig whose crown can be 70m or more across. Forests of mighty kauri trees are found on Erromango, while cloud forests dripping with moss and moisture are a magnificent feature of many highland areas.

Vanuatu has around 20 species of palm, of which 14 are endemic. Orchids festoon the trees in many areas, such as along the beaches in northeastern Santo. All up, Vanuatu has 158 orchid species.

Less enchanting are the introduced weeds. Lantana and the widespread American 'mile-a-minute' vine are the worst. The latter was brought from the US as a camouflage plant during WWII, but it's been left to overrun everything.

FAUNA

Cats, dogs, cattle, horses, pigs and goats were all introduced to Vanuatu and have since gone wild. Rats are the bane of village life and do much damage to the copra industry.

Native land mammals are restricted to four flying fox species and eight bat species. What Vanuatu lacks in native mammals, it makes up for in marine life, with over 300 species of coral and more than 450 species of reef fish.

The country's largest resident mammal is the dugong, or sea cow, which is the world's only herbivorous marine mammal. It's at the easternmost limit of its range in Vanuatu.

Of Vanuatu's 121 bird species, Santo is home to the biggest variety, with 55 species including all seven of the country's endemics. Of these, the Santo mountain starling is rarest, being found only in the higher mountains of the island. In contrast, the endemic white-eye is widespread and common throughout Vanuatu.

One very interesting species is the mound-building, fowl-like megapode (namalao in Bislama). It normally uses the heat generated from rotting vegetation to incubate its eggs. But in actively volcanic areas such as here and in the Solomon Islands (see the boxed text 'Megapodes' in that chapter) it simply lays its eggs in the hot soil.

There are 19 native lizards, all small skinks and geckoes, and one land snake – the harmless Pacific boa, which grows to 2.5m. While the yellow-bellied and banded sea snakes are both extremely venomous, their small mouths and teeth aren't at all suitable for savaging humans.

The saltwater (or estuarine) crocodiles that appear from time to time around the northernmost islands have probably swum down from the Solomon Islands after losing their bearings during cyclones.

Conservation Areas

Vanuatu has three official conservation areas: Vatthe and Loru on Santo, and the kauri reserve near Happy Lands on Erromango. For information on these areas, see the relevant sections later in this chapter or contact the **Environment Unit** (☎ 25302, fax 23565; PMB 9063) in the Georges Pompidou Building in Port Vila, or their **Luganville office** (☎ 36153).

Local chiefs and kastom landholders often proclaim conservation areas as a means of protecting some valuable resource, such as turtles or coconut crabs, from overexploitation.

GOVERNMENT & POLITICS

Vanuatu has a Westminster-style constitution. The first decade of independence was reasonably stable as far as Vanuatu's political groupings were concerned: the major players were the Vanua'aku Party (VP) and the Union of Moderate Parties (UMP), with the former consistently winning government.

Since 1991, however, it's been a very different, chaotic story of Machiavellian proportions: charges of nepotism and other political crimes, rivals becoming allies and vice versa, splits within parties and leaders being ousted have all been commonplace, making you wonder who had time to run the country.

The main political parties to date have been the VP, UMP, the National United Party (NUP), the Vanuatu Republican Party (VRP) and the Melanesian Progressive Party (MPP). Since 1998 alone, there have been four prime ministers: Donald Kalpokas (VP), Serge Vohor (UMP), Barak Sope (MPP) and currently Edward Natapei, who has headed the UMP since 2001.

Vanuatu's head of state is the president, who is elected by parliament and the National Council of Chiefs (Malfatu Mauri) for five years. Malfatu Mauri also advises parliament on all constitutional matters relating to Vanuatu's traditional customs.

In addition, there are presidents of the six provincial governments – see Useful Organisations in the Facts for the Visitor section for a breakdown of the provincial government areas.

ECONOMY

Vanuatu's economy is essentially agricultural, with about 80% of the population primarily engaged in subsistence and cash-crop farming of crops such as taro, yams, coconuts, cocoa, kava and vegetables.

You'd think that Vanuatu's vast ocean area would be a rich fishing resource. Yet although there is a thriving domestic fishing industry, export earnings are negligible.

Australia is Vanuatu's main export destination, with other major customers being (in order) Japan, New Caledonia, the European Union and New Zealand.

The value of Vanuatu's imports is more than four times that of its exports. The principal imports are consumer goods, in particular rice, clothing, processed food, electrical goods and vehicles. The principal suppliers are (in order) Australia, New Zealand, Japan, France and New Caledonia.

VANUATU

Agriculture

Vanuatu's fertile volcanic soil is among its greatest assets – agriculture earns around 85% of the country's export income. Copra (dried coconut meat), beef and cocoa are the major export earners. The huge domestic demand for kava – the preferred national beverage – has made it the fastest-growing agricultural commodity. Drinkers in Vila and Luganville alone consume over 500 tonnes of kava root each year.

Tourism

Tourism is the country's second-largest foreign exchange earner. Air arrivals in 2001 totalled 53,300; the average length of stay was seven days. In the same year there were visits from 52,760 cruise-ship passengers, an increase of 73% from 1997. Most people arriving by cruise ship spend only a day or two on land. Another thousand or so visitors arrived by yacht.

Over 60% of the country's tourists come from Australia, with another 14% from New Zealand and 7% from New Caledonia.

Foreign Aid

With its recurrent trade deficit, Vanuatu's economic survival depends on aid donations from other countries – although increasingly these contributions are in the form of expertise rather than cash. The most generous aid donors have been Australia, the European Development Fund, France, New Zealand and the UK.

POPULATION & PEOPLE

Vanuatu's population in 2002 was estimated at around 200,000, of which all but 3500 were Ni-Vanuatu. (Although some islands have a strong Polynesian heritage, the Ni-Vanuatu population as a whole is overwhelmingly Melanesian.) The 'others' included about 1500 Europeans, with the remainder being mainly Asians and other Pacific Islanders.

Two-thirds of the population lives on Efate, Santo, Malekula and Tanna, and around 80% of people on these islands live in rural areas, in villages of less than 50 people. On most islands the population is concentrated along narrow coastal strips, or on offshore islets. A recent trend is the drift into towns, particularly Vila, by young Ni-Vanuatu in a usually vain search for jobs. This drift saw Vila's population double to 36,000 in the 10 years to 2002.

ARTS

Vanuatu's rich artistic heritage is testament to its extraordinarily creative people, especially remarkable considering the country's relatively low population density. Given that its people are spread over 83 islands, it's not surprising that Vanuatu's art and traditions vary from island to island; this diversity contributes to the country's unique cultural identity.

The most common subject matters represented in Vanuatuan arts are the human form and traditional interpretations of what ancestral figures looked like. The most important artefacts are made for *nimangki* (grade-taking) ceremonies (see Society later in this chapter).

Island Fuel to the Rescue?

Falling world prices for copra over the past four years has meant dozens of deserted coconut plantations around Vanuatu and reduced export earnings, obviously not good news for the country. However, a private, local 'Island Fuel' project currently under way may help tip the balance of payments back in Vanuatu's favour.

In a (coco)nutshell, Island Fuel is 67% coconut oil (obtained from copra) and 33% specially processed diesel and can only be used in diesel vehicles (coconut oil can't be used on its own because it starts to solidify below 22°C). Coconut oil is a clean fuel that does not contribute to the greenhouse effect. It emits 50% less particle matter than conventional diesel and is biodegradable. It also yields more kilometres per litre than fossil fuel and costs less. Island Fuel has been trialled on some of Vila's minibuses and the results so far have been positive.

So why is it not being embraced, or at least heartily patted on the back? There are numerous hurdles, including convincing the government that lost revenue through import duties on diesel will be more than recouped through more money staying in the economy and increased employment opportunities in the fuel's production. Also, it's still early days: there's more research to be done into the viability of setting up the project on a national scale.

It's a very exciting prospect for a country that currently imports 1.2 billion vatu worth of diesel per annum, not to mention the positives of an environmentally friendly fuel.

Islanders often believe that ritual objects are taken over by malevolent spirits during or after the ceremony. For this reason, such artefacts may be destroyed as soon as the ceremony for which they were made is completed.

Carvings

While wood is the main carved material in the archipelago, objects are also made from tree fern, stone and coral. Serious carving is almost entirely created for ceremonies, while items for sale to tourists are usually small copies of the real thing. In terms of the tourist trade, the best carvings come from northern Ambrym.

Clubs & Weapons Bows and arrows, ceremonial spears and clubs for pig killing are still carved. War clubs are made to traditional designs that seldom vary from generation to generation, let alone carver to carver. To alter a basic shape is considered a breach of *kastom*, especially as the design is often attributed to a cultural hero of the distant past. Another type of club is used for pig killing. These are shaped like mattocks, with two stylised faces carved on either side.

Bowls Large platters and bowls are used to pound yams and kava in, or to serve *laplap* (the Vanuatu national dish). Some, such as those from the Shepherd Islands, are carved to depict birds or fish.

Fern Figures Statues made from tree ferns are made on Ambrym, Malekula and Gaua. They represent both male and female ancestral figures and are carved for *nimangki* ceremonies. Tree fern statues are often painted in several different colours, the choice depending on the grade being taken.

Traditional Dress

Most Ni-Vanuatu wear European clothing as part of their daily lives, but they invariably exchange this for traditional dress whenever they attend clan ceremonies.

Local Variations In *kastom*-oriented parts of Tanna and Pentecost, men still wear *nambas* (penis wrappers) every day, while women dress in grass skirts. On Santo, the men wear *mal mal* (loincloths), while some women wear an apron of leaves. In southern Malekula, the Small Nambas women traditionally wear raffia skirts woven from banana-tree fibres.

In other parts of Vanuatu, grass skirts are fashioned from the bark of the *burao*, or wild hibiscus tree. Once it's stripped, the bark is placed in sea water, dried, measured into lengths and, if necessary, dyed.

Headdresses & Masks The wearing of elaborate headgear is a major aspect of traditional ceremonies, especially on Ambrym, Ambae, Maewo and Malekula. Only men who have advanced far up the ceremonial ladder may wear such items.

Masks are usually made from tree-fern material and represent the faces of demons and ancestral spirits. Others are constructed out of clay reinforced with coconut fibres and layered onto a wickerwork frame.

Painted fern face-masks in southern Malekula are decorated with feathers and carved pigs' tusks.

Musical Instruments

Panpipes, usually complete with seven small bamboo flutes, are found all over Vanuatu. Ambrym people play a long, geometrically carved musical pipe, while in Santo a simple three-holed flute is used.

On many islands, large triton shells are blown as a means of communication. Unlike Polynesians further east, Ni-Vanuatu make a hole in the side of the shell and use that to blow through.

The *tamtam* (slit-gongs, slit-drums) is Vanuatu's most interesting musical device. *Tamtam* are carved logs with hollowed-out slits that enable them to be used as drums. The typical *tamtam* has a representation of a human face carved above the drum part – some in northern Ambrym have rooster faces. *Tamtam* are traditionally made from the wood of the breadfruit tree, which isn't the best hardwood but does give the best sound.

Visual Arts & Crafts

Painting Styles of painting practised in Vanuatu include bark art in the Banks Islands. Body painting is also popular throughout the country as part of various traditional ceremonies.

Petroglyphs and rock paintings are the country's most ancient forms of pictorial art. The former are common and widespread, though their meanings have been lost and their main significance these days is to archaeologists. Several islands have caves where the walls are decorated with hand stencils and simple paintings of animals.

VANUATU

Sand Drawing On several northern islands, villagers do beautiful sand drawings to leave messages or illustrate local legends, songs or ceremonies. The most elaborate and picturesque versions of this art form come from Ambrym, though you can see it done as far north as the Banks.

The artist first draws the foundation design, usually a sequence of squares or rectangles in the sand. Then they begin to circle with a finger, making elicate loops and circles without raising the finger until the design is finished.

Pottery This was once a widespread industry and many finds of ceramics dating back to around AD 500 have been made. Today, however, the only remaining traditional potters live in two isolated villages, Wusi and Linduri, in southwestern Santo. The craft is restricted to women.

Weaving
Baskets and mats are made throughout the country, as are fish, bird and shellfish traps. Weaving is done mostly by women, with pandanus leaves and *burao* stalks being the most favoured materials. Wicker, coconut leaves and rattan are used when a more robust item is required.

SOCIETY
There is immense variety in Vanuatu's culture and customs. Dances, funerals, weddings, initiations, systems of authority, artistic styles, and animal and crop husbandry all differ from island to island, and often from one district to another on the larger islands. Yet there are common themes, particularly the acceptance of the obligation to pay for all services rendered.

Village Life
While townspeople's lives in Vanuatu have altered considerably in recent times, village life is much as it has always been. Women spend up to 10 hours a day in the family garden, while men spend about the same in cash cropping, fishing, hunting, boat building, artefact carving and discussing council matters. While the women prepare the evening meal, the men talk in the *nakamal* (men's clubhouse) and drink kava.

There is a constant flow of people moving from larger towns back to their traditional homes. The chance to earn money may not be so good in the villages, but the cost of living is much less: there is ancestral land to grow food on, pigs to hunt in the forest, and no crime.

Tabu
You'll frequently hear the word *tabu*, from which comes the English 'taboo'. The expression means 'sacred' as well as 'forbidden'. In its simplest form, it can mean 'no entry' when written across a doorway.

Village life is beset by *tambu* (the plural form) in the more *kastom*-oriented areas. Many of these relate to traditional ceremonies. Women and uninitiated men are barred from seeing parts of certain ceremonies, while others are restricted to women.

Women in particular must endure some rather unusual *tambu*. For example, in some areas a woman may not stand higher than a male. Nor may a woman step over a smouldering fire because while she's standing in its smoke it may rise higher than a man.

Menstruation and birth are surrounded by all sorts of restrictions. Most traditional villages have an area set aside for women to go to during menstruation and childbirth. For a woman living in a *kastom*-oriented village to continue gardening and cooking while menstruating is a serious breach of rules.

Dances & Ceremonies
Traditional dances in Vanuatu involve either impersonation or participation. Impersonation dances require more rehearsal as each dancer pretends to be an ancestor or legendary figure, wearing elaborate masks or headdresses, such as in the Rom dances of Ambrym.

In participatory dances, several people – or even several villages – take part to enact traditional themes such as hunting, war or death. See The Nekowiar & Toka under Tanna later in this chapter.

Chiefs
Women can attain much status in their communities, but only men can become chiefs. A Ni-Vanuatu chief acts as a justice of the peace and as a delegate to speak for the people of the village. His word is law in most villages. Even senior bureaucrats and politicians must do what the chief says when they're visiting their home villages.

In most northern areas chiefs achieve their rank by holding a series of lavish feasts. In contrast, chiefs from the Shepherd Islands southwards either inherit their titles or are elected.

Nimangki
From Epi northwards, status and power are earned by taking grades through the *nimangki*

system. In this process men earn respect by publicly disposing of their wealth in a series of elaborate ceremonies.

Each step up the village social ladder is accompanied by the ritual killing of pigs. Because a boar takes between six and seven years to grow a good set of tusks (the prized article) only men wealthy enough to own a large number of pigs can hope to reach society's highest levels.

Southern Malekulan males can take up to 35 grades, while on Ambae only four are required. Women from southern Malekula also take grades, though far fewer than their menfolk.

Nakamal

In most parts of northern and central Vanuatu, the *nakamal* is a two-roomed hut used as a men's clubhouse and clan museum. Elsewhere it's just the place where men meet at sunset to talk and to drink kava – it may be an open-ended hut, or even a space under a large tree.

A traditional *nakamal* must never be entered without the permission of one of its members. They are usually strictly *tabu* to women, including tourists, particularly in *kastom*-oriented areas. However, this is not the case in Vila.

Marriage

A young man cannot begin to look for a wife until he has built himself a house. In the past he might have paid up to 100 pigs for a wife. However, nowadays the maximum bride price for the entire country has been set by the council of chiefs at 80,000Vt. The groom may also have to pay compensation of up to 20,000Vt to the mother of the bride for the loss of a worker.

LANGUAGE

Vanuatu is a veritable Tower of Babel – it claims the highest concentration of different languages per head of population of any country in the world. Of the 106 indigenous languages, eight are extinct, 17 are considered endangered, and the remaining 81 are still actively spoken. The country's many local tongues developed because its people have lived in small, isolated communities, separated by difficult terrain or sea.

English and French are both widely spoken and are the principal languages of education, while Bislama, a form of pidgin English, is the national lingua franca.

Bislama Basics

Hello.	*Halo.*
Hello. (two people)	*Halo tufala.*
Hello. (three people) (from English 'all together')	*Halo trifala/olgeta.*
Hello. (more than three)	*Halo olgeta.*
Good morning.	*Gud morning.*
Good afternoon.	*Gud aftenun.*
Good night.	*Gud naet.*
How are you?	*Olsem wanem?*
Thank you (very much).	*Tangkiu (tumas)/Ta.*
Do you speak English?	*Yu save tok tok long Inglis?*
I'm sorry but I only understand a little bit of Bislama.	*Sore, be mi no save tumas Bislama yet.*
What's your name?	*Wanem nem blong yu?*
My name is...	*Nem blong mi...*
I come from...	*Mi kam long...*

Facts for the Visitor

SUGGESTED ITINERARIES

With only seven days to spend in Vanuatu, the average visitor is content to spend their time in and around Vila, plus do a two- or three-day trip to Tanna. Two weeks are easily filled if you add (for example) a scuba-diving trip to Santo, a visit to Malekula to see *kastom* dancing or a bushwalking tour on Ambrym or Erromango. Allow three weeks or more if you want to do all these things.

PLANNING
When to Go

The most pleasant time to visit is during the dry season from May to October. Visitor numbers peak over the Australian school holiday periods in June/July and September.

Maps

The most up-to-date map of Vanuatu is the 1:200,000 map published by South Pacific Maps in 2001, distributed in Australia through **Hema Maps** (☎ *07-3340 0000*). Copies are available from the Drug Store in Port Vila (1065Vt).

What to Bring

Summer clothing is generally suitable year-round. However, Efate and islands to the south can have cool nights between May and October, so be sure to pack at least a light jumper. Warm clothing is also handy after diving, for sea travel and for travelling in the open backs of 4WD taxis. A light raincoat and/or umbrella won't go astray, as it often rains, even in the dry season.

TOURIST OFFICES
Local Tourist Offices
The only official tourism office in the country is in Vila: **National Tourism Office** *(NTO;* ☎ *22813, 22515;* W *www.vanuatutourism .com)*. See the listing under Port Vila to obtain more information.

Tourist Offices Abroad
The Vanuatu NTO is represented in the following countries only:

Australia
NSW: (☎ 02-9959 3599, e info@thesalesteam .com.au) The Sales Team Marketing Group, Suite 602a, Level 6, 97-103 Pacific Hwy, North Sydney 2060
Queensland: (☎ 07-3221 2566, e brisbane .sales@airvanuatu.com.au) Level 5, 293 Queen St, Brisbane 4000
New Caledonia (☎ 28 6677, e axxessga@ affratel.nc) Axxess Travel, Lot 36 rue de Verdun, Noumea
New Zealand (☎ 6844 1781, e vanuatu@travelt alk.co.nz) Craig Andrew Reid & Associates, PO Box 7240, Taradale, Auckland

VISAS & DOCUMENTS
Every visitor must have a passport that is valid for at least four months from the date of arrival, as well as a return or onward ticket. Immigration staff may also ask for proof that you have sufficient funds to support yourself while in the country.

Entry visas are not required for nationals of the British Commonwealth and European Union countries. A number of other countries are also exempt; have a look at W www.vanuatutourism.com/visa_info.htm to see if you need a visa.

Whether you require a visa or not you're allowed an initial stay of up to 30 days. This can be extended one month at a time for up to four months.

Nonexempt visitors should contact the **Principal Immigration Officer** *(☎ 22354, fax 25492; PMB 092, Port Vila)* to organise their visa application (2500Vt fee). This must be finalised *before* arrival in the country. Of all Vanuatu's honorary consuls, the only one who can organise visas outside Vanuatu is Mr William Longwah in Australia (see Vanuatuan Representatives following).

Visa extensions are free and straightforward; this process requires leaving your passport and onward ticket with the Immigration Department in Vila or Luganville for about three days.

For driving licence requirements see Car & Motorcycle under Getting Around later in this chapter.

EMBASSIES & CONSULATES
Vanuatuan Representatives
Vanuatu does not have embassies or consulates overseas. Its honorary consuls include:

Australia (☎ 02-9597 4046) Mr William Longwah, 54 Eden St, Arncliffe, NSW 2205
France (☎ 01 40 53 82 25) Mr Daniel Martin, 9 rue Daru, 75008 Paris
Japan (☎ 422-477 792) Mr Bunnosuke Yoshioka, 4-22-36 Mure Mitaka, Tokyo 181-0002

Contact details for other honorary consuls can be obtained from the **Foreign Affairs Department** *(☎ 22347; PMB 9051, Port Vila)*.

Embassies & Consulates in Vanuatu
All the diplomatic representations to Vanuatu are in Port Vila:

Australia (☎ 22777) PO Box 111, KPMG House, rue Pasteur
China (☎ 22598) PMB 071, rue d'Auvergne
France (☎ 22353) PO Box 60, Lini Hwy
New Zealand (☎ 22933) PO Box 161, Lini Hwy
UK (☎ 23100) PO Box 567, KPMG House, rue Pasteur

CUSTOMS
Visitors aged over 15 may bring in 200 cigarettes, 100 cigarillos, 50 cigars or 250g of tobacco. You may also bring in 2L of wine and two bottles of spirits (maximum 1.5L), 250mL of *eau de toilette*, 100mL of perfume and other items up to a value of 50,000Vt.

All plants, fruit, seeds, meat, fish, shellfish, dairy and poultry products must be declared on arrival. No firearms or ammunition may be brought into the country.

MONEY
Currency
Vanuatu's currency is the *vatu* (Vt). There are 200, 500, 1000 and 5000Vt banknotes, and coins worth 1, 2, 5, 10, 20, 50 and 100Vt.

There are no limits on the amount of money you may bring into or take out of the country.

The *vatu* isn't a familiar currency overseas, so it's best to change leftover funds back to your own currency before leaving Vanuatu.

Exchange Rates

To check current exchange rates, see W www .oanda.com.

country	unit		vatu
Australia	A$1	=	91Vt
Canada	C$1	=	100Vt
euro zone	€1	=	154Vt
Fiji	F$1	=	73Vt
Japan	¥100	=	112Vt
New Zealand	NZ$1	=	79Vt
Pacific franc	100 CFP	=	128Vt
Samoa	ST1	=	46Vt
Solomon Islands	S$1	=	18Vt
Tonga	T$1	=	62Vt
UK	£1	=	222Vt
USA	US$1	=	133Vt

Exchanging Money

The three commercial banks operating in Vanuatu are the ANZ Bank, Westpac and the local National Bank of Vanuatu (NBV). All have their main offices in central Vila, as well as branches in Luganville. The NBV also has a branch at Bauerfield International Airport, open to greet all incoming international flights. The ANZ has several ATMs around downtown Vila, one at Bauerfield International Airport and one at its Luganville branch, while Westpac has one in Vila.

There are also private moneychangers in Vila and Luganville.

The major duty-free shops, restaurants and hotels in Vila should have no difficulties with cash and travellers cheques in major international currencies. However, the few hotels outside the capital may only be willing to accept Australian or US dollars.

Always take plenty of *vatu* when travelling in rural Vanuatu as you won't be able to change foreign currencies in villages. Carry a good reserve of coins and smaller denomination notes for such things as taxi fares and small purchases.

Major credit cards are accepted by the larger tourist-oriented businesses in Vila and Luganville, but don't expect to be able to use them elsewhere.

Costs

Vila is by no means a cheap place to visit, particularly if you're eating out all the time and staying in a reasonable hotel. For those on a budget, the cheapest dorm beds you'll find cost 1500Vt per person; if you're self-catering allow another 1500Vt per couple for food. When you start thinking about eating out, transport beyond Vila and tours, things really start adding up: it's easy to spend 5000Vt per person daily without doing very much at all.

Mid-range accommodation costs in the 5000Vt to 10,000Vt bracket for singles and doubles, while the top-end resorts will set you back between 10,000Vt and 20,000Vt. If you're eating out three meals a day, budget for around 5000Vt on meals, give or take a little depending on how much you like to drink.

Daily costs come down somewhat once you head to the outer islands, although the big expense can be getting to the islands. Air fares from Port Vila cost in most cases between 7000Vt and 12,000Vt. Once there, typical daily expenses are 7000Vt, including accommodation, meals and activities, although if you're prepared to do a lot of walking and not go on tours, you could spend as little as 2000Vt.

Bear in mind that all of the above prices can vary depending on what time of year you're travelling, whether you've booked through an agent, how long you're staying, if you're on a special package and so on.

Tipping & Bargaining

Tipping and bargaining are not customary practices in Vanuatu and may cause offence.

POST & COMMUNICATIONS
Post

Vanuatu has no street postal delivery service, so you must write to either a post office box or Private Mail Bag (PMB) or use the poste restante service in Vila. All major rural administrative centres have post offices.

Telephone & Fax

A microwave network connects all of the major islands. In addition, HF and VHF tele-radio services are provided to many isolated communities.

Public card-operated telephones (there are no coin-operated ones) for both local and international calls are available in most important centres. Postal agencies usually sell TeleCards. The system is easy as pie to use: just follow the instructions on the back of the card.

Local and international fax facilities are available at Vila's general post office and the Telecom Vanuatu office in Luganville.

VANUATU

Calls within Vanuatu To use the HF teleradio network, dial ☎ 22759 in Vila; to use the VHF network, dial ☎ 22221 in Vila and ☎ 36248 in Luganville. When making such a call it's a good idea to have a Bislama speaker on hand to help you out.

The cheapest time (off-peak) to make a domestic call is between 6pm and 6am Monday to Friday and all weekend; you'll be charged 20Vt every four minutes. During peak times, it costs 20Vt every two minutes.

There are no area codes in Vanuatu.

Service Messages Villages without telephone or teleradio services can usually be contacted by sending a service message over **Radio Vanuatu** *(in Vila ☎ 22999, in Luganville ☎ 36851)*.

International Calls The code for international calls from Vanuatu is ☎ 00. Vanuatu's international telephone code is ☎ 678.

There are two zones for international call rates from Vanuatu: neighbourhood (Australia, New Zealand, New Caledonia and Fiji); and the rest of the world. To call within the 'neighbourhood' costs 133Vt per minute during peak times (6am to 6pm Monday to Friday) and 108Vt per minute off-peak. The rates to everywhere else are 216/168Vt for peak/off-peak.

Many larger hotels have IDD phones, but you pay through the nose for these services.

You cannot make international reverse-charge calls from Vanuatu.

Email & Internet Access
You can access the Internet easily at a few places in Vila and Luganville. Many hotels and resorts also offer Internet access, albeit at inflated prices. Once you get to the more remote islands, however, there are no opportunities to get online.

DIGITAL RESOURCES
The World Wide Web is a rich resource for travellers. A good place to start your trip planning and Web explorations is the **Lonely Planet website** *(W www.lonelyplanet.com)*. Of particular value is the Pacific Islands branch of the Thorn Tree bulletin board, where you can ask questions before you go, or dispense advice when you get back.

There aren't that many great websites dedicated to Vanuatu, however, you could try the **National Tourism Office** *(W www .vanuatutourism.com)* or **Ja'sons South Pacific Islands** *(W www.pi-travel.co.nz)*.

BOOKS
If you're after more in-depth information on Vanuatu, Lonely Planet also publishes *Vanuatu* and *Diving & Snorkeling Guide to Vanuatu*.

The following is just a wee taste of books available from other publishers.

History
To Kill a Bird with Two Stones, by Jeremy MacClancy, is an exceptionally good history of Vanuatu. It takes the country from its earliest beginnings through the Condominium period (the 'two stones' of the title) right up to independence.

Also recommended is *Ethnology of Vanuatu: an early twentieth century study*, by Felix Speiser. This impressive, well-illustrated work contains the results of a scientific expedition to the country in 1910 to1912 by Dr Speiser, a professor at the University of Basel, Switzerland.

Arts & Customs
Arts of Vanuatu, by Joel Bonnemaison (ed) et al, is an essential reference. This lavishly illustrated work explores the rich diversity of Vanuatu's unique cultural identity, looking at it in both historical and contemporary contexts.

Novels
James Michener's novel *Tales of the South Pacific* gives a very good picture of life in Santo when US forces were garrisoned there during WWII.

Gwendoline Page's very readable *Coconuts and Coral* is a detailed and often amusing account of life in the New Hebrides during the 1960s as seen by a young English family.

NEWSPAPERS & MAGAZINES
The major newspapers are the thrice-weekly *Trading Post* and the twice-weekly *Port Vila Presse*. Both cost 100Vt.

Air Vanuatu's in-flight magazine *Island Spirit* has general facts and reasonable articles about the country.

RADIO & TV
The government-owned Radio Vanuatu provides trilingual FM, AM and SW services throughout the country. All services operate continuously from 6am to 10pm and offer international and local news bulletins. You'll find it at 98FM and 1125AM. You can also pick up the BBC at 99FM.

Local TV is available on a single channel from around 4.30pm to 11.30pm daily.

TIME

Vanuatu time is GMT/UMT plus 11 hours, which is one hour ahead of Australian Eastern Standard Time. Noon in Vila is 1am in London, 8pm in New York and 11am in Sydney. Local time is the same as in New Caledonia, but one hour behind Fiji and New Zealand.

HEALTH

The major medical facilities are in Vila and Luganville, both of which have good-sized hospitals and well-stocked pharmacies. There is also a decompression chamber for divers in Vila. Many remote rural areas have no health facilities apart from aid posts, if that. See Health in the Regional Facts for the Visitor chapter for more information.

Water

Domestic water supplies in main urban centres are normally quite safe for drinking, although in some areas (eg, Luganville and Lamap) it should be boiled towards the end of a long dry season.

In rural areas, drinking water obtained from springs is generally OK. Water from other sources should be purified before drinking. You can generally buy bottled water everywhere, but it's wise to always have an emergency bottle on hand.

Mosquito-Borne Diseases

Malaria is Vanuatu's major health risk. It is extremely important to avoid mosquito bites – you should also consider taking malarial prophylactics. Dengue fever is another potential health risk.

SOCIAL GRACES

Villages are amazingly clean and tidy, and even though their small huts and shared facilities mean a village is more like a camping ground than a suburban street as we know it, you cannot wander around like you might in a camping ground. So stick to the road, perhaps wait outside a village until somebody approaches you – that won't take long – and check that any road you are on isn't private property.

Villagers are very friendly and hospitable, but life is expensive for them. The cost of educating their children is a huge burden that is way beyond many people, so always pay your way fairly. Trading a trinket or a packet of cigarettes for a lobster just isn't fair. It can be tricky. Sometimes offering money just doesn't work and it's impossible to lug around enough jars of peanut butter, torches and other worthwhile goodies. Phonecards are a good alternative as gifts.

Islanders seldom wear scant or revealing clothing, and women's thighs are always covered. Try to ensure that what you wear shows due respect. You should not treat somebody as an equal until you've gauged their response to you. You may be talking to a chief, even though he looks 15, or a sorcerer, and you might offend someone you really don't want to offend. Always observe things that are *tabu*, for example, *nakamal* in rural villages are often off limits to women. Some areas keep women 'in their place'. It's polite to grin and bear it. See Tabu under Society earlier in this chapter.

USEFUL ORGANISATIONS

Staff at the various provincial government offices will be happy to advise you on travel in their area or region. However, these offices, with the exception of Sanma and Shafa, are sometimes difficult to contact directly – you'll often find that the phone is disconnected, or it's constantly engaged. This is an instance where a 'service message' over Radio Vanuatu can be very useful (see Post & Communications earlier in this chapter).

The provinces and their headquarters are as follows:

Malampa Province (Malekula, Ambrym & Paama; ☎ 48403, 48491, 48643) PO Box 22, Lakatoro, Malekula

Penama Province (Pentecost, Ambae & Maewo; ☎ 38348, 38414, 38415) Saratamata, Ambae

Sanma Province (Espiritu Santo & Malo; ☎ 36712) PO Box 239, Luganville, Santo

Shefa Province (Efate, Epi & The Shepherd Islands; ☎ 22752) PMB 9078, Port Vila

Tafea Province (Tanna, Erromango, Aneityum, Aniwa & Futuna; ☎ 68664, 68638) PO Box 28, Isangel, Tanna

Torba Province (The Banks & Torres Islands; ☎ 38550) Sola, Vanua Lava

Women intending to travel solo to the outer islands should contact the **Vanuatu National Council of Women** (☎ 23108; PO Box 975), next to the National Museum in Vila, for information on cultural matters relating to women as well as for help with transport and accommodation.

DANGERS & ANNOYANCES

Your belongings will normally be quite safe in your hotel room. However, petty theft is on the increase and you should never leave any

VANUATU

valuables, wallets or handbags lying about unattended. Clothing, footwear, snorkelling gear and other useful items are also at risk of theft.

BUSINESS HOURS

Government offices generally open Monday to Friday from 7.30am to 11.30am, and 1.30pm to 4.30pm, and sometimes Saturday morning. Shops normally begin trading at 7.30am and go through until around 6pm or 7pm; only some close for the midday siesta. Saturday shopping generally ceases between 11.30am and midday, although Chinese stores tend to remain open all weekend.

PUBLIC HOLIDAYS & SPECIAL EVENTS

In addition to New Year's Day, Easter, Ascension Day, Assumption Day and Christmas (see the Regional Facts for the Visitor chapter for dates), Vanuatu celebrates:

Father Walter Lini Remembrance Day
  21 February
Custom Chiefs' Day 5 March
Labour Day 1 May
Children's Day 24 July
Independence Day 30 July
Rom Dance Ceremony August
Constitution Day 5 October
National Unity Day 29 November
Family Day 26 December

Independence Day festivities are Vanuatu's most important annual event. Other notable events of cultural interest include the following (contact the NTO for exact dates as they change yearly):

February
Jon Frum Day Held at Sulphur Bay, Tanna, includes festivities, dancing and parades

April–June
Naghol This land-diving ceremony occurs in several villages in southern Pentecost (see the boxed text 'The Land Divers of South Pentecost' later in this chapter)

August–October
Nekowiar This clan-alliance ceremony is held on Tanna over a period of three days every year

ACTIVITIES

It's very easy to be very lazy in Vanuatu, but at the same time it's also difficult to ignore the chance for excellent diving, snorkelling, hiking, fishing, kayaking and sailing, and to get immersed in the country's culture and natural environment.

Swimming

Although the swimming close to Vila is not that brilliant, further afield there are hundreds of beaches. Many of the sandy ones are black (a legacy of the nation's volcanoes) while others are brilliant white. Sharks, stonefish and strong currents are a danger in some areas. Always seek local advice before plunging in.

Diving

Vanuatu's many scuba sites include several world-class dives. Some are spotlighted in the special section 'South Pacific Diving', earlier in this book. Vila has the best range of underwater topography in a small area, while Santo has the best wreck, coral and fish dives.

For contact details of specialist dive-tour operators in Vila and Luganville, see the sections on Efate and Santo later in this chapter.

Hiking

The country has many fine walks, including strenuous overnight hikes on Erromango, Ambrym, Santo, Gaua and Malekula. When planning a walk you can organise it yourself in conjunction with a guide from where you're staying or through tour operators such as Tamaso Aliat Wi Tours and The Adventure Centre in Vila (for contact details see Organised Tours under Getting Around later in this chapter).

When walking on jungle paths always wear long pants to protect yourself from stinging plants – ignore this advice at your peril. Sandals and runners are not suitable for jungle hiking or volcano climbs.

Guides are generally required for walks off the beaten track – hiring one will cost around 3000Vt per day.

ACCOMMODATION

The following is a summary of accommodation options in Vanuatu (in order of expense). In Vila and Luganville, you're usually limited to guesthouses, motels and resorts.

Bungalows Quaint thatched cubby houses with little verandas and pandanus leaf walls, often set in gorgeous surroundings. Good idea to BYO toilet paper, earplugs (the roosters generally stir at around 4am) and torch. They cost anywhere between 1800Vt and 4500Vt, and generally include all meals.

Camping While there are no official camping grounds, many bungalows and guesthouses are happy for you to use their grounds and facilities for a minimal fee.

Guesthouses Usually concrete buildings without much character, but with fully-equipped kitchens so you can cook for yourself. Usually cost between 1000Vt and 1500Vt.

Nakamal Very basic, open, roofed meeting areas that may not cost anything more than an evening's talk with the locals. BYO bedding, water and protection against mosquitoes, fleas and rats. Meals can usually be supplied for around 200Vt each.

Resorts & Motels Impressive selection in and around Vila and, to a lesser extent, on Santo and Tanna. There are a handful of motels that cost under 7000Vt for a double, several motels in the 7000Vt to 10,000Vt price bracket, while most top-end resorts start at around 15,000Vt per double.

Resthouses & Women's Club Houses Basic accommodation with a bed (of sorts) usually provided, meals cooked for you (200Vt each) and conveniences out there somewhere. BYO bedding, mosquito net and water. Cost between 500Vt and 1000Vt.

FOOD & DRINK

Thanks largely to its French influence, Vila is well known in the Pacific for its international cuisine. The main supermarkets all carry a good range of local and imported food and drink, including alcohol.

Restaurants are scarce outside Luganville and Vila, although most rural guesthouses provide decent meals. The larger villages have general stores, but their choice of grocery lines is often limited. Some also have markets where you can buy cheap, fresh produce.

Kava drinking is an evening ritual throughout the country – it's available in most villages, and there are plenty of kava bars in Vila and Luganville. See the boxed text 'Kava' in the Regional Facts for the Visitor chapter.

SHOPPING
Handicrafts

Vanuatu offers a wide range of traditional and contemporary handicrafts and artefacts, with woven leaf products and wood carvings being most popular. The major handicraft outlets in Vila, where examples of all the nation's art forms are available. Elsewhere, purchasing is usually by direct contact with village artisans.

Objects must be fumigated if they are made from tree ferns, have soil or feathers on them,

or have fresh borer holes. If necessary you can arrange this yourself at one of the country's two **quarantine stations**: near Bauerfield International Airport in Vila (☎ 23130) and at Luganville's main wharf (☎ 36728). The process takes a minimum of 24 hours and costs from 800Vt.

You'll require a Cites (Convention on International Trade in Endangered Species) exemption form for objects made from tree ferns or parts of animals, including shell and coral. If the seller can't organise this, go to the **Environment Unit** (☎ 25302) in the Georges Pompidou Building in central Vila and make an application.

The export of all magic stones and antiques – that is, artefacts more than 50 years old – is banned. If your purchase could possibly be taken for a restricted item, make sure you obtain a certificate proving that it's been made recently.

Duty-Free

Vila is the country's only duty-free port. When making duty-free purchases you must produce your passport and onward or return ticket. The shop will deliver the goods to you on departure at the airport or main wharf.

Getting There & Away

AIR

The following airlines have regular scheduled flights to Vanuatu:

Air Pacific (☎ 22836, W www.airpacific.com, Lini Hwy) South Pacific Travel is Air Pacific's agent (see Travel Agencies following)

Air Vanuatu (☎ 23848, W www.airvanuatu.com) rue de Paris

Aircalin (☎ 22019, W www.aircalin.nc, Lini Hwy) Aircalin is the New Caledonian airline

Qantas Airways (W www.qantas.com.au) Acts as the sales agent for Air Vanuatu in all areas outside Australia, New Zealand, Fiji and New Caledonia

For further information see the introductory Getting There & Away chapter earlier in this book.

Airports

Vanuatu's major international airport, Bauerfield, is 6km north of Port Vila. It has an ANZ

ATM, a National Bank of Vanuatu branch that's usually open for currency exchange whenever there's an international flight coming or going, a café, and duty-free shopping (it's cheaper in town).

Departure Tax

There is a 2500Vt airport tax charged to all international passengers (except for children under two) leaving Vanuatu. This should be included in your ticket price, but it doesn't hurt to double-check.

Australasia

Air Vanuatu only operates direct flights from Brisbane and Sydney to Port Vila. Return fares from Sydney start from A$780/870 in the low/high season; from Brisbane it's A$670/750. A typical fare from Melbourne, going via Sydney, is A$900/1000.

Hideaway Holidays (☎ 02-9743 0253; W www.hideawayholidays.com.au) is a fantastic South Pacific specialist offering a range of flight/accommodation deals to Vanuatu. Packages start at around A$1199 for seven nights.

Air Vanuatu has direct flights from Auckland to Vila, as well as flights via Nadi and Noumea. Return low-season fares start from NZ$948 for the direct flights, from NZ$1282 for the indirect.

Talpacific Holidays (☎ 09-914 8728; W www.travelarrange.co.nz) is a good South Pacific travel agent.

The Pacific

Connections from other Pacific islands to Vanuatu are rare. There are flights from Fiji (Air Pacific) and Noumea (Aircalin), but if you are travelling to/from other Pacific islands you will need to get connecting flights in New Zealand, Fiji or Noumea. Your best bet if you're travelling around the Pacific is to purchase an air pass for the region – see the regional Getting There & Away chapter earlier in this book.

SEA
Cruise Ship

Vila hosts a cruise ship on average about once or twice a fortnight. The South Sea Shipping (☎ 22205, fax 23304; e southsea@vanuatu.com.vu) company, upstairs from Tropik Bistrot in Vila, is the agent for the two ships that currently visit the country from Sydney. These ships are P&O's *Pacific Sky* and *Pacific Princess*.

Yacht

The best sources of general information on yachting matters are the Vanuatu Cruising Yacht Club (☎ 24634; Lini Hwy), at the northern end of downtown Vila, and Waterfront Bar & Grill (☎ 23490; Lini Hwy), opposite Iririki.

Touring yachts are not permitted to make landfall in or depart from Vanuatu until they have cleared customs and immigration at Vila, Luganville, Lenakel (Tanna) or Sola (Vanua Lava), the country's authorised ports of entry. There are hefty fines for disobeying this rule. There is a landing fee of 7000Vt for the first 30 days and 100Vt per day thereafter.

Getting Around

All the major islands receive scheduled air services from Vila or Luganville. While the national road network continues to grow, many remote areas can only be reached by footpath or boat.

AIR

Vanair is Vanuatu's only domestic air carrier. You can check current prices and schedules with its head office (☎ 22643, fax 23910; rue Pasteur; open 7.30am-5pm Mon-Fri, to 11am Sat) in central Vila, or at its Luganville office (☎ 36421; Main St).

Vanair offers scheduled flights to 28 airfields (often with grass or coral runways) using its small fleet of 20-seat Twin Otters. While the service is generally very reliable, delays of an hour or more are not uncommon. 'Milk-run' flights (ie, one that picks up and drops off people and supplies on a number of islands), particularly, can leave you guessing.

If you book your flights directly with Vanair you will receive a 20% discount. Children between two and 12 fly half-price. Students are granted a 25% discount on presentation of satisfactory proof, such as an International Student Identity Card (ISIC).

It pays to book your seat well in advance, particularly on the more popular routes such as Vila to Luganville and Tanna, and it's very important to always reconfirm your flight.

Discover Vanuatu Pass

Vanair's 'Discover Vanuatu Pass' gives you the chance to fly a combination of sectors within 30 days for US$236. The specified destinations are Craig Cove on Ambrym, Norsup on Malekula, Luganville and Tanna.

BUS

Public minibuses carrying up to 14 passengers operate in Vila, Luganville and, to a much lesser extent, eastern Santo and eastern Malekula. You'll know them by the red 'B' fixed to their numberplates.

These vehicles are a little like taxis, only much cheaper. In the towns they don't run fixed routes, but zoom all over the place at the whim of their passengers. You simply flag them down by the roadside, and they'll stop if there's a spare seat.

CAR & MOTORCYCLE
Road Rules

There's a speed limit of 50km/h in Vila and Luganville, but once out of town there are no formal restrictions – speed in rural areas is usually dictated by road conditions (often pretty terrible). Vehicles drive on the right, as in France. Always give way to traffic coming from the right, and be wary of people or animals on the road in rural areas.

Rental

You can hire cars and 4WD vehicles in Vila and Luganville, and scooters in Vila. The minimum age for renting a car is 23; for a scooter it's 17, provided you hold a valid driving licence.

An International Driver's Licence is not needed to drive in Vanuatu; most current national driving licences suffice. However, you must have held your licence for at least a year, in some cases longer.

BOAT

Travelling around Vanuatu by boat is an adventurous and cheaper option for those with plenty of time. You can travel to just about every island; in most cases it's about half the cost of flying. Conditions and facilities on board some boats, particularly those built primarily for cargo, are pretty basic, and on longer journeys it can become very unpleasant if the sea is rough. Still, travelling by boat can be a great way to get a different perspective on the country and is often an excellent way to meet locals.

If you're planning to travel to many of the islands by boat, especially the more far-flung ones, suss out whether there are beds or not, and make sure you bring a pillow, sleeping bag and mat. Also, ask if meals and water are included in the price, or whether you have to BYO supplies.

Many of the boats don't really run to a schedule as such, but they do work to a kind

of pattern, conducting round trips of various islands every week, fortnight or month.

A new operator is the **Lady Deema** (☎ 27 926; e *ladydeema@hotmail.com*). It provides a comfortable service and mainly sails between Santo and Vila, with some services to Malekula and Tanna. It's likely to visit other islands soon. You can book through The Adventure Centre in Vila (see Organised Tours following).

Another recommended service about to commence at the time of writing, and with the same contact details as the *Lady Deema*, is the catamaran ferry **Island Explorer**. It will offer a regular service to Pentecost, Malekula, Maewo and Ambrym, with trips also planned to the Banks Group.

A more rudimentary option is Sea-Link's cargo ship **MV Tina 1** (☎ 36517; e *sealink@ vanuatu.com.vu*), which sails weekly from Santo to Vila via Pentecost, Ambrym, Paama and Epi, then returns via Epi, Ambrym and Malekula.

To visit the far north, there's the copra vessel **MV Keidi** (☎ 36530; *LCM Store, Main St, Luganville*), which sails from Santo to Gaua, Vanua Lava, Moto Lava and the Torres Islands every four weeks. In between, it visits Ambae and Maewo.

Then there's **MV** *Havannah* (☎ 22666; *Surata Tamaso Travel, Vila*) which travels from Noumea in New Caledonia to Vila, Malekula and Santo before returning to Noumea, or to Vila via Tanna and return. Each service is usually once a month.

Canoe & Speedboat

When Ni-Vanuatu talk of speedboats, they mean outboard-powered dinghies or small work-boats. Canoes are simply dugout craft with outriggers, usually powered by paddles. Except on the shorter routes, speedboats have generally replaced canoes as commuter craft. Speedboat prices can be very high, and a longish journey on which you're the only passenger can really damage the budget – wait for the scheduled services rather than chartering if you can.

TAXI

Most islands with roads have taxis. In Vila and Luganville these are mostly conventional sedans, while in rural areas they're 4WD trucks or utilities. Taxis and public transport trucks have a red 'T' on their number plates.

The minimum charge in urban areas is 100Vt, and for a straight point-to-point charter you can expect to pay around 100Vt per kilometre. However, in some rural areas, such as south Pentecost, you'll be charged a lot more than that.

Taxis in Vila and Luganville should have their meters on for trips within the town area. If the meter is off, ask that it be switched on. For longer journeys you can negotiate a price with the driver (make sure they stick to it).

A day charter will generally cost between 8000Vt and 12,000Vt, depending on factors such as road conditions and distance. In addition, you may be expected to provide lunch for the driver. Always ask your hotel to recommend someone, rather than take pot luck down at the taxi rank.

At bush airfields, the best source of information on local taxis is the Vanair clerical staff. Taxis are usually conspicuous by their absence on Sunday and public holidays in rural areas.

ORGANISED TOURS

There's a wide variety of tours on offer, particularly on Efate and Santo. These include traditional culture, yacht cruises, scuba diving, bushwalking, bus tours and kayaking. Between them, the major inbound tour operators (all in central Vila) have details of most tours throughout the country.

Adventures in Paradise (☎ 25200,
 e paradise@vanuatu.com.vu)
Island Safaris Vanuatu (☎ 23288,
 w www.islandsvanuatu.com)
Rainbow Adventure Tours (☎/fax 26117)
Tamaso Aliat Wi Tours (☎ 25600, w www
 .vanuatutourism.com/tamaso_aliat3.htm)
The Adventure Centre (☎ 22743,
 w www.adventurevanuatu.com)

Efate

pop 42,130 • area 915 sq km
James Cook named this island after Lord Sandwich, the British patron of his voyage. However, the islanders' own name for it, Efate (ef-**art**-ay), has prevailed. Efate has two of the country's best deep-water anchorages, Vila Bay and Havannah Harbour, as well as the principal airport and national capital, Port Vila.

Havannah Harbour was the site of the first European settlement on Efate. For a time it was the island's commercial centre, but in the 1880s most of its malaria-ravaged residents decamped for the healthier climate of Vila Bay. In 1906 Vila was declared the seat of the newly proclaimed Condominium government.

PORT VILA
pop 36,000
Built around horseshoe-shaped Vila Bay, Vila climbs steep hillsides that offer stunning views over the bay and Iriri and Ifira islands. Its beautiful harbour combined with a faded French atmosphere make it one of the South Pacific's most attractive towns.

Information
Tourist Offices The **National Tourism Office** (NTO; ☎ 22813, 22515; Lini Hwy; open 7.30am-4.30pm Mon-Fri, 8am-noon Sat) is a small information centre opposite the Banque ANZ Pacifique. The helpful staff can assist with accommodation bookings, tours and information on the outer islands.

Money Foreign exchange is mainly handled by the **ANZ Bank**, **Banque ANZ Pacifique** (both open 8am-3pm Mon-Fri), and **Westpac** (open 8.30am-4pm Mon-Fri), which are all on Lini Hwy.

Goodies Money Exchange (cnr Lini Hwy & rue Pasteur; open 8am-5.30pm Mon-Fri, 8am-4pm Sat, 8.30am-noon Sun) generally gives the best rates.

Post & Communications Vila's **General Post Office** (GPO; Lini Hwy; open 7.30am-4.30pm Mon-Fri, 7.30am-11.30am Sat) has a poste restante service and Internet facilities (25Vt per minute). There are several card-operated phone boxes outside, as well as more private phone and fax booths inside.

The **Underwater Post Office** (3m below surface, Hideaway Island Marine Sanctuary, Port Vila) is definitely the most novel PO in the Pacific: don your diving gear and buy a waterproof postcard stamped by a PO worker (diver...).

Naviti Internet Café (Lini Hwy; 25Vt/min; open 7.30am-6.30pm Mon-Fri, 8am-noon Sat) is the best bet for using the Internet.

Travel Agencies Vila's out-bound operators include **South Pacific Travel** (☎ 22836; e spts@vanuatu.com.vu; Lini Hwy) and **Surata Tamaso Travel** (☎ 22666; e tamaso-tours@vanuatu.com.vu; Lini Hwy). Both can arrange and confirm bookings on any airline around the world.

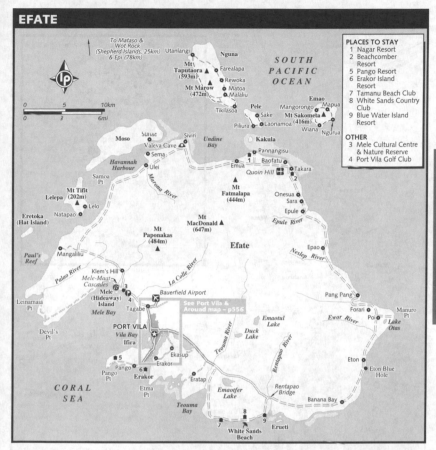

EFATE

To Mataso &
Wot Rock
(Shepherd Islands; 25km)
& Epi (78km)

Utanlangi

Nguna

**SOUTH
PACIFIC
OCEAN**

Mt
Taputaora
(593m)

Farealapa

Rewoka

Mt Marow
(472m)

Matoa

Malaliu

Tikilasoa

Pele

Sake

Piliura

Laonamoa

Mangorongo

Mapua

Mt Sakometa
(416m)

Wiana

Ngurua

Emao

Moso

Suuae

Siviri

Valeva Cave

Sema

*Undine
Bay*

Kakula

Pannangisu

Havannah
Harbour

Ulei

Maranu River

Emua

Baofatu

Quoin Hill

Takara

Samoa
Pt

Mt
Fatmalapa
(444m)

Onesua

Sara

Mt Tifit
(202m)

Lelepa

Lelo

Natapao

Eretoka
(Hat Island)

Mt
MacDonald ▲
(647m)

Epule

Epule River

Mt
Paponakas
(484m)

Efate

Epao

Neslep River

Paul's
Reef

Mangaliliu

Palao River

Klem's Hill

Mele-Maat
Cascades

Mele
(Hideaway)
Island

La Colle River

Bauerfield Airport

Pang Pang

Forari

Poi

Manuro
Pt

Ewor River

Lake
Otas

Leinamaia
Pt

Tagabe

Teouma River

Emaotul
Lake

Duck
Lake

Rentapao River

PORT VILA

Vila Bay

Ifira

See Port Vila &
Around map – p556

Eton

Eton Blue
Hole

Devil's
Pt

Ekasup

Erakor

Eratap

Emaotfer
Lake

Rentapao
Bridge

Banana Bay

**CORAL
SEA**

Pango
Pt

Pango

Erakor

Etma
Pt

*Teouma
Bay*

White Sands
Beach

Erueti

PLACES TO STAY
1 Nagar Resort
2 Beachcomber
  Resort
5 Pango Resort
6 Erakor Island
  Resort
7 Tamanu Beach Club
8 White Sands Country
  Club
9 Blue Water Island
  Resort

OTHER
3 Mele Cultural Centre
  & Nature Reserve
4 Port Vila Golf Club

0   5   10km
0   3   6mi

VANUATU

Medical Services East of downtown, **Vila Central Hospital** (☎ 22100) has a dentist, several private practitioners and a dispensary, and is open for outpatients during normal business hours.

ProMedical (☎ 25566) is a private, 24-hour paramedic service, which also operates a **decompression chamber** for divers.

There are three well-stocked pharmacies in central Vila, the best being the **Drug Store** (*Lini Hwy; open 7.30am-6pm Mon-Fri, to noon Sat, 8.30am-noon Sun*) opposite the Westpac Bank.

National Museum of Vanuatu

This excellent museum and cultural centre (☎ 22129; *Lini Hwy; adult/child 500/100Vt; open 9am-4.30pm Mon-Fri, to noon Sat*), which is on rue d'Artois across from the entrance of Parliament House, is home to quite a large and well-displayed selection of traditional artefacts, including items such as *tamtam*, massive outrigger canoes, ceremonial headdresses and examples of Lapita and Wusi pottery.

Market

Vila's waterfront market is open round-the-clock from Monday through to noon on Saturday. The goods being offered here include a wide range of fruit and vegetables (all at rock-bottom prices), flowers, firewood, jewellery, wood carvings, as well as other touristy souvenirs. The produce is seasonal, so keep your eye out for delicious goodies such as wild raspberries and mangoes around November, and passionfruit from the months of March to May.

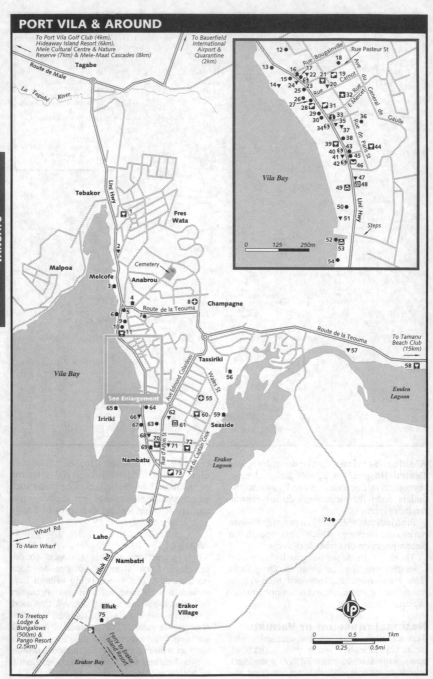

PORT VILA & AROUND

To Port Vila Golf Club (4km),
Hideaway Island Resort (6km),
Mele Cultural Centre & Nature
Reserve (7km) & Mele-Maat Cascades (8km)

To Bauerfield
International
Airport &
Quarantine
(2km)

Route de Male

Tagabe

La Tagabé River

Lini Hwy

Tebakor

Fres
Wata

Malpoa

Melcofe

Anabrou

Cemetery

Route de la Teouma

Champagne

Route de la Teouma

To Tamanu
Beach Club
(15km)

Tassiriki

Vila Bay

See Enlargement

Wailes St

Ave Edmond Colardeau

Seaside

Emden
Lagoon

Ririki

Nambatu

Rue d'Artois St

Ave du Captain Cook

Erakor
Lagoon

Wharf Rd

To Main Wharf

Laho

Nambatri

Elluk Rd

Elluk

Erakor
Village

To Treetops
Lodge &
Bungalows
(500m) &
Pango Resort
(2.5km)

Ferry to Erakor
Island Resort

Erakor Bay

Vila Bay

Rue Bougainville

Rue Pasteur St

Rue Bougainville

Ave du Carnot

Rue E Metcel

Rue du General de Gaulle

Rue de Paris St

Lini Hwy

Steps

0   125   250m

0   0.5   1km
0   0.25   0.5mi

PORT VILA & AROUND

PLACES TO STAY
- 3 Whispering Coral
- 4 Vila Hibiscus Motel
- 6 Chantilly's on the Bay; Tilly's; Cutting Edge Adventures
- 16 Olympic Hotel
- 56 Le Meridien; Palms Casino
- 59 Poppy's on the Lagoon
- 65 Iririki Island Resort
- 69 Kaiviti Village Motel
- 75 Crowne Plaza

PLACES TO EAT
- 2 Harbour View Restaurant
- 14 Rossi Restaurant
- 20 Natapoa Take Away
- 22 El Gecko
- 24 Lapita Café; Exotic Arts
- 35 Hana's Delicatessen
- 37 Centrepoint Supermarket
- 41 Jill's Café
- 47 Au Péché Mignon
- 51 Sea View Restaurant & Takeaway; ANZ ATM
- 57 Vila Chaumières
- 62 Ebisu Restaurant
- 66 Waterfront Bar & Grill; South Pacific Travel
- 68 Tropik Bistrot; South Sea Shipping
- 71 Chez Genevieve

OTHER
- 1 Crow's Nest Kava Bar
- 5 Surata Tamaso Travel; Tamaso Aliat Wi Tours
- 7 Georges Pompidou Building
- 8 Pro Medical
- 9 Shefa Provincial Council
- 10 Helikopta Kampani
- 11 Port Vila Pub; Public Toilet
- 12 Radio Vanuatu
- 13 Vanuatu Cruising Yacht Club
- 15 Aircalin
- 17 Philippe Metois Photography
- 18 Vanair
- 19 UK & Australian High Commissions
- 21 Smuggler's Niteclub
- 23 Goodies Money Exchange
- 25 Public Library
- 26 Island Safaris
- 27 Tranquillity Island Dive
- 28 New Zealand High Commission (upstairs)
- 29 Adventures in Paradise
- 30 Immigration Department (upstairs)
- 31 French Embassy
- 32 Police Station
- 33 National Tourism Office
- 34 Banque ANZ Pacifique
- 36 Air Vanuatu; National Bank of Vanuatu
- 38 Hebrida Market Place; L'atelier
- 39 Le Flamingo
- 40 Westpac Bank
- 42 ANZ Bank
- 43 Drug Store
- 44 Club Vanuatu
- 45 The Adventure Centre; Sailaway Cruises
- 46 General Post Office
- 48 Naviti Internet Café
- 49 Taxi Rank
- 50 Market; Public Toilet
- 52 Iririki Wharf
- 53 Taxi Stand
- 54 Meridian Charters
- 55 Vila Central Hospital
- 58 Chez Etienne
- 60 Red Light Nakamal
- 61 National Museum of Vanuatu; Vanuatu National Council of Women
- 63 Parliament House
- 64 Rainbow Adventure Tours
- 67 Nautilus Scuba
- 70 Club 21
- 72 Ronnie's Nakamal
- 73 People's Republic of China Embassy
- 74 Ekasup Cultural Village

Iririki

Little Iririki, an island 300m from Vila's waterfront, is connected to the mainland by a free, 24-hour ferry service. You're welcome on the island during daylight hours, or longer if eating/drinking at the Iririki Island Resort restaurant/bar (see Places to Stay). Kayaks, catamarans and snorkelling gear can be hired.

Swimming & Snorkelling

There are a few small sandy beaches on Erakor and Iririki islands where the swimming and snorkelling's not bad. The best option for snorkelling not too far from town is Mele (Hideaway Island; see its listing in the Around Port Vila section).

Diving

The main dive-tour operators based in and around town include:

Hideaway Island Resort & Marine Sanctuary (☎ 22963, W www.hideaway.com.vu) Mele
Nautilus Scuba (☎ 22398, W www.nautilus .com.vu) Lini Hwy
Tranquillity Island Dive (☎ 25020, W www.south pacdivecruise.com.vu/resort.html) Lini Hwy

All three operators offer a range of PADI courses, including introductory ones for beginners, which cost from 6000Vt. Single dives for certified divers start at around 3800Vt. You can also dive with Sailaway Cruises, which offers scuba diving on its tours (see Organised Tours following).

Organised Tours

For details of the main inbound operators see Organised Tours in the Getting Around section earlier in this chapter.

Sea Trips There's plenty of boat operators vying for your *vatu* with various trips on offer.

Meridian Charters (☎ 83352), just south of downtown, is well regarded, particularly for its two-hour sunset cruise (4000Vt including alcohol and nibbles, Tuesday to Sunday).

Sailaway Cruises (☎ 25155; Lini Hwy; W www.pacificislandtravel.com/vanuatu/crui ses/sailaway.html) is a good option if you are interested in a yacht cruise beyond Vila Bay. Its regular day cruises (7900Vt) include stops for diving and snorkelling on superb coral gardens at Eretoka (Hat Island) and Paul's Rock.

Cutting Edge Adventures (☎ 22176; Lini Hwy; e cutting@vanuatu.com.vu), at Chantilly's on the Bay, offers excellent half- to 10-day trips in inflatable kayaks to various islands around the Efate coast. Half/full day rates are around 3800/7400Vt, including a guide.

Bus Tours Most inbound operators offer bus tours. You'll pay from 5000Vt for a round trip of Efate, a short day tour. Progress is normally fairly slow because of the poor road conditions, so you may only stop four or five times en route.

Cultural Tours Most tour operators offer **Melanesian feast** nights in nearby villages, with **Ekasup Cultural Village** being one of the best. These cost upwards of 3000Vt and are a good opportunity to sample traditional cooking, listen to string bands and watch *kastom* dancing.

Places to Stay – In & Around Vila

Vila and its surrounds has a dizzying number of accommodation options, far too many to be listed here. For alternatives to the following, contact the NTO. There is a handful of other places to stay outside Vila described under Around the Island later in this chapter.

Budget Like a big, inviting family home, **Whispering Coral** (☎/fax 26515; singles/doubles without bathroom from 3000/3500Vt) has a lovely waterfront garden on Vila Bay. There's no sign so it is a little tricky to find, but it's off Lini Highway just north of the Trading Post office. The price includes breakfast.

Treetops Lodge & Bungalows (☎ 22944; e swedcons@vanuatu.com.vu; dorm beds 1500Vt, singles/doubles from 2500/3000Vt), 4km south of the post office on the road to Pango, has a Robinson Crusoe feel to it. It's a relaxed place with a great communal kitchen/living area set up on the veranda. The price includes breakfast.

Vila Hibiscus Motel (☎/fax 28289; e vila hibiscusmotel@vanuatu.com.vu; dorm beds 1500Vt, singles/doubles from 3900/4500Vt) is fresh, spotless and highly recommended, especially for its central location which is a five-minute walk north of town. The private rooms have their own kitchen, bathroom and TV; larger (huge, actually) family units are particularly good value (8800Vt per four people).

Both **Hideaway Island Resort** and **Erakor Island Resort** offer good dormitory-style accommodation (in among more swish offerings). They charge 2280Vt and 2800Vt, respectively for a dorm bed (the standard is much better at Erakor). See their full listings following for more details.

Mid-Range The friendly, down-to-earth **Kaiviti Village Motel** (☎ 24684, fax 24685; e kaiviti@vanuatu.com.vu; Lini Hwy; studio singles/doubles with kitchenettes 8400Vt) is in a good location about a 10-minute walk south of downtown. It has a swimming pool, bar, air-con ground-floor rooms and upstairs rooms with balconies and ceiling fans. There are also double-storey apartments that are good value for groups (15,500Vt for six people).

Olympic Hotel (☎ 22464, fax 22953; e olympichotel@vanuatu.com.vu; singles/doubles with fridge 6500Vt, studio with kitchenette 7200Vt), up near Goodies Money Exchange on Lini Hwy, is the place to head if you want to stay right in the middle of town. It's worth paying the extra 700Vt for the very spacious studios. All rooms have air-con, and children under 12 can stay for free.

Pango Resort (☎ 22701, fax 22693; e pangoresort@vanuatu.com.vu; self-contained singles/doubles from 10,000Vt) is a delightful spot tucked away down near Pango Point (200/1500Vt by bus/taxi). The bungalows are superb and there's a swimming pool, bar and good Italian restaurant.

Hideaway Island Resort (☎ 22963, fax 23867; e hideaway@vanuatu.com.vu; dorm beds 2280Vt, singles/doubles without bathroom 4800/6840Vt, ocean view bungalows from 8640/12,000Vt) is a low-key, unpretentious place in a delightful island setting, best known for the great snorkelling literally on its doorstep. It has its own restaurant and bar near the water's edge, and a water sports desk and dive centre. The standard rooms aren't anything special, but they are worth it just to stay on the island. It's 10km northwest of Vila (200/1500Vt by minibus/taxi); a free ferry service connects the resort with the mainland.

Top End You're likely to get substantial discounts and special deals through your travel agent for most, if not all, of the following places.

Iririki Island Resort (☎ 23388, fax 23880; e info@iririki.com; garden-view bungalow singles/doubles from 19,800Vt) is on beautiful Iririki in Vila Bay. It's the most central of

Vila's large resorts, and is connected to town by a free 24-hour ferry service. The resort has terrific views, 70 air-con bungalows – some are waterfront (35,700Vt) – a swimming pool, day spa and water sports centre, and a great restaurant and bar with regular happenings. They also have a no-children policy, perhaps to maintain a romantic air for the many couples who tie the knot here.

Chantilly's on the Bay (☎ 27079, fax 28 111; e chantillys@vanuatu.com.vu; Lini Hwy; air-con singles/doubles from 18,000Vt) is a sparkling new boutique hotel about a 10 minute-walk north of central Vila. It's in a nautically influenced, brilliantly white building sitting pretty on Vila Bay. All 20 rooms have terrific bay views from individual balconies, and come with kitchenette, cable TV and Internet connection. There's also a swimming pool and a very good restaurant (see Places to Eat).

Erakor Island Resort (☎ 26983, fax 22983; e erakor@vanuatu.com.vu; dorm beds 2800Vt, waterfront bungalows with ceiling fan from 24,000Vt) is located on its own lovely 6.4-hectare island and connected to the mainland by a free 24-hour ferry. All of the bungalows are on the waterfront and wonderful, the bar and restaurants are good and there are complimentary water sports for guests (catamaran, outrigger canoes, snorkelling gear).

Poppy's on the Lagoon (☎/fax 23425; e poppys@vanuatu.com.vu; garden/pool view bungalows 14,500Vt, 1-/2-bedroom lagoon view suites 15,500/18,000Vt) receives rave reports from travellers. It's on the shores of Erakor Lagoon, about a 15-minute walk from downtown. Run in a very friendly and professional manner, this village-like setup has three swimming pools, all with children's shallows, and top-notch, spotless accommodation (complete with kitchens, some with disabled access).

There are two massive chain resorts in Vila – **Le Meridien** (☎ 22040, fax 23340; w www.lemeridien-portvila.com; singles/doubles 15,750Vt, lagoon view 18,900Vt); and the **Crowne Plaza** (☎ 22313, fax 22665; w www.crowneplaza.com; singles/doubles from 16,900Vt). Both overlook Erakor Lagoon and have what you'd expect: swimming pools, private beaches, golf courses, tennis courts, water sports, restaurants and bars. Le Meridien is the more atmospheric of the two, while children under 13 get a good deal at Crowne, with free meals and an excellent kid's club.

Places to Eat

As with accommodation options, you're spoilt for choice in the culinary department in and around Vila. The following is just a taste of what's on offer.

Snacks Right on the water next to the market, **Sea View Restaurant & Takeaway** (☎ 27207; takeaway burgers from 200Vt, evening mains 650-1350Vt; open 9am-10pm daily) is the best place for fast food in town, mainly because of its great views. Upstairs is the restaurant which, while not exactly cheap, is good value.

Lapita Café (Lini Hwy; meals 260-850Vt; open 8.30am-4.30pm Mon-Fri, to 3pm Sat), close to the public library, specialises in island food (the delish pumpkin in coconut sauce is a must).

Natapoa Take Away (rue de Paris; meals around 300Vt; open 6.30am-7pm Mon-Fri, to 6pm Sat) is a cute little place, popular with locals and good for huge stir-fries and great serves of spring rolls.

Centrepoint Supermarket (Lini Hwy; open daily) has takeaway lunches (near the bakery in the supermarket) for rock-bottom prices. Try the beef stew (180Vt) or rolls with various fillings (from 150Vt).

Cafés A few doors south of the NTO is **Hana's Delicatessen** (Lini Hwy; open 8am-5pm Mon-Fri, to noon Sat), the best place for coffee and one of the finest casual lunch venues in town. Its excellent gourmet fare includes delicious salads (around 900Vt), sushi, baguettes, pies and pasties, as well as scrumptious cakes and other delicatessen delights.

Au Péché Mignon (Lini Hwy; open 6am-6pm Mon-Fri, to 2pm Sat) certainly rivals Hana's in the sweets department. This (very) French patisserie, just south of the post office, is a terrific spot for a coffee and sweet treat.

El Gecko (☎ 25597; Lini Hwy; sandwiches from 400Vt, mains 1100-1550Vt; open 6.30am-6pm daily, dinner Fri only), next to Goodies, offers relaxed courtyard dining as well as a more formal indoor area. The food here is very good.

Jill's Café (Lini Hwy; meals 400-700Vt; open 7am-6pm Mon-Fri, to 1.30pm Sat), between the Westpac and ANZ banks, is great for a big American-style breakfast (hash browns, pancakes, waffles) as well as Mexican and other American tucker.

VANUATU

Restaurants – Vila At Chantilly's on the Bay (see Places to Stay), **Tilly's** (☎ 27079; Lini Hwy; mains 1600-2200Vt; open 7am-late daily) is definitely up there with the best. Drink in the superb bay views with excellent food and impeccable service. It also offers a great tapas menu and caters for children.

Tropik Bistrot (☎ 26484; Lini Hwy; mains 1400-1950Vt; open 6pm-late Mon-Sat) is another tres bon restaurant. Just north of Kaiviti Village Motel, its nondescript exterior belies a candle-lit gem of an interior. The food is French and fabulous.

Waterfront Bar & Grill (☎ 23490; Lini Hwy; mains 1500-2900Vt; open 11am-late daily), opposite Iririki, is a terrific island-style place with yachts lining its sea wall. It's the place for yachties and anyone else who digs fresh seafood, steak, a touch of Mexican and/or beer.

Rossi Restaurant (☎ 22528; off Lini Hwy; mains 1100-2330Vt; open 7am-late daily), on the waterfront in the centre of town, is a Vila dining institution. It promises a good variety of fresh fish and other seafood, great service and a welcoming ambience.

Harbour View Restaurant (☎ 23668; mains 700-1800Vt; open 11am-2pm, 6pm-10pm daily) is arguably the best Chinese restaurant in town. It overlooks Vila Bay about 1.5km north of downtown and serves up a large selection of Cantonese cuisine, including particularly yummy sizzling plates.

Ebisu Restaurant (☎ 23612; rue d'Artois; mains 1000-1700Vt; open 11.30am-1.30pm, 6.30pm-11pm daily), up near the National Museum, is the only place in Vanuatu specialising in Japanese cuisine… and it does a good job of it, too.

Chez Genevieve (☎ 27386; rue d'Artois; mains 470-1000Vt; open daily) is a good option at the cheaper end of the price scale. A few hundred metres south of Ebisu, the service here is excellent and the French- and Italian-inspired food is good.

Restaurants – Around Vila Sitting over the waters of palm-fringed and flood-lit Emden Lagoon, gorgeous **Vila Chaumières** (☎ 22866; mains 1400-2250Vt; open for lunch & dinner daily) is one of the most romantic venues in the Pacific. The fare is mostly French with some English staples thrown in. Be sure to book, and ask for a waterside table.

Tamanu Beach Club (☎ 27279; mains 1750-2500Vt; open for lunch and dinner daily), 15km southeast of Vila, is another superb out-of-towner. Relaxed but sophisticated, it offers open-air dining beside the pounding ocean.

Entertainment

Vila's nightlife is not exactly thronging, but there are a few good bars. Not to worry – after a few kava you will probably just feel like curling up anyway.

Kava Bars There are well over 100 kava bars or nakamal in Vila, with most being little more than iron sheds. The sunset kava cup, served in a coconut shell or plastic bowl, is a ritual for many Ni-Vanuatu and expats. Good options include **Crow's Nest Kava Bar** about 20 minutes' walk north of central Vila, **Ronnie's Nakamal** in Nambatu and **Red Light Nakamal** near the hospital. The going rate is 50Vt for a small 'shell' and 100Vt for a larger one.

Although kava is generally and traditionally reserved for men, female expatriates and tourists are welcome at most nakamal in Vila.

Bars, Clubs & Gaming Lounges On the northern edge of central Vila, **Port Vila Pub** (open 11.30am-3am Tues-Sat, from 5pm Sun & Mon) is the town's only true 'pub'. There's a good beer garden where you can also hoe into a huge steak.

Waterfront Bar & Grill (see Places to Eat) is deservedly one of the most popular places for a tipple. A relaxed, inviting atmosphere is guaranteed and there's live entertainment most nights.

Chez Etienne (open 5pm-late Tues-Sun), overlooking Emden Lagoon, is a cool bar-and-billiards haunt with good music. This terrific spot away from town doesn't really get going until about 11pm. The one-way taxi fare is 2000Vt.

Smuggler's Niteclub (rue de Paris; admission free before 9pm, then 500Vt; open 7.30pm-3am Tues-Sat) is your best bet for getting down. **Le Flamingo**, a once very popular nightclub close to the Westpac Bank, was closed down but is rumoured to be reopening.

Palms Casino (open 12.30pm-3.30am daily) is at Le Meridien and there are also pokies at **Club 21** (The Melanesian Port Vila; Lini Hwy; open 5pm-11pm daily) and **Club Vanuatu** (rue de Paris; open 10am-1am daily).

Shopping

Hebrida Market Place *(Lini Hwy; open 8am-5pm Mon-Fri, to 12.30pm Sat)*, just north of the Drug Store, is jam-packed with hand-painted clothes and is also good for woven bags and mats.

L'atelier, in the Hebrida Market Place, is a wonderful place to start looking for wooden carvings and handicrafts. A good selection can also be found at **Exotic Arts** *(Lini Hwy; open 10am-3.30pm Mon-Fri, to 1.30pm Sat)*, near the public library, Lapita Café and Goodies.

Philippe Metois Photography *(Lini Hwy; open 8.30am-noon, 1.30pm-5pm Mon-Fri, 8.30am-noon Sat)*, close to Goodies, has gorgeous shots of Vanuatu for sale – unframed prints start at 1250Vt, framed at 10,000Vt.

The **Vanuatu Cultural Centre** is at the **National Museum** and it has produced some excellent CDs, including *Ol Voes Blong Vanuatu* (Voices of Vanuatu), that make great mementos. These are available at the museum and various shops (2300Vt).

There are a number of shops which sell **duty-free** products on Lini Highway between the market and the northern end of the central business district. In general, these are reasonable for alcohol and perfume, but not so great on electrical goods.

Getting There & Away

See Getting There & Away and Getting Around earlier in this chapter for details of airline and shipping services to and from Vila.

Getting Around

To/From the Airport Airport shuttle buses cost 400Vt per person to/from Vila, and taxis 1000Vt. Alternatively, if you don't have much luggage, you can catch a minibus for 100Vt.

Minibus The cheapest way around Vila is by minibus (see Bus under Getting Around earlier in this chapter). The main roads are usually thick with minibuses between 6am and 7.30pm. Fares are a uniform 100Vt wherever you go within the wider town area. To travel further afield to such places as Erakor and Hideaway islands costs 200Vt.

Car & Motorcycle Vila has a number of car hire companies including **Avis** *(☎ 22570; Bauerfield International Airport)*, **Budget** *(☎ 23170; Lini Hwy, Nambatu)* and **Discount Rentals** *(☎ 23242; Lini Hwy, Nambatu)*.

As an example of costs, a one-day hire of Budget's cheapest four-seater costs 5660Vt (including VAT). Petrol generally costs about 100Vt per litre.

Budget also hires out scooters, as does **Nautilus Scuba** *(☎ 22398; Ⓦ www.nautilus.com.vu; Lini Hwy)*. Prices are typically 2800Vt for a half-day and 4100Vt for 24 hours.

Taxi There are over 200 taxis operating in Vila, and as there's sufficient work for only around 70, the service tends to be very competitive (see Taxi under Getting Around earlier in this chapter).

Vila's main taxi stands are beside the market and Iririki Wharf.

AROUND PORT VILA
Erakor

At the mouth of Erakor Lagoon lies Erakor, one of the island jewels of Vila. Erakor has a white sandy beach near its lovely resort (see Places to Stay under Port Vila earlier in this chapter). A free 24-hour ferry service links the island to a small jetty on the mainland, just south of Crowne Plaza Resort.

Mele (Hideaway Island)

About 9km north of Vila, there's a signposted dirt road on the left that leads down to Mele Beach; barely 200m across the water is Hideaway Island accessed by a free ferry service.

The dense vegetation covering the island's two hectares is punctuated by the beachfront bungalows of Hideaway Island Resort. Just offshore is the best snorkelling close to Vila; you'll find swarms of colourful, friendly fish.

There's a 500Vt entrance fee for all day-trippers, payable at the water-sports desk at the end of the jetty. You can hire snorkelling gear (800Vt/day), kayaks and catamarans (1000/1500Vt per hour). On the downside, the small coral beach in front of the restaurant gets very crowded on busy days.

For more details see Hideaway Island Resort under Places to Stay in Port Vila earlier in this chapter.

Mele-Maat Cascades

These beautiful cascades *(adult/child 1000/500Vt; open daily)* are nearby Mele, immediately before the hairpin bend at the base of Klem's Hill. You'll find pool after pool of clear, aqua water shaded by rainforest leading up to the main, 20m-high waterfall (the swimming hole at the base was badly damaged in an earthquake in 2002). It takes about 20 minutes to walk to the top with the help of guide ropes. Be prepared for wet feet, slippery, moss-covered rocks and a lovely cool swim (there are toilets and change rooms at the entrance).

Mele Cultural Centre & Nature Reserve

About 1km south of the cascades, this reserve (adult/child 600/300Vt; open 9am-4.30pm daily) is a terrific place to learn about Vanuatu's culture and its natural environment, especially if you don't get a chance to visit some of the other islands.

Port Vila Golf Club

The clubhouse for Vanuatu's principal golf course is on the main road to Mele. Visitors are welcome – club hire, trolley and green fees (18 holes) cost 3300Vt.

AROUND THE ISLAND

The coastal route around Efate is 138km, which doesn't sound very far but, given the poor pot-holed condition of most of the road, it ends up taking about six hours, including a few stops.

If you are hiring a car, drive *very* carefully: the steep hills in the northwest are particularly hairy. If it's been raining a lot, it would pay to check that a conventional vehicle will get all the way around. Remember that well-stocked stores and fuel stations are scarce outside Vila.

The following places, just a sample of what's on offer, are listed in an anticlockwise direction from Vila. Major points of interest closer than 11km to town are described in the previous Around Port Vila section.

White Sands Beach

Just past Efate's largest river, **Teouma River** (approach bridge with care as it was badly damaged by an earthquake in 2002), there's a right-hand turn that takes you down to the coastal road.

White Sands Beach, fringed with screw-trunked pandanus palms, is rather exposed but does have a few good **snorkelling** and **swimming** spots.

Tamanu Beach Club (☎ 27279, fax 24470; e tamanu@vanuatu.com.vu; singles/doubles from 7500Vt) is a couple of kilometres west of White Sands Beach. While it doesn't have a great swimming beach, this small resort of five luxurious French colonial-style bungalows is gorgeous and rooms are fan-cooled.

There's a very good **restaurant** (see Restaurants – Vila's Outskirts earlier in this chapter) overlooking the beach.

White Sands Country Club (☎ 22090, fax 27221; e whitesan@vanuatu.com.vu; singles/doubles 11,250Vt) is the place to head if you live and breathe golf. It has 10 fan-cooled bungalows nestled amongst coconut trees, a pool, tennis court, restaurant and bar and, most importantly, an 18-hole golf course. The price includes breakfast.

Rentapao River

Cutting Edge Adventures offers excellent half-day **kayaking** trips here – see Organised Tours under Port Vila earlier in this chapter for more details.

Blue Water Island Resort (☎ 27606, fax 27604; e bluewateresort@vanuatu.com.vu; garden view singles/doubles 7000Vt), 3km before the river's bridge, is a large development of 49 bungalows wrapped around a blue lagoon. The price includes breakfast, and there's a restaurant, bar, swimming pool and excellent open-air **aquarium** (nonguest adult/child 600/300Vt). If you're game, you can get in and swim with loads of fish and massive sea turtles; opposite them, in a separate pool, are beautiful reef sharks.

Eton Blue Hole

Continue on around to the east coast and you'll find this lovely **swimming** and **snorkelling** spot near Eton. There are toilets and a change room. The entrance fee is 300Vt per person.

Takara

Although a windswept spot, Takara is fairly popular with Vila residents on weekends. From the beach there's a fine view of the nearby island of **Emao**, an extinct volcano. Looking beyond Emao you can see towering, pinnacle-shaped **Mataso** with smaller **Wot Rock** on the right. In the distance are the beckoning, misty outlines of the rest of the **Shepherds Islands**.

Beachcomber Resort (☎ 23576, fax 26458; e beachc@vanuatu.com.vu; singles/doubles 5400Vt) has basic accommodation in brick bungalows (sleeping up to six and the price includes breakfast), a restaurant, great ocean views and a hot, indoor mineral pool.

Baofatu

Two US WWII fighter planes lie in the shallows close to this French-speaking village. They ran out of fuel coming in to land at

Quoin Hill, a former American WWII airstrip. Matanawora World War II Relics is located here. Contact **Tamaso Aliat Wi Tours** (☎ *25600; adult/child 4200/2100Vt*) to arrange a tour, which includes swimming and snorkelling around one of the planes.

Paonangisu

This village is the best place to ask about a speedboat ride across to the islands of **Nguna, Pele** and **Kakula**. The boats usually leave from nearby Emua and should be arranged in advance (either through Nagar Resort, following, or a tour operator) to suit the tides.

Nagar Resort (☎ *23221, fax 27289; bungalows per person 4500Vt*) boasts gorgeous grounds on the waterfront, with a fine view of the islands. There are four tiny but cute bungalows (shared bathroom), as well as two larger self-contained family bungalows. Its licensed **restaurant** *(meals 450-1500Vt)* is the best place to stop for lunch on a round-island trip; it's lovely to eat alfresco under the trees.

A **taxi** to here from Vila costs 4000Vt. Alternatively, you may be able to get a lift with one of the tour coaches on their round-Efate trips.

Siviri

A road bears northwards off the main road through a coconut grove to Siviri, half a kilometre beyond the main road. Just before the village, behind the pumphouse, is **Valeva Cave** *(admission per person 100Vt)*. This small, moist cavern has many interesting formations as well as a freshwater lake. Permission to enter may be gained at the pumphouse.

Ulei

Pronounced 'oo-lay', this village is on the site of the former Havannah Harbour settlement, Efate's main European base until the early 1880s. During WWII, US warships grouped in the harbour's protected waters prior to the critical Battle of the Coral Sea in mid-1942. Later, the US used the area as a naval base.

On the seaward side of the road near central Ulei is the **American Pool**, a concrete reservoir that served as a water source for visiting ships.

Klem's Hill

There's a parking bay here, 200m above sea level, with superb views of coconut plantations, the ocean, Vila and Hideaway Island, but you may be asked to pay 100Vt for a squiz.

Tanna

pop 28,200 ● area 565 sq km

Tanna means 'Earth' in Tannese. And the earth here offers its best: from lush undisturbed rainforests, heady night-perfumed flowers, coffee plantations, plains where wild horses roam, mighty mountains, hot springs, waterfalls, and over it all, fuming furious Mt Yasur, one of the world's most accessible volcanoes (see the boxed text 'Visiting Mt Yasur' later in this chapter).

The Tannese are passionate about their island. Local chiefs form marine and wildlife sanctuaries; there are gardening, surfing, cycling, walking or volcano enthusiasts everywhere; and very serious quarantine controls; the island has no nasty bugs, so everything's grown without insecticides, herbicides or pesticides, and they want to keep it that way. Christianity, cargo cult and *kastom* are important and all natural phenomena have a fourth dimension of spirituality and mystique.

Learn about the fascinating Jon Frum cult (see the boxed text 'The Jon Frum Movement' later in this chapter), meet *kastom* villagers wearing *namba* (traditional sheath) and grass-skirts, watch age-old festivals or just laze on a tropical island beach and watch the sun set.

The Nekowiar & Toka

Everyone describes the Toka, an awe-inspiring dance, as one of Vanuatu's major cultural events. However, it is only one section of a huge, three-day ceremony called the Nekowiar, an alliance-making process between neighbouring villages, bringing leaders together to organise marriages.

The preparations for the Nekowiar are exhaustive. Three dances are practised at the rehearsal site, the men scour the bush and villages for pigs and kava, and beauty magic takes over: using powders mixed with coconut oil, everyone colours their face a deep red, with black and yellow stripes down their nose and across to their ears. Finally up to 2000 people assemble while the hosts display around 100 pigs, tied by the feet and suspended on poles.

It begins with the host village's young men dancing. When the women respond to a dance invitation, the **Napen-Napen** begins. This spectacular dance by the women represents their toil in the fields, and continues throughout the first night, with the women

VANUATU

VANUATU

arrayed in red, yellow, blue, green and mauve grass skirts.

The **Toka** begins the next morning and reaches its climax that night (and may go on all night). All the male guests take part. If the Toka dancers make a circle and capture a woman, she's tossed up and down between them. Tourists may watch, but should remain well back.

On the third day the chief of the host village produces the **Kweriya**, a 3m bamboo pole with white-and-black feathers wound around it and hawk's feathers on top. It announces that the **Nao** – the host village's dance – is to begin. The men's dance enacts events such as hunting and wrestling.

The climax is in the afternoon. Pigs, kava roots, woven mats, grass skirts, and massive quantities of *laplap* are brought out. The pigs

are ceremonially clubbed, cooked and a huge feast begins.

The Nekowiar is usually held between August and October. If you get a chance to go, do so. You may need to camp out, like the villagers, and it costs 5000Vt to watch, plus 10,000Vt to video it. Contact the NTO for more details.

Organised Tours

You can get package deals in Vila that typically include air fares, transfers, accommodation, all meals and visits to Mt Yasur and a *kastom* village (about 35,000Vt).

Wherever you stay, your host will have the full range of tours on the island available for you to choose from. If you prefer to make your own arrangements, they will organise transport.

TANNA

1 White Grass Ocean Resort & Restaurant
2 Tanna Evergreen Bungalows
3 Friendly Bungalows
4 Nikiti Guesthouse
5 Port Resolution Yacht Club & Restaurant
6 Turtle Bay Inn & Vulcain Restaurant
7 Entry Gate to Mt Yasur Crater
8 Jungle Oasis; Volcano Adventure Lodge

The Jon Frum Movement

In 1936 it was claimed that the brother of the god of Mt Tukosmera, Jon Frum, came from the sea at Green Point and announced himself to some kava drinkers. He told them there would be an abundance of wealth and no more epidemics – so long as all Europeans left Tanna.

When US troops landed on Efate and Santo, many Tannese went to work for them. They saw huge quantities of transport equipment, refrigerators and radios and endless supplies of Coca-Cola and cigarettes. But most of all, the Tannese met generous African–Americans who were surely Tannese in disguise. Jon Frum must be American.

Keen to hear his message, some supporters made imitation radio aerials out of tin cans and wire. Others built an airfield in the bush and constructed wooden aircraft to entice his cargo planes to land. Still others erected wharves where his ships could berth.

The Red Cross sign meant free medical treatment. Small red crosses were erected all over Tanna and remain a feature in Jon Frum villages.

The movement has at times been vigorously opposed by missionaries and officials. Even now, some cult villages refuse to pay taxes or use government schools.

When will he come? 'How long have Christians waited?' they ask. 'Nearly 2000 years, yet we've waited only 65!'

Getting There & Away

Vanair provides return flights between Vila and Tanna at least daily. Twice-weekly services also land at Aniwa, Aneityum, Futuna and Erromango.

The MV *Havannah* has a return service from Vila usually once a month (6700Vt).

For more details, see the Air and Boat sections, both under Getting Around earlier in this chapter.

Getting Around

Tanna has a good network of unsealed roads and 4WD tracks; all the major attractions are linked by roads to Lenakel, the capital.

Taxis and the local bus meet each incoming flight. The fare to Lenakel is 1000/200Vt by taxi/bus. Ring ☎ 68647 to ask the bus to pick you up. A one-way taxi charter from Lenakel to Port Resolution will cost around 6000Vt.

AROUND THE ISLAND

The following is an overview of Tanna's main attractions.

Northwestern Tanna

Near the Tanna Airport, little **Imanaka** is a Jon Frum village with dances on Friday night. Visitors are welcome but should come with a tour group. The entry fee is 300Vt.

Up the coastal road the country is flat and used to be covered with hardy grasses that turned white in summer – hence its name White Grass Plains. The area is now covered with green ground cover but it is still the haunt of wild horses. They're wonderful to see.

Just north of the White Grass Ocean Resort, small sandy bays and a large blue hole in the reef make good **swimming** spots.

Tanna Evergreen Bungalows (☎ 68774, 68846, fax 68846; ✉ Tevergreen@vanuatu.com .vu; singles/doubles without bathroom 4000/ 6850Vt) is a five-minute walk from Tanna Airport. Six bungalows hide coolly in lush forest, between hammocks that string from the trees. There's a bar and an alfresco dining room.

White Grass Ocean Resort (☎ 68688, fax 68677; ⊠ www.whitegrassvanuatu.com.vu; singles/doubles 10,875/15,000Vt), a short walk further along the coast, has 12 comfortable, beachfront self-contained bungalows (price includes breakfast and transfers), a delightful à la carte restaurant (meals 600Vt to 1500Vt) and bar, and a turtle and bird sanctuary. This place does a good job of combining all the luxuries with Vanuatu's laid-back, warm hospitality.

Lenakel Around 1000 people live in Lenakel, which has mains electricity. The best-stocked store is the Tafea Co-op with processed food, alcohol and clothing. There are also several excellent bakeries.

A **covered market** across from the co-op and an **open market** near the wharf are both open Monday, Thursday afternoon and Friday.

Places to Stay & Eat On the bay behind the Tafea Co-op, **Tafea Guesthouse** (☎ 68695, fax 68846; ✉ Tevergreen@vanuatu.com.vu; beds 1500Vt) is a rambling, dingy colonial building, but there's a reasonable kitchen.

Lenakel Cove Resort (☎ 68860, fax 68861; dorm beds/singles/doubles 2500/5000/7500Vt) offers spacious Melanesian bungalows with en suites, in a stunning garden overlooking the soccer stadium. Horses can be hired (from beginners up) as can guides for jungle trail rides. The resort's restaurant (meals 300Vt to 1200Vt) has a bar and the owner runs film, band, dance and karaoke nights.

Uma Dining Room (☎ 68768; meals 700Vt) serves tasty meals like local fish in coconut cream with sweet potato chips and island cabbage.

Southwestern Tanna

A short walk from **Isangel** is the small Jon Frum settlement **Imai**.

Bethel Seventh-Day Adventists hold Saturday baptisms on the small black-sand beach at **Ebul Bay**. Visitors are welcome to watch.

Kastom reigns supreme in **Yakel**. Villagers wear only *namba* and grass skirts, although they change into Western clothing when visiting other areas. The children don't attend school, or travel and you see little sign of the modern age. The major exception is the village truck. As many as 600 men share the open-air *nakamal*, under a huge banyan, to drink kava, while dancing nights occur on a regular basis.

Central Tanna

Vanuatu's main **coffee-growing** area is in the Middle Bush. Tanna Coffee Development Co in **Fetukai** is the major producer. Visitors are welcome to inspect the plantation and factory, but enquire first through your bungalow.

Loanialu Lookout, on top of the main range on the road from Lenakel to Port Resolution, offers a magnificent view of the Mt Yasur. On a clear day Aniwa and Futuna can be seen in the distance.

Eastern Tanna

There's a health centre, mission, education centre, two stores and a cardphone at **White Sands**.

Sulphur Bay used to be a major centre of the Jon Frum cult until a philosophical rift occurred between two chiefs. Like other Jon Frum villages, it's built around a square ceremonial ground. The church to one side houses the movement's most sacred red cross. Beside it is an unpainted post dedicated to Christ, and used to heal backaches. If you ask, you'll be shown the grave of Nampus, a

Jon Frum prophet of the 1950s. Entry to the village is 500Vt.

When Lake Isiwi broke its banks it formed a hot spring on the black-sand beach, providing hydrotherapy if you jump out of the spring into the surf. Ask for permission to use it.

Places to Stay & Eat Close to the beach at White Sands, **Nikiti Guesthouse** (☎ 68616; beds & meals per person 2500Vt) has five beds in a bungalow.

Friendly Bungalows (in Vila ☎ 22666, fax 24275, in Tanna fax 68638; dorm beds/doubles 1500/5000Vt) is set in beautiful grounds on a black-sand beach, although it's isolated from major attractions. It has pleasant self-contained bungalows and a slightly run-down dormitory. The licensed **restaurant** specialises in local cooking, but meals are expensive (675Vt for a light breakfast, 1650Vt for a three-course dinner such as salad, baked fish and cake).

Southeastern Tanna

The entry gate to Mt Yasur is near **Imayo**, a *kastom* village that is visited by tour groups.

The impressive **Imayo Waterfall** lies deep in the rainforest, but the hike takes three hours each way and is suitable only for experienced bushwalkers. Ask at Jungle Oasis, in nearby **Loanengo**, about guides.

Mt Yasur Towering above you, Mt Yasur darkens the sky with great clouds of ash-laden smoke. This gritty material has smothered the vegetation, reducing the landscape to a prehistoric desert; the gaunt shapes of surviving pandanus palms add to the surrealistic view.

Mt Yasur (admission 2000Vt) is one of the world's most accessible active volcanoes. In fact, 4WD vehicles can get to within 150m of the crater rim. The entry fee helps local villagers buy food when the ash rain ruins their crops. When the volcano is playing at levels 3 and 4, you should not go up to the rim.

Places to Stay & Eat At Loanengo, **Jungle Oasis** (☎ 68676; singles/doubles 2000/2500Vt) is set in a romantic botanical garden, where fireflies light the paths and Mt Yasur thunders in the background. Transfers from the airport cost 4000Vt (shared) and the price includes breakfast.

Volcano Adventure Lodge (☎ 68676; singles/doubles 3600/4300Vt), next door, is another friendly place. It has four bungalows, each sleeping four, and the price includes breakfast.

Visiting Mt Yasur

The level of activity within Mt Yasur fluctuates between dangerous and relatively calm, but when it's hot… it's hot. This is what you may experience when the mountain is flexing its muscle.

Stumbling up the rough 150m path from the car park to the crater rim (where there's no safety fence, by the way), your introduction to the turmoil within consists of whiffs of sulphur accompanied by whooshing and roaring noises. Then you're on the barren ash rim looking down into a dark central crater about 300m across and 100m deep.

At the bottom, three vents seem to be taking it in turns to spit showers of molten rock and smoke, like monstrous Roman candles. When the biggest one blows there's an ear-splitting explosion that causes heads to disappear into collars. The earth trembles and a fountain of fiery magma soars skywards above the rim. After this come progressively smaller roars until eventually all is quiet, except for the sound of rocks thudding back into the crater. At night you can see glowing boulders as big as trucks somersaulting back down into what looks like the embers of a vast campfire.

Then, just when you're getting used to it, you hear a great 'gasp', then bang. The ground shakes again as great lumps of red-hot magma shoot high overhead. Black smoke boils upwards in a dense, writhing column, and you may see brief flashes of lightning within. Down below, magma splashes in the central vent before subsiding again.

You realise why tourists have been badly singed, lost their cameras in flight, and one tourist and two guides died. It is important to take heed of your guide about how close to go.

Some visitors find Mt Yasur a terrifying experience; it's definitely unforgettable and shouldn't be missed. At night, the fireworks are more spectacular, and you can see the potentially deadly flying lava bombs coming…

Still game? Take a good torch and warm clothing, and do have your personal affairs sorted out before you go.

Both places have dining rooms (meals 600Vt to 1000Vt) where lunch is typically chicken curry with rice.

Ianakun Bungalows are being built high up in Isarkei, where you can watch Mt Yasur's fireworks display from the balcony. Contact Jungle Oasis for details.

Port Resolution This beautiful bay, with its magnificent cliffs is Tanna's best place to **anchor**. Wide flower-lined paths lead to the beach: one comes out near the bay at **Yewao Point**. This is a marine sanctuary where, just before the coral reef finishes, the water is calm and offers excellent snorkelling. Further around the bay is a *tabu* rocky outcrop where, it is believed, people's spirits go when they die.

Another path brings you onto a top **surf beach** starting at **Yatana** and running into **Yankaren Para** with deep heavy swells along 2.5km of white-sand beach. Surfing groups from Australia come here, and a surfing film was made in 2002.

Places to Stay & Eat Set among gorgeous coconut palms on a cliff top, **Port Resolution Yacht Club** (☎ 68791, fax 68676; e white grasstanna@vanuatu.com.vu; singles/doubles 2000/3000Vt) has marvellous views over to rugged Mt Melen. Its Melanesian bungalows sleep up to four people; bathrooms are shared and the price includes breakfast in its rates. Transfers from the airport cost 3100/5700Vt for one/two passengers. The restaurant of the club (meals 500Vt to 1500Vt) has cold drinks, and sometimes even beer. There is an extensive menu which includes lobster, Melanesian fish salad, and chicken all smoked in a local oven.

Sharks Bay This tiny bay attracts dozens of **yellow reef sharks** that you can observe from the rocky shore.

Turtle Bay Inn (Relais Baie de Tortues; ☎ 68850, fax 68885; e info@vanuatupara dise.com; singles/doubles 3500/6000Vt) is the perfect spot if you are looking for total seclusion and relaxation with a touch of island luxury. This very French establishment has electricity, hot showers and spacious bungalows. The price includes breakfast in its rates.

Vulcain Restaurant (set 3-course meals 1500Vt, snacks 500Vt), at the inn, serves Mediterranean and local cuisine.

VANUATU

Erromango

pop 1700 • area 975 sq km

The 'Island of Mangoes' is a mountainous, mainly forested island, with almost all of its inhabitants living in a few villages on its rugged coast.

By the 1840s Erromango had a well-earned reputation as a dangerous place for Europeans. The villagers had a penchant for warfare and cannibalism, and didn't hesitate to attack the whalers, sandalwooders, missionaries and blackbirders who landed on their shores. Five white missionaries were murdered here between 1839 and 1872. Today, Erromangans will tell you that the dramatic depopulation of their island (from 10,000 people in the 1820s to less than 400 a century later) was God's punishment for killing the missionaries.

Not many tourists visit Erromango; those who do mainly have walking in mind. Another reason is to see the island's giant kauris, which in itself requires some hard walking. June to August can be cool and wet, particularly in upland areas, so it's wise to take appropriate clothing.

Getting There & Away

The island's airfields are at Dillons Bay and Ipota. Vanair has three weekly flights from Vila to Tanna via both airfields.

The MV *Havannah* service to Tanna sometimes calls in at Erromango.

For more details see the Air and Boat sections, both under Getting Around earlier in this chapter.

Getting Around

There's a road between Dillons Bay and the airfield (600Vt), and old logging roads from Dillons Bay to Potnarvin (often impassable), and from Ipota into the southern forests.

You can hire speedboats at Dillons Bay, Potnarvin and Ipota. It costs upwards of 10,000Vt for a charter from Dillons Bay to Potnarvin.

AROUND THE ISLAND
Dillons Bay

With 500 people, Dillons Bay is Erromango's largest settlement, and it's also called Unpongkor. The gardens at Dillons Bay spread from the village to the huge crystal clear **swimming hole** formed by the Williams River as it turns to the sea. The path takes you through

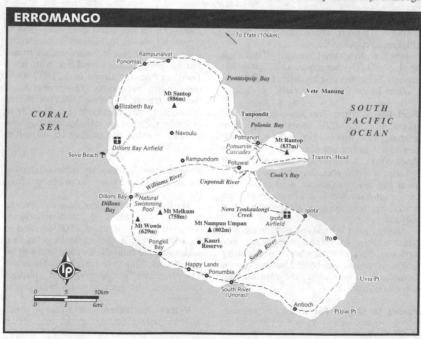

ERROMANGO

Mystery Island

'Welcome to Paradise', the pilot will say as you clamber out of his tiny plane onto Aneityum's grass airstrip on Mystery Island. And it's true: this beautiful sandy islet is surrounded by a broad sandbank and dazzling coral in an azure sea, just like in the movies. Garden paths crisscross the island, many leading to little thatched dunnies.

Aneityum people believe Mystery Island, known locally as Inyeug, to be the home of ghosts, so no one will live there. The area has been designated a marine sanctuary, with a ban on fishing, except for sport. **Snorkelling** is fantastic in the sea at the end of the runway, or go out to the reef proper in a canoe.

Mystery Island Guesthouse (☎ 68896, 68672; beds 2250Vt) has three bedrooms and a kitchen. Someone will come over from Aneityum each day to look after you and bring you supplies, but it's a good idea to bring extra food. Another two bungalows and a small bar/restaurant are planned to open in 2003. Vanair operates two round-trips per week connecting Vila, Tanna, Futuna and Aneityum. Except on cruise-ship days (about every six weeks), you'll probably have this island paradise to yourself.

a rainforest where you'll see the sandalwood trees that were once plentiful. In the vicinity is a **rock** that shows the outline of Williams, the first missionary to be killed. They laid the body, which was short and stout, on the rock and chipped around it prior to cooking and eating it.

You can do several guided **walks** from Dillons Bay. William Mete at Meteson's Guesthouse (see following) can arrange tours, transport and guides for several walks, such as the trip via Happy Lands to the **kauri reserve**.

A three- or four-day walk down south and across to Ipota offers the experienced hiker magnificent scenery. A guide will cost about 1500Vt per day, plus food.

At the mouth of Williams River, **Meteson's Guesthouse** (☎/fax 68792; e islands@vanuatu.com.vu; singles/doubles 4220/5640Vt) has been renovated and extended to sleep 10. Chief William is very knowledgeable about the island and Mrs Mete cooks excellent meals (250Vt). The price includes breakfast.

Eastern Erromango

It's an interesting full-day walk from Dillons Bay across undulating country to the east coast. If you decide to bypass Potnarvin and go straight to Ipota, cross the Unpotndi River at the small village of Potuwai, where you should be able to find a guide.

Potnarvin is a pleasant settlement of 250 people that stretches along a long black-sand beach with good surf and pretty **cascades** 1km inland. Towering over the village is **Mt Rantop** (837m). Below the mountain, on its southern side, is a long white-sand beach with coral shallows.

The new **Potnarvin Guesthouse** (☎ 68792; singles/doubles 3000/5000Vt) is a simple concrete building.

If you haven't already found a guide, arrange for one here. The south road is mostly level as far as **Cook's Bay**, where you follow the shore to Ipota. There's some nice coastal scenery, but it is rugged going, so leave yourself plenty of time.

Ipota and its airstrip were built by a French logging company in 1969, and today 150 people live there. **Ipota Guesthouse** (☎ 68792; singles/doubles 3000/5000Vt) has been recently renovated.

Malekula

pop 24,000 • area 2023 sq km

Shaped like a 'sitting dog', Malekula has two highland areas connected by a narrow section called 'the dog's neck'. The uplands, intersected by valleys, rise to over 800m in the southern centre. This area and the southwest coast are extremely rugged and inhospitable.

Twenty-eight languages are spoken, making Malekula linguistically and culturally very diverse and a favoured stamping ground for anthropologists. Two of its major cultural groups are the Big Nambas, and Small Nambas, the names originating from the size of the men's *namba*. A southern *kastom* group, traditionally called Man Bush, has also lately been named Small Nambas.

Hiking

There are two major hikes across Malekula that both combine natural and cultural treasures

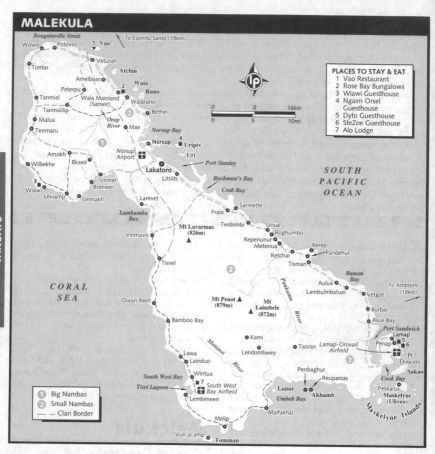

MALEKULA

Bougainville Strait
To Espiritu Santo (18km)
Wowo Potovro
1 Vao
Veturah
Tontar Atchin
Amelboas 2 Wala
Peterpu Rano
Tanmial Wala Mainland Walarano
Tanmalilip (Sanwir) Bethel
Malua Orap Mae
Tenmaru River Norsup Bay
Amokh Norsup 4 Uripiv
Williekhe I Bkaeir Norsup Uri
3 Unmet Airport Lakatoro Port Stanley
Wiawi Brenwei Litslits Bushman's Bay
Leviamp Unmakh Larevet Crab Bay
Lambumbu Sarmette
Bay Fralo Tenbimbi Unua
Vinmavis Mt Lavarmas Roghumbo
(826m) Repenunur Rerep
Metenua Pandehur
Tisvel Retchar Tisman
Banam
Bay
Aulua Vetgot
Dixon Reef Mt Penot Mt Lambulmbatuei
(879m) Laimbele Burbar
(872m) Asuk Bay
Bamboo Bay Port Sandwich
Kami Lamap
Lawa Lendombwey Taoran Lamap-Orovail Penap
Lainduo Airfield Pt
Wintua Penbaghur Doucere
South West Bay 7 South West Reupanias Sakao
Tisri Lagoon Bay Airfield Lanur Cook Bay
Lembinwen Umbeb Bay Akhamb Peskarus
Melip Malfakhal Maskelyne
(Ulíveo)
Vun'ai'amp Tomman Maskelyne Islands

To Ambrym
(18km)

SOUTH
PACIFIC
OCEAN

CORAL
SEA

Pankumа
River

Matanoi
River

PLACES TO STAY & EAT
1 Vao Restaurant
2 Rose Bay Bungalows
3 Wiawi Guesthouse
4 Ngaim Orsel
Guesthouse
5 Dyto Guesthouse
6 SteZoe Guesthouse
7 Alo Lodge

0   8   16km
0   5   10mi

1 Big Nambas
2 Small Nambas
— Clan Border

---

such as magnificent scenery, World Heritage caves, waterfalls and *kastom* villages. The one across the dog's head was recently documented by the Australian Heritage Foundation. For a one- or a two-week hiking package contact **The Adventure Centre** (☎ 22743; W *www.adventurevanuatu.com; Lini Hwy, Port Vila*).

Getting There & Away

Vanair flights go via Norsup at least twice daily on the Vila/Luganville route. Three times a week there's a flight into Lamap from both Vila and Luganville, and a similar service to South West Bay. A twice-weekly loop links Norsup with Ambrym, Paama and Epi.

Boat services to Malekula are offered by *Lady Deema*, *Island Explorer*, MV *Tina 1* and MV *Havannah*. The typical fare from Vila is around 6700Vt. See Boat under the

Getting Around section earlier in this chapter for more details.

Getting Around

To/From the Airport Vanair offers Norsup/Lamap and Norsup/South West Bay flights three days a week. There are no flights between Lamap and South West Bay.

It costs 300/100Vt by taxi/minibus from Norsup airport into Lakatoro.

Public Transport You can find taxis in Norsup, Lakatoro and Lamap. A truck goes along the east coast between Lakatoro and Lamap (1000Vt) on weekdays, leaving Lamap at 5am; returning from Lakatoro at 1pm. On weekends charter the **truck** (☎ 48594; 15,000Vt). Don't baulk at the price – it's a fabulous half-day journey along a stunning coastline.

Trucks run more frequently between Lakatoro and the north charging 200Vt from Norsup to Veturah. The loop run around the 'dog's head' departs once a day from Lakatoro for 500Vt.

Speedboats are the only form of transport in the south.

AROUND THE ISLAND

The following concentrates on the major points of interest.

The Dog's Head

There's a number of tours and activities at this end of Malek ula, including a demanding half-day return walk to the Botko Big Nambas **cannibal site** deep in the forest behind Wala Mainland – it's complete with a stone fireplace, stone tables where corpses were dismembered, and many bones.

There are also tours to see Small Nambas *kastom* **dancing** on Rano, or at Amelboas, and to Big Nambas dances at Unmet and Mae.

Norsup In northern Malekula, Norsup was the centre for French administration, and is still mainly French-speaking. It's a run-down sort of place, with very little left except a **hospital** (☎ 48410), a store, a bakery and a **post office**. There's a market every day except Sunday. About 800m offshore is small, French-speaking Norsup (the island), where there's excellent white sand beaches and good **snorkelling**.

North of Norsup, **Walarano** is a good place to buy carvings, particularly of dolphins and canoes.

Further north at **Wala Mainland** (also known as Sanwir) you can stay at **Rose Bay Bungalows** (☎/fax 48602; e Rosebay@vanuatu.com.vu; per person including meals 3000Vt, dorm B&B 1800Vt). Near the mouth of Orap River, this is a charming group of traditional bungalows with en suites, set in gardens on a small black-sand bay. Taxis/buses from Norsup Airport cost 900/200Vt per person.

Vao Traditional customs have survived well on Vao. **Initiation** is an important rite for young boys. Once they are circumcised, they live in a special initiates' hut where they are taunted and teased for a month. They must grin and bear it, otherwise they'll be forbidden to marry.

Some footpaths on Vao are for males only. Others are for females. The chief will arrange an escort to ensure you don't breach any *tabu*.

Vao has many old *natsaro* (traditional dancing grounds) lined with stone monoliths and ancient *tamtam*, where your guide may demonstrate drumming.

The islanders make fascinating wooden masks, clubs and ceremonial bowls.

Small **Vao Restaurant** (☎ 48895) serves island meals.

Unmet, Brenwei & Bkaeir The residents of Unmet and Brenwei are Christian, but they've built a *nakamal* at Unmet for tourists that's one of the best places to see Big Nambas *kastom* dancing.

Bkaeir is the most *kastom*-oriented of the Big Nambas villages; it's a good place to see traditional houses and watch *kastom* dancing. You can walk here from **Wiawi** on the coast, but the hike is hard going and takes about four hours. Guides can be hired in Wiawi, where there's the small **Wiawi Guesthouse** (1500Vt). Otherwise, phone the villagers shared number at Unmet (☎ 48464) for a guide or 4WD truck to take you there.

Eastern Malekula

Lakatoro This attractive place, with many shady trees and a lot of development going on, is Malampa province's administrative capital and main town.

The village is on two levels divided by a steep slope. On the top level, the **Malampa Provincial Council** (☎ 48503) can tell you about tours and accommodation.

Lakatoro has mains electricity, a general store, ANZ and NBV banks, a post office and a bakery. There is also a **cultural centre** that holds dance performances.

Places to Stay & Eat Next door to the general store, **LTC Holiday Units** (☎ 48554, fax 48656; units without/with air-con 4000/6750Vt) comprises eight self-contained, Western-style units, all sparkling new with fridges and en suites.

MDC Guesthouse (☎ 48508; rooms without/with air-con 2500/5000Vt), at the other end of town, is a modern motel (two-storey!) with spacious rooms and shared kitchen and facilities.

Maxi Restaurant (meals 300Vt; open 7.30am-4.30pm Mon-Fri) is clean and spacious. It serves a few dishes like steak and rice, and will open for dinner if you book.

Uripiv & Uri Both these islands have a **marine sanctuary** proclaimed by the chief.

VANUATU

They have everything for the **snorkeller** – beautiful coral, small colourful fish, turtles and even giant clams.

Ngaim Orsel Guesthouse (☎ 48564, 48566; beds 1500Vt, meals around 250Vt), on Uripiv, is a very friendly place set in the middle of an old *natsaro* filled with exotic plants. There's a bungalow, library and quaint new house with three bedrooms.

You can get to the islands by **canoe** or **speedboat** from the Lakatoro jetty. There are plenty of canoes going across between 4pm and 4.30pm, when it costs 100Vt for a ride. Otherwise, a speedboat charter is 1500Vt.

Vetgot By far the main attraction here is the Small Nambas *kastom* **dancing** put on by the men and women of the Hefa Sar Culture Club. A programme of eight dances costs 3000Vt per person.

Banam Bay Bungalows were ruined by a cyclone in 2000. They are hoping to rebuild. Ask **Island Safaris** (☎ 23288; w www.islands vanuatu.com; back of arcade, Lini Hwy, Port Vila) for the latest.

Transport to Vetgot costs 3500/300Vt by taxi/truck from the Lamap-Orovail Airfield and at least 6000/600Vt by taxi/truck from Lakatoro.

Lamap This town is a derelict shadow of its former self when it was the principal French government centre. It has a **hospital**, store, **post office** and **NBV bank**.

The town's busiest operation is the **Roman Catholic mission**. There's a large, modern church in its grounds, with several interesting wall paintings modelled on traditional sand drawing designs.

Taxis and **speedboats** are available for hire. It costs 500Vt from the Lamap-Orovail Airfield by taxi.

It's a pleasant, 45-minute **walk** from Lamap to the wharf at **Port Sandwich**, however, don't swim or even paddle at the small golden beach there, no matter how tempting – this is the worst place for shark attacks. There are also tours to Small Nambas *kastom* dances at Labreau and Penap.

Places to Stay & Eat On the road to the airport are two new, pleasant places:

Dyto Guesthouse (☎ 48663; per person 1000Vt) has two bedrooms, a pleasant kitchen and very clean facilities. BYO food, but the owner, who also arranges transport and tours, will make sure you don't starve.

Ste Zoe Guesthouse (☎ 48663; beds 1500Vt) is on the hill overlooking the beach, 2km from the airport. Kamille, the school principal, will look after you and arrange tours. You can buy **meals** (200Vt to 500Vt).

The Maskelynes The road from Lamap ends at a pleasant sandy beach, **Point Doucere**, the major landing for **canoes** and **speedboats** going out to the Maskelynes.

These islands are gorgeous. Most have coral reefs with excellent **snorkelling** and **diving**, but be *very* careful of strong currents.

Uliveo is the hub of the Maskelynes and its main village is **Peskarus**. It's a friendly busy place and beautiful to stroll around. Tours include: Ringi Te Suih Marine Conservation Area; the Giant Clam Garden; mangrove discovery; swimming and snorkelling at Sakao Beach; and visits to Lutes and Hemanguru to see school children dancing.

Nagol Bungalows (☎ 48930, 48519; e is lands@vanuatu.com.vu; singles/doubles 2480/4560Vt) has three traditional rooms on the shore between the mangroves in Peskarus. The owners cook excellent **meals** (400Vt to 1900Vt), introduce you to village life and arrange tours. The price includes breakfast.

Transport from the Lamap-Orovail Airfield to Peskarus by truck and boat costs 4500Vt.

South West Bay

The ancient traditions of the Small Nambas people are well preserved in southwestern Malekula. *Nakamal* and dancing grounds are being opened to tourists and grade-taking is on the increase. While there are no full-*kastom* people left, you can learn about their traditions on tours from Wintua.

Wintua Looking out over South West Bay's broad expanse while still behind forested hills is Wintua. You can do a day walk into the hills to three mainly *kastom* villages – **Looranba'an**, **Veremboas** and **Mendua** – where you can see *kastom* activities by arrangement (5000Vt for a *kastom* dance).

Alo Lodge (☎/fax 48659; rooms 4000Vt) is near the South West Bay Airfield. George Thompson, the owner, meets most flights and can arrange transport, guides, deep-sea fishing or tours. The guesthouse has four bedrooms, and a wide veranda for dining. The price includes breakfast, but bring some emergency food.

There are regular Vanair **flights** to South West Bay (if the airfield is not under water).

Ambrym

pop 8000 • area 680 sq km
While Vanuatu's southern islands are paradise, you could easily think Ambrym was the devil's playground. Craig Cove is a sad mix of concrete buildings by a rocky bay, where the cargo boat MV *Saraika* lies half-submerged, rusting. Don't despair. As you travel elsewhere the landscape opens up.

Most tourists visit Ambrym to see the twin volcanoes of Mt Marum and Mt Benbow. Other attractions include Vanuatu's best fern carvings and *tamtam*, and the Rom dances of northern and western Ambrym.

Ambrym is called the Black Island because of its dark volcanic soils. It is an appropriate name, particularly within the enormous central caldera, which is totally devoid of vegetation. The island is often devastated by cyclones, and its volcanoes have wiped out whole villages in the years of 1913, 1929 and 1950, while lesser eruptions occurred in the years of 1937, 1946, 1979 and 1993. Drifting ash creates serious problems by disrupting the fruiting of food plants and increasing soil acidity.

Traditional Culture
Ambrym is considered Vanuatu's sorcery centre as magic is said to be strongest on islands with active volcanoes. Sorcerers – *man blong majik* or *man blong posen* – are treated with respect. Many islanders have seen too many unexplained happenings to regard a sorcerer with anything but awe.

Ambrym is also the island for **sand drawers** with 180 sand designs, each referring to a specific object, legend, dance or creature.

The Rom Dance The island's most striking ceremony, takes place over several weeks every August in the north as part of grade-taking. It was in danger of dying out in the south, but is being revived for tourists.

The Rom costume consists of a tall, conical, brightly painted mask, and a cloak of banana leaves.The dancer is represented as a spirit, so each costume is burned after the dance in case the spirit haunts or impersonates the dancer. Consequently, very few Rom outfits exist although the National Museum in Vila has one.

Getting There & Away
Ambrym's airfields are at Craig Cove in the southwest and Ulei in the southeast. Planes

VANUATU

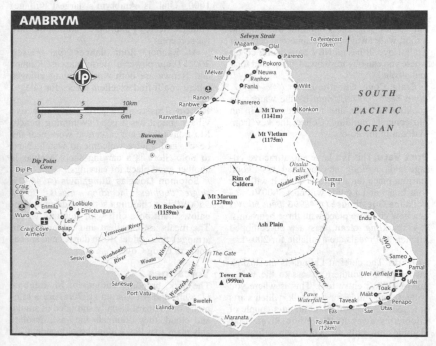

planes call in to Craig Cove from Vila or Luganville six times weekly, while three call in to Ulei.

Sea-Link's MV *Tina 1* stops along Ambrym's west coast each week on its journeys from Santo to Vila. Another, more comfortable service about to commence is **Island Explorer** (☎ 27926; e *ladydeema@hotmail.com*).

Getting Around
A 4WD road connects Craig Cove with Maranata, in the south, and Endu, on the east coast. From there a narrow path goes north to Wilit. There are roads around the northern tip, then a track from Melvar to Ranvetlam.

The terrain along the northwest coast is very rough, with no established path. Most people travel between Craig Cove and Ranvetlam by speedboat (10,000Vt each way).

AROUND THE ISLAND
Southwestern Ambrym
Volcano tours run out of Craig Cove, Sanesup, Port Vatu and Lalinda (see Volcano Tours following for details).

The villagers at **Lolibulo** will perform the Rom dance by arrangement (4500Vt), and there are tours to *kastom* villages.

Craig Cove District Several very small villages are scattered around the airfield, and a short walk away is the commercial centre of Craig Cove. It has an **NBV bank** and a **co-op** where you can buy fresh bread, processed food and alcohol.

Craig Cove Guesthouse (☎/fax 48507; *dorm beds 1000Vt*), right by the water, has cooking facilities and four bedrooms in an old concrete building. Collect the key from William in the co-op.

Port Vatu This is a large and attractive village laid out along the coast road. It's a good starting place for a volcano walk. It will take four hours and a guide will cost 3000Vt.

Paline Guesthouse (☎ 48996; *beds 500Vt*) is a new concrete place with three bedrooms. It's sparkling clean, has a well-equipped kitchen and **meals** are available for 200Vt.

Lalinda The chief at Lalinda is the *kastom* owner of the southern access to the volcanoes (1000Vt entry fee). This is where you collect your guide for the walk, which starts at a vehicle drop-off point about a couple of kilometres away at **Woketebo River**. Take a guide, not only for your own safety but

because the villagers worry about you. Besides, the local guide, Jimmy Penuel, is a volcano consultant for *National Geographic*.

The taxi to Lalinda is 4500Vt from Craig Cove.

Northern Ambrym
Most of Ambrym's northern coast is extremely rocky. In some places high volcanic cliffs rise straight out of the sea. Only Olal, Magam, Parereo and Ranon have beaches.

The island's best carvings come from the north. Dance clearings in the villages usually have several tall *tamtam* standing around as permanent sentinels. You'll find sand artists in most villages along the coast from Ranvetlam to Konkon.

The sacred custom of the north is that there is no fishing, hunting or other activities from September 1 to January 31 – the yam planting season. Volcano trips are only available from the south during these months. Outside these months, volcano trips are the major attraction as Ranvetlam offers the easiest route up Marum (see Volcano Tours following for details).

Olal & Around With its population around 1000, Olal is Ambrym's largest village. Taxis can be hired here to visit surrounding villages. Nearby **Pokoro** is a traditional centre for sorcerers.

At Ranhor, **Rom dances** (*per person 3000Vt*) are powerful performances. Ranhor and Neuwa are both wood-carving villages where you'll find excellent pieces for sale.

Ranon This is not a particularly attractive village, but it has a good **swimming beach**. Most days there are carvers at work near the beach, and you're welcome to watch. Next to Solo Store is a carving shop. **Melvar** is another good place for carvings.

Solomon Douglas Bungalows (☎ 48405; *singles/doubles including meals 3500/ 5500Vt*) is a charming set of traditional bungalows built on a cliff with stunning views. The meals are excellent and the owner can arrange tours, guides, Rom dances and speedboats to Craig Cove.

Volcanoes
The dark, brooding outlines of Mt Benbow (1159m) and Mt Marum (1270m) are a kilometre or so apart. Usually shrouded in smoke and cloud, they dominate the vast, desolate **ash plain** that lies within the old caldera. At

night, the sky above them glows red from the infernos below.

Columns of white smoke pour from Mt Benbow's central crater. However, Mt Marum has recently become more active, spewing molten rock and dense black smoke from its vents. Since 1998 it's been closely monitored and evacuation plans have been worked out, just in case.

Hiking If you wish to explore the volcanoes, you must be fit, reasonably acclimatised and used to walking on steep terrain, as conditions can be difficult. The path takes you up steep slopes, with thick jungle that can tear at you. There's no shade on the barren ash surfaces in the caldera, where the heat can be terrific. Skin protection (including a broad-rimmed hat) and plenty of water are essential; loose-fitting cotton clothing is the most comfortable.

The slopes around both volcanoes are covered with a dry slippery crust. You'll need strong walking boots capable of kicking toe holes in the crust otherwise your backside might become a toboggan down a very high, steep ridge. Ankle support is necessary as there's some boulder hopping.

The weather can change very rapidly, the wind can be icy and the surfaces are extremely slippery when they're wet.

Access Points The best starting points for walks to the volcanoes are Lalinda and Ranvetlam. Many people prefer to camp overnight on the ash plain as it's a long eight- or nine-hour day from either end. You'll definitely need two days if you want to climb both volcanoes.

Volcano Tours One of the best walks in the South Pacific is run by **Isaiah Bong** (☎ 48405, Renvetlam) who operates a walking tour from Ranvetlam down to Craig Cove, climbing both volcanoes and spending a night on the ash plain (tents and food provided).

Alternatively, you can do an eight-hour day walk from Ranvetlam to either one of the volcanoes (one/two people 5500/7000Vt) through Solomon Douglas Bungalows in Ranon.

Starting at Sanesup or ,Lalinda in the south, if you're fit, you might do the return walk to one of the Mt Marum external vents and climb to the summit of Mt Benbow in a day. The cost for this through the **Milee Sea Bungalows** (☎ 48596) in Sanesup is 9500/15,000Vt for one/two people, including transport to the drop-off point.

Espiritu Santo

pop 30,900 • area 3677 sq km
Although officially named Espiritu Santo – Spanish for the Holy Spirit – this island is called Santo by almost everyone. (Luganville, the island's principal settlement, is also generally referred to as Santo.)

The island's drawcard is its world-class scuba diving, particularly the wreck of the SS *President Coolidge*. There's also no shortage of good (if not tough) walking, great beaches and an interesting history (see History at the start of this chapter). Most tourist facilities are concentrated in and around Luganville, where there are several motels and resorts.

Santo is Vanuatu's largest island (116km long, 59km wide) and is also home to the country's four highest peaks: Mt Tabwemasana, Mt Kotamtam, Mt Tawaloala and Santo Peak, all over 1700m. They rise from the mountainous spine that runs almost the full length of the island's west coast. In contrast, the much flatter southern and eastern coastal strips have been largely developed for cattle grazing (Santo carries the bulk of Vanuatu's beef-cattle herd) and plantations.

Santo is still an important centre for *ni-mangkl* ceremonies. Although most people living along the southern and eastern seaboards wear European clothing, in other less accessible parts many people still dress as *kastom* demands.

Diving & Snorkelling
There are at least 20 worthwhile dive sites in the channels within 20km south and southwest of Luganville. Santo's wreck and coral diving are generally superior to Efate's. Vanuatu's most famous wreck dive is the SS *President Coolidge*, which lies in 21m to 67m of water just east of Luganville. A well-known snorkelling spot is **Million Dollar Point** – see Around the Island for more.

The local dive tour specialists are:

Allan Power Dive Tours (☎ 36822, ℮ apower@ mail.vanuatu.com.vu) Main St. Across from Hotel Santo
Aquamarine (☎ 36196, ℮ aquamrne@vanuatu .com.vu) Near Santo Chinese Restaurant
Bokissa Island Dive (☎ 36913, ℮ reservations@ bokissa.vu) Bokissa Eco Island Resort
Pro Dive Santo (☎ 36911, ℮ prodive@vanuatu .com.vu) Aore Island. Just across Segond Channel

VANUATU

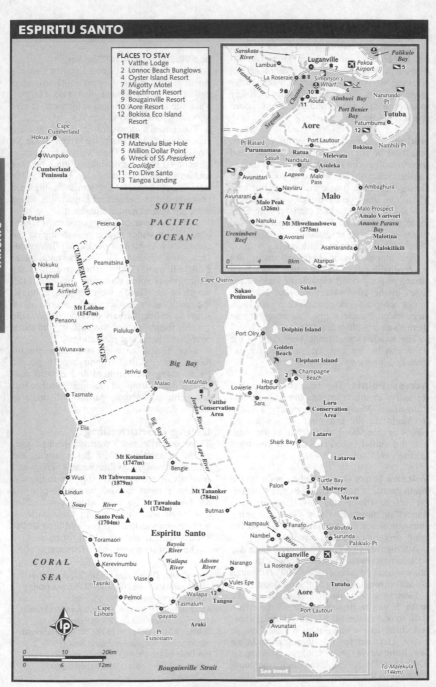

SS President Coolidge: A Scuba Sensation

On the morning of 26 October 1942, the SS *President Coolidge* sank after hitting two 'friendly' American mines in Segond Channel. A luxury liner, she had been refitted as a troopship and was carrying over 5000 men, all but two of whom survived.

The ship is now famous amongst the scuba set as the world's largest diveable WWII wreck. With a moderate current and visibility up to 40m, conditions are normally excellent for diving. Swimming along and through the wreck you can view the trappings of a 1930s luxury liner as well as the hardware of a WWII troopship.

One of the most famous dives on the *Coolidge* is the 'Lady', a bas-relief of a woman and a unicorn that once hung above the fireplace in the elegant smoking lounge. There's still a barber chair still bolted to the floor of the beauty salon and the swimming pool is still there at 50m (of course, the most frequent joke is that it's still full of water...).

The *Coolidge* should *only* be attempted by experienced divers with an experienced guide, as most of the dives require decompression diving and knowledge of the wreck. At 202m long it's far too big to be explored on a single dive. In fact, the experts recommend at least four.

All four operators can dive the SS *President Coolidge* as well as a number of other wrecks and reefs. Single shore/boat dives usually start at around 3600/5000Vt.

Organised Tours

Two recommended tour operators are **Heritage Tours** (☎ 36862, mobile 40968) and **Paradise Tours** (☎ 37159). They offer a range of standard half-day and day tours in their minibuses and can also tailor to your interests (eg, hiking, WWII touring).

A typical day trip includes visiting Fanafo, Matantas, Champagne Beach and the Matevulu Blue Hole for 4000Vt per person (minimum two passengers). Whether you book with one of the above operators or through your hotel tour desk, be sure to agree on where you want to go as not all guides have access to Champagne Beach due to *kastom* disputes.

Getting There & Away

Air Santo had five operational airfields during WWII, but now only Pekoa, 6km from Luganville, remains in use; wartime pilots knew it as Bomber Two. The island's only other commercial strip is at Lajmoli, on the northwest coast.

There are about two return flights daily between Santo and Vila; tickets cost 12,280Vt one way (including taxes). Pekoa is the main feeder airport for the northern islands.

Sea There are numerous options for sea travel to Santo, including *Lady Deema*, *Island Explorer* and MV *Tina 1*. The typical fare from Port Vila to Santo is 6500Vt. See Boat under Getting Around earlier in this chapter.

Luganville has full customs and immigration facilities for yachts at the main wharf. Segond Channel is the town's main anchorage. Most yachts prefer to anchor off Aore Resort, where a number of moorings are provided.

Getting Around Santo has a reasonable network of unsealed roads connecting Luganville with the southwest, north and east coasts; elsewhere you have to travel by boat or hoof it.

To/From the Airport The minibus fare between Pekoa Airport and Luganville is 200Vt, while taxis charge from 500Vt shared.

Air Vanair has one flight weekly from Luganville to Lajmoli airfield (6090Vt).

Minibus Regular minibus services connect Luganville and Port Olry. As their main function is to run workers to and from town, the best way to catch a ride is to stand by the roadside before 7am, if you're heading in, and after 5pm, on the outward run. The fare is 500Vt each way.

Car You can hire cars directly through **Hotel Santo** (☎ 36250; Main St) for 3800Vt per day plus 38Vt per kilometre. Hotel Santo also has an office for **Santo 4WD Rental** (☎ 37259, 44259) from where you can hire a 4WD for 11,500Vt per day. Insurance costs extra.

Taxi & Truck There are plenty of taxis and public transport trucks operating around Luganville. As in Vila, competition is fierce and tourists are fair game for some operators.

VANUATU

LUGANVILLE
pop 10,750

The country's largest town after Vila is Luganville, Vanuatu's north capital. Before WWII, Luganville was a scattered collection of buildings separated by coconut plantations. Then the Americans came and changed its face forever.

Today, the town's wide main street sprawls along several kilometres of waterfront. It's a sleepy, dilapidated place, with numerous ageing Quonset huts and rusting steel sea walls remaining as evidence of more prosperous days. Things get pretty quiet here after dark, at which time it's probably best that solo female travellers don't go out alone.

Information
Money Luganville is the only town other than Vila with commercial banking facilities. These are provided by the **ANZ Bank**, **Westpac** and the **NBV bank**, all on the main street. The ANZ has an ATM.

A good place to change money after banking hours is at the **Santo Sports Club** *(Main St; open 9am-midnight daily)*.

Post & Communications The post office *(open 7.30am-11.30am, 1.15pm-4.30pm Mon-Fri, 7.30am-11.30am Sat)* has a phonecard telephone outside. You'll also find public phones (and fax facilities) at **Telecom Vanuatu's office** *(rue La Pérouse; open 7.30am-11.30am, 1.15pm-4pm Mon-Fri)*.

The best place in town to email is at **Computer & Network Services** *(25Vt per min; open 7.30am-11.30am, 1.30pm-5pm Mon-Fri, 8am-11.30am Sat)*, close to the Vanair office.

Medical Services The **Northern District Hospital** *(☎ 36345)* is perched above the town in Le Plateau. There's a **pharmacy** *(☎ 36213)* at the hospital and two smaller ones with limited supplies on Main Street.

Luganville Market
Villagers come from all over southern and eastern Santo to sell their garden produce at the **Luganville Market** *(Main St)* near the Sarakata Bridge. It's open round-the-clock daily.

Places to Stay – Budget
Unity Park Motel *(☎ 36052; e locm@vanuatu.com.vu; Main St; dorm singles/doubles 1350/2100Vt, private from 2400Vt)* has shared

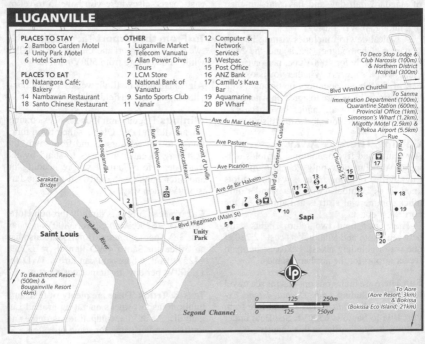

LUGANVILLE

PLACES TO STAY	OTHER	12 Computer &
2 Bamboo Garden Motel	1 Luganville Market	Network
4 Unity Park Motel	3 Telecom Vanuatu	Services
6 Hotel Santo	5 Allan Power Dive	13 Westpac
	Tours	15 Post Office
PLACES TO EAT	7 LCM Store	16 ANZ Bank
10 Natangora Café;	8 National Bank of	17 Camillo's Kava
Bakery	Vanuatu	Bar
14 Nambawan Restaurant	9 Santo Sports Club	19 Aquamarine
18 Santo Chinese Restaurant	11 Vanair	20 BP Wharf

To Deco Stop Lodge & Club Narcosis (100m) & Northern District Hospital (300m)

Blvd Winston Churchil

To Sanma Immigration Department (100m), Quarantine Station (600m), Provincial Office (1km), Simonson's Wharf (1.2km), Migotty Motel (2.5km) & Pekoa Airport (5.5km)

Rue

Ave du Mar Leclerc

Ave Pastuer

Ave Picanon

Ave de Bir Hakeim

Rue Bougainville

Cook St

Rue La Pérouse

Rue d'Entrecasteaux

Rue Dumont d'Urville

Blvd du General de Gaulle

Churchil St

Paul Gauguin

Sarakata Bridge

Blvd Higginson (Main St)

Sapi

Unity Park

Saint Louis

Sarakata River

To Beachfront Resort (500m) & Bougainville Resort (4km)

Segond Channel

0   125   250m
0   125   250yd

To Aore (Aore Resort; 3km) & Bokissa (Bokissa Eco Island; 21km)

VANUATU

kitchen and bathroom facilities, laundry, very basic but clean rooms and is popular with the budget set.

Bamboo Garden Motel (☎ 36837; e valiant@vanuatu.com.vu; singles/doubles 1500/2500Vt), opposite the market, is a cheerily painted, homely little place with a shared balcony and kitchen. The single rooms are tiny but cute; if you're after a double, request the larger room with its own bathroom.

Migotty Motel (☎ 36494; fan-cooled singles/doubles 3000/4000Vt) is an out-of-towner near the airport with an appealing coastal outlook. It's good value.

Places to Stay – Mid-Range

Hotel Santo (☎ 36250, fax 36749; e hotel santo@vanuatu.com.vu; Main St; singles/doubles with fan 5500/6500Vt, with air-con 9440/10,540Vt) is in a retro '70s building in the centre of town. It has a swimming pool, bar and restaurant, lovely staff, comfortable rooms and a relaxed vibe.

Deco Stop Lodge (☎ 36175, fax 36101; e deco@vanuatu.com.vu; dorm beds 3500Vt, singles/doubles from 6500Vt), sitting pretty on the ridge behind Luganville with fine views of Segond Channel, is a good-value place with a great social atmosphere (especially when booked out by diving groups). There's a restaurant, bar and inviting swimming pool. The price includes breakfast.

The Beachfront Resort (☎ 36881, fax 36882; e bfresort@vanuatu.com.vu; singles/doubles from 4500/6500Vt) is a friendly, low-key spot on the southern outskirts of town with motel-style fan-cooled bungalows, all with kitchenettes, and a restaurant, bar and laundry.

Places to Stay – Top-End

The following are all in the vicinity of Luganville, not in the town itself.

Bougainville Resort (☎ 36257, fax 36647; e charles@vanuatu.com.vu; singles/doubles with fan 8000/9000Vt), about 5km from the centre of town, is a tropical garden oasis carved out of the surrounding jungle. It's a delightful spot, with 18 airy bungalows, a bar, swimming pool and the most sophisticated restaurant on Santo (see Places to Eat following). The price includes breakfast. A minibus/taxi from town costs 100/300Vt.

Aore Resort (☎ 36705; fax 36703; e aore@vanuatu.com.vu; singles/doubles from 6750/10,500Vt, family rooms from 10,500Vt, children under 12 free), on Aore (pronounced

'ow-ree') Island, seems a world away from Luganville 3km across the channel. It's a terrific, unpretentious place with a swimming pool, bar and restaurant (mains around 1550Vt), a pretty outlook over moored yachts, and kayaks, snorkelling gear and mountain bikes available. The price includes breakfast. There is a free ferry for guests, which leaves at four set times daily from BP Wharf; for nonguests it costs 250Vt return (or free if you eat at the restaurant).

Bokissa Eco Island Resort (☎ 36913, fax 36855; e holiday@bokissa.vu; bungalows per person including all meals 10,000Vt) is on Bokissa, about 10km southeast of Luganville. The air-con bungalows front the ocean and are surrounded by shady old trees; hammocks dot the place and there's snorkelling at your doorstep. There's also a swimming pool, a library, a dive operator and plenty of activities and tours on offer. Unscheduled transfers from the mainland (3000Vt return, 30 minutes each way) leave from Simonsen's wharf.

Places to Eat

Natangora Café (Main St; meals 350-600Vt; open 7.30am-4.30pm Mon-Fri, 8am-1pm Sat) specialises in breakfasts, home-roasted coffee, hamburgers, ice cream and home-made pastries and cakes. Its pleasant alfresco setting, good food and reasonable prices make it popular with expats and Ni-Vanuatu alike. Pop into the **bakery** down the eastern side of the café for yummy French batards (40Vt).

Nambawan Restaurant (Main St; dinner mains 1350-1650Vt, open breakfast, lunch & dinner daily) is a new, friendly place with pleasant outdoor and indoor eating areas. The daily 250Vt specials (eg, chicken and rice) are good value.

Santo Chinese Restaurant (☎ 36452; mains 480-1800Vt; open lunch & dinner daily) is down a dim side street just east of the ANZ Bank. This is a no-frills, good-value place with plenty of character, and plates heaving under generous serves.

Bougainville Resort (☎ 36257, fax 36647; e charles@vanuatu.com.vu; dinner mains 1550-1700Vt; open breakfast, lunch & dinner daily) has a restaurant that offers one of Santo's few opportunities for a gourmet experience. The broad veranda with its dreamy view is a particularly good spot to dine.

Entertainment

Apart from eating out, the entertainment scene is pretty light-on in Luganville.

Santo Sports Club (☎ 36373; open 9am-midnight daily) is a good spot for a beer and cheapish pub-style meal on the balcony. There's also a satellite television if you need a TV fix.

Club Narcosis at the Deco Stop Lodge (see Places to Stay) can be fun, especially if you're into pool – there's a comp every Friday from 7.30pm.

Camillo's, one of about 40 licensed kava bars in Luganville, is well worth a visit. You'll be welcome at most others too – just look for a red or green light outside.

Getting Around

You'll have no difficulty finding a minibus between 7am and 5.30pm, but it's a different story outside these hours. The standard rate anywhere around town is 100Vt.

Taxis and public transport trucks can be found waiting at the market or on Main Street. If walking around Luganville at night, carry a torch so you can see the holes!

AROUND THE ISLAND

The following, while by no means a complete inventory of all Santo's offerings, is a rundown on its main attractions, the most interesting and accessible of which are in the southeast and northeast of the island.

Southeastern Santo

Fanafo You can visit this interesting group of villages independently, but it's best if you take a guided tour or at least make prior arrangements. When you arrive, ask for Chief Tabou Rusa and he will detail someone to act as guide (500Vt per car). One of the things you may be shown is the grave of Jimmy Stevens, as well as various relics associated with him.

Chief Tabou Rusa has a basic **guesthouse** in Fanafo that makes a good base for a day-return walk to **Butmas**, a village up in the hills. Many traditional supporters of Jimmy Stevens left Fanafo after his death and went to live in Butmas.

Fanafo's Christians wear ordinary clothes, while *kastom*-oriented males of all ages are naked except for their *mal mal*. You may also see small girls wearing leaves and older females in grass skirts.

To get to Fanafo turn left at the T-junction 22.4km northwest of Luganville.

Million Dollar Point Heading towards Palikulo Point from Luganville, and just

where the main coastal road turns to the north, a well-defined track runs southwards to the nearby beach. This astounding spot is where hundreds of tonnes of US military equipment were dumped at the end of WWII. At low tide you'll find coral-encrusted axles and other metal objects littering the beach for a kilometre in either direction.

It's usually a great **snorkelling** spot owing to the generally shallow depth and excellent visibility, although at certain times of the year currents can be strong – check with one of the local dive operators if you're concerned. Also, we've received several reports of theft from here so don't leave valuables in cars or lying around. The entrance fee is 500Vt per car.

Matevulu Blue Hole Further north, about 20km out of Luganville, there's a track on the left that takes you up the former US wartime airstrip, Fighter One. The main track turns left towards the Matevulu Agricultural College about halfway along the strip, but continue up the strip to the end. Here you swing left and follow the track around to the crystal-clear Matevulu Blue Hole. (It can be a bit tricky to get here, so ask for additional help from your hotel if you're directionally challenged.)

There are several 'blue holes' on Santo and they're so named for very good reason – their colour is stunningly, well, blue. This is the largest such feature on Santo, being about 50m across and 18m deep. Not surprisingly, it's a great spot for swimming and scuba diving.

Oyster Island Resort Back on the main road, about 400m north of the turn-off to the Matevulu Blue Hole, the track on your right heads down to a landing area where you can catch the boat across to the beautiful **Oyster Island Resort** (☎/fax 36283; e oysteril@vanuatu.com.vu; singles/doubles 4000/4500Vt). This charming hideaway consists of eight simple, Melanesian-style bungalows in a beautiful, serene waterfront setting. The prices shown include breakfast. The lovely owners have several tours on offer (eg, hiking to a traditional village, canoeing up the Matevulu River). There's a **restaurant** that is open daily (mains 1250Vt to 2200Vt) that specialises in seafood; reservations are advisable.

Getting there costs 300Vt by the regular Luganville–Port Olry minibus service (see

Getting Around at the start of Espiritu Santo) or 2000Vt by taxi each way. To summon the boat across, bang on the gas cylinder.

Northeastern Santo

Loru Conservation Area Covering 220 hectares, this fine park *(admission per person 500Vt)* contains one of the last patches of lowland forest remaining on Santo's east coast. There are several excellent **nature walks**, many **coconut crabs** and a **bat cave**, which the villagers use as a cyclone shelter. The turn-off (right-hand side) is 41km north of Luganville; from here head to Kole 1 village and ask for a guide to take you to the **information centre**.

Accommodation is available in a basic **bungalow** *(per person 500Vt)* with cooking facilities. There's currently no way of making an advance booking; crossing your fingers for a vacancy might help.

Lonnoc Beach Bungalows In a beautiful coastal setting 55km from Luganville is **Lonnoc Beach Bungalows** *(☎/fax 36141; singles/doubles 3100/4200Vt)*. A good spot to drop out for a few days, its traditional-style bungalows line the beachfront – try to score one with a private bathroom and veranda. The price includes breakfast.

There's a small bar and restaurant with a good vegetarian selection (nonguests welcome, but let them know you're coming), a sandy swimming beach and a stunning view of **Elephant Island** out the front. It runs a daily return bus service to Luganville for 500Vt each way (departing 6.30am, returning from town around 4pm).

Champagne Beach The road past Lonnoc Beach Bungalows stops at Champagne Beach, which is as lovely as the brochures say describes it. Cruise ships drop anchor here every four weeks or so between May and October and for a few hours it's just like Queensland's Gold Coast as up to 1500 passengers come ashore to splash and sunbathe. Apart from cruise-ship days and weekends, however, you're likely to have it all to yourself.

There is, of course, the inevitable *kastom* fee – although in this case there are two of them, so you must place 500Vt per car in each of the honesty boxes on the way in. Two local men claim to be the beach's rightful landholder and each wants payment for the right to use it.

Matantas & the Vatthe Conservation Area Matantas is split into two parts, with one being Baha'i and the other Seventh-Day Adventist. You'll see the **information centre** for the conservation area on the left as you arrive. If there's no-one at the centre, bang on the bamboo *tamtam* or walk further into Matantas and ask for Purity.

There's a cemetery surrounded by a low, mortared stone wall in the centre of Matantas, reputedly used as a fortified camp by Quirós when he landed here in 1606. Also of interest is a tree that was damaged by shellfire in September 1980 at the end of the Santo rebellion, when the Papua New Guinea gunboat *Madang* shelled Matantas, forcing the rebel villagers to accept Vanuatu's authority.

The Vatthe Conservation Area is one of Santo's highlights for anyone who likes trees, birds and hiking. Covering about 45 sq km, it stretches along the coast from north of Matantas to the **Jordan River**, and inland to the top of a 400m-high limestone scarp. Half of the park is covered by Vanuatu's largest, reasonably intact, alluvial lowland forest, which was the main reason for its protection in 1996.

Various walks (and other activities) can be arranged through the information centre, from a quiet two-hour stroll to a two-day effort that includes the highest point on the scarp – 449m **Mt Wimbo**. You're expected to take a guide for most walks/activities.

Vatthe Lodge *(☎/fax 36153; rooms per person 2000Vt; meals 500-1500Vt)* is next door to the information centre and has several basic but lovely island-style bungalows with shared bathrooms, pebble floors, hurricane lamp lighting and mosquito nets.

A transport charter to Matantas from Luganville costs 6000Vt (one way). If there's a truck going that way it will cost only about 500Vt per person – to find out about this, contact the Vatthe Lodge.

If you are travelling independently, the best way to get there is via the east coast road, turning off 4.6km south of Hog Harbour. (Take the left fork just past Lowerie – the right heads toward Port Olry.) From the turn-off, this road intersects with the (very rough) road down to Fanafo after approximately 11km. Continue on straight and you'll arrive at the edge of a high scarp after 8km or so – down to Matantas it's a very steep one-way track with nowhere to pull over, so honk your horn as you descend, to warn any oncoming traffic.

VANUATU

Pentecost

pop 15,500 • area 438 sq km
Pentecost gets its name because it was first seen by Europeans on Whit Sunday. The island is famous for the ritual of men in the south diving from high towers to bless the yam harvest (*naghol*) – see the boxed 'The Land Divers of South Pentecost'.

Getting There & Away
Pentecost has two airfields: Sara in the north and Lonorore in the southwest. Vanair has three return flights weekly to both airports from Vila and Luganville via Ambae.

Sea services to Pentecost include *Island Explorer* and MV *Tina 1*. The typical fare from Port Vila to Laone is 5000Vt. See Boat under Getting Around earlier in this chapter.

Getting Around
There's a 4WD road down the west coast and another across from Pangi to Bunlap. They are extraordinarily bad – just ruts hanging onto cliff faces. By the time you add the driver's danger money it's a staggering 30,000Vt to get from Laone down to Pangi.

MV *Tina 1* goes from Laone to Pangi (1000Vt) twice a week, with fantastic views of coastal villages thrown in.

Organised Tours Most tourists come on day trips by air to see the land diving. Any agent in Vila can arrange visits. Entry fees, including camera permits, are around 20,000Vt (transport and accommodation are on top of that).

To organise your own tour, speak to **Chief Willy Orion** (☎/fax 38448, ☎ 38444) in Salap.

AROUND THE ISLAND
The bulk of Pentecost's tourist attractions are at the southern end of the island, especially around *naghol* time. For information on the central and northern regions, contact the NTO or the Penama provincial government office (see Useful Organisations in the Facts for the Visitor section).

Southwestern Pentecost
Around Lonorore Airfield There's a snack bar and cardphone at the airport, a **post office** and **clinic** nearby, and the new pleasant **Airport Resthouse** (☎ 38356; beds 500Vt), in case you are stranded. A **land-dive tower**

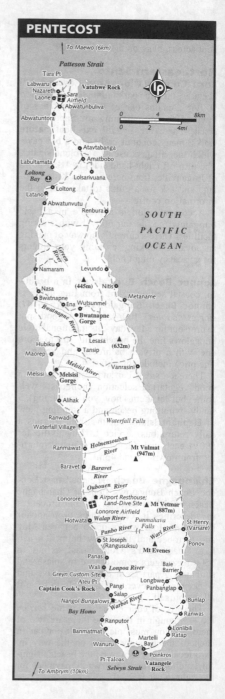

PENTECOST

To Maewo (6km)

Patteson Strait

Tara Pt
Labwaru
Nazareth
Laone
Sara Airfield
Abwatunbuliva
Abwatuntora

Vatubwe Rock

0   4   8km
0   2   4mi

Atavtabanga
Labultamata
Amatbobo
Loltong Bay
Lolsarivuana
Latano
Loltong
Abwatunvutu
Renbura

SOUTH PACIFIC OCEAN

Namaram
Levundo
Green River
(445m)
Nitis
Nasa
Metaname
Bwatnapne
Ena
Wutsunmel
Bwatnapne River
Bwatnapne Gorge
Hubiku
Lesasa
(632m)
Maorep
Tansip
Melsisi River
Vanrasini
Melsisi
Melsisi Gorge
Alihak
Ranwadi
Waterfall Falls
Waterfall Village
Ranmawat
Holnensouban River
Mt Vulmat (947m)
Baravet
Baravet River
Oubouen River
Lonorore
Airport Resthouse;
Land-Dive Site
Mt Vetmar (887m)
Lonorore Airfield
Hotwata
Walap River
Punmahava Falls
St Henry (Varsare)
Panbo River
Wari River
Ponov
St Joseph (Rangusuksu)
Mt Evenes
Panas
Wali
Lonpoa River
Baie Barrier
Greyn Custom Site
Longbwe
Ateu Pt
Pangi
Panbanglap
Captain Cook's Rock
Salap
Warbot River
Bunlap
Nangol Bungalows
Bay Homo
Ranputor
Ranwas
Lonlibili
Banmatmat
Martelli Bay
Ratap
Wanuru
Pt Taloas
Selwyn Strait
Poinkros
Vatangele Rock
To Ambrym (10km)

The Land Divers of South Pentecost

Many centuries ago a woman tried to flee her husband Tamalié, who pursued her up a huge banyan. She leapt, supposedly to her death. He leapt after her realising, too late, that she had tied vines to her ankles.

Local women re-enacted their sister's dive. However, this made the wind whistle eerily through the trees – a sign that Tamalié's spirit was distressed. So the elders ruled that only men could make the jump.

A full-sized tower, which takes several weeks to erect, is vertical for 16m, then leans backwards. Tree trunks, saplings and branches from the surrounding bush are bound around a tall tree stump with vines, and secured to neighbouring trees. The soil in front of the tower is cleared of rocks, then loosened to reduce the chance of injury.

Each diver carefully selects his own vines. If they are 10cm too long he will crush his skull; too short and he'll be jerked back against the tower (bones have occasionally been broken or a spleen ruptured). Women must not see the tower being built. On the day, they must remain at least 20m away.

Fathers teach their young sons to dive from their shoulders. Boys practice diving from boulders into the sea. At age eight they are circumcised, after which time they can make their first jump.

The Dive

Between 20 and 60 males per village will dive. The youngest go first, leaping from as high as 9m. Before diving, each man tells the crowd his most intimate thoughts. The people below stop their singing and dancing, and stand quietly; these could be his last words.

Finally the diver claps his hands, crosses his arms and leans forward. In slow motion, falling, he arches his back. The vines abruptly stop his downward rush. Only his hair will have touched the soil, to fertilise the yam crop. The crowd roars its appreciation, and dances and stomps and whistles in tribute.

The final dive, from the tower's narrow pointed peak, is the responsibility of the 'chief of the tower'. He must lunge far enough outwards to avoid hitting any parts jutting out below him.

Men dive wearing red *namba*; their women dance in white grass skirts made from wild hibiscus. It's a powerful and awesome sight.

is built on a hill near the end of the runway each year.

For transport around the south, ring **John** (☎ *38444, 38399*). He's very reliable.

Panas Two **land-dive towers** are erected annually on the hills between here and nearby Wali. Another tower is built at **St Joseph** (Rangusuksu).

Melten Women's Council Guesthouse (☎ *38327; per person including meals 1500Vt*) has three twin rooms in a pretty village across from a white coral beach. The swimming is good, but beware of sharks. If you ring, leave a message for Evelyn.

Pangi & Salap These villages spread along the stony shore of pretty **Bay Homo**. Pangi has a kava bar, **ANZ bank**, **clinic**, a large store, and you can hire taxis and speedboats. Swimming and snorkelling are safe because of the reef.

Land-diving, organised by **Chief Willy** (☎ *38444; 20,000Vt*) occurs twice, in April and May.

If you're very fit, you can hike from Salap to Bunlap via small *kastom* villages, spend a night at Bunlap, then return along the 4WD road. Walking conditions are difficult and strenuous – Chief Willy will arrange guides.

Places to Stay & Eat The Pangi women's club runs the very clean **Pangi Guesthouse** (☎ *38327; per person including meals 1000Vt*) up behind the store. If you ring, ask for Roslyn. Pangi also boasts a **restaurant** that is open weekdays from 6am to 10pm (meals 150Vt).

Nangol Bungalows (☎/*fax 38448,* ☎ *38 444; per person including meals 4200Vt*), just south of Salap, has a relaxing setting on the beach, next to a river. Enjoy bread baked on the open fire, or river prawns in coconut cream. The dining room (meals from 500Vt to 1000Vt) is on the beach.

Getting There & Away A speedboat or taxi ride to Ranwas costs 4000Vt from Salap. Transport from the airport by truck or boat is 3000Vt.

VANUATU

Southeastern Pentecost

Ranwas This is a charming village perched on a high ridge overlooking the sea. From here a slippery path heads north for 30 minutes to Bunlap or Baie Barrier. Chief Willy can arrange a tour to the two *kastom* villages **Lonlibili** and **Ratap**, just south of Ranwas. Be there to watch the sun come up.

Bunlap This large, full *kastom* village lies up a steep hillside. At its Ranwas end are three *nakamal* and two *natsaro* ringed with coral stones. The traditional leaf houses are built so low their roofs almost touch the ground.

Attempts to introduce Christianity, as recently happened at neighbouring **Baie Barrier**, have failed. Most villagers wear *namba* and grass skirts, although the children dress to attend school, and the local language is used.

The **Bunlap Guesthouse** *(per person including meals 2000Vt)* offers an ace opportunity to stay among these very traditional people.

The men build two or three land-dive towers here each year. However, as this is not a commercial spot there is no guarantee you'll be invited to watch.

Banks & Torres Islands

Despite its beauty and fascinating culture, very few visitors make it to this part of Vanuatu. Those who do can expect glorious isolated beaches, snorkelling with visibility to 50m, friendly villagers, amazing scenery with volcanoes, hot springs, you name it... but very few facilities.

There are 62 islands in the Banks and Torres groups, only 13 of which are inhabited. The others are either sandy islets or jagged volcanic rocks poking out of the sea.

There are four airfields in the area, but little motor transport. Be prepared for lots of walking and wild boat trips. Shops often run out of supplies so bring emergency food and water. Your own mosquito net would also not go astray.

Getting There & Away

Vanua Lava, Gaua and Mota Lava are serviced by Vanair twice weekly from Luganville, with one flight calling in to the Torres group if there's demand. Flights go in any order, some landings may be omitted, and schedules change unexpectedly. It's best to be ready to dash to the airstrip should a plane appear.

The cargo ship MV *Keidi* visits the Banks and Torres every four weeks. From Santo it takes one week to Torres (3000Vt including meals and bed; 1500Vt to Gaua). See Boat under Getting Around earlier for more details.

BANKS ISLANDS
pop 7700 • area 746 sq km
This scattered, mainly volcanic chain includes two islands with active volcanoes: Gaua and Vanua Lava.

Gaua
Gaua is also called Santa Maria. It offers spectacular hikes to a crater lake, volcano, falls and caves. The highest point, **Mt Garet** (797m), rises 115m above the floor of a semi-active volcanic crater. At the base of the crater is very pretty sulphur-tinted **Lake Letas**.

Gaua's northeastern coast, where most of the population lives, is fringed by extensive coral gardens and has a few small, sandy bays. An **Arts Festival** is held every two years. In 2005 a Woman's Art Festival will be held in Maseri, 2km from the airport.

At **Lakona Bay** on the west coast (two hours by boat from the airport) you can hear the amazing **water music** created by the local women who clap under the water in the ocean. High cliffs fall straight into the sea on this rugged side.

Stone Relics Everywhere on Gaua is evidence of more populous times. You'll find long stretches of dry-stone walls and rock foundations of houses everywhere. Equally interesting are the obelisks and stone stages where chiefs delivered justice, and stone bowls piled up at the bases of banyans.

Rocks about 1.5m high were occasionally carved, and treated as powerful gods. One of the island's more famous relics is a particularly large **monolith** about 2m across with remarkable petroglyphs that cover almost the entire surface. It's in the south, a three- to four-hour walk from Gaua Airport.

Things to See & Do It's a fascinating half-day walk from Lembot to **Lake Letas** through an incredibly huge **banyan** – the path winds for 35m through its roots past the stone foundations of an old *nakamal*. It may be possible to hire an aluminium motorboat to travel around the lake (5000Vt). If so, you can visit three boiling mud pools: grey, brown and blue!

The **volcano** hike is best done over two days. A dinghy is left at the lake to get you across to Mt Garet. It's a demanding climb from the lake up to the volcano and you'll need boots to handle the sharp gravel (costs are about 15,000/20,000Vt for one/two people for tents, food, guides, boat and entry fees).

A full-day hike to **Siri Falls** usually starts from Lambal. It's mainly good walking to the lake, but the final detour is long and difficult.

The best **snorkelling** is out from Vatles Rock at Bushman Bay, which has great **deep-sea fishing**. Chief Richard, who lives by the creek there, will show you around.

Charles at Wongrass Bungalows (see following) is your best contact to arrange hikes or tours.

Places to Stay & Eat Five minutes walk from the airport, **Wongrass Bungalows** (☎ 38 504; per person including meals 3600Vt) has three bedrooms in a thatched building set in a pretty garden. **Meals** are excellent; try the crispy fried fish with *taro* chips.

For a walk on the wild side, the new **Kaska Bay Guesthouse** (☎ 22339; ⓔ abann@ vanuatu.com.vu; per person including meals 2000Vt) is perched on a rocky outcrop surrounded by wind and sea. Transport from the airport by boat costs 500Vt, or it's an easy walk to the French School, then down to the coast (40 minutes).

Kerllui Guesthouse (☎ 22339; ⓔ abann@ vanuatu.com.vu; per person including meals 2000Vt) has three tiny new bungalows and a gracious curved **restaurant** on grassy flats by sparkling Lembot River.

Getting Around Vanair flies into Gaua on Saturday and Tuesday from Santo. From the airport, an 8km road runs down the coast to Mbarevit near the mouth of the Mbe Salomul River. It's 1500Vt by taxi (if it's not in pieces) or 2000Vt by speedboat if it's high tide.

Vanua Lava
One of the Banks group's dramatic sights is at **Waterfall Bay** on the west coast of Vanua Lava. Here, two spectacular waterfalls, known collectively as **Sara Falls**, tumble over the cliff straight into a large pool near the sea.

Once you could hunt **saltwater crocodiles** on Vanua Lava, but the 1972 cyclone devastated the population and only two remain – one is estimated to be 6m long, the other 2m.

Sola The administrative headquarters for Torba province is located in Sola, so it has government offices, a co-op, post office and NBV bank. Electricity is available during restricted hours. There is also a **police station** (☎ 38556). You can arrange boat trips to Moto, Moto Lava, Ureparapara and around Vanua Lava; contact John at the **Torba Provincial Council** (☎ 38550).

Wilkin's Guesthouse (☎ 38550; per person including meals 2000Vt) has two bungalows on a white-sand beach. A nearby **restaurant** sells meals and kava.

Nearby is the **Leumerous Guesthouse** (☎ 38 556, 38823; per person including meals 2500Vt), that has thatched bungalows set in botanical-like gardens.

Getting Around A taxi normally meets each flight (600Vt to Sola), otherwise it's a 40-minute walk.

TORRES ISLANDS
pop 950 • area 105 sq km
This small archipelago stretches for 42km and consists of six main islands, four of which are populated.

Dazzling white-sand beaches are the general rule. Surfing is particularly good, especially when the southeast trade winds are blowing. Loh and Toga are good places to see megapode birds, known locally as scrub hens, which lay their eggs in the warm sand.

The airport is on **Linua**, which is unpopulated except for the tourist accommodation. South, across a tidal sandbank, is **Loh**. Tegua and Hiu to the north both offer excellent **snorkelling**. Just south is Toga where most of the people live. No islands are more than 4km apart, so the people mainly get around in **outrigger canoes**.

The president of the tourism council, **David Andrew** (☎ 38573; Loh, Torres Islands), can help with all inquiries and arrange accommodation and transport.

Places to Stay & Eat
Five minutes from the airport, **Kamilisa Guesthouse** (☎ 38573, 38565; per person including meals 2000Vt) has two rooms right on the lagoon. The owner offers good service and delicious lobster meals. Butterfly lovers will find this place amazing.

Joseph Baley Bungalow (☎ 38573; per person including meals 2000Vt) is on a fantastic very white-sand beach on Loh. People have spent a week here and loved every minute.

Fresh fruit, vegetables and seafood are plentiful, but the stores have very limited, and expensive, stocks.

VANUATU

Wallis & Futuna

Wallis and Futuna are two forgotten specks, sitting 230km apart in the immense Pacific blue. For those in search of serenity, the islands' laidback lifestyle is just right.

The territory's name should have been Uvea & Futuna but Captain Wallis, fresh from 'discovering' Tahiti, dropped by and his name stuck. Except for their French ownership there's actually little connection between the islands: Wallis is surrounded by a wide lagoon, while its people have ancestral connections with Tonga; Futuna has no lagoon, and its people trace their ancestry back to Samoa. The island of Alofi, near Futuna, is uninhabited.

Facts about Wallis & Futuna

HISTORY

Wallis and Futuna were populated when the great Lapita settlement wave moved across the Pacific between 1500 BC and 500 BC. Objects found on Futuna have been dated to 800 BC, although it's probable there are even older sites. These early settlers practised agriculture and fishing, and they brought the first pigs to the islands. Later Futuna came under the influence of Samoa while Wallis suffered repeated invasions from Tonga, starting around 1400 AD. The ferocity of the Tongan invasions ensured their position in the island's oral histories.

The Dutch explorers Jacques le Maire and William Schouten chanced upon Futuna in 1616 and named the island Hoorn, after their home port (the same Hoorn after which Cape Horn at the southern tip of South America is named). The next visitor, the English navigator Samuel Wallis who had recently discovered Tahiti, arrived at Uvea in 1767. Again the island is renamed but Wallis' name, unlike Hoorn, has stuck.

In the first half of the 19th century the islands became popular stops for whaling ships, followed by traders, bêche-de-mer gatherers and, inevitably, missionaries. The first Catholic Marist missionaries, including Pierre Bataillon on Wallis and Pierre Chanel on Futuna, arrived in 1837. In 1841 Chanel was murdered by King Niuluki, an action which probably had more to do with

At a Glance

Capital City (& Island): Mata'Utu (Wallis)
Population: 15,500
Time: 12 hours ahead of GMT
Land Area: 274 sq km (169 sq miles)
Number of Islands: Three major islands, 20 smaller ones
International Telephone Code: ☎ 681
GDP/Capita: US$2000
Currency: Cour de Franc Pacifique (100 CFP = US$0.97)
Languages: Wallisian, Futunan & French
Greeting: *Malo* (Wallisian), *Maro* (Futunan), *Bonjour* (French)

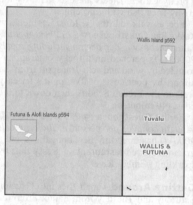

Wallis Island p592

Futuna & Alofi Islands p594

Tuvalu

WALLIS & FUTUNA

Highlights

- **Lalolalo crater lake** – the sheer-sided and perfectly circular lake on Wallis
- **Talietumu & Tonga Toto** – excavated archaeological sites on Wallis which have uncovered Tongan settlements
- **Visiting hallowed sights** – the many churches on both islands, particularly the kaleidoscope interior of St Joseph's on Wallis, the triple-towered Sausau Church on Futuna and the chapel dedicated to St Pierre Chanel, the Pacific's saint, on Futuna
- **Alofi** – the picture-perfect beach and almost untouched forest interior of this uninhabited island

Saint Pierre Chanel of Oceania

Pierre Louis Marie Chanel was born into a French peasant family in 1802, and trained as a priest. He embarked for the Pacific islands with the newly formed Catholic Society of Mary (Marist) in 1836 and, the following year, was the first missionary to set foot on Futuna. The ruling king, Niuluki, welcomed him.

As the missionaries gained converts and thus decayed the traditional power structure of the island, Niuluki became less keen on the newcomers. When Niuluki's own son asked to be baptised, the king issued an edict that the missionaries cease their activities. On 28 April 1841, a band of warriors, probably condoned by Niuluki, attacked Pierre Chanel and killed him.

Despite this (or perhaps because of it) the island soon became fully Christian as other Marist priests took up the challenge.

Pierre Chanel was declared venerable in 1857, beatified in 1889 and finally canonised as the patron saint of Oceania in 1954. He is also recognised as the first martyr to lay his life down for Oceania (Rev. John Williams had been dead two years at this stage but he was a Protestant – and that doesn't count).

the decaying traditional power structure than religion but which, nevertheless, was to make St Pierre Chanel the Pacific's first saint (see the following boxed text 'Saint Pierre Chanel of Oceania'). In the second half of the century France gradually began to assume control of the islands, officially taking control over the years 1886 to 1888.

Things remained quiet until WWII when Wallis & Futuna was the only French colony to side with the collaborationist Vichy government, despite pressure from New Caledonia. The arrival of war in the Pacific ended that phase and in May 1942 the 5000 Wallisians suddenly found 2000 American forces coming ashore. Airstrips were built – the one at Hihifo is still in use today. At its peak there were 6000 Americans on Wallis and their presence deeply influenced traditional culture.

On 29 July 1961, Wallis & Futuna officially became a French *Territoire d'Outre-Mer* (overseas territory). These days, there appears to be little local sentiment in favour of independence from France.

GEOGRAPHY & GEOLOGY

The group consists of three major islands and about 20 islets, approximately 300km west of Samoa and 600km northeast of Fiji.

Wallis is low lying and is the creation of volcanic eruptions, a fact clearly attested to by the many volcano craters, most of them now lakes. The highest bump on the landscape is Mt Lulu Fakahega (145m). Wallis' shallow lagoon can only be entered by one of four passes, the Honikulu Pass. About 15 small islets – some volcanic stumps, others classic sandy *motu* (islands) – are dotted around the lagoon.

Futuna and neighbouring Alofi lie 230km to the southwest of Wallis. The result of geological upheavals, they're much more mountainous than Wallis. Futuna's highest point is Mt Puke (524m); on Alofi it's Mt Kolofau (417m). Fringing reefs embrace both islands while in places the mountainous interior plunges straight into the sea.

Both Wallis and Futuna sit close to the meeting point of the Pacific and the Indo-Australian continental plates and are subject to earthquake activity, most recently in the disastrous quake of 1993.

CLIMATE

The dry season (May to October) sees average temperatures hovering around 27°C (81°F). In the hotter wet season (November to April) temperatures reach 30°C (86°F) around February, and cyclones can eventuate.

ECOLOGY & ENVIRONMENT

Deforestation has left only a fraction of the original forests intact (15% on Wallis, 30% on Futuna). The problem is not due to international logging concerns but more to the use of wood as the main fuel source. The deforested, steep slopes of Futuna are particularly prone to erosion, and increased runoff poses a threat to coral reefs and vital fisheries. On Alofi most of the tropical jungle still stands.

All three islands have a problem with the giant *Achatina fulica* (African snails) that arrived 20 years ago, hitchhiking in on the bottom of containers from New Caledonia. The snails damage crops and are proving impossible to eradicate.

FLORA & FAUNA

There are no native animals or plants of particular significance although Wallis does have an endemic lizard and Futuna three endemic subspecies of land birds (white-collared kingfisher, Polynesian thriller and Fijian thrush). Many ocean birds, such as sterns and frigate birds, breed on some of the islets.

Pigs were bought to the islands with the first settlers. They play a key role as a customary exchange during festivals, communions, weddings and traditional celebrations and, due to their customary value, are highly priced. Until the late 1980s, pigs roamed free but a royal decree put an end to such ways (except on Alofi where they still have a free range).

GOVERNMENT & POLITICS

Wallis & Futuna is a straightforward colony and France basically calls the shots, but there are three kings – one from Wallis and two from the ancient Futunan kingdoms of Sigave and Alo – as well as a 20-member territorial assembly, elected for five years.

The Council of the Territory, a six-member government cabinet consisting of the three kings and three other members appointed by the French Prefect (High Administrator), is advised by the territorial assembly. Wallis & Futuna elects one senator to the French Senate and one deputy to the French National Assembly.

Custom plays an important role in territorial and local politics and the kings' customary authority is generally respected. A king can be replaced if he loses the allegiance of his people. The king of Wallis, Tomasi Kulimoetoke, has reigned for more than 40 years but on Futuna the two kings come and go frequently.

ECONOMY

Wallis & Futuna's economy is almost totally based on French assistance. Its exports are 'negligible' – an armful of copra, a basketful of trochus shells and a handful of handicrafts. Imports, however, are plentiful – lots of shiny new cars, cans of beer, food and fine French wine. Balancing the books on that equation is the French government and its employees and the many citizens of Wallis & Futuna who have left the islands and work overseas, principally in New Caledonia. Apart from fishing and subsistence agriculture, working on the islands essentially means working for the government.

POPULATION & PEOPLE

The islands have a population of approximately 15,500: 10,200 on Wallis and 5300 on Futuna, but there is an even larger population living overseas. It's estimated about 20,000 Wallisians and Futunans live in New Caledonia.

As well as the indigenous population, about 800 *papalagi* (expats), mainly French, live on Wallis and 100 on Futuna.

A large proportion of the islands' indigenous population still live in traditional, oval-shaped, open-sided, thatch-roofed *fale* (houses). Social organisation on Wallis is matrilineal – property is handed down on the female side of the family.

ARTS

Beautiful *tapa* (cloth made from mulberry and breadfruit trees) featuring traditional motifs is produced on both islands. Futuna *tapa*, called *siapo*, is marked with predominantly geometric patterns whereas Wallis *tapa*, known as *gatu*, depicts 'land and sea' designs. (See Women's Business in the South Pacific Arts special section.)

Mats made from pandanus leaves are widely used. *Pareo*, or *manou* in local French, often come in bright colours.

Wood carving is an important activity – majestically large *tano'a*, the multilegged wooden bowls used for making kava, are carved on Futuna. Local woodcarving artists of note include Mika Initia, Suve Suva and Soane Hoatau.

Traditional dances are regularly performed. The year's big event is on the eve of 14 July when a competition is held involving traditional dancers from several villages. The ancient *soamako* (war dances) are particularly impressive.

The islands' best known artist is the late Soane Michon; prints of his work are for sale. Look out also for paintings by the native artist, Soane Patita Takaniua.

RELIGION

Wallis & Futuna is conservative and very Catholic. A Sunday church service, usually at around 7am, is well worth going along to: lots of colour, lots of flowers and wonderful singing.

A huge number of often impressively large churches are found round the two islands, and even uninhabited Alofi and the small islands around the Wallis lagoon have chapels and oratories.

LANGUAGE

Virtually no English is spoken on Wallis and even less on Futuna, so being able to speak some French really helps. See the French Language appendix in this book for some useful phrases.

Reflecting the historical connections of the islands, Wallisian is very similar to Tongan and Futunan is similar to Samoan. See Language in the Samoa and Tonga chapters for pronunciation tips.

Wallisian Basics

Hello (in the morning).	*Malo te ma'uli.*
Hello (later).	*Malo te kataki.*
Goodbye (to someone who is leaving).	*'Alu la.*
Goodbye (if you are leaving).	*Nofo la.*
How are you?	*'E lelei pe?*
I'm well.	*Ei, 'e lelei pe.*
Thank you.	*Malo te ofa.*
Yes.	*Ei.*
No.	*Oho.*

Futunan Basics

Hello (in the morning).	*Malo le ma'uli.*
Hello (later).	*Malo le kataki.*
Goodbye (to someone who is leaving).	*'Ano la.*
Goodbye (if you are leaving).	*Nofo la.*
How are you?	*E ke malie fa'i?*
I'm well.	*Lo, e kau malie fa'i.*
Thank you.	*Malo.*
Yes.	*Lo.*
No.	*E'ai.*

Facts for the Visitor

SUGGESTED ITINERARIES

There's not much flexibility to visiting the islands as the number of flights coming through Wallis & Futuna each week is very limited. A day is sufficient to see either island, although, of course, lazing on the beach can stretch those time limits.

TOURIST OFFICES

With very few tourists, there's understandably no official tourist offices on Wallis & Futuna.

VISAS & EMBASSIES

There are no overseas diplomatic representatives and since Wallis & Futuna is a French Territory, French embassies abroad represent the islands. Visa regulations are the same as for France's other Pacific territories – see Embassies & Consulates in the Tahiti & French Polynesia or New Caledonia chapters for diplomatic representation.

MONEY

As in Tahiti & French Polynesia and New Caledonia, the Cour de Franc Pacifique (CFP) is the local currency, tied to the euro. And like the other two countries, prices on Wallis & Futuna are high in comparison to other Pacific nations. For exchange rates, see Money in the Tahiti & French Polynesia chapter. It's wise to bring some CFP with you – there's no bank at the Wallis airport.

The **Banque de Wallis et Futuna** (BWF) branch in Fenuarama, the new shopping centre in Mata'Utu, can advance cash to Visa and MasterCard holders. It will change foreign currency but exacts a horrific 1000 CFP commission on each travellers cheque exchange. It has the territory's only ATM.

Credit cards are accepted in most hotels and at car rental agencies but not in most shops.

POST & COMMUNICATIONS

There are post offices located in Mata'Utu and Vaitupu on Wallis, plus one in Leava on Futuna.

Public phones require a telecard (1000, 3000 or 5000 CFP). Wallis & Futuna's international telephone code is ☎ 681.

There's an Internet cafe, K PRIM, in the Fenuarama shopping complex in Mata'Utu. On Futuna you can use the hotel terminals.

DIGITAL RESOURCES

Well, where doesn't have a website? Wallis & Futuna's official site (W www.wallis.co.nc) is for Francophones only. Useful sites for English speakers are W www.wallis-islands .com and W www.wallis-and-futuna.com.

BOOKS

Wallis et Futuna – Hommes et Espaces (CTRDP, Noumea, 1994) is an excellent book on the country, written in French. It can be bought from La Palme d'Or bookshop in Mata'Utu.

NEWSPAPERS & MAGAZINES

The locally published *Fenua* is a weekly news magazine. French magazines are available in several supermarkets.

RADIO & TV

RFO (Reseau France Outre-mer), the French global radio and television network, operates a

WALLIS & FUTUNA

24-hour local radio station and one TV channel which broadcasts from 6am to around midnight. Satellite TV is available in a few hotels.

TIME
Wallis & Futuna is just west of the International Date Line and 12 hours ahead of GMT. When it's noon on Wallis or Futuna it is noon in Auckland, 10am in Sydney, midnight in London (ie, just coming into the same day) and 4pm the previous day in Los Angeles.

HEALTH
The French government funds the health services and hospital treatment is free. There is a public hospital in Mata'Utu on Wallis, and in Leava on Futuna.

The water is drinkable on Wallis and Futuna, but should be treated on Alofi.

BUSINESS HOURS
Shops are open Monday to Friday and many open on weekends, but they tend to shut for a long, lazy lunch.

PUBLIC HOLIDAYS & SPECIAL EVENTS
Most holidays and festivals are the French dates also celebrated in New Caledonia and Tahiti & French Polynesia (see Public Holidays in the Regional Facts for the Visitor chapter). In addition, 29 July commemorates the day when Wallis & Futuna became a French territory; St Pierre Chanel Day is 28 April.

ACTIVITIES
The diving club **Te U Hauhaulele** (☎ 72 19 42) organises weekend trips to the outer reef. Good diving spots are the *Trou du Diable*, or Devil's Hole, near Nukuhione islet and Fatumanini Pass at the western edge of the lagoon. Other water activities – picnic excursions to the islets, fishing in the lagoon, windsurfing and sailing – can be arranged via **Fiafia o te tai** (☎ 72 29 67).

Snorkellers should head for the reef fringes, such as around Matala'a beach on Wallis, Faioa islet off Wallis, Vele beach on Futuna and around the lagoon on Alofi.

Golf is played on a six-hole course, although by playing the same holes in different directions they manage to make it feel bigger.

French or not, one of the most popular sports on Wallis is *kilikiti*, the Polynesian version of cricket. See the boxed text 'The Civilising Influence of Cricket' in the Samoa chapter.

ACCOMMODATION
The few hotels (about 50 rooms altogether) are rarely full. Nevertheless, booking ahead secures you a room, but, equally important, it means you get picked up (1500 CFP) at the airport. The website at W www.wallis-and -futuna.com lists all accommodation.

Hotels generally offer comfortable rooms or bungalows, with air-con and private bathrooms. Some have terraces overlooking the lagoon or a swimming pool. Prices range from 7000 CFP for a single room to 16,000 CFP for a two-person bungalow; a French-style breakfast is included.

FOOD
Where food is concerned, you're unlikely to forget that the islands are a French colony – you do eat well. Opportunities to sample the local cuisine are limited; you're more likely to be breakfasting on a baguette or croissant and strong coffee and enjoying an equally French-influenced lunch and dinner.

All supermarkets and most shops are well stocked with imported food including meat, fish, fruit and vegetables. Fresh local produce is increasingly available in the shops, and there's now a Sunday market at Akaaka on Wallis selling local products. Many islanders barter food – if someone catches a fish they don't need it's given to a friend or neighbour, who tosses back a bunch of bananas or a basket of taro. Visitors, however, will find their stomachs are filled mainly with imported goods – chances are that the pork or fish you munch in a local restaurant has come from Europe or elsewhere in the Pacific.

DRINKS
The water is safe to drink and bottled water is readily available in most shops. There's no shortage of wine or beer either. A can of beer in a bar or restaurant costs 350 CFP or 400 CFP; in a shop you'll pay 180 CFP for a Fiji Bitter or 190 CFP for a Foster's Lager.

Kava drinking is still an important everyday event on Futuna, and if you drive around the island after dusk you'll see *fale* after *fale* where men are involved in the ritualistic preparation and drinking of this popular Pacific intoxicant. See the boxed text 'Kava' in the Regional Facts for the Visitor chapter.

ENTERTAINMENT
Videos can be hired on both Wallis and Futuna. Occasional dance performances occur and Wallis has a couple of relaxed weekend discos.

Getting There & Away

AIR

Aircalin (Air Calédonie International; [W] www
.aircalin.nc) flies three times a week to/from
New Caledonia (52,000/60,000 CFP return
fare in low/high season; three hours each
way); two of the flights return to Noumea
(New Caledonia) via Nadi in Fiji (1¾ hours).
For local Aircalin contact details, see the following Getting Around section.

None of the South Pacific air passes include Wallis & Futuna.

SEA

There are no regular ferries nor cruise ships
docking.

Yachts are not inclined visit Wallis that
often, despite its welcoming lagoon. Because
there is not much room around the Mata'Utu
wharf, yachts are encouraged to moor near
the petroleum wharf at Halalo in the south
of Wallis.

Getting Around

Aircalin (☎ 72 28 80, fax 72 27 11 in Wallis, ☎ 72
32 04, fax 72 34 39 in Futuna; [W] www.aircalin
.nc) flies between the islands four times a
week (45 minutes, 17,800 CFP return). It is
best to book in advance. Check the website
for the latest schedules.

There are plans to complement inter-island
flights with a ferry service but, at the time of
updating, the ferry was lying idle.

There is no public transport on either of
the islands; if you want wheels you had better rent a car (around 7500 CFP/day). There
are lots of motorcycles and but very few
bicycles.

Wallis Island

pop 10,200 • area 77.9 sq km
Surrounded by an island-dotted barrier reef,
Wallis Island is the larger and more heavily
populated of the Wallis & Futuna duo. The
lagoon islands, the churches and the perfectly
shaped crater lakes are all interesting, but
Wallis also has one of the largest and most
extensive archaeological sites in the whole
of the Pacific.

MATA'UTU

pop 1300
Mata'Utu is the main administrative centre –
a snoozy town sprawling up the hill from
the lagoon; it's a long walk from anywhere
to anywhere. Mata'Utu has no street names,
and there's no tourist office or other information source.

The waterfront is dominated by **Mata'Utu**
or **Our Lady of Good Hope Cathedral**, looking across the open green to the lagoon. The
twin-towered cathedral is a grey and stolid
looking building but inside it's surprisingly
light and bright. The Maltese cross centred
between the two towers is the royal insignia
of Wallis. The adjacent **King's Palace**, with
its two-storey verandahs running all the way
around, almost looks like an Australian country residence.

South of the King's Palace is the post
office, the gendarmerie, the Fenuarama and
Uvea shopping centres, the residence of the
French Administrator, the wharf and, further
still, the territory's administrative centre.

The **BWF bank** (open 8am-12.15pm &
1.30pm-4pm Mon-Fri) is in the new Fenuarama shopping complex. Here, too, you'll
find a pharmacy.

AROUND THE ISLAND

For a good look over the whole island, head
for **Mt Lulu Fakahega** (145m). You can drive
to the top, where there's a small abandoned
chapel. Footpaths meander down to the west
coast road from the summit.

The 35km island-circuit road is unsealed
and at times fairly rough. It never actually
runs along the coast although in a few places
there are detours that run along the water's
edge. Starting from Mata'Utu and going
clockwise around the island, the route passes
Lake Kikila, the only lake that is not in a volcano crater. Built in 1991, the **Church of the
Sacred Heart** at Faga'uvea is unmissable –
it's like a multitiered lighthouse towering up
beside the road.

In Mala'efo'ou, the **Church of St Joseph**
is the oldest church on the island. It has a
beautiful interior covered in a kaleidoscope
of decorations. Many of them are inspired
by traditional 'land and sea' tapa designs. A
side road leads to the impressive **Talietumu**
archaeological site. This huge and beautifully restored site was a fortified Tongan
settlement, dating from around 1450 AD. A
wide defensive wall with entrance passages
surrounds tree-dotted lawns and a numbe

of other structures, including large platforms and a circular stockade base.

In the southwest of the island, the striking **Lake Lanutavake** lies just off the road. Nearby, the **St Pierre Chanel Chapel** overlooks another crater lake.

Lake Lalolalo is the most spectacular of the Wallis crater lakes. The eerie lake is an almost perfect circle with sheer rocky cliffs falling 30m down to the inky, 80m-deep lake waters. Tropic birds are often seen gliding effortlessly across the lake. It's said that the American forces dumped equipment into the lake at the end of WWII. Just to the west hides another crater, this one without a lake; another crater lake (Lake Lano) lies a short walk north.

Back along the coast are several quite pretty little beaches. Unfortunately the water here is very shallow, the bottom is muddy and it's a favourite basking spot for stingrays. The attraction here is the **Tonga Toto** archaeological site. The name could be translated as 'the blood of Tongans'; an alternative name for the area is the *marais sanglant* or 'swamp of blood', all indicating that the Tongan invasion was not an easy one. This fortified settlement includes impressive walls and a paved footpath running down to the water.

Continue to the northern end of the island to the coastal villages of **Vailala**, where there's a bit of beach, and Vaitupu with its large **Church of St Peter & Paul**.

AROUND THE LAGOON

Some lagoon islands are high volcanic islands, others are sandy-reef-created *motu*. Since there are virtually no useable beaches

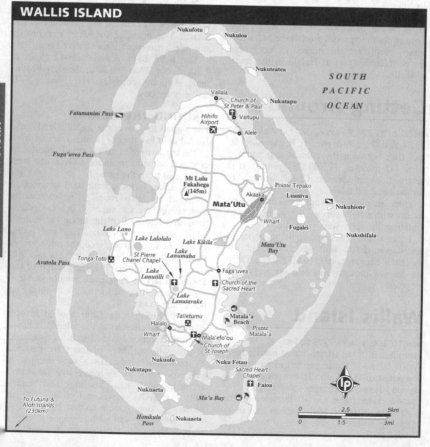

WALLIS ISLAND

on the main island, the lagoon islands are popular excursions for swimming and picnics. None of the lagoon islands are inhabited but many of them have small chapels or oratories. **Faioa** at the southern end of the lagoon probably has the finest beaches.

Nukuhione, with its long, curving sandspit, is a popular excursion and lies on the eastern edge of the reef. Just south is **Nukuhifala**, which also has good beaches. Up at the northern end of the lagoon, **Nukufotu** is noted for its bird population.

PLACES TO STAY & EAT

There are just three hotels. **Hôtel Lomipeau** (☎ 72 20 21, fax 72 26 95; e hotel.lomipeau@ wallis.co.nz; singles/doubles/triples 10,500/ 11,500/13,000 CFP) and **Hôtel Moana Ho'ou** (☎ 72 21 35, fax 72 21 35; singles/doubles 85000/9500 CFP) are both in Mata'Utu. **Hôtel L'Albatros** (☎ 72 20 99, fax 72 18 27; singles/doubles 12,750/16,000 CFP) is near the airport.

Small snack bars are dotted around the island but most serious dining takes place in or around Mata'Utu. A few restaurants boast an open-air dining area and a menu with all the French regulars, accompanied by a fine wine list. Expect to pay above 2000 CFP for a substantial meal. **Restaurant Lomipeau** (3-course meals 2650 CFP), attached to the hotel of the same name, specialises in seafood, and **La Terrasse de Liku** (☎ 72 27 37; mains 2000-2200 CFP), just north of Mata'Utu centre, is also recommended.

There's a **supermarket** in the Fenuarama shopping complex.

SHOPPING

Uvea and nearby **Fenuarama** shopping centres in Mata'Utu have souvenir shops such as **Perle d'Uvea** or **La Palme d'Or/Curios des Îles** (which specialises in books). Beautiful postcards are sold in **Foto Fenua**.

GETTING AROUND

Wallis's Hihifo airport is 6km from Mata'Utu. There are no taxis or other transport, but if you're stuck somebody will offer you a ride. All hotels offer airport transfer for 1500 CFP.

Since there's no public transport, it's a case of rent wheels or walk. Cars can be rented from **Pacific Auto Location** (☎ 72 28 32, fax 72 29 33) and **Pacific Dihn Motoka** (☎ 72 20 23, fax 72 26 57). Check out w www.wallis -and-futuna.com. You could probably rent a scooter or bicycle if you ask around.

Futuna & Alofi

Futuna: pop 5300 • area 64 sq km
Alofi: pop 0 • area 51 sq km
Futuna seems at first to be merely a quieter version of Wallis, but there's many differences. The island is more mountainous and has no lagoon, and the population has strong Samoan links, in contrast to Wallis' ties with Tonga. The languages betray these connections although the people of the two islands understand each other quite easily. Futuna is also a much more traditional island, less influenced by the modern world. There are two districts on Futuna, Alo and Sigave; the main centre is Leava, situated in the Sigave district.

Uninhabited Alofi, with its tropical forest and beach, is a piece of paradise. A strait less than 2km wide separates the two islands.

LEAVA
pop 950
Everything of note is concentrated in Leava, the island's major centre, on the south coast. There are a couple of supermarkets, a post office, a BWF branch (open irregular hours), the island's administrative headquarters (there's even a library), the police station and a wharf.

AROUND THE ISLANDS
The 33km Futuna circuit is solid concrete, except for the unsealed northeast coast. This route starts at Leava and goes clockwise.

The **Sausau Church**, is an impressive sight with its three circular towers. It was built in just eight months after its predecessor was destroyed in the catastrophic 1993 earthquake.

On the island circuit look, for the many fale fono, the oval-shaped, open-walled structures where village men gather in the evening to prepare and drink kava – many of them are utilitarian concrete and corrugated-iron structures. The fine fale fono in the village of **Vaisei** is traditional, with substantial wood pillars and beams lashed together with sennit (intricately patterned rope made from coconut fibre) and topped by a coconut palm roof.

After reaching the north point of the island, the road passes the natural rock formations at **Pointe Matapu** and the lava rock formations of **Pointe des Pyramides**. At Poi, the green-trimmed, three-tiered tower **Pierre Chanel Church** has enough pews to easily seat a couple of thousand worshippers. The chapel includes relics of the saint, including some of his clothes and the war club said to have dispatched him.

FUTUNA & ALOFI ISLANDS

Soon after Poi, the road climbs away from the north coast over the hills to drop down to the south coast. The impressive blue-and-white **Leava Church** has a fine ceiling with carved wood figures of men. The figures lean out from the side walls, supporting the roof rafters with an outstretched arm. Like much Futuna carving, a chainsaw was a principal instrument.

About 4km further there's a less inspiring sight – a roadside dump where garbage is tipped down the cliffside in an unsightly, smelly example of administrative stupidity.

No road crosses the interior, but there is a network of footpaths winding up into the central hills. With enough time you might even find a way up **Mt Puke** (524m).

Boats run across to uninhabited **Alofi** from Vele beach beside the airport (4000 CFP for the whole boat; 15 minutes). Alofi has an idyllic beach; all elements of the postcard ensemble of white sand, clear water and shady trees are there. People come from Futuna to tend gardens and check on their pigs. There's a series of open *fale*, each with a solar cell to provide lighting, for overnight accommodation but people usually just stay for the day. Alofi even has a small **church** – Sacré Coeur.

PLACES TO STAY & EAT

The two hotels on Futuna both have a bar-restaurant: lovely **Somalama Park Hôtel** (☎ 72 32 20, fax 72 31 75; e somalama@wallis.co.nc; singles/doubles 10,500/11,500 CFP) is in Toloke in the northeast; **Hôtel Fiafia** (☎ 72 32 20, fax 72 31 75; rooms 7000/11,500 CFP) is close to Leava.

Futuna's shops and supermarkets may not be quite as well stocked as those on Wallis, but compared to almost any other Pacific island of this size they're quite amazing. Snack bars come and go.

SHOPPING

Futuna is noted for its *tapa* work and wood carving. A number of places around the island display artisan's signs. *Tano'a* sell for about 5000 CFP to 10,000 CFP per 10cm-diameter bowl. In the *fale fono* there are often *tano'a* measuring more than a metre in diameter! This is obviously a boy thing – 'you think yours is big? You should see the size of my kava bowl!'

GETTING AROUND

Futuna's grass airstrip is 12.5km from Leava. Ask at the hotels about renting a car.

Glossary

'aiga – Samoan for *kainga*
'ainga – see *kainga*
'ava – Samoan for *kava*
ahima'a – earth/stone oven
ahu – raised altar or chiefly backrest found on ancient *marae* (Polynesia)
aitu – spirit, ghost (Polynesia)
Anglophone – English-speaking person (New Caledonia, Solomon Islands, Vanuatu)
ariki – (aliki, ali'i, ari'i) paramount chief; members of a noble family
atoll – low-lying island built up from successive deposits of coral
atua – god or gods (Polynesia)
aualuma – society of unmarried women (western Polynesia)
aumanga – (aumaga in Samoa, Tokelau) society of untitled men who do most of the fishing and farming (Polynesia)
Austronesians – people or languages from Indonesia, Malaysia and the Pacific islands

banyan – huge fig tree
barrier reef – a long, narrow coral reef lying offshore and separated from the land by a lagoon of deep water that shelters the land from the sea; see also *fringing reef*
bêche-de-mer – lethargic, bottom-dwelling sea creature
beka – Fijian for *peka*
betel nut – round, greenish-orange nut of the Areca palm chewed for its narcotic effect (Solomons, northern Vanuatu)
bigman – chief (Solomons, Vanuatu)
bilibili – bamboo raft (Fiji)
bilo – vessel made from half a coconut shell and used for drinking *kava* (Fiji)
biu – treehouse for initiated boys (Solomon Islands)
blackbirding – a 19th-century recruitment scheme little removed from outright slavery
bonito – blue-fin tuna
borrow pits – pits dug out to provide landfill (Tuvalu)
bougna – traditional *Kanak* meal of yam, *taro* and sweet potatoes with chicken, fish or crustaceans, wrapped in banana leaves and cooked in coconut milk in an earth oven (New Caledonia)
breadfruit – large, starchy fruit with a coarse green skin
bringue – family event with friends (French Polynesia)
bula – Fijian greeting

burao – wild hibiscus tree
bure – thatched dwelling (Fiji)

cagou – New Caledonia's national bird
Caldoche – white people born in New Caledonia whose ancestral ties go back to the convicts or the early French settlers
cargo cults – religious movements whose followers hope for the imminent delivery of vast quantities of modern wealth (cargo), from either supernatural forces or the inhabitants of faraway countries
case – traditional *Kanak* house (New Caledonia); see also *grande case*
cassava – edible, starch-yielding root
chef – customary leader of a clan (New Caledonia)
ciguatera – food poisoning caused by eating infected tropical fish
clan – tribe; grouping of people with a real or reputed descent from a common ancestor
coconut crab – huge, edible land crab
copra – dried coconut kernel from which oil is extracted
coral – rock-like structure composed of the dead, calcified remains of many generations of tiny sea creatures called coral polyps
la coutume – custom (New Caledonia); see *kastom*

dalo – Fijian for *taro*
drop-off – diving term for a steep drop in the ocean floor
drua – double-hulled canoe (Fiji)
dugong – herbivorous sea mammal

'ei – necklace (Cook Islands)
El Niño – weather phenomenon that brings wet weather to the eastern Pacific and droughts to the west; see also *La Niña*
expat – expatriates

fafine – see *vahine*
faka – (fa'a) according to (a culture's) customs and tradition, eg, *fa'a Samoa* or *faka Pasifika*
fakaleiti – (fa'afafine in Samoa) man who dresses and lives as a woman (Tonga)
fale – house with thatched roof and open sides, but often used to mean any building
fale fono – meeting house, village hall or parliament building
fale umu – kitchen huts
fanua – Samoan for *fenua*

fare – see *fale*
fatele – traditional music and dance performance (Tuvalu)
fenua – land
fiafia – dance performance (Samoa)
fono – governing council (Polynesian)
Francophone – French-speaking person (New Caledonia, Solomons, Vanuatu)
French Territories – French Polynesia (including Tahiti), Wallis & Futuna and New Caledonia
fringing reef – coral reef along the shore of an island without enclosing a lagoon; see also *barrier reef*
fumarole – small volcanic or thermal fissure in the ground from which steam, smoke or gas arises
fusi – cooperative stores (Tuvalu)

gîte – group of bungalows used for tourist accommodation (French territories)
global warming – warming of the Earth due to the greenhouse effect
grade-taking – process by which Melanesian men progress through a series of castes, proving their worth through feasts and gifts; see *nimangki*
grande case – big house where tribal chiefs meet; see also *case*.
guano – sea-bird manure and dead bodies, rich in phosphate and nitrates

heilala – Tonga's national flower
honu – turtle (French Polynesia)
horue – surfing (French Polynesia)
hôtel de ville – see *mairie*

ika – (**i'a**) fish
inati – sharing (Tokelau)

kai – food
kainga – (**kaiga, 'aiga, 'ainga**) extended family (Polynesia)
kaloama – juvenile goatfish (Niue)
Kanak – indigenous New Caledonians
kanaka – people (Polynesia)
kaokioki – (**kaleve** in Tokelau) beer-like fermented coconut drink
kastom – custom; rules relating to traditional beliefs (Solomons, Vanuatu)
kastom ownership – traditional ownership of land, objects or reef
katuali – black-and-grey-striped sea kraits (Niue)
kava – mud-coloured, mildly intoxicating drink made from the roots of the *Piper methysticum* plant

kikau – thatch-roofed
kirikiti (**kilikiti**) – cricket with many players on each side (French Polynesia, Samoa, Tokelau, Tuvalu and Wallis & Futuna)
koutu – ancient open-air royal courtyard (Cook Islands)
kumara – (**kumala, 'umala**) sweet potato
kuri – (**kuli**) dogs

La Niña – weather phenomenon related to (and often following) *El Niño* which brings wet weather to the western Pacific and droughts to the east
Lapita – ancestors of the Polynesians
laplap – Vanuatu national dish
lava-lava – sarong-type garment; wide piece of cloth worn as a skirt by women and men
leeward – on the downwind side, sheltered from the prevailing winds
lei – see *'ei*
lovo – traditional feast (Fiji)

mahimahi – dolphin fish
mahu – French Polynesian word for *fakaleiti*
maire – aromatic leaf (Cook Islands)
mairie – town hall (French Polynesia, New Caledonia)
makatea – geological term for a raised coral island; coral coastal plain around an island
mal mal – *T-piece* of cotton on *tapa* cloth worn by male dancers (Vanuatu)
malo – Polynesian greeting
man blong majik/posen – sorcerers
mana – personal spiritual power
manatee – see *dugong*
maneapa – community meeting house (Tuvalu)
mangrove – tropical tree that grows in tidal mud flats and extends looping roots along the shoreline
manu – birds
Maohi – (**Maori**) indigenous people (Cook Islands, Society Islands)
marae – (**malae, me'ae**) community village green (western Polynesia); pre-Christian sacred site (eastern Polynesia); ceremonial meeting ground (Cook Islands)
masi – bark cloth with designs printed in black and rust (Fiji)
matai – (**mataiapo** in the Cook Islands) senior male, political representative of a family (Samoa, Tokelau and Tuvalu)
matrilineal – relating to descent and/or inheritance along the female line
meke – dance performance that enacts stories and legends (Fiji)

Melanesia – islands of the western Pacific comprising Papua New Guinea, Solomon Islands, Vanuatu, New Caledonia and Fiji; the name is Greek for 'Black Islands'
métro – someone from France (New Caledonia)
Micronesia – islands of the northwestern Pacific, including Palau, Northern Mariana Islands, Guam, FSM, Marshall Islands, Nauru and Kiribati; the name is Greek for 'Small Islands'
moa – chicken
moai – large stone statues (Easter Island)
motu – island, islet
muu-muu – (**Mother Hubbard, mission dress**) long, loose-fitting dress introduced to the Pacific by the missionaries

naghol – land-diving ritual (Vanuatu)
nahnmwarki – district chief (Pohnpei)
nahs – traditional ceremonial house (Pohnpei)
nakamal – men's clubhouse (New Caledonia, Vanuatu)
namalao – fowl-like megapode
namba – traditional sheath (Vanuatu)
natsaro – traditional dancing ground (Vanuatu)
nguzunguzu – carved wooden canoe figurehead (Solomons)
nimangki – status and power earned by *grade-taking* (Vanuatu)
nipa palm – palm tree whose foliage is used for thatching and basketry
niu – coconut
Ni-Vanuatu – people from Vanuatu
noddy – tropical tern, or aquatic bird, with black and white or dark plumage
noni – age-defying juice (French Polynesia)
nono – small gnats, sandflies (French Polynesia)
nuku – (**nu'u**) village (Polynesian)

ono – barracuda
ota – raw fish marinated in coconut milk and lime juice (Niue)
outrigger – float mounted parallel to the hull of a canoe to make it more stable

pa'anga – the currency of Tonga
pae pae – paved floor of a *marae*
palangi – (**palagi**) white person, Westerner (Polynesia)
pandanus – common plant whose sword-shaped leaves are used to make mats, baskets and *tapa*
papaya – see *pawpaw*

Papuans – ancient people who are among the ancestors of modern Melanesians
pareu – (**parpa, pareo**) Cook Island, French Polynesian, New Caledonian and Vanuatuan for *lava-lava*
pawpaw – sweet-tasting fruit
peka – (**pe'a** in Samoa) bat, small bird
pelagic – creatures living in the upper waters of the open ocean
petroglyph – design carved in stone
pilou – *Kanak* dance, performed for important ceremonies or events
pirogue – dugout canoe
Polynesia – the huge triangle of ocean and islands bounded by Hawaii, New Zealand and Easter Island. Includes the Cook Islands, French Polynesia, Niue, Pitcairn Island, Samoa, American Samoa, Tokelau, Tonga, Tuvalu and Wallis & Futuna. The name is Greek for 'Many Islands'.
Polynesian Outliers – the islands of eastern Melanesia and southern Micronesia which are populated by Polynesians
popaa – Westerner (French Polynesia)
puaka – (**pua'a**) pig (Polynesia)
pukao – topknot
pulenuku – (**pulenu'u**) head man, village mayor (Polynesia)
purse seine – large net generally used between two boats that is drawn around a school of fish, especially tuna; boats that use this method are called *purse seiners*

quonset hut – WWII military storage shed made from corrugated iron

rack rates – normal walk-in room rates without discounts
rae rae – French Polynesian for *fakaleiti*
rangatira – (**ragatira** in Samoa, **ra'atira** in Tahiti) chief, nobility (Polynesia)
ratu – chief (Fiji)
reef – ridge of coral, rock or sand lying just below the sea's surface; see *barrier reef* and *fringing reef*
rori – French Polynesian for *bêche-de-mere*

sa – sacred, forbidden; holy day, holy time (Samoa and Tuvalu)
sakau – see *kava*
sake – Japanese rice wine
Saudeleur – tyrannical royal dynasty which ruled ancient Pohnpei
sea slug – see *bêche-de-mer*
sevusevu – presentation of a gift to a village chief and, by extension, to the ancestral gods and spirits (Fiji)

siapo – Samoan for *tapa*
skrab dak – (**scrab faol**) megapode bird (Solomon Islands)
snack – cheap cafe (French Territories)
sour toddy – see *kaokioki*
sulu – Fijian and Tuvaluan for *lava-lava*
swim-through – hole or tunnel large enough to swim through

ta'ovala – distinctive woven pandanus mats worn around the waist in Tonga
tabu – see *tapu*
tagimoucia – national flower of Fiji
tamaaraa – traditional-style feast
tambu (p) – *tabu* (Vanuatu)
tamtam – slit-gong, slit-drum; made from carved logs with a hollowed-out section (Vanuatu)
tanata – (**tangata**) people (Polynesia)
tano'a – multi-legged wooden bowl used for mixing *kava* (Wallis & Futuna)
tapa – see *masi*
tapu – sacred, prohibited
taro – plant with green heart-shaped leaves, cultivated for both its leaf and edible rootstock
tatau – tattoo
taulasea – traditional healer (Samoa)
taupo – ceremonial virgin (Samoa)
taupou – title bestowed by high-ranking chief upon a young woman of his family (Polynesia)
taupulega – village council of elders and *matai* (Tokelau)
tiki – carved human figure (Polynesia)
tivaevae – (**tifaifai** in French Polynesia) colourful intricately sewn appliqué works (Cook Islands)
to'ona'i – Sunday lunch (Samoa)
T-piece – small piece of cloth covering only the groin area (Solomons, Vanuatu)
trade winds – near-constant winds that blow from the northeast in the North Pacific and from the southeast in the South Pacific
trepang – see *bêche-de-mer*
tridacna clam – giant clam, *Tridagna gigas*

trochus – shellfish
tufanga – (**tufuga** in Samoa, **tahua** in Tahiti) priest, expert (Polynesia)
tui – (**tu'** in Tonga) paramount king (central Pacific)
tumunu – hollowed-out coconut-tree stump used to brew bush-beer; also bush-beer drinking sessions

uga – coconut crab
ulihega – bait fish (Niue)
umete – wooden dishes (French Polynesia)
umu – earth oven
umukai – feast of foods cooked in an *umu*

vahine – woman (Polynesia)
vaka – (**va'a**) canoe
vale – Fijian for *fale*
vanua – Melanesian for *fenua*

wantok – one talk; the western Melanesian concept that all those who speak your language are allies (Solomon Islands)
windward – side of an island which faces the prevailing wind; opposite of *leeward*

yam – starchy tuber
yaqona – Fijian for *kava*

Abbreviations

CFP – the cour de franc Pacifique; the local currency in France's three Pacific territories
EEZ – Exclusive Economic Zone
GDP – Gross Domestic Product
GMT – Greenwich Mean Time
ISIC – International Student Identity Card
LMS – London Missionary Society
PADI – Professional Association of Dive Instructors
RFO – Radio France Outre-Mer
RTW – Round-The-World ticket
SPF – South Pacific Forum
SPTO – South Pacific Tourism Organisation
USP – University of the South Pacific

Appendix I – Climate Charts

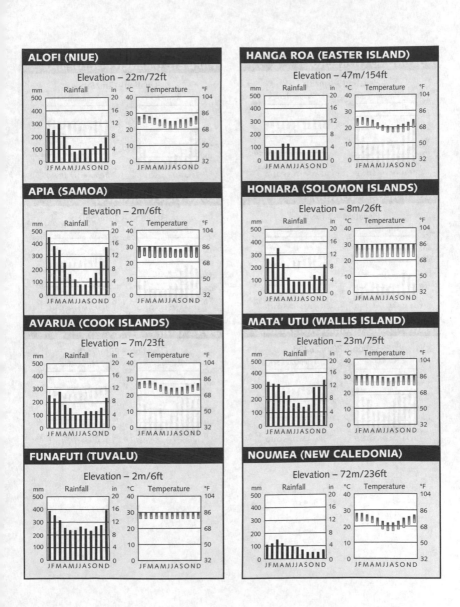

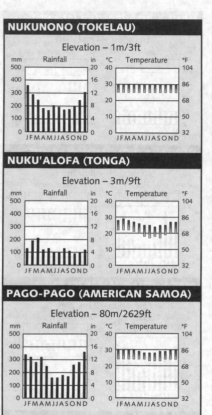

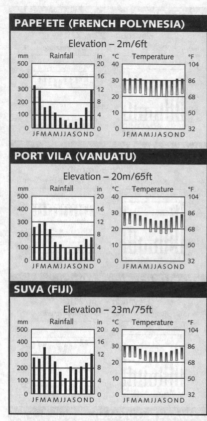

Appendix II – Telephones

DIAL DIRECT

You can dial directly from most countries in the South Pacific to almost anywhere in the world. This is usually cheaper than going through the operator.

To call abroad you simply dial the international access code (IAC) for the country you are calling from (most commonly ☎ 00 in the Pacific but see the following table), the international telephone code (ITC) for the country you are calling, the local area code (if there is one, and usually dropping the leading zero if there is one) and then the number.

If, for example, you are in the Cook Islands (international access code ☎ 00) and want to make a call to the US (international telephone code ☎ 1), San Francisco (area code ☎ 212), number ☎ 123 4567, then you dial ☎ 00-1-212-123 4567.

To call from Fiji (IAC ☎ 05) to Australia (ITC ☎ 61), Sydney (area code ☎ 02), number ☎ 123 4567, then you dial ☎ 05-61-2-1234 5678 (dropping the zero from Sydney's area code).

There are no area codes in any of the countries of the South Pacific.

Telephone Codes

Country	ITC (☎)	IAC (☎)	Country	ITC (☎)	IAC (☎)
American Samoa	684	00	Pitcairn Island	872-144-5372	
Cook Islands	682	00	Samoa	685	00
Easter Island	56-32	N/A	Solomon Islands	677	00
Fiji	679	05	Tokelau	690	00
French Polynesia	689	00	Tonga	676	00
Hawaii	1-808	011	Tuvalu	688	00
New Caledonia	687	00	Vanuatu	678	00
Niue	683	00	Wallis & Futuna	681	19
Papua New Guinea	675	05			

Other country codes include: Australia ☎ 61, Canada ☎ 1, France ☎ 33, Germany ☎ 49, Hong Kong ☎ 852, Indonesia ☎ 62, Japan ☎ 81, Malaysia ☎ 60, New Zealand ☎ 64, Singapore 65, South Africa ☎ 27, UK ☎ 44, USA ☎ 1

ITC – International Telephone Code (to call *into* that country)

Appendix III – Language

PACIFIC LANGUAGES

The Austronesian family of languages is the most widely distributed in the world. It includes all Polynesian and Micronesian languages, many Melanesian and Southeast Asian languages as well as the Malagasy language from Madagascar, off the African coast. While the words for common concepts such as 'land', 'ancestors' or 'fish' are the same in many Pacific languages, there is also considerable diversity, particularly in ancient and culturally-diverse Melanesia, where over a thousand different languages exist.

At the other end of the scale, the last area to be settled, Polynesia, is the most linguistically homogenous. Here, inter-island travel ensured that the languages of Polynesia would almost be dialects of one language. James Cook's Tahitian translator, Tupaia, had little trouble understanding Maori in the Cook Islands or New Zealand, and travellers to the Pacific may find that they have a head start in a new Polynesian language if they've already learned a few words in another.

Prior to the arrival of the missionaries, no written languages existed in the Pacific (with the possible exception of the *rongorongo* script of the Rapa Nui; see the boxed text 'Rongorongo' in the Easter Island chapter). Without a written language, oral traditions were very important in all Pacific cultures.

A common feature of Polynesian languages is the dropped consonant. This is an effect similar to that heard in the Cockney accent, where the letter 't' is not pronounced when it falls within a word, eg, 'butterfly' is pronounced 'bu-er-fly', and 'bottle' is pronounced 'bo-ul'. This momentary closing of the throat is called a glottal stop, and is written as an apostrophe. Thus in Tahiti, where the 'k' sound is dropped, the place name Havaiki becomes Havai'i (ha-vai-ee) and *kumara* becomes 'umara. Cook Islanders drop 'h', so that Havaiki becomes 'Avaiki.

Another feature of Pacific languages that troubles English speakers is the soft 'ng' sound. This is pronounced as the 'ng' in the English word 'singer' – without sounding the hard 'g' as in 'finger'. The name for the country Tonga, for example, is pronounced 'tong-ah' not 'ton-gah'. To make it even more difficult, some Pacific languages spell this sound simply 'g' (the Samoan word *lagi* is pronounced 'pah-lang-i').

English is widely spoken throughout the Pacific, and will be understood in the main towns and cities of almost every country. Exceptions are the French territories (New Caledonia, Wallis & Futuna and French Polynesia, including Tahiti), where French is the first or second language. Some French (even bad French) is very useful in these territories, and to help you make your bad French better, an extensive French language guide is given later in this appendix.

The hundreds of languages of Melanesia have led to the development of 'business' or pidgin languages for communication across language barriers. PNG, the Solomon Islands and Vanuatu all use pidgin languages that mix English, French and German with Melanesian words.

No Pacific languages use an 's' to denote plurals (as the English language does), but this rule is happily broken almost everywhere. For example, a Samoan hotel owner will offer to show you around their *fales* (huts), or a Vanuatuan trader will offer to sell you some *tamtams* (slit drums). In this book we've stuck to the rules and relied on the context to make the meaning clear.

For useful phrases in Pacific languages, see the Language sections in the individual country chapters. For a more comprehensive overview of the languages of the region, get a copy of Lonely Planet's *South Pacific* and *Pidgin* phrasebooks.

FRENCH

French is the major non-indigenous language in French Polynesia (including Tahiti), New Caledonia and Wallis & Futuna. It will also prove useful in Vanuatu.

There are a few peculiarities of French pronunciation you should remember: **ai** is pronounced as the 'e' in 'pet', **eau/au** as the 'au' in 'caught', **ll** as the 'y' in 'yet', **ch** as 'sh', **qu** as 'k', and **r** is rolled from the back of the throat; conson ants at the end of words are usually silent; when **n** or **m** occur at the end of a word they indicate nasalisation of the preceding vowel.

Essentials

Hello/Good morning..	*Bonjour*
Good evening.	*Bonsoir.*
Goodbye.	*Au revoir.*

How are you?	*Comment allez-vous?*
I'm fine (thanks).	*Je vais bien (merci).*
What's your name?	*Comment vous appelez-vous?*
My name is ...	*Je m'appelle ...*
Yes	*Oui.*
No.	*Non.*
Please.	*S'il vous plaît.*
Thank you (very much).	*Merci (beaucoup).*
You're welcome.	*Je vous en prie.*
Excuse me.	*Excusez-moi.*
I'm sorry.	*Pardon.*
I understand.	*Je comprends.*
I don't understand.	*Je ne comprends pas.*
Could you please write that down?	*Est-ce que vous pouvez l'écrire?*

Getting Around

When does ... leave/arrive?	*À quelle heure part/arrive le ...?*
the bus	*le bus*
the boat/ferry	*le bateau/le bac*
Where is ...?	*Où est ...?*
the bus station	*la gare routière*
the bus stop	*l'arrêt d'autobus*
the ticket office	*le guichet*
I'd like to hire ...	*Je voudrais louer ...*
a bicycle	*un vélo*
a car	*une voiture*
a guide	*un guide*
I want to go to ...	*Je voudrais aller à ...*
How do I get to ...?	*Comment peut-on aller à ...?*
Is it near/far?	*Est-ce près/loin d'ici?*
(Go) straight ahead.	*(Allez) tout droit.*
(Turn) left/right.	*(Tournez à) gauche/ droite.*

Around Town

Where is ...?	*Où est ...?*
I'm looking for ...	*Je cherche ...*
a bank	*une banque*
a bookshop	*une librairie*
a chemist (pharmacy)	*une pharmacie*
a clothing store	*un magasin de vêtements*
the hospital	*l'hôpital*
a laundry	*une laverie*
the market	*le marché*
a newsagents	*une agence de presse*
the police	*la police*

the post office	*le bureau de poste*
a telephone box	*une cabine téléphonique*
the tourist office	*l'office de tourisme*
What time does it open/close?	*Quelle est l'heure d'ouverture/ de fermeture?*
How much is it?	*C'est combien?*
breakfast	*le petit déjeuner*
lunch	*le déjeuner*
dinner	*le dîner*
set dish of the day	*le plat du jour*
bakery	*la boulangerie*
butcher	*la boucherie*
cafe-style snack bar	*la brasserie*
food shop	*l'alimentation*
grocery store	*l'épicerie*
restaurant	*le restaurant*
shop	*le magasin*
supermarket	*le supermarché*
I'm a vegetarian.	*Je suis végétarien* (m)/ *végétarienne* (f).

Accommodation

I'm looking for ...	*Je cherche ...*
a youth hostel	*une auberge de jeunesse*
a camping ground	*un camping*
a hotel	*un hôtel*
I'd like ...	*Je voudrais ...*
a bed	*un lit*
a single room	*une chambre simple*
a double room	*une chambre double*
How much is it ...?	*C'est combien ...?*
per night	*par nuit*
per person	*par personne*

Times & Dates

At what time?	*À quelle heure?*
What time is it?	*Quelle heure est-il?*
When?	*Quand?*
today	*aujourd'hui*
tonight	*ce soir*
tomorrow	*demain*
yesterday	*hier*
Monday	*lundi*
Tuesday	*mardi*
Wednesday	*mercredi*
Thursday	*jeudi*
Friday	*vendredi*
Saturday	*samedi*
Sunday	*dimanche*

Health

I need a doctor.	*J'ai besoin d'un médecin.*
Where's a hospital?	*Où est l'hôpital?*
I'm diabetic/ asthmatic.	*Je suis diabétique/ asthmatique.*
I'm pregnant.	*Je suis enceinte.*
I'm allergic to ... antibiotics penicillin	*Je suis allergique ... aux antibiotiques à la pénicilline*

antiseptic	*l'antiseptique*
aspirin	*l'aspirine*
condoms	*des préservatifs*
contraceptive	*le contraceptif*
diarrhoea	*la diarrhée*
medicine	*le médicament*
nausea	*la nausée*
sanitary napkins	*des serviettes hygiéniques*
sunscreen	*de la crème haute protection*
tampons	*des tampons*

Emergencies

Help!	*Au secours!*
Fire!	*Au feu!*
Call a doctor!	*Appelez un médecin!*
Call the police!	*Appelez la police!*
Leave me alone!	*Fichez-moi la paix!*
I'm lost.	*Je me suis égaré/ égarée. (m/f)*

Numbers

1	*un*
2	*deux*
3	*trois*
4	*quatre*
5	*cinq*
6	*six*
7	*sept*
8	*huit*
9	*neuf*
10	*dix*
11	*onze*
12	*douze*
13	*treize*
14	*quatorze*
15	*quinze*
16	*seize*
17	*dix-sept*
18	*dix-huit*
19	*dix-neuf*
20	*vingt*
21	*vingt-et-un*
30	*trente*
40	*quarante*
50	*cinquante*
60	*soixante*
70	*soixante-dix*
80	*quatre-vingts*
90	*quatre-vingt-dix*
100	*cent*
1000	*mille*
2000	*deux mille*

Thanks

R Akker, Coral Anderson, Dorte Andersen, Jacinda Anderson, Lois Anderson, Cathy Sue Anunsen, Gerry & Vi Barker, Marian Barnes, Felix Baumann, Brad Beecroft, William Berg, Edwin Bergenhuizen, France Betbeder, Markus Birsfelder, Nicola Blay, Mike Blennerhassett, Leah Bloomfield, Bev Blythe, A D Blythen, Sergio Moya Boom, Roland Brandenburg, Chris & Tom Brayton, Michael Bridge, Chris Briggs, Emmanuele Brissat, Margaret Brown, Klemens Bruckner, Richard Brunt, Ivar Bruun, Jolene Buchanan, Shyrel Burt, Ian Byles, Yvette Carman, Rusty Cartmill, Narelle Castles, Jeff Catherwood, Ingrid Champion, Daniel Christen, Scott Christensen, Roy Clark, Racheal Cramer, Hollis Dana, Ed Davids, Sandra Davidson, Nicole Demosky, Tony Densham, Andrew Dorkins, Rueben Driedger, Manuel Pete Duenas, Phillip East, Dave Edwards, J Edwards, Ken E Edwards, Bernd Eisele, Elissa Arkinstall, Nivine Emeran, Eric Estolelting, Caroline Ewing.

Katharina Faleovalu, Ferdinand Fellinger, Julie Fenwick, Geert Fijnaut, Jim Flewelling, Pamela Flick, Paul Franckowiak, Chris Freer, David Frid, Mike Galvin, Michael Ganin, Maria Gaspar, Chrissen Gemmill, Duncan Gilroy, Line Glemmestad, Phil Goddard, Paul Griffiths, Reg & Brenda Hamilton, Marika Hammarstrom, Anita Harris, Paul Harris, Leeane Harvey, Jennifer Heebink, Anna Heino, Peter Hendrie, Thijs Heslenfeld, Gavin Hirst, Tim Hogard, Bill Hoskins, Mike Houlding, Lisa Humphrey, William Hurrey, Per Hylle, Brian Jackson, Meryem Jammes, Jan Jasiewicz, Ann Jeffrey, Amanda Jobbins, Belinda & Ferre Johann, Sian Jones, James Jordin, Merrilyn Kennedy, Warren & Venetia King, Bruce & Susan Kirkham, Max Koerndl, Silke Korbl, Barry Kowal, Thomas R Kraemer, Barbara Krantz, Jorg & Sara Krebs, Juergen Kretschmer, Margarete Kuderna,.

Louis Lagrave, Harriet Lamb, Gerhard Lammel, Christy Lanzl, Patricia Laporte, Klaus Latta, Pascal Laurin, Craig Lawrence, Diana Lea, Mike Lebson, Kathryn Lewis, Chris Little, Henry Long, Laura Losee, Chris Lowden, Sita Luca, Kirsten Lund Larsen, Mirna Macchini, Sally Mack, Philip K Maini, Tomas Maltby, Susie Markham, Michael Marquardt, Allegra Marshall, Jennifer Anne Mathers, Stuart Matthews, Frank Mayberry, Kelly McCarthy, Dr Rob McDougall, Nicola McGioff, Kat Mclean, Hilary McNamara, Angela McWhirter, Terry Meanwell, Amanda Menard, Sheryl Mills, Dorothy & Sam Miser, Sara Molan, Rick Moloney, Gregory Mooney, Patrick Morgan, John Morley, Karen Munro, Robin Nahum, Victoria Nason, Paul Neville, Glenn & Sandi Newell, Jens P Nielsen, Trine Nielsen, Fernando Odriozola, Angela Ottaway, Toby Ottaway, Bill Owens.

Matt Papaphotis, James Parry, Keith Parsons, Craig Patton, Charles Paul, Claudia Paul Magus, Jonathan Peppiatt, Mark Perkins, Tracey Phillips, Mahannah Pike, Chris Pouney, Lawrence Powell, John Prime, Freda Prouty, Graham Quigg, Marek Rajnic, Marianne Reimann, Laura Reyno, Nicole M. Reynolds, Lindsay Rieger, Joseph Ross, Tobias Rossel, Esma Rubini, Todd Rufner, Frankfurier Rundschau, Roy Safanda, Fia Salapo, Martine E Saunders, Jean-Francois Sauvage, Vernon Scarborough, Brandy Schoenburger, Martin Searle, Peter Selwyn, Neilesh Shelat, Joanne Sims, David Sinn, A. F. Siraa, Tim Snowden, Sven Sprzagala, Richard Stacey, Siegfried Stapf, Eric Steinert, Karin Steinkamp, Georgia Stone, Stefan Strasser, Scott Sutton, Tania Sweet, Kara Szifris.

George Talbot, Joe Taschetta, Jochen Tekotte, Astrid ten Oever, Glyn Thomas, Russell Thomas, Julie Thorpe, Sophie Tibbs, Sue & Drew Tierney, James Tobin, Paul Tribble, Maryanne Twomey, Andy Ulery, Mathias Ulmer, Caroline & Herman van denWall Bake, Matia Martina Vercikova, Gavin Vessey, Eldad Vizel, Arlinde Vletter, Cees Vletter, Alan Wald, Lise Waldek, Andy Walters, Gabrielle Watson, G Weeks, Wolfgang Weitlaner, C Wellwood, Jennifer Welte, Sally Weston, E.G. Whitlam, Donna Widdison, Christina Willesen, Craig Williams, Lincoln Young.

Index

Abbreviations

Text

Bold indicates maps.

Boxed Text

MAP LEGEND

CITY ROUTES

Freeway	Freeway	====	Unsealed Road
Highway	Primary Road		One Way Street
Road	Secondary Road		Pedestrian Street
Street	Street		Stepped Street
Lane	Lane	)==	Tunnel

REGIONAL ROUTES

	Freeway
	Primary Road
	Secondary Road
	Minor Road

BOUNDARIES

	International
	State/Province
	Disputed
	Cliff

HYDROGRAPHY

	River/Creek		Dry Lake/Salt Lake
	Canal		Spring/Rapids
	Lake		Waterfalls

TRANSPORT ROUTES & STATIONS

	Train		Walking Trail
	Cable Car, Chairlift		Walking Tour
	Ferry, Transport		Pier or Jetty

AREA FEATURES

	Airport		Forest	+ + + Cemetery	Plaza
	Building		Marine Reserve	Beach	Reef
	Park, Gardens		Market	Swamp	Sports Ground

POPULATION SYMBOLS

✪ CAPITAL	National Capital	● CITY	City	● Village	Village
◉ CAPITAL	Provincial Capital	● Town	Town		Urban Area

MAP SYMBOLS

■	Place to Stay	▼ Place to Eat	● Point of Interest

✚ ✈	Airfield/Airport	⊟ ▢	Cinema/Pub	▦ ✉	Museum/Mine	✪	Shopping Centre
⚓	Airplane Wreck	◥ ⚓	Dive Site/Surf Beach	⚑ ♆	Monument/Fountain	▥	Stately Home
⊕ ⚓	Anchorage/Shipwreck	✚	Hospital/Clinic	☪	Mosque	▣	Swimming Pool
▣	Archaeological Site	▢	Embassy	▤	National Park	⊟ ⊟	Taxi/Bus Terminal
⊖	Bank	●	Golf Course	●	Snorkelling	⊠	Telephone
⌂ ☼	Cave/Lookout	▣	Internet Cafe	●	Petrol Station	⊕	Tourist Information
✚	Church	▥ ▥	Swami/Sikh Temple	▣ ⊠	Police/Post Office	▲ ▲	Volcano/Mountain

Note: not all symbols displayed above appear in this book

LONELY PLANET OFFICES

Australia
Locked Bag 1, Footscray, Victoria 3011
☎ 03 8379 8000 fax 03 8379 8111
email: talk2us@lonelyplanet.com.au

UK
72-82 Rosebery Ave, London, EC1R 4RW
☎ 020 7841 9000 fax 020 7841 9001
email: go@lonelyplanet.co.uk

USA
150 Linden St, Oakland, CA 94607
☎ 510 893 8555 TOLL FREE: 800 275 8555
fax 510 893 8572
email: info@lonelyplanet.com

France
1 rue du Dahomey, 75011 Paris
☎ 01 55 25 33 00 fax 01 55 25 33 01
email: bip@lonelyplanet.fr
www.lonelyplanet.fr

World Wide Web: www.lonelyplanet.com or AOL keyword: lp
Lonely Planet Images: www.lonelyplanetimages.com